CRIMINAL JUSTICE ILLUMINATED

Capital Punishment
A Balanced Examination

Evan J. Mandery, JD
Assistant Professor
John Jay College of Criminal Justice
New York, New York

JONES AND BARTLETT PUBLISHERS
Sudbury, Massachusetts
BOSTON   TORONTO   LONDON   SINGAPORE

World Headquarters
Jones and Bartlett Publishers
40 Tall Pine Drive
Sudbury, MA 01776
978-443-5000
info@jbpub.com
www.jbpub.com

Jones and Bartlett Publishers Canada
2406 Nikanna Road
Mississauga, ON L5C 2W6
Canada

Jones and Bartlett Publishers International
Barb House, Barb Mews
London W6 7PA
United Kingdom

Production Credits
Publisher—Public Safety Group: Kimberly Brophy
Acquisitions Editor: Chambers Moore
Production Manager: Amy Rose
Associate Production Editor: Carolyn F. Rogers
Editorial Assistant: Jaime Greene
Marketing Manager: Matthew Bennett
Marketing Associate: Laura Kavigian
Cover and Text Design: Anne Spencer
Photo Research: Kimberly Potvin
Cover Image: photo © AP Photo; column © Ron Chapple/Thinkstock/Alamy Images
Chapter Opener Image: © Masterfile
Composition: Auburn Associates, Inc.
Printing and Binding: Malloy, Inc.
Cover Printing: Malloy, Inc.

Library of Congress Cataloging-in-Publication Data

Mandery, Evan J.
  Capital punishment : a balanced examination / Evan J. Mandery.— 1st ed.
    p. cm.
  Includes bibliographical references and index.
  ISBN 0-7637-3308-3 (casebound)
  1. Capital punishment—United States. 2. Capital punishment—Moral and ethical aspects.
I. Title.
  KF9227.C2M35 2004
  345.73′0773—dc22
                           2004014553

Printed in the United States of America
08 07 06 05 04   10 9 8 7 6 5 4 3 2 1

Contents

PART I Moral Considerations

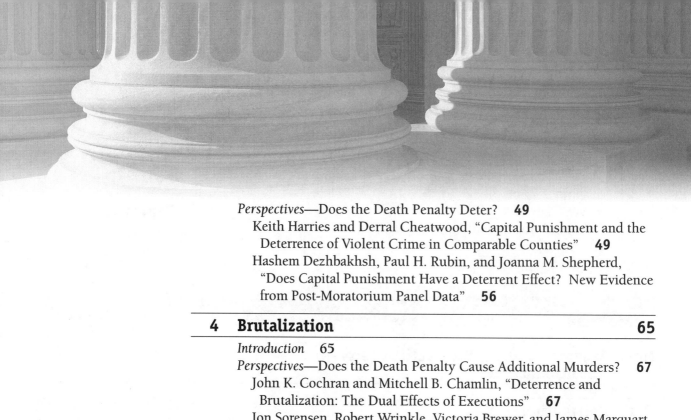

PART II Constitutional Considerations

The Death Penalty as Applied in America—
An Introduction   **155**

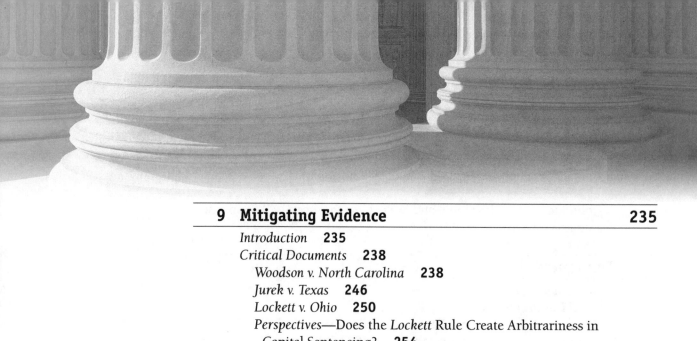

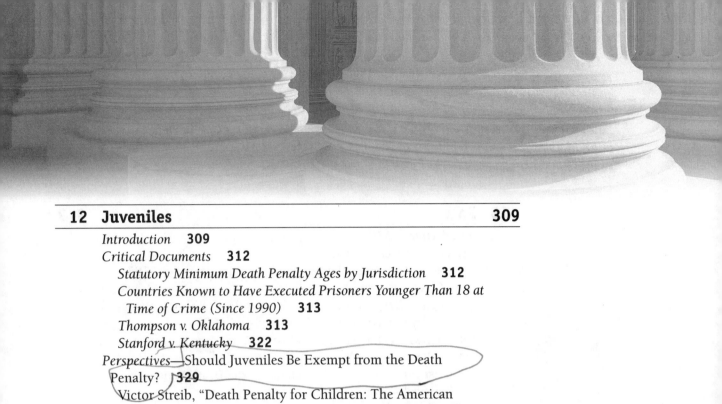

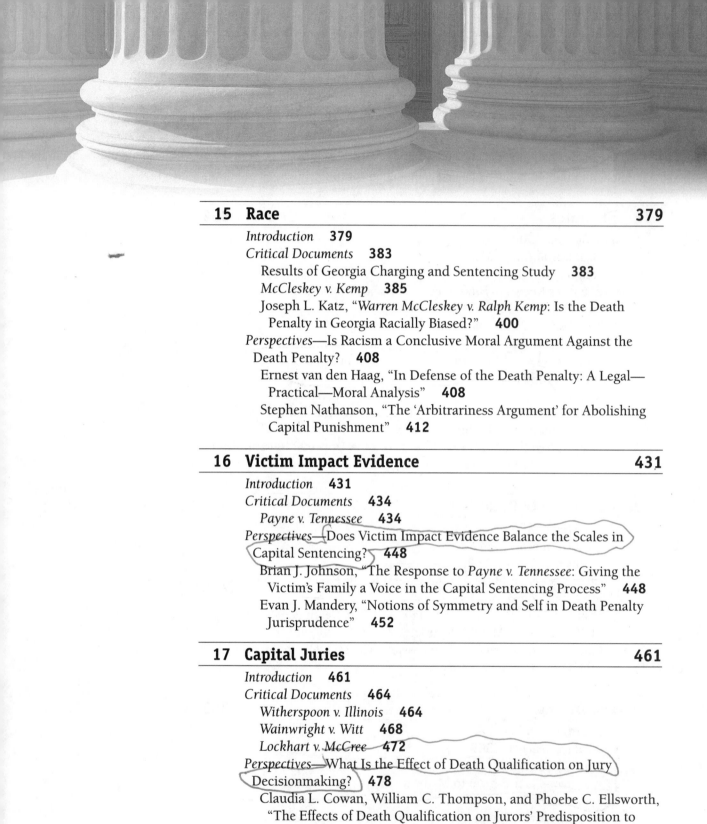

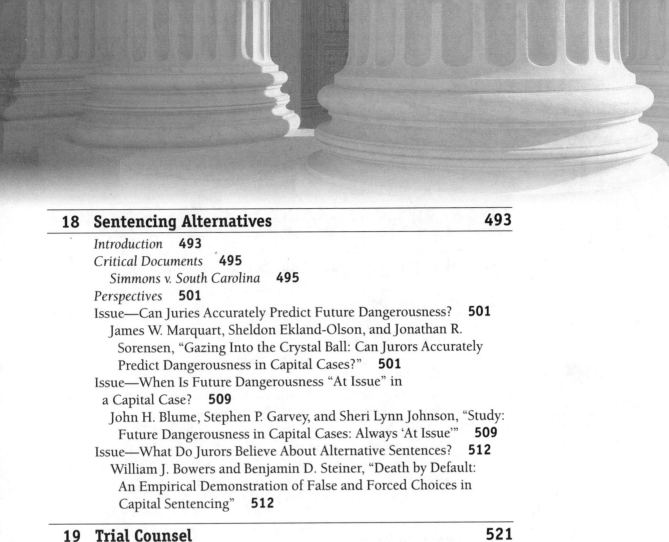

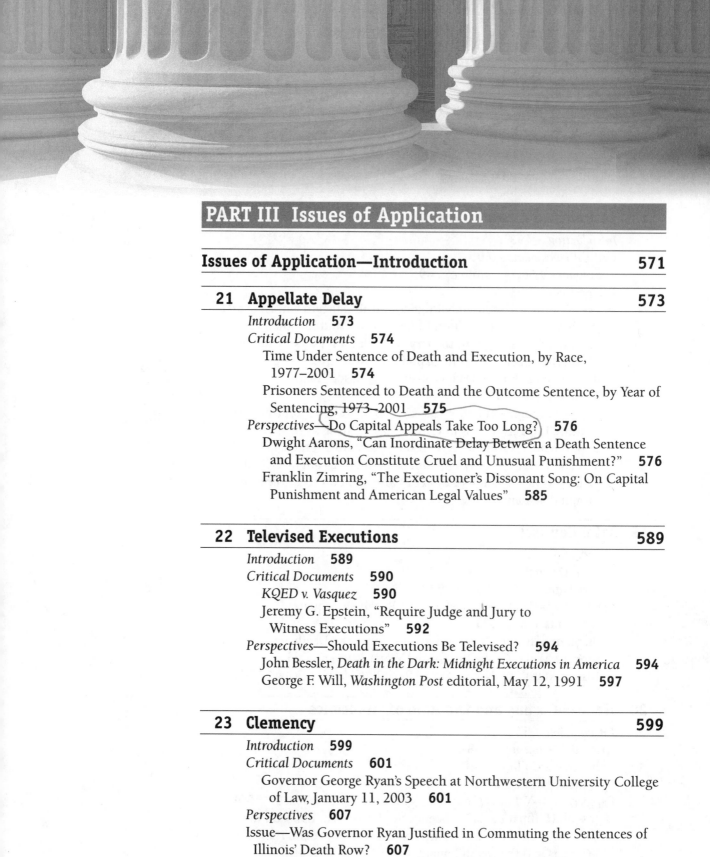

PART III Issues of Application

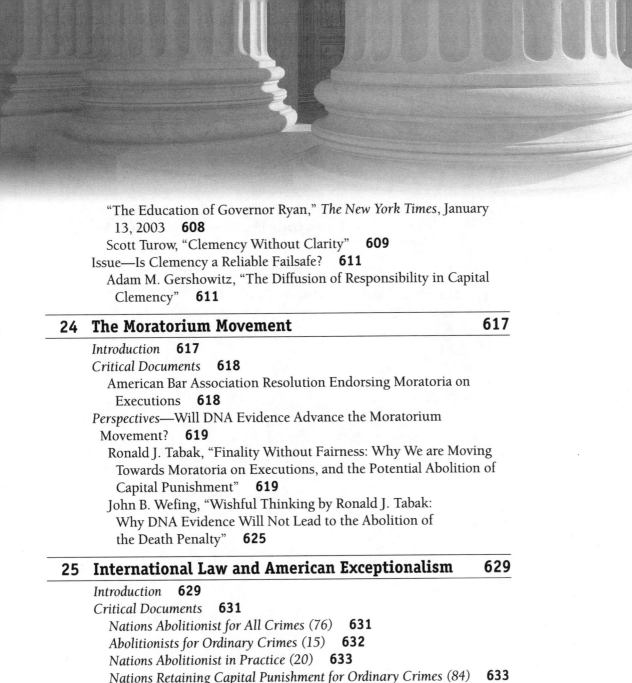

In 1998, while an associate at Shearman & Sterling, I began working on the appeal of William Thomas Knotts, an inmate on death row in Alabama. Mr. Knotts was convicted of the brutal murder of Helen Rhodes, whom he shot in the course of robbing her home, in the presence of her two-year-old son. The murder was gruesome, as is every case you will read in this book. But there was mitigating evidence. William committed the crime at the age of seventeen, he had been abused badly as a child—beaten often and sometimes locked in his room for days at a time without food, and evidence suggested that he had suffered brain damage in a car accident. Who could say whether he deserved to die? I thought he did not, but reasonable arguments could be made on either side. The Alabama jury recommended that William be given life imprisonment. The judge disagreed and imposed a sentence of death. When I began working on the case, I viewed the death penalty as a violation of human rights. I argued passionately that William be spared.

Meeting and getting to know a death row inmate put a human face on an academic issue and permanently changed the way I regard the death penalty. No one meeting William could believe that he had been offered the same opportunities and had the same capacity to reason as someone raised in a secure home and family. I was equally affected, though, by meeting Helen Rhodes' husband, who opposed the death penalty, and whom I tried to persuade to testify on William's behalf. Mr. Rhodes was a Christian and a peaceful man; when I spoke to him he had been raising his son alone for more than ten years. He wished no further ill upon William. But he also wished that the event be put behind him for all time. The mere thought of his wife's death caused him obvious pain. All of this moved me, too, as it would have moved anyone.

I arrived at John Jay College of Criminal Justice in the fall of 2000 with an open mind and the aim of teaching and writing about the death penalty. I opposed the death penalty, but I did not dismiss lightly my experience with Mr. Rhodes or the opinion of the overwhelming majority of Americans who supported (and continue to support) capital punishment. So I read as widely as I could, and listened to students and colleagues.

One thing that struck me in reading and teaching about the death penalty was the absence of books presenting a balanced examination of the subject. The overwhelming weight of scholarship on the death penalty comes from the abolitionist side. This is not to say that abolitionists have the better argument in every case, only that the great majority of research either comes from opponents of capital punishment or reaches conclusions that militate against the death penalty. In researching and writing this book, I have tried hard to find credible pro-death penalty scholarship.

This book, in short, is a balanced, policy-oriented examination of the death penalty as practiced in the United States. The book considers, in turn, the moral-

ity of the death penalty, the constitutional issues of its implementation in America, and some of the hard questions concerning its applications, such as how long capital appeals take and whether or not the delay—sometimes referred to as the "death row phenomenon"—can be defended. Each chapter begins with a primer on the issue at hand—the data and critical documents necessary to make an educated assessment—and then continues with essays offering differing viewpoints.

The approach of the book is issue specific. The chapter on deterrence, for example, does not consider at any length whether deterrence is a legitimate or sufficient justification for public policy—a serious question, to be sure. Rather, the text considers exclusively the evidence on whether the death penalty deters. It fosters what I sometimes describe as horizontal thinking (the evidence of deterrence), rather than vertical thinking (whether deterrence is a valid or sufficient justification for capital punishment). The aim here is to evaluate arguments on their own terms.

This may strike some as artificial. People don't ordinarily reach an opinion on a moral issue by tallying up the arguments in its favor and against. People are guided generally by core moral beliefs. I expect most death penalty opponents would not change their mind if it were proved to a certainty that the death penalty deters, just as most proponents would not waver were it conclusively shown that the death penalty did not deter or that it caused additional murders. Most abolitionists are guided by a belief that the death penalty violates human dignity, most proponents by the belief that the death penalty is the ultimate affirmation of human dignity.

But people debate the issue piecemeal and an open-minded examination of the individual issues can be enlightening. This has been my own experience. Eight years ago, before I began working on William's case, I would have ranked racism and the risk of executing innocent persons as my top reasons for opposing the death penalty. Today they are at the very bottom of my list. Not to say that these aren't serious concerns—they are—but I worry much more today about the ability of courts and juries to make meaningful distinctions between those who deserve to die and those who do not, the overzealousness of prosecutors, and the competence of the attorneys assigned to represent the condemned. Examining capital punishment has required me to think about some basic philosophical questions—are there situations in which I would take another human life, and how do I distinguish the cases in which I would from those that I think are morally intolerable? These distinctions are often hard to draw.

Of course, the point is not how my views have evolved, the point is that evolution is possible. I hope the dialogue here germinates the seeds of an evolution in your own thinking, no matter what direction it takes you.

I welcome feedback of any kind from all readers of the book. I am interested to hear from students and teachers what aspects of the book they find useful and what they feel can be improved. I try to keep abreast of developments in the field, but I am obliged to any authors who make me aware of new research and articles. I would like very much if future editions of this book could serve as a forum for debate.

I can be reached at John Jay College of Criminal Justice, 899 Tenth Avenue, New York, New York 10019. My email addresses are emandery@jjay.cuny.edu and emandery@hotmail.com.

In editing the cases and readings presented in the book, I have prioritized readability over most other concerns. I have liberally omitted brackets, ellipses, and citations, and have even changed the occasional word if I thought it would help to minimize confusion. I have preserved the original numbering of Supreme Court cases, even if some sections have been omitted. However, articles that were previously published elsewhere, I have renumbered with impunity. None of these changes are remotely material. I mention this only to caution the reader against citing to this text. The best practice, as always, is to refer to the original documents. Supreme Court citations are presented with the cases. References to original versions of articles, as appropriate, are listed at the end of the book in The Authors and Their Contributions.

A Note to Students and Teachers

Thanks to the members of the death penalty community, supporters and abolitionist alike, for supporting this project. In the course of researching and writing this book, I reached out to all kinds of people whose perspective I thought might add somethiing to the book. Everyone I contacted graciously allowed me to reprint their work.

Professor Jeffrey L. Kirchmeier of the City University of New York School of Law reviewed an early version of this manuscript and offered helpful comments and support. Thanks to my research assistant Katie Taylor, to Carolyn Rogers of Jones & Bartlett for her competence and good cheer, to my parents, and most importantly to Jennifer DeYoung, who takes second seat to no one in the department of good cheer.

This book is dedicated to Seymour Goldstein and his spirit (alive and well in his wife, Roz). Sy hated the death penalty, but liked a good argument even better, and would have embraced the spirit of this text.

Acknowledgments

The focus of this book is the death penalty in the modern era, the beginning of which is marked by the Supreme Court's 1972 decision in *Furman v. Georgia*, holding unconstitutional the death penalty as then applied in Georgia. At the time, Georgia's sentencing statute gave juries unguided discretion to impose or decline to impose the death penalty. *Furman* marked the first occasion on which the Court exercised oversight over death-sentencing procedures, an effort that continues to this day.

Introduction

This is not to say that the Court was unconcerned with the death penalty prior to *Furman*. To the contrary, in the four decades preceding *Furman*, the Court reversed or vacated convictions in 43 death penalty cases. The first of these reversals, *Powell v. Alabama*, is considered one of the seminal decisions of constitutional criminal procedure. *Powell* considered the plight of the "Scottsboro Boys," a group of young black men accused of raping a white woman, and sentenced to die by an all-white jury following a quick trial in an emotionally charged atmosphere. The Supreme Court reversed the convictions of the Scottsboro Boys and ordered a new trial. As with each of the reversals preceding *Furman*, though, the concern was not the death penalty itself. In *Powell*, the issue was whether the defendants had received constitutionally adequate counsel under the Sixth and Fourteenth Amendments. In succeeding cases, the Court raised questions about race-based jury selection, coerced confessions, and prosecutorial misconduct. The Court showed a sensitivity to cases in which the defendant's sentence was death, but all of its decisions were based on questions of constitutional procedure applicable to criminals generally.

It was not until 1971 that the Court dealt with the death-sentencing process as an independent entity. In *McGautha v. California*, a 1971 case, the Court rejected a challenge to California's sentencing scheme under the due process clause of the Fourteenth Amendment. The California death-sentencing scheme, like the Georgia scheme later considered by the Court in *Furman*, gave juries unguided discretion to choose between life and death. In rejecting McGautha's challenge, the Court noted that during the early history of the death penalty, many states had mandatory death penalties for certain kinds of crimes, and that some juries, resistant to impose capital punishment, acquitted defendants who were guilty but whose offenses were inappropriate for the death penalty. Discretion was introduced to capital sentencing as a means of combating this problem of jury nullification. A discretionary scheme legitimated the exercise of mercy by juries without causing undeserved acquittals.

In *Furman*, the Court considered—and upheld—a challenge to Georgia's death-sentencing scheme based upon the Constitution's prohibition of cruel and unusual punishments. In so doing, the Court shifted the primary focus of litigation concerning the death penalty to the Eighth Amendment. *Furman* divided the Court—each of the justices voting with the majority wrote separately to explain his reasoning—it is the longest collection of opinions in the history of the Court. It seems fair to say, though, that the Justices were each concerned with the many different kinds of arbitrariness generated by a sentencing scheme vesting juries with unguided discretion and with the death penalty generally. The death penalty in Georgia was arbitrary in the most literal sense—it was impossible to predict which defendants would get the death penalty and which would not—and to the extent that predictions were possible, they proved only that a host of irrelevant factors infected the process—race, economics, geography, and quality of counsel to name a few. Over the succeeding 30 years, the Court has through its decisions incrementally defined what procedures are required to ensure that a defendant is not arbitrarily sentenced to die.

The most significant of these decisions is *Gregg v. Georgia*, a 1976 case in which the Court upheld the constitutionality of Georgia's revised death-sentencing scheme. Following *Furman*, Georgia revised its death-sentencing statute in three main ways: First, Georgia narrowed the class of murderers subject to capital punishment by requiring that at least one of ten specified statutory aggravating circumstances be proved beyond a reasonable doubt. Second, it bifurcated trials, dividing capital proceedings into a separate guilt phase and sentencing phase where the jury weighs the aggravating evidence against the mitigating evidence. Third, it required automatic appeal of death sentences to the Georgia Supreme Court with the court required to consider, among other things, whether the sentence is disproportionate compared to sentences imposed in similar cases. In *Gregg*, the Court held that these reforms adequately guided juror discretion so as to ensure against arbitrary sentences.

On the same day the Court decided *Gregg*, it rejected in *Woodson v. North Carolina* a mandatory sentencing scheme, enacted by North Carolina and several other states as a response to *Furman*. Though mandatory sentences are predictable and necessarily counter arbitrariness, the Court rejected the North Carolina approach on the basis of another principle: death, because of its finality, requires an individualized assessment of whether a defendant deserves to die. A year later, the Court ruled the death penalty unconstitutional for rape, holding that the sentence was excessive for the crime, an analysis the Court does not ordinarily undertake outside of the death penalty context. *Coker v. Georgia* opened the door to a flood of challenges from petitioners sentenced to death that the death penalty was disproportionate for their own kind of crime or because of some special status they possessed—for example, their youth or mental retardation.

Gregg, Woodson, and *Coker* are the cornerstones of the Supreme Court's death penalty jurisprudence, the source of three main—arguably sometimes contradictory—principles from which all else flows: (1) death-sentencing schemes must

not produce arbitrary results; (2) death-sentencing schemes must allow for consideration of the individual and any mitigating evidence he or she offers; and (3) death sentences must not be excessive to the crime or class of individuals to which the defendant belongs. Subsequent Court decisions are efforts to flesh out the answers to these questions in specific circumstances.

In defining the contours of a constitutional death penalty under the Eighth Amendment, morality plays some role. The Court has said explicitly that moral judgments are relevant, and no doubt the justices' own ethical beliefs inform their views on cases. But the Court has said that the primary inquiry is objective—the Court attempts to assess "evolving standards of decency" in determining whether the death penalty is appropriate for a crime or particular criminal. In assessing this question, the Court is guided to some small extent by the history of the death penalty, and to a much larger extent by the death penalty as practiced in America.

Whether the Court has asked the right questions—and whether it has offered the right answers to these questions—are the inquiries that shape this book. The remainder of this introduction offers a very short glimpse of the history of the death penalty and a somewhat more detailed examination of the key questions concerning the death penalty as practiced in the United States today—which states have it, upon whom is it imposed, and why do Americans support it in such large numbers. Part I of the book examines the moral debate about the death penalty, relevant to the Supreme Court and its Eighth Amendment jurisprudence, and of course to individuals in forming their own opinions about the death penalty. Part II of the book considers the legal debate about the death penalty and the key questions involved there: whether arbitrariness is a sufficient argument against capital punishment, and, if the decision is made to have capital punishment, what procedures and restrictions should be put in place to ensure that it is used in as fair a manner as possible. Here the focus is prescriptive as much as descriptive. The section presents the Court's answers to these questions, but devotes equal or greater attention to assessing whether the Court's approach to answering these questions is logical, and whether the Court is succeeding in achieving its own goals. The book concludes in Part III by considering some questions attendant to the application of the death penalty.

I. *A Short History of the Death Penalty in America*

In 1608 the Jamestown colony of Virginia executed Captain George Kendall on evidence of his spying for Spain, and in so doing embraced a long, worldwide tradition of capital punishment. The Greeks, Romans, Egyptians, Persians, Chinese, Phoenicians, and Israelites all practiced capital punishment—generally for murder, but sometimes for less serious offenses such as blasphemy, adultery, and the practicing of magic. English law embraced the death penalty. English common

law recognized eight capital crimes: treason, petty treason, murder, larceny, robbery, burglary, rape, and arson. Over time the British enacted more and more capital laws until, by 1820, the death penalty extended to more than 200 offenses including forgery and a host of property offenses.

American colonists brought the death penalty with them to America, though they restricted its use, particularly in the northern colonies. The first laws of Massachusetts recognized but twelve capital crimes—including idolatry, blasphemy, and witchcraft. The Quaker founders of Pennsylvania limited the death penalty to murderers and traitors. The colony of South Jersey did not authorize capital punishment at all.

While the colonies embraced capital punishment less enthusiastically than the motherland, the death penalty was undeniably a fact of life in colonial America. As the colonies grew, they increasingly relied upon the death penalty as a means of maintaining order. In some instances, England required individual colonies to enact the death penalty as a check against crime. By the time of the Revolutionary War, many colonies had expanded the reach of their statutes to make treason, piracy, rape, sodomy, and even some property crimes punishable by death.

For this and other reasons, it seems clear that the Eighth Amendment of the Bill of Rights was not intended to abolish capital punishment. The cruel and unusual punishments clause has its roots in the English Bill of Rights of 1689. The English clause was enacted as a response to the Bloody Assizes, a savage response by King James II to the Monmouth Rebellion. The framers of the United States Constitution wanted to avoid some of the harsher punishments used abroad. But when the United States Constitution was adopted in 1789, branding and whipping were still common in the colonies, as was capital punishment. The Fifth Amendment, adopted on the same day as the Eighth Amendment, explicitly contemplates the death penalty: "No person shall be held for a capital or otherwise infamous crime, unless on a presentment or indictment of a Grand Jury." Later it adds: "Nor shall any person be deprived of life, liberty, or property without due process of law."

The first major transformation in the scope of the death penalty occurred towards the end of the 18th century when Pennsylvania divided murder by degrees. Previously, Anglo-Saxon law had treated all malicious homicide—that is any killing not justified or excused—in the same manner. Under the Pennsylvania definition, first-degree murder was a premeditated killing or any killing committed during the course of an arson, rape, burglary, or robbery. Only first-degree murders were punishable by death, but for all such offenses, the death penalty was mandatory. Most states adopted the division of murders into degrees over the next four decades.

Southern states relied upon the death penalty as a tool for keeping slaves in check. Slave stealing, inciting slaves to insurrection, and concealing a slave with intent to free him were all punishable by death in North Carolina. Many south-

ern criminal codes were explicitly racist. Georgia's rape statute provided for the death penalty for a slave or freeman of color who raped a white female; a white man convicted of raping a slave or woman of color was subject to a fine or imprisonment at the court's discretion. Even after the Emancipation Proclamation ended the so-called "Black Codes" of southern states, the situation did not altogether improve: in the 1890s, for example, lynchings exceeded legal executions—more than half of the 1540 lynchings during this period were of black men.

Benjamin Rush, a physician and signatory to the Declaration of Independence, initiated the first abolition movement in the late 1780s. In the 1830s and 1840s abolitionist activity revived, coinciding with the end of public executions. Much of this sentiment went hand in hand with slavery abolition movements. Michigan, Wisconsin, and Rhode Island abolished the death penalty during this time, but the movement again lost momentum with the start of the Civil War. In the last part of the 19th century, a progressive reform movement revived the push for abolition, and by World War I thirteen states had abolished the death penalty, but again the momentum towards abolition was interrupted by the war.

Over the succeeding forty years, public support for the death penalty strengthened, fueled in part by fear of immigrants and fifth columnists. By 1920, five states that had abolished the death penalty reinstated it. Approximately 1600 people were executed in the United States during the 1930s, more than during the two preceding centuries combined. In total, since the first days of the British Colonies in America, some 15,000 executions have been confirmed in the United States. Some estimates put the number closer to 22,500.

The abolition movement coalesced again in the 1950s, sparked in part by the passionate and public attack on the death penalty by Albert Camus. The burgeoning civil rights movement focused attention on the treatment of blacks in all areas, including the criminal justice system, which necessarily subjected the death penalty to further scrutiny. In 1957, polls showed that only a bare majority of Americans supported the death penalty. By 1966, that number had fallen to 42%. The NAACP challenged the treatment of black prisoners in the South and cultivated a cadre of volunteer attorneys to represent death row prisoners. By the late 1960s, the NAACP had achieved a *de facto* moratorium on executions. This state of affairs was constitutionalized by the *Furman* decision in 1972. The Court's decision in *Gregg* opened the door to further executions. The first occurred in 1977, and continued at an accelerating rate through the late 1990s, from whence they have leveled off, as reflected in **Table I-1**.

II. *The Death Penalty in America Today*

The death penalty is currently authorized by 38 states and the federal government. In 2002, 69 men and two women were executed in thirteen states—33 in

Table I-1	Executions since 1977		
Year	Number of executions	Year	Number of executions
1977	1	1991	14
1979	2	1992	31
1981	1	1993	38
1982	2	1994	31
1983	5	1995	56
1984	21	1996	45
1985	18	1997	74
1986	18	1998	68
1987	25	1999	98
1988	11	2000	85
1989	16	2001	66
1990	23	2002	71

the state of Texas alone, making it by far the most active death penalty state in the nation. Oklahoma carried out the next most executions with 7.

A total of 3557 prisoners were under sentence of death at the end of 2002. California has the largest death row—614 prisoners are under sentence of death—followed by Texas. During 2002, 159 prisoners were sentenced to die, the smallest number of admissions since 1973. Texas is again the leader with 37 of the admissions to death row, followed by California (14), Alabama (11), Florida (10), and Pennsylvania (9), as shown in **Table I-2.**

The number of prisoners under sentence of death rose steadily from 1972, when the Supreme Court issued its decision in *Furman*, through 2001, when the figure finally leveled off. This initial pooling followed by a leveling is as one might expect. Given that capital appeals average approximately 10 years (appellate delay is the subject of Chapter 21), pooling almost necessarily occurs during the initial years following the reinstatement of the death penalty because some prisoners will enter death row, but none will leave. After enough time has passed to process some appeals, there begins to be some outflow. If the rate of death sentences remains the same, pooling should slow. If the rate of executions equals the rate of sentences there should then be a leveling off. If the rate of executions exceeds the rate death sentences are imposed, the number of persons under sentence of death should decline.

As noted, in 2002, 159 death sentences were imposed and 71 executions carried out. These numbers would suggest an increase in the death-sentenced

Table I-2	Executions and Prisoners Under Sentence of Death as of December 31, 2002			
Executions during 2002		**Number of prisoners under sentence of death**		**Jurisdictions without death penalty**
Texas	33	California	614	Alaska
Oklahoma	7	Texas	450	District of Columbia
Missouri	6	Florida	366	Hawaii
Georgia	4	Pennsylvania	241	Iowa
Virginia	4	North Carolina	206	Maine
Ohio	3	Ohio	205	Massachusetts
Florida	3	Alabama	191	Michigan
South Carolina	3	Illinois	159	Minnesota
Alabama	2	Arizona	120	North Dakota
Mississippi	2	Georgia	112	Rhode Island
North Carolina	2	Oklahoma	112	Vermont
Louisiana	1	Tennessee	95	West Virginia
California	1	Louisiana	86	Wisconsin
		25 other jurisdictions	600	
Total	71	Total	3557	

pool. This is only true, however, if execution is the only possible way off death row, which it is not. There is the possibility that an inmate prevails on his habeas petition or his sentence is commuted or, as becomes increasingly relevant as the death-row population ages, a prisoner may die. In 2002, 25 persons died while under sentence of death—21 by natural causes, 3 by suicide, and 1 at the hands of another prisoner. Another 83 prisoners had their death sentences overturned by appellate courts. Thus a total of 179 prisoners exited death row in 2002—71 by execution, 25 by death, and 83 by prevailing on appeal—exceeding by 20 the number of sentences imposed and explaining the down tick in the number of prisoners under sentence of death, depicted in **Figure I-1**.

Two items are striking in **Table I-3**, which tracks the outcome of cases in which prisoners have been sentenced to death: the first is that even among death-sentenced defendants, executions are a rarity—barely 11% of prisoners sentenced to die since 1973 have been executed. The second is that prisoners remain on death row for a long time. More than half of the prisoners sentenced to death in 1990 are still on death row. In 1974, 149 defendants were sentenced to die—two are still on death row.

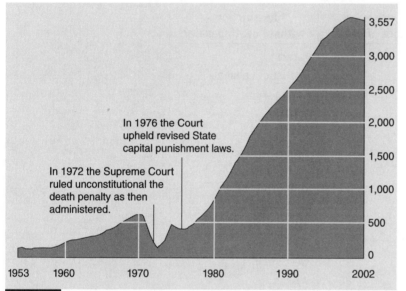

In 1972 the Supreme Court ruled unconstitutional the death penalty as then administered.

In 1976 the Court upheld revised State capital punishment laws.

Figure I-1 Prisoners under sentence of death, 1953–2002.

Since 1977, Texas, Virginia, Missouri, Oklahoma, and Florida have executed 544 prisoners, representing more than two thirds of the 820 executions that have been carried out since *Gregg*. Examining the geographic distribution of the modern death penalty, as shown in **Table I-4**, reveals that capital punishment in America is by and large a southern phenomenon.

Lethal injection is the most common method of execution, employed by 37 states, as shown in **Table I-5**. Nine states authorize electrocution, four states lethal gas, three states hanging, and three states firing squad. That this total exceeds the number of death penalty states (and indeed the number of states) is explained by the fact that 17 states authorize more than one method of execution—generally at the election of the condemned.

Tables I-6 and **I-7** present some demographic characteristics of prisoners under sentence of death. Two facts immediately stand out—blacks and men are represented in gross disproportion to their share of the general population. These anomalies differ, though in one significant respect—men are overrepresented in comparison to the share of murders they commit, blacks are underrepresented. Men have committed about 90% of all known murders since 1990. Blacks committed more than half the murders known to police during the same period.

The issue of race and the death penalty is discussed in Chapter 15. One thing seems fair to say with respect to race: if the death penalty is racist, the explanation is more complicated than has commonly been offered. That blacks commit a disproportionate share of murder does not disprove racism—it may be that police and prosecutors selectively target blacks and that the death penalty reinforces this discrimination. But it is also true that the kind of racism that has been identified by scholars—discrimination by race of victim—benefits blacks in a peculiar manner. Because blacks tend to kill blacks and because, according to statistics, prosecutors and juries value white lives more than black lives, blacks

Table I-3 — Prisoners Sentenced to Death and Outcome of Sentence, 1973–2002

| Year of sentence | Number sentenced to death | | | Number of prisoners removed from under sentence of death | | | | | Under sentence of death 12/31/2002 |
| | | | | Appeals or higher court overturned | | | | | |
		Execution	Other death	Death penalty statute	Conviction	Sentence	Sentence commuted	Other or unknown reasons	
1973	42	2	0	14	9	8	9	0	0
1974	149	10	4	65	15	30	22	1	2
1975	298	6	4	171	24	67	21	2	3
1976	233	14	5	136	17	43	15	0	3
1977	137	19	3	40	26	32	7	0	10
1978	185	36	6	21	36	65	8	0	13
1979	151	28	13	2	28	59	5	1	15
1980	173	45	13	3	30	50	7	0	25
1981	224	54	13	0	42	74	6	1	34
1982	265	58	17	0	38	71	8	1	72
1983	252	60	17	1	27	62	8	2	75
1984	285	58	14	2	44	65	7	8	87
1985	266	39	7	1	42	72	5	3	97
1986	300	59	20	0	45	54	7	5	110
1987	289	44	19	5	39	61	2	6	113
1988	290	45	12	1	32	58	4	0	138
1989	259	35	10	0	31	50	6	0	127
1990	252	33	9	0	35	40	2	0	133
1991	267	29	10	0	32	34	5	0	157
1992	287	29	10	0	24	39	7	0	178
1993	289	30	13	0	17	25	6	0	198
1994	315	28	10	0	23	30	3	0	221
1995	318	26	12	0	15	26	1	0	238
1996	320	15	8	0	20	33	2	0	242
1997	276	5	4	0	20	18	1	0	228
1998	300	8	6	1	14	15	1	0	255
1999	279	2	5	0	13	7	1	0	251
2000	231	3	2	0	3	6	0	0	217
2001	163	0	1	0	3	2	0	0	157
2002	159	0	1	0	0	0	0	0	158
Total, 1973–2002	7254	820	268	463	744	1196	176	30	3557

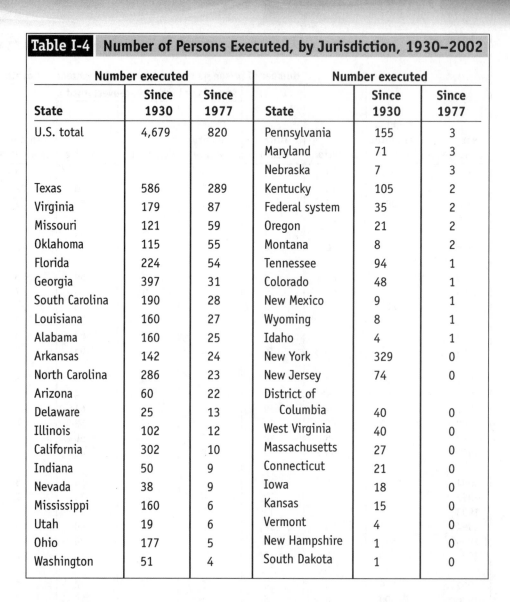

Table I-4	**Number of Persons Executed, by Jurisdiction, 1930–2002**				
	Number executed			**Number executed**	
State	**Since 1930**	**Since 1977**	**State**	**Since 1930**	**Since 1977**
U.S. total	4,679	820	Pennsylvania	155	3
			Maryland	71	3
			Nebraska	7	3
Texas	586	289	Kentucky	105	2
Virginia	179	87	Federal system	35	2
Missouri	121	59	Oregon	21	2
Oklahoma	115	55	Montana	8	2
Florida	224	54	Tennessee	94	1
Georgia	397	31	Colorado	48	1
South Carolina	190	28	New Mexico	9	1
Louisiana	160	27	Wyoming	8	1
Alabama	160	25	Idaho	4	1
Arkansas	142	24	New York	329	0
North Carolina	286	23	New Jersey	74	0
Arizona	60	22	District of Columbia	40	0
Delaware	25	13	West Virginia	40	0
Illinois	102	12	Massachusetts	27	0
California	302	10	Connecticut	21	0
Indiana	50	9	Iowa	18	0
Nevada	38	9	Kansas	15	0
Mississippi	160	6	Vermont	4	0
Utah	19	6	New Hampshire	1	0
Ohio	177	5	South Dakota	1	0
Washington	51	4			

may benefit from discrimination. They may be overrepresented on death row when compared to their presence in the population at large, but they are underrepresented when compared to the share of murders they commit.

The gender effect is most often explained by noting that women do not commit the kinds of murders that juries generally regard as most aggravated. Juries and prosecutors tend to target killers of vulnerable victims or police officers and people who kill in an especially cruel manner; most women murder in

Table I-5 Method of Execution by State

Lethal injection		Electrocution	Lethal gas
Alabama	Nevada	Alabama	Arizona
Arizona	New Hampshire	Arkansas	California
Arkansas	New Jersey	Florida	Missouri
California	New Mexico	Kentucky	Wyoming
Colorado	New York	Nebraska	
Connecticut	North Carolina	Oklahoma	
Delaware	Ohio	South Carolina	
Florida	Oklahoma	Tennessee	
Georgia	Oregon	Virginia	
Idaho	Pennsylvania		
Illinois	South Carolina		
Indiana	South Dakota	**Hanging**	**Firing squad**
Kansas	Tennessee	Delaware	Idaho
Kentucky	Texas	New Hampshire	Oklahoma
Louisiana	Utah	Washington	Utah
Maryland	Virginia		
Mississippi	Washington		
Missouri	Wyoming		
Montana			

situations stemming from domestic violence. This neutral explanation suggests that the discrimination in favor of women (or against men) is not invidious. If there is a real difference in the kinds of murders men and women commit, then the differences in sentencing of the two groups is not inherently discriminatory. Professor Joseph Katz makes the same argument about race in Chapter 15. He offers data showing that blacks tend to murder while committing other felonies, and shows that these kinds of crimes are generally regarded by society as more aggravated. But although race discrimination is generally perceived as an evil of death sentencing, gender discrimination is not. To be sure, there are good arguments to be made in favor of this disparity: one may question Professor Katz's data or conclusion, or note that the motive behind the preferential treatment of women is benign while the motive behind the harsher treatment of black killers is malevolent. All that can be said conclusively is that when the data is examined, the question is much more complicated than it appears at first glance.

	Demographic Characteristics of Prisoners under Sentence
Table I-6	**of Death, 2002**

Characteristic	Total at year end	Admissions	Removals
Total number under sentence of death	3557	159	179
	(%)	(%)	(%)
Gender			
Male	98.6	96.9	97.2
Female	1.4	3.1	2.8
Race			
White	54.3	52.2	67.0
Black	43.7	45.9	31.8
All other races	2.0	1.9	1.2
Hispanic origin			
Hispanic	11.5	14.9	9.5
Non-Hispanic	88.5	85.1	90.5
Education			
8th grade or less	14.7	21.4	14.5
9th–11th grade	37.1	34.9	36.2
High school graduate/GED	38.5	37.3	36.2
Any college	9.7	6.3	13.1
Marital status			
Married	221	25.8	23.9
Divorced/separated	20.8	16.7	22.0
Widowed	2.8	6.8	3.1
Never married	54.3	50.7	50.9

With respect to age, it is clear that capital murderers are young. But there is no anomaly here: murderers are young generally—the murder rate is highest among 18–24-year-olds. The striking number in Table I-7 is the 74 persons under sentence of death for crimes committed while under the age of eighteen. The question of executing juveniles is raised in Chapter 12.

Table I-7	Age at Time of Arrest for Capital Offense and Age of Prisoners Under Sentence of Death at Year End 2002			
	Prisoners under sentence of death			
	At time of arrest		**On December 31, 2002**	
Age	**Number**	**Percent**	**Number**	**Percent**
Total number under sentence of death on 12/31/02	3299	100%	3557	100%
17 or younger	74	2.2	0	0.1
18–19	355	10.8	4	4.3
20–24	894	27.1	153	12.7
25–29	745	22.6	452	17.0
30–34	540	16.4	606	17.4
35–39	355	10.8	619	19.6
40–44	178	5.4	696	12.7
45–49	99	3.0	450	8.5
50–54	40	1.2	304	4.9
55–59	14	0.4	174	1.7
60–64	2	—	59	1.1
65 or older	3	0.1	40	
Mean age	28 yrs.		39 yrs.	
Median age	27 yrs.		39 yrs.	

III. *Public Opinion and the Death Penalty in America*

At least on the surface, public opinion in the United States overwhelmingly supports capital punishment. This statement must be made with qualification because polling data is malleable. The form in which questions about capital punishment are asked affects responses. For example, the baseline Gallup question is, "Are you in favor of the death penalty for a person convicted of murder?" When Gallup asked this question in May 2003, 74% of respondents expressed support for the death penalty; 24% said they opposed it. The question, "If you could choose between the following two approaches, which do you think is the better penalty for murder: the death penalty or life imprisonment with absolutely no possibility of parole?" generated results that called the baseline number into question. A slight majority (53%) said they favored the death penalty, and 44% favored life imprisonment. How much this result undermines the reliability of the response to the initial question is unclear. It may be that respondents to the baseline question—which Gallup has asked almost annually since 1953 (the historical results of these polls are presented in **Table I-8**)—do not initially contemplate the possibility of life without parole as an alternative sentence or change opinion when it is called to mind. It may also be that people do not believe life imprisonment is truly ever without the possibility of parole. It seems fair to say though, as with all poll questions, the manner in which questions about the death penalty are phrased has some impact on responses.

It also seems fair to say that there is a committed, ideological-based core of support for the death penalty that is not responsive to changes in forms of ques-

Table I-8 — Death Penalty Opinion

Q. Are you in favor of the death penalty for a person convicted of murder?

Year	For (%)	Against (%)	No opinion (%)	Year	For (%)	Against (%)	No opinion (%)
1953	68	25	7	January 1985	72	20	8
1956	53	34	13	November 1985	75	17	8
1957	47	34	18	1986	70	22	8
1960	53	36	11	1988	79	16	5
1965	45	43	12	1991	76	18	6
1966	42	47	11	1994	80	16	4
1967	54	38	8	1995	77	13	10
1969	51	40	9	1999	71	22	7
1971	49	40	11	2000	66	28	6
March 1972	50	41	9	2001	68	28	6
November 1972	57	32	11	May 2002	72	25	3
1976	66	26	8	October 2002	70	25	6
1978	62	27	11	May 2003	74	24	2
1981	66	25	9				

Gallup, 1953–2003

tions (see **Table I-9**). Three quarters of Americans express support for the death penalty despite the belief that the death penalty is unfairly applied and not highly effective, if effective at all. A majority of Americans believe that the death penalty does not deter murder. As many believe the death penalty is applied unfairly as believe it is applied fairly. More than eight in ten believe that at least some innocent people have been executed since the death penalty was reinstated following *Gregg*.

Why the support for the death penalty despite the persistent and serious reservations about its efficacy? The answer, at least in part, is that support for capital

Table I-9	Public Reservations about the Death Penalty

Do you feel the death penalty acts as a deterrent to murder—that it lowers the murder rate or not?[a]

Yes	43%
No	52%
No opinion	6%

From what you know, do you think that the death penalty is or is not applied fairly?[b]

Applied fairly	42%
Not applied fairly	42%
Depends	8%
Not sure	8%

Since the death penalty was reinstated in the 1970s, do you think many innocent people have been wrongly executed, only some, very few, or none?[c]

Many	8%
Some	33%
Very few	41%
None	11%
Don't know	7%

[a]ABC News/*Washington Post*, April 20–24, 2001; survey of 1003 adults nationwide.
[b]NBC News/*Wall Street Journal*, July 27–28, 2000; survey of 500 voters nationwide.
[c]*Newsweek*, June 1–2, 2000; survey of 750 adults nationwide.

punishment is based on fundamental views of justice. When people are asked the open-ended question of why they support the death penalty for murder, the most common answer by far—almost half of all responses—is that punishment should fit the crime (see **Table I-10**). Another 6% say convicted murderers deserve it; another 3% cite Biblical reasons. Thus almost six of ten people cite reasons that have nothing to do with efficiency. If people are to be given the death penalty because it is what they deserve—that is, for retributive reasons—whether the penalty deters or not is beside the point. Mistaken applications of the death penalty are of limited relevance. Because the death penalty gives murderers what they deserve, applying the death penalty increases the measure of justice distributed by the system. The only concern that might arise would be if large numbers of people are being executed in error, or so a retributivist's thinking might go.

It is, of course, an entirely separate matter whether retribution or any of the other articulated bases of support are compelling reasons to support the death

Table I-10 Reported Reasons for Favoring the Death Penalty	
Question: Why do you favor the death penalty for murder?	**(%)**
An eye for an eye/they took a life/fits the crime	48
Save taxpayers money/cost associated with prison	20
Deterrent for potential crimes/set an example	10
They deserve it	6
Support/believe in death penalty	6
Depends on the type of crime they commit	6
They will repeat their crime/keep them from repeating it	6
Biblical reasons	3
Relieves prison overcrowding	2
If there's no doubt the person committed the crime	2
Life sentences don't always mean life in prison	2
Don't believe they can be rehabilitated	2
Serve justice	1
Fair punishment	1
Would help/benefit families of victims	1
Other	3
No opinion	1

penalty. Part I of the book is devoted to analyzing each of these arguments on its own terms. For example, for the 10% of people who express support for the death penalty because it deters, Chapter 3 examines the evidence in favor of and against deterrence. The discussion here is not whether someone's view should be guided by utilitarian concerns such as deterrence, but whether, if they are guided by such views, the evidence should lead them to support the death penalty.

Some people have posited that support for the death penalty is borne of ignorance. In his concurrence in *Furman v. Georgia*, Justice Thurgood Marshall dismissed public support for the death penalty as uninformed and, hence, irrelevant to assessing contemporary standards of decency. Given information about the death penalty, Marshall wrote, "the great mass of citizens would conclude that the death penalty is immoral and therefore unconstitutional." The so-called Marshall hypothesis is that support for the death penalty is uninformed and that opinions are subject to persuasion.

Marshall's hypothesis presents an empirical question. Support for his proposition is less than convincing. To an individual whose support is based on retribution, one would expect that increased knowledge would have little or no impact on his opinion. The data consistently bears this out. Retributivists continue to express support for the death penalty even when informed of the so-called "facts" about capital punishment. (Marshall himself predicted this result; his reply is that retribution is not a legitimate aim of the criminal justice system.)

Opinions of nonretributivists are more malleable, though here too the evidence is mixed. One research design is to survey students in a death penalty course at the beginning of the semester and again at the end. If the Marshall hypothesis is valid, one would expect to find diminished support for the death penalty at the end of the course, particularly if the instructor is an opponent of the death penalty. I have maintained data of this kind over the four years I have taught about the death penalty. To be sure, some students change opinions. But a more powerful effect of education is to make people more invested in their own views and more convinced of the correctness of their beliefs, a result that persistently appears in other studies. Even in studies where malleability of opinion exceeds hardening, the death penalty retains majority support even after the subject's "education." I don't put "facts" and "education" in quotes pejoratively. I do it to draw attention to an obvious problem with testing the Marshall hypothesis: agreeing on what information may be presented as conclusively proved. Some "facts" that researchers offer to subjects are undeniably true—the death penalty has been abolished by a majority of Western European nations; poor people are much more likely to be sentenced to die than rich people. Other statements that have been presented in research are more debatable. One leading study on the Marshall hypothesis informed subjects (in addition to the preceding two facts) that "studies have *not* found that abolishing the death penalty has any significant effect on the murder rate in a state" and that "the death penalty costs the taxpayer less than life imprisonment."

Is it fair to classify these claims as facts and not beliefs? Does the death penalty's ineffectiveness as a deterrent belong in the same class of statements as the roundness of the Earth? My own judgment is that it does not. The higher cost of the death penalty comes close to an axiom, in my view, certainly closer than the absence of a deterrent effect (but this is only my weighing of the evidence). The central aim of this book is to enable readers to make precisely these judgments with unbiased data and balanced viewpoints, and to show the weakness of the cursory, one-sided approach that has often been taken when discussing the so-called facts about the death penalty. Even true facts require qualification. Though I believe the death penalty is more expensive than life imprisonment, the death penalty might be reformed to change this condition—appeals could be shortened, the defendant's right to present mitigating evidence could be restricted. And some facts need context. The poor are certainly more likely to receive the death penalty than the rich, just as blacks are disproportionately represented on death row, a fact also commonly relied upon by abolitionists. But it is also true that blacks and the poor commit a disproportionate share of murders. This is not to say that race or economic discrimination is not a problem or a valid argument against the death penalty, just that the data needs to be considered in context. The "facts" are not so clear as may seem at first blush. So it is with almost every aspect of capital punishment. The death penalty is not an isolated institution, it is practiced in a society rife with inequalities of many kinds; it is only to be expected that it reproduces some of these conditions. Again, this is not a defense of the death penalty, just an appeal to open-minded people to consider it in the fullness of its social and historical context.

The lack of evidence for the Marshall hypothesis is consistent with the demography of opinion, presented in **Table I-11**. Age, education, income, community membership, and politics have no correlation with attitudes. If the Marshall hypothesis were correct, one would expect to see education—or one of the proxies for education—correlate positively with opposition to the death penalty, but there is no evidence for any of this. The response might be that it is education about the death penalty that counts, not education generally, but this is not entirely convincing—one would also expect better educated people to be better read and more generally aware of social issues. The factors that do have some predictive value in the demographic data—gender and race—have no apparent relationship to education. According to the 2000 census, there is no material difference between the educational attainment of men and women. Blacks attend college less often than whites, though the gap has narrowed substantially over the past

Table I-11 Demographic Factors and Support for the Death Penalty

Question: Are you in favor of the death penalty for a person convicted of murder?

	Yes, in favor (%)	No, not in favor (%)	Don't know/ refused (%)
National	72	25	3
Sex			
Male	80	19	1
Female	64	31	5
Race			
White	77	21	2
Nonwhite	53	41	6
Black	47	49	4
Age			
18 to 29 years	73	26	1
30 to 49 years	75	22	3
50 to 64 years	67	32	1
50 years and older	68	27	5
65 years and older	69	23	8
Education			
College postgraduate	65	31	4
College graduate	79	20	1
Some college	70	28	2
High school graduate or less	73	22	5
Income			
$75,000 and over	74	24	2
$50,000 to $74,999	72	26	2
$30,000 to $49,999	68	29	3
$20,000 to $29,999	69	31	0
Under $20,000	77	18	5
Community			
Urban area	66	31	3
Suburban area	73	24	3
Rural area	76	21	3

Table I-11 continued			
Region			
East	68	29	3
Midwest	69	29	2
South	72	23	5
West	80	19	1
Politics			
Republican	75	22	3
Democrat	67	29	4
Independent	73	24	3

fifty years. It seems doubtful that education plays any role in shaping attitudes. Support or opposition to the death penalty appears to be a core belief.

On the other hand, if support for the death penalty is a core value, one would expect to find little change in support for the death penalty over time, absent some change in the demographics of the community. In fact, as presented earlier in Table I-9, public opinion has fluctuated rather dramatically since Gallup began surveying in the 1950s. One of the interesting puzzles in the death penalty universe is explaining these variations.

Demographic changes do not provide an adequate explanation. Women have not changed as a portion of the population since the early surveys. Minority population has changed somewhat. Blacks represented approximately 10% of the population in 1950; they represent approximately 12% today. This is not enough to materially alter the data, and in any case would predict lower support for the death penalty when, in fact, support has generally trended upwards. Furthermore the fluctuations in intragender and intrarace attitudes over time have paralleled almost precisely the fluctuations in the population as a whole (in other words, they are positively correlated).

One explanation that has been advanced is that support for the death penalty correlates with crime rates. The explanation is simple: when crime rates go up, people turn to harsher punishments—simple, but somewhat unsatisfying for at least three reasons. First, while crime rates and support for the death penalty mostly trend in the same direction, some notable exceptions can be found—homicide rates dropped sharply during the early 1980s while support for the death penalty rose. Second, if support for the death penalty derives from fear of crime, one would expect crime victims to be more likely to support the death penalty. No support for this can be found in the data: research persistently shows that crime victims are no more likely to support the death penalty than ordinary citizens. Finally, the crime-rate explanation doesn't make intuitive sense. If people perceive that the death penalty works, that is, that it deters crime, why would they abandon it when crime rates go down? It is not as if crime rates go to zero. So long as there is one murder in the community, one would imagine people who believe in deterrence to be calling for harsher penalties. And, of course, people who believe in retribution will always be demanding just deserts.

This is a question for future research. I will posit my own theory: support for the death penalty correlates with perceptions of the reliability of sentencing. Following the *Gregg* decision, support for the death penalty spiked upward for the first time in two decades. This could be attributed to the belief that *Gregg* reduced arbitrariness in death sentencing (whether this is true or not is the subject of Chapter 9). Some data suggests marginally diminishing support for the death penalty in the early 21st century. This is attributable to publicity surrounding DNA evidence and mistaken convictions. Of course this is merely a theory.

It is certainly true that support for the death penalty diminishes when it is applied to groups perceived to be less responsible than ordinary adults. **Table I-12** presents data on public opinion in 2001 on the death penalty for juveniles, the mentally infirm, and women. (The wisdom and constitutionality of applying the death penalty to juveniles, the mentally retarded, and the insane is discussed in Chapters 11–13.) The Supreme Court has ruled the death penalty unconstitutional for the mentally retarded and those who become insane while awaiting execution; the mentally ill and children are still eligible for capital punishment. Chapters 11–13 consider whether the Supreme Court has been consistent in these rulings and whether they are based on sound policy.

IV. *Questions About the Death Penalty in America*

If nothing else, the preceding discussion suggests the complexity of the questions that might be asked about the death penalty. One might ask is it just, or why

Table I-12	Attitudes Toward the Death Penalty for Selected Groups		
Question: Do you favor or oppose the death penalty for...?			
	Favor (%)	Oppose (%)	Don't know (%)
Juveniles	26	69	5
The mentally retarded	13	82	5
The mentally ill	19	75	5
Women	68	29	3

people believe it to be just, or whether if people were better informed they would believe it to be just. The research agenda of some scholars is devoted to answering just one facet of these questions.

The focus here is on the death penalty as public policy, so the book devotes more attention to the basic question—is it just?—than to the metaquestions such as why people consider it to be just. In considering the justness of the death penalty, one could spend a lifetime debating the proper grounds for the discussion; for example, should utilitarian considerations govern or pure retributive concerns? The focus here is on the quality of each argument on its own terms. The book does not consider in any detail whether utilitarian concerns should trump retributive concerns; it considers at great length the quality of the utilitarian arguments: Does the death penalty in fact deter? Does it save money versus life imprisonment? In that sense, the book presents what might be termed a segmented ethical examination, which is just one of several valid ways of critically examining an issue.

In assessing the body of constitutional law governing the death penalty, the agenda is set by the Supreme Court itself. The Court rejected the death penalty in *Furman* and reapproved it in *Gregg* based on concern with arbitrariness and, later, satisfaction that the concern had been addressed. So it seems reasonable to ask whether the Court has in fact reduced arbitrariness. Arbitrariness can be understood in different senses. The book considers many of the questions that might be asked. Are death sentences predictable? In other words, do the most deserving people receive the death penalty? Should certain groups of people be categorically excluded? Do insidious factors such as race infect the death sentencing process and, if so, is this an argument against capital punishment? Are trial procedures set up in such a manner as to produce predictable results? Is predictability always desirable? If unpredictability stems from empowering the juries to grant mercy, is this different from the unpredictability stemming from overzealous or improperly motivated prosecutors and juries?

One final thought: strongly held views offer a convenient way to avoid engaging many of these questions. If one categorically opposes the death penalty in all cases, whether the death penalty is implemented in a racist fashion is beside the point—it is unjust if it is racist, it is unjust if it is not racist. This is an approach one might take to the contents of this book. The far more interesting intellectual exercise is to consider the evidence on its own terms—regardless of one's views on the death penalty, to objectively assess whether the evidence of racism is convincing and sufficient grounds for change, and to ask the ultimate conditional question: If a death penalty is to be imposed, what procedures must be put in place, if any, to ensure that it is imposed in a fair manner? This is not to encourage people to toss aside their moral compasses, just to examine the material here with an open mind.

Moral Considerations

■ Moral Arguments About the Death Penalty— An Introduction

The moral debate over capital punishment is strikingly and uniquely robust. In most matters of public policy, people on either side usually can find some consensus among them. In the debate over affirmative action, for example, it is not seriously disputed that affirmative action leads to violations of the right to equal treatment. Those who nevertheless support affirmative action believe that it is permissible, or required, to depart from the principle of merit in order to achieve broader social aims: they believe that preferential treatment is required to compensate past wrongs, or to create role models to attract young minorities to professions previously viewed as unavailable to them, or that the whole notion of merit and qualification is itself riddled with prejudice. But across one axis there is agreement: affirmative action departs from the principle of merit in selection and substitutes grounds generally regarded as unacceptable, namely race and sex. In the best of all worlds, both sides agree, affirmative action would be unnecessary.

Death penalty proponents and abolitionists share no such common ground.

Many different kinds of arguments are made about the death penalty. They are usefully divided into three broad classes: utilitarian arguments, retributive arguments, and egalitarian arguments. Utilitarian arguments are appeals to the common good. Such arguments are forward looking; they seek to punish offenders for the future benefit that might be gained from punishment: for the deterrent effect the punishment might have against other prospective offenders and the offender himself, and for the benefit to public safety gained by incapacitating the offender. In short, utilitarian arguments consider the costs and benefits of competing forms of punishment.

Retributive arguments, by contrast, are appeals to desert. These arguments are backwards looking—the future benefit that might be gained from punishment is irrelevant, all that matters is that the offender is given what he deserves. To retributivists, the costs and benefits of punishment are inconsequential. Religious arguments might usefully be grouped under this heading. The ultimate source of authority in religious arguments is God, whereas retributivists appeal to rea-

1

son, but the ultimate aim of retributivists and those appealing to religion is the same—to do the right thing regardless of the consequences.

Egalitarian arguments are appeals to equity; people in the same position should be treated the same. There is some logic to thinking of egalitarian arguments as a subset of retributive arguments: all people, of course, deserve to be treated fairly. But in the context of the death penalty, at least, egalitarian arguments are persuasive (or unpersuasive) in a different way than basic retributive arguments. Several studies have shown a strong race-of-victim effect in the administration of the death penalty in America: people who kill whites are far more likely to receive the death penalty than people who kill blacks. Some proponents of capital punishment offer a classic retributivist response: this means only that justice is not being done in cases in which the murder victim is black. Pointing to an injustice in other similar cases—that is, too little punishment—does not mean that an injustice has been done in this case. Other proponents reject the desirability of equity entirely: evenhandedness is not generally a goal of the criminal justice system. Police and prosecutors do not succeed in capturing all offenders, and all convicted defendants are not treated the same way. Yet no one seriously contends that the distribution of criminal penalties should be halted because it is antiegalitarian. It thus seems useful to consider egalitarian arguments as a separate grouping.

These are the clearly differentiable modes of discourse, the different battlefields upon which this war is fought. Neither side is inclined to give an inch in any theater. Some advocates may emphasize the significance of retributive arguments, others utilitarian concerns, but neither side has made any meaningful concessions. Abolitionists tend to say, "It violates the dignity of man for the state to take a human life. Thus the death penalty would be wrong even if it did deter and save money, but in any case it does not deter and costs more than life imprisonment." Opponents say things like "The death penalty gives murderers what they deserve, and thus would be the proper punishment even it causes a brutalization effect—that is, even if it led to more murders—but in any case it does not lead to more murders; it deters murder and saves the public the cost of keeping inmates in prison for long terms." And so it goes. The only subject of consensus is that the death penalty is conclusively incapacitating. Executed defendants will never kill again, though even here there is debate. Abolitionists dispute that incapacitation is a special concern for murderers. Some evidence suggests that they are no more likely to recidivate than other kinds of criminals; hence, abolitionists say people who emphasize incapacitation should either support the death penalty for all criminals or none.

The object of this section is to evaluate each kind of argument on its own merit. This is the more interesting and constructive way to debate the issue. If someone tells you they support the death penalty because the Bible teaches an eye for an eye, it is far more effective to be able to respond by offering competing passages from the Old Testament than to argue that religion should have no place in public policy discourse. I term the first kind of argument horizontal, the second vertical. The succeeding sections all approach the issues horizontally. Whether or not deterrence as a legitimate aim of the criminal justice system is discussed, but the focus of this part of the book is on the quality of the competing studies that have examined the issue and what lessons, if any, may be drawn from the data.

The data on public opinion, discussed in the Introduction to the book, suggest that most people's opinions on capital punishment are heavily influenced by vertical arguments. Theists are far more likely to support the death penalty than atheists (although, paradoxically, the Roman Catholic Church opposes capital punishment). Blacks, perhaps more sensitive to issues of race and equity, are more likely to oppose the death penalty than whites. So in some sense horizontal arguments are beside the point, because often people will argue past one another on this issue. But in another significant sense, arguments of this kind are even more important: if people are committed to a worldview, if they are strictly utilitarian for example, and if they can be persuaded on their own terms that their position is mistaken, say by conclusive evidence of deterrence or savings, then their minds can be changed.

Chapters 1 and 2 consider retributive concerns and religious arguments. Chapters 3 through 6 address the utilitarian issues of deterrence, risk of recidivism, and cost. Chapter 7 considers the risk of executing innocents, which has both utilitarian and retributive consequences.

Retribution

■ Retribution—Introduction

Retribution is the notion that punishment is imposed because it is deserved. Murderers are to be given the death penalty because that is the penalty they have earned by their offense. The philosopher Immanuel Kant wrote that retribution is grounded in respect for the autonomy of the offender. If a criminal is punished to deter others from committing a similar crime, then they are being treated as a means to an end. If a criminal is punished too little or not at all, perhaps because of some mitigating factor in his personal history, then the notion of his free will is denied. Modern theorists offer competing formulations of retribution and different bases for its grounding, but all stand in contrast to consequentialist defenses of the death penalty. The death penalty is right or wrong, regardless of whether it deters crime or what its cost. It is right even if it serves no other purpose than to give the criminal his due. As Kant famously put it, "Even if a civil society were to dissolve itself by common agreement, the last murderer remaining in prison must first be executed." Kant's teachings are excerpted in the Critical Documents section that follows.

This is unquestionably a powerful idea, and public support for the death penalty is—at least on the surface—largely based on notions of retribution. In most polls, "an eye for an eye" or "punishment should fit the crime" is the plurality reason offered by proponents for their support of capital punishment. In a 2001 Gallup poll, 48% of respondents cited retribution as the basis for their support, more than twice the level of support offered for any other justification.

The concern is the quality of the argument on its own terms. If retribution is the true currency of justice, does it dictate support for the death penalty? Here we ask the horizontal question, as we do throughout the book: should a retributivist support capital punishment? The retributive argument for the death penalty has considerable appeal. Murderers have committed the most serious offense imaginable; they deserve to be treated in the most severe manner.

One objection to retributive theory is that it presumes a baseline condition of equality in society that is not present in practice. An essential presupposition of retribution is that the offender is fully responsible for his crime. Yet, the United States executes juveniles and the mentally ill. Hugo Adam Bedau suggests that it is hypocritical for retributive defenders of the death penalty not to object with equal force to the execution of these less responsible individuals. The retributivist response to this claim is that even the young and the mentally ill understand the difference between right and wrong, and so long as they do understand this difference it is just to hold them accountable for their actions.

Professor Bedau's argument raises an important point about retribution—it has both a positive and negative component. Retribution requires that offenders be given as much punishment as they deserve but no more than they deserve. Neither abolitionists nor defenders of the death penalty consider the full implications of retributivism. Abolitionists often point to the execution of innocents as a retributive injustice and cause for abolishing the death penalty without recognizing the retributive injustice of not giving defendants deserving the death penalty their due. Defenders of the death penalty sometimes make the same mistake and demand the death penalty on retributive grounds without acknowledging the problem of innocence and the difficulty in determining with certainty which defendants deserve to die and which do not, each a serious concern from the standpoint of retribution.

Another commonly raised objection is that while retribution offers a compelling definition of who should be punished—the guilty and no one else—it is less effective at defining the quantity of punishment that the offender should receive. Why does the murderer deserve death and not life imprisonment without the possibility of parole? It is not useful to rely upon *lex talionis*—"an eye for an eye"—to resolve this question. We do not generally think that rapists deserve to be raped, nor that car thieves deserve to be punished by having their cars taken from them. For some crimes, it is not even possible to imagine the equivalent punishment. How would one defraud a fraud? What would be the appropriate punishment for a traitor or a kidnapper or an embezzler? Albert Camus argued that the death penalty is too much punishment for murderers:

> *An execution is not simply death. It is just as different from the privation of life as a concentration camp is from prison. It adds to death a rule, a public premeditation known to the future victim, an organization which is itself a source of moral sufferings more terrible than death. Capital punishment is the most premeditated of murders, to which no criminal's deed, however calculated can be compared. For there to be an equivalency, the death penalty would have to punish a criminal who had warned his victim of the date at which he would inflict a horrible death on him and who, from that moment onward, had confined him at his mercy for months. Such a monster is not encountered in private life.*

One response to the uncertainty of the appropriate quantity of punishment might be to say that criminals deserve the punishment the law provides, a legalistic notion of retributivism. If the law says that car thieves are to be punished by twenty years in prison, and the law is known within the community, and the thief chooses to steal anyway, then this is the punishment the offender deserves. This also means that murderers deserve death in Texas, but not in Massachusetts, and that what they deserve may change from year to year as new legislators enter office. This is an unsatisfying and arbitrary notion of retributivism. Even the most devoted retributivists generally concede that the calculation of punishment requires a more nuanced formula than either legalistic retributivism or *lex talionis* provide.

The leading modern solution to this problem has been a notion of proportionate retributivism. Penalties are ranked in order of harshness; crimes are ranked in order of severity. The most severe crime is paired with the harshest punishment, the second most severe crime is paired with the second harshest punishment, and so on until all crimes have been paired with proportionate punishments. This method dictates relative levels of desert—a murderer deserves a harsher punishment than a thief—but this method does not dictate any absolute levels of punishment. If murder is the most severe crime, the murderer may justly receive a 10-year prison term if that is the harshest punishment the society deems just, and every other criminal, thieves included, should receive less severe penalties.

In the debate that follows, Claire Finkelstein argues that even proportionate retributivism does not dictate support for the death penalty. Finkelstein notes that proportionate retributivists do not believe that all forms of punishment are acceptable—virtually everyone agrees that torture is unacceptable. But there is no objective theory by which to determine which acts are morally acceptable and which are not. If torture is off limits, Finkelstein argues, then surely the death penalty is too. Finkelstein posits that the death penalty is fundamentally at odds with the retributivist's recognition of the physical integrity of human beings. Michael Davis responds by arguing that it may be possible to construct a common standard of humanness: that we can determine with certainty what punishments are morally tolerable within a particular society. Davis argues that in the contemporary United States, early death—which is what capital punishment inflicts—is not so rare as to be inhumane.

■ Retribution—Critical Documents

Immanuel Kant, "The Right of Punishing" from *Metaphysics of Morals*

Judicial or juridical punishment is to be distinguished from natural punishment, in which crime as vice punishes itself, and does not as such come within the cognizance of the legislator. Juridical punishment can never be administered merely as a means for promoting another good either with regard to the criminal himself or to civil society, but must in all cases be imposed only because the individual on whom it is inflicted has committed a crime. For one man ought never to be dealt with merely as a means subservient to the purpose of another, nor be mixed up with the subjects of real right. The penal law is a categorical imperative; and woe to him who creeps through the serpent-windings of utilitarianism to discover some advantage that may discharge him from the justice of punishment.

But what is the mode and measure of punishment which public justice takes as its principle and standard? It is just the principle of equality, by which the pointer of the scale of justice is made to incline no more to the one side than the other. It may be rendered by saying that the undeserved evil which any one commits on another is to be regarded as perpetrated on himself. Hence it may be said: "If you slander another, you slander yourself; if you steal from another, you steal from yourself; if you strike another, you strike yourself; if you kill another, you kill yourself." This is the right of retaliation (jus talionis); and, properly understood, it is the only principle which in regulating a public court, as distinguished from mere private judgment, can definitely assign both the quality and the quantity of a just penalty. All other standards are wavering and uncertain; and on account of other considerations involved in them, they contain no principle conformable to the sentence of pure and strict justice.

It may appear, however, that difference of social status would not admit the application of the principle of retaliation, which is that of "like with like." But although the application may not in all cases be possible according to the letter, yet as regards the effect it may always be attained in practice, by due regard being given to the disposition and sentiment of the parties in the higher social sphere. Thus a pecuniary penalty on account of a verbal injury may have no direct proportion to the injustice of slander; for one who is wealthy may be able to indulge himself in this offence for his own gratification. Yet the attack committed on the honour of the party aggrieved may have its equivalent in the pain inflicted upon the pride of the aggressor, especially if he is condemned by the judgment of the court, not only to retract and apologize, but to submit to some meaner ordeal, as kissing the hand of the injured person.

But whoever has committed murder, must die. There is, in this case, no juridical substitute or surrogate, that can be given or taken for the satisfaction of justice. There is no likeness or proportion between life, however painful, and death; and therefore there is no equality between the crime of murder and the retaliation of it but what is judicially accomplished by the execution of the criminal. His death, however, must be kept free from all maltreatment that would make the humanity suffering in his person loathsome or abominable. Even if a civil society resolved to dissolve itself with the consent of all its members—as might be supposed in the case of a people inhabiting an island resolving to separate and scatter themselves throughout the whole world—the last murderer lying in the prison ought to be executed before the resolution was carried out. This ought to be done in order that every one may realize the desert of his deeds, and that blood-guiltiness may not remain upon the people; for otherwise they might all be regarded as participators in the murder as a public violation of justice.

■ Retribution—Perspectives

■ Issue—Does Retribution Demand the Death Penalty?

Claire Finkelstein, "Death and Retribution"

I. *Introduction*

It is often supposed that a theory of punishment predicated on desert lends support to the death penalty. What leads to this assumption is a prior thought about the appropriate punishment for murder: If we are to punish murderers as they deserve, we will inflict on them what they inflicted on their victims, namely death. This association between a desert-based theory of punishment, known as retributivism, and the death penalty appears not only in academic writings on the subject, but in popular views of punishment as well. Public rhetoric in support of the death penalty, for example, is nearly always retributivist. Politicians urging its use in a particular case will more readily speak of justice and desert than of future dangerousness or setting an example for others. They evidently think the retributivist argument for death more appealing than the utilitarian arguments that might be made in its favor.

In my view, however, the faith that death penalty proponents place in the retributivist theory of punishment is misplaced. In this essay I argue that retributivism fails to justify the use of death as punishment, and, moreover, that a desert-based theory of punishment is particularly ill-suited to such a task. I shall not argue against retributivism as a theory of punishment per se. My more limited suggestion is that even if retributivism succeeds in justifying the practice of punishment overall, it cannot provide a compelling reason for including the penalty of death in that practice.

II. *The Basic Retributivist Argument for the Death Penalty*

Retributivism is the theory of punishment that asserts that punishment is justified because, and only to the extent that, the criminal deserves to be punished in virtue of the wrongfulness of his act. Traditionally, the core of the retributivist's argument for any specific penalty is the doctrine of *lex talionis*, the idea that a person deserves to experience the suffering or moral evil he has inflicted on his victim. Taken literally, *lex talionis* is an absurd doctrine—no one thinks we should rape rapists, assault assailants, or burgle the homes of burglars. This difficulty making sense of *lex talionis* has accordingly led some retributivists to suggest that retributivism is most compelling as a general justification for the institution as a whole, without thinking of it as containing a further theory of the measure of punishment. But in the absence of its accompanying doctrine of *lex talionis*, or any other way of giving content to the notion of desert, the retributivist will remain unable to justify any specific penalty, including the death penalty. Given that retributivism is absurd if accompanied by a literal interpretation of *lex talionis*, and vacuous (for our purposes) if articulated without *lex talionis*, the retributivist must attempt to cast his defense of the death penalty in terms of a more approximate system for matching crimes with punishments, one that does not insist that the punishment exactly fit the crime.

Most retributivists who argue in favor of the death penalty attempt to do just this. That is, they abandon *lex talionis* in favor of a similar idea, namely that a criminal deserves to suffer some approximate match for what he inflicted on his victim. But this approach turns out to be more problematic than one might have thought. Begin by considering just how approximate the doctrine must be to work. It is not only that presently we are unwilling to inflict some of the more extreme harms, like rape and torture, that criminals sometimes inflict on their victims. The prohibited list also includes more modest harms, such as forcing a member of a fraternity to imbibe too much alcohol or requiring a rogue cop to remove his clothes and walk half a mile in winter along a public road, both harms that such perpetrators have inflicted on their victims. Indeed, once one begins to consider all the deviant forms of behavior our criminal codes outlaw, it is clear that the vast majority of criminal acts are not ones we feel entitled to impose by way of punishment. There are really only several criminal acts that we regard as yielding acceptable forms of punishment: false imprisonment, theft, and in some states murder. The retributivist who wishes to match crimes with punishments must come up with a theory that would limit the deserved penalty to the three forms of criminal conduct listed above.

There are two possible strategies available to the retributivist in order to accomplish this end. The first distributes punishments proportionately, so that the worst crimes are matched with the worst penalties, and so on down the line. This method dictates only relative levels of desert, rather than requiring any particular objective measure of what criminal acts deserve what treatment. We might call this version of retributivism the "proportionate penalty" theory. One can think of this strategy as an alternative to lax talons or as an interpretation of it; the label is unimportant. For the sake of clarity, let us treat *lex talionis* as the theory that calls for a strict equivalence between crime and punishment. Proportionate penalty will thus be a modification of the basic *lex talionis* doctrine. Whatever its other merits, this latter approach will not help the retributivist to argue for the death penalty—the method does not provide an argument that we ought to include a given penalty on the list of acceptable penalties. It merely insists on taking available punishments—that is, punishments we are already willing to inflict—and imposing them on perpetrators in order of severity according to the seriousness of the criminal acts performed.

The second, and more promising strategy is to attempt to establish a moral equivalence between crimes and permissible punishments. This strategy asserts that the perpetrator should suffer an amount equivalent to the harm or moral evil inflicted on the victim, but the kind of harm or moral evil involved need not match. That is, instead of either assigning the same harm or evil as punishment that the offender inflicted on his victim, or fixing penalties proportionately by making sure that the right intervals obtain between levels of punishments, we can match crimes with punishments on an absolute scale, but establish only a rough moral equivalence between the two. We would seek to inflict on the perpetrator by way of punishment the nearest morally permissible form of punishment to the act the perpetrator committed. Let us call this version of retributivism the "moral equivalence" theory of justified punishment.

Arguably, Kant suggested a moral equivalence approach to punishment on at least one occasion:

> *A monetary fine on account of a verbal injury, for example, bears no relation to the actual offence, for anyone who has plenty of money could allow himself such an offence whenever he pleased. But the injured honour of one individual might well be closely matched by the wounded pride of the other, as would happen if the latter were compelled by judgment and right not only to apologize publicly, but also, let us say, to kiss the hand of the former, even though he were of lower station.*

The moral equivalence theory has no way of identifying which penalties are morally permissible and which are not. That is, whatever other lessons we should draw from Kant's view on punishment, we should understand him as believing that a perpetrator can be treated in a way that is morally commensurate with the harm and suffering he inflicted on the victim, without having to inflict that very same punishment on him. And while Kant does not articulate the theory in this way, the basic strategy of such views is to try to distinguish what a person deserves, in some absolute sense, from what it is permissible for society to inflict on him by way of punishment. The moral equivalence theory thus maintains that while a criminal who locks his victim in the trunk of a car before killing her may "deserve" to be locked in a trunk himself before being executed, it is not permissible for us to inflict such a punishment on him. The moral equivalence theory suggests that we eliminate forms of treatment that are impermissible from our roster of available punishments, and within that constraint, attempt to match the offender's criminal act as closely as possible with the punishment we inflict on him.

But the moral equivalence theory is woefully incomplete. By itself it has no way of identifying which penalties are morally permissible and which are not. How do we know, for example, that locking a perpetrator in the trunk of a car and then killing him is impermissible, but that simply executing him is not? The moral equivalence theory needs to be supplemented by another moral theory, one that tells us which penalties are morally permissible and which are not.

Let us suppose the moral equivalence theorist manages to supply such an account and that we accept the theory in that form. Still, it is not clear that the moral equivalence theory can be used to defend the death penalty. There are at least two problems with that view. First, even in this modified form, there clearly are some penalties we think of as morally unacceptable but which are less severe than death. And if we wish to rule out those penalties, we will be compelled to rule out death as well. Consider torture. It is difficult to see torture as off-limits on the grounds that it is unacceptably severe, because it is actually most plausible to think of torture as less severe than death. The moral equivalence theorist's own method makes it clear why this is so: If penalties are to be the equivalent of crimes, then we should rank penalties the way we rank crimes. But we think of murder as a more heinous crime than any non-lethal assault. So torture should be a less severe penalty than death. But if torture is an unacceptable penalty, it should follow that death is unacceptable as well, given that death is a more severe penalty than torture. Let us call this argument on behalf of the abolitionist the "severity response."

Admittedly there are some problems with the severity response. First, the death penalty proponent might dispute the claim that death is more severe than torture. Torture is more severe, he might argue, because it is more uncivilized and more brutal than death. That torture is widely regarded by everyone, on all sides of the argument, as unacceptable but death is not seems to bear out the death penalty proponent's intuition on this point. But what about the fact that most perpetrators themselves would choose torture instead of death? The death penalty proponent might say that the criminal's own preferences cannot be the measure of the severity of a punishment. It is perfectly possible, for example, that a given criminal would prefer to spend a night in jail than to pay a small fine, because he is very attached to money and does not particularly mind confinement. But this would not show that the night in jail is a less severe penalty than the fine. There are also those who would prefer death to life imprisonment without parole. Yet surely these preferences do not imply that life imprisonment is a more severe penalty, even for those defendants.

Against this (and on behalf of the abolitionist), it might be noted that we can speak of the pain of having a tooth pulled and compare it favorably to the pain of having a severe burn, without its being infallibly true that everyone would choose the former over the latter. We are entitled to think of incarceration as "painful" because we assess that treatment in general terms. It need not be the case that everyone who has ever been "punished" by way of incarceration found that treatment painful. There are many penalties we would readily classify as less severe than torture and death that we do not hesitate to say are impermissible to impose.

Finally, the death penalty proponent might object to the severity argument by pointing out that severity does not correlate terribly well with impermissibility. There are many penalties we would readily classify as less severe than torture and death that we do not hesitate to say are impermissible to impose. There is, for example, great resistance to the recent turn toward shame sanctions, such as forcing a convicted sex offender to display a sign outside of his dwelling revealing his status or forcing him to affix sex offender license plates to his car. It is also questionable whether it is permissible to sterilize repeat sex offenders, or to force female adolescent offenders to subject themselves to mandatory birth control measures like Depo-Provera. If the abolitionist's severity argument were correct, however, we would have to take the lowest unacceptable penalty on the list of penalties and say that any penalty more severe than it would be morally unacceptable. This strategy would quickly rule out most sentences currently inflicted for felonies, since many objectionable shame sanctions are less severe than most terms of imprisonment.

On behalf of the abolitionist once again, and against this counter argument, we might say that perhaps we are wrong to reject shame sanctions and other minor interferences with liberty. Indeed, the above argument suggests a compelling reason to allow them, namely, that imposing them may enable us to avoid inflicting more severe penalties that involve significantly greater loss of liberty. If, for example, we have the choice between a shame sanction—like a sign or a license plate—and a period of incarceration, and if both penalties are equally effective from the standpoint of deterrence, we arguably have an obligation to inflict the shame sanction, since it is the less invasive penalty. On balance, then, the argument we offered above on the abolitionist's behalf seems to me a good one—that if we reject torture because it is too severe, we should reject death as a penalty because it is more severe. This argument, however, seems to require that we revise our intuitions about a number of lesser penalties.

Because neither proponents nor abolitionists offers an account of severity or even particularly attempts to explain its stance on death, the debate between proponent and opponent seems arbitrary. It quickly reduces to the question of whether we think death an excessively harsh penalty—and that is not a terribly nuanced ground on which to settle the matter.

But we should not be too hasty to declare the argument a draw. The result is that the death penalty proponent bears the burden of proof. The retributivist is particularly affected by this burden of proof claim, for by his lights killing a person is such an evil act that the killer incurs a tremendous moral debt, repayable only with the murderer's own life. It would seem to follow that an executioner, or society more generally, who takes a person's life must incur this same moral debt, unless his act is morally justified. In the absence of such a justification, the executioner, and society as his accomplice, is no better than a murderer.

III. *Conventional Retributivism*

There is another version of the retributivist's argument we must at least briefly consider, according to which principles of desert should be understood as grounded in contractarian agreement. This view enjoys a substantial advantage over ordinary retributivism. The version of retributivism that is grounded in consent stands in an entirely different position relative to that presumption against punishment with which we began. Here the presumption, if anything, works the other way around: We seem entitled to assume, at least as an initial matter, that a treatment to which a person has consented is one it is morally acceptable to inflict on him. If it can indeed be shown that there is a consensual basis for treating the worst criminals as deserving of death, it will be much less difficult to justify inflicting it on them.

According to the view we are now considering, the reason the person who commits a particularly vicious murder deserves to die is that he has agreed to the norms that dictate this treatment. I suggest we call this "conventional retributivism," since this account makes the notion of desert, which lies at the heart of the retributivist approach, dependent on the prior agreement of those who will be affected by it. There are two versions of this kind of approach. According to the first version, we can actually think of the criminal as agreeing to his own punishment, since the criminal act itself constitutes the criminal's acceptance of the punishment that is later imposed on him. This is what I shall call the "voluntarist" theory of punishment. The central thought of the voluntarist account is that the criminal gives his tacit consent to be punished by performing the criminal act in the first place.

There are some problems with this account. First, it is not at all clear that the consent that attaches to the voluntarily performed act should be thought to transfer to a consequence of that act the agent foresees but does not intend. Second, the voluntarist argument justifies far more than we are comfortable allowing by way of legitimate punishment. This is because justifications for punishment based on consent lack a principle of proportionality that would limit the level of punishment that could be imposed for a particular crime. Thus it would be perfectly acceptable to assign the death penalty for a minor traffic offense, as long as the offender was aware of the risk of receiving that penalty when he voluntarily broke the law. Although someone might be prepared to embrace this consequence of a consensual account, it seems a deeply objectionable feature of this theory, because it would put the consensual account out of sync with our prevailing practices of punishment. This is a problem that should worry the retributivist, since retributivism trades particularly heavily on intuitions about which penalties "fit" with which acts, it does not appear to be open to the retributivist to dispense with proportionality concerns.

There is, however, a second version of conventional retributivism. On this version, instead of thinking of consent as operating act-by-act, and therefore looking for a way of establishing the criminal's consent to the actual punishment he suffers, we should understand the entity to which the criminal consents as a general institution, or set of principles, which in turn provide a justification for a particular treatment of a given offender. The consent, that is, operates at the level of what Rawls calls the "basic structure," instead of at the level of the institution's particular response to the performance of a given prohibited act.

The question we must now ask is whether this "consensual" account of punishment would favor the death penalty. The question is whether individuals in an antecedent position of choice would have chosen the death penalty as part of the most rational means of dealing with those who commit the worst violations of the beneficial social rules that have been adopted. The argument that they would goes as follows. Each person enters into society because he fears for his bodily security and longevity. Putative members of society would choose to include the death penalty in the schedule of available penalties for the worst crimes since, assuming the death penalty deters, they would thereby increase the expected benefits of a system of punishment. The argument for the death penalty, then, is that it increases each person's expected security.

Against the above argument, however, one should note that every member of society must also take into account the possibility that he will be subject to the death penalty, either because he chooses to commit a crime for which the death penalty is authorized, or because he is wrongfully thought to have committed such a crime. The death penalty thus also decreases each person's expected security. Thus the increased security provided by the deterrent benefits of having the death penalty must be balanced for each rational individual against the decreased personal security the death penalty also involves. Rational agents selecting rules for the governance of society would choose to have a death penalty if it turned out that the added deterrent benefits of having that penalty, over and above the deterrent benefits of life sentences, were greater than the decreased security to each person from the possibility of being subject to the death penalty themselves. Arguably it would be rational for contracting agents to include the death penalty in the rules governing punishment.

But what about the person who is erroneously put to death? For him, there is no net increase in expected security. As it turns out, his bodily security will have been destroyed by the existence of the death penalty. He would probably have done considerably better if he had lived with the increased threat of being the victim of a violent crime, and avoided the death penalty (even if he had to spend the rest of his life in prison anyway). And arguably since each person knows *ex ante* that he may end up in this position *ex post*, he cannot regard the death penalty as rationally motivated.

So whether rational agents in a contractarian scheme would agree to the death penalty under the circumstances is a complicated matter. If the *ex ante* expected security of the death penalty is positive, on one view this would be sufficient to make it rational for putative members of society to agree to it, even if the death penalty could end up leaving any given individual worse off than if he had not agreed to it. On another view, however, for putative members of society to agree to the death penalty, each person must believe that no matter how things turn out, he will be better off under the death penalty regime than he would be in its absence. Let us make a very implausible assumption, namely, that the deterrent benefits from the death penalty are so great as to leave even the person put to death under its rule better off than he would be in a society that did not include the death penalty in its available punishments. On this hypothesis, the difference between the two forms of the consensual account would disappear, and we have reason to think that the consensual approach to punishment would endorse the death penalty.

But even if rational agents can regard their expected security as improved by the existence of the death penalty (and indeed even if the death penalty meets the stronger condition of leaving all members of society better off than they would be in its absence), it need not be the case that rational individuals would institute it. For there are deontological norms to which the retributivist is committed, and these arguably counsel against legitimizing an agreement with a person to put him to death. To see this, consider a different, but instructive example, the case of the "Kidney Society."

Suppose everyone were at some small risk of finding himself with two failing kidneys. In order to protect against the risk of needing a kidney and having access to none, a group of people enter into an agreement to supply one another with a kidney by lottery, should one of the members of the group end up in this situation. The terms of the agreement specify that if any member of the group finds himself needing a kidney to survive, a lottery would be held to determine who would supply that individual with the needed kidney. Once a person is chosen by lot to supply the kidney, he would have no choice but to yield, and a kidney could be removed, by force if need be, in order to supply the needed kidney to the person with dual kidney failure. In this case, we could say that there is no benefit to the person who must have his kidney removed as the upshot of the lottery. He is clearly better off with two kidneys than with one. From his perspective, the gamble has not turned out to be worth it. But there was a benefit to him in entering into the agreement with others in the first place. We can therefore hypothesize that if he thinks the danger of dual kidney failure sufficiently great, and the loss to himself of being the one to be chosen by lot to donate a kidney either sufficiently remote or sufficiently bearable, he may regard the terms of the Kidney Society's agreement beneficial on the whole, making it fair to enforce its terms when he resists its application to himself. Like the increased net security we hypothesized the death penalty might provide, the members of the Kidney Society enjoy an increase in the net expected health benefits they experience, even counting the "costs" of having to provide a kidney.

Yet there are reasons to suppose that forcibly removing an objector's kidney would not be justifiable on consensual grounds, for it is not at all clear that rational agents concerned to maximize their long-term well-being would embrace the kidney scheme, or that ultimately it would be rational for individuals to ensure against kidney loss in this way. Despite the fact that each person can regard himself as better off living in a society in which he has insurance against dual kidney failure, at the risk of having to provide one of two extraneous kidneys himself, rational agents might not prefer a social scheme that provides them with such benefits. Rational agents might not want to select the "meta-regime" in which it was permissible to attack a non-consenting donor in the way necessary to enforce the Kidney Society lottery, even if the donation were one that the donor had putatively agreed to *ex ante* by signing up for the Kidney Society. One has only to reflect on the extreme discomfort we would have enforcing the kidney donation agreement if the person who had drawn the short straw in the lottery objected. Would we be willing to enforce such an agreement, solely on the grounds that the unlucky lottery participant had benefited from the insurance such a scheme gave him up until now? It goes without saying that no court in this country would order specific performance for such an agreement. Even if organ donation agreements were not void as contrary to public policy, the most one could expect to win against a recalcitrant donor would be monetary damages for the failure to turn over his kidney.

Presumably what bothers us about enforcing a kidney lottery is that we think the person who draws the short straw in the lottery has rights to bodily integrity, rights that he did not, and could not, contract away in the initial agreement to enter the lottery. While we might imagine contracting away some substitute for one's kidney—monetary compensation, for example—we cannot quite understand one's own bodily organs as themselves subject to voluntary renunciation. Indeed, a retributivist ought to have particularly strong objections to seeing rights to bodily integrity as the subject of a contract between rational agents, for it is usually because of the retributivist's view of the robustness of such rights on the victim's part that he is so confident of his judgment that the murderer deserves to die for violating them.

IV. *Conclusion*

If the retributivist seeks to defend the death penalty by claiming that an offender deserves to suffer precisely the treatment he has inflicted on his victim, the theory will prove absurd and morally repugnant: We simply are not prepared to rape the rapist and assault the assailant. So he must try to find the "moral equivalent" of the offender's criminal act instead, ruling out immoral acts and restricting available penalties to morally acceptable forms of punishment. But which acts are morally acceptable? Many penalties we currently consider morally impermissible, such as torture, are actually less severe than death. And that suggests that whatever method the moral equivalence theorist uses to eliminate torture could also be used to eliminate death. So unless the retributivist is prepared to allow that criminals can be tortured, it will be hard for him to employ a moral equivalence strategy to argue for the death penalty. And in the absence of a clear justification for using death as a punishment, the death penalty is morally impermissible, given that there is a presumption against the infliction of any painful, involuntary treatment.

There is, however, another possibility for justifying the death penalty along retributivist lines, and this is to combine the basic retributivist approach with a consensual theory of punishment: Criminals would be subject to an agreed upon roster of deserved penalties, allocated according to general moral principles they endorse. On this strategy, it would not be necessary to justify the death penalty per se, since a treatment to which an offender has himself consented is at least presumptively morally acceptable. The most compelling version of what I have been calling conventional retributivism sees the offender as having agreed to norms that govern the institution under which he is punished.

But it is very implausible that rational agents primarily concerned with protecting and prolonging their lives would consent to an institution of punishment that contained such a terrible penalty, even if it provided them with positive net expected security. Rational agents would be unlikely to agree to equip one another with the power to put members of their own society to death, despite the benefits in expected security we are now assuming they would garner. They would thereby alienate the strong rights to bodily integrity whose protection was their primary motivation for entering into civil society, the same set of rights that arguably lies behind the retributivist's conception of desert for punishment in the first place.

Michael Davis, "A Sound Retributive Argument for the Death Penalty"

Claire Finkelstein's primary conclusion is that "retributivism fails to justify the use of death as punishment." By "justify," Finkelstein seems to mean no more than "show to be morally permitted." I shall justify the death penalty in a somewhat stronger sense. I shall show statutory provision of the death penalty to be not only sometimes morally permitted but, all else equal, something that reason sometimes recommends. I shall not, however, argue that morality (or reason) requires it. I do not believe that countries such as Canada and Mexico, or states such as Wisconsin and Michigan, are engaged in immoral conduct because they do not punish murder with death.

I. *Two Kinds of Retribution*

Finkelstein begins her discussion of retributivism with an oversight that may explain how she missed the argument I am about to make. While recognizing that the literal form of *lex talionis*—the criminal deserves in punishment the same harm that the crime caused—is not a popular position even among staunch retributivists, she still seems to suppose that all forms of retributivism must proportion punishment to the harm done (at least for the major intentional crimes). The retributivist "would seek to inflict on the perpetrator by way of punishment the nearest morally permissible form of punishment to the act the perpetrator committed." This is the "moral equivalence" ("nearest") form of *lex talionis*.

All forms of the *lex talionis* use the harm the crime does as a major component when determining equivalence. All forms of the *lex talionis*, therefore, have trouble with the enormous diversity of crimes characteristic of any sophisticated legal system. Too many crimes do no harm—in any useful sense of "harm." Any retributivism must be able to assign penalties to many "harmless" crimes, everything from attempted murder to reckless driving, from failure to place a tax stamp on a liquor bottle to conspiracy to commit embezzlement. For that reason, a number of retributivists have tried to understand punishment as taking back (or canceling) the unfair advantage the criminal gets from the crime as such (or, at least, the value of that unfair advantage) rather than as returning something like the harm he did. Here is an example of the method by which that sort of retributivism would assign penalties to crimes:

1. Prepare a list of penalties consisting of those evils (a) which no rational person would risk except for some substantial benefit and (b) which may be inflicted through the (relatively just) procedures of the criminal law.

2. Strike from the list all inhumane penalties.

3. Type the remaining penalties (by evil imposed), rank them within each type (by amount of that evil), and then combine rankings into a scale.

4. List all crimes.

5. Type the crimes (by interest protected), rank them within each type (by degree of protection), and then combine rankings into a scale.

6. Connect the greatest penalty with the greatest crime, the least penalty with the least crime, and the rest accordingly.

7. Thereafter, type and grade new (humane) penalties as in step 3 and new crimes as in step 5, and then proceed as above.

The harm a crime actually does plays no part in this assignment of (maximum) penalties. The "harm" in prospect, if the evil in question is "harm" in any interesting sense, does have a part, but one constrained by considerations of type and grade, that is, by relationships internal to a system of criminal justice.

In a society much like ours, the initial list of penalties might include: death, loss of liberty, pain, loss of property, loss of opportunities (for example, revocation of driver's license or franchise), mutilation, and shame. These are the most persuasive penalties we can impose.

II. *Torture, Death, and Severity*

Finkelstein need not object to this seven-step method. She can restate one of her arguments in its terms: Death, she might say, cannot pass the test set by step 2—or, at least, cannot if torture fails (as almost everyone now agrees it does). Death must fail if torture does because torture is not as severe a penalty as death. Since step 2 excludes death if it excludes torture, and it does exclude torture, the death penalty cannot be justified (or, at least, is no more justifiable than torture is).

If that is the argument she would make for striking death from the list, all I need to do is provide one plausible example of a jurisdiction in which death can be justified as a penalty even though torture cannot be.

Consider, then, a jurisdiction, such as Illinois, in which the statutory penalty for armed robbery, aggravated arson, and similar serious non-lethal crimes is 6–30 years imprisonment, the statutory penalty for simple first-degree murder is 20–60 years imprisonment, and the statutory penalty for multiple murders is life imprisonment without parole. We may, I think, agree that someone who commits several first-degree murders on one occasion in an exceptionally brutal way deserves a penalty significantly more severe than the penalty for simple multiple murder (assuming the more severe penalty is both possible and otherwise permissible). That is, there is enough difference between these two categories of crime that we should (if possible and permissible) assign the more serious a substantially higher penalty. We want to give the criminal a reason not to be brutal even if he is going to murder several people, a reason that—as a rational person—he should find significant. Death is such a penalty.

But (Finkelstein might respond) you have not yet explained why we should not choose life-imprisonment-with-torture instead of death. Any rational person should consider torture (added to life imprisonment) a significant reason not to do what he might do if the penalty were only life imprisonment. If your theory justifies the use of torture, it is (presumptively) refuted, since everyone agrees torture is not justified. If, on the other hand, you cannot justify torture, how are you to justify the more severe penalty of death without begging the question of death's moral permissibility?

The reason why we cannot justify the use of torture instead of the death is, of course, that torture has been struck from the list of available penalties; it is inhumane. But, in order to explain why death is not also off the list, the defender of the death penalty needs a theory of inhumane penalties (one that does not beg questions about the death penalty's moral permissibility). There is such a theory, one that explains why penalties can be morally permissible at one time and not at another, why death can be humane even if torture clearly is not, one general enough not to beg our question.

III. *Humaneness*

We do not object to a penalty (such as torture) as inhumane simply because of its severity. The penalty, considered as a physical act, a certain quantity of pain or the like, never changes—though objections do. Nor do we object to a penalty as inhumane because of what we are willing to suffer. We are sometimes willing to suffer inhumane penalties ourselves (for example, a few hours of torture to avoid long imprisonment). We seem to object to a penalty as inhumane only when use of that penalty on anyone, especially someone else (against his will), shocks us; when, that is, we cannot comfortably bear its general use. Shock is neither rational nor irrational. The person who does not find shocking what everyone else does is eccentric, insensitive, or callous. She is not necessarily irrational. We think she needs to let go more, to feel more, or to live better, not to be cured or caged. Shock at this or that is not a basic evaluation all rational persons must share; nor is it the inevitable consequence of what all rational persons do share. For example, much that might turn most of us pale does not bother a surgeon. What shocks us seems to be a consequence of how we live, of what we do and do not experience.

Though I may say a penalty is inhumane because it shocks me, a penalty is not inhumane just because it shocks me. A penalty is inhumane (in a particular society) if its use shocks all or almost all; humane, if its use shocks at most a few; and neither clearly humane nor clearly inhumane, if its use shocks many but far from all. We suppress inhumane penalties (in part at least) because we do not want to be shocked by their use.

But shock as such is morally indifferent whereas humaneness seems to be morally important. What is the connection between shock and morality? The connection seems to be this: to treat a person in a way that we generally find shocking is to treat her as we ourselves do not want to be treated, as we would not treat most other persons, as we might not even be willing to treat animals. It is, in short, to degrade her, to treat her as less than a person. If morality requires us to treat each person as a person (and that, it seems to me, is relatively uncontroversial), then we do something (at least prima facie) morally wrong if we inflict on a person (against her will) a penalty that we find shocking.

IV. *How is a Common Standard of Humaneness Possible?*

Making humaneness a function of shock in this way may seem puzzling. Shock, I said, is neither rational nor irrational. If what is inhumane depends upon most of us agreeing about what shocks us, how does it happen that there is so much agreement about what is inhumane?

The puzzle is not hard to solve. Ways of life shape our sensibilities in certain ways. A shared way of life, because it shapes a common sensibility, also forges a standard of humaneness. We are made to agree. Imprisoning someone for months or years would shock most people in a society of nomads. In such a society, the gentlest detention would be inhumane. Imprisoning does not shock us only because we are every day penned in houses, workshops, and offices and often spend years in the same city or town. Although we admit imprisonment to be a great evil, we do not think of it as an inhumane punishment.

There is then some relationship between "progress" and what is or is not inhumane. Insofar as technological progress has meant the disappearance of certain evils from daily life, it has meant as well a change of sensibility and so a change in what society should lay aside as inhumane ("cruel and unusual," as the courts say). Public executions came to shock our humanity about the time it became rare for ordinary people to die in the street. During the last few decades, most death-penalty states switched from execution by (private) hanging, gassing, or electrocution to execution by (private) lethal injection. Why? Perhaps because death by injection is more like the hospital death we are now accustomed to (hanging, gassing, and electrocution resembling more the industrial accidents that, happily, have become relatively rare).

What then of the death penalty itself? If what I have said so far is right, the death penalty will shock enough of us only when it has become rare enough for people to die unwillingly before old age (such an early death being the evil that the death penalty imposes). How rare is "rare enough"? That is a question for social science. What is clear, I think, is that early death is not rare enough in the United States today to make the death penalty as shocking as it needs to be to be inhumane here. Certainly, death by lethal injection does not shock most of us in the way even fifty lashes with a whip does.

V. *The Kidney Society*

I have admitted that criminal desert is not the only constraint on how we can justifiably punish. Humaneness is another. I may seem thereby to have opened myself to Finkelstein's final argument, the one resting on "deontological norms [apart from desert] to which the retributivist is committed." She makes her argument using a single example, the Kidney Society. I agree with her intuition that "we" would object to the violation of bodily integrity necessary to make the Kidney Society's version of social insurance work. We would not require specific performance even if we would enforce the contract by assessing damages for a failure to perform. What I deny is the relevance of that intuition to the death penalty. The death penalty does not involve the same violation of bodily integrity as removing a human kidney. Death by lethal injection is much closer in that respect to forced medication (something that does not shock us) than to the Kidney Society's forced mutilation. In any case, our intuitions here rest on the same sensitivities as our intuitions of humaneness. Our intuitions of humaneness need not make sense according to some abstract theory of what resembles what. They are what they are, and that is the end of it—until they change.

Finkelstein might, I suppose, still respond that we should reject the death penalty whenever a less severe penalty is available. Torture is a less severe penalty. Therefore, we should reject the death penalty.

To this last (desperate) argument, I would respond that torture is not available—for the reasons already given. It is inhumane (even though less severe). Is there an alternative to the death penalty, another penalty significantly more severe than life imprisonment without parole but not inhumane? Some of the other penalties on our original list, all those that significantly add to life imprisonment without parole—torture, flogging, and so on—are also inhumane (and so, are not available). The remainder of the list, though available, does not significantly add to life imprisonment without parole. Why should someone who contemplates brutally murdering a number of people care whether, in addition to life imprisonment without parole, his punishment would include loss of his driver's license or his right to vote?

If the death penalty is the only penalty Illinois has that is both available and significantly more severe than life imprisonment, Illinois is left with the death penalty as the only way to distinguish aggravated multiple murder from lesser forms of multiple murder. Since we have good reason to want to proportion punishment to criminal desert, Illinois has a retributive justification to use death as a penalty, because of the markedly greater criminal desert of aggravated multiple murder.

Of course, this argument presupposes that Illinois' statutory scheme is (relatively) just otherwise and that Illinois cannot achieve the distinction between aggravated and lesser crimes by reducing the penalty for lesser crimes. Although I believe that Illinois' statutory scheme is too severe overall, even though it is otherwise relatively just, its being so does not matter here. Even if Illinois' penalties are too severe overall, nothing in Finkelstein's argument, or in the retributive method I outlined here, rules out the possibility that a statutory scheme like Illinois' might be justified somewhere sometime. If lesser penalties will not preserve enough order, the legal system will either have to impose heavier penalties overall or, after trying to improve enforcement, subside into disorder. What scheme of penalties is sufficient to preserve order is not something to be settled by an abstract argument such as Finkelstein's. Finkelstein's argument is refuted.

Religion

2

■ Religion—Introduction

The role of religion in shaping attitudes about capital punishment is paradoxical: most major religious groups in the United States oppose capital punishment, but most of the adherents to these religions profess support for the death penalty.

Fifteen religious groups in the United States have over 1 million adherents (this includes atheists, and the fast-growing legions of neopagans). The churches of American Baptists, Methodists, Eastern Orthodox, Presbyterians, Episcopalians, the Reformed Church in America, and the United Church of Christ are all abolitionist. The position of the Roman Catholic Church, as expressed in its 1995 encyclical *Evangelium Vitae*, excerpted in the Critical Documents section of this chapter, and through modifications to the catechism announced in 1997, is that the death penalty is permissible in instances where it is "the only possible way of effectively defending human lives against the unjust aggressor." The catechism adds that such instances are "practically non-existent in today's world given the resources for restraining criminals." The Qur'an supports the death penalty, but there is a strong tradition of mercy within Islam. Conservative branches of Judaism support the death penalty, but most liberal branches do not. The Evangelical Lutheran Church in America is abolitionist; the Missouri Synod of the Lutheran Church is retentionist, as are American Baptists and the Church of Latter-day Saints.

Despite the weight of authority, most people who express a religious belief support capital punishment. In a 2000 survey, Catholics and Protestants were more likely to support the death penalty than ordinary citizens (see **Table 2-1**). Overall, 63 percent supported the death penalty. Sixty-six percent of Catholics and 64 percent of Protestants supported the death penalty. Fifty-seven percent of Jewish respondents expressed support for capital punishment. While support for the death penalty among Protestants and Catholics has remained fairly constant over the past 20 years, both in absolute terms and relative to the national norms, support among Jews has diminished. In 1978, Jews supported the death penalty with greater conviction than the average citizen. That effect has all but disappeared in the data.

The debate in the Judeo-Christian tradition over whether the Old and New Testaments condone capital punishment has some striking parallels to modern de-

Table 2-1	Religion and Support for the Death Penalty					
	1978		1990		2000	
Religion	Support (%)	Oppose (%)	Support (%)	Oppose (%)	Support (%)	Oppose (%)
National	66	28	74	19	63	29
Protestant	67	27	75	19	64	27
Catholic	68	27	76	18	66	27
Jewish	79	21	74	15	57	36
None	58	38	72	24	60	32

bates over modes of constitutional interpretation. Generally speaking, retentionists find support for capital punishment directly from the text of the Bible. The Old Testament explicitly refers to capital punishment in several instances—retentionists argue that the passages should be given their plain meaning. Abolitionists contend that the relevant exercise is to divine the true meaning of the text; passages need to be read in conjunction with the whole of the Bible or interpreted in historical context. John Howard Yoder, an abolitionist, puts it this way:

> The first task of the biblical interpreter, as I have already said, is not to read a text as if "from scratch," or as if its meanings were self-evident to every well-intentioned reader, but rather to protect the text from misuse, even to "liberate" its original meaning from the deposit of interpretations which have already been laid over it by centuries of readers.

Obvious parallels can be drawn to constitutional discourse. Textualists, such as the former Supreme Court Justice Hugo Black, argue that the language of the Constitution must be given its plain meaning. Originalists argue that the real exercise is to discern the true meaning of the drafters of the Constitution. The debate for textualists is over the natural meaning of the language in question; for originalists the issue is whose intent matters and how that intent is to be discerned. The ground rules of the debate are crucial because, especially in the case of the Bible and capital punishment, the rules go a long way to determining who has the better argument. Judaism, Michael Walzer wrote, "is not found in the text so much as in the interpretations of the text."

That the Old Testament endorses capital punishment is not seriously debated. The story of Noah contains what appears to be a divine command endorsing capital punishment:

> Whoever sheds the blood of Man
> In Man shall his blood be shed
> For in the image of God
> He made Man. (Genesis 9:6)

The Old Testament specifically calls for the death penalty as punishment for many crimes including murder, rape of an engaged woman, kidnapping, adultery, fornication by women, incest, male homosexuality, sodomy with animals, idolatry, sorcery, and rebelliousness on the part of a son. But the Old Testament also put in place strict procedural rules before any execution could be carried out. Ignorance of the law was a valid defense, circumstantial evidence was excluded, and witnesses were precluded from testifying on the basis of hearsay. Juries sentencing a defendant to die were required to attend the execution. Most significantly, a person could not be convicted of a capital crime on the basis of the testimony of a single witness.

Many of these requirements have modern analogs. One of the suggestions of the Illinois Capital Punishment Commission—upon whose recommendations Governor George Ryan commuted the death sentences of more than 100 death row inmates in January 2003 (discussed in Chapter 23)—parallels the biblical requirement of corroboration. The commission recommended that "capital punishment not be available when a conviction is based solely upon the testimony of a single eyewitness." Chapter 22 offers a proposal by Jeremy Epstein, a former United States attorney, to revive the biblical requirement that sentencing juries be present at the execution of the defendant. Some scholars suggest that these requirements are collectively so onerous that if implemented the death penalty would rarely, if ever, be imposed.

Whether the New Testament supports capital punishment is less certain. The clearest reference to the use of the death penalty in the New Testament is in John's Gospel (8:1–11). In this passage, a woman accused of adultery is brought before Jesus. Most biblical interpreters agree that the intention of the scribes who brought the accused woman before Jesus was to challenge the authority Jesus had been exercising while teaching in the temple. Jesus responded to the situation by saying, famously, "Let him that is without sin cast the first stone." Abolitionists argue that this is a repudiation of capital punishment; it suggests that the executioner must be beyond reproach. It might be just for God to exact death as punishment for sin, but it is beyond the ability of mortals to make a life-and-death judgment of this kind. Retentionists argue that the passage is properly understood as an effort by Jesus to evade the trap set for him by his detractors.

Abolitionists say that although support for capital punishment is undeniably found in some parts of the Bible in general, and many places in the Old Testament specifically, the text is better understood more as an account of existing conditions than as a recipe for reform. As Gardner Hanks puts it in the debate found in the Perspectives section of this chapter, Genesis 9:6 is "descriptive" not "prescriptive." John Howard Yoder writes, "This is not legislation for a government to apply. It is wisdom, a prediction, a description, of how things are in fact, in primitive and ancient societies." Abolitionists further argue—Gardner Hanks makes this point effectively—that as a whole the Old Testament is a story of a "repeating cycle of redemption," a worldview with which capital punishment is inherently in tension.

Some abolitionists go a step further. For example, in *Dead Man Walking*, Sister Helen Prejean argues against biblical support for capital punishment by noting the—by modern standards, absurd—litany of crimes for which the Old Testament approved of capital punishment. "I couldn't worship a god who is less compassionate than I am." Some retentionists take great offense at arguments of this kind, saying that Prejean has effectively substituted her own code of morality for God's teachings. As one pro-death penalty advocacy group puts it, "Prejean has abandoned biblical text for only one reason: the text conflicts with her personal belief. It is not uncommon for persons of faith to create a god in their own image, to give that god their values, instead of accepting those values which are inherent to the deity."

The claim that retentionists are strict interpretivists and abolitionists are intentionalists is a generalization. Notable exceptions can be found, especially with respect to New Testament teachings, which are not as clearly supportive of capital punishment as those in the Old Testament. Ezekiel 33:11 is often cited by abolitionists:

> As I live, says the Lord God, I have no pleasure in the death of the wicked, but that the wicked turn away from his way and live; turn back, turn back your evil ways; for why will you die, O House of Israel?

On its surface, the passage seems to plainly condemn capital punishment. Professor Lloyd R. Bailey offers this contrary analysis:

> To some readers, this may seem clear enough! God not only takes no "pleasure" in the death of the wicked but prefers that they "turn back." Such understanding might indeed be justified if one could read the Bible atomistically, that is, one verse at a time, with the understanding that the verse has a self-contained eternal truth. However, if the prophet is speaking to a specific audience about a particular problem, and if his response covers several verses (or even a chapter), then the modern interpreter must hear him out and look for the central idea.

Professor Bailey's argument rings of interpretivism. This is not to say that one mode of argument is right or wrong, or one conclusion justified and another not. It is only to point out that each side in the debate has relied upon different methods of interpretation in different situations.

In the debate that concludes this chapter, Kerby Anderson argues that capital punishment is the ultimate expression of human dignity and that the moral principles upon which it is based precede the Old Testament. Gardner Hanks argues that neither the Old nor New Testament offer support for capital punishment. Hanks acknowledges textual support for capital punishment in the Old Testament, but argues that on the whole it teaches that true justice is not possible in a system administered by mere human beings. Ultimate justice is for God to discern. In the New Testament, every execution that occurs is arbitrary and unjust. Hanks argues that this should lead Christians to view the death penalty with great distrust.

■ Religion—Critical Documents

Ioannes Paulus PP. II, "*Evangelium Vitae*—On the Value and Inviolability of Human Life" (1995)

2. Man is called to a fullness of life, which far exceeds the dimensions of his earthly existence, because it consists in sharing the very life of God. The loftiness of this

supernatural vocation reveals the greatness and the inestimable value of human life even in its temporal phase. Life on earth is not an "ultimate" but a "penultimate" reality; even so, it remains a sacred reality entrusted to us, to be preserved with a sense of responsibility and brought to perfection in love and in the gift of ourselves to God and to our brothers and sisters.

3. Every individual, precisely by reason of the mystery of the Word of God who was made flesh is entrusted to the maternal care of the Church. Therefore every threat to human dignity and life must necessarily be felt in the Church's very heart; it cannot but affect her at the core of her faith in the Redemptive Incarnation of the Son of God, and engage her in her mission of proclaiming the Gospel of life in all the world and to every creature.

Today this proclamation is especially pressing because of the extraordinary increase and gravity of threats to the life of individuals and peoples, especially where life is weak and defenseless. In addition to the ancient scourges of poverty, hunger, endemic diseases, violence and war, new threats are emerging on an alarmingly vast scale.

The Second Vatican Council forcefully condemned a number of crimes and attacks against human life. Thirty years later, taking up the words of the Council and with the same forcefulness I repeat that condemnation in the name of the whole Church, certain that I am interpreting the genuine sentiment of every upright conscience: "Whatever is opposed to life itself, such as any type of murder, genocide, abortion, euthanasia, or wilful self-destruction, whatever violates the integrity of the human person, such as mutilation, torments inflicted on body or mind, attempts to coerce the will itself; whatever insults human dignity, such as subhuman living conditions, arbitrary imprisonment, deportation, slavery, prostitution, the selling of women and children; as well as disgraceful working conditions, where people are treated as mere instruments of gain rather than as free and responsible persons; all these things and others like them are infamies indeed. They poison human society, and they do more harm to those who practice them than to those who suffer from the injury. Moreover, they are a supreme dishonour to the Creator."

7. "God did not make death, and he does not delight in the death of the living." The Gospel of life, proclaimed in the beginning when man was created in the image of God for a destiny of full and perfect life, is contradicted by the painful experience of death which enters the world and casts its shadow of meaninglessness over man's entire existence. Death came into the world as a result of the devil's envy and the sin of our first parents. And death entered it in a violent way, through the killing of Abel by his brother Cain: "And when they were in the field, Cain rose up against his brother Abel, and killed him." This first murder is presented with singular eloquence in a page of the Book of Genesis which has universal significance: it is a page rewritten daily, with inexorable and degrading frequency, in the book of human history.

And yet God, who is always merciful even when he punishes, "put a mark on Cain, lest any who came upon him should kill him." He thus gave him a distinctive sign, not to condemn him to the hatred of others, but to protect and defend him from those wishing to kill him, even out of a desire to avenge Abel's death. Not even a murderer loses his personal dignity, and God himself pledges to guarantee this. And it is precisely here that the paradoxical mystery of the merciful justice of God is shown forth. As Saint Ambrose writes: "God drove Cain out of his presence and sent him into exile far away from his native land, so that he passed from a life of human kindness to one which was more akin to the rude existence of a wild beast. God, who preferred the correction rather than the death of a sinner, did not desire that a homicide be punished by the exaction of another act of homicide."

12. In fact, while the climate of widespread moral uncertainty can in some way be explained by the multiplicity and gravity of today's social problems, and these can sometimes mitigate the subjective responsibility of individuals, it is no less true that we are confronted by an even larger reality, which can be described as a veritable structure of sin. This reality is characterized by the emergence of a culture which denies solidarity and in many cases takes the form of a veritable "culture of death." This culture is actively fostered by powerful cultural, economic and political currents which encourage an idea of society excessively concerned with efficiency.

34. Life is always a good. This is an instinctive perception and a fact of experience, and man is called to grasp the profound reason why this is so. Why is life a good? This question is found everywhere in the Bible, and from the very first pages it receives a powerful and amazing answer. The life which God gives man is quite different from the life of all other living creatures, inasmuch as man, although formed from the dust of the earth is a manifestation of God in the world, a sign of his presence, a trace of his glory. Man has been given a sublime dignity, based on the intimate bond which unites him to his Creator: in man there shines forth a reflection of God himself.

55. This should not cause surprise: to kill a human being, in whom the image of God is present, is a particularly serious sin. Only God is the master of life! Yet from the beginning, faced with the many and often tragic cases which occur in the life of individuals and society, Christian reflection has sought a fuller and deeper understanding of what God's commandment prohibits and prescribes. There are in fact situations in which values proposed by God's Law seem to involve a genuine paradox. This happens for example in the case of legitimate defense, in which the right to protect one's own life and the duty not to harm someone else's life are difficult to reconcile in practice. Unfortunately it happens that the need to render the aggressor incapable of causing harm sometimes involves taking his life. In this case, the fatal outcome is attributable to the aggressor whose action brought it about, even though he may not be morally responsible because of a lack of the use of reason.

56. This is the context in which to place the problem of the death penalty. The problem must be viewed in the context of a system of penal justice ever more in line with human dignity and thus, in the end, with God's plan for man and society. The primary purpose of the punishment which society inflicts is "to redress the disorder caused by the offence." Public authority must redress the violation of personal and social rights by imposing on the offender an adequate punishment for the crime, as a condition for the offender to regain the exercise of his

or her freedom. In this way authority also fulfills the purpose of defending public order and ensuring people's safety, while at the same time offering the offender an incentive and help to change his or her behavior and be rehabilitated.

It is clear that, for these purposes to be achieved, the nature and extent of the punishment must be carefully evaluated and decided upon, and ought not go to the extreme of executing the offender except in cases of absolute necessity: in other words, when it would not be possible otherwise to defend society. Today however, as a result of steady improvements in the organization of the penal system, such cases are very rare, if not practically non-existent.

57. If such great care must be taken to respect every life, even that of criminals and unjust aggressors, the commandment "You shall not kill" has absolute value when it refers to the innocent person. And all the more so in the case of weak and defenseless human beings, who find their ultimate defense against the arrogance and caprice of others only in the absolute binding force of God's commandment.

Therefore, by the authority which Christ conferred upon Peter and his Successors, and in communion with the Bishops of the Catholic Church, I confirm that the direct and voluntary killing of an innocent human being is always gravely immoral.

The deliberate decision to deprive an innocent human being of his life is always morally evil and can never be licit either as an end in itself or as a means to a good end. It is in fact a grave act of disobedience to the moral law, and indeed to God himself, the author and guarantor of that law; it contradicts the fundamental virtues of justice and charity.

As far as the right to life is concerned, every innocent human being is absolutely equal to all others. This equality is the basis of all authentic social relationships which, to be truly such, can only be founded on truth and justice, recognizing and protecting every man and woman as a person and not as an object to be used. Before the moral norm which prohibits the direct taking of the life of an innocent human being "there are no privileges or exceptions for anyone. It makes no difference whether one is the master of the world or the 'poorest of the poor' on the face of the earth. Before the demands of morality we are all absolutely equal."

■ Religion—Perspectives

■ Issue—Does the Bible Support Capital Punishment?

Kerby Anderson, "Should Christians Support the Death Penalty?"

I. *Old Testament Examples*

Throughout the Old Testament we find many cases in which God commands the use of capital punishment. We see this first with the acts of God Himself.

God was involved, either directly or indirectly, in the taking of life as a punishment for the nation of Israel or for those who threatened or harmed Israel.

One example is the flood of Noah in Genesis. God destroyed all human and animal life except that which was on the ark. Another example is Sodom and Gomorrah, where God destroyed the two cities because of the heinous sin of the inhabitants. In the time of Moses, God took the lives of the Egyptians' first-born sons and destroyed the Egyptian army in the Red Sea.

The Old Testament is replete with references and examples of God taking life. In a sense, God used capital punishment to deal with Israel's sins and the sins of the nations surrounding Israel.

The Old Testament also teaches that God instituted capital punishment in the Jewish law code. According to Genesis 9:6, capital punishment is based upon a belief in the sanctity of life. It says, "Whoever sheds man's blood by man his blood shall be shed, for in the image of God, He made man."

The Mosaic Law set forth numerous offenses that were punishable by death. The first was murder. In Exodus, God commanded capital punishment for murderers. Premeditated murder was punishable by death. A second offense punishable by death was involvement in the occult. This included sorcery, divination, acting as a medium, and sacrificing to false gods. Third, capital punishment was to be used against perpetrators of sexual sins such as rape, incest, or homosexual practice.

Notice that the principle in Genesis 9:6 is not tied to the theocracy. Instead, the principle of *Lex talionis* (a life for a life) is tied to the creation order. Capital punishment is warranted due to the sanctity of life. Even before we turn to the New Testament, we find this universally binding principle that precedes the Old Testament law code.

II. *New Testament Principles*

Some Christians believe that capital punishment does not apply to the New Testament and church age.

First we must acknowledge that God gave the principle of capital punishment even before the institution of the Old Testament law code. Capital punishment was instituted by God because humans are created in the image of God. The principle is not rooted in the Old Testament theocracy, but rather in the creation order. It is a much broader biblical principle that carries into the New Testament. Even so, some Christians argue that in the Sermon on the Mount Jesus seems to be arguing against capital punishment. But is He?

In the Sermon on the Mount, Jesus is not arguing against the principle of a life for a life. Rather He is speaking to the issue of our personal desire for vengeance. He is not denying the power and responsibility of the government. In the Sermon on the Mount, Jesus is speaking to individual Christians. He is telling Christians that they should not try to replace the power of the government. Jesus does not deny the power and authority of government, but rather He calls individual Christians to love their enemies and turn the other cheek.

Some have said that Jesus set aside capital punishment when He did not call for the woman caught in adultery to be stoned. But remember the context. The Pharisees were trying to trap Jesus between the Roman law and the Mosaic law. If

He said that they should stone her, He would break the Roman law. If He refused to allow them to stone her, He would break the Mosaic law. Jesus's answer avoided the conflict: He said that he who was without sin should cast the first stone. Since He did teach that a stone be thrown, this is not an abolition of the death penalty.

In other places in the New Testament we see the principle of capital punishment being reinforced. The fact that the Apostle Paul used the image of the sword further supports the idea that capital punishment was to be used by government in the New Testament age as well. Rather than abolish the idea of the death penalty, Paul uses the emblem of the Roman sword to reinforce the idea of capital punishment.

The New Testament did not abolish the death penalty; it reinforced the principle of capital punishment.

III. *Capital Punishment and Deterrence*

Is capital punishment a deterrent to crime? At the outset, we should acknowledge that the answer to this question should not change our perspective on this issue. A Christian's belief in capital punishment should be based upon what the Bible teaches not on a pragmatic assessment of whether or not capital punishment deters crime.

That being said, however, we should try to assess the effectiveness of capital punishment. But even if we are not absolutely sure of its deterrent effect, the death penalty should be implemented. If it is a deterrent, then implementing capital punishment certainly will save lives. If it is not, then we still will have followed biblical injunctions and put convicted murderers to death.

IV. *Capital Punishment and Discrimination*

Many people oppose capital punishment because they feel it is discriminatory. The charge is somewhat curious since most of the criminals that have been executed in the last decade are white rather than black. Nevertheless, a higher percentage of ethnic minorities are on death row.

But even if we find evidence for discrimination in the criminal justice system, notice that this is not really an argument against capital punishment. It is a compelling argument for reform of the criminal justice system. It is an argument for implementing capital punishment carefully. In fact, most of the social and philosophical arguments against capital punishment are really not arguments against it at all. These arguments are really arguments for improving the criminal justice system. If discrimination is taking place and guilty people are escaping penalty, then that is an argument for extending the penalty, not doing away with it.

Gardner C. Hanks, *Against the Death Penalty: Christian and Secular Arguments Against Capital Punishment*

I. *Life for Life? Old Testament Perspectives*

The Bible is a source of values for many people in North America. The Old Testament is at the center of the Jewish faith and along with the New Testament speaks powerfully to all serious Christians.

Christians who defend capital punishment scripturally most often do so with references to the Old Testament. God told Noah after the flood, "Whoever sheds the blood of a human, by a human shall that person's blood be shed." This passage is frequently cited by death penalty advocates. These advocates also point to the many places in the Law where the death penalty is not only sanctioned but seemingly required.

It cannot be denied that certain Old Testament texts endorse capital punishment. Individual passages, however, need to be read in the context of the whole message of the Bible. When viewed in its entirety, the Old Testament is the story of a repeating cycle of redemption. God creates humans in his own image. Then comes human sin. God's forgiveness and reinstatement, human sin again, followed by God's forgiveness and reinstatement, and so on. This pattern, which mitigates against the final solution of the death penalty, begins with the fall of Adam and Eve and is seen clearly in the Genesis story of the first murder.

A. The First Murder Cain and Abel were two brothers, the sons of Adam and Eve. Cain became jealous of his brother when God looked more favorably on Abel's sacrifice than on Cain's. Cain lured his brother to an isolated place and then murdered him. In modern terminology, this was a first-degree murder: premeditated and cold-blooded. Cain then tried to cover up the murder, but the Lord uncovered the crime.

However, the Lord God did not take Cain's life for the murder. Instead, the punishment chosen was separation from the community by banishment. At the time the Bible was written this was a severe punishment. Personal identity was so tied into community life that to be severed from the community was second only to death.

However, God softened the punishment. He gave Cain protection. He declared that anyone who killed Cain would be required to suffer seven times the punishment given to Cain. God gave Cain a special mark to show this protection. Although Cain was punished severely, the story ends not with Cain's death, but with the birth of Cain's son Enoch. So God's answer to the murder of Abel was not death but a new life.

B. Noah and the Rule of Blood How then do we move from the forgiveness and regeneration of Cain to the harsh words of God to Noah in Genesis? The text in question is part of God's blessing and instructions to Noah and his family after the Flood. Up until this time human beings were not allowed to eat meat. Now, as the "golden age" of creation ended, God broke the harmony between humans and animals. Humans could now kill animals for food. However there were limitations. The first was that humans could not eat the blood of animals, and the second was that they could not take human life, as they could an animal's life.

God told Noah that there would be a reckoning for killing other human beings. The text of Genesis 9:6 follows. "Whoever sheds the blood of a human, by a human shall that person's blood be shed." The passage certainly is descriptive of how life was at the time. The murder of a family member could bring the beginning of prolonged revenge-seeking in the form of a blood feud.

However, this raises a question. Is the text in Genesis 9:6 prescriptive or merely descriptive? Does this text tell us how God wants things to be or just how things are? In answering this question, the passage should not be taken out of context. The final line in the poetic text, a line rarely quoted by death penalty proponents, is important. "For in his own image God made humankind." Nothing is said about a person losing this image-bearing characteristic when sin, even a murder, is committed. The killing of a murderer is as much the destruction of the image of God as is the killing of any other human being.

C. Moses the Murderer One remarkable characteristic of the Old Testament narratives is the brutal honesty with which human nature is pictured. All human beings in the Old Testament are shown as deeply flawed. The stories abound with liars, cheaters, cowards, thieves, and murderers. Think of the three greatest human characters in the history of ancient Israel: Abraham nearly murdered his own son; Moses and David were both killers.

The story of the murder committed by Moses is told in Exodus. Moses, brought up in the royal household of an Egyptian princess, somehow discovered that he was actually a Hebrew. We can only imagine what he must have gone through psychologically at this point in his life. It must have been traumatic for him to find that he was not really a member of the Egyptian upper classes but instead a member of a clan of slaves. A modern equivalent might be for the son of a Fortune 500 family to discover he is really an adopted child from the ghetto.

To find out more about himself and his people, Moses went to visit the work camps where his relatives were laboring. During this visit, he began to identify with the slaves. When he saw one of the laborers being mistreated by an Egyptian overseer, he became incensed. But his response was calculated; he did not fly into a fit of rage and act on sheer impulse. The Bible tells us, "He looked this way and that, and seeing no one he killed the Egyptian and hid him in the sand."

Again, by modern standards this killing would probably be considered first-degree murder. The killing was calculated, and under Noachian law, to kill an Egyptian was as wrong as to kill a fellow Israelite. In spite of this, God was merciful. Life for life was not required of Moses. Like Cain, Moses was punished with exile. He was removed from all that he knew, from the protection of both his natural and his adoptive people. Yet God mitigated the punishment through his providential meeting with the daughters of Jethro, the priest of Midian. The rest of the story is well known. Moses returned from exile to become the greatest leader the Israelites were ever to have, and one of the greatest lawgivers the world has ever known.

D. The Law Given Moses' own history, it is ironic that Christian death penalty proponents find their strongest biblical support in the law he gave the Israelites. Capital punishment is a prominent part of the code of conduct contained in the Old Testament. The death penalty is invoked for many crimes, including murder, rape of an engaged woman, kidnapping, adultery, fornication by women, incest, male homosexuality, having sex with animals, idolatry, sorcery, false witness in a capital case, prophecy in the name of other gods, false prophecy, cursing one's parents, and rebelliousness on the part of a son.

For those of us who live in a more pluralistic, scientific, and less patriarchal society, the list seems excessive. Few of even the most adamant Jewish or Christian death penalty proponents would advocate the death penalty for all the offenses listed above. So this list must be viewed from a historical perspective if it is to teach us anything about how we should approach modern capital punishment.

First, we must recognize that capital punishment in the Old Testament was seen as a form of religious sacrifice. Much as sacrificing an animal paid God back for less-serious crimes, human sacrifice through the death penalty restored the balance of justice after a more serious crime had been committed. This belief predated the Mosaic law and can still be heard in arguments for the death penalty today. For example, the idea that the death penalty must exist to "balance out" murder or "to make things right" is a secular expression of this belief.

Before the law existed, families were responsible for seeking the human sacrifice that would atone for a serious crime committed against one of its members. This system led to an unregulated cycle of violence, in which families could be trapped into continuous and deadly conflict with each other.

Old Testament scholars have long recognized that the Mosaic law was meant to be a limitation on violence rather than an endorsement of it. The written laws came into Israel's history at a time when the community was passing from a nomadic, tribal society to a more stable, agricultural society with a more centralized government. In general the laws reflect a movement away from the blood feud and negotiation between families as a method of social control to a more "bureaucratic" approach to justice, with priests or village elders acting as judges.

Thus while the law may appear to be excessively violent by modern standards, it actually was intended to reduce the level of violence. When Exodus says, "life for a life, eye for eye, tooth for tooth," the law actually means, "No more than a life for a life; no more than an eye for an eye; no more than a tooth for a tooth." Before the law, clans could choose to seek revenge at whatever level they wished.

The law made justice less dependent on personal whims and social power. The message behind the law was that God is working through the community and will provide both victims and offenders with justice. Relatives of a victim who has been murdered, raped, or maimed are too emotionally involved to rationally decide what is best for the community. The law put a definite limit on the allowable retaliation for a crime. At the same time it provided victims with justice.

This is seen in the one text of the Old Testament that most clearly mandates the death penalty—Numbers 35:30–34. The passage calls for the death penalty for a murderer and does not allow ransom in place of it. Ransom, of course, would be more possible for the rich and powerful family than for the poor. This text then puts the rich murderer and the poor murderer on the same level. The rich person cannot murder the poor person with impunity, because the penalty is death. Here God is telling us that a life is a life.

If nothing else, the law slowed down the process of revenge. Unlike the blood feud, where retaliation could be carried out whenever and however the offended party wished, the law required that there be a process at which witnesses would bring forth testimony about what had occurred. In the Deuteronomic code, there were three important provisions about these witnesses. The first provision was that there must be more than one witness in order for a person to be convicted. Given that the methods of modern criminology were not available and that cases were handled with dispatch, it can be assumed that "witnesses" in the Deuteronomic code refers primarily to eyewitnesses. It is a high standard to require this degree of proof, having at least two eyewitnesses. Murder is frequently committed in secret.

The second Deuteronomic rule regarding witnesses was that they must also act as the executioners in capital cases. Unlike modern society, which holds its executions in private, Old Testament society held public executions. Those who provided the testimony to bring about a death sentence were expected to help carry it out. "The hands of the witnesses shall be the first raised against the person to execute the death penalty."

The final Deuteronomic provision for witnesses regarded the penalty for false testimony and followed the ninth commandment. The serious implications of bearing false witness would make witnesses careful to tell the truth as clearly and as simply as possible, without embellishments or inferences. With these provisions for witnessing, the Mosaic law was intended to be as fair as possible to the accused person. Indeed if the standards for testimony used in the Deuteronomic law were applied in our own criminal justice system, it is doubtful that there would be many convictions in death penalty cases.

E. Conclusion While the Old Testament does not forbid the death penalty, it imposes stringent criteria for its use. The Old Testament is concerned for justice and belief in a God who ultimately prefer to restore rather than to punish. This worked against widespread executions.

In addition, one of the great lessons of the Old Testament is that all nations, all social systems, even those special in God's eyes, fail to live up to his standards. True justice will not be found in any system that depends on human administration. People who are rich and powerful will always be treated better within the criminal justice system than those who are poor and weak. With this realization, we now turn to God's powerful new covenant made through the life and execution of the Son of man, the quintessential representative of the poor and the weak—those who suffer most at the hands of human justice systems.

II. *One Without Sin: New Testament Perspectives*

Whereas the Old Testament allowed the death penalty under certain stringent conditions, the New Testament closed off all possibility of any support for capital punishment. In the New Testament, Jesus creates the kingdom of God, a new social order not dependent on the use of political, social, or police power. Under this new social arrangement, love—not violence—is paramount. Since killing and revenge are incompatible with love it should be obvious that capital punishment cannot be part of the reign of God inaugurated through Jesus Christ.

A. Jesus Stops an Execution There can be no question about Jesus' attitude toward the death penalty. He did not deal with some controversial issues. But in the story of John, he did speak about capital punishment. Jesus was teaching in the temple when the scribes and Pharisees approached him with a woman caught in the act of adultery. According to the law, adultery was a capital offense. Apparently they were not too concerned about evenhanded justice since they did not also bring the man who committed adultery with this woman.

Jesus realized that their purpose for bringing the problem to him was to trap him into saying something inappropriate and blasphemous. So he didn't hurry his answer. Finally he told them, "Let anyone among you who is without sin be the first to throw a stone at her."

The merciful reasonableness of Jesus' approach to the problem diluted the blood lust of the crowd. They were forced to think about what they were doing. Ashamed of themselves, they slipped away. Jesus then told the woman that he, too, did not condemn her. "Go, and do not sin again." The approach that Jesus took to capital crime was in accordance with his approach to sin, forgiveness, and redemption in general. For Jesus, sin was sin; there was no sin worse than any other. All sin represented the human desire to control others, to make others into objects that exist only for our own benefit. Sin is our unholy desire "to be like God" in the sense that it is the human obsession to be in charge, to be at the center of the universe.

According to Jesus, this sinfulness could come out in acts or words or even thoughts. In the Sermon on the Mount, he equates murder with verbal insults and anger. In the same way, for Jesus there was no difference between actually committing adultery and harboring lustful thoughts. In either case, we belittle the importance of another human being.

In this sense, the law that Jesus gave us was a more stringent law than the Mosaic law of the Old Testament. But the answer Jesus made to all sin, whether that sin came out in the form of an angry word or a murder, was a merciful forgiveness that challenged the mind-set of violence and vengeance. "Love your enemies and pray for those who persecute you," Jesus told his followers.

Thus the response Jesus gave to the crowd who wanted to execute the adulteress was simply a logical extension of his approach to sinfulness in general. We have the right to kill only when we ourselves are blameless. Since we are never blameless, we never have the right to kill. Instead, our reaction to sin must be forgiveness, even as we ask for the forgiveness of our own sins. If we cannot forgive others, then we have no right to expect anyone, including God, to forgive our sins. Jesus made this explicit in Matthew. "For if you forgive others their trespasses, your heavenly Father will also forgive you; but if you do not forgive others, neither will your Father forgive your trespasses."

B. The Most Famous Execution That Christians should oppose the death penalty is clear in what Jesus taught during his ministry, and it can also be found in the example set by his own death. When Christians are tempted to think that support for capital punishment is compatible with their faith, they should consider carefully that they serve a Lord who himself was the victim of the death penalty.

The Hollywood portrayals of the death of Jesus have made us think of it in terms of heroes and villains. Jesus is seen as the hero; Caiaphas, Pilate, and Herod are shown as villains. Caiaphas is a scheming and power-mad politician. Pilate is a weak and vacillating judge. Herod is the mad king more interested in Jesus' ability to perform miracles than in the facts of his criminal case.

Such portrayals may lead us to believe that Jesus' trial was held in an uncivilized society, and that his death may have been avoided if a more reasonable and less capricious legal system had been in place. We may come out of such movies, for example, wishing that Jesus had been tried under the American judicial system—that our system could never have committed such a blatant injustice.

The facts, however, are quite different. Jesus Christ was tried in the most moral country of his time. He was tried under a system of justice that, while harsh, was systematic and strove to be fair. This fact has much to teach us about the fallibility of human morality and justice, even at their best.

Throughout the Roman Empire, the Jewish population was known as one of the most moral elements of society. The moral value of the Jewish population to the Roman Empire was recognized by exempting Jews from certain religious obligations they could not follow under Jewish law. These laws and the moral separateness of the Jews also at times led to resentment which could boil up into vicious pogroms and other measures against them. As with all moral people, the Jewish population was viewed with a mixture of respect, distrust, guilt, and hatred.

The Sanhedrin, the Jewish legislative body that tried Jesus, included some of these teachers of the law as well as the political leaders of the Jewish people in Judea. Because the trial was also held at the time of Passover, we surmise that the Jewish leaders would have been especially careful to follow the law to the greatest degree possible.

The reports of the trial in Matthew and Mark, however, do seem to contain deviations from rules for sessions of the Sanhedrin. The meeting was not held at the prescribed place; the meeting was held at night; the verdict was not postponed by a day; and the rules of evidence were abused. The account in Luke tells a different story of a daytime trial. Experts have suggested that the meeting reported in Matthew and Mark may have been a pretrial hearing and that Luke reports the true trial.

Whatever happened, the Bible does not tell of an uproar because of a serious violation of the law, something that would surely have occurred if zealous teachers of the law had been aware of such violations. Perhaps there are two explanations for this. Either the laws were not broken, or the violations were held to be minor. In either case it seems clear that the chief Jewish leaders felt that Jesus had received a fair hearing that did not violate the law in any substantial way.

But what then of the Roman law? Although the Roman legal system could be harsh, its principles were based on a desire for fairness, especially for Roman citizens. Paul's appeals for justice based on his Roman citizenship in Acts indicate the power that citizens held under the law. Principles of Roman law have influenced legal systems from that time forward. In fact, some principles of Roman law are still found in American jurisprudence.

The Pilate pictured in the Bible was hardly an example of Roman virtue. Yet, it is also obvious that he felt he needed a better reason than first given by the Jewish leaders to execute Jesus. When the trial opened, he found that Jesus was not in violation of any Roman law. Although he was willing to have him flogged to appease the Jewish leadership, he found no cause to condemn Jesus to death.

Pilate was finally convinced to crucify Jesus for reasons more political than legal. While Jesus had done nothing that warranted the death penalty, the claims being made about him made him dangerous. Caiaphas and his followers recognized that Pilate would have to act if Jesus was seen as a real danger to Roman rule. Thus, Pilate finally chose to condemn Jesus as "King of the Jews."

The execution of Jesus, then, demonstrates the flawed nature of all human systems of morality and law. When principles come into conflict with perceived practical needs, principles are often laid aside. Jesus' death should not lead to the condemnation of the Jewish leaders (much less the Jewish people) or the Roman leadership. Instead, it points to the injustice that contaminates all nations and their systems of justice.

In Christian theology, Jesus' death on the cross is much more than an example of human injustice. Jesus' death is in some mysterious way redemptive. In the Old Testament, animal sacrifice and capital punishment were meant to atone for individual sins, thereby reestablishing the moral balance that sin destroyed. According to the New Testament, Christ's death atoned for all human sin: past, present, and future. First John 2:2 states, "He is the atoning sacrifice for our sins, and not for ours only but also for the sins of the whole world."

Jesus' death removed the need for the animal sacrifices required in the Old Testament; his death was the final and all-redeeming sacrifice. Similarly, his death also removed the need for the human sacrifice of capital punishment. Because Jesus has righted the moral balance for all time, we no longer have to make sacrifices, either animal or human, to make things right. This is what frees his disciples to forgive those who have broken the moral order.

To support the death penalty, then, is to bring into question the efficacy of Christ's sacrifice. Society may still protect itself by separating the dangerous criminal from other people. Yet from a Christian point of view, this should be done as a redemptive act, not as a punitive one. The death penalty, which has no redemptive purpose, then, must not be used.

C. The Authorities and the Sword There are an overwhelming number of scriptural passages against the death penalty in the Gospels. For this reason, Christian death penalty proponents rarely appeal to the Gospels to support their belief. The one New Testament passage to which they may appeal is Romans 13:3–4.

> *For rulers are not a terror to good conduct, but to bad. Do you wish to have no fear of the authority? Then do what is good, and you will receive its approval; for it is God's servant for your good. But if you do what is wrong, you should be afraid, for the authority does not bear the sword in vain! It is the servant of God to execute wrath on the wrongdoer.*

This passage appears to lend some support for capital punishment. This is true, however, only if the text is read out of context. The word that has been translated "sword" in this passage is *machaira*, a symbol of authority but not the weapon used by the Romans in carrying out executions.

The early Christian church was a revolutionary movement. Some of the epistles—both of Paul and of other writers—show that, like most revolutionary movements, the church was attracting people who felt that the new social order gave them the right to do whatever they liked. Their behavior endangered the position of the church. Paul warned the churches that, to the degree it was possible without violating the law of God, Christians should obey the government.

For Paul, the state was a necessary structure in a fallen world. Through its police power, it kept a semblance of peace and therefore had the right to use reasonable force to carry out this function. At the time Paul was writing, however, Christians could not participate in government as officials, because they would not take the oath of allegiance to the emperor. They believed that such an oath of allegiance would have run counter to their allegiance to Jesus as Lord.

Romans 13 was written to a group of people who were not participants in government. They were people who had to live under the authority of a government over which they had no control. Given this situation, Paul suggested that they adopt a nonprovocative attitude toward the state.

Thus Paul's endorsement of governmental use of force in Romans 13 is not ringing. Taken in the context of the rest of Paul's writings and of the New Testament as a whole, Romans 13 only counsels Christians to submit to the authorities but does not allow them to participate in the state's unchristian actions. As such, it cannot be said that Romans 13 represents Paul's approval of the government's use of capital punishment.

D. Conclusion Through his teaching and his actions, Jesus Christ showed his disapproval of capital punishment. Every execution that occurs in the New Testament is arbitrary and unjust. Christ himself stopped one execution and was the victim of another. These facts in and of themselves should lead Christians to view the death penalty unfavorably.

While early Christians recognized the need for the state to sometimes use force in restraining evil, their view was that the utility of force was limited and its use should be curtailed. The failure of the Christian community to endorse governmental violence made it highly suspect in the eyes of the Roman empire. This led to conflict with the government and to the martyrdom of many early Christians.

The New Testament shows that the earliest Christians viewed the death penalty primarily from the perspective of potential victims, not supporters or enforcers. The subsequent history of the post-apostolic church reinforces the view that the earliest Christians opposed the death penalty and that this view came directly from their understanding that this was the position taken by Christ himself.

Deterrence

■ Deterrence—Introduction

In some polls, the most often cited reason for supporting the death penalty is the belief that it deters crime. In a *Newsweek* survey conducted in 2000, 34% of respondents cited deterrence as the main reason they supported the death penalty, ranking higher than all other reasons, including "an eye for an eye" and closure for victims. At the same time, a majority of people do not believe the death penalty is a deterrent. Even among supporters of the death penalty, there is considerable doubt of its efficacy. One in three death penalty supporters believes the death penalty is not a deterrent, and a substantial majority believe that it is at most a minor deterrent. Some, however, have questioned precisely how important a factor it truly is in shaping attitudes. Professors Phoebe Ellsworth and Lee Ross suggest that death penalty supporters claim their position is based upon deterrence because it is more socially acceptable than retribution and has the appearance of being scientific.

Deterrence is not a robust explanation of support for capital punishment. People say they support capital punishment because it deters, but in truth they would support capital punishment even if it were proved to their satisfaction that it did not deter. The famous capital punishment defender Ernest van den Haag reports that the well-known abolitionist Hugo Adam Bedau told him in correspondence that he would oppose the death penalty even if it were proved that each execution deterred 100,000 murders. The inverse might also be true. Some abolitionists have candidly said they would oppose capital punishment even if it were shown that it did deter murder. Ambiguities in public opinion notwithstanding, whether the death penalty deters is a crucially important question from a public policy standpoint, certainly more significant than cost. Criminal justice systems do not exist to save money; however, they do exist, at least in part, to deter crime.

At the outset, a distinction must be drawn between the two classical forms of deterrence—specific and general. Specific deterrence is the use of criminal penalties to deter the defendant from reoffending; in other words, to teach him a lesson. General deterrence is the use of criminal sanctions to dissuade other potential offenders from committing criminal acts. One of the few things that can be conclusively said about the death penalty is that it is an excellent specific deterrent (if it makes sense to think of an execution as a deterrent). Executed defendants never commit criminal acts again. Whether it is an effective general deterrent is a more difficult question to answer.

The intuition behind the use of capital punishment for deterrence is that the harsher the penalty, the more it deters. Professor van den Haag has said, "Our penal system rests on the proposition that more severe penalties are more deterrent than less severe penalties." But it isn't entirely clear how much the severity of the sanction contributes to deterrence. The certainty of punishment and the swiftness with which the sanction is delivered also enhance deterrence. The publicity of punishment matters, too. Harsh punishment imposed in secret is no deterrent to others. It might be that a swift and certain punishment of moderate severity deters more than a delayed, uncertain harsher penalty. The death penalty is imposed infrequently in America, and when it is imposed, it is slow to be delivered.

Other possibilities can be imagined. It might be that beyond a certain threshold harsher penalties do not lead to increased deterrence. It is possible that at some point extreme punishment becomes incomprehensibly extreme to a potential offender. Being executed seems dramatically harsh; being sentenced to prison for fifty years seems dramatically harsh, too. The deterrence argument behind the death penalty is based on the notion that potential offenders will not commit capital crimes because of a marginal increase in penalty—from, say, fifty years in prison, to death.

It is possible too that the use of capital punishment actually encourages homicide. Some scholars have suggested that violence in movies, television, and video games desensitizes people to violence and is at least partially responsible for the significant increase in homicide rates during the second half of the 20th century. The death penalty might conceivably send a message that the government condones violence. This is generally referred to as the "brutalization effect" of the death penalty. Scholars have found inconclusive evidence that homicide rates spike following executions, suggesting the validity of the brutalization hypothesis. This evidence is discussed further in Chapter 4.

The deterrence and brutalization effects are not mutually exclusive. It might be that the death penalty deters some murders and causes some others. The question of deterrence then becomes whether the magnitude of one effect is greater than the other.

These questions do not lend themselves to convenient study. Prior to 1975, most researchers studied the deterrence question by comparative analysis. They compared murder rates in contiguous states that had different death penalty laws, or murder rates in an individual state before and after the implementation of the death penalty, or murder rates immediately following executions, theorizing that the deterrent or antideterrent effect of the death penalty would be most pronounced during periods when capital punishment was most in the public consciousness.

Professor Thorsten Sellin conducted the most famous of the comparative studies on the issue of deterrence. Sellin compared the homicide rates in contiguous states with and without the death penalty from 1920 through 1963. Sellin found no compelling evidence of deterrence. For the years in question, Michigan (without capital punishment), Indiana, and Ohio (both with capital punishment) each had aggregate homicide rates of 3.5 per 100,000 population. Sellin found similar results in other contiguous states. He also found similar results studying police killings and prison murders. It is sometimes argued that the death penalty is useful in shaping the course of criminal conduct; it deters criminals from carrying weapons and discourages them from using the weapons in the face of arrest. In the case of prison murders, the thought is that because inmates have little to fear from the criminal justice system, they can only be deterred by the threat of capital punishment. Sellin found no evidence to support either of these conclusions in his comparative analysis. Some other studies have approached the issue in a longitudinal fashion. One team of researchers examined whether homicide rates increased after the death penalty was abolished in various countries including Austria, Canada, Denmark, England, Israel, and Switzerland. The researchers found ambiguous evidence: in some countries homicide rates increased, in other countries the rates decreased.

Of course, comparative studies have obvious deficiencies. Geographical and temporal contiguity are built-in controls of sorts. States abutting one another as well as individual countries over different time periods presumably have similar economic conditions and racial demographics, but these are only imperfect controls; myriad variables have been hypothesized to affect crime rates, including unemployment, age demographics, and expenditure on police. To draw more definitive conclusions about the deterrent effect of the death penalty, a researcher must control for the effect of these other variables.

In 1975, Professor Isaac Ehrlich published the first study of deterrence that employed multiple regression analysis. Ehrlich controlled for the impact of unemployment, per capita income, and age demographics (generally speaking, young people commit more crime) in analyzing homicide rates between 1933 and 1969. Ehrlich concluded that "an additional execution per year over the period in question may have resulted, on average, in seven or eight fewer murders." Professor Ehrlich's study gained immediate influence. It is cited in the majority opinion in *Gregg*.

Most importantly, Professor Ehrlich's study loosed a spate of scientific analysis of deterrence. One line of research critiqued the methodology employed by Professor Ehrlich. These detractors argued, among other things, that Professor Ehrlich's analysis failed to consider the possible impact of a host of other factors including racial discord in the United States, the Vietnam War, and the increased prevalence of handgun ownership. A host of other researchers including William Bowers and Glenn Pierce; Brian Forst; Jon Sorensen, Robert Wrinkle, Victoria Brewer and James Marquart; and William Bailey employed multiple regression analysis without finding any statistically significant deterrent effect. One methodological advance was to limit analyses to those types of murder likely to be deterred by the death penalty. For example, William Bailey and Ruth Peterson found no effect of the death penalty on the killing of police officers in the United States from 1973 through 1984. Other studies have focused on the difference between stranger and nonstranger homicide, with the thought that nonstranger homicide is likely to be less sensitive to the certainty and severity of criminal sanctions.

In 1989, the American Society of Criminology—the largest association of criminologists in the United States—adopted a resolution calling for the abolition of capital punishment, relying in part upon its review of death penalty research and the absence of "consistent evidence of crime deterrence through execution." In a survey presented in this chapter's Critical Documents section, more than 80% of the past presidents of the American Society of Criminology, the Academy of Criminal Justice Sciences, and the Law and Society Association said they believe the death penalty is no more effective at deterring homicide than long prison sentences.

The retentionist case has been strengthened by a series of studies finding evidence of deterrence through regression analysis. Teams of researchers at Clemson University, Emory University, University of Colorado, and the University of Houston have all published studies reporting statistically significant evidence of deterrence. The Perspectives section of this chapter offers two different studies, each employing different methodologies and reaching different conclusions. Keith Harries and Derral Cheatwood compare murder rates in contiguous counties with different death penalty laws (generally counties at the edges of states with different death penalty rules). The proximity of the counties offers built-in controls for variables that might affect crime rates. Harries and Cheatwood find no evidence of a deterrent effect. Hashem Dezhbakhsh, Paul Rubin, and Joanna Shepherd, employing a regression analysis, find that each execution results in an average of eighteen fewer murders.

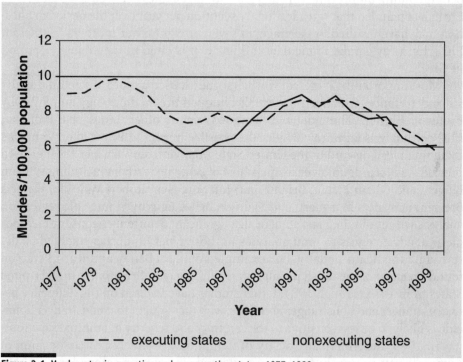

Figure 3-1 Murder rates in executing and nonexecuting states, 1977–1999.

■ Deterrence—Critical Documents

Michael L. Radelet and Ronald L. Akers, "Deterrence and the Death Penalty: The Views of the Experts"

The goal of this research is to determine if there is consensus among expert criminologists on whether the death penalty has been, is, or could be a general deterrent to criminal homicide. To assess expert opinion, we surveyed 67 of the 70 current and former presidents of three professional criminology organizations: The American Society of Criminology, Academy of Criminal Justice Sciences, and Law and Society Association. Over 80 percent of these experts believe the existing research fails to support a deterrence justification for capital punishment. Over three-quarters believe that increasing the frequency of executions, or decreasing the time spent on death row before execution, would not produce a general deterrent effects.

I. *Methodology*

To assess what the "experts" think about the deterrent effect of the death penalty, we must first answer the question of how to define "expert." One plausible definition is anyone who has published peer-reviewed research on the death penalty and deterrence. Surely those who have been active researchers in an area over many years are experts. However, such an approach has limited utility because 1) it is possible that only death penalty abolitionists, for whatever reasons, are motivated to conduct such research, 2) there would be a problem in differentially weighing the opinions of scholars who have published several acclaimed deterrence studies in major criminology journals from those whose research is less abundant or respected, and 3) surveying researchers in the field of deterrence would ask them to, in effect, evaluate their own work.

For this project we define "expert" as one who has achieved visibility and recognition as a leader among criminologists in the United States. Our operational definition is one who has been recognized by peers to the extent of being elected to the highest office in scholarly organizations. We contacted all present and former presidents of the country's top academic criminological societies. This small and elite group includes many of the country's most respected criminologists. As such, although few of these scholars have done research on capital punishment in general or deterrence in particular, they are generally well versed in central criminological issues, such as crime causation, crime prevention, and criminal justice policy. The presidents of three associations were surveyed: the American Society of Criminology, Academy of Criminal Justice Sciences, and the Law and Society Association.

The American Society of Criminology (ASC), founded in 1941, is the country's largest association of professional and academic criminologists, with a 1994 membership of 2,500, dominated by academics from graduate and research institutions. The Academy of Criminal Justice Sciences (ACJS), founded in 1963 includes 2,400 members. Its primary goal is the advancement of the criminal justice system through research and education. Its membership overlaps to a considerable extent with the ASC, but its leadership does not. Only one person in the history of the two societies has served as president of both. The Law and Society Association (L&SA), founded in 1964, includes more law professors and legal scholars among its 1,400 members than either the ASC or ACJS. Again there is overlapping membership with ASC and some with ACJS, but no one has served as president of L&SA and either of the other two. These three associations are all interdisciplinary and publish what are among the most respected scholarly journals in criminology and criminal justice: *Criminology* (ASC), *Justice Quarterly* (ACJS), and *Law and Society Review* (L&SA). Each organization elects officers, including a president, by a ballot sent to all members. To be elected president, one must generally have high visibility in the field, be well-respected, and have been active in programmatic and organizational activities.

Through letters and phone calls we were able to identify which of the former presidents of these organizations were still living, and to obtain addresses for each. A total of 71 individuals was identified: 29 from the Academy of Criminal Justice Sciences, 27 from the American Society of Criminology, and 15 from the Law and Society Association. As noted, one person had served as president of two of the associations, reducing our sample to 70. A total of 67 responded to our questionnaire (95.7 percent): 27 from ACJS, 26 from the ASC, and 15 from L&SA.

The presidents were asked to answer the questions "on the basis of your knowledge of the literature and research in criminology." We did not ask for their personal opinions on the death penalty. Eleven questions relating to deterrence issues were included on the questionnaire, and the responses to all eleven are reported below.

II. *Results*

A. General Questions on Deterrence The first question to be explored concerns the general question of how the presidents of the criminological associations generally view the deterrence question. **Table 3-2** begins by replicating the question asked in the Gallup polls, "Do you feel that the death penalty acts as a deterrent to the commitment to murder—that it lowers the murder rate, or what?" It can be seen that the experts are more than twice as likely as the general population to believe that the death penalty does not lower the murder rate. Among the 64 experts who voiced opinions on this question, 56 (87.5 percent) believe the death penalty does not have deterrent effects.

We next compared the beliefs of our experts to those of top criminal justice administrators, specifically to the beliefs of the police chiefs surveyed by Peter D. Hart Research Associates in 1995. Overall there is widespread agreement between the criminologists and the police chiefs on the deterrent value of the death penalty (or lack thereof), with the criminologists even less likely than the chiefs to see any deterrent value. All of the criminologists, and 85 percent of the police chiefs, believe it is totally or largely accurate that "Politicians support the death penalty as a symbolic way to show they are tough on crime." Almost 87 percent of the criminologists and 57 percent of the chiefs find it totally or largely accurate to say "Debates about the death penalty distract Congress and state legislatures from focusing on real solutions to crime problems." None of the criminologists, and only about a quarter of the chiefs, believe there is any accuracy in the statement, "The death penalty significantly reduces the number of homicides." These statements indicate that both academic criminologists and po-

| Table 3-2 | Comparison of Responses of Criminologists and General Public to Identical Questions on Deterrence | | |

Q. Do you feel that the death penalty acts as a deterrent to the commitment to murder—that it lowers the murder rate, or what?

	Criminology Presidents	Gallup 1985	Gallup 1991
Yes	11.9%	62%	51%
No	83.6	31	41
No Opinion	4.5	7	8
N (responses)	67.0	1,523	990

lice chiefs view the death penalty as more effective in political rhetoric than as a criminal justice tool.

Table 3-3 asks general questions about deterrence in two different ways. We developed the wording for these questions ourselves, so no comparisons with other opinion polls are possible. However, we believe these questions word the issue more precisely than the questions taken from other surveys. Given the widespread availability of "life without parole" as an alternative to the death penalty, the first question displayed in Table 3-3 is perhaps the clearest statement of the deterrence issue as actually faced by researchers and policy makers today.

B. The Question of Reform Proponents of the death penalty might concur with the critics of the deterrence argument, but say that the lack of a clear deterrent

| Table 3-3 | Responses of Criminologists to General Questions on Deterrence |

Q. Overall, over the last twenty years, the threat or use of the death penalty in the United States has been a stronger deterrent to homicide than the threat or use of long (or life) prison sentences.

Strongly agree	0
Agree	4.5%
Disagree	43.3
Strongly disagree	49.3
No response	3.0

Q. Overall, how would you evaluate the empirical support for the deterrent effects of the death penalty?

Strong support	0
Moderate support	4.5%
Weak support	44.8
No support	49.3
No response	1.5

effect is a result of the fact that only a small proportion of those on death row are executed each year, or that the wait on death row between condemnation and execution is too long. Increasing the frequency and decreasing the celerity of the death penalty could produce a deterrent effect. The experts responding to our survey, however, disagree with such a position. Almost eighty percent disagree or strongly disagree with the statement, "If the frequency of executions were to increase significantly, more homicides would be deterred than if the current frequency of executions remained relatively stable." Nearly three quarters (73.2 percent) of the experts disagreed or strongly disagreed with the position that decreasing the time on death row would deter more homicides. Much of the research that informs these experts' opinions was done with data from the 1930's, 1940's, and 1950's, when the frequency of executions was higher and the average time spent on death row was shorter than it is today. Hence, criminologists do have some research at their disposal that would enable accurate predictions of what would happen if these proposed death penalty reforms were actually enacted.

C. Support for the Brutalization Hypothesis In a final question, the experts were asked how they felt about the so-called "brutalization hypothesis." This argument suggests that the death penalty tends to devalue human life and send a message that tells citizens that killing people under some circumstances is appropriate. However, this hypothesis does not have widespread support among experts. Two-thirds (67.1 percent) of the respondents either disagree or strongly disagree with the statement, "Overall, the presence of the death penalty tends to increase a state's murder rate rather than to decrease it."

The responses to this item help us address some possible reservations about our overall findings: Is there anti-capital punishment bias among our respondents? Were the responses made based on an understanding of the research or are our respondents merely liberal academics who object to the death penalty on moral grounds and would report opinions that might undermine it, even if the empirical evidence showed otherwise? The responses to the question on brutalization suggest that the answers to these questions are negative. If our respondents simply respond to any question in a way that buttresses the abolitionist position, there should be strong agreement with the notion that the death penalty actually increases the homicide rate, since this is an anti-capital punishment argument. It appears, instead, that the respondents were responding on the grounds we asked—their appraisal of existing research. The brutalization hypothesis, in fact has not been tested very well and the research supporting it remains more suggestive than definitive. As on the other questions, our respondents appear to be reacting to the state of knowledge on this question, not to their personal preferences.

III. *Conclusions*

The results of this project clearly show that there is a wide consensus among America's top criminologists that the death penalty does, or can do, little to reduce rates of criminal violence in our society. These results chisel away at one of the most important justifications for the death penalty in modern society.

The study also suggests that political debates about how to reduce criminal violence in America should shift away from debates about the death penalty.

Politicians or prosecutors who continue to support the death penalty on deterrence grounds may be able to point to their "gut" feelings or to individual studies that support their position. Our findings support a shift in political discussions about crime away from the death penalty and in the direction of more promising crime reducing policies.

■ Deterrence—Perspectives

■ Issue—Does the Death Penalty Deter?

Keith Harries and Derral Cheatwood, "Capital Punishment and the Deterrence of Violent Crime in Comparable Counties"

The deterrence argument for capital punishment claims that the existence of the death penalty and the use of that penalty will deter violent crime within the political jurisdiction in which the law exists and is applied. If that is true, then in two fundamentally similar jurisdictions that differ only in the existence and use of capital punishment, the level of violent crime in the jurisdiction that employs the death penalty should be lower than the level in the jurisdiction that does not.

Past comparative research has suggested that this is not the case. However, most of the research on deterrence has relied on large units of analysis, seldom smaller than states or nations, with the attendant problems of data aggregation and comparability of units. The larger the jurisdictions, the more heterogeneous they become and the less sure we can be of controlling for extraneous factors or guaranteeing true comparability between the entities examined. To counteract these problems, the research reported in this chapter employs socioeconomic and capital punishment variables for 1,725 counties in the United States and for a smaller select sample of 293 matched pairs of counties. The use of counties not only significantly expands the sample size but also addresses the problem of data aggregation by dealing with more compact and homogenous units. At the same time, employing 293 pairs of contiguous counties confronts the issue of comparability by directly contrasting political entities that are inherently similar in terms of their human and physical geographies, their regional settings, and their broad developmental characteristics.

Differences between the pairs of matched counties on those economic and sociodemographic characteristics that have proven significant correlates of serious violent crime are then tested as predictors of differences in the violent crime rate between the counties. Further, each contiguous pair consists of counties in two different states, so the use of capital punishment will vary across each pair. This variation, then, is also tested as a predictor of the difference in the level of violent crime between the two adjacent counties. By studying matched counties in which the existence of capital punishment statutes or the level of use of those statutes varies, we should have improved the conditions to test deterrence theory in comparative settings. Based upon the weight of the prior research, we posit that neither the existence of a provision for capital punishment at the state level, the use of the provision as demonstrated by the number of inmates sentenced to death, nor the enactment of that provision as demonstrated by the actual number of executions in the state since 1976, has the effect of deterring violent crime at the county level.

I. *Sample and Methodology*

The original full data set consists of 1,725 counties drawn from the County and City Data Book for 1988. This constitutes all counties in the United States with populations of 20,000 or more. Data on key variables, including race, gender, and age composition, are reported in the County and City Data Book only for counties of that size or larger. This, of course, produces some bias in the data, unavoidable given the data available. The benefits derived from the larger sample of more homogenous counties (compared to states or nations) seems to justify use of the sample, even taking these problems into account.

The final sample sought for the research was a specific set of counties in the United States that inherently controlled for a number of fundamental variables. A method to assure comparability on the dimensions of geography, regional context, and historical development and yet allow variance in state patterns in the use of capital punishment, is to select all pairs of counties in the United States that share a majority of a contiguous border across a state line. This is certainly not a common technique, and the procedure for determining such pairs is described below. We must note that a more precise or formal description is given first, but must also acknowledge that the criterion used is somewhat difficult to visualize.

In 1990, we located every pair of counties in the United States that mutually shares 45 percent or more of their borders across a state line. We originally planned to use counties that shared a majority of their mutual boundaries, that is, 50 percent or more. But in a surprising number of cases, determining precisely this "50 percent" measure proved to be difficult, since one county would share almost exactly that amount with two other counties. To account for this, we adopted the more forgiving 45 percent figure.

First, we looked at every county that had a border on a state line. If 45 percent or more of that border was shared by a county across that state line, we then asked whether that second county also shared 45 percent of its border with the first county. So, for example, over 45 percent of the southern border of York County, Pennsylvania, and 45 percent of the northern border of Baltimore County, Maryland, are shared. In some cases, one county shared one border with two other counties or shared two borders across two states (when on the "corner" of a state, for example). In these cases, a die was rolled to determine which pair of counties would be used in the analysis. As a result, no county was included more than once.

This process of matching enabled us to do two things. First, in comparing these counties, we controlled for the features discussed above. The topography, climate, and general ethnic, economic, and social history of any specific portion of northern Mississippi and southern Tennessee, for example, are virtually indistinguishable. The same is true for the topography, climate, and history of northeastern Virginia compared to southwestern Maryland, or the panhandle of Florida compared to southern Alabama. Yet some measures of southerness would place Mississippi, Tennessee, and Virginia together, while separating Maryland from Virginia. And cross-state comparisons would find the suburbs of Washington, D.C. in the same classification as villages in the Shenandoah Valley, or Miami, Florida, grouped with Leonia (population 200), Florida. Our sample of contiguous counties addresses this problem by comparing Hardeman County, Tennessee directly with Benton County, Mississippi, Montgomery County, Maryland, with Loudoun County, Virginia, and Holmes County, Florida, with Geneva County, Alabama. Geographic factors that may have had a significant effect on social or historical development (specifically rivers or lakes) are dealt with in the analysis.

Second, such matching enables us to identify counties that share these geographic, climatic, and developmental features, yet that exist in jurisdictions that differ (by virtue of being in different states) on the presence of a capital punishment statute (in some cases), or on the number of inmates on death row or the number of persons executed since 1976 in all cases.

Again, an example illustrates the methodology. Cowley County in Kansas shares over 45 percent of its southern border with the northern border of Kay County in Oklahoma. These counties are small enough in size that they are relatively homogenous in the socio-demographic characteristics of their population, yet they are separated by the legal codes of the two states in which they lie. Oklahoma allows for capital punishment; Kansas did not when this project was undertaken. Further, even if two states have provisions for capital punishment, they will vary in the degree to which they sentence their citizens to death and the degree to which they carry out those sentences.

Incidentally, the comparison of contiguous counties in two states, only one of which has the death penalty, allows for a limited test of the displacement hypothesis. If the homicide offender is the logical actor required by deterrence theory, then the existence of the death penalty should prompt offenders to change the location of their crime when possible. If this were the case, an offender should choose an abolitionist state in which to commit a felony if it required nothing more than crossing a county line. This should be particularly true in our case, since our crime data include the supposedly more planned offense of robbery. However, our data allow only for a limited consideration of this question. If crime rates are higher in abolitionist states' counties, it could imply either that deterrence works or that displacement is occurring, and we would not be in a position to make even tentative claims regarding displacement. However, if crime rates are not higher in abolitionist states, then the nature of the sample involved would clearly imply that displacement is not occurring.

After eliminating duplicated counties, we found 786 such counties, or 393 matched pairs, in the United States. Again, however, not all of these have adequate data for analysis. The final study, then, is based on 293 matched pairs of these counties, comparing 586 counties in all.

The variables included in the analysis have been drawn from the literature on the correlates of violent crime at a variety of geographic scales, ranging from cities to nation-states. A set of 13 key variables that recur repeatedly in the literature on violent crime were selected from the *County and City Data Book* for 1988. These variables were: population, population per square mile, percent non-white, male-female ratio, percentage aged 15 to 24, percentage aged 24 to 34, percentage of female-headed households, infant deaths per 1,000 births, percentage with 12+ years education, percentage below the poverty level, percentage of owner-occupied homes, unemployment rate, and per capita income. In addition, the number of violent crimes was taken from this source and the county violent crime rate computed as the dependent variable.

Both methodological considerations and recent work by Bailey and Peterson support the use of violent crime rates rather than capital murder rates as the dependent variable. Bailey and Peterson used a monthly time-series analysis of executions and execution publicity effects, on rates of Type I (most serious) Uniform Crime Reports (UCR) crimes (with the exception of murder and arson) to test the premise that "capital punishment may affect other crimes that put victims' lives at risk." The results indicate an impact of executions on rates of robbery, burglary, and—(most especially)—aggravated assault. Indeed, this research finds stronger deterrent effects for these crimes than have been found for murder.

Methodologically, the availability of the data and the theoretical operation of deterrent effects (if any) in real-world populations both argue for the use of violent crime rates. Only the violent crime rate is reported in the County and City Data Book, and using murder data for smaller counties would necessitate not only using another data source, but in some cases aggregating data over periods of 5–10 years (or more) to ensure capturing at least one murder in small counties. Given all these considerations, the general violent crime rate remains the dependent variable employed.

It is beyond the scope here to discuss the abundance of research that supports the inclusion of the chosen independent variables. The centrality of density or urbanization to levels of violence across a geographic scale is well documented, and two variables were coded as potential measures of this: population and population density. We assumed that population density is the most obvious measure, in that it is a crude metric of potential interactions between people, including those that involve criminal violence. However, we remained open to the possibility that the absolute number of people in the geographic area may be the critical factor and left in a measure to allow for this.

The recurrent association of violent crime with measures of race, age, and gender is captured with figures on percentage nonwhite, the male-to-female ratio, and the percentage of the population aged 15–34 (computed from two variables in the data). The literature on violent crime clearly indicates that the ages from 15 to 34 are those of highest involvement. Similarly, one of the most consistent correlates of criminal involvement is failure in school, measured by the percentage of the population with 12 years or more of education.

The final six variables are all surrogate measures of economic well-being. All have been used in various studies as economic measures. Some are quite obvious, specifically the percentage below the poverty level, the unemployment rate and per capita income. The remaining three have been shown to be reliable indicators of the real level of economic deprivation in ways that might be hidden by more obvious monetary measures, specifically: infant deaths per 1,000, percentage of female headed households, and percentage of owner-occupied homes.

Finally, from *Death Row, USA,* published by the NAACP Legal Defense Fund, each county was coded as to whether it was in a state with or without a death penalty statute, the number of people being held on death row as of spring 1992 in the state in which each county appears, and the number of people executed in each county's state since 1976.

II. *Findings*

A first series of multiple regressions was run on the full set of 1,725 counties without inclusion of the capital punishment variables. A second set of equations was then computed with the capital punishment variables included. The purpose was to see what variables appeared to the important without the capital punishment measures in the analysis. Again these analyses are only preliminary to the central analyses of the data for the matched pairs.

Tests of intercorrelation and examination of a number of preliminary multiple regressions led to the inclusion of 9 of the original 13 independent variables in the final multivariate analyses of the full county sample: population density (DENSITY), males per 100 females (SEXRATIO), percentage of female households (%FEMHEAD), infant deaths per 1,000 births (INFTDETH), percentage below poverty level (%POVERTY), percentage of owner-occupied housing (%OWN-HOME), the unemployment rate (UNEMPLOY), per capita income (PERCAPIN), and percentage age 15 to 34 (%15TO34).

Thus, from the original 13 variables percentage age 25 to 34 were combined into 1 variable, and 3 variables (population, percentage with 12+ years of education and percentage nonwhite) were dropped. The latter variable, percentage nonwhite, is one of the more common correlates in the literature but was deleted because of its high correlation with the percentage of female households and the fact that when substituted in the multiple regressions for percentage of female households, its effect was less than the factor for which it was substituted. The same is true for the education measure (percentage with 12+ years of education), which was highly correlated with per capita income, yet was not as influential in the multiple regression analysis, and population which had a similar relationship to the measure of density.

From these nine variables, six enter in the first regression equation, with the rate of violent crime as the dependent or "predicted" variable (see **Table 3-4**). Of these six, three explain 36 percent of the variance in the homicide rate, while the remaining three variables that enter add less than an additional 1 percent. Pragmatically, then the key variables in predicting the violent crime rate in the larger sample are the percentage of female-headed households, the percent of owner-occupied housing, and personal income per capita. The most significant of these is the percentage of female-headed households, which alone accounts for 25 percent of the variance. Of the remaining variables, two have signs opposite those expected, the percentage age 15 to 34 and the percentage living in poverty.

The addition of the capital punishment variables to the analysis of the full sample produces few changes (see **Table 3-5**). The first three factors in both equations are the same, and the percentage of variance explained is identical. However, the number of inmates on death row enters as the fourth variable, and adds 2.9 percent to the level of statistical explanation. The remaining two variables in the

Table 3-4	Predictors of Violent Crime Rate in 1,725 Counties		
Variable	**Beta**	**R^2**	**Cumulative R^2**
%FEMHEAD	.436	.250	.250
%OWNHOME	−.285	.086	.336
PERCAPIN	.114	.028	.364
DENSITY	.062	.004	.368
%POVERTY	−.088	.002	.370
%15TO34	−.061	.002	.372

Note: Beta represents the correlation between the variable and the violent crime rate. For example, a 1% increase in FEMHEAD is associated with a .436% increase in violent crime rate. A 1% increase in OWNHOME is associated with a .285% decrease in violent crime rate. R^2 represents the percentage by which the variable explains the variance in the violent crime rate.

equation also appeared in the first multiple regression, although their order has changed. Neither of them adds substantially to the predictive power of the model.

The significance of the capital punishment variable that enters the equation, however, is in its sign. The rate of violent crime is positively related to the number of inmates on death row. It certainly may be the case that more violent areas produce more candidates for death row, but these data clearly do not support the position that placing people on death row or executing them is correlated with lower rates of violent crime.

The important tests for our purposes, however, are those that now include the capital punishment variables in the matched county pairs.

To examine this, we have created independent or predictor variables that are computed as the differences between the matched counties on the variables used in the previous analyses, with the dependant variable computed as the difference in the county violent crime rates.

These difference variables are employed as predictor variables in a regression, and the results appear in **Table 3-6**. The most obvious finding for our research is that none of the capital punishment variables appear. In keeping with findings from other research, the difference in population density between the two coun-

Table 3-5	Predictors of Violent Crime Rate in 1,725 Counties with Capital Punishment Variables Included		
Variable	**Beta**	**R^2**	**Cumulative R^2**
%FEMHEAD	.478	.250	.250
%OWNHOME	−.235	.086	.336
PERCAPIN	.069	.028	.364
#DEATHROW	.194	.029	.393
%POVERTY	−.160	.007	.400
DENSITY	.090	.006	.406

Table 3-6	Socio-Economic and Capital Punishment Differences as Predictors of Differences in Violent Crime Rates Among 293 Matched County Pairs		
Variable	Beta	R^2	Cumulative R^2
Diff. DENSITY	.7613	.632	.632
Diff. %FEMHEAD	.2354	.028	.660
Diff. INFTDEATH	−.1129	.015	.675
Diff. %POVERTY	−.1091	.008	.683

ties enters first, followed by the difference in the percentage of female headed households, the difference in the infant death rate, and the difference in the percentage below the poverty line.

In order to examine the effect that the differences in the existence of capital punishment statutes, the number of people on death row, or the number of people executed since 1976 have on the difference in the violent crime rate in these matched counties, we forced the capital punishment variables into the equation first. Taken together, they produced an R^2 of .0176, in essence accounting for less than 2 percent of the variation. After these variables, the four factors reported above enter in the same order in roughly the same magnitude. Moreover, the relationship between the difference in the number of inmates on death row or the number executed and the difference in the violent crime rate in these matched pairs is again positive.

III. *Conclusion and Discussion*

There is, then, virtually no support here for a deterrence effect of capital punishment at the county level. Not the existence of a capital punishment statute at the state level, the presence of individuals on death row, nor the execution of individuals correlates with lower crime rates at the county level. Whatever the process for the deterrent effect of capital punishment is supposed to be—however the use of the death penalty at the state level is supposed to translate itself to individuals—it is not manifesting itself at the level of counties.

Indeed, what correlations do appear between capital punishment variables and violent crime are positive. As one increases, so does the other. Two arguments could account for our data. On the one hand, the data may support a just-deserts model. If there is more violent crime, there will be more people to sentence and execute, a logical or justified conclusion within that framework. On the other hand, a brutalization argument also fits the data. Two dimensions of this model could be relevant, both of which have also found empirical support in other research. It may be that frequent executions by the state create an atmosphere for the legitimation of violence, so that individuals come to decide for themselves that someone they personally define as a transgressor deserves to be killed. This research was designed to test the deterrence argument rather than evaluate brutalization effects or just-deserts, however, so while the data certainly fit a brutalization model better, we must be somewhat reserved in claims for support for that idea.

On the contrary, the deterrence model argues that the presence and enactment of capital punishment statutes will produce lowered levels of violent crime. Even if one suggests this will only occur over time, then the measure of the number of people executed by state since 1976 accounts for this difference. However, while our data provide some support for a brutalization or just-deserts argument, they clearly do not support deterrence as a function of capital punishment.

The positive correlation found also offers a strong challenge to a displacement argument. The contiguous counties we looked at offered excellent opportunities for displacement to occur; indeed, it is difficult to think of a more potentially ideal setting. The positive association between crime rates and the death penalty variables appears to dictate rejection of the idea that rational criminals move their activities from death penalty jurisdictions to non-death penalty jurisdictions when it is convenient to do so.

One of the more intriguing findings, albeit unrelated to the initial concerns of the study, is the predominance of the percentage of female headed households as a primary determinant of the level of violent crime at the county level, both in the general sample and in the smaller congruent-county sample. This is a finding that we can only suggest deserves further investigation, and we note that other research finds similar importance in the percentage of female households for certain types of crime, although some research finds a negative effect from the same variable.

Taken together, our finding that sociodemographic factors are significant in predicting county-level rates of violent crime and the finding that the capital punishment variables are not significant again confirm the conclusion that structural factors and the cultural conditions that accompany them are far more important in determining the level of violent crime in a locality than are the actions of agencies of social control.

The decision of whether a model of justice based on a just-deserts philosophy is called for is a moral question and not one based upon data, since such a model does not rest on empirically testable beliefs that behaviors will change. Deterrence inherently rests on a belief that behavior will change and is, as a result, not supported. Whether a just-deserts model is justified by our findings may be a question for moral philosophy, theory, or politics. But our findings clearly offer no support for a deterrent effect of capital punishment.

Hashem Dezhbakhsh, Paul H. Rubin, and Joanna M. Shepherd, "Does Capital Punishment Have a Deterrent Effect? New Evidence from Post-Moratorium Panel Data"

Evidence on the deterrent effect of capital punishment is important for many states that are currently reconsidering their position on the issue. We examine the deterrent hypothesis using county-level, post-moratorium panel data and a system of simultaneous equations. The procedure we employ overcomes common aggregation problems, eliminates the bias arising from unobserved heterogeneity, and provides evidence relevant for current conditions. Our results suggest that capital punishment has a strong deterrent effect; each execution results, on average, in 18 fewer murders—with a margin of error of plus or minus 10. Tests show that results are not driven by tougher sentencing laws, and are also robust to many alternative specifications.

I. *Introduction*

The acrimonious debate over capital punishment has continued for centuries. An important issue in this debate is whether capital punishment deters murders. Psychologists and criminologists who examined the issue initially reported no deterrent effect. Economists joined the debate with the pioneering work of Ehrlich. Ehrlich's regression results, using U.S. aggregate time-series for 1933–1969 and state level cross-sectional data for 1940 and 1950, suggest a significant deterrent effect, which sharply contrasts with earlier findings. The policy importance of the research in this area is borne out by the considerable public attention that Ehrlich's work has received. The Solicitor General of the United States, for example, introduced Ehrlich's findings to the Supreme Court in support of capital punishment.

Coinciding with the Supreme Court's deliberation on the issue, Ehrlich's finding inspired an interest in econometric analysis of deterrence, leading to many studies that use his data but different regression specifications—different regressors or different choice of endogenous vs. exogenous variables. The mixed findings prompted a series of sensitivity analyses on Ehrlich's equations, reflecting a further emphasis on specification.

Data issues, on the other hand, have received far less attention. Most of the existing studies use either time-series or cross-section data. The studies that use national time-series data are affected by an aggregation problem. Any deterrence from an execution should affect the crime rate only in the executing state. Aggregation dilutes such distinct effects. Cross sectional studies are less sensitive to this problem, but their static formulation precludes any consideration of the dynamics of crime, law enforcement, and judicial processes. Moreover, cross sectional studies are affected by unobserved heterogeneity which cannot be controlled for in the absence of time variation. The heterogeneity is due to jurisdiction-specific characteristics that may correlate with other variables of the model, rendering estimates biased. Several authors have expressed similar data concerns or called for new research based on panel data. Such research will be timely and useful for policy making.

We examine the deterrent effect of capital punishment using a system of simultaneous equations and county-level panel data that cover the post-moratorium period. This is the most disaggregated and detailed data used in this literature. Our analysis overcomes data and econometric limitations in several ways. First, the disaggregate data allow us to capture the demographic, economic, and jurisdictional differences among U.S. counties, while avoiding aggregation bias. Second, by using panel data, we can control for some unobserved heterogeneity across counties, therefore avoiding the bias that arises from the correlation between county-specific effects and judicial and law enforcement variables. Third, the large number of county-level observations extends our degrees of freedom, thus broadening the scope of our empirical investigation. The large data set also increases variability and reduces colinearity among variables. Finally, using recent data makes our inference more relevant for the current crime situation and more useful for the ongoing policy debate on capital punishment.

III. *Empirical Results*

A. Regression Results The coefficient estimates for the murder supply equation obtained using the two-stage least squares method and controlling for county-level fixed effects are reported in **Table 3-7.** Various models reported in Table 3-7 differ in the way the perceived probabilities of arrest, sentencing and execution are measured. These three probabilities are endogenous to the murder supply equation; the tables present the coefficients on the predicted values of these probabilities.

For model 1 in Table 3-7 the conditional execution probability is measured by executions at t divided by number of death sentences at t + 6. For model 2 this probability is measured by number of executions at t + 6 divided by number of death sentences at t. The two ratios reflect forward looking and backward looking expectations, respectively. The displacement lag of six years reflects the lengthy waiting time between sentencing and execution, which averages six years for the period we study. For probability of sentencing given arrest we use a two-year lag displacement, reflecting an estimated two year lag between arrest and sentencing. Therefore, the conditional sentencing probability for model 1 is measured by the number of death sentences at t divided by the number of arrests for murder at t − 2. For model 2 this probability is measured by number of death sentences at t + 2 divided by number of arrests for murder at t. Given the absence of an arrest lag, no lag displacement is used to measure the arrest probability. It is simply the number of murder-related arrests at t divided by the number of murders at t.

For model 3 we use an averaging rule. We use a six year moving average to measure the conditional probability of execution given a death sentence. Specifically, this probability at time t is defined as the sum of executions during (t + 2, t + 1, t, t − 1, t − 2, and t − 3) divided by the sum of death sentences issued during (t − 4, t − 5, t − 6, t − 7, t − 8, and t − 9). The six-year window length and the six-year displacement lag capture the average time from sentence to execution for our sample. In a similar fashion, a two-year lag and a two-year window length is used to measure the conditional death sentencing probabilities. Given the absence of an arrest lag, no averaging or lag displacement is used when computing arrest probabilities.

Strictly speaking, these measures are not the true probabilities. However, they are closer to the probabilities as viewed by potential murderers than would be the "correct" measures. Our formulation is consistent with Sah's argument that criminals form perceptions based on observations of friends and acquaintances. We draw on the capital punishment literature to parameterize these perceived probabilities.

Models 4, 5, and 6 are similar to models 1, 2, and 3 except for the way we treat undefined probabilities. When estimating models 1, 2, and 3 we observed that in several years some counties had no murders, and some states had no death sentences. This rendered some probabilities undefined because of a zero denominator. Estimates in models 4–6 are obtained excluding these observations. Alternatively, and to avoid losing data points, for any observation (county/year) where the probabilities of arrest or execution are undefined due to this problem, we substituted the relevant probability from the most recent year when the probability was not undefined. We look back up to four years, because in most cases this eradicates the problem of undefined probabilities. The assumption

Table 3-7: Two-Stage Least Squares Regression Results for Murder Rate

Estimated Coefficients

Regressors	Model 1	Model 2	Model 3	Model 4	Model 5	Model 6
Deterrent Variables:						
Probability of Arrest	−4.037	−10.096	−3.334	−2.264	−4.417	−2.184
	(6.941)**	(17.331)**	(6.418)**	(4.482)**	(9.830)**	(4.568)**
Conditional Probability of Death Sentence	−21.841	−42.411	−32.115	−3.597	−47.661	−10.747
	(1.167)	(3.022)**	(1.974)**	(.2475)	(4.564)**	(.8184)
Conditional Probability of Execution	−5.170	−2.888	−7.396	−2.715	−5.201	−4.781
	(6.324)**	(6.094)**	(10.285)**	(4.389)**	(19.495)**	(8.546)**
Other Crimes:						
Aggravated Assault Rate	.0040	.0059	.0049	.0053	.0086	.0064
	(18.038)**	(23.665)**	(22.571)**	(29.961)**	(47.284)**	(35.403)**
Robbery Rate	.0170	.0202	.0188	.0110	.0150	.0116
	(39.099)**	(51.712)**	(49.506)**	(35.048)**	(54.714)**	(41.162)**
Economic Variables:						
Real Per Capita Personal Income	.0005	.0007	.0006	.0005	.0004	.0005
	(14.686)**	(17.134)**	(16.276)**	(20.220)**	(14.784)**	(19.190)**
Real Per Capita Unemployment Insurance Payments	−.0064	−.0077	−.0033	−.0043	−.0054	−.0038
	(6.798)**	(8.513)**	(3.736)**	(5.739)**	(7.317)**	(5.080)**
Real Per Capita Income Maintenance Payments	.0011	-.0020	.0024	.0043	.0002	.0027
	(1.042)	(1.689)*	(2.330)**	(5.743)**	(.2798)	(3.479)**
Demographic Variables:						
% of Population that is African-American	.0854	−.1114	.1852	.1945	.0959	.1867
	(2.996)**	(4.085)**	(6.081)**	(9.261)**	(4.956)**	(7.840)**
% of Population that is a Minority other than African-American	−.0382	.0255	−.0224	−.0338	−.0422	−.0237
	(7.356)**	(.7627)	(4.609)**	(7.864)**	(9.163)**	(5.536)**
% of Population that is Male	.3929	.2971	.2934	.2652	.3808	.2199
	(7.195)**	(3.463)**	(5.328)**	(6.301)**	(8.600)**	(4.976)**
% of Population that is age 10–19	−.2717	−.4849	.0259	−.2096	−.6516	−.1629
	(4.841)**	(8.021)**	(.4451)	(5.215)**	(15.665)**	(3.676)**
% of Population that is age 20–29	−.1549	−.6045	−.0489	−.1315	−.5476	−.1486
	(3.280)**	(12.315)**	(.9958)	(3.741)**	(15.633)**	(3.971)**
Population Density	−.0048	−.0066	−.0036	−.0044	−.0041	−.0046
	(22.036)**	(24.382)**	(17.543)**	(30.187)**	(27.395)**	(30.587)**
NRA Membership Rate, (% state pop. in NRA)	.0003	.0004	−.0002	.0008	.0006	.0008
	(1.052)	(1.326)	(.6955)	(3.423)**	(3.308)**	(3.379)**
Intercept	6.393	23.639	−12.564	10.327	17.035	10.224
	(.4919)	(6.933)**	(.9944)	(.8757)	(8.706)**	(1.431)
F-Statistic	217.90	496.29	276.46	280.88	561.93	323.89
Adjusted R^2	.8476	.8428	.8624	.8256	.8062	.8269

underlying such substitution is that criminals will use the most recent information available in forming their expectations. So a person contemplating committing a crime at time t will not assume that he will not be arrested if no crime was committed, and hence no arrest was made, during this period. Rather, he will form an impression of the arrest odds based on arrests in recent years. Models 4–6 use this substitution rule to compute probabilities when they are undefined.

The results in Table 3-7 suggest the presence of a strong deterrent effect. The estimated coefficient of the execution probability is negative and highly significant in all six models. This suggests that an increase in perceived probability of execution given that one is sentenced to death will lead to a lower murder rate. The estimated coefficient of the arrest probability is also negative and highly significant in all six models. This finding is consistent with the proposition set forth by the economic models of crime that suggests an increase in the perceived probability of apprehension leads to a lower crime rate.

For the sentencing probability, the estimated coefficients are negative in all models and significant in three of the six models. It is not surprising that sentencing has a weaker deterrent effect, given that we are estimating the effect of sentencing, *holding the execution probability constant*. What we capture here is a measure of the "weakness" or "porosity" of the state's criminal justice system. The coefficient of the sentencing probability picks up not only the ordinary deterrent effect, but also the porosity signal. The latter effect may, indeed, be stronger. For example, if criminals know that the justice system issues many death sentences but the executions are not carried out, then they may not be deterred by an increase in probability of a death sentence. In fact, a study by Leibman, Fagan and West reports that nearly seventy percent of all death sentences issued between 1973 and 1995 were reversed on appeal at the state or federal level. Also, six states sentence offenders to death but have performed no executions. This reveals the indeterminacy of a death sentence and its ineffectiveness when it is not carried out. Such indeterminacy affects the deterrence of a death sentence.

The murder rate appears to increase with aggravated assault and robbery, as the estimated coefficients for these two variables are positive and highly significant in all cases. This is in part because these crimes are caused by the same factors that lead to murder, and so measures of these crimes serve as additional controls. In addition, this reflects the fact that some murders are the byproduct of robbery or aggravated assault. Additional demographic variables are included primarily as controls, and we have no strong theoretical predictions about their signs. Estimated coefficients for per capita income are positive and significant in all cases. This may reflect the role of illegal drugs in homicides during this time period. Drug consumption is expensive, and may increase with income. Those in the drug business are disproportionately involved in homicides because the business generates large amounts of cash, which can lead to robberies, and because normal methods of dispute resolution are not available. An increase in per capita unemployment insurance payments is generally associated with a lower murder rate.

Other demographic variables are often significant. More males in a county is associated with a higher murder rate, as is generally found. An increase in percentage of the teen-age population, on the other hand, appears to lower the murder rate. The fraction of the population that is African American is generally associated with higher murder rates, and the percentage that is minority other than African American is generally associated with a lower rate.

The estimated coefficient of population density has a negative sign. One might have expected a positive coefficient for this variable; murder rates are higher in large cities. However, this may not be a consistent relationship: the murder rate can be lower in suburbs than it is in rural areas, although rural areas are less densely populated than suburbs. But the murder rate may be higher in inner cities where the density is higher than the suburbs. Glaeser and Sacerdote also report that crime rates are higher for cities with 25,000–99,000 persons than for cities with between 100,000–999,999 persons and then higher for cities over 1,000,000, although not as high as for the smaller cities. Because there are relatively few counties containing cities of over 1,000,000, our measure of density may be picking up this nonlinear relationship. They explain the generally higher crime rate in cities as a function of higher returns, lower probabilities of arrest and conviction, and the presence of more female headed households.

Finally, the estimates of the coefficient of the NRA membership variable are positive in five of the six models and significant in half of the cases. A possible justification is that in counties with a large NRA membership guns are more accessible, and they can therefore serve as the weapon of choice in violent confrontations. The resulting increase in gun use, in turn, may lead to a higher murder rate.

The most robust findings in these tables are as follows: The arrest, sentencing, and execution measures all have a negative effect on murder rate, suggesting a strong deterrent effect as the theory predicts. Other violent crimes tend to increase murder. The demographic variables have mixed effects; murder seems to increase with the proportion of the male population. Finally, the NRA membership variable has positive and significant estimated coefficients in all cases, suggesting a higher murder rate in counties with a strong NRA presence.

We do not report estimates of the coefficients of the other equations in the system because we are mainly interested in the equation that provides direct inference about the deterrent effect. Nevertheless, the first stage regressions do produce some interesting results. Expenditure on the police and judicial/legal system appears to increase the productivity of law enforcement. Police expenditure has a consistently positive effect on the probability of arrest; expenditure on the judicial/legal system has a positive and significant effect on the conditional probability of receiving a death penalty sentence. The partisan influence variable also has a consistently positive and significant impact on the probability of receiving a death sentence and of execution. This result indicates that the more Republican the state, the more common are death row sentences and executions. The expenditure on the judicial/legal system has a negative and significant effect on the conditional probability of execution. This result implies that more spending on appeals and public defenders results in fewer executions.

B. Effect of Tough Sentencing Laws One may argue that the documented deterrent effect reflects the overall toughness of the judicial practices in the executing states. For example, these states may have tougher sentencing laws that serve as a deterrent to various crimes including murder. To examine this argument, we constructed a new variable measuring "judicial toughness" for each state, and estimated the correlation between this variable and the execution variable.

The inclusion of the toughness variable did not change the significance or sign of the estimated execution coefficient. Moreover, the toughness variable has an insignificant coefficient estimate in four of the six regressions. The low correlation between execution probability and the toughness variable, along with the observed robustness of our results to inclusion of the toughness variable suggest that the deterrent finding is driven by executions and not by tougher sentencing laws.

C. Magnitude of the Deterrent Effect The statistical significance of the deterrent coefficients suggests that executions reduce the murder rate. But how strong is the expected trade-off between executions and murders? In other words, how many potential victims can be saved by executing an offender? Neither aggregate time-series nor cross-sectional analyses can provide a meaningful answer to this question. Aggregate time-series data, for example, cannot impose the restriction that execution laws are state-specific and any deterrent effect should be restricted to the executing state. Cross-sectional studies, on the other hand, capture the effect of capital punishment through a binary dummy variable that measures an overall effect of the capital punishment laws instead of a marginal effect.

Panel data econometrics provides the appropriate framework for a meaningful inference about the trade-off. Here an execution in one state is modeled to affect the murders in the same state only. Moreover, the panel allows estimation of a marginal effect rather than an overall effect.

We evaluate this quantity for the U.S. using the most recent period that our sample covers. The resulting estimate is 18 with a margin of error of 10 and therefore a corresponding 95% confidence interval (8-28). This implies that each additional execution has resulted, on average, in 18 fewer murders, or in at least 8 fewer murders. In calculating the trade-off estimate we use the population of the states with a death penalty law, since only residents of these states can be deterred by executions.

D. Robustness of Results While we believe that our econometric model is appropriate for estimating the deterrent effect of capital punishment, the reader may want to know how robust are our results. To provide such information, we examine the sensitivity of our main finding—that capital punishment has a deterrent effect on capital crimes—to the econometric choices we have made. In particular, we evaluate the robustness of our deterrence estimates to changes in aggregation level, functional form, sampling period, modeling death penalty laws, and endogenous treatment of the execution probability.

Overall, we estimate 55 models; the estimated coefficient of the execution probability is negative and significant in 49 of these models and negative but insignificant in four models. The above robustness checks suggest that our main finding that executions deter murders is not sensitive to various specification choices.

V. *Concluding Remarks*

Our results suggest that the legal change allowing executions beginning in 1977 has been associated with significant reductions in homicide. An increase in any of the three probabilities of arrest, sentencing, or execution tends to reduce the crime rate. In particular, our most conservative estimate is that the execution of each offender seems to save, on average, the lives of 18 potential victims. (This estimate has a margin of error of plus and minus 10.) Moreover, we find robbery and aggravated assault associated with increased murder rates. A higher NRA presence, measured by NRA membership rate, seems to have a similar murder-increasing effect. Tests show that results are not driven by "tough" sentencing laws, and are also robust to various specification choices. Our main finding, that capital punishment has a deterrent effect, is robust to choice of functional form (double-log, semi-log, or linear), state level vs. county level analysis, sampling period, endogenous vs. exogenous probabilities, and level vs. ratio specification of the main variables. Overall, we estimate 55 models; the estimated coefficient of the execution probability is negative and significant in 49 of these models and negative but insignificant in four models.

Finally, a cautionary note is in order: deterrence reflects social benefits associated with the death penalty, but one should also weigh in the corresponding social costs. These include the regret associated with the irreversible decision to execute an innocent person. Moreover, issues such as the possible unfairness of the justice system and discrimination need to be considered when making a social decision regarding capital punishment. Nonetheless, our results indicate that there are substantial costs in deciding not to use capital punishment as a deterrent.

Brutalization

■ Brutalization—Introduction

"Brutalization" is the term given to the notion that the death penalty may encourage murder by desensitizing citizens to violence. This is sometimes referred to as "antideterrence" or "counterdeterrence," because the result of the effect is an *increase* in the number of murders. However, these putatively synonymous terms are somewhat misleading. The intuition behind brutalization and general deterrence are not the same.

General deterrence is based upon the presumption that a potential criminal makes the decision whether or not to commit a crime based on a cost-benefit calculation. This worldview of potential criminals is the defining characteristic of what is known as "rational-choice theory" in the literature of criminology. People contemplating crime weigh the potential gain from the offense against the likely costs. In so doing they make the familiar calculation: the cost is the product of the likelihood of being detected and the severity of the resulting punishment. Increasing the penalties for an offense increases the cost to a potential defendant, making that kind of crime less attractive. Reducing the police force decreases the chance of a potential defendant being detected, making crime in general more attractive. Deterrence theory presumes that potential criminal defendants are rational and quite sophisticated.

The brutalization thesis is operating on an entirely different notion of criminal behavior. The thought here is that violence by the government and in television and movies desensitizes people to violence and leads them to commit crime they otherwise would not commit. This views the nature of criminal behavior as being decidedly antirational. Murderers are not committing crime on the basis of cost-benefit calculations; they are murdering because they have been taught at a conscious or subconscious level that murder is an acceptable form of behavior. The brutalization thesis views the criminal as a product of his environment. The criminal does what he has been programmed to do.

Brutalization and deterrence are not mutually exclusive. It is entirely possible that the death penalty may deter some potential criminals while leading others to commit crimes they might not otherwise commit. Some researchers have found evidence for deterrence but not brutalization, some for brutalization but not deterrence, some for both, some for neither. Part of the difficulty in assessing the aggregate impact of the death penalty on crime may be the impossibility of separating these effects. Suppose the murder rate in a jurisdiction does not change following the implementation of the death penalty. It may be that the death penalty has neither a deterrent nor a brutalizing effect—hence there is no change. It may also be that the deterrent and brutalizing effects are of equal and opposite force, canceling each other out. It is the difference between an object untouched by outside forces, and an object being pushed upon by equal opposing forces. Both are stationary, but these are different situations. Identifying which is the case is problematic.

Even if isolating the brutalization effect from the deterrence effect were possible, studying the brutalization effect would still be challenging. One possible method entails asking criminals why they committed crimes, but subjective methodologies are notoriously unreliable. Defendants have no incentive to tell the truth. In many or most cases they may not know the truth themselves. Not all of the defendants possess the self-awareness to know what led them to crime. In many or most cases, it might very well have been a host of factors.

Professors William Bowers and Glenn Pierce of Northeastern University attacked the problem by applying this intuition: If the brutalization effect exists, it is likely to be most pronounced immediately following an execution. The more prominent the execution is in the public consciousness, Bowers and Pierce say, the more pronounced its impact is likely to be, if the execution has any impact at all. Bowers and Pierce employed a longitudinal methodology: they studied 692 executions and all homicides in New York State between 1906 and 1963. They found spikes in the murder rate following executions. On average, Bowers and Pierce concluded that each execution led to three additional homicides in the nine months following the execution.

Bowers and Pierce offer this explanation for their findings:

> *The lesson of the execution may be to devalue the life by the example of human sacrifice. Executions demonstrate that it is correct and appropriate to kill those who have gravely offended us. The fact that such killings are to be performed only by duly appointed officials on duly convicted offenders is a detail that may get obscured by the message that such offenders deserve to die. If the typical murderer is someone who feels that he has been betrayed, dishonored, or disgraced by another person—and we suggest that such feelings are far more characteristic of those who commit murder than is a rational evaluation of costs and benefits—then it is not hard to imagine that the example executions provide may inspire a potential murderer to kill the person who has greatly offended him. In effect, the message of the execution may be lethal vengeance, not deterrence.*

The Perspectives section of this chapter offers a sample of the different conclusions made by researchers. Studying murders in California following a highly publicized execution, John Cochran and Mitchell Chamlin find a short-term drop in nonstranger felony-murders and an increase in argument-based stranger homicides. Their results suggest offsetting deterrence and brutalization effects. Jon Sorensen and his team of researchers, studying the effects of executions in Texas, find no support for either the brutalization or deterrent effects.

Brutalization—Perspectives

Issue—Does the Death Penalty Encourage Murder?

John K. Cochran and Mitchell B. Chamlin, "Deterrence and Brutalization: The Dual Effects of Executions"

On April 21, 1992, California drew wide national attention when Robert Alton Harris, a white male convicted of two counts of first-degree murder and sentenced to death, was executed in the gas chamber at San Quentin. Harris's execution was the first use of the death penalty since Aaron Mitchell's execution in April 1967, and marked the end of 25-year moratorium on capital punishment in the state. Because the Harris execution generated tremendous statewide and national publicity, it provides us with opportunity to examine the deterrent and/or brutalization effects, if any, of capital punishment.

Beyond the publicity received, the Harris execution is especially useful for these purposes because it is the first post-*Furman* execution in the state. As such, it is symbolically important, perhaps even more so than any subsequent execution. Finally, Harris was the only post-*Furman* offender to be executed in the gas chamber. These characteristics of the Harris execution combine to suggest that its effect, deterrent and/or brutalizing, should be most profound.

Using weekly time-series data on the level and type of criminal homicide incidents in the state from 1989 through 1995, we exploit the quasi-experimental qualities of this naturally occurring "experiment" to assess the impact of Harris's execution on the incidence of homicide. Unlike earlier studies on the effects of the reintroduction of executions, this study follows the lead of Cochran and his associates by disaggregating criminal homicides into various forms of murder highly likely to be affected by capital punishment: felony-murders of nonstrangers for which we predict a deterrent effect, and argument-murders of strangers, for which we predict a brutalization effect.

Cochran et al. observed that Oklahoma's execution of Charles Troy Coleman exerted an "abrupt, permanent" brutalization effect on the weekly level of stranger-argument homicides. Yet, because these authors limited their study to an impact assessment of the Coleman execution, they were unable to consider whether the effects they observed were truly permanent and endured after subsequent executions and/or the passage of time. Their observations may have been a mere historical artifact. In the present study we can address this limitation by assessing the enduring quality of these potential effects over a subsequent execution.

Our findings reveal, as predicted, that the period following the execution of Harris showed a significant decrease in nonstranger felony-murders and a significant increase in argument-based murders of strangers. Moreover, the increase in argument-based stranger murders associated with the Harris execution endured over a subsequent execution, while the observed decrease in nonstranger felony murders associated with the original execution apparently transferred to the subsequent execution.

I. *Deterrence and Brutalization*

There are two opposing arguments regarding the impact of executions on homicide levels. One is the deterrence argument which claims that executions deter potential offenders and thus lead to a decrease in homicides during postexecution periods. According to the other argument, executions brutalize members of society such that potential offenders are inspired by the execution, which is said to legitimize lethal vengeance. Under this brutalization argument, levels of homicide are hypothesized to increase after the execution. Thus the deterrence and the brutalization argument make opposite predictions about the impact of executions.

Traditionally each of these arguments has been tested against the null hypothesis of no impact of executions; the null hypothesis is rejected only occasionally. The great majority of studies aimed at assessing the impact of capital punishment consistently fail to find more than chance-only associations. A small minority of studies have found evidence of a deterrent effect; a handful of others have found support for the brutalization thesis.

Nevertheless, the weight of the current evidence has led most criminologists to reject the validity of both arguments. Thus, although some studies support one or the other of these arguments, the most consistently observed finding in this area is that the death penalty has no significant, measurable effect on homicides.

We suggest that these arguments may have been dismissed prematurely. In fact, we argue that both claims may be valid and that executions can lead to both deterrent and brutalization effects. That is, executions deter some forms of criminal homicides while encouraging others through brutalization. The net effect, consistent with the extant research, is that these two opposing effects tend to cancel each other out, leading to an overall null effect. These dual, opposing effects can be observed only when criminal homicides are properly disaggregated into more homogeneous forms.

The deterrence argument assumes that criminal behavior, including homicide, results when rational actors assess the costs and benefits of various alternative courses of action, and that they voluntarily select the behavioral option which provides the greatest apparent ratio of benefits to costs. One can question the assumption that killers exercise rational judgment and thus are sensitive to the objective costs of homicide. We know, for instance, that many homicides are acts of passion involving precipitation by the victim, intoxicated parties, affronts to honor, rage, jealousy, and/or frustration, and are face-saving contests which tend to escalate uncontrollably toward lethal violence and a fatal outcome. These characterizations do not square with most persons' conceptualization of rationality as assumed by deterrence/rational choice theorists.

For some subsets of criminal homicides, however, the assumption of rationality is not so far-fetched; felony-murders are primary among these. In felony-murders, offenders enter the felony situation, typically an armed robbery, with at least a tacit understanding that lethal force may be necessary during the commission of the crime and that additional costs may be incurred. Thus felony-murders are a form of instrumental homicide for which it is reasonable to accept the assumption of rationality necessary for deterrent effects. As a result, such murders are potentially deterrable by the threat of capital punishment. The deterrent potential, however, is likely to be manifested only for those executions which receive significant media attention.

The brutalization argument claims that executions actually increase postexecution homicides because of the "beastly example" that an execution presents. According to the brutalization argument, executions devalue human life. An execution may not deliver a lesson of deterrence, but instead may illustrate the legitimacy of lethal vengeance.

This lesson in the legitimacy of lethal vengeance is premised on the idea that potential offenders do not identify with the condemned—a necessary condition for deterrence. Instead they identify with the executioner and see characteristics of deservedness in the condemned which they then apply to others in their life. Thus the brutalization effect of executions is restricted to those homicides in which victims are most likely to be viewed as deserving.

Many scholars believe that argument-based homicides are the form of criminal homicide most likely to include "deserving" victims because of the affronts to honor and the efforts to save face common in these "situated transactions." Like the potential deterrent effects of executions, however, this brutalization effect depends on the degree to which potential offenders are made aware of the "lethal vengeance" lesson; that is, the brutalization effect also requires high levels of execution publicity.

In sum, we argue here that highly publicized executions tend to deter felony-murders, but they also tend to brutalize argument-based killings.

II. *The Contingent Effects of Informal Social Controls*

Criminologists have long recognized the connections between formal and informal social controls and their joint influences on behavior. Researchers in this area contend that threats of formal sanctions can activate informal control systems; in turn, the control capacity of the formal sanctions is augmented and enhanced. That is, formal sanctions have greater specific deterrent value when they operate jointly with the informal controls implied in the social relations among persons known to one another.

As applied to the current study, the general deterrent effect of executions (formal control) on the level of felony-murders (which are deemed instrumental and rational) should be strongest in incidents involving nonstrangers (informal control). We acknowledge that some nonstranger relationships provide unique opportunities for criminal victimizations and also may be special sources of criminal motivation. Generally, however, these situations are characterized by preexisting attachments in which the ties that bind serve as informal social controls that constrain the likelihood of offending. Thus the general deterrent effect of executions on felony-murders is strengthened especially in circumstances involving nonstrangers.

Alternatively, the crime-reducing effect of capital punishment on nonstranger felony homicides may operate through a different process. For instance, many motivated offenders may purposively exploit the criminal opportunities provided by their relations with others. Family, friends, and acquaintances, because of the motivated offenders' knowledge about their daily routines, guardianship, target attractiveness, and the like, may become the preferred targets for victimization such as robbery, rape, or burglary. This information alluring between victim and offender, however, cuts both ways: the nonstranger victims also may know their assailants' identities. Thus the offenders may find it necessary to kill potential witnesses against them to avoid detection. Such victims also may be more inclined to offer resistance to known assailants, which also could precipitate their murder.

In either case, nonstranger felony homicides are likely to decrease after publicized executions. The threat of execution may persuade these offenders to select different targets for their crimes, namely strangers, where the need to kill witnesses or resistors is much less powerful. If this is the case, then nonstranger felony homicides should decrease after publicized executions. These crimes, in turn, may be displaced onto robberies, rapes, burglaries, and so on, involving strangers.

We also argue that informal social controls dampen or attenuate the brutalization effect of executions. According to Cochran et al., "a brutalization effect is most likely to occur in those 'situated transactions' where inhibitions against the use of violence are already absent or considerably relaxed, such as situations that involve affronts by strangers." Here, in the absence of effective informal control, the lesson regarding the appropriateness of lethal vengeance against deserving others, as taught by the execution example, is free to be followed in full force. Affronts by family, friends, or acquaintances constrain this brutalization effect because they include some measure of informal social control. Such is not the case with affronts among persons known to one another. Thus in this study we assess two hypotheses regarding the impact of highly publicized executions: (1) a deterrent effect on nonstranger felony-murders and (2) a brutalization effect on argument-based homicides among strangers.

III. *Data and Methods*

We use autoregressive integrated moving-average analyses to assess the effects, if any, of the Harris execution on the level of total, felony, felony-stranger, felony-nonstranger, argument, stranger-argument, and nonstranger-argument homicides in California. For each of these seven forms of homicide, we produced weekly time-series data covering the years 1989 through 1995 (N = 364 weeks) from the Supplementary Homicide Reports (SHR). Official codes and designations used in the SHR are employed in our disaggregations of these incidents. Homicides in which the circumstances and/or the victim-offender relationship were unknown were excluded from our disaggregated analyses; we coded incidents with multiple offenders and/or multiple victims as nonstranger homicides if any victim-offender pair was nonstranger.

IV. *Results*

The data shows that the Harris execution had no appreciable impact on the weekly level of total, felony, stranger-felony, argument, or nonstranger-argument homicides in California. These null findings are not surprising; they are largely consistent with those reported by others. Moreover, they are consistent with our predictions. Recall our theoretical assertion that highly publicized executions have both deterrent and brutalization effects, depending on the form of homicide examined; that these opposing effects may negate one another statistically unless the measure of homicide is disaggregated properly; and finally, that these opposing effects are also contingent on the presence or absence of informal social controls as evidenced by the nature of the victim-offender relationship.

In sum, we argue that the presence of social ties between victim and offender (nonstrangers) is a source of informal social control which strengthens the deterrent effect of executions on instrumental homicides (felony-murders). Conversely, the absence of such ties (as between strangers) enhances the brutalization effect of executions on expressive (argument-based) homicides. Hence we anticipate and observe null effects of the Harris execution on the weekly level of those homicides which are not characterized by these contingencies.

On the other hand, the findings reveal two statistically significant effects of the Harris execution. As predicted, the Harris execution was followed by a small but significant decrease in the level of nonstranger felony-murders. Thus the joint effects of formal social control (the execution) and informal social control (the presence of a victim-offender relationship) may have reduced the weekly level of nonstranger felony-murders in California by more than two per month.

This small deterrent effect of the Harris execution on the weekly level of nonstranger felony-murders is more than offset by a strengthening of the brutalization effect on the level of argument-based homicides among strangers. Specifically, the reintroduction of executions in California was followed by a significant increase in the weekly level of stranger-argument homicides, an increase of almost four such homicides per month.

In sum, California's return to the death penalty with the highly publicized execution of Robert Alton Harris, after a 25-year hiatus apparently may have produced two simultaneous but opposing effects: a deterrent effect on nonstranger felony-murders and a brutalization effect on argument-based stranger homicides. These effects nullify one another under broader aggregations of these offense data, such that the net effect of the Harris execution on the weekly level of homicides per se is null. These findings are consistent with our predictions and, in part, with the current research literature in this area.

V. Discussion

The effects, if any, of capital punishment on the level of criminal homicide have long been debated. To date, however, the social scientific community and its research literature have not provided much compelling information on this issue. The traditional research strategy has been simply to assess whether capital punishment/executions deter criminal homicide. The results, although mixed, suggest that they do not. More recently, scholars have altered their research methodologies to allow for the consideration of a rival effect, the brutalization effect. Using these designs, they have assessed whether executions produce a deterrent or a brutalization effect. These effects are viewed as competitive and mutually exclusive, such that evidence which supports (for example) brutalization invalidates deterrence.

Starting with the work of Cochran and his colleagues, some criminologists now are beginning to understand that these effects may not be mutually exclusive and that executions can produce both effects simultaneously. That is, highly publicized executions can deter some forms of homicide while brutalizing others. This is precisely what we found in regard to California's reintroduction of the death penalty with the executions of Robert Alton Harris in April 1992 and David Edwin Mason, 16 months later, in August 1993.

To observe these dual but opposing effects, however, one needs a research design in which the data on the offense are first disaggregated into more homogeneous forms. Failure to follow this step introduces an offense aggregation bias into the analyses, which in turn contaminates the results. Such a bias has been a common feature of research on the impact of capital punishment. It is time for criminologists to abandon this simplistic tradition.

Similarly, we have shown that it is time for criminologists to address the contingent nature of these dual effects. Both the deterrent and the brutalization effect of executions are contingent on the nature of the victim-offender relationship. Deterrence/rational choice theorists working in other areas have acknowledged the integrated nature of formal and informal sanction threats; ours is the first study to employ these ideas to assess the impact of capital punishment. As we predicted, the deterrent effect of capital punishment was evident only for instrumental crimes (felony-murders), in which informal social controls also operate (as measured by the presence of a prior victim-offender relationship). We also noted the contingent nature of the brutalization effect, in which the absence of informal social controls (as measured by the absence of a prior victim-offender relationship) allowed the execution message regarding the appropriateness of lethal vengeance to be expressed in full force.

What, then, are the policy implications of this study? Some may be more obvious than others. For instance, do these findings support the retention or the abolition of capital punishment? On the one hand, retention is supported by the apparent deterrent effects we observed, especially in conjunction with other bases of support for capital punishment such as retribution, incapacitation, and satisfaction of public opinion. On the other hand, abolition is supported by the apparent brutalization effects we also observed—again, in conjunction with other bases of opposition for capital punishment such as irreversibility and the discriminatory nature of its application. The brutalization effect appears to be a relatively permanent consequence of a state's return to capital punishment; the deterrent effect apparently requires additional repeated applications to maintain its influence. Moreover, both of these effects are contingent on the influence of social ties and informal social controls: deterrence is enhanced and brutalization effects are mitigated where such controls are present.

Perhaps, then, the obvious policy implications of this study involve efforts at community building. A more communitarian society might reduce criminal activity so effectively as to obviate the perceived need for drastic measures of control such as capital punishment. We urge other criminologists to begin assessing these ideas more fully.

Jon Sorensen, Robert Wrinkle, Victoria Brewer, and James Marquart, "Capital Punishment and Deterrence: Examining the Effect of Executions on Murder in Texas"

After thoroughly reviewing the empirical literature, Ruth Peterson and William Bailey concluded that the lack of evidence for any deterrent effect of capital punishment was incontrovertible. According to them, no credible empirical studies had ever been able to demonstrate that the severity, certainty, or celerity of capital punishment reduced the rate of homicide. However, they did envision situations that might present unique opportunities to engage the deterrence hypothesis.

One such opportunity presented itself in Texas in recent years. By far the most active death penalty state, Texas has accounted for more than a third of all executions in the United States since the reimplementation of capital punishment in the years following *Furman*. In 1997 alone, Texas executed a record number of 37 capital murderers, accounting for half of the 74 U.S. executions in that year. Texas has provided an ideal natural experiment to engage the deterrence hypothesis.

One study of the effect of capital punishment on homicide rates in Texas from 1933 through 1980 found no support for the deterrence hypothesis. Although this study did not include the effects of any post-*Furman* executions in Texas, an update of their research extended the period studied through 1986. Decker and Kohfeld then found that executions were actually followed by an increase in homicide rates, supporting the brutalization hypothesis. Their studies, however, included a limited number of control variables, an aggregate measure of homicide, and the use of years as the unit of analysis. Their updated study captured few of the executions that were to occur in the post-*Furman* era. The study reported here advances the work of Decker and Kohfeld by examining the deterrence hypothesis in Texas from 1984 through 1997, capturing the most active period of executions in a jurisdiction during the post-*Furman* period. It also simultaneously incorporates the methodological strengths of recent studies to provide one of the most compelling tests of the deterrence hypothesis completed thus far.

I. *Data and Methods*

To examine the deterrence hypothesis during the modern era, data that spanned the years from 1984 through 1997 were collected from official sources. The year 1984 was chosen as the beginning of the data collection period because of the availability of specific data on homicides and the onset of executions. Because no executions took place until December 1982, the period before the onset of executions was eliminated from our analyses due to a lack of variance in the independent variable.

The number of executions served as the independent variable. The number of executions was tabulated from ledgers provided by the Texas Department of Criminal Justice–Institutional Division. The dependent variables included rates of murder and rates of felony murder. Information on the number of murders was collected from the Texas Department of Public Safety–Uniform Crime Reporting Division. The murder rate was based on the number of murders and nonnegligent manslaughters occurring in Texas during the period studied. Excluded from this category were negligent manslaughters, accidental homicides, justifiable homicides committed by citizens and police officers, and executions performed by the state. Murders involving burglary, robbery, or sexual assault were coded as felony murders. Information on control variables that have most often been found to be related to homicide rates in previous studies was also collected.

Information related to homicide in general, including the percentage of the state population living in metropolitan areas, the percentage of the population aged 18 through 34, and the unemployment rate, were culled from the *Statistical Abstracts of the United States*. The number of physicians per 100,000 residents was also coded from the *Statistical Abstracts of the United States* and is included as a proxy for the availability of emergency services, which could prevent an aggravated assault from turning deadly. Other variables that are typically included in homicide studies are the percentage of Blacks and the percentage of divorced individuals. They were excluded from this study because both were constant over the time period studied. Furthermore, these variables were not significant predictors of homicide rates in a recent deterrence study.

Additional information was collected from alternate sources. The percentage of murders resulting in convictions was collected from the *Annual Reports of the Texas Judicial Council* as an additional measure of the certainty of punishment. The rate of incarceration per 100,000 in the state was gathered from the Bureau of Justice Statistics. The incarceration rate was included to control for possible incapacitation effects resulting from a vast increase in Texas's prison population during the time period studied. Information on the percentage of Texas residents who are on Aid to Families with Dependent Children (AFDC) was gathered. Although a direct relationship between welfare and homicide rates is typically expected, a recent study found that AFDC is an indicator of available resources that act to mitigate the harshness of poverty, thereby decreasing homicide rates.

Control variables were also calculated from the Supplemental Homicide Report data. The percentage of homicides resulting from gunshots was included as a proxy for the availability of firearms. Temporal variables were included to account for surges and lulls in the homicide rate. A high- and low-season variable specified months that were found to be significantly higher or lower in general homicide rates. High season included the months of July and August, whereas low season included only the month of February. Because the state experienced a record number of executions in 1997, an indicator of that year was also included as a control variable.

II. *Analysis and Findings*

The data illustrates the episodic nature of executions. After the first execution, which was that of Charlie Brooks, was carried out in December 1982, the next one did not take place until James Autry was executed in March 1984. A small wave of executions, which peaked at 10 in 1986, followed. A slump in executions then occurred, with an average of four per year being carried out during 1988 through 1991. The ascendance of executions in 1992 signaled the beginning of a more substantial wave of executions, with an average of 15.5 executions per year during 1992 through 1995.

A legal challenge to Texas's procedures for speeding up the appellate processing of capital cases resulted in a moratorium on executions. With the exception of the voluntary execution of Joe Gonzalez in September 1996, executions were halted to await a decision of the Texas Court of Criminal Appeals on the legality of the new procedures. Executions resumed in February 1997, after the court's pronouncement that the expedited appellate procedures were constitutional. The next wave of executions in Texas would be of historical significance. In dispatching 37 backlogged cases, Texas reached a new record for the number of executions carried out in the state during a single year.

The rate of murder in the state from 1984 through 1991 showed no discernible trend in relation to the execution rate. Although there was a slight decrease in murder rates in 1987 through 1989 after the execution wave of the mid-1980s that could be attributed to a deterrent effect, the homicide rate only began to increase in 1990 and 1991, which was after a 2-year lull in executions during the late 1980s. Although the increase could be attributed to the earlier lull in executions and hence support the deterrence hypothesis, the considerable lag in its increase would suggest that any deterrent effect, or lack thereof, occurred only after a considerable time and is of limited significance.

The greatest amount of support for the deterrence hypothesis is found when the decrease in murder rates is paired with the increase in executions during the 1990s. During the execution wave of the 1990s, the murder rate declined substantially in the state. In the same year that the state reached a historical high in executions, the murder rate fell below what was experienced in decades. Although this seems to provide a strong support for the deterrence hypothesis, the downward trend in homicide rates does not appear to be disturbed by the moratorium on executions in 1996, as the deterrence hypothesis would predict; instead, the downward trend continued.

Furthermore, murder rates have been declining throughout the United States during this same period, which suggest that factors unrelated to executions were responsible for this pattern.

To test for the influence of other causal factors, control variables were included along with executions and used to predict general murder rates and felony murder rates across the monthly series of data from 1984 through 1997. In the first model, the general murder rates were regressed on executions and the control variables. The number of executions was not related to murder rates over the 14-year period that was studied. Control variables positively related to murder rates included the percentage of the population in metropolitan areas, the percentage of the population age 18 to 34, the murder conviction rate, and the high season. The low season, February, was the only variable with a significant negative relation to murder rates. Inclusion of these variables produced a high degree of fit to the data with an overall R^2 of .75.

III. *Conclusions*

This study found that recent evidence from the most active execution state in the nation lent no support to the deterrence hypothesis. The number of executions did not appear to influence either the rate of murder in general or the rate of felony murder in particular. At the same time, no support was found for the brutalization hypothesis. Executions did not reduce murder rates; they also did not have the opposite effect of increasing murder rates. The inability to reject the null hypothesis supports findings from the vast majority of studies on deterrence and capital punishment. From the data presented, it appears that other factors are responsible for the variations and trends in murder rates.

Although appropriate methodology and statistics were employed in the analysis, a number of criticisms could be raised concerning our failure to find evidence of a deterrent effect. Missing data are particularly troubling when data are disaggregated to calculate felony murder rates. Cases that are missing data on the circumstances surrounding a homicide in the SHR are likely to turn into felony murders when their circumstances are finally uncovered. Furthermore, it may be that the deterrent effects of executions on potential offenders can never be adequately ascertained, because measuring crimes that did occur is only a proxy for how many that were prevented. We also concede that the findings are limited to the sampled time period and the jurisdiction studied.

Considering these limitations, any research that makes a claim concerning the deterrence hypothesis should be treated with caution. However, because we confirmed the findings of previous studies and because the Texas context was so uniquely suited for finding any potential deterrent effects, there is little reason to question the findings.

Once this argument is accepted, several implications can arise. Some may infer, for example, that these results suggest the repeal of the death penalty because it fails to serve the penological function that is so often offered in its defense. Others would argue that various other goals must also be taken into consideration before making this determination, such as whether the public supports its use, whether it serves the goals of retribution, whether it saves money over life imprisonment, whether it serves to provide justice to the families of victims, and whether it serves the interests of the criminal justice system in general. However, these justifications have also been challenged by research. Along with the steady stream of consistent findings on the failure of capital punishment in all of these areas, this study cannot help but support the abolitionist argument.

Incapacitation

■ Incapacitation—Introduction

One thing that can be said for the death penalty is that it is conclusively incapacitating. Executed murderers never murder again. But this is surely not a sufficient argument for the death penalty. Cutting off the hands of thieves and castrating rapists are also conclusively incapacitating punishments. So too the death penalty for jaywalking ensures against recidivism. Some people might support cutting off the hands of thieves, but presumably all would balk at the idea of executing jaywalkers. One objection would be retributive: death is more punishment than a jaywalker deserves. But we also can isolate objections to executing jaywalkers based solely on grounds of incapacitation: penalties less severe than death are adequate to specifically deter jaywalkers, and it is not clear that jaywalkers are more likely to jaywalk again by virtue of having jaywalked before.

This second point is important. Like all utilitarian arguments, the incapacitation defense of capital punishment looks forward: the aim is to eliminate offenders who pose a special ongoing risk to society. Some criminal behavior is habituated, some is not. Some sex offenders are highly likely to recidivate. A husband who kills in the heat of passion after finding his wife in bed with another man is presumably no more likely to kill in the future than anyone else. To kill jaywalkers in the name of incapacitation requires the answer to an empirical question: are there habitual jaywalkers or does everyone jaywalk about as often as everyone else? If the answer is that someone who has jaywalked is no more likely to jaywalk again by virtue of having jaywalked before, then from the standpoint of incapacitation there is no convincing argument to incapacitate jaywalkers. If we were to execute the captured jaywalker, we may as well execute everyone in society because every other person is just as likely to jaywalk in the future as the person executed. Such a course of action trivializes the notion of incapacitation.

Executing jaywalkers also amounts to a gross retributive injustice, although this concern has nothing to do with the merits of the incapacitation argument. This slippage between incapacitation and retribution is only natural and can be seen in arguments by both sides of the debate. In his excellent text on the death penalty, Robert Bohm, an abolitionist, offers this argument against executing all capital offenders:

To ensure that no convicted capital offender killed again, all convicted capital offenders would have to be executed. There are several problems with such a strategy. First, innocent people have been executed. If all capital offenders were executed to prevent any one of them from killing again, it would be impossible to rectify the injustices done to the innocent people executed, their families and friends, and to a society that considered such acts immoral.

On the other side of the issue, Justice For All, a leading pro-death penalty organization offers:

The argument that murderers are the least likely of all criminals to repeat their crimes is not only irrelevant, but also increasingly false. Six percent of young adults paroled in 1978 after having been convicted of murder were arrested for murder again within six years of release. Murderers have so violated the human rights of their victims and of society that it should be a moral imperative that they never again have that opportunity.

Each of these arguments is convincing to some extent, but neither is grounded in the notion of incapacitation. Professor Bohm's invocation of the specter of executing innocents may either be viewed as a utilitarian or a retributive argument, but it is not purely addressed to incapacitation (though Professor Bohm goes on to offer extensive evidence about the risk or lack of risk that capital murderers pose to society). Justice For All's argument starts down an incapacitative path, but quickly detours into pure retribution. This does not make either of these arguments wrong—the only point here is that the natural way to argue about the necessity of incapacitation is to invoke other kinds of concerns.

The aim here, as always, is to consider the issue in a purely horizontal fashion: do capital murderers present a special ongoing risk to society? Two related questions present themselves: Are capital murderers more likely to murder again (or more likely to commit other felonies) than other murderers? Are capital murderers more likely to murder again (or more likely to commit other felonies) than average citizens? If the answer to the first question is that capital murderers are no more likely to recidivate than other murderers, it leaves open whether this suggests all murderers should be executed or none. If the answer to the second question is that capital murderers are no more likely to recidivate than ordinary citizens, it certainly suggests that incapacitation is not a highly relevant concern.

These questions are difficult to study for an obvious reason: with one notable exception discussed in the following text, capital murderers are generally not released into the general prison population or into society. It may be possible, however, to draw some lessons from the behavior of defendants sentenced to life without parole (LWOP). If LWOP-sentenced prisoners recidivate at a higher rate than other prisoners, this suggests they may be special risks and more legitimately regarded as requiring incapacitation.

LWOP-sentenced prisoners are an especially interesting population because they are, in some sense, beyond deterrence. Absent the death penalty, LWOP-sentenced prisoners have nothing to fear from criminal sanctions. Of course they do have something to fear from internal prison sanctions: crime or misbehavior may cause them to lose privileges or to be placed in isolation cells. Some data suggest that LWOP prisoners actually commit fewer crimes in prison than other inmates. Raymond Paternoster hypothesizes that this may be attributed to their habituation to prison life. Non-LWOP prisoners are by definition a more transient population. This result, if robust, has important implications for the deterrence argument. It suggests that criminals are more effectively deterred by socialization than by harsher sanctions.

The case of LWOP prisoners also invites an interesting question for death penalty proponents. Presume that some LWOP-sentenced prisoner has already been administratively punished—say his privileges have been taken away and he has been placed in solitary confinement. At some point, there might be no sanction other than death with which to threaten the inmate. Even if the death penalty is opposed on other grounds, might it be necessary to retain capital punishment to deter the otherwise undeterrable offender?

Of course, the point of discussing LWOP inmates is what their behavior suggests about the necessity of incapacitation. There are two separate issues: the risk capital murderers pose to the prison population and the risk they pose to the public at large.

Thorsten Sellin approached the issue of risk posed to the prison population by examining prison assaults. In the jurisdiction that he studied, Sellin found that of the 600 prison assaults that occurred in 1965, 61 resulted in death (8 staff members, 53 inmates). Of the 59 prison murderers (some had multiple victims, hence the number of offenses exceeds the number offenders), 20 were serving sentences for previous capital offenses at the time of the prison murders. (Several of these offenses were committed by inmates guilty of crimes such as rape, kidnapping, and assault, which are no longer capitally chargeable.) Convicted robbers committed the plurality of the murders—32%—convicted murderers ranked next with 27% of the total. By examining the issue retrospectively rather than prospectively studying different prison populations, we are left with some unanswered baseline questions. It would be especially useful to know what percentage of the prison population murderers represented at various times in order to assess whether the percentages are proportionate to the population or not. And none of this data enable us to make reliable predictions about which individual prisoners represent special threats. A study of life-sentenced defendants in Texas, presented in the Perspectives section of this chapter, suggests that future violent behavior is positively correlated with three offense-related factors: involvement in a robbery–murder, multiple victims in the original offense, and a prior attempted murder or assault. The study also suggests a positive correlation with three offender-related factors: membership in a prison gang, a prior prison term, and age upon entering prison.

Scant data exist on the behavior of murderers following release into society. Relying on data from the National Council on Crime and Delinquency (NCCD), Hugo Bedau reported that of 2646 murderers released between 1900 and 1977, 16 were reincarcerated for a subsequent homicide and 88 for a subsequent felony. The NCCD data cover only one year following release. Considering this, the absolute risk of recidivism seems significant. In a more recent study, 5% of released Georgia murderers committed subsequent murders within seven and a half years

Table 5-1	Criminal History Profile of Various Races of Prisoners Under Sentence of Death							
	Number of prisoners under sentence of death				Percent of prisoners under sentence of death			
	All	White	Black	Hispanic	All (%)	White (%)	Black (%)	Hispanic (%)
U.S. total	3593	1679	1520	339	100	100	100	100
Prior felony convictions								
Yes	2129	962	951	188	64.0	61.7	68.1	58.9
No	1199	598	446	131	36.0	38.3	31.9	41.1
Not reported	265							
Prior homicide convictions								
Yes	285	132	126	23	8.1	8.0	8.5	6.9
No	3245	1521	1361	312	91.9	92.0	91.5	93.1
Not reported	63							
Legal status at time of capital offense								
Charges pending	232	126	94	12	7.1	8.3	6.9	3.9
Probation	328	140	149	32	10.1	9.2	10.9	10.3
Parole	572	233	255	76	17.6	15.3	18.7	24.4
Prison escapee	38	23	11	3	1.2	1.5	0.8	1.0
Incarcerated	88	39	42	6	2.7	2.6	3.1	1.9
Other status	21	11	8	1	0.6	0.7	0.6	0.3
None	1970	953	802	181	60.6	62.5	58.9	58.2
Not reported	344							

2000

of their release. Neither of these studies distinguishes between capital murderers and noncapital murderers. It might be argued that the studies suggest a compelling case for incapacitating all murderers. (Although this is not an implementable policy; the Supreme Court rejected a mandatory death penalty for murder in *Woodson v. North Carolina*, discussed in Chapter 9.) But the results of the studies suggest nothing at all about the relative threat capital murderers present to society on an ongoing basis. The question remains whether capital murderers are more likely to recidivate than ordinary murderers and average citizens.

History offered a unique opportunity to test this question. In 1972, the Supreme Court ruled the death penalty as applied in Georgia unconstitutional. (This history is covered extensively in Chapter 8.) As a result of the Supreme Court's decision in *Furman v. Georgia*, the sentences of all death row inmates in the United States were commuted to life imprisonment with the possibility of parole. Several studies tracked the behavior of the *Furman*-commuted inmates.

Table 5-2	Rate of Recidivism of State Prisoners Released in 1994, by Most Serious Offense for Which Released				

Most serious offense for which released	Percent of all released prisoners (%)	Percent of released prisoners who, within 3 years, were:			
		Rearrested (%)	Reconvicted (%)	Returned to prison with a new prison sentence (%)	Returned to prison with or without a new prison sentence (%)
All released prisoners	100	67.5	46.9	25.4	51.8
Violent offenses	22.5	61.7	39.9	20.4	48.8
Homicide	1.7	40.7	20.5	10.8	31.4
Kidnapping	0.4	59.4	37.8	25.1	29.5
Rape	1.2	46.0	27.4	12.6	43.5
Other sexual assault	2.4	41.4	22.3	10.5	36.0
Robbery	9.9	70.2	46.5	25.0	54.7
Assault	6.5	65.1	44.2	21.0	51.2
Other violent	0.4	51.7	29.8	12.7	40.9
Property offenses	33.5	73.8	53.4	30.5	56.4
Burglary	15.2	74.0	54.2	30.8	56.1
Larceny/theft	9.7	74.6	55.7	32.6	60.0
Motor vehicle theft	3.5	78.8	54.3	31.3	59.1
Arson	0.5	57.7	41.0	20.1	38.7
Fraud	2.9	66.3	42.1	22.8	45.4
Stolen property	1.4	77.4	57.2	31.8	62.4
Other property	0.3	41.1	47.6	28.5	40.0
Drug offenses	32.6	66.7	47.0	25.2	49.2
Possession	7.5	67.5	46.6	23.9	42.6
Trafficking	20.2	64.2	44.0	24.8	46.1
Other/unspecified	4.9	75.5	60.5	28.8	71.8
Public-order offenses	9.7	62.2	42.0	21.6	48.0
Weapons	3.1	70.2	46.6	24.3	55.5
Driving under the influence	3.3	51.5	31.7	16.6	43.7
Other public order	3.3	65.1	48.0	24.4	43.6
Other offenses	1.7	64.7	42.1	20.7	66.9

In the most comprehensive of these studies, James Marquart and Jonathan Sorensen tracked the behavior of 558 *Furman*-commuted inmates for a 15-year period. Almost half (239 of 558) of the inmates were paroled. Marquart and Sorensen found that approximately 20% of the releasees returned to prison for new offenses or technical violations. Only one of the releasees murdered again;

two committed rapes. The releasees committed a total of 29 felonies. On the basis of this evidence, Marquart and Sorensen argued that "these prisoners did not represent a significant threat to society." This study is presented in the Critical Documents section. No subsequent study has challenged Marquart and Sorensen's methodology or findings, though their conclusion seems debatable. If we took 558 people at random and followed them for fifteen years, we would be surprised to find 2 felons among them, I expect, let alone 29. This is a somewhat persuasive, if not compelling, case for incapacitation. At the same time, while the numbers are higher than we might expect on average, they also do not suggest a crisis. Murderers are not prone to recidivating in mass numbers.

Tables 5-1 and **5-2** present data on recidivism by released state prisoners and the criminal history of prisoners under sentence of death. The data unquestionably suggest such individuals pose some future risk. The question is whether the relative risk they do pose is of sufficient magnitude to justify the use of capital punishment as a measure for permanent incapacitation.

■ Incapacitation—Critical Documents

James W. Marquart and Jonathan R. Sorensen, "A National Study of the Furman-Commuted Inmates: Assessing the Threat to Society From Capital Offenders"

On June 29, 1972, a sharply splintered Supreme Court struck down the capital sentencing statutes of Georgia and Texas. *Furman* invalidated the death sentences of hundreds of inmates awaiting execution in thirty states and the District of Columbia. The capital offenders affected by the decision had their death sentences commuted to life imprisonment and were subsequently "released" into the general prisoner population to serve the remainder of their sentences.

The *Furman* decision represents an "ideal" natural experiment for testing such predictions of future dangerousness. Most recently, studies in Texas and Kentucky concluded that the *Furman*-commuted inmates in those states did not represent a disproportionate threat to either the custodial staff, or if released, to the general community. In both states, recidivism among ex-capital offenders was not proportionally higher than among offenders convicted of similar crimes.

This study examines the prison and release behavior of all capital offenders commuted by *Furman*. What happened to the former death row prisoners? How accurate were the long-term predictions of violence? If released, did these offenders repeat their crimes and return to prison? Providing answers to these and other questions bears directly on the justification for capital punishment in many states today—particularly those states whose current capital statutes have a "future-dangerousness" provision. Such a provision reflects the premise that incapacitation of capital offenders protects society from future violence inflicted by those offenders. This study is a descriptive analysis of the institutional and post-release behavior of 558 *Furman*-commuted inmates in thirty states and the District of Columbia.

I. *Methodology*

The first stage in this research was to obtain a list of inmates commuted by Furman. Douglas Lyons of the NAACP Legal Defense Fund prepared a "List of Persons on Death Row at Time of Furman." The list contained thirty states and 613 inmates whose capital sentences were set aside by the Furman ruling. We obtained a copy, telephoned each state department of corrections, developed a contact person, and explained our research goals.

Once the research was formally approved we forwarded code sheets to the contact persons for data collection. These sheets covered six data categories:

1. current status (e.g., still in prison, paroled, deceased);
2. previous felony convictions;
3. total number of prior incarcerations;
4. prison disciplinary history;
5. victim information for the crime for which the defendant received the death penalty; and
6. whether the crime was committed in the commission of another felony.

Data on 558 prisoners was obtained from twenty-nine states and the District of Columbia.

II. *General Characteristics of the Furman-Commuted Offenders*

According to our data, there were 558 inmates (excluding Illinois) on death row awaiting execution in 1972 who were commuted as a result of Furman. Of these inmates, 474 (85%) were capital murderers, eighty-one (14%) were rapists, and four (1%) were sentenced to death for armed robbery. In terms of race and ethnicity, 309 (55%) prisoners were black, 240 (43%) were white, eight (1%) were hispanic, and one was an American Indian. As expected, the capital offenders were overwhelmingly male (only two were female), with a median age of thirty-two years in 1972.

We asked each state prison system to provide data on the prisoners' prior criminal history. According to our contact persons, these data were gleaned from initial classification interviews and cross-checked with FBI and local state police records. **Table 5-3** presents this information.

Table 5-3 Criminal History of the *Furman*-Commutees	White	Nonwhite	Total
Prior Record			
Convicted of UCR offense	56.9%	52.7%	54.5%
Convicted of UCR property offense	46.3%	38.8%	42.1%
Convicted of UCR violent offense	24.5%	28.7%	26.8%
Prior adult prison incarceration	45.5%	33.1%	38.6%
Prior jail term	31.7%	29.2%	30.3%
Prior juvenile incarceration	22.1%	24.7%	23.6%

These data reveal that the majority of commuted offenders had been convicted of a prior UCR offense. They were not first offenders. However, these conviction data also show that property crimes were their main criminal activity. Nearly three-quarters had no prior convictions for violent UCR offenses. Specifically, 97% had no previous conviction for murder, 96% for rape, 87% for armed robbery, and 85% for aggravated assault. Additionally, 61% of these inmates had never been incarcerated in an adult correctional institution. In short, the typical *Furman*-commutee was a southern male black murderer without a lengthy history of serious violence or repeated trips to prison.

III. *Offense Data*

In this section we compare the death row population in 1972 with aggregate UCR arrest data for homicide from the years 1968–1972. These latter data, while less than ideal, serve as a crude "control" group. Where possible we relate our findings to prior research that also serves as a "control." The first section examines the capital murderers, while the second focuses on the rapists.

A. The *Furman* Murderers **Table 5-4** compares the *Furman*-releasees with persons arrested for murder during the preceding five years.

While not offering conclusive evidence, these data provide support for the differential sentencing of capital offenders—in this case murderers. Clearly, capital juries consistently sentenced to death those defendants who killed whites. While a direct comparison between the groups is not possible, the differential treatment of male and female homicide offenders has been shown repeatedly and exists in pre-*Furman* and post-*Furman* periods. In the five years prior to 1972,

Table 5-4	Comparison of *Furman*-Murderers, Persons Arrested for Murder Only 1968–1972, and the Current Death Row Population		
	Furman	Arrestees	Current Death Row
Offender Characteristics			
Sex			
Male	99.6%	84.3%	98.9%
Female	0.4%	15.7%	1.1%
Race			
White	47.5%	36.8%	51.8%
Non-white	52.5%	63.2%	48.2%
Victim Characteristics			
Sex			
Male	67.4%	78.0%	56.0%
Female	32.6%	22.0%	44.0%
Race			
White	80.2%	44.4%	61.9%
Non-white	19.8%	55.6%	38.1%

16% of those arrested for murder were women, yet less than 1% were on death row at the time of the Furman decision.

Table 2 also presents data on those currently housed on death row. Today's death row population is somewhat dissimilar from the *Furman* prisoners. The majority of death row inmates are white males. Interestingly, 38% of today's victims were non-white, as compared to 20% in the *Furman* era. Perhaps prosecutors are more sensitive to minority victims of felony-murders than they were two or even three decades ago. Authorities may simply be more willing to prosecute these cases today.

To obtain a more focused picture of the capital murderer, we collected data on the victims of the *Furman* murderers. **Table 5-5** presents data on these crimes.

These data indicate that white and non-white offenders were quite similar in terms of the number of victims, and the sex and age of the victim. By far the most striking difference between white and non-white murderers was the victim's race. White offenders killed whites in almost every circumstance. However, non-white offenders "crossed over" 65% of the time and were subsequently sentenced to death. This pattern of differential sentencing is also evident in Table 2. Less than half of the homicide victims during the five years prior to *Furman* were white. However, victims of offenders on death row were overwhelmingly (80%) white. Based on the victim's race, our data suggest bias and arbitrariness in the processing of capital murder cases. If racial discrimination occurs through interaction with other variables, one would expect that non-white and white offenders on death row would have different background characteristics. Data would show that non-whites are less violent than whites, or that the circumstances of the crime were not as grave for non-whites to become death row inmates. However, data in this paper reveal that non-whites typically had more violence in their back-

Table 5-5	Victim-Offender Relationship By Race of Offender		
	White Offenders	**Non-white Offenders**	**Total**
Offense Characteristics			
Multiple victims	20.3%	16.7%	18.4%
Sex of victim			
Male	64.7%	69.9%	67.4%
Female	35.3%	30.1%	32.6%
Median age of victim	38	34	37
Race of victim			
White	95.2%	65.5%	80.5%
Non-white	4.8%	34.5%	19.5%
Victim-offender relationship			
Stranger	42.0%	60.8%	52.3%
Law enforcer	13.0%	13.9%	13.5%
Acquaintance	29.0%	20.5%	24.3%
Family	15.9%	4.8%	9.9%
Committed during a felony	50.0%	64.4%	58.0%

grounds and their capital offenses were more serious in that they occurred in the course of another felony.

B. The *Furman* Rapists In the first several decades following the Civil War Reconstruction era, executions consisted mainly of lynchings of blacks convicted of crimes against whites. Our data reveal a clear pattern of discrimination. Of the eighty rapists on death row at the time of the *Furman* decision, all were incarcerated in southern prison systems. Furthermore, sixty-eight (85%) were non-white. The victims of these offenses were overwhelmingly white (91% of the instances). Most of these offenses (81%) involved a lone victim, who was unknown to the assailant (78% of the offenses). Most of the rapists lacked a prior record. Only 5% had a previous rape conviction, while 29% had been confined in an adult penitentiary for any crime. Nationwide, during 1968–1972, an average of 51% of persons arrested for rape were non-white. Of the *Furman*-commuted offenders, 85% were non-white.

IV. *Institutional Behavior*

Custodial officers, psychiatrists and prison administrators feared the release of the *Furman*-commuted inmates into the general prisoner population. Many believed that these former death row prisoners were different than other inmates and represented a unique security risk. In this section, we analyze the institutional disciplinary behavior of the *Furman* offenders from 1972–1987.

A. Serious Rule Violations The definition of serious rule violations and the classification of these offenses vary between states. To insure coder reliability, we designated three major generic categories of offenses: offenses against other prisoners such as murder and fighting with weapons; offenses against prison staff such as striking a guard; and offenses against institutional order such as inciting riots or work strikes.

The data indicate that over a fifteen-year period, slightly less than one-third of the former death row inmates committed serious prison rule violations. Over one-half (84 or 51.9%) of those inmates committing serious rule violations were involved in only one rule violation, and another quarter (38 or 23.5%) were involved in only two rule violations. These data demonstrate, at least among these violators, that most serious infractions were one-time events or situations. In short, most of the *Furman* inmates were not violent menaces to the institutional order. As a group, they were not a disproportionate threat to guards and other inmates.

B. Chronic Rule Violators A small group of chronic offenders, forty inmates (7.4% of the total for whom disciplinary information was available) were involved in three or more serious rule violations, accounting for more than one-half of the total serious rule violations. Each of these forty inmates (thirty-six murderers and four rapists) committed an average of 5.1 serious rule violations over the fifteen-year period. This finding supports previous studies which have shown that within the prison community, as in the free world, a small group of offenders accounts for the majority of offenses.

C. Violent Rule Violators For the purposes of this study, violent rule violators were defined as those prisoners who committed murders and weapon-related aggravated assaults on prison staff or other inmates. Overall, the *Furman* offenders committed six killings in the institutional setting. All six institutional killers were serving time for capital murder. Two of these murderers were again sentenced to death, one for the murder of an inmate in Florida, and the other for the murder of a correctional officer in Ohio. Of the other fifty-nine serious acts of violence, thirty-eight inmates were involved. We investigated the differences between inmates committing serious violent acts and those who did not.

Neither offense characteristics nor the offender's race, age, or prior criminal history significantly differed between those who committed violent acts and those who did not. In short, no variable served as a predictor of these violent acts.

V. *Parole Behavior*

Perhaps the greatest fear expressed after the *Furman* decision was that commuted inmates would someday be released to society and commit more heinous crimes. This section describes the behavior following release of the former death-row inmates. The following section compares rates of recidivism of *Furman*-commuted murderers and rapists to recidivism rates for offenders convicted of similar crimes who were not originally sentenced to death.

A. The Parolees Of the 558 *Furman*-commuted inmates, 315 (56.5%) have not been released from prison. Of those, thirty-nine died, and three escaped and have not been recaptured. Two hundred forty-three (44%) of the capital offenders have been released to society. Of these, 191 (78.6%) have not been returned to prison: 147 are on their original parole, 19 discharged their sentences, 17 successfully completed their parole, 6 died in the community, and 2 were pardoned. Fifty-two (21%) of the releasees returned to prison for technical violations or new offenses. Of these, forty-two are currently incarcerated, eight have been re-paroled, and two have died in prison.

How have the *Furman*-releasees fared on parole? Did these capital offenders present a great risk to society? **Table 5-6** reports the percentages of the murderers and rapists who were released and returned to prison or recidivated.

The released *Furman*-commuted offenders have lived a combined total of 1,282 years in the community while committing twelve violent offenses—approximately two violent offenses per year for the released inmates or nine violent offenses per 1,000 releasees per year. Recidivism occurred an average of 3.4 years after release for murderers and 2.5 years for rapists. Of the 239 paroled offenders, one killed again. Two rapists raped again.

To determine if this level of recidivism is excessive for these criminals, we compared them to a like group of offenders, specifically other murderers. Bedau cites various data on the release behavior of paroled murderers. The data show that, overall, only a small percentage (less than 1%) of released murderers were returned to prison for committing a subsequent homicide. For example, of 11,532 murderers released between 1971 and 1975, twenty-six committed new homicides in the first year after release from prison. However, our data reveal that after five years on parole, only one murderer committed a second murder while in the larger society. Though these data are not conclusive, they do suggest that the capital murderers on parole do not represent a disproportionate threat to the larger society.

Table 5-6	Total Recidivism By Offense	
Release Outcome	**Murderers**	**Rapists**
Total Released	188 (43.4%)	51 (64.6%)
Mean Time in Community	5.3 years	5.6 years
Recidivated	38 (20.2%)	13 (25.5%)
Technical Violations	15 (8.0%)	4 (7.8%)
Misdemeanor	3 (1.6%)	0
New Felony Offense	20 (10.6%)	9 (17.6%)
Murder	1	0
Rape	0	2
Robbery	4	2
Aggravated Assault	1	2
Burglary	4	2
Larceny-Theft	3	0
Possession of firearms	2	0
Drugs	4	1
Indecency with a child	1	0

The data in this study parallel other recidivism research on murderers in general. While murderers on parole appear to rarely repeat their original crime, more research on these released offenders is needed.

Given the amount of time these parolees have spent in the free community (an average of five years), their overall post-release behavior takes on great significance when evaluating the incapacitation effect of the death penalty. Murder is the prime concern. Incapacitation advocates would insist that the execution of every *Furman*-offender would have prevented the one subsequent murder referred to above. Further, the executions would have prevented six prison murders (four inmates and two guards). This evidence supports permanent incapacitation as a means to prevent future capital crimes. However, four inmates on death row at the time of *Furman* were innocent according to a study by Bedau and Radelet. These four individuals could possibly have been executed had it not been for *Furman*.

At the same time, incapacitation advocates might argue that the death row experience itself was prophetic and acted as a deterrent that kept more of the *Furman*-releasees from killing again. That is, the *Furman* inmates were so close to death that they straightened up their act out of fear. Although this possibility seems far-fetched and self-serving it is a viable explanation for the behavior of some prisoners. For example, a *Furman* inmate in Texas, a double murderer who has never been released from prison, wrote us and explained that his good prison conduct and overall positive outlook on life was the direct result of his time spent on death row. Moreover, this capital murderer has over the years completed more than a dozen furloughs successfully.

While execution would certainly have prevented seven additional murders, our data also show that 551 prisoners, or 98%, did not kill either in prison or in the free community. The vast majority served their time in prison with few challenges to the prison staff. Moreover, most of those released on parole were not menaces to the social order. The death row experience alone cannot account for deterring 551 inmates spread across thirty states. What can account for this fact?

In 1972, the average age of the *Furman* inmates was thirty-one years. These inmates were generally older than other "incoming" prisoners. Some had spent five, six, or even seven years on death row prior to commutation and this confinement eased their adjustment upon return to the general prisoner population. If anything, the death row experience was a learning experience. While confined on "the row," these prisoners learned how to survive in prison and how to "do time." When released to the general prisoner population in 1972, they were already "prisonized" and acclimated to institutional life. This minor adjustment translated into relatively few disciplinary infractions. The disciplinary data reported earlier support this point. The *Furman* prisoners represented an "older" cadre of convicts well adapted to the penitentiary.

We also suggest that the commutees as a group were older upon release to the free community. Excluding time on death row, the average time spent in prison before release was nine and one-half years. Therefore, these prisoners as a group were over forty years old when released from prison. We are suggesting that the most important variable explaining the *Furman*-offenders' low rate of recidivism in the free community is age, or the aging process and its effect on future criminal activity. In other words, the dual effects of long prison terms (incapacitation) and aging on these offenders—presumably the high risk offenders—effectively reduced their potential for future criminal activity.

VI. *Conclusions*

H.L.A. Hart asked: "What is the weight and character of the evidence that the death penalty is required for the protection of society?" This question, in our opinion, is the most salient one in any discussion of the utility of capital punishment. Seven (1.3%) *Furman*-commuted prisoners were responsible for seven additional murders. Certainly execution of all 558 prisoners would have prevented these killings. However, such a "preemptive strike" would not have greatly protected society. In addition, four innocent prisoners would have been put to death. The question then becomes whether saving the lives of the seven victims was worth the execution of four innocent inmates.

The data in this paper suggest that these prisoners did not represent a significant threat to society. Most have performed well in the prison; those few who have committed additional violent acts are indistinguishable from those who have not. Therefore, over-prediction of secondary violence is indicated. More than two-thirds of the *Furman* inmates, using a very liberal definition of violence, were false positives—predicted to be violent but were not. We cannot conclude from these data that their execution would have protected or benefited society.

There are numerous policy implications to be drawn from the data presented in this paper. We do not suggest that every commuted capital offender can be released into free society. Some, albeit a minority, certainly need long-term confinement in maximum security facilities. Life-without-parole statutes are not the answer either because the indiscriminate warehousing of these prisoners would not have prevented numerous killings in free society. What we are suggesting is that the great majority of the *Furman* inmates were not violent predators in the prison or free society. The data presented in this paper suggest that current capital sentencing schemes predicated on their incapacitation effect, as is the practice of many states today that include a prediction of future dangerousness to justify executions, cannot accomplish their goals accurately or with a sense of fair play.

■ Incapacitation—Perspectives

■ Issue—Are Capital Murderers a Greater Threat Than Noncapital Murderers?

Jon Sorensen and Robert D. Wrinkle, "No Hope for Parole: Disciplinary Infractions Among Death-Sentenced and Life-Without-Parole Inmates"

In the last two decades, life-without-parole (LWOP) statutes enacted by a majority of states have created an ever-increasing population of inmates with little hope for release. Also, for death-sentenced (DS) inmates, the trend in recent years has been to house them on death row for several years before execution. Many observers believe that an inmate population—capital inmates—with so little or nothing to lose will be unruly and violent during their long periods of incarceration. The present study examined the level of rule violations and violent acts during incarceration committed by capital inmates (LWOP and DS) and a comparison group of second-degree murderers serving long, indeterminate sentences (life-with-parole, or LWP).

As a general rule, long-term inmates tend to avoid trouble and spend their time constructively. Most recent research suggests that an inverse relationship exists between sentence length and disciplinary infractions. Prison officials usually deem prisoners serving life sentences to be the most manageable prisoners.

Most previous research, however, has referred to long-term inmates, not inmates who have no hope of release. Some have contended that newer life-sentenced inmates serving longer terms have less to lose and will behave predictably worse than previous generations of lifers. Some have predicted that LWOP statutes, in particular, will result in a "new breed of superinmates prone to violence and uncontrollable."

DS inmates often are seen as even more potentially dangerous than life-sentenced capital murderers. One of the most touted rationales for sentencing a select group of capital offenders to death is to incapacitate them, thereby preventing future acts of violence, "because if a capital murderer were sentenced to life imprisonment, he may some day kill a fellow prisoner or member of the prison staff, the assumption being that he is, more than a prisoner sentenced for some other crime, prone to homicidal violence."

Although there is reason to suspect that capital inmates pose a threat to others in the institutions in which they are housed, little research evidence exists to support such claims. The current research compares the behavior of LWOP and DS capital murderers to that of a group of LWP inmates sentenced to long terms for second-degree murder.

I. *Method*

The sample included all male inmates sentenced to the Missouri Department of Corrections (MDOC) for capital murder since the reimposition of the death penalty in 1977. As of January 1993, there were 416 male capital murderers incarcerated in the MDOC, 93 (22.4%) of them sentenced to death and 323 (77.6%) sentenced to life without the possibility of parole. As a comparison group, a sample of second-degree murderers was selected by choosing every fifth inmate from a list provided by the MDOC for the same time period. This systematic sampling procedure resulted in a sample of 232 inmates.

II. Results

Table 5-7 presents descriptive variables for the DS, LWOP, and LWP inmates. The three groups did not differ significantly in time served but did differ significantly with respect to age and ethnicity, LWP inmates were significantly younger and included a significantly higher percentage of African Americans than the other two groups. These latter findings were not unexpected, given that most of the murders were intraracial and that killers of Whites were given more severe penalties than killers of African Americans in Missouri during this period of time

Table 5-8 presents data pertaining to overall rule infractions for the DS, LWOP, and LWP inmates. There were significant group differences with respect to prevalence, and to the rate for the first 3 years, DS and LWOP inmates were significantly, respectively, less likely to be involved in overall rule infractions than were LWP inmates. There were no significant differences in rates of overall infractions between the groups after 3 years of incarceration.

Next, the influence of other variables on group differences in overall rule infractions was explored. A regression model predicting the total number of rules infractions was significant. Time served, age, and race were significantly related to overall rates of infractions in the predicted directions (age negatively, and time served and race positively). Type of sentence did not contribute significantly to the prediction of rule-violating behavior.

Table 5-9 presents the number and rate of assaultive rule violations. As was true for overall rule infractions, DS and LWOP inmates were no more likely than LWP inmates to have committed violent offense against others within the insti-

Table 5-7	Descriptive Variables for Death-Sentenced, Life-Without-Parole, and Life-With-Parole Inmates		
		Type of Sentence	
Variable	DS	LWOP	LWP
Mean years served	6.62	6.66	7.13
Mean age at admission	31.27	29.19	26.90
Percentage African American	47.31	52.32	62.07

Table 5-8	Rule Infractions Among Death-Sentenced, Life-Without-Parole, and Life-With-Parole Inmates		
		Type of Sentence	
Overall Rule Infractions	**DS**	*LWOP*	*LWP*
Prevalence	86.02	90.71	100.00
Frequency	9.97	11.66	13.48
Overall yearly rate	1.53	1.88	2.09
Rate after first 3 years	1.45	1.65	1.98
Rate after 3 years	1.70	1.50	1.82

tution. None of the between-group comparisons involving the variables in Table 3 was statistically significant.

Next the same regression approach presented above was used to predict the total number of assaultive infractions. Similar to the model predicting overall infractions, type of sentence was not predictive of assaultive behavior. Age and time served were significant, but race had no influence.

III. *Discussion*

The findings from this study do not provide support for the expectation that DS and LWOP inmates would commit more infractions than LWP inmates. Type of sentence did not have an effect on the overall number or rate of rule infractions. Although it appeared that LWP inmates were more likely to commit rule violations in the bivariate analyses, the differences between the groups disappeared in the regression models, suggesting that they resulted from the influence of other variables. DS and LWOP inmates also were no more likely to have been involved in assaultive behavior than were the LWP inmates.

Table 5-9	Types of Assaultive Rule Infractions Committed by Death-Sentenced, Life-Without-Parole, and Life-With-Parole Inmates		
		Type of Sentence	
Assaultive Rule Infractions	**DS**	*LWOP*	*LWP*
Prevalence	23.66	17.65	22.41
Frequency	.43	.40	.41
Yearly rate	.06	.06	.06
Number of			
Murder/manslaughters	1	4	3
Assaults	24	73	76
Forcible Sexual Assaults	1	0	5
Minor Sexual Assaults	14	52	11

These findings suggest that capital inmates, both DS and LWOP, are no more of a threat to others in the institution than are murderers serving long-term sentences with the possibility of parole. This supports studies that have found that the carrot of parole does not greatly influence institutional behavior. It also supports studies that have found that DS inmates and capital inmates in general do not present a disproportionate threat to the prison population.

The findings are counter to predictions based on concerns that LWOP inmates are an irrepressible group of inmates prone to disruptive and violent behavior. They also are not in agreement with predictions made by many about DS inmates, who are often seen as being too dangerous to be permitted to reside within the confines of the regular prison environment.

Matt DeLisi and Ed A. Munoz, "Future Dangerousness Revisited"

I. *Introduction*

One of the most dramatic discretionary processes in criminal justice is the decision to sentence an offender to death. At the sentencing phase, a primary concern of jurors or judges is the criminal propensity and risks that an offender poses. Many questions are considered. If this individual were one day released from prison, would he likely commit another heinous offense? Is life imprisonment veracious, or is it likely that this defendant will be released from prison? Is this offender so volatile that he is a likely danger to correctional staff, medical practitioners, and other inmates? Does the extensive criminal record of this defendant guarantee that he will similarly victimize others in the future? In short, is this individual too dangerous to take a chance on his potential future crimes? In over 20 jurisdictions across the United States, affirmative answers to these very questions can be used as aggravating factors in determining a sentence of death.

II. *Empirical Background*

To date, investigations of the institutional and post-release misconduct of condemned or formerly condemned offenders are decisively unsupportive of the future dangerousness doctrine. Marquart and Sorensen monitored 47 Texas inmates whose death sentences were commuted by governors following *Furman*. They found that condemned offenders were generally compliant and that a small cadre of inmates committed most prison infractions. After release from prison, only 8% of the formerly condemned offenders committed new felonies. Similarly, Vito and Wilson tracked 17 Kentucky inmates who were eventually paroled after the commutation of their death sentence; 65% of these ($n = 11$) were so compliant on parole that they were placed on inactive supervision. Only four inmates were re-arrested, none for an additional homicide.

Marquart and Sorensen later conducted a national study of condemned inmates whose sentences were commuted. They found that these 558 offenders committed six homicides while incarcerated, but that the majority of inmates served their sentences with few incidents of misconduct. A subset of the original sample as ultimately released from prison to the community; 79% were completely crime-free during their release. The remaining 21% of the parolees recidivated and were re-incarcerated. Cunningham and Reidy disaggregated Texas Department of Corrections data and compared the base rates of violence of released death row inmates, inmates serving a life sentence, high security inmates, and other inmates. They found that former death row inmates had the lowest involvement in serious violent prison rule violations. Lifers, others, and high security inmates constituted much greater threats than formerly condemned offenders.

Utilizing data from the Missouri Department of Corrections, Sorensen and Wrinkle compared the prison misconduct careers of 93 condemned inmates, 323 inmates serving life imprisonment without the possibility of parole, and 232 inmates sentenced to life with parole. Like earlier studies, they found that most inmates, regardless of their sentence, were generally compliant during imprisonment and that a handful of volatile inmates committed most of the serious infractions. Sorensen and his colleagues later found that demographic indicators such as age and race were much more related to assaultive behavior in prison than capital offender status.

Sorensen and Pilgrim later examined the infraction records of over 10,000 convicted murderers in Texas. Generally, they found that criminal history measures such as prison history, gang membership, and prior involvement in "felony murder" crimes, such as the contemporaneous commission of armed robbery and murder, significantly impacted prison violence. However, once again, the majority of capital murder defendants did not pose significant risks to correctional staff and other inmates. Finally, Reidy and his collaborators retrospectively studied the prison misconduct careers of 39 Indiana inmates whose death sentences were reduced to capital life between 1972 and 1999. They found that the prevalence rate of violence in prison for former death row inmates was 20.5%. Moreover, they found that 60% of the formerly condemned offenders were never placed in administrative segregation for committing serious violations during their stay in the general prison population. They concluded that contrary to the public perception of their future dangerousness, most death row inmates were cooperative and rather manageable.

Perhaps the relatively low levels of misconduct among condemned vis-à-vis general prisoners are a consequence of the unique characteristics of death row. For example, Arriaga described death row as an arena of deprivation, depersonalization, and demoralization. Condemned offenders are virtually denied human interaction and many states mandate that death row offenders spend 23 hours per day in their cells. Compared to other incarcerated persons, condemned offenders have restricted recreation, visitation, and work opportunities and scarce opportunities to engage other inmates. Although there is considerable state variation in terms of the deprivations experienced by condemned offenders, death row is, generally speaking, a stark environment. Although the conditions of death row cannot explain why formerly condemned prisoners have low recidivism levels once released from prison, the punitive level of social control on death row could explain their low rates of misconduct while imprisoned.

There are additional hypotheses for the relatively low levels of violence engaged in by condemned offenders. Cunningham and Vigen have suggested that, contrary to conventional wisdom, death row inmates have much to lose by engaging in prison misconduct. Many are pursuing appeals or post-conviction reviews of their sentence, processes that could be compromised by further violent behavior. Also, some capital defendants have little to no prior criminal record and have been convicted of a relatively out of character, isolated event such as a "passion killing." Hence, further violence is not expected from an individual whom, prior to his or her capital offense, ostensibly did not engage in criminal activity.

Another explanation is that the future dangerousness doctrine itself is problematic. Condemned offenders might demonstrate low levels of institutional and post-release violence because the courts simply cannot predict future dangerousness. Obviously, further understanding of the institutional behavior of condemned and non-condemned offenders is needed to further assess future dangerousness. The current study seeks to accomplish this in two ways. First, previous studies are geographically limited because they are disproportionately based on Texas data. Therefore the replication of prior findings in other jurisdictions and geographic areas is important. To redress this, the current research employs a large, heterogeneous sample of offenders from a new geographic area, Arizona. Second, the current research empirically examines the relationship between sentence type and institutional violence controlling for a battery of diagnostic, offense, and demographic characteristics with robust multivariate models. This will isolate the potentially independent effects on sentence type of prison misconduct and build upon the extant literature that generally uses retrospective, descriptive data analysis.

III. *Methodology*

A. Data Data are derived from the official prison records of inmates committed to the Arizona Department of Corrections. Prison classification and diagnostic personnel compile an encyclopedia dossier for each inmate in their custody. This report contains demographic information, primary charge and felony classification, length and type of sentence, admission and expected release dates (if applicable), housing and facility transfers, escape and absconding information, work and prison industry history, and parole history. In an effort to appropriately classify inmates according to their needed level of custody, programming, and treatment, the prison diagnostic unit creates quantitative scales that measure inmates according to a variety of risks such as institutional, security-threat group, and escape.

B. Sample A simple random sample of 1,005 inmates was selected from a sampling frame of nearly 27,000 inmates (the state prison population). Of these, 893 inmates were serving determinate sentences ranging from 1 and 70 years, 43 inmates were serving a life sentence, and 69 inmates had been sentenced to death. The latter offenders were oversampled to ensure enough cases for statistical analyses. The total sample was 83% male and 17% female. Forty six percent of the inmates were White, 29% were Hispanic, 16% were Black, 7% were Native American, and 2% were Asian American. These demographic estimates did not appreciably differ from the prison population parameters; 92% male, 8% female; 45% White, 24% Hispanic, 15% Black, 5% Native American, and 1% Asian American.

C. Independent Variables

 i. Demographic Factors

By and large, investigators have found that age, race, and sex significantly influence prison misconduct just as they influence involvement in crime. Specifically, scholars have found that racial minorities, particularly Blacks, engage in more prison misconduct than Whites.

A more robust and less controversial finding is the link between age and assorted forms of prison misconduct. Myriad studies have documented that younger inmates are more volatile, problematic, and prone to commit violations in prison than older inmates

Gender differences in prison misconduct are a clear example of the differences between substantive and statistical significance. On one hand, male inmates are overwhelmingly more dangerous than female inmates, evidenced by their involvement in the most severe forms of violence such as murder, hostage taking, and rioting. On the other hand, female inmates are subject to greater social control in correctional facilities, resulting in inflated official misconduct records for women.

Finally, fewer studies have examined the relationship between educational attainment and prison violence, and to date, the findings are mixed. It is hypothesized that educational attainment is inversely related to involvement in prison violence.

ii. Offense Type/Severity

An important criticism of capital punishment is the seemingly arbitrary relationship between the severity and legal classification of the capital offense and the resultant imposition of a death sentence. A variety of extra-legal factors can differentiate killings that result in a first degree murder convictions with special circumstances, first degree murder convictions without special circumstances, second degree murder convictions, or manslaughter. Prior research has examined the future dangerousness of murderers whose cases reflected these different charges and sentencing outcomes. Terms for first degree murder, second degree murder, and manslaughter convictions were introduced as controls.

iii. Diagnostic/Criminal History

An extensive literature has documented the positive relationship between criminal record and institutional misconduct; chronic offenders or "career criminals" with extensive arrest, conviction, violence, and prison history tend to disproportionately violate prison order. Interval scales ranging from 1 = Very Low Risk to 5 = Very High Risk are created from the inmate's criminal, incarceration, and substance abuse history to classify each offender according to their needed supervision level.

Measures used to determine institutional classification are weapons history, confinement history, gang/security-threat group history, probation and parole history, substance abuse history, alcohol and drug treatment needs, and institutional risk.

D. Dependent Variable The dependent variable is the sum of eight criminal offenses that are roughly commensurate with the Part I Index offenses in the *Uniform Crime Reports*. They are murder, rape, rioting, hostage taking, aggravated assault, escape, arson, and weapons possession. Unfortunately, there is no scholarly consensus about which offenses underlie future dangerousness, however the current violations are similar to those from earlier studies.

III. *Results*

The central finding is that death row inmates were significantly involved in serious prison violence, more so than any other type of inmate. Moreover, there was a significant negative relationship between serving a life sentence and serious prison violence, rendering lifers the least violent offenders in prison. Inmates serving determinate sentences were neither more nor less involved in serious misconduct than their peers serving more punitive sanctions. That persons sentenced to death will continue to engage in serious and violent crime while incarcerated is fully consistent with the future dangerousness doctrine and thereby directly in opposition to the extant literature.

Some of the more unexpected results occurred among the demographic variables. Although age was inversely related to prison violence for all three equations, none of these effects achieved statistical significance. Similarly, there were no statistically significant sex differences for violent prison misconduct. Having said this, it is important to notice the more substantive effects between sex and inmate status by examining the distributions across sentence types. None of the condemned offenders (0%) in this study were female. Only three of 43 (7%) inmates serving life imprisonment were female. However, nearly one in five inmates (171/893 = 19%) serving a determinate sentence was female. Therefore, while regression analyses did not produce significant effects for male and female inmates, it is clear that the most serious offenders, according to sentence severity, were male. For all three regressions, minority inmates engaged in significantly more violent prison misconduct than white inmates. This is supportive of prior research. Finally, less educated inmates were more likely to engage in prison violence than inmates who have completed more years of school.

With the exception of one regression where first degree murder was negatively related to prison violence, severity of offense was unrelated to involvement in prison violence. Otherwise, violent prison misconduct did not depend on the legal classification of the inmate's instant offense, whether first or second degree murder or manslaughter.

Overall, the most robust predictors of prison violence were diagnostic measures based on prior criminal record. Inmates with extensive weapons history were more than three standard deviation units above the mean levels of prison violence. More dramatic was the relationship between confinement history and prison violence. Inmates with multiple prior stints in prison were nearly seven standard deviation units above the mean levels of prison violence. Whereas prior prison record was an important predictor, prior *punishment* history was not. Inmates who had been adjudicated and sentenced to community corrections such as probation were not significantly likely to commit serious prison violations. As expected, gang-affiliated inmates committed more prison violence than inmates not involved in gangs.

Inmates who had more extensive substance abuse histories were less involved in prison violence, however inmates with more acute drug and alcohol treatment needs were more involved in prison violence. These seemingly contradictory findings probably indicate the temporal component of addiction. Offenders may report substantial drug histories, however these histories can be dated. Conversely, offenders with current addictions and the need for immediate treatment constitute a more grave, contemporaneous risk. The composite measure of institutional risk was, predictably, significantly related to engaging in prison violence. This suggests that the prison classification unit appropriately assessed the risks that various inmates pose to prison safety. Finally, time served was positively related to prison violence. This makes intuitive sense because the more time served correlates to more opportunities to engage in misconduct and be cited by correctional staff.

IV. *Discussion*

The personification of the future dangerousness doctrine is Kenneth McDuff. A chronic delinquent, McDuff was on parole for burglary in 1966 when he and a drinking companion happened upon three teenagers in a park. Intoxicated and armed, McDuff commandeered their car and abducted the three youths (two males and one female). He summarily executed the males; then proceeded to rape, rob, torture, and ultimately, kill the young girl. McDuff became known as the "Broomstick Killer" because he used the blunt instrument to bludgeon the young girl. For these crimes, McDuff was convicted and sentenced to death.

Like over 500 condemned offenders nationwide, McDuff's death sentence was commuted to life imprisonment following the 1972 *Furman* ruling. McDuff would remain incarcerated for the next 17 years until severe crowding in the Texas prison system, his relatively pliant conduct in prison, his middle-age status, and other factors resulted in his parole release in 1989. Within one year, McDuff was re-incarcerated after menacing two young African Americans with a knife (McDuff was an avowed racist, alcoholic, and cocaine addict). After a brief incarceration, McDuff was re-released again. Over the next several years, he would engage in an array of criminal activity including the abduction, rape, robbery, torture, and murder of several women. Estimates vary, but law enforcement officials and investigators have linked the serial killer to as many as nine abduction/homicides in Texas. Convicted and returned to death row, Kenneth McDuff was finally executed in November 1998.

The indignant, sullen, unrepentant, and frighteningly recidivistic McDuff was exceptional, however. Retrospective analysis of condemned offenders from prior studies revealed a story far different from McDuff's. Most capital offenders adjusted well to prison and complied with its rules. Moreover, formerly condemned offenders behaved well while on parole and were more likely to be re-incarcerated for technical violations or minor crimes rather than violent ones. If analyzed by the same method, the current data would have produced similar results. Only three inmates killed again while incarcerated: a condemned inmate who totaled 37 total prison violations including one escape; a "lifer" who totaled 95 violations including two escapes, two threatening staff, nine assaults, two weapons violations, and two incidents of arson; and an inmate serving a 2-year sentence who amassed 46 prison violations (21 for disobeying staff). Respectively, 1.4% (1/69) of condemned offenders, 2.3% (1/43) of lifers, and 0.1% (1/893) of other inmates killed while incarcerated. These prevalence numbers are low and resemble those from prior research. However, multivariate analyses here portray an entirely different situation than prior research. Condemned offenders were more dangerous than other inmates, evidenced by their significant involvement in the most serious forms of prison misconduct. This relationship persisted controlling for 15 demographic, offense type, criminal history, and diagnostic variables.

Obviously, no research design is perfect and the current study was potentially limited by the reliance on official misconduct data. Prior research indicated that correctional staff differentially cited inmates for misconduct based on their ascribed characteristics. This could be the case here. Although officer discretion is minimized when discussing the most serious forms of misconduct, it is simply unknown to what degree official biases affected the recording of misconduct.

Finally, the lack of structural variables describing the correctional facilities within which the inmates lived was an important limitation of these data. For example, one could argue that the current findings had less to do with individual dangerousness and more to do with the social control and environment experienced by condemned versus other inmates. Nevertheless and despite these admonitions, the current study employed a large probability sample, included many empirically important statistical controls, and utilized a robust data analysis technique.

Cunningham and Reidy have claimed that prison is fundamentally different than free society and that prison violence does not predictably follow from preconfinement violence or the capital offense of conviction. This statement contradicts both the current findings and scores of evidence suggesting that individuals with extensive criminal records, consistent adverse contacts with the criminal justice system, antisocial personality disorders, and histories of violence are most likely to engage in misconduct while imprisoned. It is unclear why prior criminality was largely unrelated to previous studies of future dangerousness/ condemned offenders but critical to the larger study of institutional misconduct. Future research should sample sufficient numbers of condemned, life imprisonment, and other inmates from new jurisdictions to assess this further.

V. Conclusion

Although future dangerousness has important legal value, it could be interpreted as a superfluous concept. Criminals who are convicted of the most heinous crimes are marked for death *for what they have done.* Therefore it is rather curious that so much emphasis is placed on the probabilistic prediction of future conduct and social scientists ability to do so when it is known with certainty what has already occurred. However, prior conduct is not the only consideration in the capital punishment debate. A defendant's probable future criminal behavior is a critically important issue to juries, courtroom officers, and citizens. More needs to be known about future dangerousness. The current study provides fresh evidence that condemned offenders will indeed continue to behave violently even within the confines of death row. That finding was unexpected, should prove to be controversial, and should serve as the impetus for additional research.

Cost

Cost—Introduction

It is unclear what role considerations of cost play in shaping public attitudes about the death penalty. In some recent polls, savings to taxpayers ranks only behind retribution as a basis for supporting the death penalty. One in five supporters of capital punishment cite savings to taxpayers as a basis for their support. Other data suggest that cost is not a dispositive consideration. Many proponents would support capital punishment even if it were demonstrated to them that life-without-parole (LWOP) inmates were the less expensive alternative.

The debate over comparative cost is complicated by the fact that assessing the cost of the death penalty depends in part on the rights to which capital defendants are afforded. Not everyone agrees on what those rights should be. In arguing that the death penalty is more expensive, abolitionists rely in part on the fact that capital litigation is more expensive. Capital defendants have what is sometimes called "super due process," including the right to present unlimited mitigating evidence, possession of more extensive appellate rights, and the opportunity to seek gubernatorial clemency. In the Perspectives section of this chapter, John McAdams argues that abolitionists have effectively created a catch-22: they fight for greater protections for defendants at trial and during appeal, while arguing that death penalty prosecutions are too expensive to be justified.

The issue considered here is whether, given existing protections, the cost of a capital case from indictment to execution exceeds the cost of a noncapital case from indictment to the natural death of the inmate. This may seem unsatisfying not only to death penalty proponents who believe capital defendants are afforded more rights by the law than they should be, but also to those who believe it is unjustifiable to spend any money to keep convicted murderers alive in prison. Nevertheless, of the many questions that might be asked about cost, this seems the most relevant for at least three reasons. One, none of the procedural rights afforded defendants are likely to change in the foreseeable future—certainly not the right to present unlimited mitigating evidence, guaranteed by *Lockett v. Ohio*, or the right to bifurcated trials, approved by *Gregg*—which add significantly to the marginal additional cost in capital trials. Two, there is no other way to meaningfully discuss the issue than to consider the world as it is. It is possible that no two people will agree precisely as to what reduced rights capital defendants should be entitled. Three, proponents don't generally allow for the implications of the inverse of the McAdams's concern: many conservatives believe that prison conditions are better than they should be. Worsening prison conditions might reduce the cost of life imprisonment, but death penalty proponents don't generally take this into account when assessing the relative cost of death sentences and life prison terms. So it seems fair to distill the issue into a single question: is the death penalty as currently constituted more or less expensive than the alternatives?

The general framework for thinking about the cost issue is set out in **Figure 6-1**. There is an up-front cost to seeking death sentences. Capital litigation is significantly more expensive than noncapital litigation (the reasons for this are discussed below). During the period of incarceration—for the capital defendant, from conviction through execution; for the noncapital defendant, from conviction through natural death—it is somewhat more expensive to keep prisoners on death row than in the general population (the reasons for this are again discussed below). There are also some costs associated with executions. Following executions, savings result. The executed defendant costs the state nothing further, while the state must bear the ongoing cost of incarcerating the noncapital defendant to his natural death. So the question is whether the additional expense of seeking a death sentence and imprisoning the death-sentenced inmate outweighs the savings derived from the avoided cost of incarcerating executed capital defendants to the end of their natural lives. Generally speaking, both sides agree that this question is the framework within which this issue should be considered. From there, the two sides differ only in their estimates of costs.

In the Critical Documents section of this chapter, Philip Cook's team from Duke University offers some specific numbers to fill in this conceptual framework based upon their study of the death penalty in North Carolina. Professor Cook concludes that the extra cost of prosecuting a case capitally versus not capitally is approximately $2.1 million.

1. Cost of Capital Trials Versus Noncapital Trials

Why do capital trials cost more? The main reason is the added expense of jury selection and bifurcated trials. The separate penalty phase hearing creates an additional litigated question of fact: whether the aggravating evidence outweighs the mitigating evidence. Pretrial expenses are generally greater in capital cases. Investigation of mitigating evidence is expensive. Both the state and defense frequently hire private investigators. More complicated trials mean more complicated motion practice. Both sides routinely hire experts. It is common to have psychiatrists, medical examiners, neurologists, and criminologists testify during the

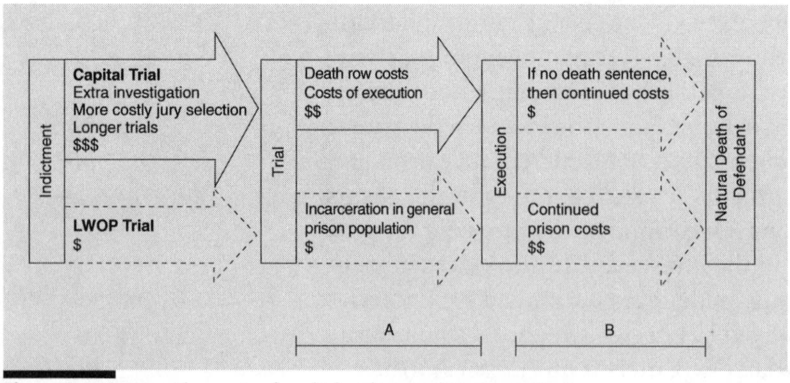

Figure 6-1 Comparative costs of capital and noncapital prosecutions.

penalty phase, each at considerable expense. Because of the separate penalty phase, capital trials last longer. This places increased demands on courts and means extra money spent on attorneys. Some states require two attorneys for capital defendants.

Juries in capital cases must be screened for attitudes about capital punishment. Some jurors who are against capital punishment and some who are automatically in favor of capital punishment must be excluded from the jury. This matter is discussed in more detail in Chapter 15. The extra voir dire associated with eliminating predisposed jurors creates additional expense. Longer voir dire means longer trials, which means more court time and more attorney time. Lawyers in capital cases are often allowed more peremptory challenges than in ordinary cases. Attorneys frequently retain experts in connection with the screening process, a legitimate expense because the consequences are high if a death penalty supporter or opponent slips into the jury.

An additional cost associated with capital trials is the reduced likelihood of plea bargaining. The overwhelming majority of criminal cases are resolved through plea bargaining. Death cases are resolved far less often through this method; according to one estimate, such cases are resolved ten times less often than other felony cases.

It is also worth noting that the additional costs of a capital trial are borne regardless of whether a death verdict results. If a capital trial does not result in a death verdict, the extra cost of the trial is a deadweight loss. The state bears the higher costs of the capital trial, but gets none of the offsetting benefit of a reduced prison term resulting from execution. Of course, capital sentencing rates vary from jurisdiction to jurisdiction.

2. Relative Costs of Incarceration

Following a capital conviction, the defendant is incarcerated on death row. It is generally thought that maintaining this population, as with most special prison populations, is somewhat more expensive than maintaining an ordinary prisoner. Some costs also attach to the execution, although these costs (electricity, drugs, interment) are not likely to materially affect the debate. Following execution the government's financial obligation to the prisoner ends.

On the other side of the ledger is the cost of maintaining a noncapital defendant. This depends in part on the length of the alternative sentence. If the alternative to a death sentence in a particular jurisdiction is a prison term of one year, this may seem like bad public policy, but it will make the death penalty appear relatively more expensive. In some states, but not all, life without parole is the alternative to death. Most studies that examine the issue, including the North Carolina study presented in the following section, have compared the cost of the death penalty to the cost of a sentence of life without parole.

3. Deferred Savings and the Time Value of Money

Capital prosecutions create the certainty of greater costs through trial because of extra investigation, more costly jury selection, and longer trials. If the capital prosecution results in a death sentence, some savings are achieved following the execution of the defendant. The savings must be discounted by two factors.

First, the savings must be discounted by the fact that it is somewhat more costly to maintain the prisoner prior to his execution. The longer the period between trial and execution (represented as span A in Figure 6-1) relative to the period between execution and the natural death of the defendant (span B in Figure 6-1), the less savings the death penalty produces. If murderers are generally old and likely to die anyway, it does not save much to execute them.

Second, the savings must be discounted by the fact that they are deferred. Society does not begin to enjoy the savings from death sentences until after the execution. According to some estimates, the average time a prisoner spends on death row is 12 years (again, see span A in Figure 6-1). We need to introduce one basic economic concept to frame this debate properly. As a general proposition, we would rather pay a dollar in ten years than a dollar today. This is the notion of the time value of money. The dollar in hand can be invested. There is the chance that events may obviate the need for the dollar to be spent. Of course, there are offsetting uncertainties. With respect to the death penalty, there is the chance that prison costs will rise faster than the pace of inflation, making the deferred savings relatively more valuable. But ordinarily people and governments are less concerned with deferred expenses than with immediate expenses, and less pleased with deferred benefits than immediate benefits. If capital trials resulted in quick executions this would be one thing, having to wait ten years to enjoy the cost benefit is another.

It also merits mention that prisoners maintained in jail die far earlier than their natural life expectancy because of poor health care, stress, and risk of murder in prison. This also offsets the savings that might be seen as resulting from the death penalty. On the other hand, if the death penalty deters, there may be positive externalities (or indirect economic benefits, such as the decline in smoking resulting from a cigarette tax) attaching to the death penalty that are difficult to quantify.

The following Perspectives section includes Professor McAdams's argument mentioned previously, and an essay by Richard Dieter, Executive Director of the Death Penalty Information Center in Washington, D.C., who argues that political grandstanding precludes a meaningful assessment of the true costs of capital punishment.

Cost—Critical Documents

Philip J. Cook and Donna B. Slawson, "The Costs of Processing Murder Cases in North Carolina"

Our objective in this report is to provide useful estimates of the costs of adjudicating capital cases in North Carolina. The "super due process" protections accorded the defendant in capital cases ensure that the typical capital case in North Carolina, as in other states, is more expensive at every stage of adjudication than it would have been if the State had not sought the death penalty. While this assertion is not in dispute, there is considerable uncertainty about the magnitude of the cost premium in capital cases. Several estimates from other states have been disseminated, but these estimates are for various reasons of limited use.

It should be noted that this report is not a comprehensive evaluation of the death penalty. Our focus is on the costs to state and county government. We do not consider the costs of adjudication borne by the federal government, or by private individuals. Nor do we consider the possible benefits of the death penalty, with one exception—the savings in the cost of incarceration. Our intent, then, is simply to put a price on the death penalty that is relevant to the state's taxpayers and their elected officials. The value of what they are buying at this price is left for others to determine.

I. *Trial Court Costs*

Our analysis of the extra costs of adjudicating murder cases capitally begins with the initial determination of guilt and sentencing. Capital cases tend to impose greater burdens on the defense, prosecution, and trial courts than do similar cases that are prosecuted and tried noncapitally. We estimate this difference using data on a sample of murder cases.

A. Data Collection We began by identifying the prosecutorial districts with the most murder cases. The top nine districts accounted for about 40 percent of a murder cases in the state in 1990. We then visited the Clerk of Superior Court in each of the eight counties. Identifying the sample cases by number, we copied information concerning the calendar of events in the case, the ultimate disposition, the names of the attorneys, and payments made by the courts. We also visited with the DAs and Public Defenders and sent them questionnaires concerning the time that they and their assistants had devoted to each case in the sample. We also sought copies of fee orders submitted by court-appointed defense attorneys.

This procedure produced fairly complete information on the murder cases in the sampling frame, which we ultimately defined as the cases where the DA sought a conviction for first or second-degree murder. In particular, a case is included in the sample if it meets the following criteria: 1) The defendant was indicted for murder; and 2) The case was ultimately disposed of by a guilty plea to first or second degree murder, or by a murder trial (either capital or noncapital). We succeeded in obtaining data on over 70 percent of such cases for the eight counties.

As it turned out, this procedure did not produce an adequate sample of cases that had been tried capitally. For that reason, we decided to incorporate cases from counties outside our sample of eight. State-wide lists of capital cases during 1990 and 1991 were provided by the AOC and the Appellate Defender's Office. These lists included 76 new cases from 42 different counties.

Since our purpose is to compare the costs of adjudicating capital and noncapital murder cases, we exercised considerable care in classifying the sample cases. Our operating definition of a *"capital case" is a case that was prosecuted as such through the guilt phase of the trial.*

B. Items Included in Trial Court Costs The items included in our tabulation of costs are summarized here:

1. Defense costs
- Payments for time and expenses of court-appointed lawyers;
- Time of attorneys in the Public Defender's Office;

- Payments to expert witnesses and private investigators;
- Time of PD investigator and other support staff.

2. Prosecution costs
   - Time of DA and ADAs; time of DA's investigator;
   - Payments to expert prosecution witnesses;
   - Time of victim-witness coordinator and other support staff.

3. Courtroom costs
   - Number of days for pretrial motions;
   - Number of days for jury selection, guilt phase, and sentencing phase;
   - Payments to members of jury pool, expenses for meals and lodging.

The items denominated in time, including days in court and the time of attorneys in the DA and PD offices are assigned monetary value.

The quality of data we collected is uneven. Information on payments to court-appointed private defense attorneys and expert witnesses is generally accurate, since it was usually possible to obtain copies of the fee orders or other documentation. Data on the number of days in court are derived from the fee orders or from the court docket sheets, where available; these sources required some interpretation, but we believe the errors tend to be small and more or less random.

Most problematic of the important cost items are the hours of time spent by the attorneys for the prosecution and the defense on each case. Attorneys in the DA and PD offices do not ordinarily keep time logs, so that the data they provided us were estimates from their recollection, aided perhaps by their written records of the sequence of events. While these recollections are bound to be somewhat inaccurate, we have no reason to believe that they are biased either up or down. On the average, then, the errors may tend to cancel out.

We do not take account of possible differences in pretrial release arrangements. Defendants in capital cases spend more time in jail awaiting trial than do defendants in murder cases that are not being prosecuted capitally. But we do not believe that this difference is important to the overall (cohort-based) difference in cost between capital and noncapital murder cases, since if the defendant is eventually convicted and sent to prison, whatever pretrial time was spent in jail is usually credited toward completion of the prison term.

Another omission from our accounting is the costs to the state and local law enforcement. DAs rely on law enforcement investigators to help develop cases for trial. It has been argued that the extent of the police investigation required by the DA's office will be greater if the DA intends to try the defendant capitally than for a similar murder case that is being prosecuted noncapitally. Since our data collection effort did not include the police, we have no basis for testing this claim.

C. Results for Capital and Noncapital Cases The most valid method for comparing the costs of capital and noncapital cases would be to conduct an experiment in which a series of aggravated murder cases are randomly divided between capital and noncapital prosecution, and the costs for each are tabulated following completion of the trials. Such an experiment would no doubt be unconstitutional. Our method is to compare costs for actual capital and noncapital murder cases, while acknowledging that in the absence of a true experiment, these two groups may not be strictly comparable. For example, the cases in our capital sample are more likely than the noncapital-murder trial cases to involve one or more additional felony charges (in addition to murder). On the average, then, capital cases may be more complex and require more time consuming investigation and presentation at trial than noncapital murder cases.

It is also true that the capital murder cases are less likely to involve a retained attorney; thus one reason why the state's costs of defending capital murder cases are relatively high is that the capital cases have a higher percentage of indigent defendants. Of course, some defendants who could afford retained counsel in a noncapital case would not be able to afford the extra cost of defending a capital case. If this is the explanation for the higher percentage of indigent defendants in capital cases, then it should not be netted out in estimating the extra costs of capital cases. These differences should be kept in mind in interpreting our results.

We now present our results for the costs of murder trials, beginning with the total and then for each of the important components. **Table 6-1** reports the distributions of total costs for trials in our three samples.

We see that capital trials are much more costly than noncapital trials on the average; the average (mean) capital trial that ends with the guilt phase costs $57,000, 3.4 times the mean of the noncapital trials ($17,000), while the average bifurcated capital trial is 5.0 times as costly at $84,000. What is also evident from these statistics is the considerable variability in costs from trial to trial within the same category. For example, the least expensive capital trial was less costly to the state than the median noncapital trial. The most expensive trial in the entire sample was a bifurcated capital trial costing the state $180,000; the least expensive was a noncapital case costing just $8,000.

We now report the statistics for several of the important components of the total cost: the length of the trial, the number of attorney hours devoted to the defense, and the number of attorney hours devoted to prosecution. The means and medians for these statistics are listed in **Table 6-2**. **Table 6-3** tabulates the relevant percentages depicted in these charts.

Table 6-1	Costs of Murder Trials		
	Capital Trial/ Bifurcated	**Capital Trial/ Guilt Phase Only**	**Noncapital Murder Trial**
Minimum	$24,777	$9,802	$7,766
25th %ile	$46,826	$32,140	$10,946
50th %ile	$75,552	$47,736	$13,762
75th %ile	$110,792	$72,721	$22,896
Maximum	$179,736	$137,500	$30,952
Mean	$84,099	$57,290	$16,697
#of Observations	32	26	19

Table 6-2	Average Time Expended for Trial, Defense, and Prosecution: Comparison of Three Samples		
	Capital Trial/ Bifurcated	Capital Trial/ Guilt Phase only	Noncapital Murder Trial
Length of Trial (days)	14.6 (n = 32)	10.6 (n = 26)	3.8 (n = 19)
Defense Attys Time (hours)	613 (n = 28)	447 (n = 20)	150 (n = 12)
Prosecution Time (hours)	282 (n = 32)	186 (n = 26)	61 (n = 19)

II. *Alternative Estimates of the Trial Costs per Death Sentence*

In this section we provide alternative estimates of the trial-related costs of capital adjudication. By the "single case" perspective, we define the cost of the death penalty as the difference in the costs of successfully prosecuting a single case as a capital case and as a noncapital case. By the "cohort" perspective, we take account of the cost-implications of the State's low "batting average" in capital prosecutions: in a majority of instances where the State prosecutes a case capitally, the death penalty is not imposed, and if imposed, never carried out. The cohort perspective thus examines the costs of prosecuting death penalty cases as a group.

A. Single Case Perspective As we have seen, the average cost to the state and county of a bifurcated capital trial is about $84,000. If these same cases had instead been adjudicated and tried noncapitally how much would they have cost on the average? The answer suggested by our data is $17,000, since that is the average cost of the noncapital murder trials in our sample. But our noncapital murder trial sample may not be a valid "control group" for the capital trial sample; in particular, we know that the noncapital defendants were less likely to be indigent or to be charged with one or more other felonies in addition to the murder. There may be other differences in the inherent complexity or costliness of these cases as well.

Table 6-3	Percentage Breakdown of Total Costs: Comparison of Three Samples		
	Capital Trial/ Bifurcated	Capital Trial/ Guilt Phase only	Noncapital Murder Trial
Courtroom	32.5%	34.7%	40%
Defense	43.9%	41.5%	30.3%
Prosecution	22.2%	22.7%	24.2%
Witness Fees and Other	1.4%	1.1%	5.5%
Total	100%	100%	100%

While there is no perfect way of dealing with this comparability problem, we have attempted to "control for" the intrinsic characteristics of the cases by use of regression analysis, a common statistical technique for taking a number of different characteristics into account simultaneously. The result is that, other things equal, bifurcated capital trials cost 3.8 times as much as noncapital murder trials, while capital trials that end with the guilt phase cost 2.5 times as much as noncapital murder trials. The average cost of our noncapital murder cases for which the state paid for the defense was $19,685; multiplying this number by the factor estimated from the regression equation yields an estimate for the average cost of bifurcated capital trials of indigent defendants as $75,000, and for capital trials that end with the guilt phase as $49,000. The excess costs can be calculated by subtracting $19,685 from each of these, yielding $55,000 and $29,000 respectively. Note that these regression-based estimates are somewhat less than the difference in means. The reason is that our regression adjusts for two sources of systematic difference between capital and noncapital cases: whether the defendant is indigent for purposes of financing his or her defense, and whether the defendant is tried on more than one felony charge. This approach is conservative, in the sense that the regression adjustment implicitly assumes that indigency and number of charges are determined independent of whether the case is prosecuted capitally, an assumption that is not always correct. Therefore the true differential may lie somewhere between two types of estimates.

B. Cohort Perspective In North Carolina during 1991 and 1992 there were 94 defendants tried capitally. Here is the distribution of outcomes:

- 29 (31%) Sentence of death imposed by jury
- 30 (32%) Capital trial, sentence of life imposed by jury
- 35 (37%) Capital trial, defendant acquitted or sentenced by judge

We see that only 31 percent of the capital trials resulted in the imposition of the death sentence. Yet all of these trials, regardless of outcome, were more costly than they would have been if they had proceeded noncapitally. Thus the single-case approach understates the average cost to the state per death sentence imposed. Based on these numbers, we assume that for every 100 capital trials, there are 31 in which the death penalty is imposed by the jury, 32 in which the jury imposes a life sentence after finding the defendant guilty of murder in the first degree, and 37 in which the jury acquits or convicts of a noncapital crime. If all 100 of these cases were tried noncapitally, then the total excess costs would be the sum of the excess costs for the 63 bifurcated trials, and the excess costs for the capital trials that end with the guilt phase. This total excess cost is divided by 31 (the number of death sentences imposed) to calculate the excess costs per death sentence imposed. The calculations are shown in **Table 6-4**, using both approaches developed above. The middle column of this table uses the sample averages as the basis for estimating excess costs; the result is an estimate of $185,000 per death sentence. The last column uses the excess cost estimates derived from the regression analysis, with a result of $148,000 per death sentence.

The extra costs to the trial courts of capital adjudication do not end with the original disposition of the case. Historically, at least, death-sentenced defen-

Table 6-4 Excess Costs for Capital Murder Trials		
	Excess Cost Based on Sample Averages (per case)	Cost Estimate Based on Regression Analysis (per case)
Capital Trial/ Bifurcated	$67,402	$55,500
Capital Trial/ Guilt Phase only	$40,593	$29,200
Excess cost per death sentence*	$185,428	$147,700

dants have been far more likely to win a new trial from the appeals courts than are other murder convicts. And there is a substantial probability that a death-sentence case will be remanded for resentencing, which requires much the same costly effort as a retrial. These new trials and new sentencing hearings are part of the cost of adjudicating the death penalty.

To quantify the extra costs resulting from subsequent trials and sentencing proceedings, we begin by reporting on the relative frequencies of such events in North Carolina. During the years 1979 to 1985 there were 69 death sentences imposed. Of these, 9 were remanded for a new trial on direct appeal, while 18 were remanded for a new sentencing hearing. Subsequently a number of the cases that were affirmed on direct appeal have been granted relief through the appeals process and remanded to the trial courts, while nine of those that received a new trial or new sentencing as a result of direct appeal have cycled back a second time following a new death sentence and new remand. By October 1992, this cohort of 69 capital cases had a total of 33 new sentencing hearings and 12 new trials—*two such events for every three death sentences imposed.* For the sake of comparison, we also tracked the appeals history of murder convictions that resulted in life imprisonment during the same period, 1979–1985. Of 161 such cases, just nine (6 percent) were remanded for a new trial.

Given these results, we see that the differential cost to the trial courts of imposing a death sentence includes the expected cost of this case returning to the court for subsequent trial or resentencing. Our estimate is:

Extra costs due to likelihood of retrial or resentencing =

(likelihood of retrial) × *(average cost of capital trial)* + *(likelihood of resentencing)* × *(average cost of resentencing)* =

$(17.4\%) \times (\$84,099) + (47.8\%) \times (\$68,138) = \$47,203.$

From this figure we subtract the cost of retrials in life-sentenced cases, which works out to just $933 per case. The difference ($47,203 − $933) is $46,270. We can combine this result with the excess costs of the original trial, which yields a total of either $194,000 or $232,000, depending on which of the estimates is used. The "bottom line," then, is that the extra costs to the public of prosecution, defense, and trial are about $200,000 per death sentence imposed. This estimate does not include the costs of appeals or imprisonment, which are the topics of subsequent sections of this report.

III. *Postconviction Costs*

Postconviction proceedings can extend over many years as convictions are reviewed by various state and federal courts. Here, we offer estimates of the costs incurred by North Carolina taxpayers during this process.

A. Direct Appeal Every defendant who is convicted of murder in the first degree and who is sentenced either to death or to life imprisonment has a right to appeal the conviction to the Supreme Court of North Carolina. We estimate the amount of time spent both by the Court and by prosecuting and defending attorneys during the appeal of such cases.

B. The Supreme Court of North Carolina Survey There are several reasons why adjudicating direct appeals of death cases might consume more of the Supreme Court's time than would life cases. First, appellate briefs in death cases tend to be more lengthy than those filed in life cases. Second, proportionality review by the Court is a step required in death cases but not life cases. Third, certain issues, such as the death-qualification procedures required during jury selection in capital trials, are typically not subjects for review in cases where the defendant received a life sentence at the trial level. Appellate attorneys tend to use more time for oral argument, and justices tended to spend more time evaluating death cases after oral argument than life cases. A summary of the cost data for these cases is presented in **Table 6-5**.

Table 6-5	Time Spent Processing Murder Cases on Direct Appeal, 9/91 to 8/92: SCNC Justices and Law Clerks (in hours)				
		N	Mean	Median	Range
Justices	Life	19	12.3	11.4	1.8 to 31.5
	Death	12	19.5	19.6	6.4 to 31.5
Law Clerks	Life	19	59.7	44.3	3.0 to 212.0
	Death	12	74.3	72.1	17.3 to 176.3

Applying the dollar values attributable to each of these positions, the following total costs for each of these samples are obtained (**Table 6-6**):

Table 6-6	Costs of Adjudicating Life and Death Cases on Direct Appeal: SCNC Justices and Law Clerks			
		Mean Cost	Median Cost	Range
Justices	Life	$1,143	$1,102	$170 to $3,053
	Death	$1,887	$1,894	$622 to $3,053
Law Clerks	Life	$1,429	$1,240	$84 to $5,940
	Death	$2,083	$2,021	$483 to $4,939
Total	Life	$2,572	$2,620	$541 to $8,032
	Death	$3,970	$3,753	$1,105 to $7,992

As expected, the average costs of time devoted by justices and clerks to death cases exceeded that for life cases, although the differences are not large. The mean cost is higher by 54 percent ($3,970/$2,572), while the median estimate is higher by 43 percent ($3,753/$2,619).

C. Proceedings Following the Direct Appeal If no relief is granted on direct appeal, capital defendants have recourse to subsequent review in the federal and state courts. To estimate the full cost of these postconviction proceedings requires a sample of cases where the death sentence was actually carried out. There are only five such cases in the modern era in North Carolina. We were able to obtain some cost data on just three of them. In addition, we have obtained data on the costs of the recent *Maynard* case, which came close to execution before the Governor commuted the sentence.

Capital costs are not calculated routinely by the Department of Corrections, but we were able to estimate them for a new medium security unit. In July 1992, the DOC opened the Brown Creek Correctional Facility. This prison is a medium security, dormitory type facility. Construction was budgeted at $17.5 million. The DOC Central Engineering Division provided an estimate of the facility's useful life as 50 years, with significant renovations being made at 20 and 40 years, each entailing costs amounting to 25% of original construction expense. From these numbers we estimated that the annual capital cost per inmate is $746. This result will change somewhat with changes in assumptions about interest and inflation rates. But whatever we assume about inflation and interest rates, within reason, it remains true that capital costs of incarceration are small relative to operating costs.

D. Cost Saving from Shorter Incarceration for Death-Sentenced Defendants The present value of the extra 10 or 15 years in prison can be calculated under different assumptions concerning the level of custody (**Table 6-7**). If all these years are spent in medium security, then the costs are somewhat higher than if the last five years are spent in minimum custody, as would normally be the case in North Carolina prisons. Of these four estimates, we believe that the smallest is the best guide to the future, since it best comports with experience and current practice. For the "single case" perspective, then, our best estimate is that an execution saves $166,000 in incarceration costs.

Table 6-7	Costs of Differential Prison Time, Life vs. Death	
Time Until Execution	**Complete Term in Medium Security**	**Complete Last Five Years in Minimum Security**
Execution After Five Years	$288,481	$266,714
Execution After Ten Years	$187,687	$165,920

The cohort *perspective* is also relevant, and yields a far smaller number. The key to estimating the correctional savings for a cohort of death-sentenced defendants is knowing the percentage of these defendants who will ultimately be executed. Recent history suggests that this percentage is quite low—only four (5.8 percent) of the 69 defendants sentenced to death between 1979 and 1985 have been executed to date (March 1993). Of the 26 who remain on death row, it is impossible to predict with confidence how many will ultimately be executed, and even if we could predict correctly, the resulting percentage would not serve as a reliable guide to the future. Our approach is to offer cost estimates for what we consider a reasonable range of possible execution probabilities for future death-sentenced defendants, namely 10–30 percent.

Our calculation of cohort cost savings is based on the assumption that death-sentenced defendants who are not executed will serve 20 years in prison on the average, the last five years of which will be in minimum security. Thus there will be no "savings" for those not executed. The results are as follows (**Table 6-8**):

Table 6-8	Cost Savings From Differential Prison Time, Cohort Perspective	
Execution Percentage	**Cost Saving Per Defendant (10 Year Execution)**	**Cost Saving Per Defendant (5 Year Execution)**
10	$16,592	$26,671
20	$33,184	$53,343
30	$49,776	$80,014

The estimated cost savings depend critically on the percentage of defendants executed, and the elapsed time from sentence to execution. For example, assuming an elapsed time of 10 years and a 20 percent execution rate yields an estimate of $33,000 per death sentence imposed; if the execution rate is only 10 percent, the cost saving falls to $17,000.

IV. Summing Up the Costs

To estimate the net cost to the North Carolina public of adjudicating a case capitally, we now combine the estimates from the above sections. **Table 6-9** tells the story.

From the single case perspective, the cost of the death penalty is about $163,000 per case. The largest entry in this calculation, $255,000 for postconviction proceedings, is also the most uncertain. We base this estimate on the average of the two recent cases for which we were able to obtain relatively complete information. It is difficult to predict whether these two cases will provide a reliable

Table 6-9	Extra Costs to the North Carolina Public of Capital Cases	
	Single Case Perspective (per case)	**Cohort Perspective (per death penalty imposed)**
Trial	$67,402	$194,000
Direct Appeal	$6,977	$13,561
Postconviction	$255,000	> > $25,500
Imprisonment	($165,920)	($16,600)
Total	$163,459	> > $216,461

guide to the costs of future postconviction litigation for cases that are concluded by carrying out the death penalty (or, as in the *Maynard* case, coming close). The other entries are more straightforward. The estimate for the differential trial cost assumes that the defendant is indigent. The savings from cutting short the period of imprisonment is estimated on the assumption that the execution occurred after 10 years. Hence, our first conclusion is this:

> *The extra costs to the North Carolina public of adjudicating a case capitally through to execution, as compared with a noncapital adjudication that results in conviction for first degree murder and a 20-year prison term, is about $163,000.*

The single case approach is a useful beginning in understanding the costs of the death penalty, but it is not directly relevant to policy decisions. Much of the extra costs of death penalty adjudication are generated by cases that stop short of execution. For every death penalty imposed by a jury there are several others that are prosecuted capitally but tried to a lesser conclusion. And in only a small percentage of cases in which the death penalty is imposed, is the defendant ultimately executed. In policy debate over, say, whether the legislature should change the domain of the death penalty, the relevant cost figure includes the extra costs from all such cases. The second column of Table 6-10 reports these extra costs, calculated on a "per death penalty imposed" basis. The entries require some explanation.

As in the single case estimate, the most problematic entry is for postconviction adjudication costs. The entry here indicates that these costs are much greater than $25,500, which is 10 percent of the postconviction costs for the single case approach. The logic here is straightforward. Suppose that there is one execution for every ten death penalties imposed, and that postconviction costs for that execution are $255,000 (as indicated above). The postconviction cost *per death penalty imposed* is the average (over 10 cases) of the $255,000 and the costs of postconviction proceedings for the nine other capital cases. We have little basis for estimating the postconviction costs of these other cases. A rough calculation suggests that these other postconviction proceedings may add $58,000 or so to the overall average, in which case the cost of postconviction proceedings per death penalty imposed would be $84,000 and the total cost would be $274,000. In Table 6-9, we simply indicate that the true number is much larger than the one given here. The entry for incarceration cost savings is also based on the assumption that 10 percent of death row inmates are ultimately executed.

As explained above, the entries for trial cost and direct appeal incorporate the likelihood that death sentenced cases return to the trial courts for retrial or resentencing. Our second conclusion is this:

> *The extra cost to the North Carolina public of prosecuting a case capitally, as compared with a noncapital prosecution, is more than $216,000 per death penalty imposed. This estimate takes into account the likelihood that the jury will actually impose the death penalty, and if so, that the appellate courts will return the case to Superior Court for retrial or resentencing.*

It should be noted that there is another natural way to report the cohort costs of the death sentence. Instead of reporting these costs per death penalty imposed, we could report these costs *per execution*. Notice that if we carry through our assumption that there is only one execution for every ten death-sentenced defendants, then the answer emerges directly:

> *The extra cost per execution of prosecuting a case capitally is more than $2.16 million.*

Of course the assumption that 10 percent of death-sentenced defendants will be executed is open to question. For those who believe that the probability of execution will prove higher than 10 percent in the future, we calculate the implications of higher percentages in **Table 6-10**.

Our calculations hold constant the cost of trial and direct appeal (from Table 6-9), while varying the likelihood that the death sentence will be carried out. In these calculations, the cost per death penalty does not change much, but the cost per execution is quite sensitive to the execution percentage. Still, for any reasonable imputation of the postconviction costs for other capital cases, the extra cost per execution will exceed $800,000 even if the execution probability is as high as an unprecedented 30 percent.

It is possible to use our data to make a rough estimate of the statewide costs incurred over a particular time period. As noted, over the two-year period 1991 and 1992 there were a total of 94 defendants tried capitally. Of these, 29 were sentenced to death. These capital trials would have cost the state and counties about $4.3 million less if they had proceeded noncapitally. If the death-sentenced cases follow a postconviction track similar to that of cases from previous years, the cost to the state will total about $2.8 million for appeals and postconviction proceedings, and $1.4 million for retrials and resentencing proceedings ordered by the appellate courts. If 10 percent of the death-sentenced defendants will be executed, the savings in imprisonment costs will be about $0.5 million. Combining all these figures gives an overall extra cost of about $8.0 million, or an average of $4.0 million for the two years.

We conclude with a reminder that these estimates do not include federal or private costs, but rather are limited to those that are a direct burden on state and local government. Our numbers indicate that burden is substantial. But we leave it to others to judge whether the benefits of executing some murderers are such that it is worthwhile to expend so much public resources on the effort.

Table 6-10	Effects of Execution Probability On Cost Per Execution			
Execution Percentage	Postconviction Costs per Death Penalty	Imprisonment Savings per Death Penalty	Total Costs per Death Penalty	Total Costs per Execution
10	> > $25,500	($16,592)	> > $216,461	> > $2.16 million
20	> > $51,000	($33,184)	> > $225,377	> > $1.13 million
30	> > $76,500	($49,776)	> > $234,285	> > $0.78 million

■ Cost—Perspectives

■ Issue—Is the Cost of the Death Penalty Relative to Other Forms of Punishment a Valid Argument Against Capital Punishment?

Richard C. Dieter, "What Politicians Don't Say About the High Costs of the Death Penalty"

Throughout the United States, police are being laid off, prisoners are being released early, the courts are clogged, and crime continues to rise. The economic recession has caused cutbacks in the backbone of the criminal justice system. In Florida, the budget crisis resulted in the early release of 3,000 prisoners. In Texas, prisoners are serving only 20% of their time and rearrests are common. Georgia is laying off 900 correctional personnel and New Jersey has had to dismiss 500 police officers. Yet these same states, and many others like them, are pouring millions of dollars into the death penalty with no resultant reduction in crime.

The exorbitant costs of capital punishment are actually making America less safe because badly needed financial and legal resources are being diverted from effective crime fighting strategies. Before the Los Angeles riots, for example, California had little money for innovations like community policing, but was managing to spend an extra $90 million per year on capital punishment. Texas, with over 300 people on death row, is spending an estimated $2.3 million per case, but its murder rate remains one of the highest in the country.

The death penalty is escaping the decisive cost-benefit analysis to which every other program is being put in times of austerity. Rather than being posed as a single, but costly, alternative in a spectrum of approaches to crime, the death penalty operates at the extremes of political rhetoric. Candidates use the death penalty as a facile solution to crime which allows them to distinguish themselves by the toughness of their position rather than its effectiveness.

The death penalty is much more expensive than its closest alternative—life imprisonment with no parole. Capital trials are longer and more expensive at every step than other murder trials. Pre-trial motions, expert witness investigations, jury selection, and the necessity for two trials—one on guilt and one on sentencing—make capital cases extremely costly, even before the appeals process begins. Guilty pleas are almost unheard of when the punishment is death. In addition, many of these trials result in a life sentence rather than the death penalty, so the state pays the cost of life imprisonment on top of the expensive trial.

The high price of the death penalty is often most keenly felt in those counties responsible for both the prosecution and defense of capital defendants. A single trial can mean near bankruptcy, tax increases, and the laying off of vital personnel. Trials costing a small county $100,000 from unbudgeted funds are common and some officials have even gone to jail in resisting payment.

Nevertheless, politicians from prosecutors to presidents choose symbol over substance in their support of the death penalty. Campaign rhetoric becomes legislative policy with no analysis of whether the expense will produce any good for the people. The death penalty, in short, has been given a free ride. The expansion of the death penalty in America is on a collision course with a shrinking budget for crime prevention. It is time for politicians and the public to give this costly punishment a hard look.

I. *The Financial Costs of the Death Penalty*

Death penalty cases are much more expensive than other criminal cases and cost more than imprisonment for life with no possibility of parole. In California, capital trials are six times more costly than other murder trials. A study in Kansas indicated that a capital trial costs $116,700 more than an ordinary murder trial. Complex pre-trial motions, lengthy jury selections, and expenses for expert witnesses are all likely to add to the costs in death penalty cases. The irreversibility of the death sentence requires courts to follow heightened due process in the preparation and course of the trial. The separate sentencing phase of the trial can take even longer than the guilt or innocence phase of the trial. And defendants are much more likely to insist on a trial when they are facing a possible death sentence. After conviction, there are constitutionally mandated appeals which involve both prosecution and defense costs.

Most of these costs occur in every case for which capital punishment is sought, regardless of the outcome. Thus, the true cost of the death penalty includes all the added expenses of the "unsuccessful" trials in which the death penalty is sought but not achieved. Moreover, if a defendant is convicted but not given the death sentence, the state will still incur the costs of life imprisonment, in addition to the increased trial expenses.

For the states which employ the death penalty, this luxury comes at a high price. In Texas, a death penalty case costs taxpayers an average of $2.3 million, about three times the cost of imprisoning someone in a single cell at the highest security level for 40 years. In Florida, each execution is costing the state $3.2 million. In financially strapped California, one report estimated that the state could save $90 million each year by abolishing capital punishment. The New York Department of Correctional Services estimated that implementing the death penalty would cost the state about $118 million annually.

II. *The Cost to Local Governments*

An increasingly significant consequence of the death penalty in the United States is the crushing financial burden it places on local governments. Economic recessions have made it clear that there is no unlimited source of government largesse. Counties, which bear the brunt of the costs of death penalty trials, are also the primary deliverers of local health and human services in the public sector. Hard choices have to be made among the demands of providing essential services, creative crime reduction programs such as community policing, and the vigorous pursuit of a few death penalty cases.

As Scott Harshbarger, Attorney General of Massachusetts, put it: "Virtually every major program designed to address the underlying causes of violence and to support the poor, vulnerable, powerless victims of crime is being cut even further to the bone. In this context, the proposition that the death penalty is a needed addition to our arsenal of weapons lacks credibility and is, as a sheer matter of equity, morally irresponsible. If this is really the best we can do, then our public value system is bankrupt and we have truly lost our way."

While state and national politicians promote the death penalty, the county government is typically responsible for the costs of prosecution and the costs of the criminal trial. In some cases, the county is also responsible for the costs of defending the indigent. Georgia, Alabama and Arkansas, for example, provide little or no funding for indigent defense from the state treasury. In Lincoln County, Georgia, citizens have had to face repeated tax increases just to fund one capital case.

Even where the state provides some of the money for the counties to pursue the death penalty, the burden on the county can be crushing. California, for example, was spending $10 million a year reimbursing counties for expert witnesses, investigators and other death-penalty defense costs, plus $2 million more to help pay for the overall cost of murder trials in smaller counties. (Now, even that reimbursement is being cut.) But many financially strapped smaller counties still could not afford to prosecute the complicated death-penalty cases. Some small counties have only one prosecutor with little or no experience in death-penalty cases, no investigators, and only a single Superior Court judge.

In Sierra County, California, authorities had to cut police services in 1988 to pick up the tab of pursuing death penalty prosecutions. The County's District Attorney, James Reichle, complained, "If we didn't have to pay $500,000 a pop for Sacramento's murders, I'd have an investigator and the sheriff would have a couple of extra deputies and we could do some lasting good for Sierra County law enforcement." The county's auditor, Don Hemphill, said that if death penalty expenses kept piling up, the county would soon be broke. Just recently, Mr. Hemphill indicated that another death penalty case would likely require the county to lay off 10 percent of its police and sheriff force.

With more death row inmates and more executions than any other state, Texas is also experiencing the high costs of executions. Norman Kinne, Dallas County District Attorney, expressed his frustration at the expense:

> *Even though I'm a firm believer in the death penalty, I also understand what the cost is. If you can be satisfied with putting a person in the penitentiary for the rest of his life. I think maybe we have to be satisfied with that as opposed to spending $1 million to try and get them executed. I think we could use the money better for additional penitentiary space, rehabilitation efforts, drug rehabilitation, education, and especially devote a lot of attention to juveniles.*

Some state appeals courts are overwhelmed with death penalty cases. The California Supreme Court, for example, spends more than half its time reviewing death cases. The Florida Supreme Court also spends about half its time on death penalty cases. Many governors spend a significant percentage of their time reviewing clemency petitions and more will face this task as executions spread. As John Dixon, Chief Justice (Retired) of the Louisiana Supreme Court, said: "The people have a constitutional right to the death penalty and we'll do our best to make it work rationally. But you can see what it's doing. Capital punishment is destroying the system."

III. *Alternatives for Reducing Crime*

While direct causes for a decrease in crime are difficult to pinpoint, many experts have attributed New York's success to an increasingly popular concept known as community policing. Community policing is a strategy for utilizing police officers not just as people who react to crime, but also as people who solve problems by becoming an integral part of the neighborhoods they serve.

Compared to community policing and other successful programs, the death penalty, for all its cost, appears to have no effect on crime. A *New York Times* editorial noted recently that the number of executions in this country "constituted less than .001 percent of all murderers and were only .000004 percent of all violent criminals. Even if U.S. executions were multiplied by a factor of 10 they would still constitute an infinitesimal element of criminal justice." The public seems to agree: Only 13 percent of those who support capital punishment believe it deters crime.

IV. *Political Manipulation of the Death Penalty*

What drives this high spending on such an ineffective program? The answer lies partly in the promotion by politicians who hope to benefit by advocating the death penalty. Even though it fails to meet the cost-benefit test applied to other government programs, many politicians use capital punishment to distinguish themselves from their opponents. Politicians have generally not posed the death penalty as one alternative among a limited number of crime fighting initiatives for which the people must ultimately pay. Rather, the death penalty is used to play on the public's fear of crime and to create an atmosphere in which the extreme view wins. The rhetoric then becomes policy and the people pay.

V. *The Death Penalty in State Politics*

The death penalty is almost the exclusive function of the states rather than the federal government. It is not surprising, then, that some of the most blatant attempts at political manipulation of the death penalty have occurred on the level of state politics. Florida and Texas are two states with the largest death rows and most active execution chambers. They were also the scene of recent gubernatorial races featuring candidates boasting of their ability to secure more executions than their opponent. In 1990, Florida's Governor Bob Martinez campaigned with background shots of smirking serial killer Ted Bundy, while reminding the voters how many death warrants he had signed. Martinez was defeated by Democrat Lawton Chiles who also favors the death penalty.

The 1990 governor's race in Texas presented a variety of candidates vying to demonstrate their greater support of the death penalty. As populist Democrat Jim Hightower put it, the race boiled down to one issue: "Who can kill the most Texans?"

Former governor Mark White portrayed his toughness by walking through a display of large photos of the people executed during his term. Attorney General Jim Mattox insisted that he was the one who should be given credit for the 32 executions carried out under his watch. Meanwhile, the Republican candidate, Clayton Williams, showed pictures of a simulated kidnapping of young children from a school yard and then touted his backing of a separate law to impose the death penalty for killing children. His ad ended with the slogan: "That's the way to make Texas great again."

Politicians are quick to capitalize on an opportunity to promote the death penalty. In Arizona, state Representative Leslie Johnson called for the death penalty for child molesters after a particularly horrendous crime in Yuma. On the floor of the House, Johnson proposed the quick fix: "If we do away with these people, if we do have the death penalty and if you are a sex offender, you're just out of here—dead, gone. And if we get a few innocent people, fine and dandy with me. I'll take the percentage, folks, because I don't want to put my children at risk anymore."

In Kentucky, Commonwealth Attorney Ernest Jasmin made a name for himself by obtaining a death sentence against the killer of two teenagers from Trinity High School. He then campaigned as the Trinity Prosecutor, taking ads in the high school newspaper and campaigning with one of the victim's parents frequently at his side.

In Nebraska, attorney general Don Stenberg took the unusual step of attaching a personal letter to his Supreme Court brief urging the execution of Harold Otey, whom he described as a "vicious killer" who "still smirks at the family of the victim." While pushing publicly for Otey's death, Stenberg also sat as one of three decision makers at Otey's clemency hearing and two of his staff presented gruesome details of the murder.

In sum, there has been a steady stream of politicians attempting to capitalize on the death penalty issue in recent years. Real solutions to crime get overshadowed in the tough talk of capital punishment. When some of the politicians are successful, the death penalty gets implemented or expanded and the people begin to pay the high costs. Somewhere down the road there may be an execution, but the crime rate continues to increase. Politicians do the people a disservice by avoiding the hard economic choices that have to be made between the death penalty and more credible methods of reducing violence.

VI. *Conclusion*

The death penalty is parading through the streets of America as if it were clothed in the finest robes of criminal justice. Most politicians applaud its finery; others stare in silence, too timid to proclaim that the emperor has no clothes. Instead of confronting the twin crises of the economy and violence, politicians offer the death penalty as if it were a meaningful solution to crime. At the same time, more effective and vital services to the community are being sacrificed. Voters should be told the truth about the death penalty. They should understand that there are programs that do work in reducing crime, but the resources to pay for such programs are being diverted into show executions. Being sensible about crime is not being soft on crime. Too much is at stake to allow political manipulation to silence the truth about the death penalty in America.

John McAdams, "It's Good, and We're Going to Keep It: A Response to Ronald Tabak"

It seems productive to dismiss a variety of arguments commonly used by death penalty opponents—arguments obviously specious and misguided.

One such class of arguments seeks to hold the death penalty responsible for the mischief that death penalty opponents themselves have caused. Sometimes, these arguments remind me of the famous (and doubtless apocryphal) case in an English court where a defendant was accused of a heinous crime. He was accused of killing his mother and father, and he was clearly guilty. He threw himself on the mercy of the court and asked for compassion on the grounds that he was an orphan.

Thus we have opponents of the death penalty pointing out, quite correctly, that it has cost more to execute a guilty murderer than to keep him in prison for life. For example, Bill Ryan, Chairman of the Illinois Death Penalty Moratorium Project recently claimed:

> *Over the past 22 years since the death penalty was reinstated, Illinois taxpayers have spent more than $800 million to send 260 men and women to death row. This amount is over and above what it would have cost to sentence each of the 260 to prison for life without parole.*

As Radelet, Bedau, and Putnam put it:

> *A criminal justice system (like Michigan's or Canada's) that never raises the controversial question of the death penalty in a murder case is far less expensive to operate than a system (like California's or Texas's) that regularly raises the issue in every case of aggravated murder.*

Why has it been so expensive to execute people? Because activist anti-capital punishment lawyers seek, and liberal activist judges grant, endless rounds of appeal.

Along similar lines, the abolitionist Ronald Tabak laments "geographic disparities" in the administration of the death penalty. The majority of executions are indeed in a few, mostly Southern, states. In reality, the willingness of states to execute prisoners is a function of political ideology, with the more liberal states being loath to impose capital punishment. Note the irony. Liberals, where they have political power, make it difficult or impossible to execute murderers, and then complain about "regional disparity" when other states continue to do so.

Death penalty opponents insist that it is "capricious" because some prisoners are executed while others get a lesser punishment in spite of having committed a virtually identical crime. Yet Ronald Tabak complains about the fact that the U.S. Congress has successfully limited federal habeas corpus appeals. The attitude of the anti-death penalty crowd toward the appeals process seems to be the same as that of the Gore campaign toward the recent vote count in Florida: we will just keep doing it until it yields the result we want. Yet the unbridled appeals process places a large premium on having especially clever counsel, having the right sort of activist anti-death penalty judges in the ranks of those who will hear the endless appeals, and other factors that are unequally distributed among those convicted of murder.

Indeed, Ronald Tabak believes that the fact that a convicted murderer was battered as a child is a good reason for a jury, during the "penalty phase" of the trial, to decide not to assess a death penalty. This is an example of how the bifurcated trial, a "reform" put in place in the wake of *Furman*, may well have increased capriciousness. When the penalty phase of the trial turns into a blatant attempt to manipulate the emotions of the jury, inequities are likely to result.

Running like a mantra through Ron Tabak's argument is the phrase, "The public needs to understand." He opines that it is "important the public understand." I am afraid this is indicative of the elitism that is so endemic among death penalty opponents. They cannot accept that the public does understand, indeed understands better than the activist elites.

Innocence

■ Innocence—Introduction

No concern tempers American support for the death penalty more than the specter of the execution of an innocent person. This fear is the most common reason cited by opponents of the death penalty as the basis for their position, and it is the concern that gives retentionists the most pause about their position. Eighty percent of Americans believe that an innocent person has been executed within the past five years. When Illinois Governor George Ryan commuted the sentences of all death-row inmates in his state at the end of his term in 2002, the justification he offered most frequently was his fear that his state had, and would again, execute an innocent person. This belief is so powerful that it is plausible to argue—though it has not been proven—that perceptions of the reliability of the capital-sentencing process might be the most influential factor in determining public support for the death penalty.

It is entirely sensible that concern for executing the innocent assumes such a prominent place in the death penalty debate. From any moral standpoint, the execution of an innocent person is intolerable. For a retributivist, the execution of an innocent is a gross injustice, as the person executed deserved no punishment at all.

The retributivist might argue, though, that the death penalty is justified despite the small risk of executing innocents by the gain in retributive justice resulting from murderers getting the full punishment they deserve. For a utilitarian, the calculation is complex. On the surface, such a tragic mistake represents the loss of a productive member of society. On the other hand, there might be some offsetting benefit to the exercise of the death penalty, and executions in general. If the utilitarian believes that the death penalty deters or is necessary to incapacitate dangerous felons, he might support capital punishment even if it were foreseeable that some (presumably small) number of innocent people might be lost. But innocence would still be a serious concern for the utilitarian because executing innocents diminishes the deterrent effect of the death penalty and leads the state to spend money on the trial and execution of individuals who are not threats to society. No one on either side of the debate over capital punishment desires the execution of an innocent person. The debate is over the extent of the measures that should be taken to prevent the execution of an innocent, and whether the risk of a mistake is a conclusive argument against capital punishment.

The first question to ask is how many innocent people have been executed, and how many more are likely to be executed under existing procedures? To answer this question we must define "innocence," a problematic matter. Is innocence defined as innocence of the crime charged, innocence of *any* crime, or not deserving of death for the crime committed? Under either definition, innocence is difficult to measure; under the latter, it might be a metaphysical impossibility. Later chapters lay out in detail the procedures followed by capital juries. Generally speaking, juries are first asked to determine whether one or more of several specific aggravating factors are present in a case. If such a factor is present, the defendant is legally eligible for the death penalty. It is then for the jury to decide whether the aggravating factors outweigh the mitigating evidence in the defendant's case. The presence of an aggravating factor is a factual question. It is possible, though highly unlikely, to determine *after* a trial that a jury erred in determining an aggravating factor to have been present. But the weighing of the aggravating evidence against the mitigating evidence is a value judgment. We might find flaws in the procedures surrounding the jury's determination, but the determination itself—as a value judgment—is essentially unassailable. Though this distinction seems critical and obvious, scholars have not always been careful in differentiating between these contrasting conceptions of innocence.

Even if innocence is defined in the narrower and more tangible sense of being innocent of the crime charged, measuring the frequency of error in capital cases is daunting. At least in this context, unlike determinations of death eligibility, an answer exists. Whether a defendant deserves death is an opinion. Whether a defendant committed a murder or some other felony is a question of fact. He or she either did or did not do it. As a practical matter, though, the difference is largely academic. Society can never know for sure whether a defendant has committed a crime. A verdict of guilt is essentially a guess based upon evidence available at trial. A subsequent assessment of innocence is also a guess, though perhaps a more educated guess based upon evidence available after the time of trial.

One can imagine circumstances in which subsequent evidence makes the verdict of guilt seem highly unreliable: DNA evidence could prove that blood found on the victim belonged to someone other than the defendant, or someone else might confess to the crime for which the defendant has been convicted. But even these situations cannot offer certainty. Accepting DNA evidence as factual requires believing the expert witnesses supplying the evidence and rejecting the conclusion—no matter how superficially unlikely—that the defendant participated in the crime despite the DNA evidence. Accepting a competing confession requires crediting one story over another. Corroborating facts might offer greater confidence. Perhaps the confessor offers information that only the perpetrator of the crime would be in a position to know. This is more the stuff of movies. In almost every case, only God knows the truth.

Some researchers have tried to find specific instances in which it is highly likely that the defendant was innocent. Other efforts have been aimed at evaluating the reliability of capital sentencing procedures so that we can make some educated guesses about the aggregate likelihood of error. This latter research does not make it possible to point to a particular case and say that an injustice has been done. Rather, the abolitionist can use the results of such studies to say something like, "Given what we know of the reliability of jury verdicts and capital procedures, it is likely that between 10 and 20 of the 3500 inmates currently under sentence of death in the United States are innocent of the crime charged."

The following debate presents the most famous attempt to identify innocent individuals convicted of capital crimes and executed. Professors Hugo Adam Bedau and Michael Radelet identified 350 cases of wrongful conviction for homicide or capital rape in the set of, what they term, "potentially capital cases." The set of potentially capital cases includes not just cases that resulted in a death sentence, but cases that might have resulted in the death penalty but for what the authors call "adventitious factors." These factors include the verdict, the sentencing decision of the trial court, or where the crime occurred. In their response, Stephen Markman and Paul Cassell identify a variety of putative weaknesses in Bedau and Radelet's study; some of the alleged flaws seem unavoidable, others do not. Bedau and Radelet rely on subjective or anecdotal evidence to identify cases of mistaken executions; this seems unavoidable. Just as it is impossible to know with metaphysical certainty whether someone is guilty, so too it is impossible to conclusively prove innocence. Their decision, however, to include potentially capital cases and not to differentiate among errors in cases prior to 1977 and after is a matter of choice and of moment. When the Supreme Court upheld the revised Georgia death penalty statute in 1977—after ruling an earlier version unconstitutional in 1973—it did so relying upon certain provisions in the revised statute that were designed to offer greater reliability. Only 31 of the 350 miscarriages of justice identified by Bedau and Radelet occurred between 1977 and 1986 (the last year of their study). This suggests the important conclusion that errors are occurring less frequently in the post-*Gregg* world than in the pre-*Furman* world. Bedau and Radelet respond that none of the *Gregg* reforms—such as bifurcated trials and the requirement of finding aggravating factors—are likely to reduce error.

The most significant research into the reliability of death-sentencing procedures is a study by a team of researchers headed by Professor James Liebman at Columbia University. Professor Liebman, Jeffrey Fagan, and Valerie West found that more than two thirds of fully reviewed state capital cases were reversed by courts because of serious errors. That means that at some point in the history of a capital case, in two of three instances a reviewing court found error with the conduct of the trial. In a follow-up to their study, the Columbia team found that the more frequently a state or county imposes death verdicts, the more likely the verdicts are to be tainted by error. They also found that error is more likely to occur in states with greater African-American populations, in states with more poverty, and in states where trial judges are subject to popular election. Excerpts from *A Broken System* are included in the Critical Documents section of this chapter.

The findings of the Liebman team are sobering, but the data alone do not prove that innocent people are being executed. Some retentionists argue that the verdict of guilt went undisturbed in the overwhelming majority of the cases studied by Liebman's team. Only a quarter of the capital convictions were set aside, and most of these defendants were retried and resentenced. The Liebman team responds, reasonably, that errors in sentencing are quite disturbing, and that the error rates they assess are a valid measure of the risk that an innocent or undeserving person will be executed.

The fact remains that neither the Liebman team nor Bedau and Radelet nor any other researcher has produced a case where there is consensus that the wrong man has been put to death. They offer compelling evidence of innocent men nearly being put to death and disturbing evidence of unreliable procedures, but no concrete example, and certainly no case since 1977, of any person actually executed where grave doubts exist as to guilt. In his book, *The Contradictions of Capital Punishment*, Franklin Zimring writes, "The absence of such a poster child actually executed is a puzzle if not an embarrassment to the critics of the death penalty system. Moreover, the absence of an unambiguously innocent defendant who has been executed might be regarded as a challenge to those who believe on actuarial grounds that innocent defendants are missed by the current system." The embarrassing failure by abolitionists to produce a clear case of an innocent being executed suggests that the system, circuitous and plodding as it is, might actually be working. Bedau and Radelet respond that this is merely good fortune—it is a mistake to label the haphazard manners in which these errors have been caught as a *system*. But the perception remains.

It seems fair in sum to say this: It is likely that the overwhelming majority of people executed did commit the act with which they were charged. Some of these people might not have deserved death, but legal calculations of desert are by necessity subjective to some extent. It is one thing if a mistake has been made as to the presence of an aggravating factor or an element of the offense. But eligibility for death is another matter. If we ask enough groups whether a particular defendant deserves to die, it is only inevitable that some will say no.

The availability of DNA evidence has somewhat changed the picture, but the perception of its impact might be greater than the reality. DNA evidence is an enormously useful tool in demonstrating error, but it is available in only a small fraction of cases. The Innocence Project at Cardozo Law School is the most significant organization in the country offering pro bono representation to inmates challenging their convictions on the basis of DNA evidence. To date, the project has helped to reverse the convictions of one hundred defendants. However, a minority of these exonerated inmates were on death row. DNA evidence may be a double-edged sword in the debate over capital punishment. Errors exposed by DNA question the reliability of the capital sentencing process. But the correction of these errors creates a perception of the reliability that is exaggerated beyond the truth. In most cases, DNA evidence is not available. Overall, this new technology does not materially change the risk of error.

So if the risk of error is inevitable but incalculable, how do these two facts affect the policy debate on capital punishment? Bedau and Radelet argue that it is a conclusive argument against capital punishment; the significant risk of executing innocents is not offset by any significant benefit. Markman and Cassell say executing an innocent is a statistical unlikelihood in the post-*Gregg* world, and the incapacitation and deterrence benefits of capital punishment are substantial. This chapter concludes with a piece in which I argue that although executing innocents is a serious concern, it is unlikely that mistakes are going uncorrected by virtue of the death penalty. Because it takes so long to execute death-sentenced inmates, it is likely that an error, if detectable, will be caught while the inmate is on death row. This is not an argument for the death penalty. Rather, it questions if the risk of executing innocents is a conclusive argument against the death penalty, and why it is not also a conclusive argument against other highly punitive sanctions such as life imprisonment without parole.

■ Innocence—Critical Documents

James S. Liebman, Jeffrey Fagan, and Valerie West, "A Broken System: Error Rates in Capital Cases, 1973–1975"

The modern death-sentencing era began with the implementation of new capital statutes designed to satisfy *Furman*. Unfortunately, no central repository of detailed information on post-*Furman* death sentences exists. In order to collect that information, we undertook a painstaking search, beginning in 1991 and accelerating in 1995, of all published state and federal judicial opinions in the U.S. conducting direct and habeas review of state capital judgments, and many of the available opinions conducting state post-conviction review of those judgments. We then (1) checked and catalogued all the cases the opinions revealed, and (2) collected hundreds of items of information about each case from the published decisions and the NAACP Legal Defense Fund's quarterly death row census, and (3) tabulated the results. Nine years in the making, our central findings thus far are these:

- Between 1973 and 1995, approximately 5,760 death sentences were imposed in the U.S. Only 313 (5.4%) of those resulted in an execution during the period.
- Of the 5,760 death sentences imposed, 4,578 (79%) were finally reviewed on "direct appeal" by a state high court. Of those, 1,885 (41%) were thrown out because of "serious error," i.e., error that the reviewing court concludes has seriously undermined the reliability of the outcome or otherwise "harmed" the defendant.
- Nearly all of the remaining death sentences were then inspected by state post-conviction courts. Our data reveal that state post-conviction review is an important source of review in states such as Florida, Georgia, Indiana, Maryland, Mississippi, North Carolina, and Tennessee. In Maryland, at least 52% of capital judgments reviewed on state post-conviction during the study period were overturned due to serious error; the same was true of at least 25% of the capital judgments that were similarly reviewed in Indiana, and at least 20% of those reviewed in Mississippi.
- Of the death sentences that survived state direct and post-conviction review, 599 were finally reviewed in a first habeas corpus petition during the 23-year study period. Of those 599, 237 (40%) were overturned due to serious error.
- The "overall success rate" of capital judgments undergoing judicial inspection, and its converse, the "overall error rate," are crucial factors in assessing the effectiveness of the capital punishment system. The "overall

success rate" is the proportion of capital judgments that underwent, and passed, the three-stage judicial inspection process during the study period. The "overall error rate" is the reverse: the proportion of fully reviewed capital judgments that were overturned at one of the three stages due to serious error. Nationally, over the entire 1973–1995 period, the overall error-rate in our capital punishment system was 68%.

■ "Serious error" is error that substantially undermines the reliability of the guilt finding or death sentence imposed at trial. Each instance of that error warrants public concern. The most common errors are (1) egregiously incompetent defense lawyering (accounting for 37% of the state postconviction reversals), and (2) prosecutorial suppression of evidence that the defendant is innocent or does not deserve the death penalty (accounting for another 16%–19%, when all forms of law enforcement misconduct are considered). As is true of other violations, these two count as "serious" and warrant reversal only when there is a reasonable probability that, but for the responsible actor's miscues, the outcome of the trial would have been different.

■ The seriousness of these errors is also revealed by what happens on retrial, when the errors are cured. In our state post-conviction study, an astonishing 82% of the capital judgments that were reversed were replaced on retrial with a sentence less than death, or no sentence at all. In the latter regard, 7% of the reversals for serious error resulted in a determination on retrial that the defendant was not guilty of the capital offense.

■ The 68% rate of capital error found by the three stage inspection process is much higher than the error rate of less than 15% found by those same three inspections in noncapital criminal cases.

■ Appointed federal judges are sometimes thought to be more likely to overturn capital sentences than state judges, who almost always are elected in capital-sentencing states. In fact, state judges are the first and most important line of defense against erroneous death sentences. They found serious error in and reversed 90% (2,133 of the 2,370) capital sentences that were overturned during the study period.

■ Finding all these errors takes time. Calculating the amount of time using information in published decisions is difficult. Only a small percentage of direct appeals decisions report the sentence date. By the end of the habeas stage, however, a larger proportion of sentencing dates is reported in one or another decision in the case. Accordingly, it is possible to get a good sense of timing for only the 599 cases that were finally reviewed on habeas corpus. Among those cases:

1. It took an average of 7.6 years after the defendant was sentenced to die to complete federal habeas consideration in the 40% of habeas cases in which reversible error was found.

2. In the cases in which no error was detected at the third inspection stage and an execution occurred, the average time between sentence and execution was 9 years. Matters did not improve over time. In the last 7 study years (1989–95), the average time between sentence and execution rose to 10.6 years.

- High rates of error, and the time consequently needed to filter out all that error, frustrate the goals of the death penalty system. In general, where the rate of serious reversible error in a state's capital judgments reaches 55% or above (as is true for the vast majority of states), the state's capital punishment system is effectively stymied-with its proportion of death sentences carried out falling below 7%.

The recent rise in the number of executions is not inconsistent with these findings. Instead of reflecting improvement in the quality of death sentences under review, the rising number of executions may simply reflect how many more sentences have piled up for review. If the error-induced pile-up of cases is the cause of rising executions, their rise provides no proof that a cure has been found for disturbingly high error rates. To see why, consider a factory that produces 100 toasters, only 32 of which work. The factory's problem would not be solved if the next year it made 200 toasters (or added 100 new toasters to 100 old ones previously backlogged at the inspection stage), thus doubling its output of working products to 64. With, now, 136 duds to go with the 64 keepers, the increase in the latter would simply mask the persistence of crushing error rates. The decisive question, therefore, is not the number of death sentences carried out each year, but the proportion.

- In contrast to the annual number of executions, the proportion of death row inmates executed each year has remained remarkably stable-and extremely low. Since post-*Furman* executions began in earnest in 1984, the nation has executed an average of about 1.3% of its death row inmates each year; in no year has it ever carried out more than 2.6% of those on death row.

Implications of Central Findings

To help appreciate these findings, consider a scenario that might unfold immediately after any death sentence is imposed in the U.S. Suppose the defendant, or a relative of the victim, asks a lawyer or the judge, "What now?"

Based on almost a quarter century of experience in thousands of cases in 28 death-sentencing states in the U.S. between 1973 and 1995, a responsible answer would be: "The capital conviction or sentence will probably be overturned due to serious error. It'll take nine or ten years to find out, given how many other capital cases being reviewed for likely error are lined up ahead of this one. If the judgment is overturned, a lesser conviction or sentence will probably be imposed."

As anyone hearing this answer would probably conclude as a matter of sheer common sense, all this error, and all the time needed to expose it, are extremely burdensome and costly:

- Capital trials and sentences cost more than noncapital ones. Each time they have to be done over—as happens 68% of the time—that difference grows exponentially.
- The error-detection system all this capital error requires is itself a huge expense-apparently millions of dollars per case.
- Many of the resources currently consumed by the capital system are not helping the public, or victims, obtain the valid death sentences for egregious offenses that a majority support. Given that nearly 7 in 10 capital judgments have proven to be seriously flawed, and given that 4 out of 5

capital cases in which serious error is found turn out on retrial to be more appropriately handled as non-capital cases (and in a sizeable number of instances, as non-murder or even non-criminal cases), it is hard to escape the conclusion that large amounts of resources are being wasted on cases that should never have been capital in the first place.

- Public faith in the courts and the criminal justice system is another casualty of high capital error rates. When most capital-sentencing jurisdictions carry out fewer than 6% of the death sentences they impose, and when the nation as a whole never executes more than 2.6% of its death population in a year, the retributive and deterrent credibility of the death penalty is low.

- When condemned inmates turn out to be innocent—an error that is different in its consequences, but is not evidently different in its causes, from the other serious error discussed here—there is no accounting for the cost: to the wrongly convicted; to the family of the victim, whose search for justice and closure has been in vain; to later victims whose lives are threatened—and even taken—because the real killers remain at large; to the public's confidence in law and legal institutions; and to the wrongly executed, should justice miscarry at trial, and should reviewing judges, harried by the amount of error they are asked to catch, miss one.

If what were at issue here was the fabrication of toasters (to return to our prior example), or the processing of social security claims, or the pre-takeoff inspection of commercial aircraft—or the conduct of any other private—or public-sector activity—neither the consuming and the taxpaying public, nor managers and investors, would for a moment tolerate the error-rates and attendant costs that dozens of states and the nation as a whole have tolerated in their capital punishment system for decades. Any system with this much error and expense would be halted immediately, examined, and either reformed or scrapped.

The question this Report poses to taxpayers, public managers and policymakers, is whether that same response is warranted here, when what is at issue is not the content and quality of tomorrow's breakfast, but whether society has a swift and sure response to murder, and whether thousands of men and women condemned for that crime in fact deserve to die.

■ Innocence—Perspectives

■ Issue—What is the Risk of Executing the Innocent and Is It a Conclusive Argument Against Capital Punishment?

Hugo Adam Bedau and Michael L. Radelet, "Miscarriages of Justice in Potentially Capital Cases"

Few errors made by government officials can compare with the horror of executing a person wrongly convicted of a capital crime. At least since 1762, when it was established that Jean Calas was innocent of the murder for which he was put to death in Toulouse, France, opponents of the death penalty have cited the possibility of executing the innocent as a compelling reason to abolish the death penalty. In 1775, Jeremy Bentham offered as his chief objection against capital punishment its "irremissibility," citing in support of this objection "the melancholy affair of Calas." Today in this country, death penalty proponents are readier to acknowledge that the possibility of such errors can never be eliminated as long as we continue to use the death penalty. They go on to claim, however, that the "moral advantages" of capital punishment outweigh the "moral drawbacks," and thus that society is rationally "warranted" in taking this risk.

Yet the risk of executing the innocent is largely unknown. Few empirical studies have addressed the issue of wrongful convictions. In recent years, some death penalty proponents have asked its critics to make "a credible effort to assign a probability to the risk of executing an innocent person." A necessary condition of such an estimate is an accurate and comprehensive study of erroneous convictions in which the defendant was, or might have been, sentenced to death. As a contribution to this task, we present 350 cases in which defendants convicted of capital or potentially capital crimes in this century, and in many cases sentenced to death, have later been found to be innocent. Our findings prompt us to echo the words of an earlier investigator who noted that the catalogue of erroneous convictions "could be extended, but if what has already been presented fails to convince the reader of the fallibility of human judgment then nothing will."

The earliest effort in this country to identify cases in which the innocent were executed (or almost executed) was conducted in 1912 by the American Prison Congress. After devoting almost a year to this task, the Congress concluded that there were no such cases. The methodology of this study, however, was quite primitive. A letter of inquiry was sent to the warden of each prison in the United States and Canada, asking whether he had "personal knowledge" of any such errors. The response rate was not reported; all responses received were in the negative. The one exception was from the warden of the Leavenworth prison in Kansas, who reported "one or two persons who may, in my opinion, have been executed wrongfully." There is no evidence that the Congress investigated this response.

No investigator has ever undertaken systematic investigation into all cases where errors were alleged, or examined all known executions for evidence of error. We do not find it surprising that we have found no instance in which the government has officially acknowledged that an execution carried out under lawful authority was in error. As we shall see, failure by the authorities to acknowledge error is not very convincing evidence that errors have not occurred.

The primary aim of this article is to reach a better understanding of the miscarriages of justice in capital or potentially capital cases that have occurred in the United States during this century. To this end, we undertook as our main task the construction, on uniform principles, of a catalogue of cases in which such grave errors occurred. In order to convey to the reader the full scope and variety of the cases we have examined, we shall explain our criteria, the rationale behind their choice, and the consequences that adoption and application of these criteria had in shaping our catalogue.

I. *Methodology*

This article grew out of an effort that was initiated twenty-five years ago, as mentioned above, by one of the present authors. In that research, as revised three years later, seventy-four cases involving eighty-five defendants were reported, including eighty-one defendants erroneously convicted between 1883 and 1962. By 1982, about fifty or so additional miscarriages in potentially capital cases had been identified.

We began our collaboration on this project in late 1983. Our intent was to transform the project from one of casual collection into a sustained and systematic attempt to identify as many cases as possible. We used several search procedures. We examined the *New York Times Index* for every year since 1900. In 1984, we placed announcements of our research project in three national newsletters: one for criminologists, one for litigating defense attorneys in capital cases, and one for opponents of the death penalty. These announcements invited readers who knew about relevant cases to contact us; a dozen or so new cases were brought to our attention in this way. We also undertook to reread most of the social science literature and government documents on the death penalty in America that have been published in this century; we investigated many relevant cases mentioned in these sources but that had been previously overlooked. We also examined the capital punishment holdings of the New York Public Library, the Ehrmann archive at Northeastern University, the Espy archive, the papers of Marion Wright (the former head of North Carolinians Against the Death Penalty). In addition, we made special efforts to examine the personal papers of those who had done previous systematic research on this subject.

In January 1984, we sent letters to forty-seven governors and to the mayor of the District of Columbia. Each letter explained the project and included summaries of the cases (if any) already in our files from the jurisdiction in question. Overall, these efforts resulted in the discovery of very few additional cases. This experience taught us that no jurisdiction keeps a public list of its erroneous convictions, even in murder cases.

II. *The Concept of a Potentially Capital Case*

This study focuses on those cases in which the defendant was erroneously convicted of a capital crime and sentenced to death. But we do not confine our catalogue to the central core of cases in which an innocent person was sentenced to death, much less to the few cases in which we believe an innocent defendant was executed. To do so would exclude several types of cases, involving defendants also convicted "beyond a reasonable doubt," that shed light on how our criminal justice system has treated the most serious felony defendants during this century. Thus, we extended our examination to include what we call "potentially capital" cases.

The first extension that we make beyond the central core of cases is to include those in which the sentencer, empowered by statute to impose a punishment of imprisonment rather than of death, imposed this lesser sentence. The great majority of the defendants included in our catalogue who were convicted of first-degree murder in death penalty jurisdictions fall into this category. We include such cases because the trial court could have sentenced the convicted defendant to death.

The second extension beyond the death-sentence cases is to include those in which the trial court convicted the defendant of a noncapital version of a crime that has both capital and noncapital forms. The classic example is the decision to convict a defendant of second-degree murder rather than first-degree murder. Not only is it typically within a trial court's authority to choose to convict the defendant of second-rather than first-degree murder, it is also true that trial courts are often inconsistent and unpredictable in their decisions of this sort. Such cases include, for example, defendants who pleaded guilty in order to avoid the risk of a death sentence, but who were later exonerated when it was shown that the guilty plea was falsely given. In some of these cases, the evidence indicates that the defendant feared that insisting on innocence would increase the likelihood of a death sentence if convicted.

The third extension is more debatable; it is to include some cases in which the defendant was tried and convicted of a crime that is not punishable by the death penalty only because it had been previously abolished for that crime in the defendant's jurisdiction. Because murder has been a capital crime in most American jurisdictions during this century, we have included in our catalogue of potentially capital crimes all wrongful homicide convictions in abolition states, such as Michigan and Wisconsin, which do not punish any form of homicide with the death penalty. Of the 350 cases in our catalogue, twenty-four were contributed by jurisdictions that had abolished the death penalty.

In general, then, our inclusion of *potentially* capital cases draws attention to the way in which each case did culminate in a death sentence, or might have, except for some relatively adventitious factor: the verdict of the trial court, the sentencing decision of the trial court, or the jurisdiction in which the crime occurred.

Although our concept of a potentially capital crime extends the notion of a capital crime beyond the narrowest sense of the term, our practice also restricts its possible extension in two ways. First, we have confined the jurisdiction-without-capital-punishment category to crimes of criminal homicide, even though roughly ten percent of all the persons executed (and an uncalculated larger percentage of all those sentenced to death) in this century were convicted of capital crimes other than homicide. Rape, robbery, kidnapping, and burglary have all been statutory capital crimes in several jurisdictions in this country at various times during this century

Second, we have restricted our catalogue by excluding all wrongful convictions for capital or potentially capital crimes other than homicide and rape. Stressing the central role of homicide convictions hardly needs comment; criminal homicide is the paradigm capital crime. We also included rape (but only if the defendant was sentenced to death) because nearly all of the executions in the United States in this century other than for murder have been for rape, and because there have been some flagrant cases of wrongful conviction for this crime.

Given the evidence at our disposal and the appropriate criteria of error, these decisions yield a set of 350 cases. They are distributed by type of convic-

Table 7-1	Miscarriages of Justice in Potentially Capital Cases (N = 350)
Type of Crime	**Number of Cases**
Homicide	326
First-degree murder (1)	200
Second-degree murder (2)	73
Other homicide (3)	14
Unspecified (4)	39
Rape (R)	24

tion in **Table 7-1**. The final dispositions by trial court after the erroneous convictions for the 350 defendants are reported in **Table 7-2**.

An inspection of the annual distribution of our cases (not presented in a table) shows that in virtually every year in this century, in some jurisdiction or other, at least one person has been under death sentence who was later proved to be innocent. Based on this evidence, it is virtually certain that at least some of the nearly 2,000 men and women currently under sentence of death in this country are innocent.

The racial distribution of our 350 defendants shows that 151, or 43 percent, are known to be black. Since the proportion of blacks in the general population in this century has been about ten percent, the data suggest that blacks are much more likely than whites to be erroneously convicted of a potentially capital crime. Because black Americans are more likely than whites to be arrested and indicted for felony offenses, it appears that the risk of a miscarriage of justice falls disproportionately on blacks when compared to their representation in the population, but not in comparison to their arrest rates.

III. *The Concept of a Miscarriage of Justice*

"Miscarriage of justice" is a concept open to various definitions and applications. Because it has no standard or preferred use, we need to explain as precisely as possible how we define and use the concept in this article.

In this article, we use the term "miscarriage of justice" to refer only to those cases in which: (a) the defendant was convicted of homicide or sentenced to death

Table 7-2	Final Disposition by Type of Sentence (N = 350)
Type of Sentence	**Number of Cases**
Error corrected before sentencing (1)	5
Prison term less than life (2)	67
Life term (25 years or more) (3)	139
Death	139
Not executed (4)	116
Executed (5)	23

for rape; *and* (b) when either (i) no such crime actually occurred, *or* (ii) the defendant was legally and physically uninvolved in the crime. We have three main reasons for adopting these relatively strict criteria.

First, we are primarily concerned with *wrong-person mistakes*—the conviction and execution of the *factually* "innocent"—and not with the erroneous conviction of those who are *legally* innocent (as in cases of killing in self-defense). Second, if we can show—as, indeed, we can—that the number of erroneous convictions is substantial in potentially capital cases in which the central (even if not the only) error was convicting the wholly innocent, that will suffice to reinforce an important lesson: Our criminal justice system is fallible and the gravest possible errors in its administration can be documented.

Finally, and most importantly, if the concept of miscarriage of justice in capital cases is extended to include all those cases in which errors and mistakes accompany the arrest, trial, conviction, or sentencing of someone who indeed is involved in the crime then it is unclear whether *any* capital case can be regarded as free of mistake.

The problem of adequately defining a capital crime—a crime in which the guilty defendant "deserves" the death penalty—is not new; it is virtually as old as the history of the death penalty itself. No empirical research, such as ours, could hope to investigate all the kinds of "mistakes" that occur, once it is granted that the very concept of a mistake has become blurred beyond recognition. We reduce this problem, if we do not entirely avoid it, by excluding all cases in which, so far as we can tell, the errors do not include the conviction of a person both legally and factually innocent.

IV. *The Evidence for Miscarriages of Justice*

Having specified the criteria used to delimit the class of cases that involve the miscarriages of justice of concern to us, we now review the kinds of evidence we have relied upon to decide whether a given case should be included in our catalogue. Apart from those few cases where it was later established that no capital crime was committed, or that the defendant had an ironclad alibi, or that someone else was incontrovertibly guilty, there is no quantity or quality of evidence that could be produced that would definitively prove innocence. The most one can hope to obtain is a consensus of investigators after the case reaches its final disposition. Consensus can be measured in degrees, and the cases that we have included in our catalogue are those in which we believe a majority of neutral observers, given the evidence at our disposal, would judge the defendant in question to be innocent. This belief is largely untested because, in the great majority of our cases (apart from those in which the state has in some manner acknowledged its error), no previous scholarly investigator has weighed the evidence or reported any evaluation of it.

The evidence of innocence falls broadly into two main categories. First, decisions by actors in the criminal justice system or in one of the branches of state government may indicate a belief that the conviction was in error. Second, indications from others not acting in any official role, or by persons acting outside their official roles, may point to an erroneous conviction. Eighty-eight percent of our cases fall into the first category; thus, in the vast majority of cases, we can point to one or more government actions that demonstrate an official recognition that the conviction was in error. Although it would be going too far to regard such action as equivalent to *official admission* of error in all cases—and especially as the admission that a wholly innocent person had been convicted—it is reasonable to regard most of these cases in this manner, and to try to distinguish all the cases in which at least some official action has been recorded from those in which no such action has occurred.

Probably the most persuasive form that official admission of error can take is the award of *indemnity*. Indemnity usually takes the form of a special act by the state legislature to award a sum of money to the wrongly convicted person. Indemnity is rarely obtained; we find it in only twenty-nine of our cases. We regard indemnity as a sufficient basis for inclusion of a case in our catalogue.

A defendant who has obtained indemnity has usually received a prior award of executive *pardon*. Far more defendants are pardoned than are ever indemnified. Unindemnified defendants in sixty-four of our cases received a pardon. By itself, of course, a pardon is not a wholly reliable sign that an innocent person was convicted. We therefore regard a pardon, standing alone, as a good indicator of innocence, but neither a necessary nor a sufficient ground for including a case in our catalogue.

Sometimes the executive branch takes official action in a form *other than a pardon*. Indeed, in sixty-five of our cases, a convicted defendant was released without a formal pardon, even though it is clear that the reason for release was the belief by the governor or his advisors that the prisoner was innocent. The release decision in these cases typically takes one of two forms: commutation of sentence to time served, followed by outright release or parole.

Far more difficult to evaluate is *reversal* of the conviction. For our purposes, a reversal is a significant indication of serious error either when the defendant is *acquitted* following retrial or when the indictment is dismissed.

But not all the evidence on which we have relied has been provided by government officials who have corrected their errors or those of other officials. Just as the government can err in the first instance by convicting the innocent, the government can also err in failing to pardon, retry, or grant acquittal to a deserving defendant. Few if any public figures like to admit errors publicly, especially if it is thought that such an admission might threaten their careers. When we cannot point to any government official or body that has examined the evidence, reached a decision that error occurred, and intervened on behalf of justice for the defendant, we rely on any of four other kinds of evidence.

On several occasions (in thirteen of the cases), *another person confessed*. Not uncommonly, such confessions failed to lead to an arrest and conviction of the real culprit. Many such confessions are false or dubious, and thus they must be evaluated with extreme caution. In a few cases, however, there was little or no evidence of guilt, and *another person was implicated* by evidence other than a confession. No doubt the strongest cases of this sort occur when the second person was not only implicated, but was tried and convicted on persuasive evidence, and the wrongly convicted defendant was set free.

In six cases, we base our judgment on *the opinion of a state official*, usually the warden of the prison in which the prisoner was serving time or awaiting execution.

Finally, in some fifteen cases we have only *the weight of the evidence*. Sometimes this includes the unshaken conviction by the defense attorney and others who studied the case that the convicted defendant was innocent.

V. *The Causes of Error*

Miscarriages of justice are caused by a wide variety of factors. We have organized our set of cases into four main categories: (1) errors caused by the police prior to trial; (2) errors created by the prosecution before or during trial; (3) errors caused by witnesses giving depositions or testifying against the defendant; and (4) sundry other causes that enter in the proceedings against the defendant.

VI. *The Discovery of Error*

There is no common or typical route by which an innocent defendant can be vindicated, and vindication, if it ever comes, will not necessarily come in time to benefit the defendant. The criminal justice system is not designed to scrutinize its own decisions for a wide range of factual errors once a conviction has been obtained. Our data show that it is rare for anyone within the system to play the decisive role in correcting error. Even when actors in the system do get involved, they often do so on their own time and without official support or encouragement. Far more commonly, the efforts of persons on the fringe of the system, or even wholly outside it, make the difference. The coincidences involved in exposing so many of the errors and the luck that is so often required suggest that only a fraction of the wrongly convicted are eventually able to clear their names.

Some who read the descriptions of our cases might erroneously argue that these data prove that "the system works." To be sure, many innocent defendants have used the system, notably the appellate courts, to win their freedom. But in the bulk of the cases, the defendant has been vindicated not *because* of the system, but *in spite* of it. The system provides at most the avenues and forums for vindication, not the impetus for it. Most victims of miscarriage, like other felony defendants found guilty, have expended all their financial resources trying to avoid conviction. Once convicted and imprisoned, few have attorneys who are willing or able to continue to fight for them. In short, the lesson taught by our data is how lucky these few erroneously convicted defendants were to have been eventually cleared. To think that these cases show that "the system works" is to ignore that, once a defendant is convicted, there is no *system* to which he can turn and on which he can rely to verify and rectify substantive error. The convicted defendant can initiate an appeal based on procedural error in his trial, or on newly discovered evidence, but not on his factual guilt or innocence. This leaves most erroneously convicted defendants with no place to turn for vindication.

Table 7-3 summarizes the agony of error in our 350 cases, using as a yardstick the amount of time spent by the defendant in prison before the error was recognized and rectified.

VII. *Execution of the Innocent*

We include in our catalogue twenty-three cases of persons we believe to be innocent defendants who were executed. Chronologically, these cases divide very unequally; all but four occurred in the first half of the period under study (i.e., before 1943) and nearly half (ten) occurred in the first quarter of the period (i.e., before 1922).

Table 7-3	The Agony of Error	

DEFENDANTS' ACTUAL PUNISHMENT

	Number of Cases (N = 350)	Percent
Released from Confinement	315	90.0
After serving 0–5 years (1)	187	53.4
After serving 6–10 years (2)	65	18.6
After serving 11–15 years (3)	24	6.9
After serving 16 or more years (4)	39	11.1
Not Released from Confinement	31	8.9
Died while serving sentence (5)	8	2.3
Executed (6)	23	6.6
Unknown (7)	4	1.1

From these figures, one might be tempted to infer that the problem of executing the innocent has diminished with the passage of time. The temptation should be resisted: A mere decrease in the absolute number of people wrongfully executed tells very little; a trend can be seen only by determining whether the *proportion* of erroneous executions has changed over time. Between 1900 and 1942, of an estimated 5,229 lawful executions in the United States, nineteen erroneous executions constitute 0.36 percent of the total. Between 1943 and 1985, of the 1,863 executions, four erroneous executions constitute 0.22 percent of the total, roughly one-third less than the proportion in the earlier period. Between 1900 and 1922, of an estimated 2,465 executions, we show ten in error, or 0.40 percent of the total—only slightly greater than for the entire 1900–1942 period and roughly twice that for the years 1943–1985. We advise caution in inferring a trend because the differences in these proportions are quite small. In addition, we must repeat that we have not—nor has anyone else—examined *all* of the more than 7,000 executions during this century in light of *all* the available evidence. Until this is done, proposing trends in the execution of the innocent is idle speculation.

VIII. *Error and the Abolition of the Death Penalty*

Evaluating the argument against the death penalty based on the fact that innocent defendants have been and will be executed requires some care. As it is *certain* that there are and will be such cases, death penalty proponents cannot evade the problem. Ernest van den Haag, one of this country's most vocal death penalty proponents, agrees, but then argues that the benefits of capital punishment outweigh this liability. His rationale requires that the alleged benefits of capital punishment (e.g., retribution and incapacitation) be accurately assessed, and then shown to outweigh its known liabilities (e.g., cost, arbitrariness, and the risk of errors). But since there is no consensus in our society over the weight to be assigned to each variable in this equation, we are doomed to disagree over how to compute it.

The van den Haag rationale also necessitates the impossible task of estimating the odds of executing the innocent. A 1 percent error rate, for example, might be acceptable to those who tend to favor the death penalty, whereas an arbitrarily selected higher rate—say 5 percent—would not be. Even if the odds could be calculated, it would be incorrect to use such a restricted notion of erroneous execution when debating whether or not to retain the death penalty. The criminal law defines innocence much more broadly than the narrow definition used in our research. Thus, a priori, the odds of executing the legally innocent (i.e., all those defendants who lack mens rea) are many times greater than are the odds of executing those who literally had nothing to do with causing the victim's death. Nonetheless, for reasons we have outlined below, any attempt to calculate the odds of executing the innocent, whatever the definition, is doomed to fail.

In any event, van den Haag's defense of the death penalty despite his concession that some innocent defendants will be executed can be criticized on grounds other than the impossibility of performing the calculations his argument requires. One could accept his cost-benefit logic for the sake of the argument, and still point to at least three objections. First, there is little or no empirical evidence on behalf of any of the alleged benefits of the death penalty that make it superior to long-term imprisonment. Second, van den Haag's comparison of the death penalty with other activities that cause the death of the innocent (building houses, driving a car, playing golf or football) is misleading for two reasons. Those who participate in the latter voluntarily consent to their exposure to risk, whereas there is no reason to believe that the *innocent* defendant has consented to the risk of being executed. Furthermore, the intention of capital punishment is to kill the convicted, whereas this is not the intention of the practices to which van den Haag draws a parallel. Third, and most importantly, we need to consider basic issues of individual rights in a democratic society. We suspect that those who reason as van den Haag does might see the issue differently were they the innocent defendants facing the executioner. The right to life of all innocent citizens is beyond dispute. A worker cannot be required to risk certain death by being forced to repair a malfunctioning nuclear reactor, even if by doing so he or she would save hundreds of lives. The American military cannot order draftees to become kamikaze pilots, regardless of what benefits might ensue. Only volunteers—those who willingly risk or waive their right to life—could be asked to do such jobs. Given the irremediability of the death penalty and the availability of an adequate alternative punishment, the execution of *any* defendant is unnecessary and cannot be justified even if there were substantial benefits of capital punishment.

Defenders of the death penalty will dispute this conclusion. They could argue that abolitionists have forgotten the risk that elimination of the death penalty would force society to bear: the risk of recidivist crimes by persons previously convicted of murder but not incapacitated from future offenses by execution. Every time a guilty person is convicted of murder but not sentenced to death and executed, society runs the risk that such a person may kill again, or commit other crimes—against a fellow inmate, a prison visitor, a prison employee, or even the general public. Evidence suggests that although the number of such crimes is not large, it exceeds the number of known innocents who have been executed. If this is indeed true, why should society run what appears to be the greater of the two risks?

An adequate reply to this important objection is complex. First, it is not possible to know which risk is greater merely by knowing the difference between the two aggregate numbers (those wrongfully executed and those victims of recidivist murderers). The proper way to determine which risk is greater is to take a fixed population of persons condemned but not executed (e.g., all those spared execution by the 1972 *Furman* decision), and determine (1) how many were wrongfully convicted and (2) how many of the others, truly guilty, committed subsequent murder. Second, by abolishing mandatory death penalties, society has implicitly agreed to run the risk of recidivism by convicted murderers, whatever that risk may be, since the effect of discretionary death sentencing is that only a small fraction of all those convicted of murder are sentenced to death and executed. Third, as things currently stand, society runs *both* the risk of executing the innocent *and* the risk of recidivist murder, whereas it is only necessary that society run one or the other. To that extent, our current practice seems irrational unless it can be shown that a combination of these two risks is lower than either risk taken alone. Fourth, it is virtually impossible to imagine our society not running some risk of recidivist murder. Not only is the mandatory death penalty unconstitutional, but few American jurisdictions in this century enacted and enforced a truly mandatory death penalty even for murder during the years when it was a constitutionally permissible option. On the other hand, many nations and several American jurisdictions have decided not to run the risk of executing the innocent. Thus, the question we should really ask is this: Which is more rational, running the risk of recidivist murder for 100 percent of convicted murderers (as abolitionists evidently believe), or (as defenders of the death penalty seem to prefer) running the risk for 95 percent or more of convicted murderers plus the risk of executing the innocent for the remaining 5 percent or less?

But even this does not state the true problem accurately. In addition to the two risks under discussion, there are other risks associated with the deterrent and incapacitative effects of the death penalty that must be taken into account. For example, some have argued persuasively that the "brutalizing" effect of the death penalty is measurably greater than its deterrent and incapacitative effects. Abolishing the death penalty involves running a slightly greater risk of recidivist murder than at present plus the alleged risk of lesser deterrence, whereas retaining or expanding the death penalty involves preserving or increasing the risks of brutalization and of executing the innocent. Although no adequate calculation of the relative risks involved is possible, the fact of erroneous death sentences and executions, the absence of any convincing evidence favoring the superior deterrent effect of the death penalty, and the low incidence of recidivism seems to us to show that abolition is the better policy.

IX. *The Risk of Error*

Criminologists have long referred to what they call "the dark figure of crime"—the unknown number of crimes actually committed in a community during a given period, unknown because neither arrest records nor victim reports mention them. Our research naturally leads to speculation about what might be called "the dark figure of innocence"—the number of cases per year or per jurisdiction in which undetected substantive error occurs in potentially capital cases.

Does the paucity of known and documented cases in which an innocent defendant was executed show that the criminal justice system, at least where the death penalty is concerned, works satisfactorily? Is the discovery of a case in which an innocent person is executed bound to be rare because so few cases of this sort have actually occurred? Is it possible that the availability of the death penalty spurs the system to work more reliably than it otherwise might?

Our results lead us to believe that the small number of cases in our catalogue in which major doubts remain about the guilt of the executed is an indication not of the reliability and fairness of the system, but rather of its power and finality. For a variety of reasons, very few cases in this century have managed to attract the sustained interest of persons in a position to undertake the research necessary to challenge successfully a guilty verdict meted out to a defendant later executed. Rarely are funds available to investigate executions of the allegedly innocent. Once the defendant is dead, the best source of evidence is gone, as is the main motive to reinvestigate. Further, the limited resources of those who might challenge the deceased's guilt are quickly absorbed by the legal battles involved in trying to save the lives of others still on death row. The result is that, as time passes, relevant evidence of a miscarriage remains undiscovered. Finally, officials and citizens involved in a death penalty case, from arrest to denial of commutation, tend to close ranks and resist admission of error. No forum save that of public opinion exists to present evidence in favor of the belief that some innocent person went to his death.

X. *Possible Remedies*

Three major reforms that are feasible have already occurred: abolishing the mandatory death penalty; assuring automatic appellate review of all death sentences; and confining the death penalty to murder and other forms of criminal homicide. Only one further major reform remains available: abolishing the death penalty entirely. This, too, is a feasible step to take, as the history of the abolition of this punishment in some American jurisdictions and elsewhere in the world adequately demonstrates. Granted, we have no evidence that ending the death penalty would reduce the likelihood of wrongful conviction in what are now potentially capital cases. But no evidence is needed to support the claim that complete abolition of the death penalty would eliminate the worst of the possible consequences that accrue from wrongful convictions in what are now capital cases.

We agree with the observation of a supporter of the death penalty who writes: "To say that someone deserves to be executed is to make a godlike judgment with no assurance that it can be made with anything resembling godlike perspicacity." The research presented in this article underscores the all-too-human errors that afflict the actual attempt to render such judgments.

Stephen J. Markman and Paul G. Cassell, "Protecting the Innocent: A Response to the Bedau-Radelet Study"

Given the fallibility of human judgments, the possibility exists that the use of capital punishment may result in the execution of an innocent person. This terrible prospect raises the issue of whether the risk of error in administering the death penalty is sufficiently high both to outweigh the potential benefits of capital punishment and to offend the moral sensibilities that must support a free society's criminal justice system. Despite occasional claims that specific individuals have been put to death for crimes they did not commit, the risk of executing the innocent has never been the subject of thorough and rigorous empirical study. Recently, however, two opponents of the death penalty, Hugo Adam Bedau and Michael L. Radelet, have published the results of "sustained and systematic" research purporting to show that the use of capital punishment entails an intolerable risk of mistaken executions. According to the authors, 350 persons have been wrongly convicted of capital or "potentially capital" crimes in the United States during this century; and twenty-three innocent persons have actually been executed. These alarming conclusions cannot be taken at face value. Not only is the Bedau-Radelet study severely flawed in critical respects, it wholly fails to demonstrate an unacceptable risk of executing the innocent. To the contrary, it confirms—as convincingly as may be possible—the view that the risk is too small to be a significant factor in the debate over the death penalty. Because of these shortcomings, the study deserves a response, lest it gain currency to the detriment of clear thinking on the subject for years to come.

The response presented here proceeds along two lines. The first is directed at the relevance and validity of the study itself. The study suffers from a number of flaws. The most serious of these are the authors' reliance on material irrelevant to the risk of wrongful executions and their method of determining innocence. With respect to relevance, only about seven percent of the study deals with cases of allegedly erroneous executions. Moreover, even as regards these cases, the authors' decision to include cases from the early part of this century, long before the adoption of the extensive contemporary system of safeguards in the death penalty's administration, skews their analysis of capital punishment under contemporary circumstances. With respect to methodology, the authors' method is overly subjective. It is also one-sided in its description of the cases of alleged error. Indeed, with respect to some of the allegedly mistaken executions, there appears to be little resemblance between the authors' descriptions and the actual cases.

The second line of response rebuts the argument that capital punishment should be abolished because the risk of erroneous execution is unacceptably high. That argument fails for several reasons. First, no sound reason exists for believing that there is currently an intolerable risk of executing an innocent person. Over the past fifteen years, procedural protections have been adopted to reduce as much as possible the likelihood that error will be committed or, if committed, that it will go undetected. More to the point, the authors present no credible evidence that any innocent person has been executed during this period; and they do not claim that any individual now awaiting execution is innocent. In addition, the argument undervalues the important reason why the great majority of Americans and their legislators recently have determined that capital punishment should be reinstated, notwithstanding society's inability to administer the death penalty with "godlike perspicacity." That reason is to save lives. Through a combination of deterrence, incapacitation, and the imposition of just punishment, the death penalty serves to protect a vastly greater number of innocent lives than may be lost through its erroneous application. Society would be guilty of a self-destructive "failure of nerve" if it were to forego the use of an appropriate and effective punishment simply because it is not humanly possible to eliminate the risk of mistake entirely.

I. *Flaws in the Bedau-Radelet Study*

A. The Misleading Nature of the Study The authors assert that 350 Americans have been wrongly convicted of capital or "potentially capital" crimes during this century. The category of "potentially capital" cases, however, consists in large measure of cases in which the death penalty was not available or was not the sentence given. The authors justify including these "potentially capital cases" on the ground that, "except for some relatively adventitious factor," they might have culminated in a death sentence. This approach seriously misstates the magnitude of the problem of wrongful capital convictions. The authors have pointed to only 200 allegedly wrongful convictions for first-degree murder during this century. In only 139 of these cases were the defendants actually sentenced to death. More to the point, the death sentence was carried out in only twenty-three of the 350 cases cited by the authors. Thus, strictly speaking, only 6.6 percent of the study is relevant to the issue of wrongful executions. Moreover, the authors cite but a single allegedly erroneous execution during the past twenty-five years—that of James Adams. A review of that case demonstrates, however, that Adams was unquestionably guilty. Thus, Bedau and Radelet have made no persuasive showing that anyone has been wrongly executed since new capital punishment procedures were instituted in the wake of *Furman v. Georgia*. In short, what the authors have done could be compared to studying traffic deaths before the adoption of traffic signals.

The authors also mislead readers through their presentation of the data. Presumably, the issue is whether the magnitude of the risk of executing innocent persons makes capital punishment unwise as a matter of policy. The size of this risk can only be evaluated, however, by dividing the number of innocent persons who have been executed by the total number of persons executed. The number of persons wrongly convicted of capital crimes and sentenced to death is less significant for at least two reasons: First, if these persons were not executed, their erroneous convictions and death sentences have no bearing on the wisdom of executing persons properly convicted of capital crimes. Second, focusing on trial court dispositions alone completely ignores the procedural protections for detecting erroneous convictions that are available through direct appeal and collateral attack.

B. The Subjectivity of the Study The overwhelming problem with the Bedau-Radelet study is the largely subjective nature of its methodology and therefore of its conclusions. The linchpin of the study is the claim that the authors have identified "350 cases in which defendants convicted of capital or potentially capital crimes in this century, and in many cases sentenced to death, have later been found to be innocent." This claim raises the critical question of the meaning of the phrase "found to be innocent." The use of this phrase—and its variant, "proved to be innocent"—clearly suggests a high degree of certainty in the determination of innocence. The use of the passive voice, however, belies that the authors themselves made many of the findings; and neither the standard they use to determine innocence nor the proof they offer to meet that standard permits such assurance.

The authors' standard is simply their belief, arrived at after reviewing the information available to them regarding each case, that "a majority of neutral observers, given the evidence at the authors' disposal, would judge the defendant in question to be innocent." The authors' dubious method of finding convicted individuals to have been innocent strikes the neutral observer reading the authors' very brief discussion of wrongful executions. There one reads the following:

> The evidence for judgment of error in these cases will naturally interest many, but what we can report will satisfy only a few. In the notorious cases, we have relied on the judgment of other scholars whose investigative work convinces us that error did indeed occur. Nothing we can say here will cause the controversy that still surrounds each of these cases to abate. In some of the more obscure cases, we have relied entirely on the opinions of officials whose views we believe deserve to be taken seriously. In none of these cases, however, can we point to the implication of another person or to the confession of the true killer, much less to any official action admitting the execution of an innocent person.

Given this admission, a neutral observer is entitled to be skeptical that this study contributes to a better understanding of the prevalence of error in the administration of the death penalty. The use of such questionable methodology invites readers to suspend use of their critical faculties and simply accept the results of this study on faith—faith that in fact the authors have sufficient information to make a judgment in each of these cases and faith that they, rather than the jurors and judges who considered the evidence admitted at trial, have made the correct judgment. Such faith hardly seems justified, given Bedau and Radelet's tendency to rely upon sources that either do not support their statements and conclusions or contradict them. These errors and other aspects of the study give the impression that it is more an argumentative tract than a fair-minded inquiry.

Examination of individual cases in which the authors claim that an innocent person was executed heightens the reader's skepticism. Consider, for example, the case of James Adams. According to the authors, Adams was erroneously executed in 1984. This case is particularly important because it is the only alleged example of an innocent person's execution since *Furman v. Georgia*. Consideration of all the evidence demonstrates beyond a reasonable doubt that Adams was guilty of the crime for which he was executed. The authors are able to maintain that Adams was the victim of a "miscarriage of justice" only by resorting to a distorted view of the evidence, derived solely from the defendant's brief before the Clemency Board, and by ignoring the compelling evidence directly linking him to the murder. Moreover, as is shown by the following brief review of some of the other alleged examples of erroneous executions, the authors' misrepresentation of the Adams case is not an aberration. They show similar disregard of the evidence in many other cases.

The authors state that "critics who seize on the weakest cases and generalize from them to the whole set will miss the forest for a few trees." Our examination reveals, however, that there are not enough "trees" to make up a copse, let alone a "forest."

II. *Flaws in the Argument for Abolition*

Even if Bedau and Radelet's study could be taken at face value, it would not provide a rational basis for rejecting capital punishment.

A. The Risk of Erroneous Execution The use of capital punishment entails some risk that an innocent person will be executed. Proponents of the death penalty have commonly taken the position that this risk is not great. The Bedau-Radelet study confirms this view. After "sustained and systematic" research, they point to only twenty-three out of more than 7000 executions as erroneous. Their judgments of error are unconvincing with respect to the twelve cases in which sufficient facts are available to test them. Their methodology makes their conclusion in the other eleven cases suspect as well. Assuming, however, for the sake of argument that as many as twenty-three innocent persons have been executed, the rate of error would be only about one-third of one percent over the past eighty-seven years. Moreover, even accepting the authors' claims, this miniscule rate of error has been reduced by more than one-third since 1943.

But, say Bedau and Radelet, "evaluating the argument against the death penalty based on the fact that innocent defendants have been and will be executed requires some care." This is so, they add, because "our total of twenty-three wrongful executions is not an estimate, and it cannot serve as a basis for a reasonable estimate, of the total number of wrongful executions in the United States during this century." The true number is far greater, they hint; but "any attempt to calculate the odds of executing the innocent is doomed to fail." It must be remembered, however, that Bedau and Radelet are the ones who argue that existing law should be changed. Accordingly, they bear the burden of justifying their argument by producing credible evidence that the use of capital punishment entails a significant risk of executing the innocent. This they have failed to do, and their assertion that the task is impossible is no substitute. Responsible social policy should be based on the best information available, not—as the authors apparently would have it—on speculation as to what the information would show if it were available.

B. Safeguards Against Erroneous Execution The safeguards that exist to protect criminal defendants, especially those charged with capital crimes, lessen the risk of erroneous execution. In particular, a number of statutory protections have arisen since *Furman*. Although the specific provisions of statutes governing capital punishment vary among jurisdictions, these statutes generally share a number of features, most of which are intended to safeguard against erroneous imposition of the death penalty. The important provisions of a typical death penalty statute are as follows.

First, the statutes limit imposition of capital punishment to the most serious offenses against society—intentional crimes that involve the taking of human life. Second, the defendant must be notified in advance of the state's intention to seek the death penalty and of the aggravating factors the state proposes to prove as justifying a sentence of death. Third, if the trial results in a guilty verdict, a post-verdict hearing must be held to determine the penalty. Fourth, in order to justify the death penalty's imposition, the state must prove beyond a reasonable doubt the existence of at least one statutorily specified aggravating factor that is not outweighed by any mitigating factors. Fifth, the jury must unanimously determine, on the basis of its findings concerning aggravating and mitigating factors, whether the death penalty is justified. Sixth, the state's highest court automatically reviews all death sentences to ensure that there is an adequate legal basis for imposing the death penalty, that the sentence was not imposed as a result of passion or prejudice, and that the sentence is not excessive or disproportionate to the penalty imposed in similar cases. Seventh, the defendant may also seek a new trial on the basis of newly discovered evidence that she or he was not guilty.

C. The Effect of Safeguards in Recent Years According to Bedau and Radelet, ninety-four defendants have been the subjects of "miscarriages of justice" in capital or potentially capital cases since 1960. However, only twenty-six of these persons were sentenced to death. Only two were executed, and the authors give unconvincing reasons for concluding that these executions were erroneous. There is, in short, no persuasive evidence that any innocent person has been put to death in more than twenty-five years. Equally significant, Bedau and Radelet do not include in their catalogue any individual on death row at the end of their study.

The likely explanation for the absence of errors in capital cases during the past quarter century is the greater care taken by the courts to assure the correct resolution of such cases and, particularly, the pains-taking reviews that occur in cases in which the death sentence is actually imposed. The point is illustrated by the very few "miscarriages of justice" claimed by Bedau and Radelet to have occurred in the decade after the Supreme Court upheld the constitutionality of the death penalty.

D. The Benefits of Capital Punishment A thorough inquiry into the significance of the risk of executing an innocent person in the debate over capital punishment should attempt to evaluate capital punishment's benefits. Bedau and Radelet simply despair of this effort, concluding that "since there is no consensus in our society over the weight to be assigned to each variable in the death penalty equation, we are doomed to disagree over how to compute it." However, an assessment of the costs and benefits leads to the conclusion that the minute risk of executing an innocent person is substantially outweighed by the protection that capital punishment affords to society through incapacitation, deterrence, and just punishment.

The purpose of the criminal law is not merely to control behavior—a tyrant can do that—but also to promote respect for that which should be respected, especially the lives, the moral integrity, and even the property of others. In a country whose principles forbid it to preach, the criminal law is one of the few available institutions through which it can make a moral statement and, thereby, hope to promote this respect. To be successful, what it says—and it makes this moral statement when it punishes—must be appropriate to the offense and, therefore, to what has been offended. If human life is to be held in awe, the law forbidding the taking of it must be held in awe; and the only way it can be made to be awful or awe inspiring is to entitle it to inflict the penalty of death.

One could argue that the execution of innocent defendants undermines the death penalty's capacity to provide the incapacitation, deterrence, and just punishment necessary to protect the innocent lives of others. With respect to incapacitation, for example, if an innocent person is executed for murder, the true culprit is likely to remain at large, free to kill again. Likewise, the threat of capital punishment theoretically may not deter persons from murdering if they perceive the threat to be directed indiscriminately at the innocent as well as at the guilty. Infliction of the death penalty upon innocent persons is also clearly not just punishment.

The force of these arguments depends, however, on the frequency with which persons are executed for capital offenses they did not commit and, to the extent that the arguments relate to deterrence and just punishment, on the degree of public knowledge of the number of mistaken executions. If such miscarriages of justice are relatively common, then capital punishment—in addition to taking the lives of innocent defendants—might well be ineffective in protecting innocent life generally. On the other hand, if such occurrences are unusual, then these consequences are unlikely. In fact, erroneous executions appear to be extremely rare if not nonexistent.

Ultimately, the Bedau-Radelet study offers little to opponents of capital punishment. The eighty-four percent of Americans who support the death penalty do so not because they believe its administration is perfect, but because they believe it to be prudently administered in a manner consistent with the society's interest in justice and the protection of the innocent. Nothing presented by Bedau and Radelet undermines that conviction.

Hugo Adam Bedau and Michael L. Radelet, "The Myth of Infallibility: A Reply to Markman and Cassell"

Paucity of space here denies us the opportunity to reply in detail to Markman and Cassell's criticisms, but the discrepancy between their characterizations and what we actually asserted, argued, and implied is so great that it warrants at least a brief response.

I. *Subjective Methodology*

Markman and Cassell complain again and again about what they call our "methodology." They do not mean by this what we called our "methodology," namely, the methods we used to obtain information about alleged cases of wrongful conviction. Nor do they offer an alternative "methodology" that they regard as superior to ours. Our practice was simply to review all the information we could find about a given case, citing our sources so others could follow our trail, before including or excluding the case from our catalogue. Although they disagree with our evaluation of the evidence for innocence in several borderline cases, their critique of our evaluation appears to us to have involved no departures in principle from our own practice. Their criticisms would establish a flaw in our methodology only if their disagreements were based on evidence or reasoning available to them because they relied on a different (and to this extent superior) "methodology." Mere disagreement with our evaluation in any given case does not impeach our "methodology"; if anything, it vindicates it.

II. *Compelling Evidence and Unanimous Juries*

Markman and Cassell contend that in the Adams case, our article "ignores the compelling evidence that convinced a unanimous jury of his guilt beyond a reasonable doubt," and that in this and other cases, we alone have judged the convicted defendants to be innocent. Their charge is false and misleading. First, in 160 of our cases, we point to appellate courts that reversed convictions, to trial juries that acquitted defendants previously convicted, or to prosecutors who decided not to retry the defendant whose conviction had been reversed, as evidence of a prior miscarriage of justice. So we did indeed give weight to the "considered judgment of the juries and judges," although we did not take it as conclusive evidence of guilt—any more than we treated acquittals at retrial as conclusive evidence of innocence. There are only forty-one cases, including the twenty-three where we believe that the defendant was executed in error, in which we cannot point to some official nullification of the conviction. We remain convinced that the trial courts in these forty-one cases were in error—just as various government officials, juries, and courts in effect agreed that the trial courts had erred in the other 309 cases.

Second, we of course recognize that in all of the 350 cases, as in the Adams case, a trial court accepted a plea of guilty or rendered a guilty verdict. Nonetheless, we believe that the defendant was innocent in every one of these cases. Markman and Cassell write as if the trial court is the final authority on the factual question of the defendant's guilt. Worse, they write as if part of the evidence against the defendant is the fact that a trial court judged the defendant to be guilty "beyond a reasonable doubt." Since many of these unanimous juries (and some unanimous appellate courts) have been demonstrably in factual error, we are unpersuaded by the ostensibly "compelling evidence" that persuaded the trial court in the first instance in each of our 350 cases. The issue our research undertook to investigate is whether trial courts, including unanimous juries, in potentially capital cases are always factually correct in their judgments of guilt "beyond a reasonable doubt." We have demonstrated that they are not.

Third, we do not ignore "compelling evidence" in the Adams case or in any other. Markman and Cassell, as their discussion of the Adams case shows, prefer instead simply to restate the case for the prosecution, as though that by itself impeaches our judgment. Unlike our critics, we attempted to refer readers to all major sources where information could be obtained, not simply to those sources that buttress our conclusions. All our critics show is the inadequacy of our case summaries for their own purposes. Suffice it to say here that nothing these critics have noted removes the very serious doubts in the Adams case, or in any other case included in our catalogue.

III. *Execution of the Innocent*

We of course anticipated that subsequent investigators might disagree with us on some borderline cases, either on the basis of their interpretation of the available record (which is all that Markman and Cassell rely on) or on the basis of evidence not available to us. We agree with our critics that we have not "proved" these executed defendants to be innocent; we never claimed that we had. It is completely unclear to us what Markman and Cassell would count as "proof" in such cases—except possibly the discovery that no potentially capital crime had even occurred. As we noted, the kinds of evidence to which we could and did point— such as confessions by another person or alibi evidence—are not definitive. How, for example, we or anyone else should now set about trying to "prove" that Joe Hill was not guilty in 1915 of the murder for which he was executed, is an interesting but unresolvable question. Our claim that he is to be counted among the innocent is of course contestable; we did not set ourselves up as a Court of Final Judgment in Capital Cases. We reiterate, however, that we believe all 350 defendants to have been innocent, and we shall continue in this belief until shown otherwise with adequate evidence.

IV. *The Risk of Executing the Innocent*

Markman and Cassell make much of our professed inability to compute an estimate of the risk of erroneous execution. They argue that computing (or estimating) this risk is a necessary condition for any argument against the death penalty. Lest there be any confusion on the matter, we must stress two points. We, like other opponents of the death penalty, oppose executions of the guilty as well as executions of the innocent—which presumably even friends of the death penalty deplore. So our personal rejection of capital punishment, on moral grounds and on grounds of social policy, does not turn on estimating the risk of executing the innocent. We believe likewise that social policy on the death penalty should turn not only on the risk of executing innocents, or even on the other important generalizations that our research established, but should turn on other political and moral considerations as well.

V. *Statutory Safeguards to Prevent Miscarriages*

Markman and Cassell point to seven statutory provisions, most of which they claim "are intended to safeguard against erroneous imposition of the death penalty." These seven are a mixed bag. The first (limitation of capital punishment to murder) has nothing to do with the intention to reduce the risk of wrongful execution, and it is hypocritical for Markman and Cassell to point to it when the Department of Justice itself is on record elsewhere as currently favoring the death penalty for several nonhomicidal crimes. The fourth (jury required to find at least one aggravating circumstance not cancelled or outweighed by any mitigating circumstance) is severely flawed, given what is known about how juries actually use their "guided discretion" in sentencing. The sixth standard (judicial override of jury recommended sentence) is similarly unworthy of praise given what is known about its actual operation.

VI. *Conclusion*

The Department of Justice under the Reagan Administration has made quite clear its support for the death penalty, and the critique of our research by Markman and Cassell is but one more indication of that support. We view this hostile attention as evidence of how influential the Department thinks our research may prove to be. Since Markman and Cassell begin their critique by conceding that human judgments are not infallible and that "the possibility exists" that innocent defendants will be executed, they evidently concede one of the basic assumptions of our research. The fundamental questions in dispute are thus how to measure the risk of such error, the extent to which our research enables one to make that measurement, the role this risk should play in a rational assessment of the death penalty, and the adequacy of the evidence to convince the unbiased observer that such errors have indeed occurred. In their zeal to attack our research, our critics have failed to shed light on these important issues. Their efforts appear to spring largely from unacknowledged political roots; as a result, they either obfuscate the issues or merely trumpet the limits of our research as though we had failed to state them in the first place.

The basic problem with Markman and Cassell's response is that it seems bent on defending the criminal justice system in every regard that bears on the death penalty and its administration. This inflexible stance requires our critics to deny that anyone actually innocent has ever been executed, lest the criminal justice system itself be charged with such an error. It is an effort to protect the myth of systemic infallibility: the myth that prosecutors in capital cases never indict an innocent person; that if they do the trial courts can be counted on to acquit; that if the courts convict they sentence to prison rather than to death; that if courts do convict and sentence to death the appellate courts may be relied on to rectify an erroneous conviction; and that if the appellate courts fail then the chief executive will come to the rescue. We do not believe this myth, we do not sympathize with the effort to protect it, and we trust that anyone who studies our research will agree with us in rejecting the myth. We stand firmly behind every conclusion reached in our original essay.

Evan J. Mandery, "Innocence as a Death Penalty Issue"

This risk of executing an innocent person is a matter that gives the public serious pause, as well it should. The execution of an innocent person is a serious matter. The incarceration of an innocent person is also a serious matter, though, and virtually all abolitionists, of which I am one, have said very little about why risk of error is a conclusive moral argument against the death penalty but not a conclusive argument against incarceration. Why is innocence a death penalty issue?

Abolitionists generally rely upon the familiar "death is different" mantra. Professors Bedau and Radelet acknowledge that they "have no evidence that ending the death penalty would reduce the likelihood of wrongful conviction in what are now potentially capital cases." Abolition of the death penalty, they say, "would eliminate the worst of the possible consequences that accrue from wrongful convictions in what are now capital cases." Laurie Anne Whitt, Alan Clarke, and Eric Lambert put it this way:

> For the average person, as well as the philosopher, death's irrevocability makes the problem of innocence greater than if the same innocent person were languishing in prison. Rightly or wrongly, the innocent at the gallows excites more passion than the guiltless languishing away in prison. So long as the wrongfully executed person lives, the error can be rectified—if only partially and belatedly. But the state cannot correct error, or make restitution, posthumously.

The descriptive part of this claim cannot be objected to: people perceive the plight of the executed innocent to be more compelling than the incarcerated blameless. I have relied upon this argument myself in conversation. But the plight of the ordinary incarcerated innocent is serious too. All of the philosophical arguments raised about the problem of innocence apply with equal force to incarceration as to execution. It is retributively unfair to incarcerate the innocent. A rule-utilitarian would disfavor jailing the innocent, just as she would disfavor executing the innocent. In each debate, the question becomes—for the utilitarian—whether the offsetting benefits of incarceration and executions outweigh the costs, which include the risk to innocents—and for the retributivists—whether the quantum of justice gained by giving the guilty what they deserve outweighs the justice lost by punishing the innocent. Whether death is different in a way that makes a difference in this debate is a more problematic question than it appears at first glance.

Are innocent convicts worse off in a regime with the death penalty than they are in a regime without capital punishment? The death penalty affects the plight of the innocent-convicted in four ways: (1) it shortens the amount of time during which a mistake can be discovered and corrected, (2) in instances where mistakes are caught and corrected before execution, it changes (presumably worsens) the conditions under which they are incarcerated while they are alive, (3) in instances where mistakes are caught after execution, the mistakes cannot be corrected in any meaningful way, and (4) in instances where mistakes are not corrected, the innocent are killed rather than spend the remainder of their lives on death row.

If innocence is to be examined as a death penalty issue, it is the combination of first and second effects that are most serious and deserving of study. The question is this: How much is the chance of an error being discovered diminished by virtue of the death penalty? In instances where mistakes are corrected the question is how much worse are prison conditions on death row than for the general population? Some mistakes will never be corrected. In these cases, the question is how much worse is it to be executed than to live on death row?

The answer to the question of how much the chance of discovering an error is diminished by virtue of the death penalty is undeniably some, but I expect not much, and less than it was in the past. Even under a death penalty regime some chance exists, of course, that a mistaken conviction will be corrected. Depending on one's view, this chance is quite substantial. According to the most recent Bureau of Justice Statistics report, prisoners spend an average of more than ten years in jail between sentence and execution. The chance of catching an error during this period is equal under a death-penalty regime and a regime without capital punishment. The difference is that in a death penalty regime an error cannot be corrected during the time after the execution (although it still could be caught). So the impact of the death penalty on the innocence issue is that errors that are caught between the time of execution and the defendant's otherwise natural death cannot be corrected. (See **Figure 7-1** below.)

How many errors are likely to surface between the years when the defendant is executed and when he would otherwise naturally die? This is a question for study. It seems fair to say, though, that the number is lower for those convicted today than it was for those convicted, say, twenty years ago. If a defendant were convicted twenty years ago and executed with average expediency, he would have

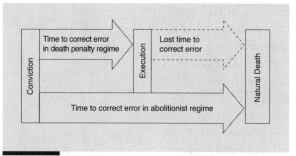

Figure 7-1 Marginal difference in error correction under death penalty regime.

missed out on the possibility of being exonerated by DNA evidence. The question is whether there is some technological improvement in the offing that defendants convicted today will not be able to benefit from if he is executed in the normal course of business. The answer to this question is, of course, unknowable, but it seems unlikely. In the absence of such a technological change, the sole issue is whether the average time between conviction and execution is sufficient for a defendant to gain access to potentially exculpatory evidence, find a competent lawyer to present it, and present it to a court. These are serious questions—I have heard lawyers for the Innocence Project and other groups that offer representation to convicted inmates tell of decade-long battles to gain access to rape kits and other evidence with the potential to exonerate. But even if the answer is that ten years is not enough time, that is an argument for further delaying executions not an argument against the death penalty.

If the answer is, as I expect, that very few errors are missed and uncorrected as a result of the death penalty, the question then is whether the cost imposed on the innocent is too much to bear. There are two such costs. One is the cost imposed upon defendants whose errors are caught and corrected: they spend their jail time on death row instead of the general population and under constant threat of death. This is a serious cost, the intuition behind Albert Camus' famous argument that the death penalty is disproportionate for murder because of the time the condemned must spend anticipating his execution. This wrong may be reparable to some extent—perhaps by money damages—though almost no states offer meaningful compensation to those wrongfully convicted and exonerated. The other cost is that imposed upon the innocent whose errors are not corrected: they lose the years between execution and natural death, time that would be spent on death row. This is a serious cost, too. I have never met a death row inmate who did not prefer the possibility of life without parole over execution.

I wonder, though, whether the magnitude of these costs is sufficient to materially affect either the utilitarian or retributive calculus on the merits of capital punishment. It seems hard to imagine a utilitarian who otherwise supports the death penalty opposing capital punishment because of the small decrease in the chance of catching an error, the moderate cost imposed on the very small number of people whose wrongful convictions are reversed, and the cost imposed on defendants whose wrongful convictions are never caught. This last cost seems incalculable. The thought of an innocent person being executed is repugnant. I do not know, though, how much more or less repugnant is the thought of an innocent person spending their life in jail; this cost has not led us to refrain from incarcerating putative offenders with impunity. I could at least imagine the argument that it would be preferable to be executed than to live without hope, although it is only in retrospect that we know that the error was not caught for this group of people, so they might have had some hope while they lived, hope that we know after the fact will go unrealized, but prospectively might have offered some quality of life.

I expect that if the issue were framed in this way the cost would not be enough to affect the debate one way or the other. People would support or oppose the death penalty for the usual reasons. I oppose it because it does not deter and because I believe all life should be treated with respect. This is not to say that the risk of executing innocents is irrelevant. It is an important consideration. Some innocent will be executed. Given that the death penalty offers no demonstrable benefit to offset this intolerable cost it is, to my mind, a conclusive argument. But it is extraordinarily unlikely that an error will go uncorrected by virtue of the death penalty. The death penalty exacerbates the costs of a mistake; it has not been shown that it causes mistakes. For this reason, I am not sure that innocence is best thought of as a death penalty issue. To my mind it is an issue that is better considered in the general debate on incarceration.

I worry that the current reliance on innocence as an argument against the death penalty has a potential unintended negative impact. Focusing exclusively on death row inmates may divert attention from the fact that it is also a serious issue for incarceration. If I were evaluating the death penalty, I would devote scarce resources to the crucial questions whether the death penalty deters and whether it actually encourages violence. I would urge studying the frequency of mistaken convictions if I were assessing the costs and benefits of persistent reliance on long-term sentences (including but not limited to the death penalty). The costs of mistakes here are serious too, the offsetting benefits are not as obvious as is presumed, and innocent convicts not on death row have less access to high-quality legal representation than those on death row.

Constitutional Considerations

II

■ The Death Penalty as Applied in America— An Introduction

Even if one concedes that capital punishment is moral in concept, it is an entirely separate issue whether the death penalty as implemented in the United States works well. "Working well" is the vaguest of notions; efficiency is in the eye of the beholder. Some might say the system works well if defendants are executed swiftly and in the cheapest manner possible. Others might deem a death penalty system maximally efficient if it went to the greatest possible lengths to ensure that not a single innocent person was executed.

To some extent, the Supreme Court itself has defined the terms of this debate. In its decisions, the Court has placed great emphasis on limiting arbitrariness in death sentencing. Arbitrariness is a broad concept itself. The death penalty is arbitrary in many different ways: It is geographically arbitrary—defendants in states without the death penalty are treated differently than defendants in states that do have the death penalty. It is economically arbitrary—rich people have access to better representation. The death penalty is arbitrary by gender, as the death penalty is rarely sought and imposed against women. It is arbitrary by race—people who kill whites are more likely to receive the death penalty than those who murder blacks. Finally, the death penalty is arbitrary in the most basic sense—it is ultimately within the jury's discretion to impose the death penalty or not, and they need not explain the basis of their decision. A jury may grant mercy to one defendant but not to another. People generally regard this last kind of arbitrariness as a strength of the criminal justice system.

This section begins by presenting several early Supreme Court decisions that established the constitutional parameters of the modern death penalty. As is evident in the first of these cases, *Furman v. Georgia*, even the justices of the Supreme Court had very different views about what kinds of arbitrariness should concern the law.

Prior to *Furman*, virtually all states left the decision of whether a particular defendant should be sentenced to die to the unguided discretion of the judge and jury. In *McGautha v. California*, a 1971 case, the Court rejected a challenge under the due process clause of the Fourteenth Amendment to unguided discretion in death sentencing. However, only two years later, the Court found in *Furman* that untrammeled discretion violated the Eighth Amendment's guarantee against cruel and unusual punishments, made applicable to the states through the Fourteenth Amendment.

The *Furman* decision had monumental consequences—the death sentences of more than 600 condemned prisoners were commuted to life *with* the possibility of parole—but the decision was not the product of consensus. All nine justices wrote separate opinions. Collectively, the opinions totaled more than 50,000 words, the longest collection of opinions in the history of the Supreme Court. None of the five justices voting with the majority joined in any of the others' opinions. Justices Stewart and White emphasized the infrequency with which the death penalty was imposed: for Justice Stewart this was a moral failing, for Justice White it undermined the deterrent value of the death penalty. Justice Douglas emphasized the racially discriminatory manner in which the death penalty was imposed. Justices Brennan and Marshall offered rationales that suggested the death penalty was categorically wrong, not just as applied in Georgia.

While *Furman* was not the product of consensus, it seems fair to say that each of the justices in the majority shared a concern with arbitrariness understood as unpredictability. This is a particular sense of arbitrariness, the notion that in an efficient system it should be possible to make somewhat accurate predictions about which defendants will receive the death penalty and which will be spared. Presumably, in a system functioning well, defendants who commit the most severe crimes will receive the death penalty more often than defendants who commit less aggravated offenses. It is the absence of this regularity that Justice Stewart seems to be reacting to when he writes that "death sentences are cruel and unusual in the same way that being struck by lightning is cruel and unusual." Is this a moral argument? If, in a particular jurisdiction, police officers gave speeding tickets to drivers who drove up to twenty miles per hour over the speed limit, but not to drivers who drove more than twenty miles per hour over the speed limit, we would likely call this system inequitable or irrational, but probably not immoral (because the speeders *did* speed). It is these kinds of arguments with which this section is concerned.

Following *Furman*, the overwhelming majority of states that had the death penalty in place before *Furman* revised their statutes and reinstituted the death penalty. The revisions fall into two broad classifications: some states instituted a mandatory death penalty; others attempted to curb the jury's discretion by implementing guidelines.

The Supreme Court rejected the mandatory death penalty approach in *Woodson v. North Carolina*, excerpted in Chapter 9, holding that the mandatory sentencing procedure did not allow for "particularized consideration of relevant aspects of the character and record of each convicted defendant before the imposition upon him of a sentence of death." *Woodson* is a cornerstone of modern death penalty jurisprudence. In *Lockett v. Ohio*, also excerpted in Chapter 9, the Court carried *Woodson* through to its logical extension: a defendant must be allowed to present any mitigating evidence that he deems relevant. The principle of *Woodson* and *Lockett* is that a jury must base a death sentence on the particular circumstances of a defendant's life. This seems just from the standpoint of the individual, but the decisions arguably create arbitrariness (understood as unpredictability), even as the Court condemns it. If jurors are required to hear all mitigating evidence, then a particular jury might grant mercy to a defendant on the basis of an idiosyncratic reaction to some proffered item of mitigating evidence. Whether *Woodson* and *Lockett* are in tension with *Furman* and *Gregg*—and whether the tension is defensible—is the subject of Chapter 9.

Georgia responded to *Furman* by adopting three measures designed to curb the discretion of the jury: First, Georgia narrowed the class of murderers subject to capital punishment by requiring that at least one of ten specified statutory aggravating circumstances be proved beyond a reasonable doubt. Second, it bifurcated trials, dividing capital proceedings into a separate guilt phase and sentencing phase where the jury weighs the aggravating evidence against the mitigating evidence. Third, it required automatic appeal of death sentences to the state supreme court with the court required to consider, among other things, whether the sentence is disproportionate compared to sentences imposed in similar cases.

In *Gregg v. Georgia*, decided on the same day as *Woodson*, the Supreme Court held by a vote of 7–2 that the revised Georgia statute sufficiently curbed discretion so that juries could no longer "wantonly and freakishly" impose death sentences. For the most part, most states implementing or reimplementing the death penalty have followed the Georgia approach. Some states vest ultimate discretion in the judge rather than the jury. The Supreme Court approved that approach in *Proffitt v. Florida*, another of the *Gregg*-companion cases. Texas focused jury discretion further by identifying five offenses punishable by death and asking the jury three tightly focused questions (whether the defendant's conduct was deliberate, whether the defendant constituted a continuing threat to society, and whether the conduct of the defendant was unreasonable in response to any provocation). At no point is the jury invited to weigh aggravating and mitigating evidence. The Supreme Court approved this approach in *Jurek v. Texas*, another *Gregg*-companion case, holding that the third statutory question invited the jury to consider the defendant's mitigating circumstances. This opportunity was critical to the Court's thinking. In the final *Gregg*-companion case, *Roberts v. Louisiana*, the Court rejected the Louisiana statute, which took the Texas approach of identifying a small set of death-eligible offenses, but did not invite the consideration of mitigating evidence.

That so many states followed the basic Georgia approach of aggravating factors and bifurcated trials is not so much an endorsement of Georgia's thinking as it is a product of practicality. The Supreme Court decides concrete cases. It does not offer advisory opinions; it passes judgment on the constitutionality of the scheme that is immediately before it. A state attorney general might speculate that the Court would have approved the revised scheme with, say, bifurcated trials and proportionality review but not a system of aggravating factors, but it would only be speculation. Florida, Texas, and Louisiana did successfully implement variations of the Georgia system, and in *Pulley v. Harris*, the Supreme Court approved California's death-sentencing scheme, which did not include appellate proportionality review. But the safest route for a state to ensure that its scheme would pass constitutional muster was to emulate a scheme that had already been approved by the Supreme Court, and that is what most states did. There is, thus, striking consistency among state death penalty statutes.

It seems reasonable then to ask whether the Georgia approach has worked. And, as it was Justices White and Stewart who changed sides from *Furman* to *Gregg*, and as Justices White and Stewart identified the infrequency and unpredictability of the imposition of the death penalty as its major flaws, it seems reasonable to define "working" as whether the Georgia approach has generated predictable outcomes. Chapter 8 considers whether the death penalty has succeeded in generating greater reliability in death sentencing. Chapter 9 considers whether the Court's decisions in *Woodson* and *Lockett*—requiring the individualized consideration of mitigating evidence—are reconcilable with *Gregg*.

Of course, these are not the only questions to be asked. The racial arbitrariness emphasized by Justice Douglas is patently undesirable. Chapter 15 examines the distribution of the death penalty with regard to race and the legal and policy conclusions to be drawn from the data. Chapter 19 considers what might be termed the "economic arbitrariness" of the death penalty. Of what quality are the lawyers appointed by the court to represent defendants charged with capital crimes? To what quality representation are such defendants entitled?

Most people believe that certain kinds of defendants, the very young and the retarded, for example, should not be eligible for the death penalty, a belief the Supreme Court has credited. Creating exceptions for certain classes of people creates another kind of arbitrariness: in the United States someone who commits murder at the age of 16 years is eligible for the death penalty, while someone 15 years old is not. The succeeding chapters consider the validity of these different categories of defendants. Chapters 10 through 14 offer debates over the execution of rapists, juveniles, the retarded, felony–murderers, and reformed defendants.

Arbitrariness

■ Arbitrariness—Introduction

In *Furman v. Georgia*, the Supreme Court by a 5–4 vote struck down Georgia's death penalty scheme, which gave juries unguided discretion to determine death sentences. Georgia responded to *Furman* by regulating the sentencing process. In *Gregg*, the Supreme Court by a 7–2 vote upheld the revised Georgia statute as constitutional. The two justices who switched sides between *Furman* and *Gregg* (Stewart and White) each expressed concern in *Furman* with the infrequency and randomness with which juries imposed the death penalty. For Justice Stewart the arbitrariness was a matter of fairness. For Justice White the concern was utilitarian—a randomly and infrequently imposed death penalty could not possibly deter. But because each found the unpredictability of the original statute fatal, it seems only fair to ask whether the revised Georgia statute has created greater rationality.

Georgia reformed its death-sentencing scheme in three significant ways: (1) it bifurcated trials; (2) it created a set of statutory aggravating factors, at least one of which must be found by the jury to be proved beyond a reasonable doubt; and (3) it required the automatic appeal of all death sentences to the Georgia State Supreme Court to determine whether the sentence was disproportionate compared to sentences imposed in similar cases.

Of the three reforms, the scheme of aggravating factors is much more significant from the standpoint of the defendant and in reducing arbitrariness than either proportionality review or bifurcated trials. There can be little debate that appellate proportionality review, whatever the Supreme Court envisioned it to be, has not amounted to a significant right for defendants. Most states have reduced proportionality review to a perfunctory exercise: the state supreme court determines whether a death sentence has ever been given in any case with facts similar to the appellant's. Only a handful of death sentences have been reversed under this standard. Some state schemes do not include proportionality review at all. In *Pulley v. Harris*, the Supreme Court upheld the California death sentencing statute, which does not include proportionality review.

The value of separating the guilt and penalty phases of capital trials is more debatable. Bifurcation certainly creates the appearance of regularity; the jury spends part of the trial considering exclusively whether the defendant deserves the death penalty. From the defendant's standpoint, bifurcated trials might be less advantageous than single-phase trials. In a single-phase trial, all of the mitigating and aggravating evidence is before the jury when they decide guilt and penalty. The potential benefit to defendants from bifurcating trials is that the jury will not hear all of the aggravating evidence when it decides guilt. If the relevant aggravating factor is based upon the prior conduct of the defendant (prior felony offenses, for example) or the risk he poses to society (future dangerousness is a common aggravator) then bifurcation keeps some aggravating evidence from the jury when it decides guilt. But if the aggravating factor relates to the manner in which the crime was committed, as many aggravating factors do (the "outrageously and wantonly vile" aggravator mentioned in *Gregg* is common among state statutes) then the jury by necessity hears much of the aggravating evidence during the prosecutor's case-in-chief. Bifurcation keeps some, but not all, aggravating evidence from the jury during the guilt phase.

The countering benefit from single-phase trials for defendants is that the jury might hear mitigating evidence during the guilt phase that, in a bifurcated trial, it would not hear until the penalty phase. Conceivably, a jury might nullify—that is, acquit a defendant it would otherwise have convicted—if the presentation of the mitigating evidence were deferred. Although some or much aggravating evidence slips into the penalty phase in a bifurcated trial, the jury is not likely to hear much mitigating evidence during the penalty phase. If the mitigating evidence relates to some ongoing physical condition of the defendant—a mental impairment, for example—or to some aspect of the crime itself—such as rendering assistance to the victim—then it may be revealed during the guilt phase as part of the description of the crime. But most mitigating evidence relates to the defendant's character and upbringing. The abuse a defendant suffered as a child or his history of alcoholism is not likely to be relevant to any guilt-phase issues.

So in some sense the defendant gets the worst of both worlds in a bifurcated system: the jury hears most of the aggravating evidence during the guilt phase, but very little of the mitigating evidence. In a single-phase trial, the entirety of the aggravating evidence is before the jury during the guilt phase, but so is the entirety of the mitigating evidence. In a bifurcated trial, much of the aggravating evidence is before the jury during the guilt phase, but little of the mitigating evidence (**Figure 8-1**). Whether a particular procedure is advantageous to one party or the other is a separate question from whether the procedure is likely to generate greater predictability in outcomes. It isn't obvious what the effect would be other than to ensure that fewer defendants are (unfairly) spared by virtue of the jury's premature consideration of mitigating evidence. The effect of bifurcated trials has not been empirically examined, and is not much discussed in the literature, so the preceding argument, whether of intuitive appeal or not, must be classified as unproved.

The significance of statutory aggravating factors is more obvious. Justice Stewart emphasized the significance of aggravating factors in his opinion in *Gregg*:

> *No longer can a jury do as* Furman's *jury did: reach a finding of the defendant's guilt and then, without discretion, decide whether he should live or die. . . . While some jury discretion still exists, the discretion to be exercised is controlled by clear and objective standards so as to produce non-discriminatory application.*

No scholar has seriously challenged the theoretical usefulness of aggravating factors in regularizing death sentencing. The question is how useful aggravating factors have proved in practice.

Aggravating factors have the potential to rationalize death sentencing in three ways. First, they can narrow the universe of defendants eligible for the death penalty. This function is significant in light of the Court's decision in *Woodson* rejecting mandatory death penalties. Second, aggravating factors can help to ensure that similar cases are treated similarly. Professors Carol and Jordan Steiker term this function "channeling." Third, aggravating factors can help to rationalize the death-sentencing process by working to ensure that the penalty is reserved for the most culpable defendants.

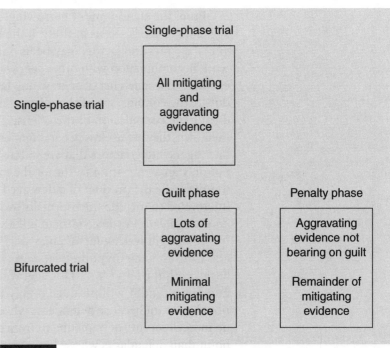

Figure 8-1 Effect of bifurcated trials on presentation of aggravating and mitigating evidence.

Different aggravators are differently suited to these different aims. Generally speaking, factors written in objective terms are better suited to channeling than factors written in subjective terms. For example, the aggravating factor "the offense of murder was outrageously and wantonly vile" almost certainly produces less predictable outcomes than the aggravating factor "whether the defendant physically tortured his victim during the commission of the offense." "Outrageous" and "wanton" are subjective terms; what is outrageous and wanton is ultimately a matter of opinion. Most jurors would probably consider torture to be outrageously and wantonly vile, but they might differ whether certain conduct short of torture met the standard. If, for example, the defendant murdered the victim in the presence of the victim's child, it might be difficult to predict whether a jury would consider that to be outrageously and wantonly vile conduct. On the other hand, it is clear this does not meet the standard of physical torture. Whether it should be included as conduct worthy of the death penalty is another matter. The object here is predictability.

The "outrageously and wantonly vile" aggravator might also perform poorly at the narrowing function. One objection commonly raised against aggravators such as "outrageously and wantonly vile" and "heinous, atrocious, and cruel" is that they are so vague and broad that every murder might be construed as falling within their rubric. For an aggravating factor to serve the function of narrowing, it must eliminate at least one defendant by its application. "Used a weapon during the commission of the offense" might not be a rational aggravating factor and might not eliminate many defendants, but it does serve the function of narrowing because it winnows the defendants who kills their victims by scaring them to death, unlikely as this case might be. The question with "outrageously and wantonly vile" and "heinous, atrocious, and cruel" is whether they eliminate any defendants at all.

From the standpoint of narrowing, it is important also to consider the list of aggravating factors in its entirety. If the list is long enough, even though the individual aggravating factors may be useful in narrowing, any one aggravator might work in combination with other aggravators to defeat the narrowing purpose. For example: if a state's list of aggravating factors included the factor "used a weapon during the commission of the offense" and also the factor "did not use a weapon during the commission of the offense," even though the factors may narrow on their own, they are useless in combination. The example is extreme, but many states have aggravating factors that are in tension with one another. In some states it is not only an aggravating factor for the murder to involve torture, but also for the murder to be the product of a depraved indifference to human life, a factor often interpreted to include the especially swift killing of a person. So it may be an aggravating factor in some states to kill a victim either especially slowly or quickly.

Some aggravating factors may perform well by some standards but not others. Consider this hypothetical aggravating factor: "the defendant's last name began with the letter 'A.'" This aggravator narrow the universe of death-eligible murderers, and it will produce highly predictable results, but it fails on the rationality count because defendants whose last names begin with the letter "A" are no more deserving of punishment from either a retributive or public policy standpoint than defendants whose last names begin with other letters.

The question remains: how is the success of the *Gregg*-reforms to be measured? In the debate that follows, Professors Carol and Jordan Steiker argue that the Supreme Court has, through its subsequent decisions, allowed the *Gregg*-reforms to be so weakened as to render them toothless. The Steikers argue that the Court has tolerated vague aggravating factors and overly broad lists of aggravating factors so as to preclude their narrowing and channeling effect.

Professor McCord, also an abolitionist, argues that while the Steikers may accurately describe the Supreme Court's jurisprudence subsequent to *Gregg*, the question of the efficacy of the *Gregg* reforms is essentially an empirical one. The Court's objection to the pre-*Furman* Georgia scheme was that it generated arbitrary, unpredictable results. Professor McCord compares jury verdicts in the pre-*Furman* and post-*Gregg* worlds and finds some evidence that jury verdicts are more predictable in the modern system. Defendants in the most aggravated cases are more likely to receive the death penalty than they were pre-*Furman*, and defendants in the least aggravated cases are less likely to receive the death penalty than they were pre-*Furman*.

■ Arbitrariness—Critical Documents

Furman v. Georgia
408 U.S. 238 (1972)

Per Curiam
The Court holds that the imposition and carrying out of the death penalty in these cases constitute cruel and unusual punishment in violation of the Eighth and

Fourteenth Amendments. The judgment in each case is therefore reversed insofar as it leaves undisturbed the death sentence imposed, and the cases are remanded for further proceedings.

Mr. Justice Douglas, concurring.

It has been assumed in our decisions that punishment by death is not cruel, unless the manner of execution can be said to be inhuman and barbarous. The generality of a law inflicting capital punishment is one thing. What may be said of the validity of a law on the books and what may be done with the law in its application do, or may, lead to quite different conclusions. It would seem to be incontestable that the death penalty inflicted on one defendant is "unusual" if it discriminates against him by reason of his race, religion, wealth, social position, or class, or if it is imposed under a procedure that gives room for the play of such prejudices.

There is evidence that the provision of the English Bill of Rights of 1689, from which the language of the Eighth Amendment was taken, was concerned primarily with selective or irregular application of harsh penalties and that its aim was to forbid arbitrary and discriminatory penalties of a severe nature.

The words "cruel and unusual" certainly include penalties that are barbaric. But the words, at least when read in light of the English proscription against selective and irregular use of penalties, suggest that it is "cruel and unusual" to apply the death penalty—or any other penalty—selectively to minorities whose numbers are few, who are outcasts of society, and who are unpopular, but whom society is willing to see suffer though it would not countenance general application of the same penalty across the board.

There is increasing recognition of the fact that the basic theme of equal protection is implicit in "cruel and unusual" punishments. "A penalty should be considered 'unusually' imposed if it is administered arbitrarily or discriminatorily." The same authors add that "the extreme rarity with which applicable death penalty provisions are put to use raises a strong inference of arbitrariness." The President's Commission on Law Enforcement and Administration of Justice recently concluded:

> *There is evidence that the imposition of the death sentence and the exercise of dispensing power by the courts and the executive follow discriminatory patterns. The death sentence is disproportionately imposed and carried out on the poor, the Negro, and the members of unpopular groups.*

A study of capital cases in Texas from 1924 to 1968 reached the following conclusions:

> *Application of the death penalty is unequal: most of those executed were poor, young, and ignorant. Seventy-five of the 460 cases involved co-defendants, who, under Texas law, were given separate trials. In several instances where a white and a Negro were co-defendants, the white was sentenced to life imprisonment or a term of years, and the Negro was given the death penalty. Another ethnic disparity is found in the type of sentence imposed for rape. The Negro con-*

> *victed of rape is far more likely to get the death penalty than a term sentence, whereas whites and Latins are far more likely to get a term sentence than the death penalty.*

Furman, a black, killed a householder while seeking to enter the home at night. Furman shot the deceased through a closed door. He was 26 years old and had finished the sixth grade in school. Pending trial, he was committed to the Georgia Central State Hospital for a psychiatric examination on his plea of insanity tendered by court-appointed counsel. The superintendent reported that a unanimous staff diagnostic conference had concluded "that this patient should retain his present diagnosis of Mental Deficiency, Mild to Moderate, with Psychotic Episodes associated with Convulsive Disorder." The physicians agreed that "at present the patient is not psychotic, but he is not capable of cooperating with his counsel in the preparation of his defense"; and the staff believed "that he is in need of further psychiatric hospitalization and treatment."

We cannot say from facts disclosed in these records that these defendants were sentenced to death because they were black. Yet our task is not restricted to an effort to divine what motives impelled these death penalties. Rather, we deal with a system of law and of justice that leaves to the uncontrolled discretion of judges or juries the determination whether defendants committing these crimes should die or be imprisoned. Under these laws no standards govern the selection of the penalty. People live or die, dependent on the whim of one man or of 12.

Those who wrote the Eighth Amendment knew what price their forebears had paid for a system based, not on equal justice, but on discrimination. In those days the target was not the blacks or the poor, but the dissenters, those who opposed absolutism in government, who struggled for a parliamentary regime, and who opposed governments' recurring efforts to foist a particular religion on the people. But the tool of capital punishment was used with vengeance against the opposition and those unpopular with the regime. One cannot read this history without realizing that the desire for equality was reflected in the ban against "cruel and unusual punishments" contained in the Eighth Amendment.

In a Nation committed to equal protection of the laws there is no permissible "caste" aspect of law enforcement. Yet we know that the discretion of judges and juries in imposing the death penalty enables the penalty to be selectively applied, feeding prejudices against the accused if he is poor and despised, and lacking political clout, or if he is a member of a suspect or unpopular minority, and saving those who by social position may be in a more protected position. In ancient Hindu law a Brahman was exempt from capital punishment, and under that law, "generally, in the law books, punishment increased in severity as social status diminished." We have, I fear, taken in practice the same position, partially as a result of making the death penalty discretionary and partially as a result of the ability of the rich to purchase the services of the most respected and most resourceful legal talent in the Nation.

The high service rendered by the "cruel and unusual" punishment clause of the Eighth Amendment is to require legislatures to write penal laws that are even-handed, nonselective, and nonarbitrary, and to require judges to see to it that general laws are not applied sparsely, selectively, and spottily to unpopular groups.

A law that stated that anyone making more than $50,000 would be exempt from the death penalty would plainly fall, as would a law that in terms said that blacks, those who never went beyond the fifth grade in school, those who made less than $3,000 a year, or those who were unpopular or unstable should be the only people executed. A law which in the overall view reaches that result in practice has no more sanctity than a law which in terms provides the same.

Thus, these discretionary statutes are unconstitutional in their operation. They are pregnant with discrimination and discrimination is an ingredient not compatible with the idea of equal protection of the laws that is implicit in the ban on "cruel and unusual" punishments.

Any law which is nondiscriminatory on its face may be applied in such a way as to violate the Equal Protection Clause of the Fourteenth Amendment. Such conceivably might be the fate of a mandatory death penalty, where equal or lesser sentences were imposed on the elite, a harsher one on the minorities or members of the lower castes. Whether a mandatory death penalty would otherwise be constitutional is a question I do not reach. I concur in the judgments of the Court.

Mr. Justice Brennan, concurring.

The basic concept underlying the Cruel and Unusual Punishments Clause is nothing less than the dignity of man. While the State has the power to punish, the Clause stands to assure that this power be exercised within the limits of civilized standards.

At bottom, then, the Clause prohibits the infliction of uncivilized and inhuman punishments. The State, even as it punishes, must treat its members with respect for their intrinsic worth as human beings. A punishment is "cruel and unusual," therefore, if it does not comport with human dignity.

This formulation, of course, does not of itself yield principles for assessing the constitutional validity of particular punishments. Nevertheless, even though "this Court has had little occasion to give precise content to the Clause," there are principles recognized in our cases and inherent in the Clause sufficient to permit a judicial determination whether a challenged punishment comports with human dignity.

The primary principle is that a punishment must not be so severe as to be degrading to the dignity of human beings. More than the presence of pain, however, is comprehended in the judgment that the extreme severity of a punishment makes it degrading to the dignity of human beings. The barbaric punishments condemned by history, "punishments which inflict torture, such as the rack, the thumbscrew, the iron boot, the stretching of limbs and the like," are, of course, "attended with acute pain and suffering." When we consider why they have been condemned, however, we realize that the pain involved is not the only reason. The true significance of these punishments is that they treat members of the human race as nonhumans, as objects to be toyed with and discarded. They are thus inconsistent with the fundamental premise of the Clause that even the vilest criminal remains a human being possessed of common human dignity.

In determining whether a punishment comports with human dignity, we are aided also by a second principle inherent in the Clause—that the State must not arbitrarily inflict a severe punishment. This principle derives from the notion that the State does not respect human dignity when, without reason, it inflicts upon some people a severe punishment that it does not inflict upon others. Indeed, the very words "cruel and unusual punishments" imply condemnation of the arbitrary infliction of severe punishments. And, as we now know, the English history of the Clause reveals a particular concern with the establishment of a safeguard against arbitrary punishments.

A third principle inherent in the Clause is that a severe punishment must not be unacceptable to contemporary society. Rejection by society, of course, is a strong indication that a severe punishment does not comport with human dignity. In applying this principle, however, we must make certain that the judicial determination is as objective as possible.

The question under this principle, then, is whether there are objective indicators from which a court can conclude that contemporary society considers a severe punishment unacceptable. Accordingly, the judicial task is to review the history of a challenged punishment and to examine society's present practices with respect to its use. Legislative authorization, of course, does not establish acceptance. The acceptability of a severe punishment is measured, not by its availability, for it might become so offensive to society as never to be inflicted, but by its use.

The final principle inherent in the Clause is that a severe punishment must not be excessive. A punishment is excessive under this principle if it is unnecessary: The infliction of a severe punishment by the State cannot comport with human dignity when it is nothing more than the pointless infliction of suffering. If there is a significantly less severe punishment adequate to achieve the purposes for which the punishment is inflicted, the punishment inflicted is unnecessary and therefore excessive.

The test, then, will ordinarily be a cumulative one: If a punishment is unusually severe, if there is a strong probability that it is inflicted arbitrarily, if it is substantially rejected by contemporary society, and if there is no reason to believe that it serves any penal purpose more effectively than some less severe punishment, then the continued infliction of that punishment violates the command of the Clause that the State may not inflict inhuman and uncivilized punishments upon those convicted of crimes.

The punishment challenged in these cases is death. Death, of course, is a "traditional" punishment, one that "has been employed throughout our history," and its constitutional background is accordingly an appropriate subject of inquiry. The question is whether the deliberate infliction of death is today consistent with the command of the Clause that the State may not inflict punishments that do not comport with human dignity. I will analyze the punishment of death in terms of the principles set out above and the cumulative test to which they lead: It is a denial of human dignity for the State arbitrarily to subject a person to an unusually severe punishment that society has indicated it does not regard as acceptable, and that cannot be shown to serve any penal purpose more effectively than a significantly less drastic punishment. Under these principles and this test, death is today a "cruel and unusual" punishment.

Death is a unique punishment in the United States. In a society that so strongly affirms the sanctity of life, not surprisingly the common view is that death is the ultimate sanction. This natural human feeling appears all about us. There has been no national debate about punishment, in general or by imprisonment, comparable to the debate about the punishment of death. No other punishment has been so continuously restricted, nor has any State yet abolished prisons, as some have abolished this punishment.

The only explanation for the uniqueness of death is its extreme severity. Death is today an unusually severe punishment, unusual in its pain, in its finality, and in its enormity. No other existing punishment is comparable to death in terms of physical and mental suffering. Although our information is not conclusive, it appears that there is no method available that guarantees an immediate and pain-less death. Since the discontinuance of flogging as a constitutionally permissible punishment, death remains as the only punishment that may involve the con-scious infliction of physical pain. In addition, we know that mental pain is an inseparable part of our practice of punishing criminals by death, for the prospect of pending execution exacts a frightful toll during the inevitable long wait be-tween the imposition of sentence and the actual infliction of death.

The unusual severity of death is manifested most clearly in its finality and enormity. Death, in these respects, is in a class by itself.

Death is truly an awesome punishment. The calculated killing of a human being by the State involves, by its very nature, a denial of the executed person's humanity. The contrast with the plight of a person punished by imprisonment is evident. An individual in prison does not lose "the right to have rights." A pris-oner remains a member of the human family. Moreover, he retains the right of access to the courts. His punishment is not irrevocable. Apart from the common charge, grounded upon the recognition of human fallibility, that the punish-ment of death must inevitably be inflicted upon innocent men, we know that death has been the lot of men whose convictions were unconstitutionally secured in view of later, retroactively applied, holdings of this Court. The punishment it-self may have been unconstitutionally inflicted, yet the finality of death precludes relief. An executed person has indeed "lost the right to have rights." As one 19th century proponent of punishing criminals by death declared, "When a man is hung, there is an end of our relations with him. His execution is a way of saying, 'You are not fit for this world, take your chance elsewhere.'"

In comparison to all other punishments today, then, the deliberate extin-guishment of human life by the State is uniquely degrading to human dignity. I would not hesitate to hold, on that ground alone, that death is today a "cruel and unusual" punishment, were it not that death is a punishment of longstand-ing usage and acceptance in this country. I therefore turn to the second princi-ple—that the State may not arbitrarily inflict an unusually severe punishment.

The outstanding characteristic of our present practice of punishing criminals by death is the infrequency with which we resort to it. The evidence is conclu-sive that death is not the ordinary punishment for any crime.

There has been a steady decline in the infliction of this punishment in every decade since the 1930's, the earliest period for which accurate statistics are available. In the 1930's, executions averaged 167 per year; in the 1940's, the average was 128; in the 1950's, it was 72; and in the years 1960–1962, it was 48. There have been a total of 46 executions since then, 36 of them in 1963–1964. Yet our population and the number of capital crimes committed have increased greatly over the past four decades. The contemporary rarity of the infliction of this punishment is thus the end result of a long-continued decline.

When a country of over 200 million people inflicts an unusually severe punishment no more than 50 times a year, the inference is strong that the punishment is not being regularly and fairly applied. To dispel it would indeed require a clear showing of nonarbitrary infliction.

Although there are no exact figures available, we know that thousands of murders and rapes are committed annually in States where death is an authorized punishment for those crimes. However the rate of infliction is characterized—as "freakishly" or "spectacularly" rare, or simply as rare—it would take the purest sophistry to deny that death is inflicted in only a minute fraction of these cases. How much rarer, after all, could the infliction of death be?

When the punishment of death is inflicted in a trivial number of the cases in which it is legally available, the conclusion is virtually inescapable that it is being inflicted arbitrarily. Indeed, it smacks of little more than a lottery system. The States claim, however, that this rarity is evidence not of arbitrariness, but of informed selectivity: Death is inflicted, they say, only in "extreme" cases.

Informed selectivity, of course, is a value not to be denigrated. Yet presumably the States could make precisely the same claim if there were 10 executions per year, or five, or even if there were but one. That there may be as many as 50 per year does not strengthen the claim. When the rate of infliction is at this low level, it is highly implausible that only the worst criminals or the criminals who commit the worst crimes are selected for this punishment. No one has yet suggested a rational basis that could differentiate in those terms the few who die from the many who go to prison. Crimes and criminals simply do not admit of a distinction that can be drawn so finely as to explain, on that ground, the execution of such a tiny sample of those eligible. Certainly the laws that provide for this punishment do not attempt to draw that distinction; all cases to which the laws apply are necessarily "extreme." Nor is the distinction credible in fact. If, for example, petitioner Furman or his crime illustrates the "extreme," then nearly all murderers and their murders are also "extreme."

Although it is difficult to imagine what further facts would be necessary in order to prove that death is, as my Brother Stewart puts it, "wantonly and freakishly" inflicted, I need not conclude that arbitrary infliction is patently obvious. I am not considering this punishment by the isolated light of one principle. The probability of arbitrariness is sufficiently substantial that it can be relied upon, in combination with the other principles, in reaching a judgment on the constitutionality of this punishment.

When there is a strong probability that an unusually severe and degrading punishment is being inflicted arbitrarily, we may well expect that society will disapprove of its infliction. I turn, therefore, to the third principle. An examination of the history and present operation of the American practice of punishing criminals by death reveals that this punishment has been almost totally rejected by contemporary society.

Our practice of punishing criminals by death has changed greatly over the years. One significant change has been in our methods of inflicting death. Although this country never embraced the more violent and repulsive methods employed in England, we did for a long time rely almost exclusively upon the gallows and the firing squad. Since the development of the supposedly more humane methods of electrocution late in the 19th century and lethal gas in the 20th, however, hanging and shooting have virtually ceased. Our concern for decency and human dignity, moreover, has compelled changes in the circumstances surrounding the execution itself. No longer does our society countenance the spectacle of public executions, once thought desirable as a deterrent to criminal behavior by others. Today we reject public executions as debasing and brutalizing to us all.

Also significant is the drastic decrease in the crimes for which the punishment of death is actually inflicted. While esoteric capital crimes remain on the books, since 1930 murder and rape have accounted for nearly 99% of the total executions, and murder alone for about 87%. In addition, the crime of capital murder has itself been limited. In consequence, virtually all death sentences today are discretionarily imposed. Finally, it is significant that nine States no longer inflict the punishment of death under any circumstances, and five others have restricted it to extremely rare crimes.

Thus, although "the death penalty has been employed throughout our history," in fact the history of this punishment is one of successive restriction. What was once a common punishment has become, in the context of a continuing moral debate, increasingly rare. The evolution of this punishment evidences, not that it is an inevitable part of the American scene, but that it has proved progressively more troublesome to the national conscience. The result of this movement is our current system of administering the punishment, under which death sentences are rarely imposed and death is even more rarely inflicted.

The progressive decline in, and the current rarity of, the infliction of death demonstrate that our society seriously questions the appropriateness of this punishment today. The States point out that many legislatures authorize death as the punishment for certain crimes and that substantial segments of the public, as reflected in opinion polls and referendum votes, continue to support it. Yet the availability of this punishment through statutory authorization, as well as the polls and referenda, which amount simply to approval of that authorization, simply underscores the extent to which our society has in fact rejected this punishment. When an unusually severe punishment is authorized for wide-scale application but not, because of society's refusal, inflicted save in a few instances, the inference is compelling that there is a deep-seated reluctance to inflict it. Indeed, the likelihood is great that the punishment is tolerated only because of its disuse. The objective indicator of society's view of an unusually severe punishment is what society does with it, and today society will inflict death upon only a small sample of the eligible criminals. Rejection could hardly be more complete without becoming absolute. At the very least, I must conclude that contemporary society views this punishment with substantial doubt.

The final principle to be considered is that an unusually severe and degrading punishment may not be excessive in view of the purposes for which it is inflicted. This principle, too, is related to the others. When there is a strong probability that the State is arbitrarily inflicting an unusually severe punishment that is subject to grave societal doubts, it is likely also that the punishment cannot be shown to be serving any penal purpose that could not be served equally well by some less severe punishment.

The States' primary claim is that death is a necessary punishment because it prevents the commission of capital crimes more effectively than any less severe punishment. The first part of this claim is that the infliction of death is necessary to stop the individuals executed from committing further crimes. The sufficient answer to this is that if a criminal convicted of a capital crime poses a danger to society, effective administration of the State's pardon and parole laws can delay or deny his release from prison, and techniques of isolation can eliminate or minimize the danger while he remains confined.

The more significant argument is that the threat of death prevents the commission of capital crimes because it deters potential criminals who would not be deterred by the threat of imprisonment. The argument is not based upon evidence that the threat of death is a superior deterrent. Indeed, as my Brother Marshall establishes, the available evidence uniformly indicates, although it does not conclusively prove, that the threat of death has no greater deterrent effect than the threat of imprisonment. The States argue, however, that they are entitled to rely upon common human experience, and that experience, they say, supports the conclusion that death must be a more effective deterrent than any less severe punishment. Because people fear death the most, the argument runs, the threat of death must be the greatest deterrent.

It is important to focus upon the precise import of this argument. It is not denied that many, and probably most, capital crimes cannot be deterred by the threat of punishment. Thus the argument can apply only to those who think rationally about the commission of capital crimes. Particularly is that true when the potential criminal, under this argument, must not only consider the risk of punishment, but also distinguish between two possible punishments. The concern, then, is with a particular type of potential criminal, the rational person who will commit a capital crime knowing that the punishment is long-term imprisonment, which may well be for the rest of his life, but will not commit the crime knowing that the punishment is death. On the face of it, the assumption that such persons exist is implausible.

In any event, this argument cannot be appraised in the abstract. We are not presented with the theoretical question whether under any imaginable circumstances the threat of death might be a greater deterrent to the commission of capital crimes than the threat of imprisonment. We are concerned with the practice of punishing criminals by death as it exists in the United States today. Proponents of this argument necessarily admit that its validity depends upon the existence of a system in which the punishment of death is invariably and swiftly imposed. Our system, of course, satisfies neither condition. A rational person contemplating a murder or rape is confronted, not with the certainty of a speedy death, but with the slightest possibility that he will be executed in the distant future. The risk of death is remote and improbable; in contrast, the risk of long-term imprisonment is near and great. In short, whatever the speculative validity of the assumption that the threat of death is a superior deterrent, there is no reason to believe that as currently administered the punishment of death is necessary to deter the commission of capital crimes. Whatever might be the case were all or substantially all eligible criminals quickly put to death, unverifiable possibilities are an insufficient basis upon which to conclude that the threat of death today has any greater deterrent efficacy than the threat of imprisonment.

There is, however, another aspect to the argument that the punishment of death is necessary for the protection of society. The infliction of death, the States urge, serves to manifest the community's outrage at the commission of the crime. It is, they say, a concrete public expression of moral indignation that inculcates respect for the law and helps assure a more peaceful community. Moreover, we are told, not only does the punishment of death exert this widespread moralizing influence upon community values, it also satisfies the popular demand for grievous condemnation of abhorrent crimes and thus prevents disorder, lynching, and attempts by private citizens to take the law into their own hands.

The question, however, is not whether death serves these supposed purposes of punishment, but whether death serves them more effectively than imprisonment. There is no evidence whatever that utilization of imprisonment rather than death encourages private blood feuds and other disorders. Surely if there were such a danger, the execution of a handful of criminals each year would not prevent it. The assertion that death alone is a sufficiently emphatic denunciation for capital crimes suffers from the same defect. If capital crimes require the punishment of death in order to provide moral reinforcement for the basic values of the community, those values can only be undermined when death is so rarely inflicted upon the criminals who commit the crimes. Furthermore, it is certainly doubtful that the infliction of death by the State does in fact strengthen the community's moral code; if the deliberate extinguishment of human life has any effect at all, it more likely tends to lower our respect for life and brutalize our values. That, after all, is why we no longer carry out public executions.

There is, then, no substantial reason to believe that the punishment of death, as currently administered, is necessary for the protection of society. The only other purpose suggested, one that is independent of protection for society, is retribution. Shortly stated, retribution in this context means that criminals are put to death because they deserve it.

As administered today, however, the punishment of death cannot be justified as a necessary means of exacting retribution from criminals. When the overwhelming number of criminals who commit capital crimes go to prison, it cannot be concluded that death serves the purpose of retribution more effectively than imprisonment. The asserted public belief that murderers and rapists deserve to die is flatly inconsistent with the execution of a random few. As the history of the punishment of death in this country shows, our society wishes to prevent crime; we have no desire to kill criminals simply to get even with them.

In sum, the punishment of death is inconsistent with all four principles: Death is an unusually severe and degrading punishment; there is a strong probability that it is inflicted arbitrarily; its rejection by contemporary society is virtually total; and there is no reason to believe that it serves any penal purpose more effectively than the less severe punishment of imprisonment. The function of these principles is to enable a court to determine whether a punishment comports with human dignity. Death, quite simply, does not.

Mr. Justice Stewart, concurring.

The penalty of death differs from all other forms of criminal punishment, not in degree but in kind. It is unique in its total irrevocability. It is unique in its rejection of rehabilitation of the convict as a basic purpose of criminal justice. And it is unique, finally, in its absolute renunciation of all that is embodied in our concept of humanity.

For these and other reasons, at least two of my Brothers have concluded that the infliction of the death penalty is constitutionally impermissible in all circumstances under the Eighth and Fourteenth Amendments. Their case is a strong one. But I find it unnecessary to reach the ultimate question they would decide.

It is clear that these sentences are "cruel" in the sense that they excessively go beyond, not in degree but in kind, the punishments that the state legislatures have determined to be necessary. It is equally clear that these sentences are "unusual" in the sense that the penalty of death is infrequently imposed for murder, and that its imposition for rape is extraordinarily rare. But I do not rest my conclusion upon these two propositions alone.

These death sentences are cruel and unusual in the same way that being struck by lightning is cruel and unusual. For, of all the people convicted of rapes and murders in 1967 and 1968, many just as reprehensible as these, the petitioners are among a capriciously selected random handful upon whom the sentence of death has in fact been imposed. My concurring Brothers have demonstrated that, if any basis can be discerned for the selection of these few to be sentenced to die, it is the constitutionally impermissible basis of race. But racial discrimination has not been proved, and I put it to one side. I simply conclude that the Eighth and Fourteenth Amendments cannot tolerate the infliction of a sentence of death under legal systems that permit this unique penalty to be so wantonly and so freakishly imposed.

Mr. Justice White, concurring.

The facial constitutionality of statutes requiring the imposition of the death penalty for first-degree murder, for more narrowly defined categories of murder, or for rape would present quite different issues under the Eighth Amendment than are posed by the cases before us. In joining the Court's judgments, therefore, I do not at all intimate that the death penalty is unconstitutional *per se* or that there is no system of capital punishment that would comport with the Eighth Amendment. That question, ably argued by several of my Brethren, is not presented by these cases and need not be decided.

The narrower question to which I address myself concerns the constitutionality of capital punishment statutes under which (1) the legislature authorizes the imposition of the death penalty for murder or rape; (2) the legislature does not itself mandate the penalty in any particular class or kind of case, but delegates to judges or juries the decisions as to those cases, if any, in which the penalty will be utilized; and (3) judges and juries have ordered the death penalty with such infrequency that the odds are now very much against imposition and execution of the penalty with respect to any convicted murderer or rapist. It is in this context that we must consider whether the execution of these petitioners would violate the Eighth Amendment.

I begin with what I consider a near truism: that the death penalty could so seldom be imposed that it would cease to be a credible deterrent or measurably to contribute to any other end of punishment in the criminal justice system. It is perhaps true that no matter how infrequently those convicted of rape or murder are executed, the penalty so imposed is not disproportionate to the crime and those executed may deserve exactly what they received. It would also be clear that executed defendants are finally and completely incapacitated from again committing rape or murder or any other crime. But when imposition of the penalty reaches a certain degree of infrequency, it would be very doubtful that any existing general need for retribution would be measurably satisfied.

Most important, a major goal of the criminal law—to deter others by punishing the convicted criminal—would not be substantially served where the penalty is so seldom invoked that it ceases to be the credible threat essential to influence the conduct of others. For present purposes I accept the morality and utility of punishing one person to influence another. I accept also the effectiveness of punishment generally and need not reject the death penalty as a more effective deterrent than a lesser punishment. But common sense and experience tell us that seldom-enforced laws become ineffective measures for controlling human conduct and that the death penalty, unless imposed with sufficient frequency, will make little contribution to deterring those crimes for which it may be exacted.

The imposition and execution of the death penalty are obviously cruel in the dictionary sense. But the penalty has not been considered cruel and unusual punishment in the constitutional sense because it was thought justified by the social ends it was deemed to serve. At the moment that it ceases realistically to further these purposes, however, the emerging question is whether its imposition in such circumstances would violate the Eighth Amendment. It is my view that it would, for its imposition would then be the pointless and needless extinction of life with only marginal contributions to any discernible social or public purposes. A penalty with such negligible returns to the State would be patently excessive and cruel and unusual punishment violative of the Eighth Amendment.

It is also my judgment that this point has been reached with respect to capital punishment as it is presently administered under the statutes involved in these cases. Concededly, it is difficult to prove as a general proposition that capital punishment, however administered, more effectively serves the ends of the criminal law than does imprisonment. But however that may be, I cannot avoid the conclusion that as the statutes before us are now administered, the penalty is so infrequently imposed that the threat of execution is too attenuated to be of substantial service to criminal justice.

The death penalty is exacted with great infrequency even for the most atrocious crimes and that there is no meaningful basis for distinguishing the few cases in which it is imposed from the many cases in which it is not. The short of it is that the policy of vesting sentencing authority primarily in juries—a decision largely motivated by the desire to mitigate the harshness of the law and to bring community judgment to bear on the sentence as well as guilt or innocence—has so effectively achieved its aims that capital punishment within the confines of the statutes now before us has for all practical purposes run its course.

In this respect, I add only that past and present legislative judgment with respect to the death penalty loses much of its force when viewed in light of the recurring practice of delegating sentencing authority to the jury and the fact that a jury, in its own discretion and without violating its trust or any statutory policy, may refuse to impose the death penalty no matter what the circumstances of the crime. Legislative "policy" is thus necessarily defined not by what is legislatively authorized but by what juries and judges do in exercising the discretion so regularly conferred upon them. In my judgment what was done in these cases violated the Eighth Amendment. I concur in the judgments of the Court.

Mr. Justice Marshall, concurring.

A punishment may be deemed cruel and unusual for any one of four distinct reasons. First, there are certain punishments that inherently involve so much physical pain and suffering that civilized people cannot tolerate them—*e.g.*, use of the rack, the thumbscrew, or other modes of torture. Regardless of public sentiment with respect to imposition of one of these punishments in a particular case or at any one moment in history, the Constitution prohibits it. These are punishments that have been barred since the adoption of the Bill of Rights.

Second, there are punishments that are unusual, signifying that they were previously unknown as penalties for a given offense. If these punishments are intended to serve a humane purpose, they may be constitutionally permissible. Prior decisions leave open the question of just how much the word "unusual" adds to the word "cruel." I have previously indicated that use of the word "unusual" in the English Bill of Rights of 1689 was inadvertent, and there is nothing in the history of the Eighth Amendment to give flesh to its intended meaning.

Third, a penalty may be cruel and unusual because it is excessive and serves no valid legislative purpose. The decisions previously discussed are replete with assertions that one of the primary functions of the cruel and unusual punishments clause is to prevent excessive or unnecessary penalties, these punishments are unconstitutional even though popular sentiment may favor them.

Fourth, where a punishment is not excessive and serves a valid legislative purpose, it still may be invalid if popular sentiment abhors it. For example, if the evidence clearly demonstrated that capital punishment served valid legislative purposes, such punishment would, nevertheless, be unconstitutional if citizens found it to be morally unacceptable. A general abhorrence on the part of the public would, in effect, equate a modern punishment with those barred since the adoption of the Eighth Amendment. There are no prior cases in this Court striking down a penalty on this ground, but the very notion of changing values requires that we recognize its existence.

In order to assess whether or not death is an excessive or unnecessary penalty, it is necessary to consider the reasons why a legislature might select it as punishment for one or more offenses, and examine whether less severe penalties would satisfy the legitimate legislative wants as well as capital punishment. If they would, then the death penalty is unnecessary cruelty, and, therefore, unconstitutional.

There are six purposes conceivably served by capital punishment: retribution, deterrence, prevention of repetitive criminal acts, encouragement of guilty pleas and confessions, eugenics, and economy. These are considered *seriatim* below.

A. The concept of retribution is one of the most misunderstood in all of our criminal jurisprudence. The principal source of confusion derives from the fact that, in dealing with the concept, most people confuse the question "why do men in fact punish?" with the question "what justifies men in punishing?" Men may punish for any number of reasons, but the one reason that punishment is morally good or morally justifiable is that someone has broken the law. Thus, it can correctly be said that breaking the law is the *sine qua non* of punishment, or, in other words, that we only tolerate punishment as it is imposed on one who deviates from the norm established by the criminal law.

The fact that the State may seek retribution against those who have broken its laws does not mean that retribution may then become the State's sole end in punishing. Our jurisprudence has always accepted deterrence in general, deterrence of individual recidivism, isolation of dangerous persons, and rehabilitation as proper goals of punishment. Retaliation, vengeance, and retribution have been roundly condemned as intolerable aspirations for a government in a free society.

To preserve the integrity of the Eighth Amendment, the Court has consistently denigrated retribution as a permissible goal of punishment. It is undoubtedly correct that there is a demand for vengeance on the part of many persons in a community against one who is convicted of a particularly offensive act. At times a cry is heard that morality requires vengeance to evidence society's abhorrence of the act. But the Eighth Amendment is our insulation from our baser selves. The "cruel and unusual" language limits the avenues through which vengeance can be channeled. Were this not so, the language would be empty and a return to the rack and other tortures would be possible in a given case.

B. The most hotly contested issue regarding capital punishment is whether it is better than life imprisonment as a deterrent to crime.

While the contrary position has been argued, it is my firm opinion that the death penalty is a more severe sanction than life imprisonment. Admittedly, there are some persons who would rather die than languish in prison for a lifetime. But, whether or not they should be able to choose death as an alternative is a far different question from that presented here—*i.e.*, whether the State can impose death as a punishment. Death is irrevocable; life imprisonment is not. Death, of course, makes rehabilitation impossible; life imprisonment does not. In short, death has always been viewed as the ultimate sanction, and it seems perfectly reasonable to continue to view it as such.

It must be kept in mind, then, that the question to be considered is not simply whether capital punishment is a deterrent, but whether it is a better deterrent than life imprisonment.

There is no more complex problem than determining the deterrent efficacy of the death penalty. "Capital punishment has obviously failed as a deterrent when a murder is committed. We can number its failures. But we cannot number its successes. No one can ever know how many people have refrained from murder because of the fear of being hanged." This is the nub of the problem and it is exacerbated by the paucity of useful data. The United States is more fortunate than most countries, however, in that it has what are generally considered to be the world's most reliable statistics.

Thorsten Sellin, one of the leading authorities on capital punishment, has urged that if the death penalty deters prospective murderers, the following hypotheses should be true:

(a) Murders should be less frequent in states that have the death penalty than in those that have abolished it, other factors being equal. Comparisons of this nature must be made among states that are as alike as possible in all other respects—character of population, social and economic condition, etc.—in order not to introduce factors known to influence murder rates in a serious manner but present in only one of these states.

(c) Murders should increase when the death penalty is abolished and should decline when it is restored.

(d) The deterrent effect should be greatest and should therefore affect murder rates most powerfully in those communities where the crime occurred and its consequences are most strongly brought home to the population.

(e) Law enforcement officers would be safer from murderous attacks in states that have the death penalty than in those without it.

Sellin's evidence indicates that not one of these propositions is true. Sellin's statistics demonstrate that there is no correlation between the murder rate and the presence or absence of the capital sanction. He compares States that have similar characteristics and finds that irrespective of their position on capital punishment, they have similar murder rates. In the New England States, for example, there is no correlation between executions and homicide rates. The same is true for Midwestern States, and for all others studied. Both the United Nations and Great Britain have acknowledged the validity of Sellin's statistics.

In sum, the only support for the theory that capital punishment is an effective deterrent is found in the hypotheses with which we began and the occasional stories about a specific individual being deterred from doing a contemplated criminal act. These claims of specific deterrence are often spurious, however, and may be more than counterbalanced by the tendency of capital punishment to incite certain crimes.

The United Nations Committee that studied capital punishment found that "it is generally agreed between the retentionists and abolitionists, whatever their opinions about the validity of comparative studies of deterrence, that the data which now exist show no correlation between the existence of capital punishment and lower rates of capital crime."

In light of the massive amount of evidence before us, I see no alternative but to conclude that capital punishment cannot be justified on the basis of its deterrent effect.

C. Much of what must be said about the death penalty as a device to prevent recidivism is obvious—if a murderer is executed, he cannot possibly commit another offense. The fact is, however, that murderers are extremely unlikely to commit other crimes either in prison or upon their release. For the most part, they are first offenders, and when released from prison they are known to become model citizens. Furthermore, most persons who commit capital crimes are not executed. With respect to those who are sentenced to die, it is critical to note that the jury is never asked to determine whether they are likely to be recidivists. In light of these facts, if capital punishment were justified purely on the basis of preventing recidivism, it would have to be considered to be excessive; no general need to obliterate all capital offenders could have been demonstrated, nor any specific need in individual cases.

D. The three final purposes which may underlie utilization of a capital sanction—encouraging guilty pleas and confessions, eugenics, and reducing state expenditures—may be dealt with quickly. If the death penalty is used to encourage guilty pleas and thus to deter suspects from exercising their rights under the Sixth Amendment to jury trials, it is unconstitutional.

Moreover, to the extent that capital punishment is used to encourage confessions and guilty pleas, it is not being used for punishment purposes.

In light of the previous discussion on deterrence, any suggestions concerning the eugenic benefits of capital punishment are obviously meritless. As I pointed out above, there is not even any attempt made to discover which capital offenders are likely to be recidivists, let alone which are positively incurable.

As for the argument that it is cheaper to execute a capital offender than to imprison him for life, even assuming that such an argument, if true, would support a capital sanction, it is simply incorrect. A disproportionate amount of money spent on prisons is attributable to death row. Condemned men are not productive members of the prison community, although they could be, and executions are expensive. Appeals are often automatic, and courts admittedly spend more time with death cases.

When all is said and done, there can be no doubt that it costs more to execute a man than to keep him in prison for life.

E. There is but one conclusion that can be drawn from all of this—i.e., the death penalty is an excessive and unnecessary punishment that violates the Eighth Amendment. The statistical evidence is not convincing beyond all doubt, but it is persuasive. It is not improper at this point to take judicial notice of the fact that for more than 200 years men have labored to demonstrate that capital punishment serves no purpose that life imprisonment could not serve equally well. And they have done so with great success. Little, if any, evidence has been adduced to prove the contrary. The point has now been reached at which deference to the legislatures is tantamount to abdication of our judicial roles as factfinders, judges, and ultimate arbiters of the Constitution. We know that at some point the presumption of constitutionality accorded legislative acts gives way to a realistic assessment of those acts. This point comes when there is sufficient evidence available so that judges can determine, not whether the legislature acted wisely, but whether it had any rational basis whatsoever for acting. We have this evidence before us now. There is no rational basis for concluding that capital punishment is not excessive. It therefore violates the Eighth Amendment.

In addition, even if capital punishment is not excessive, it nonetheless violates the Eighth Amendment because it is morally unacceptable to the people of the United States at this time in their history.

While a public opinion poll obviously is of some assistance in indicating public acceptance or rejection of a specific penalty, its utility cannot be very great. This is because whether or not a punishment is cruel and unusual depends, not on whether its mere mention "shocks the conscience and sense of justice of the people," but on whether people who were fully informed as to the purposes of the penalty and its liabilities would find the penalty shocking, unjust, and unacceptable.

In other words, the question with which we must deal is not whether a substantial proportion of American citizens would today, if polled, opine that capital punishment is barbarously cruel, but whether they would find it to be so in the light of all information presently available.

It has often been noted that American citizens know almost nothing about capital punishment. Some of the conclusions arrived at in the preceding section and the supporting evidence would be critical to an informed judgment on the morality of the death penalty.

This information would almost surely convince the average citizen that the death penalty was unwise, but a problem arises as to whether it would convince him that the penalty was morally reprehensible. This problem arises from the fact that the public's desire for retribution, even though this is a goal that the legislature cannot constitutionally pursue as its sole justification for capital punishment, might influence the citizenry's view of the morality of capital punishment. The solution to the problem lies in the fact that no one has ever seriously advanced retribution as a legitimate goal of our society. Defenses of capital punishment are always mounted on deterrent or other similar theories. This should not be surprising. It is the people of this country who have urged in the past that prisons rehabilitate as well as isolate offenders, and it is the people who have injected a sense of purpose into our penology. I cannot believe that at this stage in our history, the American people would ever knowingly support purposeless vengeance. Thus, I believe that the great mass of citizens would conclude on the basis of the material already considered that the death penalty is immoral and therefore unconstitutional.

But, if this information needs supplementing, I believe that the following facts would serve to convince even the most hesitant of citizens to condemn death as a sanction: capital punishment is imposed discriminatorily against certain identifiable classes of people; there is evidence that innocent people have been executed before their innocence can be proved; and the death penalty wreaks havoc with our entire criminal justice system.

Assuming knowledge of all the facts presently available regarding capital punishment, the average citizen would, in my opinion, find it shocking to his conscience and sense of justice. For this reason alone capital punishment cannot stand.

There is too much crime, too much killing, too much hatred in this country. If the legislatures could eradicate these elements from our lives by utilizing capital punishment, then there would be a valid purpose for the sanction and the public would surely accept it. It would be constitutional. As the Chief Justice and Mr. Justice Powell point out, however, capital punishment has been with us a long time. What purpose has it served? The evidence is that it has served none. I cannot agree that the American people have been so hardened, so embittered that they want to take the life of one who performs even the basest criminal act knowing that the execution is nothing more than bloodlust. This has not been my experience with my fellow citizens. Rather, I have found that they earnestly desire their system of punishments to make sense in order that it can be a morally justifiable system.

Mr. Chief Justice Burger, with whom Mr. Justice Blackmun, Mr. Justice Powell, and Mr. Justice Rehnquist join, dissenting.

I

If we were possessed of legislative power, I would either join with Mr. Justice Brennan and Mr. Justice Marshall or, at the very least, restrict the use of capital punishment to a small category of the most heinous crimes. Our constitutional inquiry, however, must be divorced from personal feelings as to the morality and efficacy of the death penalty, and be confined to the meaning and applicability of the uncertain language of the Eighth Amendment. It is essential to our role as a court that we not seize upon the enigmatic character of the guarantee as an invitation to enact our personal predilections into law.

The Eighth Amendment forbids "cruel and unusual punishments." In my view, these words cannot be read to outlaw capital punishment because that penalty was in common use and authorized by law here and in the countries from which our ancestors came at the time the Amendment was adopted. It is inconceivable to me that the framers intended to end capital punishment by the Amendment.

Before recognizing such an instant evolution in the law, it seems fair to ask what factors have changed that capital punishment should now be "cruel" in the constitutional sense as it has not been in the past. It is apparent that there has been no change of constitutional significance in the nature of the punishment itself. Twentieth century modes of execution surely involve no greater physical suffering than the means employed at the time of the Eighth Amendment's adoption. And although a man awaiting execution must inevitably experience extraordinary mental anguish, no one suggests that this anguish is materially different from that experienced by condemned men in 1791, even though protracted appellate review processes have greatly increased the waiting time on "death row." To be sure, the ordeal of the condemned man may be thought cruel in the sense that all suffering is thought cruel. But if the Constitution proscribed every punishment producing severe emotional stress, then capital punishment would clearly have been impermissible in 1791.

However, the inquiry cannot end here. For reasons unrelated to any change in intrinsic cruelty, the Eighth Amendment prohibition cannot fairly be limited to those punishments thought excessively cruel and barbarous at the time of the adoption of the Eighth Amendment. A punishment is inordinately cruel, in the sense we must deal with it in these cases, chiefly as perceived by the society so characterizing it. Nevertheless, the Court up to now has never actually held that a punishment has become impermissibly cruel due to a shift in the weight of accepted social values; nor has the Court suggested judicially manageable criteria for measuring such a shift in moral consensus.

The Court's quiescence in this area can be attributed to the fact that in a democratic society legislatures, not courts, are constituted to respond to the will and consequently the moral values of the people.

I do not suggest that the validity of legislatively authorized punishments presents no justifiable issue under the Eighth Amendment, but, rather, that the primacy of the legislative role narrowly confines the scope of judicial inquiry. Whether or not provable, and whether or not true at all times, in a democracy the legislative judgment is presumed to embody the basic standards of decency prevailing in the society. This presumption can only be negated by unambiguous and compelling evidence of legislative default.

III

There are no obvious indications that capital punishment offends the conscience of society to such a degree that our traditional deference to the legislative judgment must be abandoned. It is not a punishment such as burning at the stake that everyone would ineffably find to be repugnant to all civilized standards. Nor is it a punishment so roundly condemned that only a few aberrant legislatures have retained it on the statute books. Capital punishment is authorized by statute in 40 States, the District of Columbia, and in the federal courts for the commission of certain crimes. On four occasions in the last 11 years Congress has added to the list of federal crimes punishable by death. In looking for reliable indicia of contemporary attitude, none more trustworthy has been advanced.

One conceivable source of evidence that legislatures have abdicated their essentially barometric role with respect to community values would be public opinion polls, of which there have been many in the past decade addressed to the question of capital punishment. Without assessing the reliability of such polls, or intimating that any judicial reliance could ever be placed on them, it need only be noted that the reported results have shown nothing approximating the universal condemnation of capital punishment that might lead us to suspect that the legislatures in general have lost touch with current social values.

Counsel for petitioners rely on a different body of empirical evidence. They argue, in effect, that the number of cases in which the death penalty is imposed, as compared with the number of cases in which it is statutorily available, reflects a general revulsion toward the penalty that would lead to its repeal if only it were more generally and widely enforced. It cannot be gainsaid that by the choice of juries—and sometimes judges—the death penalty is imposed in far fewer than half the cases in which it is available. To go further and characterize the rate of imposition as "freakishly rare," as petitioners insist, is unwarranted hyperbole. And regardless of its characterization, the rate of imposition does not impel the conclusion that capital punishment is now regarded as intolerably cruel or uncivilized.

It is argued that in those capital cases where juries have recommended mercy, they have given expression to civilized values and effectively renounced the legislative authorization for capital punishment. At the same time it is argued that where juries have made the awesome decision to send men to their deaths, they have acted arbitrarily and without sensitivity to prevailing standards of decency.

The selectivity of juries in imposing the punishment of death is properly viewed as a refinement on, rather than a repudiation of, the statutory authorization for that penalty. Legislatures prescribe the categories of crimes for which the death penalty should be available, and, acting as "the conscience of the community," juries are entrusted to determine in individual cases that the ultimate punishment is warranted. Juries are undoubtedly influenced in this judgment by myriad factors. It is hardly surprising that juries have been increasingly meticulous in their imposition of the penalty. But to assume from the mere fact of relative infrequency that only a random assortment of pariahs are sentenced to death, is to cast grave doubt on the basic integrity of our jury system.

It would, of course, be unrealistic to assume that juries have been perfectly consistent in choosing the cases where the death penalty is to be imposed, for no human institution performs with perfect consistency. There are doubtless prisoners on death row who would not be there had they been tried before a different jury or in a different State. In this sense their fate has been controlled by a fortuitous circumstance. However, this element of fortuity does not stand as an indictment either of the general functioning of juries in capital cases or of the integrity of jury decisions in individual cases. There is no empirical basis for concluding that juries have generally failed to discharge in good faith the responsibility described in *Witherspoon*—that of choosing between life and death in individual cases according to the dictates of community values.

The rate of imposition of death sentences falls far short of providing the requisite unambiguous evidence that the legislatures of 40 States and the Congress have turned their backs on current or evolving standards of decency in continuing to make the death penalty available.

IV

Capital punishment has also been attacked as violative of the Eighth Amendment on the ground that it is not needed to achieve legitimate penal aims and is thus "unnecessarily cruel." As a pure policy matter, this approach has much to recommend it, but it seeks to give a dimension to the Eighth Amendment that it was never intended to have and promotes a line of inquiry that this Court has never before pursued.

The Eighth Amendment was included in the Bill of Rights to guard against the use of torturous and inhuman punishments, not those of limited efficacy.

There is no authority suggesting that the Eighth Amendment was intended to purge the law of its retributive elements, and the Court has consistently assumed that retribution is a legitimate dimension of the punishment of crimes. It would be reading a great deal into the Eighth Amendment to hold that the punishments authorized by legislatures cannot constitutionally reflect a retributive purpose.

The less esoteric but no less controversial question is whether the death penalty acts as a superior deterrent. Those favoring abolition find no evidence that it does. Those favoring retention start from the intuitive notion that capital punishment should act as the most effective deterrent and note that there is no convincing evidence that it does not. Escape from this empirical stalemate is sought by placing the burden of proof on the States and concluding that they have failed to demonstrate that capital punishment is a more effective deterrent than life imprisonment. Numerous justifications have been advanced for shifting the burden, and they are not without their rhetorical appeal. However, these arguments are not descended from established constitutional principles, but are born of the urge to bypass an unresolved factual question. Comparative deterrence is not a matter that lends itself to precise measurement; to shift the burden to the States is to provide an illusory solution to an enormously complex problem. If it were proper to put the States to the test of demonstrating the deterrent value of capital punishment, we could just as well ask them to prove the need for life imprisonment or any other punishment. Yet I know of no convincing evidence that life imprisonment is a more effective deterrent than 20 years' imprisonment, or even that a $10 parking ticket is a more effective deterrent than a $5 parking ticket. In fact, there are some who go so far as to challenge the notion that any punishments deter crime. If the States are unable to adduce convincing proof rebutting such assertions, does it then follow that all punishments are suspect as being "cruel and unusual" within the meaning of the Constitution? On the contrary, I submit that the questions raised by the necessity approach are beyond the pale of judicial inquiry under the Eighth Amendment.

V

The critical factor in the concurring opinions of both Mr. Justice Stewart and Mr. Justice White is the infrequency with which the penalty is imposed. This factor is taken not as evidence of society's abhorrence of capital punishment—the inference that petitioners would have the Court draw—but as the earmark of a deteriorated system of sentencing. It is concluded that petitioners' sentences must be set aside, not because the punishment is impermissibly cruel, but because juries and judges have failed to exercise their sentencing discretion in acceptable fashion.

While I would not undertake to make a definitive statement as to the parameters of the Court's ruling, it is clear that if state legislatures and the Congress wish to maintain the availability of capital punishment, significant statutory changes will have to be made. Since the two pivotal concurring opinions turn on the assumption that the punishment of death is now meted out in a random and unpredictable manner, legislative bodies may seek to bring their laws into compliance with the Court's ruling by providing standards for juries and judges to follow in determining the sentence in capital cases or by more narrowly defining the crimes for which the penalty is to be imposed.

Real change could clearly be brought about if legislatures provided mandatory death sentences in such a way as to deny juries the opportunity to bring in a verdict on a lesser charge; under such a system, the death sentence could only be avoided by a verdict of acquittal. If this is the only alternative that the legislatures can safely pursue under today's ruling, I would have preferred that the Court opt for total abolition.

It seems remarkable to me that with our basic trust in lay jurors as the keystone in our system of criminal justice, it should now be suggested that we take the most sensitive and important of all decisions away from them. I could more easily be persuaded that mandatory sentences of death, without the intervening and ameliorating impact of lay jurors, are so arbitrary and doctrinaire that they violate the Constitution. The very infrequency of death penalties imposed by jurors attests their cautious and discriminating reservation of that penalty for the most extreme cases.

VI

Since there is no majority of the Court on the ultimate issue presented in these cases, the future of capital punishment in this country has been left in an uncertain limbo. Rather than providing a final and unambiguous answer on the basic constitutional question, the collective impact of the majority's ruling is to demand an undetermined measure of change from the various state legislatures and the Congress. While I cannot endorse the process of decision making that has yielded today's result and the restraints that that result imposes on legislative action, I am not altogether displeased that legislative bodies have been given the opportunity, and indeed unavoidable responsibility, to make a thorough re-evaluation of the entire subject of capital punishment. If today's opinions demonstrate nothing else, they starkly show that this is an area where legislatures can act far more effectively than courts.

The legislatures are free to eliminate capital punishment for specific crimes or to carve out limited exceptions to a general abolition of the penalty, without adherence to the conceptual strictures of the Eighth Amendment. The legislatures can and should make an assessment of the deterrent influence of capital punishment, both generally and as affecting the commission of specific types of crimes. If legislatures come to doubt the efficacy of capital punishment, they can abolish it, either completely or on a selective basis. If new evidence persuades them that they have acted unwisely, they can reverse their field and reinstate the penalty to the extent it is thought warranted. An Eighth Amendment ruling by judges cannot be made with such flexibility or discriminating precision.

The world-wide trend toward limiting the use of capital punishment, a phenomenon to which we have been urged to give great weight, hardly points the way to a judicial solution in this country under a written Constitution. Rather, the change has generally come about through legislative action, often on a trial basis and with the retention of the penalty for certain limited classes of crimes. Virtually nowhere has change been wrought by so crude a tool as the Eighth Amendment. The complete and unconditional abolition of capital punishment in this country by judicial fiat would have undermined the careful progress of the legislative trend and foreclosed further inquiry on many as yet unanswered questions in this area.

Mr. Justice Blackmun, dissenting.

Cases such as these provide for me an excruciating agony of the spirit. I yield to no one in the depth of my distaste, antipathy, and, indeed, abhorrence, for the death penalty, with all its aspects of physical distress and fear and of moral judgment exercised by finite minds. That distaste is buttressed by a belief that capital punishment serves no useful purpose that can be demonstrated. For me, it violates childhood's training and life's experiences, and is not compatible with the philosophical convictions I have been able to develop. It is antagonistic to any sense of "reverence for life." Were I a legislator, I would vote against the death penalty for the policy reasons argued by counsel for the respective petitioners and expressed and adopted in the several opinions filed by the Justices who vote to reverse these judgments.

My problem, however, is the suddenness of the Court's perception of progress in the human attitude since decisions of only a short while ago.

To reverse the judgments in these cases is, of course, the easy choice. It is easier to strike the balance in favor of life and against death. It is comforting to relax in the thoughts—perhaps the rationalizations—that this is the compassionate decision for a maturing society; that this is the moral and the "right" thing to do; that thereby we convince ourselves that we are moving down the road toward human decency; that we value life even though that life has taken another or others or has grievously scarred another or others and their families; and that we are less barbaric than we were in 1879, or in 1890, or in 1910, or in 1947, or in 1958, or in 1963, or a year ago, in 1971, when *Wilkerson, Kemmler, Weems, Francis, Trop, Rudolph*, and *McGautha* were respectively decided.

This, for me, is good argument, and it makes some sense. But it is good argument and it makes sense only in a legislative and executive way and not as a judicial expedient.

I do not sit on these cases, however, as a legislator, responsive, at least in part, to the will of constituents. Our task here, as must so frequently be emphasized and re-emphasized, is to pass upon the constitutionality of legislation that has been enacted and that is challenged. This is the sole task for judges. We should not allow our personal preferences as to the wisdom of legislative and congressional action, or our distaste for such action, to guide our judicial decision in cases such as these. The temptations to cross that policy line are very great. In fact, as today's decision reveals, they are almost irresistible.

Although personally I may rejoice at the Court's result, I find it difficult to accept or to justify as a matter of history, of law, or of constitutional pronouncement. I fear the Court has overstepped. It has sought and has achieved an end.

Mr. Justice Powell, with whom the Chief Justice, Mr. Justice Blackmun, and Mr. Justice Rehnquist join, dissenting.

Perhaps enough has been said to demonstrate the unswerving position that this Court has taken in opinions spanning the last hundred years. On virtually every occasion that any opinion has touched on the question of the constitutionality of the death penalty, it has been asserted affirmatively, or tacitly assumed, that the Constitution does not prohibit the penalty. No Justice of the Court, until today, has dissented from this consistent reading of the Constitution. The petitioners in these cases now before the Court cannot fairly avoid the weight of this substantial body of precedent merely by asserting that there is no prior decision precisely in point. *Stare decisis*, if it is a doctrine founded on principle, surely applies where there exists a long line of cases endorsing or necessarily assuming the validity of a particular matter of constitutional interpretation. Those who now resolve to set those views aside indeed have a heavy burden.

Petitioners seek to avoid the authority of the foregoing cases, and the weight of express recognition in the Constitution itself, by reasoning which will not withstand analysis. We are not asked to consider the permissibility of any of the several methods employed in carrying out the death sentence. Nor are we asked, at least as part of the core submission in these cases, to determine whether the penalty might be a grossly excessive punishment for some specific criminal conduct. Either inquiry would call for a discriminating evaluation of particular means, or of the relationship between particular conduct and its punishment. Petitioners' principal argument goes far beyond the traditional process of case-by-case inclusion and exclusion. Instead the argument insists on an unprecedented constitutional rule of absolute prohibition of capital punishment for any crime, regardless of its depravity and impact on society. In calling for a precipitate and final judicial end to this form of penalty as offensive to evolving standards of decency, petitioners would have this Court abandon the traditional and more refined approach consistently followed in its prior Eighth Amendment precedents. What they are saying, in effect, is that the evolutionary process has come suddenly to an end; that the ultimate wisdom as to the appropriateness of capital punishment under all circumstances, and for all future generations, has somehow been revealed.

The prior opinions of this Court point with great clarity to reasons why those of us who sit on this Court at a particular time should act with restraint before assuming, contrary to a century of precedent, that we now know the answer for all time to come.

"Rigorous observance of the difference between limits of power and wise exercise of power—between questions of authority and questions of prudence—requires the most alert appreciation of this decisive but subtle relationship of two concepts that too easily coalesce. No less does it require a disciplined will to adhere to the difference. It is not easy to stand aloof and allow want of wisdom to prevail, to disregard one's own strongly held view of what is wise in the conduct of affairs. But it is not the business of this Court to pronounce policy. It must observe a fastidious regard for limitations on its own power, and this precludes the Court's giving effect to its own notions of what is wise or politic. That self-restraint is of the essence in the observance of the judicial oath, for the Constitution has not authorized the judges to sit in judgment on the wisdom of what Congress and the Executive Branch do."

Petitioners' contentions are premised, as indicated above, on the long-accepted view that concepts embodied in the Eighth and Fourteenth Amendments evolve. They present, with skill and persistence, a list of "objective indicators" which are said to demonstrate that prevailing standards of human decency have progressed to the final point of requiring the Court to hold, for all cases and for all time, that capital punishment is unconstitutional.

Any attempt to discern contemporary standards of decency through the review of objective factors must take into account several overriding considerations which petitioners choose to discount or ignore. In a democracy the first indicator of the public's attitude must always be found in the legislative judgments of the people's chosen representatives. Mr. Justice Marshall's opinion today catalogues the salient statistics. Forty States, the District of Columbia, and the Federal Government still authorize the death penalty for a wide variety of crimes. That number has remained relatively static since the end of World War I. That does not mean, however, that capital punishment has become a forgotten issue in the legislative arena. As recently as January, 1971, Congress approved the death penalty for congressional assassination. In 1965 Congress added the death penalty for presidential and vice presidential assassinations. Additionally, the aircraft piracy statute passed in 1961 also carries the death penalty.

This recent history of activity with respect to legislation concerning the death penalty abundantly refutes the abolitionist position.

The second and even more direct source of information reflecting the public's attitude toward capital punishment is the jury.

During the 1960's juries returned in excess of a thousand death sentences, a rate of approximately two per week. Whether it is true that death sentences were returned in less than 10% of the cases as petitioners estimate or whether some higher percentage is more accurate, these totals simply do not support petitioners' assertion at oral argument that "the death penalty is virtually unanimously repudiated and condemned by the conscience of contemporary society." It is also worthy of note that the annual rate of death sentences has remained relatively constant over the last 10 years and that the figure for 1970—127 sentences—is the highest annual total since 1961. It is true that the sentencing rate might be expected to rise, rather than remain constant, when the number of violent crimes increases as it has in this country. And it may be conceded that the constancy in these statistics indicates the unwillingness of juries to demand the ultimate penalty in many cases where it might be imposed. But these considerations fall short of indicating that juries are imposing the death penalty with such rarity as to justify this Court in reading into this circumstance a public rejection of capital punishment.

One must conclude, contrary to petitioners' submission, that the indicators most likely to reflect the public's view—legislative bodies, state referenda and the juries which have the actual responsibility—do not support the contention that evolving standards of decency require total abolition of capital punishment. Indeed, the weight of the evidence indicates that the public generally has not accepted either the morality or the social merit of the views so passionately advocated by the articulate spokesmen for abolition. But however one may assess the amorphous ebb and flow of public opinion generally on this volatile issue, this type of inquiry lies at the periphery—not the core—of the judicial process in constitutional cases. The assessment of popular opinion is essentially a legislative, not a judicial, function.

Petitioners seek to salvage their thesis by arguing that the infrequency and discriminatory nature of the actual resort to the ultimate penalty tend to diffuse public opposition. We are told that the penalty is imposed exclusively on uninfluential minorities—"the poor and powerless, personally ugly and socially unacceptable." It is urged that this pattern of application assures that large segments of the public will be either uninformed or unconcerned and will have no reason to measure the punishment against prevailing moral standards.

Apart from the impermissibility of basing a constitutional judgment of this magnitude on such speculative assumptions, the argument suffers from other defects. If, as petitioners urge, we are to engage in speculation, it is not at all certain that the public would experience deep-felt revulsion if the States were to execute as many sentenced capital offenders this year as they executed in the mid-1930's. It seems more likely that public reaction, rather than being characterized by undifferentiated rejection, would depend upon the facts and circumstances surrounding each particular case.

As Mr. Justice Marshall's opinion today demonstrates, the argument does have a troubling aspect. It is his contention that if the average citizen were aware of the disproportionate burden of capital punishment borne by the "poor, the ignorant, and the underprivileged," he would find the penalty "shocking to his conscience and sense of justice" and would not stand for its further use.

Certainly the claim is justified that this criminal sanction falls more heavily on the relatively impoverished and underprivileged elements of society. The "have-nots" in every society always have been subject to greater pressure to commit crimes and to fewer constraints than their more affluent fellow citizens. This is, indeed, a tragic byproduct of social and economic deprivation, but it is not an argument of constitutional proportions under the Eighth or Fourteenth Amendment. The same discriminatory impact argument could be made with equal force and logic with respect to those sentenced to prison terms. The Due Process Clause admits of no distinction between the deprivation of "life" and the deprivation of "liberty." If discriminatory impact renders capital punishment cruel and unusual, it likewise renders invalid most of the prescribed penalties for crimes of violence. The root causes of the higher incidence of criminal penalties on "minorities and the poor" will not be cured by abolishing the system of penalties. Nor, indeed, could any society have a viable system of criminal justice if sanctions were abolished or ameliorated because most of those who commit crimes happen to be underprivileged. The basic problem results not from the penalties imposed for criminal conduct but from social and economic factors that have plagued humanity since the beginning of recorded history, frustrating all efforts to create in any country at any time the perfect society in which there are no "poor," no "minorities" and no "underprivileged." The causes underlying this problem are unrelated to the constitutional issue before the Court.

Petitioner urges that capital punishment is cruel and unusual because it no longer serves any rational legislative interests. Before turning to consider whether any of the traditional aims of punishment justify the death penalty, I should make clear the context in which I approach this aspect of the cases.

First, I find no support—in the language of the Constitution, in its history, or in the cases arising under it—for the view that this Court may invalidate a category of penalties because we deem less severe penalties adequate to serve the ends of penology.

Secondly, if we were free to question the justifications for the use of capital punishment, a heavy burden would rest on those who attack the legislatures' judgments to prove the lack of rational justifications.

I come now to consider, subject to the reservations above expressed, the two justifications most often cited for the retention of capital punishment. The concept of retribution—though popular for centuries—is now criticized as unworthy of a civilized people. Yet this Court has acknowledged the existence of a retributive element in criminal sanctions and has never heretofore found it impermissible.

While retribution alone may seem an unworthy justification in a moral sense, its utility in a system of criminal justice requiring public support has long been recognized. Lord Justice Denning, now Master of the Rolls of the Court of Appeal in England, testified on this subject before the British Royal Commission on Capital Punishment:

Many are inclined to test the efficacy of punishment solely by its value as a deterrent: but this is too narrow a view. Punishment is the way in which society expresses its denunciation of wrong doing: and, in order to maintain respect for law, it is essential that the punishment inflicted for grave crimes should adequately reflect the revulsion felt by the great majority of citizens for them. The truth is that some crimes are so outrageous that society insists on adequate punishment, because the wrong-doer deserves it, irrespective of whether it is a deterrent or not.

Deterrence is a more appealing justification, although opinions again differ widely. Indeed, the deterrence issue lies at the heart of much of the debate between the abolitionists and retentionists. Statistical studies, based primarily on trends in States that have abolished the penalty, tend to support the view that the death penalty has not been proved to be a superior deterrent. Some dispute the validity of this conclusion, pointing out that the studies do not show that the death penalty has no deterrent effect on any categories of crimes. On the basis of the literature and studies currently available, I find myself in agreement with the conclusions drawn by the Royal Commission following its exhaustive study of this issue:

> *Prima facie the penalty of death is likely to have a stronger effect as a deterrent to normal human beings than any other form of punishment, and there is some evidence (though no convincing statistical evidence) that this is in fact so. But this effect does not operate universally or uniformly, and there are many offenders on whom it is limited and may often be negligible. It is accordingly important to view this question in a just perspective and not base a penal policy in relation to murder on exaggerated estimates of the uniquely deterrent force of the death penalty.*

As I noted at the outset of this section, legislative judgments as to the efficacy of particular punishments are presumptively rational and may not be struck down under the Eighth Amendment because this Court may think that some alternative sanction would be more appropriate. While the evidence and arguments advanced by petitioners might have proved profoundly persuasive if addressed to a legislative body, they do not approach the showing traditionally required before a court declares that the legislature has acted irrationally.

I now return to the overriding question in these cases: whether this Court, acting in conformity with the Constitution, can justify its judgment to abolish capital punishment as heretofore known in this country. It is important to keep in focus the enormity of the step undertaken by the Court today. Not only does it invalidate hundreds of state and federal laws, it deprives those jurisdictions of the power to legislate with respect to capital punishment in the future, except in a manner consistent with the cloudily outlined views of those Justices who do not purport to undertake total abolition. Nothing short of an amendment to the United States Constitution can reverse the Court's judgments.

With deference and respect for the views of the Justices who differ, it seems to me that all these studies—both in this country and elsewhere—suggest that, as a matter of policy and precedent, this is a classic case for the exercise of our oft-announced allegiance to judicial restraint. I know of no case in which greater gravity and delicacy have attached to the duty that this Court is called on to perform whenever legislation—state or federal—is challenged on constitutional grounds. It seems to me that the sweeping judicial action undertaken today reflects a basic lack of faith and confidence in the democratic process. Many may regret, as I do, the failure of some legislative bodies to address the capital punishment issue with greater frankness or effectiveness. Many might decry their failure either to abolish the penalty entirely or selectively, or to establish standards for its enforcement. But impatience with the slowness, and even the unresponsiveness, of legislatures is no justification for judicial intrusion upon their historic powers.

Mr. Justice Rehnquist, with whom the Chief Justice, Mr. Justice Blackmun, and Mr. Justice Powell join, dissenting.

The Court's judgments today strike down a penalty that our Nation's legislators have thought necessary since our country was founded. My Brothers Douglas, Brennan, and Marshall would at one fell swoop invalidate laws enacted by Congress and 40 of the 50 state legislatures, and would consign to the limbo of unconstitutionality under a single rubric penalties for offenses as varied and unique as murder, piracy, mutiny, highjacking, and desertion in the face of the enemy. Whatever its precise rationale, today's holding necessarily brings into sharp relief the fundamental question of the role of judicial review in a democratic society. How can government by the elected representatives of the people co-exist with the power of the federal judiciary, whose members are constitutionally insulated from responsiveness to the popular will, to declare invalid laws duly enacted by the popular branches of government?

The courts in cases properly before them have been entrusted under the Constitution with the last word, short of constitutional amendment, as to whether a law passed by the legislature conforms to the Constitution. But just because courts in general, and this Court in particular, do have the last word, the admonition of Mr. Justice Stone dissenting in *United States v. Butler* must be constantly borne in mind:

> *While unconstitutional exercise of power by the executive and legislative branches of the government is subject to judicial restraint, the only check upon our own exercise of power is our own sense of self-restraint.*

Rigorous attention to the limits of this Court's authority is likewise enjoined because of the natural desire that beguiles judges along with other human beings into imposing their own views of goodness, truth, and justice upon others. Judges differ only in that they have the power, if not the authority, to enforce their desires. This is doubtless why nearly two centuries of judicial precedent from this Court counsel the sparing use of that power.

A separate reason for deference to the legislative judgment is the consequence of human error on the part of the judiciary with respect to the constitutional issue before it. Human error there is bound to be, judges being men and women, and men and women being what they are. But an error in mistakenly sustaining the constitutionality of a particular enactment, while wrongfully depriving the individual of a right secured to him by the Constitution, nonetheless does so by simply letting stand a duly enacted law of a democratically chosen legislative body. The error resulting from a mistaken upholding of an individual's constitutional claim against the validity of a legislative enactment is a good deal more serious. For the result in such a case is not to leave standing a law duly enacted by a representative assembly, but to impose upon the Nation the judicial fiat of a majority of a court of judges whose connection with the popular will is remote at best.

The task of judging constitutional cases cannot for this reason be avoided, but it must surely be approached with the deepest humility and genuine deference to legislative judgment. Today's decision to invalidate capital punishment is, I respectfully submit, significantly lacking in those attributes.

Gregg v. Georgia
429 U.S. 153 (1976)

Judgment of the Court, and opinion of Mr. Justice Stewart, Mr. Justice Powell, and Mr. Justice Stevens, announced by Mr. Justice Stewart.

The issue in this case is whether the imposition of the sentence of death for the crime of murder under the law of Georgia violates the Eighth and Fourteenth Amendments.

I

The petitioner, Troy Gregg, was charged with committing armed robbery and murder. In accordance with Georgia procedure in capital cases, the trial was in two stages, a guilt stage and a sentencing stage. The evidence at the guilt trial established that on November 21, 1973, the petitioner and a traveling companion, Floyd Allen, while hitchhiking north in Florida were picked up by Fred Simmons and Bob Moore. Their car broke down, but they continued north after Simmons purchased another vehicle with some of the cash he was carrying. While still in

Florida, they picked up another hitchhiker, Dennis Weaver, who rode with them to Atlanta, where he was let out about 11 P.M. A short time later the four men interrupted their journey for a rest stop along the highway. The next morning the bodies of Simmons and Moore were discovered in a ditch nearby.

The jury found the petitioner guilty of two counts of armed robbery and two counts of murder. At the penalty stage, which took place before the same jury, neither the prosecutor nor the petitioner's lawyer offered any additional evidence. Both counsel, however, made lengthy arguments dealing generally with the propriety of capital punishment under the circumstances and with the weight of the evidence of guilt. The trial judge instructed the jury that it could recommend either a death sentence or a life prison sentence on each count. The judge further charged the jury that in determining what sentence was appropriate the jury was free to consider the facts and circumstances, if any, presented by the parties in mitigation or aggravation. Finally, the judge instructed the jury that it "would not be authorized to consider imposing the penalty of death" unless it first found beyond a reasonable doubt one of these aggravating circumstances:

> One—That the offense of murder was committed while the offender was engaged in the commission of two other capital felonies, to-wit the armed robbery of Simmons and Moore.

> Two—That the offender committed the offense of murder for the purpose of receiving money and the automobile described in the indictment.

> Three—The offense of murder was outrageously and wantonly vile, horrible and inhuman, in that they involved the depravity of the mind of the defendant.

Finding the first and second of these circumstances, the jury returned verdicts of death on each count. The Supreme Court of Georgia affirmed the convictions and the imposition of the death sentences for murder.

II

Before considering the issues presented it is necessary to understand the Georgia statutory scheme for the imposition of the death penalty. The Georgia statute, as amended after our decision in *Furman* retains the death penalty for six categories of crime: murder, kidnapping for ransom or where the victim is harmed, armed robbery, rape, treason, and aircraft hijacking. The capital defendant's guilt or innocence is determined in the traditional manner, either by a trial judge or a jury, in the first stage of a bifurcated trial.

After a verdict, finding, or plea of guilty to a capital crime, a presentence hearing is conducted before whoever made the determination of guilt. The sentencing procedures are essentially the same in both bench and jury trials. At the hearing:

> *The judge or jury shall hear additional evidence in extenuation, mitigation, and aggravation of punishment, including the record of any prior criminal convictions and pleas of guilty or pleas of nolo contendere of the defendant, or the absence of any prior conviction and pleas: Provided, however, that only such evidence in aggravation as the State has made known to the defendant prior to his trial shall be admissible. The judge or jury shall also hear argument by the de-*

fendant or his counsel and the prosecuting attorney regarding the punishment to be imposed.

The defendant is accorded substantial latitude as to the types of evidence that he may introduce. Evidence considered during the guilt stage may be considered during the sentencing stage without being resubmitted.

In the assessment of the appropriate sentence to be imposed the judge is also required to consider or to include in his instructions to the jury "any mitigating circumstances or aggravating circumstances otherwise authorized by law." The scope of the nonstatutory aggravating or mitigating circumstances is not delineated in the statute. Before a convicted defendant may be sentenced to death, however, except in cases of treason or aircraft hijacking, the jury, or the trial judge in cases tried without a jury, must find beyond a reasonable doubt one of the 10 aggravating circumstances specified in the statute. The sentence of death may be imposed only if the jury (or judge) finds one of the statutory aggravating circumstances and then elects to impose that sentence. If the verdict is death, the jury or judge must specify the aggravating circumstance(s) found. In jury cases, the trial judge is bound by the jury's recommended sentence.

In addition to the conventional appellate process available in all criminal cases, provision is made for special expedited direct review by the Supreme Court of Georgia of the appropriateness of imposing the sentence of death in the particular case. The court is directed to consider "the punishment as well as any errors enumerated by way of appeal," and to determine:

(1) Whether the sentence of death was imposed under the influence of passion, prejudice, or any other arbitrary factor, and

(3) Whether, in cases other than treason or aircraft hijacking, the evidence supports the jury's or judge's finding of a statutory aggravating circumstance, and

(4) Whether the sentence of death is excessive or disproportionate to the penalty imposed in similar cases, considering both the crime and the defendant.

If the court affirms a death sentence, it is required to include in its decision reference to similar cases that it has taken into consideration.

A transcript and complete record of the trial, as well as a separate report by the trial judge, are transmitted to the court for its use in reviewing the sentence. The report is in the form of a $6\frac{1}{2}$-page questionnaire, designed to elicit information about the defendant, the crime, and the circumstances of the trial. It requires the trial judge to characterize the trial in several ways designed to test for arbitrariness and disproportionality of sentence. Included in the report are responses to detailed questions concerning the quality of the defendant's representation, whether race played a role in the trial, and, whether, in the trial court's judgment, there was any doubt about the defendant's guilt or the appropriateness of the sentence. A copy of the report is served upon defense counsel. Under its special review authority, the court may either affirm the death sentence or remand the case for resentencing. In cases in which the death sentence is affirmed there remains the possibility of executive clemency.

III

We address initially the basic contention that the punishment of death for the crime of murder is, under all circumstances, "cruel and unusual" in violation of the Eighth and Fourteenth Amendments of the Constitution. We later consider the sentence of death imposed under the Georgia statutes at issue in this case.

The Court on a number of occasions has both assumed and asserted the constitutionality of capital punishment. But until *Furman*, the Court never confronted squarely the fundamental claim that the punishment of death always, regardless of the enormity of the offense or the procedure followed in imposing the sentence, is cruel and unusual punishment in violation of the Constitution. Although this issue was presented and addressed in *Furman*, it was not resolved by the Court. Four Justices would have held that capital punishment is not unconstitutional *per se;* two Justices would have reached the opposite conclusion; and three Justices, while agreeing that the statutes then before the Court were invalid as applied, left open the question whether such punishment may ever be imposed. We now hold that the punishment of death does not invariably violate the Constitution.

C

The imposition of the death penalty for the crime of murder has a long history of acceptance both in the United States and in England. The common-law rule imposed a mandatory death sentence on all convicted murderers. And the penalty continued to be used into the 20th century by most American States, although the breadth of the common-law rule was diminished, initially by narrowing the class of murders to be punished by death and subsequently by widespread adoption of laws expressly granting juries the discretion to recommend mercy.

It is apparent from the text of the Constitution itself that the existence of capital punishment was accepted by the Framers. At the time the Eighth Amendment was ratified, capital punishment was a common sanction in every State. Indeed, the First Congress of the United States enacted legislation providing death as the penalty for specified crimes. The Fifth Amendment, adopted at the same time as the Eighth, contemplated the continued existence of the capital sanction by imposing certain limits on the prosecution of capital cases.

Four years ago, the petitioners in *Furman* and its companion cases predicated their argument primarily upon the asserted proposition that standards of decency had evolved to the point where capital punishment no longer could be tolerated. The petitioners in those cases said, in effect, that the evolutionary process had come to an end, and that standards of decency required that the Eighth Amendment be construed finally as prohibiting capital punishment for any crime regardless of its depravity and impact on society. This view was accepted by two Justices. Three other Justices were unwilling to go so far; focusing on the procedures by which convicted defendants were selected for the death penalty rather than on the actual punishment inflicted, they joined in the conclusion that the statutes before the Court were constitutionally invalid.

The petitioners in the capital cases before the Court today renew the "standards of decency" argument, but developments during the four years since *Furman* have undercut substantially the assumptions upon which their argument rested. It is now evident that a large proportion of American society continues to regard it as an appropriate and necessary criminal sanction.

The most marked indication of society's endorsement of the death penalty for murder is the legislative response to *Furman*. The legislatures of at least 35 States have enacted new statutes that provide for the death penalty for at least some crimes that result in the death of another person. And the Congress of the United States, in 1974, enacted a statute providing the death penalty for aircraft piracy that results in death. These recently adopted statutes have attempted to address the concerns expressed by the Court in *Furman* primarily (i) by specifying the factors to be weighed and the procedures to be followed in deciding when to impose a capital sentence, or (ii) by making the death penalty mandatory for specified crimes. But all of the post-*Furman* statutes make clear that capital punishment itself has not been rejected by the elected representatives of the people.

The jury also is a significant and reliable objective index of contemporary values because it is so directly involved. It may be true that evolving standards have influenced juries in recent decades to be more discriminating in imposing the sentence of death. But the relative infrequency of jury verdicts imposing the death sentence does not indicate rejection of capital punishment *per se*. Rather, the reluctance of juries in many cases to impose the sentence may well reflect the humane feeling that this most irrevocable of sanctions should be reserved for a small number of extreme cases. Indeed, the actions of juries in many States since *Furman* are fully compatible with the legislative judgments, reflected in the new statutes, as to the continued utility and necessity of capital punishment in appropriate cases. At the close of 1974 at least 254 persons had been sentenced to death since *Furman,* and by the end of March 1976, more than 460 persons were subject to death sentences.

As we have seen, however, the Eighth Amendment demands more than that a challenged punishment be acceptable to contemporary society. The Court also must ask whether it comports with the basic concept of human dignity at the core of the Amendment. Although we cannot "invalidate a category of penalties because we deem less severe penalties adequate to serve the ends of penology," the sanction imposed cannot be so totally without penological justification that it results in the gratuitous infliction of suffering.

The death penalty is said to serve two principal social purposes: retribution and deterrence of capital crimes by prospective offenders.

In part, capital punishment is an expression of society's moral outrage at particularly offensive conduct. This function may be unappealing to many, but it is essential in an ordered society that asks its citizens to rely on legal processes rather than self-help to vindicate their wrongs.

Retribution is no longer the dominant objective of the criminal law, but neither is it a forbidden objective nor one inconsistent with our respect for the dignity of men. Indeed, the decision that capital punishment may be the appropriate sanction in extreme cases is an expression of the community's belief that certain crimes are themselves so grievous an affront to humanity that the only adequate response may be the penalty of death.

Statistical attempts to evaluate the worth of the death penalty as a deterrent to crimes by potential offenders have occasioned a great deal of debate. The results simply have been inconclusive. As one opponent of capital punishment has said:

> *After all possible inquiry, including the probing of all possible methods of inquiry, we do not know, and for systematic and easily visible reasons cannot know, what the truth about this 'deterrent' effect may be. The inescapable flaw is that social conditions in any state are not constant through time, and that social conditions are not the same in any two states. If an effect were observed (and the observed effects, one way or another, are not large) then one could not at all tell whether any of this effect is attributable to the presence or absence of capital punishment. A 'scientific'—that is to say, a soundly based—conclusion is simply impossible, and no methodological path out of this tangle suggests itself.*

Although some of the studies suggest that the death penalty may not function as a significantly greater deterrent than lesser penalties, there is no convincing empirical evidence either supporting or refuting this view. We may nevertheless assume safely that there are murderers, such as those who act in passion, for whom the threat of death has little or no deterrent effect. But for many others, the death penalty undoubtedly is a significant deterrent. There are carefully contemplated murders, such as murder for hire, where the possible penalty of death may well enter into the cold calculus that precedes the decision to act. And there are some categories of murder, such as murder by a life prisoner, where other sanctions may not be adequate.

The value of capital punishment as a deterrent of crime is a complex factual issue the resolution of which properly rests with the legislatures, which can evaluate the results of statistical studies in terms of their own local conditions and with a flexibility of approach that is not available to the courts. Indeed, many of the post-*Furman* statutes reflect just such a responsible effort to define those crimes and those criminals for which capital punishment is most probably an effective deterrent.

In sum, we cannot say that the judgment of the Georgia Legislature that capital punishment may be necessary in some cases is clearly wrong. Considerations of federalism, as well as respect for the ability of a legislature to evaluate, in terms of its particular State, the moral consensus concerning the death penalty and its social utility as a sanction, require us to conclude, in the absence of more convincing evidence, that the infliction of death as a punishment for murder is not without justification and thus is not unconstitutionally severe.

Finally, we must consider whether the punishment of death is disproportionate in relation to the crime for which it is imposed. There is no question that death as a punishment is unique in its severity and irrevocability. When a defendant's life is at stake, the Court has been particularly sensitive to insure that every safeguard is observed. But we are concerned here only with the imposition of capital punishment for the crime of murder, and when a life has been taken deliberately by the offender, we cannot say that the punishment is invariably disproportionate to the crime. It is an extreme sanction, suitable to the most extreme of crimes.

We hold that the death penalty is not a form of punishment that may never be imposed, regardless of the circumstances of the offense, regardless of the character of the offender, and regardless of the procedure followed in reaching the decision to impose it.

IV

We now consider whether Georgia may impose the death penalty on the petitioner in this case.

A

While *Furman* did not hold that the infliction of the death penalty *per se* violates the Constitution's ban on cruel and unusual punishments, it did recognize that the penalty of death is different in kind from any other punishment imposed under our system of criminal justice. Because of the uniqueness of the death penalty, *Furman* held that it could not be imposed under sentencing procedures that created a substantial risk that it would be inflicted in an arbitrary and capricious manner. Indeed, the death sentences examined by the Court in *Furman* were "cruel and unusual" in the same way that being struck by lightning is cruel and unusual.

Furman mandates that where discretion is afforded a sentencing body on a matter so grave as the determination of whether a human life should be taken or spared, that discretion must be suitably directed and limited so as to minimize the risk of wholly arbitrary and capricious action.

It is certainly not a novel proposition that discretion in the area of sentencing be exercised in an informed manner. We have long recognized that "for the determination of sentences, justice generally requires that there be taken into account the circumstances of the offense together with the character and propensities of the offender."

Jury sentencing has been considered desirable in capital cases in order "to maintain a link between contemporary community values and the penal system." But it creates special problems. Much of the information that is relevant to the sentencing decision may have no relevance to the question of guilt, or may even be extremely prejudicial to a fair determination of that question. This problem, however, is scarcely insurmountable. Those who have studied the question suggest that a bifurcated procedure—one in which the question of sentence is not considered until the determination of guilt has been made—is the best answer.

But the provision of relevant information under fair procedural rules is not alone sufficient to guarantee that the information will be properly used in the imposition of punishment, especially if sentencing is performed by a jury. Since the members of a jury will have had little, if any, previous experience in sentencing, they are unlikely to be skilled in dealing with the information they are given. To the extent that this problem is inherent in jury sentencing, it may not be totally correctable. It seems clear, however, that the problem will be alleviated if the jury is given guidance regarding the factors about the crime and the defendant that the State, representing organized society, deems particularly relevant to the sentencing decision.

The idea that a jury should be given guidance in its decisionmaking is also hardly a novel proposition. Juries are invariably given careful instructions on the law and how to apply it before they are authorized to decide the merits of a lawsuit.

While some have suggested that standards to guide a capital jury's sentencing deliberations are impossible to formulate, the fact is that such standards have been developed. When the drafters of the Model Penal Code faced this problem, they concluded "that it is within the realm of possibility to point to the main circumstances of aggravation and of mitigation that should be weighed and weighed against each other when they are presented in a concrete case." While such standards are by necessity somewhat general, they do provide guidance to the sentencing authority and thereby reduce the likelihood that it will impose a sentence that fairly can be called capricious or arbitrary. Where the sentencing authority is required to specify the factors it relied upon in reaching its decision, the further safeguard of meaningful appellate review is available to ensure that death sentences are not imposed capriciously or in a freakish manner.

In summary, the concerns expressed in *Furman* that the penalty of death not be imposed in an arbitrary or capricious manner can be met by a carefully drafted statute that ensures that the sentencing authority is given adequate information and guidance. As a general proposition these concerns are best met by a system that provides for a bifurcated proceeding at which the sentencing authority is apprised of the information relevant to the imposition of sentence and provided with standards to guide its use of the information.

We do not intend to suggest that only the above described procedures would be permissible under *Furman* or that any sentencing system constructed along these general lines would inevitably satisfy the concerns of *Furman,* for each distinct system must be examined on an individual basis. Rather, we have embarked upon this general exposition to make clear that it is possible to construct capital-sentencing systems capable of meeting *Furman*'s constitutional concerns.

B

We now turn to consideration of the constitutionality of Georgia's capital-sentencing procedures. In the wake of *Furman,* Georgia amended its capital punishment statute, but chose not to narrow the scope of its murder provisions. Thus, now as before *Furman,* in Georgia "a person commits murder when he unlawfully and with malice aforethought, either express or implied, causes the death of another human being." All persons convicted of murder "shall be punished by death or by imprisonment for life."

Georgia did act, however, to narrow the class of murderers subject to capital punishment by specifying 10 statutory aggravating circumstances, one of which must be found by the jury to exist beyond a reasonable doubt before a death sentence can ever be imposed. In addition, the jury is authorized to consider any other appropriate aggravating or mitigating circumstances. The jury is not required to find any mitigating circumstance in order to make a recommendation of mercy that is binding on the trial court, but it must find a *statutory* aggravating circumstance before recommending a sentence of death.

These procedures require the jury to consider the circumstances of the crime and the criminal before it recommends sentence. No longer can a Georgia jury do as Furman's jury did: reach a finding of the defendant's guilt and then, without guidance or direction, decide whether he should live or die. Instead, the jury's attention is directed to the specific circumstances of the crime: Was it committed in the course of another capital felony? Was it committed for money? Was it committed upon a peace officer or judicial officer? Was it committed in a particularly heinous way or in a manner that endangered the lives of many persons? In addition, the jury's attention is focused on the characteristics of the person who committed the crime: Does he have a record of prior convictions for capital offenses? Are there any special facts about this defendant that mitigate against imposing capital punishment? As a result, while some jury discretion still exists, "the discretion to be exercised is controlled by clear and objective standards so as to produce non-discriminatory application."

As an important additional safeguard against arbitrariness and caprice, the Georgia statutory scheme provides for automatic appeal of all death sentences to the State's Supreme Court. That court is required by statute to review each sentence of death and determine whether it was imposed under the influence of passion or prejudice, whether the evidence supports the jury's finding of a statutory aggravating circumstance, and whether the sentence is disproportionate compared to those sentences imposed in similar cases.

In short, Georgia's new sentencing procedures require as a prerequisite to the imposition of the death penalty, specific jury findings as to the circumstances of the crime or the character of the defendant. Moreover, to guard further against a situation comparable to that presented in *Furman,* the Supreme Court of Georgia compares each death sentence with the sentences imposed on similarly situated defendants to ensure that the sentence of death in a particular case is not disproportionate. On their face these procedures seem to satisfy the concerns of *Furman.* No longer should there be "no meaningful basis for distinguishing the few cases in which the death penalty is imposed from the many cases in which it is not." The petitioner contends, however, that the changes in the Georgia sentencing procedures are only cosmetic, that the arbitrariness and capriciousness condemned by *Furman* continue to exist in Georgia—both in traditional practices that still remain and in the new sentencing procedures adopted in response to *Furman.*

First, the petitioner focuses on the opportunities for discretionary action that are inherent in the processing of any murder case under Georgia law. He notes that the state prosecutor has unfettered authority to select those persons whom he wishes to prosecute for a capital offense and to plea bargain with them.

The existence of these discretionary stages is not determinative of the issues before us. At each of these stages an actor in the criminal justice system makes a decision which may remove a defendant from consideration as a candidate for the death penalty. *Furman,* in contrast, dealt with the decision to impose the death sentence on a specific individual who had been convicted of a capital offense. Nothing in any of our cases suggests that the decision to afford an individual defendant mercy violates the Constitution. *Furman* held only that, in order to minimize the risk that the death penalty would be imposed on a capriciously selected group of offenders, the decision to impose it had to be guided by standards so that the sentencing authority would focus on the particularized circumstances of the crime and the defendant.

The petitioner further contends that the capital sentencing procedures adopted by Georgia in response to *Furman* do not eliminate the dangers of arbitrariness and caprice in jury sentencing. He claims that the statute is so broad and vague as to leave juries free to act as arbitrarily and capriciously as they wish. While there is no claim that the jury in this case relied upon a vague or overbroad provision to establish the existence of a statutory aggravating circumstance, the petitioner looks to the sentencing system as a whole (as the Court did in *Furman* and we do today) and argues that it fails to reduce sufficiently the risk of arbitrary infliction of death sentences. Specifically, *Gregg* urges that the statutory aggravating circumstances are too broad and too vague, that the sentencing procedure allows for arbitrary grants of mercy, and that the scope of the evidence and argument that can be considered at the presentence hearing is too wide.

The petitioner attacks the seventh statutory aggravating circumstance, which authorizes imposition of the death penalty if the murder was "outrageously or wantonly vile, horrible or inhuman in that it involved torture, depravity of mind, or an aggravated battery to the victim," contending that it is so broad that capital punishment could be imposed in any murder case. It is, of course, arguable that any murder involves depravity of mind or an aggravated battery. But this language need not be construed in this way, and there is no reason to assume that the Supreme Court of Georgia will adopt such an open-ended construction. In only one case has it upheld a jury's decision to sentence a defendant to death when the only statutory aggravating circumstance found was that of the seventh, and that homicide was a horrifying torture-murder.

The petitioner next argues that the requirements of *Furman* are not met here because the jury has the power to decline to impose the death penalty even if it finds that one or more statutory aggravating circumstances are present in the case. This contention misinterprets *Furman*. Moreover, it ignores the role of the Supreme Court of Georgia which reviews each death sentence to determine whether it is proportional to other sentences imposed for similar crimes. Since the proportionality requirement on review is intended to prevent caprice in the decision to inflict the penalty, the isolated decision of a jury to afford mercy does not render unconstitutional death sentences imposed on defendants who were sentenced under a system that does not create a substantial risk of arbitrariness or caprice.

Finally, the Georgia statute has an additional provision designed to assure that the death penalty will not be imposed on a capriciously selected group of convicted defendants. The new sentencing procedures require that the State Supreme Court review every death sentence. In performing its sentence-review function, the Georgia court has held that "if the death penalty is only rarely imposed for an act or it is substantially out of line with sentences imposed for other acts it will be set aside as excessive." The court on another occasion stated that "we view it to be our duty under the similarity standard to assure that no death sentence is affirmed unless in similar cases throughout the state the death penalty has been imposed generally."

The provision for appellate review in the Georgia capital-sentencing system serves as a check against the random or arbitrary imposition of the death penalty. In particular, the proportionality review substantially eliminates the possibility that a person will be sentenced to die by the action of an aberrant jury. If a time comes when juries generally do not impose the death sentence in a certain kind of murder case, the appellate review procedures assure that no defendant convicted under such circumstances will suffer a sentence of death.

V

The basic concern of *Furman* centered on those defendants who were being condemned to death capriciously and arbitrarily. Under the procedures before the Court in that case, sentencing authorities were not directed to give attention to the nature or circumstances of the crime committed or to the character or record of the defendant. Left unguided, juries imposed the death sentence in a way that could only be called freakish. The new Georgia sentencing procedures, by contrast, focus the jury's attention on the particularized nature of the crime and the particularized characteristics of the individual defendant. While the jury is permitted to consider any aggravating or mitigating circumstances, it must find and identify at least one statutory aggravating factor before it may impose a penalty of death. In this way the jury's discretion is channeled. In addition, the review function of the Supreme Court of Georgia affords additional assurance that the concerns that prompted our decision in *Furman* are not present to any significant degree in the Georgia procedure applied here.

For the reasons expressed in this opinion, we hold that the statutory system under which Gregg was sentenced to death does not violate the Constitution. Accordingly, the judgment of the Georgia Supreme Court is affirmed.

Mr. Justice White, with whom the Chief Justice and Mr. Justice Rehnquist join concurring in the judgment.

Petitioner also argues that decisions made by the prosecutor—either in negotiating a plea to some lesser offense than capital murder or in simply declining to charge capital murder—are standardless and will inexorably result in the wanton and freakish imposition of the penalty condemned by the judgment in *Furman*. I address this point separately because the cases in which no capital offense is charged escape the view of the Georgia Supreme Court and are not considered by it in determining whether a particular sentence is excessive or disproportionate.

Petitioner's argument that prosecutors behave in a standardless fashion in deciding which cases to try as capital felonies is unsupported by any facts. Petitioner simply asserts that since prosecutors have the power not to charge capital felonies they will exercise that power in a standardless fashion. This is untenable. Absent facts to the contrary, it cannot be assumed that prosecutors will be motivated in their charging decision by factors other than the strength of their case and the likelihood that a jury would impose the death penalty if it convicts. Unless prosecutors are incompetent in their judgments, the standards by which they decide whether to charge a capital felony will be the same as those by which the jury will decide the questions of guilt and sentence. Thus defendants will escape the death penalty through prosecutorial charging decisions only because the offense is not sufficiently serious; or because the proof is insufficiently strong. This does not cause the system to be standardless any more than the jury's decision to impose life imprisonment on a defendant whose crime is deemed insufficiently serious or its decision to acquit someone who is probably guilty but whose guilt is not established beyond a reasonable doubt. Thus the prosecutor's charging decisions are unlikely to have removed from the sample of cases considered by the Georgia Supreme Court any which are truly "similar." If the cases really were "similar" in relevant respects, it is unlikely that prosecutors would fail to prosecute them as capital cases; and I am unwilling to assume the contrary.

Petitioner's argument that there is an unconstitutional amount of discretion in the system which separates those suspects who receive the death penalty from those who receive life imprisonment, a lesser penalty, or are acquitted or never charged, seems to be in final analysis an indictment of our entire system of justice. Petitioner has argued, in effect, that no matter how effective the death penalty may be as a punishment, government, created and run as it must be by humans, is inevitably incompetent to administer it. This cannot be accepted as a proposition of constitutional law. Imposition of the death penalty is surely an awesome responsibility for any system of justice and those who participate in it. Mistakes will be made and discriminations will occur which will be difficult to explain. However, one of society's most basic tasks is that of protecting the lives of its citizens and one of the most basic ways in which it achieves the task is through criminal laws against murder. I decline to interfere with the manner in which Georgia has chosen to enforce such laws on what is simply an assertion of lack of faith in the ability of the system of justice to operate in a fundamentally fair manner.

Mr. Justice Brennan, dissenting.

In *Furman*, I read "evolving standards of decency" as requiring focus upon the essence of the death penalty itself and not primarily or solely upon the procedures under which the determination to inflict the penalty upon a particular person was made. That continues to be my view.

This Court inescapably has the duty, as the ultimate arbiter of the meaning of our Constitution, to say whether, when individuals condemned to death stand before our Bar, "moral concepts" require us to hold that the law has progressed to the point where we should declare that the punishment of death, like punishments on the rack, the screw, and the wheel, is no longer morally tolerable in our civilized society. My opinion in *Furman* v. *Georgia* concluded that our civilization and the law had progressed to this point and that therefore the punishment of death, for whatever crime and under all circumstances, is "cruel and unusual" in violation of the Eighth and Fourteenth Amendments of the Constitution.

I shall not again canvass the reasons that led to that conclusion. I emphasize only that foremost among the "moral concepts" recognized in our cases and inherent in the Clause is the primary moral principle that the State, even as it punishes, must treat its citizens in a manner consistent with their intrinsic worth as human beings—a punishment must not be so severe as to be degrading to human dignity. A judicial determination whether the punishment of death comports with human dignity is therefore not only permitted but compelled by the Clause.

In *Furman,* I set forth at some length my views on the basic issue presented to the Court in these cases. The death penalty, I concluded, is a cruel and unusual punishment prohibited by the Eighth and Fourteenth Amendments. That continues to be my view.

I have no intention of retracing the "long and tedious journey," that led to my conclusion in *Furman.* My sole purposes here are to consider the suggestion that my conclusion in *Furman* has been undercut by developments since then, and briefly to evaluate the basis for my Brethren's holding that the extinction of life is a permissible form of punishment under the Cruel and Unusual Punishments Clause.

Since the decision in *Furman,* the legislatures of 35 States have enacted new statutes authorizing the imposition of the death sentence for certain crimes, and Congress has enacted a law providing the death penalty for air piracy resulting in death. I would be less than candid if I did not acknowledge that these developments have a significant bearing on a realistic assessment of the moral acceptability of the death penalty to the American people. But if the constitutionality of the death penalty turns, as I have urged, on the opinion of an *informed* citizenry, then even the enactment of new death statutes cannot be viewed as conclusive. In *Furman,* I observed that the American people are largely unaware of the information critical to a judgment on the morality of the death penalty, and concluded that if they were better informed they would consider it shocking, unjust, and unacceptable. A recent study, conducted after the enactment of the post-*Furman* statutes, has confirmed that the American people know little about the death penalty, and that the opinions of an informed public would differ significantly from those of a public unaware of the consequences and effects of the death penalty.

Even assuming, however, that the post-*Furman* enactment of statutes authorizing the death penalty renders the prediction of the views of an informed citizenry an uncertain basis for a constitutional decision, the enactment of those statutes has no bearing whatsoever on the conclusion that the death penalty is unconstitutional because it is excessive. An excessive penalty is invalid under the Cruel and Unusual Punishments Clause "even though popular sentiment may favor" it. The inquiry here, then, is simply whether the death penalty is necessary to accomplish the legitimate legislative purposes in punishment, or whether a less severe penalty—life imprisonment—would do as well.

The two purposes that sustain the death penalty as nonexcessive in the Court's view are general deterrence and retribution. In *Furman,* I canvassed the relevant data on the deterrent effect of capital punishment. The state of knowledge at that point, after literally centuries of debate, was summarized as follows by a United Nations Committee:

It is generally agreed between the retentionists and abolitionists, whatever their opinions about the validity of comparative studies of deterrence, that the data which now exist show no correlation between the existence of capital punishment and lower rates of capital crime.

The available evidence, I concluded in *Furman,* was convincing that "capital punishment is not necessary as a deterrent to crime in our society."

The Solicitor General in his *amicus* brief in these cases relies heavily on a study by Isaac Ehrlich, reported a year after *Furman,* to support the contention that the death penalty does deter murder. Since the Ehrlich study was not available at the time of *Furman* and since it is the first scientific study to suggest that the death penalty may have a deterrent effect, I will briefly consider its import.

The Ehrlich study focused on the relationship in the Nation as a whole between the homicide rate and "execution risk"—the fraction of persons convicted of murder who were actually executed. Comparing the differences in homicide rate and execution risk for the years 1933 to 1969, Ehrlich found that increases in execution risk were associated with increases in the homicide rate. But when he employed the statistical technique of multiple regression analysis to control for the influence of other variables posited to have an impact on the homicide rate, Ehrlich found a negative correlation between changes in the homicide rate and changes in execution risk. His tentative conclusion was that for the period from 1933 to 1967 each additional execution in the United States might have saved eight lives.

The methods and conclusions of the Ehrlich study have been severely criticized on a number of grounds. It has been suggested, for example, that the study is defective because it compares execution and homicide rates on a nationwide, rather than a state-by-state, basis. The aggregation of data from all States—including those that have abolished the death penalty—obscures the relationship between murder and execution rates. Under Ehrlich's methodology, a decrease in the execution risk in one State combined with an increase in the murder rate in another State would, all other things being equal, suggest a deterrent effect that quite obviously would not exist. Indeed, a deterrent effect would be suggested if, once again all other things being equal, one State abolished the death penalty and experienced no change in the murder rate, while another State experienced an increase in the murder rate.

The most compelling criticism of the Ehrlich study is that its conclusions are extremely sensitive to the choice of the time period included in the regression analysis. Analysis of Ehrlich's data reveals that all empirical support for the deterrent effect of capital punishment disappears when the five most recent years are removed from his time series—that is to say, whether a decrease in the execution risk corresponds to an increase or a decrease in the murder rate depends on the ending point of the sample period. This finding has cast severe doubts on the reliability of Ehrlich's tentative conclusions. Indeed, a recent regression study, based on Ehrlich's theoretical model but using cross-section state data for the years 1950 and 1960, found no support for the conclusion that executions act as a deterrent.

The Ehrlich study, in short, is of little, if any, assistance in assessing the deterrent impact of the death penalty. The evidence I reviewed in Furman remains convincing, in my view, that "capital punishment is not necessary as a deterrent to crime in our society." The justification for the death penalty must be found elsewhere.

The other principal purpose said to be served by the death penalty is retribution. The notion that retribution can serve as a moral justification for the sanction of death finds credence in the opinion of my Brothers Stewart, Powell, and Stevens, and that of my Brother White in *Roberts v. Louisiana.* It is this notion that I find to be the most disturbing aspect of today's unfortunate decisions.

The concept of retribution is a multifaceted one, and any discussion of its role in the criminal law must be undertaken with caution. On one level, it can be said that the notion of retribution or reprobation is the basis of our insistence that only those who have broken the law be punished, and in this sense the notion is quite obviously central to a just system of criminal sanctions. But our recognition that retribution plays a crucial role in determining who may be punished by no means requires approval of retribution as a general justification for punishment. It is the question whether retribution can provide a moral justification for punishment—in particular, capital punishment—that we must consider.

This statement is wholly inadequate to justify the death penalty. As my Brother Brennan stated in *Furman,* "there is no evidence whatever that utilization of imprisonment rather than death encourages private blood feuds and other disorders." It simply defies belief to suggest that the death penalty is necessary to prevent the American people from taking the law into their own hands.

In a related vein, it may be suggested that the expression of moral outrage through the imposition of the death penalty serves to reinforce basic moral values—that it marks some crimes as particularly offensive and therefore to be avoided. The argument is akin to a deterrence argument, but differs in that it contemplates the individual's shrinking from antisocial conduct, not because he fears punishment, but because he has been told in the strongest possible way that the conduct is wrong. This contention, like the previous one, provides no support for the death penalty. It is inconceivable that any individual concerned about conforming his conduct to what society says is "right" would fail to realize that murder is "wrong" if the penalty were simply life imprisonment.

The foregoing contentions—that society's expression of moral outrage through the imposition of the death penalty pre-empts the citizenry from taking the law into its own hands and reinforces moral values—are not retributive in the purest sense. They are essentially utilitarian in that they portray the death penalty as valuable because of its beneficial results. These justifications for the death penalty are inadequate because the penalty is, quite clearly I think, not necessary to the accomplishment of those results.

There remains for consideration, however, what might be termed the purely retributive justification for the death penalty–that the death penalty is appropriate, not because of its beneficial effect on society, but because the taking of the murderer's life is itself morally good. Some of the language of the opinion of my Brothers Stewart, Powell, and Stevens appears positively to embrace this notion of retribution for its own sake as a justification for capital punishment.

Of course, it may be that these statements are intended as no more than observations as to the popular demands that it is thought must be responded to in order to prevent anarchy. But the implication of the statements appears to me to be quite different—namely, that society's judgment that the murderer "deserves" death must be respected not simply because the preservation of order requires it, but because it is appropriate that society make the judgment and carry it out. It is this latter notion, in particular, that I consider to be fundamentally at odds with the Eighth Amendment. The mere fact that the community demands the murderer's life in return for the evil he has done cannot sustain the death penalty, for as Justice Stewart, Powell, and Stevens remind us, "the Eighth Amendment demands more than that a challenged punishment be acceptable to contemporary society." To be sustained under the Eighth Amendment, the death penalty must "comport with the basic concept of human dignity at the core of the Amendment," the objective in imposing it must be "consistent with our respect for the dignity of other men." Under these standards, the taking of life "because the wrongdoer deserves it" surely must fall, for such a punishment has as its very basis the total denial of the wrongdoer's dignity and worth.

The death penalty, unnecessary to promote the goal of deterrence or to further any legitimate notion of retribution, is an excessive penalty forbidden by the Eighth and Fourteenth Amendments. I respectfully dissent from the Court's judgment upholding the sentences of death imposed upon the petitioners in these cases.

■ Arbitrariness—Perspectives

■ Issue—Has the Supreme Court Reduced Arbitrariness in Death Sentencing?

Carol S. Steiker and Jordan M. Steiker, "Sober Second Thoughts: Reflections on Two Decades of Constitutional Regulation of Capital Punishment"

I. *Introduction*

In 1972, the Supreme Court in *Furman* abolished the death penalty as it was then administered in the United States. In 1976, the Court in *Gregg* and its quartet of accompanying cases sustained some new death penalty statutes that appeared to address many of the concerns voiced in *Furman*. In doing so, the Court embarked on a course of continuing constitutional regulation of capital punishment in America.

Virtually no one thinks that the constitutional regulation of capital punishment has been a success. But oddly, and we think significantly, critics of the Court's death penalty jurisprudence fall into two diametrically opposed camps. On the one hand, some critics claim that the Court's work has burdened the administration of capital punishment with an overly complex, absurdly arcane, and minutely detailed body of constitutional law that, in the words of Learned Hand in a slightly different context, "obstructs, delays, and defeats" the administration of capital punishment. This set of critics notes the sheer volume of death penalty litigation, the labyrinthine nature of the doctrines that such litigation has spawned, the frequency with which federal courts overturn state-imposed death sentences, and the lengthy delays that occur between the imposition of death sentences and their execution.

On the other hand, a different set of critics claims that the Court has turned its back on regulating the death penalty and no longer even attempts to meet the concerns about the arbitrary and discriminatory imposition of death that animated its "constitutionalization" of capital punishment in *Furman*. These critics note that the Court's intervention has done little or nothing to remedy the vast overrepresentation on death row of the young, poor, and mentally retarded or the continuing influence of race on the capital sentencing decision. Under this view, in the anguished words of Justice Blackmun, who twenty years after his dissent in *Furman* radically changed course and argued for the abolition of the death penalty, the Court has done no more than "tinker with the machinery of death."

We thus have chosen to read *Furman* and *Gregg* together as a way of identifying the Supreme Court's concerns and goals regarding its constitutional regulation of capital punishment. We stop with *Gregg* and its companion cases, because the seeds of all of the rest of the Court's capital jurisprudence can be traced to the themes that it sounded in 1972 and 1976. Since 1976, the Supreme Court's pronouncements on capital punishment have been essentially backward-looking; majority and dissenting Justices alike have cast their positions in terms of what *Furman* and *Gregg* command and permit. This is not to deny that the morass of *Furman* and the tentative, provisional tone of the 1976 decisions left future Justices a wide margin of deniability; nonetheless, it seems likely that the Court itself would think it fair to measure the success of its capital punishment jurisprudence against the concerns articulated in *Furman* and *Gregg*. We think that these concerns can fairly be grouped around four ideas: desert (the problem of overinclusion), fairness (the problem of underinclusion), individualization, and heightened procedural reliability.

A. Desert At the time of the Court's decision in *Furman*, virtually every death penalty jurisdiction in the United States afforded sentencers absolute discretion to impose either death or life imprisonment (or sometimes merely a term of years) for certain crimes.

One problem with such broad discretionary schemes identified by the *Furman* and *Gregg* Courts was that the state and federal legislatures that drafted such statutes were never required to articulate a theory about the most deathworthy crimes or defendants. The Justices in *Furman* repeatedly noted that the number of those actually sentenced to death represented only a tiny fraction of those eligible to be executed by the broad net cast by the state statutes at issue in the case. Such sentencing systems provide no guarantee that each imposition of the death penalty reflected the larger community's considered judgment—as articulated through its elected representatives—about who deserved to die. This failure can be thought of as a problem of "overinclusion": without narrower statutory mandates, individual sentencers might return sentences of death in otherwise "ordinary" cases and thus perhaps run afoul of the larger community's moral standards.

B. Fairness Related to, but conceptually distinct from, the concern about desert in capital sentencing is the concern about fairness. Even if every defendant sentenced to death under a capital sentencing scheme "deserved" to die according to the larger community's considered judgment, the scheme could still be subject to challenge on the basis that it treated others, just as "deserving" as the condemned defendant, more leniently for no reason, or for invidious reasons. Thus, a sentencing scheme could avoid the problem of "overinclusion" (the failure to distinguish the deserving from the undeserving), but still present the problem of "underinclusion" (the failure to treat equally deserving cases alike).

The problems of overinclusion and underinclusion are related at a general conceptual level in that both are concerned with treating like cases alike. Overinclusion (the execution of a defendant in the absence of expressed legislative will) treats the defendant more harshly than he deserves, whereas underinclusion (the failure to execute some other defendants in the presence of expressed legislative will) treats other defendants more leniently than they deserve. The problems are related at a practical level as well: both overinclusion and underinclusion are necessarily aggravated by the kind of wholly discretionary, completely standardless decisionmaking that prevailed in the capital sentencing context prior to *Furman*. Moreover, the most obvious remedies for overinclusion will also help ameliorate the problem of underinclusion (and vice versa).

Despite these connections, desert and fairness concerns remain conceptually and practically distinct, as the *Furman* and *Gregg* Courts recognized. The problem of ascribing desert, and thus avoiding over inclusion, is largely the realm of the legislature, which speaks as the voice of the larger community. The *Furman* Court fueled its concerns about desert by observing the sheer infrequency with which sentencers imposed the death penalty: such rarity of imposition, the Court observed, suggested that the death penalty was not serving any useful function in society and that it no longer reflected any considered community judgment or "legislative will." Unlike its concerns about desert, the *Furman* Court's concerns about fairness were fueled not by the sheer infrequency of the imposition of the death penalty, but rather by the patterns of its imposition.

Justice Douglas's concurring opinion in *Furman* presents the clearest expression of the fairness concern—what he himself called the "equal protection" theme "implicit" in the Eighth Amendment proscription of cruel and unusual punishments.

C. Individualization Ironically, the *Furman* and *Gregg* Courts' commitment to individualized sentencing began not in contrast to, but rather as an outgrowth of, their concerns about desert and fairness. Each of the three concerns or commitments (desert, fairness, and individualization) reflects different facets of the basic norm of equal treatment, the idea that like cases should be treated alike. As the pluralities explained in *Woodson* and *Roberts v. Louisiana*, the third and fourth companion cases to *Gregg*, mandatory death penalty statutes run afoul of the basic norm of equal treatment because they erroneously rely on the flawed belief that "every offense in a like legal category calls for an identical punishment without regard to the past life and habits of a particular offender." In other words, in order to treat like cases alike, sentencers must have access to information about relevant likenesses and differences.

Ultimately, Justice Brennan failed to convince his brethren that respect for humanity required the abolition of capital punishment altogether. However, his lengthy *Furman* concurrence did begin to develop a notion of human dignity that formed the basis of the Court's requirement of individualized sentencing—a requirement that later became a pillar of Eighth Amendment law separate and distinct from, and in some tension with, the *Furman* Court's predominant concerns about desert and fairness.

D. Heightened Procedural Reliability Like its commitment to individualized capital sentencing, the Court's concern for heightened procedural reliability in capital cases built on Justice Brennan's solo concurrence in *Furman*. Just as Justice Brennan elaborated the notion of "human dignity" implicit in the Court's "evolving standards of decency" formulation of the Eighth Amendment, he also singlehandedly constructed the now-familiar "death is different" argument. Arguing that death as a punishment differs in kind, and not merely degree, from all other punishments, Justice Brennan attempted to demonstrate that its "uniqueness" as a punishment, both in severity and finality, rendered it cruel and unusual in all circumstances. No other Justices in *Furman* joined in that conclusion (although, arguably, Justice Marshall agreed with it).

Four years later, however, a plurality of the Court echoed Brennan's *Furman* concurrence in *Woodson* when it noted, in language that would be repeated many times in future cases: Death, in its finality, differs more from life imprisonment than a 100-year prison term differs from one of only a year or two. Because of that qualitative difference, there is a corresponding difference in the need for reliability in the determination that death is the appropriate punishment in a specific case.

II. *Ending Back at the Beginning: The Return to Pre-*Furman *Capital Sentencing*

We now turn to the current regulatory approach that has emerged from *Furman* and the 1976 decisions. To illustrate the complexity of current doctrine as well as its relatively minimal demands on states seeking to administer the death penalty, we organize the Court's jurisprudence around four doctrinal areas that correspond to the concerns of *Furman* and the 1976 cases that we described above.

This organization enables us to perform three important tasks. First, it allows us to rise above the morass of extraordinarily complicated doctrine and get a "bird's-eye view" of the entire landscape of constitutional death penalty regulation. Only by doing so can we see clearly the entirety of what states must do to impose the death penalty within the bounds of current constitutional constraints. Second, examining doctrine within our framework helps explain why so much capital litigation persists despite the limited nature of the Court's actual demands. Within each of our categories, we trace the distinctive misunderstandings and evasions that account for ongoing, yet avoidable constitutional litigation. Third, and finally, by examining the Court's present doctrines in light of the concerns reflected in the early death penalty decisions, we are able to perform an internal critique of the Court's capital jurisprudence—to evaluate its success in light of its own purported goals.

A. Narrowing One body of doctrine is designed to ensure that only those who are most deserving of the death penalty are eligible to receive it. Given the observed rarity of death sentences in relation to serious violent crimes, including murder, this doctrine—which we call "narrowing"—seeks to force communities, speaking through state legislatures, to designate in advance those offenders most deserving of death. By forcing states to articulate their theories of the "worst" offenders, the narrowing doctrine purportedly guards against "overinclusion"— that is, the application of the death penalty in circumstances in which, notwithstanding the sentencer's decision, the sentence is not deserved according to wider community standards.

As the Court has elaborated this idea, state legislatures can narrow the class of the death-eligible in one of two ways. First, statutes can fulfill this narrowing requirement at the penalty phase of a capital trial by requiring the prosecution to prove the existence of some "aggravating factor" beyond what is required for conviction of capital murder. Second, statutes can narrow at the guilt phase of the capital trial by confining their definitions of capital murder to a certain subset of offenses more serious than the class of all murders. Finally, as an additional failsafe beyond these forms of legislative narrowing, courts can further narrow the class of the death-eligible through some sort of post-sentencing proportionality review. Courts can either perform this review "wholesale" by excluding entire groups of offenders or offenses from the ambit of the death penalty based on insufficient culpability or harm, or they can undertake case-by-case examinations of facts to ensure that each sentence imposed is actually deserved in light of a particular jurisdiction's general sentencing practices.

Despite the promise that the narrowing doctrine would significantly reduce the problem of overinclusion, the doctrine as elaborated by the Court has done no such thing. As the following section will illustrate, death-eligibility remains remarkably broad—indeed, nearly as broad as under the expansive statutes characteristic of the pre-*Furman* era.

1. Aggravating Circumstances

In evaluating the states' approaches, the Court has insisted that a state scheme must "genuinely narrow the class of persons eligible for the death penalty and must reasonably justify the imposition of a more severe sentence on the defendant compared to others found guilty of murder." This language, however, has been more bark than bite. First, the Court has approved aggravating circumstances that arguably encompass every murder, such as Arizona's circumstance that asks whether the defendant committed the offense in an "especially heinous, cruel or depraved manner" and Idaho's circumstance that asks whether "by the murder, or circumstances surrounding its commission, the defendant exhibited utter disregard for human life."

A second, and more significant, failing of the Court's approach is that the Court has placed no outer limit on the number of aggravating factors that a state may adopt. Thus, even if a state adopts aggravating factors that, taken individually, meaningfully narrow the class of the death-eligible, the factors collectively might render virtually all murderers death-eligible. This concern is not merely an idle possibility. Several states have enumerated ten or more aggravating circumstances, each individually sufficient to support a capital sentence. Indeed, most states adopting capital statutes after *Furman* have looked for guidance to the Model Penal Code, which lists eight aggravating circumstances, including the notoriously vague "especially heinous, atrocious or cruel" factor that has generated litigation in numerous jurisdictions.

The experience in Georgia reflects the general failure of states to achieve any meaningful narrowing through the enumeration of aggravating circumstances. The most detailed study of death-eligibility within a state—conducted by the famous Baldus group—found that approximately eighty-six percent of all persons convicted of murder in Georgia over a five-year period after the adoption of Georgia's new statute were death-eligible under that scheme. Perhaps more revealing is the Baldus study's conclusion that over ninety percent of persons sentenced to death before *Furman* would also be deemed death-eligible under the post-*Furman* Georgia statute. The Baldus group's work strongly suggests that Georgia has not articulated a carefully circumscribed theory of what the state might regard as the "worst" murders.

2. Proportionality Review

One important qualification should be made to the general observation that meaningful narrowing is neither required by Court decisions nor secured by state statutory schemes. The most significant source of narrowing in current doctrine stems not from the enumeration of aggravating circumstances (or from more limited definitions of capital offenses) but rather from the Court's proportionality decisions, which preclude the imposition of the death penalty when the Court has discerned an overwhelming societal consensus against that punishment for particular crimes. Most notably, in *Coker*, the Court ruled only one year after the 1976 decisions that the Eighth Amendment barred states from imposing the death penalty for the crime of rape. This decision remains the most significant source of protection against overinclusion in the administration of the death penalty.

Coker, though, stands as an exception to the Court's general reluctance to narrow the class of death-eligible defendants through constitutionally imposed proportionality limitations. Although the Court held in 1982 that the death penalty was disproportionate as applied to a perpetrator who had not killed, attempted to kill, or intended to kill, the Court subsequently retracted that standard and sustained the proportionality of the death penalty for major participants in dangerous felonies who exhibit reckless indifference to human life. Thus, the death penalty remains available for persons convicted of felony-murder regardless whether the defendant intended to commit, attempted to commit, or actually committed murder. Indeed, states have executed several "non-triggermen" since *Furman*, and a substantial number of states presently make the death penalty available for participants in dangerous felonies in which an accomplice intentionally or even accidentally kills.

In addition to its reluctance to narrow the availability of the death penalty based on mitigating aspects of the offense, the Court has declined to exempt certain classes of offenders from death-eligibility based on personal characteristics—such as youth and retardation—that tend to lessen culpability. In *Stanford v. Kentucky*, the Court rejected the claim that an emerging national consensus precluded the imposition of the death penalty for offenders who were sixteen or seventeen years old at the time of the offense. Conceding that few juvenile offenders had been sentenced to death over the past several decades, the Court maintained that such evidence could not support the proposition that society overwhelmingly disapproved of the death penalty's application to juveniles.

Apart from *Coker*, then, the Court's proportionality decisions suggest strongly that the "narrowing" of the class of offenders and offenses subject to the death penalty should be accomplished primarily, as in the pre-*Furman* regime, by sentencer discretion guided by statutory criteria rather than court mandate. Given that the statutory criteria (in the form of aggravating and mitigating circumstances) do not themselves accomplish any significant narrowing, this approach is essentially indistinguishable from the standardless discretion embodied in the pre-1972 statutes.

B. Channeling   As discussed above, *Furman* and the 1976 decisions sought not merely to ensure that the death penalty was imposed only on deserving offenders, but also to ensure that similarly situated offenders would be treated equally. Overinclusion, of course, constitutes one kind of inequality, but it is not the only kind. Inequality also results if some—but not all—deserving offenders receive the death penalty, especially if there is no principled basis for distinguishing between those who receive the penalty and those who do not.

The 1976 decisions appeared to suggest that the most promising means of avoiding this sort of inequality was to focus, or "channel," the sentencer's discretion on the relevant decisionmaking criteria. Notwithstanding the 1976 decisions' seeming endorsement of channeling as a separate constitutional requirement, subsequent doctrine has veered sharply in the direction of Justice Harlan. The Supreme Court has emphatically disclaimed any separate requirement to channel discretion apart from the requirement that states narrow the class of death-eligible offenders. Accordingly, under current doctrine, once a state has limited the death penalty to some sub-class or sub-classes of murderers, the state can give the sentencer absolute and unguided discretion to decide between death and some lesser punishment. Indeed, a state could constitutionally achieve the "narrowing" function at the guilt phase of a capital trial and ask one simple question at the punishment phase: life or death?

The collapsing of the channeling requirement into the narrowing function fundamentally ignores a crucial concern of *Furman*. As argued above, it is undoubtedly true that narrowing the class of the death-eligible was a central goal of *Furman* because it addressed the problem of overinclusion—imposition of the death penalty in a particular case in which the defendant did not deserve death in light of general community standards. But *Furman* was at least equally concerned with underinclusion—the failure of juries to impose death in cases in which it is truly deserved. Indeed, underinclusion, rather than overinclusion, was the principal target of the NAACP's pre-*Furman* efforts to subject state capital punishment statutes to constitutional scrutiny.

Narrowing the class of the death-eligible in no way addresses the problem of underinclusion, because open-ended discretion after death-eligibility permits, even invites, the jury to act according to its own unaccountable whims. Without guiding the sentencer at all points of its decisionmaking, there simply is no guarantee that the "equal protection" concerns highlighted in *Furman* will be meaningfully addressed.

Once channeling the sentencer's consideration of mitigating evidence becomes impermissible, it is difficult to see a basis to insist on channeling the sentencer's consideration of aggravating evidence. If the sentencer may refuse to impose a death sentence for any reason or no reason at all (and nothing guides the sentencer in that decision), there is no effective means of preventing underinclusion. In such circumstances, guiding the sentencer in its consideration of aggravating evidence will not meaningfully contribute to "equality" in sentencing, because the absolute discretion afforded the sentencer at the critical moment of decision will render insignificant whatever guidance has been achieved on the aggravating side. This tension between *Gregg*'s seeming insistence on channeling and *Woodson*'s seeming insistence on uncircumscribed consideration of mitigating evidence constitutes the central dilemma in post-*Furman* capital punishment law.

The Court's focus on narrowing as the sole constitutionally required means of addressing arbitrariness in capital sentencing—to the exclusion of both channeling and proportionality review—has yielded an additional significant consequence for death penalty doctrine. Because states need not channel sentencing discretion (and need not require sentencers to explicitly weigh enumerated aggravating and mitigating factors), the punishment decision need not have any structure at all. Under current doctrine, a state could choose to limit death-eligibility through its definition of capital murder (as several states have), and then simply ask the sentencer to decide punishment in light of any aggravating or mitigating factors that the sentencer deems significant. Although no state has yet chosen to leave the punishment phase unstructured to this degree, such a scheme would clearly withstand constitutional scrutiny given current doctrine. Indeed, such a scheme would also avoid much of the complicated litigation that has arisen as a result of states' decisions to design more elaborate sentencing proceedings.

The apparent constitutional permissibility of such a scheme seems odd given the Court's strong emphasis in the 1976 decisions on the creation of a separate structured punishment phase in the post-*Furman* statutes it sustained. In those decisions, the Court did not explicitly indicate that a bifurcated proceeding with a carefully designed punishment phase was constitutionally indispensable. Nonetheless, a casual (and even a careful) observer of the interaction between the Court's decisions and statutory developments following *Furman* would likely have regarded such a proceeding as the new hallmark of permissible death penalty schemes. That current doctrine would permit a state to enact a statute defining nineteen or so categories of capital murder and to provide for a punishment phase structured around one general question—life or death—reveals the extent to which the Court has retreated from the more ambitious regulatory efforts that its 1976 decisions seemed to embrace and indeed to require.

C. Mitigation In its rejection of mandatory sentencing in the 1976 decisions, the Court made clear that a defendant was entitled to an "individualized" proceeding that would facilitate the sentencer's consideration of mitigating evidence. Those opinions did not, however, answer two crucial questions concerning the scope of that right. First, the opinions did not specify what kinds of evidence could be regarded as "mitigating" so as to trigger the defendant's right to offer the evidence. Thus, litigation was inevitable in those states that through statute or practice limited the sentencer's consideration to certain kinds of mitigating evidence. Second, the opinions did not define the extent to which states are permitted to structure the sentencer's consideration of mitigating evidence. Most states, including Georgia, invited the sentencer to evaluate mitigating evidence at the end of the decisionmaking process in answering the fundamental question of life or death. Other states, such as Texas and Oregon, permitted the sentencer to consider mitigating evidence only in the context of answering specific fact-based questions.

Current doctrine has rendered both of these uncertainties moot, because all death-penalty schemes presently permit unconstrained consideration of mitigating evidence. Accordingly, virtually all of the current litigation concerning the individualization requirement is backward-looking, gauging the constitutionality of statutory provisions and state practices that are no longer in force. Ironically, then, the past twenty years of intricate litigation over states' fulfillment of the individualization requirement is coming to an end only because states have voluntarily reproduced the open-ended consideration of mitigating factors that was a central feature of the pre-*Furman* statutes.

D. Death is Different One of the central themes of *Gregg* and its companion cases concerned the need for "heightened reliability" in capital cases. According to the Court, the qualitative difference between death and all other punishments justifies a corresponding difference in the procedures appropriate to capital versus non-capital proceedings. The Court echoed the "death is different" principle in a number of subsequent cases, but close examination of the Court's decisions over the past twenty years reveals that the procedural safeguards in death cases are not as different as one might suspect. Although the Court has carved out a series of protections applicable only to capital trials, it has done so in an entirely ad hoc fashion and left untouched a substantial body of doctrine that relegates capital defendants to the same level of protection as non-capital defendants.

The Court has invoked the notion of heightened reliability to permit voir dire concerning racial prejudice in cases involving interracial murders; to invalidate a death sentence based in part on a pre-sentence report that was not made available to defense counsel; to prevent prosecutors from deliberately misleading jurors about the consequences of their decision by misstating the scope of appellate review; to require the inclusion of a lesser-included offense instruction in cases in which the evidence would support a guilty verdict for a non-capital offense; and to permit the defendant to inform the jury of the real consequences of a "life" sentence when the state argues that the defendant would be dangerous in the future and "life" means life without possibility of parole as a matter of state law. The Court also has invoked the "death is different" doctrine in post-trial proceedings to overturn a sentence based on a prior conviction that was later invalidated, and to suggest that some post-trial judicial consideration of newly-discovered evidence of innocence may be mandated when the inmate makes a "truly persuasive" showing of actual (as opposed to legal) innocence.

The decisions described above, taken together with the cases elaborating the requirement of individualized sentencing, represent the sum total of the Court's applications of its death-is-different doctrine. It should be apparent from the brief summary of these decisions that the doctrine does not reflect a systematic effort to regulate the death penalty process so much as a series of responses to particular circumstances in which the Court deemed a state rule or practice manifestly unreliable or unfair.

In sum, despite Justice Scalia's protestations that the Court has embarked on an elaborate scheme of death-penalty regulation—what he termed in one opinion a "Federal Rules of Death Penalty Evidence"—the Court's death-is-different doctrine is nothing more than a modest, ad hoc series of limitations on particular state practices. As with the Court's other death penalty doctrines, the seemingly intricate and demanding constraints appear quite marginal upon closer inspection.

It is quite understandable that advocates of capital punishment, as well as institutional actors charged with implementing state capital schemes, would look at the past twenty-five years of federal constitutional regulation and see an obstructionist Court imposing a confusing morass of hyper-technical rules. Judged by the volume of cases the Court has heard, the intricacy of the Court's resulting opinions, and the malleability of the emerging doctrines, the Court has assumed a prominent and seemingly powerful role in regulating the death penalty. As in other areas of extensive public law litigation, the Court appears also to have institutionalized a role for highly specialized lawyers who, in this context, regard a conviction and sentence of death as merely the beginning of an intensive and time-consuming process of state and federal appeals.

Despite this perception, contemporary death penalty law is remarkably undemanding. The narrowing, channeling, and individualization requirements can be simultaneously and completely satisfied by a statute that defines capital murder as any murder accompanied by some additional, objective factor or factors and that provides for a sentencing proceeding in which the sentencer is asked simply whether the defendant should live or die. No longer can death be imposed for the crime of rape, but beyond that, the state can seek the death penalty against virtually any murderer. As for the requirement of heightened reliability, it surfaces unpredictably at the margins of state capital schemes. Ironically, in the post-*Furman* regime, the doctrine of heightened reliability, rather than the death penalty itself, seems to strike like lightning, randomly and with little effect.

The resemblance of this hypothetical scheme to the pre-*Furman* regime is striking in itself, but all the more striking because of the widespread perception that death penalty law is extremely demanding. Our fundamental claim is that virtually all of the complexity of death penalty law over the past twenty years stems from a failure in translation rather than an insistence on fulfilling the ambitious goals of *Furman* and the 1976 decisions. This communication gap, in which the Court rarely identified in clear and unanimous terms the minimal obligations of states in the post-*Furman* era, and in which states failed to respond quickly (or in some cases at all) to obvious, correctable defects in their statutes in light of those minimal obligations, has left us with the worst of all possible regulatory worlds. The resulting complexity conveys the impression that the current system errs, if at all, on the side of heightened reliability and fairness. And the fact of minimal regulation, which invites if not guarantees the same kinds of inequality as the pre-*Furman* regime, is filtered through time-consuming, expensive proceedings that ultimately do little to satisfy the concerns that led the Court to take a sober second look at this country's death penalty practices in the first place. In short, the last twenty years have produced a complicated regulatory apparatus that achieves extremely modest goals with a maximum amount of political and legal discomfort.

III. *Final Reflections*

We have argued that the Supreme Court's chosen path of constitutional regulation of the death penalty has been a disaster, an enormous regulatory effort with almost no rationalizing effect. If this claim is true, one has to wonder why the Court has neither abandoned its efforts altogether nor pursued one of the alternatives.

Perhaps the Justices have retained current death penalty doctrine despite its failings as a house because at some level they appreciate its success as a facade. The Court's doctrine can be said to work as a facade to the extent that it is successful at making participants in the criminal justice system and the public at large more comfortable with the death penalty than they otherwise would be or should be.

This argument is of a kind that legal scholars designate, not always with completely shared definitions, as "legitimation" theory. The use of the verb "to legitimate" in this context is distinct from the two primary dictionary definitions of the word—the first being what one might call "formal" legitimation ("to give legal status or authorization to"), as in "the Supreme Court legitimated an act of Congress by upholding it against constitutional challenge"; and the second being what one might call "normative" legitimation ("to show or affirm to be justified"), as in "the Supreme Court's documentation of coercive police interrogation techniques legitimated its conclusion that Miranda warnings were necessary to prevent involuntary confessions." Rather, the distinctive sense of legitimation to which we refer derives from the work of the sociologist Max Weber, and it might best be described as an "empirical" or "phenomenological" sense of the word. The Weberian idea of legitimation focuses on an individual's (or a group's) experience of belief in the normative legitimacy of a social phenomenon, such as a set of relationships, a form of organization, or an ongoing custom or practice, whatever might "really" be the case. Thus, the Weberian definition of legitimation might be, in Webster's dictionary parlance, "to induce the belief of normative justification." We use it in the more particular sense of inducing a false or exaggerated belief in the normative justifiability of something in the social world—that is, of inducing belief in the absence of or in contradiction to evidence of what the phenomenon is "really" like.

We think that legitimation arguments at all three levels of generality can be made about the Supreme Court's Eighth Amendment jurisprudence. These arguments range from the powerful to the plausible to the speculative, in inverse relation to the level of generality. At the most specific "internal" level of generality, powerful evidence suggests that death penalty law makes actors within the criminal justice system more comfortable with their roles by inducing an exaggerated belief in the essential rationality and fairness of the system. At the next level of generality, we believe it is plausible, even probable, that death penalty law makes members of the public at large more comfortable with the use of capital punishment than they would be in the absence of such law. At the greatest level of generality, one could speculate that if death penalty law legitimates capital punishment as a social practice, then it also legitimates the social order as a whole by making palatable the most awesome exercise of state power.

Two separate compelling arguments support the claim that the Court's death penalty law has an "internal" legitimation effect. First, the Court's focus on controlling the discretion of capital sentencers creates a false aura of rationality, even science, around the necessarily moral task of deciding life or death. Robert Weisberg has argued convincingly that the Court's attempt to tame the "existential moment" of decision in the capital sentencing process has had the effect of reducing the anxiety that judges and juries feel about exercising their sentencing power.

The second "internal" legitimation argument focuses on how the Court's constitutionalization of capital punishment has diluted sentencing judges' and jurors' sense of ultimate responsibility for imposing the death penalty. The Supreme Court's Eighth Amendment jurisprudence has itself recognized the ways in which knowledge of a lack of final responsibility for imposing the death sentence can impermissibly bias a sentencing jury's decision. In *Caldwell v. Mississippi*, for example, the Court reversed a death sentence imposed after the prosecutor was permitted to argue to the sentencing jury that its decision to impose the death sentence would be reviewed by the state supreme court. Such an argument, opined the Court, impermissibly denigrated the jury's sense of "awesome responsibility" for imposing the death penalty, especially because it was simply not true that appellate courts could redo the moral calculus assigned to the sentencing jury. Yet what the Court's Eighth Amendment law forbids the prosecutor or judge to tell a seated sentencing jury is exactly what the law itself "tells" every potential juror.

The public's vague and incomplete knowledge about an intricate scheme of constitutional regulation of the death penalty thus acts as a society-wide *Caldwell* argument. The public develops a strong but false sense that many levels of safeguards protect against unjust or arbitrary executions. They are thus likely to accept any executions that finally make it through the system as being more than fair enough. The Supreme Court's death penalty law, by creating an impression of enormous regulatory effort while achieving negligible regulatory effects, effectively obscures the true nature of our capital sentencing system, in which the pre-*Furman* world of unreviewable sentencer discretion lives on, with much the same consequences in terms of arbitrary and discriminatory sentencing patterns.

The legitimating effect of the Court's Eighth Amendment jurisprudence is very real and leads us to think that we may have started with the wrong question. Instead of asking why the Court's doctrine has persisted despite its failure as regulation, perhaps we should be asking whether that doctrine has any effect besides its failure as regulation.

The short history of death penalty law thus illustrates in a profound way how institutions—even institutions as young and as frequently scrutinized as the constitutional regulation of capital punishment under the Eighth Amendment—can take on lives of their own and find a place for themselves different from the one envisioned by their creators. Both the death penalty abolitionists who self-consciously litigated *Furman* and *Gregg*, believing that their arguments would lead to the end of capital punishment in America, and the coalition of centrist Justices who took on a more limited reformist mission post-*Furman* and *Gregg*, would no doubt be surprised to observe the extent to which current death penalty law acts to legitimate capital punishment - by denying contradictions between individualized consideration and fairness over a range of cases, by masking the moral choice and wide discretion of capital sentencers, and by promoting the appearance of intensive regulation despite its virtual absence. It is deeply ironic that the impulse to abolish and reform the death penalty has produced a body of law that contributes substantially to the stabilization and perpetuation of capital punishment as a social practice. We are left with the worst of all possible worlds: the Supreme Court's detailed attention to death penalty law has generated negligible improvements over the pre-*Furman* era, but has helped people to accept without second thoughts - much less "sober" ones—our profoundly failed system of capital punishment.

David McCord, "Judging the Effectiveness of the Supreme Court's Death Penalty Jurisprudence According to the Court's Own Goals: Mild Success or Major Disaster?"

I. *Introduction*

Opponents of the death penalty have long taken the Supreme Court to task for not ruling that the penalty is per se unconstitutional. But there also has been a longstanding breed of less absolutist critics. These critics are willing to assume arguendo that regulation rather than abolition is a proper stance for the Court. They then argue that the Court's chosen means of regulation have proven ineffective to remedy the very evils that prompted the Court to undertake regulation of capital punishment in the first place. The most complete and high-profile presentation of this critique occurs in a provocative article in a recent issue of the *Harvard Law Review*. There, Professors Carol S. and Jordan M. Steiker seek to perform an "internal" critique of Supreme Court death penalty jurisprudence: an examination of whether the Court has achieved the goals that it has set for itself since it began to regulate state death penalty law more than two decades ago. After exhaustive and thoughtful analysis, the authors come to a damning conclusion: "The Supreme Court's chosen path of constitutional regulation of the death penalty has been a disaster, an enormous regulatory effort with almost no rationalizing effect." If Steiker and Steiker are correct, they have succeeded in exposing the fact that the Court's regulatory effort is the juridical equivalent of the Emperor's new clothes—costly, yet embarrassingly ineffective for the goals Steiker and Steiker attribute to the Court: decreasing "overinclusion"—the imposition of death sentences on defendants who are not among the "worst" murderers; decreasing "underinclusion"—the imposition of death sentences on only some, rather than all, equally culpable murderers; and increasing "individualization" of sentencing by considering all aspects of the defendant's character;

all through "heightened procedural reliability." I will argue that despite the virtues of their article, Steiker and Steiker are wrong in two important ways.

First, they, along with other critics I will call "academic underinclusionists," have wrongly concluded that minimizing *all* underinclusion has been one of the Court's concerns. The correct view, I will contend, is that the Court has had only one primary goal for its regulation of capital punishment: decreasing overinclusion, with particular interest in minimizing invidious overinclusion due to racial bias. I will argue that the Court's regulatory efforts have prompted responses from the states that, at least on their faces, seem to have the potential to partially achieve the Court's goal.

The question then becomes, of course, whether these state responses have actually succeeded in producing such improved results. I will contend that the second way in which I believe Steiker and Steiker have erred is by not substantiating their claim that the Court has legitimated state death penalty systems having the same potential to operate arbitrarily as the pre-*Furman* systems. Beyond that, I will argue that they have not proven that post-*Furman* systems are in fact systematically operating in as arbitrary a fashion, even accepting Steiker and Steiker's assertion that the Court is opposed to all underinclusion. In fact, the best available evidence strongly suggests that post-*Furman* systems are operating *less* arbitrarily with respect to both overinclusion and underinclusion, and that this improvement is likely due in significant part to the Court's regulatory efforts.

Before I begin my task, though, a bit of a disclaimer is in order. The analysis that Steiker and Steiker perform, and that I will undertake in response, is of a very traditional scholarly sort—trying to figure out what a body of legal doctrine says, what the policy goals behind it are, and whether it seems to be fulfilling those goals. The same type of analysis could be applied to a body of contract, tort, or property law. But the death penalty seems different to many people: it evokes such intense emotions in some opponents that scholarly analysis seems beside the point. Lest those opponents take me as an apologist for the death penalty, let me state my position for the record: I do not believe the death penalty should exist. Nor do I want to be understood as arguing that the Court has done an excellent job in choosing and implementing the goals it is seeking to foster through its death penalty jurisprudence. I do insist, though, that the topic is fair game for traditional, dispassionate legal analysis, that such analysis in this instance turns out to be quite illuminating, and that when the analysis cuts in the Court's favor, one must call it as one sees it.

II. *Steiker and Steiker's Mistake Regarding Underinclusion*

A. Steiker and Steiker's Argument As the authors themselves recognize, it is crucial to their enterprise to correctly identify the concerns that the Court would itself choose to analyze its performance. Here, then, are the concerns Steiker and Steiker identify: "We think that these concerns can fairly be grouped around four ideas: desert (overinclusion), fairness (underinclusion), individualization, and heightened procedural reliability."

Having identified these concerns, Steiker and Steiker go on to demonstrate how, in their view, the Court's jurisprudence has failed to result in improved capital punishment systems that assuage any of the four concerns. As to overinclusion, Steiker and Steiker claim that the Court has failed to require states to narrow significantly the class of death-eligible defendants. As to underinclusion, the authors argue that the Court has failed to require the sentencer's decision to be "channeled" at the "critical moment when it decides whether to impose a death sentence." This leaves standardless discretion in the sentencer, which inevitably leads to like cases being treated differently. The authors also are critical of the Court's approach to achieving its goal of individualization. Although the Court has certainly opened the door to all individualizing mitigating evidence, it also has concomitantly permitted arbitrariness into the process by the very same means. Nor has the Court required states to channel the sentencer's consideration of individualizing evidence. Finally, as to heightened procedural reliability, the Court has failed, according to Steiker and Steiker, to go as far as it should in requiring states to treat death differently procedurally. Thus, Steiker and Steiker contend that the Court's capital jurisprudence has been an ineffective disaster. However, I believe Steiker and Steiker have erred in their identification of the Court's alleged concern with underinclusion, which substantially undermines the subsequent critique.

B. Underinclusion Depicted Steiker and Steiker are certainly operating on the basis of received wisdom when they contend that the Court is concerned with the problem of underinclusion. Several other academic underinclusionists have concluded that the Court views underinclusion as a vice. The most well-known are Professors David Baldus, George Woodworth, and Charles Pulaski (hereinafter "BWP"), who refer to the same problem as that of "excessiveness," or, even more descriptively, "comparative excessiveness." BWP performed thorough and influential research on a body of several hundred pre- and post-*Furman* cases to study the extent of the underinclusion problem in Georgia. It is crucial to understand what academic underinclusionists mean when they refer to underinclusion, particularly as it differs from overinclusion. While I will discuss the BWP statistical work later, the easiest visual aid to use in understanding the issue is one created by Professor Arnold Barnett about a decade ago.

Professor Barnett examined Georgia murder convictions between March 28, 1973, and June 30, 1978, and analyzed the variables that appeared to him to account for whether or not death sentences were imposed. He concluded that the likelihood of a death sentence depended upon how the case scored on each of three variables: certainty that the killing was deliberate; relationship between defendant and victim; and vileness of killing (which involved two sub-inquiries: whether there was a plausible claim of self-defense, and whether the killing was particularly horrific in any of fourteen specified ways). He developed a protocol for each of the three variables that permitted him to assign a score of 0, 1, or 2 as to the first and third variables, and 0 or 1 as to the second (0 having little or no tendency to lead to a death sentence, 1 having a moderate tendency, and 2 having a strong tendency—thus, the best (least death-prone) score a case could get was 0, 0, 0, and the worst (most death-prone) score a case could get was 2, 1, 2). He then analyzed what proportion of defendants in cases having identical scores received the death sentence. His chart is reproduced in **Figure 8-2**, although I have added letters for easy reference. The score of each case on Barnett's three variables is in parentheses on the bottom line of each box. The first number on the top line is the proportion of cases in that box in which the defendant was sentenced to death. Next to the proportion, in parentheses, is the fraction on which the proportion is based—the numerator is the number of defendants in that category who received the death sentence, and the denominator is the number of cases in that category. For example, in box K, there were fifty-nine defendants whose cases scored 1, 1, 1, and fifteen of them received the death sentence, a proportion of .25.

There are three important things to note about Barnett's diagram. First, it generally reflects a common-sense continuum, from a nonexistent or very low death sentencing rate in the lower-scored cases (boxes A-J), through a signifi-

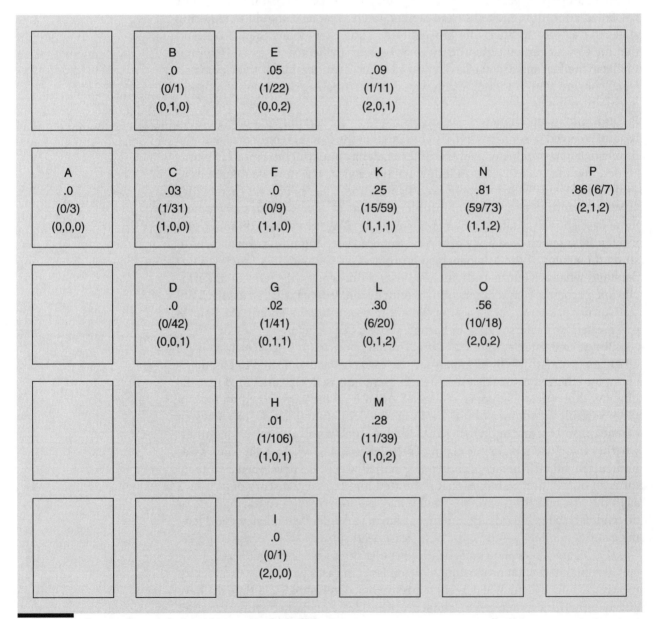

Figure 8-2 Death sentencing rates for Barnett's categories of defendants.

cant but not preponderant rate in moderate-scored cases (boxes K-M), to a preponderant rate in high-scored cases (boxes N-P). The second thing to note is how well the diagram illustrates the clear cases of overinclusion: unless Barnett's analysis failed to pick up on some key aggravating aspect of the cases—always a possibility when using a factors-type analysis—the imposition of the death sentence on one defendant in each of boxes C, E, G, H, and J seems clearly to be arbitrary in that it is unlikely that those defendants were among the worst murderers in Georgia during that time span. For those defendants, Justice Stewart's famous aphorism that "these death sentences are cruel and unusual in the same way that being struck by lightning is cruel and unusual" seems apt.

The third important thing to note about Barnett's diagram is how prevalent underinclusion is compared with overinclusion. I draw the dividing line separating overinclusion and underinclusion between boxes J and K. In all the boxes A-J, the death sentencing rate is below ten percent, while in all the boxes K-P, the death sentencing rate is at least twenty-five percent. To me, this indicates that the death-sentenced defendants in boxes K-P were not overincluded—their crimes were of a nature that evoked death sentences with regularity. If my dividing line is right, then there are 109 instances of underinclusion in boxes K-P, compared with only five cases of overinclusion in boxes A-J. This means that underinclusion is a much more prevalent aspect of the system than is overinclusion.

Academic underinclusionists do not demand perfect evenhandedness of the system. BWP set the threshold for evenhanded sentencing as above .80, i.e., in over eighty percent of similar cases, the sentence was death. Thus, they are willing to accept the evenhandedness of the death sentences in cases in boxes P (.86 ratio) and N (.81 ratio). The true underinclusion problem, according to academic underinclusionists, inheres in boxes K-M and O, where there is both a significant death sentencing rate and a significant number of defendants who are spared the ultimate sanction. The diagram thus well illustrates the core concern of the academic underinclusionists (including Steiker and Steiker)—a concern that they believe the Court shares. And, admittedly, academic underinclusionists do have significant language from the Court's opinions on which to rely. Nevertheless, to really understand what the Court is getting at by these statements, one must recognize that there are three different reasons for underinclusion, and that the Court views the validity of these reasons in quite different ways.

C. The Causes of Underinclusion Steiker and Steiker suggest that there are only two possible reasons for the failure to treat equally deserving cases alike: "for no reason, or for invidious reasons." Obviously, both of these are illegitimate reasons—no rational person wants to see a defendant sentenced to death because of the result of a coin toss, or because of racial or class bias. However, the landscape of underinclusion has more features than these two, as will be apparent by examining a set of Georgia cases that have been studied extensively.

During the five-year period covered by Barnett's study, there were about 2,000 defendants in Georgia convicted of murder or voluntary manslaughter. Of these, 594 defendants received either life or death sentences after jury trials, or were sentenced to death after pleading guilty to murder. These 594 formed the basis for Barnett's analysis. In 194 of those cases, there was a single death penalty trial, and in twelve additional cases, there were two or more penalty trials. The upshot is a total of 206 penalty trials with 112 death sentences imposed. The obvious challenge arising from the data is to explain the factors that resulted in some defendants being sentenced to death, and others not. Barnett and BWP made herculean efforts to isolate factors about the cases from which explanations could be inferred. I will now, instead, identify factors about the system that account for the underinclusion.

Only about thirty percent of homicide cases (594 out of approximately 2,000) resulted in murder convictions. Thus, there was a seventy percent underinclusion rate "off-the-top" as to whether the death sentence would be sought. This underinclusion must be due in part to what I will call "prosecutorial charging underinclusion"—the prosecutor chose not to seek a murder conviction. The reasons for prosecutorial underinclusion can conceptually be divided into three categories: (1) merits-based—the prosecutor did not personally believe that the case warranted a murder conviction, and/or the prosecutor did not believe the jury could be convinced to return a murder verdict; (2) mundane—which includes a whole host of variables that are endemic to a prosecutor's job, e.g., a key witness disappeared or changed stories, the prosecutor had a case overload and needed to plea bargain, the prosecutor had to offer a deal to one co-defendant to obtain testimony against another, etc.; and (3) invidious—the prosecutor's decision not to seek a murder conviction was based on illegitimate discriminatory motives, most likely racial or class bias.

The seventy percent off-the-top underinclusion rate also must be in part a result of what I will call "guilt-determiner underinclusion"—the prosecutor sought a murder conviction, but the trier of fact (usually a jury) returned a manslaughter verdict. This underinclusion can be divided into two categories: (1) merits-based—the trier of fact felt that the facts warranted the lesser conviction; and (2) invidious—the trier of fact reduced the level of the conviction for illegitimate discriminatory motives.

Of the 594 cases that resulted in murder convictions, prosecutors sought death sentences in only about one-third of them. Of the 400 instances in which the death penalty was not sought, 123 can be explained by the fact that the defendant was not death-eligible because there was no statutory aggravating factor present. This leaves about 270 cases of what I will call "prosecutorial sentencing underinclusion." Again, the universe of possible causes of prosecutorial underinclusion can be divided into three categories: merits-based, mundane, and invidious.

The data also show that the sentencers declined to impose death sentences in ninety instances out of 203, a "sentencer underinclusion" rate of about forty-five percent. This underinclusion can theoretically be divided into the same two categories as guilt-determiner underinclusion: merits-based—the sentencer felt that the case did not warrant a death sentence, and invidious—the sentencer declined to impose a death sentence for illegitimate motives. This describes a richer and more true-to-life understanding of underinclusion than is presented by Steiker and Steiker. The richer understanding of underinclusion has important implications for understanding the Court's death penalty jurisprudence. A necessary prelude to examining that jurisprudence, though, is a paean to the virtues of merit-based underinclusion.

D. The Legitimacy of Merits-Based Underinclusion Our system is *designed* to be merits-based underinclusive at the guilt/innocence stage. The old adage that it is better for ten guilty persons to go free than for one innocent person to be convicted is premised on the belief that when the individual's stake is so high, the risk of error should fall on the side of underinclusion by a fairly large margin. This underinclusion sentiment is reflected in the criminal justice system by two primary devices, which I will refer to as "traditional underinclusion mechanisms": the requirement of proof of guilt beyond a reasonable doubt, and the requirement of a supermajority vote of the jury for conviction (unanimity in most jurisdictions). The Court has held that both of these traditional underinclusion mechanisms are mandated by the Constitution, which means they must reflect a laudable policy goal. Thus, at the guilt/innocence stage, merits-based underinclusion is indisputably a virtue, not a vice.

The virtue of merits-based underinclusion at the sentencing stage *in general* is a less straightforward proposition. Where the system is, by definition, not dealing with innocent persons, there are undeniable benefits to consistency in terms of actual fairness, the appearance of fairness, and general deterrence. Equally undeniably, however, there should always be a place for individualization in the sentencing process, as even quite rigid sentencing guidelines recognize. The clearest underinclusion mechanism at sentencing is simple mercy—the defendant may deserve a certain sentence, but there is nonetheless some reason, perhaps inarticulable, not to give it to the defendant.

As to *capital* sentencing, the urge for merits-based underinclusion is strong, and its wellsprings parallel those that animate the desire for underinclusion at the guilt/innocence stage. The state's extinguishing of the defendant's life seems qualitatively different and more drastic than any other punishment that can be imposed—to most of us, death *is* different.

State death sentencing procedures are chock-full of underinclusion mechanisms. These devices are at their most potent in states where the jury is the sentencer. Twenty-eight of the thirty-eight death penalty states fall into this category. In eighteen of those states, the jury must unanimously find that at least one statutory aggravating circumstance has been proven by the state. In all twenty-eight jury sentencing states, the jury must unanimously vote for a death sentence.

The beyond-a-reasonable-doubt standard is almost, but not quite, as prevalent as the unanimity requirement. Most states employ these traditional underinclusion mechanisms in combination. The most underinclusive combination, found in three states, is a unanimity requirement as to the aggravating circumstances, coupled with a requirement that the aggravating circumstances unanimously be found to outweigh the mitigating circumstances beyond a reasonable doubt. The most common combination, found in eleven states, is a unanimity requirement as to the aggravating circumstances that must be found beyond a reasonable doubt, followed by a requirement that the jury unanimously find for death after considering the aggravating and mitigating circumstances. Every jury-sentencing state has opted to employ at least one, and usually more than one, underinclusion mechanism.

The non-jury-sentencing states give the sentencing decision to the trial judge. The unanimity requirement is, of course, inapplicable to a one-person sentencer. However, some of these states do employ burden of persuasion underinclusion mechanisms.

There is no definitive research examining whether death sentencing underinclusion mechanisms have an actual underinclusive effect, and, if so, how much. Yet, common sense suggests that there is such an effect. In particular, it seems that the requirement for unanimity in jury sentencing states should have a powerful underinclusive effect. There is, in fact, some data to support this hunch: death sentencing rates tend to be lower in jury sentencing states than in judge-sentencing states.

Georgia, a jury-sentencing state, employs the most common combination of traditional underinclusion mechanisms. Since there are three causes of underinclusion—merits-based, invidious, and mundane—Barnett's chart becomes at once both more problematic and more meaningful. Now, rather than simply labeling disparities where the death sentencing rates range from .25 to .56, as underinclusive and thus undesirable, we have to ask what kinds of underinclusion are at work. If, as I have argued, underinclusion mechanisms can have merits-based underinclusive effects, then it seems likely that some of the non-death sentences in those boxes are underincluded for that reason.

I am not alone in believing that such underinclusion is legitimate and desirable: a broad-ranging consensus supports the desirability of merits-based underinclusion in death sentencing. Many state legislators who support the death penalty have included underinclusion mechanisms in their states' death penalty statutes. Further, state legislators have included these mechanisms voluntarily, as the Supreme Court has never even hinted that states are required to adopt such mechanisms. On the other side of the debate, death penalty opponents, who have lost the fight to abolish the death penalty, would surely, as a fallback position, want to have as many underinclusion mechanisms as possible incorporated in any death penalty statute. Thus, I believe that it is hardly open to debate that merits-based underinclusion in death sentencing is a virtue, not a vice.

E. Supreme Court Underinclusiveness Jurisprudence

1. Mundane and Merits-Based Underinclusion

The Court has not wanted to regulate prosecutorial underinclusiveness resulting from mundane causes, perhaps because it recognizes that it has no effective way—short of declaring the death penalty unconstitutional per se—to regulate this sort of prosecutorial behavior.

The Court also has sought to prevent states from curtailing the power of guilt-determiners to exercise merits-based underinclusion. The key precedent in this area is *Beck v. Alabama*, in which the Court found a state law that prohibited lesser-included offense instructions unconstitutional. Giving the guilt-determiner the option of convicting of a lesser included offense provides the opportunity to underinclude. *Beck* establishes the constitutional necessity that the guilt-determiner be provided with that opportunity.

As with guilt-determiner underinclusion, the Court has actively sought to prohibit states from curtailing merits-based sentencer underinclusion. This practice is illustrated by several important lines of authority, starting with the 1968 decision of *Witherspoon v. Illinois*. *Witherspoon* clearly shows the Court embracing death sentence underinclusion by prohibiting the state from employing a device—exclusion of death-dubious jurors—that would have tended to minimize the chances of underinclusion.

The *Woodson* line of cases illustrates the same point. The effect of a mandatory sentence is to negate the possibility of underinclusion as to any defendant who falls into that category. The Court's unwillingness to tolerate such mandatory schemes clearly illustrates its dislike for devices that would eliminate the possibility of underinclusion.

The *Lockett/Eddings* doctrine requiring the sentencer to consider all the mitigating evidence offered by the defendant also undermines Steiker and Steiker's conclusion that the Court is not concerned with underinclusion. The purpose of the requirement is to give the sentencer every possible basis to underinclude a particular defendant.

These lines of authority, taken together, constitute strong evidence that the Court has consistently viewed merits-based sentencer underinclusion as a virtue, and has taken steps to prohibit states from minimizing it. However, it is the line of authority embodied in *McCleskey v. Kemp*, that is the real nail in the coffin of Steiker and Steiker's argument that the Court has viewed all underinclusion, whatever its source, as a vice. Steiker and Steiker discuss *McCleskey* under the fourth of their concerns, heightened procedural regularity. However, *McCleskey* is much more pertinent to underinclusion because it is the only important case in which the Court has ever been starkly confronted with the opportunity to view underinclusion as a vice calling for a constitutional remedy.

Although not the most famous portion of the opinion, the Court did consider whether McCleskey's death sentence could stand in view of the fact that others with similar culpability had not been sentenced to death. In essence, the Court considered whether underinclusion rendered the death sentence unconstitutional. The Court declined to find a constitutional defect: "Absent a showing that the Georgia capital punishment system operates in an arbitrary and capricious manner, McCleskey cannot prove a constitutional violation by demonstrating that other defendants who may be similarly situated did not receive the death penalty." A clearer rejection of the notion that the Court believes capital underinclusion, regardless of its source, to be unconstitutional can hardly be imagined.

These lines of authority not only serve to prohibit states from minimizing the opportunity for merits-based sentencer underinclusion, but also indirectly foster merits-based underinclusion by prosecutors at both the charging and sentencing stages. Tender-hearted prosecutors can defend decisions not to seek death sentences by saying, "While the case may have warranted it, I wasn't completely sure," or, more likely, "I didn't think the sentencer would go for death, so why spend all that extra money?" Even hard-nosed prosecutors can't ignore fiscal concerns, nor do they like to be perceived as having "lost" a case where they sought a death sentence, but the sentencer returned a nondeath verdict. Thus, maintaining the power of the sentencer to underinclude likely has a "trickle-down" effect on prosecutors.

2. The Court's Real and Only Underinclusion Concern: Invidious Underinclusion
Despite the Court's broad pronouncements that state death penalty systems are required to operate evenhandedly, by process of elimination it is clear that *invid-*

ious underinclusion is the *only* sort of underinclusion with which the Court has ever really been concerned.

In understanding the Court's concern with evenhandedness, it is important to recognize the racially charged milieu in which members of the Court made their initial comments about the subject back in *Furman*. For as many years as they had been on the Court, these justices had seen a steady stream of death penalty cases from the South in which (1) African-Americans were seemingly disproportionately represented as defendants; and (2) many of the defendants had been sentenced to death for rape of white women. In this milieu, it seems quite likely that judicial comments about evenhandedness are in fact coded references to concerns about invidious racial discrimination against African-American defendants.

Fifteen years after *Furman*, the *McCleskey* Court dealt invidious discrimination claims in capital cases a near-mortal blow. The BWP study was about the most compelling scenario that could have been conceived—short of race-of-defendant disparities—to induce the Court to condemn a capital punishment system on the basis of invidious racial discrimination. Nevertheless, the argument only induced four justices to that conclusion. To the majority, McCleskey's proof of invidious discrimination simply was not strong enough. While this was a great defeat for death penalty opponents, the Court did in fact adhere to the position that invidious discrimination, if proven, would be unconstitutional.

The most charitable interpretation of the dubious holding that the proof was insufficient is that the Court may have been worried that a contrary conclusion would send the states "back to the drawing board" to come up with systems having some internal review mechanism promoting more consistency. This would, of course, have the concomitant effect of leaving less room for merits-based underinclusion. Perhaps this concern was in Justice Powell's mind when he wrote for the majority: "Discretion in the criminal justice system offers substantial benefits to the criminal defendant. Of course, 'the power to be lenient also is the power to discriminate,' but a capital punishment system that did not allow for discretionary acts of leniency 'would be totally alien to our notions of criminal justice.'"

3. The Court's Primary Concern: Minimizing Overinclusion

I have demonstrated that the Court's dual concerns with respect to underinclusion have been to maximize the opportunities for the merits-based variety, while minimizing the instances of the invidious kind. This is consistent with the Court's primary goal of minimizing overinclusion.

To summarize my argument so far, the academic underinclusionists are wrong in identifying one of the Court's goals as rectifying states' "failure to treat equally deserving cases alike" (again, except for invidious underinclusion). Rather, the Court has tried to *preserve* the power of prosecutors and sentencers to underinclude in potential capital cases. I will argue next that not only have Steiker and Steiker misidentified one of the Court's goals, but they also have not proven their claim that the Court's jurisprudence has failed to achieve any measurable degree of success as to its chosen goals. Indeed, the available evidence points in the opposite direction.

III. *Steiker and Steiker Have Not Proven That the Court's Regulatory Effort Has Been an Ineffective Disaster and Have Ignored Evidence to the Contrary*

Steiker and Steiker's argument for the ineffectiveness of the Court's capital punishment jurisprudence has both a premise and a conclusion. The *premise* is that the Court has not imposed significant requirements or prohibitions mandating states to create systems having stricter standards than pre-*Furman* systems, but, through the *Lockett/Eddings* doctrine, has actually forced states back toward pre-*Furman*-like systems. This means that while present systems *appear* to be more nonarbitrarily selective and provide for more structured and informed decisionmaking, they have virtually the same potential to operate in a systematically arbitrary fashion. I believe this premise is flawed because there are at least two significant ways that current systems not only appear to provide for less arbitrary decision making, but actually do so: the required statutory narrowing of death-eligibility, and sentencing hearings that permit the defendant to present mitigating evidence.

The conclusion of Steiker and Steiker's syllogism is that because the Court's jurisprudence leaves virtually the same potential for arbitrariness as in pre-*Furman* systems, the jurisprudence has been "a disaster, an enormous regulatory effort with almost no rationalizing effect." Even assuming, arguendo, that their premise is correct, Steiker and Steiker's conclusion is flawed. The Steikers' argument consistently leaps from the *could be* to the *is*: because current state systems, minimally regulated by the Court, *invite* arbitrary application, the Court's jurisprudence *is* an ineffective disaster. Steiker and Steiker miss an indispensable logical step: they have to prove that systems with virtually the same potential to operate in systematically arbitrary fashions are actually living down to that potential. The authors do not even attempt such proof, and in fact, they ignore important evidence to the contrary.

A. The Flaw in Steiker and Steiker's Premise Steiker and Steiker minimize the winnowing effect of aggravating circumstances in Georgia, citing BWP's work showing that most post-*Furman* Georgia murderers are death-eligible because their cases involve at least one aggravating circumstance. While it is true that the aggravating circumstance requirement's winnowing effect is not huge, neither is it de minimis: BWP found that of the 606 jury-trial murder convictions in their post-*Furman* study, 123 defendants were immune from the death penalty because no aggravating circumstance existed. This is an exclusion rate of twenty percent that did not exist pre-*Furman*. Admittedly, these excluded defendants would have been unlikely candidates for death even under the pre-*Furman* system. But that also means that they would have been candidates from which one could expect instances of overinclusion. If, as I have argued, the Court has always been primarily concerned with overinclusion, then the Court should consider it a victory to have forced Georgia to define these defendants out of the death-eligible pool. In this respect, the post-*Furman* Georgia system is demonstrably more nonarbitrarily selective than the pre-*Furman* system.

Prior to 1970, a death penalty trial in Georgia was unitary, meaning that the jury deliberated on both guilt and sentence at the close of the state's case. In 1970, two years before *Furman*, the Georgia Legislature mandated bifurcated proceedings in death penalty cases. This was a step forward, but BWP had this to say about those sentencing proceedings: "Prior to *Furman*, the sentencing phase of Georgia's bifurcated procedure was a perfunctory affair." Of sentencing hearings during the five years after *Gregg*, BWP had this to say: "After *Furman* and, perhaps more importantly, after *Lockett* the evidence offered during the sentencing phase of capital cases in Georgia became much more extensive." Here, then, is another way in which the difference between the pre- and post-*Furman* worlds is not just a chimera—the sentencer in Georgia got significantly more relevant information in the post-*Furman* era.

B. The Flaw in Steiker and Steiker's Conclusion Despite the demonstrable rationalizing effects of the statutory narrowing of death eligibility and more complete sentencing hearings, Steiker and Steiker correctly argue that the potential for arbitrary overinclusion still exists. After all, no human-judgment-driven system is perfect. Nevertheless, to prove that this potential is being realized to the same extent as in the pre-*Furman* era, Steiker and Steiker would have to present something more than assumption and conjecture. This they do not do.

1. Empirical Evidence of the Decline in Overinclusion—BWP's Georgia Study

When it comes to empirical analysis of the real-world effects of a death penalty system, the work of BWP in Georgia towers above all others, and is the only substantial research effort that has compared a pre-*Furman* system with a post-*Furman* system. The BWP data, although used by BWP to measure underinclusion, can easily be adapted to examine overinclusion.

BWP sorted 293 death-eligible (guilty of murder) pre-*Furman* cases into six culpability levels (with level one being least culpable, and level six being most culpable) based upon numerous factors. They then calculated the death sentencing rate within each level. Their results are set forth in **Figure 8-3**. The data is easy to understand: at level one, for example, only one out of 110 defendants was sentenced to death, a rate of .01; while at level six, ten out of ten defendants were sentenced to death, a rate of 1.00.

The chart clearly illustrates some overinclusion, although exactly how much depends upon what cutoff one establishes for the dividing line between overinclusion and underinclusion. To me, the .23 rate at level three does *not* illustrate overinclusion—almost a quarter of the murderers in that level were determined unanimously by juries to be among the "worst" murderers. On the other hand, any defendant in a level where the death sentencing rate falls below .10 (ten percent) has figuratively been "struck by lightning." The data in this chart does not require any thinner parsing: using the .10 cutoff, the proportion of overincluded defendants to the whole 293-person population is .03 (9/293). This rate is quite low in and of itself. However, the proportion of overinclusive death sentences within the category of the death-sentenced is significant—nine of the forty-four death sentences were overinclusive, a proportion of .20 (twenty percent).

Case Culpability Level (lowest to highest)	Death-Sentence Rate
1	.01 (1/110)
2	.08 (8/95)
3	.23 (10/43)
4	.53 (8/15)
5	.35 (7/20)
6	1.00 (10/10)

Figure 8-3 Death sentencing rates for BWP categories of pre-*Furman* defendants.

BWP performed the same analysis on 606 Georgia murder convictions in the five years following the 1973 enactment of the new Georgia death penalty statute prompted by *Furman*. The lack of any aggravating circumstance removed 123 defendants from death penalty eligibility, which left 483 eligible cases. The BWP figures for those cases are shown in **Figure 8-4**.

Here, more discrimination concerning where to draw the cutoff for over-inclusion is appropriate. Specifically, were the death-sentenced defendants at level two, where the rate is .14, overincluded? If we adopt a .10 cutoff, thereby deeming level two's death-sentenced defendants to *not* have been overincluded, then there is a significant improvement from the pre-*Furman* data: only six of the 606 defendants (remember, the 123 defendants who were convicted of first-degree murder but were not death-eligible because of the lack of an aggravating circumstance have to be included to make a valid comparison, because they would have been death-eligible pre-*Furman*) were overincluded, a proportion of .001 (compared to the pre-*Furman* proportion of .03); and only six of the 112 death sentences were overinclusive, a proportion of .05 (com-

Case Culpability Level (lowest to highest)	Death-Sentence Rate
1	.02 (6/276)
2	.14 (9/65)
3	.38 (18/47)
4	.65 (22/34)
5	.85 (23/27)
6	1.00 (34/34)

Figure 8-4 Death sentencing rates for BWP categories of post-*Furman* defendants.

pared to the pre-*Furman* proportion of .20). If we draw the cutoff higher, say at .15 (which would be reasonable), or .20 (which would be too high, but nevertheless would make no difference with these data, because the .14 rate at level two jumps to .38 at level three), the improvement still exists, although it becomes less significant. There also are fifteen defendants out of the 606-person population who were overincluded, a proportion of .025. While that improvement may be a modest one compared with the pre-*Furman* proportion of .03, such modesty could be because there really was not a great deal of improvement that could be made—the three-percent pre-*Furman* overinclusion rate may be about as close to "perfect" operation as any human-judgment-driven system is likely to get. However, another comparison shows more significant improvement in the post-*Furman* era—the overincluded defendants as a proportion of the death-sentenced defendants is .13 (fifteen of 112), rather than the pre-*Furman* .20 rate.

2. Some New Evidence That Overinclusion Is Not a Widespread Defect in Georgia's Sentencing

To determine whether BWP's findings about the decrease in overinclusion in Georgia were an artifact of the 1970s, I analyzed more recent cases in Georgia in which defendants received death sentences. I chose the twenty-five cases most recently decided by the Georgia Supreme Court on direct appeal. This sample includes almost one-quarter of the inmates on Georgia's death row, and covers Georgia Supreme Court opinions from early 1988 through late 1995.

I begin with a general comment: the facts in every one of the twenty-five cases (except one) serve immediate notice that the case is something more than a run-of-the-mill homicide. Six recurring exacerbating motifs (hereinafter "exacerbators") are apparent. By far the most commonly occurring (fifteen cases) is what I will call "overkill": the method of killing is particularly repulsive because the defendant inflicted more damage than was necessary to cause death. Four cases involve more than fifteen stab wounds; three involve multiple gunshot wounds inflicted in other than a continuous burst; two involve repeated bludgeoning; one involves both ligature and manual strangulation; and four involve a potpourri of methods, such as beating with a baseball bat, shooting, and dismembering (although the victim may have been dead at the time of dismembering).

After overkill, the second exacerbator is kidnap/rape/murder (four cases). The third is multiple homicide (six cases). The fourth is that the defendant's prior criminal record clearly indicated that he had not learned his lesson (three cases). The fifth exacerbator is that defendant was on a crime spree in which he committed serious crimes other than the homicide that resulted in the death sentence (seven cases). The sixth exacerbator is that the defendant killed a child (two cases). There is only one of the twenty-five cases that does not contain at least one of these exacerbating motifs, and many cases involve more than one.

The exacerbators are, of course, only a rough-and-ready indicator that these death sentences were not overinclusive. A more illuminating test would be to try to estimate what percentage of similar cases resulted in death sentences. I analyzed the cases in two ways. First, I applied the Barnett method. Second, I used a method developed by BWP that categorizes cases based upon the following factors: the number of persons killed by defendant; whether the defendant committed a serious contemporaneous offense; whether there were serious aggravating circumstances; whether defendant had a prior record; whether there were mitigating circumstances; and whether there were minor aggravating circumstances. The two methods are complementary in that each considers significant factors that the other does not, or uses the factors differently in the analysis. I considered a case worthy of further discussion in terms of overinclusion if its ratio did not rise to the level of .30 using either method. The results of my analyses appear in summary form in **Figure 8-5**.

There are four cases—all involving intrafamily killings—that require closer examination for overinclusion because they do not rise to the .30 ratio under either the Barnett or BWP criteria: cases 7, 13, 15, and 18.

Case 15 is the lowest scoring of all the cases—garnering only a .01 ratio in the Barnett analysis, and a .00 under the BWP analysis-yet it is the easiest one to understand why a death sentence was

Case #	Barnett Ratio	BWP Ratio	Exacerbators
1	.28	.68	Overkill; kidnap/rape; child victim
2	.56	.32	Double homicide
3	.81	.60	Overkill
4	—	.25	Prior record; spree
5	.56	.03	Overkill
6	.28	.60	Overkill
7	.01	.00?	—
8	.28	.32	Double homicide
9	.56	—	Overkill
10	.81	.69	Overkill; spree
11	.86	.69	Kidnap/rape; spree
12	.28	.89	Overkill
13	.28	.03	Overkill
14	.56	.69	Overkill; spree
15	.01	.00	Child victim
16	.28	.60	Overkill; spree
17	.81	.60	Overkill
18	.05	.03	Overkill
19	.28	.88	Double homicide
20	.30	.88	Double homicide; spree
21	.81	.25	Kidnap/rape; prior record
22	.28	.32	Triple homicide; 2 child (?) victims
23	.56	.42	Overkill
24	.28	.32	Double homicide
25	.81	.69	Overkill; spree

Figure 8-5 Levels of culpability in recent Georgia death sentences.

imposed. What the case really shows are the limitations of both the Barnett and BWP analyses. In this case, the defendant's ten-year-old son annoyed him by playing with a toy tractor after the defendant asked him to stop. Defendant found his shotgun (which the family had hidden), and shot the boy while the child begged for his life. Defendant then stated, "I couldn't learn him nothing by beating him with a belt, so I guess I learned him something this time." The defendant was, though, quite drunk at the time. The case scores only 1, 0, 1 under the Barnett criteria because, the defendant knew the victim, there was no claim of self-defense, and the case does not meet any of the criteria for the vileness sub-inquiry concerning the horrific nature of the killing. The case scores low under the BWP criteria because the only factor working against the defendant is a serious aggravating circumstance (victim pled for life). The case did not involve a serious contemporaneous felony, the defendant had no prior record, the defendant presented the mitigator of drunkenness, and there was no minor aggravating circumstance. Neither analysis captures the significance of the victim being a child, the trivialness of the "provocation," or the defendant's subsequent boasting about the homicide. Common sense indicates that this is actually quite an aggravated case, and that many—if not most—juries would impose death sentences in similar cases.

The hardest case in which to explain the death sentence as not overinclusive is number 7. In this case, the defendant broke into his ex-wife's house armed with a gun. When she and her son arrived home, the son tried to shoot the defendant, but the gun wouldn't fire. Defendant hit his ex-wife at least fifty times, then dragged her outside, pulled her head back by her hair, and shot her in the forehead. This case is the only one of the twenty-five that does not involve an exacerbator. Further, the case's Barnett score of 1, 0, 1 places it in a category where only one of 106 cases resulted in a death sentence. Under BWP analysis, it falls into a box where the ratio is .00 (unless this qualifies as an "execution-style" killing, in which case it moves to a box with a .42 ratio). What all this shows is that despite the appalling nature of the case, it is a fairly typical domestic killing. The other twenty-four cases demonstrate that death sentences are not imposed in domestic killings unless there are multiple homicides (as in cases 2, 22, and 24), overkill (as in cases 12, 13, 14, 18 and 23), or a child victim (as in case 15). None of these factors are present here. Although the case does involve an armed burglary, and an arguably cold, execution-style slaying, it may represent an instance of overinclusion.

My conclusion from analyzing these cases is that, with one possible exception, the Georgia system has not been overinclusive over the past six years. This conclusion accords with the very low rate of overinclusion illustrated by the BWP study of 1973–1978. Even though neither BWP nor I examined cases from 1979–1988 for overinclusion, I feel fairly confident in asserting that Georgia's post-*Furman* system has not exhibited a significant degree of overinclusion. Whether the same can be said for other states is an open question, but perhaps the Georgia data provides hope that what is true in Georgia is also true elsewhere.

3. Empirical Evidence of the Decline in Underinclusion

BWP specifically set out to compare underinclusion in the pre-and post-*Furman* cases. Their standard for judging underinclusion was if the frequency with which death sentences occur in other cases classified as similar is less than .35. If the death-sentencing rate among similar cases exceeds .80, they classify a death-sentence case as presumptively evenhanded." Using an "overall culpability" index based upon seventeen legitimate case characteristics and regression analysis, BWP studied a sample of pre- and post-*Furman* cases. BWP found:

> *In comparison to the pre-*Furman *figure, there is more selectivity in the post-*Furman *system. For example, only 29 percent of the post-*Furman *death-sentence cases possessed culpability scores equal to or less than the culpability score of the 95th percentile life-sentence cases, a decline from the comparable pre-*Furman *figure of 61 percent. Only 13 percent of the post-*Furman *death sentences appear in categories of cases with death-sentencing rates of less than .35, and more than half of the post-*Furman *death sentences occurred in cases for which the death-sentencing rate among similar cases exceeds .80.*

One also should note from the two BWP charts above that the death-sentencing rate rose in the three crucial midlevel categories that give rise to the underinclusion concern—from .23 to .38 in level three; from .53 to .65 in level four; and from .35 to .85 in level five—indeed, the level five proportion moved from the brink of presumptive excessiveness to above the threshold for presumptive evenhandedness. Steiker and Steiker fail to acknowledge the existence of this evidence; indeed, they cite the very BWP book in which this data appears for support of their position.

Whether we should be heartened by this decline in underinclusion is another question. A decline in merits-based underinclusion would be a mixed blessing: while it would make the system more evenhanded, it also would tend to show that the system is not erring as much as it perhaps should on the side of not imposing death in debatable cases. A decline in mundane underinclusion would be neutral. A decline in invidious underinclusion would be welcome, but there is no significant evidence of such a decline due to anything the Court has done.

4. Are the Post-Furman Declines in Overinclusion and Underinclusion Attributable to the Court's Jurisprudence?

A last hope for Steiker and Steiker's conclusion might be that, even assuming these improvements in overinclusion and underinclusion exist, they were *not* a result of the Court's death penalty regulatory jurisprudence, but instead resulted from some *other* factor(s). But BWP considered this possibility, and rejected the conclusion that the Court's efforts had not played a significant role in the process. BWP noted that improvements in the system began immediately and abruptly after the Georgia Legislature retooled the death penalty statutes in the wake of *Furman*.

BWP hypothesized four changes other than the statutory reforms prompted by *Furman* that might have accounted for the improvements: better record-keeping in the state system; a general trend toward consistency and reasonableness on the parts of prosecutors and juries, perhaps from better education and improved living standards; initially greater selectivity by prosecutors and judges due to the fear that the Court would exercise close supervision over the new system; and a general decline in racial discrimination. While believing that each of these alternative hypotheses probably had some explanatory power, BWP concluded that the impact of the statutory reforms was nonetheless important: "We remain persuaded, therefore, that Georgia's 1973 statutory reforms contributed significantly to the decline of excessiveness that we observe in our post-*Furman* data." Those statutory reforms were, of course, a direct product of the Court's death penalty jurisprudence. This hardly supports Steiker and Steiker's conclusion that the Court's efforts—judged through the lens of its own concerns—have been an ineffective disaster in Georgia. The Georgia data gives reason to suspect that the same ameliorative effect has occurred in other states.

IV. *Conclusion*

Steiker and Steiker begin the second paragraph of their article with the observation, "Virtually no one thinks that the constitutional regulation of capital punishment has been a success." If the authors had said "*complete* success," surely no one, including the Supreme Court justices, would disagree. But the Court would not—and should not—agree that its efforts have been an ineffective disaster. The best available evidence shows that the Court's regulatory death penalty jurisprudence *has* been successful in decreasing overinclusion, which is the primary vice that the Court has seen in death penalty systems for the last quarter of a century. One can argue that the Court was wrong to focus (or focus so exclusively) on minimizing overinclusion, or that the Court could have devised better ways to achieve that goal. But let's give credit where credit is due—the populations of death rows since 1972 very likely comprise a more carefully selected and "worse" collection of malefactors than before 1972. This is not an insignificant achievement. So, while death penalty opponents rue the Court's failure to regulate death more severely, I doubt that there is one experienced capital defense lawyer in this country who would rather return to the pre-*Furman* era. Perhaps not even many prosecutors would want to return to the days before *Furman*, when such an unguided power of life and death rested in their hands.

Mitigating Evidence

9

■ Mitigating Evidence—Introduction

In *Woodson v. North Carolina*, the Supreme Court rejected a mandatory death penalty for all defendants convicted of first-degree murder or felony murder. The North Carolina approach was ostensibly a valid response to the *Furman* concern with arbitrariness. All murderers would be treated equally under a mandatory scheme, addressing Justice Stewart's concern with the "freakishness" with which death was imposed, and Justice Douglas's concern with discriminatory application. More defendants would be executed, addressing Justice White's concern that the death penalty was imposed too infrequently to serve the aim of deterrence. The Court nevertheless rejected the mandatory scheme because it failed to allow for individualized consideration of the appropriateness of the death penalty. No such requirement constrains state governments or the federal government from imposing mandatory minimum noncapital sentences on defendants. Death is different, according to the *Woodson* Court:

> The penalty of death is qualitatively different from a sentence of imprisonment, however long. Death, in its finality, differs more from life imprisonment than a 100-year prison term differs from one of only a year or two. Because of that qualitative difference, there is a corresponding difference in the need for reliability in the determination that death is the appropriate punishment in a specific case.

Prior to imposing a sentence of death, the judge or jury must consider the particular aspects of the character and record of each convicted defendant. Justice Stewart wrote for the majority:

> We believe that in capital cases the fundamental respect for humanity underlying the Eighth Amendment...requires consideration of the character and record of the individual offender and the circumstances of the particular offense as a constitutionally indispensable part of the process of inflicting the penalty of death.

A corollary of *Woodson* is that the defendant must be allowed to present mitigating evidence on his own behalf. The Georgia scheme, approved in *Gregg* on the same day the Court rejected the North Carolina scheme, authorized the jury "to consider any other appropriate aggravating or mitigating circumstances."

Gregg and *Woodson* left unresolved the question of how much mitigating evidence the defendant has a right to present. In *Lockett v. Ohio* (1978), the Court answered that a defendant could present as much mitigating evidence as he wants. Once a jury returned a verdict of guilt and found an aggravating factor to be present, the Ohio death penalty statute required the trial judge to impose a death sentence unless he found, by a preponderance of the evidence, that: (1) the victim had induced or facilitated the offense, (2) it was unlikely that the defendant would have committed the offense but for the fact that he "was under duress, coercion, or strong provocation," or (3) the offense was "primarily the product of the defendant's psychosis or mental deficiency." Lockett argued that the Ohio statute did not permit the sentencing judge to consider as mitigating evidence her age, her lack of intent to cause death, and her minor role in the offense. The Supreme Court agreed.

Lockett followed the logic of *Woodson*, holding that a defendant must be permitted to offer any aspect of his character or record or any of the circumstances of the offense that he deemed relevant. Justice Burger echoed the *Woodson* Court's notion of the distinctiveness of death as a punishment. He wrote:

> *Given that the imposition of death by public authority is so profoundly different from all other penalties, we cannot avoid the conclusion that an individualized decision is essential in capital cases. The need for treating each defendant in a capital case with the degree of respect due the uniqueness of the individual is far more important than in noncapital cases.*

Lockett merges two distinct issues: the quantity of mitigating evidence the defendant must be allowed to present, and how much consideration the jury must give to the evidence as presented. *Lockett* suggests that the defendant must be allowed to present any mitigating evidence he wants. Whether constraints can be placed on the jury's consideration of the offered evidence is another matter.

Lockett favorably cites the Texas death penalty statute, approved by the Court in *Jurek*. The Texas statute made no reference to mitigating evidence. Like the Ohio statute, the Texas statute required the death penalty to be imposed in cases of aggravated murder unless the jury affirmatively answered one of three narrow questions. The *Lockett* Court held that the second of these questions—"whether there is a probability that the defendant would commit criminal acts of violence that would constitute a continuing threat to society"—had been broadly interpreted by the Texas courts so as to allow the jury to consider whatever mitigating evidence the defendant might see fit to offer. The *Lockett* Court thus reconciles *Jurek* and *Lockett* as consistent, but it is at least arguable that the favorable reference to *Jurek* opens the door for states to restrict the manner in which mitigating evidence is considered, if not the quantity and kind of evidence that is offered.

Subsequent Court decisions have carried the *Woodson-Lockett* doctrine through to its furthest possible extension. In *Eddings v. Oklahoma*, 1982 decision, the Court held that a trial judge violated the rule of *Lockett* by failing to consider evidence of the defendant's troubled childhood and his emotional disturbance. In *Skipper v. Oklahoma*, the trial court refused to allow the defendant to introduce evidence of his good behavior in prison during the seven months he spent in jail awaiting trial. The Court held that this deprival also violated the requirements of *Lockett*, even though the behavior at issue occurred after the crime. (The relevance of this kind of evidence is debatable from a retributive standpoint. The point is considered at length in the discussion of victim impact evidence in Chapter 16.)

In *Hitchcock v. Dugger*, a 1987 decision concerning the Florida death penalty, the Court held that nonstatutory mitigating evidence must be considered. The Florida statute enumerates certain mitigating circumstances. Under the Florida scheme, the jury renders an advisory verdict as to whether the specified mitigating circumstances outweigh the specified aggravating circumstances. The trial judge only considered the mitigating evidence offered by *Hitchcock* that bore directly on the statutorily enumerated circumstances. The Court held that this too violated *Lockett*. The sentencer is not required to give effect to mitigating evidence, but all mitigating evidence offered by the defendant must be considered. Moreover, juror unanimity as to a single mitigating factor is not required to grant mercy to the defendant. If each juror believes that the mitigating evidence cumulatively outweighs the aggravating evidence, this is sufficient to spare the defendant, regardless of whether the jurors agree on which particular mitigating factor has been proved.

Lockett and its progeny are in some tension with *Furman* and *Gregg*. The thrust of *Furman* and *Gregg* is to reduce arbitrariness in sentencing. The *Lockett* line condones, indeed requires, unpredictability. These cases hold that the defendant must be allowed to present any mitigating evidence he deems relevant and that the jury must be allowed to give effect to this evidence, even if the individual jurors do not agree on the presence of particular mitigating factors. This requirement opens the door to randomness.

Justice Scalia puts it in starker terms:

> To acknowledge that "there is perhaps an inherent tension" between this line of cases and the line stemming from Furman, is rather like saying that there was perhaps an inherent tension between the Allies and the Axis Powers in World War II. And to refer to the two lines as pursuing "twin objectives," is rather like referring to the twin objectives of good and evil. They cannot be reconciled.

Whether this inconsistency is defensible is the subject of debate. The reason this kind of randomness is not uniformly condemned is that the error generated by *Lockett*'s breadth is different in kind from the error generated from the unguided discretion existing prior to the *Furman* decision. Recall David McCord's distinction between over-inclusiveness and under-inclusiveness. In the pre-*Furman* world, states ran the risk of sentencing undeserving defendants to die. McCord argues that the Supreme Court is more concerned with eliminating this overinclusiveness than with underinclusiveness. The *Lockett* rule does not cause an undeserving defendant to die. The only error it can create is that an otherwise deserving defendant is spared the death penalty. *Lockett* is, in part, about allowing juries the freedom to grant mercy. Some people say that randomness deriving from mercy is defensible. It is worth asking whether this distinction has force.

In one of the following readings, Jeffrey Kirchmeier argues that the Supreme Court's approach to mitigation is in inherent conflict with its concern for arbitrariness. Kirchmeier suggests that the only way to resolve the current paradox of death sentencing is to either adopt a mandatory sentencing scheme or, as he prefers, to abandon the death penalty entirely. Christopher Smith argues that a mandatory death penalty cannot eliminate arbitrariness or discrimination because the jury decision is but one of several decision points in the death-sentencing process.

■ Mitigating Evidence—Critical Documents

Woodson v. North Carolina
428 U.S. 280 (1976)

Judgment of the Court, and opinion of Mr. Justice Stewart, Mr. Justice Powell, and Mr. Justice Stevens, announced by Mr. Justice Stewart.

The question in this case is whether the imposition of a death sentence for the crime of first-degree murder under the law of North Carolina violates the Eighth and Fourteenth Amendments.

I

The petitioners were convicted of first-degree murder as the result of their participation in an armed robbery of a convenience food store, in the course of which the cashier was killed and a customer was seriously wounded.

The North Carolina General Assembly in 1974 followed the court's lead and enacted a new statute that was essentially unchanged from the old one except that it made the death penalty mandatory. The statute now reads as follows:

> *Murder in the first and second degree defined; punishment—A murder which shall be perpetrated by means of poison, lying in wait, imprisonment, starving, torture, or by any other kind of willful, deliberate and premeditated killing, or which shall be committed in the perpetration or attempt to perpetrate any arson, rape, robbery, kidnapping, burglary or other felony, shall be deemed to be murder in the first degree and shall be punished with death. All other kinds of murder shall be deemed murder in the second degree, and shall be punished by imprisonment for a term of not less than two years nor more than life imprisonment in the State's prison.*

It was under this statute that the petitioners, who committed their crime on June 3, 1974, were tried, convicted, and sentenced to death.

North Carolina, unlike Florida, Georgia, and Texas, has thus responded to *Furman* by making death the mandatory sentence for all persons convicted of first-degree murder. In ruling on the constitutionality of the sentences imposed on the petitioners under this North Carolina statute, the Court now addresses for the first time the question whether a mandatory death penalty for a broad category of homicidal offenses constitutes cruel and unusual punishment.

Central to the application of the Eighth Amendment is a determination of contemporary standards regarding the infliction of punishment. As discussed in *Gregg*, indicia of societal values identified in prior opinions include history and traditional usage, legislative enactments, and jury determinations.

In order to provide a frame for assessing the relevancy of these factors in this case we begin by sketching the history of mandatory death penalty statutes in the United States. At the time the Eighth Amendment was adopted in 1791, the States uniformly followed the common-law practice of making death the exclusive and mandatory sentence for certain specified offenses. Although the range of capital offenses in the American Colonies was quite limited in comparison to the more than 200 offenses then punishable by death in England, the Colonies at the time of the Revolution imposed death sentences on all persons convicted of any of a considerable number of crimes, typically including at a minimum, murder, treason, piracy, arson, rape, robbery, burglary, and sodomy. As at common law, all homicides that were not involuntary, provoked, justified, or excused constituted murder and were automatically punished by death. Almost from the outset jurors reacted unfavorably to the harshness of mandatory death sentences. The States initially responded to this expression of public dissatisfaction with mandatory statutes by limiting the classes of capital offenses.

This reform, however, left unresolved the problem posed by the not infrequent refusal of juries to convict murderers rather than subject them to automatic death sentences. In 1794, Pennsylvania attempted to alleviate the undue severity of the law by confining the mandatory death penalty to "murder of the first degree" encompassing all "wilful, deliberate and premeditated" killings. Other jurisdictions soon enacted similar measures, and within a generation the practice spread to most of the States.

Despite the broad acceptance of the division of murder into degrees, the reform proved to be an unsatisfactory means of identifying persons appropriately punishable by death. Although its failure was due in part to the amorphous nature of the controlling concepts of willfulness, deliberateness, and premeditation, a more fundamental weakness of the reform soon became apparent. Juries continued to find the death penalty inappropriate in a significant number of first-degree murder cases and refused to return guilty verdicts for that crime.

The inadequacy of distinguishing between murderers solely on the basis of legislative criteria narrowing the definition of the capital offense led the States to grant juries sentencing discretion in capital cases. Tennessee in 1838, followed by Alabama in 1841, and Louisiana in 1846, were the first States to abandon mandatory death sentences in favor of discretionary death penalty statutes. This flexibility remedied the harshness of mandatory statutes by permitting the jury to respond to mitigating factors by withholding the death penalty. By the turn of the century, 23 States and the Federal Government had made death sentences discretionary for first-degree murder and other capital offenses. During the next two decades 14 additional States replaced their mandatory death penalty statutes. Thus, by the end of World War I, all but eight States, Hawaii, and the District of Columbia either had adopted discretionary death penalty schemes or abolished the death penalty altogether. By 1963, all of these remaining jurisdictions had replaced their automatic death penalty statutes with discretionary jury sentencing.

The history of mandatory death penalty statutes in the United States thus reveals that the practice of sentencing to death all persons convicted of a particular offense has been rejected as unduly harsh and unworkably rigid. The two crucial indicators of evolving standards of decency respecting the imposition of punishment in our society—jury determinations and legislative enactments—both point conclusively to the repudiation of automatic death sentences.

Still further evidence of the incompatibility of mandatory death penalties with contemporary values is provided by the results of jury sentencing under discretionary statutes. In *Witherspoon v. Illinois*, the Court observed that "one of the most important functions any jury can perform" in exercising its discretion to choose "between life imprisonment and capital punishment" is "to maintain a link between contemporary community values and the penal system." Various studies indicate that even in first-degree murder cases, juries with sentencing discretion do not impose the death penalty "with any great frequency." The actions of sentencing juries suggest that under contemporary standards of decency death is viewed as an inappropriate punishment for a substantial portion of convicted first-degree murderers.

Although it seems beyond dispute that, at the time of the *Furman* decision in 1972, mandatory death penalty statutes had been renounced by American juries and legislatures, there remains the question whether the mandatory statutes adopted by North Carolina and a number of other States following *Furman* evince a sudden reversal of societal values regarding the imposition of capital punishment. In view of the persistent and unswerving legislative rejection of mandatory death penalty statutes beginning in 1838 and continuing for more than 130 years until *Furman*, it seems evident that the post-*Furman* enactments reflect attempts by the States to retain the death penalty in a form consistent with the Constitution, rather than a renewed societal acceptance of mandatory death sentencing. The fact that some States have adopted mandatory measures following *Furman* while others have legislated standards to guide jury discretion appears attributable to diverse readings of this Court's multi-opinioned decision in that case.

North Carolina's mandatory death penalty statute for first-degree murder departs markedly from contemporary standards respecting the imposition of the punishment of death and thus cannot be applied consistently with the Eighth and Fourteenth Amendments' requirement that the State's power to punish "be exercised within the limits of civilized standards."

B

A separate deficiency of North Carolina's mandatory death sentence statute is its failure to provide a constitutionally tolerable response to *Furman*'s rejection of unbridled jury discretion in the imposition of capital sentences. Central to the limited holding in *Furman* was the conviction that the vesting of standardless sentencing power in the jury violated the Eighth and Fourteenth Amendments. It is argued that North Carolina has remedied the inadequacies of the death penalty statutes held unconstitutional in *Furman* by withdrawing all sentencing discretion from juries in capital cases. But when one considers the long and consistent American experience with the death penalty in first-degree murder cases, it becomes evident that mandatory statutes enacted in response to *Furman* have simply papered over the problem of unguided and unchecked jury discretion.

As we have noted *supra,* there is general agreement that American juries have persistently refused to convict a significant portion of persons charged with first-degree murder of that offense under mandatory death penalty statutes. In view of the historic record, it is only reasonable to assume that many juries under mandatory statutes will continue to consider the grave consequences of a conviction in reaching a verdict. North Carolina's mandatory death penalty statute provides no standards to guide the jury in its inevitable exercise of the power to determine which first-degree murderers shall live and which shall die. And there is no way under the North Carolina law for the judiciary to check arbitrary and capricious exercise of that power through a review of death sentences. Instead of rationalizing the sentencing process, a mandatory scheme may well exacerbate the problem identified in *Furman* by resting the penalty determination on the particular jury's willingness to act lawlessly. While a mandatory death penalty statute may reasonably be expected to increase the number of persons sentenced to death, it does not fulfill *Furman's* basic requirement by replacing arbitrary and wanton jury discretion with objective standards to guide, regularize, and make rationally reviewable the process for imposing a sentence of death.

C

A third constitutional shortcoming of the North Carolina statute is its failure to allow the particularized consideration of relevant aspects of the character and record of each convicted defendant before the imposition upon him of a sentence of death. In *Furman*, members of the Court acknowledged what cannot fairly be denied—that death is a punishment different from all other sanctions in kind rather than degree. A process that accords no significance to relevant facets of the character and record of the individual offender or the circumstances of the particular offense excludes from consideration in fixing the ultimate punishment of death the possibility of compassionate or mitigating factors stemming from the diverse frailties of humankind. It treats all persons convicted of a designated offense not as uniquely individual human beings, but as members of a faceless, undifferentiated mass to be subjected to the blind infliction of the penalty of death.

This Court has previously recognized that "for the determination of sentences, justice generally requires that there be taken into account the circumstances of the offense together with the character and propensities of the offender." Consideration of both the offender and the offense in order to arrive at a just and appropriate sentence has been viewed as a progressive and humanizing development. While the prevailing practice of individualizing sentencing determinations generally reflects simply enlightened policy rather than a constitutional imperative, we believe that in capital cases the fundamental respect for humanity underlying the Eighth Amendment requires consideration of the character and record of the individual offender and the circumstances of the particular offense as a constitutionally indispensable part of the process of inflicting the penalty of death.

This conclusion rests squarely on the predicate that the penalty of death is qualitatively different from a sentence of imprisonment, however long. Death, in its finality, differs more from life imprisonment than a 100-year prison term differs from one of only a year or two. Because of that qualitative difference, there is a corresponding difference in the need for reliability in the determination that death is the appropriate punishment in a specific case.

For the reasons stated, we conclude that the death sentences imposed upon the petitioners under North Carolina's mandatory death sentence statute violated the Eighth and Fourteenth Amendments and therefore must be set aside.

Justice Rehnquist, dissenting.

The plurality relies first upon its conclusion that society has turned away from the mandatory imposition of death sentences, and second upon its conclusion that the North Carolina system has "simply papered over" the problem of unbridled jury discretion which two of the separate opinions in *Furman*, identified as the basis for the judgment rendering the death sentences there reviewed unconstitutional. The third "constitutional shortcoming" of the North Carolina statute is said to be "its failure to allow the particularized consideration of relevant aspects of the character and record of each convicted defendant before the imposition upon him of a sentence of death."

I do not believe that any one of these reasons singly, or all of them together, can withstand careful analysis. Contrary to the plurality's assertions, they would import into the Cruel and Unusual Punishments Clause procedural requirements which find no support in our cases. Their application will result in the invalidation of a death sentence imposed upon a defendant convicted of first-degree murder under the North Carolina system, and the upholding of the same sentence imposed on an identical defendant convicted on identical evidence of first-degree murder under the Florida, Georgia, or Texas systems—a result surely as "freakish" as that condemned in the separate opinions in *Furman*.

II

The plurality is simply mistaken in its assertion that "the history of mandatory death penalty statutes reveals that the practice of sentencing to death all persons convicted of a particular offense has been rejected as unduly harsh and unworkably rigid." This conclusion is purportedly based on two historic developments: the first a series of legislative decisions during the 19th century narrowing the class of offenses punishable by death; the second a series of legislative decisions during both the 19th and 20th centuries, through which mandatory imposition of the death penalty largely gave way to jury discretion in deciding whether or not to impose this ultimate sanction. The first development may have some relevance to the plurality's argument in general but has no bearing at all upon this case. The second development, properly analyzed, has virtually no relevance.

There can be no question that the legislative and other materials discussed in the plurality's opinion show a widespread conclusion on the part of state legislatures during the 19th century that the penalty of death was being required for too broad a range of crimes, and that these legislatures proceeded to narrow the range of crimes for which such penalty could be imposed. If this case involved the imposition of the death penalty for an offense such as burglary or sodomy, the virtually unanimous trend in the legislatures of the States to exclude such offenders from liability for capital punishment might bear on the plurality's Eighth Amendment argument. But petitioners were convicted of first-degree murder, and there is not the slightest suggestion that there had been any turning away at all, much less any such unanimous turning away, from the death penalty as a punishment for those guilty of first-degree murder.

The second string to the plurality's analytical bow is that legislative change from mandatory to discretionary imposition of the death sentence likewise evidences societal rejection of mandatory death penalties. The plurality simply does not make out this part of its case, however, in large part because it treats as being of equal dignity with legislative judgments the judgments of particular juries and of individual jurors.

There was undoubted dissatisfaction, from more than one sector of 19th century society, with the operation of mandatory death sentences. One segment of that society was totally opposed to capital punishment, and was apparently willing to accept the substitution of discretionary imposition of that penalty for its mandatory imposition as a halfway house on the road to total abolition. Another segment was equally unhappy with the operation of the mandatory system, but for an entirely different reason. As the plurality recognizes, this second segment of society was unhappy with the operation of the mandatory system, not because of the death sentences imposed under it, but because people obviously guilty of criminal offenses were *not* being convicted under it. Change to a discretionary system was accepted by these persons not because they thought mandatory imposition of the death penalty was cruel and unusual, but because they thought that if jurors were permitted to return a sentence other than death upon the conviction of a capital crime, fewer guilty defendants would be acquitted.

So far as the action of juries is concerned, the fact that in some cases juries operating under the mandatory system refused to convict obviously guilty defendants does not reflect any "turning away" from the death penalty, or the mandatory death penalty. Given the requirement of unanimity with respect to jury verdicts in capital cases, a requirement which prevails today, it is apparent that a single juror could prevent a jury from returning a verdict of conviction. Occasional refusals to convict, therefore, may just as easily have represented the intransigence of only a small minority of 12 jurors as well as the unanimous judgment of all 12. The fact that the presence of such jurors could prevent conviction in a given case, even though the majority of society, speaking through legislatures, had decreed that it should be imposed, certainly does not indicate that society as a whole rejected mandatory punishment for such offenders; it does not even indicate that those few members of society who serve on juries, as a whole, had done so.

Nor do the opinions in *Furman* which indicate a preference for discretionary sentencing in capital cases suggest in the slightest that a mandatory sentencing procedure would be cruel and unusual. The plurality concedes, as it must, that following *Furman* 10 States enacted laws providing for mandatory capital punishment. These enactments the plurality seeks to explain as due to a wrongheaded reading of the holding in *Furman*. But this explanation simply does not wash. While those States may be presumed to have preferred their prior systems reposing sentencing discretion in juries or judges, they indisputably preferred mandatory capital punishment to no capital punishment at all. Their willingness to enact statutes providing that penalty is utterly inconsistent with the notion that they regarded mandatory capital sentencing as beyond "evolving standards of decency." The plurality's glib rejection of *these* legislative decisions as having little weight on the scale which it finds in the Eighth Amendment seems to me more an instance of its desire to save the people from themselves than a conscientious effort to ascertain the content of any "evolving standard of decency."

III

The second constitutional flaw which the plurality finds in North Carolina's mandatory system is that it has simply "papered over" the problem of unchecked jury discretion. The plurality states that "there is general agreement that American juries have persistently refused to convict a significant portion of persons charged with first-degree murder of that offense under mandatory death penalty statutes." The basic factual assumption of the plurality seems to be that for any given number of first-degree murder defendants subject to capital punishment, there will be a certain number of jurors who will be unwilling to impose the death penalty even though they are entirely satisfied that the necessary elements of the substantive offense are made out.

In North Carolina jurors unwilling to impose the death penalty may simply hang a jury or they may so assert themselves that a verdict of not guilty is brought in; in Louisiana they will have a similar effect in causing some juries to bring in a verdict of guilty of a lesser included offense even though all the jurors are satisfied that the elements of the greater offense are made out. Such jurors, of course, are violating their oath, but such violation is not only consistent with the majority's hypothesis; the majority's hypothesis is bottomed on its occurrence.

For purposes of argument, I accept the plurality's hypothesis; but it seems to me impossible to conclude from it that a mandatory death sentence statute such as North Carolina enacted is any less sound constitutionally than are the systems enacted by Georgia, Florida, and Texas which the Court upholds.

In Georgia juries are entitled to return a sentence of life, rather than death, for no reason whatever, simply based upon their own subjective notions of what is right and what is wrong. In Florida the judge and jury are required to weigh legislatively enacted aggravating factors against legislatively enacted mitigating factors, and then base their choice between life or death on an estimate of the result of that weighing. Substantial discretion exists here, too, though it is somewhat more canalized than it is in Georgia. Why these types of discretion are regarded by the plurality as constitutionally permissible, while that which may occur in the North Carolina system is not, is not readily apparent. The freakish and arbitrary nature of the death penalty described in the separate concurring opinions of Justices Stewart and White, in *Furman* arose not from the perception that so *many* capital sentences were being imposed but from the perception that so *few* were being imposed. To conclude that the North Carolina system is bad because juror nullification may permit jury discretion while concluding that the Georgia and Florida systems are sound because they *require* this same discretion, is, as the plurality opinion demonstrates, inexplicable.

The Texas system much more closely approximates the mandatory North Carolina system which is struck down today. The jury is required to answer three statutory questions. If the questions are unanimously answered in the affirmative, the death penalty *must* be imposed. It is extremely difficult to see how this system can be any less subject to the infirmities caused by juror nullification which the plurality concludes are fatal to North Carolina's statute. Justices Stewart, Powell, and Stevens apparently think they can sidestep this inconsistency because of their belief that one of the three questions will permit consideration of mitigating factors justifying imposition of a life sentence. It is, however, as those Justices recognize, far from clear that the statute is to be read in such a fashion. In any event, while the imposition of such unlimited consideration of mitigating factors may conform to the plurality's novel constitutional doctrine that "a jury must be allowed to consider on the basis of all relevant evidence not only why a death sentence should be imposed, but also why it should not be imposed," the resulting system seems as likely as any to produce the unbridled discretion which was condemned by the separate opinions in *Furman*.

The plurality also relies upon the indisputable proposition that "death is different" for the result which it reaches in Part III-C. But the respects in which death is "different" from other punishment which may be imposed upon convicted criminals do not seem to me to establish the proposition that the Constitution requires individualized sentencing.

One of the principal reasons why death is different is because it is irreversible; an executed defendant cannot be brought back to life. This aspect of the difference between death and other penalties would undoubtedly support statutory provisions for especially careful review of the fairness of the trial, the accuracy of the fact-finding process, and the fairness of the sentencing procedure where the death penalty is imposed. But none of those aspects of the death sentence is at issue here. Petitioners were found guilty of the crime of first-degree murder in a trial the constitutional validity of which is unquestioned here. And since the punishment of death is conceded by the plurality not to be a cruel and unusual punishment for such a crime, the irreversible aspect of the death penalty has no connection whatever with any requirement for individualized consideration of the sentence.

The second aspect of the death penalty which makes it "different" from other penalties is the fact that it is indeed an ultimate penalty, which ends a human life rather than simply requiring that a living human being be confined for a given period of time in a penal institution. This aspect of the difference may enter into the decision of whether or not it is a "cruel and unusual" penalty for a given offense. But since in this case the offense was first-degree murder, that particular inquiry need proceed no further.

The plurality's insistence on individualized consideration of the sentencing, therefore, does not depend upon any traditional application of the prohibition against cruel and unusual punishment contained in the Eighth Amendment. The punishment here is concededly not cruel and unusual, and that determination has traditionally ended judicial inquiry in our cases construing the Cruel and Unusual Punishments Clause. What the plurality opinion has actually done is to import into the Due Process Clause of the Fourteenth Amendment what it conceives to be desirable procedural guarantees where the punishment of death, concededly not cruel and unusual for the crime of which the defendant was convicted, is to be imposed. This is squarely contrary to *McGautha*, and unsupported by any other decision of this Court.

I agree with the conclusion of the plurality, and with that of Mr. Justice White, that death is not a cruel and unusual punishment for the offense of which these petitioners were convicted. Since no member of the Court suggests that the trial which led to those convictions in any way fell short of the standards mandated by the Constitution, the judgments of conviction should be affirmed. The Fourteenth Amendment, giving the fullest scope to its "majestic generalities," is conscripted rather than interpreted when used to permit one but not another system for imposition of the death penalty.

Jurek v. Texas
428 U.S. 262 (1976)

Judgment of the Court, and opinion of Mr. Justice Stewart, Mr. Justice Powell, and Mr. Justice Stevens, announced by Mr. Justice Stevens.

The issue in this case is whether the imposition of the sentence of death for the crime of murder under the law of Texas violates the Eighth and Fourteenth Amendments to the Constitution.

I

Jerry Lane Jurek, was charged by indictment with the killing of Wendy Adams "by choking and strangling her with his hands, and by drowning her in water by throwing her into a river in the course of committing and attempting to commit kidnapping of and forcible rape upon the said Wendy Adams." At the conclusion of the trial the jury returned a verdict of guilty.

Texas law requires that if a defendant has been convicted of a capital offense, the trial court must conduct a separate sentencing proceeding before the same jury that tried the issue of guilt. Any relevant evidence may be introduced at this proceeding, and both prosecution and defense may present argument for or against the sentence of death. The jury is then presented with two (sometimes three) questions, the answers to which determine whether a death sentence will be imposed.

During the punishment phase of the petitioner's trial, several witnesses for the State testified to the petitioner's bad reputation in the community. The petitioner's father countered with testimony that the petitioner had always been steadily employed since he had left school and that he contributed to his family's support.

The jury then considered the two statutory questions relevant to this case. The jury unanimously answered "yes" to both questions, and the judge, therefore, in accordance with the statute, sentenced the petitioner to death. The Court of Criminal Appeals of Texas affirmed the judgment.

We granted certiorari, to consider whether the imposition of the death penalty in this case violates the Eighth and Fourteenth Amendments of the United States Constitution.

II

The petitioner argues that the imposition of the death penalty under any circumstances is cruel and unusual punishment in violation of the Eighth and Fourteenth Amendments. We reject this argument for the reasons stated today in *Gregg*.

III

A

After this Court held Texas' system for imposing capital punishment unconstitutional in *Branch v. Texas*, decided with *Furman*, the Texas Legislature narrowed the scope of its laws relating to capital punishment. The new Texas Penal Code limits capital homicides to intentional and knowing murders committed in five situations: murder of a peace officer or fireman; murder committed in the course of kidnapping, burglary, robbery, forcible rape, or arson; murder committed for remuneration; murder committed while escaping or attempting to escape from a penal institution; and murder committed by a prison inmate when the victim is a prison employee.

In addition, Texas adopted a new capital-sentencing procedure. That procedure requires the jury to answer three questions in a proceeding that takes place subsequent to the return of a verdict finding a person guilty of one of the above categories of murder. The questions the jury must answer are these:

(1) whether the conduct of the defendant that caused the death of the deceased was committed deliberately and with the reasonable expectation that the death of the deceased or another would result;

(2) whether there is a probability that the defendant would commit criminal acts of violence that would constitute a continuing threat to society; and

(3) if raised by the evidence, whether the conduct of the defendant in killing the deceased was unreasonable in response to the provocation, if any, by the deceased.

If the jury finds that the State has proved beyond a reasonable doubt that the answer to each of the three questions is yes, then the death sentence is imposed. If the jury finds that the answer to any question is no, then a sentence of life imprisonment results. The law also provides for an expedited review by the Texas Court of Criminal Appeals.

While Texas has not adopted a list of statutory aggravating circumstances as have Georgia and Florida, its action in narrowing the categories of murders for which a death sentence may ever be imposed serves much the same purpose. In fact, each of the five classes of murders made capital by the Texas statute is encompassed in Georgia and Florida by one or more of their statutory aggravating circumstances. For example, the Texas statute requires the jury at the guilt-determining stage to consider whether the crime was committed in the course of a particular felony, whether it was committed for hire, or whether the defendant was an inmate of a penal institution at the time of its commission. Thus, in essence, the Texas statute requires that the jury find the existence of a statutory aggravating circumstance before the death penalty may be imposed. So far as consideration of aggravating circumstances is concerned, therefore, the principal difference between Texas and the other two States is that the death penalty is an available sentencing option—even potentially—for a smaller class of murders in Texas. Otherwise the statutes are similar. Each requires the sentencing authority to focus on the particularized nature of the crime.

But a sentencing system that allowed the jury to consider only aggravating circumstances would almost certainly fall short of providing the individualized sentencing determination that we today have held in *Woodson*, to be required by the Eighth and Fourteenth Amendments. For such a system would approach the mandatory laws that we today hold unconstitutional in *Woodson* and *Roberts v. Louisiana*. A jury must be allowed to consider on the basis of all relevant evidence not only why a death sentence should be imposed, but also why it should not be imposed.

Thus, in order to meet the requirement of the Eighth and Fourteenth Amendments, a capital-sentencing system must allow the sentencing authority to consider mitigating circumstances. In *Gregg*, we today hold constitutionally valid a capital-sentencing system that directs the jury to consider any mitigating factors, and in *Proffit v. Florida* we likewise hold constitutional a system that directs the judge and advisory jury to consider certain enumerated mitigating circumstances. The Texas statute does not explicitly speak of mitigating circumstances; it directs only that the jury answer three questions. Thus, the constitutionality of the Texas procedures turns on whether the enumerated questions allow consideration of particularized mitigating factors.

The second Texas statutory question asks the jury to determine "whether there is a probability that the defendant would commit criminal acts of violence that would constitute a continuing threat to society" if he were not sentenced to death. The Texas Court of Criminal Appeals has yet to define precisely the meanings of such terms as "criminal acts of violence" or "continuing threat to society." In the present case, however, it indicated that it will interpret this second question so as to allow a defendant to bring to the jury's attention whatever mitigating circumstances he may be able to show:

> In determining the likelihood that the defendant would be a continuing threat to society, the jury could consider whether the defendant had a significant criminal record. It could consider the range and severity of his prior criminal conduct. It could further look to the age of the defendant and whether or not at the time of the commission of the offense he was acting under duress or under the domination of another. It could also consider whether the defendant was under an extreme form of mental or emotional pressure, something less, per-

haps, than insanity, but more than the emotions of the average man, however inflamed, could withstand.

In the only other case in which the Texas Court of Criminal Appeals has upheld a death sentence, it focused on the question of whether any mitigating factors were present in the case. In that case the state appellate court examined the sufficiency of the evidence to see if a "yes" answer to question 2 should be sustained. In doing so it examined the defendant's prior conviction on narcotics charges, his subsequent failure to attempt to rehabilitate himself or obtain employment, the fact that he had not acted under duress or as a result of mental or emotional pressure, his apparent willingness to kill, his lack of remorse after the killing, and the conclusion of a psychiatrist that he had a sociopathic personality and that his patterns of conduct would be the same in the future as they had been in the past.

Thus, Texas law essentially requires that one of five aggravating circumstances be found before a defendant can be found guilty of capital murder, and that in considering whether to impose a death sentence the jury may be asked to consider whatever evidence of mitigating circumstances the defense can bring before it. It thus appears that, as in Georgia and Florida, the Texas capital-sentencing procedure guides and focuses the jury's objective consideration of the particularized circumstances of the individual offense and the individual offender before it can impose a sentence of death.

B

As in the Georgia and Florida cases, however, the petitioner contends that the substantial legislative changes that Texas made in response to *Furman* decision are no more than cosmetic in nature and have in fact not eliminated the arbitrariness and caprice of the system held in *Furman* to violate the Eighth and Fourteenth Amendments.

The petitioner first asserts that arbitrariness still pervades the entire criminal justice system of Texas—from the prosecutor's decision whether to charge a capital offense in the first place and then whether to engage in plea bargaining, through the jury's consideration of lesser included offenses, to the Governor's ultimate power to commute death sentences. This contention fundamentally misinterprets the *Furman* decision, and we reject it for the reasons set out in our opinion today in *Gregg*.

Focusing on the second statutory question that Texas requires a jury to answer in considering whether to impose a death sentence, the petitioner argues that it is impossible to predict future behavior and that the question is so vague as to be meaningless. It is, of course, not easy to predict future behavior. The fact that such a determination is difficult, however, does not mean that it cannot be made. Indeed, prediction of future criminal conduct is an essential element in many of the decisions rendered throughout our criminal justice system. The decision whether to admit a defendant to bail, for instance, must often turn on a judge's prediction of the defendant's future conduct. And any sentencing authority must predict a convicted person's probable future conduct when it engages in the process of determining what punishment to impose. For those sentenced to prison, these same predictions must be made by parole authorities. The task that a Texas jury must perform in answering the statutory question in issue is thus basically no different from the task performed countless times each day throughout the American system of criminal justice. What is essential is that the jury have before it all possible relevant information about the individual defendant whose fate it must determine. Texas law clearly assures that all such evidence will be adduced.

IV

We conclude that Texas' capital-sentencing procedures, like those of Georgia and Florida, do not violate the Eighth and Fourteenth Amendments. By narrowing its definition of capital murder, Texas has essentially said that there must be at least one statutory aggravating circumstance in a first-degree murder case before a death sentence may even be considered. By authorizing the defense to bring before the jury at the separate sentencing hearing whatever mitigating circumstances relating to the individual defendant can be adduced, Texas has ensured that the sentencing jury will have adequate guidance to enable it to perform its sentencing function. By providing prompt judicial review of the jury's decision in a court with statewide jurisdiction, Texas has provided a means to promote the evenhanded, rational, and consistent imposition of death sentences under law. Because this system serves to assure that sentences of death will not be "wantonly" or "freakishly" imposed, it does not violate the Constitution. Accordingly, the judgment of the Texas Court of Criminal Appeals is affirmed.

Lockett v. Ohio
438 U.S. 586 (1978)

Mr. Chief Justice Burger delivered the opinion of the Court.

We granted certiorari in this case to consider, among other questions, whether Ohio violated the Eighth and Fourteenth Amendments by sentencing Sandra Lockett to death pursuant to a statute that narrowly limits the sentencer's discretion to consider the circumstances of the crime and the record and character of the offender as mitigating factors.

Lockett was charged with aggravated murder. The jury found Lockett guilty as charged. Once a verdict of aggravated murder with specifications had been returned, the Ohio death penalty statute required the trial judge to impose a death sentence unless, after "considering the nature and circumstances of the offense" and Lockett's "history, character, and condition," he found by a preponderance of the evidence that (1) the victim had induced or facilitated the offense, (2) it was unlikely that Lockett would have committed the offense but for the fact that she "was under duress, coercion, or strong provocation," or (3) the offense was "primarily the product of [Lockett's] psychosis or mental deficiency."

Lockett challenges the constitutionality of Ohio's death penalty statute on a number of grounds. We find it necessary to consider only her contention that her death sentence is invalid because the statute under which it was imposed did not permit the sentencing judge to consider, as mitigating factors, her character, prior record, age, lack of specific intent to cause death, and her relatively minor part in the crime.

Essentially she contends that the Eighth and Fourteenth Amendments require that the sentencer be given a full opportunity to consider mitigating circumstances in capital cases and that the Ohio statute does not comply with that requirement. She relies, in large part, on the plurality opinions in *Woodson*, and the joint opinion in *Jurek*, but she goes beyond them.

We begin by recognizing that the concept of individualized sentencing in criminal cases generally, although not constitutionally required, has long been accepted in this country. Consistent with that concept, sentencing judges traditionally have taken a wide range of factors into account. That States have authority to make aiders and abettors equally responsible, as a matter of law, with principals, or to enact felony-murder statutes is beyond constitutional challenge. But the definition of crimes generally has not been thought automatically to dictate what should be the proper penalty. And where sentencing discretion is granted, it generally has been agreed that the sentencing judge's "possession of the fullest information possible concerning the defendant's life and characteristics" is "highly relevant—*if not essential*—to the selection of an appropriate sentence."

Although legislatures remain free to decide how much discretion in sentencing should be reposed in the judge or jury in noncapital cases, the plurality opinion in *Woodson*, after reviewing the historical repudiation of mandatory sentencing in capital cases, concluded that:

> *In capital cases the fundamental respect for humanity underlying the Eighth Amendment requires consideration of the character and record of the individual offender and the circumstances of the particular offense as a constitutionally indispensable part of the process of inflicting the penalty of death.*

That declaration rested "on the predicate that the penalty of death is qualitatively different" from any other sentence. We are satisfied that this qualitative difference between death and other penalties calls for a greater degree of reliability when the death sentence is imposed. The mandatory death penalty statute in *Woodson* was held invalid because it permitted *no* consideration of "relevant facets of the character and record of the individual offender or the circumstances of the particular offense." The plurality did not attempt to indicate, however, which facets of an offender or his offense it deemed "relevant" in capital sentencing or what degree of consideration of "relevant facets" it would require.

We are now faced with those questions and we conclude that the Eighth and Fourteenth Amendments require that the sentencer, in all but the rarest kind of capital case, not be precluded from considering, *as a mitigating factor*, any aspect of a defendant's character or record and any of the circumstances of the offense that the defendant proffers as a basis for a sentence less than death. We recognize that, in noncapital cases, the established practice of individualized sentences rests not on constitutional commands, but on public policy enacted into statutes. The considerations that account for the wide acceptance of individualization of sentences in noncapital cases surely cannot be thought less important in capital cases. Given that the imposition of death by public authority is so profoundly different from all other penalties, we cannot avoid the conclusion that an individualized decision is essential in capital cases. The need for treating each defendant in a capital case with that degree of respect due the uniqueness of the individual is far more important than in noncapital cases. A variety of flexible techniques—probation, parole, work furloughs, to name a few—and various postconviction remedies may be available to modify an initial sentence of confinement in noncapital cases. The nonavailability of corrective or modifying mechanisms with respect to an executed capital sentence underscores the need for individualized consideration as a constitutional requirement in imposing the death sentence.

There is no perfect procedure for deciding in which cases governmental authority should be used to impose death. But a statute that prevents the sentencer in all capital cases from giving independent mitigating weight to aspects of the defendant's character and record and to circumstances of the offense proffered in mitigation creates the risk that the death penalty will be imposed in spite of factors which may call for a less severe penalty. When the choice is between life and death, that risk is unacceptable and incompatible with the commands of the Eighth and Fourteenth Amendments.

The Ohio death penalty statute does not permit the type of individualized consideration of mitigating factors we now hold to be required by the Eighth and Fourteenth Amendments in capital cases. Its constitutional infirmities can best be understood by comparing it with the statutes upheld in *Gregg*, *Proffit*, and *Jurek*.

In upholding the Georgia statute in *Gregg*, Justices Stewart, Powell, and Stevens noted that the statute permitted the jury "to consider any aggravating or mitigating circumstances," and that the Georgia Supreme Court had approved "open and far-ranging argument" in presentence hearings. *Jurek* involved a Texas statute which made no explicit reference to mitigating factors. Rather, the jury was required to answer three questions in the sentencing process, the second of which was "whether there is a probability that the defendant would commit criminal acts of violence that would constitute a continuing threat to society." The statute survived the petitioner's Eighth and Fourteenth Amendment attack because three Justices concluded that the Texas Court of Criminal Appeals had broadly interpreted the second question—despite its facial narrowness—so as to permit the sentencer to consider "whatever mitigating circumstances" the defendant might be able to show. None of the statutes we sustained in *Gregg* and the companion cases clearly operated at that time to prevent the sentencer from considering any aspect of the defendant's character and record or any circumstances of his offense as an independently mitigating factor.

In this regard the statute now before us is significantly different. Once a defendant is found guilty of aggravated murder with at least one of seven specified aggravating circumstances, the death penalty must be imposed unless, considering "the nature and circumstances of the offense and the history, character, and condition of the offender," the sentencing judge determines that at least one of the mitigating circumstances is established by a preponderance of the evidence.

The Ohio Supreme Court has concluded that the mitigating circumstances in Ohio's statute are "liberally construed in favor of the accused." But even under the Ohio court's construction of the statute, only the three factors specified in the statute can be considered in mitigation of the defendant's sentence. We see, therefore, that once it is determined that the victim did not induce or facilitate the offense, that the defendant did not act under duress or coercion, and that the offense was not primarily the product of the defendant's mental deficiency, the Ohio statute mandates the sentence of death. The absence of direct proof that the defendant intended to cause the death of the victim is relevant for mitigating purposes only if it is determined that it sheds some light on one of the three statutory mitigating factors. Similarly, consideration of a defendant's comparatively minor role in the offense, or age, would generally not be permitted, as such, to affect the sentencing decision.

The limited range of mitigating circumstances which may be considered by the sentencer under the Ohio statute is incompatible with the Eighth and Fourteenth Amendments. To meet constitutional requirements, a death penalty statute must not preclude consideration of relevant mitigating factors.

Accordingly, the judgment under review is reversed to the extent that it sustains the imposition of the death penalty, and the case is remanded for further proceedings.

Mr. Justice White, concurring in part, dissenting in part, and concurring in the judgments of the Court.

With all due respect, I dissent. I continue to be of the view that it does not violate the Eighth Amendment for a State to impose the death penalty on a mandatory basis when the defendant has been found guilty beyond a reasonable doubt of committing a deliberate, unjustified killing. Moreover, I greatly fear that the effect of the Court's decision today will be to compel constitutionally a restoration of the state of affairs at the time *Furman* was decided, where the death penalty is imposed so erratically and the threat of execution is so attenuated for even the most atrocious murders that "its imposition would then be the pointless and needless extinction of life with only marginal contributions to any discernible social or public purposes." By requiring as a matter of constitutional law that sentencing authorities be permitted to consider and in their discretion to act upon any and all mitigating circumstances, the Court permits them to refuse to impose the death penalty no matter what the circumstances of the crime. This invites a return to the pre-*Furman* days when the death penalty was generally reserved for those very few for whom society has least consideration. I decline to extend *Woodson* in this respect.

It also seems to me that the plurality strains very hard and unsuccessfully to avoid eviscerating the handiwork in *Proffit v. Florida* and *Jurek v. Texas* and surely it calls into question any other death penalty statute that permits only a limited number of mitigating circumstances to be placed before the sentencing authority or to be used in its deliberations.

I nevertheless concur in the judgments of the Court reversing the imposition of the death sentences because I agree with the contention of the petitioners, ignored by the plurality, that it violates the Eighth Amendment to impose the penalty of death without a finding that the defendant possessed a purpose to cause the death of the victim.

Mr. Justice Rehnquist, concurring in part and dissenting in part.

As my Brother White points out in his dissent, the theme of today's opinion, far from supporting those views expressed in *Furman* which did appear to be carried over to the *Woodson* cases, tends to undercut those views. If a defendant as a matter of constitutional law is to be permitted to offer as evidence in the sentencing hearing any fact, however bizarre, which he wishes, even though the most sympathetically disposed trial judge could conceive of no basis upon which the jury might take it into account in imposing a sentence, the new constitutional doctrine will not eliminate arbitrariness or freakishness in the imposition of sentences, but will codify and institutionalize it. By encouraging defendants in capital cases, and presumably sentencing judges and juries, to take into consideration anything under the sun as a "mitigating circumstance," it will not guide sentencing discretion but will totally unleash it. It thus appears that the evil described by the *Woodson* plurality—that mandatory capital sentencing "papered over the problem of unguided and unchecked jury discretion"—was in truth not the unchecked discretion, but a system which "papered over" its exercise rather than spreading it on the record.

■ Mitigating Evidence—Perspectives

■ Issue—Does the *Lockett* Rule Create Arbitrariness in Capital Sentencing?

Jeffrey L. Kirchmeier, "Aggravating and Mitigating Factors: The Paradox of Today's Arbitrary and Mandatory Capital Punishment Scheme"

A little over twenty years ago, the modern era of capital punishment in the United States began when the Supreme Court, having struck down death penalty statutes four years earlier, upheld several states' new capital statutory schemes. Thus began the Court's attempt to develop a reasoned, consistent, and nonarbitrary system of inflicting the punishment of death.

In the Supreme Court's drive to eliminate arbitrary discretion from the use of capital punishment in America, the Court has struggled to create a fair system. In this struggle, the Court has defined two important Eighth Amendment principles: (1) the requirement that the discretion of a capital sentencer be channeled and the group of defendants eligible for death be narrowed; and (2) the requirement that a sentencer be able to consider any aspect of a defendant's crime or character that is mitigating, thus providing for individualized sentencing. In embracing these two principles, the Court has rejected both mandatory death penalty schemes and schemes that give total unbridled discretion to the sentencer. The Court instead has attempted to walk the line between such systems.

Individual Supreme Court Justices have reasoned that the two principles are inconsistent and that allowing individual sentencing—and the consideration of any mitigating factor the defendant argues—undermines any attempts by the Court to eliminate arbitrariness. While Justices Scalia and Blackmun both have argued that these two principles are incompatible, they each propound a different solution. Justice Blackmun agreed with the Court's decisions in prior cases that both principles are necessary to a constitutional death penalty. Therefore, because the goals cannot both be satisfied, he reasoned, the death penalty is unconstitutional. Former Justice Powell came to a similar conclusion after his retirement.

Justice Scalia, however, concluded that the mitigation principle was not as important as the channeled discretion requirement and, therefore, could be eliminated. In short, Justice Scalia stated that the principle of *Furman*—that arbitrariness must be eliminated in capital sentencing—is the only requirement of the Eighth Amendment. Thus, he has held that mitigating factors, like aggravating factors, must be specifically designated by the legislatures, or perhaps even eliminated. Justice Thomas has come to a similar conclusion.

This is an evaluation of the Court's jurisprudence regarding the criteria—generally in the form of aggravating and mitigating factors—for selecting which defendants are sentenced to death and which ones are not. The Court has moved toward a mandatory death penalty by limiting the use of mitigating circumstances and by permitting expansive aggravating factor statutes. Simultaneously, the Court has retreated from concerns about arbitrariness by permitting capital sentencers to consider several arbitrary factors.

I. *The Progression Toward an Arbitrary Death Penalty*

Of course, all first-degree murders are horrible. Yet, because the Court has rejected a mandatory death penalty scheme, the Court has attempted to develop a fair system for evaluating each first-degree murder and defendant to determine which defendants receive the death penalty and which ones receive life in prison.

Several of the Justices have noted continuing problems with arbitrariness in the present capital punishment scheme. In a concurring opinion in *Walton v. Arizona*, Justice Scalia concluded that the two underlying principles of modern death penalty jurisprudence—guided discretion and individualized sentencing—are incompatible. While accepting the concerns of *Furman*, Justice Scalia rejected the holdings of *Woodson* and *Lockett* that provided for individualized sentencing by requiring that the defendant be allowed to introduce any mitigating evidence. He noted that the mitigation requirement "quite obviously destroys whatever rationality and predictability the requirement that states channel the sentencer's discretion with clear and objective standards was designed to achieve." Thus, he concluded that "the mandatory imposition of death—without sentencing discretion—for a crime which States have traditionally punished with death cannot possibly violate the Eighth Amendment." He announced he would no longer follow *Lockett* and *Woodson*. Although Justice Scalia's position is far from commanding a majority of the Court, Justice Thomas has expressed similar concerns.

Although the Court has explained the importance of prohibiting courts from limiting mitigating factors, Justice Scalia is correct that the requirement of unlimited mitigating factors does allow a great deal of sentencing discretion. As the Court has noted in the context of the issue of racial discrimination in capital sentencing, "Of course, the power to be lenient also is the power to discriminate."

II. *The Progression Toward a Mandatory Death Penalty*

Although today the death penalty is arbitrarily applied in various ways, the death penalty system also is moving closer to a mandatory scheme. The death penalty is not applied to every murderer, but the death penalty system is creeping closer and closer to such a goal, through political pressures and through the Court's failure to address the trend.

The Supreme Court clearly has held that mandatory death penalty schemes are unconstitutional. The trend in legislatures to broaden death penalty statutes, as well as some of the Court's more recent cases, however, illustrate a progression toward a mandatory system of capital punishment. It appears that the Court has become exhausted with regulating this area of the law and therefore has allowed a broadening of the application of the death penalty. This trend is illustrated by the Court's willingness to allow mitigating factors to be limited and by the Court's tolerance for broad statutes that include numerous and open-ended sentencing factors.

In the early Supreme Court opinions that addressed limitations on the consideration of mitigating factors, the Court's language was sweeping in the condemnation of limits put upon consideration of mitigating evidence offered by defendants. The Court, however, retreated from this position in *Johnson v. Texas*.

In *Johnson*, the Court addressed Texas's capital sentencing statute, which does not list aggravating and mitigating factors. Instead, the jury in *Johnson* was asked during the capital sentencing phase to answer two special issues in accordance with the statute: (1) whether Johnson's conduct was "committed deliberately and with the reasonable expectation that the death of the deceased or another would result," and (2) whether there was a probability that Johnson "would commit criminal acts of violence that would constitute a continuing threat to society." The court instructed the jury that if it answered "yes" to both questions, the court would sentence Johnson to death; otherwise, the court would sentence him to life in prison. Both answers were "yes," and Johnson was sentenced to death.

Johnson was nineteen at the time of the murder, and the issue before the Supreme Court was "whether the Texas special issues allowed adequate consideration of petitioner's youth." The Court upheld the death sentence. It reasoned that *Lockett* and *Eddings* require only "that a jury be able to consider in some manner all of a defendant's relevant mitigating evidence," not that "a jury be able to give effect to mitigating evidence in every conceivable manner in which the evidence might be relevant." The Court thus implied that a state could limit the consideration of mitigating factors as long as the factors could be considered in at least one way. This holding is contrary to the rule developed from *Lockett* and *Eddings*.

Another way that the death penalty has moved closer to a mandatory scheme is through broad statutes that make it more likely that all murderers will be sentenced to death. States have created death penalty statutes that are broad in three ways. First, the statutes contain specific aggravating factors that are vague and overbroad. Second, many statutes permit arbitrary factors that make it more likely that the death penalty will be imposed. Third, most death penalty statutes include a long list of aggravating factors that include such a broad range of circumstances that they cover almost every first-degree murder case.

Although the present system has made some small progress toward achieving a fairer sentencing system, it has not come close to the goals envisioned by the Court in *Furman*. Under the Court's jurisprudence, the constitutional problems of the present arbitrary and mandatory system render it a failure.

III. *Resolving the Paradox*

There is no perfect procedure for deciding in which cases governmental authority should be used to impose death. But after rejecting capital sentencing statutes that gave sentencers complete discretion and after rejecting mandatory capital sentencing statutes, the Court has developed an Eighth Amendment jurisprudence that has embraced the evils of both of those systems. Over twenty years after *Furman*, death penalty statutes continue to be broadened to increase the likelihood that defendants will be sentenced to death, resulting in a death penalty that contains many similarities to harsh mandatory death penalty schemes. At the same time, the Court has permitted a system of sentencing factors that tolerates a substantial amount of arbitrary discretion, including the systemic factors discussed above, as well as prosecutorial discretion and racial bias.

Although it may seem paradoxical to claim that a system is both mandatory and arbitrary, that is the system we currently have. While obviously it is not completely one or the other, the system has the constitutional faults of both. We are left to wonder whether we would have only half of the constitutional problems we now face if the Court were to embrace one or the other completely.

No Justice or commentator suggests a return to the *McGautha* days when juries had almost complete and unfettered discretion in determining who received a death sentence. As Professor David McCord has suggested, attorneys probably do not want to return to such a system either. In many ways, however, we now have that system. Perhaps the present system is worse than the old system in the sense that the present system has the false appearance of being a fair and nonarbitrary system. Although Professor McCord argued that the present system works, Professors Carol Steiker and Jordan Steiker have argued that "the Supreme Court's detailed attention to death penalty law has generated negligible improvements over the pre-*Furman* era, but has helped people to accept without second thoughts—much less 'sober' ones—our profoundly failed system of capital punishment." One may ask who is correct. Do we have a better system or only a system that allows the public to pretend that the system works?

The paradox is that McCord and the Steikers each are correct. Some narrowing has occurred, but it has not occurred in a significant or rational way. The system is better than the *McGautha* era because the present capital sentencing statutes eliminate some first-degree murders from the capital sentencing pool. The system is not better than the *McGautha* era because it is arbitrary in selecting who is eliminated from the pool and because it eliminates only a few defendants before reopening the system to unlimited arbitrariness.

The two best alternatives to the constitutional paradox of today's arbitrary mandatory death sentencing scheme are the solutions that individual Supreme Court Justices have suggested. In short, "Capital punishment must be imposed fairly, and with reasonable consistency, or not at all." One option is to impose it "fairly" by following the suggestion of Justices Scalia and Thomas by completely embracing a mandatory death penalty. Such a system would need to go beyond Justice Scalia's upholding of arbitrary factors, like victim impact evidence, by requiring a mandatory death sentence for all first-degree murderers. To permit the consideration of vague aggravating factors would open the door to arbitrariness, so under the proposed system every first-degree murderer or a clearly defined group would need to receive a death sentence. Although such a system would increase the harshness of today's death penalty, its arbitrariness would be eliminated.

The other option is to follow Justices Blackmun and Powell, who both originally voted to uphold today's death penalty scheme, and subsequently concluded that the death penalty should be imposed "not at all." Holding the death penalty unconstitutional would acknowledge that all attempts to impose the ultimate punishment in a fair manner have failed and that the only constitutional alternative is to abandon the punishment altogether.

Instead of embracing one of these two options, the Court has left us with a compromise and only the appearance of a fair process. In short, the Court's constitutional interpretation is one that has neither the stomach for the harshness of a mandatory death penalty nor the willingness to counter public opinion.

The question is which of the two choices is the better option—a mandatory death penalty or no death penalty. Perhaps part of the answer lies in examining the underlying reasoning for the positions taken by Justices Scalia and Blackmun, who both recognize the same problems but come to radically different conclusions.

Justice Scalia believes in the moral philosophies supporting capital punishment. For example, in one dissent Scalia argued that potential jurors who state during voir dire that they always will vote for the death penalty should be permitted to sit as jurors, while jurors who always will vote against the death penalty should be struck for cause. In that opinion, Justice Scalia quoted Immanuel Kant in what may be his own view regarding retribution and the death penalty: "Even if a civil society resolved to dissolve itself with the consent of all its members the last Murderer lying in the prison ought to be executed before the resolution was carried out. This ought to be done in order that every one may realize the desert of his deeds."

In contrast, before Justice Blackmun came to the conclusion that the death penalty is unconstitutional, he noted his moral distaste for capital punishment. Indeed, in his *Furman* dissent, even though he voted to uphold the death penalty, he stated: "I yield to no one in the depth of my distaste, antipathy, and, indeed, abhorrence, for the death penalty, with all its aspects of physical distress and fear and of moral judgment exercised by finite minds." He added that for him, "it violates childhood's training and life's experiences, and is not compatible with the philosophical convictions I have been able to develop."

Perhaps the decision of whether to eliminate today's death penalty scheme altogether or to replace it with a mandatory death penalty scheme depends upon the principles and philosophies underlying the constitutionality of the death penalty per se and whether such principles justify the harshness of mandatory death sentences. In other words, if the death penalty is absolutely necessary to American society, we must accept a mandatory death penalty. If, however, it is not so necessary that it justifies such harshness, it must be abandoned. Other factors that must be evaluated include aspects that undermine the constitutionality of the Court's capital punishment system. Such factors include claims of racial bias, lack of federal review, no constitutional right to state post-conviction review, inadequate funding for capital defense, and poor representation by capital defense counsel.

However, even without considering other factors affecting the constitutionality of the death penalty per se, the logical correct path is evident merely from the evolution of the present system. This view is illustrated by the conversion of Justice Powell, who wrote several opinions upholding the death penalty, including the Court's opinion in *McCleskey v. Kemp*. Justice Powell did not believe that executions are never justified; however, his experience on the Court in attempting to regulate the punishment "taught him that the death penalty cannot be decently administered." Similarly, other judges have also concluded that the death penalty system does not work in practice and should be abolished.

Examining only the process used in implementing the death penalty, one notes that the United States has tried mandatory sentencing, unguided sentencing discretion, and guided sentencing discretion. The last two approaches clearly have been failures. Furthermore, mandatory death sentences have not worked historically. Additionally, as discussed above, scholars have failed to create a workable alternative to the present system, which is both mandatory and arbitrary in nature.

Because all attempts to impose the death penalty with a fair consistency have failed, the only alternative, as the Court has stated, is to apply it "not at all." The Court has never tried true abolition of the death penalty. After twenty years, it is time to take a new direction away from the failed experiment. Perhaps Justice Powell recognized the final paradox of today's death penalty: By attempting to save the constitutionality of the death penalty by imposing guidelines and permitting discretion at the same time, the Court has doomed the process and the punishment to being the ultimate failure in the United States criminal justice system.

Christopher E. Smith, "The Constitution and Criminal Punishment: The Emerging Visions of Justices Scalia and Thomas"

Consistent with their view that federal courts should defer to the policies and judgments of state governmental officials, Justices Scalia and Thomas have generally opposed judicial scrutiny of and interference with the imposition of the death penalty. In a careful study of Justice Scalia's decisions on capital punishment, one scholar concluded that "Scalia seems to believe that there are virtually no constitutional limits on a state's imposition of the death penalty."

Justice Scalia's desire to end judicial limitations on the factors considered by judges and juries when deciding whether to impose the death penalty was presented most forcefully in a concurring opinion in *Walton v. Arizona*. Justice Scalia argued there was an inherent conflict between *Furman*, which attempted to channel the sentencer's discretion, and cases which required sentencers to consider mitigating evidence instead of imposing mandatory sentences and prevented states from limiting consideration of mitigating circumstances. According to Justice Scalia, "the practice which in *Furman* had been described as the discretion to sentence to death and pronounced constitutionally prohibited, was in *Woodson* and *Lockett* renamed the discretion not to sentence to death and pronounced constitutionally required." He even applied his characteristic biting sarcasm to ridicule the two conflicting doctrines:

> To acknowledge that "there perhaps is an inherent tension" between this line of cases and the line stemming from Furman is rather like saying that there was perhaps an inherent tension between the Allies and the Axis Powers in World War II. And to refer to the two lines as pursuing "twin objectives" is rather like referring to the twin objectives of good and evil. They cannot be reconciled.

Justice Scalia also enunciated a narrow view of the Eighth Amendment, which, consistent with his other opinions, provided little guidance to judges: When punishments other than fines are involved, the Amendment explicitly requires a court to consider not only whether the penalty is severe or harsh, but also whether it is "unusual." If it is not, then the Eighth Amendment does not prohibit it, no matter how cruel a judge might think it to be. Moreover, the Eighth Amendment's prohibition is directed against cruel and unusual punishments. It does not, by its terms, regulate the procedures of sentencing as opposed to the substance of punishment. Thus, the procedural elements of a sentencing scheme come within the prohibition, if at all, only when they are of such a nature as systematically to render the infliction of cruel punishment "unusual."

He also contended that mandatory death sentences for capital crimes "cannot possibly violate the Eighth Amendment, because it will not be 'cruel' (neither absolutely nor for a particular crime) and it will not be 'unusual' (neither in the sense of being a type of penalty that is not traditional nor in the sense of being rarely or 'freakishly' imposed)." Because the "*Woodson-Lockett* line of cases bears no relation whatever to the text of the Eighth Amendment," he rejected any claim that they might deserve protection under stare decisis. In other cases, Justice Scalia attacked judicial requirements and limits (the "channeling" of mitigating discretion) on the factors judges and juries consider during sentencing.

Justice Scalia's preference for permitting states to decide criminal punishment without excessive supervision by the federal courts was also included in the Court's decision concerning the death penalty for juveniles and people with mental retardation. Justice Scalia later attracted majority support endorsing capital punishment for individuals convicted of murder at sixteen and seventeen years old. Justice Scalia's opinion relied on the originalist and majoritarian approaches, which he regularly favors. He noted capital punishment was applied to teenagers at the time the Bill of Rights was drafted and adopted. He also noted a majority of states authorizing capital punishment permit such punishment for murderers at age sixteen and above.

When Justice Thomas joined the Supreme Court, his opinions in death penalty cases echoed many of Justice Scalia's themes. Justice Thomas objected to the tension between the Court's desire in *Furman* to prevent capricious death penalty decisions and the Court's requirement in *Penry* that juries may consider mitigating evidence. Justice Thomas took Justice Scalia's objection a step further by asserting that consideration of mitigating factors and abolition of mandatory death penalties contribute to racial discrimination. Justice Thomas stated, "To withhold the death penalty out of sympathy for a defendant who is a member of a favored group is not different from a decision to impose the penalty on the basis of a negative bias." He also reiterated Justice Scalia's theme regarding majoritarian preferences manifested by elected officials to guide policy decisions affecting capital punishment: "I believe this Court should leave it to elected state legislators, 'representing organized society,' to decide which factors are 'particularly relevant to the sentencing decision.'"

Justices Scalia and Thomas stand out in the Rehnquist Court as the two justices least likely to support an individual's Eighth Amendment and death penalty claims and most likely to assert themselves in concurring and dissenting opinions.

What are the implications of the opinions of Justice Scalia and Justice Thomas? First, it is highly questionable whether these justices would recognize an Eighth Amendment violation in any situation other than a case of excessive fines. Justice Scalia's repeated emphasis on his view that punishments must be cruel and unusual and his rejection of a proportionality requirement in the Eighth Amendment might permit approval of all punishments no matter how cruel or disproportionate as long as they are not unusual.

Second, as implied by their approach to interpreting the Eighth Amendment, Justices Scalia and Thomas explicitly espouse a significant reduction, if not a nearly complete withdrawal, of the federal judiciary's supervision over criminal punishment imposed and applied by state officials.

Third, the current reduction in federal judicial review for capital cases, which comports with the views of Justices Scalia and Thomas and reflects recent changes in habeas jurisprudence, increases the risk of executing innocent persons.

Fourth, Justices Scalia and Thomas may be correct that the Court's death penalty jurisprudence which seeks to require, through the use of mitigating and aggravating factors, individualized decisions in capital cases creates an inherent conflict with the *Furman* decision's concerns about excessive discretion. By advocating the permissibility of mandatory death penalty statutes, however, Justices Thomas and Scalia fundamentally misapprehend the complex factors and multiple discretionary decisions that may produce capriciousness and discrimination. They focus on the sentencing decision itself and argue that problems caused by *Furman*'s clash with *Woodson* and *Lockett* would be resolved by eliminating the sentencer's discretion. This myopic preoccupation with discretion at a single decision point ignores the consequences of discretion at earlier stages in the proceedings, such as the prosecutor's decision about whether to seek the death penalty, the prosecutor's trial strategy and arguments, and the jury's biases in making determinations about guilt. Moreover, a focus on the sentencer's decision ignores the consequences of inadequate legal representation that may disproportionally affect poor defendants. Justice Thomas is self-deluded to believe that mandatory death sentences would reduce racial discrimination in capital sentencing. The formalistic view of the criminal justice process evident in Justice Scalia's and

Justice Thomas's arguments about discretion blind these justices to the cumulative impact of discretion and other factors on capital punishment decisions. Because scholars have documented how Supreme Court justices' attitudes and backgrounds affect their decisions, George Kannar has argued that Justice Scalia's religious background has contributed to his formalistic approach to criminal justice. Justice Thomas, a former seminary student whose childhood orientation and involvement with religion is most like Justice Scalia's, may have also shaped his views based on his religious background.

It remains to be seen whether future changes in the Court's composition will make Justice Scalia's and Justice Thomas's views about the Eighth Amendment and criminal punishment more influential. They apparently remain committed to the notion of laying the groundwork through their outspoken opinions for future jurisprudential changes that may limit judicial supervision of criminal punishment.

Rape and Proportionality

10

■ Rape and Proportionality—Introduction

The Supreme Court has held that capital punishment is constitutional provided that the statute authorizing the use of the death penalty adequately guides the discretion of the sentencer. Whether the death penalty is appropriate for all kinds of offenses and all kinds of offenders is a separate legal and ethical question.

The legal consideration is that it is not immediately apparent what provision of the Constitution one might rely upon in arguing that the death penalty is unconstitutional for certain classes of defendants facing the death penalty. The Eighth Amendment provides: "Excessive bail shall not be required, nor excessive fines imposed, nor cruel and unusual punishments inflicted." This language lends itself most naturally to a reading that certain methods of punishment—torture, for example—might be prohibited by the Constitution. A reading that certain kinds of people are exempt from certain kinds of punishment seems more strained. Either the death penalty is constitutional or it is not. Nothing in the plain language of the Eighth Amendment appears to preclude a state from deciding upon whom to impose a noncruel punishment.

This is the position of the Supreme Court in all cases outside the death penalty context. In *Solem v. Helm*, a 1983 decision, the Supreme Court held that the Eighth Amendment proscribed a life sentence without the possibility of parole for a seventh nonviolent felony. Helm was convicted in 1979 of writing a bad check for $100. He had six previous nonviolent felony convictions. The bounced check triggered a South Dakota recidivist statute that required LWOP for a defendant with Helm's record. The Court found the sentence disproportionate for Helm's crime under the cruel and unusual punishments clause. But in *Harmelin v. Michigan*, a 1991 decision involving a stiff penalty for drug possession, the Court overturned *Solem*. Writing for the majority, Justice Scalia found that the Eighth Amendment did not contain a blanket proportionality guarantee:

> *We think it enough that those who framed and approved the Federal Constitution chose, for whatever reason, not to include within it the guarantee against disproportionate sentences that some State Constitutions contained. It is worth noting, however, that there was*

> *some good reason for that choice—a reason that reinforces the ne-*
> *cessity of overruling* Solem. *While there are relatively clear histor-*
> *ical guidelines and accepted practices that enable judges to determine*
> *which* modes *of punishment are "cruel and unusual," proportion-*
> *ality does not lend itself to such analysis.*

Despite this decision, proportionality review remains an important aspect of the Supreme Court's death penalty jurisprudence. It is, as Justice Scalia wrote in *Harmelin*, "one of several respects in which we have held that 'death is different,' and have imposed protections that the Constitution nowhere else provides." Under the rubric of proportionality review, the death penalty has been deemed unconstitutional for the insane, the severely retarded, the very young, and for rapists and some kinds of felony-murderers.

The doctrine of proportionality review for death-sentenced defendants was established in a 1977 case, *Coker v. Georgia*, excerpted later in this chapter, which ruled the death penalty unconstitutional for rapists of adult victims. A Georgia jury sentenced Anthony Coker to die for the rape at knifepoint of Elnita Caver. Coker had prior convictions for rape, murder, and kidnapping, all capital felonies under Georgia law. Coker contended that, despite his prior convictions, the death penalty was unconstitutional as the immediate crime for which he was being punished was a rape not involving the taking of life.

It is important to distinguish here between the two kinds of proportionality review. One of the reforms of the Georgia death penalty statute following *Furman* is the automatic appeal of all death sentences to the state supreme court to determine "whether the sentence is disproportionate compared to those sentences imposed in similar cases." The notion of proportionality review in *Gregg* is that a death sentence might be disproportionate if a defendant is treated differently than other similarly-situated defendants. This is generally referred to as "comparative proportionality review." Coker's argument is that the death penalty is inappropriate for an entire class of offenders. This is sometimes referred to as "inherent proportionality review."

The Supreme Court might have found, as it later did in *Harmelin*, that the Eighth Amendment only restricted methods of punishment and, given the procedural protections required by *Gregg*, offered no substantive protection to Coker. Having decided to engage in the analysis, the Court might have approached proportionality review by relying upon subjective moral judgments. The Justices could have made individual assessments of whether the death penalty could ever be an appropriate punishment for the kind of crime considered.

However, the Court took a different approach. Subjective assessments did play some role in the decision in *Coker*. Justice White, writing for the majority, had a clear view that rape is not as culpable a crime as murder: "Life is over for the victim of the murderer; for the rape victim, life may not be nearly so happy as it was, but it is not over and normally is not beyond repair." But the lasting legacy of *Coker* is the precedent that the primary consideration in proportionality analysis is the "objective evidence of the country's present judgment concerning the acceptability of death" for a particular crime. The relevant objective evidence includes state legislative enactments and jury verdicts. As the Supreme

Court considers the appropriateness of the death penalty for a host of crimes and classes of criminals over the succeeding decades, objective evidence is the battleground over which the war is fought.

Fair minds can debate the validity of Justice White's subjective opinion about the relative harm caused by rapists and murderers. If it is not valid, death penalty opponents must consider whether they should nevertheless express support for *Coker*. It does have the effect of narrowing the scope of the death penalty and sets a precedent for narrowing it further still. At the same time, it seems that one could reasonably oppose the death penalty, but believe that if it *does* exist, rapists should not be exempt from it in aggravated cases.

One can also debate the helpfulness of the Court's approach to the entire issue. An obvious objection to the *Coker* approach to proportionality review is that it substantiates fluctuations in public opinion. The evidence of consensus against the death penalty for rape was overwhelming in 1977—Georgia is the only state in which Coker could have been subject to capital punishment. But the Supreme Court has sometimes found the death penalty disproportionate on less compelling evidence of consensus than in *Coker*. This point is discussed extensively in Chapters 11 and 12, in connection with the death penalty for felony-murder and juvenile offenders. In *Enmund v. Florida*, for example, the Court found the death penalty disproportionate for felony-murderers although one-third of the states approved of the death penalty for criminals similar to Enmund.

Another concern is that *Coker* relies upon a class-oriented approach to proportionality. It seems fair to say that the average murderer is more culpable than the average rapist, but it is easy to imagine a highly aggravated rape that is more culpable than some murders, and a minimally aggravated murder that is not as troubling as some rapes. The class-oriented approach in *Coker* might lead to sparing some defendants deserving of death. Proportionality of this kind might lead to some unsatisfying applications—the Court's decisions concerning the death penalty for juveniles a notable example. The Court has generally relied upon bright-line rules, even though they might not always produce just results. It hardly seems to make sense to exclude the death penalty for someone who committed a crime one day shy of his sixteenth birthday, but permit it for someone one day older.

Another problem is that proportionality review might have the effect of immortalizing temporary trends among state legislatures. If the death penalty temporarily falls out of fashion for a particular crime or type of criminal, this might lead to a ruling that it is unconstitutional for this class of offender, regardless of whether opinion or evidence about the usefulness of the penalty subsequently changes. This point is raised by Justice Burger in his *Coker* dissent and is discussed at greater length in Chapter 13, in connection with the death penalty for the mentally retarded. In *Atkins*, the Court struck down the death penalty for such persons, even though a majority of states still permitted such executions.

This chapter and the succeeding four chapters consider at the same time two parallel issues—the appropriateness of the death penalty for a particular class of criminals and the wisdom of the Court's general approach to the issue of proportionality. The discussion begins with a debate over the death penalty for rapists. *Coker* leaves open the question whether the death penalty might be constitutional for child rapists. Following *Coker*, three states—Tennessee, Florida, and

Mississippi—retained laws allowing for the execution of a child rapist. The supreme courts of Florida and Mississippi struck down their state statutes. In 1995, Louisiana adopted the death penalty for child rape. Currently, two states—Tennessee and Louisiana—authorize the death penalty for the rape of a child.

Elizabeth Gray argues that societal standards of decency have evolved to the point where the death penalty is proportional to the crime of rape against a child. Gray takes particular exception with the Court's claim that the harm caused by rapists is less than the harm caused by murderers. Pallie Zambrano argues that the death penalty should be unconstitutional for all rapists, including child rapists, because none have the intention to kill. Zambrano rests much of her argument on the small number of states to reinstitute the death penalty for child rape.

The significance of these trends is debatable. What does it mean that only three states reinstituted the death penalty for rape following *Gregg*? What does it mean that so few states reinstituted the death penalty for child rapists following *Coker*? Both sides have reasonable arguments to make. The failure to act certainly suggests that the punishment is not favored by state legislatures. But that does not mean states might not later choose to adopt the death penalty for a certain crime or class of offenders after examining the experience of other states. *Coker* and its progeny inhibit this kind of (for lack of a better word) evolution in the law.

■ Rape and Proportionality—Critical Documents

Coker v. Georgia
433 U.S. 584 (1977)

Mr. Justice White announced the judgment of the Court and filed an opinion in which Mr. Justice Stewart, Mr. Justice Blackmun, and Mr. Justice Stevens, joined.

Georgia Code Ann. §26-2001 (1972) provides that "a person convicted of rape shall be punished by death or by imprisonment for life, or by imprisonment for not less than one nor more than 20 years." Punishment is determined by a jury in a separate sentencing proceeding in which at least one of the statutory aggravating circumstances must be found before the death penalty may be imposed. Petitioner Coker was convicted of rape and sentenced to death. Both the conviction and the sentence were affirmed by the Georgia Supreme Court. Coker was granted a writ of certiorari, limited to the single claim, rejected by the Georgia court, that the punishment of death for rape violates the Eighth Amendment, which proscribes "cruel and unusual punishments" and which must be observed by the States as well as the Federal Government.

I

While serving various sentences for murder, rape, kidnapping, and aggravated assault, petitioner escaped from the Ware Correctional Institution near

Waycross, Georgia, on September 2, 1974. At approximately 11 o'clock that night, petitioner entered the house of Allen and Elnita Carver through an unlocked kitchen door. Threatening the couple with a "board," he tied up Mr. Carver in the bathroom, obtained a knife from the kitchen, and took Mr. Carver's money and the keys to the family car. Brandishing the knife and saying "you know what's going to happen to you if you try anything, don't you," Coker then raped Mrs. Carver. Soon thereafter, petitioner drove away in the Carver car, taking Mrs. Carver with him. Mr. Carver, freeing himself, notified the police, and not long thereafter petitioner was apprehended. Mrs. Carver was unharmed.

Petitioner was charged with escape, armed robbery, motor vehicle theft, kidnapping, and rape. Counsel was appointed to represent him. Having been found competent to stand trial, he was tried. The jury returned a verdict of guilty, rejecting his general plea of insanity. A sentencing hearing was then conducted in accordance with the procedures dealt with at length in *Gregg*, where this Court sustained the death penalty for murder when imposed pursuant to the statutory procedures. The jury was instructed that it could consider as aggravating circumstances whether the rape had been committed by a person with a prior record of conviction for a capital felony and whether the rape had been committed in the course of committing another capital felony, namely, the armed robbery of Allen Carver. The court also instructed, pursuant to statute, that even if aggravating circumstances were present, the death penalty need not be imposed if the jury found they were outweighed by mitigating circumstances, that is, circumstances not constituting justification or excuse for the offense in question, "but which, in fairness and mercy, may be considered as extenuating or reducing the degree" of moral culpability or punishment. The jury's verdict on the rape count was death by electrocution. Both aggravating circumstances on which the court instructed were found to be present by the jury.

II

In sustaining the imposition of the death penalty in *Gregg*, the Court firmly embraced the holdings and dicta from prior cases to the effect that the Eighth Amendment bars not only those punishments that are "barbaric" but also those that are "excessive" in relation to the crime committed. Under *Gregg*, a punishment is "excessive" and unconstitutional if it (1) makes no measurable contribution to acceptable goals of punishment and hence is nothing more than the purposeless and needless imposition of pain and suffering; or (2) is grossly out of proportion to the severity of the crime. A punishment might fail the test on either ground. Furthermore, these Eighth Amendment judgments should not be, or appear to be, merely the subjective views of individual Justices; judgment should be informed by objective factors to the maximum possible extent. To this end, attention must be given to the public attitudes concerning a particular sentence—history and precedent, legislative attitudes, and the response of juries reflected in their sentencing decisions are to be consulted. In *Gregg*, after giving due regard to such sources, the Court's judgment was that the death penalty for deliberate murder was neither the purposeless imposition of severe punishment nor a punishment grossly disproportionate to the crime. But the Court reserved the question of the constitutionality of the death penalty when imposed for other crimes.

III

That question, with respect to rape of an adult woman, is now before us. We have concluded that a sentence of death is grossly disproportionate and excessive punishment for the crime of rape and is therefore forbidden by the Eighth Amendment as cruel and unusual punishment.

A

As advised by recent cases, we seek guidance in history and from the objective evidence of the country's present judgment concerning the acceptability of death as a penalty for rape of an adult woman. At no time in the last 50 years have a majority of the States authorized death as a punishment for rape. In 1925, 18 States, the District of Columbia, and the Federal Government authorized capital punishment for the rape of an adult female. By 1971 just prior to the decision in *Furman*, that number had declined, but not substantially, to 16 States plus the Federal Government. *Furman* then invalidated most of the capital punishment statutes in this country, including the rape statutes, because, among other reasons, of the manner in which the death penalty was imposed and utilized under those laws.

With their death penalty statutes for the most part invalidated, the States were faced with the choice of enacting modified capital punishment laws in an attempt to satisfy the requirements of *Furman* or of being satisfied with life imprisonment as the ultimate punishment for *any* offense. Thirty-five States immediately reinstituted the death penalty for at least limited kinds of crime. This public judgment as to the acceptability of capital punishment, evidenced by the immediate, post-*Furman* legislative reaction in a large majority of the States, heavily influenced the Court to sustain the death penalty for murder in *Gregg*.

But if the most marked indication of society's endorsement of the death penalty for murder is the legislative response to *Furman*, it should also be a telling datum that the public judgment with respect to rape, as reflected in the statutes providing the punishment for that crime, has been dramatically different. In reviving death penalty laws to satisfy *Furman*'s mandate, none of the States that had not previously authorized death for rape chose to include rape among capital felonies. Of the 16 States in which rape had been a capital offense, only three provided the death penalty for rape of an adult woman in their revised statutes—Georgia, North Carolina, and Louisiana. In the latter two States, the death penalty was mandatory for those found guilty, and those laws were invalidated by *Woodson* and *Roberts*. When Louisiana and North Carolina, responding to those decisions, again revised their capital punishment laws, they re-enacted the death penalty for murder but not for rape; none of the seven other legislatures that to our knowledge have amended or replaced their death penalty statutes since July 2, 1976, including four States (in addition to Louisiana and North Carolina) that had authorized the death sentence for rape prior to 1972 and had reacted to *Furman* with mandatory statutes, included rape among the crimes for which death was an authorized punishment.

Georgia argues that 11 of the 16 States that authorized death for rape in 1972 attempted to comply with *Furman* by enacting arguably mandatory death penalty legislation and that it is very likely that, aside from Louisiana and North Carolina, these States simply chose to eliminate rape as a capital offense rather than to *require* death for *each* and *every* instance of rape. The argument is not without force; but 4 of the 16 States did not take the mandatory course and also did *not* continue rape of an adult woman as a capital offense. Further, as we have indicated, the legislatures of 6 of the 11 arguably mandatory States have revised their death penalty laws since *Woodson* and *Roberts* without enacting a new death penalty for rape. And this is to say nothing of 19 other States that enacted nonmandatory, post- *Furman* statutes and chose not to sentence rapists to death.

It should be noted that Florida, Mississippi, and Tennessee also authorized the death penalty in some rape cases, but only where the victim was a child and the rapist an adult. The Tennessee statute has since been invalidated because the death sentence was mandatory. The upshot is that Georgia is the sole jurisdiction in the United States at the present time that authorizes a sentence of death when the rape victim is an adult woman, and only two other jurisdictions provide capital punishment when the victim is a child.

The current judgment with respect to the death penalty for rape is not wholly unanimous among state legislatures, but it obviously weighs very heavily on the side of rejecting capital punishment as a suitable penalty for raping an adult woman.

B

It was also observed in *Gregg* that "the jury is a significant and reliable objective index of contemporary values because it is so directly involved," and that it is thus important to look to the sentencing decisions that juries have made in the course of assessing whether capital punishment is an appropriate penalty for the crime being tried. Of course, the jury's judgment is meaningful only where the jury has an appropriate measure of choice as to whether the death penalty is to be imposed. As far as execution for rape is concerned, this is now true only in Georgia and in Florida; and in the latter State, capital punishment is authorized only for the rape of children.

According to the factual submissions in this Court, out of all rape convictions in Georgia since 1973—and that total number has not been tendered—63 cases had been reviewed by the Georgia Supreme Court as of the time of oral argument; and of these, 6 involved a death sentence, 1 of which was set aside, leaving 5 convicted rapists now under sentence of death in the State of Georgia. Georgia juries have thus sentenced rapists to death six times since 1973. This obviously is not a negligible number; and the State argues that as a practical matter juries simply reserve the extreme sanction for extreme cases of rape and that recent experience surely does not prove that jurors consider the death penalty to be a disproportionate punishment for every conceivable instance of rape, no matter how aggravated. Nevertheless, it is true that in the vast majority of cases, at least 9 out of 10, juries have not imposed the death sentence.

IV

These recent events evidencing the attitude of state legislatures and sentencing juries do not wholly determine this controversy, for the Constitution contemplates that in the end our own judgment will be brought to bear on the question of the acceptability of the death penalty under the Eighth Amendment. Nevertheless, the legislative rejection of capital punishment for rape strongly confirms our own judgment, which is that death is indeed a disproportionate penalty for the crime of raping an adult woman.

We do not discount the seriousness of rape as a crime. It is highly reprehensible, both in a moral sense and in its almost total contempt for the personal integrity and autonomy of the female victim and for the latter's privilege of choosing those with whom intimate relationships are to be established. Short of homicide, it is the "ultimate violation of self." It is also a violent crime because it normally involves force, or the threat of force or intimidation, to overcome the will and the capacity of the victim to resist. Rape is very often accompanied by physical injury to the female and can also inflict mental and psychological damage. Because it undermines the community's sense of security, there is public injury as well.

Rape is without doubt deserving of serious punishment; but in terms of moral depravity and of the injury to the person and to the public, it does not compare with murder, which does involve the unjustified taking of human life. Although it may be accompanied by another crime, rape by definition does not include the death of or even the serious injury to another person. The murderer kills; the rapist, if no more than that, does not. Life is over for the victim of the murderer; for the rape victim, life may not be nearly so happy as it was, but it is not over and normally is not beyond repair. We have the abiding conviction that the death penalty, which "is unique in its severity and irrevocability," is an excessive penalty for the rapist who, as such, does not take human life.

This does not end the matter; for under Georgia law, death may not be imposed for any capital offense, including rape, unless the jury or judge finds one of the statutory aggravating circumstances and then elects to impose that sentence. For the rapist to be executed in Georgia, it must therefore be found not only that he committed rape but also that one or more of the following aggravating circumstances were present: (1) that the rape was committed by a person with a prior record of conviction for a capital felony; (2) that the rape was committed while the offender was engaged in the commission of another capital felony, or aggravated battery; or (3) the rape "was outrageously or wantonly vile, horrible or inhuman in that it involved torture, depravity of mind, or aggravated battery to the victim." Here, the first two of these aggravating circumstances were alleged and found by the jury.

Neither of these circumstances, nor both of them together, change our conclusion that the death sentence imposed on Coker is a disproportionate punishment for rape. Coker had prior convictions for capital felonies—rape, murder, and kidnapping—but these prior convictions do not change the fact that the instant crime being punished is a rape not involving the taking of life.

It is also true that the present rape occurred while Coker was committing armed robbery, a felony for which the Georgia statutes authorize the death penalty. But Coker was tried for the robbery offense as well as for rape and received a separate life sentence for this crime; the jury did not deem the robbery itself deserving of the death penalty, even though accompanied by the aggravating circumstance, which was stipulated, that Coker had been convicted of a prior capital crime.

We note finally that in Georgia a person commits murder when he unlawfully and with malice aforethought, either express or implied, causes the death of another human being. He also commits that crime when in the commission of a felony he causes the death of another human being, irrespective of malice. But even where the killing is deliberate, it is not punishable by death absent proof of aggravating circumstances. It is difficult to accept the notion, and we do not, that the rapist, with or without aggravating circumstances, should be punished more heavily than the deliberate killer as long as the rapist does not himself take the life of his victim. The judgment of the Georgia Supreme Court upholding the death sentence is reversed, and the case is remanded to that court for further proceedings not inconsistent with this opinion.

Mr. Justice Powell, concurring in the judgment in part and dissenting in part.

I concur in the judgment of the Court on the facts of this case, and also in the plurality's reasoning supporting the view that ordinarily death is disproportionate punishment for the crime of raping an adult woman. Although rape invariably is a reprehensible crime, there is no indication that petitioner's offense was committed with excessive brutality or that the victim sustained serious or lasting injury. The plurality, however, does not limit its holding to the case before us or to similar cases. Rather, in an opinion that ranges well beyond what is necessary, it holds that capital punishment always—regardless of the circumstances—is a disproportionate penalty for the crime of rape.

Today, in a case that does not require such an expansive pronouncement, the plurality draws a bright line between murder and all rapes—regardless of the degree of brutality of the rape or the effect upon the victim. I dissent because I am not persuaded that such a bright line is appropriate. "There is extreme variation in the degree of culpability of rapists." The deliberate viciousness of the rapist may be greater than that of the murderer. Rape is never an act committed accidentally. Rarely can it be said to be unpremeditated. There also is wide variation in the effect on the victim. The plurality opinion says that "life is over for the victim of the murderer; for the rape victim, life may not be nearly so happy as it was, but it is not over and normally is not beyond repair." But there is indeed "extreme variation" in the crime of rape. Some victims are so grievously injured physically or psychologically that life is beyond repair.

It has not been shown that society finds the penalty disproportionate for all rapes. In a proper case a more discriminating inquiry than the plurality undertakes well might discover that both juries and legislatures have reserved the ultimate penalty for the case of an outrageous rape resulting in serious, lasting harm to the victim. I would not prejudge the issue. To this extent, I respectfully dissent.

Mr. Chief Justice Burger, with whom Mr. Justice Rehnquist joins, dissenting.

In striking down the death penalty imposed upon the petitioner in this case, the Court has overstepped the bounds of proper constitutional adjudication by substituting its policy judgment for that of the state legislature. I accept that the Eighth Amendment's concept of disproportionality bars the death penalty for minor crimes. But rape is not a minor crime.

The Court today holds that the State of Georgia may not impose the death penalty on Coker. In so doing, it prevents the State from imposing any effective punishment upon Coker for his latest rape. The Court's holding, moreover, bars Georgia from guaranteeing its citizens that they will suffer no further attacks by this habitual rapist. In fact, given the lengthy sentences Coker must serve for the crimes he has already committed, the Court's holding assures that petitioner—as well as others in his position—will henceforth feel no compunction whatsoever about committing further rapes as frequently as he may be able to escape from confinement and indeed even within the walls of the prison itself. To what extent we have left States "elbow-room" to protect innocent persons from depraved human beings like Coker remains in doubt.

My first disagreement with the Court's holding is its unnecessary breadth. The narrow issue here presented is whether the State of Georgia may constitutionally execute this petitioner for the particular rape which he has committed, in light of all the facts and circumstances shown by this record. The plurality opinion goes to great lengths to consider societal mores and attitudes toward the generic crime of rape and the punishment for it; however, the opinion gives little attention to the special circumstances which bear directly on whether imposition of the death penalty is an appropriate societal response to Coker's criminal acts: (a) On account of his prior offenses, Coker is already serving such lengthy prison sentences that imposition of additional periods of imprisonment would have no incremental punitive effect; (b) by his life pattern Coker has shown that he presents a particular danger to the safety, welfare, and chastity of women, and on his record the likelihood is therefore great that he will repeat his crime at the first opportunity; (c) petitioner escaped from prison, only a year and a half after he commenced serving his latest sentences; he has nothing to lose by further escape attempts; and (d) should he again succeed in escaping from prison, it is reasonably predictable that he will repeat his pattern of attacks on women—and with impunity since the threat of added prison sentences will be no deterrent.

Unlike the plurality, I would narrow the inquiry in this case to the question actually presented: Does the Eighth Amendment's ban against cruel and unusual punishment prohibit the State of Georgia from executing a person who has, within the space of three years, raped three separate women, killing one and attempting to kill another, who is serving prison terms exceeding his probable lifetime and who has not hesitated to escape confinement at the first available opportunity? Whatever one's view may be as to the State's constitutional power to impose the death penalty upon a rapist who stands before a court convicted for the first time, this case reveals a chronic rapist whose continuing danger to the community is abundantly clear.

Mr. Justice Powell would hold the death sentence inappropriate in *this* case because "there is no indication that petitioner's offense was committed with excessive brutality or that the victim sustained serious or lasting injury." Apart from the reality that rape is inherently one of the most egregiously brutal acts one human being can inflict upon another, there is nothing in the Eighth Amendment that so narrowly limits the factors which may be considered by a state legislature in determining whether a particular punishment is grossly excessive. Surely recidivism, especially the repeated commission of heinous crimes, is a factor which may properly be weighed as an aggravating circumstance, permitting the imposition of a punishment more severe than for one isolated offense.

Despite its strong condemnation of rape, the Court reaches the inexplicable conclusion that "the death penalty is an excessive penalty" for the perpetrator of this heinous offense. This, the Court holds, is true even though in Georgia the death penalty may be imposed only where the rape is coupled with one or more aggravating circumstances. The process by which this conclusion is reached is as startling as it is disquieting.

The analysis of the plurality opinion is divided into two parts: (a) an "objective" determination that most American jurisdictions do not presently make rape a capital offense, and (b) a subjective judgment that death is an excessive punishment for rape because the crime does not, in and of itself, cause the death of the victim. I take issue with each.

The plurality opinion bases its analysis, in part, on the fact that "Georgia is the sole jurisdiction in the United States at the present time that authorizes a sentence of death when the rape victim is an adult woman." Surely, however, this statistic cannot be deemed determinative, or even particularly relevant. As the opinion concedes, two other States—Louisiana and North Carolina—have enacted death penalty statutes for adult rape since this Court's 1972 decision in *Furman*. If the Court is to rely on some "public opinion" process, does this not suggest the beginning of a "trend"?

More to the point, however, it is myopic to base sweeping constitutional principles upon the narrow experience of the past five years. Considerable uncertainty was introduced into this area of the law by this Court's *Furman* decision. Failure of more States to enact statutes imposing death for rape of an adult woman may thus reflect hasty legislative compromise occasioned by time pressures following *Furman*, a desire to wait on the experience of those States which did enact such statutes, or simply an accurate forecast of today's holding.

The question of whether the death penalty is an appropriate punishment for rape is surely an open one. It is arguable that many prospective rapists would be deterred by the possibility that they could suffer death for their offense; it is also arguable that the death penalty would have only minimal deterrent effect. It may well be that rape victims would become more willing to report the crime and aid in the apprehension of the criminals if they knew that community disapproval of rapists was sufficiently strong to inflict the extreme penalty; or perhaps they would be reluctant to cooperate in the prosecution of rapists if they knew that a conviction might result in the imposition of the death penalty. Quite possibly, the occasional, well-publicized execution of egregious rapists may cause citizens to feel greater security in their daily lives; or, on the contrary, it may be that members of a civilized community will suffer the pangs of a heavy conscience because such punishment will be perceived as excessive. We cannot know which among this range of possibilities is correct, but today's holding forecloses the very exploration we have said federalism was intended to foster. It is difficult to believe that Georgia would long remain alone in punishing rape by death if the next decade demonstrated a drastic reduction in its incidence of rape, an increased cooperation by rape victims in the apprehension and prosecution of rapists, and a greater confidence in the rule of law on the part of the populace.

The subjective judgment that the death penalty is simply disproportionate to the crime of rape is even more disturbing than the "objective" analysis . The plurality's conclusion on this point is based upon the bare fact that murder necessarily results in the physical death of the victim, while rape does not. However, no Member of the Court explains why this distinction has relevance, much less constitutional significance.

The clear implication of today's holding appears to be that the death penalty may be properly imposed only as to crimes resulting in death of the victim. This casts serious doubt upon the constitutional validity of statutes imposing the death penalty for a variety of conduct which, though dangerous, may not necessarily result in any immediate death, *e.g.*, treason, airplane hijacking, and kidnapping. In that respect, today's holding does even more harm than is initially apparent. We cannot avoid taking judicial notice that crimes such as airplane hijacking, kidnapping, and mass terrorist activity constitute a serious and increasing danger to the safety of the public. It would be unfortunate indeed if the effect of today's holding were to inhibit States and the Federal Government from experimenting with various remedies—including possibly imposition of the penalty of death—to prevent and deter such crimes.

Whatever our individual views as to the wisdom of capital punishment, I cannot agree that it is constitutionally impermissible for a state legislature to make the "solemn judgment" to impose such penalty for the crime of rape. Accordingly, I would leave to the States the task of legislating in this area of the law.

■ Rape and Proportionality—Perspectives

■ Issue—Is the Death Penalty a Proportionate Punishment for Child Rapists?

Elizabeth Gray, "Death Penalty and Rape: An Eighth Amendment Analysis"

> "Death is factually different. Death is final. Death is irremediable. Death is unknowable; it goes beyond the world. Death is different because even if exactly the same discretionary procedures are used to decide issues of five years versus ten years, or life versus death, the result will be more arbitrary on the life or death choice."
> —Anthony Amsterdam, Oral Argument to the Supreme Court in Gregg v. Georgia.

Of course, death is different. Life imprisonment is different from a year in prison. It's different in that it deters more than any other kind of punishment.

There are some categories of criminals who cannot be deterred any other way. As the ultimate sanction, capital punishment is unique. It is different in the sense that it deters more and thereby saves more innocent lives. It is unique in that it upholds the basic values of our society symbolically and internalizes them for us more than any other punishment.

A careful analysis of Supreme Court jurisprudence reveals that the imposition of the death penalty for the rape of a child may not violate the Eighth Amendment. The death penalty is an appropriate punishment for the rape of a child in narrow circumstances where specific aggravating circumstances are present. Such aggravating circumstances may include the commission of a rape by an offender already serving a life sentence, the rape of a child while the perpetrator knowingly engages in criminal activities known to carry a grave risk of death, the rape of a child during an attempted murder, or where the rape is outrageously and wantonly vile, horrible, inhuman such that it involved depravity of the mind of the defendant. The use of the death penalty to punish defendants that rape children in these specific circumstances is supported by historical developments, legislative judgments, sentencing decisions of juries and by the satisfaction of the two chief purposes of capital punishment, retribution and deterrence.

The historical context of the death penalty supports the notion that it is an acceptable punishment for child rapists. Capital rape laws have existed since the first colonies organized. They were not unanimously endorsed by all of the colonies or by all of the states. However, the lack of universal endorsement of a particular mode of punishment alone, does not brand such punishment unconstitutional. The natural advancement of our society supports legislatures in experimenting with criminal sanctions to find what works. As our society advances, we learn what crimes are most devastating, and what may work to stop the criminals who commit them. The process is ongoing. The rape of a child, under the above mentioned aggravated circumstances is most reprehensible. As Justice Burger explained in his dissent in *Coker*, "the reserve strength of our federal system ... allows state legislatures within broad limits to experiment with laws to achieve socially desirable results."

In *State v. Wilson*, the Louisiana Supreme Court upheld the constitutionality of the death penalty as applied to offenders who rape children under the age of twelve. As Justice Bleich noted in *Wilson*, the fact that Louisiana is the only state that presently punishes child rapists in this fashion is not determinative because it may be that this statute is the beginning of a trend, which is an evolution of a standard for dealing with this heinous crime. The evidence of such a trend has already surfaced. Lawmakers in Pennsylvania, Massachusetts, and California are considering the death penalty for child rapists. Such legislative movements indicate that lawmakers are unsatisfied with the punishments now in place for child rapists, and have determined that a different punishment is needed. Judgments are being made by them that the crime of rape, when committed against a child warrants the death penalty.

The sentencing decisions of juries also supports capital punishment for the rape of a child. Between 1955 and the *Coker* decision in 1977, there were seventy-two executions for rape in this country. The analysis in *Coker* emphasized that in nine times out of ten juries chose not to impose the death penalty for the rape of an adult woman. However, because the death penalty is not warranted under particular facts does not dictate the conclusion that it should never be allowed. If no one had ever been sentenced to die for the commission of a rape, the inference that society deemed it an inappropriate sanction for the crime of child rape might be reasonable. As Justice Powell articulated in his concurrence in *Coker*, the infrequency with which death sentences are imposed reflects that juries recognize the sentences should only be applied in extreme cases. The death penalty is not an appropriate sanction for all defendants convicted of raping a child, and it is not appropriate for all defendants convicted of murder. The rarity with which it is imposed indicates that the essence of the procedural protections guaranteed by *Furman* do work. Juries recognize the severity of their decision and impose the ultimate penalty only when the gravity of the crime makes it appropriate.

The use of the death penalty to punish child rapists also serves the purposes of deterrence and retribution. As Solicitor General Robert H. Bork made clear in his oral argument to the Supreme Court, "there are some categories of criminals who cannot be deterred any other way. Capital punishment deters more and thereby saves more innocent lives." An example is Anthony Ehrlich Coker and the circumstances under which his rape was committed. He was serving a life sentence for rape and murder. He escaped from prison and raped again. He is in the category of rapists that cannot be deterred any other way. The purpose of retribution is also satisfied. Retribution is sensitive to contemporary community morality. Our society has evolved to find the death penalty proportional to the crime of rape against a child.

In the final analysis, the Constitution contemplates that the Supreme Court's own subjective judgment will finalize the acceptability of the death penalty under the Eighth Amendment. The subjective principles that were enunciated by the majority decision in *Coker* about rape are questionable by modern standards. The crime of rape is reprehensible. Committed against a child, it is deserving of public outrage. Justice White stated in *Coker*, "rape by definition does not include the death or even serious injury to another person." The society we live in today does not accept such a theory on the effect of rape. Regarding the rape of a child, such a suggestion is ludicrous. Over twenty years have passed since the *Coker* decision. A tremendous amount of public awareness and resulting outcry has taken place with regard to sexual crimes and crimes against children. The subjective judgments imposed by the Supreme Court Justices will undoubtedly be far more sensitive to the injury caused by child rapists, and less tolerant of efforts to neutralize the punishment demanded for the crime.

The rape of a child is indeed as shocking as an intent to kill. The twenty years since the *Coker* decision have been marked by a heightened sense of societal sensitivity to the physical and emotional damage which the crime of rape causes in the lives of victims and their families. State legislatures may choose to respond by revisiting the efficacy of the death penalty as punishment for such depravity. So long as the statutes are enacted with the appropriate procedural protections mandated by *Furman* and its progeny, such statutes should withstand constitutional scrutiny.

Pallie Zambrano, "The Death Penalty is Cruel and Unusual Punishment for the Crime of Rape— Even the Rape of a Child"

In 1995, Louisiana amended its criminal code to allow for the sentence of death to be imposed when a person is convicted of raping a child under the age of twelve. In 1996, Georgia followed suit and amended its penal code to become the second and only other state to impose such a severe penalty for the crime of rape.

At a time when politicians are basing their political campaigns on law and order platforms, including proposals that the death penalty be instituted for rape and child molestation, we as a society, and in particular the courts, are being faced with the question of whether death should be imposed on a citizen convicted of raping a child.

The Supreme Court held in *Enmund v. Florida* that when there is no intent to kill in a crime, the imposition of the death penalty constitutes cruel and unusual punishment. Though Wilson and Bethley—charged under the revised Louisiana statute—may have raped their victims, they had no intent to kill their victims. The level of culpability is not as great for the crime of rape as it is for the crime of murder. As devastated as a rape victim may be, "sensitive response" by family, friends and professionals will assist the victim back to a "livable life." A murder takes away human life and, therefore, imposition of the death penalty may be justified. But the rapist does not kill and though the crime is despicable, it is not deserving of the punishment of death. Though the rape of a child is more heinous than the rape of an adult, it is still only rape and absent the intention to kill the victim the defendant should not be sentenced to die.

The United States Supreme Court identified three factors to guide courts in determining whether a sentence meets the Eighth Amendment's burden: 1) the gravity of the offense and harshness of the penalty, 2) the sentences imposed on other criminals for the same offense in the same jurisdiction, and 3) the sentences imposed on criminals for the same offense in other jurisdictions. Looking at the statutes of other states is a good way to determine if a penalty is excessive, and looking at the other states' statutes in this situation reveals that Georgia is the only state to agree with Louisiana that the death penalty is an appropriate punishment for raping a child. Twenty years after the United States Supreme Court held the death penalty was cruel and unusual punishment for the rape of an adult woman, only two states have revised their laws in an attempt to get around the Supreme Court's ruling. The other forty-eight states follow *Coker* and do not allow imposition of the death penalty solely for the crime of rape.

In fact in 1981, the Florida Supreme Court found that the holding in *Coker* was controlling for the rape of a child. When a defendant convicted of raping an eleven-year-old girl was sentenced to die, he appealed to Florida's Supreme Court. The court relied first on the reasoning in *Coker*, where the Court found that "rape is without doubt deserving of serious punishment; but in terms of moral depravity it does not compare with murder. Rape by definition does not include the death of or even the serious injury to another person. The murderer kills; the rapist, if no more than that, does not." The Florida court concluded that the reasoning of the Justices in *Coker* compelled them to find that "a sentence of death is grossly disproportionate and excessive" for the crime of rape and, therefore, forbidden by the Eighth Amendment as cruel and unusual. Even though the Florida case involved the rape of an eleven-year-old girl, *Coker* was found to control.

The only difference in Louisiana's law and the death penalty statute that the Court found unconstitutional in *Coker* is the specification of the age of the victim. No life must be lost before the death penalty can be imposed under Louisiana's law. As the Court specified in *Coker* and in *Enmund*, the crime of rape alone is not enough to allow the perpetrator to be sentenced to die. The Louisiana Court found the class of offenders is sufficiently limited to those who rape a child under the age of twelve and not every rapist will be subject to the death penalty. But as previously discussed, the death penalty is too severe a punishment for the crime of rape regardless of the victim's age.

The previous rulings by the Supreme Court have held not only that the death penalty is cruel and unusual for the crime of rape, but that it is cruel and unusual for any crime when a life is not taken. But "far more convincing than *Gregg*, or *Coker* or *Enmund*, or any of the others, the American public has spoken— through its legislatures and juries. That public has told us that, however heinous it may regard the rape of a child, death is not an acceptable punishment." It must be remembered that the question is not "whether we condone rape or murder, for surely we do not; it is whether capital punishment for rape is a punishment no longer consistent with our own self-respect."

The Supreme Court has already declared that the imposition of the death penalty for rape is unconstitutional. In fact, it went as far as to say that absent the taking of a life, the death penalty is too severe a punishment for any crime. The raping of a child is no doubt heinous, but it does not involve a taking of a life and, therefore, imposition of the death penalty would be too severe. When someone is sentenced to die for raping a child under either Georgia's or Louisiana's laws, the United States Supreme Court should grant certiorari in order to declare once and for all that the death penalty is cruel and unusual punishment for the crime of rape no matter what the age of the victim. Relying on precedent, the Justices should find that despite the despicable nature of the crime of rape, even of a child, it does not qualify as a crime deserving of the punishment of death.

Felony-Murder

11

■ Felony-Murder—Introduction

Coker invited other defendants to search, in their own cases, for evidence that societal standards of decency condemned the use of the death penalty against them. Over succeeding years, defendants offered two kinds of proportionality arguments: claims based on the crime the defendant committed (as Coker successfully argued) or the nature of his participation in the crime, and claims based on some status—for example, age or mental health—he holds or held at the time of the offense. The Supreme Court next returned to proportionality review in *Enmund v. Florida*, a 1982 decision dealing with the death penalty for felony-murderers.

The felony-murder doctrine is a departure from the normal principles of criminal law. Ordinarily, criminal liability is predicated upon the defendant's state of mind (*mens rea*) and degree of participation in the offense. To be guilty of intentional homicide, a defendant must have intended and caused the death of the victim—except in the case of felony-murder. Under the felony-murder doctrine, a defendant's intention to commit a felony may substitute for the intention to kill. For example, Jones and Smith conspire to rob a store. In the course of the robbery, Smith shoots and kills the storeowner. Jones is guilty of felony-murder because Jones's intention to commit the robbery satisfies the *mens rea* requirement for murder. This is true even if Jones did not know Smith was carrying a gun or even if Jones specifically told Smith he did not want anyone to be hurt during the robbery. It is even true if Smith did not carry a gun. If the storeowner had a heart condition and suffered a fatal heart attack when threatened by Smith, then Smith and Jones are both guilty of felony-murder.

The doctrine is controversial for obvious reasons. It might be retributively unfair to sentence someone for a crime he did not intend to commit. Harsh penalties for felony-murder do not deter behavior by potential criminals who truly do not intend to commit a murder. An argument could be made that people who commit felony-murder deserve to be punished as murderers based upon the foreseeable risk that death might result during the course of the felony. However, the statistics are less than compelling in supporting this argument. Consider **Table 10-1**, which offers a measure of the risk that a homicide will result from a felony. The data, taken from Philadelphia crime reports over a five-year period, suggest that the aggregate risk that a felony will result in death is less than one tenth of 1%.

Table 10-1	Relation of Felonies to Homicides—Philadelphia, 1948–1952		
Offense	Number of crimes reported	Number accompanied by homicide	Percentage (%)
Robbery	6432	38	.59
Rape	1133	4	.35
Burglary	27,669	1	.003
Auto Theft	10,315	2	.019
Total	45,549	45	.009

The felony-murder doctrine is even more controversial in the context of capital punishment. In many states, it is an aggravating factor that a murder was committed contemporaneously with other felony offenses. Thus, a defendant's intention to commit a felony may substitute as the mental state for murder and as the aggravating circumstance that makes him eligible for death.

In the perspectives section below, Professor Richard Rosen argues that the felony-murder doctrine is in direct conflict with the Supreme Court's death penalty jurisprudence. The felony-murder doctrine shifts emphasis away from the defendant's *mens rea*, while the Supreme Court requires—in connection with the death penalty—a heightened review of all aspects of the crime and the defendant's character. Professor Rosen expresses reservations about the wisdom of a class-oriented proportionality analysis, advocating a more individualized approach, a point discussed further in Chapter 12 in connection with the death penalty for juveniles. Professor David McCord argues that, in practice, lower courts have been consistent in restricting capital punishment only to the most aggravated felony-murder cases. He nevertheless agrees that it would be desirable to establish safeguards—such as a requirement of positive knowledge—to ensure that the death penalty net is not cast too widely.

Professors Rosen and McCord's arguments are crucial to considering the fair scope of the death penalty, but are beside the point to the Supreme Court. The Supreme Court established in *Coker* an empirical framework for analyzing standards of decency. The Court primarily looks to objective evidence—specifically, legislative judgments and jury verdicts. One question is whether the Court has been internally consistent in the quantity of evidence it requires to find the sentence of death disproportionate for a class of offenders. The evidence of consensus in *Enmund* is far less convincing than the evidence against the death penalty for rape in *Coker*.

Enmund drove the getaway car in a robbery that resulted in the gruesome deaths of Thomas and Eunice Kersey. Under Florida law, this made Enmund a constructive aider and abettor in the crime, hence a principal in first-degree murder. Florida law placed no weight on the fact that Enmund neither killed nor was present at the killings, nor did it consider whether Enmund had intended or anticipated that the Kerseys might be killed. Enmund's state of mind was at most negligent—it was foreseeable to someone in his position that death might result from the robbery. This was sufficient under Florida law to qualify Enmund for the death penalty.

In *Coker*, the evidence of societal consensus against the death penalty was convincing. Georgia was the only state that would have executed Coker on his facts. In *Enmund*, the evidence was more ambiguous. In 1982, eight states authorized the death penalty for participation in a robbery in which another participant in the crime committed murder. Nine other states allowed execution for an unintended felony-murder if sufficient aggravating circumstances outweighed mitigating circumstances. Six of these nine states made it a statutory mitigating factor that the defendant was not the triggerman and was only a minor participant. Hence, seventeen states might conceivably have allowed someone like Enmund to be executed. Writing for the majority, Justice White put it this way:

> *Only about a third of American jurisdictions would ever permit a defendant who somehow participated in a robbery where a murder occurred to be sentenced to die. Moreover, of the eight States which have enacted new death penalty statutes since 1978, none authorize capital punishment in such circumstances.*

This is the first of several vagaries in the Court's empirical analysis. Justice White says "only about a third" of jurisdictions would permit someone like Enmund to die. The numerator in this calculation is clearly 17. The denominator chosen by Justice White is either 50 or 51, depending on whether or not he is including the District of Columbia. But 50 and 51 are not the only numbers he could have selected. Thirty-six, the number of states then authorizing the death penalty, is another obvious possibility. Had this been the denominator, someone like Enmund could have been executed in almost half of the included states, hardly a consensus against his execution.

The defense of using all states as the denominator is that if a state does not have the death penalty, then it certainly would not elect to have the death penalty for the class of criminals being considered. But this doesn't necessarily follow. A person could reasonably say that she is against the death penalty, but that if she were forced to live in a world with the death penalty, then rapists should not be beyond its reach. The proper denominator isn't obvious. In subsequent proportionality decisions, the Court uses different denominators at different times. Mostly the Justices use whichever number best suits their purposes at the moment.

The second part of Justice White's argument introduces another ambiguity into proportionality analysis. Justice White notes that none of the last eight states to reintroduce the death penalty included nontriggerman felony-murderers within the ambit of their statutes. He seems to be attaching weight to the trend against the death penalty for felony-murderers. Another argument against the Court's empirical proportionality analysis is that it immortalizes temporary fluctuations in public opinion. It might be true that in 1977 only one state authorizes the death penalty for rape. That isn't to say that support for the death penalty for rape might not increase if the states were left on their own. Under the existing jurisprudence, such support will never reappear. If the death penalty for rape is ruled unconstitutional, no state will reenact the death penalty for rape. This is Justice Burger's argument in his dissent in *Coker*. States, he argues, should be free to experiment. Immortalizing short-term trends prevents states from learning whether particular kinds and levels of punishment are effective.

Under existing doctrine, proportionality review acts as a one-way ratchet—increasing support for a penalty will not result in extraconstitutionality, as something is either constitutional or it is not, but decreasing support for a penalty might result in its permanent unconstitutionality. This is a large part of Justice Scalia's objection to proportionality review. In *Harmelin v. Michigan*, he wrote:

> *The Eighth Amendment is not a ratchet, whereby a temporary consensus on leniency for a particular crime fixes a permanent constitutional maximum, disabling the States from giving effect to altered beliefs and responding to changed social conditions.*

Reliance upon trends only exacerbates the ratchet effect. *Coker* made the death penalty unconstitutional for rape on the basis of the established views of all jurisdictions. Justice White's opinion suggests the possibility that the death penalty might be ruled unconstitutional in certain cases on the basis of the views of a smaller subset of states. This reliance upon trends, fair or not, plays an increasingly prominent role in the Court's proportionality analysis. It is particularly prominent in the debate over capital punishment for the mentally retarded, as discussed in Chapter 13.

Enmund and *Tison v. Arizona* are excerpted in this chapter's Critical Documents. In *Tison*, the Supreme Court held that the Eighth Amendment does not preclude the execution of a major participant in a felony-murder who does not kill or intend to kill but has a mental state of reckless indifference to human life. There are certainly material differences in the culpability of Tison and Enmund, and it is worth discussing whether either or both are deserving of the death penalty in light of the arguments of Professors Rosen and McCord. The difference in evidence of societal values is less clear. Seventeen states would have allowed Enmund to be executed. Justice O'Connor says in *Tison* that 11 of the states authorizing capital punishment forbade imposition of the death penalty even though the defendant was a major participant in the felony murder. So the number in *Tison* is at most 25, including the 2 states that require the defendant's participation to be substantial (thus including Tison, but not Enmund), and 4 states that require a showing of recklessness or extreme indifference (again including Tison but not Enmund). Justice O'Connor seems to arrive at a final calculation of 21 states that would authorize killing Tison but not Enmund. The Court's holding is that on the basis of these 4 additional states that would permit the execution of Tison versus Enmund, there is not sufficient evidence of a consensus against the execution of someone such as Tison. There are important differences between of Tison and Enmund's cases. However, it seems worth asking, both here and in the following proportionality discussions, whether the Court's purportedly objective analysis is able to generate results that are truly objective.

■ Felony-Murder—Critical Documents

Enmund v. Florida
458 U.S. 782 (1982)

Justice White delivered the opinion of the Court.

I

The facts of this case, taken principally from the opinion of the Florida Supreme Court, are as follows. On April 1, 1975, at approximately 7:45 A.M., Thomas and Eunice Kersey, aged 86 and 74, were robbed and fatally shot at their farmhouse in central Florida. The evidence showed that Sampson and Jeanette Armstrong had gone to the back door of the Kersey house and asked for water for an over-heated car. When Mr. Kersey came out of the house, Sampson Armstrong grabbed him, pointed a gun at him, and told Jeanette Armstrong to take his money. Mr. Kersey cried for help, and his wife came out of the house with a gun and shot Jeanette Armstrong, wounding her. Sampson Armstrong, and perhaps Jeanette Armstrong, then shot and killed both of the Kerseys, dragged them into the kitchen, and took their money and fled.

Two witnesses testified that they drove past the Kersey house between 7:30 and 7:40 A.M. and saw a large cream- or yellow-colored car parked beside the road about 200 yards from the house and that a man was sitting in the car. Another witness testified that at approximately 6:45 A.M. he saw Ida Jean Shaw, petitioner's common-law wife and Jeanette Armstrong's mother, driving a yellow Buick with a vinyl top, which belonged to her and petitioner Earl Enmund. Enmund was a passenger in the car along with an unidentified woman. At about 8 A.M. the same witness saw the car return at a high rate of speed. Enmund was driving, Ida Jean Shaw was in the front seat, and one of the other two people in the car was lying down across the back seat.

Enmund, Sampson Armstrong, and Jeanette Armstrong were indicted for the first-degree murder and robbery of the Kerseys. Enmund and Sampson Armstrong were tried together. The prosecutor maintained in his closing argument that "Sampson Armstrong killed the old people." The judge instructed the jury that "the killing of a human being while engaged in the perpetration of or in the attempt to perpetrate the offense of robbery is murder in the first degree even though there is no premeditated design or intent to kill." The jury found both Enmund and Sampson Armstrong guilty of two counts of first-degree murder and one count of robbery and recommended the death penalty for both defendants.

As recounted above, the Florida Supreme Court held that the record supported more than the inference that Enmund was the person in the car by the side of the road at the time of the killings, waiting to help the robbers escape. This was enough under Florida law to make Enmund a constructive aider and abettor and hence a principal in first-degree murder upon whom the death penalty could be imposed. It was thus irrelevant to Enmund's challenge to the death sentence that he did not himself kill and was not present at the killings; also beside the point was whether he intended that the Kerseys be killed or anticipated that lethal force would or might be used if necessary to effectuate the robbery or a safe escape. We have concluded that imposition of the death penalty in these circumstances is inconsistent with the Eighth and Fourteenth Amendments.

Thirty-six state and federal jurisdictions presently authorize the death penalty. Of these, only eight jurisdictions authorize imposition of the death penalty solely for participation in a robbery in which another robber takes life. Of the remaining 28 jurisdictions, in 4 felony-murder is not a capital crime. Eleven States require some culpable mental state with respect to the homicide as a prerequisite to conviction of a crime for which the death penalty is authorized. Of these 11 States, 8 make knowing, intentional, purposeful, or premeditated killing an element of capital murder. Three other States require proof of a culpable mental state short of intent, such as recklessness or extreme indifference to human life, before the death penalty may be imposed. In these 11 States, therefore, the actors in a felony murder are not subject to the death penalty without proof of their mental state, proof which was not required with respect to Enmund either under the trial court's instructions or under the law announced by the Florida Supreme Court.

Four additional jurisdictions do not permit a defendant such as Enmund to be put to death. Of these, one State flatly prohibits capital punishment in cases where the defendant did not actually commit murder. Two jurisdictions preclude the death penalty in cases such as this one where the defendant "was a principal in the offense, which was committed by another, but his participation was relatively minor, although not so minor as to constitute a defense to prosecution." One other State limits the death penalty in felony murders to narrow circumstances not involved here.

Nine of the remaining States deal with the imposition of the death penalty for a vicarious felony murder in their capital sentencing statutes. In each of these States, a defendant may not be executed *solely* for participating in a felony in which a person was killed if the defendant did not actually cause the victim's death. For a defendant to be executed in these States, typically the statutory aggravating circumstances which are present must outweigh mitigating factors. To be sure, a vicarious felony murderer may be sentenced to death in these jurisdictions absent an intent to kill if sufficient aggravating circumstances are present. However, six of these nine States make it a statutory *mitigating* circumstance that the defendant was an accomplice in a capital felony committed by another person and his participation was relatively minor. By making minimal participation in a capital felony committed by another person a mitigating circumstance, these sentencing statutes reduce the likelihood that a person will be executed for vicarious felony murder. The remaining three jurisdictions exclude felony murder from their lists of aggravating circumstances that will support a death sentence. In each of these nine States, a nontriggerman guilty of felony murder cannot be sentenced to death for the felony murder absent aggravating circumstances above and beyond the felony murder itself.

Thus only a small minority of jurisdictions—eight—allow the death penalty to be imposed solely because the defendant somehow participated in a robbery in the course of which a murder was committed. Even if the nine States are included where such a defendant could be executed for an unintended felony murder if sufficient aggravating circumstances are present to outweigh mitigating circumstances—which often include the defendant's minimal participation in the murder—only about a third of American jurisdictions would ever permit a defendant who somehow participated in a robbery where a murder occurred to be sentenced to die. Moreover, of the eight States which have enacted new death penalty statutes since 1978, none authorize capital punishment in such circumstances. While the current legislative judgment with respect to imposition of the death penalty where a defendant did not take life, attempt to take it, or intend to take life is neither "wholly unanimous among state legislatures," nor as compelling as the legislative judgments considered in *Coker*, it nevertheless weighs on the side of rejecting capital punishment for the crime at issue.

Society's rejection of the death penalty for accomplice liability in felony murders is also indicated by the sentencing decisions that juries have made. The evidence is overwhelming that American juries have repudiated imposition of the death penalty for crimes such as petitioner's. First, according to the petitioner, a search of all reported appellate court decisions since 1954 in cases where a defendant was executed for homicide shows that of the 362 executions, in 339 the person executed personally committed a homicidal assault. In 2 cases the person executed had another person commit the homicide for him, and in 16 cases the facts were not reported in sufficient detail to determine whether the person executed committed the homicide. The survey revealed only 6 cases out of 362 where a nontriggerman felony murderer was executed. All six executions took place in 1955. By contrast, there were 72 executions for rape in this country between 1955 and this Court's decision in *Coker* in 1977.

That juries have rejected the death penalty in cases such as this one where the defendant did not commit the homicide, was not present when the killing took place, and did not participate in a plot or scheme to murder is also shown by petitioner's survey of the Nation's death-row population. As of October 1, 1981, there were 796 inmates under sentences of death for homicide. Of the 739 for whom sufficient data are available, only 41 did not participate in the fatal assault on the victim. Of the 40 among the 41 for whom sufficient information was available, only 16 were not physically present when the fatal assault was committed. These 16 prisoners included only 3, including petitioner, who were sentenced to die absent a finding that they hired or solicited someone else to kill the victim or participated in a scheme designed to kill the victim. The figures for Florida are similar.

The dissent criticizes these statistics on the ground that they do not reveal the percentage of homicides that were charged as felony murders or the percentage of cases where the State sought the death penalty for an accomplice guilty of felony murder. We doubt whether it is possible to gather such information, and at any rate, it would be relevant if prosecutors rarely sought the death penalty for accomplice felony murder, for it would tend to indicate that prosecutors, who represent society's interest in punishing crime, consider the death penalty excessive for accomplice felony murder. The fact remains that we are not aware of a single person convicted of felony murder over the past quarter century who did not kill or attempt to kill, and did not intend the death of the victim, who has been executed, and that only three persons in that category are presently sentenced to die. Nor can these figures be discounted by attributing to petitioner the argument that "death is an unconstitutional penalty absent an intent to kill," and observing that the statistics are incomplete with respect to intent. Petitioner's argument is that because he did not kill, attempt to kill, *and* he did not intend to kill, the death penalty is disproportionate as applied to him, and the statistics he cites are adequately tailored to demonstrate that juries—and perhaps prosecutors as well—consider death a disproportionate penalty for those who fall within his category.

Although the judgments of legislatures, juries, and prosecutors weigh heavily in the balance, it is for us ultimately to judge whether the Eighth Amendment permits imposition of the death penalty on one such as Enmund who aids and abets a felony in the course of which a murder is committed by others but who does not himself kill, attempt to kill, or intend that a killing take place or that lethal force will be employed. We have concluded, along with most legislatures and juries, that it does not.

We have no doubt that robbery is a serious crime deserving serious punishment. It is not, however, a crime "so grievous an affront to humanity that the only adequate response may be the penalty of death." "It does not compare with murder, which does involve the unjustified taking of human life. Although it may be accompanied by another crime, robbery by definition does not include the death of or even the serious injury to another person. The murderer kills; the robber, if no more than that, does not. Life is over for the victim of the murderer; for the robbery victim, life is not over and normally is not beyond repair." As was said of the crime of rape in *Coker*, we have the abiding conviction that the death penalty, which is "unique in its severity and irrevocability," is an excessive penalty for the robber who, as such, does not take human life.

Here the robbers did commit murder; but they were subjected to the death penalty only because they killed as well as robbed. The question before us is not the disproportionality of death as a penalty for murder, but rather the validity of capital punishment for Enmund's own conduct. The focus must be on *his* culpability, not on that of those who committed the robbery and shot the victims, for we insist on "individualized consideration as a constitutional requirement in imposing the death sentence." Enmund himself did not kill or attempt to kill; and, as construed by the Florida Supreme Court, the record before us does not warrant a finding that Enmund had any intention of participating in or facilitating a murder. Yet under Florida law death was an authorized penalty because Enmund aided and abetted a robbery in the course of which murder was committed. It is fundamental that "causing harm intentionally must be punished more severely than causing the same harm unintentionally." Enmund did not kill or intend to kill and thus his culpability is plainly different from that of the robbers who killed; yet the State treated them alike and attributed to Enmund the culpability of those who killed the Kerseys. This was impermissible under the Eighth Amendment.

In *Gregg* the opinion announcing the judgment observed that "the death penalty is said to serve two principal social purposes: retribution and deterrence." We are quite unconvinced, however, that the threat that the death penalty will be imposed for murder will measurably deter one who does not kill and has no intention or purpose that life will be taken. Instead, it seems likely that "capital punishment can serve as a deterrent only when murder is the result of premeditation and deliberation," for if a person does not intend that life be taken or contemplate that lethal force will be employed by others, the possibility that the death penalty will be imposed for vicarious felony murder will not "enter into the cold calculus that precedes the decision to act."

It would be very different if the likelihood of a killing in the course of a robbery were so substantial that one should share the blame for the killing if he somehow participated in the felony. But competent observers have concluded that there is no basis in experience for the notion that death so frequently occurs in the course of a felony for which killing is not an essential ingredient that the death penalty should be considered as a justifiable deterrent to the felony itself. This conclusion was based on three comparisons of robbery statistics, each of which showed that only about one-half of one percent of robberies resulted in homicide. The most recent national crime statistics strongly support this conclusion.

As for retribution as a justification for executing Enmund, we think this very much depends on the degree of Enmund's culpability—what Enmund's intentions, expectations, and actions were. American criminal law has long considered a defendant's intention—and therefore his moral guilt—to be critical to "the degree of his criminal culpability," and the Court has found criminal penalties to be unconstitutionally excessive in the absence of intentional wrongdoing.

For purposes of imposing the death penalty, Enmund's criminal culpability must be limited to his participation in the robbery, and his punishment must be tailored to his personal responsibility and moral guilt. Putting Enmund to death to avenge two killings that he did not commit and had no intention of committing or causing does not measurably contribute to the retributive end of ensuring that the criminal gets his just deserts.

Because the Florida Supreme Court affirmed the death penalty in this case in the absence of proof that Enmund killed or attempted to kill, and regardless of whether Enmund intended or contemplated that life would be taken, we reverse the judgment upholding the death penalty and remand for further proceedings not inconsistent with this opinion.

Justice O'Connor, with whom The Chief Justice, Justice Powell, and Justice Rehnquist join, dissenting.

The evidence at trial showed that at approximately 7:30 A.M. on April 1, 1975, Sampson and Jeanette Armstrong approached the back door of Thomas and Eunice Kersey's farmhouse on the pretext of obtaining water for their overheated car. When Thomas Kersey retrieved a water jug to help the Armstrongs, Sampson Armstrong grabbed him, held a gun to him, and told Jeanette Armstrong to take his wallet. Hearing her husband's cries for help, Eunice Kersey came around the side of the house with a gun and shot Jeanette Armstrong. Sampson Armstrong, and perhaps Jeanette Armstrong, returned the fire, killing both of the Kerseys. The Armstrongs dragged the bodies into the kitchen, took Thomas Kersey's money, and fled to a nearby car, where the petitioner, Earl Enmund, was waiting to help the Armstrongs escape. The court concluded that the evidence clearly showed that the petitioner was an accomplice to the capital felony and that his participation had not been "relatively minor," but had been major in that he "planned the capital felony and actively participated in an attempt to avoid detection by disposing of the murder weapons."

Following the analysis set forth in *Coker*, the petitioner examines the historical development of the felony-murder rule, as well as contemporary legislation and jury verdicts in capital cases, in an effort to show that imposition of the death penalty on him would violate the Eighth Amendment. This effort fails, however, for the available data do not show that society has rejected conclusively the death penalty for felony murderers.

The petitioner and the Court turn to jury verdicts in an effort to show that, by present standards at least, capital punishment is grossly out of proportion to the crimes that the petitioner committed. Surveying all reported appellate court opinions since 1954 involving executions, the petitioner has found that of the 362 individuals executed for homicide, 339 personally committed the homicidal assault, and two others each had another person commit the homicide on his behalf. Only six persons executed were "non-triggermen." A similar trend can be seen in the petitioner's survey of the current death row population. Of the 739 prisoners for whom sufficient data are available, only 40 did not participate in the homicidal assault, and of those, only 3 (including the petitioner) were sentenced to death absent a finding that they had collaborated with the killer in a specific plan to kill.

Impressive as these statistics are at first glance, they cannot be accepted uncritically. So stated, the data do not reveal the murder or fraction of homicides that were charged as felony murders, or the number or fraction of cases in which the State sought the death penalty for an accomplice guilty of felony murder. Consequently, we cannot know the fraction of cases in which juries rejected the death penalty for accomplice felony murder. Even accepting the petitioner's facts as meaningful, they may only reflect that sentencers are especially cautious in imposing the death penalty, and reserve that punishment for those defendants who are sufficiently involved in the homicide, whether or not there was specific intent to kill.

Finally, as the petitioner acknowledges, the jury verdict statistics cannot be viewed in isolation from state death penalty legislation. The petitioner and the Court therefore review recent legislation in order to support the conclusion that society has rejected capital felony murder. Of the 35 States that presently have a death penalty, however, fully 31 authorize a sentencer to impose a death sentence for a death that occurs during the course of a robbery.

The Court's curious method of counting the States that authorize imposition of the death penalty for felony murder cannot hide the fact that 23 States permit a sentencer to impose the death penalty even though the felony murderer has neither killed nor intended to kill his victim. While the Court acknowledges that eight state statutes follow the Florida death penalty scheme, it also concedes that 15 other statutes permit imposition of the death penalty where the defendant neither intended to kill or actually killed the victims.

Thus, in nearly half of the States, and in two-thirds of the States that permit the death penalty for murder, a defendant who neither killed the victim nor specifically intended that the victim die may be sentenced to death for his participation in the robbery-murder. Far from "weighing very heavily on the side of rejecting capital punishment as a suitable penalty for" felony murder, these legislative judgments indicate that our "evolving standards of decency" still embrace capital punishment for this crime.

As I noted earlier, the Eighth Amendment concept of proportionality involves more than merely a measurement of contemporary standards of decency. It requires in addition that the penalty imposed in a capital case be proportional to the harm caused and the defendant's blameworthiness. Critical to the holding in *Coker*, for example, was that "in terms of moral depravity and of the injury to the person and to the public, rape does not compare with murder, which involves the unjustified taking of human life."

Although the Court disingenuously seeks to characterize Enmund as only a "robber," it cannot be disputed that he is responsible, along with Sampson and Jeanette Armstrong, for the murders of the Kerseys. There is no dispute that their lives were unjustifiably taken, and that the petitioner, as one who aided and abetted the armed robbery, is legally liable for their deaths. Quite unlike the defendant in *Coker*, the petitioner cannot claim that the penalty imposed is "grossly out of proportion" to the harm for which he admittedly is at least partly responsible.

Tison v. Arizona
481 U.S. 137 (1987)

Justice O'Connor delivered the opinion of the Court.

I

Gary Tison was sentenced to life imprisonment as the result of a prison escape during the course of which he had killed a guard. After he had been in prison a number of years, Gary Tison's wife, their three sons Donald, Ricky, and Raymond, Gary's brother Joseph, and other relatives made plans to help Gary Tison escape again. The Tison family assembled a large arsenal of weapons for this purpose. Plans for escape were discussed with Gary Tison, who insisted that his cellmate, Randy Greenawalt, also a convicted murderer, be included in the prison break. The following facts are largely evidenced by petitioners' detailed confessions given as part of a plea bargain according to the terms of which the State agreed not to seek the death sentence. The Arizona courts interpreted the plea agreement to require that petitioners testify to the planning stages of the breakout. When they refused to do so, the bargain was rescinded and they were tried, convicted, and sentenced to death.

On July 30, 1978, the three Tison brothers entered the Arizona State Prison at Florence carrying a large ice chest filled with guns. The Tisons armed Greenawalt and their father, and the group, brandishing their weapons, locked the prison guards and visitors present in a storage closet. The five men fled the prison grounds in the Tisons' Ford Galaxy automobile. No shots were fired at the prison.

After leaving the prison, the men abandoned the Ford automobile and proceeded on to an isolated house in a white Lincoln automobile that the brothers had parked at a hospital near the prison. At the house, the Lincoln automobile had a flat tire; the only spare tire was pressed into service. After two nights at the house, the group drove toward Flagstaff. As the group traveled on back roads and secondary highways through the desert, another tire blew out. The group decided to flag down a passing motorist and steal a car. Raymond stood out in front of the Lincoln; the other four armed themselves and lay in wait by the side of the road. One car passed by without stopping, but a second car, a Mazda occupied by John Lyons, his wife Donnelda, his 2-year-old son Christopher, and his 15-year-old niece, Theresa Tyson, pulled over to render aid.

As Raymond showed John Lyons the flat tire on the Lincoln, the other Tisons and Greenawalt emerged. The Lyons family was forced into the backseat of the Lincoln. Raymond and Donald drove the Lincoln down a dirt road off the highway and then down a gas line service road farther into the desert; Gary Tison, Ricky Tison, and Randy Greenawalt followed in the Lyons' Mazda. The two cars were parked trunk to trunk and the Lyons family was ordered to stand in front of the Lincoln's headlights. The Tisons transferred their belongings from the Lincoln into the Mazda. They discovered guns and money in the Mazda which they kept, and they put the rest of the Lyons' possessions in the Lincoln.

Gary Tison then told Raymond to drive the Lincoln still farther into the desert. Raymond did so, and, while the others guarded the Lyons and Theresa Tyson, Gary fired his shotgun into the radiator, presumably to completely disable the vehicle. The Lyons and Theresa Tyson were then escorted to the Lincoln and again ordered to stand in its headlights. Ricky Tison reported that John Lyons begged, in comments "more or less directed at everybody," "Jesus, don't kill me." Gary Tison said he was "thinking about it." John Lyons asked the Tisons and Greenawalt to "give us some water . . . just leave us out here, and you all go home." Gary Tison then told his sons to go back to the Mazda and get some water. Raymond later explained that his father "was like in conflict with himself. What it was, I think it was the baby being there and all this, and he wasn't sure about what to do."

The petitioners' statements diverge to some extent, but it appears that both of them went back towards the Mazda, along with Donald, while Randy Greenawalt and Gary Tison stayed at the Lincoln guarding the victims. Raymond recalled being at the Mazda filling the water jug "when we started hearing the shots." Ricky said that the brothers gave the water jug to Gary Tison who then, with Randy Greenawalt went behind the Lincoln, where they spoke briefly, then raised the shotguns and started firing. In any event, petitioners agree they saw Greenawalt and their father brutally murder their four captives with repeated blasts from their shotguns. Neither made an effort to help the victims, though both later stated they were surprised by the shooting. The Tisons got into the Mazda and drove away, continuing their flight. Physical evidence suggested that Theresa Tyson managed to crawl away from the bloodbath, severely injured. She died in the desert after the Tisons left.

Several days later the Tisons and Greenawalt were apprehended after a shootout at a police roadblock. Donald Tison was killed. Gary Tison escaped into the desert where he subsequently died of exposure. Raymond and Ricky Tison and Randy Greenawalt were captured and tried jointly for the crimes associated with the prison break itself and the shootout at the roadblock; each was convicted and sentenced.

The State then individually tried each of the petitioners for capital murder of the four victims as well as for the associated crimes of armed robbery, kidnapping, and car theft. Each of the petitioners was convicted of the four murders under these accomplice liability and felony-murder statutes.

Arizona law provided for a capital sentencing proceeding, to be conducted without a jury, to determine whether the crime was sufficiently aggravated to warrant the death sentence. The judge found three statutory aggravating factors:

(1) the Tisons had created a grave risk of death to others (not the victims);

(2) the murders had been committed for pecuniary gain;

(3) the murders were especially heinous.

The judge found no statutory mitigating factor. Importantly, the judge specifically found that the crime was *not* mitigated by the fact that each of the petitioners' "participation was relatively minor." Rather, he found that the "participation of each petitioner in the crimes giving rise to the application of the felony murder rule in this case was very substantial." The trial judge also specifically found that each "could reasonably have foreseen that his conduct would cause or create a grave risk of death." The judge sentenced both petitioners to death.

II

Enmund explicitly dealt with two distinct subsets of all felony murders in assessing whether Enmund's sentence was disproportional under the Eighth Amendment. At one pole was Enmund himself: the minor actor in an armed robbery, not on the scene, who neither intended to kill nor was found to have had any culpable mental state. Only a small minority of States even authorized the death penalty in such circumstances and even within those jurisdictions the death penalty was almost never exacted for such a crime. The Court held that capital punishment was disproportional in these cases. *Enmund* also clearly dealt with the other polar case: the felony murderer who actually killed, attempted to kill, or intended to kill. The Court clearly held that the equally small minority of jurisdictions that limited the death penalty to these circumstances could continue to exact it in accordance with local law when the circumstances warranted. The Tison brothers' cases fall into neither of these neat categories.

Petitioners argue strenuously that they did not "intend to kill" as that concept has been generally understood in the common law. We accept this as true. As petitioners point out, there is no evidence that either Ricky or Raymond Tison took any act which he desired to, or was substantially certain would, cause death.

On the other hand, it is equally clear that petitioners also fall outside the category of felony murderers for whom *Enmund* explicitly held the death penalty disproportional: their degree of participation in the crimes was major rather than minor, and the record would support a finding of the culpable mental state of reckless indifference to human life. We take the facts as the Arizona Supreme Court has given them to us.

Raymond Tison brought an arsenal of lethal weapons into the Arizona State Prison which he then handed over to two convicted murderers, one of whom he knew had killed a prison guard in the course of a previous escape attempt. By his own admission he was prepared to kill in furtherance of the prison break. He performed the crucial role of flagging down a passing car occupied by an innocent family whose fate was then entrusted to the known killers he had previously armed. He robbed these people at their direction and then guarded the victims at gunpoint while they considered what next to do. He stood by and watched the killing, making no effort to assist the victims before, during, or after the shooting. Instead, he chose to assist the killers in their continuing criminal endeavors, ending in a gun battle with the police in the final showdown.

Ricky Tison's behavior differs in slight details only. Like Raymond, he intentionally brought the guns into the prison to arm the murderers. He could have foreseen that lethal force might be used, particularly since he knew that his father's previous escape attempt had resulted in murder. He, too, participated fully in the kidnapping and robbery and watched the killing after which he chose to aid those whom he had placed in the position to kill rather than their victims.

These facts not only indicate that the Tison brothers' participation in the crime was anything but minor; they also would clearly support a finding that they both subjectively appreciated that their acts were likely to result in the taking of innocent life. The issue raised by this case is whether the Eighth Amendment prohibits the death penalty in the intermediate case of the defendant whose participation is major and whose mental state is one of reckless indifference to the value of human life. *Enmund* does not specifically address this point. We now take up the task of determining whether the Eighth Amendment proportionality requirement bars the death penalty under these circumstances.

Like the *Enmund* Court, we find the state legislatures' judgment as to proportionality in these circumstances relevant to this constitutional inquiry. The largest number of States still fall into the two intermediate categories discussed in *Enmund*. Four States authorize the death penalty in felony-murder cases upon a showing of culpable mental state such as recklessness or extreme indifference to human life. Two jurisdictions require that the defendant's participation be substantial and the statutes of at least six more, including Arizona, take minor participation in the felony expressly into account in mitigation of the murder. These requirements significantly overlap both in this case and in general, for the greater the defendant's participation in the felony murder, the more likely that he acted with reckless indifference to human life. At a minimum, however, it can be said that all these jurisdictions, as well as six States which *Enmund* classified along with Florida as permitting capital punishment for felony murder *simpliciter*, and the three States which simply require some additional aggravation before imposing the death penalty upon a felony murderer, specifically authorize the death penalty in a felony-murder case where, though the defendant's mental state fell short of intent to kill, the defendant was a major actor in a felony in which he knew death was highly likely to occur. On the other hand, even after *Enmund*, only 11 States authorizing capital punishment forbid imposition of the death penalty even though the defendant's participation in the felony murder is major and the likelihood of killing is so substantial as to raise an inference of extreme recklessness. This substantial and recent legislative authorization of the death penalty for the crime of felony murder regardless of the absence of a finding of an intent to kill powerfully suggests that our society does *not* reject the death penalty as grossly excessive under these circumstances.

Moreover, a number of state courts have interpreted *Enmund* to permit the imposition of the death penalty in such aggravated felony murders. We do not approve or disapprove the judgments as to proportionality reached on the particular facts of these cases, but we note the apparent consensus that substantial participation in a violent felony under circumstances likely to result in the loss of innocent human life may justify the death penalty even absent an "intent to kill."

Against this backdrop, we now consider the proportionality of the death penalty in these midrange felony-murder cases for which the majority of American jurisdictions clearly authorize capital punishment and for which American courts have not been nearly so reluctant to impose death as they are in the case of felony murder *simpliciter*.

A critical facet of the individualized determination of culpability required in capital cases is the mental state with which the defendant commits the crime. Deeply ingrained in our legal tradition is the idea that the more purposeful is the criminal conduct, the more serious is the offense, and, therefore, the more severely it ought to be punished.

A narrow focus on the question of whether or not a given defendant "intended to kill," however, is a highly unsatisfactory means of definitively distinguishing the most culpable and dangerous of murderers. Many who intend to, and do, kill are not criminally liable at all—those who act in self-defense or with other justification or excuse. Other intentional homicides, though criminal, are often felt undeserving of the death penalty—those that are the result of provocation. On the other hand, some nonintentional murderers may be among the most dangerous and inhumane of all—the person who tortures another not caring whether the victim lives or dies, or the robber who shoots someone in the course of the robbery, utterly indifferent to the fact that the desire to rob may have the unintended consequence of killing the victim as well as taking the victim's property. This reckless indifference to the value of human life may be every bit as shocking to the moral sense as an "intent to kill." Indeed it is for this very reason that the common law and modern criminal codes alike have classified behavior such as occurred in this case along with intentional murders. *Enmund* held that when "intent to kill" results in its logical though not inevitable consequence—the taking of human life—the Eighth Amendment permits the State to exact the death penalty after a careful weighing of the aggravating and mitigating circumstances. Similarly, we hold that the reckless disregard for human life implicit in knowingly engaging in criminal activities known to carry a grave risk of death represents a highly culpable mental state, a mental state that may be taken into account in making a capital sentencing judgment when that conduct causes its natural, though also not inevitable, lethal result.

The petitioners' own personal involvement in the crimes was not minor, but rather, as specifically found by the trial court, "substantial." Far from merely sitting in a car away from the actual scene of the murders acting as the getaway driver to a robbery, each petitioner was actively involved in every element of the kidnapping-robbery and was physically present during the entire sequence of criminal activity culminating in the murder of the Lyons family and the subsequent flight. The Tisons' high level of participation in these crimes further implicates them in the resulting deaths. Accordingly, they fall well within the overlapping second intermediate position which focuses on the defendant's degree of participation in the felony.

Only a small minority of those jurisdictions imposing capital punishment for felony murder have rejected the possibility of a capital sentence absent an intent to kill, and we do not find this minority position constitutionally required. We will not attempt to precisely delineate the particular types of conduct and states of mind warranting imposition of the death penalty here. Rather, we simply hold that major participation in the felony committed, combined with reckless indifference to human life, is sufficient to satisfy the *Enmund* culpability requirement. The Arizona courts have clearly found that the former exists; we now vacate the judgments below and remand for determination of the latter in further proceedings not inconsistent with this opinion.

Justice Brennan, with whom Justice Marshall joins, and with whom Justice Marshall and Justice Stevens join except as to the last paragraph, dissenting.

The facts on which the Court relies are not sufficient, in my view, to support the Court's conclusion that petitioners acted with reckless disregard for human life.

The evidence in the record overlooked today regarding petitioners' mental states with respect to the shootings is not trivial. For example, while the Court has found that petitioners made no effort prior to the shooting to assist the victims, the uncontradicted statements of both petitioners are that just prior to the shootings they were attempting to find a jug of water to give to the family. While the Court states that petitioners were on the scene during the shooting and that they watched it occur, Raymond stated that he and Ricky were still engaged in repacking the Mazda after finding the water jug when the shootings occurred. Ricky stated that they had returned with the water, but were still some distance ("farther than this room") from the Lincoln when the shootings started, and that the brothers then turned away from the scene and went back to the Mazda. Neither stated that they anticipated that the shootings would occur, or that they could have done anything to prevent them or to help the victims afterward. Both, however, expressed feelings of surprise, helplessness, and regret. This statement of Raymond's is illustrative:

> *Well, I just think you should know when we first came into this we had an agreement with my dad that nobody would get hurt because we the brothers wanted no one hurt. And when this killing of the kidnap victims came about we were not expecting it. And it took us by surprise as much as it took the family the victims by surprise because we were not expecting this to happen. And I feel bad about it happening. I wish we could have done something to stop it, but by the time it happened it was too late to stop it. And it's just something we are going to live with the rest of our lives. It will always be there.*

The discrepancy between those aspects of the record on which the Court has chosen to focus and those aspects it has chosen to ignore underscores the point that a reliable and individualized *Enmund* determination can be made only by the trial court following an evidentiary hearing.

Notwithstanding the Court's unwarranted observations on the applicability of its new standard to this case, the basic flaw in today's decision is the Court's failure to conduct the sort of proportionality analysis that the Constitution and past cases require. Creation of a new category of culpability is not enough to distinguish this case from *Enmund*. The Court must also establish that death is a proportionate punishment for individuals in this category. In other words, the Court must demonstrate that major participation in a felony with a state of mind of reckless indifference to human life deserves the same punishment as intending to commit a murder or actually committing a murder. The Court does not attempt to conduct a proportionality review of the kind performed in past cases raising a proportionality question, but instead offers two reasons in support of its view.

One reason the Court offers for its conclusion that death is proportionate punishment for persons falling within its new category is that limiting the death penalty to those who intend to kill "is a highly unsatisfactory means of definitively distinguishing the most culpable and dangerous of murderers." To illustrate that intention cannot be dispositive, the Court offers as examples "the person *who tortures* another not caring whether the victim lives or dies, or the robber *who shoots* someone in the course of the robbery, utterly indifferent to the fact that the desire to rob may have the unintended consequence of killing the victim as well as taking the victim's property." Influential commentators and some States have approved the use of the death penalty for persons, like those given in the Court's examples, *who kill* others in circumstances manifesting an extreme indifference to the value of human life. Thus an exception to the requirement that only intentional murders be punished with death might be made for persons who actually commit an act of homicide; *Enmund*, by distinguishing from the accomplice case "those who kill," clearly reserved that question. But the constitutionality of the death penalty for those individuals is no more relevant to this case than it was to *Enmund*, because this case, like *Enmund*, involves accomplices *who did not kill*. Thus, although some of the "most culpable and dangerous of murderers" may be those who killed without specifically intending to kill, it is considerably more difficult to apply that rubric convincingly to those who not only did not intend to kill, but who also have not killed.

It is precisely in this context—where the defendant has not killed—that a finding that he or she nevertheless intended to kill seems indispensable to establishing capital culpability. It is important first to note that such a defendant has not committed an *act* for which he or she could be sentenced to death. The applicability of the death penalty therefore turns entirely on the defendant's mental state with regard to an act committed by another. Factors such as the defendant's major participation in the events surrounding the killing or the defendant's presence at the scene are relevant insofar as they illuminate the defendant's mental state with regard to the killings. They cannot serve, however, as independent grounds for imposing the death penalty.

Second, when evaluating such a defendant's mental state, a determination that the defendant acted with intent is qualitatively different from a determination that the defendant acted with reckless indifference to human life. The difference lies in the nature of the choice each has made. The reckless actor has not *chosen* to bring about the killing in the way the intentional actor has. The person who chooses to act recklessly and is indifferent to the possibility of fatal consequences often deserves serious punishment. But because that person has not chosen to kill, his or her moral and criminal culpability is of a different degree than that of one who killed or intended to kill.

The importance of distinguishing between these different choices is rooted in our belief in the "freedom of the human will and a consequent ability and duty of the normal individual to choose between good and evil." To be faithful to this belief, which is "universal and persistent in mature systems of law," the criminal law must ensure that the punishment an individual receives conforms to the choices that individual has made. Differential punishment of reckless and intentional actions is therefore essential if we are to retain "the relation between criminal liability and moral culpability" on which criminal justice depends. The State's ultimate sanction—if it is ever to be used—must be reserved for those whose culpability is greatest.

The Court's second reason for abandoning the intent requirement is based on its survey of state statutes authorizing the death penalty for felony murder, and on a handful of state cases. On this basis, the Court concludes that "only a small minority *of those jurisdictions imposing capital punishment for felony murder* have rejected the possibility of a capital sentence absent an intent to kill, and we do not find this minority position constitutionally required." The Court would thus have us believe that "the majority of American jurisdictions clearly authorize capital punishment" in cases such as this. This is not the case. First, the Court excludes from its survey those jurisdictions that have abolished the death penalty and those that have authorized it only in circumstances different from those presented here. When these jurisdictions are included, and are considered with those jurisdictions that require a finding of intent to kill in order to impose the death sentence for felony murder, one discovers that approximately three-fifths of American jurisdictions do not authorize the death penalty for a non-triggerman absent a finding that he intended to kill. Thus, contrary to the Court's implication that its view is consonant with that of "the majority of American jurisdictions," the Court's view is itself distinctly the minority position.

Second, it is critical to examine not simply those jurisdictions that authorize the death penalty in a given circumstance, but those that actually *impose* it. Evidence that a penalty is imposed only infrequently suggests not only that jurisdictions are reluctant to apply it but also that, when it is applied, its imposition is arbitrary and therefore unconstitutional. Thus, the Court in *Enmund* examined the relevant statistics on the imposition of the death penalty for accomplices in a felony murder.

The Court today neither reviews nor updates this evidence. Had it done so, it would have discovered that, even including the 65 executions since *Enmund*, "the fact remains that we are not aware of a single person convicted of felony murder over the past quarter century who did not kill or attempt to kill, and did not intend the death of the victim, who has been executed." Of the 64 persons on death row in Arizona, all of those who have raised and lost an *Enmund* challenge in the Arizona Supreme Court have been found either to have killed or to have specifically intended to kill. Thus, like Enmund, the Tisons' sentence appears to be an aberration within Arizona itself as well as nationally and internationally. The Court's objective evidence that the statutes of roughly 20 States appear to authorize the death penalty for defendants in the Court's new category is therefore an inadequate substitute for a proper proportionality analysis, and is not persuasive evidence that the punishment that was unconstitutional for Enmund is constitutional for the Tisons.

Our Constitution demands that the sentencing decision itself, and not merely the procedures that produce it, respond to the reasonable goals of punishment. But the decision to execute these petitioners, and like other decisions to kill, appears responsive less to reason than to other, more visceral, demands.

This case thus illustrates the enduring truth of Justice Harlan's observation that the tasks of identifying "those characteristics of criminal homicides and their perpetrators which call for the death penalty, and of expressing these characteristics in language which can be *fairly* understood and applied by the sentencing authority appear to be beyond present human ability." The persistence of doctrines (such as felony murder) that allow excessive discretion in apportioning criminal culpability and of decisions (such as today's) that do not even attempt "precisely to delineate the particular types of conduct and states of mind warranting imposition of the death penalty," demonstrates that this Court has still not articulated rules that will ensure that capital sentencing decisions conform to the substantive principles of the Eighth Amendment. Arbitrariness continues so to infect both the procedure and substance of capital sentencing that any decision to impose the death penalty remains cruel and unusual. I adhere to my view that the death penalty is in all circumstances cruel and unusual punishment prohibited by the Eighth and Fourteenth Amendments, and dissent.

■ Felony-Murder—Perspectives

■ Issue—Should Felony-Murderers Be Exempt from the Death Penalty?

Richard Rosen, "Felony Murder and the Eighth Amendment"

I. *Introduction*

This article examines the tension between two antithetical criminal law doctrines: the felony murder rule and the modern jurisprudence of capital punishment. A tension has developed between these two doctrines because they are, fundamentally, polar opposites. On the one hand, the felony murder rule, in its starkest form, provides that any participant in a specified felony that results in a death shall be punished as a murderer, no matter how accidental or unforeseeable the death, nor how attenuated the defendant's connection to the death. As such, the rule long has been criticized as a singular exception to the normal principles of criminal law, which require that liability for a particular offense be predicated on the individual defendant's mens rea and degree of participation in the specific offense charged.

On the other hand, the Supreme Court's modern jurisprudence of death is based on a heightened refinement, not an exception, to these principles. This refinement requires an even more searching inquiry into all of the relevant aspects of the crime and the defendant than usually is found in criminal law to ensure the reliability and correctness of the decision to impose death.

The purpose here is not to rehash the many criticisms of the felony murder rule. Rather, the focus is on the difficulties engendered by the continued use of the rule, in one form or the other, in those states that impose the death penalty; on the attempts made by the Supreme Court to ameliorate the harshness of the felony murder rule as it applies to felony accomplices in capital cases; and on additional but as yet unexplored ways to analyze the norms of the Eighth Amendment in the felony murder context.

II. *Felony Murder in the Age of Eighth Amendment Capital Punishment Law*

In its requirements for narrowing and individualization, as well as in its overall goal of restricting the reach of the death penalty to the most deserving offenders, the Eighth Amendment superstructure that the Court has constructed mirrors the development of the common law of homicide, at least in regard to non-felony murder. The early development of the concept of malice as a dividing line between manslaughter and murder, and the later division of murder into degrees were both attempts to narrow the class of homicide defendants eligible for the death penalty. Similarly, the shift in the twentieth century from mandatory to discretionary death penalties reflected a consensus in favor of individualized consideration of the character of the offender and the circumstances of the offense.

Furman was a declaration that these earlier efforts were insufficient to satisfy the Eighth Amendment. As subsequent decisions made clear, the Court would require both further narrowing and more intensely focused individualized considerations in an attempt to avoid the problems identified in *Furman*. In non-felony murder cases, this added refinement and order offers some assurance, however incomplete, that the death penalty will be reserved for the more culpable homicide defendants. This is because both the further narrowing of the class and the intense individualized scrutiny are applied to a class of offenders from which the least culpable homicide defendants already have been eliminated from eligibility for the death penalty. Both those who kill accidentally, without malice or without premeditation and deliberation, and those who do not participate in the killing sufficiently to be aiders and abettors under the usual norms of the criminal law are already ineligible for the death penalty, even before the procedures required by the Court are brought to bear. In short, non-felony murder capital defendants are afforded two levels of individualized scrutiny. The first level arises when the jury determines the defendant's culpability for first degree, or capital, murder, and the second level occurs when the sentencer, whether judge or jury, examines the case by using the procedures required by the Eighth Amendment.

The felony murder rule disrupts this pattern of individualized scrutiny as well as all meaningful narrowing. In Justice O'Connor's words, felony murder is not limited to murder "as it is ordinarily envisioned." Some of these defendants indeed may be among the most culpable offenders—for example, the cold-blooded executioner of a store clerk during a robbery—but many are not. The rule makes no distinctions.

The felony murder rule disregards the normal rules of criminal culpability and provides homicide liability equally for both the deliberate rapist/killer and the robber whose victim dies of a heart attack, as well as for the robber's accomplice who is absent from the scene of the crime. In its traditional form, still used in some jurisdictions, the felony murder rule can make the defendant guilty of murder when an officer or victim mistakenly kills a third person or an accomplice during the felony, or even when the defendant is involved in a traffic accident while fleeing the felony, resulting in death. A defendant who undertakes a felony only after extracting promises from his co-felon that no one will be hurt likewise is subject to the full force of the rule when the co-felon breaks the promise. In these situations, the felony murder rule has the potential to equate any participant in the felony with the cold-blooded deliberate killer, no matter how unforeseeable the death or how attenuated that defendant's participation in the felony or the events leading to death.

Therefore, notwithstanding all of the procedural requirements imposed upon the states, the possibility always exists that, with the felony murder rule as a basis for a capital sentence, some minimally culpable felony murder defendants, like accidental killers or attenuated accomplices to the felony, will be sentenced to die, even while many cold-blooded premeditated killers will be allowed to live.

III. *Case-Specific Disproportionality Review for Felony Murder Accomplices*

Consider a death sentence imposed on a defendant who just misses fitting into all of the preclusive disproportionality categories recognized by the Court. The defendant is 16 years old. He is not insane, and he is convicted of being an accomplice to an accidental felony murder. *Coker* offers no protection because a death has occurred. *Stanford* leaves him death-eligible despite his youth. The defendant always can be too involved in the felony to be shielded from the death penalty by *Tison*. Is this defendant among those "worst" murderers for whom the Court wishes to reserve the death penalty?

The only sensible answer is a negative one. A death sentence in these circumstances would be grossly disproportionate to the individual culpability and blameworthiness of this defendant. This result can only be reached, however, if a court considers the disproportionality of the death sentence in light of the totality of the circumstances surrounding the case. Since 1976, the Supreme Court, preoccupied with experimenting with the fashioning of various bright-line disproportionality rules, never has openly conducted a case-specific disproportionality review in a capital case.

The Court has neither explained why it has thus limited its disproportionality review in capital cases to the categorical method nor why it has never used this approach in noncapital cases. The reason for this differentiation between approaches in capital and noncapital cases is discernible from the opinions in *Solem v. Helm*. Two strains unite the several opinions in *Helm*. One strain is that disproportionality is a special concern in capital cases. The other strain is a desire to limit the practice of disproportionality review.

The categorical rules the Court has developed in capital cases minimize the inherent contradictions between these two concerns. The categorical rules give special protections to broad groups of potential capital defendants and, at the same time, minimize and simplify the burdens on the courts. In most cases, it is not a difficult task at either the trial or appellate level to determine whether a defendant falls on one side or the other of the bright line, e.g., whether the defendant was under 16 at the time of the crime. The real disproportionality inquiry is the initial decision about whether to adopt a rule.

The categorical rules, however, are only tools to help the courts prevent disproportionality; they are not ends in themselves. Categorical rules are broad and inflexible, and no matter how many categorical rules the Court decides to adopt, some death penalties would still be grossly disproportionate and outside the reach of the rules. Because a defendant does not fall into one of the rigid categories of defendants for whom the death penalty is proscribed does not mean either that the death sentence is proportionate or that the court has reviewed the defendant's case for disproportionality. It merely means that the death sentence imposed in the particular case is not disproportionate for the particular reason embodied in the particular rule.

Even a death penalty imposed for a deliberated and premeditated murder may be grossly disproportionate under the Eighth Amendment. After all, *Gregg* did not hold that any death sentence imposed for deliberate murder is ipso facto proportionate, only that a death penalty is not invariably disproportionate to the crime in that situation. For example, some defendants commit euthanasia in order to end the suffering of a loved one. These defendants can be, and sometimes are, convicted of first-degree premeditated and deliberated murder. Given the wide variety of aggravating circumstances used by the states, these types of murderers are not ineligible automatically for the death penalty.

These defendants would not be protected necessarily by any of the present categorical disproportionality rules, nor is an appropriate bright line to cover this situation easy to conceive. A death sentence imposed on a mercy-killer obviously is not proportionate just because the Supreme Court has not provided a categorical rule to cover this situation. This situation requires what occurs in appropriate noncapital cases—a true disproportionality inquiry, based on all of the circumstances of the case.

If the Supreme Court had envisaged solving the disproportionality problem in capital cases at one time solely by using categorical rules of preclusion, it obviously has given up this hope in the past several years. The Court's retreat from the *Enmund* rule in *Tison* does not stand alone but should be read together with the Court's refusal to erect a categorical barrier to the execution of juveniles in *Stanford*. Like *Stanford*, *Tison* is not a decision to create a new categorical rule but a decision to reject the adoption of, or, in the case of *Tison*, the continuation of, a specific rule.

Stanford did not hold that a death sentence for a 16-year-old, or mentally retarded defendant is necessarily proportionate. The Court carefully phrased its denial holding that age was not alone sufficient to render the death penalty disproportionate. *Tison* should be read the same way. Simply because a court can say that a defendant was recklessly indifferent does not mean that a death penalty is not grossly disproportionate. Only by considering all of the factors in a case can a court make this decision.

In the felony murder area, this type of case-specific review might be largely redundant, at least for accomplices, if the *Enmund* categorical rule were still the law. However, *Tison* now governs and it does little to obviate the need for a case-specific disproportionality review for felony murder accomplices.

This case-specific disproportionality review would differ only slightly from the procedure previously used by the Supreme Court to determine the appropriateness of a requested categorical rule. Although the court would have to examine a broader range of circumstances than if a categorical rule were being invoked, a court responding to such a challenge would, like the Supreme Court has in the past, have to make its own determination of the issue after seeking guidance from objective factors.

Perhaps the greatest change in case-specific disproportionality review would have to come in the court's consideration of legislative enactments. Although decisions in other cases can provide some guidance in a case-specific challenge, this guidance is not available with legislative enactments. As Justice O'Connor pointed out in her concurrence in *Thompson*, legislative enactments that permit a death penalty for a given defendant do not necessarily demonstrate a legislative choice that the defendant in question should die—they instead may indicate that a legislature simply has not considered the question.

The Court has examined legislative enactments to determine if the legislatures, as representatives of the American people, approve or disapprove of the death penalty in question. This examination may be of use when the Court looks to the determinative effect of a single factor but it is totally inappropriate under a totality of circumstances approach. It is probable that the legislatures did intend to include most felony murders and deliberate murders among those who are eligible for execution. In some cases, however, such as the 16-year-old, mentally ill felony murderer, or a mercy killer, it would be absurd to say that a legislature has chosen deliberately to include these defendants among those to be executed. Rather, it would be far more accurate to say that the legislative enactments are simply not relevant to a court's determination of disproportionality because the legislators in all probability did not even consider the death penalty under such circumstances.

In sum, it is clear that there is a compelling need for courts to develop a jurisprudence of effective case-specific disproportionality review not only for a felony murder accomplice but for any capital defendant. As broad as they are, the categorical rules are clearly insufficient to guarantee the quest for proportionality that is at the heart of the Court's entire Eighth Amendment venture.

IV. *Conclusion*

The courts, of course, could ignore the contradictions and could allow the execution of even the least culpable felony murder accomplices while many cold-blooded deliberate killers are allowed to live. To do so however, would contradict the Supreme Court's entire effort to provide some rationality in our choice of who is to die.

This article offers two suggestions: first eliminate the use of felony murder as a narrowing device when the defendant's conviction is predicated on felony murder; and second, conduct case specific proportionality review in felony murder capital cases. Both suggestions are rooted in the existing Eighth Amendment jurisprudence.

A proper application of the Eighth Amendment narrowing requirement in felony murder cases together with the entire edifice of procedural protections required by the Court in capital cases, would minimize the chance that a demonstrably undeserving felony murder defendant would receive the death penalty. History and common sense teach us, however, that some of these defendants inevitably will be sentenced to death.

The statistics cited in *Enmund* are still valid—few felony murderers who did not intend to kill are ever sentenced to death. Yet the question after *Tison* is: for which of these defendants will a death penalty be grossly disproportionate under the Eighth Amendment? With no bright-line rule in effect, the court can answer this question only by conducting an intense scrutiny of all of the circumstances of the case. The Eighth Amendment demands no less.

David McCord, "State Death Sentencing for Felony Murder Accomplices under the *Enmund* and *Tison* Standards"

I. *Introduction*

Criminals often act in groups when committing violent felonies and sometimes kill innocent victims. In most jurisdictions, a killing in the course of such felonies justifies a murder conviction for each and every accomplice, whether or not that accomplice participated in the killing act. Occasionally, felony murders are so terrible that prosecutors in these jurisdictions seek, and sentencers impose, death sentences.

But the question inevitably arises: death sentences on whom? On all members of the criminal group, no matter what their roles in the actual killing? On only the most culpable members? If only on the most culpable, how are degrees of culpability to be judged? What about the possibility of executing a defendant who was present at the scene, but who was not actually involved in any wrongdoing? These questions have loomed large in death penalty jurisprudence since the Supreme Court undertook to specify the minimum culpability necessary for group felony murderers to be eligible to be sentenced to death.

Because the Court has not revisited the topic since 1987, and the vast bulk of death sentences are imposed in state systems, the parameters for death eligibility in group felony murder cases have been developed by state courts. Indeed, there are scores of state decisions establishing the parameters of death eligibility for group felony murderers. Nevertheless, no scholar has analyzed this body of doctrine to assess how the jurisprudential guidelines of *Enmund* and *Tison* are playing out in the nitty-gritty of state death penalty jurisprudence.

II. *Felony Murder in Supreme Court Death Penalty Jurisprudence*

As a starting point, an overview of the Supreme Court's death penalty jurisprudence is useful. In retrospect, the Supreme Court's primary goal with respect to death sentencing has been to minimize the incidence of "overinclusion." A death sentence is "overinclusive" when it is imposed in circumstances where it is disproportionately harsh given the nature of the crime committed and the defendant's personal characteristics. The Court has taken two separate paths toward minimizing overinclusion.

First, the Court has limited the kinds of crimes for which capital punishment can be imposed, ruling a death sentence disproportionate to all crimes except murder, and requiring that death eligibility be limited to murders that can, by some rational criterion, be deemed "worse" than most. To effectuate these rules, the Court requires that states adopt a mechanism for identifying these "worst" murders, which most states have done by specifying "aggravating circumstances." The Court further requires states to specifically define aggravating circumstances to prevent the use of vague phrases such as "heinous, atrocious, and cruel" that arguably cover every wrongful homicide.

The Court's second line of precedent prohibits a state from judging "worstness" merely on the facts of the offense, without considering the personal characteristics of the defendant that might counsel for leniency. The Court has promulgated two bright-line rules: an age limit of sixteen, and the exclusion of the profoundly or severely retarded from death eligibility. More generally, the Court requires that a defendant be given the opportunity at the sentencing phase to present all possible mitigating evidence related to the defendant's character, record, or circumstances of the offense.

The *Enmund-Tison* line of precedent, which seeks to specify the minimum culpability supporting death eligibility for felony murder accomplices, comprises portions of both lines of precedent. Requiring that a murder be particularly aggravated before the culprits are death eligible, the felony murder trilogy demonstrates the Court's belief that some instances, in which the defendant neither personally killed nor had a high culpable mental state with respect to his accomplice's killing, are simply not aggravated enough to be death eligible. With respect to the second line of precedent—individualization by focusing not just on the crime, but on the character of the defendant—the cases require that the sentencer scrutinize the culpability of the actions and mental states of each defendant in group felony murder scenarios for whom the state seeks the death sentence, rather than condemning one accomplice vicariously for the actions of another.

III. *The Database of State Cases*

A. Selecting the Cases I generated my case database by examining every case between *Enmund* and *Tison* that cited *Enmund* (the " *Enmund* era"), and every case after *Tison* that cited *Tison* ("the *Tison* era"), through calendar year 1999. After discarding all cases that had *Enmund* or *Tison* cites, but no real issue of death eligibility for group felony murder, I ended up with a database of cases involving 189 defendants.

B. The Contemporaneous Felonies About eighty percent of the cases involved robberies; about thirty percent home burglaries; about twenty-five percent kidnappings; and about twenty percent sexual assaults. The sum of these percentages adds up to far more than one hundred because many of the felonious groups committed multiple crimes during the incident that resulted in the murder(s)— for example, robbing a store and then kidnapping and raping a clerk before killing her; or breaking into a home, kidnapping a man and woman, raping the woman, and killing the man. Additionally, about a quarter of the cases involved multiple homicides.

C. The Two Kinds of Cases I have divided the case sample into two categories: "at-least-prior-positive-knowledge," and "less-than-prior-positive-knowledge" cases. By at-least-prior-positive-knowledge cases I mean those in which there was direct evidence to support a finding that the defendant was the actual killer, attempted to kill, had intent that another cohort kill, or had specific knowledge well ahead of time that a cohort would kill. These cases are easy as a matter of law application: there is no doubt under *Enmund* or *Tison* that the defendant is death eligible.

On the other hand, a "less-than-prior-positive-knowledge" case is one in which the death sentence apparently rested on the "anticipated/contemplated" language from *Enmund*, or on the fifth basis of death eligibility in *Tison*—major participation in a dangerous felony plus reckless indifference to human life. These cases, of course, test the validity of the *Enmund/Tison* rule.

In ninety of the sample cases (forty-seven of which were from the *Enmund* era, and forty-three from the *Tison* era)—about forty-eight percent of the total—the appellate court found sufficient evidence from which to conclude that the defendant was the actual killer of the victim(s).

In twenty-one cases, the defendant was found to have attempted to kill. This includes two sub-categories of cases. In some, the defendant and another cohort inflicted serious injuries on the victim(s) such that it was impossible to tell which injuries actually caused the death(s). Thus, the defendant at least attempted to kill, and may have actually killed. In the second category of cases, the defendant harmed a victim with intent to kill, but was unsuccessful in causing death, although a different victim was murdered during the felony. In these cases, the defendant's moral culpability is indistinguishable from that of an actual killer.

Fourteen cases found that although the defendant did not harm the victim, s/he clearly intended that a cohort(s) kill the victim(s). While intent can be a slippery mental state to prove, the evidence in every case included here left no doubt of the defendant's intention. In nine cases there was direct evidence that the defendant knew a cohort intended to kill the victim because the cohort announced this intention well in advance of the felony.

The at-least-prior-knowledge cases are "easy" in terms of applying the legal rule: all such defendants are indisputably death eligible. One should not, however, be quickly convinced that all the defendants in those categories are in fact death eligible. The correctness of the death eligibility finding hinges on the correctness of the underlying factual determination that the defendant killed, attempted to kill, intended to kill, or knew the killing would occur. These factual findings, like any others, can be erroneous.

The issue of executing the innocent is usually discussed in terms of single perpetrator cases where the "wrong person" was convicted; that is, a person who was not at the scene of, and had nothing to do with, the murder. Such an innocent person is obviously not death eligible. But less obviously, a defendant who participated as an accomplice to a violent felony during which a murder was committed, but who personally does not meet the minimum *Enmund/ Tison* standard of culpability, is "innocent" of the death penalty in the sense of being ineligible for it. Accordingly, just as cases of "wrong person" innocence are significant in number, it seems certain that there are also a significant number of defendants in group felony murder scenarios who have had the crucial factual *Enmund/Tison* minimum culpability issue incorrectly decided against them.

The primary causes of erroneous factual determinations in single perpetrator death penalty cases are mistaken eyewitness identification and perjury. The potential for mistaken eyewitness identification in group felony murder cases is probably less than in single perpetrator cases because the authorities usually apprehend all those involved, and the interconnections among the defendants tend to assure that the police have not caught someone who was completely uninvolved in the criminal incident that culminated in the murder. This assertion is premised on not only logic and common sense, but also on the observation that in my case database, claims of alibi were rare almost to the point of nonexistence.

But while the potential for error due to mistaken eyewitness identification is lower in group felony murder scenarios, the potential for error based on witness perjury is significantly higher. A substantial percentage of group felony murder cases involve one or more cohorts striking a deal with the prosecution for a lesser sentence in return for testimony regarding another individual against whom the prosecution has chosen to seek the death penalty. Among the case sample, at least twenty-nine cases concern "turncoat" cohorts who provided crucial evidence against the defendant that contributed to the eventual death sentence.

In addition to the possibility of perjury by turncoat cohorts, there are other sorts of perjury—or mistake—that are as possible in group criminality cases as in single perpetrator cases. In at least seventeen of the sample cases, the non-cohort eyewitnesses identified the defendant; in at least seven cases a jailhouse informant testified that the defendant had admitted involvement in the murder; finally, in at least twenty-five cases the defendant's fate was sealed by testimony from acquaintances that the defendant had confessed to the murders. Chances are good that at least some witnesses in each category were lying or mistaken. Further, the potential for false confessions, either from coercion or for some other reason, is no less problematic here than in single perpetrator cases (at least twenty-five sample defendants confessed involvement to the police sufficient to seal their death eligibility). Thus, it seems certain that even seemingly "easy" cases under the *Enmund- Tison* standard probably have led, and certainly will lead, to the execution of defendants who were not in fact death eligible.

D. "Less-Than-Positive-Knowledge" Cases In only fifty-five sample cases the defendant's death sentence rested on evidence establishing less-than-positive-knowledge. Inasmuch as there are currently well in excess of 3000 convicts on death row, most of whom have arrived there since *Enmund* was decided in 1982, these cases represent less than two percent of the total death row population; the forty-two cases in which the death sentences were upheld represent closer to one percent of the total death row population. Common sense dictates that considerably more than one or two percent of death eligible homicides are committed in ambiguous group felony murder scenarios. It seems fair to deduce, then, either that prosecutors are reticent about seeking death sentences in less-than-positive-knowledge cases, or that sentencers are hesitant to impose death in such circumstances, or both. The prevalence of prosecutors' plea bargains with highly culpable cohorts in exchange for direct testimony implicating another against whom the prosecution has chosen to seek the death penalty is strong evidence supporting prosecutorial reticence. The prosecutorial theory seems to be that it is necessary to sacrifice the possibility of obtaining death sentences against all the cohorts in return for increasing the likelihood of getting a death sentence against at least one of them.

One could argue that this reticence is largely a result of the *Enmund/Tison* floor on death eligibility, but that would probably be an incorrect conclusion. In reality, prosecutors sought death sentences relatively infrequently in ambiguous group felony murder scenarios even before *Enmund*, almost certainly because they knew that sentencers were unlikely to impose a death sentence absent direct evidence of the defendant's participation in the murder, either by physical actions or through a highly culpable mental state. Thus, the ultimate moral of the story may be that the *Enmund/Tison* standards have had only marginal overall effects because they only apply in cases where prosecutors are unlikely to seek death sentences anyway for purely practical reasons. Surely, however, the effects are not marginal with respect to a defendant who has been death-sentenced on the basis of less-than-positive-knowledge.

IV. *Conclusions and Proposals*

Despite the ambiguities of the *Enmund/Tison* doctrine, the state appellate courts have developed a relatively consistent body of doctrine. Just because it is relatively consistent, though, does not mean that it is the best that can be done. My research has revealed three cases where death sentences were improper because there was no ironclad evidence that the defendants were even at the murder scene, at least eleven cases of wrongly imposed death sentences in less-than-positive-knowledge cases, with the potential that an indeterminable number of at-least-positive-knowledge cases were wrongly held death eligible due to incorrectly found facts. Implementation of the following proposals by state legislatures could significantly reduce many of the bases on which such mistakes were made.

1. Require at least prior positive knowledge for death eligibility. Defendants who intentionally kill, attempt to kill, intend that a cohort kill, or know well in advance that a cohort will kill all stand on the same base moral level. If we are going to have capital punishment, then four mental states can undebatably be treated as equally justifying death eligibility. A culpable mental state comprised of recklessness—even if it is extreme—has not traditionally been treated as conferring equal culpability. It is still true that much of the populace does not consider recklessness to be of equal heinousness. Why not err on the side of caution and set the minimum degree of culpability necessary for death eligibility at the level of at-least-prior-positive-knowledge that a cohort will kill? Montana reached this conclusion under its state constitution. I urge other states to follow suit.

2. Even in at-least-prior-positive-knowledge cases, require safeguards against casting the death eligibility net too widely. I have three proposals in this regard: (1)

require clear corroboration of a turncoat cohort's testimony before a defendant is death eligible; (2) require the same for the testimony of a jailhouse informant; and (3) require that the sentencer be absolutely certain that the defendant had at least prior positive knowledge before imposing a death sentence.

3. On the other hand, do not follow the New Jersey approach, which casts the net of death eligibility too narrowly. New Jersey has a statute that permits death eligibility only for the actual killer, or for someone who hired a contract killer. This is an incorrect approach to the problem. There is no moral distinction to be drawn between the actual killer and one who attempted to kill, intended to kill, or knew in advance that the killing was going to occur. A statute like New Jersey's injects arbitrariness into the system.

4. If death eligibility premised on less-than-prior-positive-knowledge is to be retained, make clear that the defendant's presence at the murder scene is an absolute prerequisite, and that the sentencer must be absolutely convinced of it before imposing a death sentence. As explained earlier, it is unjust to infer that the defendant shared in the killing actions of his cohort unless the defendant was present and failed to exercise a restraining influence. Further, absolute certainty of the defendant's presence—not just a belief beyond a reasonable doubt—is necessary to minimize the possibility of unjust death sentences.

5. If death eligibility premised on less-than-prior-positive-knowledge is to be retained, it should never be found in cases of simple robbery gone quickly awry. As likewise argued earlier, there is no basis for imputing extreme indifference to human life in a simple robbery gone quickly and fatally awry. The planned duration of the crime is short, the potential punishment for the robbery is not so severe as to engender a large probability that a cohort will kill to eliminate a witness, the defendant usually has no reason to believe the cohort to have lethal propensity, and the defendant has no opportunity to restrain in the spur of the moment.

6. Appellate courts should apply reasoned—but not knee-jerk-intra-case proportionality review. Occasionally, appellate courts take a peek at the sentences the defendant's cohorts received, and adjust the defendant's sentence to something less than death on the basis of an unnamed doctrine that could be described as intra-case proportionality review. There is a knee-jerk way to use this doctrine that may be harmful, and a reasoned way to use it that is beneficial.

The knee-jerk use of intra-case proportionality review is that if any of the cohorts received a sentence less than death, none of them are eligible to receive a death sentence. While this reduces the number of death sentences, this reduction comes at too great a cost of injecting patent arbitrariness into the system. Imagine two virtually identical robbery/murder cases, each with two cohorts. In the first case, the prosecutor strikes a deal with Cohort #1 in which he receives a life sentence in exchange for testifying against Cohort #2, who receives the death penalty. In the second case, the prosecutor successfully seeks death sentences against both cohorts. If a court were to engage in intra-case proportionality review, it would reduce the sentence of Cohort #2 in the first case, while upholding both death sentences in the second case. These differences in treatment would not be due to the merits of the cases, but rather to the vagaries of the prosecution's tactics. Under this knee-jerk approach, even the most culpable of the cohorts would be death ineligible.

On the other hand, a reasoned use of intra-case proportionality review is for an appellate court to check to see if any cohorts who were as or more culpable than the defendant received sentences less than death; if so, defendant's sentence should also be less than death. Such a downward adjustment is particularly warranted where the cohort's lesser sentence is due to a plea bargain. While even this reasoned use of intra-case proportionality review injects some systemic arbitrariness, the benefits of undoing the arbitrariness within the group of co-felons outweighs the systemic concerns.

7. The burden of persuasion for major participation with reckless indifference should be absolute certainty. This goes along with the absolute certainty standard already proposed regarding the at-least-positive-knowledge cases, and the defendant's presence at the scene for purposes as a necessary component of major participation.

These reforms would make death sentencing for felony murder accomplices more just and predictable. They would not, however, completely eliminate wrongful death sentences for felony murder accomplices. There is only one reform that can accomplish that goal, and it has my highest recommendation: abolish capital punishment.

Juveniles

12

■ Juveniles—Introduction

Whether the death penalty should apply to juveniles brings into focus the main objection to the Court's class-oriented approach to proportionality: exclusion based upon bright line rules leads to sparing some people deserving of the death penalty. This concern was also discussed in conjunction with rape. In most cases, rapists may be less culpable than murderers, but there are certainly some rapists who are more culpable than some murderers. So it is with juvenile offenders. Juveniles are, on the whole, less culpable than adult offenders, but some juvenile murderers are more culpable than some adult murderers. Exempting the entire class of rapists or juveniles spares some highly culpable defendants from the death penalty.

Consider the placement of rapists on an imaginary culpability index ranging from no culpability to maximal criminal responsibility. Murderers would be higher on the scale than rapists, but, in the view of some, there would be overlap between the groups. The worst rapist is higher on the scale than some less blameworthy murderers. Imagine also an aggregate level of culpability that renders the defendant deathworthy. More murderers than rapists would meet this threshold, but some of each group would meet it. The exclusion of rapists, then, is imperfect. It is somewhat overinclusive—it spares some people who deserve to die. It is also somewhat underinclusive—it fails to spare some defendants who do not deserve to die. By contrast, an exclusion of jaywalkers might be perfect in avoiding overinclusion—even the most egregious jaywalker would not reach the level of the least responsible murderer or rapist, and certainly no jaywalker deserves to die for their transgressions.

When rapists are categorically exempted from the death penalty two consequences follow. No rapists falling below the death-qualifying level of culpability will ever be executed—a good result for retributivists—but some rapists exceeding the death-qualifying level of culpability will be spared from death. If murderers were exempted from the death penalty, the same two consequences would follow. Some defendants not deserving death would be spared; some defendants deserving death would also be spared. The thought behind sparing rapists and not murderers is that fewer rapists are deserving of death, hence there will be minimal error with an exclusion based on rape. The ideal result from a retributive standpoint is that only defendants deserving of death be given the death penalty.

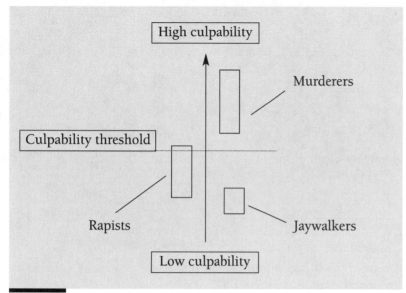

Figure 12-1 Hypothetical culpability index for rapists, murderers, and jaywalkers.

Exempting entire classes of people leads to sparing some defendants who deserve to die. So the question is whether the dividing line defines a perfect set, such as jaywalkers—that is, a set composed entirely of defendants not deserving of the death penalty—and if it is imperfect, to what degree?

The problems with the group-oriented approach parallel the considerations governing the reliance upon rules in the law rather than standards. A speed limit of 55 miles per hour, a bright line rule, may be overinclusive and underinclusive. In traffic or heavy rain, driving 55 miles per hour can be reckless. Late at night on an empty road, 70 miles per hour may be a perfectly safe speed to drive. Under the 55-mile per hour speed limit, some undeserving people may be punished (except for legal retributivists, who believe that the act of violating the law is itself deserving of punishment), and some culpable people may escape punishment. An alternative would be to post signs that say, "No driving at unreasonable speeds." This would do better at capturing the universe of deserving offenders, but would lead to obvious problems of its own: drivers would not always know what the law tolerated and what it did not, trials would become more expensive, judges and juries would be required to decide what was reasonable in a particular circumstance, and expert witnesses might be required.

The Supreme Court might have taken the *Harmelin* approach in death penalty proportionality, allowing states and individual juries to decide what punishment is deserved. The premise of capital proportionality review is that state legislatures and juries sometimes make mistakes and allow undeserving defendants to be subject to the death penalty. The Court takes a rule-oriented approach to identifying these categories of undeserving defendants. The standard-based approach would require the Court to make individual assessments of culpability, not something in which the Supreme Court normally engages. On the other hand, the rule-oriented approach is overbroad. Some defendants undeservedly sentenced by juries to die are spared; some defendants deserving death are spared too.

Some exemptions generate more of the least desired kind of error than others. Let's call an exemption "perfectly tailored" if it generates no seriously undesirable error. What exemptions are likely to be perfectly tailored? Imagine the Supreme Court ruled that the Eighth Amendment precluded the execution of defendants whose last name began with "A." By chance, this would likely spare some defendants who did not deserve death. It would also spare many people deserving of death. We don't generally think of last names as bearing on culpability. By contrast, if the Court exempted nontriggerman defendants who admitted guilt and attempted to aid the victim after the crime, this would create a well-tailored set. These are factors that correlate with culpability in an individual case. The distinctions drawn in *Enmund* and *Tison* seem better tailored than *Coker*. *Enmund* and *Tison* either exempt or don't exempt defendants based upon specific factors regarding the manner in which they committed their crime. The factors come closer to doing justice in the individual case. All the Court relied upon in *Coker* was his status as a rapist. It certainly seems relevant to know whether Coker tortured his victim or had a history of prior offenses or if he showed remorse. If the Court had exempted first-time rapists who did not brandish deadly force, this would have been a better-tailored approach to the issue.

If *Enmund* and *Tison* are in fact more satisfying than *Coker* because they draw distinctions based upon facts of the individual crime, then distinctions based on status might be considered even less satisfying. We can imagine certain groups of people for whom the death penalty is never appropriate. It is almost universally agreed that the insane should not be executed because they lack the ability to understand the punishment that is being inflicted upon them. It isn't possible, however, to make any such blanket statement about juveniles (except for the youngest of the young). On the whole, juvenile murderers might be less responsible than adult murderers. But some teenagers might be able to tell right from wrong and commit crimes that we think are more heinous than those some adults commit. In the debate below, Joseph Hoffman argues against the blanket exemption of juveniles from the death penalty. Bright line rules, he says, lead to retributive injustices. Some deserving defendants will be spared. In short, a dividing line based upon age is not well tailored. He argues further that the costs of employing a standard to determine whether the offender is deathworthy is affordable in the case of juveniles because there are so few cases in which the death penalty is sought against children. Victor Streib argues that the purposes of punishment are almost never served by the execution of children. Even the oldest, most culpable child lacks the moral development to be held accountable for his crime by death. Furthermore, children, impetuous by nature, are unlikely to be deterred by the threat of death.

The Supreme Court first addressed the proportionality of the juvenile death penalty in *Thompson v. Oklahoma*, excerpted in the Critical Documents section of this chapter. Thompson was 15 years old when he murdered his former brother-in-law. Under Oklahoma law, in order to certify a juvenile to stand trial as an adult, the trial judge must find that there are no reasonable prospects of rehabilitating the child within the juvenile justice system. Thompson's attorney argued his client's youth as a mitigating circumstance. The jury nevertheless sentenced Thompson to die. Justice Stevens wrote for a four-judge plurality and found that societal standards of decency did not support Thompson's execution. The familiar issues of calculation arise again. Stevens noted that 14 states did not have the death penalty and that 18 others expressly established minimum ages of at least 16. The 19 remaining states (including the District of Columbia) had no minimum age in their statutes. It would hence be legal in these states for a 15-year-old to receive the death penalty. Justice Stevens dismissed these states because they had "not expressly confronted the question of establishing a minimum age for imposition of the death penalty." It seems worth asking in considering the opinion whether it is fair to dismiss the 19 no-minimum states as having not confronted the issue, but to include the 14 states that did not have the death penalty.

Justice O'Connor concurred in *Thompson*, but did not find evidence of a consensus against the execution of a 15-year-old. She found the Oklahoma statute unconstitutional because it failed to set any minimum age at all, hence creating "a considerable risk that the Oklahoma legislature either did not realize its actions would have the effect of rendering 15-year-old defendants death-eligible or did not give the question the serious consideration that would have been reflected in the explicit choice of some minimum age for death-eligibility." Justice O'Connor changes sides and votes with the majority in *Stanford v. Kentucky*, excerpted below, finding that the Eighth Amendment does not preclude the execution of 16-year-olds or 17-year-olds.

We see in the various opinions and dissents a failure to agree on the most basic terms of the debate. Justice Scalia—in the minority in *Thompson*, then the majority in *Stanford*—and the faction opposed to him, fundamentally disagree as to how states opposed to the death penalty are to be counted. These fundamental conflicts recur throughout the course of proportionality jurisprudence.

In the court of public opinion, the death penalty for juveniles does not fare well. Americans oppose the death penalty for juveniles by more than two to one. The worldwide consensus is even stronger. The death penalty for juveniles is almost a uniquely American phenomenon. It is condemned by the United Nations Convention on the Rights of the Child and several other international treaties and agreements. Since 1990, there have been 33 executions of persons who committed crimes while less than 18 years old, of which 19 were conducted in the United States.

Juveniles—Critical Documents

Table 12-1 Statutory Minimum Death Penalty Ages by Jurisdiction			
Age 16 or Less	**Age 17**	**Age 18**	**None Specified**
Alabama (16)	Georgia	California	Arizona
Arkansas (14)	New Hampshire	Colorado	Idaho
Delaware (16)	North Carolina	Connecticut	Louisiana
Florida (16)	Texas	Federal System	Montana
Indiana (16)		Illinois	Pennsylvania
Kentucky (16)		Kansas	South Carolina
Mississippi (16)		Maryland	South Dakota
Missouri (16)		Nebraska	
Nevada (16)		New Jersey	
Oklahoma (16)		New Mexico	
Utah (14)		New York	
Virginia (14)		Ohio	
Wyoming (16)		Oregon	
		Tennessee	
		Washington	

Table 12-2	**Countries Known to Have Executed Prisoners Younger Than 18 at Time of Crime (Since 1990)**

Congo (Democratic Republic)
Iran
Nigeria
Pakistan
Saudi Arabia
United States of America
Yemen

Thompson v. Oklahoma
487 U.S. 815 (1987)

Justice Stevens announced the judgment of the Court and delivered an opinion in which Justice Brennan, Justice Marshall, and Justice Blackmun join.

Petitioner was convicted of first-degree murder and sentenced to death. The principal question presented is whether the execution of that sentence would violate the constitutional prohibition against the infliction of "cruel and unusual punishments" because petitioner was only 15 years old at the time of his offense.

I

Because there is no claim that the punishment would be excessive if the crime had been committed by an adult, only a brief statement of facts is necessary. In concert with three older persons, petitioner actively participated in the brutal murder of his former brother-in-law in the early morning hours of January 23, 1983. The evidence disclosed that the victim had been shot twice, and that his throat, chest, and abdomen had been cut. He also had multiple bruises and a broken leg. His body had been chained to a concrete block and thrown into a river where it remained for almost four weeks. Each of the four participants was tried separately and each was sentenced to death.

II

In confronting the question whether the youth of the defendant—more specifically, the fact that he was less than 16 years old at the time of his offense—is a sufficient reason for denying the State the power to sentence him to death, we first review relevant legislative enactments, then refer to jury determinations, and finally explain why these indicators of contemporary standards of decency confirm our judgment that such a young person is not capable of acting with the degree of culpability that can justify the ultimate penalty.

III

Justice Powell has repeatedly reminded us of the importance of the experience of mankind, as well as the long history of our law, recognizing that there *are* differences which must be accommodated in determining the rights and duties of children as compared with those of adults. Examples of this distinction abound in our law: in contracts, in torts, in criminal law and procedure, in criminal sanctions and rehabilitation, and in the right to vote and to hold office. Oklahoma recognizes this basic distinction in a number of its statutes. Thus, a minor is not eligible to vote, to sit on a jury, to marry without parental consent, or to purchase alcohol or cigarettes. Like all other States, Oklahoma has developed a juvenile justice system in which most offenders under the age of 18 are not held criminally responsible. Its statutes do provide, however, that a 16- or 17-year-old charged with murder and other serious felonies shall be considered an adult. Other than the special certification procedure that was used to authorize petitioner's trial in this case "as an adult," apparently there are no Oklahoma statutes, either civil or criminal, that treat a person under 16 years of age as anything but a "child."

The line between childhood and adulthood is drawn in different ways by various States. There is, however, complete or near unanimity among all 50 States and the District of Columbia in treating a person under 16 as a minor for several important purposes. In no State may a 15-year-old vote or serve on a jury. Further, in all but one State a 15-year-old may not drive without parental consent, and in all but four States a 15-year-old may not marry without parental consent. Additionally, in those States that have legislated on the subject, no one under age 16 may purchase pornographic materials (50 States), and in most States that have some form of legalized gambling, minors are not permitted to participate without parental consent (42 States). Most relevant, however, is the fact that all States have enacted legislation designating the maximum age for juvenile court jurisdiction at no less than 16. All of this legislation is consistent with the experience of mankind, as well as the long history of our law, that the normal 15-year-old is not prepared to assume the full responsibilities of an adult.

Most state legislatures have not expressly confronted the question of establishing a minimum age for imposition of the death penalty. In 14 States, capital punishment is not authorized at all, and in 19 others capital punishment is authorized but no minimum age is expressly stated in the death penalty statute. One might argue on the basis of this body of legislation that there is no chronological age at which the imposition of the death penalty is unconstitutional and that our current standards of decency would still tolerate the execution of 10-year-old children. We think it self-evident that such an argument is unacceptable: indeed, no such argument has been advanced in this case. If, therefore, we accept the premise that some offenders are simply too young to be put to death, it is reasonable to put this group of statutes to one side because they do not focus on the question of where the chronological age line should be drawn. When we confine our attention to the 18 States that have expressly established a minimum age in their death penalty statutes, we find that all of them require that the defendant have attained at least the age of 16 at the time of the capital offense.

The conclusion that it would offend civilized standards of decency to execute a person who was less than 16 years old at the time of his or her offense is consistent with the views that have been expressed by respected professional organizations, by other nations that share our Anglo-American heritage, and by the leading members of the Western European community.

IV

The second societal factor the Court has examined in determining the acceptability of capital punishment to the American sensibility is the behavior of juries.

While it is not known precisely how many persons have been executed during the 20th century for crimes committed under the age of 16, a scholar has recently compiled a table revealing this number to be between 18 and 20. All of these occurred during the first half of the century, with the last such execution taking place apparently in 1948. The road we have traveled during the past four decades—in which thousands of juries have tried murder cases—leads to the unambiguous conclusion that the imposition of the death penalty on a 15-year-old offender is now generally abhorrent to the conscience of the community. Department of Justice statistics indicate that during the years 1982 through 1986 an average of over 16,000 persons were arrested for willful criminal homicide (murder and nonnegligent manslaughter) each year. Of that group of 82,094 persons, 1,393 were sentenced to death. Only 5 of them, including the petitioner in this case, were less than 16 years old at the time of the offense. Statistics of this kind can, of course, be interpreted in different ways, but they do suggest that these five young offenders have received sentences that are "cruel and unusual in the same way that being struck by lightning is cruel and unusual."

V

Although the judgments of legislatures, juries, and prosecutors weigh heavily in the balance, it is for us ultimately to judge whether the Eighth Amendment permits imposition of the death penalty on one such as petitioner who committed a heinous murder when he was only 15 years old.

It is generally agreed "that punishment should be directly related to the personal culpability of the criminal defendant." There is also broad agreement on the proposition that adolescents as a class are less mature and responsible than adults. We stressed this difference in explaining the importance of treating the defendant's youth as a mitigating factor in capital cases:

> But youth is more than a chronological fact. It is a time and condition of life when a person may be most susceptible to influence and to psychological damage. Our history is replete with laws and judicial recognition that minors, especially in their earlier years, generally are less mature and responsible than adults. Particularly during

> *the formative years of childhood and adolescence, minors often lack the experience, perspective, and judgment expected of adults.*

To add further emphasis to the special mitigating force of youth, Justice Powell quoted the following passage:

> *Adolescents, particularly in the early and middle teen years, are more vulnerable, more impulsive, and less self-disciplined than adults. Crimes committed by youths may be just as harmful to victims as those committed by older persons, but they deserve less punishment because adolescents may have less capacity to control their conduct and to think in long-range terms than adults. Moreover, youth crime as such is not exclusively the offender's fault; offenses by the young also represent a failure of family, school, and the social system, which share responsibility for the development of America's youth.*

Thus, the Court has already endorsed the proposition that less culpability should attach to a crime committed by a juvenile than to a comparable crime committed by an adult. The basis for this conclusion is too obvious to require extended explanation. Inexperience, less education, and less intelligence make the teenager less able to evaluate the consequences of his or her conduct while at the same time he or she is much more apt to be motivated by mere emotion or peer pressure than is an adult. The reasons why juveniles are not trusted with the privileges and responsibilities of an adult also explain why their irresponsible conduct is not as morally reprehensible as that of an adult.

The death penalty is said to serve two principal social purposes: retribution and deterrence of capital crimes by prospective offenders. Given the lesser culpability of the juvenile offender, the teenager's capacity for growth, and society's fiduciary obligations to its children, retribution is simply inapplicable to the execution of a 15-year-old offender.

For such a young offender, the deterrence rationale is equally unacceptable. The Department of Justice statistics indicate that about 98% of the arrests for willful homicide involved persons who were over 16 at the time of the offense. Thus, excluding younger persons from the class that is eligible for the death penalty will not diminish the deterrent value of capital punishment for the vast majority of potential offenders. And even with respect to those under 16 years of age, it is obvious that the potential deterrent value of the death sentence is insignificant for two reasons. The likelihood that the teenage offender has made the kind of cost-benefit analysis that attaches any weight to the possibility of execution is so remote as to be virtually nonexistent. And, even if one posits such a cold-blooded calculation by a 15-year-old, it is fanciful to believe that he would be deterred by the knowledge that a small number of persons his age have been executed during the 20th century. In short, we are not persuaded that the imposition of the death penalty for offenses committed by persons under 16 years of age has made, or can be expected to make, any measurable contribution to the goals that capital punishment is intended to achieve. It is, therefore, "nothing more than the purposeless and needless imposition of pain and suffering," and thus an unconstitutional punishment.

VI

Petitioner's counsel and various *amici curiae* have asked us to "draw a line" that would prohibit the execution of any person who was under the age of 18 at the time of the offense. Our task today, however, is to decide the case before us; we do so by concluding that the Eighth and Fourteenth Amendments prohibit the execution of a person who was under 16 years of age at the time of his or her offense.

The judgment of the Court of Criminal Appeals is vacated, and the case is remanded with instructions to enter an appropriate order vacating petitioner's death sentence.

Justice O'Connor, concurring in the judgment.

The plurality and dissent agree on two fundamental propositions: that there is some age below which a juvenile's crimes can never be constitutionally punished by death, and that our precedents require us to locate this age in light of the "evolving standards of decency that mark the progress of a maturing society." I accept both principles. The disagreements between the plurality and the dissent rest on their different evaluations of the evidence available to us about the relevant social consensus. Although I believe that a national consensus forbidding the execution of any person for a crime committed before the age of 16 very likely does exist, I am reluctant to adopt this conclusion as a matter of constitutional law without better evidence than we now possess. Because I conclude that the sentence in this case can and should be set aside on narrower grounds than those adopted by the plurality, and because the grounds on which I rest should allow us to face the more general question when better evidence is available, I concur only in the judgment of the Court.

I

Both the plurality and the dissent look initially to the decisions of American legislatures for signs of a national consensus about the minimum age at which a juvenile's crimes may lead to capital punishment. Although I agree with the dissent's contention, that these decisions should provide the most reliable signs of a society-wide consensus on this issue, I cannot agree with the dissent's interpretation of the evidence.

The most salient statistic that bears on this case is that every single American legislature that has expressly set a minimum age for capital punishment has set that age at 16 or above. When one adds these 18 States to the 14 that have rejected capital punishment completely, it appears that almost two-thirds of the state legislatures have definitely concluded that no 15-year-old should be exposed to the threat of execution. Where such a large majority of the state legislatures have unambiguously outlawed capital punishment for 15-year-olds, and where no legislature in this country has affirmatively and unequivocally endorsed such a practice, strong counterevidence would be required to persuade me that a national consensus against this practice does not exist.

The dissent argues that it has found such counterevidence in the laws of the 19 States that authorize capital punishment without setting any statutory minimum age. If we could be sure that each of these 19 state legislatures had deliberately chosen to authorize capital punishment for crimes committed at the age of 15, one could hardly suppose that there is a settled national consensus opposing such a practice. In fact, however, the statistics relied on by the dissent may be quite misleading. When a legislature provides for some 15-year-olds to be processed through the adult criminal justice system, and capital punishment is available for adults in that jurisdiction, the death penalty becomes at least theoretically applicable to such defendants. This is how petitioner was rendered death eligible, and the same possibility appears to exist in 18 other States. As the plurality points out, however, it does not necessarily follow that the legislatures in those jurisdictions have deliberately concluded that it would be appropriate to impose capital punishment on 15-year-olds (or on even younger defendants who may be tried as adults in some jurisdictions).

There is no indication that any legislative body in this country has rendered a considered judgment approving the imposition of capital punishment on juveniles who were below the age of 16 at the time of the offense. It nonetheless is true, although I think the dissent has overstated its significance, that the Federal Government and 19 States have adopted statutes that appear to have the legal effect of rendering some of these juveniles death eligible. That fact is a real obstacle in the way of concluding that a national consensus forbids this practice. It is appropriate, therefore, to examine other evidence that might indicate whether or not these statutes are inconsistent with settled notions of decency in our society.

In previous cases, we have examined execution statistics, as well as data about jury determinations, in an effort to discern whether the application of capital punishment to certain classes of defendants has been so aberrational that it can be considered unacceptable in our society. In this case, the plurality emphasizes that four decades have gone by since the last execution of a defendant who was younger than 16 at the time of the offense, and that only 5 out of 1,393 death sentences during a recent 5-year period involved such defendants. Like the statistics about the behavior of legislatures, these execution and sentencing statistics support the inference of a national consensus opposing the death penalty for 15-year-olds, but they are not dispositive.

A variety of factors, having little or nothing to do with any individual's blameworthiness, may cause some groups in our population to commit capital crimes at a much lower rate than other groups. The statistics relied on by the plurality, moreover, do not indicate how many juries have been asked to impose the death penalty for crimes committed below the age of 16, or how many times prosecutors have exercised their discretion to refrain from seeking the death penalty in cases where the statutory prerequisites might have been proved. Without such data, raw execution and sentencing statistics cannot allow us reliably to infer that juries are or would be significantly more reluctant to impose the death penalty on 15-year-olds than on similarly situated older defendants.

Nor, finally, do I believe that this case can be resolved through the kind of disproportionality analysis employed in the plurality opinion. Granting the plurality's premise—that adolescents are generally less blameworthy than adults who commit similar crimes—it does not necessarily follow that all 15-year-olds are incapable of the moral culpability that would justify the imposition of capital punishment. Nor has the plurality educed evidence demonstrating that 15-year-olds as a class are inherently incapable of being deterred from major crimes by the prospect of the death penalty.

Legislatures recognize the relative immaturity of adolescents, and we have often permitted them to define age-based classes that take account of this qualitative difference between juveniles and adults. These characteristics, however, vary widely among different individuals of the same age, and I would not substitute our inevitably subjective judgment about the best age at which to draw a line in the capital punishment context for the judgments of the Nation's legislatures.

II

The case before us today raises some of the same concerns that have led us to erect barriers to the imposition of capital punishment in other contexts. Oklahoma has enacted a statute that authorizes capital punishment for murder, without setting any minimum age at which the commission of murder may lead to the imposition of that penalty. The State has also, but quite separately, provided that 15-year-old murder defendants may be treated as adults in some circumstances. Because it proceeded in this manner, there is a considerable risk that the Oklahoma Legislature either did not realize that its actions would have the effect of rendering 15-year-old defendants death eligible or did not give the question the serious consideration that would have been reflected in the explicit choice of some minimum age for death eligibility. Were it clear that no national consensus forbids the imposition of capital punishment for crimes committed before the age of 16, the implicit nature of the Oklahoma Legislature's decision would not be constitutionally problematic. In the peculiar circumstances we face today, however, the Oklahoma statutes have presented this Court with a result that is of very dubious constitutionality, and they have done so without the earmarks of careful consideration that we have required for other kinds of decisions leading to the death penalty. In this unique situation, I am prepared to conclude that petitioner and others who were below the age of 16 at the time of their offense may not be executed under the authority of a capital punishment statute that specifies no minimum age at which the commission of a capital crime can lead to the offender's execution.

The conclusion I have reached in this unusual case is itself unusual. I believe, however, that it is in keeping with the principles that have guided us in other Eighth Amendment cases. It is also supported by the familiar principle—applied in different ways in different contexts—according to which we should avoid unnecessary, or unnecessarily broad, constitutional adjudication. The narrow conclusion I have reached in this case is consistent with the underlying rationale for that principle, which was articulated many years ago by Justice Jackson: "We are not final because we are infallible, but we are infallible only because we are final." By leaving open for now the broader Eighth Amendment question that both the plurality and the dissent would resolve, the approach I take allows the ultimate moral issue at stake in the constitutional question to be addressed in the first instance by those best suited to do so, the people's elected representatives.

Justice Scalia, with whom The Chief Justice and Justice White join, dissenting.

I

I begin by restating the facts since I think that a fuller account of William Wayne Thompson's participation in the murder, and of his certification to stand trial as an adult, is helpful in understanding the case. The evidence at trial left no doubt that on the night of January 22–23, 1983, Thompson brutally and with premeditation murdered his former brother-in-law, Charles Keene, the motive evidently being, at least in part, Keene's physical abuse of Thompson's sister. As Thompson left his mother's house that evening, in the company of three older friends, he explained to his girlfriend that "we're going to kill Charles." Several hours later, early in the morning of January 23, a neighbor, Malcolm "Possum" Brown, was awakened by the sound of a gunshot on his front porch. Someone pounded on his front door shouting: "Possum, open the door, let me in. They're going to kill me." Brown telephoned the police, and then opened the front door to see a man on his knees attempting to repel blows with his arms and hands. There were four other men on the porch. One was holding a gun and stood apart, while the other three were hitting and kicking the kneeling man, who never attempted to hit back. One of them was beating the victim with an object 12 to 18 inches in length. The police called back to see if the disturbance was still going on, and while Brown spoke with them on the telephone the men took the victim away in a car.

Several hours after they had left Thompson's mother's house, Thompson and his three companions returned. Thompson's girlfriend helped him take off his boots, and heard him say: "We killed him. I shot him in the head and cut his throat and threw him in the river." Subsequently, the former wife of one of Thompson's accomplices heard Thompson tell his mother that "he killed him. Charles was dead and Vicki didn't have to worry about him anymore." During the days following the murder Thompson made other admissions. One witness testified that she asked Thompson the source of some hair adhering to a pair of boots he was carrying. He replied that was where he had kicked Charles Keene in the head. Thompson also told her that he had cut Charles' throat and chest and had shot him in the head. Another witness testified that when she told Thompson that a friend had seen Keene dancing in a local bar, Thompson remarked that that would be hard to do with a bullet in his head. Ultimately, one of Thompson's codefendants admitted that after Keene had been shot twice in the head Thompson had cut Keene "so the fish could eat his body." Thompson and a codefendant had then thrown the body into the Washita River, with a chain and blocks attached so that it would not be found. On February 18, 1983, the body was recovered. The Chief Medical Examiner of Oklahoma concluded that the victim had been beaten, shot twice, and that his throat, chest, and abdomen had been cut.

II

The history of this case demonstrates William Wayne Thompson is not a juvenile caught up in a legislative scheme that unthinkingly lumped him together with adults for purposes of determining that death was an appropriate penalty for him and for his crime. To the contrary, Oklahoma first gave careful consideration to whether, in light of his young age, he should be subjected to the normal criminal system at all. That question having been answered affirmatively, a jury then considered whether, despite his young age, his maturity and moral responsibility were sufficiently developed to justify the sentence of death. In upsetting this particularized judgment on the basis of a constitutional absolute, the plurality pronounces it to be a fundamental principle of our society that no one who is as little as one day short of his 16th birthday can have sufficient maturity and moral responsibility to be subjected to capital punishment for any crime. As a sociological and moral conclusion that is implausible; and it is doubly implausible as an interpretation of the United States Constitution.

Turning to legislation at the state level, one observes the same trend of *lowering* rather than raising the age of juvenile criminal liability. As for the state status quo with respect to the death penalty in particular: The plurality chooses to "confine its attention" to the fact that all 18 of the States that establish a minimum age for capital punishment have chosen at least 16. But it is beyond me why an accurate analysis would not include within the computation the larger number of States (19) that have determined that no minimum age for capital punishment is appropriate, leaving that to be governed by their general rules for the age at which juveniles can be criminally responsible. A survey of state laws shows, in other words, that a majority of the States for which the issue exists (the rest do not have capital punishment) are of the view that death is not different insofar as the age of juvenile criminal responsibility is concerned. And the latter age, while presumed to be 16 in all the States can, in virtually all the States, be less than 16 when individuated consideration of the particular case warrants it. Thus, what Oklahoma has done here is precisely what the majority of capital-punishment States would do.

The statistics of executions demonstrate nothing except the fact that our society has always agreed that executions of 15-year-old criminals should be rare, and in more modern times has agreed that they (like all other executions) should be even rarer still. There is no rational basis for discerning in that a societal judgment that no one so much as a day under 16 can *ever* be mature and morally responsible enough to deserve that penalty; and there is no justification except our own predeliction for converting a statistical rarity of occurrence into an absolute constitutional ban. One must surely fear that, now that the Court has taken the first step of requiring individualized consideration in capital cases, today's decision begins a second stage of converting into constitutional rules the general results of that individuation.

Because I think the views of this Court on the policy questions discussed in Part V of the plurality opinion to be irrelevant, I make no attempt to refute them. It suffices to say that there is another point of view, suggested in the following passage written by our esteemed former colleague Justice Powell, whose views the plurality several times invokes for support: "Minors who become embroiled with the law range from the very young up to those on the brink of majority. Some of the older minors become fully 'street-wise,' hardened criminals, deserving no greater consideration than that properly accorded all persons suspected of crime."

III

In my view the concurrence also does not fulfill its promise of arriving at a more "narrow conclusion" than the plurality, and avoiding an "unnecessarily broad" constitutional holding. To the contrary, I think it hoists on to the deck of our Eighth Amendment jurisprudence the loose cannon of a brand new principle. If the concurrence's view were adopted, henceforth a finding of national consensus would no longer be required to invalidate state action in the area of capital punishment. All that would be needed is uncertainty regarding the existence of a national consensus, whereupon various protective requirements could be imposed, even to the point of specifying the process of legislation. If 15-year-olds must be explicitly named in capital statutes, why not those of extremely low intelligence, or those over 75, or any number of other appealing gups as to which the existence of a national consensus regarding capital punishment may be in doubt for the same reason the concurrence finds it in doubt here, viz., because they are not specifically named in the capital statutes?

I respectfully dissent from the judgment of the Court.

Stanford v. Kentucky
492 U.S. 361 (1989)

Justice Scalia announced the judgment of the Court and delivered the opinion of the Court with respect to Parts I, II, III, and IV-A, and an opinion with respect to Parts IV-B and V, in which The Chief Justice, Justice White, and Justice Kennedy join.

These two consolidated cases require us to decide whether the imposition of capital punishment on an individual for a crime committed at 16 or 17 years of age constitutes cruel and unusual punishment under the Eighth Amendment.

I

The first case involves the shooting death of 20-year-old Barbel Poore in Jefferson County, Kentucky. Petitioner Kevin Stanford committed the murder on January 7, 1981, when he was approximately 17 years and 4 months of age. Stanford and his accomplice repeatedly raped and sodomized Poore during and after their commission of a robbery at a gas station where she worked as an attendant. They then drove her to a secluded area near the station, where Stanford shot her point-blank in the face and then in the back of her head. The proceeds from the robbery were roughly 300 cartons of cigarettes, two gallons of fuel, and a small amount of cash. A corrections officer testified that petitioner explained the murder as follows: "He said, 'I had to shoot her, she lived next door to me and she would recognize me. I guess we could have tied her up or something or beat her up and tell her if she tells, we would kill her.' Then after he said that he started laughing."

The second case before us today, involves the stabbing death of Nancy Allen, a 26-year-old mother of two who was working behind the sales counter of the convenience store she and David Allen owned and operated in Avondale, Missouri. Petitioner Heath Wilkins committed the murder on July 27, 1985, when he was approximately 16 years and 6 months of age. The record reflects that Wilkins' plan was to rob the store and murder "whoever was behind the counter" because "a dead person can't talk." While Wilkins' accomplice, Patrick Stevens, held Allen, Wilkins stabbed her, causing her to fall to the floor. When Stevens had trouble operating the cash register, Allen spoke up to assist him, leading Wilkins to stab her three more times in her chest. Two of these wounds penetrated the victim's heart. When Allen began to beg for her life, Wilkins stabbed her four more times in the neck, opening her carotid artery. After helping themselves to liquor, cigarettes, rolling papers, and approximately $450 in cash and checks, Wilkins and Stevens left Allen to die on the floor.

II

The thrust of both Wilkins' and Stanford's arguments is that imposition of the death penalty on those who were juveniles when they committed their crimes falls within the Eighth Amendment's prohibition against "cruel and unusual punishments." Wilkins would have us define juveniles as individuals 16 years of age and under; Stanford would draw the line at 17.

In determining what standards have "evolved," however, we have looked not to our own conceptions of decency, but to those of modern American society as a whole. As we have said, "Eighth Amendment judgments should not be, or appear to be, merely the subjective views of individual Justices; judgment should be informed by objective factors to the maximum possible extent."

III

First among the objective indicia that reflect the public attitude toward a given sanction are statutes passed by society's elected representatives. Of the 37 States whose laws permit capital punishment, 15 decline to impose it upon 16-year-old offenders and 12 decline to impose it on 17-year-old offenders. This does not establish the degree of national consensus this Court has previously thought sufficient to label a particular punishment cruel and unusual. In invalidating the death penalty for rape of an adult woman, we stressed that Georgia was the *sole* jurisdiction that authorized such a punishment. In striking down capital punishment for participation in a robbery in which an accomplice takes a life, we emphasized that only eight jurisdictions authorized similar punishment.

Since a majority of the States that permit capital punishment authorize it for crimes committed at age 16 or above, petitioners' cases are more analogous to *Tison* than *Coker, Enmund, Ford,* and *Solem.* In *Tison*, which upheld Arizona's imposition of the death penalty for major participation in a felony with reckless indifference to human life, we noted that only 11 of those jurisdictions imposing capital punishment rejected its use in such circumstances. As we noted earlier, here the number is 15 for offenders under 17, and 12 for offenders under 18. We think the same conclusion as in *Tison* is required in this case.

IV

A

Wilkins and Stanford argue, however, that even if the laws themselves do not establish a settled consensus, the application of the laws does. That contemporary society views capital punishment of 16- and 17-year-old offenders as inappropriate is demonstrated, they say, by the reluctance of juries to impose, and prosecutors to seek, such sentences. Petitioners are quite correct that a far smaller number of offenders under 18 than over 18 have been sentenced to death in this country. From 1982 through 1988, for example, out of 2,106 total death sentences, only 15 were imposed on individuals who were 16 or under when they committed their crimes, and only 30 on individuals who were 17 at the time of the crime. And it appears that actual executions for crimes committed under age 18 accounted for only about two percent of the total number of executions that occurred between 1642 and 1986. As Wilkins points out, the last execution of a person who committed a crime under 17 years of age occurred in 1959. These statistics, however, carry little significance. Given the undisputed fact that a far smaller percentage of capital crimes are committed by persons under 18 than over 18, the discrepancy in treatment is much less than might seem. Granted, however, that a substantial discrepancy exists, that does not establish the requisite proposition that the death sentence for offenders under 18 is categorically unacceptable to prosecutors and juries. To the contrary, it is not only possible, but overwhelmingly probable, that the very considerations which induce petitioners and their supporters to believe that death should *never* be imposed on offenders under 18 cause prosecutors and juries to believe that it should *rarely* be imposed.

B

This last point suggests why there is also no relevance to the laws cited by petitioners and their *amici* which set 18 or more as the legal age for engaging in various activities, ranging from driving to drinking alcoholic beverages to voting. It is, to begin with, absurd to think that one must be mature enough to drive carefully, to drink responsibly, or to vote intelligently, in order to be mature enough to understand that murdering another human being is profoundly wrong, and to conform one's conduct to that most minimal of all civilized standards. But even if the requisite degrees of maturity were comparable, the age statutes in question would still not be relevant. They do not represent a social judgment that all persons under the designated ages are not responsible enough to drive, to drink, or to vote, but at most a judgment that the vast majority are not. These laws set the appropriate ages for the operation of a system that makes its determinations in gross, and that does not conduct individualized maturity tests for each driver, drinker, or voter. The criminal justice system, however, does provide individualized testing. In the realm of capital punishment in particular, "individualized consideration is a constitutional requirement," and one of the individualized mitigating factors that sentencers must be permitted to consider is the defendant's age. Twenty-nine States, including both Kentucky and Missouri, have codified this constitutional requirement in laws specifically designating the defendant's age as a mitigating factor in capital cases. Moreover, the determinations required by juvenile transfer statutes to certify a juvenile for trial as an adult ensure individualized consideration of the maturity and moral responsibility of 16- and 17-year-old offenders before they are even held to stand trial as adults. The application of this particularized system to the petitioners can be declared constitutionally inadequate only if there is a consensus, not that 17 or 18 is the age at which most persons, or even almost all persons, achieve sufficient maturity to be held fully responsible for murder; but that 17 or 18 is the age before which *no one* can reasonably be held fully responsible. What displays society's views on this latter point are not the ages set forth in the generalized system of driving, drinking, and voting laws cited by petitioners and their *amici*, but the ages at which the States permit their particularized capital punishment systems to be applied.

V

Having failed to establish a consensus against capital punishment for 16- and 17-year-old offenders through state and federal statutes and the behavior of prosecutors and juries, petitioners seek to demonstrate it through other indicia, including public opinion polls, the views of interest groups, and the positions adopted by various professional associations. We decline the invitation to rest constitutional law upon such uncertain foundations. A revised national consensus so broad, so clear, and so enduring as to justify a permanent prohibition upon all units of democratic government must appear in the operative acts (laws and the application of laws) that the people have approved.

We also reject petitioners' argument that we should invalidate capital punishment of 16- and 17-year-old offenders on the ground that it fails to serve the legitimate goals of penology. According to petitioners, it fails to deter because juveniles, possessing less developed cognitive skills than adults, are less likely to fear death; and it fails to exact just retribution because juveniles, being less mature and responsible, are also less morally blameworthy. In support of these claims, petitioners and their supporting *amici* marshall an array of socioscientific evidence concerning the psychological and emotional development of 16- and 17-year-olds.

If such evidence could conclusively establish the entire lack of deterrent effect and moral responsibility, resort to the Cruel and Unusual Punishments Clause would be unnecessary; the Equal Protection Clause of the Fourteenth Amendment would invalidate these laws for lack of rational basis. But as the adjective "socioscientific" suggests (and insofar as evaluation of moral responsibility is concerned perhaps the adjective "ethicoscientific" would be more apt), it is not demonstrable that no 16-year-old is "adequately responsible" or significantly deterred. It is rational, even if mistaken, to think the contrary. The battle must be fought, then, on the field of the Eighth Amendment; and in that struggle socioscientific, ethicoscientific, or even purely scientific evidence is not an available weapon. The punishment is either "cruel *and* unusual" (*i.e.*, society has set its face against it) or it is not. The audience for these arguments, in other words, is not this Court but the citizenry of the United States. It is they, not we, who must be persuaded. For as we stated earlier, our job is to *identify* the "evolving standards of decency"; to determine, not what they *should* be, but what they *are*. We have no power under the Eighth Amendment to substitute our belief in the scientific evidence for the society's apparent skepticism. In short, we emphatically reject petitioner's suggestion that the issues in this case permit us to apply our "own informed judgment," regarding the desirability of permitting the death penalty for crimes by 16- and 17-year-olds.

We reject the dissent's contention that our approach, by "largely returning the task of defining the contours of Eighth Amendment protection to political majorities," leaves "constitutional doctrine to be formulated by the acts of those institutions which the Constitution is supposed to limit." To say, as the dissent says, that "it is for *us* ultimately to judge whether the Eighth Amendment permits imposition of the death penalty,"—and to mean that as the dissent means it, *i.e.*, that it is for *us* to judge, not on the basis of what we perceive the Eighth Amendment originally prohibited, or on the basis of what we perceive the society through its democratic processes now overwhelmingly disapproves, but on the basis of what we think "proportionate" and "measurably contributory to acceptable goals of punishment"—to say and mean that, is to replace judges of the law with a committee of philosopher-kings.

We discern neither a historical nor a modern societal consensus forbidding the imposition of capital punishment on any person who murders at 16 or 17 years of age. Accordingly, we conclude that such punishment does not offend the Eighth Amendment's prohibition against cruel and unusual punishment. The judgments of the Supreme Court of Kentucky and the Supreme Court of Missouri are therefore affirmed.

Justice O'Connor, concurring in part and concurring in the judgment.

Last Term, in *Thompson*, I expressed the view that a criminal defendant who would have been tried as a juvenile under state law, but for the granting of a petition waiving juvenile court jurisdiction, may only be executed for a capital offense if the State's capital punishment statute specifies a minimum age at which the commission of a capital crime can lead to an offender's execution and the defendant had reached that minimum age at the time the crime was committed. As a threshold matter, I indicated that such specificity is not necessary to avoid constitutional problems if it is clear that no national consensus forbids the imposition of capital punishment for crimes committed at such an age. Applying this two-part standard in *Thompson*, I concluded that Oklahoma's imposition of a death sentence on an individual who was 15 years old at the time he committed a capital offense should be set aside. Applying the same standard today, I conclude that the death sentences for capital murder imposed by Missouri and

Kentucky on petitioners Wilkins and Stanford respectively should not be set aside because it is sufficiently clear that no national consensus forbids the imposition of capital punishment on 16- or 17-year-old capital murderers.

In *Thompson* I noted that "the most salient statistic that bears on this case is that every single American legislature that has expressly set a minimum age for capital punishment has set that age at 16 or above." It is this difference between *Thompson* and these cases, more than any other, that convinces me there is no national consensus for bidding the imposition of capital punishment for crimes committed at the age of 16 and older.

The day may come when there is general legislative rejection of the execution of 16- or 17-year-old capital murderers that a clear national consensus can be said to have developed. Because I do not believe that day has yet arrived, I concur.

Justice Brennan, with whom Justice Marshall, Justice Blackmun, and Justice Stevens join, dissenting.

I believe that to take the life of a person as punishment for a crime committed when below the age of 18 is cruel and unusual and hence is prohibited by the Eighth Amendment.

The Court's discussion of state laws concerning capital sentencing gives a distorted view of the evidence of contemporary standards that these legislative determinations provide. Currently, 12 of the States whose statutes permit capital punishment specifically mandate that offenders under age 18 not be sentenced to death. When one adds to these 12 States the 15 (including the District of Columbia) in which capital punishment is not authorized at all, it appears that the governments in fully 27 of the States have concluded that no one under 18 should face the death penalty. A further three States explicitly refuse to authorize sentences of death for those who committed their offense when under 17, making a total of 30 States that would not tolerate the execution of petitioner Wilkins. Congress' most recent enactment of a death penalty statute also excludes those under 18.

In 19 States that have a death penalty, no minimum age for capital sentences is set in the death penalty statute. The notion that these States have consciously authorized the execution of juveniles derives from the congruence in those jurisdictions of laws permitting state courts to hand down death sentences, on the one hand, and, on the other, statutes permitting the transfer of offenders under 18 from the juvenile to state court systems for trial in certain circumstances.

I would not assume, however, in considering how the States stand on the moral issue that underlies the constitutional question with which we are presented, that a legislature that has never specifically considered the issue has made a conscious moral choice to permit the execution of juveniles. On a matter of such moment that most States have expressed an explicit and contrary judgment, the decisions of legislatures that are only implicit, and that lack the "earmarks of careful consideration that we have required for other kinds of decisions leading to the death penalty," must count for little. I do not suggest, of course, that laws of these States cut *against* the constitutionality of the juvenile death penalty—

only that accuracy demands that the baseline for our deliberations should be that 27 States refuse to authorize a sentence of death in the circumstances of petitioner Stanford's case, and 30 would not permit Wilkins' execution; that 19 States have not squarely faced the question; and that only the few remaining jurisdictions have explicitly set an age below 18 at which a person may be sentenced to death.

The application of these laws is another indicator the Court agrees to be relevant. The fact that juries have on occasion sentenced a minor to death shows, the Court says, that the death penalty for adolescents is not categorically unacceptable to juries. This, of course, is true; but it is not a conclusion that takes Eighth Amendment analysis very far. Just as we have never insisted that a punishment have been rejected unanimously by the States before we may judge it cruel and unusual, so we have never adopted the extraordinary view that a punishment is beyond Eighth Amendment challenge if it is sometimes handed down by a jury. Both in absolute and in relative terms, imposition of the death penalty on adolescents is distinctly unusual.

Our cases recognize that objective indicators of contemporary standards of decency in the form of legislation in other countries is also of relevance to Eighth Amendment analysis. Many countries, of course—over 50, including nearly all in Western Europe—have formally abolished the death penalty, or have limited its use to exceptional crimes such as treason. Within the world community, the imposition of the death penalty for juvenile crimes appears to be overwhelmingly disapproved.

Justice Scalia forthrightly states in his plurality opinion that Eighth Amendment analysis is at an end once legislation and jury verdicts relating to the punishment in question are analyzed as indicators of contemporary values. A majority of the Court rejected this revisionist view as recently as last Term. Justice Scalia's approach would largely return the task of defining the contours of Eighth Amendment protection to political majorities. But the very purpose of a Bill of Rights was to withdraw certain subjects from the vicissitudes of political controversy, to place them beyond the reach of majorities and officials and to establish them as legal principles to be applied by the courts. Our cases make clear that public perceptions of standards of decency with respect to criminal sanctions are not conclusive. A penalty also must accord with the dignity of man, which is the basic concept underlying the Eighth Amendment.

There can be no doubt at this point in our constitutional history that the Eighth Amendment forbids punishment that is wholly disproportionate to the blameworthiness of the offender. Proportionality analysis requires that we compare "the gravity of the offense," understood to include not only the injury caused, but also the defendant's culpability, with "the harshness of the penalty." In my view, juveniles so generally lack the degree of responsibility for their crimes that is a predicate for the constitutional imposition of the death penalty that the Eighth Amendment forbids that they receive that punishment.

Legislative determinations distinguishing juveniles from adults abound. These age-based classifications reveal much about how our society regards juveniles as a class, and about societal beliefs regarding adolescent levels of responsibility. To be sure, the development of cognitive and reasoning abilities and of empathy, the acquisition of experience upon which these abilities operate and upon which the capacity to make sound value judgments depends, and in general the process of maturation into a self-directed individual fully responsible for his or her actions, occur by degrees. But 18 is the dividing line that society has generally drawn, the point at which it is thought reasonable to assume that persons have an ability to make, and a duty to bear responsibility for their, judgments. Insofar as age 18 is a necessarily arbitrary social choice as a point at which to acknowledge a person's maturity and responsibility, given the different developmental rates of individuals, it is in fact "a conservative estimate of the dividing line between adolescence and adulthood.

There may be exceptional individuals who mature more quickly than their peers, and who might be considered fully responsible for their actions prior to the age of 18, despite their lack of the experience upon which judgment depends. In my view, however, it is not sufficient to accommodate the facts about juveniles that an individual youth's culpability may be taken into account in the decision to transfer him or her from the juvenile to the adult court system for trial, or that a capital sentencing jury is instructed to consider youth and other mitigating factors. I believe that the Eighth Amendment requires that a person who lacks that full degree of responsibility for his or her actions associated with adulthood not be sentenced to death. Juveniles very generally lack that degree of blameworthiness that is, in my view, a constitutional prerequisite for the imposition of capital punishment under our precedents concerning the Eighth Amendment proportionality principle.

There are strong indications that the execution of juvenile offenders violates contemporary standards of decency: a majority of States decline to permit juveniles to be sentenced to death; imposition of the sentence upon minors is very unusual even in those States that permit it; and respected organizations with expertise in relevant areas regard the execution of juveniles as unacceptable, as does international opinion. These indicators serve to confirm in my view my conclusion that the Eighth Amendment prohibits the execution of persons for offenses they committed while below the age of 18, because the death penalty is disproportionate when applied to such young offenders and fails measurably to serve the goals of capital punishment. I dissent.

◼ Juveniles—Perspectives

◼ Issue—Should Juveniles Be Exempt from the Death Penalty?

Victor Streib, "Death Penalty for Children: The American Experience with Capital Punishment for Crimes Committed While under Age Eighteen"

Within the seamless web of the law and the empirical reality of capital punishment, what role does the youth of the offender play? If it is assumed that "children have a very special place in life which law should reflect," does it necessarily follow that "civilized societies will not tolerate the spectacle of execution of children?"

A number of policies and presumptions underlie the continuing debate over the appropriateness of capital punishment for crimes by adults. Perhaps the most complete list has been provided by Justice Thurgood Marshall: "There are six purposes conceivably served by capital punishment: retribution, deterrence, prevention of repetitive criminal acts, encouragement of guilty pleas and confessions, eugenics, and economy." Each should be considered in the context of crimes committed by persons under age eighteen.

The goal of societal retribution or legal vengeance achieved through execution of a child seems difficult to justify. However, capital punishment can be characterized as an understandable expression of societal outrage at particular crimes. Even if the execution of an adult solely for revenge is constitutionally permissible, this justification of capital punishment is less appealing when the object of righteous vengeance is a child. The spectacle of our society seeking legal vengeance through execution of a child raises fundamental questions about the nature of children's moral responsibility for their actions and about society's moral responsibility to protect and nurture children.

Probably the most complex issue is whether capital punishment is more effective than life imprisonment as a deterrent to crime. This key issue has been the subject of extensive research, but no consistent conclusions have been drawn by members of the Supreme Court.

When applied to children, the key issues are adolescents' perception of death and whether that perception acts as a more significant deterrent to criminal acts than life imprisonment. Even less is known about death as a deterrent for adolescents than is known about death as a deterrent for adults. Many social scientists would agree that adolescents live for today with little thought of the future consequences of their actions. The defiant attitudes and risk-taking behaviors of some adolescents are probably related to their developmental stage of defiance about danger and death. Some adolescents may play games of chance with death from a feeling of omnipotence. They typically have not learned to accept the finality of death. Adolescents tend to view death as a remote possibility; old people die, not teenagers. Consider, for example, teenagers' propensity to flirt with death through reckless driving, ingestion of dangerous drugs, and other similar "death-defying" behavior. The meager research on this issue suggests the conclusion that threatening a child with death probably does not have the same impact as threatening an adult with death. Even if some percentage of adults are deterred by the death penalty, the deterrent effect tends to lose much of its power when imposed upon an adolescent.

No one can deny that execution of a child will prevent repetitive criminal acts by that particular child. The death penalty does, however, seem an unnecessarily harsh solution to the problem of recidivism. Not only are murderers "extremely unlikely to commit other crimes either in prison or upon their release," but irreversibly abandoning all hope of the reform of a child is squarely in opposition to the fundamental premises of juvenile justice and comparable socio-legal systems. While the specific deterrence argument may be somewhat persuasive in the case of the 45-year-old habitual criminal, it is singularly inappropriate and defeatist when applied to the 16-year-old child.

Using capital punishment as leverage to encourage guilty pleas and confessions seems not only a questionable justification for this ultimate sanction but also unnecessary in a child's case. The threat of life imprisonment for an adolescent who has fifty to sixty years yet to live is so overwhelming that it should provide whatever leverage the government might need.

Finally, the issue of using capital punishment for eugenic purposes or to improve the human race seems unworthy of serious consideration. In any event, the less severe alternatives of sterilization and/or life imprisonment would seem to be required by the Constitution.

This brief consideration of the purposes served by capital punishment for children is inconclusive at best, as is such a consideration vis-à-vis adults. Most of the justifications for capital punishment of adults lose whatever persuasiveness they have when applied to the case of an offender under age eighteen.

The notion of a governmental agency imposing the death penalty upon a child through its judicial system raises the deepest questions about the demands of justice versus the special nature of childhood. Even if the Eighth Amendment does not inherently proscribe death as a punishment for particularly aggravated murder by mature adults, the unique legal, psychological, and social status of persons under age eighteen should be incorporated into this area of constitutional interpretation. The response to this article's opening question should be that the United States counts itself among "civilized societies which will not tolerate the spectacle of execution of children."

Joseph L. Hoffmann, "On the Perils of Line-Drawing: Juveniles and the Death Penalty"

I focus here exclusively on the question whether a ban on the death penalty for juveniles is consistent with the fundamental retributive goal of ensuring that every person who commits a crime receives his or her "just deserts," or the punishment that is appropriate in light of the harm caused by the crime and the offender's culpability.

The debate, in retributive terms, has boiled down to two competing claims. The advocates of a ban have argued that most juveniles do not deserve to die for their crimes, and that a ban on the juvenile death penalty will therefore serve the ends of justice. The opponents of a ban have argued in response that at least some juveniles deserve to die for their crimes, and that a ban will therefore frustrate the ends of justice. Given the concededly small number of "death-deserving" juvenile murderers, and the inherent risk, absent a ban, of improper exercises of capital sentencing discretion, the advocates of a ban often have seemed to hold the higher ground with respect to the issue of retributive justice.

The debate about retributive justice described above badly misses the mark, however, because each side has relied entirely on cardinal proportionality to justify its position. I demonstrate that modern retributive theory, which properly demands both cardinal and ordinal proportionality, compels the Court to reject a ban on the juvenile death penalty, at least if such a ban is to be accomplished by means of a "bright line" based on the chronological age of the murderer. Those who advocate a ban on the juvenile death penalty may be able to base their constitutional claim on some set of alternative values, such as utilitarian considerations of rehabilitation or deterrence, or the symbolic value of extending mercy to murderers who are juveniles. In retributive terms, however, a ban would produce serious injustice.

In terms of retributive justice, what is most troubling about a "bright line" ban on the juvenile death penalty is not the fact that a small number of "death-deserving" juvenile murderers would escape the death penalty and receive some other lengthy prison sentence. Rather, what is most troubling, or should be, is the fact that such "death-deserving" juvenile murderers would be treated differently from nonjuvenile murderers whose desert was exactly the same as, or even less than, that of the ineligible juvenile murderers, but who would nevertheless be eligible for and receive the death penalty. The sole basis for this life-versus-death difference in punishment would be the chronological age of the murderer at the time of the crime.

The use of chronological age to draw a "bright line" and prohibit the death penalty for juveniles inevitably would produce results that, viewed in retributive justice terms, can only be described as "arbitrary" and "freakish." After all, age itself is not the factor that renders the imposition of the death penalty against most juveniles arguably unjust. Rather, age is simply a "proxy," and an imperfect one at that, for a combination of factors that determines the relative culpability of a juvenile murderer. These factors include maturity, judgment, responsibility, and the capability to assess the possible consequences of one's conduct. Because age only imperfectly reflects this complex combination of factors, the adoption of a "bright line" ban on the death penalty for juveniles, defined in terms of age, necessarily violates the concept of ordinal, or comparative, proportionality, which is an important component of retributive justice. In the end, this means that the advocates of such a constitutional ban must demonstrate other reasons to adopt it, and these other reasons must be important enough to outweigh the serious injustice such a ban would produce.

I. Why Line-Drawing Is Perilous: The Concepts of Cardinal and Ordinal Proportionality

A. An Introduction to the Problem The problem with drawing a "bright line" prohibiting the death penalty for juveniles on the basis of chronological age can perhaps best be illustrated by example. Consider the facts of *Tison v. Arizona*. Ricky and Raymond Tison, brothers, grew up in a "rather amoral" home environment under the malevolent influence of their father, Gary Tison, described as "one of the premier sociopaths of recent Arizona history." According to the *Tison* Court, Ricky Tison was twenty years old at the time of the crime; Raymond was nineteen. Because Arizona had set no minimum age for either the waiver of juvenile offenders into the adult court system or for the death penalty, however, the age of the Tison brothers was irrelevant except as a potential mitigating factor under *Lockett* and *Eddings*, at the capital sentencing hearing.

A slightly altered version of the *Tison* facts illustrates the problem created if a "bright line" prohibits imposition of the death penalty on murderers below a given age. If Ricky had been eighteen years old at the time of the crime and

Raymond only seventeen, it would be difficult to justify sentencing Ricky to death while sparing Raymond solely because he was a minor. The Court stated in *Tison* that the brothers were equally and sufficiently culpable to warrant the death penalty. Because they were equally culpable, they should be punished equally.

The hypothetical and real cases described above are troubling not only, or even primarily, because of a feeling that the nonjuvenile murderer in each case, considered independently, did not deserve the death penalty. What is most troubling about these cases is that they raise difficult issues of comparative justice, in the context of the most severe punishment that society can impose against a person who has been convicted of a crime. These cases therefore will, or should, make one think more carefully about the basic principles of retributive justice and, especially, about the relationship between just deserts and equality.

B. Fundamentals of Retributive Justice Retributivism, or retributive justice, is a theory of punishment that has undergone a vigorous revival in the United States during the last ten years.

i. The Cardinal and Ordinal Requirements of Proportionality The central concept within the theory of retributive justice is proportionality. Proportionality involves two closely related requirements. The first requirement is that punishment in order to be just must be proportional to the seriousness of the crime. Seriousness, in turn, is based on the harm caused or threatened by the crime and the culpability of the offender. If an offender acts intentionally, and there are no mitigating circumstances, he or she is deemed fully responsible for the crime. In such a case, the seriousness of the crime will depend upon the harm caused. Even so, however, it does not necessarily follow that a proportional punishment must correspond precisely to the harm caused, in the sense of *lex talionis*. Instead, a proportional punishment will be defined in terms of whatever the particular society views as appropriate for the crime. This kind of proportionality, which deals with the relationship between the seriousness of a given offender's crime and the punishment imposed against the offender, is called "cardinal" proportionality.

Proportionality also imposes a second requirement, however, and it is a requirement no less important in terms of retributive justice than the requirement of cardinal proportionality. This is the requirement that offenders whose "just deserts" are equal, in terms of the seriousness of their crimes, receive equal punishments, and offenders whose "just deserts" are different are punished differently. This kind of proportionality, which deals with comparisons between the deserts and punishments of different offenders, is called "ordinal" or "comparative" proportionality.

If one could identify the single "just" punishment for each crime and the person who committed it, in terms of cardinal proportionality, and if one could design a sentencing system that would impose only such "just" punishments, then such a system necessarily would also satisfy the requirement of ordinal proportionality. Cardinal proportionality, however, can never be such an exact science. At least in terms of cardinal proportionality, we cannot say that any particular punishment is the single "just" punishment for a given offender and crime. Cardinal proportionality thus serves as a crude limiting device, not as a precise measure of punishment.

Ordinal proportionality, on the other hand, permits us to make more precise judgments about the "justice" or "injustice" of punishments imposed against two or more offenders. Once a given offender receives a particular punishment from within the range of punishments that satisfy the requirement of cardinal proportionality, then we may conclude whether the particular punishment imposed against another offender is ordinally proportional. The imposition of punishment against the first offender provides a frame of reference for assessing the "justice" of the second offender's punishment.

ii. *The Relationship Between Cardinal and Ordinal Proportionality* This difference in precision between the kinds of judgments we can make about the cardinal and ordinal proportionality of punishments might suggest that, in some fundamental way, the two kinds of proportionality are theoretically distinct.

A helpful way of thinking about the relationship between desert and equality, and about the closely related concepts of cardinal and ordinal proportionality, is by analogy. For instance, consider the judging of a gymnastics competition. The particular score a gymnast receives for her performance can be analogized to the punishment imposed against an offender who commits a crime. And, much like the retributive theory of punishment, we could agree on a principle of "just scoring." Under this principle a gymnast's score should be based solely on her "just deserts," or on a combination of the "difficulty" of her chosen routine and the quality or "worthiness" of her individual performance.

When the first gymnast in the competition completes her performance, the judges must decide what score to assign to that performance. One obvious problem for the judges will be to establish a correspondence between the elements of "difficulty" and "worthiness" and the ten-point scale used for scoring the performances. But even if we assume that the judges are given some fixed criteria for deciding the weight to be given to the various aspects of each performance, and some fixed standards for converting the "difficulty" and "worthiness" of each performance into a score between zero and ten points, the judges must still decide exactly how "worthy" the first gymnast's performance has been. How will the judges decide the "worthiness" of the first performance?

The process of determining the "worthiness" of the first performance, and of then assigning a score to that performance, resembles the process of determining the range of cardinally proportional punishments for a given offender and crime. An experienced gymnastics judge evaluates the first gymnast's performance against the background of all of the performances the judge has seen before, and thereby makes a rough judgment about the "worthiness" of the performance. The judge uses this rough judgment, in conjunction with the fixed scoring standards, to assign a score to the performance. The background of the judge's experience establishes limits on the score that may "justly" be given to the first gymnast. As with cardinal proportionality, however, these "justice" limits are likely to be imprecise. Assuming, for example, that the first gymnast performed fairly well, there would be nothing inherently "unjust" about giving her a score of 6.5, or a 7.0, or a 7.5, or even an 8.0. All we can say, with any degree of certainty, is that it would be "unjust," in terms of the judge's past experience and our principle of "just scoring," for the judge to give the first gymnast a 4.0, or a 10.0, for a pretty good performance.

The situation changes significantly when the second gymnast completes her performance. Now the judge has a specific basis, or frame of reference, for evaluating the "worthiness" of the second gymnast's performance. For example, if the judge ignored some facet of the first gymnast's performance, such as the positioning of her left hand during a certain maneuver then the judge must also ignore the same facet of the second gymnast's performance. This makes the judge's task similar to the process of evaluating the ordinal proportionality of a particular set of punishments. Any difference in the gymnasts' scores must, in order to satisfy our principle of "just scoring," be justified in terms of either a difference in the "worthiness" of the performances, or in their "difficulty," if the content of the two routines was different.

Although it would not be inherently "unjust" for the judge to assign any score between 6.5 and 8.0 to the first gymnast's performance, it undoubtedly would violate our principle of "just scoring" for the judge to give the second gymnast the same score as the first, if the second gymnast's performance was less "worthy" than that of the first. Alternatively, if the two performances were exactly the same in terms of their "difficulty" and "worthiness," surely we would insist that the judge give both gymnasts the same score.

The gymnastics analogy highlights both aspects of the relationship between cardinal and ordinal proportionality. First, the analogy illustrates the theoretical connection between the two concepts, both of which necessarily involve comparative judgments. This theoretical connection suggests that a retributive theory of punishment must incorporate both kinds of proportionality. Second, the analogy emphasizes the point that, although cardinal and ordinal proportionality involve similar comparative processes, it is generally much more difficult to determine whether a particular punishment is cardinally proportional than it is to determine whether a series of punishments satisfies ordinal proportionality.

II. *The State of the Debate on a Ban*

The difference in precision between judgments based on cardinal and ordinal proportionality explains why the opponents of a ban on the juvenile death penalty have missed the mark, thus far, with their argument from retributive justice. By focusing on the cardinal proportionality aspect of retributive justice, opponents of a ban effectively concede the point before the debate begins. Even assuming that a murder is serious enough to merit the death penalty as a matter of retributive justice, a life sentence would in most cases also be within the broad range of cardinally proportional punishments for such a crime, because it would not be "grossly lenient" in relation to the seriousness of the crime.

In fact, it is very difficult to conclude that the imposition of a life sentence for even a particularly heinous murder committed by a juvenile violates the requirement of cardinal proportionality. Thus, the advocates of a ban on the juvenile death penalty have the upper hand, if the debate is cast solely in terms of cardinal proportionality.

Despite this weakness in the cardinal proportionality argument against a "bright line" ban on the juvenile death penalty, however, the ordinal proportionality argument is quite strong. It is hard to deny that, the imposition of the death penalty against Ricky Tison but not against Raymond, under the hypothetical facts described above, would be as "arbitrary" and "freakish" as being struck by lightning. The only difference between the two brothers that could explain the life-and-death difference in punishments, by hypothesis, would be the accident of birth that Ricky appeared a year before Raymond was born.

The problem with using age as a "bright line" in the juvenile death penalty cases is that age, standing alone, is not the reason why it is at least arguably unjust to impose the death penalty on many juveniles. If age corresponded perfectly to the combination of relevant factors, then its use as a "bright line" would not be problematic. Because age is not a "perfect" proxy, however, its use as a "bright line" necessarily produces ordinal disproportionality, or comparative injustice.

III. *Line-Drawing and the Death Penalty*

There are several areas within the context of death penalty law in which the Supreme Court has approved the use of a bright line rule. These areas, however, differ fundamentally from the context of the juvenile death penalty. Previously, whenever line-drawing has been approved by the Court in a capital case, the bright line has been drawn carefully so as to correspond perfectly with the very characteristics that made imposition of the death penalty "unjust" in the particular case. These perfect bright lines do not implicate comparative justice concerns in the same way that the proposed bright line ban on the juvenile death penalty does.

In *Coker*, *Enmund*, *Tison*, and *Ford*, the Court drew bright lines and said, in effect: "No defendant who is on the other side of this line may be put to death." These bright lines were justifiable because in each case the bright line defined a class of defendants none of whom could be said, in retributive terms, to deserve to receive the death penalty, or to be executed, for their crimes. To put it another way, in each of the aforementioned cases, the Court drew a bright line that corresponded precisely to the very characteristics that made the death penalty inappropriate, in retributive terms, for the class of relevant defendants.

The four cases, in other words, involved so-called "perfect" line-drawing. In *Coker*, for example, it was the very fact that the defendants had not killed their respective victims when they raped them that made the death penalty unjust. In *Enmund* and in *Tison*, it was precisely the defendant's relative lack of culpability with respect to the victim's death that made the death penalty unjust.

The juvenile death penalty issue differs fundamentally from the kinds of issues raised in *Coker*, *Enmund*, *Tison*, and *Ford*. In the juvenile death penalty context, chronological age is not the very characteristic that renders the death penalty necessarily inappropriate, in retributive terms, for the entire class of relevant defendants. Instead, age is only a "proxy," and an imperfect one at that, for a combination of factors that renders the death penalty an unjust punishment for some juvenile murderers. These factors, noted previously, include immaturity, poor judgment, lack of responsibility, and inability to evaluate carefully the possible consequences of one's conduct.

Age is an imperfect proxy because, as even the advocates of a bright line admit, not all juveniles fit the model of the immature, easily influenced "child" who may not, in retributive terms, deserve the death penalty. Because chronological age is only an imperfect proxy for the combination of factors truly relevant to a juvenile murderer's culpability, it is clear that at least some members of the class of juvenile murderers do not properly, as a matter of "just deserts," belong on the "death-ineligible" side of the line. This is particularly true as one approaches the presumptively "mature" age of eighteen. Thus, to the extent that age fails to reflect accurately the combination of factors that is truly relevant to the retributive justice of imposing the death penalty, a bright line based on age will produce ordinal disproportionality and comparative injustice.

IV. *Line-Drawing and Age in Other Contexts*

Bright lines based on age appear throughout the law in such areas as voting, driving, gambling, marriage, and military and jury service. Naturally, questions arise as to whether these other age-based bright lines create similar serious problems of comparative injustice. Although other age-based bright lines exist, the problems of comparative injustice in such other contexts are far less serious than in the death penalty context.

There are at least four important reasons why these other kinds of bright lines based on chronological age are different from the kind of bright line proposed in the juvenile death penalty cases.

First, punishment issues, unlike other issues involving the distribution of governmental benefits or burdens, involve the placing of blame, and therefore implicate comparative justice considerations to a much greater extent than do other issues.

Second, even if one could identify some other context in which comparative justice mattered just as much as in the context of punishment, age may simply be a better "proxy" for the relevant combination of factors in some other context than it is in the context of the juvenile death penalty, thus making its use as a proxy more easily justified in terms of comparative justice. For example, age may correspond more closely with the factors that are relevant to military service, such as physical maturity, than it does with those factors relevant to culpability for criminal conduct.

Third, and perhaps most importantly, the relative costs and benefits of using an individualized, case-by-case approach to resolve the issue in question represents a crucial distinction between the juvenile death penalty context and virtually every other context in which age limits have been imposed. It would be absurd to suggest that, because some unusually mature seventeen-year-olds are treated unjustly by a minimum voting age of eighteen, we should require an individualized determination of every seventeen-year-old's right to vote. The costs of holding such individualized hearings would greatly outweigh whatever injustice might be produced by the use of a bright line minimum voting age. The same point can be made about virtually every other age limit under the law.

In the context of the juvenile death penalty, however, the situation is quite different. The number of cases requiring individualized resolution is very small, and the importance of ensuring "just" results is very great.

Fourth, and finally, in such contexts as voting, driving, drinking, gambling, and marriage, there is a "rough" justice in saying to a juvenile, "I realize that you may be just as mature as an older person, and therefore just as qualified to engage in whatever specific behavior is at issue. The chronological age limit is arbitrary, and operates unjustly in your particular case. But this is a bright line that you will eventually cross, just as everyone has who came before you in terms of age. Therefore, you must wait your turn, and eventually you too will be allowed to vote, drive, drink, gamble, and marry." Many bright lines based on age, although justifiable primarily on the basis of administrative efficiency, nonetheless operate with this kind of rough equality. Such rough equality may be acceptable, at least where we are less than confident that we can correctly resolve the issue in question, on a case-by-case basis, without incurring prohibitive costs.

As a general matter, however, a defendant is, and can be, subjected to the death penalty decision only once. Thus, it does no good to say to the eighteen year old who receives the death penalty, "I realize the seventeen year old who committed the same crime as you did is as mature as you are, but he cannot receive the death penalty solely because of his chronological age. Someday he, too, will be eighteen years old, and he can then receive the death penalty." The rough equality that obtains in such contexts of voting, driving, drinking, gambling, and marriage is absent in the death penalty context.

For these reasons, the use of age as a bright line in the juvenile death penalty context is quite different from the use of age to draw bright lines in other contexts. The analogies to the minimum ages for driving, voting, gambling, marriage, and military and jury service are inappropriate and misleading. The nature of punishment generally, and of the death penalty in particular, should make one particularly wary about the use of age, or any other "imperfect" proxy, as a bright line.

The Mentally Retarded

■ The Mentally Retarded—Introduction

Insanity and mental retardation are distinct concepts. Insanity is not a medical term, though the concept is more or less synonymous with mental illness or psychosis. The notion of insanity is that some people are unfit to be at large because of the danger they pose to others. Insanity is a basis for civil incapacitation. It is also a defense of criminal responsibility, and may undermine the capacity of an individual to perform certain legal functions such as the making of a will. Though the finding is almost always premised upon mental illness, insanity is a social and legal construct. Section 4.01 of the Model Penal Code provides this standard for the insanity defense:

> *A person is not responsible for criminal conduct if at the time of such conduct as a result of mental disease or defect he lacks substantial capacity either to appreciate the criminality (wrongfulness) of his conduct or to conform his conduct to the requirements of the law.*

Under the Model Penal Code formulation, mental illness is a prerequisite to a legal determination of insanity.

Retardation, by contrast, is not an illness. The mentally ill have disturbed thought processes and emotions, and limited ability to learn. Their intellectual, functional, and emotional development is inhibited. Very often, they have low IQ scores. The retarded can, however, tell the difference between right and wrong, or, at least, their condition does not keep them from understanding the difference. They might perceive the world in a distorted manner, they might be unable to express themselves articulately, they might be unable to fully control their actions, but nothing about their condition precludes the retarded from appreciating the wrongfulness of criminal conduct.

This is the critical difference between the retarded and the insane. The insane do not deserve punishment because they cannot tell right from wrong. From the standpoint of retribution it is at least defensible to punish the retarded. Some people say the retarded are as able to tell right from wrong as other citizens, some say they are less able, but no one says they are categorically unable, and certainly a person's IQ is not the determinant of their moral capacity. Just as Joseph Hoffmann argued in connection with the execution of juveniles, reliance upon a bright line rule based upon IQ could lead to retributive injustices. Cathleen Herasimchuk, a former district attorney, made precisely this argument against a proposed Texas statute exempting murderers with an IQ of 65 or less from the death penalty:

> *Responsibility in the criminal justice system is based on moral blame-worthiness, not intellectual achievements. Moral culpability is composed of much more than sheer IQ. This proposed statute, however, adopts a definition of mental retardation that relies almost exclusively upon a numerical IQ test. We used to measure the culpable blameworthiness of an act by the entirety of a person's state of mind: his factual knowledge, intellectual understanding, intent, his spiritual and moral development. In sum, his full character and background.*

Herasimchuk's argument, similar to Professor Hoffmann's before, is that the system should "trust the jurors in these cases to determine whether the mental retardation, mental illness or any other possible mitigating factor calls for a sentence less than death." The argument has considerable appeal.

However, it must be noted that a defendant or defense attorney's decision to offer evidence of diminished mental capacity during the penalty phase of a capital trial is a double-edged sword. Evidence of retardation is mitigating, as it can serve to diminish the culpability of the defendant in the eyes of some jurors, and the general deterrence effect could be seen as weaker with the retarded. But evidence of retardation is also subject to an aggravating inference. In many state schemes, future dangerousness is an aggravating factor. The retarded might seem less subject to specific deterrence—they cannot easily be taught a lesson, thus they might be an ongoing threat to the community, hence, require incapacitation.

The Supreme Court first addressed the proportionality of the death penalty for the retarded in a 1989 case, *Penry v. Lynaugh*. Penry brutally raped and murdered Pamela Carpenter. He beat her and stabbed her with a pair of scissors. The jury sentenced Penry to die despite copious evidence of his retardation. Penry was diagnosed as having organic brain damage, caused either by brain trauma at birth, or by subsequent beatings and injuries to his brain. His IQ was between 50 and 63, his mental age that of a 6-year-old, and he had the social maturity of a 9- or 10-year-old. Various doctors disagreed over the extent and cause of Penry's mental limitations, but each doctor agreed that Penry "was a person of extremely limited mental ability, and that he seemed unable to learn from his mistakes."

The Court conducted the familiar examination of objective evidence of society's regard for a particular punishment. It found no consensus against the execution of the mentally retarded. At the time of *Penry*, only one state, Georgia, and the federal government specifically exempted the retarded from the ambit of their capital sentencing statutes. Writing for the majority, Justice O'Connor said that this evidence, even if taken in connection with the 14 states that rejected capital punishment completely, did not rise to the level of consensus present in *Coker* and other cases.

Following *Penry*, several states amended their death penalty statutes to exclude the retarded. From 1990 through 2001, 14 states voted to exclude the retarded. New York and Nebraska reinstated the death penalty in 1995 and 1998 respectively and expressly exempted the retarded. By the time the Supreme Court revisited the issue in 2002, 20 states permitted the execution of the retarded, 18 states and the federal government excluded the execution of the retarded, and 12 states rejected capital punishment entirely. If only the views of states that authorize capital punishment are considered, a slim majority—20 of 39—condoned the execution of the retarded.

In *Atkins v. Virginia*, reprinted in the Critical Documents section of this chapter, the majority of the Court held that this evidence was sufficient to demonstrate a national consensus against the execution of the retarded. Justice Stevens signaled a critical and controversial shift in the manner in which the Court's objective analysis is conducted. "It is not so much the number of these states that is significant," he wrote, "but the consistency of the direction of change."

By its decision, the Court further reduces the quantum of evidence required to demonstrate a national consensus. It is now not required to show absolute numbers against punishment for a particular class of offenders, a trend is enough. Whether evidence of this kind should suffice for proportionality review is a matter for discussion. And just as the Court never established in absolute terms what quantum of evidence demonstrated a consensus against the death penalty for a particular class of offenders, the Court has not said what evidence is required to demonstrate a trend. This is particularly problematic because if such a trend as two or three states taking consecutive similar action, then trends will be found routinely, often no more than the product of chance.

One could argue that it was an inevitability following *Penry* that a trend by the majority would emerge. Because only one state precluded the execution of the retarded, a trend could not have emerged in the opposite direction. And as such a short time elapsed between *Penry* and *Atkins* it is unlikely that a state would choose to exclude the retarded and then reverse itself on the basis of experience. This is what Justice Scalia meant when he wrote in dissent that "few, if any, of the States have had sufficient experience with these laws to know whether they are sensible in the long term." Furthermore, *Penry* is a veritable invitation to states to reform their statutes. It is easy to assume some states deferred consideration of the issue of the death penalty for retarded offenders pending the Court's decision in *Penry*.

If one credits any aspect of this argument about the inevitability of a trend against executing the retarded, then the relevant question might be whether the magnitude of the trend is adequately impressive to demonstrate consensus given these baseline expectations. One could reasonably attach greater weight to the 20 states that continued to condone the execution of the retarded following *Penry*. Unquestionably, *Atkins* effectively reduces the amount of evidence required to demonstrate a consensus against capital punishment for a particular crime or class of criminals.

Relying on trend evidence is unfair in yet another sense: it immortalizes temporary fluctuations in public opinion. It is entirely possible that left to their own devices, a trend might reemerge among the states in favor of executing the retarded. This will never happen following *Atkins*. Once the Court deconstitutionalizes the death penalty for a group, a state legislature has no incentive to reauthorize capital punishment for that group. A countertrend can never emerge.

So *Atkins* settles the constitutional issue of the disproportionality of the death penalty for the retarded once and for all, though its appropriateness remains a relevant public policy question. *Atkins* leaves it to the states to define retardation and establish the scope of the exemptions—as it leaves it to the states to determine the standard of insanity. If the Supreme Court follows past practice, states will have considerable leeway in determining how many people are protected by the ruling in *Atkins*. Perceptions of the soundness of the policy considerations underlying the *Atkins* decision will shape the contours of state policies.

In the debate that follows, the group Human Rights Watch argues that the execution of the retarded is a violation of human rights. They say the retarded lack the moral sophistication to be held fully and retributively accountable for their actions, and they are not capable of being deterred in the same manner as ordinary citizens. Human Rights Watch is a nonprofit, nongovernmental organization dedicated to the protection of human rights worldwide. Professor Barry Latzer argues against affording special protection to the retarded qua retarded. Like Professor Hoffmann argued in connection with juveniles, Latzer says that drawing a bright-line rule in this context produces retributive injustice. Some retarded persons are deserving of the death penalty. Latzer also points to an apparent inconsistency in the position of protectors of the retarded. Advocates argue that the retarded should be regarded as responsible human beings and, for purposes of treatment, be dealt with as individuals. In the case of the death penalty, however, the emphasis is on commonalities. Arguing against the death penalty for the retarded, advocates emphasize the shared traits of the retarded and their collective lack of moral development.

■ The Mentally Retarded—Critical Documents

Atkins v. Virginia
536 U.S. 304 (2002)

Justice Stevens delivered the opinion of the Court.

Those mentally retarded persons who meet the law's requirements for criminal responsibility should be tried and punished when they commit crimes. Because of their disabilities in areas of reasoning, judgment, and control of their impulses, however, they do not act with the level of moral culpability that characterizes the most serious adult criminal conduct. Moreover, their impairments can jeopardize the reliability and fairness of capital proceedings against mentally retarded defendants. Presumably for these reasons, in the 13 years since we decided *Penry v. Lynaugh* (1989), the American public, legislators, scholars, and judges have deliberated over the question whether the death penalty should ever be imposed on a mentally retarded criminal. The consensus reflected in those deliberations informs our answer to the question presented by this case: whether such executions are "cruel and unusual punishments" prohibited by the Eighth Amendment.

I

Petitioner, Daryl Renard Atkins, was convicted of abduction, armed robbery, and capital murder, and sentenced to death. At approximately midnight on August 16, 1996, Atkins and William Jones, armed with a semiautomatic handgun, abducted Eric Nesbitt, robbed him of the money on his person, drove him to an automated teller machine in his pickup truck where cameras recorded their withdrawal of additional cash, then took him to an isolated location where he was shot eight times and killed.

Jones and Atkins both testified in the guilt phase of Atkins' trial. Each confirmed most of the details in the other's account of the incident, with the important exception that each stated that the other had actually shot and killed Nesbitt. Jones' testimony which was both more coherent and credible than Atkins', was obviously credited by the jury and was sufficient to establish Atkins' guilt. At the penalty phase of the trial, the State introduced victim impact evidence and proved two aggravating circumstances: future dangerousness and "vileness of the offense." To prove future dangerousness, the State relied on Atkins' prior felony convictions as well as the testimony of four victims of earlier robberies and assaults.

In the penalty phase, the defense relied on one witness, Dr. Evan Nelson, a forensic psychologist who had evaluated Atkins before trial and concluded that he was "mildly mentally retarded."[3] His conclusion was based on interviews with people who knew Atkins, a review of school and court records, and the administration of a standard intelligence test which indicated that Atkins had a full scale IQ of 59. The jury sentenced Atkins to death.

Atkins did not argue before the Virginia Supreme Court that his sentence was disproportionate to penalties imposed for similar crimes in Virginia, but he did contend "that he is mentally retarded and thus cannot be sentenced to death." The majority of the state court rejected this contention, relying on our holding in *Penry*. Because of the gravity of the concerns expressed by the dissenters, and in light of the dramatic shift in the state legislative landscape that has occurred in the past 13 years, we granted certiorari to revisit the issue that we first addressed in the *Penry* case.

---

[3] The American Association of Mental Retardation (AAMR) defines mental retardation as follows: "*Mental retardation* refers to substantial limitations in present functioning. It is characterized by significantly subaverage intellectual functioning, existing concurrently with related limitations in two or more of the following applicable adaptive skill areas: communication, self-care, home living, social skills, community use, self-direction, health and safety, functional academics, leisure, and work. Mental retardation manifests before age 18." The American Psychiatric Association's (APA) definition is similar. "Mild" mental retardation is typically used to describe people with an IQ level of 50–55 to approximately 70.

II

Proportionality review under those evolving standards should be informed by objective factors to the maximum possible extent. We have pinpointed that the "clearest and most reliable objective evidence of contemporary values is the legislation enacted by the country's legislatures."

We also acknowledged in *Coker* that the objective evidence, though of great importance, did not "wholly determine" the controversy, "for the Constitution contemplates that in the end our own judgment will be brought to bear on the question of the acceptability of the death penalty under the Eighth Amendment." Thus, in cases involving a consensus, our own judgment is "brought to bear," by asking whether there is reason to disagree with the judgment reached by the citizenry and its legislators.

Guided by our approach in these cases, we shall first review the judgment of legislatures that have addressed the suitability of imposing the death penalty on the mentally retarded and then consider reasons for agreeing or disagreeing with their judgment.

III

The parties have not called our attention to any state legislative consideration of the suitability of imposing the death penalty on mentally retarded offenders prior to 1986. In that year, the public reaction to the execution of a mentally retarded murderer in Georgia apparently led to the enactment of the first state statute prohibiting such executions. In 1988, when Congress enacted legislation reinstating the federal death penalty, it expressly provided that a "sentence of death shall not be carried out upon a person who is mentally retarded." In 1989, Maryland enacted a similar prohibition. It was in that year that we decided *Penry*, and concluded that those two state enactments, "even when added to the 14 States that have rejected capital punishment completely, do not provide sufficient evidence at present of a national consensus."

Much has changed since then. Responding to the national attention received by the Bowden execution and our decision in *Penry*, state legislatures across the country began to address the issue. In 1990 Kentucky and Tennessee enacted statutes similar to those in Georgia and Maryland, as did New Mexico in 1991, and Arkansas, Colorado, Washington, Indiana, and Kansas in 1993 and 1994. In 1995, when New York reinstated its death penalty, it emulated the Federal Government by expressly exempting the mentally retarded. Nebraska followed suit in 1998. There appear to have been no similar enactments during the next two years, but in 2000 and 2001 six more States—South Dakota, Arizona, Connecticut, Florida, Missouri, and North Carolina—joined the procession. The Texas Legislature unanimously adopted a similar bill, and bills have passed at least one house in other States, including Virginia and Nevada.

It is not so much the number of these States that is significant, but the consistency of the direction of change. Given the well-known fact that anticrime legislation is far more popular than legislation providing protections for persons guilty of violent crime, the large number of States prohibiting the execution of mentally retarded persons (and the complete absence of States passing legislation reinstating the power to conduct such executions) provides powerful evidence that today our society views mentally retarded offenders as categorically less culpable than the average criminal. The evidence carries even greater force when it is noted that the legislatures that have addressed the issue have voted overwhelmingly in favor of the prohibition. Moreover, even in those States that allow the execution of mentally retarded offenders, the practice is uncommon. Some States, for example New Hampshire and New Jersey, continue to authorize executions, but none have been carried out in decades. Thus there is little need to pursue legislation barring the execution of the mentally retarded in those States. And it appears that even among those States that regularly execute offenders and that have no prohibition with regard to the mentally retarded, only five have executed offenders possessing a known IQ less than 70 since we decided *Penry*. The practice, therefore, has become truly unusual, and it is fair to say that a national consensus has developed against it.[21]

To the extent there is serious disagreement about the execution of mentally retarded offenders, it is in determining which offenders are in fact retarded. In this case, for instance, the Commonwealth of Virginia disputes that Atkins suffers from mental retardation. Not all people who claim to be mentally retarded will be so impaired as to fall within the range of mentally retarded offenders about whom there is a national consensus. As was our approach in *Ford v. Wainwright*, with regard to insanity, "we leave to the States the task of developing appropriate ways to enforce the constitutional restriction upon its execution of sentences."

IV

This consensus unquestionably reflects widespread judgment about the relative culpability of mentally retarded offenders, and the relationship between mental retardation and the penological purposes served by the death penalty. Additionally, it suggests that some characteristics of mental retardation undermine the strength of the procedural protections that our capital jurisprudence steadfastly guards.

As discussed above, clinical definitions of mental retardation require not only subaverage intellectual functioning, but also significant limitations in adaptive skills such as communication, self-care, and self-direction that became manifest before age 18. Mentally retarded persons frequently know the difference between right and wrong and are competent to stand trial. Because of their impairments, however, by definition they have diminished capacities to understand and process

---

[21] Additional evidence makes it clear that this legislative judgment reflects a much broader social and professional consensus. For example, several organizations with germane expertise have adopted official positions opposing the imposition of the death penalty upon a mentaly retarded offender. In addition, representatives of widely diverse religious communities in the United States, reflecting Christian, Jewish, Muslim, and Buddhist traditions, have filed an *amicus curiae* brief explaining that even though their views about the death penalty differ, they all "share a conviction that the execution of persons with mental retardation cannot be morally justified." Moreover, within the world community, the imposition of the death penalty for crimes committed by mentally retarded offenders is overwhelmingly disapproved. Finally, polling data shows a widespread consensus among Americans, even those who support the death penalty, that executing the mentally retarded is wrong. Although these factors are by no means dispositive, their consistency with the legislative evidence lends further support to our conclusion that there is a consensus among those who have addressed the issue.

information, to communicate, to abstract from mistakes and learn from experience, to engage in logical reasoning, to control impulses, and to understand the reactions of others. There is no evidence that they are more likely to engage in criminal conduct than others, but there is abundant evidence that they often act on impulse rather than pursuant to a premeditated plan, and that in group settings they are followers rather than leaders. Their deficiencies do not warrant an exemption from criminal sanctions, but they do diminish their personal culpability.

In light of these deficiencies, our death penalty jurisprudence provides two reasons consistent with the legislative consensus that the mentally retarded should be categorically excluded from execution. First, there is a serious question as to whether either justification that we have recognized as a basis for the death penalty applies to mentally retarded offenders.

With respect to retribution—the interest in seeing that the offender gets his "just deserts"—the severity of the appropriate punishment necessarily depends on the culpability of the offender. Since *Gregg*, our jurisprudence has consistently confined the imposition of the death penalty to a narrow category of the most serious crimes. Pursuant to our narrowing jurisprudence, which seeks to ensure that only the most deserving of execution are put to death, an exclusion for the mentally retarded is appropriate.

With respect to deterrence—the interest in preventing capital crimes by prospective offenders—it seems likely that capital punishment can serve as a deterrent only when murder is the result of premeditation and deliberation. The theory of deterrence in capital sentencing is predicated upon the notion that the increased severity of the punishment will inhibit criminal actors from carrying out murderous conduct. Yet it is the same cognitive and behavioral impairments that make these defendants less morally culpable—for example, the diminished ability to understand and process information, to learn from experience, to engage in logical reasoning, or to control impulses—that also make it less likely that they can process the information of the possibility of execution as a penalty and, as a result, control their conduct based upon that information. Nor will exempting the mentally retarded from execution lessen the deterrent effect of the death penalty with respect to offenders who are not mentally retarded. Such individuals are unprotected by the exemption and will continue to face the threat of execution.

The reduced capacity of mentally retarded offenders provides a second justification for a categorical rule making such offenders ineligible for the death penalty. The risk "that the death penalty will be imposed in spite of factors which may call for a less severe penalty," is enhanced, not only by the possibility of false confessions, but also by the lesser ability of mentally retarded defendants to make a persuasive showing of mitigation in the face of prosecutorial evidence of one or more aggravating factors. Mentally retarded defendants may be less able to give meaningful assistance to their counsel and are typically poor witnesses, and their demeanor may create an unwarranted impression of lack of remorse for their crimes. As *Penry* demonstrated, moreover, reliance on mental retardation as a mitigating factor can be a two-edged sword that may enhance the likelihood that the aggravating factor of future dangerousness will be found by the jury. Mentally retarded defendants in the aggregate face a special risk of wrongful execution.

Our independent evaluation of the issue reveals no reason to disagree with the judgment of "the legislatures that have recently addressed the matter" and concluded that death is not a suitable punishment for a mentally retarded criminal. We are not persuaded that the execution of mentally retarded criminals will measurably advance the deterrent or the retributive purpose of the death penalty. Construing and applying the Eighth Amendment in the light of our "evolving standards of decency," we therefore conclude that such punishment is excessive and that the Constitution "places a substantive restriction on the State's power to take the life" of a mentally retarded offender.

The judgment of the Virginia Supreme Court is reversed and the case is remanded for further proceedings not inconsistent with this opinion.

Chief Justice Rehnquist, with whom Justice Scalia and Justice Thomas join, dissenting.

I agree with Justice Scalia, that the Court's assessment of the current legislative judgment regarding the execution of defendants like petitioner more resembles a *post hoc* rationalization for the majority's subjectively preferred result rather than any objective effort to ascertain the content of an evolving standard of decency. I write separately, however, to call attention to the defects in the Court's decision to place weight on foreign laws, the views of professional and religious organizations, and opinion polls in reaching its conclusion.

In my view, two sources—the work product of legislatures and sentencing jury determinations—ought to be the sole indicators by which courts ascertain the contemporary American conceptions of decency for purposes of the Eighth Amendment. They are the only objective indicia of contemporary values firmly supported by our precedents. More importantly, however, they can be reconciled with the undeniable precepts that the democratic branches of government and individual sentencing juries are, by design, better suited than courts to evaluating and giving effect to the complex societal and moral considerations that inform the selection of publicly acceptable criminal punishments.

I fail to see how the views of other countries regarding the punishment of their citizens provide any support for the Court's ultimate determination. *Stanford's* reasoning makes perfectly good sense, and the Court offers no basis to question it. For if it is evidence of a *national* consensus for which we are looking, then the viewpoints of other countries simply are not relevant.

There are strong reasons for limiting our inquiry into what constitutes an evolving standard of decency under the Eighth Amendment to the laws passed by legislatures and the practices of sentencing juries in America. Here, the Court goes beyond these well-established objective indicators of contemporary values. Believing this view to be seriously mistaken, I dissent.

Justice Scalia, with whom the Chief Justice and Justice Thomas join, dissenting.

Today's decision is the pinnacle of our Eighth Amendment death-is-different jurisprudence. Not only does it, like all of that jurisprudence, find no support in the text or history of the Eighth Amendment; it does not even have support in current social attitudes regarding the conditions that render an otherwise just death penalty inappropriate. Seldom has an opinion of this Court rested so obviously upon nothing but the personal views of its members.

Before today, our opinions consistently emphasized that Eighth Amendment judgments regarding the existence of social "standards" "should be informed by objective factors to the maximum possible extent" and "should not be, or appear to be, merely the subjective views of individual Justices."

The Court pays lipservice to these precedents as it miraculously extracts a "national consensus" forbidding execution of the mentally retarded. The bare number of States alone—*18*—should be enough to convince any reasonable person that no "national consensus" exists. How is it possible that agreement among 47% of the death penalty jurisdictions amounts to "consensus"? Our prior cases have generally required a much higher degree of agreement before finding a punishment cruel and unusual on "evolving standards" grounds. In *Coker*, we proscribed the death penalty for rape of an adult woman after finding that only one jurisdiction, Georgia, authorized such a punishment. In *Enmund*, we invalidated the death penalty for mere participation in a robbery in which an accomplice took a life, a punishment not permitted in 28 of the death penalty States (78%). In *Ford*, we supported the common-law prohibition of execution of the insane with the observation that "this ancestral legacy has not outlived its time," since not a single State authorizes such punishment. In *Solem v. Helm*, we invalidated a life sentence without parole under a recidivist statute by which the criminal "was treated more severely than he would have been in any other State." What the Court calls evidence of "consensus" in the present case (a fudged 47%) more closely resembles evidence that we found *inadequate* to establish consensus in earlier cases. *Tison v. Arizona* upheld a state law authorizing capital punishment for major participation in a felony with reckless indifference to life where only 11 of the 37 death penalty States (30%) prohibited such punishment. *Stanford* upheld a state law permitting execution of defendants who committed a capital crime at age 16 where only 15 of the 36 death penalty States (42%) prohibited death for such offenders.

Moreover, a major factor that the Court entirely disregards is that the legislation of all 18 States it relies on is still in its infancy. The oldest of the statutes is only 14 years old; five were enacted last year; over half were enacted within the past eight years. Few, if any, of the States have had sufficient experience with these laws to know whether they are sensible in the long term. It is myopic to base sweeping constitutional principles upon the narrow experience of a few years.

The Court attempts to bolster its embarrassingly feeble evidence of "consensus" with the following: "It is not so much the number of these States that is significant, but the *consistency* of the direction of change." But in what *other* direction *could we possibly* see change? Given that 14 years ago *all* the death penalty statutes included the mentally retarded, *any* change (except precipitate undoing of what had just been done) was *bound to be* in the one direction the Court finds significant enough to overcome the lack of real consensus. That is to say, to be accurate the Court's " *consistency*-of-the-direction-of-change" point should be recast into the following unimpressive observation: "No State has yet undone its exemption of the mentally retarded, one for as long as 14 whole years." In any event, reliance upon "trends," even those of much longer duration than a mere 14 years, is a perilous basis for constitutional adjudication.

The Court's thrashing about for evidence of "consensus" includes reliance upon the margins by which state legislatures have enacted bans on execution of the retarded. Presumably, in applying our Eighth Amendment "evolving-standards-of-decency" jurisprudence, we will henceforth weigh not only how many States have agreed, but how many States have agreed *by how much*. Of course if the percentage of legislators voting for the bill is significant, surely the number of people *represented* by the legislators voting for the bill is also significant: the fact that 49% of the legislators in a State with a population of 60 million voted *against* the bill should be more impressive than the fact that 90% of the legislators in a state with a population of 2 million voted *for* it. (By the way, the population of the death penalty States that exclude the mentally retarded is only 44% of the population of all death penalty States. This is quite absurd. What we have looked for in the past to "evolve" the Eighth Amendment is a consensus of the same sort as the consensus that *adopted* the Eighth Amendment: a consensus of the sovereign States that form the Union, not a nose count of Americans for and against.

Even less compelling (if possible) is the Court's argument that evidence of "national consensus" is to be found in the infrequency with which retarded persons are executed in States that do not bar their execution. To begin with, what the Court takes as true is in fact quite doubtful. It is not at all clear that execution of the mentally retarded is "uncommon." *If*, however, execution of the mentally retarded *is* "uncommon"; and if it is not a sufficient explanation of this that the retarded comprise a tiny fraction of society (1% to 3%); then surely the explanation is that mental retardation is a constitutionally mandated mitigating factor at sentencing. For that reason, even if there were uniform national sentiment in *favor* of executing the retarded in appropriate cases, one would still expect execution of the mentally retarded to be "uncommon."

But the Prize for the Court's Most Feeble Effort to fabricate "national consensus" must go to its appeal (deservedly relegated to a footnote) to the views of assorted professional and religious organizations, members of the so-called "world community," and respondents to opinion polls. I agree with the Chief Justice that the views of professional and religious organizations and the results of opinion polls are irrelevant. Equally irrelevant are the practices of the "world community," whose notions of justice are (thankfully) not always those of our people. "We must never forget that it is a Constitution for the United States of America that we are expounding. Where there is not first a settled consensus among our own people, the views of other nations, however enlightened the Justices of this Court may think them to be, cannot be imposed upon Americans through the Constitution."

Beyond the empty talk of a "national consensus," the Court gives us a brief glimpse of what really underlies today's decision: pretension to a power confined *neither* by the moral sentiments originally enshrined in the Eighth Amendment (its original meaning) *nor even* by the current moral sentiments of the American people. "The Constitution," the Court says, "contemplates that in the end *our own judgment* will be brought to bear on the question of the acceptability of the death penalty under the Eighth Amendment." The arrogance of this assumption of power takes one's breath away. And it explains, of course, why the Court can be so cavalier about the evidence of consensus. It is just a game, after all. In the end, it is the *feelings* and *intuition* of a majority of the Justices that count—the perceptions of decency, or of penology, or of mercy, entertained by a majority of the small and unrepresentative segment of our society that sits on this Court. The genuinely operative portion of the opinion, then, is the Court's statement of the reasons why it agrees with the contrived consensus it has found, that the "diminished capacities" of the mentally retarded render the death penalty excessive.

The Court gives two reasons why the death penalty is an excessive punishment for all mentally retarded offenders. First, the "diminished capacities" of the mentally retarded raise a "serious question" whether their execution contributes to the "social purposes" of the death penalty, viz., retribution and deterrence. (The Court conveniently ignores a third "social purpose" of the death penalty—incapacitation of dangerous criminals and the consequent prevention of crimes that they may otherwise commit in the future, but never mind; its discussion of even the other two does not bear analysis.) Retribution is not advanced, the argument goes, because the mentally retarded are *no more culpable* than the average murderer, whom we have already held lacks sufficient culpability to warrant the death penalty. Who says so? Is there an established correlation between mental acuity and the ability to conform one's conduct to the law in such a rudimentary matter as murder? Are the mentally retarded really more disposed (and hence more likely) to commit willfully cruel and serious crime than others? In my experience, the opposite is true: being childlike generally suggests innocence rather than brutality.

Assuming, however, that there is a direct connection between diminished intelligence and the inability to refrain from murder, what scientific analysis can possibly show that a mildly retarded individual who commits an exquisite torture-killing is "no more culpable" than the "average" murderer in a holdup-gone-wrong or a domestic dispute? Or a moderately retarded individual who commits a series of 20 exquisite torture-killings? Surely culpability, and deservedness of the most severe retribution, depends not merely (if at all) upon the mental capacity of the criminal (above the level where he is able to distinguish right from wrong) but also upon the depravity of the crime—which is precisely why this sort of question has traditionally been thought answerable not by a categorical rule of the sort the Court today imposes upon all trials, but rather by the sentencer's weighing of the circumstances (both degree of retardation and depravity of crime) in the particular case. The fact that juries continue to sentence mentally retarded offenders to death for extreme crimes shows that society's moral outrage sometimes demands execution of retarded offenders. By what principle of law, science, or logic can the Court pronounce that this is wrong? There is none. Once the Court admits (as it does) that mental retardation does not render the offender morally *blameless*, there is no basis for saying that the death penalty is *never* appropriate retribution, no matter *how* heinous the crime. As long as a mentally retarded offender knows "the difference between right and wrong," only the sentencer can assess whether his retardation reduces his culpability enough to exempt him from the death penalty for the particular murder in question.

As for the other social purpose of the death penalty that the Court discusses, deterrence: That is not advanced, the Court tells us, because the mentally retarded are "less likely" than their non-retarded counterparts to "process the information of the possibility of execution as a penalty and control their conduct based upon that information." Of course this leads to the same conclusion discussed earlier— that the mentally retarded (because they are less deterred) are more likely to kill— which neither I nor the society at large believes. In any event, even the Court does not say that *all* mentally retarded individuals cannot "process the information of the possibility of execution as a penalty and control their conduct based upon that information"; it merely asserts that they are "less likely" to be able to do so. But surely the deterrent effect of a penalty is adequately vindicated if it successfully deters many, but not all, of the target class. Virginia's death penalty, for example, does not fail of its deterrent effect simply because *some* criminals are unaware that Virginia *has* the death penalty.

The Court throws one last factor into its grab bag of reasons why execution of the retarded is "excessive" in all cases: Mentally retarded offenders "face a special risk of wrongful execution." "Special risk" is pretty flabby language (even flabbier than "less likely")—and I suppose a similar "special risk" could be said to exist for just plain stupid people, inarticulate people, even ugly people. If this unsupported claim has any substance to it (which I doubt) it might support a due process claim in all criminal prosecutions of the mentally retarded; but it is hard to see how it has anything to do with an *Eighth Amendment* claim that execution of the mentally retarded is cruel and unusual.

Today's opinion adds one more to the long list of substantive and procedural requirements impeding imposition of the death penalty imposed under this Court's assumed power to invent a death-is-different jurisprudence. None of those requirements existed when the Eighth Amendment was adopted, and some of them were not even supported by current moral consensus. They include prohibition of the death penalty for "ordinary" murder, for rape of an adult woman, and for felony murder absent a showing that the defendant possessed a sufficiently culpable state of mind; prohibition of the death penalty for any person under the age of 16 at the time of the crime; prohibition of the death penalty as the mandatory punishment for any crime; a requirement that the sentencer not be given unguided discretion; a requirement that the sentencer be empowered to take into account all mitigating circumstances; and a requirement that the accused receive a judicial evaluation of his claim of insanity before the sentence can be executed. There is something to be said for popular abolition of the death penalty; there is nothing to be said for its incremental abolition by this Court.

This newest invention promises to be more effective than any of the others in turning the process of capital trial into a game. One need only read the definitions of mental retardation adopted by the AAMR and the APA to realize that the symptoms of this condition can readily be feigned. And whereas the capital defendant who feigns insanity risks commitment to a mental institution until he can be cured (and then tried and executed), the capital defendant who feigns mental retardation risks nothing at all. The mere pendency of the present case has brought us petitions by death row inmates claiming for the first time, after multiple habeas petitions, that they are retarded.

I respectfully dissent.

■ The Mentally Retarded—Perspectives

■ Issue—Should the Mentally Retarded Be Exempt from the Death Penalty?

Human Rights Watch, "Beyond Reason: The Death Penalty and Offenders with Mental Retardation"

Since the death penalty was reinstated in 1976, at least thirty-five people with mental retardation have been executed in the United States. The exact number of people with this disability who are on death row awaiting execution is not known; experts believe there may be two or three hundred. Because of their mental retardation, these men and women cannot understand fully what they did wrong and many cannot even comprehend the punishment that awaits them. While they have the bodies of adults, in crucial ways their mental function is more like that of children.

A few people with mental retardation will commit acts of terrible violence. None, however, is capable of mature, calculated evil. Accountability can be achieved, and public safety protected, without putting offenders with mental retardation to death. Indeed, none of the penological goals set forth by death-penalty proponents requires the execution of offenders with mental retardation.

I. *Mental Retardation: An Overview*

People with mental retardation in the U.S., currently estimated to number between 6.2 and 7.5 million, have historically been victimized both by their disability and by public prejudice and ignorance. Mental retardation is a lifelong condition of impaired or incomplete mental development. According to the most widely used definition of mental retardation, it is characterized by three criteria: significantly subaverage intellectual functioning; concurrent and related limitations in two or more adaptive skill areas; and manifestation before age eighteen.

A. **Subaverage intellectual functioning** Intelligence quotient (I.Q.) tests are designed to measure intellectual functioning. An I.Q. score provides a rough numerical assessment of an individual's present level of mental functioning in comparison with that of others. The vast majority of people in the United States have I.Q.s between 80 and 120, with an I.Q. of 100 considered average. To be diagnosed as having mental retardation, a person must have an I.Q. below 70–75, in the bottom 2 percent of the American population.

Although all persons with mental retardation have significantly impaired mental development, their intellectual level can vary considerably. An estimated 89 percent of all people with retardation have I.Q.s in the 51–70 range. An I.Q. in the 60 to 70 range is approximately the scholastic equivalent to the third grade.

For the lay person or non-specialist, the significance of a low I.Q. is often best communicated through the imprecise but nonetheless descriptive reference to "mental age." When a person is said to have a mental age of six, this means he or she received the same number of correct responses on a standardized I.Q. test as the average six-year-old child.

The threshold I.Q. level for a diagnosis of mental retardation has been progressively lowered over the years, in part because of awareness of the damaging social prejudice suffered by those labeled "retarded." In 1959, the American Association on Mental Deficiency set 85 as the I.Q. below which a person was considered to be retarded. In 1992, the renamed American Association on Mental Retardation lowered the mental retardation "ceiling" to an I.Q. of 70–75, but many mental health specialists argue that people with I.Q.s of up to 80 may also have mental retardation. Flexibility in the I.Q. standard is important because tests given at different times may show slight variations due to differences in the tests and because of testing error.

B. Limitations in adaptive skills Mental retardation entails significant limitations in two or more of the basic skill areas necessary to cope with the requirements of everyday life, e.g., communication, self-care, home living, social skills, community use, self-direction, health and safety, functional academics, leisure, and work. Although there are significant variations among those with mental retardation, in terms of their ability to function and their skill levels, all have significant limitations in their "effectiveness in meeting the standards of maturation, learning, personal independence, and/or social responsibility that are expected for his or her age level and cultural group." For instance, an adult with mental retardation may have trouble driving a car, following directions, participating in hobbies or work of any complexity, or behaving in socially appropriate ways. He or she may have trouble sitting or standing still, or may smile constantly and inappropriately. Limitations in everyday coping skills may be more or less severe, ranging from individuals who can live alone with intermittent support, to individuals who require extensive hands-on assistance and guidance, to individuals who require constant supervision and care. For most people with mental retardation, limited adaptive skills make ordinary life extremely difficult unless a caring family or social support system exists to provide assistance and structure.

Offenders with mental retardation who have been convicted of committing capital crimes typically grew up poor and without networks of special support and services—often without even a supportive, loving family. They functioned as best they could without professional assistance, often required to fend for themselves while still teenagers. If they were able to work, it was at basic menial tasks.

C. Manifestation before the age of eighteen Mental retardation is present from childhood. It can be caused by any condition which impairs development of the brain before, during, or after birth. The causes are numerous: hereditary factors; genetic abnormalities (e.g., Down's syndrome); poor prenatal care; infections during pregnancy; abnormal delivery; illness during infancy; toxic substances (e.g., consumption of alcohol by the pregnant mother; exposure of the child to lead, mercury or other environmental toxins); physical abuse; and malnutrition, among others. Regardless of the cause, part of the definition of mental retardation is that it manifests itself during an individual's developmental period, usually deemed to be birth through age eighteen. Many psychiatrists argue that the age before which signs of retardation must become manifest should be raised from eighteen to twenty-two, to reflect the difficulties in obtaining accurate age records for many people with this disability and the differing rates at which people develop.

An ordinary adult cannot suddenly "become" mentally retarded. An adult may, for reasons related to accident or illness, suffer a catastrophic loss in intellectual functioning and adaptive skills, but this would not make him or her "mentally retarded," since by definition mental retardation starts during childhood. One implication of this is that mental retardation is virtually impossible for an adult to fake: when evaluating whether an adult is mentally retarded, testers look not only at I.Q. test results, but also at school reports, childhood test records, and other evidence that would show whether his or her intellectual and adaptive problems developed during childhood.

With help from family, social workers, teachers, and friends, many mentally retarded people succeed in simple jobs, maintain their own households, marry, and give birth to children of normal intelligence. But, although support and services can improve the life functioning and opportunities for a person with retardation, they cannot cure the condition.

II. *Characteristics and Significance of Mental Retardation*

Although mental retardation of any degree has profound implications for a person's cognitive and social development, it is a condition which in many cases is not readily apparent. While some of the mentally retarded, such as those whose retardation is caused by Down's syndrome or fetal alcohol syndrome, have characteristically distinctive facial features, most cannot be identified by their physical appearance alone. Unless their cognitive impairment is unusually severe (e.g., an I.Q. below 40), persons with mental retardation may be thought of as "slow" but the full extent of their impairment is often not readily appreciated, particularly by people who have limited contact with or knowledge of them. Many capital offenders with mental retardation did not have their condition diagnosed until trial or during post-conviction proceedings.

A person with mental retardation, according to one expert, "is always the least smart person in any group. This leads to fear, dependence and an experience of terrible stigma and devaluation." Since mentally retarded people are often ashamed of their own retardation, they may go to great lengths to hide their retardation, fooling those with no expertise in the subject. They may wrap themselves in a "cloak of competence," hiding their disability even from those who want to help them, including their lawyers.

The fact that many people with mental retardation can and do live relatively "normal" lives with their families or in the community, coupled with the fact that most of them do not look different from people with average intellectual capabilities, can make it difficult for the public to appreciate the significance of their condition. But, as the late Justice Brennan noted, "Every individual who has mental retardation—irrespective of his or her precise capacities or experiences—has a substantial disability in cognitive ability and adaptive behavior." Like all human beings, people with mental retardation deserve to be treated with dignity and respect, and deserve the chance to live lives that are as normal as possible— but they also require special acknowledgment of their vulnerabilities and their mental incapacities.

A person with mental retardation will have limitations of a greater or lesser extent in every aspect of cognitive functioning. Many of these limitations, of course, characterize children. But while children will outgrow these limitations as their brains develop and mature, people with mental retardation will not. In limiting a person's cognitive development and ability to learn, mental retardation also limits the ability to understand abstract concepts, including moral concepts. While most defendants with mental retardation who have committed a crime know they have done something wrong, they often cannot explain why the act was wrong. The inability to comprehend abstract concepts may include the inability to fully understand the meaning of "death" or "murder."

Since they often face abuse, taunts, and rejection because of their low intelligence, people with mental retardation can be desperate for approval and friendship. Eager to be accepted and eager to please, people with mental retardation are characteristically highly suggestible.

Low intelligence and limited adaptive skills also mean that people with mental retardation often miss social "cues" that other adults understand. They may act in ways that seem suspicious, even when they have done nothing wrong. When questioned by police or other authority figures, they often smile inappropriately, fail to remain still when ordered to do so, or act agitated and furtive when they should be calm and polite. Others may fall asleep at the wrong moment.

Many, if not most, of the people with mental retardation convicted of capital murder are doubly and triply disadvantaged. In general, America's prison population is made up disproportionately of poor people, minorities, the mentally ill, and those who were abused as children. Not surprisingly, the mentally retarded people who become enmeshed in the criminal justice system usually share one or more of these characteristics: many of them come from poor families, suffered from severe abuse as children, and/or face mental illness in addition to their retardation.

A history of severe childhood abuse is particularly common among defendants with mental retardation convicted of capital murder. The long-term negative effects of childhood abuse may be even greater for people whose cognitive abilities are impaired and whose ability to navigate in the world is already seriously compromised by mental retardation.

Many capital defendants with mental retardation also suffer from mental illness. Although the two conditions are often confused, they are different disorders. Mental illness almost always includes disturbance of some sort in emotional life; intellectual functioning may be intact, except where thinking breaks with reality (as in hallucinations). A person who is mentally ill can have a very high I.Q., while a mentally retarded person always has a low I.Q. A person who is mentally ill may improve or be cured with therapy or medication, but mental retardation is a permanent state. The percentage of mentally retarded people who are also mentally ill is not known with any certainty; estimates vary from 10 percent to 40 percent. Persons who suffer from both mental illness and mental retardation are particularly disadvantaged in dealing with the criminal justice system because each condition can compound the effects of the other.

III. *Mental Retardation and Criminal Culpability*

An adult with mental retardation who commits a murder should be held legally accountable (assuming the retardation is not so profound as to render him or her incompetent to stand trial). But punishment must be proportionate to both the seriousness of the crime and the defendant's degree of moral culpability.

Although there are different degrees of mental retardation, in all cases the condition entails serious limitations on the ability to appreciate the consequences and gravity of one's actions and to exercise mature control over one's conduct. An offender with mental retardation should thus never be placed in the category of the most culpable offenders for whom the death penalty is ostensibly reserved.

Human Rights Watch believes that the moral indefensibility of executing a child extends equally to someone who, by virtue of his or her retardation, has cognitive abilities and moral comprehension similar to that of a child.

IV. *Mental Retardation and the Purposes of Capital Punishment*

The central purposes of the death penalty, according to its proponents, are retribution, deterrence, and incapacitation. None justifies the execution of persons with mental retardation.

For the goal of retribution to be satisfied, an offender must "deserve" his punishment because he chose to commit a crime and knew what he was doing. Since mental retardation precludes the high moral blameworthiness that is supposed to be a prerequisite of capital punishment, executing an offender with mental retardation cannot be justified as giving him his "just deserts."

Imposing the death penalty on persons with mental retardation is also not necessary to advance the putative goal of deterrence. People with that disability are generally unable to anticipate consequences of their actions and assess their options; there is no basis for believing their eligibility for the death penalty deters their commission of capital crimes. If offenders with mental retardation were excluded from capital punishment, other offenders would still be liable to the death penalty.

Finally, the death penalty is not the only means available to society to incapacitate people who pose a danger to society. Secure confinement of dangerous mentally retarded offenders adequately protects public safety.

Barry Latzer, "Misplaced Compassion: The Mentally Retarded and the Death Penalty"

In spring 2000, two men planned and carried out a grisly robbery murder of a Wendy's fast food restaurant in Flushing, Queens, New York. The pair, who entered the store with a bag containing bullets, masks, duct tape and a gun, forced the terrified employees to lie on their stomachs in a basement freezer. After binding and gagging the victims and covering their heads with plastic garbage bags, they methodically shot seven of them, killing five. We know exactly what happened because one of the shooters, Craig Godineaux, related the ghastly details in open court as a prelude to his plea of guilty. Godineaux, who admitted that he had personally killed three of the employees and wounded two, received life sentences, while his co-perpetrator faces the death penalty.

The sole reason for the different treatment is that New York State law (and now the Federal Constitution) categorically forbid the execution of the mentally retarded and the Queens County District Attorney concluded that Godineaux was retarded. No one suggested that Godineaux was incompetent or incapacitated. His own lawyer said that he fully understood what he had done. Indeed, his chilling account of the crime was detailed and precise, down to his own involvement in its planning and execution.

Atkins and laws like New York's are virtual guarantees of unequal justice. Without an individualized assessment of the effects of Godineaux's retardation on his criminal conduct there is no way to determine if he was morally responsible enough to be given the same punishment as his collaborator. Such a determination requires a weighing of the extent of defendant's impediment and its impact upon the crime against the reprehensibility of the offense—precisely the type of moral judgment that should be left to a jury.

I am aware that to many readers it will probably seem uncharitable if not downright hardhearted to present arguments in favor of the execution of the mentally retarded. How could anyone argue for such an irreversibly harsh punishment for someone with the mind of a six-and-one-half-year-old child?

To this I offer three brief answers. First, I do not favor execution of the mentally retarded unless they are fully responsible for the most heinous of crimes known to the penal law—murder in the first degree with aggravating circumstances. Of course, this begs the question whether such individuals ever can be "fully responsible" for their crimes. I think they can, most of the time, and furthermore, I believe that juries composed of lay persons are quite capable of determining when they can and cannot.

Second, I think that blanket exemptions from the death penalty for all retarded murderers are inconsistent with virtually all other policies for treating the retarded, and what is more, are incompatible with both capital jurisprudence (which requires individually tailored sentences) and fundamental principles of criminal law (which demand punishment in accordance with the offender's moral blameworthiness).

Finally, I believe that the concern for preferential treatment of the retarded may be based on a misunderstanding of mental retardation. Retardation is not a mental illness. Except for a tiny percentage, the retarded are not "crazy." They are not delusional. They are not psychopaths. They are not dangerous or out of control. They are, in the vernacular, "slow," or "dull-witted" or "dumb." Sometimes (approximately 6% of the retarded) they are profoundly or severely disabled, but when this is the case, they will almost certainly be excused for their harmful acts on grounds of legal insanity. Excusal in such cases is appropriate.

What is inappropriate is the assumption that retardation handicaps one to the point at which ordinary criminal punishment becomes inhumane. Indeed, no responsible person or organization (certainly not the AAMR) makes such an argument. To the contrary, organizations to promote the interests of the retarded readily concede that persons with retardation *should* be held responsible for their crimes, just like everyone else. It is only with the sentence of death that they favor an exception, arguing—inconsistently in my view—that capital punishment of the retarded is immoral.

My ultimate response to those who would call my position inhumane, is this: It is not inhumane to impose on morally responsible people constitutionally acceptable punishments that (retributively speaking) "fit" their crimes. I can appreciate the many arguments (though I do not agree with them) that the death penalty is inherently immoral. I cannot appreciate the arguments that it is only (or especially) immoral when applied to otherwise deserving murderers with retardation.

I. The Deathworthiness of the Retarded

The argument against the execution of the retarded has its roots in Justice Brennan's dissent in Penry. Justice Brennan was not saying there that the retarded should never be held responsible for their crimes. Rather, he argued that the moral blameworthiness of such a defendant can never rise to the level required for the imposition of the harshest constitutionally acceptable penalty. In simplest terms, for Brennan, the mentally retarded can never be deathworthy.

On close scrutiny, this position is indefensible. It is completely inconsistent with enlightened contemporary prescriptions for the treatment of the retarded (including Brennan's own), which require case-by-case determinations. Second, it is totally at odds with one of the most fundamental precepts of death penalty jurisprudence—the individualized sentencing requirement. Finally, Brennan's analysis is utterly incompatible with the principle of proportionality because it favors reducing an offender's sentence on the basis of characteristics that are all too often unrelated to culpability, or worse, actually serve to aggravate the crime.

Throughout the first half of the twentieth century the mentally retarded were considered a menace—"a principal source of criminal and immoral behavior." This conclusion—encapsulated in Justice Holmes's notorious "three generations of imbeciles" aphorism—was founded on crude generalizations about the effects of mental disorders. By the 1960s, these views had come to be considered an embarrassment. Sympathy for the mentally incapacitated led to a "general movement toward fuller recognition of the rights of retarded people in all areas of American law." Gross (and inaccurate) generalizations were replaced by more refined assessments which differentiated retardation from mental illness, and recognized differences among the retarded in terms of the extent of the disability.

A major thrust of the more enlightened approach to retardation prevalent since the 1950s has been to individualize treatment rather than prescribe broad measures for all persons with retardation. For instance, the federal Education of the Handicapped Act, which specifically included the mentally retarded in its definition of handicapped, requires that school authorities devise an "individualized educational program" that is "tailored to the unique needs of the handicapped child." Brennan's proposal, though intended to help the retarded by immunizing them from harsh punishment, must be seen in the light of these developments. It is nothing if not paternalistic, and despite its beneficent aims, is a throwback to an earlier era.

One cannot help but contrast Brennan's sensitivity to paternalistic legislation involving women, which he decried for "putting women, not on a pedestal, but in a cage." Sex discrimination laws also were based on gross generalizations about group incapacities and were likewise designed to "protect" the vulnerable class from such activities as unhealthful working conditions. How far a cry is it from laws meliorating the punishment of all retarded capital murderers to laws keeping retarded persons from, e.g., entering into risky contracts? Does society really want a legal precedent that treats all mentally retarded defendants as less than fully responsible?

A proper analysis of the moral culpability—more precisely, the deathworthiness—of a mentally retarded murderer requires a close examination of the effects of retardation. To accomplish this, we will rely on the work of James W. Ellis and Ruth A. Luckasson. Their oft-cited article, "Mentally Retarded Criminal Defendants," provides an overview of issues involving the retarded defendant in criminal cases. This article was published three years before the Penry decision and was not colored by the authors' views on the death penalty. Ellis and Luckasson enumerated six deficiencies of people with retardation: communication and memory, impulsivity and attention, moral development, denial of disability, lack of knowledge of basic facts, and motivation. This list was accompanied by a warning against judgments in gross.

> *Mentally retarded people are individuals. Any attempt to describe them as a group risks false stereotyping and therefore demands the greatest caution. Nevertheless, some characteristics occur with sufficient frequency to warrant certain limited generalizations. Several of these traits have important implications for the criminal justice system, and therefore merit close attention to determine if they exist in an individual criminal case.*

Note that the authors do not say that the six listed characteristics are invariably present in a retarded defendant, but rather, that *individualized* assessment is required "to determine if they exist." This point cannot be overstated: if Ellis and Luckasson are correct, it would be wrong to base policy on the assumption that these traits are always or nearly always present among retarded defendants. With this in mind, I now examine the six characteristics in order to explore the impact each might have on the deathworthiness of a murderer with retardation.

First are communication and memory problems. According to Ellis and Luckasson, "many mentally retarded people have limited communication skills. Therefore, it would not be unusual for a mentally retarded individual to be unresponsive to a police officer or other authority or to be able to provide only garbled or confused responses when questioned."

These particular deficiencies are unlikely to significantly affect deathworthiness. In the early stages of a case, they may make investigators inappropriately suspicious about a retarded interviewee. At trial, such a defendant may make a poor witness. His lawyer may also find it difficult to communicate with him. These are legitimate concerns for the guilt-determination process, but assuming, as we do, that guilt was correctly determined, defects in communication skills and memory are not relevant to the appropriateness of a death sentence.

By contrast, the second characteristic of the retarded—deficits in attention or impulse control—is likely to be relevant to sentencing. However, impulsiveness might not be a characteristic of a particular retarded defendant. Even if it were, the circumstances of the offense might not offer an opportunity for such a trait to play itself out. Some retarded defendants plan their crimes. Some act alone. Without examining the facts of each case, there simply is no way to determine whether impulsiveness caused by retardation was a significant factor in a homicide. Conceding that retardation may make a murderer nondeathworthy, there is no good reason to go further and conclude that it must or even that it invariably will.

Factor three, the lack of moral development of the retarded, *sounds* relevant to deathworthiness—until one grasps its meaning. Lack of moral development means (according to Ellis and Luckasson) a propensity to assign blame or to assume it for oneself where nonretarded people would not because elements of blameworthiness (e.g., that the party held responsible was the harm-causing agent) are absent. Of course, the propensity to take the blame may lead to a false confession and a miscarriage of justice, but as with communication deficiencies, such a shortcoming is relevant to a proper determination of guilt or innocence, not to the selection of sentence for a concededly guilty party. If the retarded individual did in fact perform the criminal act, it is hard to see how his moral immaturity in the Ellis and Luckasson sense is relevant to deathworthiness.

The fourth factor—denial of disability—and the fifth—lack of knowledge of basic facts—are, at best, indirectly related to sentencing. The last factor in the Ellis and Luckasson list is "motivation." One could easily envision a retarded person—especially one with poor impulse control—engaging in criminal acts at the suggestion of a third party—acts that a nonretarded person would avoid. Thus, even if he were responsible enough to be adjudged guilty of the homicide, his unusual gullibility, due to his mental deficiency, might well lead a jury to spare his life when imposing sentence. Once again, however, this requires a case-specific assessment. Was the defendant so impaired that even a suggestion that he kill someone seemed to him perfectly acceptable? This simply cannot be answered on the basis of abstract profiles of the mentally retarded. For one thing, as I have already pointed out, there may not have been a third party.

My conclusion is that:

1. the characteristics reported by Ellis and Luckasson may or may not be present in any particular individual with retardation, and if present, will vary considerably in their impact on the conduct of the actor;

2. assuming that they are present in, and are significant to, the behavior of the actor in question, the importance of these characteristics in the commission of a particular crime also varies with the actor and the peculiar circumstances of the incident; and

3. the matters in points one and two ought to be determined on a case-by-case basis by, and lie within the competence of, lay jurors.

II. Deterrence and Retribution

It seems especially difficult to defend the proposition that a death sentence for a retarded murderer can never be just, no matter how mild the impairment and how heinous the crime. A simple hypothetical will show the weakness of this position.

Imagine that Timothy McVeigh, notorious for murdering 168 people by bombing a federal office building, had mild retardation. Would it be proper to conclude that the death penalty was not appropriate in his case without assessing the actual effects of his impairment in light of the magnitude of the harms? If this seems to be loading the dice because of the unique atrociousness of McVeigh's crime, consider Penry's case instead. While on parole after a rape conviction, Penry, who was mildly to moderately retarded, entered the home of the victim, a young woman, brutally raped and beat her and stabbed her to death with a pair of scissors. Unless one is absolutely opposed to capital punishment in all cases, it is arbitrary to assert, without knowing more about his infirmity and its relationship to the crime, that Penry does not deserve a death sentence. I do not say that death would be just deserts for Penry; I say only that the sentence is properly a matter for the sentencing authority, and that the range of sentencing options—including death—should not be arbitrarily restricted.

With respect to deterrence, this is an empirical question and there is no proof that the less severely retarded (89 percent of all retarded persons) do not understand or fear death any more than there is proof that they do not fear imprisonment, a sanction all sides agree should continue to be applied to retarded offenders.

Nor do I agree that the execution of the retarded will have no effect on the deterrence of nonretarded offenders. Because of present-day societal sympathy for the retarded (undoubtedly mixed with fear and misunderstanding), the execution of the retarded might reinforce the impression that society forcefully condemns heinous murders.

III. Conclusion

The deathworthiness of a mentally retarded defendant should be a matter of individualized moral judgment not constitutional or legislative fiat. If the retarded individual is held fully responsible for his misdeeds *short* of capital murder, why should he be exempt from full punishment for the most egregious of offenses known to society? It is illogical to hold the retarded fully punishable for all crimes except the most reprehensible. Nor is there any sound reason to believe that juries are incapable of accurately assessing the deathworthiness of retarded murderers. The moral difficulties in such cases are no greater than in many other death penalty prosecutions. What is morally indefensible is the trend toward immunizing the mentally retarded criminal from capital punishment without regard to his deathworthiness.

The Insane

■ The Insane—Introduction

The insane present a special case from the standpoint of every recognized purpose of criminal punishment but one: the truly insane are impossible to deter. They cannot be taught a lesson for the purpose of specific deterrence; it is doubtful whether punishing the insane sends a useful message to others. For retributivists, it is difficult to argue that the deranged deserve to be punished because desert is premised upon free will, which is not present with the insane or present in a markedly different way. The only commonality with the sane criminal is the need for incapacitation. On the premise that the insane present a special case, there is unanimous agreement. Each of the states and the federal government recognizes some version of the insanity defense.

Every state and the federal government also bars the execution of a condemned prisoner who is in good mind at the time of the crime but subsequently becomes insane. This is a unique situation. If a condemned person were insane at the time of his offense he would have been found not guilty by reason of insanity. If he were insane at the time of trial, he would have been found incompetent to stand trial because he could not participate in his defense. Here, the condemned is rational at the time of the crime and trial, but subsequently becomes insane.

There is unanimity that the insane should not be executed, but in the case of criminals who are sane at the time of the offense, the policy arguments against execution on the basis of subsequent insanity are not as clear. Most religious teachings militate against dispatching an offender "into another world, when he is not of a capacity to fit himself for it." From the standpoint of specific deterrence there is little reason to carry out the sentence as the insane cannot be taught any further lesson. However, one might argue that there is a general deterrence benefit to carrying out the sentence. Failing to execute might contribute to a perception that the state is not serious about carrying out sentences. This effect is surely minimal. Deterrence theory presumes rationality on the part of the criminal. The thought would have to be that the potential criminal makes the marginal decision to commit a crime based on the chance that he will be caught, tried, and convicted, but that the sentence will never be carried out because the court concludes that he is insane—mistakenly, he hopes; otherwise, the criminal will enjoy very little benefit indeed.

The truly problematic question is whether criminals who become insane after trial deserve to be punished. The requirements of retribution are not obvious. Consider the hypothetical and strange case of Llewelyn, sentenced by a jury to die for the brutal murder and rape of a teenage girl. On the way out of the courtroom, an anvil falls on Llewelyn's head. He falls into a coma for thirty years. When Llewelyn awakens, he is sweet and docile, a changed man. When told of his crimes by his doctors, Llewelyn is horrified. He has no recollection of the crime; in his changed state he does not seem capable of such a violent act. The doctors testify that the anvil has miraculously corrected organic damage to Llewelyn's brain. Whereas before he had frontal lobe damage that limited his impulse control, now he is able to comport himself according to society's demands. Fit for execution, prison officials arrive to take Llewelyn from the hospital to the electric chair. His lawyers appeal for clemency. The governor wonders whether it is just to execute Llewelyn.

On one view, retribution demands that he be executed. It is Llewelyn who committed the murder; therefore, he should be held accountable. But the philosopher Derek Parfit argues that it makes as much sense to execute the reformed Llewelyn as it would to execute Llewelyn's son for his father's crimes. The reformed Llewelyn is essentially a new man. We have all done things as teenagers that we would never do again as adults and would feel rather put upon if we were forced to answer for them today. So it is with Llewelyn. Who counts in the calculation of desert—the offender as constituted at the time of offense or at the time the sentence is carried out?

The Supreme Court has offered different answers in different contexts. In *Skipper v. South Carolina*, the Supreme Court held that, under *Lockett*, a defendant must be allowed to present evidence of his adjustment to prison, even though this behavior is after the fact of his offense. In *Evans v. Muncy*, on the other hand, the Court let stand the denial of *habeas* relief to the petitioner, sentenced to die on the basis of a future dangerousness aggravator, who later helped to stop a prison riot and by all accounts saved the lives of several guards. These inconsistencies are discussed at greater length on the subject of symmetry and victim impact evidence in Chapter 16.

Yet, every state has implicitly taken the view that, at least as far as subsequent insanity is concerned, what counts is the condition of the offender at the time the sentence is carried out and that punishment is not deserved by the insane. In *Ford v. Wainwright*, excerpted in the Critical Documents section of this chapter, the Supreme Court found that contemporary standards of decency do not tolerate the execution of the insane. The Court applied the traditional *Coker* test. In this instance the evidence was overwhelming—no state allowed for the execution of the insane.

Why then was there a case at all? If no state would tolerate the execution of the insane, why was Ford forced to appeal to the Supreme Court to stay his execution? While no state tolerates the execution of the insane by statute and practice and, after *Ford*, by constitutional mandate, it remains for the individual state to determine the process by which insanity is judged. Florida allowed sanity to be determined through a nonadversarial process entirely within the executive branch. The Court favorably cited the procedures used in determining competency to stand trial and in involuntary commitment proceedings, but it did not articulate the precise procedures to be followed.

The amount of process guaranteed a defendant claiming insanity remains unclear. In *Lowenfeld v. Butler*, a 1988 case, the Supreme Court declined to stay Lowenfeld's execution, though he had submitted the affidavit of a clinical psychologist who believed it highly probable that Lowenfeld suffered from paranoid schizophrenia. The majority did not publish an opinion. The implication of the decision may be that the defendant had a constitutional right to a fair adjudication of insanity, not to be free from execution if actually insane. This may seem peculiar, but it parallels the Court's approach to dealing with residual questions of innocence as discussed in Chapter 20. In *Herrera v. Collins*, the Supreme Court places greater emphasis on the process by which guilt and innocence are judged rather than actual innocence. This is problematic, especially from a retributive standpoint if it allows undeserving people to be punished, but it has some obvious practical appeal. Only God knows whether a defendant is truly innocent or insane—the best that can be done in the corporeal world is to ensure a fair adjudication.

Another question, and the subject of the debate below, is whether an insane defendant can be compulsorily medicated in order to be made competent for execution. It is a vicious dilemma for the defendant—or the defendant's attorney—when the defendant must either voluntarily take medication and facilitate his own execution or refuse the medication and remain insane.

Outside the realm of capital punishment, the Supreme Court has held that a defendant may be treated with antipsychotic drugs against his will if the prisoner has been found to be dangerous to himself or others and if the treatment is determined to be in the prisoner's medical interest. State and federal courts have split in determining whether *Washington v. Harper* allows the medication of prisoners for the purpose of execution. In *Perry v. Louisiana*, the Louisiana Supreme Court found that, under the Louisiana state constitution, it is unconstitutional to force a defendant to take medication so that he can be executed. The Eighth Circuit Court of Appeals, however, allowed Arkansas officials to force Charles Singleton to take drugs to make him sane enough to be executed. In October 2003, the Supreme Court let that ruling stand, declining to grant *certiorari* in Singleton's case.

Below, Charles Ewing argues that any participation by physicians in the capital punishment process is antithetical to their professional obligation. Barry Latzer contends that whether an execution ultimately occurs is a matter of speculation—there is the possibility of an appeal or clemency, The relevant consideration for the physician, he says, is whether his assistance diminishes the immediate suffering of the patient.

■ The Insane—Critical Documents

Ford v. Wainwright
477 U.S. 399 (1986)

Mr. Justice Marshall announced the judgment of the Court and delivered the opinion of the Court with respect to Parts I and II and an opinion with respect

to Parts III, IV, and V, in which Justice Brennan, Justice Blackmun, and Justice Stevens join.

For centuries no jurisdiction has countenanced the execution of the insane, yet this Court has never decided whether the Constitution forbids the practice. Today we keep faith with our common-law heritage in holding that it does.

I

Alvin Bernard Ford was convicted of murder in 1974 and sentenced to death. There is no suggestion that he was incompetent at the time of his offense, at trial, or at sentencing. In early 1982, however, Ford began to manifest gradual changes in behavior. They began as an occasional peculiar idea or confused perception, but became more serious over time. After reading in the newspaper that the Ku Klux Klan had held a rally in nearby Jacksonville, Florida, Ford developed an obsession focused upon the Klan. His letters to various people reveal endless brooding about his "Klan work," and an increasingly pervasive delusion that he had become the target of a complex conspiracy, involving the Klan and assorted others, designed to force him to commit suicide. He believed that the prison guards, part of the conspiracy, had been killing people and putting the bodies in the concrete enclosures used for beds. Later, he began to believe that his women relatives were being tortured and sexually abused somewhere in the prison. This notion developed into a delusion that the people who were tormenting him at the prison had taken members of Ford's family hostage. The hostage delusion took firm hold and expanded, until Ford was reporting that 135 of his friends and family were being held hostage in the prison, and that only he could help them. By "day 287" of the "hostage crisis," the list of hostages had expanded to include "senators, Senator Kennedy, and many other leaders." In a letter to the Attorney General of Florida, written in 1983, Ford appeared to assume authority for ending the "crisis," claiming to have fired a number of prison officials. He began to refer to himself as "Pope John Paul, III," and reported having appointed nine new justices to the Florida Supreme Court.

Counsel for Ford asked a psychiatrist who had examined Ford earlier, Dr. Jamal Amin, to continue seeing him and to recommend appropriate treatment. On the basis of roughly 14 months of evaluation, taped conversations between Ford and his attorneys, letters written by Ford, interviews with Ford's acquaintances, and various medical records, Dr. Amin concluded in 1983 that Ford suffered from "a severe, uncontrollable, mental disease which closely resembles 'Paranoid Schizophrenia With Suicide Potential' "—a "major mental disorder severe enough to substantially affect Mr. Ford's present ability to assist in the defense of his life."

Ford subsequently refused to see Dr. Amin again, believing him to have joined the conspiracy against him, and Ford's counsel sought assistance from Dr. Harold Kaufman, who interviewed Ford in November 1983. Ford told Dr. Kaufman that "I know there is some sort of death penalty, but I'm free to go whenever I want because it would be illegal and the executioner would be executed." When asked if he would be executed, Ford replied: "I can't be executed because of the landmark case. I won. *Ford v. State* will prevent executions all over." These statements appeared amidst long streams of seemingly unrelated thoughts in rapid succession. Dr. Kaufman concluded that Ford had no understanding of why he was being executed, made no connection between the homicide of which he had been convicted and the death penalty, and indeed sincerely believed that he would not be executed because he owned the prisons and could control the Governor through mind waves. Dr. Kaufman found that there was "no reasonable possibility that Mr. Ford was dissembling, malingering or otherwise putting on a performance." The following month, in an interview with his attorneys, Ford regressed further into nearly complete incomprehensibility, speaking only in a code characterized by intermittent use of the word "one," making statements such as "Hands one, face one. Mafia one. God one, father one, Pope one. Pope one. Leader one."

Counsel for Ford invoked the procedures of Florida law governing the determination of competency of a condemned inmate. Following the procedures set forth in the statute, the Governor of Florida appointed a panel of three psychiatrists to evaluate whether Ford had "the mental capacity to understand the nature of the death penalty and the reasons why it was imposed upon him." At a single meeting, the three psychiatrists together interviewed Ford for approximately 30 minutes. One doctor concluded that Ford suffered from "psychosis with paranoia" but had "enough cognitive functioning to understand the nature and the effects of the death penalty, and why it is to be imposed on him." Another found that, although Ford was "psychotic," he did "know fully what can happen to him." The third concluded that Ford had a "severe adaptational disorder," but did "comprehend his total situation including being sentenced to death, and all of the implications of that penalty." He believed that Ford's disorder, "although severe, seemed contrived and recently learned." The interview produced three different diagnoses, but accord on the question of sanity as defined by state law.

This Court granted Ford's petition for certiorari in order to resolve the important issue whether the Eighth Amendment prohibits the execution of the insane.

II

A

We begin with the common law. The bar against executing a prisoner who has lost his sanity bears impressive historical credentials; the practice consistently has been branded "savage and inhuman." Blackstone explained:

> *Idiots and lunatics are not chargeable for their own acts, if committed when under these incapacities: no, not even for treason itself. Also, if a man in his sound memory commits a capital offence, and before arraignment for it he becomes mad, he ought not to be arraigned for it: because he is not able to plead to it with that advice and caution that he ought. And if, after he has pleaded, the prisoner becomes mad, he shall not be tried: for how can he make his defence? If, after he be tried and found guilty, he loses his senses before judgment, judgment shall not be pronounced; and if, after judgment, he becomes of nonsane memory, execution shall be stayed: for peradventure, says the humanity of the English law, had the prisoner been of*

*sound memory, he might have alleged something in stay of judgment
or execution.*

As is often true of common-law principles, the reasons for the rule are less
sure and less uniform than the rule itself. One explanation is that the execution
of an insane person simply offends humanity; another, that it provides no example to others and thus contributes nothing to whatever deterrence value is
intended to be served by capital punishment. Other commentators postulate religious underpinnings: that it is uncharitable to dispatch an offender "into another world, when he is not of a capacity to fit himself for it." It is also said that
execution serves no purpose in these cases because madness is its own punishment: *furiosus solo furore punitur*. More recent commentators opine that the community's quest for "retribution"—the need to offset a criminal act by a punishment
of equivalent "moral quality"—is not served by execution of an insane person,
which has a "lesser value" than that of the crime for which he is to be punished.
Unanimity of rationale, therefore, we do not find. "But whatever the reason of the
law is, it is plain the law is so." We know of virtually no authority condoning the
execution of the insane at English common law.

Further indications suggest that this solid proscription was carried to America,
where it was early observed that "the judge is bound" to stay the execution
upon insanity of the prisoner.

B

This ancestral legacy has not outlived its time. Today, no State in the Union
permits the execution of the insane. It is clear that the ancient and humane limitation upon the State's ability to execute its sentences has as firm a hold upon the
jurisprudence of today as it had centuries ago in England. The various reasons
put forth in support of the common-law restriction have no less logical, moral,
and practical force than they did when first voiced. For today, no less than before, we may seriously question the retributive value of executing a person who
has no comprehension of why he has been singled out and stripped of his fundamental right to life. Similarly, the natural abhorrence civilized societies feel at
killing one who has no capacity to come to grips with his own conscience or deity is still vivid today. And the intuition that such an execution simply offends
humanity is evidently shared across this Nation. Faced with such widespread
evidence of a restriction upon sovereign power, this Court is compelled to conclude that the Eighth Amendment prohibits a State from carrying out a sentence
of death upon a prisoner who is insane. Whether its aim be to protect the condemned from fear and pain without comfort of understanding, or to protect the
dignity of society itself from the barbarity of exacting mindless vengeance, the restriction finds enforcement in the Eighth Amendment.

V

[The Court deemed Florida's non-adversarial procedure for determining insanity unsatisfactory.] We do not here suggest that only a full trial on the issue

of sanity will suffice to protect the federal interests; we leave to the State the task of developing appropriate ways to enforce the constitutional restriction upon its execution of sentences. It may be that some high threshold showing on behalf of the prisoner will be found a necessary means to control the number of nonmeritorious or repetitive claims of insanity.

Yet the lodestar of any effort to devise a procedure must be the overriding dual imperative of providing redress for those with substantial claims and of encouraging accuracy in the factfinding determination. The stakes are high, and the "evidence" will always be imprecise. It is all the more important that the adversary presentation of relevant information be as unrestricted as possible. Also essential is that the manner of selecting and using the experts responsible for producing that "evidence" be conducive to the formation of neutral, sound, and professional judgments as to the prisoner's ability to comprehend the nature of the penalty. Fidelity to these principles is the solemn obligation of a civilized society.

The judgment of the Court of Appeals is reversed, and the case is remanded for further proceedings consistent with this opinion.

Justice Powell, concurring in part and concurring in the judgment.

The more general concern of the common law—that executions of the insane are simply cruel—retains its vitality. It is as true today as when Coker lived that most men and women value the opportunity to prepare, mentally and spiritually, for their death. Moreover, today as at common law, one of the death penalty's critical justifications, its retributive force, depends on the defendant's awareness of the penalty's existence and purpose. Thus, it remains true that executions of the insane both impose a uniquely cruel penalty and are inconsistent with one of the chief purposes of executions generally. For precisely these reasons, Florida requires the Governor to stay executions of those who "do not have the mental capacity to understand the nature of the death penalty and why it was imposed" on them.

Such a standard appropriately defines the kind of mental deficiency that should trigger the Eighth Amendment prohibition. If the defendant perceives the connection between his crime and his punishment, the retributive goal of the criminal law is satisfied. And only if the defendant is aware that his death is approaching can he prepare himself for his passing. Accordingly, I would hold that the Eighth Amendment forbids the execution only of those who are unaware of the punishment they are about to suffer and why they are to suffer it.

Petitioner's claim of insanity plainly fits within this standard. According to petitioner's proffered psychiatric examination, petitioner does not know that he is to be executed, but rather believes that the death penalty has been invalidated. The question in this case is whether Florida's procedures for determining petitioner's sanity comport with the requirements of due process. I would hold that they do not.

Justice O'Connor, with whom Justice White joins, concurring in the result in part and dissenting in part.

I am in full agreement with Justice Rehnquist's conclusion that the Eighth Amendment does not create a substantive right not to be executed while insane.

Accordingly, I do not join the Court's reasoning or opinion. Because, however, the conclusion is for me inescapable that Florida positive law has created a protected liberty interest in avoiding execution while incompetent, and because Florida does not provide even those minimal procedural protections required by due process in this area, I would vacate the judgment and remand to the Court of Appeals with directions that the case be returned to the Florida system so that a hearing can be held in a manner consistent with the requirements of the Due Process Clause. I cannot agree, however, that the federal courts should have any role whatever in the substantive determination of a defendant's competency to be executed.

I believe that one aspect of the Florida procedure for determining competency to be executed renders that procedure constitutionally deficient. If there is one "fundamental requisite" of due process, it is that an individual is entitled to an "opportunity to be heard." As currently implemented, the Florida procedure for determining competency violates this bedrock principle.

Because Florida's procedures are inadequate to satisfy even the minimal requirements of due process in this context, I would vacate the judgment below with instructions that the case be returned to Florida so that it might assess petitioner's competency in a manner that accords with the command of the Fourteenth Amendment.

Justice Rehnquist, with whom the Chief Justice joins, dissenting.

The Court today holds that the Eighth Amendment prohibits a State from carrying out a lawfully imposed sentence of death upon a person who is currently insane. This holding is based almost entirely on two unremarkable observations. First, the Court states that it "knows of virtually no authority condoning the execution of the insane at English common law." Second, it notes that "today, no State in the Union permits the execution of the insane." Armed with these facts, and shielded by the claim that it is simply "keeping faith with our common-law heritage," the Court proceeds to cast aside settled precedent and to significantly alter both the common-law and current practice of not executing the insane. It manages this feat by carefully ignoring the fact that the Florida scheme it finds unconstitutional, in which the Governor is assigned the ultimate responsibility of deciding whether a condemned prisoner is currently insane, is fully consistent with the "common-law heritage" and current practice on which the Court purports to rely.

The Court places great weight on the "impressive historical credentials" of the common-law bar against executing a prisoner who has lost his sanity. What it fails to mention, however, is the equally important and unchallenged fact that at common law it was the *executive* who passed upon the sanity of the condemned. So when the Court today creates a constitutional right to a determination of sanity outside of the executive branch, it does so not in keeping with but at the expense of "our common-law heritage."

Creating a constitutional right to a judicial determination of sanity before that sentence may be carried out, whether through the Eighth Amendment or the Due Process Clause, needlessly complicates and postpones still further any finality in this area of the law. The defendant has already had a full trial on the issue of guilt, and a trial on the issue of penalty; the requirement of still a third adjudication offers an invitation to those who have nothing to lose by accepting it to advance entirely spurious claims of insanity. A claim of insanity may be made at any time before sentence and, once rejected, may be raised again; a prisoner found sane two days before execution might claim to have lost his sanity the next day, thus necessitating another judicial determination of his sanity and presumably another stay of his execution.

Since no State sanctions execution of the insane, the real battle being fought in this case is over what procedures must accompany the inquiry into sanity. The Court reaches the result it does by examining the common law, creating a constitutional right that no State seeks to violate, and then concluding that the common-law procedures are inadequate to protect the newly created but common-law based right. I find it unnecessary to "constitutionalize" the already uniform view that the insane should not be executed, and inappropriate to "selectively incorporate" the common-law practice. I therefore dissent.

■ The Insane—Perspectives

■ Issue—Is it Ethical to Medicate the Insane for the Purpose of Execution?

Charles Patrick Ewing, "Diagnosing and Treating 'Insanity' on Death Row: Legal and Ethical Perspectives"

The Supreme Court's decision in *Ford* clearly heightens the procedural protections afforded the condemned inmate who claims to be insane and thus not fit for execution. No longer can such a claim be adjudicated solely on the basis of the unchallenged conclusions of the State's mental health experts. The conclusions of psychologists and psychiatrists regarding an inmate's sanity can and undoubtedly will be challenged in some legal forum. Otherwise, however, *Ford* will have little if any impact upon the roles currently played by these mental health professionals in this phase of the death penalty process. The legal, now constitutionally mandated, rule banning execution of the insane will continue to demand the participation of psychologists and psychiatrists in at least two ethically questionable roles—one diagnostic, the other therapeutic.

First, wherever sufficient doubt is raised regarding a convicted capital defendant's sanity, these mental health professionals will be called upon to evaluate the prisoner's mental functioning and to report their conclusions to the governmental officer or body charged with making the ultimate decision. Moreover, psychologists and psychiatrists will be called upon to help determine whether and when an insane convicted capital defendant has been restored to sanity and is thus legally fit to be executed. Second, psychologists and psychiatrists will be called upon to provide treatment for those condemned inmates found to be insane and thus unfit for execution. The goal of such treatment, of course, will be to restore the sanity of these inmates, thus rendering them fit for execution.

Can psychologists and psychiatrists fulfill these roles and, at the same time, meet their professional ethical obligations?

I. The "Diagnostic" Role Psychologists and psychiatrists who accept this role agree to help decide whether a condemned inmate is to live or die. Of course, they might argue that their conclusions with regard to an inmate's sanity do not seal the inmate's fate. Usually, a panel of mental health professionals is asked to evaluate the inmate and the ultimate determination always rests with a legal, rather than psychological or psychiatric decision-maker. Additionally, under *Ford*, the conclusions reached by psychologists and psychiatrists regarding the inmate's "sanity" will be subject to challenge and the inmate will be able to present evidence which might contradict those conclusions.

As a practical matter, however, the conclusions of psychologists and psychiatrists will carry significant weight. Indeed, if their conclusions are in accord with those reached by other colleagues who have examined the inmate, for all practical purposes the decision will be made by the examining mental health professionals. In some instances, psychologists and psychiatrists may conclude that the condemned inmate is insane and thus spare him or her from execution, at least temporarily. In other instances, however, they will conclude that the condemned inmate is "sane" and thus participate in a process which paves the way for the inmate's death. If they do their jobs honestly and objectively, psychologists and psychiatrists who participate in this function have no way of telling in advance what, if any, conclusions they will reach.

The ethical objection to such participation seems clear. Psychiatry and clinical psychology are, above all else, healing professions. From the ancient Hippocratic Oath ("The health of my patient will be my primary preoccupation") to the Principles of Medical Ethics adopted by the American Medical Association (AMA) and endorsed by the American Psychiatric Association, physicians consistently have professed their primary commitment to healing and the preservation of life. As the AMA has put it, a physician is a "member of a profession dedicated to preserving life where there is hope of doing so." Clinical psychology, though not a branch of medicine, is similarly devoted to healing and the relief of human suffering. According to the American Psychological Association, provision of clinical psychological services involves "the application of principles, methods, and procedures for understanding, predicting, and alleviating intellectual, emotional, psychological, and behavioral disability and discomfort."

To render a clinical judgment which has the practical effect of authorizing the execution of a convicted capital defendant is clearly contrary to the fundamental ethical commitments of psychology and psychiatry to healing and the relief of human suffering.

II. The Therapeutic Role Unlike the diagnostic role, the therapeutic role seems to involve professional practice arguably consistent with the ethical commitment of psychiatrists and psychologists to healing and the relief of suffering. Psychologists and psychiatrists who accept this role provide therapeutic services aimed at restoring the condemned inmate's mental health.

Beyond the first glance, however, it seems clear that assumption of the therapeutic role in this unique psycholegal context also violates the fundamental ethical principles of these healing professions. The ultimate purpose of providing psychological or psychiatric treatment of the "insane" condemned inmate is not to heal or relieve the suffering of that inmate, but to enable the state to take the inmate's life. If such treatment is successful, the end result will be the inmate's death. Professional acts that facilitate such a result are clearly incompatible with "preserving life where there is hope of doing so."

It must be recognized, of course, that refusal to provide psychological or psychiatric treatment to an "insane" condemned inmate also raises ethical and legal questions. As a legal matter, all penal inmates are entitled to necessary psychiatric and psychological treatment, and prison psychologists and psychiatrists have a legal if not ethical duty to provide such treatment. Thus, in this unique context, it would appear that these mental health professionals are caught between a rock and a hard place. Whether they refuse or agree to treat an insane condemned inmate, they would seem to betray their professional ethical commitment to healing practice. Moreover, if they refuse to treat such an inmate, they arguably violate the law.

From a legal perspective, the dilemma posed for these psychologists and psychiatrists seems susceptible to rather easy resolution. As state-licensed health care professionals, psychologists and psychiatrists are required by law to adhere to the ethical principles of their respective professions. The state, as both licensing authority and employer, cannot have it both ways. The state cannot, on the one hand, demand that these professionals practice ethically and yet, on the other hand, require them to engage in unethical practice.

As a purely ethical matter, the dilemma faced by psychologists and psychiatrists in this context may seem somewhat more troubling. In fact, however, this ethical dilemma is more apparent than real. Denying treatment to an insane condemned inmate may have the effect of prolonging the inmate's psychopathology and mental suffering, thus arguably violating the ethical norm of healing. Yet providing treatment may well lead to his or her death. The ultimate purpose in treating the insane condemned inmate is not to heal the inmate, but to enable the state to take his or her life.

A significant, if not the most significant, component of the ethical commitment to healing practice lies in the imperative to "preserve life where there is hope of doing so." Only an absolutist would invoke this imperative without qualification. There are of course, instances in which passive or even active euthanasia might be regarded as ethically appropriate. But where the healing professional's choice is between providing treatment which relieves psychological suffering but results in the death of an otherwise healthy human being, and refusing to provide such treatment, there can be little if any doubt that the latter course of (in)action is the ethically proper one.

III. *Conclusion* Psychologists and psychiatrists who participate in these legal functions violate the fundamental ethical norms of the healing professions to which they belong. Moreover, they do so for no good reason. The humanitarian motive advanced by laws forbidding execution of the presently insane is laudable, but that motive would be no less well-served were psychologists and psychiatrists to boycott these functions altogether.

The diagnostic function referred to earlier is a legal rather than psychological or psychiatric one. Psychological and psychiatric input, though generally desired by those who make and enforce these laws, is not essential. The decision regarding an inmate's insanity in this particular context could be made just as well—if not better—on the basis of lay evidence provided by those who know the inmate best and have had the greatest opportunity to observe him or her over time. Such a process might require greater procedural safeguards than those mandated by the Supreme Court. But given what is at stake, a heightened concern with due process in this context hardly seems unreasonable.

The "treatment" function now performed by psychologists and psychiatrists in this context is likewise not essential. In Great Britain, the law provides that once found to be presently insane, a condemned inmate is "exempted from execution altogether." If all American psychologists and psychiatrists refused to treat presently insane, condemned inmates until they were exempted from execution, the same humanitarian instinct that underlies the ban on executing the insane might well lead American legislatures to follow the example set by the British.

Ideally, psychologists and psychiatrists should voluntarily and individually relinquish both of these ethically objectionable roles.

Barry Latzer, "Between Madness and Death: The Medicate-to-Execute Controversy"

I. Introduction The evidence is overwhelming that Charles Laverne Singleton stabbed a grocery clerk to death in the course of a robbery. The victim knew him. She told the police officer who first arrived at the bloody scene, as well as the physician who unsuccessfully treated her, that Charles Singleton "came in the store, said this is a robbery, grabbed her around the neck, and went to stabbing her." Singleton was convicted and sentenced to death for the murder. Many years later (far too many), the Eighth Circuit Court of Appeals resolved an intriguing legal issue raised by this sad and deceptively simple case. May the state compel a mentally ill death row inmate to take medicine for his disorder where the beneficial effects of the treatment also make him sane enough to be executed?

For most of his time on death row, Charles Singleton has been taking psychotropic medication. It was first prescribed for anxiety and depression, but when, in 1987, Singleton's mental health began to deteriorate, he was medicated—sometimes voluntarily, sometimes forcibly—to control the symptoms of psychosis. Some of the Eighth Circuit judges described his situation as follows:

> He started to believe that his cell was possessed by demons and had "demon blood" in it. He reported that his brother would come to his locked prison cell and take him out of it for walks. He was under the impression that a prison doctor had planted some type of device in his right ear and that his thoughts were being stolen from him when he read the Bible.
>
> Singleton was diagnosed as likely schizophrenic and placed on antipsychotic medication. He initially took it on his own, but when he refused, he was forcibly medicated. For the next several years, Singleton continued to be treated for his psychosis. His medication was administered voluntarily at times, and at times it was administered forcibly. Whenever he was off his medication, his symptoms would resurface, and he would again experience hallucinations.

Two major U.S. Supreme Court decisions set the stage for the instant controversy. In 1986, in *Ford v. Wainwright*, the Court ruled that a capitally-sentenced inmate who has become "insane" may not be executed. Meanwhile, in 1990, in *Washington v. Harper*, the Court permitted prison authorities to order forcible administration of antipsychotic drugs on the condition that three requirements were met: the prisoner must have a serious mental illness, he must be dangerous to himself or others, and the treatment must be in the inmate's medical interest. Harper, however, involved a non-death-sentenced inmate. As the Eighth Circuit put it, the issues in Singelton's case are "whether the State may forcibly administer antipsychotic medication to a prisoner whose date of execution has been set and whether the State may execute a prisoner who has been involuntarily medicated under a *Harper* procedure."

By a 5-4 vote, the Eighth Circuit court answered both questions in the affirmative. At the heart of the court's ruling is the assertion that medication was in Singleton's interests even after the execution date was set and that, in effect, *Harper* applies to capital inmates.

The Eighth Circuit got it right. So long as the three *Harper* requirements—essentially, psychosis, dangerousness, and treatability—are satisfied, the state's compelling interest in the administration of justice outweighs the death row inmate's interest in avoiding both medication and execution.

II. Three Policy Options When a capitally-sentenced inmate becomes insane, yet treatable, three policy options are available:

A. *Medicate and Execute.* The state would medicate the inmate, forcibly if necessary, and if sanity is restored, impose the authorized punishment—the death sentence.

B. *Don't Medicate, Don't Execute.* Should the inmate refuse treatment the state would accede to his wishes, withhold the medication, and if he becomes incompetent, postpone indefinitely the imposition of the death sentence.

C. *Medicate, Don't Execute.* The state would remit the death sentence and, with the inmate's consent, provide treatment.

Option A seems bizarre: we treat the prisoner so that we may kill him. However, as I will try to show, this alternative turns out, upon reflection, to be the soundest of the three options—provided that one considers the death penalty to be morally justified.

By contrast, Option B—withhold treatment and suspend execution—would seem to be the least defensible of the three alternatives. It places the inmate in a cruel dilemma, a Hobson's choice between madness and death. Choosing needed medication, he prepares the way for his execution; eschewing medication, he faces continuing psychotic episodes.

One might object, however, that putting a prisoner in such a dilemma is no more cruel than the execution itself. In other words, if the death penalty is not unacceptably cruel, then neither is Option B. I would answer such an argument in the following way (while acknowledging that many would not accept this response): The death penalty is not cruel because it is imposed on a moral agent for having unlawfully and violently taken the life of an innocent fellow human being. The penalty is society's attempt to balance the moral disequilibrium created by the prisoner's murderous conduct. In short, the death penalty is supported by traditional retributive principles.

Option B, on the other hand, is unacceptably cruel because it turns illness into a virtual penological sanction. It accomplishes this by inducing the prisoner to exchange leniency for treatment. Thus the inmate's nearly inevitable mental breakdown is substituted for his authorized punishment. The bargain is struck: he trades his affliction for his life.

Option C would be justified if capital punishment, though legal, were immoral, for then it would never be morally preferable to execute anyone. This is, of course, the view of abolitionists, which probably explains why Option C is the favorite of the academy. If, however, one accepts (as this essay does) the premise that capital punishment is not inherently immoral, then Option C is difficult to defend. It is especially untenable in cases of exceptionally brutal or heinous crimes, where the claims of justice are hard to deny.

The most compelling argument for supporting Option C would seem to be based on mercy, or compassion, for the offender. Just as we sometimes reduce punishments for the elderly or those suffering from physical illness or injury, we might shorten the sentences of those afflicted by mental illness.

While every humane criminal justice system should provide for mercy, no rational criminal justice system that seeks justice for criminals can make mercy the principal component of sentencing policy. Mercy, by definition, seeks to alleviate the suffering which comes as a result of the offender's punishment, while justice is the very ground for that punishment and its concomitant suffering. Thus, mercy and justice are antipodal, which is why we sometimes speak of justice tempered by mercy. Insofar as general rules for sentencing are aimed at providing justice, mercy cannot be the basis for those rules. Consequently, Option C—which is based on mercy—cannot serve as the general rule for sentencing policy.

III. The Ethics of Medicating Death Row Inmates for Purposes of Execution

The American Psychiatric Association's Principles of Medical Ethics say: "A psychiatrist should not be a participant in a legally authorized execution." However, the Principles do not say what constitutes a "participant," which could range from direct involvement at the time of the execution, such as by certifying competence, to much more indirect involvement, such as treatment of the death row inmate well before the imposition of sentence.

A clarifying statement was issued by the Council on Ethical and Judicial Affairs of the AMA, the pertinent portion of which states:

> When a condemned prisoner has been declared incompetent to be executed, physicians should not treat the prisoner for the purpose of restoring competence unless a commutation order is issued before treatment begins. If the incompetent prisoner is undergoing extreme suffering as a result of psychosis or any other illness, medical intervention intended to mitigate the level of suffering is ethically permissible.

This statement measures the physician's ethical duty by the purpose of his or her conduct. If the purpose is to restore competence for execution, then treatment is disapproved. If, on the other hand, the incompetent death row inmate is experiencing "extreme suffering," then treatment is permitted.

In the ordinary state of affairs, the AMA statement is self-contradictory. The psychotic condemned inmate probably is suffering very greatly, which, according to the AMA statement, makes treatment ethical. However, treating such a patient also may be expected to make him competent, thus rendering the treatment unethical. Perhaps the way out of this is to adopt a subjective interpretation of the statement. If the psychiatrist's purpose is to alleviate the suffering and not to establish competence that would, from a subjectivist perspective, justify treatment.

Perhaps at the root of the AMA/APA contradiction is a more profound, and perhaps unresolvable, ethical dilemma: treat the death row inmate and contravene the mandate to preserve life; deny treatment and violate the duty to heal the sick and prevent suffering. As one analyst, Rochelle Salguero, puts it:

> *The physician cannot make an ethical choice. To comply with the interests of the state by providing treatment, the physician must violate a fundamental ethical prohibition, for without her treatment of the condemned, no execution would take place. Yet by refusing to treat the patient and thereby avoiding participation in the execution, the physician must forego her countervailing ethical duty to heal the sick and prevent suffering.*

However, there are compelling reasons to prefer treatment to non-treatment. The negative consequences of non-treatment are certain, immediate, and directly attributable to the doctor's intentional conduct. Denied antipsychotic medicine, the inmate/patient is nearly certain to become hallucinatory, delusional, disordered, incoherent, and manic. The symptoms will be clear and present and probably continue for as long as the physician withholds treatment. Moreover, the symptoms are a direct product of the doctor's failure to provide care.

By contrast, the negative consequence of treatment, that is, death by execution, is uncertain, remote, and not directly caused by the doctor. There is a good chance that the execution will not take place. Judicial reversals in last-minute appeals or gubernatorial clemency rulings make the application of capital penalties uncertain. The undesirable consequence may never occur at all. If it does occur, it probably will take place after a long lapse of time, perhaps months or years. Even if the patient ultimately is executed, the doctor is not directly causing his death. The execution is the act of the state, not the physician. The doctor's treatment is too remote in time and effect to be considered the immediate cause of death.

One might argue, however, that although the negative consequence of treatment is uncertain, remote, and indirect, it is so catastrophic to the patient that any other option is preferable. This may or may not be so. Is a life of madness—unremitting and relentless—better than death? I am not sure which I would choose were I faced with such a devastating choice. At the least, the preferred option certainly is not obvious.

Here is an analogy that demonstrates the physician's nonresponsibility for the inmate's death. Suppose a psychotic prison inmate has many enemies, perhaps because his crime or his institutional behavior violated some informal prisoner code of conduct. Suppose too that the authorities get wind of a threat to the inmate's life and they tell this to the psychiatrist hired to treat prisoners. Assume that the psychiatrist in turn tells the corrections administrators that if treatment is not forthcoming, the inmate will quickly deteriorate to the point at which hospitalization will be necessary. The authorities reply that in the hospital, the inmate will be safe from his fellow prisoners, whereas if successfully treated, he will remain in the prison and run a risk of being murdered. If the psychiatrist provides treatment, and sometime thereafter, the inmate is indeed murdered, can the physician be blamed for his death? Clearly not, because the death was uncertain, remote, and not directly caused by the doctor, whereas his duty to heal was clear and present. The same may be said in the death penalty situation.

I conclude that if a physician has the means to treat a patient's disorder, and especially if those means are relatively safe, low-cost and effective—as present-day antipsychotic medication usually is—then he or she has an overriding duty to provide treatment. This remains true even if in treating the patient, the physician exposes the patient to a risk of death due to causes other than the treatment. If, however, as Salguero's quotation above contends, the physician's moral dilemma cannot be resolved and he must violate an ethical canon whichever option he takes, then I do not see how he could be faulted. Where the choice is between evils—in this case, preserving life or alleviating suffering—the medical practitioner should not be blamed for choosing one bad alternative rather than another.

In sum, I believe that it is more ethical to treat the psychotic death row inmate than to withhold treatment and condemn him to madness.

Race

15

■ Race—Introduction

The history of capital punishment in the United States is divisible into a period of *de jure* discrimination (discrimination by law) and de facto discrimination (discrimination in practice). Prior to Reconstruction, state criminal codes often explicitly contemplated more severe punishments for crimes committed against whites than for crimes committed against blacks. The adoption of the Fourteenth Amendment in 1868 rendered such facial discrimination unconstitutional, but discriminatory laws lingered on state legislative books for decades. Rape in Georgia is a notable example. More importantly, constitutional protection did not prevent the possibility or reality of racism in practice.

The risk of race discrimination in capital sentencing is particularly pronounced because of the broad discretion invested in the actors—prosecutors, juries, and governors—that determine sentences. Prosecutors have discretion over whether to charge a death-eligible criminal with capital murder or to waive the death penalty through plea bargaining. Juries may decline to impose a death sentence for any reason or no reason at all; they are only limited in imposing capital sentences by the requirement of finding a statutory aggravating circumstance. Governors have absolute discretion in clemency proceedings. In any individual case, it is difficult to assess whether these actors have exercised discretion on the basis of permissible factors such as problems of proof, justifying a decision not to charge—or on impermissible factors such as race. Only the aggregate of decisions can be examined in an attempt to discern patterns.

In empirically assessing whether racism in the aggregate has infected the capital-sentencing process in a particular jurisdiction, it is important at the outset to draw a distinction between what Professors David Baldus and George Woodworth term "gross unadjusted" disparities and "adjusted" disparities. Adjusted disparities control for the effect of real differences in the populations, including differences in the aggravating and mitigating factors that legitimately impact jury decisions.

Suppose, hypothetically, a study reveals that juries deliver death sentences 75% of the time against the race of humans known as Crits, but only 25% of the time for the general population. This may suggest discrimination against Crits. But this could be merely a gross unadjusted disparity. If the researcher's data revealed that Crits committed the same kinds of murders as the rest of the population, it would strengthen the inference that Crits are the subject of discrimination. If, on the other hand, it turned out that Crits almost always tortured their victims, the unadjusted disparity would be less suggestive of racism. Baseline population differences must be accounted for in the same manner. Opponents of capital punishment often cite as evidence of racism the fact that blacks constitute 12% of the general population, but more than 40% of the death row population. This fails to control for the fact that blacks commit murder at a disproportionately high rate. Although blacks represent approximately 12% of the population, they commit more than half of all detected murders. The point is that unadjusted disparities say very little about the influence of race or any other factor one way or the other.

In 1990, the United States Government Accounting Office (GAO) surveyed 28 empirical studies conducted by 21 researchers on race and the death penalty. The largest and most significant of the studies reviewed by the GAO is Baldus, Woodworth, and Charles Pulaski's study of Georgia capital sentencing from 1973 to 1980. Baldus, Woodworth, and Pulaski examined 2400 potentially death-eligible cases, controlling for the presence or absence of hundreds of variables for legitimate case characteristics. The list included aggravating factors such as the defendant's prior record, violence displayed during the case including evidence of torture, the number of victims, motive for the murder, and mitigating factors such as the defendant's age, history of alcohol or drug abuse, and his admission of guilt. Baldus, Woodworth, and Pulaski found that defendants who killed whites were, on average, 4.3 times more likely to receive the death penalty than defendants whose victims were black. A black defendant who killed a white was 21 times more likely to receive the death penalty than a black who killed a black. At the same time, the Baldus team did not find any evidence that the *race of the defendant* impacted outcomes.

These results have been fairly persistent. Eighty-two percent of the studies reviewed by the GAO found evidence that the race of the victim did affect the outcomes. However, evidence for the influence of the race of the defendant on sentencing outcomes was "equivocal" in the opinion of the GAO.

Though the finding of victim-based disparities is common, it is not universal. At least one scholar has argued that the disparities are explainable not by racism, but by real differences between the kinds of murders that occur in cases of white or black victims. Professor Joseph Katz of Georgia State University analyzed the Baldus team's data and argued that it demonstrated rationality not prejudice. First, Katz argued that the revised Georgia statute operated rationally in the most basic sense: death-sentenced defendants had, relative to nondeath-sentenced defendants, a higher frequency of exacerbating evidence, such as mutilation or rape of the victim, and a lower frequency of mitigating evidence, such as a motivation of jealousy. Katz's argument is similar to the argument made by David McCord in Chapter 8 in regard to arbitrariness. The administration of the death penalty is operating rationally in the sense envisioned by *Furman*—death sentences are being returned more frequently in the more aggravated cases.

Next, Katz analyzed the presence of aggravating and mitigating factors by defendant and victim racial combinations. Katz found that white victim cases were in general more aggravated than black victim cases, and that black defendant–white victim cases were the most aggravated of all. For example, victims were raped in 29 of 510 (5.7%) death-eligible white victim cases, but only in 15 of 498 (3%) black victim cases and zero of 27 white defendant–black victim cases. Most significantly, in 96 of the 143 (67.1%) death-eligible cases involving black defendants and white victims, the victim was killed during an armed robbery. This compares with 74 of 367 (20.2%) in white-on-white cases, 31 of 471 (6.6%) in black-on-black cases, and 6 of 27 (22.2%) for white-on-black cases. Katz argues that the typical black defendant–white victim murder involves armed robbery and that this difference legitimizes the disparity in sentencing rates. He writes:

> *The four defendant-victim racial combinations provide the key that unlocks the race-of-victim sentencing puzzle. Each defendant-racial combination portrays a fundamentally different homicide pattern. The black defendant–white victim cases are the most aggravated of the four defendant-victim racial combinations. In 67.1% of the cases, the homicide results from an armed robbery whereas only 18.2% of the time is the homicide precipitated by a dispute. The interracial nature of this kind of homicide minimizes the possibility that the killing arose due to a family dispute, a quarrel between lovers, or arguments between friends and relatives. The victim was a stranger 70.6% of the time, and a family member or friend in only 4.9% of the cases. Multiple offenders were involved in 58.6% of the cases. Black defendant white victim killings are invariably linked to felony circumstances which legally qualifies the defendant for a death sentence.*

Katz has an important argument, often overlooked in the debate on race and the death penalty—that there are real differences in the kinds of murders committed by blacks and whites and against black victims and white victims. Whether this legitimizes the sentencing disparity between murderers of whites and blacks is another matter. Katz implies that it is legitimate—or at least defensible—to sentence blacks to die who kill whites at a higher rate because they tend to kill in the course of armed robbery. The unarticulated premise of Katz's argument is that committing a murder in the course of a felony enhances the level of culpability of a defendant. It is true that commission of a contemporaneous felony is an aggravating factor in many states. But, as discussed in Chapter 11, the felony-murder doctrine is highly controversial because it allows for the execution of some defendants who did not intend to kill. The contemporaneous felony aggravator is problematic for many of the same reasons. Whether or not Professor Katz has a convincing race-neutral explanation for the persistent race-of-victim effect, he still offers a crucial perspective. Excerpts from his analysis are presented in the Critical Documents section of this chapter.

What are the moral consequences of racism in sentencing? In the Perspectives section, Stephen Nathanson argues that racial arbitrariness is a sufficient argument against the death penalty because of the severity of the punishment and its questionable utility. Professor Nathanson's piece is in part a response to the famous death penalty defender Earnest van den Haag, who argued that while equal treatment is a worthy goal for the law, the concern is trumped by the moral obligation of retribution. That killers of whites are sentenced to death more often than those who kill blacks suggests only that the killers of blacks are not being given their due. Retributive injustices in black victim cases should not be used to justify further retributive injustices in white victim cases. The appeal to racism is particularly weak on the facts because the race effect is based upon the race of the victim, and it is the defendant who selects his victim.

That the evidence of racism in capital sentencing turns on the race of the victim and not the defendant complicates the policy debate in an interesting manner. If the framework of the discussion is how to cure the race-of-victim effect, rather than whether the victim-based evidence is a sufficient argument against capital punishment, the curiosity of the issue is revealed. On the whole, the race-of-victim effect benefits black defendants. Murderers, for the most part, tend to kill people of their own race. Blacks kill blacks; whites kill whites. Because blacks tend to kill blacks, and killers of blacks are sentenced to die less often, blacks are the principal beneficiaries of race-of-victim discrimination. The consequence of curing race-of-victim discrimination might be that blacks would be sentenced to die more often than they are now. Whether this is true depends on whether the hypothetical race-blind scheme sentences defendants at the current white victim rate or the black victim rate. Baldus and Woodworth explain:

> *If black victim cases are on average treated less punitively than white victim cases, fewer black defendants will be sentenced to death than would be the case in an evenhanded system that sentenced all cases at the white victim rate. However, if an evenhanded system sentenced all cases at the* black victim *rate, there would be no increase in the number of black defendants sentenced to death and a decline in the number of non-black defendants sentenced to death. Nevertheless, it is clear that if an evenhanded policy were applied to the black and white victim cases (at the current rate for either black or white victim cases), the* proportion *of black defendants on death row would increase.*

In any event, the troubling fact remains that a significant risk is present that race is impacting sentencing decisions in many jurisdictions.

The Supreme Court's concern with race in death sentencing extends back to *Furman*. Justice Douglas's concurrence turned heavily on the cruelty of applying the death penalty "selectively to minorities whose numbers are few, who are outcasts of society, and who are unpopular." Justice Marshall also bluntly discussed the history and ongoing evidence of discrimination. In dissent, Justice Powell acknowledged the history of discriminatory application of the death penalty, which he called "admittedly indefensible," but argues that it was not grounds for striking down the then current death penalty, especially in light of his view that the possibility of racial bias in trial and sentencing had diminished in recent years. It seems fair to say that the Court was, at the least, aware of the disturbing evidence of racism in capital sentencing.

The Court returned to the issue in 1987 in *McCleskey v. Kemp*. McCleskey, a black man sentenced to death for robbery-murder, argued that Georgia's capital sentencing process was infected with racism, violating the Fourteenth Amendment's equal protection clause and the Eighth Amendment. McCleskey based his argument almost entirely on the Baldus team's study of capital sentencing in Georgia.

The lower courts reviewing McCleskey's *habeas corpus* petition treated the Baldus study differently. The United States District Court rejected the Baldus study, relying in part on the testimony of Joseph Katz, and finding that the racial disparities in sentencing could be explained by higher levels of aggravation in the white victim cases than the black victim cases. The Eleventh Circuit, like the Supreme Court after it, accepted the validity of the Baldus team's study, but denied McCleskey's constitutional claims.

The Supreme Court rejected McCleskey's equal protection claim because he had not established "with exceptionally clear proof that the decision makers in McCleskey's case acted with discriminatory purpose." On the Eighth Amendment claim, the Court said that the Baldus study was not sufficient to support a finding that race had entered into sentencing in McCleskey's case—though such evidence is often relied upon in jury discrimination and employment discrimination cases. It remains an open question whether statistical evidence could ever suffice to make out a constitutional challenge. Scholars have differed on whether the decision leaves open such a possibility. As a practical matter, the answer is of little consequence. Federal district courts almost never grant hearings on claims of racial discrimination. The one court that did grant such a hearing between 1987 and 1999 dismissed the claim for failing to meet the *McCleskey* standard. Defendants rarely raise such claims any more.

To the extent race discrimination is viable as a legal basis for challenging a conviction, it is in the state courts, though even here receptiveness to race challenges are the exception rather than the norm. Even in states that welcome such claims, defendants have not fared well. The New Jersey Supreme Court is almost certainly the most progressive in the country in statistically analyzing claims of disproportionality and race discrimination in sentencing. The New Jersey court has expressly stated that claims of race of victim and race of defendant discrimination are cognizable under the equal protection clause of the New Jersey constitution. Even still, the court has rejected, as not proven, every claim it has heard so far.

■ Race—Critical Documents

Table 15-1	**Results of Georgia Charging and Sentencing Study**[a]	
Rank	**Variable label and name**	**Death-odds multiplier**
1	Defendant not the triggerman	.06
2	Defendant admitted guilt	.28
3	Defendant had a history of drug or alcohol abuse	.36
4	Defendant under 17 years of age	.41
5	Jealousy motive	.47
6	Family, lover, or barroom quarrel	.54
7	Defendant was retired, student, juvenile, or housewife	.54
8	Hate motive	.71

continues

	Results of Georgia Charging and Sentencing Study,	
Table 15-1	**continued**	
Rank	**Variable label and name**	**Death-odds multiplier**
9	Motive of pecuniary gain	.80
10	*Defendant was black*	.94
11	Number of prior defendant felony prison terms	1.1
12	Defendant caused risk to 2 or more people	1.1
13	One or more coperpetrators involved	1.3
14	Defendant was a female	1.3
15	Defendant had one or more convictions for violent personal crime, burglary, or arson	1.35
16	Nonproperty-related contemporaneous crime	1.4
17	Killed to avoid arrest of self or other	1.5
18	Victim was police or corrections officer on duty	1.7
19	Defendant was primary mover in planning homicide or contemporaneous offense	1.7
20	Rape/armed robbery/kidnapping plus silence witness, execution, or victim pleaded for life	1.8
21	Coperpetrator received a lesser sentence	2.2
22	Multiple shots	2.2
23	Victim was drowned	2.6
24	Victim was a stranger	2.8
25	Victim was bedridden/handicapped	2.8
26	Kidnapping involved	2.9
27	Victim was frail or weak	3.1
28	Defendant had a prior record for murder, armed robbery, rape, or kidnapping with bodily injury	4.1
29	Armed robbery involved	4.2
30	*One or more white victims*	4.3
31	Multiple stabbing	4.7
32	Victim was 12 or younger	4.8
33	Number of defendant prior murder convictions	5.2
34	Murder for hire	5.9
35	Defendant was a prisoner or escapee	7.7
36	Defendant killed two or more people	7.9
37	Mental torture involved	9.7
38	Rape involved	12.8
39	Defendant's motive was to collect insurance	20.1
40	Victim was tortured physically	27.4
41	Motive was to avenge role played by judicial officer, district attorney or lawyer	28.9

[a]From David C. Baldus, George Woodworth, and Charles A. Pulaski, "Law and Statistics in Conflict: Reflections on *McCleskey v. Kemp*" (1991).

The "death-odds multiplier" is the degree to which a defendant's chance of receiving a death sentence is enhanced or diminished by the presence of the factor in question. For example, if the model predicts that a defendant otherwise has a 10 percent chance of receiving a death sentence and the defendant admits guilt (multiplier of .28), he then has a 2.8 percent chance of a jury sentencing to die. Race factors are italicized.

McCleskey v. Kemp
481 U.S. 279 (1987)

Justice Powell delivered the opinion of the Court.

This case presents the question whether a complex statistical study that indicates a risk that racial considerations enter into capital sentencing determinations proves that petitioner McCleskey's capital sentence is unconstitutional under the Eighth or Fourteenth Amendment.

I

McCleskey, a black man, was convicted of two counts of armed robbery and one count of murder in the Superior Court of Fulton County, Georgia, on October 12, 1978. McCleskey's convictions arose out of the robbery of a furniture store and the killing of a white police officer during the course of the robbery.

McCleskey filed a petition for a writ of habeas corpus in the Federal District Court for the Northern District of Georgia. His petition raised 18 claims, one of which was that the Georgia capital sentencing process is administered in a racially discriminatory manner in violation of the Eighth and Fourteenth Amendments. In support of his claim, McCleskey proffered a statistical study performed by Professors David C. Baldus, Charles Pulaski, and George Woodworth (the Baldus study) that purports to show a disparity in the imposition of the death sentence in Georgia based on the race of the murder victim and, to a lesser extent, the race of the defendant. The Baldus study is actually two sophisticated statistical studies that examine over 2,000 murder cases that occurred in Georgia during the 1970s. The raw numbers collected by Professor Baldus indicate that defendants charged with killing white persons received the death penalty in 11% of the cases, but defendants charged with killing blacks received the death penalty in only 1% of the cases. The raw numbers also indicate a reverse racial disparity according to the race of the defendant: 4% of the black defendants received the death penalty, as opposed to 7% of the white defendants.

Baldus also divided the cases according to the combination of the race of the defendant and the race of the victim. He found that the death penalty was assessed in 22% of the cases involving black defendants and white victims; 8% of the cases involving white defendants and white victims; 1% of the cases involving black defendants and black victims; and 3% of the cases involving white defendants and black victims. Similarly, Baldus found that prosecutors sought the death penalty in 70% of the cases involving black defendants and white victims; 32% of the cases involving white defendants and white victims; 15% of the cases involving black defendants and black victims; and 19% of the cases involving white defendants and black victims.

Baldus subjected his data to an extensive analysis, taking account of 230 variables that could have explained the disparities on nonracial grounds. One of his models concludes that, even after taking account of 39 nonracial variables, defendants charged with killing white victims were 4.3 times as likely to receive a death sentence as defendants charged with killing blacks. According to this model, black defendants were 1.1 times as likely to receive a death sentence as other defendants. Thus, the Baldus study indicates that black defendants, such as McCleskey, who kill white victims have the greatest likelihood of receiving the death penalty.[5]

The District Court held an extensive evidentiary hearing on McCleskey's petition. Although it believed that McCleskey's Eighth Amendment claim was foreclosed, it nevertheless considered the Baldus study with care. It concluded that McCleskey's "statistics do not demonstrate a prima facie case in support of the contention that the death penalty was imposed upon him because of his race, because of the race of the victim, or because of any Eighth Amendment concern." As to McCleskey's Fourteenth Amendment claim, the court found that the methodology of the Baldus study was flawed in several respects.[6] Because of these defects, the court held that the Baldus study "failed to contribute anything of value" to McCleskey's claim. Accordingly, the court denied the petition insofar as it was based upon the Baldus study.

The Court of Appeals for the Eleventh Circuit, sitting en banc, carefully reviewed the District Court's decision on McCleskey's claim. The court assumed that the study "showed that systematic and substantial disparities existed in the penalties imposed upon homicide defendants in Georgia based on race of the homicide victim, that the disparities existed at a less substantial rate in death sen-

---

[5] Baldus' 230-variable model divided cases into eight different ranges, according to the estimated aggravation level of the offense. Baldus argued in his testimony to the District Court that the effects of racial bias were most striking in the midrange cases. "When the cases become tremendously aggravated so that everybody would agree that if we're going to have a death sentence, these are the cases that should get it, the race effects go away. It's only in the mid-range of cases where the decision-makers have a real choice as to what to do. If there's room for the exercise of discretion, then the racial factors begin to play a role." Under this model, Baldus found that 14.4% of the black-victim midrange cases received the death penalty, and 34.4% of the white-victim cases received the death penalty. According to Baldus, the facts of McCleskey's case placed it within the midrange.

[6] Baldus, among other experts, testified at the evidentiary hearing. The District Court "was impressed with the learning of all of the experts." Nevertheless, the District Court noted that in many respects the data were incomplete. In its view, the questionnaires used to obtain the data failed to capture the full degree of the aggravating or mitigating circumstances. The court criticized the researcher's decisions regarding unknown variables. The researchers could not discover whether penalty trials were held in many of the cases. In certain cases, the study lacked information on the race of the victim in cases involving multiple victims, on whether or not the prosecutor offered a plea bargain, and on credibility problems with witnesses. The court concluded that McCleskey had failed to establish by a preponderance of the evidence that the data were trustworthy.

The District Court noted other problems with Baldus' methodology. First, the researchers assumed that all of the information available from the questionnaires was available to the juries and prosecutors when the case was tried. The court found this assumption "questionable." Second, the court noted the instability of the various models. Even with the 230-variable model, consideration of 20 further variables caused a significant drop in the statistical significance of race. In the court's view, this undermined the persuasiveness of the model that showed the greatest racial disparity, the 39-variable model. Third, the court found that the high correlation between race and many of the nonracial variables diminished the weight to which the study was entitled.

tencing based on race of defendants, and that the factors of race of the victim and defendant were at work in Fulton County." Even assuming the study's validity, the Court of Appeals found the statistics "insufficient to demonstrate discriminatory intent or unconstitutional discrimination in the Fourteenth Amendment context, and insufficient to show irrationality, arbitrariness and capriciousness under any kind of Eighth Amendment analysis." The court noted:

> *The very exercise of discretion means that persons exercising discretion may reach different results from exact duplicates. Assuming each result is within the range of discretion, all are correct in the eyes of the law. It would not make sense for the system to require the exercise of discretion in order to be facially constitutional, and at the same time hold a system unconstitutional in application where that discretion achieved different results for what appear to be exact duplicates.*

The court concluded:

> *Viewed broadly, it would seem that the statistical evidence presented here, assuming its validity, confirms rather than condemns the system. The marginal disparity based on the race of the victim tends to support the state's contention that the system is working far differently from the one which* Furman *condemned. In pre-*Furman *days, there was no rhyme or reason as to who got the death penalty and who did not. But now, in the vast majority of cases, the reasons for a difference are well documented.*

The Court of Appeals affirmed the denial by the District Court of McCleskey's petition for a writ of habeas corpus insofar as the petition was based upon the Baldus study. We granted certiorari and now affirm.

II

McCleskey's first claim is that the Georgia capital punishment statute violates the Equal Protection Clause of the Fourteenth Amendment.[7] He argues that race has infected the administration of Georgia's statute in two ways: persons who murder whites are more likely to be sentenced to death than persons who murder blacks, and black murderers are more likely to be sentenced to death than white murderers. As a black defendant who killed a white victim, McCleskey claims that the Baldus study demonstrates that he was discriminated against because of his race and because of the race of his victim. In its broadest form,

---

[7] Although the District Court rejected the findings of the Baldus study as flawed, the Court of Appeals assumed that the study is valid and reached the constitutional issues. Accordingly, those issues are before us. As did the Court of Appeals, we assume the study is valid statistically without reviewing the factual findings of the District Court. Our assumption that the Baldus study is statistically valid does not include the assumption that the study shows that racial considerations actually enter into any sentencing decisions in Georgia. Even a sophisticated multiple-regression analysis such as the Baldus study can only demonstrate a *risk* that the factor of race entered into some capital sentencing decisions and a necessarily lesser risk that race entered into any particular sentencing decision.

McCleskey's claim of discrimination extends to every actor in the Georgia capital sentencing process, from the prosecutor who sought the death penalty and the jury that imposed the sentence, to the State itself that enacted the capital punishment statute and allows it to remain in effect despite its allegedly discriminatory application. We agree with the Court of Appeals, and every other court that has considered such a challenge, that this claim must fail.

A

Our analysis begins with the basic principle that a defendant who alleges an equal protection violation has the burden of proving "the existence of purposeful discrimination." A corollary to this principle is that a criminal defendant must prove that the purposeful discrimination "had a discriminatory effect" on him. Thus, to prevail under the Equal Protection Clause, McCleskey must prove that the decisionmakers in *his* case acted with discriminatory purpose. He offers no evidence specific to his own case that would support an inference that racial considerations played a part in his sentence. Instead, he relies solely on the Baldus study. McCleskey argues that the Baldus study compels an inference that his sentence rests on purposeful discrimination. McCleskey's claim that these statistics are sufficient proof of discrimination, without regard to the facts of a particular case, would extend to all capital cases in Georgia, at least where the victim was white and the defendant is black.

The Court has accepted statistics as proof of intent to discriminate in certain limited contexts. First, this Court has accepted statistical disparities as proof of an equal protection violation in the selection of the jury venire in a particular district. Second, this Court has accepted statistics in the form of multiple-regression analysis to prove statutory violations under Title VII of the Civil Rights Act of 1964.

But the nature of the capital sentencing decision, and the relationship of the statistics to that decision, are fundamentally different from the corresponding elements in the venire-selection or Title VII cases. Most importantly, each particular decision to impose the death penalty is made by a petit jury selected from a properly constituted venire. Each jury is unique in its composition, and the Constitution requires that its decision rest on consideration of innumerable factors that vary according to the characteristics of the individual defendant and the facts of the particular capital offense. Thus, the application of an inference drawn from the general statistics to a specific decision in a trial and sentencing simply is not comparable to the application of an inference drawn from general statistics to a specific venire-selection or Title VII case. In those cases, the statistics relate to fewer entities, and fewer variables are relevant to the challenged decisions.

Another important difference between the cases in which we have accepted statistics as proof of discriminatory intent and this case is that, in the venire-selection and Title VII contexts, the decisionmaker has an opportunity to explain the statistical disparity. Here, the State has no practical opportunity to rebut the Baldus study.

Finally, McCleskey's statistical proffer must be viewed in the context of his challenge. McCleskey challenges decisions at the heart of the State's criminal justice system. Because discretion is essential to the criminal justice process, we would demand exceptionally clear proof before we would infer that the discretion has been abused.

B

McCleskey also suggests that the Baldus study proves that the State as a whole has acted with a discriminatory purpose. He appears to argue that the State has violated the Equal Protection Clause by adopting the capital punishment statute and allowing it to remain in force despite its allegedly discriminatory application. But "discriminatory purpose" implies more than intent as volition or intent as awareness of consequences. It implies that the decisionmaker, in this case a state legislature, selected or reaffirmed a particular course of action at least in part "because of," not merely "in spite of," its adverse effects upon an identifiable group. For this claim to prevail, McCleskey would have to prove that the Georgia Legislature enacted or maintained the death penalty statute *because of* an anticipated racially discriminatory effect. In *Gregg* this Court found that the Georgia capital sentencing system could operate in a fair and neutral manner. There was no evidence then, and there is none now, that the Georgia Legislature enacted the capital punishment statute to further a racially discriminatory purpose.[20]

Nor has McCleskey demonstrated that the legislature maintains the capital punishment statute because of the racially disproportionate impact suggested by the Baldus study. As legislatures necessarily have wide discretion in the choice of criminal laws and penalties, and as there were legitimate reasons for the Georgia Legislature to adopt and maintain capital punishment, we will not infer a discriminatory purpose on the part of the State of Georgia. Accordingly, we reject McCleskey's equal protection claims.

III

McCleskey also argues that the Baldus study demonstrates that the Georgia capital sentencing system violates the Eighth Amendment. In sum, our decisions since *Furman* have identified a constitutionally permissible range of discretion in imposing the death penalty. First, there is a required threshold below which the death penalty cannot be imposed. In this context, the State must establish rational criteria that narrow the decisionmaker's judgment as to whether the circumstances of a particular defendant's case meet the threshold. Moreover, a societal consensus that the death penalty is disproportionate to a particular offense prevents a State from imposing the death penalty for that offense. Second, States cannot limit the sentencer's consideration of any relevant circumstance that

---

[20] McCleskey relies on "historical evidence" to support his claim of purposeful discrimination by the State. This evidence focuses on Georgia laws in force during and just after the Civil War. Of course, the "historical background of the decision is one evidentiary source" for proof of intentional discrimination. But unless historical evidence is reasonably contemporaneous with the challenged decision, it has little probative value. Although the history of racial discrimination in this country is undeniable, we cannot accept official actions taken long ago as evidence of current intent.

could cause it to decline to impose the penalty. In this respect, the State cannot channel the sentencer's discretion, but must allow it to consider any relevant information offered by the defendant.

IV

A

In light of our precedents under the Eighth Amendment, McCleskey cannot argue successfully that his sentence is "disproportionate to the crime in the traditional sense." He does not deny that he committed a murder in the course of a planned robbery, a crime for which this Court has determined that the death penalty constitutionally may be imposed. His disproportionality claim "is of a different sort." McCleskey argues that the sentence in his case is disproportionate to the sentences in other murder cases.

On the one hand, he cannot base a constitutional claim on an argument that his case differs from other cases in which defendants *did* receive the death penalty. On automatic appeal, the Georgia Supreme Court found that McCleskey's death sentence was not disproportionate to other death sentences imposed in the State. The court supported this conclusion with an appendix containing citations to 13 cases involving generally similar murders. Moreover, where the statutory procedures adequately channel the sentencer's discretion, such proportionality review is not constitutionally required.

On the other hand, absent a showing that the Georgia capital punishment system operates in an arbitrary and capricious manner, McCleskey cannot prove a constitutional violation by demonstrating that other defendants who may be similarly situated did *not* receive the death penalty. In *Gregg*, the Court confronted the argument that "the opportunities for discretionary action that are inherent in the processing of any murder case under Georgia law," specifically the opportunities for discretionary leniency, rendered the capital sentences imposed arbitrary and capricious. We rejected this contention: "Nothing in any of our cases suggests that the decision to afford an individual defendant mercy violates the Constitution."[28]

Because McCleskey's sentence was imposed under Georgia sentencing procedures that focus discretion "on the particularized nature of the crime and the particularized characteristics of the individual defendant," we lawfully may presume that McCleskey's death sentence was not "wantonly and freakishly" imposed, and thus that the sentence is not disproportionate within any recognized meaning under the Eighth Amendment.

---

[28] The Constitution is not offended by inconsistency in results based on the objective circumstances of the crime. Numerous legitimate factors may influence the outcome of a trial and a defendant's ultimate sentence, even though they may be irrelevant to his actual guilt. If sufficient evidence to link a suspect to a crime cannot be found, he will not be charged. The capability of the responsible law enforcement agency can vary widely. Also, the strength of the available evidence remains a variable throughout the criminal justice process and may influence a prosecutor's decision to offer a plea bargain or to go to trial. Witness availability, credibility, and memory also influence the results of prosecutions. Finally, sentencing in state courts is generally discretionary, so a defendant's ultimate sentence necessarily will vary according to the judgment of the sentencing authority. The foregoing factors necessarily exist in varying degrees throughout our criminal justice system.

B

Although our decision in *Gregg* as to the facial validity of the Georgia capital punishment statute appears to foreclose McCleskey's disproportionality argument, he further contends that the Georgia capital punishment system is arbitrary and capricious in *application*, and therefore his sentence is excessive, because racial considerations may influence capital sentencing decisions in Georgia. We now address this claim.

To evaluate McCleskey's challenge, we must examine exactly what the Baldus study may show. Even Professor Baldus does not contend that his statistics *prove* that race enters into any capital sentencing decisions or that race was a factor in McCleskey's particular case.[29] Statistics at most may show only a likelihood that a particular factor entered into some decisions. There is, of course, some risk of racial prejudice influencing a jury's decision in a criminal case. There are similar risks that other kinds of prejudice will influence other criminal trials. The question "is at what point that risk becomes constitutionally unacceptable." McCleskey asks us to accept the likelihood allegedly shown by the Baldus study as the constitutional measure of an unacceptable risk of racial prejudice influencing capital sentencing decisions. This we decline to do.

Individual jurors bring to their deliberations "qualities of human nature and varieties of human experience, the range of which is unknown and perhaps unknowable." The capital sentencing decision requires the individual jurors to focus their collective judgment on the unique characteristics of a particular criminal defendant. It is not surprising that such collective judgments often are difficult to explain. But the inherent lack of predictability of jury decisions does not justify their condemnation. On the contrary, it is the jury's function to make the difficult and uniquely human judgments that defy codification and that "build discretion, equity, and flexibility into a legal system."

McCleskey's argument that the Constitution condemns the discretion allowed decisionmakers in the Georgia capital sentencing system is antithetical to the fundamental role of discretion in our criminal justice system. Discretion in the criminal justice system offers substantial benefits to the criminal defendant. Not only can a jury decline to impose the death sentence, it can decline to convict or choose to convict of a lesser offense. Whereas decisions against a defendant's interest may be reversed by the trial judge or on appeal, these discretionary exercises of leniency are final and unreviewable. Similarly, the capacity of prosecutorial discretion to provide individualized justice is "firmly entrenched in American law." As we have noted, a prosecutor can decline to charge, offer a plea bargain, or decline to seek a death sentence in any particular case. Of course, "the power to be lenient also is the power to discriminate," but a capital punishment system

---

[29] According to Professor Baldus:

> *McCleskey's case falls in a grey area where you would find the greatest likelihood that some inappropriate consideration may have come to bear on the decision. In an analysis of this type, obviously one cannot say that we can say to a moral certainty what it was that influenced the decision. We can't do that.*

that did not allow for discretionary acts of leniency "would be totally alien to our notions of criminal justice."

C

At most, the Baldus study indicates a discrepancy that appears to correlate with race. Apparent disparities in sentencing are an inevitable part of our criminal justice system. The discrepancy indicated by the Baldus study is "a far cry from the major systemic defects identified in *Furman*."[36] As this Court has recognized, any mode for determining guilt or punishment "has its weaknesses and the potential for misuse." Specifically, "there can be no perfect procedure for deciding in which cases governmental authority should be used to impose death." Despite these imperfections, our consistent rule has been that constitutional guarantees are met when "the mode for determining guilt or punishment itself has been surrounded with safeguards to make it as fair as possible." Where the discretion that is fundamental to our criminal process is involved, we decline to assume that what is unexplained is invidious. In light of the safeguards designed to minimize racial bias in the process, the fundamental value of jury trial in our criminal justice system, and the benefits that discretion provides to criminal defendants, we hold that the Baldus study does not demonstrate a constitutionally significant risk of racial bias affecting the Georgia capital sentencing process.

V

Two additional concerns inform our decision in this case. First, McCleskey's claim, taken to its logical conclusion, throws into serious question the principles that underlie our entire criminal justice system. The Eighth Amendment is not limited in application to capital punishment, but applies to all penalties. Thus, if we accepted McCleskey's claim that racial bias has impermissibly tainted the capital sentencing decision, we could soon be faced with similar claims as to other types of penalty. Moreover, the claim that his sentence rests on the irrelevant factor of race easily could be extended to apply to claims based on unexplained discrepancies that correlate to membership in other minority groups, and even to gender. Similarly, since McCleskey's claim relates to the race of his victim, other claims could apply with equally logical force to statistical disparities that correlate with the race or sex of other actors in the criminal justice system, such as defense attorneys or judges. Also, there is no logical reason that such a claim need be limited to racial or sexual bias. If arbitrary and capricious punishment is the touchstone under the Eighth Amendment, such a claim could—at least in theory—be based upon any arbitrary variable, such as the defendant's facial characteristics, or the physical attractiveness of the defendant or the victim,[44] that some

---

[36] The Baldus study in fact confirms that the Georgia system results in a reasonable level of proportionality among the class of murderers eligible for the death penalty. As Professor Baldus confirmed, the system sorts out cases where the sentence of death is highly likely and highly unlikely, leaving a midrange of cases where the imposition of the death penalty in any particular case is less predictable.

[44] Some studies indicate that physically attractive defendants receive greater leniency in sentencing than unattractive defendants, and that offenders whose victims are physically attractive receive harsher sentences than defendants with less attractive victims.

statistical study indicates may be influential in jury decisionmaking. As these examples illustrate, there is no limiting principle to the type of challenge brought by McCleskey. The Constitution does not require that a State eliminate any demonstrable disparity that correlates with a potentially irrelevant factor in order to operate a criminal justice system that includes capital punishment. As we have stated specifically in the context of capital punishment, the Constitution does not "place totally unrealistic conditions on its use."

Second, McCleskey's arguments are best presented to the legislative bodies. It is not the responsibility—or indeed even the right—of this Court to determine the appropriate punishment for particular crimes. It is the legislatures, the elected representatives of the people, that are "constituted to respond to the will and consequently the moral values of the people." Legislatures also are better qualified to weigh and "evaluate the results of statistical studies in terms of their own local conditions and with a flexibility of approach that is not available to the courts." Capital punishment is now the law in more than two-thirds of our States. It is the ultimate duty of courts to determine on a case-by-case basis whether these laws are applied consistently with the Constitution. Despite McCleskey's wide-ranging arguments that basically challenge the validity of capital punishment in our multiracial society, the only question before us is whether in his case, the law of Georgia was properly applied. We agree with the District Court and the Court of Appeals for the Eleventh Circuit that this was carefully and correctly done in this case. Accordingly, we affirm the judgment of the Court of Appeals for the Eleventh Circuit.

Justice Brennan, with whom Justice Marshall joins, and with whom Justice Blackmun and Justice Stevens join in all but Part I, dissenting.

I

Adhering to my view that the death penalty is in all circumstances cruel and unusual punishment, I would vacate the decision below insofar as it left undisturbed the death sentence imposed in this case. Even if I did not hold this position, however, I would reverse the Court of Appeals, for petitioner McCleskey has clearly demonstrated that his death sentence was imposed in violation of the Eighth and Fourteenth Amendments.

II

At some point in this case, Warren McCleskey doubtless asked his lawyer whether a jury was likely to sentence him to die. A candid reply to this question would have been disturbing. First, counsel would have to tell McCleskey that few of the details of the crime or of McCleskey's past criminal conduct were more important than the fact that his victim was white. Furthermore, counsel would feel bound to tell McCleskey that defendants charged with killing white victims in Georgia are 4.3 times as likely to be sentenced to death as defendants charged with killing blacks. In addition, frankness would compel the disclosure that it was more likely than not that the race of McCleskey's victim would determine whether he received a death sentence: 6 of every 11 defendants convicted of killing a white person would not have received the death penalty if their victims had been black, while, among defendants with aggravating and mitigating factors comparable to McCleskey's, 20 of every 34 would not have been sentenced to die if their victims had been black. Finally, the assessment would not be complete without the information that cases involving black defendants and white victims are more likely to result in a death sentence than cases featuring any other racial combination of defendant and victim. The story could be told in a variety of ways, but McCleskey could not fail to grasp its essential narrative line: there was a significant chance that race would play a prominent role in determining if he lived or died.

The Court today holds that Warren McCleskey's sentence was constitutionally imposed. It finds no fault in a system in which lawyers must tell their clients that race casts a large shadow on the capital sentencing process. The Court arrives at this conclusion by stating that the Baldus study cannot "*prove* that race enters into any capital sentencing decisions or that race was a factor in McCleskey's particular case." Since, according to Professor Baldus, we cannot say "to a moral certainty" that race influenced a decision, we can identify only "a likelihood that a particular factor entered into some decisions," and "a discrepancy that appears to correlate with race." This "likelihood" and "discrepancy," holds the Court, is insufficient to establish a constitutional violation. The Court reaches this conclusion by placing four factors on the scales opposite McCleskey's evidence: the desire to encourage sentencing discretion, the existence of "statutory safeguards" in the Georgia scheme, the fear of encouraging widespread challenges to other sentencing decisions, and the limits of the judicial role. The Court's evaluation of the significance of petitioner's evidence is fundamentally at odds with our consistent concern for rationality in capital sentencing, and the considerations that the majority invokes to discount that evidence cannot justify ignoring its force.

III

A

It is important to emphasize at the outset that the Court's observation that McCleskey cannot prove the influence of race on any particular sentencing decision is irrelevant in evaluating his Eighth Amendment claim. Since *Furman*, the Court has been concerned with the *risk* of the imposition of an arbitrary sentence, rather than the proven fact of one. *Furman* held that the death penalty "may not be imposed under sentencing procedures that create a substantial risk that the punishment will be inflicted in an arbitrary and capricious manner." This emphasis on risk acknowledges the difficulty of divining the jury's motivation in an individual case. In addition, it reflects the fact that concern for arbitrariness focuses on the rationality of the system as a whole, and that a system that features a significant probability that sentencing decisions are influenced by impermissible considerations cannot be regarded as rational.

Defendants challenging their death sentences thus never have had to prove that impermissible considerations have actually infected sentencing decisions.

We have required instead that they establish that the system under which they were sentenced posed a significant risk of such an occurrence. McCleskey's claim does differ, however, in one respect from these earlier cases: it is the first to base a challenge not on speculation about how a system *might* operate, but on empirical documentation of how it *does* operate.

The Court assumes the statistical validity of the Baldus study, and acknowledges that McCleskey has demonstrated a risk that racial prejudice plays a role in capital sentencing in Georgia. Nonetheless, it finds the probability of prejudice insufficient to create constitutional concern. Close analysis of the Baldus study, however, in light of both statistical principles and human experience, reveals that the risk that race influenced McCleskey's sentence is intolerable by any imaginable standard.

B

The Baldus study indicates that, after taking into account some 230 non-racial factors that might legitimately influence a sentencer, the jury *more likely than not* would have spared McCleskey's life had his victim been black. The study distinguishes between those cases in which (1) the jury exercises virtually no discretion because the strength or weakness of aggravating factors usually suggests that only one outcome is appropriate;[2] and (2) cases reflecting an "intermediate" level of aggravation, in which the jury has considerable discretion in choosing a sentence. McCleskey's case falls into the intermediate range.[3] In such cases, death is imposed in 34% of white-victim crimes and 14% of black-victim crimes, a difference of 139% in the rate of imposition of the death penalty. In other words, just under 59%—almost 6 in 10—defendants comparable to McCleskey would not have received the death penalty if their victims had been black.

Furthermore, even examination of the sentencing system as a whole, factoring in those cases in which the jury exercises little discretion, indicates the influence of race on capital sentencing. For the Georgia system as a whole, race accounts for a six percentage point difference in the rate at which capital punishment is imposed. Since death is imposed in 11% of all white-victim cases, the rate in comparably aggravated black-victim cases is 5%. The rate of capital sentencing in a white-victim case is thus 120% greater than the rate in a black-victim case. Put another way, over half—55%—of defendants in white-victim crimes in Georgia would not have been sentenced to die if their victims had been black. Of the more than 200 variables potentially relevant to a sentencing decision, race of the victim is a powerful explanation for variation in death sen-

---

[2] The first two and the last of the study's eight case categories represent those cases in which the jury typically sees little leeway in deciding on a sentence. Cases in the first two categories are those that feature aggravating factors so minimal that juries imposed no death sentences in the 88 cases with these factors during the period of the study. Cases in the eighth category feature aggravating factors so extreme that the jury imposed the death penalty in 88% of the 58 cases with these factors in the same period.

[3] In the five categories characterized as intermediate, the rate at which the death penalty was imposed ranged from 8% to 41%. The overall rate for the 326 cases in these categories was 20%.

tence rates—as powerful as nonracial aggravating factors such as a prior murder conviction or acting as the principal planner of the homicide.[5]

These adjusted figures are only the most conservative indication of the risk that race will influence the death sentences of defendants in Georgia. Data unadjusted for the mitigating or aggravating effect of other factors show an even more pronounced disparity by race. The capital sentencing rate for all white-victim cases was almost *11 times* greater than the rate for black-victim cases. Furthermore, blacks who kill whites are sentenced to death at nearly *22 times* the rate of blacks who kill blacks, and more than *7 times* the rate of whites who kill blacks. In addition, prosecutors seek the death penalty for 70% of black defendants with white victims, but for only 15% of black defendants with black victims, and only 19% of white defendants with black victims. Since our decision upholding the Georgia capital sentencing system in *Gregg*, the State has executed seven persons. All of the seven were convicted of killing whites, and six of the seven executed were black. Such execution figures are especially striking in light of the fact that, during the period encompassed by the Baldus study, only 9.2% of Georgia homicides involved black defendants and white victims, while 60.7% involved black victims.

McCleskey's statistics have particular force because most of them are the product of sophisticated multiple-regression analysis. Such analysis is designed precisely to identify patterns in the aggregate, even though we may not be able to reconstitute with certainty any individual decision that goes to make up that pattern. Multiple-regression analysis is particularly well suited to identify the influence of impermissible considerations in sentencing, since it is able to control for permissible factors that may explain an apparent arbitrary pattern. While the decisionmaking process of a body such as a jury may be complex, the Baldus study provides a massive compilation of the details that are most relevant to that decision. As we held in the context of Title VII of the Civil Rights Act of 1964 last Term, a multiple-regression analysis need not include every conceivable variable to establish a party's case, as long as it includes those variables that account for the major factors that are likely to influence decisions. In this case, Professor Baldus in fact conducted additional regression analyses in response to criticisms and suggestions by the District Court, all of which confirmed, and some of which even strengthened, the study's original conclusions.

The statistical evidence in this case thus relentlessly documents the risk that McCleskey's sentence was influenced by racial considerations. This evidence shows that there is a better than even chance in Georgia that race will influence the decision to impose the death penalty: a majority of defendants in white-victim crimes would not have been sentenced to die if their victims had been black. In determining whether this risk is acceptable, our judgment must be shaped by the awareness that "the risk of racial prejudice infecting a capital sentencing proceeding is especially serious in light of the complete finality of the death sentence." In determining the guilt of a defendant, a State must prove its case beyond a reasonable doubt. That is, we refuse to convict if the chance of error is simply

---

[5] The fact that a victim was white accounts for a nine percentage point difference in the rate at which the death penalty is imposed, which is the same difference attributable to a prior murder conviction or the fact that the defendant was the "prime mover" in planning a murder.

less likely than not. Surely, we should not be willing to take a person's life if the chance that his death sentence was irrationally imposed is *more* likely than not. In light of the gravity of the interest at stake, petitioner's statistics on their face are a powerful demonstration of the type of risk that our Eighth Amendment jurisprudence has consistently condemned.

C

Evaluation of McCleskey's evidence cannot rest solely on the numbers themselves. We must also ask whether the conclusion suggested by those numbers is consonant with our understanding of history and human experience. Georgia's legacy of a race-conscious criminal justice system, as well as this Court's own recognition of the persistent danger that racial attitudes may affect criminal proceedings, indicates that McCleskey's claim is not a fanciful product of mere statistical artifice.

For many years, Georgia operated openly and formally precisely the type of dual system the evidence shows is still effectively in place. The criminal law expressly differentiated between crimes committed by and against blacks and whites, distinctions whose lineage traced back to the time of slavery. During the colonial period, black slaves who killed whites in Georgia, regardless of whether in self-defense or in defense of another, were automatically executed.

By the time of the Civil War, a dual system of crime and punishment was well established in Georgia. The state criminal code contained separate sections for "Slaves and Free Persons of Color," and for all other persons. The code provided, for instance, for an automatic death sentence for murder committed by blacks, but declared that anyone else convicted of murder might receive life imprisonment if the conviction were founded solely on circumstantial testimony *or* simply if the jury so recommended. The code established that the rape of a free white female by a black "shall be" punishable by death. However, rape by anyone else of a free white female was punishable by a prison term not less than 2 nor more than 20 years. The rape of *blacks* was punishable "by fine and imprisonment, at the discretion of the court."

History and its continuing legacy thus buttress the probative force of McCleskey's statistics. Formal dual criminal laws may no longer be in effect, and intentional discrimination may no longer be prominent. Nonetheless, "subtle, less consciously held racial attitudes" continue to be of concern, and the Georgia system gives such attitudes considerable room to operate. The conclusions drawn from McCleskey's statistical evidence are therefore consistent with the lessons of social experience.

IV

Our desire for individualized moral judgments may lead us to accept some inconsistencies in sentencing outcomes. Since such decisions are not reducible to mathematical formulae, we are willing to assume that a certain degree of variation reflects the fact that no two defendants are completely alike. There is thus a presumption that actors in the criminal justice system exercise their discretion in responsible fashion, and we do not automatically infer that sentencing patterns that do not comport with ideal rationality are suspect.

As we made clear in *Batson v. Kentucky*, however, that presumption is rebuttable. *Batson* dealt with another arena in which considerable discretion traditionally has been afforded, the exercise of peremptory challenges. Those challenges are normally exercised without any indication whatsoever of the grounds for doing so. As with sentencing, therefore, peremptory challenges are justified as an occasion for particularized determinations related to specific individuals, and, as with sentencing, we presume that such challenges normally are not made on the basis of a factor such as race. As we said in *Batson*, however, such features do not justify imposing a "crippling burden of proof," in order to rebut that presumption. The Court in this case apparently seeks to do just that. On the basis of the need for individualized decisions, it rejects evidence, drawn from the most sophisticated capital sentencing analysis ever performed, that reveals that race more likely than not infects capital sentencing decisions. The Court's position converts a rebuttable presumption into a virtually conclusive one.

It has now been over 13 years since Georgia adopted the provisions upheld in *Gregg*. Professor Baldus and his colleagues have compiled data on almost 2,500 homicides committed during the period 1973–1979. They have taken into account the influence of 230 nonracial variables, using a multitude of data from the State itself, and have produced striking evidence that the odds of being sentenced to death are significantly greater than average if a defendant is black or his or her victim is white. The challenge to the Georgia system is not speculative or theoretical; it is empirical. As a result, the Court cannot rely on the statutory safeguards in discounting McCleskey's evidence, for it is the very effectiveness of those safeguards that such evidence calls into question.

The Court next states that its unwillingness to regard petitioner's evidence as sufficient is based in part on the fear that recognition of McCleskey's claim would open the door to widespread challenges to all aspects of criminal sentencing. Taken on its face, such a statement seems to suggest a fear of too much justice. Yet surely the majority would acknowledge that if striking evidence indicated that other minority groups, or women, or even persons with blond hair, were disproportionately sentenced to death, such a state of affairs would be repugnant to deeply rooted conceptions of fairness. The prospect that there may be more widespread abuse than McCleskey documents may be dismaying, but it does not justify complete abdication of our judicial role.

In fairness, the Court's fear that McCleskey's claim is an invitation to descend a slippery slope also rests on the realization that any humanly imposed system of penalties will exhibit some imperfection. Yet to reject McCleskey's powerful evidence on this basis is to ignore both the qualitatively different character of the death penalty and the particular repugnance of racial discrimination.

It hardly needs reiteration that this Court has consistently acknowledged the uniqueness of the punishment of death. As a result, the degree of arbitrariness that may be adequate to render the death penalty "cruel and unusual" punishment may not be adequate to invalidate lesser penalties. What these relative degrees of arbitrariness might be in other cases need not concern us here; the point is that the majority's fear of wholesale invalidation of criminal sentences is unfounded.

The Court also maintains that accepting McCleskey's claim would pose a threat to all sentencing because of the prospect that a correlation might be demonstrated between sentencing outcomes and other personal characteristics. Again, such a view is indifferent to the considerations that enter into a determination whether punishment is "cruel and unusual." Race is a consideration whose influence is expressly constitutionally proscribed. We have expressed a moral commitment, as embodied in our fundamental law, that this specific characteristic should not be the basis for allotting burdens and benefits. Three constitutional amendments, and numerous statutes, have been prompted specifically by the desire to address the effects of racism. That a decision to impose the death penalty could be influenced by *race* is thus a particularly repugnant prospect, and evidence that race may play even a modest role in levying a death sentence should be enough to characterize that sentence as "cruel and unusual."

Certainly, a factor that we would regard as morally irrelevant, such as hair color, at least theoretically could be associated with sentencing results to such an extent that we would regard as arbitrary a system in which that factor played a significant role. As I have said above, however, the evaluation of evidence suggesting such a correlation must be informed not merely by statistics, but by history and experience. One could hardly contend that this Nation has on the basis of hair color inflicted upon persons deprivation comparable to that imposed on the basis of race. Recognition of this fact would necessarily influence the evaluation of data suggesting the influence of hair color on sentencing, and would require evidence of statistical correlation even more powerful than that presented by the Baldus study. The Court's projection of apocalyptic consequences for criminal sentencing is thus greatly exaggerated.

Finally, the Court justifies its rejection of McCleskey's claim by cautioning against usurpation of the legislatures' role in devising and monitoring criminal punishment. The Court is, of course, correct to emphasize the gravity of constitutional intervention and the importance that it be sparingly employed. The fact that "capital punishment is now the law in more than two thirds of our States," however, does not diminish the fact that capital punishment is the most awesome act that a State can perform. The judiciary's role in this society counts for little if the use of governmental power to extinguish life does not elicit close scrutiny.

Those whom we would banish from society or from the human community itself often speak in too faint a voice to be heard above society's demand for punishment. It is the particular role of courts to hear these voices, for the Constitution declares that the majoritarian chorus may not alone dictate the conditions of social life. The Court thus fulfills, rather than disrupts, the scheme of separation of powers by closely scrutinizing the imposition of the death penalty, for no decision of a society is more deserving of "sober second thought."

V

Warren McCleskey's evidence confronts us with the subtle and persistent influence of the past. His message is a disturbing one to a society that has formally repudiated racism, and a frustrating one to a Nation accustomed to regarding its destiny as the product of its own will. Nonetheless, we ignore him at our peril, for we remain imprisoned by the past as long as we deny its influence in the present.

It is tempting to pretend that minorities on death row share a fate in no way connected to our own, that our treatment of them sounds no echoes beyond the chambers in which they die. Such an illusion is ultimately corrosive, for the reverberations of injustice are not so easily confined. "The destinies of the two races in this country are indissolubly linked together," and the way in which we choose those who will die reveals the depth of moral commitment among the living.

The Court's decision today will not change what attorneys in Georgia tell other Warren McCleskeys about their chances of execution. Nothing will soften the harsh message they must convey, nor alter the prospect that race undoubtedly will continue to be a topic of discussion. McCleskey's evidence will not have obtained judicial acceptance, but that will not affect what is said on death row. However many criticisms of today's decision may be rendered, these painful conversations will serve as the most eloquent dissents of all.

Joseph L. Katz, "Warren McCleskey v. Ralph Kemp: Is the Death Penalty in Georgia Racially Biased?"

I. *Abstract*

I was hired by the Georgia Attorney General to analyze the Baldus team databases, and testified as to my findings at McCleskey's evidentiary hearing. In my opinion, the Supreme Court ruled properly that statistical models are inappropriate and ineffective to measure the extent (if any) of discrimination in capital sentencing decisions. This article discusses the general limitations of statistics to infer racial bias in capital cases by considering the statistical evidence presented in *McCleskey*.

II. *The Baldus, Woodworth and Pulaski Studies*

The NAACP Legal Defense Fund commissioned the Baldus team to conduct a detailed statistical study, called the Georgia Charging and Sentencing Study (GCSS), to focus on sentencing practices in Georgia after *Furman*. The purpose of the study was to empirically test whether or not the revised Georgia death sentencing system is operating fairly, and formed the basis for the statistical analyses presented to the District Court.

The second study attempted to collect information on over 500 crime related factors for a sample of 1,082 defendants convicted of voluntary manslaughter or murder in Georgia between 1973 and 1978. Drawing on information from data files at the Georgia Department of Pardons and Paroles, five second-year law students were paid $5 an hour to fill out a 42-page questionnaire for each defendant sampled. The bulk of the data on the circumstances of the offense was taken from a one or two page police or criminal investigation report. Most of the questionnaire items are categorical, indicating whether or not the coder believed a particular aggravating, mitigating or evidentiary factor occurred in the case.

III. *Limitation on the GCSS Database*

Despite the persistent data-gathering effort, the final database has serious problems. Over 100 questionnaire items associated with the crime were unknown for a significant percentage of the 1,082 cases. For instance, in 41% of the cases, it was unknown if the homicide was motivated by racial hatred. In 46% of the cases, it was unknown if the homicide had been planned for more than five minutes. In 74% of the cases, it was unknown whether the victim pleaded for his life. In 82% of the cases it was unknown if the defendant expressed pleasure with the homicide. Even the race of the victim was unknown for 62 cases. The consistency and accuracy of the data was a further problem. When identical aggravating or mitigating factors were compared in the same case between the earlier Procedural Reform Study and the later GCSS, differences were often found.

There are further structural problems with the questionnaire and the coding of items. Most crime-related factors are collected as categorical items, which ignores qualitative differences in the factors between cases. In the case of homicides with multiple offenders, the study adopted the protocol of attributing the aggravating circumstances of the crime to each offender without adjustment for his particular level of involvement. This muddling of the aggravating variables makes it more difficult for statistical models to predict or explain the sentencing outcomes for each offender. Multiple offenders are involved in 40.3% of the life sentence cases and 61.6% of death penalty cases.

To assess the reliability and face validity of the data from the two studies, I presented the coded data on the death penalty cases to the State attorneys who litigate all death penalty appeals for Georgia. After examining the data, the consensus agreed that the two studies missed important aggravating and evidentiary facts in the death penalty cases. In fact, important aggravating factors were missing from McCleskey's own case.

Murder cases are stories, not a collection of categorical aggravating, mitigating, and evidentiary factors. Even if the foils available in McCleskey's questionnaire were completely and accurately filled out, there would still be insufficient detail to enable anyone, unfamiliar with his case, to recreate the crime story.

The District Court ruled on the sufficiency of the database and found "the data base has substantial flaws and that petitioner has failed to establish by a preponderance of the evidence that it is essentially trustworthy," and "there are errors in coding the questionnaire for the case *sub judice*. This fact alone will invalidate several important premises of petitioner's experts."

IV. *Analysis of the GCSS: Is the Georgia Sentencing System Arbitrary?*

If a defendant is convicted of murder and the prosecution asks for the death penalty, then the trial moves to the penalty phase. The jury is obligated to consider the combination of all relevant aggravating, mitigating and evidentiary facts of the case before imposing a sentence. Thus, it is impossible to judge the appropriateness of a defendant's sentence based upon the knowledge of whether or not one or several particular factors occurred. However, if the revised statutes are working as designed, then death-sentenced defendants should have a relatively high frequency of incidents that tend to exacerbate homicides such as the mutilation or rape of the victim. Furthermore, death-sentenced defendants should also have a relatively low frequency of incidents that tend to excuse homicides such as the killing resulting from a family quarrel or other dispute. This is precisely the pattern that is depicted by the Georgia Charging and Sentencing Study database.

Table 15-2 below compares the incidence of important aggravating and mitigating factors of the crimes according to the offender's conviction and sentence.

The 1,082 defendants were divided into three distinct groups by crime of conviction (voluntary manslaughter or murder) and sentence: (1) defendants convicted of voluntary manslaughter and sentenced to prison for 1 to 20 years, (2) defendants convicted of murder and sentenced to life imprisonment and (3) defendants convicted of murder and sentenced to death. For several important aggravating and mitigating features of homicides, Table 15-2 displays the percentage of cases for which each of these factors occurred, broken down by crime of conviction and sentence. Table 15-2 is an abbreviated version of a more detailed exhibit with over 100 aggravating and mitigating factors that I presented to the court.

According to Table 15-2, the victim was killed during an armed robbery in 55.8% of the death sentence cases, 28.0% of the life sentence cases, and 2.8% of the voluntary manslaughter cases. On the other hand, the homicide arose as the result of a dispute in 81.4% percent of the voluntary manslaughter cases, 46.8% of the life sentence cases and only 14.1% of the death sentence cases.

Cases in which the occurrence of a factor is unknown are excluded from the percentage calculation for that factor. Admittedly, the vast number of unknown and incorrect data in the GCSS database limit the accuracy and reliability of any analysis of the data. Nevertheless, Table 15-2 shows a consistent pattern of higher percentages for aggravating factors and lower percentages for mitigating factors as the sentence increases in severity. Death sentence cases tend to exhibit the highest percentage of each aggravating factor and the lowest percentage of each mitigating factor.

Of particular interest is the third section of Table 15-2, where 77.3% of the defendants convicted of voluntary manslaughter and 78.4% of defendants convicted of murder and sentenced to life are classified as poor as compared to only 38.0% of the defendants sentenced to death. This is inconsistent with the theory that only the poor and the powerless are sentenced to death.

V. *Race of Victim Analysis*

The Georgia Charging and Sentencing Study estimated that 7% of white defendants were sentenced to death as compared to only 4% of black defendants. Therefore, death sentences were imposed on a higher percentage of whites than blacks. However, when the cases were divided up by the race of the victim, 11% of the white victim killers were sentenced to death as compared to only 1% of the black victim killers. There are two plausible explanations for this 10 percent disparity.

Baldus testified that racial factors play a role in determining who receives the death penalty in Georgia. He contends that at least part of the difference in death sentencing rates is due to institutionalized racism in the Georgia sentencing system, in that a black life is not held to be as valuable as a white life. An alternative explanation for the 10 percent disparity in death sentencing rates is that white victim homicides generally occur in more aggravated circumstances than black victim homicides. The GCSS database supports this position. **Table 15-3** displays the percentage of cases in which several of the more important aggravating and mitigating features are broken down by the victim's race.

| Table 15-2 | Comparison of Aggravating and Mitigating Crime Factors by Conviction and Sentence | | | | | |

	Voluntary Manslaughter Conviction: 1–20 Years		Murder Conviction: Life Sentence		Murder Conviction: Death Sentence	
Aggravating Factors	Count**	Percent	Count**	Percent	Count**	Percent
Victim killed during armed robbery	14/504	2.8%	118/422	28.0%	77/138	55.8%
Victim kidnapped	2/504	0.4%	27/422	6.4%	51/138	37.0%
Victim raped	1/504	0.2%	15/422	3.6%	28/138	20.3%
Victim beaten	21/502	4.2%	50/420	11.9%	28/140	20.0%
Victim witness to crime	3/501	0.6%	51/390	13.1%	56/117	47.9%
Execution style murder	24/468	5.1%	65/380	17.1%	67/125	53.6%
Victim mutilated	7/502	1.4%	43/420	10.2%	43/140	30.7%
Killing unnecessary to finish crime	7/499	1.4%	45/395	11.4%	50/119	42.0%
Victim pled for life	11/118	9.3%	32/98	32.7%	44/67	65.7%
Victim tortured	2/502	0.4%	5/420	1.2%	17/140	12.1%
Victim forced to disrobe	2/502	0.4%	20/420	4.8%	44/140	31.4%
Defendant resisted arrest	31/474	6.5%	75/403	18.6%	53/138	38.4%
Mitigating Factors						
Jealously motivated the killing	67/421	15.9%	43/392	11.0%	1/139	0.7%
Defendant enraged	389/444	87.6%	166/348	47.7%	23/109	21.1%
Family, lover, liquor, barroom fight	321/443	72.5%	150/390	38.5%	12/129	9.3%
Killing resulted from dispute	373/458	81.4%	178/380	46.8%	18/128	14.1%
Defendant remorseful	32/56	57.1%	20/74	27.0%	2/39	5.1%
Victim provoked passion in defendant	92/397	23.2%	23/391	5.9%	0/131	0.0%
Defendant/Victim Status						
Defendant poor	389/503	77.3%	327/417	78.4%	38/100	38.0%
Defendant high status	12/504	2.4%	12/416	2.9%	4/127	3.1%
Victim a stranger to defendant	38/495	7.7%	122/413	29.5%	82/140	58.6%
Victim family, friend, or intimate	272/495	54.9%	149/419	35.6%	20/140	14.3%
Victim a police officer	0/507	0.0%	13/421	3.1%	9/140	6.4%
Multiple offenders	45/500	9.2%	170/422	40.3%	85/138	61.6%
Number of cases in database	516		426		140	

* Cases in which the occurrence of a factor is unknown are excluded from the percentage calculation for that factor.

** Under the column "COUNT," the denominator indicates the number of defendants for which the factor was known and the numerator indicates the number of defendants for which the factor was indicated present in the case.

Table 15-3	Comparison of Aggravating and Mitigating Crime Factors by the Race of the Victim					
	White Victim Cases		**Black Victim Cases**			
Aggravating Factors	**Count**	**Percent**	**Count**	**Percent**	**Percent Difference**	**Z Score**
Victim killed during armed robbery	170/510	33.3%	37/498	7.4%	25.9%	10.2
Victim kidnapped	68/510	13.3%	11/498	2.2%	11.1%	6.6
Victim raped	29/510	5.7%	15/498	3.0%	2.7%	2.1
Victim beaten	63/512	12.6%	31/493	6.3%	6.3%	3.3
Victim witness to crime	92/471	19.5%	17/481	3.5%	16.0%	7.8
Execution style murder	118/465	25.4%	34/456	7.5%	17.9%	7.3
Victim mutilated	76/512	14.8%	14/493	2.8%	12.0%	6.7
Killing unnecessary to finish crime	81/474	17.1%	21/484	4.3%	12.8%	6.4
Victim pled for life	60/156	38.5%	26/117	22.2%	16.3%	2.9
Victim tortured	18/512	3.5%	6/493	3.0%	6.8%	4.3
Victim forced to disrobe	50/512	9.8%	15/493	3.0%	6.8%	4.3
Defendant resisted arrest	112/493	22.7%	42/469	9.0%	13.7%	5.8
Mitigating Factors						
Jealosy motivated the killing	29/477	6.1%	70/427	16.4%	−10.3%	−5.0
Defendant enraged	200/423	47.3%	334/428	78.0%	−30.7%	−9.3
Family, lover, liquor, barroom fight	165/468	35.3%	284/444	64.0%	−28.7%	−8.7
Killing resulted from dispute	205/464	44.2%	327/450	72.7%	−28.5%	−8.7
Defendant remorseful	21/91	23.1%	29/71	40.8%	−17.7%	−2.4
Victim provoked passion in defendant	34/451	7.5%	73/417	17.5%	−10.0%	−4.5
Defendant/Victim Status						
Defendant poor	302/469	64.4%	407/488	83.4%	−19.0%	−6.7
Defendant high status	20/493	4.1%	8/494	1.6%	2.5%	2.3
Victim a stranger to defendant	184/509	35.8%	55/483	18.8%	17.0%	9.1
Victim, family, friend, or intimate	167/509	34.6%	242/483	39.6%	−5.0%	−5.5
Victim a police officer	18/512	3.5%	3/498	0.6%	2.9%	3.2
Multiple offenders	227/507	44.8%	65/495	13.3%	31.5%	10.9
Number of cases in database**	516		504			
Death sentence percentage		11%		1%		

 * Cases in which the occurrence of a factor is unknown are excluded from the percentage calculation for that factor.

 ** The percentage calculations omit the 62 cases in which the race of the victim was unknown.

 *** The Z-value indicates the number of standard deviations the calculated percent difference is from 0.

White victim homicides have a much higher incidence of armed robberies, kidnappings, and rapes. For example, in 33.3% of the white victim cases, the victim was killed during the course of an armed robbery as compared to only 7.4% of the black victim cases. The 25.9% difference in armed robbery rates between white victim and black victim cases is approximately 10.2 standard deviations above 0%. Furthermore, white victim homicides show a greater percentage of mutilations, execution style murders, tortures, and beaten victims, features which generally aggravate homicides and increase the likelihood of a death sentence if one or more statutory aggravating factors is also present.

On the other hand, cases involving black victims are more likely to involve an enraged and remorseful defendant, who kills as the result of a fight or dispute. For instance, in 44.2% of the white victim cases, the homicide was precipitated by a dispute or fight as compared to 72.7% of the black victim homicides.

VI. *Defendant-Victim Racial Combination Analysis*

The GCSS projected that 22% of black killers of white victims, 8% of white killers of white victims, 1% of black killers of black victims, and 3% of white killers of black victims are sentenced to death. **Table 15-4** shows the incidence of important aggravating and mitigating factors broken down by the four defendant-victim racial combinations.

The four defendant-victim racial combinations provide the key that unlocks the race-of-victim sentencing puzzle. Each defendant-victim racial combination portrays a fundamentally different homicide pattern. The black defendant–white victim cases are the most aggravated of all four defendant-victim racial combinations. In 67.1% of the cases, the homicide results from an armed robbery whereas only 18.2% of the time is the homicide precipitated by a dispute. The interracial nature of this kind of homicide minimizes the possibility that the killing arose due to a family dispute, a quarrel between lovers, or arguments between friends and relatives. The victim was a stranger 70.6% of the time, and a family member or friend in only 4.9% of the cases. Multiple offenders were involved in 58.6% of the cases. Black defendant–white victim killings are invariably linked to felony circumstances which legally qualifies the defendant for a death sentence.

Of all four defendant-victim racial combinations, the black defendant–black victim homicides occur most frequently with 477 cases. Only 6.6% of the time did the homicide result from an armed robbery, whereas 73.0% of the time the killing was precipitated by a dispute. In this category of homicide, the victim is a stranger only 9.6% of the time as compared to a family member or friend 51.4% of the time. Multiple offenders are involved in only 12.4% of the cases. This kind of homicide is characterized by poor defendants (83.9%), acting alone, who kill family members, friends, or other acquaintances during a fight or argument. This type of killing tends to have mitigating circumstances which explains why few of these defendants are ever sentenced to death.

The white defendant–white victim cases reflect a mixture of two basic types of killings. Although the majority of these homicides are precipitated by disputes and fights, a significant percentage occur during the course of a felony or involve horrible brutal killings.

Table 15-4	Comparison of Aggravating and Mitigating Crime Factors by the Defendant-Victim Racial Combination							
	Black Kills White		White Kills White		Black Kills Black		White Kills Black	
Aggravating Factors	Count	Percent	Count	Percent	Count	Percent	Count	Percent
Victim killed during armed robbery	96/143	67.1%	74/367	20.2%	31/471	6.6%	6/27	22.2%
Victim kidnapped	26/143	18.2%	74/367	20.2%	10/471	6.6%	6/27	22.2%
Victim raped	14/143	9.8%	42/367	11.4%	15/471	3.2%	0/27	0.0%
Victim beaten	16/143	11.2%	15/367	4.1%	30/467	6.4%	1/26	3.8%
Victim witness to crime	47/129	36.4%	47/369	12.7%	14/457	3.1%	3/24	12.5%
Execution style murder	42/127	33.1%	76/338	22.5%	131/432	7.2%	3/24	12.5%
Victim mutilated	25/143	17.5%	51/369	13.8%	13/467	2.8%	1/26	3.8%
Killing unnecessary to finish crime	47/124	37.9%	34/350	9.7%	21/461	4.6%	0/23	0.0%
Victim pled for life	25/43	58.1%	35/113	31.0%	23/108	21.3%	3/9	33.3%
Victim tortured	3/143	2.1%	15/369	4.1%	6/467	1.3%	0/26	0.0%
Victim forced to disrobe	18/143	12.6%	32/369	8.7%	15/467	3.2%	0/26	0.0%
Defendant resisted arrest	37/141	26.2%	75/352	21.3%	37/444	8.3%	5/25	20.0%
Mitigating Factors								
Jealousy motivated the killing	0/140	0.0%	29/337	8.6%	70/403	17.4%	0/24	0.0%
Defendant enraged	22/121	18.2%	178/302	58.9%	321/409	78.5%	13/19	68.4%
Family, lover, liquor, barroom fight	10/133	7.5%	155/335	46.3%	273/420	65.0%	11/24	45.8%
Killing resulted from dispute	24/132	18.2%	181/332	54.5%	311/426	73.0%	16/24	66.7%
Defendant remorseful	3/22	13.6%	18/69	26.1%	26/67	38.8%	3/4	75.0%
Victim provoked passion in defendant	4/132	3.0%	30/319	9.4%	67/394	17.0%	6/23	26.1%
Defendant/Victim Status								
Defendant poor	93/125	74.4%	209/344	60.8%	386/460	83.9%	21/28	75.0%
Defendant high status	0/133	0.0%	20/360	5.6%	7/466	1.5%	1/28	3.6%
Victim a stranger to defendant	101/143	70.6%	83/366	22.7%	44/457	9.6%	11/26	42.3%
Victim, family, friend, or intimate	7/143	4.9%	160/366	43.7%	235/457	51.4%	7/26	26.9%
Victim a police officer	15/142	10.6%	3/370	0.8%	3/472	0.5%	0/26	0.0%
Multiple offenders	82/140	58.6%	145/367	39.5%	58/468	12.4%	8/27	29.6%
Number of cases in database**	145		371		477		28	
Death sentence percentage		22%		8%		1%		3%

* Cases in which the occurrence of a factor is unknown are excluded from the percentage calculation for that factor.

** The percentage calculations omit the 62 cases in which the race of the victim was unknown.

Only 28 cases are categorized as white defendant black victim homicides. Four of these cases are misclassified as interracial killings due to the convention adopted by the study of classifying Hispanic defendants as white but Hispanic victims as black. The relatively few incidents of white defendant black victim homicides and the uncertain data make it difficult to ascertain any distinctive pattern. Yet, one important fact is clear. This type of homicide rarely occurs in Georgia. In fact, over 95% of the black victim cases have black defendants. The black victim homicide patterns revealed by the GCSS are generally consistent with earlier studies of homicides in Atlanta, Georgia.

VII. *Conclusion*

As a whole, black victim homicides in Georgia are less aggravated and more mitigated than white victim homicides. Accordingly, a higher percentage of killers of whites are sentenced to death than killers of blacks. The racial death sentencing patterns found in Georgia are not unique to Georgia. Similar aggregate racial death sentencing patterns have been identified in Florida, Texas, Ohio, Mississippi, Oklahoma, Illinois, Arkansas, Virginia, North Carolina, and South Carolina.

But in Georgia, equal death sentencing rates by race of the victim would be more suggestive of racial bias than higher death sentencing rates for white victim cases. Furthermore, to rectify the imbalance in death sentencing rates by race, Georgia prosecutors and juries would be required to consider race along with the aggravating, mitigating, and evidentiary facts of the case before deciding to seek or impose the death penalty.

Baldus and others have argued that the low death sentencing rate for black victim cases is due, in part, to a lower value that the state of Georgia places on a black life. Following this line of reasoning, the equalization of death sentencing rates by race in Georgia would require that more death sentences be imposed on black defendants who kill black victims. But black on black homicides are the most mitigated of the four defendant-victim racial combinations.

The GCSS attempts to categorize defendants that are "similarly situated," based upon the aggravating, mitigating, and evidentiary factors in their case. Death sentencing disparities, by race, of "similarly situated" cases are interpreted as evidence of racial discrimination. A fair test of capital decisions made by Georgia prosecutors, juries, and trial judges, requires that the analysis be limited to "death eligible" defendants and all relevant information be considered that was known to the decision maker at the point in time that the capital decision was made. Yet every murder case is a unique combination of aggravating, mitigating, and evidentiary facts. The determination of these facts for a particular case is not always straightforward, as witnesses can give conflicting testimony at trial, or the prosecuting attorney and defense attorney can interpret the evidence differently. Cataloguing the facts of the case into simple categorical variables loses critical information that can mean the difference between life and death.

At the same time that the District Court denied McCleskey's claim of racial bias in the Georgia sentencing system, the court threw out McCleskey's conviction and sentence on the grounds that one of the witnesses, Offie Evans (McCleskey's cellmate), was promised leniency for his testimony against McCleskey and this promise was not divulged to the jury. The Eleventh Circuit Court of Appeals disagreed and reversed the District Court on this issue. Baldus did not collect any data concerning promises to witnesses nor concerning most of the myriad technical issues which death-sentenced litigants regularly raise on appeal. Ironically, at the same time as McCleskey's lawyers argued that Baldus had controlled for every possible factor in his 230+ variable model that could conceivably cause a death sentence, they also argued that other factors were present that served to deny McCleskey a fair trial and could have drastically changed the outcome of his trial.

The criminal justice system affords each capital defendant an opportunity to a fair trial with impartial jurors. Two hundred years of careful jurisprudence has attempted to preserve and improve the integrity of the trial process. The appellate courts rely upon voluminous records to carefully consider every aspect of a death penalty case to determine if the sentence is appropriate and if the trial conforms to the highest standards of fairness and equity. General statistics on homicide cases based on limited and incomplete data is a poor substitute for the judicial process.

■ Race—Perspectives

■ Issue—Is Racism a Conclusive Moral Argument Against the Death Penalty?

Earnest van den Haag, "In Defense of the Death Penalty: A Legal—Practical—Moral Analysis"

Three questions about the death penalty so overlap that they must each be answered. I shall ask seriatim: Is the death penalty constitutional? Is it useful? Is the death penalty morally justifiable?

I . The Constitutional Question

To regard the death penalty as unconstitutional one must believe that the standards that determine what is "cruel and unusual" have so evolved since 1868 as to prohibit now what was authorized then. What might these standards be? And what shape must their evolution take to be constitutionally defective?

A. Consensus A moral consensus, intellectual or popular, could have evolved to find execution "cruel and unusual," but it did not. Intellectual opinion is divided. Polls suggest that today most people would vote for the death penalty. Congress, reflecting this opinion, recently has legislated the death penalty for skyjacking under certain conditions. The representative assemblies of two-thirds of the states have reenacted capital punishment when previous laws were found constitutionally defective.

If however, there were a consensus against the death penalty, the Constitution expects the political process to reflect it rather than judicial decisions. Courts are meant to interpret the law made by the political process and to set constitutional limits to it—not to replace it by responding to a presumed moral consensus. Surely the "cruel and unusual" phrase was not meant to authorize the courts to become legislatures. Thus, neither a consensus of moral opinion, nor a "moral discovery" by judges is to be disguised as a constitutional interpretation. Even when revealed by a burning bush, new moral norms were not meant to become constitutional norms by means of court decisions. To be sure, the courts in the past have occasionally done away with obsolete kinds of punishment—but never in the face of legislative and popular position and reenactment. Abolitionists now press the courts to create rather than to confirm obsolescence. That courts are urged to do what so clearly is for voters and lawmakers to decide suggests that the absence of consensus for abolition is recognized by the opponents of capital punishment.

What then can the phrase "cruel and unusual punishment" mean today?

B. "Cruel" The term cruel may be understood to mean excessive, punitive without, or beyond, a rational-utilitarian purpose. Since capital punishment excludes rehabilitation and is not needed for incapacitation, the remaining rational-utilitarian purpose would be deterrence, the reduction of the rate at which the crime punished is committed by others. I shall consider this reduction further on. Here, I wish to note that if the criterion for the constitutionality of any punishment were an actual demonstration of its rational-utilitarian effectiveness, all legal punishments would be in as much constitutional jeopardy as the death penalty. Are fines for corporations deterrent? Rehabilitative? Incapacitative? Is a jail term for possession of marijuana? Has it ever been established beyond doubt that ten years in prison are doubly as deterrent as five, or at least sufficiently more deterrent?

The constitution certainly does not require a demonstration of rational-utilitarian effects for any punishment. Such a demonstration so far has not been available. To demand it for one penalty—however grave—and not for others, when it is known that no such demonstration is available, seems constitutionally unjustified. Penalties always have been regarded as constitutional if they can be plausibly intended (rather than demonstrated) to be effective (useful), and if they are not grossly excessive (i.e., unjust).

Justice, a rational but nonutilitarian purpose of punishment, requires that a sanction be proportioned to the gravity of the crime. Thus, constitutional justice authorizes, even calls for, penalties commensurate with the gravity of the crime. One cannot demand that this constitutionally required escalation stop short of the death penalty unless one furnishes positive proof of its injustice as well as ineffectiveness. If this be thought of as cruelty, then no proof exists of either aspect.

C. "Unusual" The term "unusual" is generally interpreted to mean either randomly capricious and therefore unconstitutional, or capricious in a biased, discriminatory way so as to particularly burden specifiable groups. Random arbitrariness might violate the Eighth Amendment, while biased arbitrariness would violate the Equal Protection Clause.

For the sake of argument, let me grant that either or both forms of capriciousness prevail, and that they are less tolerable with respect to the death penalty than with respect to milder penalties—which certainly are not meted out less capriciously. However prevalent, neither form of capriciousness would argue for abolishing the death penalty. Capriciousness is not inherent in that penalty, or in any penalty, but occurs in its distribution. Therefore, the remedy lies in changing the laws and procedures that distribute the penalty.

D. Unavoidable Capriciousness If capricious distribution places some convicts, or groups of convicts, at an unwarranted disadvantage, can it be remedied sufficiently to satisfy the Eighth and Fourteenth Amendments? Some capriciousness is unavoidable. Decisions of the criminal justice system often rest on such accidental factors as the presence or absence of witnesses to an act or the cleverness or clumsiness of police officers. All court decisions must rest on the available and admissible evidence for, rather than the actuality of, guilt. Availability of evidence is necessarily accidental to the actuality of whatever it is that the evidence is offered to demonstrate.

If possible, without loss of other desiderata, accident and capriciousness should be minimized. But discretionary judgments obviously cannot be avoided altogether. The framers of the Constitution certainly were aware of the unavoidable elements of discretion which affect all human decisions, including those of police officers, of prosecutors, and of the courts. Because it always was unavoidable, discretion no more speaks against the constitutionality of the criminal justice system or of any of its penalties now than it did when the Constitution was written—unless something has evolved since, to make unavoidable discretion, tolerable before, intolerable now—at least for the death penalty. I know of no such evolution; and if it had occurred I would think it up to the legislative branch of government to register it.

The Constitution, although it enjoins us to minimize capriciousness, does not enjoin a standard of unattainable perfection or exclude penalties because that standard has not been attained. Although we should not enlarge discretion *praeter necessitatem* some discretion is unavoidable and even desirable, and certainly is no reason for giving up any form of punishment.

E. Avoidable Capriciousness Capriciousness should be prevented by abolishing penalties capriciously distributed only when it is so unavoidable and excessive that penalties are randomly distributed between the guilty and the innocent. When that is not the case the abuses of discretion which lead to discrimination against particular groups of defendants or convicts certainly require correction, but not abolition of the penalty abused.

II. *Moral Issues*

A. Justice and Equality Regardless of constitutional interpretation, the morality and legitimacy of the abolitionist argument regarding capriciousness, discretion, or discrimination, would be more persuasive if it were alleged that those selectively executed are not guilty. But the argument merely maintains that some guilty, but favored, persons or groups escape the death penalty. This is hardly sufficient for letting others escape it. On the contrary, that some guilty persons or groups elude it argues for *extending* the death penalty to them.

Justice requires punishing the guilty—as many of the guilty as possible—even if only some can be punished, and sparing the innocent—as many of the innocent as possible, even if not all are spared. Morally, justice must always be preferred to equality. It would surely be wrong to treat everybody with equal justice in preference to meting out justice to some. Justice cannot ever permit sparing some guilty persons, or punishing some innocent ones, for the sake of equality—because others have been unjustly spared or punished. In practice, penalties never could be applied if we insisted that they cannot be inflicted on any guilty person unless we are able to make sure that they are equally applied to all other guilty persons. Anyone familiar with law enforcement knows that punishments can be inflicted only on an unavoidably capricious selection of the guilty.

Although it does not warrant serious discussion, the argument from capriciousness looms large in briefs and decisions. For the last seventy years, courts have tried—lamentably and unproductively—to prevent errors of procedure, or of evidence collection, or of decision-making, by the paradoxical method of letting defendants go free as a punishment, or warning, to errant law enforcers. Yet the strategy admittedly never has prevented the errors it was designed to prevent—although it has released countless guilty persons. There is no more merit in the attempt to persuade the courts to let all capital crime defendants go free of capital punishment because some have wrongly escaped it, than in attempting to persuade the courts to let all burglars go, because some have wrongly escaped detection or imprisonment.

B. The Essential Moral Question Is the death penalty morally just and/or useful? This is the essential moral, as distinguished from the constitutional, question. Discrimination is irrelevant to this moral question. If the death penalty were distributed equally and uncapriciously and with superhuman perfection to all the guilty, but were morally unjust, it would be unjust in each case.

Contrariwise, if the death penalty is morally just, however discriminatorily applied to only some of the guilty, it remains just in each case in which it is applied. The utilitarian (political) effects of unequal justice may well be detrimental to the social fabric because they outrage our passion for equality before the law. Unequal justice also is morally repellent. Nonetheless unequal justice is still justice. The guilty do not become innocent or less deserving of punishment because others escaped it. Nor does any innocent deserve punishment because others suffer it. Justice remains just, however unequal, while injustice remains unjust, however equal. While both are desired, justice and equality are not identical. Equality before the law should be extended and enforced—but not at the expense of justice.

C. Maldistribution Among the Guilty Capriciousness, at any rate, is used as a sham argument against capital punishment by abolitionists. They would oppose the death penalty if it could be meted out without any discretion. They would oppose the death penalty in a homogeneous country without racial discrimination. And they would oppose the death penalty if the incomes of those executed and of those spared were the same. Actually, abolitionists oppose the death penalty, not its possible maldistribution.

D. Maldistribution Between Guilty and Innocent What about persons executed in error? The objection here is not that some of the guilty escape, but that some of the innocent do not—a matter far more serious than discrimination among the guilty. Yet, when urged by abolitionists, this, along with all distributional arguments, is a sham. Why? Abolitionists are opposed to the death penalty for the guilty as much as for the innocent. Hence, the question of guilt, if at all relevant to their position, cannot be decisive for them. Guilt is decisive only to those who urge the death penalty for the guilty. They must worry about distribution—part of the justice they seek.

E. Miscarriages of Justice The execution of innocents believed guilty is a miscarriage of justice that must be opposed whenever detected. But such miscarriages of justice do not warrant abolition of the death penalty. Unless the moral drawbacks of an activity or practice, which include the possible death of innocent bystanders, outweigh the moral advantages, which include the innocent lives that might be saved by it, the activity is warranted. Most human activities—medicine, manufacturing, automobile and air traffic, sports, not to speak of wars and revolutions—cause the death of innocent bystanders. Nevertheless, if the advantages sufficiently outweigh the disadvantages, human activities, including those of the penal system with all its punishments, are morally justified.

Stephen Nathanson, "The 'Arbitrariness Argument' for Abolishing Capital Punishment"

I. *Introduction*
This paper defends both the relevance and the force of the arbitrariness argument against capital punishment. The heart of the argument is that the death penalty ought to be abolished because arbitrary factors play a central role in determining who is condemned to die and who is not. Sometimes race is cited as the arbitrary factor, sometimes economic status or chance. Whatever specific factors are cited, the claim is that people equally guilty are punished in different ways. These unequal sentences are evidence of the injustice of the death penalty. Because efforts to end arbitrariness in sentencing are doomed to fail, the only remedy to the problem is abolition of the death penalty.

II. Arbitrariness and the Supreme Court
Furman invalidated existing laws authorizing capital punishment, thus forcing death penalty supporters to write new laws to eliminate arbitrariness from sentencing in capital cases. A central question since *Gregg* has been whether the new laws solved the arbitrariness problem or merely papered over it. A large body of research indicates that the legal changes have failed to eliminate the arbitrariness that the Court had objected to in *Furman*. In *McCleskey*, however, the Court rejected statistical evidence of the continuing impact of race on capital sentences, thus cementing the decision it reached in *Gregg*. But critics continue to raise the arbitrariness issue, and two Supreme Court justices, Powell and Blackmun, later expressed regret for supporting the death penalty in *Gregg* and *McCleskey*. Interestingly, the history of attempts to deal with the arbitrariness issue in the United States played a role in the Supreme Court of South Africa's 1995 ruling that the death penalty violated its new constitution.

III. *Criticisms of the Arbitrariness Argument*
Death penalty supporters can respond to charges of arbitrariness in one of three ways. They can a) deny that the process is still arbitrary, b) admit the problem and work for further reform, or c) claim that the arbitrariness argument is flawed and provides no evidence that the death penalty is unjust. This last, most sweeping objection has been most forcefully expressed by Ernest van den Haag. He writes:

If the death penalty is morally just, however discriminatorily applied to only some of the guilty, it does remain just in each case in which it is applied. The guilty do not become innocent or less deserving of punishment because others escaped it.

The logic of van den Haag's view rests on his equation of doing justice with giving people what they deserve. He holds that what people deserve is the only relevant factor in determining if a punishment is just. For this reason, comparisons between the treatment of different individuals are irrelevant. If desert alone matters, unequal and discriminatory treatment do not. Given these views, van den Haag's dismissive response to the arbitrariness problem is not surprising. He writes:

The abolitionist argument regarding capriciousness, discretion, or discrimination, would be more persuasive if it were alleged that those selectively executed are not guilty. But the argument maintains that some guilty, but favored, persons or groups escape the death penalty. This is hardly sufficient for letting others escape it. On the contrary, that some guilty persons or groups elude it argues for extending the death penalty to them.

These objections present a powerful challenge to the arbitrariness argument. Underlying them is the following plausible argument:

1. The justice of a punishment is determined by whether the person deserves it.

2. What people deserve is unaffected by the treatment of other people.

3. Therefore, punishments can be just even if they are unequally applied.

Van den Haag believes that the *Furman* Court erred in deciding that arbitrariness rendered the death penalty unjust. For this reason, even if later reforms failed to eliminate arbitrariness, it does not matter.

IV. How Arbitrariness Undermines Justice

In order to show why these objections are mistaken, I will distinguish three different versions of the arbitrariness argument. I will call them the arguments from

- arbitrary severity,
- arbitrary inequality, and
- arbitrary unreliability.

While van den Haag and other critics see the arbitrariness argument only as an argument against arbitrary inequalities, the argument as a whole calls attention to *excessive* punishments in some cases and, more generally, to the *unreliability* of process of sentencing in capital cases.

A. Version 1: Arbitrary Severity Defenders of the arbitrariness argument stress the following sorts of facts:

- only a small percentage of people guilty of homicide are sentenced to die;
- persons guilty of similar crimes are often given different punishments;
- differences in sentences cannot be explained by reference to legal criteria; and
- differences in sentences can be explained by the influence of arbitrary, legally irrelevant factors.

Defenders point out, for example, that people who kill whites are more likely to be executed than people who kill blacks, even though race is not a legitimate reason to judge one crime to be worse than another. According to a 1998 survey, in the twenty years following *Gregg*, 83% of those executed were charged with the murder of a white victim, while only 1 percent of executions involved a white person who had killed a black victim. Other studies examine specific cases in order to show that similar crimes are often punished quite differently, some leading to death and others to imprisonment.

Critics reply that these instances of arbitrary treatment are irrelevant as long as those who are executed deserve their punishment. That others who are equally deserving are not executed is a form of unjust leniency, but it does not undermine the justice of executing those who deserve to die.

This reply fails because it focuses exclusively on the problem of unjust leniency for some while completely ignoring the problem of undeserved, excessive harshness in punishment for others. Van den Haag's approach to these issues rests on a false picture of the sentencing process. His view, represented in the charts below, assumes that the process begins with a group of people, all of whom deserve to die.

Stage 1

Convicted Murderers
Who Deserve to Die

This group is then subdivided into those who are sentenced to die and those who are sentenced to imprisonment.

Stage 2

	Deserve to Die
Sentenced to Die	A
Sentenced to Imprisonment	B

Based on this image of the process, it is natural to think that people who are executed have no legitimate complaint since all of them are in the "deserve to die" column. Understood in this way, it is easy to think that the only possible injustice is excessive leniency.

This interpretation overlooks the possibility that arbitrary factors may lead to punishments that are excessively harsh. It overlooks a whole category of people whose punishment is *greater* than they deserve. This occurs because the critics misunderstand both stages of the process. The charts below accurately represent the situation.

Stage 1	
Convicted Murderers	**Convicted Murderers**
Who Deserve to Die	Who Do Not Deserve to Die

The people in this group, some of whom deserve to die and some of whom do not, are then sorted into two further groups in the sentencing phase. The resulting distribution, shown in the chart below, includes a group of people that van den Haag completely overlooks.

Stage 2		
	Deserve to Die	**Do Not Deserve to Die**
Sentenced to Die	A	C
Sentenced to Imprisonment	B	D

People in group C are sentenced to die even though, by hypothesis, they do not deserve to die. This may occur because a) they are completely innocent or b) although guilty, their crime lacks the appropriate aggravating features or possesses relevant mitigating features. In neither case does the person executed deserve to die.

Why is this form of injustice overlooked by critics? One reason is that defenders of the arbitrariness argument have themselves presented it in a way that strongly suggests the first interpretation. Recall Justice Stewart's description:

> *Of all the people convicted of rapes and murders in 1967 and 1968, many just as reprehensible as these, the petitioners are among a capriciously selected random handful upon whom the sentence has in fact been imposed.*

Justice Douglas speaks of the discrimination that results in "saving those who by social position may be in a more protected position," thus emphasizing the problem of unjust leniency. These passages strongly suggest that the key problem is that some people are treated less severely than they ought to be. What is omitted is the group who, because of the influence of arbitrary factors, receive excessively harsh punishments which they do not deserve.

Critics may also overlook this group because they assume that everyone guilty of first degree murder deserves to die and thus that there is no possibility of excessive severity for them. But this is not the view of the law. The Supreme Court, in rejecting mandatory death sentences in *Woodson*, insisted on individualized consideration of each case. The arbitrariness argument, then, is not only about unequal treatment or unjust leniency. It challenges the view that all who are executed deserve to die. Two kinds of errors, then, are possible: excessive leniency and excessive harshness. The argument from arbitrary severity charges that some people are executed even though—by the law's own criteria—they do not deserve to die.

B. Version 2: Arbitrary Inequality While I have argued that critics mistakenly focus only on arbitrary inequality and ignore the problem of excessive, undeserved punishment, I do not want to suggest that the argument from arbitrary inequality is weak or trivial. It appears weak only when people assume that there is only one criterion of justice, but verdicts and sentences can be just and unjust in many different ways. As the "arbitrary inequality" argument suggests, a sentence may be unjust because it differs from others for similar crimes. In addition, however, a sentence may be unjust because it results from flawed procedures. Likewise, systems and institutions can be unjust as well as individual sentences.

Because van den Haag assumes that individual desert is the only criterion of justice, he can see no relationship between justice and equal treatment. "Justice," he writes, "remains just, however unequal." This view rests on several assumptions:

1. that we can judge the justice of punishments by focusing exclusively on individual cases;

2. that comparisons between punishments are irrelevant to evaluating their justice.

We can see that both these assumptions are false by considering cases in which a person satisfies the conditions for deserving a punishment and yet is unjustly punished.

Suppose that two drivers violate the speed limit but that only one is punished. Suppose, too, that the reason for the disparity is that one person is a friend of the arresting officer while the other is not. According to van den Haag's view, the only problem here is that the unpunished person is treated too leniently; he denies that the punished person is treated unjustly.

In spite of the abstract plausibility of this claim, I believe that virtually all of us would feel unjustly treated if we were punished while equally guilty persons were not. Imagine that both you and the driver of another car are pulled over by a police officer for speeding. The officer writes a speeding ticket that carries a $100 fine for you and then addresses the other driver. While you wait, you hear the officer say, "Joe, I didn't realize it was you. Be more careful because next time I'll give you a ticket!" It is hard to imagine that anyone would not feel aggrieved by this differential treatment, even if we acknowledge our guilt in speeding.

This type of injustice is magnified when it is not an isolated incident. Suppose that friends and relatives of police officers are never punished for speeding violations or that selective enforcement targets only certain identifiable groups of people. To take an extreme case, imagine a town in which only one person receives speeding tickets while all others go free. The unfortunate speeder is continually stopped and ticketed while others speed by. While the unfortunate speeder satisfies the criteria for deserving to be punished, there is something grossly unfair about his being the repeated victim of selective enforcement of the law. He is clearly being treated unequally, and his punishment—though deserved—is clearly not being imposed *because* he deserves it. We cannot explain the pattern of enforcement and punishment by focusing on desert because equally deserving people are allowed to go unpunished. So, injustice in this case has nothing to do with a lack of desert; rather it has to do with unequal treatment.

These examples show the need for a distinction between two kinds of justice, which Joel Feinberg has labeled *comparative* and *noncomparative* justice. Once we see that there are different forms of justice, it becomes clear that conflicts between forms of justice are possible. In the speeding driver cases, the noncomparative, desert criterion is satisfied while the comparative, equal treatment criterion is violated. The same can happen in death penalty cases. If similar cases are treated differently, then a conflict exists between the equal treatment promised by the law and the allocation of punishment according to what people deserve. These punishments are just by one criterion and unjust by the other.

When conflicts occur between comparative and noncomparative justice, how can we assess the overall justice of the punishment? Which kind of justice should take precedence in our overall judgment? While I believe there are reasons favoring comparative justice in death penalty cases, what I want to stress here is that any decision about which criterion takes precedence must appeal to reasons other than equality or desert. Simply saying that someone deserves a punishment does not settle the issue.

Even if one decides that desert-based justice is more important than equal treatment, it is important not to gloss over the conflict. If we ignore the distinction, we will remain blind to the fact that in cases of conflict, no matter what we do, one form of justice is going to be violated. Even if desert trumps equal treatment, the injustice of unequal treatment would remain.

C. Procedural Justice Those who focus only on desert as the criterion of justice ignore a third criterion that is central to the law, the criterion of procedural justice. The existence of this criterion strengthens the claim that punishments can be unjust even when deserved.

To see this, imagine a secret lottery system for punishments. When a murder occurs, someone is selected by lottery and executed for the crime. While virtually everyone punished by such a system would be innocent, it might happen occasionally that a person who has committed a murder is selected by lot and suffers the punishment that (by hypothesis) he deserves. What should we say about such a case? Is the punishment just?

In this case, it is no doubt much better that the guilty person be punished than an innocent person. Still, we ought to be troubled that the punishment is a matter of chance and that no rational procedure ties the sentence to evidence of guilt. What is lacking is *procedural* justice. Even people who are guilty ought only to be punished after a reliable process that establishes their guilt and their degree of culpability and, in the light of these, determines the appropriate punishment. For this reason, one might regard the guilty, lottery-selected murderer as a victim of injustice, even though he deserves the punishment and even though it would be a greater injustice if he were innocent.

The same point applies to other cases where people are not chosen randomly. Victims of lynchings are treated unjustly even if they are believed to be guilty. Likewise, a person may have a trial and still be a victim of procedural injustice. A guilty person can be unjustly punished if he is coerced into confessing, if his conviction is based on falsified evidence, if he lacks a competent lawyer, or if in other ways he lacks a procedure that judges him on the basis of reliable evidence that is presented under fair conditions. Even if there is a sincere belief in guilt, injustices occur when there is no fair, reliable procedure by which guilt is established.

Criteria of procedural justice, then, present us with a third relevant criterion that applies to sentencing for murder, and if we find a combination of unequal sentences and procedural flaws, this would strengthen the claim of injustice even in cases where the persons in question do deserve death.

It is surely irresponsible for people or institutions to impose punishments without taking due care that they are acting properly, and the level of care required increases with the severity of the punishment. If the members of a group execute a person without a proper trial, they are engaging in a form of casual killing. In so doing, they display their own disregard for the value of human life. Supporters of the death penalty—if they are to act consistently with a commitment to the value of human life—must take the requirements of procedural justice very seriously. Execution without procedural justice shows a reckless indifference toward the life of the person punished and is itself a close cousin of murder.

I raise the issue of procedural justice because the biggest obstacle to accepting the injustice of arbitrary inequality is a fixation on desert as the sole criterion of justice. The recognition of procedural injustices helps to shake this narrow focus. Defenders of the arbitrariness argument need not reject the desert criterion, but they remind us that desert is not the whole of justice.

D. The Justice of Systems v. the Justice of Individual Sentences While a desert-focused perspective is entirely individualistic, the arbitrariness argument is a critique of the workings of institutions. It highlights patterns of sentencing and raises concerns about systematic injustice. No system can be perfect, but when there is pervasive injustice, individual errors cannot be dismissed as occasional imperfections in a mostly just practice. Failures to provide equal justice and fair procedures casts doubt on the moral legitimacy of both individual sentences and whole systems.

One mistake in evaluating systems is to suppose that a good faith effort is sufficient for achieving justice. On this view, if no one intentionally acts unjustly, then no injustice occurs. We can see that this is incorrect by considering a system with the following features: the police strive to identify the actual perpetrators of homicides; prosecutors scrupulously try to determine the proper level of criminal charges by paying careful attention to the nature of the crime and the specifications in the law; juries strive to reach accurate decisions of guilt and innocence; sentencing authorities attempt to impose sentences in accord with the requirements of the law; and appeals courts carefully review sentences to insure that procedural and substantive justice are achieved.

Actual systems do not live up to this positive image, but even if they did, they could still be unjust. How could this be? Suppose that police officials are influenced in their investigations by the race or economic class of suspects or victims; suppose that when prosecutors make charging decisions, their view of the seriousness of a crime is affected by the race of the victim or the defendant; suppose that the quality of lawyers for defendants varies with their economic resources so that poor defendants have less effective legal representation; suppose that juries are influenced by the race or social and economic status of victims and defendants or that they fail to understand the laws governing sentencing. In other words, suppose that—in spite of people's best efforts—arbitrary factors have a significant impact on sentences for murders.

As a result, suppose that higher percentages of those who kill whites are sentenced to die than those who kill blacks, that blacks who kill whites have the highest probability of receiving a death sentence, and that those who kill blacks have a much smaller chance of a death sentence. Suppose that the low quality of legal counsel available to poor defendants leads to greater rates of conviction and more severe punishments than occurs with better off defendants who hire their own lawyers. Suppose that wealthy people are seldom sentenced to die while poor people are more frequently executed. A system with these unintended features would have the properties Justice Douglas described in *Furman* when he said that the death penalty was "selectively applied" to people who are "poor and despised, lacking political clout, or members of a suspect or unpopular minority" and that was not applied to "those who by social position may be in a more protected position."

There is strong evidence that the legal system in the United States possesses such features. Having a court-appointed attorney or low socioeconomic status ought not to determine whether a person is killed by the state, but research shows that this happens, and, as with race, this is not surprising because it is consistent with our common sense understanding that these pervasive features of social life have an impact on decisions and events in many areas.

E. Do These Facts Matter? Critics respond that we need to look at the death penalty on a case by case basis and that patterns in sentencing do not matter. These patterns are important not only because they indirectly illuminate what occurs in individual cases, but also because they are relevant to our assessment of institutions and practices. The facts about arbitrariness cast doubt on the justice of the legal system as a whole. Such considerations are ignored when people focus on individual desert alone. Nonetheless, evaluations of systems are not esoteric and play an important role in determining people's attitudes towards the institutions under which they live. While people trust, cooperate with, and even take pride in institutions that are just, when they think institutions are unjust, this calls their legitimacy into question.

It is no trivial matter that the words etched across the Supreme Court building are "Equal Justice Under Law." Those words represent a kind of promise to citizens about the way that they will be treated by the legal institutions; they express a commitment to treating all citizens by the same rules and standards. Whether the government lives up to these promises is relevant to citizens' attitudes toward the claims to loyalty and obedience that governments make on them.

If members of some groups know that those who harm them will be punished more leniently or that the punishments imposed on people like themselves are likely to be more severe than those imposed on others, they will properly view the legal system with distrust and suspicion. Since equal justice is promised to all, unequal justice is a serious defect of the system.

This is not a novel or abstruse criticism. Consistency—treating similar cases similarly—has always been regarded as a central virtue in the administration of the law, while inconsistency is a vice. Moreover, consistency is necessarily a feature of systems rather than individual cases so that there is no way to test for it in any single case; only comparisons will reveal it or its absence. If the death penalty is imposed unequally on different groups or depends on the group membership of the victim, this is an important failure. If equally deserving defendants receive different forms of punishment for reasons not related to the provisions of the law, then the system as a whole is unjust, even if the disparities and inconsistencies are unintended.

In *Furman*, the Supreme Court took these problems seriously and recognized the injustice of the death penalty system. Since *Gregg*, the Court majority has been content to disregard the patterns of arbitrariness and inequality that have persisted in spite of court-mandated reforms. This can only be seen as a retreat from their earlier commitment to systemic justice.

F. Version 3: Arbitrariness and Unreliability I now want to discuss a version of the argument that is suggested by the reasoning of death penalty opponents but not generally articulated well enough to bring out its full force. I call it the argument from *arbitrary unreliability*. According to this argument, if arbitrary factors play a significant causal role in generating sentences, then the sentences too will be arbitrary, and if the sentences are arbitrary, then we have no reason to believe that they are either accurate or just.

This argument, while related to the concerns about procedural justice raised earlier, stresses the causal connection between procedures and outcomes. In the punishment system, the outcome that we want is justice; we want people to receive the punishment which, by the standards of the law, they deserve. If our process is reliable, then we are justified in believing that the punishments imposed by the system are just. If there is evidence of unreliability, this should undermine our confidence that justice is the outcome of the system. In this version of the argument, unequal treatment for similar crimes is seen as evidence of system unreliability and erroneous outcomes.

To see the force of this argument, consider what makes a punishment *non-arbitrary*. A person is non-arbitrarily punished if it is

a) beyond a reasonable doubt that he or she committed the crime in question, and

b) beyond a reasonable doubt that the defendant and crime have the features that the law specifies as the basis for the particular punishment.

When these conditions are met, the punishment can be explained by reference to legally relevant features of the person and the crime. When irrelevant features play a primary role in determining whether and how a person is punished, these conditions are not met, and the punishment is arbitrary.

An extreme form of arbitrariness would be a lottery system. In a punishment lottery, the results are arbitrary because they are random, but randomness is not essential to arbitrariness. What make a random system arbitrary is the lack of a relationship between the punishment and guilt. A non-random process can be arbitrary too if it lacks the proper relationship between punishments and guilt.

Suppose that a good faith effort is made to determine guilt but that the process is known to be unreliable. Suppose, for argument's sake, that we have evidence that half of those punished are innocent. In this case, we have a system of arbitrary punishment because guilt beyond a reasonable doubt has not been established, and the probability of punishing innocent people is as high as the probability of punishing guilty people.

In raising this point, I have arrived at a familiar feature of the death penalty debate—the argument that the death penalty is wrong because innocent people might be executed by mistake. What is usually overlooked is that the argument from innocence is a special case of the argument from arbitrariness. Punishing the innocent in circumstances where we know that judgments of guilt are false or unreliable is one form of arbitrary punishment.

While I have used fanciful examples to raise this problem, the problem itself is far from fanciful. We think of the criterion of "guilt beyond a reasonable doubt" as relating primarily to the role of juries who are considering the evidence presented to them. But what if the evidence presented to jurors cannot be trusted? What if the system for generating evidence is itself unreliable? This is precisely the situation that led Governor George Ryan of Illinois to order a moratorium on executions. Ryan's decision was a response to the fact that while Illinois had executed 12 people for murder between 1977 and 2000, 13 people who had been sentenced to die during that same period were later shown to be innocent and were exonerated.

These problems are not limited to Illinois. According to James McCloskey, from 1973 to 1995, while 226 people were executed in the United States, 54 were released from death row because of innocence. The causes of error nationally are similar to those in Illinois. In their study of wrongful convictions for capital crimes, Hugo Bedau and Michael Radelet identify the questionable actions of police officers and prosecutors as a major cause of wrongful convictions. Similarly, the authors of a general study of wrongful convictions cite "police and prosecutorial overzealousness" as the single, most pervasive "system dynamic" in cases of erroneous convictions.

Another source of error is inadequate legal counsel. The inadequacies cited in a report by the ABA include: the appointment of lawyers who lack criminal trial experience, who do not know the special procedures for capital cases, who lack adequate resources to cover the costs of preparing and investigating their clients' cases. In numerous cases, lawyers fail to introduce mitigating factors in the sentencing phase and fail to make relevant objections during a trial so that they can be considered on appeal. These problems are widely known to officials, but they have had little political incentive to deal with them.

A welcome exception to these blasé attitudes is the decision by Judge Jed Rakoff in *U.S. v. Quinones*. Rakoff, citing the many convictions that have been overturned in recent years by DNA evidence, argues that we can infer that the legal process does not reliably differentiate the innocent from the guilty and therefore that the death penalty violates the Constitution. This view appeals directly to what I have called the argument from unreliability. Because the system cannot be trusted, we cannot trust its judgment in individual cases.

V. *The Argument from Arbitrary Unreliability Concluded*

Recall the two requirements for a non-arbitrary punishment: it must be

> a) beyond a reasonable doubt that the person punished committed the crime, and
>
> b) beyond a reasonable doubt that the defendant and the crime have the features that the law articulates as the basis for the particular punishment.

While executing innocents involves a failure of the first condition, the second condition shows that even people who are guilty of a crime can be unjustly punished. Once we see that the system is unreliable with respect to guilt and innocence, we can see that the same arbitrary factors make it unreliable with respect to whether people deserve death or a lesser punishment. Just as the system cannot be relied on to distinguish the guilty from the innocent, so it cannot be relied on to make the more subtle distinction between

> a) those who are guilty of homicide and deserve a sentence of death, and
>
> b) those who are guilty of homicide but do not deserve death.

Since death sentences are only non-arbitrary when it is beyond a reasonable doubt that a person satisfies the legal criteria for the death penalty, then the unreliability of the system to make these discriminations is grounds for rejecting the death penalty.

Note how this argument differs from the version that van den Haag's criticized. He assumed that we know who deserves to die and thus that the arbitrariness argument is simply about equally deserving people being treated unequally. As I have shown, that is not the only problem with arbitrariness. The arbitrary elements play a causal role that results in disparate sentences for similar crimes. These disparities, in addition to exhibiting instances of unequal justice, also function as evidence for the unreliability of the system. They show the failure of the system to distinguish those who deserve to die from those who do not in a reliable, principled way. As a result, we cannot be reasonably certain that those who are sentenced to die actually satisfy the legal requirements for deserving a death sentence.

Justice Blackmun reached exactly this conclusion in his dissent in *Callins*. He wrote:

> *The basic question—does the system accurately and consistently determine which defendants 'deserve' to die?—cannot be answered in the affirmative.*

Because the system for imposing the death penalty does not "accurately and consistently determine which defendants 'deserve' to die," it cannot justify us in believing that capital punishment is consistent with a proper respect for the value of human life.

VI. Replies to Critics: Michael Davis

Having explained the three versions of the arbitrariness argument, I want to reply briefly to three further objections that have been raised against it.

Michael Davis begins his two part criticism by challenging the role of statistical evidence in studies of arbitrariness. While statistical studies reveal possible arbitrariness, he says, they cannot show that the process is actually arbitrary without a different kind of evidence. He writes:

> All the studies of arbitrariness I have seen are external. The reasons a prosecutor, judge, or jury gave for her act, when reported at all, are treated as claims to be debunked using external evidence. A hundred prosecutors whose acts together have "discriminatory effect" are treated as a unit acting arbitrarily whatever their motivation and however much care they took to be fair. Any final judgment should wait until we hear their side.

Davis's argument parallels the Supreme Court's position in *McCleskey*. There the Court rejected statistical evidence for overturning an individual execution, claiming that the only relevant evidence would be evidence about the particular case. Like Davis, the Court argued that even if patterns of racial discrimination exist, it does not follow that the treatment of a specific defendant was arbitrary or discriminatory. Davis too says that statistical studies cannot show that the people made their decisions for inappropriate reasons.

Davis's objection fails for two reasons. First, he ignores studies that include "internal" evidence about the judgments of prosecutors, jurors, and judges and that support the statistical evidence of arbitrariness. Second, he ignores the possibility of unintentional discrimination. While it is worth investigating the rationales offered by people involved in the process, there is no reason to take them as definitive. Even sincere attempts to do justice can fail.

Davis has a second, more ambitious criticism of the arbitrariness argument. Having asked for non-statistical evidence, he claims that "we are unlikely ever to have" the kind of evidence that would establish arbitrariness in individual cases. "Here's why," he explains:

> Suppose we uncovered evidence of (serious) arbitrariness in a particular murder case. Such evidence would constitute grounds for appeal. Only if our evidence failed to bring about a successful appeal could we properly conclude that the death penalty was arbitrarily administered. But, if the evidence of (serious) arbitrariness were convincing, it should precipitate an appeal and that appeal should be successful. So, any system of justice that both allows appeals and conducts them reasonably well should devour evidence of distributive arbitrariness as fast as researchers produce it.

In other words, if researchers find evidence of arbitrariness in individual cases, that evidence can be used in legal appeals and, where credible, it will lead to reversals of the sentences of persons treated arbitrarily. When this occurs, the information will cease to provide evidence for the arbitrariness of the system.

As each individual case is dealt with, the system will be vindicated rather than undermined.

The trouble with this objection is that Davis's description of how this evidence would be treated is inconsistent with what we know about the actual workings of the legal system. While the process he describes sometimes occurs, there is abundant evidence that the legal system is much less responsive to evidence of arbitrariness than he supposes. Many officials—from the Supreme Court on down—are reluctant to allow new evidence to play the role that Davis describes, and the law permits them to ignore such evidence.

James McCloskey, describing how the system deals with post-conviction claims of innocence, writes:

> Once wrongly convicted and sentenced to death, the criminal justice system treats you as a leper. No one wants to touch you. In my view, those in authority seem to be more interested in finality, expediency, speed, and administrative streamlining than in truth, justice, and fairness.

In addition, the Supreme Court has denied that people have a constitutional right to legal representation in post-conviction proceedings, even in capital cases. As a result, the new evidence Davis describes might never be heard and might be inadequately presented.

The resistance of the legal system to claims by persons already convicted is strikingly revealed in the Supreme Court's 1993 decision, *Herrera v. Collins*. There, the Court ruled that new evidence of innocence need not be considered because it failed to meet the Texas 60-day deadline for submitting it.

Davis's assumption that the legal system will jump at the chance to undo arbitrariness flies in the face of the facts. We have no reason to believe that the process Davis imagines—in which evidence of arbitrariness would be "devoured" by a justice-seeking, self-correcting system—would normally occur. In a footnote comment, Davis concedes that

> if recent attempts to cut short appeals go far enough, so that even new evidence proving innocence would not be sufficient grounds to reverse a death sentence, then the conditions I am supposing would not be met.

Because this situation had already developed prior to Davis's article, this concession nullifies his original objection.

VII. Replies to Critics: Phillip Montague

Phillip Montague attacks the arbitrariness argument and the claims of unequal justice which figured in *McCleskey*. He argues that these inequalities are irrelevant by using a series of imaginary cases.

The first case involves a sheriff who sometimes must kill an aggressor in order to save an innocent person. Montague's sheriff, he tells us,

> *does not always try to prevent the deaths of those who are the targets of aggression. Sometimes he chooses, on the basis of tossing coins, to allow aggressors to kill innocent people.*

Montague notes that if we apply the perspective of comparative justice to these actions, we will conclude that

> *Sheriff acts in a comparatively unjust way in selectively killing aggressors; and presumably, he does comparative injustices to the aggressors whom he does kill.*

Montague rejects this view and claims that no injustice is done to the aggressors who are killed, even though Sheriff does not kill other equally threatening aggressors.

To strengthen his conclusion, Montague imagines the sheriff confronting the first situation in which he can save an innocent person only by killing the attacker. In this first case, the sheriff does not kill the attacker and thus allows the innocent victim to be killed. Seeking to reduce the principle of comparative justice to absurdity, Montague claims that

> *the comparative principle creates a moral presumption against Sheriff's killing any aggressors he subsequently encounters in similar other-defense situations. In other words, the comparative principle would presumptively require Sheriff to allow culpable aggressors to kill innocent persons, because he failed to do what was required of him on a particular past occasion.*

Montague thinks it is clear that the Sheriff should not act this way, and he extrapolates from these cases to draw similar conclusions about the sentencing decisions of a judge. Just as the sheriff would be wrong not to kill some attackers simply because he had failed to kill others, so likewise, a judge who fails to sentence some deserving murderers to death would be wrong to refrain from imposing death on subsequent murderers for whom death is the right punishment.

Based on these imaginary cases, he concludes that the death penalty, even if imposed randomly or selectively, can still be just in those cases in which deserving murderers are executed. Hence the Supreme Court (in *McCleskey*) correctly rejected the claim that unequal treatment is a legitimate reason to overturn a particular death sentence.

In making his argument, Montague relies on two plausible assumptions, both of which he mistakenly believes are inconsistent with the arbitrariness argument. Both of these, however, can be accepted by defenders of the arbitrariness argument, and neither assumption undermines the force of the arbitrariness argument.

The first assumption is that it is more important to protect innocent people's lives than to satisfy the claims of comparative justice. There is no reason why people concerned about comparative justice must reject this priority. They could give priority to saving innocent lives while continuing to condemn the sheriff's unequal treatment of aggressors as unjust. To attach a value to comparative justice does not require a lack of concern for protecting the lives of innocent people.

Moreover, a defender of the arbitrariness argument can grant this in the case of the sheriff without granting it in the case of the judge. The judge is not dealing with imminent danger to an innocent person. She is dealing with a defendant who has already been rendered powerless and unthreatening, and she endangers no one by sentencing this person to life imprisonment. The proponent of comparative justice can accept what Montague says about the sheriff cases while rejecting the extension to the judge case.

Montague's second assumption is that it is ridiculous to believe that a person who acts wrongly in a first instance is obligated to repeat the same mistake in subsequent cases. Of course, he is right, but it is hard to see why even the most ardent champion of comparative justice would believe that a first time error should be repeated eternally. The rational response to error is correction in subsequent cases, and one can make this correction even if one values consistency. Defenders of comparative justice need not hold the absurdities which Montague attributes to them.

Montague's arguments unwittingly support a point I made earlier—that we can speak of a system being just or unjust in addition to evaluating individual cases. Surely a systematic practice of protecting victims of only one race or killing only attackers of one race would be grossly unjust. Even if we would approve all acts that save the lives of innocent persons, we still ought to condemn the practice of only saving victims of one race or only killing attackers of another. A sheriff who was known to follow such policies should surely be replaced.

Finally, even if Montague's objections were valid, they would undermine only the argument from arbitrary inequality and would leave both the argument from arbitrary severity and the argument from arbitrary unreliability untouched. He himself seems to notice this toward the end of his discussion when he shifts his attention from imaginary cases to the real world. After reiterating his belief that if whites who deserve death are treated more leniently than blacks, it does not follow that blacks who are executed are treated unjustly, he adds,

> *The likelihood is vanishingly small that racial influences will take so limited a form in the real world. If sentencing decisions in capital cases proceeded systematically along racial lines, then racial factors are bound to influence decisions regarding arrests, arraignments, verdicts, and sentences of non whites in other cases. One could reasonably wonder, then, whether non whites sentenced to death in jurisdictions like the one in question are correctly sentenced—whether, in other words, there is a good chance that people are mistakenly sentenced to death.*

Here Montague supports the view that differential treatment provides presumptive evidence of unreliable processes and erroneous judgments. He acknowledges that if prejudice plays an important role in the process, this role will not merely result in unequal sentences; it will also generate unreliable sentences that are unreliable and potentially excessively harsh. This is the very point I have stressed in discussing arbitrary severity and arbitrary unreliability.

VIII. *Replies to Critics: Does Arbitrariness Undermine All Punishments?*

One final criticism must be considered since it frequently appears as a *coup de grace* that allegedly reduces the arbitrariness argument to absurdity. After trying to show that the arbitrariness argument is weak or irrelevant, critics then claim that even if it succeeds in establishing that the death penalty is unjust, it still fails show that it ought to be abolished.

According to this final argument, if the arbitrariness argument is a good basis for abolishing the death penalty and if (as it is reasonable to suppose) the problems that affect the death penalty—inequalities, excessive severity, unreliability—affect other punishments, then the arbitrariness argument requires us to abolish all punishment and not just capital punishment. This *reductio ad absurdum* is supposed to create a dilemma for those who argue from arbitrariness. Either they must reject all punishment or they must drop the claim that arbitrariness is a reason for rejecting the death penalty.

This objection has been raised by many critics. In footnotes to *McCleskey*, Powell cites studies that purport to show the influence of various arbitrary factors on sentencing. Like other critics, he sees the arbitrariness argument as applicable to the entire practice of criminal punishment and rejects the argument because he sees no way to limit its reach to the death penalty.

The standard reply to this objection is that "death is different" and hence needs to be treated differently from other punishments. This reply is absolutely correct. Death as a punishment is extraordinary in its severity and makes impossible any later reconsideration of a person's cases. It combines the severest harm with the least chance of correction.

But this reply is too defensive in spirit. It fails to show the absurd view that underlies the objection that if arbitrariness is a reason for abolishing capital punishment, it is a reason for abolishing all punishment. In raising this objection, critics rely on an absurd model of moral, legal, and public policy reasoning. They assume that an argument can only provide a reason for something if it provides a decisive consideration for or against it. Virtually all important positions on legal and moral matters, however, are supported and opposed on the basis of many reasons, and rational decisions on these matters always require considering multiple values and principles.

Arbitrariness and discrimination are serious problems, but they are not the only things that need to be considered in this context. One relevant factor, surely, is the likely effects of abolition. In the case of the death penalty, there is no reason to believe that anyone will be less safe without a death penalty, while in the case of punishments generally, it is plausible to suppose that the abolition of all punishment would result in many more people being victimized and harmed.

If we want to consider abolishing a punishment because it is imposed arbitrarily, then we need to consider at least two things—the arbitrariness of the punishment and the effect of abolition. In the case of capital punishment, these two factors support abolition while in the case of punishment in general, they do not. That is not an argument for complacency about arbitrariness in the imposition of other punishments, but it is a sufficient response to the claim that one could only accept the arbitrariness argument against capital punishment only if one automatically accepts the same argument against all punishment.

The strongest argument for continuing a process that contains arbitrary elements is that the practice is necessary to prevent significant evils. It is a kind of argument from necessity: "we know that these practices are flawed, but we have no better way to protect people from serious evils." To be compelling, however, this argument requires that two things be true:

- first, that the practice of punishing people for particular crimes and at particular levels of harshness actually does prevent serious evils, and
- second, that there are no better ways to accomplish this result.

Where these conditions are not met, the argument from arbitrariness provides a compelling reason to alter or abolish a practice of punishing people for specific crimes.

In thinking about punishment as a whole, there is reason to believe that it does help to protect people by deterring crimes. While fear of punishment is not the only motivation that keeps us from harming others, it can supplement and reinforce other motivations in important ways, especially in large societies where people interact with many others with whom they have no personal or ongoing relationships. In addition, there seems to be no alternative to this system of preventing harmful acts. For these reasons, we are justified in using the system of punishment even though we know that arbitrary factors play an important role in its operations and that it is far from perfectly just.

While the arbitrariness argument does not undermine the punishment system as a whole, it can undermine a particular punishment where it does apply and is supplemented by other arguments. In the case of the death penalty, there are familiar reasons for treating the punishment of death differently and for taking the arbitrary features extremely seriously.

Critics are mistaken, then, in their claim that the arbitrariness argument must be automatically extended to any and all punishments, and Justice Powell's concern about the implications of accepting the arbitrariness argument was misplaced. (After retiring from the Court, Powell himself acknowledged that he had erred in upholding the death penalty in *McCleskey*.) The critics are wrong because they construe moral reasoning as the making of simple deductions from single principles or values, while in this and all other cases, such reasoning always involves the weighing and balancing of many relevant factors. What John Rawls notes about abstract issues in the theory of justice applies to more specific instance as well. A reasoned view about the morality of the death penalty

> *cannot be deduced from self-evident premises or conditions on principles; instead, its justification is a matter of the mutual support of many considerations, of everything fitting together into one coherent view.*

IX. Conclusion I have tried to show that the problem of arbitrariness provides the basis for a powerful set of arguments against capital punishment. Most critics of the argument have misinterpreted it, seeing it only as an argument about unequal treatment. I have argued that even people who place desert at the center of their thinking need to take arbitrariness seriously because the influence of arbitrary factors leads to violations of the desert criterion itself. Even if some murderers deserve to die, there is little reason to believe that our system picks out only those murderers as the ones who will be executed. While a certain amount of arbitrariness must be accepted in any human institution, there is no justification for accepting it in the practice of punishing by death.

Victim Impact Evidence

■ Victim Impact Evidence—Introduction

Many state statutes allow victims of crimes—and, in the case of murder, surviving family members—to offer input regarding the sentencing of the offender. "Victim impact evidence" is the blanket term used to describe a range of evidence relating to the impact of the crime on the victim and his or her family. It includes direct evidence of the offense such as how the victim suffered through his personal injuries and economic loss, the psychological and economic impact of the crime upon the defendant's family, and, in some states, testimony by the family or the victim as to the type of punishment that should be imposed upon the defendant.

The latter two kinds of evidence are more problematic than the first. Testimony as to the harm inflicted upon the victim seems directly tied to the culpability of the defendant as it is the result of his own actions. Someone who breaks the arms of his victim before murdering is presumably, or at least arguably, more culpable than someone who kills quickly. But the relevance of the subsequent impact of the crime upon the family of the victim is less clear. If the consequences are known to the perpetrator, this is one thing, but if they are merely probable, or unknown and unforeseen, many argue that the outcome has no bearing on the culpability of the defendant. The relevance of testimony by family members as to appropriate sentence is even less clear. Family members are no better than the judge at assessing the appropriate sentence for an offender, and are probably worse. Admitting this kind of testimony can only be defended on grounds of closure and fairness, based on the notion that giving surviving family members say in the process of how the defendant is treated helps them heal from the crime.

The concern with family impact evidence is that it introduces arbitrariness into sentencing. Suppose Jones and Smith shoot store clerks during the course of two different robberies. Neither shooter knows either clerk. Neither has ever seen either clerk before. As it turns out, Jones's victim is an ordained minister. At trial, a parade of witnesses testifies that Jones's victim is a pillar of the community, a beloved father, selfless and charitable. Smith's victim has been violently abusing his wife. She had not reported his abuse to the authorities out of fear of reprisal by her brutal husband, but she is emboldened now, and though she knows it to have been wrong, is thankful for Smith's act.

If the survivors of these two victims testify at the trials of Jones and Smith, we see the possibility that the two defendants will be treated differently even though their crimes were the same and neither knew anything about the victim or the victim's families. In *Payne v. Tennessee*, excerpted below, Justice Rehnquist argues that victim impact evidence is not normally used in this fashion. Its purpose is not to value one human life over another. It is, he says, to impress upon the jury the gravity of the taking of any human life. Justice Souter's argument suggests that it is not unfair to hold Jones accountable for the consequences of his actions. Jones may not have known his victim to be a priest, but it is foreseeable in the taking of any human life that the victim may have a family and be a good man, and it is not unjust for the defendant to own up to this.

But the risk of arbitrariness is present—defendants who had the same mental state and committed the same crime may be treated differently. This concern is at a zenith in capital cases. In *Booth v. Maryland*, a 1987 decision and the first by the Supreme Court on the subject of victim impact evidence, the Court struck down the Maryland victim impact statute because of the risk of arbitrariness.

Booth and an accomplice broke into the home of Irvin and Rose Bronstein, an elderly couple. Booth planned to use the stolen money to buy heroin. Two days after the robbery, the Bronsteins' son found his parents' dead bodies bound and gagged. The Bronsteins had been stabbed with a knife taken from the kitchen. The jury convicted Booth on two counts of first-degree murder.

The Maryland Department of Parole and Probation prepared a presentence report that included, as required by statute, a victim impact statement. The victim impact statement included evidence of psychological problems the victims' children had suffered as a result of the crime. The Bronsteins' son had become depressed, their daughter withdrawn and distrustful. The murder had ruined the wedding of one of the Bronsteins' granddaughters. The victim impact statement included family members' opinions about the proper disposition of the case. The son said that his parents had been "butchered like animals." The daughter said that a person such as Booth could never be rehabilitated.

The Supreme Court overturned Booth's sentence. Justice Powell emphasized the requirement of *Gregg*, *Woodson*, and *Lockett* that an "individualized determination" of the appropriateness of death be based upon the "character of the individual and the circumstances of the crime." The *Booth* Court said that victim impact statements allowed for irrelevant factors to enter into the sentencing decision such as the willingness and ability of the victim's family to articulate its grief, and the relative worth of the victim's character.

Two years later, the Court reaffirmed the holding of *Booth* in *South Carolina v. Gathers*. Gathers brutally murdered Richard Haynes, a former mental patient who called himself "Reverend Minister." At closing argument, the prosecutor read to the jury from a religious tract found in Haynes' pocket, inferring from the pamphlet that Haynes had been a God-fearing man. The Supreme Court reversed Gathers' conviction, carrying the *Booth* rationale a bit closer to its fullest extension. Though victim impact evidence had not been admitted, the prosecutor had referred to qualities of Haynes that may not have been known or foreseeable to Gathers and were, therefore, irrelevant to Gathers' moral culpability.

Booth and *Gathers* were each decided by 5 to 4 majorities. Anthony Kennedy replaced Lewis Powell on the bench between the time *Booth* and *Gathers* were decided. This should have tipped the scales in favor of the dissenters in *Booth*, but Byron White, a dissenter in *Booth*, voted with the majority in *Gathers*, writing, "Unless *Booth* is to be overruled, the judgment below must be affirmed." Two years later, Justice White changed his mind and voted to overturn *Booth*. David Souter, who replaced William Brennan on the bench during that time, joined.

Thurgood Marshall wrote a stinging dissent in *Payne*, one of the last decisions in which he would participate as a Justice. Marshall argued that the Court's reversal of itself undermined the principle of *stare decisis* and the credibility of the Court. The only distinction that could be drawn between *Gathers* and *Payne* is that the composition of the Court had changed. The majority and Justice Scalia offered a powerful response to Justice Marshall's concern: *stare decisis* is more important in cases involving property and contract rights than in cases involving evidentiary rules.

The question is intriguing. The *Payne* majority's argument is essentially this: when the Court decides issues that affect economic interests, people adjust their expectations on the basis of that decision. A citizen may be ambivalent between two interpretations of the tax code. As long as he knows what the prevailing interpretation is, he can adjust his expectations and actions accordingly. The only disaster from his standpoint is if the rule is reversed without notice. People do not generally act on the basis of expectations of liberties or procedural rules. If the police fail to read a defendant his *Miranda* rights and still question him, no defendant confesses because his *Miranda* rights have been violated. He doesn't think, "My *Miranda* rights have been violated, so I may as well go ahead and confess; it will just be suppressed later anyway." So the argument goes with victim impact evidence: no defendant commits a crime knowing that the likelihood of the death penalty being imposed on him is reduced by the inadmissibility of victim impact evidence. It is possible, however, to imagine someone exercising civil liberties outside of the criminal context on the expectation of protection. People speak and pray freely, whereas they might not if the rights could be easily abridged. And there is some undeniable long-term deleterious effect to the Court changing its mind about important issues. On the other hand, we do expect the Court to be open to changing its mind. For example, at the time of *Brown v. Board of Education*, no one advocated adhering to the principle of separate but equal, articulated in *Plessy v. Ferguson*, because of *stare decisis*.

The substantive issues in *Payne* are equally fascinating. The relevance of victim impact evidence is debatable. In some ways, it is analogous to the question of how criminal attempts should be treated. Some argue that all that matters is the defendant's intent and actions; therefore, attempts should be treated the same as completed crimes, and victim impact evidence excluded. Others argue that harm matters, that it legitimately bears on what the offender deserves, and that completed crimes should be treated more severely than unsuccessful attempts, and victim impact evidence included.

Justice Souter argues that it is the foreseeability of harm that is relevant. Even if a defendant has not actually foreseen a particular harm, if it were foreseeable that harm would result, it is reasonable to hold the defendant accountable for that harm. Jones may not have known that his victim had a family, but Jones knows that men do have families. If Jones kills his victim, resulting harm to the victim's family bears on Jones's culpability. At the same time, this reintroduces the problem of the moral lottery. What is foreseeable to the defendant is that his victim will have life circumstances that will probably evoke an average amount of sympathy. It is fair to hold him accountable for no more and no less. There is the question, too, whether it is necessary to put this evidence before the jury at all. Is there any juror who does not appreciate the fullness of life and the truth that murdered victims leave behind grieving survivors?

Even if victim impact evidence is irrelevant, others argue that it should nevertheless be admitted. Defendants have an absolute right under *Lockett* to offer any mitigating evidence they see fit, no matter how remote its connection to culpability. The question of symmetry is the subject of the articles below. Brian Johnson argues that it is only fair to balance the scales and let victims have their say, even if the evidence they offer is of questionable relevance. In my own essay, I argue that victim impact evidence is an asymmetrical response to the concern with mitigating evidence. If the concern is that unlimited mitigating evidence creates one-sided arbitrariness favoring the defendant, then the symmetrical response is to allow prosecutors to offer evidence of the advantages the defendant enjoyed throughout his life. Moreover I argue that the Court has been inconsistent in deciding whether evidence subsequent to the time of offense is relevant in assessing the culpability of the defendant, and that these inconsistencies suggest a lack of agreement on how to calculate the punishment a defendant deserves.

■ Victim Impact Evidence—Critical Documents

Payne v. Tennessee
501 U.S. 808 (1991)

Justice Rehnquist delivered the opinion of the Court.

In this case we reconsider our holdings in *Booth v. Maryland* and *South Carolina v. Gathers* that the Eighth Amendment bars the admission of victim impact evidence during the penalty phase of a capital trial.

Petitioner, Pervis Tyrone Payne, was convicted by a jury on two counts of first-degree murder and one count of assault with intent to commit murder in the first degree. He was sentenced to death for each of the murders and to 30 years in prison for the assault.

The victims of Payne's offenses were 28-year-old Charisse Christopher, her 2-year-old daughter Lacie, and her 3-year-old son Nicholas. The three lived together in an apartment in Millington, Tennessee, across the hall from Payne's girlfriend, Bobbie Thomas. On Saturday, June 27, 1987, Payne visited Thomas' apartment several times in expectation of her return from her mother's house in Arkansas, but found no one at home. On one visit, he left his overnight bag, containing clothes and other items for his weekend stay, in the hallway outside Thomas' apartment. With the bag were three cans of malt liquor.

Payne passed the morning and early afternoon injecting cocaine and drinking beer. Sometime around 3 P.M., Payne returned to the apartment complex, entered the Christophers' apartment, and began making sexual advances towards Charisse. Charisse resisted and Payne became violent. The noise briefly subsided and then began, "horribly loud." The neighbor called the police after she heard a "blood curdling scream" from the Christophers' apartment.

When the first police officer arrived at the scene, he immediately encountered Payne, who was leaving the apartment building, so covered with blood that he appeared to be "sweating blood." The officer confronted Payne, who responded, "I'm the complainant."

Inside the apartment, the police encountered a horrifying scene. Blood covered the walls and floor throughout the unit. Charisse and her children were lying on the floor in the kitchen. Nicholas, despite several wounds inflicted by a butcher knife that completely penetrated through his body from front to back, was still breathing. Miraculously, he survived, but not until after undergoing seven hours of surgery and a transfusion of 1,700 cc's of blood—400 to 500 cc's more than his estimated normal blood volume. Charisse and Lacie were dead.

Charisse's body was found on the kitchen floor on her back, her legs fully extended. She had sustained 42 direct knife wounds and 42 defensive wounds on her arms and hands. The wounds were caused by 41 separate thrusts of a butcher knife. None of the 84 wounds inflicted by Payne were individually fatal; rather, the cause of death was most likely bleeding from all of the wounds.

Lacie's body was on the kitchen floor near her mother. She had suffered stab wounds to the chest, abdomen, back, and head. The murder weapon, a butcher knife, was found at her feet. Payne's baseball cap was snapped on her arm near her elbow.

Payne was apprehended later that day hiding in the attic of the home of a former girlfriend. He had blood on his body and clothes and several scratches across his chest. It was later determined that the blood stains matched the victims' blood types. The jury returned guilty verdicts against Payne on all counts.

During the sentencing phase of the trial, Payne presented the testimony of four witnesses: his mother and father, Bobbie Thomas, and Dr. John T. Hutson, a clinical psychologist specializing in criminal court evaluation work. Bobbie Thomas testified that she met Payne at church, during a time when she was being abused by her husband. She stated that Payne was a very caring person, and that he devoted much time and attention to her three children, who were being affected by her marital difficulties. She said that the children had come to love him very much and would miss him, and that he "behaved just like a father that loved his kids." She asserted that he did not drink, nor did he use drugs, and that it was generally inconsistent with Payne's character to have committed these crimes.

Dr. Hutson testified that based on Payne's low score on an IQ test, Payne was "mentally handicapped." Hutson also said that Payne was neither psychotic nor schizophrenic, and that Payne was the most polite prisoner he had ever met. Payne's parents testified that their son had no prior criminal record and had never been arrested. They also stated that Payne had no history of alcohol or drug abuse, he worked with his father as a painter, he was good with children, and he was a good son.

The State presented the testimony of Charisse's mother, Mary Zvolanek. When asked how Nicholas had been affected by the murders of his mother and sister, she responded:

> *He cries for his mom. He doesn't seem to understand why she doesn't come home. And he cries for his sister Lacie. He comes to me many times during the week and asks me, Grandmama, do you miss my Lacie? And I tell him yes. He says, I'm worried about my Lacie.*

In arguing for the death penalty during closing argument, the prosecutor commented on the continuing effects of Nicholas' experience, stating:

> *But we do know that Nicholas was alive. And Nicholas was in the same room. Nicholas was still conscious. His eyes were open. He responded to the paramedics. He was able to follow their directions. He was able to hold his intestines in as he was carried to the ambulance. So he knew what happened to his mother and baby sister.*
>
> *There is nothing you can do to ease the pain of any of the families involved in this case. There is nothing you can do to ease the pain of Bernice or Carl Payne, and that's a tragedy. There is nothing you can do basically to ease the pain of Mr. and Mrs. Zvolanek, and that's a tragedy. They will have to live with it the rest of their lives. There is obviously nothing you can do for Charisse and Lacie Jo. But there is something that you can do for Nicholas.*
>
> *Somewhere down the road Nicholas is going to grow up, hopefully. He's going to want to know what happened. And he is going to know what happened to his baby sister and his mother. He is going to want to know what type of justice was done. He is going to want to know what happened. With your verdict, you will provide the answer.*

The jury sentenced Payne to death on each of the murder counts.

We granted certiorari to reconsider our holdings in *Booth* and *Gathers* that the Eighth Amendment prohibits a capital sentencing jury from considering "victim impact" evidence relating to the personal characteristics of the victim and the emotional impact of the crimes on the victim's family.

Booth and *Gathers* were based on two premises: that evidence relating to a particular victim or to the harm that a capital defendant causes a victim's family do not in general reflect on the defendant's "blameworthiness," and that only evidence relating to "blameworthiness" is relevant to the capital sentencing decision. However, the assessment of harm caused by the defendant as a result of the crime charged has understandably been an important concern of the criminal law, both in determining the elements of the offense and in determining the appropriate punishment. Thus, two equally blameworthy criminal defendants may be guilty of different offenses solely because their acts cause differing amounts of harm. "If a bank robber aims his gun at a guard, pulls the trigger, and kills his target, he may be put to death. If the gun unexpectedly misfires, he may not. His moral guilt in both cases is identical, but his responsibility in the former is greater." The same is true with respect to two defendants, each of whom participates in a robbery, and each of whom acts with reckless disregard for human life; if the robbery in which the first defendant participated results in the death of a victim, he may be subjected to the death penalty, but if the robbery in which the second defendant participates does not result in the death of a victim, the death penalty may not be imposed.

The principles which have guided criminal sentencing—as opposed to criminal liability—have varied with the times. Whatever the prevailing sentencing philosophy, the sentencing authority has always been free to consider a wide range of relevant material. In the federal system, we observed that "a judge may appropriately conduct an inquiry broad in scope, largely unlimited either as to the kind of information he may consider, or the source from which it may come." Even in the context of capital sentencing, prior to *Booth* the joint opinion of Justices Stewart, Powell, and Stevens in *Gregg*, had rejected petitioner's attack on the Georgia statute because of the "wide scope of evidence and argument allowed at presentence hearings." The joint opinion stated: "We think that the Georgia court wisely has chosen not to impose unnecessary restrictions on the evidence that can be offered at such a hearing and think it desirable for the jury to have as much information before it as possible when it makes the sentencing decision."

We have held that a State cannot preclude the sentencer from considering "any relevant mitigating evidence" that the defendant proffers in support of a sentence less than death. Thus we have, as the Court observed in *Booth*, required that the capital defendant be treated as a "uniquely individual human being." But it was never held or even suggested in any of our cases preceding *Booth* that the defendant, entitled as he was to individualized consideration, was to receive that consideration wholly apart from the crime which he had committed. The language quoted from *Woodson* in the *Booth* opinion was not intended to describe a class of evidence that *could not* be received, but a class of evidence which *must* be received. This misreading of precedent in *Booth* has, we think, unfairly weighted the scales in a capital trial; while virtually no limits are placed on the relevant mitigating evidence a capital defendant may introduce concerning his own circumstances, the State is barred from either offering "a quick glimpse of the life" which a defendant "chose to extinguish," or demonstrating the loss to the victim's family and to society which has resulted from the defendant's homicide.

The *Booth* Court reasoned that victim impact evidence must be excluded because it would be difficult, if not impossible, for the defendant to rebut such evidence without shifting the focus of the sentencing hearing away from the defendant, thus creating a "'mini-trial' on the victim's character." In many cases the evidence relating to the victim is already before the jury at least in part because of its relevance at the guilt phase of the trial. But even as to additional evidence admitted at the sentencing phase, the mere fact that for tactical reasons it might not be prudent for the defense to rebut victim impact evidence makes the case no different than others in which a party is faced with this sort of a dilemma. As we explained in rejecting the contention that expert testimony on future dangerousness should be excluded from capital trials, "the rules of evidence generally extant at the federal and state levels anticipate that relevant, unprivileged evidence should be admitted and its weight left to the factfinder, who would have the benefit of cross-examination and contrary evidence by the opposing party."

Payne echoes the concern voiced in *Booth*'s case that the admission of victim impact evidence permits a jury to find that defendants whose victims were assets to their community are more deserving of punishment than those whose victims are perceived to be less worthy. As a general matter, however, victim impact evidence is not offered to encourage comparative judgments of this kind— for instance, that the killer of a hardworking, devoted parent deserves the death penalty, but that the murderer of a reprobate does not. It is designed to show instead *each* victim's "uniqueness as an individual human being," whatever the jury might think the loss to the community resulting from his death might be. The facts of *Gathers* are an excellent illustration of this: The evidence showed that the victim was an out of work, mentally handicapped individual, perhaps not, in the eyes of most, a significant contributor to society, but nonetheless a murdered human being. Under our constitutional system, the primary responsibility for defining crimes against state law, fixing punishments for the commission of these crimes, and establishing procedures for criminal trials rests with the States.

We are now of the view that a State may properly conclude that for the jury to assess meaningfully the defendant's moral culpability and blameworthiness, it should have before it at the sentencing phase evidence of the specific harm caused by the defendant. "The State has a legitimate interest in counteracting the mitigating evidence which the defendant is entitled to put in, by reminding the sentencer that just as the murderer should be considered as an individual, so too the victim is an individual whose death represents a unique loss to society and in particular to his family." By turning the victim into a "faceless stranger at the penalty phase of a capital trial," *Booth* deprives the State of the full moral force of its evidence and may prevent the jury from having before it all the information necessary to determine the proper punishment for a first-degree murder.

The present case is an example of the potential for such unfairness. The capital sentencing jury heard testimony from Payne's girlfriend that they met at church; that he was affectionate, caring, and kind to her children; that he was not an abuser of drugs or alcohol; and that it was inconsistent with his character to have committed the murders. Payne's parents testified that he was a good son, and a clinical psychologist testified that Payne was an extremely polite prisoner and suffered from a low IQ. None of this testimony was related to the circumstances of Payne's brutal crimes. In contrast, the only evidence of the impact of Payne's offenses during the sentencing phase was Nicholas' grandmother's description—in response to a single question—that the child misses his mother and baby sister. Payne argues that the Eighth Amendment commands that the jury's death sentence must be set aside because the jury heard this testimony. But the testimony illustrated quite poignantly some of the harm that Payne's killing had caused; there is nothing unfair about allowing the jury to bear in mind that harm at the same time as it considers the mitigating evidence introduced by the defendant. The Supreme Court of Tennessee in this case obviously felt the unfairness of the rule pronounced by *Booth* when it said: "It is an affront to the civilized members of the human race to say that at sentencing in a capital case, a parade of witnesses may praise the background, character and good deeds of Defendant (as was done in this case), without limitation as to relevancy, but nothing may be said that bears upon the character of, or the harm imposed, upon the victims."

Under the aegis of the Eighth Amendment, we have given the broadest latitude to the defendant to introduce relevant mitigating evidence reflecting on his individual personality, and the defendant's attorney may argue that evidence to the jury. Petitioner's attorney in this case did just that. For the reasons discussed above, we now reject the view—expressed in *Gathers*—that a State may not permit the prosecutor to similarly argue to the jury the human cost of the crime of which the defendant stands convicted. We reaffirm the view expressed by Justice Cardozo: "Justice, though due to the accused, is due to the accuser also. The concept of fairness must not be strained till it is narrowed to a filament. We are to keep the balance true."

We thus hold that if the State chooses to permit the admission of victim impact evidence and prosecutorial argument on that subject, the Eighth Amendment erects no *per se* bar. A State may legitimately conclude that evidence about the victim and about the impact of the murder on the victim's family is relevant to the jury's decision as to whether or not the death penalty should be imposed. There is no reason to treat such evidence differently than other relevant evidence is treated.

Payne and his *amicus* argue that despite these numerous infirmities in the rule created by *Booth* and *Gathers*, we should adhere to the doctrine of *stare decisis* and stop short of overruling those cases. *Stare decisis* is the preferred course because it promotes the evenhanded, predictable, and consistent development of legal principles, fosters reliance on judicial decisions, and contributes to the actual and perceived integrity of the judicial process. Nevertheless, when governing decisions are unworkable or are badly reasoned, "this Court has never felt constrained to follow precedent." *Stare decisis* is not an inexorable command; rather, it "is a principle of policy and not a mechanical formula of adherence to the latest decision." This is particularly true in constitutional cases, because in such cases "correction through legislative action is practically impossible." Considerations in favor of *stare decisis* are at their acme in cases involving property and contract rights, where reliance interests are involved; the opposite is true in cases such as the present one involving procedural and evidentiary rules.

Applying these general principles, the Court has during the past 20 Terms overruled in whole or in part 33 of its previous constitutional decisions. *Booth* and *Gathers* were decided by the narrowest of margins, over spirited dissents challenging the basic underpinnings of those decisions. They have been questioned by Members of the Court in later decisions and have defied consistent application by the lower courts. Reconsidering these decisions now, we conclude, for the reasons heretofore stated, that they were wrongly decided and should be, and now are, overruled. We accordingly affirm the judgment of the Supreme Court of Tennessee.

Justice O'Connor, with whom Justice White and Justice Kennedy join, concurring.

We do not hold today that victim impact evidence must be admitted, or even that it should be admitted. We hold merely that if a State decides to permit consideration of this evidence, "the Eighth Amendment erects no *per se* bar." If, in a particular case, a witness' testimony or a prosecutor's remark so infects the sentencing proceeding as to render it fundamentally unfair, the defendant may seek appropriate relief under the Due Process Clause of the Fourteenth Amendment.

That line was not crossed in this case. The State called as a witness Mary Zvolanek, Nicholas' grandmother. Her testimony was brief. She explained that Nicholas cried for his mother and baby sister and could not understand why they did not come home. I do not doubt that the jurors were moved by this testimony—who would not have been? But surely this brief statement did not inflame their passions more than did the facts of the crime.

Nor did the prosecutor's comments about Charisse and Lacie in the closing argument violate the Constitution. The prosecutor remarked that Charisse would never again sing a lullaby to her son and that Lacie would never attend a high school prom. In my view, these statements were permissible. "Murder is the ultimate act of depersonalization." It transforms a living person with hopes, dreams, and fears into a corpse, thereby taking away all that is special and unique about the person. The Constitution does not preclude a State from deciding to give some of that back.

Booth also addressed another kind of victim impact evidence—opinions of the victim's family about the crime, the defendant, and the appropriate sentence. As the Court notes in today's decision, we do not reach this issue as no evidence of this kind was introduced at petitioner's trial. Nor do we express an opinion as to other aspects of the prosecutor's conduct. As to the victim impact evidence that was introduced, its admission did not violate the Constitution. Accordingly, I join the Court's opinion.

Justice Scalia, with whom Justice O'Connor and Justice Kennedy join except as to the first paragraph, concurring.

The Court correctly observes the injustice of requiring the exclusion of relevant aggravating evidence during capital sentencing, while requiring the admission of all relevant mitigating evidence. I have previously expressed my belief that the latter requirement is both wrong and, when combined with the remainder of our capital sentencing jurisprudence, unworkable. Even if it were abandoned, however, I would still affirm the judgment here. True enough, the Eighth Amendment permits parity between mitigating and aggravating factors. But more broadly and fundamentally still, it permits the People to decide (within the limits of other constitutional guarantees) what is a crime and what constitutes aggravation and mitigation of a crime.

The response to Justice Marshall's strenuous defense of the virtues of *stare decisis* can be found in the writings of Justice Marshall himself. That doctrine, he has reminded us, "is not an imprisonment of reason." If there was ever a case that defied reason, it was *Booth*, imposing a constitutional rule that had absolutely no basis in constitutional text, in historical practice, or in logic. *Booth*'s stunning *ipse dixit*, that a crime's unanticipated consequences must be deemed "irrelevant" to the sentence, conflicts with a public sense of justice keen enough that it has found voice in a nationwide "victims' rights" movement.

Today, however, Justice Marshall demands of us some "special justification"— *beyond* the mere conviction that the rule of *Booth* significantly harms our criminal justice system and is egregiously wrong—before we can be absolved of exercising "power, not reason." I do not think that is fair. In fact, quite to the contrary, what would enshrine power as the governing principle of this Court is the notion that an important constitutional decision with plainly inadequate rational support *must* be left in place for the sole reason that it once attracted five votes.

It seems to me difficult for those who were in the majority in *Booth* to hold themselves forth as ardent apostles of *stare decisis*. That doctrine, to the extent it rests upon anything more than administrative convenience, is merely the application to judicial precedents of a more general principle that the settled practices and expectations of a democratic society should generally not be disturbed by the courts. It was, I suggest, *Booth*, and not today's decision, that compromised the fundamental values underlying the doctrine of *stare decisis*.

Justice Souter, with whom Justice Kennedy joins, concurring.

To my knowledge, our legal tradition has never included a general rule that evidence of a crime's effects on the victim and others is, standing alone, irrelevant to a sentencing determination of the defendant's culpability. Criminal conduct has traditionally been categorized and penalized differently according to consequences not specifically intended, but determined in part by conditions unknown to a defendant when he acted.

Evidence about the victim and survivors, and any jury argument predicated on it, can of course be so inflammatory as to risk a verdict impermissibly based on passion, not deliberation. But this is just as true when the defendant knew of the specific facts as when he was ignorant of their details, and in each case there is a traditional guard against the inflammatory risk, in the trial judge's authority and responsibility to control the proceedings consistently with due process, on which ground defendants may object and, if necessary, appeal.

Booth nonetheless goes further and imposes a blanket prohibition on consideration of evidence of the victim's individuality and the consequential harm to survivors as irrelevant to the choice between imprisonment and execution, except when such evidence goes to the "circumstances of the crime," and probably then only when the facts in question were known to the defendant and relevant to his decision to kill. This prohibition rests on the belief that consideration of such details about the victim and survivors as may have been outside the defendant's knowledge is inconsistent with the sentencing jury's Eighth Amendment duty "in the unique circumstance of a capital sentencing hearing to focus on the defendant as a uniquely individual human being." The assumption made is that the obligation to consider the defendant's uniqueness limits the data about a crime's impact, on which a defendant's moral guilt may be calculated, to the facts he specifically knew and presumably considered. His uniqueness, in other words, is defined by the specifics of his knowledge and the reasoning that is thought to follow from it.

To hold, however, that in setting the appropriate sentence a defendant must be considered in his uniqueness is not to require that only unique qualities be considered. While a defendant's anticipation of specific consequences to the victims of his intended act is relevant to sentencing, such detailed foreknowledge does not exhaust the category of morally relevant fact. Murder has foreseeable consequences. When it happens, it is always to distinct individuals, and, after it happens, other victims are left behind. Every defendant knows, if endowed with the mental competence for criminal responsibility, that the life he will take by his homicidal behavior is that of a unique person, like himself, and that the person to be killed probably has close associates, "survivors," who will suffer harms and deprivations from the victim's death. Just as defendants know that they are not faceless human ciphers, they know that their victims are not valueless fungibles; and just as defendants appreciate the web of relationships and dependencies in which they live, they know that their victims are not human islands, but individuals with parents or children, spouses or friends or dependents. Thus, when a defendant chooses to kill, or to raise the risk of a victim's death, this choice necessarily relates to a whole human being and threatens an association of others, who may be distinctly hurt. The fact that the defendant may not know the details of a victim's life and characteristics, or the exact identities and needs of those who may survive, should not in any way obscure the further facts that death is always to a "unique" individual, and harm to some group of survivors is a consequence of a successful homicidal act so foreseeable as to be virtually inevitable.

That foreseeability of the killing's consequences imbues them with direct moral relevance, and evidence of the specific harm caused when a homicidal risk is realized is nothing more than evidence of the risk that the defendant originally chose to run despite the kinds of consequences that were obviously foreseeable. It is morally both defensible and appropriate to consider such evidence when penalizing a murderer, like other criminals, in light of common knowledge and the moral responsibility that such knowledge entails. Any failure to take account of a victim's individuality and the effects of his death upon close survivors would thus more appropriately be called an act of lenity than their consideration an invitation to arbitrary sentencing. Indeed, given a defendant's option to introduce relevant evidence in mitigation, sentencing without such evidence of victim impact may be seen as a significantly imbalanced process.

I do not, however, rest my decision to overrule wholly on the constitutional error that I see in the cases in question. I must rely as well on my further view that *Booth* sets an unworkable standard of constitutional relevance that threatens to produce arbitrary consequences and uncertainty of application. These conclusions will be seen to result from the interaction of three facts. First, although *Booth* was prompted by the introduction of a systematically prepared "victim impact statement," *Booth*'s restriction of relevant facts to what the defendant knew and considered in deciding to kill applies to any evidence, however derived or presented. Second, details of which the defendant was unaware, about the victim and survivors, will customarily be disclosed by the evidence introduced at the guilt phase of the trial. Third, the jury that determines guilt will usually determine, or make recommendations about, the imposition of capital punishment.

A hypothetical case will illustrate these facts and raise what I view as the serious practical problems with application of the *Booth* standard. Assume that a minister, unidentified as such and wearing no clerical collar, walks down a street to his church office on a brief errand, while his wife and adolescent daughter wait for him in a parked car. He is robbed and killed by a stranger, and his survivors witness his death. What are the circumstances of the crime that can be considered at the sentencing phase under *Booth*? The defendant did not know his victim was a minister, or that he had a wife and child, let alone that they were watching. Under *Booth*, these facts were irrelevant to his decision to kill, and they should be barred from consideration at sentencing. Yet evidence of them will surely be admitted at the guilt phase of the trial. The widow will testify to what she saw, and, in so doing, she will not be asked to pretend that she was a mere bystander. She could not succeed at that if she tried. The daughter may well testify too. The jury will not be kept from knowing that the victim was a minister, with a wife and child, on an errand to his church. This is so not only because the widow will not try to deceive the jury about her relationship, but also because the usual standards of trial relevance afford factfinders enough information about surrounding circumstances to let them make sense of the narrowly material facts of the crime itself. No one claims that jurors in a capital case should be deprived of such common contextual evidence, even though the defendant knew nothing about the errand, the victim's occupation, or his family. And yet, if these facts are not kept from the jury at the guilt stage, they will be in the jurors' minds at the sentencing stage.

Booth thus raises a dilemma with very practical consequences. If we were to require the rules of guilt-phase evidence to be changed to guarantee the full effect of *Booth*'s promise to exclude consideration of specific facts unknown to the defendant and thus supposedly without significance in morally evaluating his decision to kill, we would seriously reduce the comprehensibility of most trials by depriving jurors of those details of context that allow them to understand what is being described. If, on the other hand, we are to leave the rules of trial evidence alone, *Booth*'s objective will not be attained without requiring a separate sentencing jury to be empaneled. This would be a major imposition on the States, however, and I suppose that no one would seriously consider adding such a further requirement.

But, even if *Booth* were extended one way or the other to exclude completely from the sentencing proceeding all facts about the crime's victims not known by the defendant, the case would be vulnerable to the further charge that it would lead to arbitrary sentencing results. In the preceding hypothetical, *Booth* would require that all evidence about the victim's family, including its very existence, be excluded from sentencing consideration because the defendant did not know of it when he killed the victim. Yet, if the victim's daughter had screamed "Daddy, look out," as the defendant approached the victim with drawn gun, then the evidence of at least the daughter's survivorship would be admissible even under a strict reading of *Booth*, because the defendant, prior to killing, had been made aware of the daughter's existence, which therefore became relevant in evaluating the defendant's decision to kill. Resting a decision about the admission of impact evidence on such a fortuity is arbitrary.

Booth promises more than it can deliver, given the unresolved tension between common evidentiary standards at the guilt phase and *Booth*'s promise of a sentencing determination free from the consideration of facts unknown to the defendant and irrelevant to his decision to kill. I join the Court in its partial overruling of *Booth* and *Gathers*.

Justice Marshall, with whom Justice Blackmun joins, dissenting.

Power, not reason, is the new currency of this Court's decisionmaking. Four Terms ago, a five-Justice majority of this Court held that "victim impact" evidence of the type at issue in this case could not constitutionally be introduced during the penalty phase of a capital trial. By another 5-4 vote, a majority of this Court rebuffed an attack upon this ruling just two Terms ago. Nevertheless, having expressly invited respondent to renew the attack, today's majority overrules *Booth* and *Gathers* and credits the dissenting views expressed in those cases. Neither the law nor the facts supporting *Booth* and *Gathers* underwent any change in the last four years. Only the personnel of this Court did.

In dispatching *Booth* and *Gathers* to their graves, today's majority ominously suggests that an even more extensive upheaval of this Court's precedents may be in store. The majority declares itself free to discard any principle of constitutional liberty which was recognized or reaffirmed over the dissenting votes of four Justices and with which five or more Justices *now* disagree. The implications of this radical new exception to the doctrine of *stare decisis* are staggering. The majority today sends a clear signal that scores of established constitutional liberties are now ripe for reconsideration, thereby inviting the very type of open defiance of our precedents that the majority rewards in this case. Because I believe that this Court owes more to its constitutional precedents in general and to *Booth* and *Gathers* in particular, I dissent.

This Court has never departed from precedent without "special justification." Such justifications include the advent of "subsequent changes or development in the law" that undermine a decision's rationale; the need "to bring a decision into agreement with experience and with facts newly ascertained"; and a showing that a particular precedent has become a "detriment to coherence and consistency in the law." The majority cannot seriously claim that *any* of these traditional bases for overruling a precedent applies to *Booth* or *Gathers*. It takes little real detective work to discern just what *has* changed since this Court decided *Booth* and *Gathers*: this Court's own personnel.

This truncation of the Court's duty to stand by its own precedents is astonishing. By limiting full protection of the doctrine of *stare decisis* to "cases involving property and contract rights," the majority sends a clear signal that essentially *all* decisions implementing the personal liberties protected by the Bill of Rights and the Fourteenth Amendment are open to reexamination. Taking into account the majority's additional criterion for overruling—that a case either was decided or reaffirmed by a 5-4 margin "over spirited dissent,"—the continued vitality of literally scores of decisions must be understood to depend on nothing more than the proclivities of the individuals who *now* comprise a majority of this Court.

In my view, this impoverished conception of *stare decisis* cannot possibly be reconciled with the values that inform the proper judicial function. Contrary to what the majority suggests, *stare decisis* is important not merely because individuals rely on precedent to structure their commercial activity but because fidelity to precedent is part and parcel of a conception of "the judiciary as a source of impersonal and reasoned judgments." Indeed, this function of *stare decisis* is in many respects even *more* critical in adjudication involving constitutional liberties than in adjudication involving commercial entitlements. Because enforcement of the Bill of Rights and the Fourteenth Amendment frequently requires this Court to rein in the forces of democratic politics, this Court can legitimately lay claim to compliance with its directives only if the public understands the Court to be implementing "principles founded in the law rather than in the proclivities of individuals."

Carried to its logical conclusion, the majority's debilitated conception of *stare decisis* would destroy the Court's very capacity to resolve authoritatively the abiding conflicts between those with power and those without. If this Court shows so little respect for its own precedents, it can hardly expect them to be treated more respectfully by the state actors whom these decisions are supposed to bind. By signaling its willingness to give fresh consideration to any constitutional liberty recognized by a 5-4 vote "over spirited dissent," the majority invites state actors to renew the very policies deemed unconstitutional in the hope that this Court may now reverse course, even if it has only recently reaffirmed the constitutional liberty in question.

Indeed, the majority's disposition of this case nicely illustrates the rewards of such a strategy of defiance. The Tennessee Supreme Court did nothing in this case to disguise its contempt for this Court's decisions in *Booth* and *Gathers*.

Offering no explanation for how this case could possibly be distinguished from *Booth* and *Gathers*—for obviously, there is none to offer—the court perfunctorily declared that the victim-impact evidence and the prosecutor's argument based on this evidence "did not violate either of those decisions." It cannot be clearer that the court simply declined to be bound by this Court's precedents.

Far from condemning this blatant disregard for the rule of law, the majority applauds it. It is hard to imagine a more complete abdication of this Court's historic commitment to defending the supremacy of its own pronouncements on issues of constitutional liberty.

Today's decision charts an unmistakable course. If the majority's radical reconstruction of the rules for overturning this Court's decisions is to be taken at face value—and the majority offers us no reason why it should not—then the overruling of *Booth* and *Gathers* is but a preview of an even broader and more far-reaching assault upon this Court's precedents. Cast aside today are those condemned to face society's ultimate penalty. Tomorrow's victims may be minorities, women, or the indigent. Inevitably, this campaign to resurrect yesterday's "spirited dissents" will squander the authority and the legitimacy of this Court as a protector of the powerless.

I dissent.

Justice Stevens, with whom Justice Blackmun joins, dissenting.

Justice Marshall is properly concerned about the majority's trivialization of the doctrine of *stare decisis*. But even if *Booth* and *Gathers* had not been decided, today's decision would represent a sharp break with past decisions. Our cases provide no support whatsoever for the majority's conclusion that the prosecutor may introduce evidence that sheds no light on the defendant's guilt or moral culpability, and thus serves no purpose other than to encourage jurors to decide in favor of death rather than life on the basis of their emotions rather than their reason.

Until today our capital punishment jurisprudence has required that any decision to impose the death penalty be based solely on evidence that tends to inform the jury about the character of the offense and the character of the defendant. Evidence that serves no purpose other than to appeal to the sympathies or emotions of the jurors has never been considered admissible. Thus, if a defendant, who had murdered a convenience store clerk in cold blood in the course of an armed robbery, offered evidence unknown to him at the time of the crime about the immoral character of his victim, all would recognize immediately that the evidence was irrelevant and inadmissible. Evenhanded justice requires that the same constraint be imposed on the advocate of the death penalty.

Today's majority has obviously been moved by an argument that has strong political appeal but no proper place in a reasoned judicial opinion. Because our decision in *Lockett* recognizes the defendant's right to introduce all mitigating evidence that may inform the jury about his character, the Court suggests that fairness requires that the State be allowed to respond with similar evidence about the *victim*. This argument is a classic non sequitur: The victim is not on trial; her character, whether good or bad, cannot therefore constitute either an aggravating or a mitigating circumstance.

Even if introduction of evidence about the victim could be equated with introduction of evidence about the defendant, the argument would remain flawed in both its premise and its conclusion. The conclusion that exclusion of victim impact evidence results in a significantly imbalanced sentencing procedure is simply inaccurate. Just as the defendant is entitled to introduce any relevant mitigating evidence, so the State may rebut that evidence and may designate any relevant conduct to be an aggravating factor provided that the factor is sufficiently well defined and consistently applied to cabin the sentencer's discretion.

The premise that a criminal prosecution requires an evenhanded balance between the State and the defendant is also incorrect. The Constitution grants certain rights to the criminal defendant and imposes special limitations on the State designed to protect the individual from overreaching by the disproportionately powerful State. Thus, the State must prove a defendant's guilt beyond a reasonable doubt.

Victim impact evidence, as used in this case, has two flaws. First, aspects of the character of the victim unforeseeable to the defendant at the time of his crime are irrelevant to the defendant's "personal responsibility and moral guilt" and therefore cannot justify a death sentence. Second, the quantity and quality of victim impact evidence sufficient to turn a verdict of life in prison into a verdict of death is not defined until after the crime has been committed and therefore cannot possibly be applied consistently in different cases.

The majority attempts to justify the admission of victim impact evidence by arguing that "consideration of the harm caused by the crime has been an important factor in the exercise of sentencing discretion." This statement is misleading and inaccurate. It is misleading because it is not limited to harm that is foreseeable. There is a rational correlation between moral culpability and the foreseeable harm caused by criminal conduct. But the majority cites no authority for the suggestion that unforeseeable and indirect harms to a victim's family are properly considered as aggravating evidence on a case-by-case basis.

Justice Souter argues that these harms are sufficiently foreseeable to hold the defendant accountable because "every defendant knows that the person to be killed probably has close associates, survivors, who will suffer harms and deprivations from the victim's death." But every juror and trial judge knows this much as well. Arguing in the alternative, Justice Souter correctly points out that victim impact evidence will sometimes come to the attention of the jury during the guilt phase of the trial. Thus, to justify overruling *Booth*, he assumes that the decision must otherwise be extended far beyond its actual holding.

In the case before us today, much of what might be characterized as victim impact evidence was properly admitted during the guilt phase of the trial. The fact that a good deal of such evidence is routinely and properly brought to the attention of the jury merely indicates that the rule of *Booth* may not affect the outcome of many cases.

In reaching our decision today, however, we should not be concerned with the cases in which victim impact evidence will not make a difference. We should be concerned instead with the cases in which it will make a difference. In those cases, defendants will be sentenced arbitrarily to death on the basis of evidence that would not otherwise be admissible because it is irrelevant to the defendants' moral culpability.

The notion that the inability to produce an ideal system of justice in which every punishment is precisely married to the defendant's blameworthiness somehow justifies a rule that completely divorces some capital sentencing determinations from moral culpability is incomprehensible to me. Also incomprehensible is the argument that such a rule is required for the jury to take into account that each murder victim is a "unique" human being. The fact that each of us is unique is a proposition so obvious that it surely requires no evidentiary support. What is not obvious, however, is the way in which the character or reputation in one case may differ from that of other possible victims. Evidence offered to prove such differences can only be intended to identify some victims as more worthy of protection than others. Such proof risks decisions based on the same invidious motives as a prosecutor's decision to seek the death penalty if a victim is white but to accept a plea bargain if the victim is black.

I recognize that today's decision will be greeted with enthusiasm by a large number of concerned and thoughtful citizens. The great tragedy of the decision, however, is the danger that the "hydraulic pressure" of public has played in the resolution of the constitutional issue involved. Today is a sad day for a great institution.

■ Victim Impact Evidence—Perspectives

■ Issue—Does Victim Impact Evidence Balance the Scales in Capital Sentencing?

Brian J. Johnson, "The Response to *Payne v. Tennessee*: Giving the Victim's Family a Voice in the Capital Sentencing Process"

In *Payne*, the Supreme Court reversed its position in *Booth*, by holding that the Eighth Amendment does not erect a *per se* bar to the introduction of victim impact evidence in a capital sentencing proceeding.

Unlike statutory aggravating circumstances, the Supreme Court has held that a defendant has a right to present "any relevant mitigating evidence" that he proffers in support of a sentence less than death. Although the state must show the existence of a specific aggravating circumstance for a jury to sentence a defendant to death, a defendant has an unfettered right to present any type of evidence, however remotely relevant to mitigation of a death sentence, which might tend to make the imposition of the death penalty less likely. This imbalance, which existed before *Payne*, led Justice Scalia to comment in *Booth*:

> To require, as we have, that all mitigating factors which render capital punishment a harsh penalty in the particular case be placed before the sentencing authority, while simultaneously requiring that evidence of much of the human suffering the defendant has inflicted be suppressed, is in effect to prescribe a debate on the appropriateness of the capital penalty with one side muted.

The most effective way to ensure that the relatives of murder victims are given an opportunity to be heard during a capital sentencing proceeding is to combine a narrowly written statute with a constitutional amendment that specifically provides for the right of victims to be heard during sentencing. Combining a statutory provision with a constitutional amendment sends a clear and unambiguous message to state appellate courts. The people of the state, through their elected representatives and through ratification of a constitutional amendment, deem such evidence appropriate and relevant, despite any personal opinions of members of the bench to the contrary.

Victim impact evidence is among the most powerful evidence the state can present to a jury for the purpose of sentencing a defendant to death. One of the strongest criticisms of such evidence is its strong emotional impact. The fear is that such emotionally charged evidence will overwhelm any sense of reason during the sentencing process, such that the jury will sentence a defendant based solely upon emotion.

Such an argument carries weight. However, that victim testimony is emotional is not reason enough for its *per se* exclusion. The emotional reaction is a direct result of the defendant's action; it was wrought by his own hands. It does not lie in the defendant's mouth to complain when emotion is a foreseeable consequence of his actions. Furthermore, juries have demonstrated an ability to consider mitigating factors even in the face of incredibly emotionally charged victim impact evidence in high-profile cases. Nonetheless, due to the strong emotional content of such evidence, limitations should be placed on its admission. As noted in Payne, in the event that evidence is introduced that is "so unduly prejudicial that it renders the trial fundamentally unfair, the Due Process Clause of the Fourteenth Amendment provides a mechanism for relief."

Death penalty cases are very costly, not only in terms of dollars, but in the emotional toll the lengthy trial and appeal process takes upon victims. Although a sentence of death may be expediently and emotionally gratifying to the prosecutor and the victim, that gratification must be tempered with the realities of the appeals process. If a sentence is overturned, not only is the original expense wasted, but a decision must be made whether to attempt to resentence the defendant to death and to put the victim through another emotional ordeal. Ironically, the evidence that gave the victim a voice could be used to prolong his or her agony.

An effective capital punishment system is not served by temporary victories. The goal of a statute that gives victims a voice should include the goal that the sentence withstand judicial scrutiny. The goal should not be that every capital defendant receives the death sentence, but rather that every death sentence that is imposed be upheld.

I. *Victim Impact Statute*

To ensure that a defendant's right to due process is maintained, a narrowly drawn statute should make clear that the normal rules of evidence that apply to criminal trials apply to the sentencing proceeding as well. Thus, the introduction of victim impact evidence should never be mandated by the statute. Despite its political appeal, such a provision would make a sentence more susceptible to being overturned on due process grounds. Despite the possibility that a judge with anti-capital punishment leanings might exclude victim impact testimony, the discretion of a judge to exclude prejudicial evidence must be maintained to ensure an appeal-proof sentence.

The statute should also provide that only one victim or representative shall be appointed to speak. From the victim's family point of view, this would certainly be the most unappealing aspect of a victim impact provision in a capital sentencing statute. Inevitably the victim's murder or victimization will have impacted many members of his or her family, and the natural temptation is to bring numerous family members to the stand to drive home the impact of the defendant's crime and to give them their day in court. However, with each witness paraded before the jury, the chances increase that an appellate court will view such evidence as cumulative and prejudicial. The most effective means of removing this temptation is by removing any discretion by the state or trial judge on this point.

Third, the statute should specify exactly what type of evidence is admissible by following the language of *Payne*. It should specify that the evidence is limited to showing the victim's uniqueness as an individual human being and the resulting loss to the community members by the victim's death. The statute should make clear that opinions about the defendant, the appropriate sentence, and the crime are not permitted. Despite the emotional appeal of a victim compelling the jury to, "Please give him death," the Court has not overturned the part of *Booth* that says such evidence is inadmissible.

Finally, the statute should make clear that the defendant has a right to cross-examine the witness as with any other witness. This would ensure that the defendant's right to confront witnesses is maintained, despite the potential that cross-examination might elicit testimony that is emotionally painful for the witness.

II. *Model Constitutional Amendment*

For a constitutional amendment to effectively give victims of crime a right to testify during sentencing, this right must be specifically enumerated. Furthermore, to ensure that the relatives of victims have a right to testify, the amendment must show that the drafters intended to extend the rights of victims to members of a deceased victim's family. In so doing, the amendment should make clear that the intention is not to infringe unconstitutionally upon a defendant's rights.

Model Constitutional Amendment

> *Victims of crime, including the lawful representative of a minor, incompetent, or victim of homicide, are entitled to the right to be informed of criminal proceedings, and to be present, and heard when relevant, at all crucial stages of criminal proceedings, including all sentencing and post-conviction proceedings, to the extent that these rights do not interfere with the constitutional rights of the accused.*

III. *Recent Decisions Regarding the Admissibility of Victim Impact Evidence*

Payne allows states to admit victim impact evidence during the capital sentencing phase, but the decision did not provide states with much guidance with regards to what types of victim impact evidence is admissible, or what procedures a trial court should adopt to ensure that the admission of victim impact evidence does not become so prejudicial as to render the sentencing phase fundamentally unfair. As a result, state courts are now beginning to grapple with these questions.

In *State v. Muhammad* (1996), the Supreme Court of New Jersey addressed a challenge to the capital sentencing statute, which allows the state to introduce victim impact evidence when offered to rebut a defendant's presentation of "catch-all" mitigation evidence. In addition to upholding the constitutionality of the statute under the federal and New Jersey Constitutions, the court held that a certain number of procedures must be followed before victim impact evidence can be admitted into evidence:

> *The defendant should be notified prior to the commencement of the penalty phase that the State plans to introduce victim impact evidence if the defendant asserts the catch-all factor. The State shall also provide the defendant with the names of the victim impact witnesses that it plans to call so that defense counsel will have an opportunity to interview the witnesses prior to their testimony. The greater the*

number of survivors who are permitted to present victim impact evidence, the greater the potential for the victim impact evidence to unduly prejudice the jury against the defendant. Thus, absent special circumstances, we expect that the victim impact testimony of one survivor will be adequate to provide the jury with a glimpse of each victim's uniqueness as a human being and to help the jurors make an informed assessment of the defendant's moral culpability and blameworthiness. Further, minors should not be permitted to present victim impact evidence except under circumstances where there are no suitable adult survivors and thus the child is the closest living relative.

Before a family member is allowed to make a victim impact statement, the trial court should ordinarily conduct a hearing, outside the presence of the jury, to make a preliminary determination as to the admissibility of the State's proffered victim impact evidence. The witness's testimony should be reduced to writing to enable the trial court to review the proposed statement to avoid any prejudicial content. The testimony can provide a general factual profile of the victim, including information about the victim's family, employment, education, and interests. The testimony can describe generally the impact of the victim's death on his or her immediate family. The testimony should be factual, not emotional, and should be free of inflammatory comments or references.

The trial court should weigh each specific point of the proffered testimony to ensure that its probative value is not substantially outweighed by the risk of undue prejudice or misleading the jury. Determining the relevance of the proffered testimony is particularly important because of the potential for prejudice and improper influence that is inherent in the presentation of victim impact evidence. However, in making that determination, there is a strong presumption that victim impact evidence that demonstrates that the victim was a unique human being is admissible. During the preliminary hearing, the trial court should inform the victim's family that the court will not allow a witness to testify if the person is unable to control his or her emotions. That concern should be alleviated by our requirement that the witness be permitted only to read his or her previously approved testimony. Finally, the court should also take the opportunity to remind the victim's family that the court will not permit any testimony concerning the victim's family members' characterizations and opinions about the defendant, the crime, or the appropriate sentence.

Muhammad also made clear the importance of constitutional amendment to ensure that victim impact testimony is admissible:

At times we have interpreted the State Constitution to afford New Jersey citizens broader protection of certain rights than that afforded by analogous or identical provisions of the Federal Constitution. In the absence of the Victim's Rights Amendment, we might have con-

> *tinued to hold that victim impact evidence should not be admitted during the sentencing phase of a capital case.*

IV. Conclusion

As courts and legislatures continue to accept the use of victim impact testimony, the challenge that faces courts today should not be whether such evidence should be admitted, but how. Despite criticism, it is readily apparent that a majority of courts accept the rationale of *Payne*, and reject that of *Booth*.

To suggest that the impact of a victim's murder is not relevant to a defendant's sentencing is to marginalize the crime. The very reason we place such a high price on the intentional, unjustified taking of a human life is that murder encompasses much more than the simple extinguishing of a life. Murder does not end there. It is the rending of a person from his family, friends, and community. It deprives an individual of the opportunity to make contributions to civilization a characteristic that distinguishes the human race from all other forms of life on the planet. It is for this cost that society exacts its highest penalty.

In *Booth*, Powell argued that victim impact evidence is unrelated to the blameworthiness of a particular defendant because, "defendants rarely select their victims based on whether the murder will have an effect on anyone other than the person murdered."

Rather than being an argument against impact, this argument supports its use. Any defendant charged with the degree of mental competence to be held accountable for his actions is able to appreciate that his actions will bear consequences which extend beyond the person he murders. It is this callous disregard of "whether the murder will have an effect on anyone other the person murdered" that makes the evidence of the impact of this disregard relevant.

The challenge is to construct statutes which provide victims with a voice without creating a vigilante atmosphere in the courtroom. This is best achieved with narrowly written statutes that provide minimal potential for the admission of prejudicial evidence.

As Justice Cardozo noted over sixty years ago: "But justice, though due to the accused, is due the accuser also. The concept of fairness must not be strained till it is narrowed to a filament. We are to keep the balance true."

Evan J. Mandery, "Notions of Symmetry and Self in Death Penalty Jurisprudence"

The jurisprudence of death is rife with expressions of concern for symmetry, for putting prosecutors and defense attorneys on equal footing at capital trials. Nowhere is this more evident than in the debate over the admissibility of victim impact evidence. Three of the four Justices writing opinions in *Payne* concurring with the result that victim impact evidence is not *per se* inadmissible under the Eighth Amendment relied at least in part upon symmetry as a basis for their judgment. Scholars defending the decision have advanced the same rationale. Some lower courts have interpreted this as the main lesson of *Payne*. In simplest terms the argument is this: since defendants are able to introduce any and all mitigating evidence, no matter how attenuated its connection might be to an evaluation of culpability, surviving victims should be able to do the same.

This notion of symmetry has been largely unexamined. Critics of *Payne* have generally said that balancing is not a worthwhile goal, tacitly accepting the notion that admitting victim impact evidence is analogous to allowing unrestricted mitigating evidence to enter trials. But it is not symmetrical at all. The policy objection to unrestricted mitigating evidence is that, antithetical to the principles of *Furman* and *Gregg*, it introduces an element of arbitrariness to death sentencing. *Gregg* requires the consideration of aggravating evidence to be structured. Contrarily, in the view of some, the rule of *Lockett* requires that the defendant be permitted to offer any and all mitigating evidence, no matter what its quality or relevance. Arbitrariness results—a jury may idiosyncratically credit some irrelevant mitigating evidence and thus spare a defendant deserving of death. This is unjust from a retributive standpoint, a windfall to the defendant. The defendant has received less punishment than he deserves.

Defenders of victim impact evidence say that if the defendant is allowed to offer mitigating evidence of questionable relevance, the defendant should be able to offer aggravating victim impact evidence, even if it is of questionable relevance. Victim impact evidence carries with it its own risk of arbitrariness: a jury may idiosyncratically credit some irrelevant victim impact evidence and thus sentence an undeserving defendant to die. So be it, proponents say. What is good for the goose should be good for the gander.

Defenders of victim impact evidence thus respond to the objection to mitigating evidence not by diminishing the arbitrariness that mitigating evidence supposedly introduces, but by introducing more arbitrariness into the sentencing phase, arbitrariness of a different kind. Mitigating evidence and victim impact evidence are not symmetrical in any way. Conventional mitigating evidence is premised upon an inference that runs forward in time: a defendant is less culpable because of something that has happened in the past. Most victim impact evidence is premised upon a backward-looking inference: future events—the effects of the crime upon surviving family members—enhance the culpability of the defendant.

Conventional mitigating evidence takes the view that the defendant should be sentenced on the basis of who he is at the moment of sentencing; changes he may undergo in the future—contrition, reformation—are irrelevant. Victim impact evidence takes an evolved view of self—defendants should be responsible for the future harm caused by their actions. Victim impact evidence is deemed constitutional as a symmetrical response to mitigating evidence, but they are apples and oranges.

I. *Notions of Symmetry Examined*

A. Good for the Goose Symmetry Proponents of victim impact evidence argue that if a defendant is allowed to present unlimited mitigating evidence, some or much of which is of questionable relevance, then the prosecution should not be precluded from offering victim impact evidence, even if that evidence is of questionable relevance. What is good for the goose should be good for the gander. So is this the symmetrical response? Proponents of victim impact evidence argue that it rebalances the scales unfairly tipped by the admission of unlimited mitigating evidence. But even if admitting unlimited mitigating evidence is wrong, the admission of victim impact evidence is not a wrong that counteracts the other wrong. It is just another wrong.

Recall the three main objections to the Supreme Court's approach to mitigating evidence: (1) that the requirement of *Lockett* reintroduces arbitrariness into death sentencing, (2) that not all mitigating evidence bears on culpability, and (3) that even if certain kinds of mitigating evidence do bear on culpability, they are irrelevant unless they suggest that the offender lost the basic ability to tell right from wrong. Victim impact evidence is not responsive to the third concern; it does not in any way bear on the defendant's ability to distinguish right from wrong. The first and second concerns merge in some sense. It seems fair to say that the basic objection to mitigating evidence is that it increases arbitrariness. The question is: does victim impact evidence counter this effect?

The simple answer is that victim impact evidence only increases arbitrariness in death sentencing. The concern with mitigating evidence that juries will have different reactions to mitigating evidence and hence may not treat like cases alike is present in the same way with victim impact evidence. Juries may have idiosyncratic reactions to victim impact evidence. The resulting unpredictability may be more insidious in the case of victim impact evidence than with mitigating evidence. The inference from mitigating evidence runs forward in time; the inference from victim impact evidence backwards. Victim impact evidence is a lottery in every sense: subsequent events are used to retrospectively reflect upon the culpability of the defendant. While it may be foreseeable to a murderer that his crime will have potentially devastating consequences, the precise results cannot be foreseen. They hence have no bearing on the culpability of the defendant. At least some kinds of mitigating evidence bear on the culpability of the defendant.

The arbitrariness concern is only remedied by victim impact evidence if the objection to mitigating evidence arbitrariness is that the resulting uncertainty is one-sided in favor of the defendant. No defendant will receive the death penalty who otherwise would not by virtue of a jury idiosyncratically crediting mitigating evidence that does not truly bear on culpability (call this Type I error). All that could happen is that a defendant will be unjustly spared (call this Type II error). Victim impact evidence will not reduce Type I error; it will not affect the number of defendants that are unjustly spared. It will only lead to an increase of Type II error; some defendants will be sentenced to die who otherwise would have been spared. Victim impact evidence does not diminish arbitrariness; it increases it, though the resulting additional arbitrariness will be one-sided in favor of the prosecution.

It seems doubtful that increasing arbitrariness to balance the resulting mistakes is a legitimate aim of punishment, though some parts of the Court's opinion in *Payne* hint at precisely this point. How exactly does victim impact evidence work to balance the scales? The *Payne* Court cites Justice White's concurrence in *Booth*:

> The State has a legitimate interest in counteracting the mitigating evidence which the defendant is entitled to put in, by reminding the sentencer that just as the murderer should be considered as an indi-

vidual, so too the victim is an individual whose death represents a unique loss to society and in particular to his family.

This argument seeks to correct a perceived wrong with an additional wrong.

The most direct response to the concern that mitigating evidence creates arbitrariness would be to curtail the arbitrariness by allowing state legislatures to classify the kinds of mitigating evidence that might be presented at trial. But if one proceeds on the presumption that *Lockett* precludes this course of action, what then? The symmetrical response would be to allow pre-crime defendant-based aggravating evidence. Mitigating evidence is offered for the inference that because of the defendant's upbringing or physical condition he is less responsible than the average criminal defendant. Pre-crime aggravating evidence would be offered for the inference that because of the defendant's upbringing or physical condition he is more responsible than the average criminal defendant. A prosecutor could point to a defendant's good schooling and parenting and argue that the defendant should have understood better than the average person the immorality of his actions. Contra-mitigating evidence is admissible now for rebuttal purposes. The argument here is that the symmetrical response would be to allow prosecutors to offer pre-crime defendant-based aggravating evidence as part of its case-in-chief at the sentencing phase.

The relationship between mitigating evidence and pre-crime defendant-based aggravating evidence is far more symmetrical than between mitigating evidence and victim impact evidence. Mitigating evidence and pre-crime defendant-based aggravating evidence are both offered for a forward-looking inference, that because of the defendant's particular personal history he is more or less responsible for the crime than the average person. Put another way, there is x-axis symmetry between mitigating evidence and pre-crime defendant-based aggravating evidence. **Figure 16-1** below depicts the kinds of inferences that may or may not be drawn—the circle represents the victim, the triangle the defendant. A shaded inference is permissible; an unshaded inference is impermissible. The arrow in which the direction points indicates the direction of the inference—whether it is forward or backward-looking.

The objection to both kinds of evidence is identical: the relationship between certain past events and the crime may be too attenuated to credit; certain types of personal history events should not be relevant at all. The objection to mitigating evidence is that it puts the defendant's character at issue, when some aspects of his character are not relevant to culpability. Pre-crime defendant-based aggravating evidence puts the defendant's entire character at issue. It directly addresses the concern with Type I error—fewer defendants will undeservingly be spared the death penalty by virtue of irrelevant character evidence—and it creates no additional risk of Type II error.

Pre-crime mitigating evidence and victim impact evidence are apples and

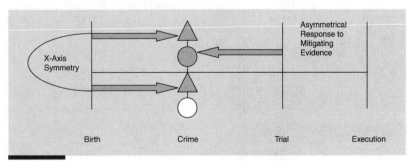

Figure 16-1 Symmetry of responses to pre-crime mitigating evidence.

oranges. Conventional mitigating evidence is offered for a forward-looking inference. Victim impact evidence is offered for a backward-looking inference. Though some conventional mitigating evidence is surely irrelevant, it all concerns a relevant moral actor, the defendant. Victim character evidence concerns a relevant actor only if the victim is a member of a class that triggers a statutory aggravating circumstance. No family impact evidence concerns any relevant moral actor.

One could imagine the response that this mischaracterizes the breadth of mitigating evidence that is offered on behalf of the defendant. The defendant is not only able to offer pre-crime evidence for its forward-looking mitigating evidence. *Ford v. Wainwright* and *Skipper v. South Carolina*, in which the Court held that evidence of adjustment to prison falls under the protection of *Lockett*, suggest that the defendant is also able to offer post-crime evidence for its backward-looking mitigating inference. Even if *Ford* is viewed as an aberration, there is still *Skipper* to answer for. In *Skipper*, the Court held that a defendant must be allowed to introduce as mitigating evidence that he had adjusted well to prison. *Skipper* thus adopts an evolving view of self: people change over time and the culpability of their different selves should be assessed separately.

Victim impact evidence, the argument might go, responds to this evolved view of self by adopting an evolved view of the victim. Just as post-crime, pre-trial evidence about the defendant is admissible for the mitigating inference that might be drawn from it, post-crime, pre-trial victim impact evidence should be admissible for the aggravating inference that might be drawn from it. The response has facial appeal, but it is not symmetrical.

But the symmetrical response to the requirement that defendants be allowed to offer post-crime, pre-trial *Skipper*-type evidence would be to admit post-crime, pre-trial aggravating evidence about the defendant. Under this rule, a prosecutor could argue that a defendant's poor adjustment to prison or his lack of contrition enhanced his culpability. This evidence would be admissible not just to rebut a defendant's claim that he had adjusted to prison or was contrite, but as part of the prosecution's case-in-chief at the sentencing phase.

The relationship between *Skipper*-type evidence and post-crime, pre-trial defendant-based aggravating evidence is symmetrical. The relationship between *Skipper*-type evidence and victim impact evidence is not. Both *Skipper*-type evidence and post-crime, pre-trial defendant based aggravating evidence are offered for backward-looking inferences: that the defendant's culpability should be diminished or enhanced because of the person into whom he has evolved. Put another way, there is x-axis symmetry between *Skipper*-type evidence and post-crime, pre-trial defendant-based aggravating evidence (**Figure 16-2**).

If the concern with *Skipper*-type evidence is that it adopts an improper view of self and increases arbitrariness by allowing irrelevant mitigat-

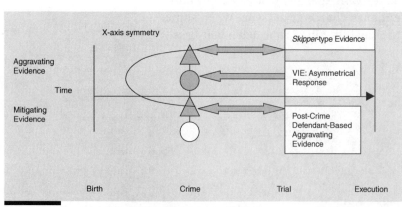

Figure 16-2 Symmetrical response to *Skipper*-type evidence.

ing evidence to be considered, admitting post-crime, pre-trial defendant-based aggravating evidence is the most direct possible response. Post-crime, pre-trial defendant-based aggravating evidence will reduce Type I error without increasing Type II error. The relationship between *Skipper*-type evidence and victim impact evidence is apples and oranges. *Skipper* evidence concerns the defendant; victim impact evidence the victim. There is at least a conceivable view of self under which *Skipper* evidence should be admissible: people evolve, they should be sentenced on the basis of who they are, not who they have been. There is no comparable argument to be made with victim impact evidence. Admitting victim impact evidence is only a counter to arbitrariness if the concern with arbitrariness is, again, that defendants get too few death sentences.

B. Structured Aggravating/Structured Mitigating Symmetry Implicit in arguments defending the admissibility of victim impact evidence on grounds of symmetry is the notion that aggravating and mitigating evidence should be treated in the same manner. This point is starkly raised in Justice Scalia's famous concurrence in *Walton v. Arizona* in which he declared that he would not "in this case or in the future vote to uphold an Eighth Amendment claim that the sentencer's discretion has been unlawfully restricted."

Justice Scalia's concurrence presents a somewhat different claim on symmetry than the argument for victim impact evidence. There the argument is that if the defendant is allowed to introduce irrelevant evidence, the prosecution should be too. Here the claim is that if the state can structure the sentencer's consideration of aggravating evidence it should also be able to structure its consideration of mitigating evidence.

The argument has facial appeal. If the state is required to define the aggravating circumstances a jury may rely upon in sentencing someone to death it seems reasonable to say the state may define the mitigating circumstances a jury may rely upon in sparing a defendant otherwise deserving of death. This is the crux of the philosophically interesting issue, but the claim on symmetry is flawed. The structuring of aggravating and mitigating evidence safeguards against different kinds of error.

Retributivists say people should receive as much punishment as they deserve. The harder question is determining the quantum of punishment that is deserved. In answering this, retributivists have turned most often to the argument that punishments should be distributed proportionately, so that the most culpable crime receives the most serious penalty, the second most culpable crime receives the second most serious penalty, and so on down the line to the least serious offender. This still leaves open the question how to determine in practice the severity of wrongs and punishments. In the case of the death penalty this question is most often answered by the jury: a defendant is punished by death if the jury says that it is what is deserved.

Retributivism poses an objective inquiry: the defendant should receive as much punishment as they deserve. Leaving the calculation to the subjective assessment of a jury leads to the two possible kinds of error discussed above: a jury might fail to sentence to die a defendant deserving of death (Type I error) or sentence an undeserving defendant to die (Type II error). The unstructured consideration of aggravating and mitigating evidence leads to different kinds of potential error. The unstructured consideration of aggravating evidence runs the risk that a jury may sentence to die a defendant that belongs to a class of offenders that does not deserve death. If aggravating circumstances are structured, Type I error will be reduced, though some Type II error may also result. If the universe of behavior covered by aggravating circumstances is defined too narrowly, some defendants deserving of death may not be sentenced to die.

The unstructured consideration of mitigating evidence creates a risk of Type II error exclusively. A jury may fail to sentence to die a death-deserving defendant, but no defendant will be sentenced to die by virtue of the unstructured consideration of mitigating evidence.

Justice Scalia's argument conflates these risks. His argument reduces to this: if States are compelled to reduce Type I error at the cost of some Type II error, they should be permitted to structure their statutes such that the consideration of mitigating evidence diminishes Type II error. The tacit assumption is that Type I error and Type II error are equally bad.

If this argument were offered in the context of determining criminal guilt it would seem patently wrong. Setting the burden of proof in criminal cases at proof beyond a reasonable doubt as opposed to, say, proof by a preponderance of the evidence, decreases Type I error at the expense of an increase in Type II error. This tradeoff is not questioned and, in fact, is constitutionally required. No one argues that because the state bears this daunting burden of proof, that the prosecution should be compensated with some offsetting advantage. Type I error is more tolerable than Type II error.

Presumably the argument is that sentencing is different because the defendant has already been judged to be guilty and is, hence, deserving of punishment. But retributivism contains a negative component equally significant as its positive component: a defendant should receive as much punishment as he deserves, and no more punishment than he deserves. To a retributivist, the imposition of excessive punishment is as much an injustice as the imposition of too little punishment. In death sentencing, the magnitude of the disparity between Type I error and Type II error is even greater than in guilt sentencing. Type I error is worse in the death penalty context since such errors cannot be reversed following the execution of the defendant.

II. *Conclusion*

A foolish consistency is the hobgoblin of little minds, so it seems fair to ask why it should be a goal of death sentencing. Criminal procedure abounds with disparities between the treatment of defendants and prosecutors. Many are constitutionally required and justifiably so. Symmetry is not a goal of itself, it is only useful if it vindicates some other legitimate objective.

The consistency advocated in *Payne* is of the most foolish kind. It is, first of all, not consistency in any meaningful sense. The objection to breadth of mitigating evidence introduced at capital trials is that much of it has no bearing on culpability and hence creates arbitrariness in sentencing. The symmetrical response would be to allow prosecutors to introduce aggravating evidence from the defendant's background. This is evidence from the same time period, offered for the same kind of inference, objectionable for the same reasons as mitigating evidence. Victim impact evidence responds to the objection to mitigating evidence by introducing a whole new kind of evidence into capital trials: backwards-looking, after-the-fact evidence that may or may not have been foreseeable to the defendant. This creates symmetry in the most trivial sense: it responds to arbitrariness that favors the defendant by introducing arbitrariness that favors the defendant.

The arbitrariness resulting from victim impact evidence is different in kind from that alleged to result from mitigating evidence. The unstructured consideration of mitigating evidence creates the risk that a defendant deserving death will be excused. The unstructured consideration of aggravating evidence, including the consideration of victim impact evidence creates a categorically different kind of risk: that an undeserving defendant will be sentenced to die. From the standpoint of retribution, this risk is greater than or equal to the risk resulting from the unstructured consideration of mitigating evidence. It is wrong to say that admitting victim impact evidence is a symmetrical response to mitigating evidence. It is dubious to claim that symmetry would even be desirable.

But what about *Skipper*? If a defendant has the constitutional right to offer post-crime mitigating evidence on his behalf, then surely it must be permissible for a state to allow the prosecution to offer post-crime evidence of the impact of the crime upon the victim's family. Again, though, the claimed symmetry is false. The symmetrical response to *Skipper* would be to allow the prosecution to offer post-crime aggravating evidence of the defendant's behavior. And again, more importantly, it is not at all obvious why symmetry would be desirable.

The real significance of *Skipper* is the insight it offers into the fundamental confusion in death penalty jurisprudence over the nature of self. The Court's approach to ordinary mitigating evidence views the person as a consonant individual. The criminal defendant is the product of who he was in the past. *Skipper* and arguably *Ford* take an evolved view of self: people can change, they should be held to answer for who they are, not who they have been. *Evans v. Muncy*, in which the Court upheld the denial of habeas relief to a petitioner sentenced under a future danger aggravator who later stopped a prison riot, and *Herrera* suggest a skepticism about this view: evidence developed subsequent to trial are irrelevant, all that matters is the determination made at the time of trial, whether demonstrably inaccurate or not. There is no consistent world view to be discerned in the case law.

One could imagine different valid answers to the question of which is the proper view of self, but the failure of the Court to articulate any coherent notion is damning. The death penalty persists almost entirely on the basis of appeals to retributive justice. Retributivists purport to give criminals what they deserve—no more, no less. To do so, they must offer a formula; they must articulate a mechanism or a permissible range of mechanisms by which desert may be calculated. In this light, the inability to answer the most rudimentary question corollary to this inquiry—from what point in time is desert to be calculated—is damning.

Capital Juries

17

■ Capital Juries—Introduction

In most states with capital punishment, the decision to impose the death penalty rests with the jury. Selection of a capital jury is thus of even greater significance than in ordinary criminal cases, and as might be expected, the procedures governing the selection process have been the subject of extensive litigation. The Supreme Court requires that prospective jurors who are categorically opposed to the death penalty must be excluded from the capital jury. Because the capital jury decides both the guilt of the defendant and the appropriate sentence, some have argued that the so-called "death-qualified" jury is partial, in that it is more likely to convict than a jury composed of a random cross section of the population.

Jury Selection Generally

In criminal cases, a panel of prospective jurors, called the *venire*, is drawn from a list of residents in the county in which the crime occurred. Voter registration rolls or driver license records are common sources for the roll. The *venire* is drawn randomly from the list of residents. The prosecutor, defense attorney, and judge then examine the members of the jury panel to determine their ability to serve on the jury. Panelists may be struck in either of two manners: the trial court grants a motion by one of the attorneys to strike a prospective jury member for cause, or an attorney exercises one of his peremptory challenges against a *venire* person.

A juror may be struck for cause if he or she is unable for any reason to render an impartial verdict in the case. For example, a juror may be struck for cause if he or she knows one of the litigants, or one of the attorneys, or has outside knowledge of the facts of the case, or a financial interest in its outcome. No limit is placed on the number of panel members that may be struck for cause. Any *venire* member who is partial must be struck regardless of how many have been struck before.

Peremptory challenges, by contrast, are limited in number. (The actual number varies from state to state.) Peremptory challenges are wildcards. A lawyer may use a peremptory challenge to strike a juror for any reason at all, except those prohibited by the Supreme Court. In *Batson v. Kentucky*, a 1986 decision, the Court held that peremptory challenges may not be exercised on the basis of race. It later held in *J.E.B. v. Alabama*, that the decision may not be based on gender. The restriction on race-based (and presumably gender-based) peremptory challenges applies equally to the prosecution and defense, according to the Court's 1992 decision in *Georgia v. McCollum*. Peremptory challenges are often based upon the intuition of the attorneys, although lawyers are increasingly relying upon experts for assistance in identifying prospective jurors who might not be sympathetic to their side.

Despite the Supreme Court's prohibition against race-based and gender-based challenges, ample evidence suggests that lawyers continue to exercise challenges on the basis of race and gender. David Baldus, George Woodworth, and a team of researchers examined jury panels in 317 capital murder trials in Philadelphia between 1981 and 1987. The Baldus and Woodworth team found widespread "discrimination in the use of peremptory challenges on the basis of race and gender by both prosecutors and defense counsel." Professor Baldus's team concluded that the Court's decisions banning such discrimination has had only "a marginal impact."

Jury Selection in Capital Cases

In capital cases, juries must be screened for attitudes about the death penalty. In an ordinary criminal case there is no reason to examine potential jurors about penalties as the sentencing decision is not in the hands of the jury. Because the capital jury decides both guilt and sentence, juror attitudes about penalties are relevant. If a potential juror is against the death penalty in all cases, or for an automatic death penalty for all murderers, then he or she is unfit to serve on the capital jury (at least for the sentencing phase) because that person is unable to follow the law, which requires a case-by-case determination of deathworthiness. All sides agree on this proposition. The harder question is what to do with jurors who are not against the death penalty in all cases, but have serious reservations about it.

Two principles are in competition here. On the one hand, the jury must be able to deliver a fair and impartial verdict. Jurors with religious or conscientious reservations about the death penalty might not be able to render an impartial verdict as to sentencing. On the other hand, the defendant is entitled to a jury that represents a fair cross section of the community. Most communities are filled with people who have reservations of some kind about the death penalty.

From a strategic standpoint, the prosecutor would like the universe of exclusion to be as large as possible. If a juror who expresses reservations about the death penalty can be struck for cause, it frees the prosecutor to use one of his or her peremptory challenges on another juror. The defendant, of course, would like to retain as many of the conscientious objectors as possible. Before the Supreme Court weighed in on the issue, state court judges varied widely in what standards they used to govern the exclusion of potential jurors who expressed reservations about the death penalty.

The Court first addressed the permissible parameters of these rulings in *Witherspoon v. Illinois*, a 1968 case, excerpted in the Critical Documents section of this chapter. An Illinois statute allowed the prosecutor to challenge for cause "any juror who shall, on being examined, state that he has conscientious scruples against capital punishment, or that he is opposed to the same." On the basis of this provision, the prosecution challenged nearly half of the prospective jurors. Witherspoon presented three unpublished studies to the Court showing that death-qualified juries were more conviction prone. The Court dismissed the studies as "too tentative," but did hold that the Illinois standard created too broad a class of excludables. The Court said that the only potential jurors to be excluded were those who would vote automatically against capital punishment, or those who could not make an impartial decision as to guilt. It is important to keep in mind that *Witherspoon* precedes *Furman* and *Gregg*. Provisions for bifurcated trials did not yet exist.

In a 1980 decision, *Adams v. Texas*, the Court stated that a potential juror could not be excluded for cause "based on his views about capital punishment unless those views would prevent or substantially impair the performances of his duties as a juror in accordance with his instruction and his oath." This suggests a somewhat broader class of potential excludables. A potential juror could be excluded without making it "unmistakably clear" that he or she would automatically vote against the death penalty. In *Wainwright v. Witt*, a 1985 decision excerpted below, the Court held that the *Adams* standard had replaced the *Witherspoon* standard and was the law of the land.

None of these decisions addressed the reality of the post-*Gregg* world of bifurcated trials. The question remained whether excluding potential jurors on the basis of attitudes that impaired the performance of their duties at the sentencing phase deprived the defendant of a fair trial at the guilt phase. In *Lockhart v. McCree*, presented in the Critical Documents section of this chapter, McCree offered social science data to show that excluding jurors under the *Witherspoon* standard produced juries that were more likely to convict than juries that were not death qualified. The Supreme Court rejected McCree's argument. The Court noted that *Witherspoon*-excludables were not a suspect classification. Excluding jurors with reservations about the death penalty was not analogous to excluding blacks or women, practices the Court had condemned. Race and gender are immutable characteristics; opposition to the death penalty is a matter of conscience. The Court also noted that McCree could not have objected to his jury but for the process of death qualification. The same twelve jurors might have ended up on McCree's jury by luck without violating McCree's rights in any way. Thus the Court held that death qualification did not deprive the defendant of a fair trial as to guilt.

This presents an essentially empirical question: whether the process of death qualification, as defined by the Supreme Court, creates juries that are more prone to convict than juries that are not death qualified. The *McCree* Court, however, dismissed the fifteen published studies presented to it showing that death-qualified jurors are more conviction prone than excludable jurors. There is also a nonempirical component to this issue: one could argue that even if death-qualified juries *are* more conviction prone, this does not necessarily deprive the defendant of a fair trial. Professor Nancy King argues below that the concept of jury nullification is not firmly rooted in the Constitution. Still, the question seems to cry out for an empirical answer. *McCree* loosed a spate of research trying to answer the concerns the Court had with the social science evidence presented to it in that case.

The overwhelming majority of studies have supported the conclusion that death-qualified juries are more likely to convict than ordinary juries. Excerpts from one of the leading studies by Claudia Cowan, William Thompson, and Phoebe Ellsworth are presented in the Perspectives section of this chapter. Professor Cowan's team concluded that death-qualified juries are more prone to convict, and concomitant with that finding, such juries are more inclined to believe prosecution witnesses and less inclined to credit defense witnesses.

If death qualification does stack the deck against capital defendants, the problem could be largely avoided by employing two juries. Justice Marshall argued in his dissent to *McCree* that two juries should be employed in capital cases: one to determine guilt, one to determine sentence. This would finesse the problem of death qualification. Marshall's proposal has not gained favor. The *McCree* majority maintained that the split jury process would be inefficient. Justice Rehnquist wrote, "It seems obvious to us that in most, if not all, capital cases much of the evidence adduced at the guilt phase of the trial will also have a bearing on the penalty phase; if two juries were to be required, such testimony would have to be presented twice, once to each jury." The majority also maintained that defendants enjoyed a potential benefit from the unitary jury: if the jury had any residual doubts about the defendant's guilt, this might have a mitigating influence in the defendant's favor during the sentencing phase.

■ Capital Juries—Critical Documents

Witherspoon v. Illinois
391 U.S. 510 (1968)

Mr. Justice Stewart delivered the opinion of the Court.

The petitioner was brought to trial in 1960 in Cook County, Illinois, upon a charge of murder. The jury found him guilty and fixed his penalty at death. At the time of his trial an Illinois statute provided:

> *In trials for murder it shall be a cause for challenge of any juror who shall, on being examined, state that he has conscientious scruples against capital punishment, or that he is opposed to the same.*

Through this provision Illinois armed the prosecution with unlimited challenges for cause in order to exclude those jurors who, in the words of the State's highest court, "might hesitate to return a verdict inflicting death." At the petitioner's trial, the prosecution eliminated nearly half the venire of prospective jurors by challenging, under the authority of this statute, any venireman who expressed qualms about capital punishment. From those who remained were chosen the jurors who ultimately found the petitioner guilty and sentenced him to death. The Supreme Court of Illinois denied post-conviction relief, and we granted certiorari to decide whether the Constitution permits a State to execute a man pursuant to the verdict of a jury so composed.

I

The issue before us is a narrow one. It does not involve the right of the prosecution to challenge for cause those prospective jurors who state that their reservations about capital punishment would prevent them from making an impartial decision as to the defendant's guilt. Nor does it involve the State's assertion of a right to exclude from the jury in a capital case those who say that they could never vote to impose the death penalty or that they would refuse even to consider its imposition in the case before them. For the State of Illinois did not stop there, but authorized the prosecution to exclude as well all who said that they were opposed to capital punishment and all who indicated that they had conscientious scruples against inflicting it.

In the present case the tone was set when the trial judge said early in the voir dire, "Let's get these conscientious objectors out of the way, without wasting any time on them." In rapid succession, 47 veniremen were successfully challenged for cause on the basis of their attitudes toward the death penalty. Only five of the 47 explicitly stated that under no circumstances would they vote to impose capital punishment. Six said that they did not "believe in the death penalty" and were excused without any attempt to determine whether they could nonetheless return a verdict of death. Thirty-nine veniremen, including four of the six who indicated that they did not believe in capital punishment, acknowledged having "conscientious or religious scruples against the infliction of the death penalty" or against its infliction "in a proper case" and were excluded without any effort to find out whether their scruples would invariably compel them to vote against capital punishment.

Only one venireman who admitted to "a religious or conscientious scruple against the infliction of the death penalty in a proper case" was examined at any length. She was asked: "You don't believe in the death penalty?" She replied: "No. It's just I wouldn't want to be responsible." The judge admonished her not to forget her "duty as a citizen" and again asked her whether she had "a religious or conscientious scruple" against capital punishment. This time, she replied in the negative. Moments later, however, she repeated that she would not "like to be responsible for deciding somebody should be put to death." Evidently satisfied that this elaboration of the prospective juror's views disqualified her under the Illinois statute, the judge told her to "step aside."

II

The petitioner contends that a State cannot confer upon a jury selected in this manner the power to determine guilt. He maintains that such a jury, unlike one chosen at random from a cross-section of the community, must necessarily be biased in favor of conviction, for the kind of juror who would be unperturbed by the prospect of sending a man to his death, he contends, is the kind of juror who would too readily ignore the presumption of the defendant's innocence, accept the prosecution's version of the facts, and return a verdict of guilt. To support this view, the petitioner refers to what he describes as "competent scientific evidence that death-qualified jurors are partial to the prosecution on the issue of guilt or innocence."

The data adduced by the petitioner, however, are too tentative and fragmentary to establish that jurors not opposed to the death penalty tend to favor the prosecution in the determination of guilt. We simply cannot conclude, either on the basis of the record now before us or as a matter of judicial notice, that the exclusion of jurors opposed to capital punishment results in an unrepresentative jury on the issue of guilt or substantially increases the risk of conviction.

III

It does not follow, however, that the petitioner is entitled to no relief. For in this case the jury was entrusted with two distinct responsibilities: first, to determine whether the petitioner was innocent or guilty; and second, if guilty, to determine whether his sentence should be imprisonment or death. It has not been shown that this jury was biased with respect to the petitioner's guilt. But it is self-evident that, in its role as arbiter of the punishment to be imposed, this jury fell woefully short of that impartiality to which the petitioner was entitled under the Sixth and Fourteenth Amendments.

The only justification the State has offered for the jury-selection technique it employed here is that individuals who express serious reservations about capital punishment cannot be relied upon to vote for it even when the laws of the State and the instructions of the trial judge would make death the proper penalty. But in Illinois, as in other States, the jury is given broad discretion to decide whether or not death *is* "the proper penalty" in a given case, and a juror's general views about capital punishment play an inevitable role in any such decision.

A man who opposes the death penalty, no less than one who favors it, can make the discretionary judgment entrusted to him by the State and can thus obey the oath he takes as a juror. But a jury from which all such men have been excluded cannot perform the task demanded of it. Guided by neither rule nor standard, "free to select or reject as it sees fit," a jury that must choose between life imprisonment and capital punishment can do little more—and must do nothing less—than express the conscience of the community on the ultimate question of life or death. Yet, in a nation less than half of whose people believe in the death penalty, a jury composed exclusively of such people cannot speak for the community. Culled of all who harbor doubts about the wisdom of capital punishment—of all who would be reluctant to pronounce the extreme penalty—such a jury can speak only for a distinct and dwindling minority.

If the State had excluded only those prospective jurors who stated in advance of trial that they would not even consider returning a verdict of death, it could argue that the resulting jury was simply "neutral" with respect to penalty. But when it swept from the jury all who expressed conscientious or religious scruples against capital punishment and all who opposed it in principle, the State crossed the line of neutrality. In its quest for a jury capable of imposing the death penalty, the State produced a jury uncommonly willing to condemn a man to die.

It is, of course, settled that a State may not entrust the determination of whether a man is innocent or guilty to a tribunal "organized to convict." It requires but a short step from that principle to hold, as we do today, that a State may not entrust the determination of whether a man should live or die to a tribunal organized to return a verdict of death. Specifically, we hold that a sentence of death cannot be carried out if the jury that imposed or recommended it was chosen by excluding veniremen for cause simply because they voiced general objections to the death penalty or expressed conscientious or religious scruples against its infliction.[21] No defendant can constitutionally be put to death at the hands of a tribunal so selected.

Whatever else might be said of capital punishment, it is at least clear that its imposition by a hanging jury cannot be squared with the Constitution. The State of Illinois has stacked the deck against the petitioner. To execute this death sentence would deprive him of his life without due process of law. Reversed.

Mr. Justice Black, with whom Mr. Justice Harlan and Mr. Justice White join, dissenting.

The opinion affirming this conviction for a unanimous Illinois Supreme Court was written by Justice Walter Schaefer, a judge nationally recognized as a protector of the constitutional rights of defendants charged with crime. It seems particularly unfortunate to me that this Court feels called upon to charge that Justice Schaefer and his associates would let a man go to his death after the trial court had contrived a "hanging jury" and, in this Court's language, "stacked the deck" to bring about the death sentence for petitioner. With all due deference it seems to me that one might much more appropriately charge that this Court has today written the law in such a way that the States are being forced to try their murder cases with biased juries. If this Court is to hold capital punishment unconstitutional, I think it should do so forthrightly, not by making it impossible for States to get juries that will enforce the death penalty.

As I see the issue in this case, it is a question of plain bias. A person who has conscientious or religious scruples against capital punishment will seldom if ever

---

[21] Just as veniremen cannot be excluded for cause on the ground that they hold such views, so too they cannot be excluded for cause simply because they indicate that there are some kinds of cases in which they would refuse to recommend capital punishment. And a prospective juror cannot be expected to say in advance of trial whether he would in fact vote for the extreme penalty in the case before him. The most that can be demanded of a venireman in this regard is that he be willing to *consider* all of the penalties provided by state law, and that he not be irrevocably committed, before the trial has begun, to vote against the penalty of death regardless of the facts and circumstances that might emerge in the course of the proceedings. If the *voir dire* testimony in a given case indicates that veniremen were excluded on any broader basis than this, the death sentence cannot be carried out even if applicable statutory or case law in the relevant jurisdiction would appear to support only a narrower ground of exclusion.

We repeat, however, that nothing we say today bears upon the power of a State to execute a defendant sentenced to death by a jury from which the only veniremen who were in fact excluded for cause were those who made unmistakably clear (1) that they would *automatically* vote against the imposition of capital punishment without regard to any evidence that might be developed at the trial of the case before them, or (2) that their attitude toward the death penalty would prevent them from making an impartial decision as to the defendant's *guilt*. Nor does the decision in this case affect the validity of any sentence *other* than one of death. Nor, finally, does today's holding render invalid the *conviction*, as opposed to the *sentence*, in this or any other case.

vote to impose the death penalty. This is just human nature, and no amount of semantic camouflage can cover it up. In the same manner, I would not dream of foisting on a criminal defendant a juror who admitted that he had conscientious or religious scruples against not inflicting the death sentence on any person convicted of murder (a juror who claims, for example, that he adheres literally to the Biblical admonition of "an eye for an eye"). Yet the logical result of the majority's holding is that such persons must be allowed so that the "conscience of the community" will be fully represented when it decides "the ultimate question of life or death." While I have always advocated that the jury be as fully representative of the community as possible, I would never carry this so far as to require that those biased against one of the critical issues in a trial should be represented on a jury.

The majority opinion attempts to equate those who have conscientious or religious scruples against the death penalty with those who do not in such a way as to balance the allegedly conflicting viewpoints in order that a truly representative jury can be established to exercise the community's discretion in deciding on punishment. But for this purpose I do not believe that those who have conscientious or religious scruples against the death penalty and those who have no feelings either way are in any sense comparable. Scruples against the death penalty are commonly the result of a deep religious conviction or a profound philosophical commitment developed after much soul-searching. The holders of such scruples must necessarily recoil from the prospect of making possible what they regard as immoral. On the other hand, I cannot accept the proposition that persons who do not have conscientious scruples against the death penalty are "prosecution prone."

It seems to me that the Court's opinion today must be read as holding just the opposite from what has been stated above. For no matter how the Court might try to hide it, the implication is inevitably in its opinion that people who do not have conscientious scruples against the death penalty are somehow callous to suffering and are, as some of the commentators cited by the Court called them, "prosecution prone." This conclusion represents a psychological foray into the human mind that I have considerable doubt about my ability to make, and I must confess that the two or three so-called "studies" cited by the Court on this subject are not persuasive to me.

I believe that the Court's decision today goes a long way to destroying the concept of an impartial jury as we have known it. I shall not contribute in any way to the destruction of our ancient judicial and constitutional concept of trial by an impartial jury by forcing the States through "constitutional doctrine" laid down by this Court to accept jurors who are bound to be biased. For this reason I dissent.

Wainwright v. Witt
469 U.S. 412 (1985)

Justice Rehnquist delivered the opinion of the Court.

This case requires us to examine once again the procedures for selection of jurors in criminal trials involving the possible imposition of capital punishment, and to consider standards for federal courts reviewing those procedures upon petition for a writ of habeas corpus.

I

Respondent Johnny Paul Witt was convicted of first-degree murder in Florida and sentenced to death.

The only claim the Eleventh Circuit found meritorious was respondent's *Witherspoon* claim. The court found the following exchange during *voir dire*, between the prosecutor and venireman Colby, to be insufficient to justify Colby's excusal for cause:

Q. Prosecutor: Now, let me ask you a question, ma'am. Do you have any religious beliefs or personal beliefs against the death penalty?

A. Colby: I am afraid personally but not—

Q. Speak up, please.

A. I am afraid of being a little personal, but definitely not religious.

Q. Now, would that interfere with you sitting as a juror in this case?

A. I am afraid it would.

Q. You are afraid it would?

A. Yes, Sir.

Q. Would it interfere with judging the guilt or innocence of the Defendant in this case?

A. I think so.

Q. You think it would.

A. I think it would.

Q. Your honor, I would move for cause at this point.

THE COURT: All right. Step down.

Defense counsel did not object or attempt rehabilitation.

The Court of Appeals construed our decisions to require that jurors expressing objections to the death penalty be given "great leeway" before their expressions justify dismissal for cause. The court concluded that the colloquy with venireman Colby reprinted above did not satisfy the *Witherspoon* standard. Colby's limited expressions of "feelings and thoughts" failed to "unequivocally state that she would automatically be unable to apply the death penalty."

More recent opinions of this Court demonstrate no ritualistic adherence to a requirement that a prospective juror make it "unmistakably clear that she would *automatically* vote against the imposition of capital punishment." In *Lockett*, prospective capital jurors were asked: "Do you feel that you could take an oath to well and truly try this case and follow the law, or is your conviction so strong that you cannot take an oath, knowing that a possibility exists in regard to capital punishment?'"

We held that the veniremen who answered that they could not "take the oath" were properly excluded. Although the *Lockett* opinion alluded to the second half of the footnote 21 standard, dealing with a juror's inability to decide impartially a defendant's guilt, the Court did not refer to the "automatically" language. Instead, it simply determined that each of the excluded veniremen had made it "unmistakably clear that they could not be trusted to abide by existing law and to follow conscientiously the instructions of the trial judge."

This Court again examined the *Witherspoon* standard in *Adams v. Texas*. *Adams* involved the Texas capital sentencing scheme, wherein jurors were asked to answer three specific questions put by the trial judge. The court was required to impose the death sentence if each question was answered affirmatively. A Texas statute provided that a prospective capital juror "shall be disqualified unless he states under oath that the mandatory penalty of death or imprisonment for life will not affect his deliberations on any issue of fact." Before deciding whether certain jurors had been properly excluded pursuant to this statute, this Court attempted to discern the proper standard for making such a determination. The Court discussed its prior opinions, noting the *Witherspoon* Court's recognition, in footnote 21, that States retained a "legitimate interest in obtaining jurors who could follow their instructions and obey their oaths." The Court concluded:

> *This line of cases establishes the general proposition that a juror may not be challenged for cause based on his views about capital punishment unless those views would prevent or substantially impair the performance of his duties as a juror in accordance with his instructions and his oath. The State may insist, however, that jurors will consider and decide the facts impartially and conscientiously apply the law as charged by the court.*

The Court went on to hold that *as applied in that case* certain veniremen had been improperly excluded under the Texas statute, because their acknowledgment that the possible imposition of the death penalty would or might "affect" their deliberations was meant only to indicate that they would be more emotionally involved or would view their task "with greater seriousness and gravity." The Court reasoned that such an "effect" did not demonstrate that the prospective jurors were unwilling or unable to follow the law or obey their oaths.

The state of this case law leaves trial courts with the difficult task of distinguishing between prospective jurors whose opposition to capital punishment will not allow them to apply the law or view the facts impartially and jurors who, though opposed to capital punishment, will nevertheless conscientiously apply the law to the facts adduced at trial. Although this task may be difficult in any event, it is obviously made more difficult by the fact that the standard applied in *Adams* differs markedly from the language of footnote 21. The tests with respect to sentencing and guilt, originally in two prongs, have been merged; the requirement that a juror may be excluded only if he would never vote for the death penalty is now missing; gone too is the extremely high burden of proof. In general, the standard has been simplified.

There is good reason why the *Adams* test is preferable for determining juror exclusion. First, although given *Witherspoon*'s facts a court applying the general principles of *Adams* could have arrived at the "automatically" language of *Witherspoon*'s footnote 21, we do not believe that language can be squared with the duties of present-day capital sentencing juries. In *Witherspoon* the jury was vested with unlimited discretion in choice of sentence. Given this discretion, a juror willing to *consider* the death penalty arguably was able to "follow the law and abide by his oath" in choosing the "proper" sentence. Nothing more was required. Under this understanding the only veniremen who could be deemed excludable were those who would never vote for the death sentence or who could not impartially judge guilt.

After our decisions in *Furman* and *Gregg*, however, sentencing juries could no longer be invested with such discretion. As in the State of Texas, many capital sentencing juries are now asked specific questions, often factual, the answers to which will determine whether death is the appropriate penalty. In such circumstances it does not make sense to require simply that a juror not "automatically" vote against the death penalty; whether or not a venireman *might* vote for death under certain *personal* standards, the State still may properly challenge that venireman if he refuses to follow the statutory scheme and truthfully answer the questions put by the trial judge. To hold that *Witherspoon* requires anything more would be to hold, in the name of the Sixth Amendment right to an impartial jury, that a State must allow a venireman to sit despite the fact that he will be unable to view the case impartially.

Finally, the *Adams* standard is proper because it is in accord with traditional reasons for excluding jurors and with the circumstances under which such determinations are made. We begin by reiterating *Adams'* acknowledgment that "*Witherspoon* is not a ground for challenging any prospective juror. It is rather a limitation on the State's power to exclude." Exclusion of jurors opposed to capital punishment began with a recognition that certain of those jurors might frustrate the State's legitimate interest in administering constitutional capital sentencing schemes by not following their oaths. *Witherspoon* simply held that the State's power to exclude did not extend beyond its interest in removing those particular jurors. But there is nothing talismanic about juror exclusion under *Witherspoon* merely because it involves capital sentencing juries. *Witherspoon* is not grounded in the Eighth Amendment's prohibition against cruel and unusual punishment, but in the Sixth Amendment. Here, as elsewhere, the quest is for jurors who will conscientiously apply the law and find the facts. That is what an "impartial" jury consists of, and we do not think, simply because a defendant is being tried for a capital crime, that he is entitled to a legal presumption or standard that allows jurors to be seated who quite likely will be biased in his favor.

As with any other trial situation where an adversary wishes to exclude a juror because of bias, then, it is the adversary seeking exclusion who must demonstrate, through questioning, that the potential juror lacks impartiality. It is then the trial judge's duty to determine whether the challenge is proper. This is, of course, the standard and procedure outlined in *Adams*, but it is equally true of any situation where a party seeks to exclude a biased juror.

We therefore take this opportunity to clarify our decision in *Witherspoon*, and to reaffirm the above-quoted standard from *Adams* as the proper standard for determining when a prospective juror may be excluded for cause because of his or her views on capital punishment. That standard is whether the juror's views would "prevent or substantially impair the performance of his duties as a juror in accordance with his instructions and his oath." We note that, in addition to dispensing with *Witherspoon*'s reference to "automatic" decisionmaking, this standard likewise does not require that a juror's bias be proved with "unmistakable clarity." This is because determinations of juror bias cannot be reduced to question-and-answer sessions which obtain results in the manner of a catechism. What common sense should have realized experience has proved: many veniremen simply cannot be asked enough questions to reach the point where their bias has been made "unmistakably clear"; these veniremen may not know how they will react when faced with imposing the death sentence, or may be unable to articulate, or may wish to hide their true feelings. Despite this lack of clarity in the printed record, however, there will be situations where the trial judge is left with the definite impression that a prospective juror would be unable to faithfully and impartially apply the law. Deference must be paid to the trial judge who sees and hears the juror.

The trial court's finding of bias was made under the proper standard and was fairly supported by the record. Since respondent has not adduced "clear and convincing evidence that the factual determination by the State court was erroneous," we reverse the judgment of the Court of Appeals. It is so ordered.

Justice Brennan, with whom Justice Marshall joins, dissenting.

The Court's reasoning does not in any way justify abandonment of the restrictions *Witherspoon* has placed on the exclusion of prospective jurors. Without a doubt, a State may inquire whether a particular juror will be able to follow his or her oath to abide by the particulars of a guided discretion sentencing approach, and upon receiving an unmistakably clear negative response the State may properly move to exclude that juror. But the existence of a guided discretion scheme in no way diminishes the defendant's interest in a jury composed of a fair cross section of the community and a jury not "uncommonly willing to condemn a man to die." Even under a guided discretion proceeding a juror must have the opportunity to consider all available mitigating evidence, and to decide against imposition of the death sentence in any individual case. The risks that *Witherspoon* sought to minimize through defining high standards of proof for exclusions based on death penalty scruples are, we correctly held in *Adams*, equally prevalent in the context of guided discretion sentencing schemes.

Like the death-qualified juries that the prosecution can now mold to its will to enhance the chances of victory, this Court increasingly acts as the adjunct of the State and its prosecutors in facilitating efficient and expedient conviction and execution irrespective of the Constitution's fundamental guarantees. One can only hope that this day too will soon pass.

Lockhart v. McCree
476 U.S. 162 (1986)

Justice Rehnquist delivered the opinion of the Court.

In this case we address the question left open by our decision nearly 18 years ago in *Witherspoon*: Does the Constitution prohibit the removal for cause, prior to the guilt phase of a bifurcated capital trial, of prospective jurors whose opposition to the death penalty is so strong that it would prevent or substantially impair the performance of their duties as jurors at the sentencing phase of the trial? We hold that it does not.

McCree was charged with capital felony murder. The trial judge at *voir dire* removed for cause, over McCree's objections, those prospective jurors who stated that they could not under any circumstances vote for the imposition of the death penalty. Eight prospective jurors were excluded for this reason. The jury convicted McCree of capital felony murder, but rejected the State's request for the death penalty, instead setting McCree's punishment at life imprisonment without parole.

The Eighth Circuit found "substantial evidentiary support" for the District Court's conclusion that the removal for cause of "*Witherspoon*-excludables" resulted in "conviction-prone" juries, and affirmed the grant of habeas relief on the ground that such removal for cause violated McCree's constitutional right to a jury selected from a fair cross section of the community.

Having identified some of the more serious problems with McCree's studies, however, we will assume for purposes of this opinion that the studies are both methodologically valid and adequate to establish that "death qualification" in fact produces juries somewhat more "conviction-prone" than "non-death-qualified" juries. We hold, nonetheless, that the Constitution does not prohibit the States from "death qualifying" juries in capital cases.

The Eighth Circuit ruled that "death qualification" violated McCree's right to a jury selected from a representative cross section of the community. But we do not believe that the fair-cross-section requirement can, or should, be applied as broadly as that court attempted to apply it. We have never invoked the fair-cross-section principle to invalidate the use of either for-cause or peremptory challenges to prospective jurors, or to require petit juries, as opposed to jury panels or venires, to reflect the composition of the community at large. The limited scope of the fair-cross-section requirement is a direct and inevitable consequence of the practical impossibility of providing each criminal defendant with a truly "representative" petit jury. We remain convinced that an extension of the fair-cross-section requirement to petit juries would be unworkable and unsound, and we decline McCree's invitation to adopt such an extension.

But even if we were willing to extend the fair-cross-section requirement to petit juries, we would still reject the Eighth Circuit's conclusion that "death qualification" violates that requirement. The essence of a "fair-cross-section" claim is the systematic exclusion of "a 'distinctive' group in the community." In our view, groups defined solely in terms of shared attitudes that would prevent or substantially impair members of the group from performing one of their duties as jurors, such as the "*Witherspoon*-excludables" at issue here, are not "distinctive groups" for fair-cross-section purposes.

We think it obvious that the concept of "distinctiveness" must be linked to the purposes of the fair-cross-section requirement. We have identified those purposes as (1) ensuring that the "commonsense judgment of the community" will act as "a hedge against the overzealous or mistaken prosecutor," (2) preserving "public confidence in the fairness of the criminal justice system," and (3) implementing our belief that "sharing in the administration of justice is a phase of civic responsibility."

Our prior jury-representativeness cases involved such groups as blacks, women, and Mexican-Americans. The wholesale exclusion of these large groups from jury service clearly contravened all three of the aforementioned purposes of the fair-cross-section requirement. Because these groups were excluded for reasons completely unrelated to the ability of members of the group to serve as jurors in a particular case, the exclusion raised at least the possibility that the composition of juries would be arbitrarily skewed in such a way as to deny criminal defendants the benefit of the common-sense judgment of the community. In addition, the exclusion from jury service of large groups of individuals not on the basis of their inability to serve as jurors, but on the basis of some immutable characteristic such as race, gender, or ethnic background, undeniably gave rise to an "appearance of unfairness." Finally, such exclusion improperly deprived members of these often historically disadvantaged groups of their right as citizens to serve on juries in criminal cases.

The group of "*Witherspoon*-excludables" involved in the case at bar differs significantly from the groups we have previously recognized as "distinctive." "Death qualification" is carefully designed to serve the State's concededly legitimate interest in obtaining a single jury that can properly and impartially apply the law to the facts of the case at both the guilt and sentencing phases of a capital trial.

Furthermore, unlike blacks, women, and Mexican-Americans, "*Witherspoon*-excludables" are singled out for exclusion in capital cases on the basis of an attribute that is within the individual's control. The removal for cause of "*Witherspoon*-excludables" in capital cases does not prevent them from serving as jurors in other criminal cases, and thus leads to no substantial deprivation of their basic rights of citizenship. They are treated no differently than any juror who expresses the view that he would be unable to follow the law in a particular case.

In sum, "*Witherspoon*-excludables," or for that matter any other group defined solely in terms of shared attitudes that render members of the group unable to serve as jurors in a particular case, may be excluded from jury service without contravening any of the basic objectives of the fair-cross-section requirement.

McCree argues that, even if we reject the Eighth Circuit's fair-cross-section holding, we should affirm the judgment below on the alternative ground, adopted by the District Court, that "death qualification" violated his constitutional right to an impartial jury. McCree does not claim that his conviction was tainted by any of the kinds of jury bias or partiality that we have previously recognized as violative of the Constitution. Instead, McCree argues that his jury lacked impartiality because the absence of "*Witherspoon*-excludables" "slanted" the jury in favor of conviction.

We do not agree. McCree's "impartiality" argument apparently is based on the theory that, because all individual jurors are to some extent predisposed towards one result or another, a constitutionally impartial *jury* can be constructed only by "balancing" the various predispositions of the individual *jurors*. Thus, according to McCree, when the State "tips the scales" by excluding prospective jurors with a particular viewpoint, an impermissibly partial jury results. We have consistently rejected this view of jury impartiality, including as recently as last Term when we squarely held that an impartial *jury* consists of nothing more than "*jurors* who will conscientiously apply the law and find the facts."

The view of jury impartiality urged upon us by McCree is both illogical and hopelessly impractical. McCree characterizes the jury that convicted him as "slanted" by the process of "death qualification." But McCree admits that exactly the same 12 individuals could have ended up on his jury through the "luck of the draw," without in any way violating the constitutional guarantee of impartiality. Even accepting McCree's position that we should focus on the *jury* rather than the individual *jurors*, it is hard for us to understand the logic of the argument that a given jury is unconstitutionally partial when it results from a state-ordained process, yet impartial when exactly the same jury results from mere chance. On a more practical level, if it were true that the Constitution required a certain mix of individual viewpoints on the jury, then trial judges would be required to undertake the Sisyphean task of "balancing" juries, making sure that each contains the proper number of Democrats and Republicans, young persons and old persons, white-collar executives and blue-collar laborers, and so on. Adopting McCree's concept of jury impartiality would also likely require the elimination of peremptory challenges, which are commonly used by both the State and the defendant to attempt to produce a jury favorable to the challenger.

Justice Marshall's dissent points out that some States which adhere to the unitary jury system do not allow the defendant to argue "residual doubts" to the jury at sentencing. But while this may justify skepticism as to the extent to which such States are willing to go to allow defendants to capitalize on "residual doubts," it does not wholly vitiate the claimed interest. Finally, it seems obvious to us that in most, if not all, capital cases much of the evidence adduced at the guilt phase of the trial will also have a bearing on the penalty phase; if two different juries were to be required, such testimony would have to be presented twice, once to each jury. As the Arkansas Supreme Court has noted, "such repetitive trials could not be consistently fair to the State and perhaps not even to the accused."

In our view, it is simply not possible to define jury impartiality, for constitutional purposes, by reference to some hypothetical mix of individual viewpoints. Prospective jurors come from many different backgrounds, and have many different attitudes and predispositions. But the Constitution presupposes that a jury selected from a fair cross section of the community is impartial, regardless of the mix of individual viewpoints actually represented on the jury, so long as the jurors can conscientiously and properly carry out their sworn duty to apply the law to the facts of the particular case. We hold that McCree's jury satisfied both aspects of this constitutional standard. The judgment of the Court of Appeals is therefore. Reversed.

Justice Marshall, with whom Justice Brennan and Justice Stevens join, dissenting.

In the wake of *Witherspoon*, a number of researchers set out to supplement the data that the Court had found inadequate in that case. The results of these studies were exhaustively analyzed by the District Court in this case, and can be only briefly summarized here. The data strongly suggest that death qualification excludes a significantly large subset—at least 11% to 17%—of potential jurors who could be impartial during the guilt phase of trial. Among the members of this excludable class are a disproportionate number of blacks and women.

The perspectives on the criminal justice system of jurors who survive death qualification are systematically different from those of the excluded jurors. Death-qualified jurors are, for example, more likely to believe that a defendant's failure to testify is indicative of his guilt, more hostile to the insanity defense, more mistrustful of defense attorneys, and less concerned about the danger of erroneous convictions. This pro-prosecution bias is reflected in the greater readiness of death-qualified jurors to convict or to convict on more serious charges. And, finally, the very process of death qualification—which focuses attention on the death penalty before the trial has even begun—has been found to predispose the jurors that survive it to believe that the defendant is guilty. The evidence thus confirms, and is itself corroborated by, the more intuitive judgments of scholars and of so many of the participants in capital trials—judges, defense attorneys, and prosecutors.

The true impact of death qualification on the fairness of a trial is likely even more devastating than the studies show. *Witherspoon* placed limits on the State's ability to strike scrupled jurors for cause, unless they state "unambiguously that they would automatically vote against the imposition of capital punishment no matter what the trial might reveal." It said nothing, however, about the prosecution's use of peremptory challenges to eliminate jurors who do not meet that standard and would otherwise survive death qualification. There is no question that peremptories have indeed been used to this end, thereby expanding the class of scrupled jurors excluded as a result of the death-qualifying *voir dire* challenged here. The only study of this practice has concluded: "For the five-year period studied a prima facie case has been demonstrated that prosecutors in Florida's Fourth Judicial Circuit systematically used their peremptory challenges to eliminate from capital juries venirepersons expressing opposition to the death penalty."

Respondent does not claim that any individual on the jury that convicted him fell short of the constitutional standard for impartiality. Rather, he contends that, by systematically excluding a class of potential jurors less prone than the population at large to vote for conviction, the State gave itself an unconstitutional advantage at his trial.

I am puzzled by the difficulty that the majority has in understanding the "logic of the argument." For the logic is precisely that which carried the day in *Witherspoon*, and which has never been repudiated by this Court—not even today, if the majority is to be taken at its word. There was no question in *Witherspoon* that if the defendant's jury had been chosen by the "luck of the draw," the same 12 jurors who actually sat on his case might have been selected. Nonetheless, because the State had removed from the pool of possible jurors all those expressing general opposition to the death penalty, the Court overturned the defendant's conviction, declaring "that a State may not entrust the determination of whether a man should live or die to a tribunal organized to return a verdict of death."

As the *Witherspoon* Court recognized, "the State's interest in submitting the penalty issue to a jury capable of imposing capital punishment" may be accommodated without infringing a capital defendant's interest in a fair determination of his guilt if the State uses "one jury to decide guilt and another to fix punishment." Any exclusion of death-penalty opponents, the Court reasoned, could await the penalty phase of a trial. The question here is thus whether the State has *other* interests that require the use of a single jury and demand the subordination of a capital defendant's Sixth and Fourteenth Amendment rights.

The only two reasons that the Court invokes to justify the State's use of a single jury are efficient trial management and concern that a defendant at his sentencing proceedings may be able to profit from "residual doubts" troubling jurors who have sat through the guilt phase of his trial. The first of these purported justifications is merely unconvincing. The second is offensive.

The additional costs that would be imposed by a system of separate juries are not particularly high.

> First, capital cases constitute a relatively small number of criminal trials. Moreover, the number of these cases in which a penalty determination will be necessary is even smaller. A penalty determination will occur only where a verdict on guilt has been returned that authorizes the possible imposition of capital punishment, and only where the prosecutor decides that a death sentence should be sought. Even in cases in which a penalty determination will occur, the impaneling of a new penalty jury may not always be necessary. In some cases, it may be possible to have alternate jurors replace any 'automatic life imprisonment' jurors who served at the guilt determination trial.

In a system using separate juries for guilt and penalty phases, time and resources would be saved every time a capital case did not require a penalty phase. The *voir dire* needed to identify nullifiers before the guilt phase is less extensive than the questioning that under the current scheme is conducted before *every* capital trial. The State could, of course, choose to empanel a death-qualified jury at the start of every trial, to be used only if a penalty stage is required. However, if it opted for the cheaper alternative of empaneling a death-qualified jury only in the event that a defendant were convicted of capital charges, the State frequently would be able to avoid retrying the entire guilt phase for the benefit of the penalty jury. Stipulated summaries of prior evidence might, for example, save considerable time. Thus, it cannot fairly be said that the costs of accommodating a defendant's constitutional rights under these circumstances are prohibitive, or even significant.

Even less convincing is the Court's concern that a defendant be able to appeal at sentencing to the "residual doubts" of the jurors who found him guilty. Any suggestion that the current system of death qualification "may be in the defendant's best interests, seems specious unless the state is willing to grant the defendant the option to waive this paternalistic protection in exchange for better odds against conviction."

On occasion, this Court has declared what I believe should be obvious—that when a State seeks to convict a defendant of the most serious and severely punished offenses in its criminal code, any procedure that "diminishes the reliability of the guilt determination" must be struck down. But in spite of such declarations, I cannot help thinking that respondent here would have stood a far better chance of prevailing on his constitutional claims had he not been challenging a procedure peculiar to the administration of the death penalty. For in no other context would a majority of this Court refuse to find any constitutional violation in a state practice that systematically operates to render juries more likely to convict, and to convict on the more serious charges. I dissent.

■ Capital Juries Perspectives

■ Issue—What is the Effect of Death Qualification on Jury Decisionmaking?

Claudia L. Cowan, William C. Thompson, and Phoebe C. Ellsworth, "The Effects of Death Qualification on Jurors' Predisposition to Convict and on the Quality of Deliberation"

I. *Introduction*

The jury is a uniquely democratic institution. A jury is seen as a fair tribunal because it represents the coalescence of a great diversity of community attitudes. The preservation of this diversity is of central importance both to the defendant, who is entitled to the collective judgment of the community, and to the community itself, whose members are entitled to an equal say on matters so fundamental as criminal justice.

The Supreme Court "repeatedly has held that meaningful community participation cannot be attained with the exclusion of minorities or other identifiable groups from jury service." The practice of "death-qualifying" capital juries by excluding those who are adamantly opposed to the death penalty is an unusual departure from this commitment to diversity. It is the sole legal rule that permits the categorical exclusion of a whole group of otherwise eligible citizens from jury service on the basis of their beliefs. The purpose of their exclusion is rooted in the traditional reliance on the same jury to determine both guilt and penalty in capital trials. This group, the "*Witherspoon* excludables," has indicated their inability to consider voting for death if the defendant were found guilty of a capital crime and are therefore barred from the determination of the penalty; for reasons of economy and convenience, they are also excluded from participation in the determination of guilt or innocence.

The effect of this exclusion is that there are two distinct types of jury that decide whether people accused of crimes are innocent or guilty. In almost all criminal cases the defendant is tried by a "mixed" jury, representing the full range of community opinion. But in capital cases, the defendant is tried by a death-qualified jury, representing a more limited spectrum of community opinion.

Legal scholars and social scientists have long been concerned with the consequences of this anomalous exclusion in capital trials. One effect, the unusually punitive nature of a jury culled of all members who express any opposition to capital punishment, was recognized by the Court in *Witherspoon*.

A second effect is the loss of representativeness. Women and blacks, whose rights to proportional representation on juries have been specifically guaranteed by the Supreme Court, are disproportionately excluded from capital juries under *Witherspoon*, and so are the poor, and members of certain religions. And, because attitudes toward the death penalty are related to other attitudes about the criminal justice system, death qualification reduces the chances that certain beliefs and viewpoints will be represented. This limitation of the diversity of the opinions and ideas may adversely affect the quality of the jury's deliberation, a point to which we shall return.

This restriction of the range of attitudes is also related to a third possible effect of death qualification: conviction proneness. In attempting to test the validity of this premise, social scientists have generally taken two different approaches. The first is to demonstrate that attitudes toward the death penalty are correlated with other attitudes more closely related to the juror's perceptions of the guilt or innocence of criminal defendants. This research has consistently found that those who favor the death penalty are likely to favor the prosecution, relative to those who oppose the death penalty. The second approach is to attempt to demonstrate the conviction proneness of death-qualified jurors more directly, by asking subjects their verdicts in real or simulated cases.

II. Method

A. Overview A group of adults qualified for jury service watched a videotape of a simulated homicide trial, which represented all major aspects of an actual criminal trial. After hearing the evidence, arguments, and instructions, the jurors gave an initial verdict. Jurors were then divided into 12-person juries and allowed to deliberate for one hour. Half the juries were composed exclusively of death-qualified jurors, subjects who had previously indicated that they were willing to consider voting to impose the death penalty (death-qualified juries). The remaining juries comprised a majority of death-qualified jurors, but also included two to four jurors who would be excluded under current law because of their views on capital punishment (mixed juries). After deliberation on either a mixed or death-qualified jury, each subject completed a postdeliberation questionnaire tapping different aspects of the jury's functioning and rendered a postdeliberation verdict.

It is important to note that there are two very different types of questions that can be addressed by this design. First, at the level of individual subjects, we can ask how the *Witherspoon*-excludable jurors differ from the death-qualified jurors.

Second, we can ask how the restriction of diversity on a death-qualified jury affects the process of that jury's deliberation.

B. Subjects Two hundred and eighty-eight adults eligible for jury service in Santa Clara or San Mateo County, California participated in the study. Each subject was paid $10 for participation.

C. Definition of Experimental Groups Juror eligibility and division into experimental groups was established in initial telephone contact with potential subjects. In the telephone interview, two questions derived from the *Witherspoon* decision were used to identify the subject groups. The experimenters explained that judges in homicide trials ask questions about the jurors' attitudes, and subjects should answer just as they would if they were being questioned prior to a real trial.

All persons who stated unambiguously that they could not vote for the death penalty in any case, were designated the *Witherspoon*-excludable group. Those who responded that they would consider imposing the death penalty in some cases became the death-qualified group.

D. The Trial Videotape After viewing simulated trial materials prepared by several other social scientists interested in jury behavior and considering creating materials of our own, we decided to use the videotape prepared by Dr. Reid Hastie for use in his research on the jury deliberation process. We found this tape to be representative of the procedures, setting, style, and issues that commonly occur in actual homicide trials. The case was complex enough to afford several plausible interpretations and verdict preferences. It resembled most real murder trials in that the fact that the defendant had killed the victim was not in controversy; rather, the evidence centered on the precise sequence of events preceding the killing, and on the defendant's state of mind at the time. Finally, the tape was far more vivid and realistic than any others we have encountered. We felt that it was highly unlikely that we could construct a better tape with our resources.

Hastie's videotape is a reenactment of an actual homicide case based on a complete transcript of the original trial. Each actor portraying a defense or prosecution witness was provided with "a summary of the case highlighting his or her testimony." The judge and the lawyers, portrayed by an actual judge and two experienced criminal attorneys, were given "unabridged copies of the judge's instructions, selections of relevant testimony, and the attorney's opening and closing arguments as they were originally presented." The attorneys were asked to develop their cases as they would for a real trial, the witnesses were asked to review their materials to get their version of the events firmly in mind, and then, for the actual taping, all actors put aside their materials.

In the trial videotape, the defendant Frank Johnson is charged with first degree murder for the stabbing of Alan Caldwell outside a neighborhood bar. The prosecution brings evidence that the defendant and victim had argued in the bar earlier that day, and that Caldwell had threatened the defendant with a straight razor. Johnson left, but returned with a friend that evening, carrying a fishing knife in his pocket. Caldwell later came into the bar, and he and the defendant went outside and began to argue loudly. Two witnesses testify that they saw Johnson stab down into Caldwell's body. The victim's razor was subsequently found folded in his left rear pocket. For the defense, Johnson testified that he had returned to the bar that evening on the invitation of his friend, and had entered only after ascertaining that Caldwell was not there. Caldwell had come in and asked him to step outside, he supposed for the purpose of patching up their quarrel. Once outside, Caldwell had hit him and come at him with a razor. He had pulled out a fishing knife that he often carried in his pocket and Caldwell had run onto the knife. Johnson's friend corroborated much of his testimony. In cross-examination the defense attorney casts doubt on the ability of the prosecution eyewitnesses to see the scuffle, and shows that medical evidence cannot establish whether the defendant stabbed down into the victim or the victim ran onto the knife.

Four verdicts are possible in this case, dependent upon the jury's findings of the facts. The defendant may be guilty of first degree murder, of second degree murder, of voluntary manslaughter, or he may be not guilty by reason of self-defense or accidental homicide.

E. Procedure All jury assignments were random subject to the following constraints: (1) juries could not contain members who were acquainted, (2) juries could not contain more than one student member, and (3) numbers of male jury members and of persons recruited from the jury list were roughly equalized across juries.

Once the subjects were settled in the jury room, the experimenter told them that their next task was to discuss the case and try to reach a verdict. S/he told them that their immediate postvideotape verdict was confidential, and that they need not feel committed to it. S/he informed them that most juries begin by taking a straw vote, and that in any case they should choose a foreman before beginning their deliberation.

The experimenter closed by informing the subjects that they had one hour in which to deliberate, and that they should try to reach a decision in that time, although s/he realized that one hour might not be long enough to reach a consensus. The purpose of this instruction was simply to assure that the subjects worked on their deliberation seriously and tried to reconcile their differences of opinion; in fact we did not expect them to reach a verdict, nor did we ask that a final vote be taken.

Subjects were then left to discuss the case.

III. *Results*

A. Sample Characteristics The subject sample was fairly representative of the suburban upper-middle-class community surrounding Stanford University, except that males and minorities were under-represented. The sample was 93% white, comprising 35.4% males and 64.6% females. Married persons were 46% of the sample; 25% were single, 19% divorced, 4% separated, and 6% widowed. The median educational level was slightly less than a baccalaureate degree. Registered Democrats were 45.3% of the sample, Republicans 33.5% and unregistered 6.8%, with the remainder divided among Independent voters and small parties. In the category of religious affiliation, 35% listed themselves as Protestant, 17% as Catholic, 9% as Jewish, 25% listed no affiliation, and 14% listed other religions. *Witherspoon*-excludable jurors did not differ significantly from death-qualified jurors in any of these characteristics with two notable exceptions. Excludables were more likely to be female and Catholic.

B. Conviction Proneness The distribution of initial verdict preferences is presented in **Table 17-1**.

Our results provide strong support for the hypothesis that death-qualified jurors are more likely to convict than are jurors excludable under the *Witherspoon* criteria. The most direct test of this hypothesis is a comparison of Guilty and Not Guilty verdicts between the two groups of jurors. Among the death-qualified jurors 22.1% voted Not Guilty while 77.9% found the defendant Guilty of some level of homicide. Among the excludable jurors, 46.7% voted Not Guilty, and 53.3%

Table 17-1	Verdict Choices of Death-Qualified and Excludable Jurors

Predeliberation ballot	Death-qualified (%)	Excludable (%)
First-degree murder	7.8	3.3
Second-degree murder	21.3	23.3
Manslaughter	48.9	26.7
Not guilty	22.1	46.7
	100	100

Postdeliberation ballot	Death-qualified (%)	Excludable (%)
First-degree murder	1	3.4
Second-degree murder	17.3	13.8
Manslaughter	68	48.3
Not guilty	13.7	34.5
	100	100

voted Guilty of some offense. This difference indicates that the departure from representativeness created by the process of restricting juries in capital cases to death-qualified jurors creates a bias against defendants in death penalty trials.

C. Other Variables and Conviction Proneness In general, personal characteristics of the jurors showed little correlation with first ballot vote. Harsher verdicts were not associated with: age, sex, level of education, previous experience on a jury panel, or the jurors' views of the level of subjective certainty that would justify a verdict of guilty.

D. Differences Between Death-Qualified and Excludable Jurors on Postdeliberation Measures

i. Perceptions of Witness Credibility

In general, as might be expected from their verdicts, death-qualified jurors were more impressed with prosecution witnesses than were excludable jurors. Two measures of credibility were taken for each witness: how believable his testimony was and how helpful it was in understanding what happened on the night of the killing. The results are presented in **Table 17-2**.

In contrast, there were no significant differences in death-qualified and excludable jurors' ratings of defense witnesses. Both groups found the defense eyewitness and the defendant relatively noncredible.

ii. Perceptions of Attorneys

Death-qualified and excludable jurors did not differ in their perceptions of the likeability, competence, or believability of the defense attorney.

iii. Memory for Judge's Instructions

In general, jurors' memory for the trial judge's instructions was not good. Overall, jurors answered only 11.77 of 18 true-false questions correctly; random

Table 17-2	Death-Qualified and Excludable Jurors' Perceptions of the Believability and Helpfulness of Prosecution Witness	

		Believability rating
		Mean
Police eyewitness:	Death-qualified	5.54
	Excludable	4.24
Arresting officer:	Death-qualified	5.59
	Excludable	5.00
Forensic pathologist:	Death-qualified	6.55
	Excludable	5.62
Prosecution eyewitness:	Death-qualified	5.18
	Excludable	4.65

		Helpfulness rating
		Mean
Police eyewitness:	Death-qualified	5.06
	Excludable	3.86
Arresting officer:	Death-qualified	3.94
	Excludable	3.52
Forensic pathologist:	Death-qualified	5.51
	Excludable	4.31
Prosecution eyewitness:	Death-qualified	4.28
	Excludable	3.72

Note: Ratings were made on a scale from 1 to 7, where 1 was not at all believable/helpful, and 7 was very believable/helpful.

guessing would result in 9 right answers. Excludable jurors did not score significantly higher than death-qualified jurors.

Though the questions were very difficult, it was clear from the videotapes of jury deliberation that many jurors failed to understand even such basic matters as the distinctions between possible verdicts, and that deliberation often failed to eliminate these misconceptions. One jury concluded that second degree murder was a premeditated killing without extreme hatred (their definition of malice aforethought). This generally poor understanding of legal instructions has also been found by other students of jury performance.

iv. Death-Qualified vs. Mixed Juries

We have argued that the preservation of diversity of opinion on a jury may affect the deliberation process in and of itself, independently of the number of Not Guilty votes. A thorough examination of this question would involve a detailed analysis of the videotapes of the jury deliberations. For the time being, however, we can compare the postdeliberation questionnaire responses of those who served on the homogeneous death-qualified juries with those who served on juries that included some excludable jurors.

v. Perceptions of Witness Credibility and Attorneys

Excludable jurors, it will be recalled, were more critical of the prosecution and if anything slightly less critical of the defense witnesses than were death-qualified jurors. When ratings of jurors on death-qualified and mixed juries were compared, the same pattern emerged.

vi. Memory for Evidence and Judge's Instructions

It will be recalled that excludable subjects did not differ significantly from death-qualified subjects in their memory for the evidence. The presence of both types of jurors on the same jury, however, significantly improved the members' memory. Subjects on mixed juries remembered more evidentiary facts correctly than did subjects on death-qualified juries.

vii. Assessments of Jury Deliberation

Excludable jurors were more critical of their juries than were death-qualified jurors. The same pattern of self-criticism was observed for mixed juries as compared with death-qualified juries.

III. *Discussion*

A. Conviction Proneness Let us begin with the bias toward conviction, where the results are conclusive. In 1968 the *Witherspoon* court decided that the data before them were insufficient to persuade them that death qualification "results in an unrepresentative jury on the issue of guilt or substantially increases the risk of conviction," but that the question was an empirical question which might be resolved by more compelling data in a future case. Since then, numerous studies have been published. All have found the same result. Empirical methods have ranged from retrospective interviews with jurors about their experiences, to national public opinion surveys, to a series of increasingly elaborate laboratory simulations. All have found the same result. As the controlled simulations become more realistic, the differences between death-qualified and excludable jurors become more pronounced.

The results of the present study add to the body of previous research in several ways. First, our videotaped trial was far more involving than any of the other stimulus materials used. Members of our simulated juries debated heatedly, and many were loath to stop when the hour was over, although they had already spent close to four hours in the study and it was getting close to dinner time. Those who had participated in real juries felt that the experience matched their actual jury experience. Second, we determined that the differences persisted after an hour's deliberation. Third, we determined that the differences between the two groups were in fact due to their excludable vs. qualified status, and not to any differences in background variables or other biases in the sample. Because our results confirmed those of the earlier, less sophisticated studies, we gain confidence that their results were not a function of particular weaknesses in the individual studies or of poor definition of the excludable group, but instead reflected true differences between death-qualified and excludable jurors.

B. Other Effects of Loss of Diversity Our study also allows us to present some initial data on some other detrimental effects of the loss of diversity on the death-qualified jury. It must be remembered that these effects are not just side effects of conviction-proneness: they exist after we have partialed out the effects of first ballot verdicts, and thus represent additional, independent effects of the homogenization of viewpoints on the jury.

Our data do indicate that participation on the more diverse juries led jurors to be more critical in their evaluations of the witnesses. When we look at individual jurors, the direction of differences is what we would expect: Death-qualified jurors trust the prosecution witnesses more than excludable jurors do, and the defense witnesses less.

Although we do not yet have data on the vigor and thoroughness of the jury's arguments, we do know that members of the death-qualified juries were more satisfied with their experience. Members of mixed juries felt that the case was more difficult and were less sure that they were being fair.

We are, of course, eagerly awaiting the further use of these data in the courts. We have tried very hard to provide the sort of research that the courts have requested and so far we are encouraged by the response. Most of the data on conviction proneness, including our own, were collected in direct response to an empirical question posed by the United States Supreme Court. As social scientists, we cannot help regarding the cases on death qualification that come before the appellate courts as test cases, not only of the Constitutional issues, but of the use of social scientific research in judicial decision making.

Nancy J. King, "Silencing Nullification Advocacy Inside the Jury Room and Outside the Courtroom"

Jurors in criminal cases occasionally "nullify" the law by acquitting defendants who they believe are guilty according to the instructions given to them in court. American juries have exercised this unreviewable nullification power to acquit defendants who face sentences that jurors view as too harsh, who have been subjected to what jurors consider to be unconscionable governmental action, who have engaged in conduct that jurors do not believe is culpable, or who have harmed victims whom jurors consider unworthy of protection. Recent reports suggest jurors today are balking in trials in which a conviction could trigger a "three strikes" or other mandatory sentence, and in "assisted suicide," drug possession, and firearms cases. Race-based nullification is also a topic of current interest.

A renaissance of academic support for jury nullification has coincided with increased visibility of the Fully Informed Jury Association ("FIJA"), a national, nonprofit organization devoted to promoting jury nullification. A wide assortment of people who disagree with or distrust some aspect of the criminal law or its enforcement support FIJA, from AIDS activists to motorcyclists against mandatory helmet laws. FIJA reaches potential jurors with its message of jury power through its newsletter, website, and handbills distributed at courthouses. This pro-nullification activity has prompted some critics to call for the judicial review of acquittals and tighter limits on evidence and argument that might encourage juries to exercise a leniency the letter of the law does not allow. But judges who seek to control nullification today must not only rein in defense counsel; they must also confront nullification's new advocates—leafletters and the jurors themselves.

They are doing just that. Prosecutors and trial judges unhappy about nullification advocacy are pursuing charges of contempt, obstruction, or tampering against those who target potential jurors with nullification propaganda. Venirepersons who admit during voir dire that they were exposed to nullification advocacy or who express doubts about or disagreement with the criminal law or its enforcement are being excluded from jury service with challenges for cause. Jurors exposed as holdouts or advocates of nullification in the jury room are being dismissed, replaced, and sometimes prosecuted. The Second Circuit Court of Appeals recently declared that trial judges have the duty to dismiss jurors who intend to nullify. One state judge published a virtual "how to" guide for other trial judges who wish to suppress nullification advocacy in their courthouses.

I. *The Constitutional Roots of Nullification*

Although scholars have been debating the constitutional roots of the power of jurors to acquit for years, the origins of jury nullification remain elusive. The Constitution is silent on the point, and while the Framers clearly considered essential the right to a jury trial in criminal cases, historical accounts of their intent regarding the extent of the criminal jury's power are inconclusive. Similarly, there is little consistency in colonial practice that would shed light on whether the new nation's judges agreed that the Constitution embodied a law-finding function for juries. Supreme Court precedent on the point is also ambiguous. This Part reviews several alternative interpretations of the jury's nullification power and considers how each would affect judicial efforts to exclude nullifiers from criminal juries.

A. Nullification as nuisance. The approach least likely to offer any impediment to the exclusion of potential nullifiers is the view that the jury's ability to acquit against the law without judicial interference is not an affirmative grant of power but rather an unavoidable result of the recognition of two other important rights: the defendant's right under the Sixth Amendment to a jury's independent assessment of the facts, and the defendant's interest in the finality of acquittals protected by the Double Jeopardy Clause. In essence, the jurors may be wrong about the law when they acquit, but identifying and correcting their error would unduly threaten these important procedural rights.

Under these explanations, nullification need not be protected, only tolerated when expedient. This theory does not present an impenetrable constitutional barrier to the exclusion of potential nullifiers from jury panels before a verdict is returned. Indeed, screening out legal skeptics during voir dire would seem to be an effective method of controlling lawless acquittals, a method that avoids interference with either the jury's factfinding or the finality of the jury's verdict.

B. The juror's fundamental right to nullify. Other explanations of nullification accord it more direct constitutional status. Among these, the theory of nullification as a juror's personal right places the strongest restraint on what judges can do directly to jurors. The idea here is that any citizen who serves as a juror in a criminal case has a civic duty and privilege to stand as a barrier of conscience between the government and the accused. While no reference to an individual right to nullify appears in the Constitution or in the Bill of Rights, at the time the Constitution was drafted and ratified, some of the most influential political thinkers believed that an essential function of the jury was to advance the moral development of each individual juror.

Jury trials could be affected profoundly if the freedom to vote against convicting a person condemned by the law was recognized as a fundamental right. To exclude a juror solely because she expresses some willingness to do what the Constitution authorizes her to do would be as suspect as excluding her from the polls because of her desire to vote for an unpopular candidate. Excluding nullifiers might still be justified if one assumes that the government has a compelling interest in securing juror adherence to the law.

C. The defendant's right to a jury that is free to nullify. The Sixth Amendment offers an alternative basis that may prohibit judges from purging nullifiers from juries. Until relatively recently, the Impartial Jury Clause guaranteed only that the jury that ultimately tried the defendant had to be reasonably unbiased. The impartiality of a jury did not depend upon the attributes of those who were not selected for the jury.

The Supreme Court modified this interpretation in a line of cases originating with *Witherspoon*. The *Witherspoon* Court recognized, for the first time, a constitutional limit on the government's right to challenge for cause. The Court agreed that the Sixth and Fourteenth Amendments allow prosecutors in capital cases to exclude any juror who could not vote to impose the death penalty, but held that those same constitutional provisions prohibit the exclusion of a juror whose doubts about the death penalty were not strong enough to prevent the juror from sentencing a defendant to death.

If the Sixth Amendment forbids prosecutors from banishing jurors with moderate doubts about the legislature's chosen punishment from juries in order to secure that punishment, then the Constitution also might bar government efforts to exclude jurors with moderate doubts about the criminal law in order to secure convictions, thus regulating a prosecutor's effort to "conviction-qualify" every jury assessing guilt just as it regulates efforts to "death-qualify" capital juries.

The Court, however, appears to have rejected such a reading. In *Lockhart v. McCree*, the Court upheld a murder conviction despite the defendant's argument that the prosecutor's challenges for cause had deprived him of an impartial verdict under the Sixth Amendment. The Court reasoned that even assuming that, as a class, those who could not impose the death penalty were less likely to convict, nothing in the Sixth Amendment prevents a court from culling them from the guilt-phase jury. Since *Lockhart*, the Court has consistently stated that *Witherspoon* error does not entitle a defendant to a new trial, only to resentencing.

What can explain the Court's interest in retaining death-option-doubters on sentencing juries, but lack of interest in retaining guilt-option-doubters on guilt-phase juries? One obvious answer would be to explain *Witherspoon* as a product of the Court's particular concern about the arbitrary imposition of the penalty of death under the Eighth Amendment, rather than a decision based in the meaning of the "impartial jury" guaranteed by the Sixth Amendment. The Court, however, has rejected this easy answer. Instead, the distinction may have other explanations. The Court may consider the kind of decisionmaking involved in a sentencing determination to be entirely different from the kind involved in a guilt determination. A jury determining guilt has a less morally complex task to perform than a jury choosing an appropriate sentence, and thus remains impartial even when jurors who are not sufficiently biased to be excluded for cause are excluded anyway. A sentencing jury's decision is less concrete, more discretionary, and more vulnerable to viewpoint stacking than is the determination of guilt or innocence. Alternatively, the Court may have concluded that the cost of requiring two different juries in capital cases, one that was not death-qualified for the guilt phase, and one that was for the sentencing phase, simply was too high to credibly impose upon the states as a federal constitutional command.

D. Jury nullification as a part of the separation of powers. Another possible source of constitutional protection against the exclusion of those who may nullify is the Jury Clause of Article III. Professors Akhil Reed Amar and Michael Stokes Paulsen each have argued that Article III delegated to the jury the power to decide certain legal questions through its general verdict of acquittal, thus providing a structural check on the power of the judiciary, the legislature, and the executive.

This approach has logical appeal. There are very few limits in the original Constitution that operate directly to protect individual citizens other than office holders. The Jury Clause in Article III is one of them. It is joined in Article I by the prohibitions against bills of attainder, ex post facto laws, and suspensions of the writ of habeas corpus, and in Article II by the power of pardon. Only the unique power of the criminal sanction warranted so many different barriers. It makes sense to construe them together, as operating alike—against punishment and in favor of leniency.

While one or more of these last three theories may offer a basis for limiting the exclusion of potential nullifiers from juries, subsequent sections will demonstrate that each suffers from the same serious flaws. There is no historical support, at least in decisions from most of the nineteenth century, for any constitutional barrier preventing the exclusion of potential nullifiers from juries in criminal cases. History aside, each of the theories that might create a constitutionally protected zone for nullification fails to offer any basis for deciding which, if any, of the many other limits on nullification are unconstitutional, potentially threatening a variety of well accepted practices. Finally, the theories offer no guidance for judges to distinguish between those reasons to nullify that are forbidden, and those that are acceptable, virtually guaranteeing the arbitrary application of nullification safeguards.

II. *The Threat to Existing Nullification Controls*

Apart from its novelty, a constitutional ban on the exclusion of nullifiers from juries would raise difficult problems of scope. The various theories that could regulate the challenge of potential nullifiers could not be confined easily to the jury selection phase of trial. Other nullification controls may become difficult to justify once one decides the Constitution prevents courts from barring legal dissenters from juries. To find that the Constitution forbids the exclusion of jurors who disagree with the law from criminal juries would require acknowledging an entirely different theory of the jury's nullification power, one that would also sweep away other well-accepted jury controls.

A. The impact of recognizing an Article III power to nullify. Consider first the argument that Article III establishes in the jury an affirmative power to nullify that may not be undercut by efforts to purge nullifiers from the jury box. Recognition of that power could change significantly the processing of federal jury trials. Under this theory, separation of powers cases rather than defendants' rights cases would provide a more appropriate analysis for distinguishing between permissible and impermissible infringement of the jury's nullification power. If one of the jury's assigned functions is to check the judiciary, the legislature, or the executive by acquitting "in the teeth of both law and facts," then only when that power is impermissibly impaired would the Constitution be violated.

For example, one might conclude that keeping jurors in the dark about nullification still permits them to tap their (albeit uninformed) consciences, but keeping people off the jury who admit that they might tap their consciences completely disables even uninformed nullification. If so, Article III could allow the judicial suppression of nullification instructions, evidence, and argument, but limit the government's ability to disqualify nullification sympathizers. It is equally plausible, however, to argue that instructing jurors that they "must" convict disables the jury's checking function as completely as excusing admitted nullifiers during voir dire. One might even argue that separation of powers principles bar no jury control short of complete preemption of the jury's verdict of acquittal through the entry of a judgment of conviction: even retrials after acquittal or the application of collateral estoppel against the defendant following one jury's determination do not prevent the jury as an institution from exercising its checking powers, since both provide a jury with a chance to nullify. Indeterminacy aside, an Article III nullification power is also inconsistent with the Supreme Court's decision to allow defendants the opportunity to waive trial by jury and be tried by a judge instead.

B. Implications of recognizing nullification as an individual right of defendant or juror. A power to nullify based on the defendant's Sixth Amendment protection would encounter similar difficulties. Sixth Amendment theories that might regulate the exclusion of potential nullifiers from criminal juries have no logical boundaries. If government is prohibited from crippling nullification through jury selection, then shouldn't other efforts to cripple jury nullification be off limits too? There is nothing in the text of the Sixth Amendment, or in its past application, that might suggest where a defendant's right to a jury that is free to nullify begins and where it ends.

C. Tolerance, rather than protection, of jury nullification provides predictable limits. Unlike each of the foregoing theories, an explanation of jury nullification that accords it no affirmative constitutional status avoids the slippery slope. Explaining jury nullification as merely the name we give to our inability or unwillingness to identify or remedy lawless acquittals neatly accounts for much of the existing precedent regarding judicial limits on nullification. So long as judges are able to distinguish between factbased reasons and extra-legal reasons for acquitting, and so long as controlling nullification neither disturbs a jury verdict nor discourages or preempts candid jury room debate about the facts, judges willingly have condemned any and all reasons for acquittal that fall outside what they perceive to be the letter of the law. For example, venirepersons who admit that they disagree with some aspect of the law during voir dire, or lawyers who insist on advancing arguments unauthorized by the law, are easy targets. In both of these contexts there is no risk of disturbing a verdict or disrupting deliberations, and questioning by the court provides a means to reduce guesswork about the position of advocate or juror. Predictably, in these contexts, nullification advocacy is not tolerated. After the verdict, when the costs of curing nullification rise, so does judicial resistance to the cure. The interest of preserving the finality of verdicts, the inability to know what really motivated a jury's decision to agree on acquittal, and the fear that trying to find out would systematically chill candid deliberations, all account for continued opposition to post-verdict regulation of criminal acquittals.

More specifically, an understanding of nullification as merely the cost of protecting the double jeopardy interest in finality and the Sixth Amendment interest in independent factfinding provides a sensible way to identify which of the potential jury controls collected earlier may be tolerated and which may not. Such an understanding would preclude, for example, a new trial after acquittal and a judge's attempt to preempt a jury's acquittal by entering judgment or partial judgment of conviction before, during, or after a jury trial. These controls fail to protect the defendant's constitutional interests in finality and independent factfinding. However, these interests would not be infringed by anti-nullification instructions, limits on nullification argument and evidence, or special interrogatories, which are presently prohibited in many jurisdictions. The exclusion of nullifiers from the jury can be analyzed according to whether that exclusion threatens factfinding or finality.

Thus, unlike the effort to confer independent constitutional status on nullification, viewing nullification as a byproduct of the protection of other constitutional rights provides a logical stopping point along the spectrum of jury controls. Of course, nullification advocates may not be troubled that recognition of a constitutional limit on the government's ability to challenge nullifiers for cause might logically lead to the abolition of other restraints on the jury's power. But all of us should be wary of threats to established procedural features of the criminal process. Other revolutions in the constitutional regulation of jury selection, such as the cross-section requirement and the Batson ban against race-based peremptory challenges, have been preceded by an outpouring of cultural, political, and jurisprudential concern about race-based inequality. There is no similarly powerful societal impetus for calling into question nearly two centuries of precedent permitting courts to exclude nullifiers from criminal juries.

III. *Conclusion*

At first glance, the existing combination of rules regarding the jury's ability to ignore its instructions has little coherence. Why should the Constitution bar judges from correcting nullification after it happens, but enable them to minimize its occurrence beforehand? The privilege that jurors now enjoy to acquit for any reason seems at odds with several judicial practices, including the custom of carefully winnowing from the jury all those who might take advantage of their veto power, and censoring those who try to tell jurors that they have such power. Yet a hard look at the Constitution for ammunition with which to defend the advocates of jury nullification against these repressive techniques yields very little. Every theory that might prohibit judges from suppressing pronullification advocacy misfires. Jury nullification is not protected by the Constitution as an independent good, but rather, is tolerated as a byproduct of the careful defense of other fundamental values. The tolerance that jury nullification presently enjoys should not, and cannot without greater cost, be transformed into a more robust affirmative grant of power.

18

Sentencing Alternatives

■ Sentencing Alternatives—Introduction

What guidance should be given capital juries in deciding whom should be sentenced to die? In particular, what should capital juries be told concerning what might happen to a defendant in the event they do not sentence him to die?

How this latter question is answered may be of particular concern to the capital defendant. The less severe the jury perceives the alternatives to the death penalty to be, the more likely—one might expect—they are to select the death penalty. From the defendant's standpoint, he would like the jury to believe that the alternative to death is severe as possible.

What matters here is not the actual penalty, but the perception of the penalty. Even if the alternative to the death penalty is life imprisonment without the possibility of parole, jurors may not believe that LWOP is really LWOP—they may credit the possibility of clemency or the risk of escape and sentence a defendant to die rather than allow society to run the risk of these contingencies. Some scholars argue that it is inherently unfair to allow jurors to consider the possibility of escape or release, but the truly unfair situation is where the jury overestimates the risk of these contingencies—in other words, the jury mistakenly believes the defendant, if spared, will serve a shorter time in jail than he is likely to serve on average.

Research suggests that juries *do* operate under misperceptions of this kind, and that these misperceptions make them more likely to impose death sentences than they would be if they knew the alternatives. A study by William Bowers and Benjamin Steiner, presented in the Perspectives section of this chapter, shows that jurors significantly underestimate the death penalty alternatives both in states with and without parole, and that these beliefs make them materially more likely to vote for the death penalty. Jurors believe that prisoners given life sentences serve, on average, seventeen years in prison before they are released. A team of researchers led by Craig Haney found that jurors do not believe that even those prisoners sentenced to LWOP will never be released from prison.

The key constitutional question here is whether, when LWOP is the alternative to a death sentence, the jury must be informed of that fact. Abolitionists point to the results of empirical research as a conclusive argument for requiring that juries be informed of sentencing alternatives. The argument is convincing; the data about juror misperception and the materiality of their mistaken beliefs is robust.

One could argue that a qualification is necessary, though. If a life sentence is the alternative to the death penalty, and a jury believes that life-sentenced defendants serve only seventeen years on average, when in fact life-sentenced defendants serve thirty years on average, this is unfair to the death-charged defendant; the jury is more likely to vote for death than they would be with full information. Similarly, if LWOP is the alternative to the death penalty, and a jury believes the alternative is a less severe sanction, then the jury is again more likely to vote for death than they would be with full information. But what should the jury know about LWOP? Surely commutation is a possibility, as is escape, even if the likelihood of either is remote. If it is unfair for the jury to believe the alternative to death is less severe than is truly the case, it is arguably also unfair for them to believe the alternative is more severe than it really is. Perhaps in appropriate cases the jury should hear testimony from experts about how long LWOP-sentenced defendants serve and how often their sentences are commuted.

The Supreme Court's answer to the question is that jurors must be informed that LWOP is the alternative if future dangerousness has been made an issue in the case. In *Simmons v. South Carolina*, a 1994 case reprinted in the Critical Documents section of this chapter, the prosecution argued that Simmons's future dangerousness was a factor for the jury to consider in deciding the appropriate punishment. Simmons requested an instruction informing the jury that life imprisonment did not include parole eligibility in his case. During deliberations, the jury sent a question to the judge asking whether the defendant would be parole eligible. The Court held that on these facts, due process required that the defendant be entitled to inform the jury of his parole ineligibility.

The Court has balanced *Simmons*, though, in a way that suggests awareness of the symmetry issue discussed above. In *Ramdass v. Angelone*, a 2000 decision, the Court ruled that state judges may decline to give an LWOP-alternative instruction if they find that a defendant given that sentence may still at some point become eligible for parole. In *California v. Ramos*, the Court upheld the constitutionality of a California law requiring that jurors be informed of the governor's power to commute sentences. The Court has also been reluctant to extend *Simmons*. In *Brown v. Texas*, the court refused to require that jurors be told of lengthy minimum sentences in states that do not have LWOP as the alternative to death. And, of course, *Simmons* itself significantly restricts juror knowledge of alternative sentences by its ruling that the obligation to inform is only triggered when future dangerousness is put at issue.

In the Perspectives below, James Marquart, Seldon Ekland-Olson, and Jonathan Sorensen examine the accuracy of juror predictions of future dangerousness in capital trials. Professor Marquart and his team conclude that juries overpredict future dangerousness; that is, they forecast that many more prisoners will be violent in the future than actually are. John Blume, Stephen Garvey, and Sheri Lynn Johnson question the wisdom of the Supreme Court's "at issue" requirement. Professor Blume and his team argue that future dangerousness is always at issue in capital cases, whether it is explicitly raised or not. Hence, they say, jurors should always be told of relevant sentencing alternatives. Given all of the empirical data, has the Supreme Court struck the correct balance? The section concludes with a study by William Bowers and Benjamin Steiner, which examines jurors beliefs about alternatives to the death penalty. Given all of the empirical data, has the Supreme Court struck the correct balance?

■ Sentencing Alternatives—Critical Documents

Simmons v. South Carolina
512 U.S. 154 (1994)

Justice Blackmun announced the judgment of the Court and delivered an opinion, in which Justice Stevens, Justice Souter, and Justice Ginsburg join.

This case presents the question whether the Due Process Clause of the Fourteenth Amendment was violated by the refusal of a state trial court to instruct the jury in the penalty phase of a capital trial that under state law the defendant was ineligible for parole. We hold that where the defendant's future dangerousness is at issue, and state law prohibits the defendant's release on parole, due process requires that the sentencing jury be informed that the defendant is parole ineligible.

I

In July 1990, petitioner beat to death an elderly woman, Josie Lamb, in her home in Columbia, South Carolina. The week before petitioner's capital murder trial was scheduled to begin, he pleaded guilty to first-degree burglary and two counts of criminal sexual conduct in connection with two prior assaults on elderly women. Petitioner's guilty pleas resulted in convictions for violent offenses, and those convictions rendered petitioner ineligible for parole if convicted of any subsequent violent-crime offense.

Prior to jury selection, the prosecution advised the trial judge that the State "obviously was going to ask you to exclude any mention of parole throughout this trial." Over defense counsel's objection, the trial court granted the prosecution's motion for an order barring the defense from asking any question during *voir dire* regarding parole. Under the court's order, defense counsel was forbidden even to mention the subject of parole, and expressly was prohibited from questioning prospective jurors as to whether they understood the meaning of a "life" sentence under South Carolina law. After a 3-day trial, petitioner was convicted of the murder of Ms. Lamb.

In its closing argument the prosecution argued that petitioner's future dangerousness was a factor for the jury to consider when fixing the appropriate punishment. The question for the jury, said the prosecution, was "what to do with petitioner now that he is in our midst." The prosecution further urged that a verdict for death would be "a response of society to someone who is a threat. Your verdict will be an act of self-defense." Petitioner sought to rebut the prosecution's generalized argument of future dangerousness by presenting evidence that, due to his unique psychological problems, his dangerousness was limited to elderly women, and that there was no reason to expect further acts of violence once he was isolated in a prison setting.

Concerned that the jury might not understand that "life imprisonment" did not carry with it the possibility of parole in petitioner's case, defense counsel asked the trial judge to clarify this point by defining the term "life imprisonment" for the jury. To buttress his request, petitioner proffered, outside the presence of the jury, evidence conclusively establishing his parole ineligibility. On petitioner's behalf, attorneys for the South Carolina Department of Corrections and the Department of Probation, Parole and Pardons testified that any offender in petitioner's position was in fact ineligible for parole under South Carolina law. The prosecution did not challenge or question petitioner's parole ineligibility. Instead, it sought to elicit admissions from the witnesses that, notwithstanding petitioner's parole ineligibility, petitioner might receive holiday furloughs or other forms of early release. Even this effort was unsuccessful, however, as the cross-examination revealed that Department of Corrections regulations prohibit petitioner's release under early release programs such as work-release or supervised furloughs, and that no convicted murderer serving life without parole ever had been furloughed or otherwise released for any reason.

Petitioner then offered into evidence, without objection, the results of a statewide public-opinion survey conducted by the University of South Carolina's Institute for Public Affairs. The survey had been conducted a few days before petitioner's trial, and showed that only 7.1 percent of all jury-eligible adults who were questioned firmly believed that an inmate sentenced to life imprisonment in South Carolina actually would be required to spend the rest of his life in prison. Almost half of those surveyed believed that a convicted murderer might be paroled within 20 years; nearly three-quarters thought that release certainly would occur in less than 30 years. More than 75 percent of those surveyed indicated that if they were called upon to make a capital sentencing decision as jurors, the amount of time the convicted murderer actually would have to spend in prison would be an "extremely important" or a "very important" factor in choosing between life and death.

Petitioner argued that, in view of the public's apparent misunderstanding about the meaning of "life imprisonment" in South Carolina, there was a reasonable likelihood that the jurors would vote for death simply because they believed, mistakenly, that petitioner eventually would be released on parole.

After deliberating on petitioner's sentence for 90 minutes, the jury sent a note to the judge asking a single question: "Does the imposition of a life sentence carry with it the possibility of parole?" Over petitioner's objection, the trial judge gave the following instruction:

> You are instructed not to consider parole or parole eligibility in reaching your verdict. Do not consider parole or parole eligibility. That is not a proper issue for your consideration. The terms life imprisonment and death sentence are to be understood in their plain and ordinary meaning.

Twenty-five minutes after receiving this response from the court, the jury returned to the courtroom with a sentence of death.

II

The Due Process Clause does not allow the execution of a person "on the basis of information which he had no opportunity to deny or explain." In this case, the jury reasonably may have believed that petitioner could be released on parole if he were not executed. To the extent this misunderstanding pervaded the jury's deliberations, it had the effect of creating a false choice between sentencing petitioner to death and sentencing him to a limited period of incarceration. This grievous misperception was encouraged by the trial court's refusal to provide the jury with accurate information regarding petitioner's parole ineligibility, and by the State's repeated suggestion that petitioner would pose a future danger to society if he were not executed. Three times petitioner asked to inform the jury that in fact he was ineligible for parole under state law; three times his request was denied. The State thus succeeded in securing a death sentence on the ground, at least in part, of petitioner's future dangerousness, while at the same time concealing from the sentencing jury the true meaning of its noncapital sentencing alternative, namely, that life imprisonment meant life without parole. We think it is clear that the State denied petitioner due process.

The State and its amici contend that petitioner was not entitled to an instruction informing the jury that petitioner is ineligible for parole because such information is inherently misleading. Essentially, they argue that because future exigencies such as legislative reform, commutation, clemency, and escape might allow petitioner to be released into society, petitioner was not entitled to inform the jury that he is parole ineligible. Insofar as this argument is targeted at the specific wording of the instruction petitioner requested, the argument is misplaced. Petitioner's requested instruction ("If you recommend that the defendant be sentenced to life imprisonment, he actually will be sentenced to imprisonment in the state penitentiary for the balance of his natural life") was proposed only after the trial court ruled that South Carolina law prohibited a plain-language instruction that petitioner was ineligible for parole under state law. To the extent that the State opposes even a simple parole-ineligibility instruction because of hypothetical future developments, the argument has little force. Respondent admits that an instruction informing the jury that petitioner is ineligible for parole is legally accurate. Certainly, such an instruction is more accurate than no instruction at all, which leaves the jury to speculate whether "life imprisonment" means life without parole or something else. The State's asserted accuracy concerns are further undermined by the fact that a large majority of States which provide for life imprisonment without parole as an alternative to capital punishment inform the sentencing authority of the defendant's parole ineligibility.

It is true that we generally will defer to a State's determination as to what a jury should and should not be told about sentencing. In a State in which parole is available, how the jury's knowledge of parole availability will affect the decision whether or not to impose the death penalty is speculative, and we shall not lightly second-guess a decision whether or not to inform a jury of information regarding parole. States reasonably may conclude that truthful information regarding the availability of commutation, pardon, and the like should be kept from the jury in order to provide "greater protection in the States' criminal Justice system than the Federal Constitution requires." Concomitantly, nothing in the Constitution prohibits the prosecution from arguing any truthful information relating to parole or other forms of early release.

But if the State rests its case for imposing the death penalty at least in part on the premise that the defendant will be dangerous in the future, the fact that the alternative sentence to death is life without parole will necessarily undercut the State's argument regarding the threat the defendant poses to society. Because truthful information of ineligibility allows the defendant to "deny or explain" the showing of future dangerousness, due process plainly requires that he be allowed to bring it to the jury's attention by way of argument by defense counsel or an instruction from the court.

III

There remains to be considered whether the South Carolina Supreme Court was correct in concluding that the trial court "satisfied in substance petitioner's request for a charge on parole ineligibility," when it responded to the jury's query by stating that life imprisonment was to be understood in its "plain and ordinary meaning."

It can hardly be questioned that most juries lack accurate information about the precise meaning of "life imprisonment" as defined by the States. For much of our country's history, parole was a mainstay of state and federal sentencing regimes, and every term (whether a term of life or a term of years) in practice was understood to be shorter than the stated term.

An instruction directing juries that life imprisonment should be understood in its "plain and ordinary" meaning does nothing to dispel the misunderstanding reasonable jurors may have about the way in which any particular State defines "life imprisonment." It is true, as the State points out, that the trial court admonished the jury that "you are instructed not to consider parole" and that parole "is not a proper issue for your consideration." Far from ensuring that the jury was not misled, however, this instruction actually suggested that parole *was* available but that the jury, for some unstated reason, should be blind to this fact. Undoubtedly, the instruction was confusing and frustrating to the jury, given the arguments by both the prosecution and the defense relating to petitioner's future dangerousness, and the obvious relevance of petitioner's parole ineligibility to the jury's formidable sentencing task.

But even if the trial court's instruction successfully prevented the jury from considering parole, petitioner's due process rights still were not honored. Because petitioner's future dangerousness was at issue, he was entitled to inform the jury of his parole ineligibility. An instruction directing the jury not to consider the defendant's likely conduct in prison would not have satisfied due process in *Skipper*, and, for the same reasons, the instruction issued by the trial court in this case does not satisfy due process.

IV

The State may not create a false dilemma by advancing generalized arguments regarding the defendant's future dangerousness while, at the same time, preventing the jury from learning that the defendant never will be released on parole. The judgment of the South Carolina Supreme Court accordingly is reversed, and the case is remanded for further proceedings.

Justice Scalia, with whom Justice Thomas joins, dissenting.

Today's judgment certainly seems reasonable enough as a determination of what a capital sentencing jury should be permitted to consider. That is not, however, what it purports to be. It purports to be a determination that any capital sentencing scheme that does *not* permit jury consideration of such material is so incompatible with our national traditions of criminal procedure that it violates the Due Process Clause. There is really no basis for such a pronouncement, neither in any near uniform practice of our people, nor in the jurisprudence of this Court.

With respect to the former I shall discuss only current practice. South Carolina is not alone in keeping parole information from the jury. Four other States in widely separated parts of the country follow that same course, and there are other States that lack any clear practice. By contrast, the parties and their *amici* point to only 10 States that arguably employ the procedure which, according to today's opinions, the Constitution requires. This picture of national practice falls far short of demonstrating a principle so widely shared that it is part of even a current and temporary American consensus.

As for our prior jurisprudence: The prior law applicable to that subject indicates that petitioner's due process rights would be violated if he was "sentenced to death on the basis of information which he had no opportunity to deny or explain." The opinions of Justice Blackmun and Justice O'Connor both try to bring this case within that description, but it does not fit.

The opinions paint a picture of a prosecutor who repeatedly stressed that petitioner would pose a threat to society *upon his release*. The record tells a different story. Rather than emphasizing future dangerousness as a crucial factor, the prosecutor stressed the nature of petitioner's crimes: the crime that was the subject of the prosecution, the brutal murder of a 79-year-old woman in her home, and three prior crimes confessed to by petitioner, all rapes and beatings of elderly women, one of them his grandmother. I am sure it was the sheer depravity of those crimes, rather than any specific fear for the future, which induced the South Carolina jury to conclude that the death penalty was Justice.

Not only, moreover, was future dangerousness not emphasized, but future dangerousness *outside of prison* was not even mentioned. Both Justice Blackmun and Justice O'Connor focus on two portions of the prosecutor's final argument to the jury in the sentencing phase. First, they stress that the prosecutor asked the jury to answer the question of "what to do with petitioner now that he is in our midst." That statement, however, was not made (as they imply) in the course of an argument about future dangerousness, but was a response to petitioner's mitigating evidence. Read in context, the statement is not even relevant to the issue in this case:

> *The defense in this case as to sentence is a diversion. It's putting the blame on society, on his father, on his grandmother, on whoever else he can, spreading it out to avoid that personal responsibility. That he came from a deprived background. That he didn't have all of the breaks in life and certainly that helps shape someone. But we are not concerned about how he got shaped. We are concerned about what to do with him now that he is in our midst.*

Both opinions also seize upon the prosecutor's comment that the jury's verdict would be "an act of self-defense." That statement came at the end of admonition of the jury to avoid emotional responses and enter a rational verdict:

> *Your verdict shouldn't be returned in anger. Your verdict shouldn't be an emotional catharsis. Your verdict shouldn't be a response to that eight-year-old kid testifying in mitigation and really shouldn't be a response to the gruesome grotesque handiwork of petitioner. Your verdict should be a response of society to someone who is a threat. Your verdict will be an act of self-defense.*

This reference to "self-defense" obviously alluded, neither to defense of the jurors' own persons, nor specifically to defense of persons outside the prison walls, but to defense of all members of society against this individual, wherever he or they might be. Thus, as I read the record (and bear in mind that the trial judge was on the lookout with respect to this point), the prosecutor did not *invite* the jury to believe that petitioner would be eligible for parole—he did not *mislead* the jury.

The rule the majority adopts in order to overturn this sentence therefore goes well beyond what would be necessary to counteract prosecutorial misconduct (a disposition with which I might agree). As a general matter, the Court leaves it to the States to strike what *they* consider the appropriate balance among the many factors that determine whether evidence ought to be admissible. One reason for leaving it that way is that a sensible code of evidence cannot be invented piecemeal. Each item cannot be considered in isolation, but must be given its place within the whole. Preventing the *defense* from introducing evidence regarding parolability is only half of the rule that prevents the *prosecution* from introducing it as well. If the rule is changed for defendants, many will think that evenhandedness demands a change for prosecutors as well. State's attorneys ought to be able to say that if, ladies and gentlemen of the jury, you do not impose capital punishment upon this defendant (or if you impose anything less than life without parole) he may be walking the streets again in eight years! Many would not favor the admission of such an argument—but would prefer it to a state scheme in which defendants can call attention to the unavailability of parole, but prosecutors cannot note its availability. This Court should not force state legislators into such a difficult choice unless the isolated state evidentiary rule that the Court has before it is not merely less than ideal, but beyond a high threshold of unconstitutionality.

When the prosecution has not specifically suggested parolability, I see no more reason why the Constitution should compel the admission of evidence showing that, under the State's current law, the defendant would be nonparolable, than that it should compel the admission of evidence showing that parolable life-sentence murderers are in fact almost never paroled, or are paroled only after age 70; or evidence to the effect that escapes of life-without-parole inmates are rare; or evidence showing that, though under current law the defendant *will* be parolable in 20 years, the recidivism rate for elderly prisoners released after long incarceration is negligible. All of this evidence may be thought relevant to whether the death penalty should be imposed, and a petition raising the last of these claims has already arrived.

As I said at the outset, the regime imposed by today's judgment is undoubtedly reasonable as a matter of policy, but I see nothing to indicate that the Constitution requires it to be followed coast to coast. I fear we have read today the first page of a whole new chapter in the "death-is-different" jurisprudence which this Court is in the apparently continuous process of composing. The heavily outnumbered opponents of capital punishment have successfully opened yet another front in their guerilla war to make this unquestionably constitutional sentence a practical impossibility.

I dissent.

■ Sentencing Alternatives—Perspectives

■ Issue—Can Juries Accurately Predict Future Dangerousness?

James W. Marquart, Sheldon Ekland-Olson, and Jonathan R. Sorensen, "Gazing Into the Crystal Ball: Can Jurors Accurately Predict Dangerousness in Capital Cases?"

No research has measured the accuracy of juror predictions of future dangerousness in capital murder trials. The criminal justice system regularly depends on three types of prediction. The first is anamnestic, with predictions based on past behavior of the individual. The second is actuarial, with predictions based on the behavior of persons with similar characteristics (e.g., drug courier profiles). The third, and perhaps most common, is clinical, with predictions based on the clinical judgment of an expert, usually a psychologist or psychiatrist.

Predictions of future behavior are routinely accepted by the criminal justice system. While all prediction is difficult, violent behavior is relatively infrequent, and the low base rate makes accurate predictions particularly problematic. As many researchers have observed, overprediction (a high rate of false positives) is the norm.

One prior study has assessed dangerousness among what is arguably the most dangerous of populations: capital offenders. Marquart and Sorensen examined the level of violent behavior over fourteen years by Texas offenders whose death sentences were reversed in *Furman*. They found that although prison personnel claimed that the group of *Furman* commutees would pose a disproportionate threat to prisoners and guards, and to citizens in the event of parole, this threat did not materialize. Over the fourteen years, one commutee committed a second murder while on parole. The majority of the offenders were model inmates; among those paroled, most adjusted to the "free world" without serious arrest or conviction.

The Texas death penalty statute studied by Marquart and Sorensen required no explicit predictions of future dangerousness. Under the current post-*Furman* statute, however, juries must make an explicit prediction about the dangerousness of the offender. The question posed here is whether such predictions are in fact related to future behavior.

I. *A Test of Jury Predictions of Dangerousness*

To test the accuracy of jury predictions of dangerousness, we compared 92 offenders sentenced to capital punishment who subsequently had their sentences commuted or reversed to capital offenders who had received a life sentence. A control group of inmates—those convicted of capital murder but sentenced to life imprisonment—was extracted from the population of murderers who entered the Texas Department of Corrections (TDC) from 1974 to 1988. This control cohort ($N = 107$) consists only of those prisoners convicted of capital murder who had their life sentences determined by juries during the punishment proceedings. Defendants found guilty of capital murder but given life imprisonment as a result of a plea bargain were not included in this analysis. Juvenile cases were also excluded from the analysis. We also excluded 19 offenders who were convicted of capital murder and sentenced to life imprisonment but for whom the jury predicted dangerousness. These 19 offenders will be included in a later analysis in this paper.

Of the final group of those released from death row ($N = 92$), the majority (82) were released by commutation; this group also includes those who were retried and sentenced to prison and those who had their original cases dismissed.

In the following sections, we shall examine the institutional and post-release behavior of the commutees during 1974–88 to determine the degree to which these offenders did in fact represent a continuing threat of violence to society.

II. *Jury Predictions of Dangerousness*

In the sentencing phase of a Texas capital murder trial, the jury must predict that the defendant will "commit criminal acts of violence that would constitute a continuing threat to society" if it is to impose capital punishment. This must be established beyond a reasonable doubt. What evidence do jurors use in reaching this conclusion?

A. Prior Record One factor juries consider is the defendant's prior criminal history (an anamnestic prediction). **Table 18-1** displays criminal data gathered from extensive case files maintained by the Board of Pardons and Parole and the TDC, and supplemented by cross-checks with records from the Texas Department of Public Safety.

Table 18-1 shows that the criminal backgrounds of former death row inmates and those who were sentenced to life were similar. These data suggest that the

Table 18-1	Prior Criminal History	
Type of past activities	**Released from death row (%)**	**Initially sentenced to life imprisonment (%)**
Prior incidents		
0	11	9
1–2	24	21
3–5	30	29
5 or more	35	41
Prior violent incidents		
0	60	69
1–2	29	25
3 or more	11	6
Convictions for UCR violent crimes		
0	82	83
1–2	15	16
3 or more	3	1
Convictions for UCR property crimes		
0	54	61
1–2	21	27
3 or more	25	12
Adult incarcerations		
0	66	69
1–2	27	28
3 or more	7	3

juries' decision to sentence to death or life was not based primarily on the defendant's prior record. In terms of prior incidents, nine out of ten inmates from both groups had some contact with the police (e.g., under investigation for a crime). Well over three-quarters of the offenders from each group had no convictions for violent assaultive behavior. If convictions for violent offenses had been the sole factor used to predict future dangerousness, only 18 percent of the death-sentenced and 17 percent of the life-sentenced (control cohort) prisoners could have been considered threats to society. Only three of the former death row and two control cohort inmates had a prior murder conviction. In addition, two-thirds of each group had never been imprisoned. These conviction data suggest that most offenders in both groups were not violent, repetitive criminals. Instead, based on conviction data, they could be best described as property offenders who eventually committed a capital homicide.

B. Instant Offense Jurors need not focus solely on a defendant's prior history of violent crime, for they are also presented with extensive and sometimes graphic details about the immediate offense.

The two groups were also very similar in the rest of the felony murder types, with no major or significant difference. From these data it is apparent that jurors did not rely solely on the type of homicide in making predictions about future dangerousness. At least 50 percent of each group were convicted of robbery-murders.

C. Expert Opinion A review of the trial transcripts suggests that juries also used psychiatric testimony in making a prediction about the defendant's future dangerousness. We reviewed twenty cases involving death-sentenced inmates in which expert clinical testimony was used. The testimony generally followed the same pattern in which defendants were labeled "sociopaths," or people who felt no remorse for their acts and were highly effective manipulators. When asked if there was a probability that the defendant would commit criminal acts of violence that would constitute a continuing threat to society, psychiatrists typically answered "yes," despite defense counsel objections that the question invaded the jury's province to answer that same question.

Some psychiatrists specialize in capital murder cases. One such psychiatrist, James P. Grigson, has been nicknamed "Dr. Death" and has testified for the prosecution in nearly one-third of the Texas cases involving death row inmates. Grigson's very strong opinions are illustrated by his testimony in cases in which the offender was sentenced to death but later received a commutation:

Prosecutor: In your opinion, will he kill again?

Grigson: Yes he certainly will if there is any way at all he was given the opportunity to, he certainly will…Well, society can restrict him, confine him; yet even in areas of confinement, this behavior killing people will continue.

Prosecutor: Can you tell us whether or not, in your opinion, having killed in the past, he is likely to kill in the future, given the opportunity?

Grigson: He absolutely will, regardless of whether he's inside an institutional-type setting or whether he's outside. No matter where he is, he will kill again.

Prosecutor: Are you telling me, then, that even if he were institutionalized, put in a penitentiary for a life sentence—would he still be a danger to guards, prisoners, and other people around him?

Grigson: Yes. He would be a danger in any type of setting, and especially to guards or to other inmates. No matter where he might be, he is a danger.

Implicit in these answers is Grigson's firm belief that there is no hope of treating, curing, or rehabilitating these offenders.

Whatever the merits of the positions taken by psychiatrists in capital murder trials, the American Psychiatric Association (APA), in *Barefoot v. Estelle* (1983), stated that predictions such as "100% certainty that the defendant will kill again" are prejudicial to the defendant. According to some psychologists, clinicians are no more accurate in their predictions than lay persons.

Psychiatrists are often presented with hypothetical situations that essentially present the facts of the case. This increasingly popular method allows psychiatrists to predict future behavior without having examined the defendant. While there is little direct evidence that such testimony affects jury decisions, it is regularly presented, and the Supreme Court has at least been willing to assume that the testimony affects jury decisions.

III. *Evidence of Dangerousness*

We next examine the behavior of the ninety-two prisoners sentenced to death in part because the jury determined they represented a continuing threat, but who were later either released into the general prisoner population or paroled to the broader community.

A. Institutional Behavior To evaluate the institutional behavior of these inmates, we compared their behavior with three comparison groups: (1) the control group of all 107 prisoners convicted of capital murder during 1974–88 who were sentenced to life imprisonment, but not predicted to be dangerous during the punishment stage of their trials; (2) the entire prison population in 1986; and (3) all inmates housed in a single high security prison (the Darrington Unit) in the TDC in 1986. If jurors acting under the current statute are effective at predicting the future dangerousness of convicted murderers, we would expect that the 92 inmates under the sentence of death who were later released from death row would have a record of more violent institutional conduct than any of the comparison groups.

It is difficult to make direct comparisons between these groups due to the differences in time spent in prison, or the "at risk" period. However, it is possible to make some general observations regarding prison behavior as well as the degree to which the commutees constituted a menace or disproportionate threat to other inmates and the custodial staff. The best indicator of a "continuing threat" concerns murders and violent assaults, especially those involving weapons. The data in **Table 18-2** reveal that the yearly rate of weapon-related rule violations for those released from death row was somewhat lower than the rate for other groups. One commuted capital murderer (Noe Beltran), however, was involved in a gang-related prison murder in July 1988. Beltran, a member of the Hispanic prison gang the Texas Syndicate (TS), and several fellow gang members murdered another TS member in a power struggle. He thus became the first inmate in Texas since the inception of state-imposed executions in 1924 to be released from death row and returned with a second death sentence. However, murder in prison was not as common as the clinical predictions promised. Nor were the death row releasees, compared to the other groups, more violently assaultive or predatory, or a disproportionate threat to other inmates and staff.

We examined the evidence of positive institutional behaviors as well as rule-breaking activity, including time-earning status or class, good time accumulated, and program enrollment. As of January 1, 1989, approximately 90 percent of both the former death row inmates and the life-sentenced control cohort who were still incarcerated held trusty status (a reward for good behavior). Two-thirds of both groups have never been in solitary confinement, a punishment

Table 18-2	Reported Serious Violent Rule Violations			
Prison rule infraction	Released from death row	Life sentence	Systemwide (1986)	Darrington (1986)
Murder of an inmate	1	0	3	1
Aggravated assault on an inmate with a weapon	4	7	266	23
Sexual abuse of an inmate by threat	0	1	48	1
Murder of an officer	0	0	0	0
Striking an officer	4	12	4144	308
Total infractions	9	20	4461	333

for serious disciplinary infractions. One former death row inmate graduated cum laude with a bachelor's degree in psychology from Sam Houston State University in May 1988. Twenty-seven percent of commuted capital offenders and 22% of the control group had clean records with no minor violations of any type recorded during their prison stay.

Despite these "glowing marks," some former death row prisoners albeit a minority, have been disciplinary problems. Eight have been identified as prison gang members, and they have been confined indefinitely in administrative segregation or high security housing areas. Six control group members have been identified as gang members and have been housed in administrative segregation wings.

B. Post-Release Behavior Of the ninety-two commutees, seventy-eight remain in prison. Of the fourteen who are no longer in prison, two died in the general prisoner population; another died while on parole in a construction accident in late 1987 more than one year after his release. The other eleven include one inmate who was transferred to a federal prison in New York in 1977 and was paroled in 1983. Four other inmates discharged their sentences. The remaining six inmates were paroled. As of April 1989, the average time spent in the broader community by these eleven inmates was 4.5 years. One of the six was returned to prison for a serious violent crime.

Of the life-sentenced control cohort, ninety-four (88%) have never been released to the free society; one died in prison. Of the remaining thirteen, four had their cases reversed or dismissed. Nine have been paroled, spending an average of four years (at this writing) in the outside community; one of the nine parolees was returned to prison. This inmate has been released and returned to prison four times over the past seven years for the possession of drugs, aggravated assault, and aggravated robbery. He is currently out on parole.

C. Jury Predictions Among Life-Sentenced Prisoners The difference between the two categories of capital offenders we are examining lies in the responses juries gave to the three questions in the sentencing phase of the bifurcated trial (See *Jurek v. Texas*, supra Chapter 9). These data show that the decision to give life versus death in Texas rests squarely on Question 2— future dangerousness. In 85 percent (N = 107) of the cases (the control cohort), the jury failed to predict that the defendant would pose a continuing threat to society.

Table 18-3 presents the prison behavior of all 126 life-sentenced inmates in response to Question 2. Of those 19 inmates jurors predicted would be a continuing violent threat, 4 (21%) engaged in violent assaultive behavior in the prison setting, while 15 (79%) did not commit any aggressive or predatory acts as prisoners. Among the inmates predicted not to be continuing threats, 10 (12%) did in fact commit violent acts. If the juries predicted no future prison violence for all cases, they would have been accurate in 110 (87%) instances, with no false positives and 13 percent false negatives. Instead, juries made correct predictions in 76 percent of the 104 cases, with 14 percent false positives and 10 percent false negatives.

It can be argued from these data that Texas juries in capital cases have some predictive power. In this sense, the law is working successfully. However, there is a good deal of hidden irony. For example, one capital offender, Noe Beltran, was given a death sentence but later received a commutation. The Texas Court of Criminal Appeals reversed his death sentence, ruling there was insufficient evidence to predict future dangerousness. In 1988, however, Beltran murdered a fellow gang member and received a new death sentence. On the other hand, in the celebrated case represented in *The Thin Blue Line* (1988), Randall Dale Adams was predicted (by Dr. James Grigson) to be a danger, spent time on death row, had his death sentence commuted to life and was recently released from prison. It is widely acknowledged that Adams is innocent. Finally, one life-sentenced capital offender who was predicted not to be a future threat has been released from prison and returned several times for committing new violent felonies. It is very difficult to resolve the implications of these findings. Predicting future dangerousness appears to depart little from gazing in a crystal ball when it comes to determining the fate of capital murderers.

IV. *Conclusion*

This paper analyzed the behavior of ninety-two persons, each of whom jurors judged to be a continuing violent threat to society. The former death row offenders

Table 18-3	Prison Behavior of Life-Sentenced Inmates Compared to Predictions		
	Predicted to be a continuing threat		
Prison behavior	**Yes**	**No**	**Deadlocked**
Violent in prison			
Yes	4 (21%)	10 (12%)	2 (9%)
No	15 (79%)	75 (88%	20 (91%)

spent an average of just over six years in the general prison population. A minority of these inmates committed a handful of violent offenses at rates comparable to or lower than other inmates. One, however, killed another prisoner in a gang-related murder. Overall these former death row prisoners were not a disproportionate threat to the institutional order, other inmates, or the custodial staff. Indeed, their total rate of assaultive institutional misconduct was lower than those of both the capital murder offenders who were given a life sentence and the general prisoner population. Further, the majority of infractions were committed by a minority of the capital prisoners; most never committed any serious rule violations after their release from death row. Likewise, most never spent time in solitary confinement.

Behavior in prison is one thing. Behavior when released may be another. Twelve former death row inmates were eventually released to free society. One committed a second homicide, a brutal slaying in some ways similar to the offense for which he was originally sentenced to death. This, of course, is a disturbing finding. At this point, on the basis of a sample of twelve, the post-prison behavior of the former death row inmates cannot be assessed.

Moreover, even if we were confident that one of twelve released prisoners would commit a future violent act, the policy implications are unclear. Should we kill all twelve persons, or all ninety-two, because an unknown minority in their midst are likely to be repeat offenders? Punishment, particularly capital punishment, on the basis of predictions of future behavior will always involve a large proportion of false positives. There is nothing to suggest a future that offers "100 percent certainty" in the prediction of violence. The data presented here indicate that overprediction is the norm. The Texas capital murder statute, as currently drawn, cannot avoid the dilemma.

Traditionally, it is argued that under the United States Constitution false positives are an anathema: Better that a hundred guilty go free than one innocent be sentenced to death. This raises the question of whether, in the context of the Texas predictive capital punishment scheme, future jurors should be told of the predictive record of their predecessors. The finding that past jurors have overpredicted violence may serve to caution future jurors in their deliberations.

The data presented in this paper suggest that jurors err in the direction of false positives when it comes to predicting future dangerousness. What we do not know on the basis of these data is whether jury decisions in Texas would be different if jurors were not required to predict dangerousness as a precondition for sentencing an offender to death.

Jurors in Texas may be reacting to the instant offense, the same way jurors do in other death-sentencing states. If so, the structure of the statute in Texas simply preserves the fiction that jurors are basing this crucial decision on anything approaching consistently valid predictions of future behavior. Even for those who have committed very violent acts in the past, the data simply do not bear out this rational, utilitarian image of capital sentencing. Further research is needed to assess whether jurors, consciously or unconsciously, decide that an offender deserves to die and then tailor their responses to the questions accordingly.

■ Issue—When is Future Dangerousness "At Issue" In a Capital Case?

John H. Blume, Stephen P. Garvey, and Sheri Lynn Johnson, "Study: Future Dangerousness in Capital Cases: Always 'At Issue'"

I. *Introduction*

Capital jurors face a hard choice. They must impose a sentence of death, or a sentence of life imprisonment, one or the other. But for many jurors the choice is even harder.

The problem is this: Even where the alternative to death is life imprisonment, and where life imprisonment means life imprisonment without any possibility of parole, jurors may nonetheless believe that the defendant, if not sentenced to death, will one day find his way to freedom. In the minds of these jurors, the choice is really between death and something less than life imprisonment, and this imagined but false choice will prompt them to cast their vote for death. Forced to choose, jurors would prefer to see the defendant executed rather than run the risk that he will someday be released.

In *Simmons*, the Supreme Court tried to craft a solution to this problem. A plurality of the *Simmons* Court held that when state law authorizes the jury to impose a life sentence without the possibility of parole, due process entitles a capital defendant to inform the jury about his parole ineligibility. But *Simmons* came with a catch: A capital defendant was entitled to this remedy only if the state placed his future dangerousness "at issue." Otherwise, the jury was to be left to its own devices, forced to rely on its own understanding, however far off the mark, of what life imprisonment really meant.

But why the "at issue" requirement? The most likely explanation is ultimately empirical. On this account, the rule in *Simmons* is designed to obviate juror misapprehension about parole ineligibility and thereby promote reliability in capital sentencing. The "at issue" requirement, in turn, reflects the empirical assumption that capital jurors worry about the defendant's future dangerousness, and thus about what a sentence of life imprisonment really means, only if the state injects the issue of future dangerous into the proceedings. If not, jurors will think little, if at all, about future dangerousness, and no remedial instruction is needed.

We disagree. Based on the results of interviews with over a hundred jurors who served on capital cases in South Carolina, all conducted in connection with the nationwide Capital Jury Project (CJP), we argue that the "at issue" requirement is misguided because the empirical assumption on which it rests is false: We find that future dangerousness is on the minds of most capital jurors, and is thus "at issue" in virtually all capital trials, no matter what the prosecution says or does not say.

II. *The Capital Jury Project*

The Capital Jury Project is a National Science Foundation-funded, multistate research effort designed to better understand the dynamics of juror decision making in capital cases. Toward that end, the CJP began in 1990 to interview in a number of different states jurors who had actually served on capital cases. Analyses of the data collected during the interviews began appearing in 1993.

Prior to the work of the CJP, our understanding of juror decision making in capital cases—and in particular of the sentencing phase of the trial—was based primarily on mock jury studies, and on inferences drawn from the conduct of individual cases. Each of these methodologies, though valuable, has limitations. Mock studies are open to a variety of criticisms, not the least of which is that the experience of mock jurors is substantially removed from that of actual jurors, perhaps especially so in capital cases. Likewise, inferences based on an individual case or series of cases may not lend themselves to generalization; worse, they may reflect little more than the preconceptions of the person drawing them.

The CJP and its individual researchers have to date conducted interviews with 916 jurors who sat on 257 capital trials in eleven different states (Alabama, California, Florida, Georgia, Kentucky, Missouri, North Carolina, Pennsylvania, South Carolina, Texas, and Virginia). The CJP's aim was to conduct interviews with at least four jurors from a randomly selected sample of cases, half of which resulted in a final verdict of death, and half in a final verdict of life imprisonment. The results we present below are based on the CJP's efforts in South Carolina.

III. *Always "At Issue"*

Our focus here is limited to the *Simmons* "at issue" requirement. But in order to set the context, we begin with a brief review of existing CJP findings that highlight the important role future dangerousness plays in capital sentencing. We then present the results of the simple analysis that lead us to urge the Court to abandon the "at issue" requirement.

A. Future Dangerousness The results that have so far emerged from the research efforts of the CJP support the following three propositions related to the role of future dangerousness in capital sentencing:

First, "jurors grossly underestimate how long capital murderers not sentenced to death usually stay in prison." In South Carolina, for example, the median juror estimate of years usually served by capital murderers not sentenced to death was only seventeen years.

Second, future dangerousness plays a highly prominent role in the jury's discussions during the penalty phase. One of the earliest CJP studies, which relied on South Carolina data, found that topics related to the defendant's dangerousness should he ever return to society (including the possibility and timing of such a return) are second only to the crime itself in the attention they receive during the jury's penalty phase deliberations. Future dangerousness overshadows evidence presented in mitigation, as well as any concern about the defendant's dangerousness in prison.

Third, these misconceptions about parole eligibility have predictable and deadly consequences. The shorter the period of time a juror thinks the defendant will be imprisoned, the more likely he or she is to vote for death on the final ballot.

Those findings suggest that a capital defendant should have a right to tell the jury how long he will remain in prison if not sentenced to death, even if the term of his imprisonment under state law is less than death, and even if the prosecution does nothing to place his future dangerousness "at issue." In other words, we believe these findings cast serious doubt on both of the requirements set forth in *Simmons*.

For now, however, we concentrate on the second requirement: Does it makes sense, in light of how capital jurors decide capital cases, to require the right *Simmons* recognizes—the right of a capital defendant to honestly tell the jury that, if its members do not sentence him to death, he will in accordance with state law never be released from prison—to turn on the prosecution's decision to put future dangerousness "at issue?"

B. Testing the Empirical Assumption Behind the "At Issue" Requirement The "at issue" requirement, as we construe it here, is based on the Court's empirical assumption that jurors only worry about future dangerousness if and when the prosecution broaches the subject. However, we would have assumed just the opposite: that capital jurors worry about future dangerousness no matter what the prosecution says. Here we put these competing assumptions to two empirical tests.

First, if the Court's assumption is correct, then we would expect the jury's discussions during the penalty phase to reflect worries about future dangerousness only when the prosecution makes a point of it; in contrast, if our assumption is correct, then we would expect the jury's discussions to reflect worries about future dangerousness even when the prosecution says nothing about it at all. Second, if the Court's assumption is correct, we would expect jurors to say that future dangerousness influenced their sentencing decisions only when the prosecution raised questions about it; in contrast, if our assumption is correct, then we would expect jurors to say that future dangerousness was a significant factor in their sentencing decisions regardless of the prosecution's focus.

One question the CJP asked jurors was the following: "How much did the prosecutor's evidence and arguments at the punishment stage of the trial emphasize the danger to the public if the defendant ever escaped or was released from prison?" The possible responses were: a "great deal," a "fair amount," "not much," and "not at all." Of the 187 South Carolina jurors we interviewed, fifty-three said that the prosecutor's evidence and argument at the penalty phase emphasized the defendant's danger to the public if he was ever released or escaped from prison "not at all." It is on this group of fifty-three that we focus the remainder of our analysis. If future dangerousness matters to this group, then it matters even when the prosecution has not placed the defendant's dangerousness "at issue."

We next look at the responses this group of jurors gave when asked a series of questions about the topics the jury discussed during the course of its penalty phase deliberations. We focus in particular on how much the jury discussed various topics related to the defendant's future dangerousness. Even among jurors who said the prosecution made no effort whatsoever to emphasize the defendant's future dangerousness, anywhere between twenty-one and thirty-two percent reported that the jury's discussions during the penalty phase focused "a great deal" on a variety of topics related to worries about the defendant's future dangerousness. Moreover, anywhere between fifty-three and sixty-six percent of these same jurors reported that the jury's discussions focused at least a "fair amount" on topics related to the defendant's future dangerousness.

Concentrating once again on those jurors who said the prosecutor emphasized "not at all" the defendant's danger to the public if he was ever released or escaped from prison, we asked how important it was to them in deciding the defendant's punishment to "keep the defendant from ever killing again." Forty-three percent said it was "very" important; twenty-six percent said it was "fairly" important. In other words, nearly seventy percent of the jurors who served on cases in which the prosecution did not put the defendant's future dangerousness "at issue" nonetheless reported that keeping the defendant from ever killing again was at least fairly important to them in deciding how to vote.

Of course, the jury's concern about "keeping the defendant from ever killing again" might include concerns about keeping him from killing again in prison, as well as outside of it. Accordingly, we also analyzed responses to a narrower question: How concerned was the juror that the defendant might get back into society if not given the death penalty. Thirty-one percent said they were "greatly concerned," and another twenty-nine percent said they were "somewhat concerned." That makes a total of sixty percent. Put differently, on an average jury in which the prosecutor emphasized the defendant's future dangerousness "not at all," seven members would be at least somewhat concerned that, unless sentenced to death, the defendant might get back into society.

IV. *Conclusion*

Under existing doctrine, due process entitles a capital defendant to inform the jurors who will decide his fate that, if not sentenced to death, he will never be eligible for parole—but only if his future dangerousness is "at issue." Yet the fact of the matter is that future dangerousness is on the minds of most capital jurors and thus "at issue" in virtually all capital trials, even if the prosecution says nothing about it. Ironically, a capital defendant is therefore better off, all else being equal, if the prosecutor argues that he will pose a danger to society—in which case the defendant would be entitled to a *Simmons* instruction—than if the prosecutor remains silent.

The better approach—one not only more closely attuned to the empirical realities of capital sentencing but also more in keeping with the spirit of *Simmons* itself—would be to eliminate the "at issue" requirement altogether.

■ Issue—What Do Jurors Believe About Alternative Sentences?

William J. Bowers and Benjamin D. Steiner, "Death by Default: An Empirical Demonstration of False and Forced Choices in Capital Sentencing"

I. *Introduction: The Challenge of* Brown v. Texas

How capital jurors should make the life or death sentencing decision is a critical issue at the core of modern capital jurisprudence. Since its 1976 decisions authorized the states' return to capital punishment, the Supreme Court has grappled with the two-sided question: To what extent can we trust jurors to understand and apply the law correctly and to what extent must they be explicitly directed in their decision-making? Once the Court has determined that some constraints are necessary, it then must decide whether they are needed only to correct misbehavior or, more fundamentally, to shape the constitutional contours of capital sentencing. What the Court decides to do, or not to do, has often depended on untested assumptions about how jurors make the critical punishment decision. Such empirical assumptions need to be informed, and sometimes revised, in light of the kind of data presented here.

In the denial of certiorari in *Brown v. Texas*, one of these perplexing empirical issues surfaced as a clear concern of four Supreme Court justices. Basically, the issue is this: Should capital jurors know how long the defendant must spend in prison before becoming eligible for parole, or how long he is apt to serve before actually being paroled, if the defendant is not given the death penalty? Texas's sentencing scheme presents a particular irony, as Justice Stevens observed in *Brown*:

> The situation in Texas is especially troubling. In Texas, the jury determines the sentence to be imposed after conviction in a significant number of noncapital felony cases. In those noncapital cases, Texas law requires that the jury be given an instruction explaining when the defendant will become eligible for parole. Thus, the Texas Legislature has recognized that, without such an instruction, Texas jurors may not fully understand the range of sentencing options available to them. Perversely, however, in capital cases, Texas law prohibits the judge from letting the jury know when the defendant will become eligible for parole if he is not sentenced to death.

Why shouldn't Texas jurors, or those from any other state, know about parole in making their capital sentencing decision? Isn't parole an even more important consideration in capital than in noncapital sentencing? Justice Stevens cites evidence from citizen surveys in a number of states that indicates people find the death penalty less attractive the longer offenders would stay in prison before becoming eligible for parole, and surmises that the Texas rule against informing jurors of parole eligibility in capital cases "tips the scales in favor of a death sentence that a fully informed jury might not impose." He concludes with a call for further study of the issue of false choice to assist the Court in its correct resolution.

Although the assumption that jurors disregard parole in their decision-making has undergirded the thinking of courts about how jurors should make capital sentencing decisions, the empirical data shows it is a false description of what jurors actually do—a legal fiction. The stage is thus set for an examination of two related empirical questions: Do capital jurors misunderstand the death penalty alternative, in the absence of being informed; and, if so, do such misunderstandings bias their sentencing decisions?

In *Simmons*, the Court first grappled with these questions, focusing on the narrow range of capital cases in which the defendant is alleged to be dangerous and the only sentencing alternative would be life without parole (LWOP). The Court held that when a defendant's future dangerousness is at issue, due process requires that a jury be informed of the fact that state law makes the defendant ineligible for parole. In reaching its decision, the *Simmons* Court relied upon evidence from public opinion research and early findings from this study of jurors' decision-making in capital cases. *Brown* invites a more comprehensive and thoroughgoing examination of the role of jurors' beliefs about the death penalty alternative in their capital sentencing decisions—an examination of the extent to which the sentencing decisions of capital jurors are "false" and "forced" choices. Such a broader empirical inquiry into the possibly pernicious influence of mistaken beliefs about the death penalty alternative is the subject of this Article.

II. *Punishment Decisions and Jurors' Estimates of the Alternative to Death*

A. The Research Methodology The data for this investigation is drawn from the Capital Jury Project (CJP), a national study of capital jurors' sentencing decisions in fifteen states. Capital jurors have been selected for interviews in a three-stage sampling procedure: (1) fifteen states have been chosen to reflect the principal variations in guided discretion capital statutes; (2) within each state, twenty to thirty full capital trials conducted since 1987 have been selected to represent both life and death sentencing outcomes; and (3) for each trial a target sample of four jurors has been systematically selected for three-to-four-hour personal interviews. The findings presented below are based on interviews completed to date, with 916 jurors from 257 capital trials in 11 states. These are states in which at least forty interviews have been completed with jurors from a minimum of ten different capital trials.

B. Jurors' Perceptions of the Death Penalty Alternative Jurors grossly underestimate how long capital murderers not sentenced to death usually stay in prison. **Table 18-4** shows that most jurors believe such offenders will usually be back on the streets even before they become eligible for parole. In fact, jurors' estimates

Table 18-4	Jurors' Median Estimates of Years Usually Served in Prison by Capital Murderers Not Given Death	
State	**Median estimate**	**Mandatory minimum**
Alabama	15 years	LWOP
California	20	LWOP
Florida	20	25
Georgia	7	15
Kentucky	10	12–25
Missouri	20	LWOP
N. Carolina	17	20
Pennsylvania	12	LWOP
S. Carolina	17	30
Texas	15	20
Virginia	16	21.75

are typically at least five years less than the mandatory minimum for parole consideration in their states.

Jurors typically think such offenders will be back in society in about 15 years. Moreover, jurors' estimates are relatively constant across states: they fall between 15 and 20 years in 8 states; Georgia, Kentucky, and Pennsylvania are the exceptions. Having parole or prohibiting it altogether makes relatively little difference in these estimates; 14.6 years is the average of the median estimates in the 7 states with parole, 16.3 years is the average in the 4 states that prohibit parole. Similarly, the length of the mandatory minimum has relatively little effect on jurors' release estimates, with the exception of Georgia.

In most states most jurors' release estimates are ill-informed suppositions or speculations, not a reflection of consensus keyed to the mandatory minimum for parole or any other specific time interval. In the evident absence of knowing or agreeing on what the death penalty alternative actually is, most jurors gravitate to estimates even below the mandatory minimum for parole.

C. The Pernicious Effect of Jurors' Misperceptions The focus now shifts from jurors' perceptions of the death penalty alternative itself to how such perceptions affect whether jurors do or do not impose the death penalty upon a defendant they have convicted of capital murder. Specifically, the analysis will consider the effect of false choices between the death penalty and what jurors wrongly believe the alternative to be. This is precisely what concerned the Court in *Simmons* and continued to concern four of its members in *Brown*.

The analysis examines and compares 3 groups of jurors, those whose estimates of the time usually served by capital murderers not sentenced to death ("release estimates") are: 0–9 years, 10–19 years, and 20 or more years. The 0–9 year estimates are well below the mandatory minimums for parole, and hence far below parole practice. The 10–19 estimates are also below the mandatory minimums in 9 of these states, and below 2 of the 3 sentencing options in Kentucky. The first two of these categories reveal the effect of what is manifestly a "false choice" in capital sentencing.

In the CJP interviews, respondents were asked what they had thought the defendant's punishment should be at four distinct stages of the trial process. These four points were: (a) after the guilt decision, but before the sentencing stage of the trial; (b) after the sentencing trial, but before sentencing deliberations; (c) at the first jury vote on punishment; and (d) at the jury's final punishment vote.

Jurors' stands on punishment at these four points in the trial process are presented in **Table 18-5** for those who estimated the alternative to be 0–9 years, 10–19 years, and 20 years or more. Specifically, the table shows the percentage who took a stand for death, for life, or were undecided on the defendant's punishment at each of the first three points during the trial, and the percentage who voted for life or for death at the final decision point.

In various ways, then, the data demonstrates the pervasive pro-death effect of jurors' underestimates of time served before release on their approach to punishment. The influence of early release perceptions is evident throughout the process, but is especially felt early in sentencing deliberations—between the end of the sentencing phase of the trial and the jury's first vote on punishment. Jurors with the most exaggerated underestimates of the death penalty alterna-

Table 18-5	Juror Stands in Punishment at Four Points in the Trial by Their Estimates of the Death Penalty Alternative		
	Estimates of years served by capital murderers not given death		
Stand on punishment			
At guilt stage of trial	0–9	10–19	20+
Death	39.2	28.8	28.2
Life	10.8	14.4	22.7
Undecided	50.0	56.8	49.1
After sentencing instructions			
Death	50.8	44.3	39.0
Life	15.9	16.9	23.2
Undecided	33.3	38.8	37.8
At 1st vote on punishment			
Death	66.7	60.8	45.5
Life	21.4	24.0	40.2
Undecided	11.9	15.2	14.3
At final punishment vote			
Death	68.5	65.1	43.1
Life	31.5	34.9	56.9

tive disproportionately take a pro-death stand early, even before the sentencing stage of the trial. Those whose mistaken estimates are not as extreme also move disproportionately to a pro-death stand, but they tend to do so later in the process.

The relevance of these findings to the Court's decision in *Simmons* is unmistakable. The data clearly shows that it is how soon jurors erroneously think such offenders usually return to society, not simply whether or not they wrongly believe such offenders will serve the rest of their lives in prison, as *Simmons* supposes, that influences capital jurors' thinking and voting on a defendant's punishment. When jurors underestimate the death penalty alternative, they are making a "false choice," whether the true alternative is life with or without parole. Whether parole is possible or release actually occurs in twenty years, thirty years, forty years, or never, when jurors mistakenly believe that capital offenders are usually back on the streets in less than twenty years, especially less than ten years, they are far more likely to vote for death.

D. Dangerousness, Release Estimates, and False Choice What about the requirement in *Simmons* that future dangerousness be argued before a capital defendant is entitled to have his jurors know what his alternative sentence would actually be? In *Simmons*, the defendant was alleged to be dangerous and the Court held that a false choice in sentencing would deprive him of the right to protect himself against such allegations. But what about defendants, unlike Simmons, who are not alleged to be dangerous by the prosecution or not thought to be dangerous by jurors? Do they not also need protection against a false choice in sentencing?

To examine the role of claims and beliefs about the defendant's possible dangerousness, jurors were asked questions concerning: (a) prosecution allegations of the defendant's future dangerousness; and (b) their own perceptions and concerns about whether the defendant would be a danger to society in the future.

First, considering prosecution allegations of the defendant's dangerousness (Panel A), it is evident that jurors' release estimates are a strong predictor of their final punishment vote, quite apart from prosecution claims of dangerousness. At each level of prosecution stressing the need to "keep the defendant from killing again" and the "danger to the public if the defendant ever escaped or was released from prison," jurors who estimate release in 20 or more years are consistently and substantially less likely to vote for death than those who thought release would come in 0–9 or 10–19 years. In every category of alleged dangerousness, they were at least nineteen percentage points less likely to vote for death than one or (usually) both groups of their more mistaken counterparts. Quite evidently, jurors' perceptions of the death penalty alternative affect their punishment decisions whether or not the prosecution stresses the defendant's dangerousness.

Moving from prosecutors' allegations to jurors' own perceptions and concerns about the defendant's dangerousness, again jurors' release estimates relate to their punishment votes, both when dangerousness is and is not an issue in the trial. On all three questions, release estimates influence final punishment votes. This holds true whether or not jurors think the evidence proved that the defendant was dangerous, however important jurors feel it is to keep the defendant from killing again, and however concerned jurors are about the defendant's possible return to society.

It is true, as *Simmons* implies, that underestimates of the alternative punishment are a strong predictor of a final vote for death when dangerousness is alleged or perceived—when the prosecutor argues that the defendant would be dangerous in the future, when jurors believe the evidence proves this, and when jurors are concerned that the defendant will return to society someday and possibly even kill again. Yet the data presented here indicates that these claims or beliefs are not necessary for mistaken early release estimates to promote death as punishment. When jurors believe such offenders will return to society sooner, they are moved to vote for death without having to believe that the offender will be dangerous to others in the future. Perhaps considerations of retribution, beyond mere incapacitation, are indeed relevant to these jurors' decision-making.

Consider the possibility that jurors' underestimates of the death penalty alternative may actually cause them to overestimate the defendant's dangerousness. Judging a person's likely future dangerousness is far from foolproof; indeed, those who have examined such assessments find that they are often unreliable because they are subject especially to "false positives" or predictions of dangerousness that do not materialize. It is axiomatic that however dangerous a convicted capital murderer may appear to be in terms of objective indicators such as his past record of criminal violence, the sooner he is released from prison, the more opportunity he will have to harm others in society. Hence, jurors who wrongly believe that such an offender would be released in less than ten years may well see him as more "dangerous," than those who believe release will come only after twenty or more years. In this way, mistaken estimates of the defendant's early parole or release from prison may be bootstrapped into capital sentencing by being surreptitiously incorporated into the constitutionally authorized judgment of future dangerousness.

The data suggests this effect. The base figures for the percentages reveal, for example, that the jurors who most underestimate the death penalty alternative are also the ones most likely to be greatly concerned about the defendant's return to society. There are two noteworthy findings. First, there is virtually no association between jurors' perceptions of the death penalty alternative and prosecution allegations of the defendant's dangerousness. Jurors who believe the defendant would return to society sooner are not more likely to report that prosecutors claimed the defendant was dangerous. Second, when it comes to jurors' own perceptions of, and concerns about, the defendant's dangerousness there is, indeed, an association with their estimates of the death penalty alternative. That is, jurors who believe release will come earlier are more likely to believe the evidence "proved" the defendant dangerous, to regard keeping the defendant from killing again as "very important" in their sentencing decision, and to be "greatly concerned" about the defendant's possible return to society in deciding on punishment.

III. *Conclusion*

The faults in capital sentencing which this data reveals are formidable and may be irremediable. There is a pervasive misimpression among jurors that convicted first-degree murderers not given the death penalty will be released on parole well before they actually are, or possibly could be under the law—a kind of hegemonic myth of early release that infects the capital sentencing decision with excessiveness, in the use of death as punishment. In order for jurors to correctly understand the true death penalty alternative in reaching their punishment decision, they will need to be convinced that their current beliefs about parole are mistaken; indeed, what they regard as mistaken is in fact true. In order to purge capital punishment decisions of unreliability and excessiveness, and to ensure the primacy of retributive purposes, jurors must have retributively appropriate sentencing options available. They must also be able to rely upon objective information about parole practices in their state in place of the erroneous personal impressions that now clearly factor into their decisions. Otherwise, they cannot make a reasoned moral judgment based on a clear understanding of the alternatives—as is constitutionally required in noncapital cases.

The evidence of false and forced choices presented here is more than a showing of disparities in sentencing outcomes; it is a demonstration of fundamental faults in the decision-making process. It is a revelation of flaws that compromise the ability of real jurors in real cases with real defendants to make reasoned moral punishment decisions. It shows that guiding jurors' discretion in the assessment of aggravating and mitigating circumstances is insufficient to curb arbitrariness and excessiveness because jurors' decisions are befouled by false and forced choices. Fundamentally, it reveals that these flaws have undermined the retributive core of the capital sentencing decision. We submit that the capital jury's "difficult and uniquely human" decisions require that the Court correct these flaws or recognize that they are sufficiently pernicious and irremediable to render the enterprise of capital punishment constitutionally unworkable.

Trial Counsel

![19](chapter number 19)

◼ Trial Counsel—Introduction

In many ways it is meaningless to speak of the death penalty without being geographically specific. One could quite reasonably support the death penalty as practiced in New York, but be adamantly opposed to capital punishment as practiced in Texas; the two systems are dramatically distinct. The Texas death-sentencing statute is far broader than its New York equivalent and more restrictive of the manner in which the jury may consider mitigating evidence. The death penalty is more frequently sought by prosecutors—Texas executed 33 inmates in 2002; a total of 6 are under sentence of death in New York, though the murder rates in the two states are roughly equivalent.

Perhaps no feature of the death penalty as practiced in the South is more distinct and controversial than the quality of lawyers assigned to represent capital defendants. In New York, those charged with capital crimes receive the highest-quality representation. The Office of the Appellate Defender, the primary supplier of representation to capital defendants, is staffed with highly experienced attorneys; competition for positions in the office is fierce. Defense counsel in Texas and other southern states are commonly paid a flat fee for representing a capital defendant, a fee that when amortized over the total number of hours that such a case requires ends up amounting to little more than minimum wage. In *Macias v. Collins*, a 1992 decision, the Fifth Circuit overturned the Texas conviction of Macias on grounds of ineffective assistance of counsel. Judge Patrick Higginbotham famously wrote, "The state paid defense counsel $11.84 per hour. Unfortunately, the justice system only got what it paid for." Stephen Bright, director of the Southern Center for Human Rights, once said, "I know a Mississippi lawyer who has spent 400 hours working on a capital trial and can only get $1000. I can make more money pumping gas than working on a capital case." A 1994 study found that in the nine southern states that constitute the "death belt," more than 10% of the attorneys who represent indigent capital defendants were subsequently disbarred, suspended, or otherwise disciplined. More than one third of these attorneys practiced civil law not criminal law, and a majority had no experience in capital cases.

Representation for the poor is obviously a serious issue. It isn't obvious, though, why poor representation is a death penalty issue. It would be one matter if incompetent representation occurred exclusively or predominantly in capital cases, but abundant evidence suggests that attorneys in ordinary criminal cases are often performing inadequately. Questionnaires of federal judges have found that the judges perceive somewhere between 10–20% of the lawyers appearing before them to be less than satisfactory. If incompetent representation is a compelling argument against the death penalty, why is it also not a convincing argument against criminal sanctions generally?

The commonly offered response is that death is different: the stakes are higher, mistakes are irreversible. In his dissent to the Court's seminal 1984 decision in *Strickland v. Washington*, Justice Thurgood Marshall argues that death is "qualitatively different" from any other sentence and because of this qualitative difference, "there is a corresponding difference in the need for reliability." One wonders, though, whether a defendant facing a sentence of 30 years would agree that the need for reliability in his own case is less than that of the capital defendant.

The constitutional protection of the right to counsel is derived from the Sixth Amendment. The Sixth Amendment provides: "In all criminal prosecutions, the accused shall enjoy the right to have the assistance of counsel for his defense." Some argue that the right to counsel is the most fundamental of all civil liberties. Judge David Bazelon has called it the "most pervasive right" because it enables a citizen to assert other rights guaranteed him by the Constitution. It is critical to the criminal defendant so that he is not condemned simply because he lacks the skills and experience to prove his own innocence.

The standard governing claims of ineffective assistance of counsel is established in *Strickland*, excerpted in the Critical Documents section of this chapter. In *Strickland*, the Court held that a prisoner must show both deficient performance by trial counsel and prejudice in order to sustain a petition based on ineffective assistance. Deficient performance is judged by an objective standard of reasonableness measured against prevailing professional norms. Prejudice means that the attorney's errors were "so serious as to deprive the defendant of a fair trial, a trial whose result is reliable." It is not enough for the petitioner to show that the trial counsel's errors "had some conceivable effect on the outcome of the proceeding." The scrutiny of trial counsel's performance is "highly deferential."

Given the high degree of deference incorporated into the standard, it is not surprising that lower courts have found a wide range of conduct by attorneys to be constitutionally adequate. Several cases had upheld convictions where attorneys slept through large portions of their trials. One Texas judge wrote, "The Constitution says that everyone's entitled to an attorney of their choice. But the Constitution does not say that the lawyer has to be awake." In *Darden v. Wainwright* and *Burger v. Kemp*, the Supreme Court upheld death sentences even where the defense attorney offered no mitigating evidence during the sentencing phase. *Burger v. Kemp* establishes the principle that so long as an attorney investigates a matter, such as evidence of mitigation, the decision not to present that evidence is presumed a strategic decision.

The Court has been similarly reluctant to find prejudice in cases where attorney misconduct is found to have existed. In *Lockhart v. Fretwell*, a 1993 case, the Court upheld a conviction where trial counsel failed to object to the use of an aggravating factor, pecuniary gain, that duplicated an element of the underlying felony conviction. The objection would have been sustained if made under *Collins v. Lockhart*, an Eighth Circuit decision. *Collins* was overturned four years later based upon the Supreme Court's 1988 decision in *Lowenfeld v. Phelps*, holding that sentencing schemes with duplicative aggravators were not unconstitutional so long as the scheme, taken as a whole, narrowed in some way. Even though the objection would have saved Fretwell, the Court found no prejudice, holding that to find otherwise would give Fretwell a "windfall."

In 1989, the Court held in *Murray v. Giarratano* that prisoners do not have a constitutional right to counsel during the habeas stage. The right to counsel extends only to trial and direct appeal. Some have argued that this places the criminal defendant in a catch-22: he has the constitutional right to competent counsel, but does not have the guarantee of access to an attorney to challenge whether he has received effective representation. A provision of a 1988 Congressional act authorizing the death penalty for drug kingpins authorized federal courts to appoint counsel for death row prisoners in federal *habeas* petitions. The 1996 Antiterrorism and Effective Death Penalty Act (AEDPA), discussed more extensively in Chapter 21, restricts review of habeas petitions by death row prisoners in states that "opt in" to AEDPA. One condition of opting in is that states provide attorneys to death row inmates at the state habeas stage.

In the Perspectives section of this chapter, Stephen Bright deplores the state of capital representation in the South. Bright is head of the Southern Center for Human Rights and one of the leading death penalty lawyers in the United States. He says that attorneys representing capital defendants are paid far too little, that the standard of conduct to which they are held is too low, and that judges often have the incentive to appoint the worst quality counsel. Joshua Marquis, a district attorney in Oregon, argues that conditions are far improved and that in his own district he is often outspent in capital cases. The differences between the two perspectives no doubt reflect differences in underlying philosophy, but also underscore the dramatic geographic differences in the manner in which capital punishment is practiced.

■ Trial Counsel—Critical Documents

Strickland v. Washington
466 U.S. 668 (1984)

Justice O'Connor delivered the opinion of the Court.

This case requires us to consider the proper standards for judging a criminal defendant's contention that the Constitution requires a conviction or death sentence to be set aside because counsel's assistance at the trial or sentencing was ineffective.

I

A

During a 10-day period in September 1976, respondent planned and committed three groups of crimes, which included three brutal stabbing murders, torture, kidnapping, severe assaults, attempted murders, attempted extortion, and theft. After his two accomplices were arrested, respondent surrendered to police and voluntarily gave a lengthy statement confessing to the third of the criminal episodes. The State of Florida indicted respondent for kidnapping and murder and appointed an experienced criminal lawyer to represent him.

Counsel actively pursued pretrial motions and discovery. He cut his efforts short, however, and he experienced a sense of hopelessness about the case, when he learned that, against his specific advice, respondent had also confessed to the first two murders. By the date set for trial, respondent was subject to indictment for three counts of first-degree murder and multiple counts of robbery, kidnapping for ransom, breaking and entering and assault, attempted murder, and conspiracy to commit robbery. Respondent waived his right to a jury trial, again acting against counsel's advice, and pleaded guilty to all charges, including the three capital murder charges.

In the plea colloquy, respondent told the trial judge that, although he had committed a string of burglaries, he had no significant prior criminal record and that at the time of his criminal spree he was under extreme stress caused by his inability to support his family. He also stated, however, that he accepted responsibility for the crimes. The trial judge told respondent that he had "a great deal of respect for people who are willing to step forward and admit their responsibility" but that he was making no statement at all about his likely sentencing decision.

Counsel advised respondent to invoke his right under Florida law to an advisory jury at his capital sentencing hearing. Respondent rejected the advice and waived the right. He chose instead to be sentenced by the trial judge without a jury recommendation.

In preparing for the sentencing hearing, counsel spoke with respondent about his background. He also spoke on the telephone with respondent's wife and mother, though he did not follow up on the one unsuccessful effort to meet with them. He did not otherwise seek out character witnesses for respondent. Nor did he request a psychiatric examination, since his conversations with his client gave no indication that respondent had psychological problems.

Counsel decided not to present and hence not to look further for evidence concerning respondent's character and emotional state. That decision reflected trial counsel's sense of hopelessness about overcoming the evidentiary effect of respondent's confessions to the gruesome crimes. It also reflected the judgment that it was advisable to rely on the plea colloquy for evidence about respondent's background and about his claim of emotional stress: the plea colloquy communicated sufficient information about these subjects, and by forgoing the opportunity to present new evidence on these subjects, counsel prevented the State from cross-examining respondent on his claim and from putting on psychiatric evidence of its own.

Counsel also excluded from the sentencing hearing other evidence he thought was potentially damaging. He successfully moved to exclude respondent's "rap sheet." Because he judged that a presentence report might prove more detrimental than helpful, as it would have included respondent's criminal history and thereby would have undermined the claim of no significant history of criminal activity, he did not request that one be prepared.

At the sentencing hearing, counsel's strategy was based primarily on the trial judge's remarks at the plea colloquy as well as on his reputation as a sentencing judge who thought it important for a convicted defendant to own up to his crime. Counsel argued that respondent's remorse and acceptance of responsibility justified sparing him from the death penalty. Counsel also argued that respondent had no history of criminal activity and that respondent committed the crimes under extreme mental or emotional disturbance, thus coming within the statutory list of mitigating circumstances. He further argued that respondent should be spared death because he had surrendered, confessed, and offered to testify against a codefendant and because respondent was fundamentally a good person who had briefly gone badly wrong in extremely stressful circumstances. The State put on evidence and witnesses largely for the purpose of describing the details of the crimes. Counsel did not cross-examine the medical experts who testified about the manner of death of respondent's victims.

The trial judge found numerous aggravating circumstances and no (or a single comparatively insignificant) mitigating circumstance. He sentenced respondent to death on each of the three counts of murder and to prison terms for the other crimes.

B

Respondent subsequently sought collateral relief on numerous grounds, among them that counsel had rendered ineffective assistance at the sentencing proceeding. He asserted that counsel was ineffective because he failed to move for a continuance to prepare for sentencing, to request a psychiatric report, to investigate and present character witnesses, to seek a presentence investigation report, to present meaningful arguments to the sentencing judge, and to investigate the medical examiner's reports or cross-examine the medical experts. In support of the claim, respondent submitted 14 affidavits from friends, neighbors, and relatives stating that they would have testified if asked to do so. He also submitted one psychiatric report and one psychological report stating that respondent, though not under the influence of extreme mental or emotional disturbance, was "chronically frustrated and depressed because of his economic dilemma" at the time of his crimes.

II

A convicted defendant's claim that counsel's assistance was so defective as to require reversal of a conviction or death sentence has two components. First, the defendant must show that counsel's performance was deficient. This requires showing that counsel made errors so serious that counsel was not functioning as the "counsel" guaranteed the defendant by the Sixth Amendment. Second, the defendant must show that the deficient performance prejudiced the defense. This requires showing that counsel's errors were so serious as to deprive the defendant of a fair trial, a trial whose result is reliable. Unless a defendant makes both showings, it cannot be said that the conviction or death sentence resulted from a breakdown in the adversary process that renders the result unreliable.

A

The proper standard for attorney performance is that of reasonably effective assistance. When a convicted defendant complains of the ineffectiveness of counsel's assistance, the defendant must show that counsel's representation fell below an objective standard of reasonableness.

More specific guidelines are not appropriate. The Sixth Amendment refers simply to "counsel," not specifying particular requirements of effective assistance. It relies instead on the legal profession's maintenance of standards sufficient to justify the law's presumption that counsel will fulfill the role in the adversary process that the Amendment envisions. The proper measure of attorney performance remains simply reasonableness under prevailing professional norms.

Representation of a criminal defendant entails certain basic duties. Counsel's function is to assist the defendant, and hence counsel owes the client a duty of loyalty, a duty to avoid conflicts of interest. From counsel's function as assistant to the defendant derive the overarching duty to advocate the defendant's cause and the more particular duties to consult with the defendant on important decisions and to keep the defendant informed of important developments in the course of the prosecution. Counsel also has a duty to bring to bear such skill and knowledge as will render the trial a reliable adversarial testing process.

These basic duties neither exhaustively define the obligations of counsel nor form a checklist for judicial evaluation of attorney performance. In any case presenting an ineffectiveness claim, the performance inquiry must be whether counsel's assistance was reasonable considering all the circumstances. Prevailing norms of practice as reflected in American Bar Association standards and the like are guides to determining what is reasonable, but they are only guides. No particular set of detailed rules for counsel's conduct can satisfactorily take account of the variety of circumstances faced by defense counsel or the range of legitimate decisions regarding how best to represent a criminal defendant. Any such set of rules would interfere with the constitutionally protected independence of counsel and restrict the wide latitude counsel must have in making tactical decisions. Indeed, the existence of detailed guidelines for representation could distract counsel from the overriding mission of vigorous advocacy of the defendant's cause. Moreover, the purpose of the effective assistance guarantee of the Sixth Amendment is not to improve the quality of legal representation, although that is a goal of considerable importance to the legal system. The purpose is simply to ensure that criminal defendants receive a fair trial.

Judicial scrutiny of counsel's performance must be highly deferential. It is all too tempting for a defendant to second-guess counsel's assistance after conviction or adverse sentence, and it is all too easy for a court, examining counsel's defense after it has proved unsuccessful, to conclude that a particular act or omission of counsel was unreasonable. A fair assessment of attorney performance requires that every effort be made to eliminate the distorting effects of hindsight, to reconstruct the circumstances of counsel's challenged conduct, and to evaluate the conduct from counsel's perspective at the time. Because of the difficulties inherent in making the evaluation, a court must indulge a strong presumption that counsel's conduct falls within the wide range of reasonable professional assistance; that is, the defendant must overcome the presumption that, under the circumstances, the challenged action "might be considered sound trial strategy." There are countless ways to provide effective assistance in any given case. Even the best criminal defense attorneys would not defend a particular client in the same way.

The availability of intrusive post-trial inquiry into attorney performance or of detailed guidelines for its evaluation would encourage the proliferation of ineffectiveness challenges. Criminal trials resolved unfavorably to the defendant would increasingly come to be followed by a second trial, this one of counsel's unsuccessful defense. Counsel's performance and even willingness to serve could be adversely affected. Intensive scrutiny of counsel and rigid requirements for acceptable assistance could dampen the ardor and impair the independence of defense counsel, discourage the acceptance of assigned cases, and undermine the trust between attorney and client.

Thus, a court deciding an actual ineffectiveness claim must judge the reasonableness of counsel's challenged conduct on the facts of the particular case, viewed as of the time of counsel's conduct. The court should recognize that counsel is strongly presumed to have rendered adequate assistance and made all significant decisions in the exercise of reasonable professional judgment.

These standards require no special amplification in order to define counsel's duty to investigate, the duty at issue in this case. Strategic choices made after thorough investigation of law and facts relevant to plausible options are virtually unchallengeable; and strategic choices made after less than complete investigation are reasonable precisely to the extent that reasonable professional judgments support the limitations on investigation. In other words, counsel has a duty to make reasonable investigations or to make a reasonable decision that makes particular investigations unnecessary. In any ineffectiveness case, a particular decision not to investigate must be directly assessed for reasonableness in all the circumstances, applying a heavy measure of deference to counsel's judgments.

The reasonableness of counsel's actions may be determined or substantially influenced by the defendant's own statements or actions. Counsel's actions are usually based, quite properly, on informed strategic choices made by the defendant and on information supplied by the defendant. In particular, what investigation decisions are reasonable depends critically on such information. For example, when the facts that support a certain potential line of defense are generally known to counsel because of what the defendant has said, the need for further investigation may be considerably diminished or eliminated altogether. And when a defendant has given counsel reason to believe that pursuing certain investigations would be fruitless or even harmful, counsel's failure to pursue those investigations may not later be challenged as unreasonable.

B

An error by counsel, even if professionally unreasonable, does not warrant setting aside the judgment of a criminal proceeding if the error had no effect on the judgment. The purpose of the Sixth Amendment guarantee of counsel is to ensure that a defendant has the assistance necessary to justify reliance on the outcome of the proceeding. Accordingly, any deficiencies in counsel's performance must be prejudicial to the defense in order to constitute ineffective assistance under the Constitution.

It is not enough for the defendant to show that the errors had some conceivable effect on the outcome of the proceeding. Virtually every act or omission of counsel would meet that test. On the other hand, we believe that a defendant need not show that counsel's deficient conduct more likely than not altered the outcome in the case.

The defendant must show that there is a reasonable probability that, but for counsel's unprofessional errors, the result of the proceeding would have been different. A reasonable probability is a probability sufficient to undermine confidence in the outcome.

In making this determination, a court hearing an ineffectiveness claim must consider the totality of the evidence before the judge or jury. Some of the factual findings will have been unaffected by the errors, and factual findings that were affected will have been affected in different ways. Some errors will have had a pervasive effect on the inferences to be drawn from the evidence, altering the entire evidentiary picture, and some will have had an isolated, trivial effect. Moreover, a verdict or conclusion only weakly supported by the record is more likely to have been affected by errors than one with overwhelming record support. Taking the unaffected findings as a given, and taking due account of the effect of the errors on the remaining findings, a court making the prejudice inquiry must ask if the defendant has met the burden of showing that the decision reached would reasonably likely have been different absent the errors.

III

Having articulated general standards for judging ineffectiveness claims, we think it useful to apply those standards to the facts of this case in order to illustrate the meaning of the general principles.

Application of the governing principles is not difficult in this case. The facts as described above make clear that the conduct of respondent's counsel at and before respondent's sentencing proceeding cannot be found unreasonable. They also make clear that, even assuming the challenged conduct of counsel was unreasonable, respondent suffered insufficient prejudice to warrant setting aside his death sentence.

With respect to the performance component, the record shows that respondent's counsel made a strategic choice to argue for the extreme emotional distress mitigating circumstance and to rely as fully as possible on respondent's acceptance of responsibility for his crimes. Although counsel understandably felt hopeless about respondent's prospects nothing in the record indicates that counsel's sense of hopelessness distorted his professional judgment. Counsel's strategy choice was well within the range of professionally reasonable judgments, and the decision not to seek more character or psychological evidence than was already in hand was likewise reasonable.

The trial judge's views on the importance of owning up to one's crimes were well known to counsel. The aggravating circumstances were utterly overwhelming. Trial counsel could reasonably surmise from his conversations with respondent that character and psychological evidence would be of little help. Respondent had already been able to mention at the plea colloquy the substance of what there was to know about his financial and emotional troubles. Restricting testimony on respondent's character to what had come in at the plea colloquy ensured that contrary character and psychological evidence and respondent's criminal history, which counsel had successfully moved to exclude, would not come in. On these facts, there can be little question, even without application of the presumption of adequate performance, that trial counsel's defense, though unsuccessful, was the result of reasonable professional judgment.

With respect to the prejudice component, the lack of merit of respondent's claim is even more stark. The evidence that respondent says his trial counsel should have offered at the sentencing hearing would barely have altered the sentencing profile presented to the sentencing judge. As the state courts and District Court found, at most this evidence shows that numerous people who knew respondent thought he was generally a good person and that a psychiatrist and a psychologist believed he was under considerable emotional stress that did not rise to the level of extreme disturbance. Given the overwhelming aggravating factors, there is no reasonable probability that the omitted evidence would have changed the conclusion that the aggravating circumstances outweighed the mitigating circumstances and, hence, the sentence imposed. Indeed, admission of the evidence respondent now offers might even have been harmful to his case: his "rap sheet" would probably have been admitted into evidence, and the psychological reports would have directly contradicted respondent's claim that the mitigating circumstance of extreme emotional disturbance applied to his case.

Failure to make the required showing of either deficient performance or sufficient prejudice defeats the ineffectiveness claim. Here there is a double failure. More generally, respondent has made no showing that the justice of his sentence was rendered unreliable by a breakdown in the adversary process caused by deficiencies in counsel's assistance. Respondent's sentencing proceeding was not fundamentally unfair.

Justice Marshall dissenting.

The majority fails to take adequate account of the fact that the locus of this case is a capital sentencing proceeding. Accordingly, I join neither the Court's opinion nor its judgment.

My objection to the performance standard adopted by the Court is that it is so malleable that, in practice, it will either have no grip at all or will yield excessive variation in the manner in which the Sixth Amendment is interpreted and applied by different courts. To tell lawyers and the lower courts that counsel for a criminal defendant must behave "reasonably" and must act like "a reasonably competent attorney," is to tell them almost nothing. In essence, the majority has instructed judges called upon to assess claims of ineffective assistance of counsel to advert to their own intuitions regarding what constitutes "professional" representation, and has discouraged them from trying to develop more detailed standards governing the performance of defense counsel. In my view, the Court has thereby not only abdicated its own responsibility to interpret the Constitution, but also impaired the ability of the lower courts to exercise theirs.

The debilitating ambiguity of an "objective standard of reasonableness" in this context is illustrated by the majority's failure to address important issues concerning the quality of representation mandated by the Constitution. It is an unfortunate but undeniable fact that a person of means, by selecting a lawyer and paying him enough to ensure he prepares thoroughly, usually can obtain better representation than that available to an indigent defendant, who must rely on appointed counsel, who, in turn, has limited time and resources to devote to a given case. Is a "reasonably competent attorney" a reasonably competent adequately paid retained lawyer or a reasonably competent appointed attorney? It is also a fact that the quality of representation available to ordinary defendants in different parts of the country varies significantly. Should the standard of performance mandated by the Sixth Amendment vary by locale? The majority offers no clues as to the proper responses to these questions.

I object to the prejudice standard adopted by the Court for two independent reasons. First, it is often very difficult to tell whether a defendant convicted after a trial in which he was ineffectively represented would have fared better if his lawyer had been competent. Seemingly impregnable cases can sometimes be dismantled by good defense counsel. On the basis of a cold record, it may be impossible for a reviewing court confidently to ascertain how the government's evidence and arguments would have stood up against rebuttal and cross-examination by a shrewd, well-prepared lawyer. The difficulties of estimating prejudice after the fact are exacerbated by the possibility that evidence of injury to the defendant may be missing from the record precisely because of the incompetence of defense counsel. In view of all these impediments to a fair evaluation of the probability that the outcome of a trial was affected by ineffectiveness of counsel, it seems to me senseless to impose on a defendant whose lawyer has been shown to have been incompetent the burden of demonstrating prejudice.

Even if I were inclined to join the majority's two central holdings, I could not abide the manner in which the majority elaborates upon its rulings. Particularly regrettable are the majority's discussion of the "presumption" of reasonableness to be accorded lawyers' decisions and its attempt to prejudge the merits of claims previously rejected by lower courts using different legal standards.

The only justification the majority itself provides for its proposed presumption is that undue receptivity to claims of ineffective assistance of counsel would encourage too many defendants to raise such claims and thereby would clog the courts with frivolous suits and "dampen the ardor" of defense counsel. I have more confidence than the majority in the ability of state and federal courts expeditiously to dispose of meritless arguments and to ensure that responsible, innovative lawyering is not inhibited. In my view, little will be gained and much may be lost by instructing the lower courts to proceed on the assumption that a defendant's challenge to his lawyer's performance will be insubstantial.

The majority suggests that, "for purposes of describing counsel's duties," a capital sentencing proceeding "need not be distinguished from an ordinary trial." I cannot agree.

"The penalty of death is qualitatively different from a sentence of imprisonment, however long. Because of that qualitative difference, there is a corresponding difference in the need for reliability in the determination that death is the appropriate punishment in a specific case."

When instructing lower courts regarding the probability of impact upon the outcome that requires a resentencing, I think the Court would do best explicitly to modify the legal standard itself. In my view, a person on death row, whose counsel's performance fell below constitutionally acceptable levels, should not be compelled to demonstrate a "reasonable probability" that he would have been given a life sentence if his lawyer had been competent; if the defendant can establish a significant chance that the outcome would have been different, he surely should be entitled to a redetermination of his fate.

If counsel had investigated the availability of mitigating evidence, he might well have decided to present some such material at the hearing. If he had done so, there is a significant chance that respondent would have been given a life sentence. In my view, those possibilities, conjoined with the unreasonableness of counsel's failure to investigate, are more than sufficient to establish a violation of the Sixth Amendment and to entitle respondent to a new sentencing proceeding. I respectfully dissent.

■ Trial Counsel—Perspectives

■ Issue—Do Capital Defendants Receive Adequate Representation?

Stephen B. Bright, "Counsel for the Poor: The Death Sentence Not for the Worst Crime but for the Worst Lawyer"

After years in which she and her children were physically abused by her adulterous husband, a woman in Talladega County, Alabama, arranged to have him killed. Tragically, murders of abusive spouses are not rare in our violent society, but seldom are they punished by the death penalty. Yet this woman was sentenced to death. Why?

It may have been in part because one of her court-appointed lawyers was so drunk that the trial had to be delayed for a day after he was held in contempt and sent to jail. The next morning, he and his client were both produced from jail, the trial resumed, and the death penalty was imposed a few days later. It may also have been in part because this lawyer failed to find hospital records documenting injuries received by the woman and her daughter, which would have corroborated their testimony about abuse. And it may also have been because her lawyers did not bring their expert witness on domestic abuse to see the defendant until 8 P.M. on the night before he testified at trial.

Poor people accused of capital crimes are often defended by lawyers who lack the skills, resources, and commitment to handle such serious matters. This fact is confirmed in case after case. It is not the facts of the crime, but the quality of legal representation, that distinguishes this case, where the death penalty was imposed, from many similar cases, where it was not.

The woman in Talladega, like any other person facing the death penalty who cannot afford counsel, is entitled to a court-appointed lawyer. But achieving competent representation in capital and other criminal cases requires much more than the Court's recognition of the vital importance of counsel and of "thoroughgoing investigation and preparation." Providing better representation today than the defendants had in Scottsboro in 1931 requires money, a structure for providing indigent defense that is independent of the judiciary and prosecution, and skilled and dedicated lawyers.

More than sixty years after *Powell* and thirty years after *Gideon*, this task remains. This essay describes the pervasiveness of deficient representation, examines the reasons for it, and considers the likelihood of improvement.

I. *The Difference a Competent Lawyer Makes in a Capital Case*

Arbitrary results, which are all too common in death penalty cases, frequently stem from inadequacy of counsel. The process of sorting out who is most deserving of society's ultimate punishment does not work when the most fundamental component of the adversary system, competent representation by counsel, is missing. Essential guarantees of the Bill of Rights may be disregarded because counsel failed to assert them, and juries may be deprived of critical facts needed to make reliable determinations of guilt or punishment. The result is a process that lacks fairness and integrity.

For instance, the failure of defense counsel to present critical information is one reason that Horace Dunkins was sentenced to death in Alabama. Before his execution in 1989, when newspapers reported that Dunkins was mentally retarded, at least one juror came forward and said she would not have voted for the death sentence if she had known of his condition. Nevertheless, Dunkins was executed.

This same failure of defense counsel to present critical information also helps account for the death sentences imposed on Jerome Holloway—who has an IQ of 49 and the intellectual capacity of a 7-year-old—in Bryan County, Georgia. It helps explain why Donald Thomas, a schizophrenic youth, was sentenced to death in Atlanta, where the jury knew nothing about his mental impairment because his lawyer failed to present any evidence about his condition. In each of these cases, the jury was unable to perform its constitutional obligation to impose a sentence based on "a reasoned *moral* response to the defendant's background, character and crime," because it was not informed by defense counsel of the defendant's background and character.

It can be said confidently that the failure to present such evidence made a difference in the Holloway and Thomas cases. After each was reversed—one of them for reasons having nothing to do with counsel's incompetence—the pertinent information was presented to the court by new counsel, the death sentence was not imposed. But for many sentenced to death, such as Horace Dunkins, there is no second chance.

In these examples, imposition of the death penalty was not so much the result of the heinousness of the crime or the incorrigibility of the defendant—the factors upon which imposition of capital punishment supposedly is to turn—but rather of how bad the lawyers were. A large part of the death row population is made up of people who are distinguished by neither their records nor the circumstances of their crimes, but by their abject poverty, debilitating mental impairments, minimal intelligence, and the poor legal representation they received.

A member of the Georgia Board of Pardons and Paroles has said that if the files of 100 cases punished by death and 100 punished by life were shuffled, it would be impossible to sort them out by sentence based upon information in the files about the crime and the offender.

Although it has long been fashionable to recite the disgusting facts of murder cases to show how deserving of death particular defendants may be, such renditions fail to answer whether the selection process is a principled one based on neutral, objective factors that provide a "meaningful basis for distinguishing the few cases in which the death penalty is imposed from the many cases in which it is not." Virtually all murders involve tragic and gruesome facts. However, the death penalty is imposed, on average, in only 250 cases of the approximately 20,000 homicides that occur each year in the United States. Whether death is imposed frequently turns on the quality of counsel assigned to the accused.

II. *The Pervasive Inadequacy of Counsel for the Poor and the Reasons for It*

Inadequate legal representation does not occur in just a few capital cases. It is pervasive in those jurisdictions which account for most of the death sentences. The American Bar Association concluded after an exhaustive study of the issues that "the inadequacy and inadequate compensation of counsel at trial" was one of the "principal failings of the capital punishment systems in the states today." Justice Thurgood Marshall observed that "capital defendants frequently suffer the consequences of having trial counsel who are ill-equipped to handle capital cases." The *National Law Journal*, after an extensive study of capital cases in six Southern states, found that capital trials are "more like a random flip of the coin than a delicate balancing of the scales" because the defense lawyer is too often "ill-trained, unprepared and grossly underpaid." Many observers from a variety of perspectives and from different states have found the same scandalous quality of legal representation.

These assessments are supported by numerous cases in which the poor were defended by lawyers who lacked even the most rudimentary knowledge, resources, and capabilities needed for the defense of a capital case. Death sentences have been imposed in cases in which defense lawyers had not even read the state's death penalty statute or did not know that a capital trial is bifurcated into separate determinations of guilt and punishment. State trial judges and prosecutors—who have taken oaths to uphold the law, including the Sixth Amendment—have allowed capital trials to proceed and death sentences to be imposed even when defense counsel fought among themselves or presented conflicting defenses for the same client, referred to their clients by a racial slur, cross-examined a witness whose direct testimony counsel missed because he was parking his car, slept through part of the trial, or was intoxicated during trial. Appellate courts often review and decide capital cases on the basis of appellate briefs that would be rejected in a first-year legal writing course in law school.

There are several interrelated reasons for the poor quality of representation in these important cases. Most fundamental is the wholly inadequate funding for the defense of indigents. Public defender programs have never been created or properly funded in many jurisdictions. The compensation provided to individual court-appointed lawyers is so minimal that few accomplished lawyers can be enticed to defend capital cases. Those who do take a capital case cannot afford to devote the time required to defend it properly. As a result, the accused are usually represented by lawyers who lack the experience, expertise, and resources of their adversaries on the prosecution side.

Many state court judges, instead of correcting this imbalance, foster it by intentionally appointing inexperienced and incapable lawyers to defend capital cases, and denying funding for essential expert and investigative needs of the defense. The minimal standard of legal representation in the defense of poor people, as currently interpreted by the Supreme Court, offers little protection to the poor person stuck with a bad lawyer.

A. The Lack of a Functioning Adversary System Many death penalty states have two state-funded offices that specialize in handling serious criminal cases. Both employ attorneys who generally spend years—some even their entire careers—handling criminal cases. Both pay decent annual salaries and provide health care and retirement benefits. Both send their employees to conferences and continuing legal education programs each year to keep them up to date on the latest developments in the law. Both have at their disposal a stable of investigative agencies, a wide range of experts, and mental health professionals anxious to help develop and interpret facts favorable to their side. Unfortunately, however, in many states both of these offices are on the same side: the prosecution.

One is the District Attorney's office in each judicial district, whose lawyers devote their time exclusively to handling criminal matters in the local court systems. These lawyers acquire considerable expertise in the trial of criminal cases, including capital cases. There are, for example, prosecutors in the District Attorney's office in Columbus, Georgia, who have been trying death penalty cases since the state's current death penalty statute was adopted in 1973. The other office is the state Attorney General's office, which usually has a unit made up of lawyers who specialize in handling the appeals of criminal cases and habeas corpus matters. Here, too, lawyers build expertise in handling capital cases.

The specialists in the offices of both the district attorneys and the attorneys general have at their call local, state, and, when needed, federal investigative and law enforcement agencies. They have a group of full-time experts at the crime laboratory and in the medical examiner's offices to respond to crime scenes and provide expert testimony when needed. If mental health issues are raised, the prosecution has a group of mental health professionals at the state mental facilities. No one seriously contends that these professional witnesses are objective. They routinely testify for the prosecution as part of their work, and prosecutors enjoy longstanding working relationships with them.

In Alabama, Georgia, Mississippi, Louisiana, Texas, and many other states with a unique fondness for capital punishment, there is no similar degree of specialization or resources on the other side of capital cases. A poor person facing the death penalty may be assigned an attorney who has little or no experience in the defense of capital or even serious criminal cases, one reluctant or unwilling to defend him, one with little or no empathy or understanding of the accused or his particular plight, one with little or no knowledge of criminal or capital punishment law, or one with no understanding of the need to document and present mitigating circumstances. Although it is widely acknowledged that at least two lawyers, supported by investigative and expert assistance, are required to defend a capital case, some of the jurisdictions with the largest number of death sentences still assign only one lawyer to defend a capital case.

In contrast to the prosecution's virtually unlimited access to experts and investigative assistance, the lawyer defending the indigent accused in a capital case may not have any investigative or expert assistance to prepare for trial and present a defense. A study of twenty capital cases in Philadelphia in 1991 and 1992 found that the court "paid for investigators in eight of the twenty cases, spending an average of $605 in each of the eight" and that the court "paid for psychologists in two of them, costing $400 in one case, $500 in the other." It is impossible even to begin a thorough investigation or obtain a comprehensive mental health evaluation for such paltry amounts.

B. The Lack of Indigent Defense Programs In many jurisdictions where capital punishment is frequently imposed, there are no comprehensive public defender systems whose resources can parallel the prosecutorial functions of the district attorneys' offices. There are no appellate defender offices that parallel the function of the capital litigation sections of the attorneys general's offices. In fact, there is no coherent system at all, but a hodgepodge of approaches that vary from county to county.

In many jurisdictions, judges simply appoint members of the bar in private practice to defend indigents accused of crimes. The lawyers appointed may not want the cases, may receive little or no compensation for the time and expense of handling them, may lack any interest in criminal law, and may not have the skill to defend those accused of a crime. As a result, the poor are often represented by inexperienced lawyers who view their responsibilities as unwanted burdens, have no inclination to help their clients, and have no incentive to develop criminal trial skills. Lawyers can make more money doing almost anything else. Even many lawyers who have an interest in criminal defense work simply cannot afford to continue to represent indigents while also repaying their student loans and meeting their familial obligations.

Some counties employ a "contract system" in which the county contracts with an attorney in private practice to handle all of the indigent cases for a specified amount. Often contracts are awarded to the lawyer—or group of lawyers—who bids the lowest. Any money spent on investigation and experts comes out of the amount the lawyer receives. These programs are well known for the exceptionally short shrift that the poor clients receive and the lack of expenditures for investigative and expert assistance.

C. Compensation of Attorneys: The Wages of Death The United States Court of Appeals for the Fifth Circuit, finding that Federico Martinez-Macias "was denied his constitutional right to adequate counsel in a capital case in which his actual innocence was a close question," observed that, "The state of Texas paid defense counsel $11.84 per hour. Unfortunately, the justice system got only what it paid for." What is unusual about the case is not the amount paid to counsel, but the court's acknowledgement of its impact on the quality of services rendered.

As we have seen, in many jurisdictions poor people facing the death penalty are not assigned specialists who work for indigent defense programs, but individual attorneys, often sole practitioners. In some jurisdictions, the hourly rates in capital cases may be below the minimum wage or less than the lawyer's overhead expenses. Many jurisdictions limit the maximum fee for a case. At such rates it is usually impossible to obtain a good lawyer willing to spend the necessary time.

Alabama limits compensation for out-of-court preparation to $20 per hour, up to a limit of $1,000. In one rare Alabama case where two lawyers devoted 246.86 and 187.90 hours respectively to out-of-court preparation, they were still paid $1000 each, or $4.05 and $5.32 per hour.

In some rural areas in Texas, lawyers receive no more than $800 to handle a capital case. Generally, the hourly rate is $50 or less. Attorneys appointed to defend capital cases in Philadelphia are paid an average of $6399 per case. In the few cases where a second attorney has been appointed, it is often at a flat rate of $500. A study in Virginia found that, after taking into account an attorney's overhead expenses, the effective hourly rate paid to counsel representing an indigent accused in a capital case was $13. In Kentucky, the limit for a capital case is $2500.

Sometimes even these modest fees are denied to appointed counsel. A capital case in Georgia was resolved with a guilty plea only after the defense attorneys, a sole practitioner and this author, agreed not to seek attorneys' fees as part of the bargain in which the state withdrew its request for the death penalty.

Not surprisingly, a recent study in Texas found that "more experienced private criminal attorneys are refusing to accept court appointments in capital cases. In many counties, the most qualified attorneys often ask not to be considered for court appointments in capital cases due to the fact that the rate of compensation would not allow them to cover the expense of running a law practice." The same unwillingness to take cases because of the low fees has been observed in other states. Consequently, although capital cases require special skills, the level of compensation is often not enough even to attract those who regularly practice in the indigent defense system.

D. The Role of Judges: Appointment and Oversight of Mediocrity and Incompetence Even if, despite the lack of indigent defense programs and adequate compensation, capable lawyers were willing to move to jurisdictions with many capital cases, forego more lucrative business, and take appointments to capital cases, there is still no assurance that those lawyers would be appointed to the cases. It is no secret that elected state court judges do not appoint the best and brightest of the legal profession to defend capital cases. In part, this is because many judges do not want to impose on those members of the profession they believe to have more important, financially lucrative things to do. But even when choosing from among those who seek criminal appointments, judges often appoint less capable lawyers to defend the most important cases.

Judges have appointed to capital cases lawyers who have never tried a case before. A study of homicide cases in Philadelphia found that the quality of lawyers appointed to capital cases in Philadelphia is so bad that "even officials in charge of the system say they wouldn't want to be represented in Traffic Court by some of the people appointed to defend poor people accused of murder." The study found that many of the attorneys were appointed by judges based on political connections, not legal ability. "Philadelphia's poor defendants often find themselves being represented by ward leaders, ward committeemen, failed politicians, the sons of judges and party leaders, and contributors to the judge's election campaigns."

An Alabama judge refused to relieve counsel even when they filed a motion to be relieved of the appointment because they had inadequate experience in defending criminal cases and considered themselves incompetent to defend a capital case. Georgia trial judges have repeatedly refused to appoint or compensate the experienced attorneys who, doing pro bono representation in postconviction stages of review, had successfully won new trials for clients who had been sentenced to death. A Georgia judge refused to appoint an expert capital litigator from the NAACP Legal Defense and Educational Fund to continue representation of an indigent defendant, even though the Legal Defense Fund lawyer had won a new trial for the client by showing in federal habeas corpus proceedings that he had received ineffective assistance from the lawyer appointed by the judge at the initial capital trial.

A newly admitted member of the Georgia bar was surprised to be appointed to handle the appeal of a capital case on her fifth day of practice in Columbus, Georgia. Two days earlier she had met the judge who appointed her when she accompanied her boss to a divorce proceeding. Only after she asked for help was a second attorney brought onto the case. Another lawyer in that same circuit was appointed to a capital case, but after submitting his first billing statement to the judge for approval was told by the judge that he was spending too much time on the case. He was summarily replaced by another lawyer and the defendant was ultimately sentenced to death. For a number of years, judges in that circuit appointed a lawyer to capital cases who did not challenge the under representation of black citizens in the jury pools for fear of incurring hostility from the community and alienating potential jurors. As a result, a number of African-Americans were tried by all-white juries in capital cases even though one-third of the population of the circuit is African-American.

The many other examples of exceptionally poor legal representation documented by the ABA, the *National Law Journal*, and others indicate that judges either are intentionally appointing lawyers who are not equal to the task or are completely inept at securing competent counsel in capital cases. The reality is that popularly elected judges, confronted by a local community that is outraged over the murder of a prominent citizen or angered by the facts of a crime, have little incentive to protect the constitutional rights of the one accused in such a killing. Many state judges are former prosecutors who won their seats on the bench by exploiting high-publicity death penalty cases. Some of those judges have not yet given up the prosecutorial attitude.

E. The Minimal Standard of Legal Representation Tolerated in Capital Cases This sad state of affairs is tolerated in our nation's courts in part because the United States Supreme Court has said that the Constitution requires no more. Instead of actually requiring *effective* representation to fulfill the Sixth Amendment's guarantee of counsel, the Court has brought the standard down to the level of ineffective practice. Stating that "the purpose of the effective assistance guarantee of the Sixth Amendment is not to improve the quality of legal representation," the Court in *Strickland* adopted a standard that is "highly deferential" to the performance of counsel. To prevail on a claim of ineffective assistance of counsel, a defendant must overcome "a strong presumption that counsel's conduct falls within the wide range of reasonable professional assistance," show that the attorney's representation "fell below an objective standard of reasonableness," and establish "prejudice," which is defined as a reasonable probability that counsel's errors affected the outcome.

As Judge Alvin Rubin of the Fifth Circuit concluded:

> *The Constitution, as interpreted by the courts, does not require that the accused, even in a capital case, be represented by able or effective counsel. Consequently, accused persons who are represented by "not-legally-ineffective" lawyers may be condemned to die when the same accused, if represented by* effective *counsel, would receive at least the clemency of a life sentence.*

Much less than mediocre assistance passes muster under the *Strickland* standard. Errors in judgment and other mistakes may readily be characterized as "strategy" or "tactics" and thus are beyond review. Indeed, courts employ a lesser standard for judging the competence of lawyers in a capital case than the standard for malpractice for doctors, accountants, and architects.

The defense lawyer in one Texas case failed to introduce any evidence about his client at the penalty phase of the trial. The attorney's entire closing argument regarding sentencing was: "You are an extremely intelligent jury. You've got that man's life in your hands. You can take it or not. That's all I have to say." A United States district court granted habeas corpus relief because of the lawyer's failure to present and argue evidence in mitigation, but the Fifth Circuit, characterizing counsel's nonargument as a "dramatic ploy," found that the attorney's performance satisfied *Strickland*. The lawyer was later suspended for other reasons. The defendant was executed.

III. *The Need for Individual Responses and Limits on the Power of the Courts*

The quality of legal representation in capital cases in many states is a scandal. However, almost no one cares. Those facing the death penalty are generally poor, often members of racial minorities, often afflicted with substantial mental impairments, and always accused of serious, terrible crimes. The crimes of which they are accused bring out anger, hatred, and a quest for vengeance on the part of most people, including judges, prosecutors, and, quite often, even those appointed to represent the accused. All of this leads to, at best, indifference and, more often, hostility toward the plight of those accused. And many outside the criminal justice system are indifferent because they are unaware of what passes for justice in the courts. There is a growing cynicism about the importance of due process and the protections of the Bill of Rights. Many of those who hold or aspire to public office find it impossible to resist the temptation to resort to demagoguery to exploit these sentiments.

But this reality does not excuse the constitutional responsibility of the judiciary and members of the legal profession to ensure that even the most despised defendants still receive the highest quality legal representation in proceedings that will determine whether they live or die. Justice William Brennan, with his usual eloquence, once observed in another context,

> It is tempting to pretend that those on death row share a fate in no way connected to our own, that our treatment of them sounds no echoes beyond the chambers in which they die. Such an illusion is ultimately corrosive, for the reverberations of injustice are not so easily confined. The way in which we choose those who will die reveals the depth of moral commitment among the living.

Unfortunately, what has been revealed about the depth of moral commitment among legislators, members of the bar, and the judiciary is very discouraging. It is unlikely that the promise of *Powell* and *Gideon* will ever be fulfilled for most of those accused of criminal violations. Legislatures are unwilling to pay the price for adequate representation, most courts are unwilling to order it, and most members of the bar are unwilling or unable to take on the awesome responsibility of providing a vigorous defense without adequate compensation.

The best hope for most of those facing the death penalty is that capable lawyers will volunteer to take their cases and provide proper representation regardless of whether they are paid adequately or at all. A member of the New York Court of Appeals, citing the ethical obligation of lawyers to recognize deficiencies in the legal system and initiate corrective measures, has urged lawyers to respond to the challenge of seeing that those who face the worst penalty receive the best representation.

Lawyers must not only respond, but in doing so they must litigate aggressively the right to adequate compensation, to the funds necessary to investigate, and for the experts needed to prepare and present a defense. Lawyers must also bring systemic challenges to indigent defense systems. Attorneys for the poor—whether in assigned counsel, contract, or public defender systems—must refuse unreasonable caseloads and insist upon the training and resources to do the job right.

And lawyers must continue to bear witness to the shameful injustices which are all too routine in capital cases. The uninformed and the indifferent must be educated and reminded of what is passing for justice in the courts. It is only by the witness of those who observe the injustices in capital cases firsthand that others in society can be accurately informed.

IV. *Conclusion*

Courts have issued many pronouncements about the importance of the guiding hand of counsel, but they have failed to acknowledge that most state governments are unwilling to pay for an adequate defense for the poor person accused of a crime. Unfortunately, the Supreme Court has not been vigilant in enforcing the promise of *Powell* and *Gideon*. Its acceptance of the current quality of representation in capital cases as inevitable or even acceptable demeans the Sixth Amendment. It undermines the legitimacy of the criminal courts and the respect due their judgments. No poor person accused of *any* crime should receive the sort of representation that is found acceptable in the criminal courts of this nation today, but it is particularly indefensible in cases where life is at stake. Even one of the examples of deficient representation described in this Essay is one more than should have occurred in a system of true justice.

Providing the best quality representation to persons facing loss of life or imprisonment should be the highest priority of legislatures, the judiciary, and the bar. However, the reality is that it is not. So long as the substandard representation that is seen today is tolerated in the criminal courts, at the very least, this lack of commitment to equal justice should be acknowledged and the power of courts should be limited. So long as juries and judges are deprived of critical information and the Bill of Rights is ignored in the most emotionally and politically charged cases due to deficient legal representation, the courts should not be authorized to impose the extreme and irrevocable penalty of death. Otherwise, the death penalty will continue to be imposed, not upon those who commit the worst crimes, but upon those who have the misfortune to be assigned the worst lawyers.

Joshua Marquis, "Not So Dire After All: *Gideon*'s Legacy"

In the 40 years since Clarence Gideon penciled an appeal that now requires appointed counsel in all cases when a defendant faces incarceration, the face of the American justice system has been transformed. Contrary to the handwringing in many circles, the promise of *Gideon* has not gone unfulfilled.

In 1963, the year the Supreme Court held that right to appointed counsel extended beyond capital cases, the cutting-edge show on TV was *The Defenders*, in which those threadbare but plucky lawyers strove mightily against enormous odds to defend their indigent clients.

But the legal landscape in the 21st century is very different. In my home state of Oregon, one of the top firms, Portland-based Stoel Rives, contributed more than $100,000 in firm resources for a single capital appeal in Alabama. The state of Oregon spent $75 million last year on indigent defense, while taxpayers paid $55 million to fund all of the state's district attorneys offices. Oregon is not unique. Contrary to the conventional wisdom, in many states the resources afforded public defenders and lawyers providing indigent defense outstrip the resources given prosecutors.

In Illinois, where the *Chicago Tribune* harshly criticized some private lawyers who botched indigent capital cases, the newspaper grudgingly admitted that the Cook County Public Defenders Office did an outstanding job despite a heavy caseload. Across America, the offices of public defenders—and prosecutors— have attracted some of the best legal talent in spite of salaries that rarely if ever match what first-year associates make at the nation's top firms.

Some point, for example, to the New Orleans public defender crisis as typical of indigent defense throughout the country. But take the case of Oregon, where recently, in case after case, almost a million dollars was spent by taxpayers to defend indigent clients charged with murder. Not only do the court-appointed lawyers get paid six figures for their legal work, but the investigators are paid only slightly less and there are many examples of out-of-state experts who are paid $20,000 or more by the state indigent defense program. Similar resources exist in states from California to Connecticut. And in Illinois, reforms have included the establishment of a multimillion-dollar fund to help indigent capital defendants.

As a district attorney who is regularly outspent at least 10-to-one in capital cases, I am confident that someone charged with murder in my state gets a first-class defense. I know that if convicted, the defendant cannot claim that the state stinted in the least in his defense. No Oregon appeals court has ever reversed a case for want of funds that the appellant claimed were denied him during the preparation or trial of his case. I'm not even permitted to know how much money is spent until all the direct and collateral appeals have been exhausted.

Justice is a work in progress and there are plenty of improvements that can be made to move closer to the unreachable goal of perfect justice. But justice is a two-way street, as the victims of crime and the state that represents them must also have their day in court: Both public defenders and prosecutors have to be adequately funded to bring justice to the accused and the victims of crime.

It's important to acknowledge the considerable strides made since a Florida drifter and habitual criminal filed a plea that drew the attention of our nation's highest court. It does a disservice to both the real changes and the fine work done by the many public defender programs to imply that an accused criminal is no better off today than Gideon was almost a half-century ago.

In addition to public funding, there is a role to be played by the private bar, too. Those law firms that attract the best law students with salaries higher than those of many chief prosecutors can offer up more pro bono work to assist public defender programs, such as the one in New Orleans, that need assistance so desperately. Many lawyers in this country have become very wealthy through their work in the legal system. It's only fair to ask that they share, as many have done, some of their talents with less lavishly funded legal enterprises.

If charged today, *Gideon* would be afforded free counsel at every stage of trial, appeal and post-conviction relief. Gideon's trumpet is now joined by an entire brass band that, like all good musicians or craftsmen of any sort, is always trying to reach the perfect note.

Habeas Corpus and the Role of Innocence

■ Habeas Corpus and the Role of Innocence— Introduction

Chapter 7 of this book considered what the risk of executing innocent persons adds to the moral case against the death penalty. The answer to that question turns, in part, on the magnitude of that risk and whether utilitarian benefits and increases in retributive justice resulting from executions offset the cost of potential errors. This was a policy issue, a question of justice in the aggregate. It is a separate question what role a claim of innocence should play in an individual case. What if a defendant is tried and convicted of capital murder, but claims that the verdict was in error? What if he discovers new evidence to support his contention? Should he be entitled to seek relief from the courts? If the state court refuses to consider his claim, should he be entitled to seek relief from the federal court? Does it violate the Constitution to execute an innocent person?

The answers to these questions depend in part on the stage to which the defendant's case has proceeded. Capital cases can be divided into four distinct main phases: (1) trial and direct review, (2) state habeas corpus review, (3) federal habeas corpus review, and (4) clemency.

Stages of Capital Proceedings

1. Trial and Direct Appeal

Capital trials are bifurcated into a guilt phase and sentencing phase. The issue in the guilt phase is whether each and every element of the offense has been proved beyond a reasonable doubt. The issue in the sentencing phase is whether at least one aggravating factor has been proved beyond a reasonable doubt and whether the aggravating factors outweigh the mitigating evidence (different states frame this question in different ways).

On appeal, the defendant may challenge the legal rulings made during his trial, including any violations of his state and federal constitutional rights that he alleges to have occurred. Only issues of law may be raised on appeal. Factual determinations may not be challenged. The jury's findings as to guilt and sentence are dispositive unless a new trial is ordered.

In most states, death-sentenced defendants have an expedited right of appeal. This means they may (or must) bypass the state intermediate court of appeals and proceed directly to the court of last resort. This right or obligation is arguably to the detriment of the capital defendant. In many instances, attorneys for capital defendants consider their primary obligation to be to stretch out the appellate proceedings as long as possible, so an expedited appellate process is not necessarily a benefit.

If the appellate court finds error, the case is often remanded for retrial. If the error pertained only to the sentencing phase, the case is remanded for a new sentencing hearing only. If the state court of last resort finds no error, the defendant may appeal to the United States Supreme Court for a writ of certiorari. A writ of certiorari is the process by which the Court designates a case for review. The Court grants writs sparingly—they are granted in fewer than 1% of the cases in which they are sought—and only in cases involving legal issues of national significance where there is a difference of opinion among the Circuit courts and state courts about the proper interpretation of the Constitution or federal law. Upon denial of certiorari, a defendant's direct appeals are exhausted.

2. State Habeas Corpus Review

This stage is sometimes called the postconviction remedies stage or collateral attack. Postconviction review is a civil proceeding, as is federal habeas corpus review, in which the prisoner, now the petitioner rather than the defendant, challenges the constitutionality of his detention. Every state has some provision for postconviction review. The processes differ from state to state though they share common features. The most significant of these is that the defendant may only raise issues that could not have been raised on direct appeal. If, for example, a defendant contends that the trial judge admitted a confession in violation of his *Miranda* rights and does not raise the objection at trial or on direct appeal, it is waived for all time because it could have been raised during direct review. (If the objection is not raised at trial, it likely is also waived by virtue of the contemporaneous objection requirement.) The most common claim raised on collateral attack is ineffective assistance of counsel. This claim is generally regarded as appropriate for postconviction review as it would be impossible for an attorney to allege his own ineffectiveness.

State habeas initiates in a state trial court, often the same court that sentenced the defendant. In cases where ineffectiveness is alleged, the petition presents a question of fact—whether the defendant's representation at trial failed to meet the *Strickland* standard and whether the defendant was prejudiced thereby. To prove such a claim the defendant ordinarily offers evidence that was not investigated or introduced by the attorney at trial. A defendant might claim, for example, that he suffered from brain damage that inhibited impulse control, and that his attorney did not develop this evidence at trial. He might offer testimony of doctors about the existence of the brain injury and the trial transcript and other evidence to show that this claim was not investigated (if it was investigated by the attorney but not offered at trial, the decision not to offer the evidence is generally presumed to be a strategic choice). It is then for the finder of fact—often the trial judge—to decide whether the attorney's conduct failed to meet the

Strickland standard and whether the outcome of the trial would likely have been different if the evidence had been investigated and offered. Just as with a regular trial, these findings of facts govern throughout the remainder of the case. Just as with a regular trial, the defendant may appeal to the state intermediate court, the state highest court, and ultimately to the United States Supreme Court arguing that the court hearing his petition improperly applied the law to his claim. After he exhausts his appeals on his state habeas petition, the defendant may initiate a federal habeas corpus petition.

3. Federal Habeas Review

The writ of habeas corpus originated in England as a means of ensuring the attendance of parties who might facilitate judicial proceedings. Over time it evolved into a means of challenging imprisonment by the Crown without judicial authorization. The term is Latin in origin, meaning "have the body." Article I, section 9, of the Constitution acknowledges the writ. It provides: "The privilege of the Writ of Habeas Corpus shall not be suspended, unless when in Cases of Rebellion or Invasion the public safety may require it." The Judiciary Act of 1789 authorized judges of federal courts "to grant writs of habeas corpus in all cases where any person may be restrained of his or her liberty in violation of the Constitution, or of any treaty or law of the United States."

In 1845, the Supreme Court held in *Ex Parte Dorr* that state prisoners did not have the right to seek habeas corpus relief. Congress extended the right to state prisoners in a new Judiciary Act, passed in 1867, the same year in which the United States adopted the Fourteenth Amendment. Initially, courts took a narrow view of the scope of the writ, restricting relief to prisoners sentenced by a court lacking appropriate jurisdiction. In *Frank v. Mangrum*, a 1915 decision, the Court held that habeas relief should be provided to state prisoners whenever the state process providing postconviction relief to the prisoner deprived the prisoner of due process of law. In 1953, in *Brown v. Allen*, the Court went further still and held that state court prisoners could challenge the constitutionality of their incarceration after exhausting their state remedies, regardless of whether the state process was adequate.

Brown was the high-water mark of habeas review. Beginning in the 1970s, in the view of some observers, the trend of Court decisions has been towards restricting the availability of habeas review, the Court's preference being for constitutional conflicts in state cases to be resolved by the state courts themselves. Three reasons are commonly offered for the Court's increasingly dimmer view of habeas: First, federal courts have greater confidence in state courts and their ability to fairly resolve state criminal matters. Second, federal courts are concerned with intruding upon state courts; this hesitancy to intrude is often referred to as promoting comity. Finally, the Supreme Court has repeatedly emphasized the need for finality in criminal matters. The possibility of reversal on habeas review creates uncertainty in the criminal process. The Antiterrorism and Effective Death Penalty Act of 1996, discussed in Chapter 21, restricted the federal habeas review process in several significant manners.

Professor James Liebman argues that the policy reasons behind habeas review apply with special force in death penalty cases. Because "the death penalty is such a uniquely final and draconian step," he writes, "it follows that the *habeas corpus* remedy is especially critical in capital cases because of the high constitutional standard of due process and the particular need for reliability in such cases." Liebman further argues that parochial interests and emotions are more likely to clash with constitutional liberties in death penalty cases than in ordinary criminal cases because the facts of the case are generally so gruesome and the community so outraged. This is precisely the situation habeas corpus review is designed to address.

Federal habeas petitions originate in the United States District Court in the district in which the prisoner is incarcerated. As with state habeas petitions, the United States District Court judge must decide a question of fact: whether the defendant is being detained in contravention of his federal constitutional rights. A defendant may appeal an unfavorable decision to the United States Circuit Court of Appeals, and ultimately to the United States Supreme Court. It might be useful to think of direct appeals, state habeas, and federal habeas, as three parallel proceedings.

4. Clemency

Every state and the federal government has some provision for granting clemency. Clemency is literally the granting of kindness or mercy. A governor—or the President in the case of the federal government—may grant the defendant a reprieve, commute the sentence by substituting a less severe punishment than death, or pardon the defendant entirely. Clemency is discussed more extensively in Chapter 23 in connection with the most sweeping and controversial grant of clemency in recent history—former Illinois Governor George Ryan's decision just before he left office in 2003 to commute the sentences of all 156 inmates on the state's death row. Though the Supreme Court has referred to clemency as part of the system of safeguards against the execution of innocents, petitioners seeking clemency are entitled to few procedural protections.

Relevance of Innocence on Federal Habeas Review

A defendant's contention of innocence is directly relevant at trial. That is the raison d' être of the criminal trial—to determine the guilt or innocence of the defendant and, if guilty, to determine the appropriate sentence. The relevance at every other stage of the capital case is less clear. On direct appeal, innocence is of no legal relevance. A convincing claim might make an appellate court judge more sympathetic to a defendant's claim; a judge could also find as a matter of law that insufficient evidence existed for a jury to find guilt proved beyond a reasonable doubt. But the factual claim of innocence is not directly significant. Appellate court judges, and the United States Supreme Court, are confined to deciding matters of law. Most state postconviction statutes have some mechanism for presenting newly discovered evidence to show that the defendant is actually innocent of the crime committed. By virtue of these provisions, a claim of innocence might be relevant at the state habeas stage. No analogous provisions exist in connection with federal habeas corpus. The sole question at federal habeas is whether the defendant is being detained in violation of his constitutional rights. No constitutional provision protects an innocent person from being punished or even executed.

This might seem bizarre on first reading, but there is logic behind it. A defendant's guilt or innocence is in some sense unknowable. Mere mortals cannot know the truth. The best that can be done is to assure a process that generates reliable results. The U.S. Constitution offers protection for such processes—the guarantee of due process, a fair trial, and a reasonably competent attorney. It does not guarantee outcomes. It is one thing for a defendant to claim that the process that governed his trial was unfair; it is an entirely other matter for him to contest the result.

One can imagine a system in which defendants who were displeased with the disposition of their cases at the state level could seek substantive relief at the federal level. Federal courts could retry defendants, thus ensuring that the guilty verdicts in their cases were extra-reliable. This is essentially the relief sought by the petitioner in *Herrera v. Collins*, reprinted in the Critical Documents section of this chapter. Leonel Herrera claimed that he was actually innocent of the crime for which he had been convicted and sought relief on that basis from the federal courts. He did not allege any procedural constitutional violation. He claimed only that the execution of an innocent person would offend the Eighth Amendment.

Some strong policy reasons dictate against Herrera's claim. Granting Herrera's argument would undermine the finality of all guilty verdicts. In all probability, the retrial would be *less* reliable than the original trial, because the second trial would undoubtedly occur years later—witnesses might have died, memories certainly would have faded, and evidence grown stale. On the other hand, it seems to offend justice to tolerate the execution of an innocent man. The *Herrera* Court allows as a theoretical matter that a truly persuasive showing of innocence might be grounds for relief. Herrera, the Court says, does not meet that threshold. So long as a state remedy such as gubernatorial clemency is available to the inmate, then the threshold he must cross to make his claim of innocence is "extraordinarily high." The Court's emphasis is clearly on process rather than substance.

Relevance of the Risk of Executing Innocents to the Constitutionality of the Death Penalty

In *U.S. v. Quinones*, a federal district court judge ruled the federal death penalty unconstitutional on the basis of the evidence of risk of error presented earlier in Chapter 5. *Quinones* held that a defendant had a constitutional right not to be sentenced under a set of procedures that were, as the judge found the federal sentencing scheme to be, likely to produce error. The emphasis in *Quinones* is on substance rather than process.

Whether *Herrera* and *Quinones* were correctly decided as a matter of law and policy is a subject of considerable debate. (*Quinones* was reversed by the Second Circuit Court of Appeals). In the Perspectives section of this chapter, Professor Joseph Hoffmann, discussing *Herrera*, argues that the Court mistakenly places the emphasis on process rather than substance. Professor Barry Latzer argues that substantive concerns might be of theoretical interest, but are irrelevant in the real world. It is impossible to know the truth about a criminal defendant with certainty. All that can be hoped for is a process that generates reliable results. Given all of the procedural protections afforded criminal defendants, Professor Latzer argues that it is bizarre to have an ongoing procedural concern with innocence. *Quinones*, he argues, was incorrectly decided as a matter of law and policy.

■ Habeas Corpus and the Role of Innocence— Critical Documents

Herrera v. Collins
506 U.S. 390 (1992)

Chief Justice Rehnquist delivered the opinion of the Court.

Petitioner Leonel Torres Herrera was convicted of capital murder and sentenced to death in January 1982. He unsuccessfully challenged the conviction on direct appeal and state collateral proceedings in the Texas state courts, and in a federal habeas petition. In February 1992—10 years after his conviction—he urged in a second federal habeas petition that he was "actually innocent" of the murder for which he was sentenced to death, and that the Eighth Amendment's prohibition against cruel and unusual punishment and the Fourteenth Amendment's guarantee of due process of law therefore forbid his execution. He supported this claim with affidavits tending to show that his now-dead brother, rather than he, had been the perpetrator of the crime. Petitioner urges us to hold that this showing of innocence entitles him to relief in this federal habeas proceeding. We hold that it does not.

On an evening in late September 1981, the body of Texas Officer David Rucker was found by a passer-by. Rucker's body was lying beside his patrol car. He had been shot in the head.

At about the same time, Police Officer Enrique Carrisalez observed a speeding vehicle traveling away from the place where Rucker's body had been found, along the same road. Carrisalez, accompanied by Enrique Hernandez, turned on his flashing red lights and pursued the speeding vehicle. After the car had stopped briefly at a red light, it signaled that it would pull over and did so. The patrol car pulled up behind it. Carrisalez took a flashlight and walked toward the car of the speeder. The driver opened his door and exchanged a few words with Carrisalez before firing at least one shot at Carrisalez' chest. The officer died nine days later.

Petitioner Herrera was tried and found guilty of the capital murder of Carrisalez in January 1982, and sentenced to death. In July 1982, he pleaded guilty to the murder of Rucker.

At petitioner's trial for the murder of Carrisalez, Hernandez, who had witnessed Carrisalez' slaying from the officer's patrol car, identified petitioner as the person who had wielded the gun. A declaration by Officer Carrisalez to the same effect, made while he was in the hospital, was also admitted. Through a license plate check, it was shown that the speeding car involved in Carrisalez' murder was registered to petitioner's "live-in" girlfriend. Petitioner was known to drive this car, and he had a set of keys to the car in his pants pocket when he was arrested. Hernandez identified the car as the vehicle from which the murderer had emerged to fire the fatal shot. He also testified that there had been only one person in the car that night.

The evidence showed that Herrera's Social Security card had been found alongside Rucker's patrol car on the night he was killed. Splatters of blood on the car identified as the vehicle involved in the shootings, and on petitioner's blue jeans and wallet were identified as type A blood—the same type which Rucker had. (Herrera has type O blood.) Similar evidence with respect to strands of hair found in the car indicated that the hair was Rucker's and not Herrera's. A handwritten letter was also found on the person of petitioner when he was arrested, which strongly implied that he had killed Rucker.

Petitioner appealed his conviction and sentence, arguing, among other things, that Hernandez' and Carrisalez' identifications were unreliable and improperly admitted. The Texas Court of Criminal Appeals affirmed and we denied certiorari. Petitioner's application for state habeas relief was denied. Petitioner then filed a federal habeas petition, again challenging the identifications offered against him at trial. This petition was denied and we again denied certiorari.

Petitioner next returned to state court and filed a second habeas petition, raising, among other things, a claim of "actual innocence" based on newly discovered evidence. In support of this claim petitioner presented the affidavits of Hector Villarreal, an attorney who had represented petitioner's brother, Raul Herrera, Sr., and of Juan Franco Palacious, one of Raul, Sr.'s former cellmates. Both individuals claimed that Raul, Sr., who died in 1984, had told them that he—and not petitioner—had killed Officers Rucker and Carrisalez. The State District Court denied this application, finding that "no evidence at trial remotely suggested that anyone other than petitioner committed the offense." The Texas Court of Criminal Appeals affirmed and we denied certiorari.

In February 1992, petitioner lodged the instant habeas petition—his second—in federal court, alleging, among other things, that he is innocent of the murders of Rucker and Carrisalez, and that his execution would thus violate the Eighth and Fourteenth Amendments. In addition to proffering the above affidavits, petitioner presented the affidavits of Raul Herrera, Jr., Raul, Sr.'s son, and Jose Ybarra, Jr., a schoolmate of the Herrera brothers. Raul, Jr., averred that he had witnessed his father shoot Officers Rucker and Carrisalez and petitioner was not present. Raul, Jr., was nine years old at the time of the killings. Ybarra alleged that Raul, Sr., told him one summer night in 1983 that he had shot the two police officers. Petitioner alleged that law enforcement officials were aware of this evidence.

The District Court dismissed most of petitioner's claims as an abuse of the writ. However, the District Court granted petitioner's request for a stay of execution so that he could present his claim of actual innocence.

The Court of Appeals vacated the stay of execution. We granted certiorari and the Texas Court of Criminal Appeals stayed petitioner's execution. We now affirm.

Petitioner asserts that the Constitution prohibits the execution of a person who is innocent of the crime for which he was convicted. This proposition has an elemental appeal, as would the similar proposition that the Constitution prohibits the imprisonment of one who is innocent of the crime for which he was convicted. After all, the central purpose of any system of criminal justice is to convict the guilty and free the innocent. But the evidence upon which petitioner's claim of innocence rests was not produced at his trial, but rather eight years later. In any system of criminal justice, "innocence" or "guilt" must be determined in some sort of a judicial proceeding. Petitioner's showing of innocence, and indeed his constitutional claim for relief based upon that showing, must be evaluated in the light of the previous proceedings in this case, which have stretched over a span of 10 years.

A person when first charged with a crime is entitled to a presumption of innocence, and may insist that his guilt be established beyond a reasonable doubt. Other constitutional provisions also have the effect of ensuring against the risk of convicting an innocent person. In capital cases, we have required additional protections because of the nature of the penalty at stake. But we have also observed that "due process does not require that every conceivable step be taken, at whatever cost, to eliminate the possibility of convicting an innocent person." To conclude otherwise would all but paralyze our system for enforcement of the criminal law.

Once a defendant has been afforded a fair trial and convicted of the offense for which he was charged, the presumption of innocence disappears. Here, it is not disputed that the State met its burden of proving at trial that petitioner was guilty of the capital murder of Officer Carrisalez beyond a reasonable doubt. Thus, in the eyes of the law, petitioner does not come before the Court as one who is "innocent," but, on the contrary, as one who has been convicted by due process of law of two brutal murders.

Claims of actual innocence based on newly discovered evidence have never been held to state a ground for federal habeas relief absent an independent constitutional violation occurring in the underlying state criminal proceeding.

This rule is grounded in the principle that federal habeas courts sit to ensure that individuals are not imprisoned in violation of the Constitution—not to correct errors of fact.

More recent authority construing federal habeas statutes speaks in a similar vein. "Federal courts are not forums in which to relitigate state trials." The guilt or innocence determination in state criminal trials is "a decisive and portentous event." "Society's resources have been concentrated at that time and place in order to decide, within the limits of human fallibility, the question of guilt or innocence of one of its citizens." Few rulings would be more disruptive of our federal system than to provide for federal habeas review of freestanding claims of actual innocence.

Petitioner is understandably imprecise in describing the sort of federal relief to which a suitable showing of actual innocence would entitle him. In his brief he states that the federal habeas court should have "an important initial opportunity to hear the evidence and resolve the merits of Petitioner's claim." Acceptance of this view would presumably require the habeas court to hear testimony from the witnesses who testified at trial as well as those who made the statements in the affidavits which petitioner has presented, and to determine anew whether or not petitioner is guilty of the murder.

The dissent would place the burden on petitioner to show that he is "probably" innocent. Although the District Court would not be required to hear testimony from the witnesses who testified at trial or the affiants upon whom petitioner relies, the dissent would allow the District Court to do so "if the petition warrants a hearing." At the end of the day, the dissent would have the District Court "make a case-by-case determination about the reliability of the newly discovered evidence under the circumstances," and then "weigh the evidence in favor of the prisoner against the evidence of his guilt."

The dissent fails to articulate the relief that would be available if petitioner were to meet its "probable innocence" standard. Would it be commutation of petitioner's death sentence, new trial, or unconditional release from imprisonment? The typical relief granted in federal habeas corpus is a conditional order of release unless the State elects to retry the successful habeas petitioner, or in a capital case a similar conditional order vacating the death sentence. Were petitioner to satisfy the dissent's "probable innocence" standard, therefore, the District Court would presumably be required to grant a conditional order of relief, which would in effect require the State to retry petitioner 10 years after his first trial, not because of any constitutional violation which had occurred at the first trial, but simply because of a belief that in light of petitioner's new-found evidence a jury might find him not guilty at a second trial.

Yet there is no guarantee that the guilt or innocence determination would be any more exact. To the contrary, the passage of time only diminishes the reliability of criminal adjudications. Under the dissent's approach, the District Court would be placed in the even more difficult position of having to weigh the probative value of "hot" and "cold" evidence on petitioner's guilt or innocence.

This is not to say that our habeas jurisprudence casts a blind eye toward innocence. In a series of cases, we have held that a petitioner otherwise subject to defenses of abusive or successive use of the writ may have his federal constitutional claim considered on the merits if he makes a proper showing of actual innocence. But this body of our habeas jurisprudence makes clear that a claim of "actual innocence" is not itself a constitutional claim, but instead a gateway through which a habeas petitioner must pass to have his otherwise barred constitutional claim considered on the merits.

Petitioner in this case is simply not entitled to habeas relief based on the reasoning of this line of cases. He does not seek excusal of a procedural error so that he may bring an independent constitutional claim challenging his conviction or sentence, but rather argues that he is entitled to habeas relief because newly discovered evidence shows that his conviction is factually incorrect.

Petitioner asserts that this case is different because he has been sentenced to death. But we have "refused to hold that the fact that a death sentence has been imposed requires a different standard of review on federal habeas corpus." We have, of course, held that the Eighth Amendment requires increased reliability of the process by which capital punishment may be imposed. But petitioner's claim does not fit well into the doctrine of these cases, since, as we have pointed out, it is far from clear that a second trial 10 years after the first trial would produce a more reliable result.

Perhaps mindful of this, petitioner urges not that he necessarily receive a new trial, but that his death sentence simply be vacated if a federal habeas court deems that a satisfactory showing of "actual innocence" has been made. But such a result is scarcely logical; petitioner's claim is not that some error was made in imposing a capital sentence upon him, but that a fundamental error was made in finding him guilty of the underlying murder in the first place. It would be a rather strange jurisprudence, in these circumstances, which held that under our Constitution he could not be executed, but that he could spend the rest of his life in prison.

Petitioner argues that our decision in *Ford v. Wainwright* supports his position. The plurality in *Ford* held that, because the Eighth Amendment prohibits the execution of insane persons, certain procedural protections inhere in the sanity determination.

Unlike petitioner here, Ford did not challenge the validity of his conviction. Rather, he challenged the constitutionality of his death sentence in view of his claim of insanity. Because Ford's claim went to a matter of punishment—not guilt—it was properly examined within the purview of the Eighth Amendment. Moreover, unlike the question of guilt or innocence, which becomes more uncertain with time for evidentiary reasons, the issue of sanity is properly considered in proximity to the execution.

This is not to say, however, that petitioner is left without a forum to raise his actual innocence claim. For under Texas law, petitioner may file a request for executive clemency. Clemency is deeply rooted in our Anglo-American tradition of law, and is the historic remedy for preventing miscarriages of justice where judicial process has been exhausted.

Executive clemency has provided the "fail safe" in our criminal justice system. It is an unalterable fact that our judicial system, like the human beings who administer it, is fallible. But history is replete with examples of wrongfully convicted persons who have been pardoned in the wake of after-discovered evidence establishing their innocence. Recent authority confirms that over the past century clemency has been exercised frequently in capital cases in which demonstrations of "actual innocence" have been made.

In state criminal proceedings the trial is the paramount event for determining the guilt or innocence of the defendant. We may assume, for the sake of argument in deciding this case, that in a capital case a truly persuasive demonstration of "actual innocence" made after trial would render the execution of a defendant unconstitutional, and warrant federal habeas relief if there were no state avenue open to process such a claim. But because of the very disruptive effect that entertaining claims of actual innocence would have on the need for finality in capital cases, and the enormous burden that having to retry cases based on often stale evidence would place on the States, the threshold showing for such an assumed right would necessarily be extraordinarily high. The showing made by petitioner in this case falls far short of any such threshold.

Petitioner's newly discovered evidence consists of affidavits. Petitioner's affidavits are particularly suspect because, with the exception of Raul Herrera, Jr.'s affidavit, they consist of hearsay.

The affidavits were given over eight years after petitioner's trial. No satisfactory explanation has been given as to why the affiants waited until the 11th hour—and, indeed, until after the alleged perpetrator of the murders himself was dead—to make their statements. Equally troubling, no explanation has been offered as to why petitioner, by hypothesis an innocent man, pleaded guilty to the murder of Rucker.

Moreover, the affidavits themselves contain inconsistencies, and therefore fail to provide a convincing account of what took place on the night Officers Rucker and Carrisalez were killed. For instance, the affidavit of Raul, Jr., who was nine years old at the time, indicates that there were three people in the speeding car from which the murderer emerged, whereas Hector Villarreal attested that Raul, Sr., told him that there were two people in the car that night. Of course, Hernandez testified at petitioner's trial that the murderer was the only occupant of the car. The affidavits also conflict as to the direction in which the vehicle was heading when the murders took place and petitioner's whereabouts on the night of the killings.

Finally, the affidavits must be considered in light of the proof of petitioner's guilt at trial—proof which included two eyewitness identifications, numerous pieces of circumstantial evidence, and a handwritten letter in which petitioner apologized for killing the officers and offered to turn himself in under certain conditions. That proof, even when considered alongside petitioner's belated affidavits, points strongly to petitioner's guilt.

This is not to say that petitioner's affidavits are without probative value. Had this sort of testimony been offered at trial, it could have been weighed by the jury, along with the evidence offered by the State and petitioner, in deliberating upon its verdict. Since the statements in the affidavits contradict the evidence received at trial, the jury would have had to decide important issues of credibility. But coming 10 years after petitioner's trial, this showing of innocence falls far short of that which would have to be made in order to trigger the sort of constitutional claim which we have assumed, arguendo, to exist. The judgment of the Court of Appeals is affirmed.

Justice O'Connor, with whom Justice Kennedy joins, concurring.

I cannot disagree with the fundamental legal principle that executing the innocent is inconsistent with the Constitution. Regardless of the verbal formula employed the execution of a legally and factually innocent person would be a constitutionally intolerable event. Dispositive to this case, however, is an equally fundamental fact: Petitioner is not innocent, in any sense of the word.

The issue before us is not whether a State can execute the innocent. It is, as the Court notes, whether a fairly convicted and therefore legally guilty person is constitutionally entitled to yet another judicial proceeding in which to adjudicate his guilt anew, 10 years after conviction, notwithstanding his failure to demonstrate that constitutional error infected his trial.

Resolving the issue is neither necessary nor advisable in this case. The question is a sensitive and, to say the least, troubling one. It implicates not just the life of a single individual, but also the State's powerful and legitimate interest in punishing the guilty, and the nature of state-federal relations.

The proper disposition of this case is neither difficult nor troubling. No matter what the Court might say about claims of actual innocence today, petitioner could not obtain relief. The record overwhelmingly demonstrates that petitioner deliberately shot and killed Officers Rucker and Carrisalez the night of September 29, 1981; petitioner's new evidence is bereft of credibility.

The conclusion seems inescapable: Petitioner is guilty. The dissent does not contend otherwise.

Unless federal proceedings and relief—if they are to be had at all—are reserved for "extraordinarily high" and "truly persuasive demonstrations of 'actual innocence'" that cannot be presented to state authorities the federal courts will be deluged with frivolous claims of actual innocence.

Petitioner has failed to make a persuasive showing of actual innocence. Not one judge—no state court judge, not the District Court Judge, none of the three judges of the Court of Appeals, and none of the Justices of this Court—has expressed doubt about petitioner's guilt. Accordingly, the Court has no reason to pass on, and appropriately reserves, the question whether federal courts may entertain convincing claims of actual innocence. That difficult question remains open. If the Constitution's guarantees of fair procedure and the safeguards of clemency and pardon fulfill their historical mission, it may never require resolution at all.

Justice Scalia, with whom Justice Thomas joins, concurring.

We granted certiorari on the question whether it violates due process or constitutes cruel and unusual punishment for a State to execute a person who, having been convicted of murder after a full and fair trial, later alleges that newly discovered evidence shows him to be "actually innocent." I would have preferred to decide that question, particularly since, as the Court's discussion shows, it is perfectly clear what the answer is: There is no basis in text, tradition, or even in contemporary practice (if that were enough) for finding in the Constitution a right to demand judicial consideration of newly discovered evidence of innocence brought forward after conviction. In saying that such a right exists, the dissenters apply nothing but their personal opinions to invalidate the rules of more than two-thirds of the States, and a Federal Rule of Criminal Procedure for which this Court itself is responsible. If the system that has been in place for 200 years (and remains widely approved) "shocks" the dissenters' consciences perhaps they should doubt the calibration of their consciences, or, better still, the usefulness of "conscience shocking" as a legal test.

I nonetheless join the entirety of the Court's opinion, including the final portion because there is no legal error in deciding a case by assuming, *arguendo*, that an asserted constitutional right exists, and because I can understand, or at least am accustomed to, the reluctance of the present Court to admit publicly that Our Perfect Constitution lets stand any injustice, much less the execution of an innocent man who has received, though to no avail, all the process that our society has traditionally deemed adequate. With any luck, we shall avoid ever having to face this embarrassing question again, since it is improbable that evidence of innocence as convincing as today's opinion requires would fail to produce an executive pardon.

Justice Blackmun, with whom Justice Stevens and Justice Souter join, except as to the last paragraph, dissenting.

Nothing could be more contrary to contemporary standards of decency, or more shocking to the conscience, than to execute a person who is actually innocent.

The Court's enumeration of the constitutional rights of criminal defendants surely is entirely beside the point. These protections sometimes fail. We really are being asked to decide whether the Constitution forbids the execution of a person who has been validly convicted and sentenced but who, nonetheless, can prove his innocence with newly discovered evidence. Despite the State of Texas' astonishing protestation to the contrary, I do not see how the answer can be anything but "yes."

The Eighth Amendment prohibits "cruel and unusual punishments." This proscription is not static but rather reflects evolving standards of decency. I think it is crystal clear that the execution of an innocent person is "at odds with contemporary standards of fairness and decency." Indeed, it is at odds with any standard of decency that I can imagine.

Respondent and the United States as amicus curiae argue that the Eighth Amendment does not apply to petitioner because he is challenging his guilt, not his punishment. The majority attempts to distinguish *Ford* on that basis. Whether petitioner is viewed as challenging simply his death sentence or also his continued detention, he still is challenging the State's right to punish him. Respondent and the United States would impose a clear line between guilt and punishment, reasoning that every claim that concerns guilt necessarily does not involve punishment. Such a division is far too facile. What respondent and the United States fail to recognize is that the legitimacy of punishment is inextricably intertwined with guilt. I believe that petitioner may raise an Eighth Amendment challenge to his punishment on the ground that he is actually innocent.

The possibility of executive clemency is *not* sufficient to satisfy the requirements of the Eighth and Fourteenth Amendments. The majority correctly points out: "A pardon is an act of grace." The vindication of rights guaranteed by the Constitution has never been made to turn on the unreviewable discretion of an executive official or administrative tribunal. Indeed, in *Ford* we explicitly rejected the argument that executive clemency was adequate to vindicate the Eighth Amendment right not to be executed if one is insane. If the exercise of a legal right turns on "an act of grace," then we no longer live under a government of laws.

The question that remains is what showing should be required to obtain relief on the merits of an Eighth or Fourteenth Amendment claim of actual innocence. I agree with the majority that "in state criminal proceedings the trial is the paramount event for determining the guilt or innocence of the defendant." I also think that "a truly persuasive demonstration of 'actual innocence' made after trial would render the execution of a defendant unconstitutional." The question is what "a truly persuasive demonstration" entails, a question the majority's disposition of this case leaves open.

I think the standard for relief on the merits of an actual-innocence claim must be higher than the threshold standard for merely reaching that claim or any other claim that has been procedurally defaulted or is successive or abusive. I would hold that, to obtain relief on a claim of actual innocence, the petitioner must show that he probably is innocent. This standard is supported by several considerations. First, new evidence of innocence may be discovered long after the defendant's conviction. Given the passage of time, it may be difficult for the State to retry a defendant who obtains relief from his conviction or sentence on an actual-innocence claim. The actual-innocence proceeding thus may constitute the final word on whether the defendant may be punished. In light of this fact, an otherwise constitutionally valid conviction or sentence should not be set aside lightly. Second, conviction after a constitutionally adequate trial strips the defendant of the presumption of innocence. The government bears the burden of proving the defendant's guilt beyond a reasonable doubt, but once the government has done so, the burden of proving innocence must shift to the convicted defendant. The actual-innocence inquiry is therefore distinguishable from review for sufficiency of the evidence, where the question is not whether the defendant is innocent but whether the government has met its constitutional burden of proving the defendant's guilt beyond a reasonable doubt. When a defendant seeks to challenge the determination of guilt after he has been validly convicted and sentenced, it is fair to place on him the burden of proving his innocence, not just raising doubt about his guilt.

It should be clear that the standard I would adopt would not convert the federal courts into "forums in which to relitigate state trials." I believe that if a prisoner can show that he is probably actually innocent, in light of all the evidence, then he has made "a truly persuasive demonstration," and his execution would violate the Constitution.

In this case, the District Court determined that petitioner's newly discovered evidence warranted further consideration. Because the District Court doubted its own authority to consider the new evidence, it thought that petitioner's claim of actual innocence should be brought in state court, but it clearly did not think that petitioner's evidence was so insubstantial that it could be dismissed without any hearing at all. I would reverse the order of the Court of Appeals and remand the case to the District Court to consider whether petitioner has shown, in light of all the evidence, that he is probably actually innocent.

I think it is unwise for this Court to step into the shoes of a district court and rule on this petition in the first instance. If this Court wishes to act as a district court, however, it must also be bound by the rules that govern consideration of habeas petitions in district court. A district court may summarily dismiss a habeas petition only if "it plainly appears from the face of the petition and any exhibits annexed to it that the petitioner is not entitled to relief." In one of the affidavits, Hector Villarreal, a licensed attorney and former state court judge, swears under penalty of perjury that his client Raul Herrera, Sr., confessed that he, and not petitioner, committed the murders. No matter what the majority may think of the inconsistencies in the affidavits or the strength of the evidence presented at trial, this affidavit alone is sufficient to raise factual questions concerning petitioner's innocence that cannot be resolved simply by examining the affidavits and the petition.

I have voiced disappointment over this Court's obvious eagerness to do away with any restriction on the States' power to execute whomever and however they please. I have also expressed doubts about whether, in the absence of such restrictions, capital punishment remains constitutional at all. Of one thing, however, I am certain. Just as an execution without adequate safeguards is unacceptable, so too is an execution when the condemned prisoner can prove that he is innocent. The execution of a person who can show that he is innocent comes perilously close to simple murder.

U.S. v. Quinones
205 F. Supp. 2d 256 (2002)

Opinion by District Judge Rakoff

In its Opinion dated April 25, 2002, the Court, upon review of the parties' written submissions and oral arguments, declared its tentative decision to grant defendants' motion to dismiss the death penalty aspects of this case on the ground that the Federal Death Penalty is unconstitutional.

In brief, the Court found that the best available evidence indicates that, on the one hand, innocent people are sentenced to death with materially greater frequency than was previously supposed and that, on the other hand, convincing proof of their innocence often does not emerge until long after their convictions. It is therefore fully foreseeable that in enforcing the death penalty a meaningful number of innocent people will be executed who otherwise would eventually be able to prove their innocence. It follows that implementation of the Federal Death Penalty Act not only deprives innocent people of a significant opportunity to prove their innocence, and thereby violates procedural due process, but also creates an undue risk of executing innocent people, and thereby violates substantive due process.

In its most recent submission, the Government raises several overall objections to this conclusion. First, the Government argues that because, in the Government's view, the Framers of the Constitution, the Congress that enacted the Federal Death Penalty Act, and the Supreme Court that addressed that Act in *Herrera v. Collins* all accepted the constitutionality of administering capital punishment despite the inherent fallibility of the judicial system, even the likelihood that innocent people may mistakenly be executed does not mean that they did not receive the process that was their due or that the statute is inherently flawed. Each component of this argument deserves attention, but each is ultimately unpersuasive.

With respect to the "Framers of the Constitution," the Government argues that, because the Fifth Amendment mandates that no person shall "be deprived of life, liberty, or property without due process of law," therefore "the drafters of the Constitution themselves assumed the existence of capital punishment, doubtless against a backdrop in which they did not expect flawless administration of the penalty." But to "assume the existence" of the death penalty is not the same as endorsing it, and to "not expect flawless administration" is not the same as countenancing the execution of numerous innocent people.

There is, indeed, no indication that the Framers of the Constitution ever considered the issue of the death penalty as a substantive matter; they were simply concerned with extending due process to the full range of existing proceedings. At the time the Constitution was drafted in 1787 the death penalty was a common punishment for a wide variety of personal and property offenses, ranging from murder and rape to fraud and theft. There was no reason to believe that federal actions would be any different. Consequently, in guaranteeing due process of law to all deprivations of life, liberty and property, the drafters of the Constitution were simply applying due process to the full panoply of anticipated actions, rather than endorsing or even commenting on any particular kind of deprivation.

Furthermore, nothing suggests that the Framers regarded due process as a static concept, fixed for all time by the conditions prevailing in 1787. Just as it is settled law that the Eighth Amendment's prohibition of "cruel and unusual punishment" must be interpreted in light of "evolving standards of decency," so too it is settled law that the Fifth Amendment's broad guarantee of "due process" must be interpreted in light of evolving standards of fairness and ordered liberty. To freeze "due process" in the precise form it took in 1787 would be to freeze it to death.

With respect to the Congress that enacted the Federal Death Penalty Act in 1994, the Government argues that it was "a Congress that well understood—and fully debated—whether the FDPA should be given effect despite the risk that innocent individuals might be sentenced to death." The Government's showing in support of these broad claims is, however, wholly inadequate, for the Government cites, not to any of the formal history of the Act, but to a few spare comments on the floor of Congress.

The simple fact is that none of the committee reports that comprise the primary legislative history of the Federal Death Penalty Act contains even a single passage supporting the Government's claim. Indeed, the total absence of the Government's hypothesized "debate" from the formal history of the Act tends, if anything, to confirm the Court's view that members of Congress had no occasion in 1994 to weigh, in Benthamite fashion, a supposed balance of innocent lives saved and innocent lives lost as a result of the imposition of the death penalty. Had they done so, moreover, the debate would have been entirely speculative, for whatever the merits of the studies supporting the deterrent effect of the death penalty, it was not until after 1994 that the most clear and compelling evidence of innocent people being sentenced to death chiefly emerged, i.e., the DNA testing that established conclusively that numerous persons who had been convicted of capital crimes were, beyond any doubt, innocent.

Moreover, even if one were to suppose, contrary to fact, that the Congress that enacted the Federal Death Penalty Act undertook a "death calculus" and somehow weighed (through sheer speculation) the number of innocent lives that would be saved by the presumed added deterrent impact of the death penalty against the number of innocent lives that would be lost by innocent people being mistakenly executed, this would not be dispositive of the issue before this Court. If protection of innocent people from state-sponsored execution is a protected liberty, and if such protected liberty includes the right of an innocent person not to be deprived, by execution, of the opportunity to demonstrate his innocence, then Congress may not override such liberty absent a far more clear and compelling need than any presented here.

Which brings us to the Supreme Court's 1993 decision in *Herrera v. Collins*. The Government proclaims that *Herrera* is "fatal to defendants' motion." These contentions are, however, entirely unsupportable.

Herrera does not address the issue presented in the instant case. The *Herrera* Court's sole holding is that a belated or successive habeas petitioner must make a persuasive showing of actual innocence to warrant habeas relief. Thus, the Government's argument here that *Herrera* "forecloses" defendants' instant claim because they have not made a showing of "actual innocence" seriously misreads

Herrera. It is only in the context of a belated or successive habeas petition that the Court in *Herrera*, in furtherance of finality and of minimizing the substantial difficulties of a belated re-trial, requires such a threshold showing. By contrast, in the pre-trial posture of the instant motion, where no such concerns are present and where both defendants are presumed innocent, no special threshold showing is required, and the Government's attempt to invent one is wholly without support.

While the Government correctly notes that both the majority and dissenting opinions in *Herrera* briefly discuss the implications for the death penalty of the inherent fallibility of any system of justice, that discussion is not informed by the ground-breaking DNA testing and other exonerative evidence developed in the years since. Rather, the essential premise of the discussion, as well captured in Justice O'Connor's crucial concurring opinion, is that "our society has a high degree of confidence in its criminal trials, in no small part because the Constitution offers unparalleled protections against convicting the innocent." In light of the subsequently-developed evidence, that "high degree of confidence" is no longer tenable, and the whole discussion has been placed on a new footing.

In sum, the Court remains unpersuaded that anything in *Herrera*, the legislative history of the Federal Death Penalty Act, or the Due Process clause itself precludes the decision here reached. If anything, the combined view of five justices in *Herrera* that execution of the innocent is constitutionally impermissible supports the instant decision.

Finally, the Government argues that the evidence on which the Court premises its legal conclusions is either unreliable, irrelevant, or both. Again, each component of this argument, upon scrutiny, proves unconvincing.

Regarding the DNA testing that has exonerated at least 12 death row inmates since 1993, the Government argues that, since such testing is now available prior to trial in many cases, its effect, going forward, will actually be to reduce the risk of mistaken convictions. This completely misses the point. What DNA testing has proved, beyond cavil, is the remarkable degree of fallibility in the basic fact-finding processes on which we rely in criminal cases. In each of the 12 cases of DNA-exoneration of death row inmates, the defendant had been found guilty by a unanimous jury that concluded there was proof of his guilt beyond a reasonable doubt; and in each of the 12 cases the conviction had been affirmed on appeal, and collateral challenges rejected, by numerous courts that had carefully scrutinized the evidence and the manner of conviction. Yet, for all this alleged "due process," the result, in each and every one of these cases, was the conviction of an innocent person who, because of the death penalty, would shortly have been executed (some came within days of being so) were it not for the fortuitous development of a new scientific technique that happened to be applicable to their particular cases.

DNA testing may help prevent some such near-tragedies in the future; but it can only be used in that minority of cases involving recoverable, and relevant, DNA samples. Other scientific techniques may also emerge in the future that will likewise expose past mistakes and help prevent future ones, and in still other cases, such as those referenced below, exoneration may be the result of less scientific and more case-specific developments, such as witness recantations or discovery of new evidence. But there is no way to know whether such exoneration will come prior to (or during) trial or, conversely, long after conviction. What is certain is that, for the foreseeable future, traditional trial methods and appellate review will not prevent the conviction of numerous innocent people.

Where proof of innocence is developed long after both the trial and the direct appeal are concluded, it is entirely appropriate that the defendant make a truly persuasive showing of innocence, as *Herrera* requires, before his case can be reopened. But given what DNA testing has exposed about the unreliability of the primary techniques developed by our system for the ascertainment of guilt, it is quite something else to arbitrarily eliminate, through execution, any possibility of exoneration after a certain point in time. The result can only be the fully foreseeable execution of numerous innocent persons.

The Government does not deny that an increasing number of death row defendants have been released from prison in recent years for reasons other than DNA testing. Nor does the Government, despite its quibbles with the Death Penalty Information Center (DPIC) website, directly contest the Court's conservative conclusion that at least 20 of these non-DNA exonerations likely involved the capital convictions of innocent persons. Instead, the Government argues that both the DNA and non-DNA exonerations are irrelevant to consideration of the Federal Death Penalty Act because the exonerated defendants were all state convicts, rather than federal. This, moreover, is no accident, argues the Government, but is rather the result of the allegedly greater protections that federal procedure generally, and the Federal Death Penalty Act in particular, afford defendants.

Upon analysis, however, the Government's distinction proves ephemeral, for several reasons. To begin with, while it is true that none of the 31 persons so far sentenced to death under the Federal Death Penalty Act has been subsequently exonerated (though five of the sentences have already been reversed), the sample is too small, and the convictions too recent, to draw any conclusions therefrom.

If anything, certain federal practices present a greater risk of wrongful capital convictions than parallel state practices. For example, federal practice, in contrast to that of many states that allow the death penalty, permits conviction on the uncorroborated testimony of an accomplice. Similarly, federal practice treats circumstantial evidence identically to direct evidence and permits conviction based solely on such evidence, whereas many states that allow the death penalty permit a conviction based solely on circumstantial evidence only if such evidence excludes to a moral certainty every other reasonable inference except guilt.

Even more fundamentally, it appears reasonably well established that the single most common cause of mistaken convictions is inaccurate eyewitness testimony. Accordingly, there is no good reason to believe the federal system will be any more successful at avoiding mistaken impositions of the death penalty than the error prone state systems already exposed.

The Court also supported its overall conclusions by reference to the unusually high rate of legal error (68%) detected in appeals (both state and federal) from death penalty convictions, as shown by the comprehensive study of those appeals released in 2000 by Professor James Liebman and his colleagues. While legal error is not a direct measure of factual error, Liebman's study was concerned with errors that the appellate courts had determined were not harmless and that therefore could be outcome-determinative. That such errors could infect nearly 7 out of every 10 capital cases strongly suggests that, at a minimum, the trial process appears to operate with less reliability in the context of capital cases than elsewhere.

In response, the Government launches an extended and remarkably personal attack on Liebman and his study, even arguing that the study is suspect because Liebman is, allegedly, an avowed opponent of the death penalty. As convincingly shown, however, in the Brief Amicus Curiae Of 42 Social Scientists filed in response, the Liebman study, commissioned at the behest of the Chairman of the U.S. Senate Judiciary Committee is by far the most careful and comprehensive study in this area, and one based, moreover, exclusively on public records and court decisions.

When it comes to something as fundamental as protecting the innocent, press releases and ad hominem attacks are no substitute for reasoned discourse, and the fatuity of the Government's attacks on Liebman's study only serves to highlight the poverty of the Government's position. At the same time, no judge has a monopoly on reason, and the Court fully expects its analysis to be critically scrutinized. Still, to this Court, the unacceptably high rate at which innocent persons are convicted of capital crimes, when coupled with the frequently prolonged delays before such errors are detected (and then often only fortuitously or by application of newly-developed techniques), compels the conclusion that execution under the Federal Death Penalty Act, by cutting off the opportunity for exoneration, denies due process and, indeed, is tantamount to foreseeable, state-sponsored murder of innocent human beings.

Accordingly, the Court grants defendant's motion to strike all death penalty aspects from this case, on the ground that the Federal Death Penalty Act is unconstitutional.

◼ Habeas Corpus and the Role of Innocence— Perspectives

◼ Issue—What Is the Legal Significance of Innocence?

Joseph Hoffmann, "Is Innocence Sufficient? An Essay on the U.S. Supreme Court's Continuing Problems with Federal Habeas Corpus and the Death Penalty"

Ever since the Court made the fundamental (and, I believe, misguided) jurisprudential choice to treat the Eighth Amendment as a "super due process clause," rather than as an invitation for the federal courts to review the merits of individual state-imposed death sentences, the Court has struggled to resolve the tension between a narrow focus on death penalty procedures and the (substantive) view that federal judges have a responsibility to prevent state-imposed death sentences from being carried out when such sentences are undeserved.

This struggle has taken place in two separate arenas—the law of the death penalty under the Eighth Amendment and the law of federal habeas corpus. In the Eighth Amendment arena, the Court's process orientation has triggered a doctrinal explosion, as the Court searches for perfect death penalty procedures that can guarantee a perfect result. In the habeas arena, the Court, motivated in large part by the growth of Eighth Amendment law, has restricted the availability of habeas relief in all cases, whether capital or noncapital, on a variety of procedural grounds. These procedural habeas restrictions, however, often can be avoided if a petitioner can present a colorable claim of actual innocence.

Thus, by a bizarre and convoluted path, the Court has reached the conclusion that the substantive merits of a death-row inmate's case are relevant to the disposition of his habeas petition. But the relevance is indirect and limited—actual innocence is sometimes a necessary, but (at least presently) never a sufficient, condition for a grant of habeas relief.

Twenty years after the Court's landmark decision in *Furman*, the Court is not much closer than it ever was to resolving the tension between procedure and substance in its death penalty jurisprudence under the Eighth Amendment. Nor is it clear that the Court will ever succeed in its quest for a satisfactory approach to the federal review of state death penalty cases. The root of the problem lies in the simple fact that the Justices are both lawyers and human beings.

Why does the allegedly conservative, pro-federalism, and anti-criminal-defendant Court continue frequently to grant review in, and often to reverse, state death penalty cases? Why does Eighth Amendment law continue to grow more and more complicated, despite the impassioned pleas from Justice Scalia to simplify and reduce these federal procedural restrictions on the states?

The answer, of course, is that the Justices are only human. This is important for two reasons. First, as human beings, the Justices know that they and their fellow human beings are imperfect—human decision makers will inevitably make mistakes. Second, as human beings, the Justices (or at least most of them) care more about reaching the right result in a death penalty case than they do in almost any other kind of case that comes before them. Perhaps the most important task any judge can ever perform is to ensure that the government not kill a person unless that person truly deserves to die. Since the Court is effectively the last decision maker in most capital cases, and since the Court's decision to allow an execution to proceed is irrevocable, the Justices (or at least most of them) feel a special responsibility for the outcome. In the words of Justice Stewart's plurality opinion in *Woodson*, death is "different"—if for no other reason than precisely because most members of the Court, and most of the rest of us as well, believe it is so.

Because they are only human, the Justices, along with most of the judges in the lower federal courts, pay much closer attention to the outcomes in capital cases than they do in other criminal cases. The experience of twenty years since *Furman* suggests that, like moths to a flame, federal judges cannot avoid getting involved in state capital cases—these cases consistently receive far closer federal scrutiny than noncapital criminal cases, even in a relatively conservative era and almost regardless of the particular federal judge's ideological or jurisprudential views. And whenever a judge finds a capital case in which he or she believes an injustice is about to be done, the judge is naturally inclined to do whatever is in his or her judicial power (and maybe even a few things that arguably are not) to rectify the perceived injustice.

The simplest and most direct way for a federal judge to reverse the outcome of a state capital case with which the judge disagrees would be to rule that the death penalty is unconstitutional as applied to the individual death-row inmate. But the Court, in a series of death penalty cases dating back to 1976, has declined to lead the lower federal courts down the path of case-by-case substantive review of state capital cases under the Eighth Amendment.

Rather, the Court has done what most lawyers tend to do—it has tried to find procedural solutions for a substantive problem. One of the basic traits of most lawyers is an extremely strong belief in the value of procedures. Lawyers and judges tend to believe (or at least tend to pretend to believe) that, at least in theory, if a procedure can be improved enough, then the results produced by that procedure will necessarily be right.

There are two major difficulties with an essentially process-oriented solution to a substantive problem, such as the problem of bad outcomes in death penalty cases. First, and most obviously, even perfect procedures cannot guarantee perfect results—which means that procedural law may wind up being pushed beyond its proper limits. If a federal judge, for instance, is disturbed by what he or she perceives to be the wrong result in a capital case, and if the only way to reverse the decision is to find a federal procedural error, then the judge will be under severe, maybe insurmountable, pressure to find (or perhaps manufacture?) such an error—even if, in the abstract, the procedures used in the state courts were well within the range of reasonable fairness. In other words, a process-oriented solution for a substantive problem can, if the matter is important enough to compel judicial action, provoke an otherwise unwarranted expansion of procedural law.

Second, given the first difficulty, the procedural law is likely eventually to expand to the point where it substantially over-regulates. The primary problem is that, every time a federal court announces a new procedural rule for the purpose of overturning a state death sentence with which the judge does not agree, the rule does not disappear after the particular case is over—rather, it becomes federal law that must be applied by other courts to other cases. As the federal law becomes increasingly more complex, procedural errors may be found in many cases even though all courts would agree that the results of those cases were correct. In the death penalty context, habeas courts often deal with cases in which the federal procedural rules were violated, but in which the result of the proceeding was nevertheless correct, and in which reversal would thus impinge on the values of federalism and comity without producing a corresponding improvement in the basic justice of the outcome. In such cases, habeas courts face severe pressure to devise and apply curative methods (such as "harmless error" doctrines) to preserve the correct result even in the face of a recognized violation of federal procedural law.

Herrera v. Collins strongly suggests that the Court is not yet prepared to hop off the endless merry-go-round that it boarded when it first chose to interpret the Eighth Amendment in death penalty cases primarily in procedural, rather than substantive, terms.

Unfortunately (for both the defendant and, in my view, the jurisprudence of the Eighth Amendment), the Court in *Herrera* never reached the question whether the Eighth Amendment prohibits the execution of a defendant who makes an adequate showing, based on newly discovered evidence, of "actual innocence." The Court did not reach this question because six of the Justices concluded that, no matter what standard might be used to define such an "adequate showing," the defendant in *Herrera* could not possibly meet the standard. Chief Justice Rehnquist identified some of the practical and legal/doctrinal problems that would follow the adoption of an "actual innocence" Eighth Amendment rule. Nevertheless, he proceeded to dispose of the case based on the "assumption, for the sake of argument," that "a truly persuasive demonstration of 'actual innocence' made after trial would render the execution of a defendant unconstitutional."

If the Court had reached the constitutional issue in *Herrera*, it might have used the case to begin the process of "substantifying" its Eighth Amendment jurisprudence. Indeed, a reading of the "tea leaves" in *Herrera* suggests that, if the issue were properly raised, a majority of the Court would interpret the Constitution to require at least a limited federal (substantive) review of a defendant's claim of innocence. The three dissenters would require such a review whenever a defendant could show that he is "probably actually innocent."

The problem is that, given the disposition of *Herrera*, the Court is highly unlikely to reach the Eighth Amendment issue anytime soon. Justice O'Connor, in particular, frankly admitted her Pollyannaish hope that the Court might be able forever to duck the question.

Resolving the issue is neither necessary nor advisable in this case. The question is a sensitive and, to say the least, troubling one. The Court has no reason to pass on, and appropriately reserves, the question whether federal courts may entertain convincing claims of actual innocence. That difficult question remains open. If the Constitution's guarantees of fair procedure and the safeguards of clemency and pardon fulfill their historical mission, it may never require resolution at all.

Unfortunately, it should be obvious to anyone (except maybe Justice O'Connor) that, no matter how good the applicable procedures, any system that relies on human beings to make decisions will eventually make a mistake. This being so, the only remaining argument against recognizing a (limited) right to federal substantive review seems to be the *Herrera* majority's claim that, "Few rulings would be more disruptive of our federal system than to provide for federal habeas review of free-standing claims of actual innocence." The Court's federalism concerns are valid, but its conclusion could not be more wrong. In truth, nothing could be more disruptive of our federal system than the present world of federal habeas litigation in capital cases—a bizarre world in which state-court judgments are stayed for years, even decades, while defendants argue procedural Eighth Amendment issues unrelated to the factual correctness of their convictions and sentences, and states' attorneys respond by raising technical habeas defenses similarly unrelated to the merits of the case.

This bizarre world of federal habeas litigation is the natural by-product of the Court's procedural Eighth Amendment orientation. It is time for the Court to recognize the fundamental interdependence of death penalty and habeas law, and bring an end to the ascending spiral of technicality and complexity that currently characterizes both bodies of law. It is time for the Court to put some "substance" back into the Eighth Amendment.

Barry Latzer, "Reflections on Innocence"

I. *Defining Innocence*

It is abidingly strange that "innocence" should be problematic in a system the principal purpose of which is to differentiate the innocent from the guilty. I take "innocence" to mean that the individual did not in fact commit the crime of which he was accused. We immediately face an ambiguity with this definition, however, because one can be innocent of a particular offense, say murder in the first degree, and still be a guilty murderer, e.g., guilty of murder in the second degree. To be precise, one should differentiate between the actor who is innocent of a particular offense, and the actor who did not commit that offense or any other closely allied crime.

The problems with the concept of innocence run much deeper than this, as an epistemological issue also presents itself. It is impossible in some cases for society or the criminal justice system to know with complete certainty whether someone is innocent. Even the actor himself—due perhaps to perception, memory or mental problems—may not know. Consider the troubling cases in which defendants voluntarily confess and are convicted, only to have overhelmingly exculpatory evidence surface later. At the time they confess, these subjects believe that they are guilty, even though it isn't true. More common are the self-deluded souls who honestly believe themselves to be innocent when they are not. The prisons seem to be crowded with such people. It is clear that the apparent earnestness of the actor is an unreliable guide to the truth, and this may be so even where the assertions are against self-interest.

Even if the actor's self-knowledge is accurate, however, society's judgment may rest on an uncertain foundation. Sometimes, the most we can say is that the probabilities are such (here we indulge in descriptive adjectives such as "overwhelming") that the defendant did not do it. The same is true about guilt. It too may be ultimately indeterminate. In some cases we can say only that the probabilities point to it.

II. *The Morality of Punishment*

This fallibility of judgment may lead us to question the morality of punishment, especially harsh punishment like life in prison or the death penalty. If society cannot be absolutely certain of the guilt of the accused, is it not unfair to imprison him for life or even execute him? To answer this, one must weigh the risk of punishing the innocent against the risks to society of refraining from punishing. Setting aside the death penalty momentarily, this is not a difficult question, especially if society provides elaborate procedural protections against convicting the innocent. All the reasons commonly offered to justify punishments—retribution for the blameworthy, deterrence of future offenders, protection of society, perhaps even reform of the defendant—would be put at risk if society simply freed those found guilty. And to what end? To avoid punishing persons for whom the evidence of guilt far outweighs the evidence of innocence. This hardly seems fair to society. Obviously, no real-world criminal justice system could long function under such a regime.

Given the procedural protections against convicting innocents and the overwhelming social interest in punishing the guilty, the punishment system—despite its risk to innocents—is morally justified. The indeterminacy of innocence should perhaps make us humble, but it should not lead to paralysis. Consequently, we will inevitably hurt a few innocents (who appeared guilty) in order to avoid even greater harms.

I think this same argument applies when the punishment is death. It is morally acceptable for society to take the life of someone found guilty of a terrible crime notwithstanding the risk that he is factually innocent. This is based on the same cost/benefit analysis presented above with respect to punishments generally.

There are four differences in the capital punishment situation, but it is debatable whether they make any difference to the outcome. First, the cost to the defendant is much greater when death is the sanction because of the terrible nature of the punishment. Second, the cost to society should the punishment be withheld also is greater, given the enormity of the crime. That is, the injustice of sparing the life of someone who has committed a heinous crime is heightened by the magnitude of the offender's desert. Third, the procedural protections against convicting the innocent (sometimes dubbed "super due process") are greater in death penalty cases. And fourth, unlike all other sanctions (except life in prison without parole), with the death penalty, rehabilitation is obviously not one of the sought after benefits.

To me, these differences have no bearing on the conclusion: the risk of injustice with its concomitant loss of deterrence outweighs the risk that the death row inmate may be innocent, especially given the elaborate protections we have established in order to reduce the risk of erroneous death sentences. Many disagree with this, primarily because they place so much weight on the enormity of the capital sanction. This is no place to debate the significance of death. Suffice it that neither philosophy nor religion can agree that this life is so superior to what follows that its termination must be the worst event, and therefore, beyond measure the cruelest punishment that could ever be imposed on a human being.

Recently, a federal judge, in the *Quinones* case, challenged the conclusion that the risk to innocents is acceptable. He based his position primarily on the recent revelations (due in some cases to DNA evidence) that a number of death row inmates were, despite all the procedural protections, innocent. He concluded that the risk of executing innocents is much greater than heretofore revealed, and, indeed, much greater than the Constitution can tolerate. I disagree with this conclusion, but because the judge's viewpoint raises such intriguing issues, it deserves careful analysis, which I offer in the concluding sections of this essay.

III. *Signifying Innocence*

In addition to its definitional and epistemological difficulties there is yet another problem with the concept of innocence, what might be called a signification problem. There is, in the criminal justice process, no proceeding which eventuates in a judgment of innocence, although there are three events that may signify *probable* innocence. The trial can determine only non-innocence (probable guilt) or non-guilt. Non-guilt is not synonymous with innocence or even probable innocence. It is ambiguous, connoting either deficiencies in the prosecution's case, factual innocence or both. Deficiencies in the prosecution's case—failures of proof—are perfectly consistent with factual guilt. If the glove don't fit, perhaps the jury must indeed acquit—but that doesn't mean that O.J. did not in fact kill two people.

IV. *The Rights of Innocents*

Six of the Supreme Court justices to express a view on this issue in *Herrera* seem to have asserted that the execution of an innocent is unconstitutional, or, in Justice O'Connor's words, "the execution of a legally and factually innocent person would be a constitutionally intolerable event." It is significant that O'Connor demands both legal *and* factual innocence. How would we identify "legal innocence?" There is no proceeding that has the function of establishing legal innocence. Absent such a proceeding, it is difficult to know what is meant by this expression.

I would suggest that the most plausible reading of Justice O'Connor's comment is that there is a constitutional right not to be executed applicable only to someone who has had his or her judgment of guilt overturned because of a claim of factual innocence. Only a proceeding with the authority to reverse the trial verdict because of proof of innocence can establish the predicate for an unconstitutional execution. This seems to me to be the closest we can come to establishing "legal innocence."

Such a definition creates an anomaly, however. No one who has had his guilty verdict reversed could thenceforth receive punishment for the crime involved. Thus, no one found legally innocent could or would be executed. Consequently, the constitutional right not to be executed has, in this situation, no value; it protects nothing. Justice O'Connor evidently arrived at the same conclusion, because she added to her *Herrera* opinion, apparently on second thought, that "the issue before us is not whether a State can execute the innocent. It is whether a fairly convicted and therefore legally guilty person is constitutionally entitled to yet another judicial proceeding in which to adjudicate his guilt anew." In other words, the real issue is whether there is a right to a proceeding to determine innocence.

Even the *Herrera* dissenters, who were much more vehement about the rights of innocents, offered this peculiar wording: "We really are being asked to decide whether the Constitution forbids the execution of a person who has been validly convicted and sentenced but who, nonetheless, can prove his innocence with newly discovered evidence." But what does it mean to say that the defendant *can* prove his innocence? That he *surely* would if given the opportunity (a hearing)? Given the need to carefully reevaluate all the material facts of a case in order to draw such a conclusion, a defendant's innocence (especially one already tried and found guilty) hardly seems knowable in advance of careful review. At best, it would seem to be an open question, one which can be answered only *after* an appropriate hearing.

But were our death row inmate granted a hearing, and were he to prove his innocence at such a proceeding, he would not be executed and the Constitution would not be violated. And if he could *not* prove his innocence at such a hearing then he would be subject to execution without violating the Constitution. One is forced to the conclusion that there is no constitutional right against the execution of a person who "can prove his innocence," because such a right has no meaning. Either it protects those who are not entitled to protection (they have not proven their innocence) or it protects those who have no need for protection (they have proven their innocence).

Thus, even for the *Herrera* dissenters, the only intelligible constitutional question is whether there is a procedural right to an innocence review hearing. If this analysis is correct, then *Herrera* does not establish the right of an innocent to not be punished. Notwithstanding the *moral* claim—I concede that the principle of retribution bars punishment of innocents—there is no *constitutional* right of nonpunishment. What *Herrera* establishes, and quite tentatively at that, is the right, a very qualified right, to a hearing at which the self-proclaimed innocent defendant (probably limited to capital defendants) may offer evidence of his innocence.

V. *Quinones*

One may fairly state the *Quinones* question thus: Does a statute which creates an undue risk of executing innocent people violate due process? To be more specific, is there a liberty interest in not having one's life terminated by the State through application of a death penalty law on the grounds that there is too great a risk that the penalty will be imposed upon innocent people? The answer, it seems to me, must be "no," for three reasons.

1. There is no traditional right not to be executed on grounds of risk to innocents. Capital punishment is "deeply rooted in this Nation's history and tradition." Anyone reading Professor Banner's excellent history of the death penalty in the United States can draw no other conclusion.

Capital punishment laws have always carried a risk of death to innocents, and no doubt always will. Furthermore, as Banner makes clear, Americans have long been aware of this risk. Yet there has never been a right to object to a death penalty law on this ground. Such a right is not only not "deeply rooted," it was, until *Quinones*, unheard of.

Moreover, the *Quinones* court made no claim that some characteristic of the federal statute it voided posed greater risks to innocents than other death penalty laws. Rather, the court rested its arguments on recent revelations that several death row inmates were apparently innocent, especially revelations predicated on DNA evidence.

According to the court, in other words, we now know more certainly than ever before that innocents are wrongfully convicted and may be put to death. This does not mean, of course, that the risks have become greater, or that the federal law is riskier than other death penalty statutes, and it certainly does not mean that the contemporary death penalty poses more danger to innocents than laws of the past. It means simply that because of DNA we are now more likely to learn about our mistakes.

2. The risk to innocents cannot accurately be determined. Deciding how much probable risk is acceptable is subjective and arbitrary. *Quinones* assumes that the risk to innocents is knowable. Is it? Limiting the question to the death penalty, to determine if the risk to innocents is unacceptable, we would first have to know whether each of our capital convictions was and is valid. Assuming this is ascertainable, we would then need to know what proportion of invalid convictions is constitutionally tolerable. In truth, these questions cannot be answered with any degree of certainty.

It is sometimes impossible for society or the criminal justice system to know with complete certainty whether someone is innocent. The best we can hope to determine is probable innocence. DNA marks a wonderful advance in this regard, but it is not a panacea. In the vast majority of cases it does not tell us who is innocent. In most cases there is no DNA evidence available. Where it is available, it may not conclusively exculpate. It may prove the presence of an innocent person at the scene of a crime, or fail to prove the presence of someone who is guilty. DNA isn't the truth machine popularized by science fiction. Extraordinarily useful though it is, it cannot begin to carry humans across the epistemological barrier to godlike certainty of human culpability.

Let us nevertheless assume that probable innocence will suffice and that through DNA and scrupulous investigation we know with sufficient certainty that a certain number of capital convictions are erroneous. What proportion of error is sufficient to constitute "an undue risk of executing innocent people?"

Judge Rakoff asserts that since the *Herrera* decision in 1993, 32 death row inmates were "exonerated," 12 of them by DNA evidence. To calculate the risk of innocence, I would think that one would need to begin with the number of death sentences imposed, not since 1993, when the 32 guilty verdicts were reversed, but since the year of sentence of the inmate presently on death row the longest. I say this because the pool of alleged innocents is most likely to be drawn from inmates sentenced to death from that date forward. According to Justice Department figures, two inmates sentenced to death in 1974 were still on death row at the end of 2000, at which point (i.e., from 1974 to 2000), 6,888 capital sentences had been imposed. Consequently, the risk of innocence may be said to be $32/6,888 = .0046$, which rounds to one-half of one percent or 1/200.

However, this is the risk that those who are *sentenced* to death are innocent, which is not the same as the risk of *executing* an innocent. Fewer than ten percent of those given death sentences from 1974 to 2000 have been executed and there is little persuasive evidence that any of these individuals were innocent. Consequently, the safest conclusion is that the risk that an innocent was (or will be) executed is unknown.

Therefore, no one can say whether the risk, whatever it is, is an "undue" one. To some, the risk of *any* unjustified execution is too great. The American public, by contrast, thinks the risks are worth taking.

3. The contemporary death penalty is narrowly tailored to serve compelling governmental interests. Let us assume that there is a judicially determinable liberty interest against wrongful execution. According to the Supreme Court's formula for substantive due process there remains an additional step in the analysis. In the words of the Supreme Court, "the Fourteenth Amendment forbids the government to infringe fundamental liberty interests unless the infringement is narrowly tailored to serve a compelling state interest."

The State has a very compelling interest, namely, the interest in administering justice, which it believes served by the death penalty. Is the death penalty narrowly enough tailored to accomplish this end? Since 1976, the Supreme Court has demanded that the penalty be applied to narrower and narrower categories of defendants, so that today, for all intents and purposes, only those who commit first degree murder with aggravating circumstances (and not even all of those murderers), are eligible. Add the many procedural requirements exclusive to capital cases and I doubt one can think of a punishment (or, for that matter *any* governmental policy) more narrowly tailored and still available as an option.

VI. *Conclusion*

I am skeptical that the Federal Death Penalty Act or state death penalty laws, because they cut off opportunities for exculpation, violate due process. All death penalties terminate these opportunities. Society assumed the risk when it approved the penalty of death that its search for truth might occasionally be inadequate. This is one of the principal reasons for the adoption of super due process for capital cases. While DNA revelations remind us that no process can be perfect, the Constitution does not require perfection. More generally, innocents will always be at risk of erroneous punishment; this does not make punishment unconstitutional or immoral.

Issues of Application

III

Issues of Application—Introduction

The book concludes by considering some issues surrounding the application of the death penalty in America, including whether executions should be televised and whether it is desirable to speed up the appellate process, if it were possible to do so.

These discussions are harder to have horizontally than some of the others in the book. For example, one's position on appellate delay might be dictated by beliefs about the risk of executing the innocent. If one were confident that no innocent people were at risk of being executed, delay might seem undesirable as it undermines the deterrent effect of the law. If one believed innocent people are at risk, delay might provide a useful opportunity to correct errors. The answer to the question of whether appeals should be curtailed depends on what steps the state takes to protect against the execution of the innocent. If capital punishment were restricted to the certainly guilty, delay would certainly be undesirable. In the piece which concludes the book, Judge Alex Kozinski and Sean Gallagher argue that in many ways the current system is the worst of all possible worlds: death sentences are unreliable and, when imposed, so long after the fact of the crime that they have no deterrent value whatsoever. Kozinski and Gallagher argue for a death penalty restricted to the most egregious cases where guilt is certain and where punishment is imposed swiftly.

Chapter 21 considers the data on appellate delay and whether the delay itself is cruel and unusual punishment. Chapter 22 considers the history of public executions and whether executions should be placed on television. Chapter 23 considers the question of clemency in general and the extraordinary decision by Governor George Ryan to commute the death sentences of the entire Illinois death row. Chapter 24 considers the future of the moratorium movement in the United States in light of the attention DNA evidence has brought to some miscarriages of justice. Chapter 25 considers some possible explanations for the United States' peculiar position in the world, as the only Western democracy retaining capital punishment. The book concludes with two extraordinary views on the future of the death penalty: Justice Kozinski's piece, and Justice Harry

Blackmun's concurrence in *Callins v. Collins*, in which he completes a two-decade evolution in his view on capital punishment. A dissenter in *Furman*, Justice Blackmun says famously in *Callins* that he "shall no longer tinker with the machinery of death."

Appellate Delay

21

■ Appellate Delay—Introduction

On average, a defendant who is ultimately executed spends more than ten years on death row. In 2000, 66 prisoners were executed in the United States. They spent an average of 11 years and 10 months under sentence of death. The data on time under sentence of death and execution, presented below in **Table 21-1**, show some consistent trends. Time between sentence and execution has been increasing steadily since *Gregg*. Between 1977 and 1983 executed prisoners had spent an average of only 51 months on death row. That number has more than doubled. The data persistently show that blacks spend more time under sentence of death than whites. The average black executed between 1977 and 2001 spent 130 months in jail, as compared to 118 months for the average white.

The average prisoner on death row at year-end of 2001 had been under sentence of death for 89 months. In some instances, the delay is extraordinary. Two of the 149 defendants sentenced to death in 1974 remained on death row as of December 31, 2001. More than 30 inmates have been on death row for longer than 25 years. The Bureau of Justice Statistics profile of death row is set out in **Table 21-2** in the Critical Documents section.

Over the past decade, death penalty proponents have made successful efforts at both the state and federal level to streamline the capital appeals process and expedite executions. The most significant of these efforts is the Antiterrorism and Effective Death Penalty Act of 1996 (AEDPA). Capital punishment proponents argued that death row inmates abused the writ of habeas corpus by filing multiple, repetitive petitions. Congress passed AEDPA to restrict the availability of federal habeas relief in several significant manners:

1. *Statute of limitations*: AEDPA established a one-year statute of limitations for the filing of habeas corpus petitions. The statute of limitations runs from the date when the judgment of conviction becomes final, which is the time of completion of direct appellate review, and is tolled while state postconviction proceedings are pending. There had previously been no time limit on when a prisoner could file for habeas relief.

2. *Restrictions on successive petitions*: AEDPA severely restricts the possibility of successive petitions. Previously a prisoner might choose to withhold some claims from a petition for a future petition. Under AEDPA, a new claim may only be

brought if it is based upon a new rule of law made retroactive to cases on collateral review or it is based upon evidence that was not previously available.

3. *Exhaustion of state remedies requirement*: AEDPA precludes a defendant from seeking relief on the basis of a claim that was not fully litigated in the state courts. Pre-AEDPA *habeas* law also required exhaustion of state remedies, but under AEDPA a federal court may dismiss a defendant's unexhausted claim on the merits rather than on a procedural basis.

4. *Presumption in favor of state court findings*: If a state court fairly judged the merits of a prisoner's federal claim, the state court's decision will not be set aside under AEDPA unless the claim was contrary to or involved an unreasonable application of clearly established case law. Prisoners are generally not entitled to fact hearing on their federal claims unless they failed to develop those facts at the state level and they can show cause for the failure and innocence.

No study has yet examined the effect of AEDPA on expedited executions. Table 21-1 does suggest that the rate of growth of capital delays has slowed. Whether this is attributable to AEDPA is another question. Whether it is desirable or not is another matter still.

In the Perspectives section of this chapter, Dwight Aarons argues that the so-called "death row phenomenon" constitutes cruel and unusual punishment. Professor Aarons applies the traditional *Coker* test to assess contemporary standards of decency and finds that while legislatures and juries have not expressed a clear view on delay, it is clear that the death row phenomenon fails to serve any legitimate penological purpose and is disfavored by the international community. Franklin Zimring warns against the rising sentiment to streamline the appellate process. Professor Zimring argues that shortening the capital appeals process would undermine the "habits of legality" that are essential to a just punishment system.

■ Appellate Delay—Critical Documents

Table 21-1	Time Under Sentence of Death and Execution, by Race, 1977–2001					
Year of execution	Number executed			Average elapsed time from sentence to execution for		
	All races[a]	White[b]	Black[b]	All races[a]	White[b]	Black[b]
Total	749	471	265	123 mo	118 mo	130 mo
1977–83	11	9	2	51 mo	49 mo	58 mo
1984	21	13	8	74	76	71
1985	18	11	7	71	65	80
1986	18	11	7	87	78	102
1987	25	13	12	86	78	96
1988	11	6	5	80	72	89

Table 21-1	Time Under Sentence of Death and Execution, by Race, 1977–2001, continued

Year of execution	Number executed			Average elapsed time from sentence to execution for		
	All races[a]	White[b]	Black[b]	All races[a]	White[b]	Black[b]
1989	16	8	8	95	78	112
1990	23	16	7	95	97	91
1991	14	7	7	116	124	107
1992	31	19	11	114	104	135
1993	38	23	14	113	112	121
1994	31	20	11	122	117	132
1995	56	33	22	134	128	144
1996	45	31	14	125	112	153
1997	74	45	27	133	126	147
1998	68	48	18	130	128	132
1999	98	61	33	143	143	141
2000	85	49	35	137	134	142
2001	66	48	17	142	134	166

Note: Average time was calculated from the most recent sentencing date.
[a]Includes American Indians and Asians.
[b]Includes Hispanics.

Table 21-2	Prisoners Sentenced to Death and the Outcome Sentence, by Year of Sentencing, 1973–2001

		Number of prisoners removed from under sentence of death							Under sentence of death 12/31/2001
				Appeal or higher courts overturned—					
Year of sentence	Number sentenced to death	Execution	Other death	Death penalty statute	Conviction	Sentence	Sentence commuted	Other or unknown reasons	Under sentence of death 12/31/2001
1973	42	2	0	14	9	8	9	0	0
1974	149	10	4	65	15	30	22	1	2
1975	298	6	4	171	24	67	21	2	3
1976	233	14	5	136	17	43	15	0	3
1977	137	19	3	40	26	32	7	0	10
1978	185	36	6	21	36	65	8	0	13
1979	151	28	13	2	28	59	5	1	15
1980	173	45	13	3	30	49	7	0	26
1981	224	53	13	0	42	74	6	1	35
1982	266	57	16	0	37	69	7	1	79
1983	253	58	16	1	26	61	7	2	82
1984	285	57	12	2	40	63	7	8	96

continued

| Table 21-2 | Prisoners Sentenced to Death and the Outcome Sentence, by Year of Sentencing, 1973–2001, continued | | | | | | | | |

| | | | | Number of prisoners removed from under sentence of death | | | | | Under |
| | | | | Appeal or higher courts overturned— | | | | | |
Year of sentence	Number sentenced to death	Execution	Other death	Death penalty statute	Conviction	Sentence	Sentence commuted	Other or unknown reasons	sentence of death 12/31/2001
1985	267	35	7	1	42	70	5	3	104
1986	300	54	19	0	45	53	6	5	118
1987	289	40	17	5	39	58	2	6	122
1988	291	42	12	1	33	55	3	0	145
1989	259	33	10	0	30	50	4	0	132
1990	253	28	8	0	34	40	2	0	141
1991	266	25	10	0	32	34	5	0	160
1992	287	26	9	0	22	38	5	0	187
1993	288	24	12	0	16	23	6	0	207
1994	317	18	8	0	21	30	2	0	238
1995	318	17	9	0	14	21	1	0	256
1996	319	11	5	0	17	33	1	0	252
1997	277	3	3	0	21	15	0	0	235
1998	303	5	4	1	8	8	1	0	275
1999	282	2	4	0	8	4	0	0	264
2000	229	0	1	0	2	0	0	0	226
2001	155	0	0	0	0	0	0	0	155
Total, 1973–2001	7096	749	243	463	714	1152	164	30	3581

Note: For those persons sentenced to death more than once, the numbers are based on the most recent death sentence.

■ Appellate Delay—Perspectives

■ Issue—Do Capital Appeals Take Too Long?

Dwight Aarons, "Can Inordinate Delay Between a Death Sentence and Execution Constitute Cruel and Unusual Punishment?"

I. *Introduction*

Opinion polls generally show that the public largely favors capital punishment, but is ambivalent about the lack of actual executions. As presently administered, however, the United States' system of capital punishment is problematic. One problem that has received relatively little forthright judicial treatment concerns the delay between the imposition of a death sentence and the execution of a capital defendant. The delay between a death sentence and execution is partly attributable to the inequalities in the present administration of the death penalty. As a practical matter, some manner of delay between the sentence and an execution is both desirable and inevitable. During this period the defendant may appeal his or her conviction and sentence, and state officials—such as the prosecutor and the governor—may decide not to go forward with the execution. It is another issue, however, when the period of delay extends beyond that which is necessary for the full litigation of the legal claims in the case.

Today, more than ever, most capital defendants will spend a considerable amount of time in restrictive confinement on death row before they are executed, if they ever are executed. This delay is not always attributable to the litigation of legal issues. While awaiting execution, capital defendants experience mental anguish. This anguish should be viewed as an ancillary, unauthorized punishment that makes no measurable contribution to acceptable goals of punishment. It is cruel punishment. Executing a defendant who has experienced years of that mental anguish would seem to be the infliction of gratuitous pain and suffering, particularly if the capital defendant has experienced a change of character while on death row. Inordinate delay, as defined in this Article, is a rare occurrence. Consequently, inmates on death row for a great length of time, who later face a serious execution date, are unusual. The execution of an inmate who has had an inordinate stay on death row, however, may be cruel and unusual punishment in violation of the Eighth Amendment.

II. *Collateral Consequences of Punishment as Violative of the Eighth Amendment*

Since *Gregg*, the Court, in seven non-capital cases, has outlined the contours of the Eighth Amendment relative to the collateral consequences of an inmate's confinement. These cases can be separated into two, sometimes overlapping, categories: One group deals with the conduct of prison officials toward the inmate, and the second group concerns the permissible conditions under which inmates may be confined. Under either theory, the Eighth Amendment is violated if the claimed deprivation is objectively cruel and unusual, and prison officials acted with the requisite culpable mental state in bringing about the deprivation.

The first group of cases addressed how inmates are personally treated. For example, in *Hudson v. McMillian* a handcuffed and orderly prisoner was denied his Eighth Amendment rights when a guard "maliciously and sadistically" punched him, causing "minor bruises and swelling of his face, mouth, and lip," loosening his teeth, and cracking his partial dental plate. The second group of cases discussed the conditions of an inmate's confinement. The Court has thus far interpreted the Eighth Amendment to cover those confinement conditions that "have a mutually enforcing effect that produces the deprivation of a single, identifiable human need such as food, warmth, or exercise" and has stated that harsh conditions of confinement do not violate the Eighth Amendment. In short, these noncapital cases establish Eighth Amendment limits on the treatment of prisoners, with a particular focus on how their incarceration affects them. These same strictures should apply in capital cases. A capital defendant's inordinate stay on death row might impose consequential effects on that inmate—which are beyond the sentence authorized by the law—and, therefore, violate the "evolving standards of decency" of Eighth Amendment jurisprudence.

Mental strain is the most obvious collateral consequence experienced by capital defendants on death row for an inordinate period of time. Typically, death row inmates are confined to their cells for the great majority of each day and have relatively limited opportunities to exercise or communicate with other inmates or individuals from outside the prison. Research on the impact of this confinement indicates that inmates exhibit several emotional and psychological stages. Capital defendants have been described as experiencing a "living death." Years ago, Albert Camus wrote of the "two deaths" that are imposed on a person sentenced to death and confined to death row. These debilitating effects have, of late, been classified by some courts as the "death row phenomenon." The death row phenomenon is an ancillary, unauthorized corollary of a death sentence. The anguish suffered during the inordinate delay makes "no measurable contribution to acceptable goals of punishment and hence is nothing more than the purposeless and needless imposition of pain and suffering." When it is experienced beyond that which is necessary, the death row phenomenon should be viewed as an excessive form of punishment. As such, a state may, over time, forfeit its ability to go forward with an apparently lawfully imposed death sentence because the execution now violates the Eighth Amendment.

III. *Defendants Alleging Time Awaiting Execution as Cruel and Unusual Punishment*

There has been an increase in executions in the United States since 1983. Despite the increase in the number of defendants executed, significantly more defendants receive a death sentence each year than are executed. Thus, at the present rate, even if the state and federal courts have abandoned the rigorous scrutiny of capital cases exemplified in the 1976 cases, it is a certainty that most individuals sentenced to death will spend several years on death row before execution, if they are ever executed. Considering the number of years that inmates typically spend on death row before execution, it was inevitable that a defendant would legally challenge this state of affairs. On March 27, 1995, Justice Stevens gave new attention to this claim. That day the Court denied Clarence Allen Lackey's petition for a writ of certiorari.

Lackey claimed that it was cruel and unusual punishment for the state to execute him after a seventeen-year delay between his conviction and date of execution. Justice Stevens described the claim asserting inordinate delay as "novel," but "not without foundation." The Justice noted that *Gregg* stated that capital punishment might satisfy retribution and deterrence, and that it was arguable whether either ground retained force for prisoners on death row for seventeen years. Justice Stevens noted that Lackey's argument drew further strength from the conclusion of the Privy Council, which had interpreted section 10 of the English Bill of Rights of 1689, the recognized precursor of the Eighth Amendment, as prohibiting long delays between the death sentence and execution. Closely related to the issue presented in Lackey's petition was the question of which portion of the delay should be considered. Justice Stevens suggested that it may be appropriate to distinguish among delays resulting from the prisoner's abuse of the judicial process by escape or repetitive, frivolous filings; his legitimate exercise of his right to review; and negligence or deliberate action by the state. In closing, Justice Stevens wrote, "Petitioner's claim, with its legal complexity and its potential for far-reaching consequences, seems an ideal example of one which would benefit from such further study in the state and federal courts."

IV. *Resolving the Inordinate Delay Claim According to Eighth Amendment Principles*

Several state capital defendants have argued in federal courts that the convicting state forfeited the right to carry out their executions. These capital defendants claimed that the delay between the commission of the crime and the fulfillment of the sentence violated the Eighth Amendment. They maintained that, due to the delay, they were no longer eligible for execution. These claims were unsuccessful. In fact, in none of the cases has a majority of a reviewing court adjudicated the merits of the inordinate delay claim. Further, no court majority in the United States has directly addressed the issue, or outlined what factors it might consider in resolving an inordinate delay claim.

To prevent his pending execution, a capital defendant has to prove that carrying out the execution after an inordinate delay between the sentence and the execution is cruel and unusual punishment. The standards promulgated in *Gregg* and *Coker*, and applied in subsequent cases, govern.

A. History, Judicial Precedent, and Inordinate Delay in Capital Cases It was not until the mid-twentieth century that the time between the imposition of a death sentence and the execution began to extend into years. In 1960, the State of Washington executed a defendant within thirty-six days of his sentence, while eleven years and ten months elapsed before California carried out one of its executions. The average length of time between sentence and execution in 1960 was about two years. This period has steadily increased. For example, in 1965 there were seven executions, and reliable figures show that forty-five months passed between sentencing and execution. More generally, from 1930 to 1970, the average length of time was about 36.7 months from the imposition of the death sentence until the defendant was executed. According to the most reliable figures, which are based on cases processed before the Antiterrorism and Effective Death Penalty Act of 1996 (AEDPA), in 1995 a capital defendant spent about eleven years on death row before being executed.

There may be several reasons for the increase in the time that an inmate spends on death row. The constitutionalization of criminal procedure and an expansive interpretation of the federal habeas corpus writ both account for generating some delay. These developments have allowed capital defendants to raise more legal issues in both state and federal fora. Just as important as the various legal issues that are cognizable in a capital case are the number of individuals sentenced to death. From 1930 to 1970 there was a national average of about 600 inmates on death row. As of July 1998, there were 3,474 death row inmates. If defendants continue to receive death sentences and are placed on death row, and if resolving each case takes a substantial amount of time, then it is inevitable that, without significantly increasing the number of judges and other court personnel who process and decide capital cases, death row inmates are today—and in the future—more likely to spend more time on death row than they ever have. Since the AEDPA was enacted, it remains to be seen whether this law will reduce the time that capital defendants spend on death row.

The steady increase in time that capital defendants spend on death row has occurred without the state courts, state legislatures, or the United States Supreme Court addressing the issue of a defendant's prolonged stay on death row.

B. Contemporary Legislative Attitudes on Inordinate Delay in Capital Cases

In ruling on the substantive limits of the Eighth Amendment, the Court has considered the statutory work product of the legislatures. Through this inquiry, the Court seeks to ensure that society, via its legislative bodies, has decided to execute a certain class of defendants. In enacting death penalty laws, state legislatures do not consider whether an execution should occur after the prisoner has spent a substantial amount of time on death row. One reason for this may be that most states passed the substance of their death penalty laws before most capital inmates spent decades on death row. It was only after *Gregg* and the lack of a substantial increase in the number of executions that legislators should have foreseen some of the legal implications of confining an inmate to death row for a substantial period.

Legislatures still have not directly addressed the issue of inordinate delay when enacting or amending capital punishment laws, despite the present likelihood that capital defendants will spend a long time on death row before their execution—if they ever are executed. Legislatures have considered a related issue of the financial costs associated with capital punishment in deciding whether to authorize such punishment. There is no evidence, however, that any of these bodies considered the issue of delay associated with the imposition of the death penalty or what effect, if any, the passage of time could have on the validity of a death sentence.

State statutes do not address the issue of inordinate delay, as apparently state legislatures do not consider the issue. Notwithstanding this dereliction, one may argue that the authorization of capital punishment, coupled with the absence of a specific state law prohibiting the state from carrying out that punishment, means that the state legislature has implicitly authorized executions, no matter the length of time the defendant spends on death row. Though this argument has a seductive appeal, one should not accept it unquestioningly. In *Thompson v. Oklahoma*, Justice O'Connor faced a similar predicament. There, the Oklahoma legislature had statutorily authorized the transfer of 15-year-old defendants from juvenile to adult proceedings. One consequence of such transfers was that juveniles could face the death penalty, as *Thompson* did. Justice O'Connor wanted more evidence that the Legislature had foreseen this possibility and, thus, concurred in the Court's judgment reversing the death sentence.

Although *Thompson* discussed the death eligibility of juvenile capital defendants, it is an appropriate analogy for inordinate delay claims. As with the question of death eligibility, an execution after an inordinate delay requires consideration of whether executing the defendant is legally permissible. In both instances external circumstances—biological age or the delay in going forward with the execution—may preclude the ultimate punishment, even though in both situations the defendant committed an aggravated homicide. It therefore seems appropriate to require that state officials clearly indicate their belief that their state has a legitimate interest in going forward with an execution notwithstanding the passage of time between the crime and the defendant's continuous incarceration since the imposition of the death sentence.

C. Penological Objectives and Inordinate Delay in Capital Cases In detecting the substantive limits of the Eighth Amendment, the Court has also considered whether executing the capital defendant achieves retribution or deterrence, which *Gregg* asserted as the legitimate goals of capital punishment.

Capital punishment may serve as a general deterrent to crime if a potential offender knows that the contemplated offense is a capital crime and, due to the certainty of execution, is unwilling to engage in that criminal activity. Several studies have concluded that, as a practical matter, the present system of capital punishment usually does not achieve general deterrence because only a small percentage of the thousands of capital trials result in death sentences, and an even smaller number of defendants are executed. Further, the delay between the commission of the offense and the actualization of the punishment serves to attenuate the connection between the crime and the punishment. Carrying out executions in relative seclusion further diminishes the educative impact that executions can have on potential capital offenders. In light of all of this, it appears that the Court probably did not mean that general deterrence—as opposed to some other utilitarian goal—was the true penological aim of capital punishment.

The distinction between general deterrence and some other utilitarian basis for capital punishment assumes greater importance when considering whether Eighth Amendment principles can preclude the execution of long-delayed death sentences. On the one hand, if general utility is the penological basis for the death penalty, then perhaps after many years on death row, during which the capital defendant has exhibited a change in character, Eighth Amendment principles militate against going forward with the execution. With a sufficiently dramatic change of character, there is less need for society to carry out a death sentence due to the metamorphosis of the defendant. Executing the offender would no longer serve a greater social utility in preventing future capital crimes than confinement. On the other hand, if general deterrence is the penological basis for capital punishment, then the passage of time and the defendant's character transformation are less relevant because punishing the defendant serves as an example to others. That is, the execution might occur so that potential offenders are discouraged from engaging in similar criminal activities lest the same fate befall them.

Delay between the commission of a capital offense and the execution affects deterrence and the other utilitarian and retributionist bases of capital punishment. The utility of the execution is affected because of the attenuated connection between the crime and the punishment. When the defendant has a personality different from the one he or she had when committing the crime, going forward with the execution may not satisfy retribution. It is an unanswered question whether society still feels sufficient outrage about the crime after the defendant has spent a considerable period on death row and in restrictive conditions of confinement. It is important to ask whether society cares about the issue because the appropriateness of the death penalty, as measured by the evolving standards of decency, is premised on both society's general acceptance of capital punishment and its approval of the death sentence in particular cases. A *lex talionis* retributionist would likely maintain that neither the passage of time nor a radical change in the character of the defendant alleviates society's duty to punish the properly convicted. Immanuel Kant captured this notion when he argued that before a civil society could disband, it had to execute the last murderer in its prisons. However, a proportional retributionist would not necessarily maintain that execution is proper in inordinate delay cases.

The modern system of capital punishment is neither singularly utilitarian nor completely retributionist. It has components of both theories. Moreover, retribution, deterrence, and other utilitarian-based theories, while characterized in Eighth Amendment jurisprudence as one-dimensional constructs, are, in reality, multifaceted. Several aspects of these theories are given currency under the present capital punishment laws. For instance, the aggravating circumstances doctrine furthers retribution. That is, the aggravating circumstances proffered by the prosecution generally focus the sentencer on the social harm caused by the defendant in committing the capital offense, as well as other seemingly socially undesirable aspects of the defendant's life. Similarly, the mitigating circumstances doctrine addresses special deterrence and other utilitarian theories. The general understanding is that if there is some reason for the sentencer to exercise mercy, then execution of that capital defendant is not necessary to deter future offenses committed by that defendant. In proffering mitigating circumstances, the defense seeks to direct the sentencer's attention to the positive attributes of the defendant and the defendant's background. Executing a capital defendant after a long delay, however, may not be the most utilitarian use of the sanction; nor may it fully achieve retribution.

D. Inordinate Delay as Violative of the Eighth Amendment Under the test established by the Court for measuring the evolving standards of decency, inordinate delay between the imposition of a sentence and the actual execution of a capital defendant may violate the Eighth Amendment. The factors that the Court considers either suggest that such delays are impermissible or do not provide a determinate answer to the question. Never in this nation's history have death row inmates routinely spent as long under a death sentence. The most relevant Court precedent suggests that the period spent awaiting execution is itself a form of punishment regulated by the Eighth Amendment. There is no statutory authority that specifically authorizes executions after a capital defendant has spent an inordinate time on death row. In addition, sentencers, when deciding on what punishment to impose, do not formally consider the likelihood that the prisoner will be on death row for an inordinate period. Penologically, an execution after an inordinate delay might achieve retribution; but the Court has disapproved of naked retribution as the sole rationale for executions. Due to the paucity of definite answers to some of the factors that the Court considers, legal developments in other nations and in international law ought to be considered on this issue. International opinion generally tolerates executions so long as they occur before too long a delay between the imposition of the death sentence and the execution.

In light of the above, keeping an inmate on death row for an inordinate period violates the Eighth Amendment. Then the question arises: How long a delay is inordinate? Considering the enormity of the issue and the procedural and substantive requirements that exist in death penalty cases, capital defendants can hardly argue with the proposition that to ensure that the conviction and sentence are proper it can take about seven to eleven years from a capital conviction to execution. Thus, when an inmate claims that the state has forfeited the right to execute him because too much time has passed between his conviction and the proposed execution date, as he has suffered severe mental strain while awaiting his execution, such claims may not be cognizable until there has been an inordinate delay between the imposition of the death sentence and the anticipated execution.

The historical background of the Eighth Amendment and the words "cruel and unusual punishment" provide slight guidance. Long ago, the Court suggested that the Eighth Amendment outlawed punishment that involved "a lingering death." Accordingly, the period must be so excessive that the pending execution, in effect, constitutes punishment unauthorized by statute or the courts because it is a lingering death. This is consistent with the present interpretation of the phrase as outlawing torturous methods of execution, which logically includes the state's conduct in bringing about the execution.

Inordinate delay claims should be ripe for review only after the inmate has been under a sentence of death for twice as long as the national average of time spent on death row. The other cases of executed defendants establish the temporal period by which an execution should occur. If the defendant has been on death row for twice as long as the national average, this is excessive, in the commonly accepted legal usage of the term. While inordinate delay need not be strictly defined as twice the national average, this proposed bright line rule represents a choice that provides a ready reference point for capital cases. The Court adopted an analogous approach in *Barker v. Wingo* for determining whether there has been a violation of a criminal defendant's Sixth Amendment right to a speedy trial. To decide the issue, courts are to consider the length and reason for the delay, the defendant's assertion of the right, and the prejudice suffered by the defendant. Today, using the most recent and reliable figures available from 1995, this limitation period would require an inmate to be incarcerated about twenty-two years before he could claim that his pending execution constitutes cruel and unusual punishment in light of the severe restrictions of confinement and mental strain suffered while awaiting execution.

On the one hand, this bright line rule would ensure that the task of determining when the Eighth Amendment has been violated is based on objective factors. On the other hand, it is quite tempting to follow the Court's lead when assessing the right to a speedy criminal trial or the constitutionality of punitive damage awards under the Due Process Clause of the Fourteenth Amendment, and conclude that the Court "need not, and indeed cannot, draw a mathematical bright line between the constitutionally acceptable and the constitutionally unacceptable that would fit every case." Such an approach eliminates the need for anything more than the observation that the defendant has been treated in a fundamentally unfair manner. The Court has, however, insisted on more precise guidelines when dealing with capital cases under the Eighth Amendment. Another concern that a bright line rule may raise is that as a case approaches the limit set by the rule, there may be a flurry of activity to ensure that the defendant's case is moved along, with an accompanying loss of meaningful review of the defendant's claims. If a bright line rule initiates processing of the case, this should be viewed as beneficial; that review should strive to ensure that the defendant's claims are meaningfully and seriously considered. Objecting to the adoption of a bright line rule seems to disregard the salutary effects of such a rule.

Unlike others who have considered the question of the long delay between the imposition of a death sentence and the inmate's execution in the United States, and either have concluded that recognition of the claim would undermine the present safeguards that are part of the capital litigation process or that the death penalty is inherently unconstitutional, I propose a rule that attempts to accommodate these concerns. I am under no delusion that my proposal is perfect, in part because, as detailed elsewhere, notwithstanding a finding that the defendant's Eighth Amendment rights have been violated, the prosecution is not prevented from seeking to have a death sentence imposed in a subsequent proceeding. Yet, as best as I know, my proposal is the first to fashion a rule that accommodates most interests at stake.

V. *Conclusion*

Unlike more recent commentators and courts that have considered the issue of inordinate delay in capital cases, I have taken the Supreme Court's pronouncements on death eligibility seriously. Starting with *Gregg*, the Court ruled that the state can use the death penalty for deterrence and retribution. To that end, the Court established standards on how to detect which class of defendants is death-eligible.

Under *Gregg's* objective criteria for measuring the evolving standards of decency, inordinate delay between the imposition of a sentence and the actual execution of a capital defendant violates the Eighth Amendment. Historically, death row inmates have not regularly spent as long under a sentence of death as they may now. The most relevant Court case presumed that the mental strain experienced while awaiting execution, without a realistic notion of when, if ever, that execution would occur, is a form of punishment. Legislatures have not explicitly considered the issue of inordinate delay; consequently, there is no statutory authority that specifically authorizes executions after a capital defendant has spent an inordinate time on death row. Presently, sentencers are not allowed to consider the likelihood that the prisoner will be on death row for an inordinate period in deciding whether to impose a death sentence. Thus, the imposition of a death sentence should not be considered a definitive statement on the issue. Finally, the only penological objective that can justify an execution after an inordinate delay is unmitigated retribution. The Court, however, has disapproved of naked retribution as the sole rationale for a death sentence.

Inordinate delay claims should be ripe for review only after the inmate has been under a sentence of death for twice as long as the national average of time spent on death row by other executed inmates. This standard is based on both the language of the Eighth Amendment and the historical tradition underlying that Amendment. Even if one adopts the view suggested by some members of the Court—that inquiring whether a form of punishment contributes to accepted goals of punishment is not a function of the Court—inordinate delay appears to be both cruel and unusual punishment. Executions after an inordinate delay are unusual because most defendants are executed before spending an inordinate time (i.e., twice as long as usual) on death row. Such executions are cruel in the constitutional sense because the condemned experience severe mental anguish while awaiting execution.

The inordinate delay claims raised by state death row prisoners could be another reason for those opposed to capital punishment to advocate its abolition. These claims can also serve as an occasion to examine the administration of capital punishment in the United States or in a particular jurisdiction. I have chosen the latter course. It is an open question whether other actors in the capital litigation process—namely prosecutors, judges, governors, and others authorized to settle for a sentence other than death—will take the United States Supreme Court decisions on death eligibility seriously when presented with the next claim of inordinate delay made by a capital defendant.

Franklin Zimring, "The Executioner's Dissonant Song: On Capital Punishment and American Legal Values"

This essay concerns the implications of the practice of capital punishment on American legal values and procedures. Any death penalty, in my view, conflicts with substantive principles of human dignity, but my argument here addresses a narrower theme: the ways in which attempts to reduce delays in death penalty cases are undermining general legal norms of fairness and due process. The problem I describe is not a temporary phenomenon associated with the transition to a more efficient regime. Instead, the clash between the operational needs of an execution system and the principles and procedures of American legal culture is fundamental. Either the basic rules and values will change or the practice of execution will remain infrequent, conflict-laden, and problematic. Capital punishment can only be regarded as normal state behavior by reimagining basic principles of fairness in criminal justice.

In exploring the wide shadow that death penalty cases cast over American legal values, I am obviously rejecting a discrete conception of capital punishment held by some proponents of execution. In their view, capital punishment is a question of the appropriate sanction to be imposed on the most serious form of murder, a matter of principal importance to one part of the administration of criminal justice. In contrast, this essay reflects a belief that the conduct of death penalty cases has serious implications for the larger realm of criminal procedure. Recent cases before the U.S. Supreme Court illustrate the pressure that facilitating executions places on legal sentiments and values. They suggest that capital punishment, though it is different in a qualitative way from other criminal sanctions, may subvert due process and fairness values broadly throughout the criminal justice system.

I. *The Frustrating Impact of Delay*

What makes capital punishment a particular problem for criminal justice is that any pending legal challenge delays the imposition of the punishment. By contrast, a term of imprisonment normally begins right after sentencing, and jail confinement often starts after arrest. Even the most protracted appeal process in such circumstances usually does not postpone punishment. So allowing the legal process to go on is costless with respect to ensuring the imposition of imprisonment. The prisoner is not winning a battle against the state as a function of the appeal.

But no meaningful legal appeal can proceed without delay in the schedule of an execution. Even though the prisoner remains in custody, the punishment provided for the crime will not be imposed as long as any part of the review of the case is not complete. This situation creates two instrumental incentives in the appellate legal process. First, it encourages any defendant who wishes to avoid execution to do so by prolonging the process. Second, it makes the state representatives anxious to bring the legal review process to a close. As long as the appeal process is active, the state's penal purposes are frustrated. In such circumstances, the objective of a capital punishment regime must be to minimize the scrutiny of the legal system and to make the review process as short as possible.

From the perspective of a capital punishment regime, the operational danger of setting up a new categorical target for postconviction litigators, such as mental retardation, is quite severe. The substantive problem of allowing the ultimate penalty for a person profoundly disabled in judgment and cognitive ability is equally severe. A judicial system that recognizes the exemption will bog down in the extra hearings many defendants will gain. An operationally efficient capital punishment system will be morally compromised by its failure to protect those undeserving of death. These are the kind of hard choices that produce sharp and close divisions among the Justices in cases such as *Penry* and *Atkins*.

II. *Executing the Innocent*

The clash between operational necessity and moral legitimacy is most strikingly evident in the 1993 decision, *Herrera v. Collins*. The petitioner in *Herrera* had been convicted in the murder of a police officer and sentenced to death in 1982. Ten years later, after exhausting state remedies and fully prosecuting one federal habeas corpus petition, Herrera brought another federal habeas action alleging that he had proof of his actual innocence of the crime for which he was sentenced to death. He argued that executing a person for a crime he did not commit would constitute cruel and unusual punishment, and that he was entitled to an evidentiary hearing to establish his innocence.

The Court's opinion, by Chief Justice Rehnquist, rejected Herrera's claim without deciding the question of whether the execution of an innocent person would constitute an Eighth Amendment violation: "We may assume, for the sake of argument in deciding this case, that in a capital case a truly persuasive demonstration of 'actual innocence' made after a trial would render the execution of the defendant unconstitutional." The opinion holds that the proof offered by the defendant falls short of such a "persuasive demonstration" and therefore does not require the Court to decide whether the assumed constitutional standard should become an actual constitutional rule.

Two concurring opinions joined in by three Justices go further in supporting some constitutional protection against the execution of the probably innocent defendant, so that one might count as many as six of the nine Justices as supporting some form of Eighth Amendment protection in extreme cases. But why is the concession that executing the innocent might be a constitutional error so grudgingly made by all but the three dissenters? Why are the proper procedural channels and waiver rules so important not only to Justices Scalia and Thomas (who reject any constitutional protection), but also to the Chief Justice, who will only "assume for the sake of argument" that there is some constitutional problem with hanging the wrong man?

What we have here is a head-on collision between the operating needs of the capital punishment system and the sentiments and norms of Anglo-American criminal justice. As a substantive matter, nothing could be worse for a criminal justice system in the United States than the execution of an innocent person. No matter the procedural history that might precede such an event, no set of circumstances would seem to justify or excuse the outcome. The strongest reason for last-gasp hearings and procedures is to save the innocent from execution. Yet a rule that provided a right to a fresh hearing when new evidence might cast doubt on guilt would provide a procedural avenue of delay that many death row inmates would try to use. The few reversals that might result would be accompanied by scores of two-year delays tacked on at the end of a long and convoluted process.

In *Herrera*, the Court could not forthrightly endorse a basic sentiment of American justice without placing the efficient performance of the capital punishment regime in substantial jeopardy. This is the only plausible explanation for the ambivalent and indecisive analysis of most of the majority Justices in *Herrera* on a basic issue of principle.

III. *An Inevitable Conflict*

Is the conflict between fairness and certainty, on the one hand, and operational efficiency, on the other, inevitable in a legal system with capital punishment? As a logical matter, the answer to this question is no. One path away from the conflict would be to reduce the amount of time necessary to assure just outcomes in capital trials and appeals. Given that the passage of time prejudices the capital punishment system, why not invest resources in excellent lawyers, quick trials, and expeditious appeals in capital cases?

In practice, however, such a formula is unlikely to be implemented. The political units that maintain criminal justice systems are unwilling to make the heavy investment in defense services that faster, high-quality justice would require, and this is particularly true of the states where death sentences and executions are most common. Moreover, limiting the acceleration of the process to procedures that would ensure fairness would not reduce the anger and hostility of prosecutors toward judicial review. With more than three thousand persons on death row nationwide, even the best case trial and appeal systems would produce a ten-year lag between trial and execution if a defendant wished to delay death. A delay of that length would generate the same frustration and tension observable in the current system.

Legal rights for persons accused of crime are never politically popular, and due process is a particular source of contention when fear of crime is a conspicuous part of the urban social landscape. Rules of substantive and procedural legality are cumbersome and inconvenient for those charged with the investigation and prosecution of crime. Francis Allen has recently reviewed the manifold threats to what he calls the "habits of legality" that currently operate in American society and government. I would add to his list of dangers the possibility that compromises of due process in capital cases will undermine procedural guarantees throughout the criminal justice system. Even though capital cases are infrequent, and even though the special tension between judicial review and punitive closure only occurs in capital cases, insensitivity to considerations of legality can carry over from capital cases to the rest of criminal justice.

Such insensitivity is, to some extent, contagious no matter where in the justice system it occurs. But compromising principles in capital cases carries more than general contagion. Because death is the system's largest punishment, when rights are forfeited in capital cases, there is a momentum toward permitting the same compromises when the penal stakes are more modest. If the capital defendant cannot claim a right, who can?

Hostility to the delay produced in capital cases may also result in broad curtailment of legal remedies because capital cases cannot permissibly be singled out for special prejudice. In habeas corpus, for example, while the real target of both legislative and judicial restriction was death cases, the curtailment of the federal great writ in all state criminal cases was the means employed to achieve the restriction in death cases. This was a process of letting the tail wag the dog in collateral review of state criminal justice.

The destructive influence of capital cases on rights and remedies in other criminal cases is a historical process come full circle. The capital case was always a leading indicator of the direction in which due process guarantees would be extended. The constitutional right to counsel was extended in state capital cases a full generation before it was extended to state felonies. But even with that time gap, the flow from *Powell v. Alabama* in 1935 to *Gideon v. Wainwright* in 1963 was obvious. So there is symmetry if not poetic justice when capital cases now serve as leading indicators of a contraction in defendants' rights and the scope of judicial review.

Hostile reactions to delay are by no means the sole reason for restrictions on due process protections in the criminal justice system. But the contribution of the death penalty cases to the contraction of the scope of judicial review in habeas corpus, the growth of "harmless error" doctrine, and recent enthusiasms for enforcing procedural default rules is evident and very important. Further, when formalism neutralizes moral claims for procedural protection in capital cases, there can be no persuasive moral claim to protection in lesser cases. The behavior of the Supreme Court in capital cases thus becomes a portent of moral regression in criminal justice generally.

22

Televised Executions

■ Televised Executions—Introduction

The notion of televising executions is controversial in contemporary America, though this preference for privacy is an historical exception rather than the rule. In the early years of the United States, executions were publicized as a matter of course. Hanging days were well attended by the community, often by thousands of people, though they were not spectacles. Hangings were solemn events, surrounded by elaborate ceremony. The condemned would often be compelled to wear a special robe and marched to the gallows along established routes lined with crowds. Ministers delivered speeches. The condemned often delivered remarks of their own, generally contrite, occasionally defiant. In *The Death Penalty: An American History*, Stuart Banner offers this account of public executions:

> Hangings were not macabre spectacles staged for a bloodthirsty crowd. A hanging was normally a somber event, like a church service. Hanging day was a dramatic portrayal, in which everyone could participate, of the community's desire to suppress wrongdoing. It was a powerful symbolic statement of the gravity of crime and its consequences. The whole ceremony was public, outdoors, and as conspicuous as any event could possibly be.

The policy benefit of public executions is obvious: they maximize the deterrent effect of capital punishment. The more it is known that the death penalty will be used, and the more humiliating the manner in which it is imposed, the greater its value in dissuading potential criminals. The offsetting cost to public executions is that some criminals may be martyred, especially those whose execution is controversial or who comport themselves in an especially sympathetic manner. Banner writes, "In the eighteenth century, sympathy had been accepted as an unfortunate but unavoidable aspect of capital punishment, but in the early nineteenth century people began to complain about it and to suggest that it provided a reason for abolishing public executions." It was also argued that viewing executions made citizens more prone to violence, an analogous argument to the contemporary concern with the brutalization effect of the death penalty. These complaints became more and more common as the nineteenth century wore on. In the 1830s, several northeastern states including New York and Massachusetts abolished public executions. Hangings moved into the jail yard. By 1860, public hanging had been abolished entirely in the northern United States. Most southern states followed suit by the end of the century. The few holdout states abolished public executions, partially by necessity, with the adoption of the electric chair.

Jail yard executions remain the status quo, though the policy debate—the trade-off between increased deterrence and the risk of desensitizing people to violence—is of continued relevance today. The debate flares up from time to time in contemporary society. In 1991, the public television station KQED sought permission to videotape and televise the execution of Robert Alton Harris by the state of California. Excerpts from Judge Schanacke's decision denying such permission appear in the Critical Documents section of this chapter.

The issue returned a decade later when Timothy McVeigh, sentenced to die for the 1995 Oklahoma City bombing that killed 168 people, requested that his execution be broadcast on television in a public letter to *The Oklahoman* newspaper. McVeigh said he had no objection to his execution being broadcast on closed-circuit television, as it was, but that the limited broadcast would keep others from witnessing his death. He wrote:

> Because the closed-circuit telecast of my execution raises these fundamental equal access concerns, and because I am not otherwise opposed to such a telecast, a reasonable solution seems obvious: Hold a true "public execution"—allow a public broadcast.

McVeigh's request was endorsed by Phil Donahue, among others. Donahue argued that "the free press establishment has an obligation to show this issue."

Below, John Bessler argues that executions must be televised to let the public fully scrutinize the propriety of capital punishment. George Will wonders whether televised executions will further desensitize Americans to violence. The Critical Documents section includes a proposal by Jeremy Epstein to require judges and juries to witness executions. The proposal is controversial, but has its roots in the procedures attending to capital punishment prescribed in the Old Testament.

■ Televised Executions—Critical Documents

KQED v. Vasquez
U.S. District Court for the Northern District of California (1991)
Opinion of Judge Robert H. Schnacke

In our courts, which are constitutionally mandated to conduct public trials, the press and the public are entitled to equal access. But neither the public nor the press have been found to have the right to bring cameras, still or television, into a courtroom. Indeed, until a very recent determination to allow limited testing of television in a few federal courtrooms, all federal courtrooms are under a mandate from the Supreme Court not to do so.

In California, quite clearly executions aren't public. Penal Code Section 3605 imposes clear limits on the persons who are to attend. While the press can't be arbitrarily excluded, that doesn't mean the media attendance may not be subject to reasonable restrictions.

A great many reasons have been advanced for excluding cameras. Some may very well question how compelling those reasons are. But it's sufficient to say that whatever exclusions are appropriate for a public hearing such as a court trial, ought to be more compelling that those that are necessary to exclude them from a private execution.

The warden is designated under California law to operate and control the prison and to supervise executions. These are questions and activities that require the expertise of people who are trained in such matters. It's really not a place for intrusion by well-meaning amateurs.

We heard from a number of wardens and they all agree that managing a prison isn't an easy task. They all agree that the internal tensions that are created by a large number of criminals combined in close quarters presents, in the best of times, a wide range of problems and dangers. And, as they've pointed out, it's particularly true at times of executions. They all agree that the prison population becomes extremely tense, hostile and aggressive during the period surrounding any planned or actual execution.

The wardens were unanimous in the fact that none has ever permitted cameras at an execution. There's no evidence that any prison anywhere has ever permitted cameras in the United States. All but one of the wardens who testified presented a number of reasons why cameras ought to be excluded.

First of all, the prison personnel who participate in the execution process frequently want their identities concealed. They fear, and apparently with some justification, that harm may come to themselves or to their families in retaliation from the prisoners, or their associates, or from gangs, or from any element of the public that is possibly hysterically offended by the fact of the execution, and the prison personnel deserve protection. They might well be disclosed, their identities revealed by a camera in the area at the time of an execution, and no rational way appears to prevent cameras that are there from getting either intentional or inadvertent photographs of the prison personnel.

The witnesses to executions, the warden further pointed, out aren't allowed to bring with them any heavy objects of any sort which might create any kind of threat to others. Cameras obviously are such heavy objects. Television cameras are heavier than still cameras in many cases.

The security of prisons is something that, as I say, has to be left to the people who are responsible for dealing with the problems that arise if security is breached and prisons very jealously guard their right to maintain security. People entering the prison or even the prison grounds are subject to search and strict limitations. And the warden is really not required to trust anybody.

In California we have a gas chamber, it's glass enclosed and it's sealed during the execution process, it's filled with a lethal gas. Now, any heavy objects striking the chamber could conceivably cause a leakage of that gas into the witness area or very least as threat of creating a fear of possible break in the seal which would require some long delay or examination of the chambers that would make it difficult to carry on the execution expeditiously.

Some of the wardens had a real fear they expressed that the circulation of a photograph of an execution within the prison even after the time of the execution, and more seriously the display on television of a live broadcast of the event within the prison, could spark severe prisoner reaction that might be dangerous to the safety of prison personnel.

Mr. Procunier, formerly a warden at San Quentin was the only person who ever had responsibilities in connection with prison or with executions who indicated any doubts about the risk involved in cameras in the execution chamber. He testified that he had not at any of the prisons, and he's been at a great many of them, he's moved from one to another and had significant positions in each of them, never in any of those prisons has he ever permitted cameras to be present at an execution. When he was asked why, he said "No one ever asked." Apparently he encountered press far less aggressive than they seem to have become lately, at least. But more significantly when he was asked how much risk he would tolerate in the execution procedure, he said flatly "None."

In my view, prison officials are the experts. Their reasonable concerns must be accommodated and I find that the concerns that they have expressed are reasonable. They not unreasonably see risks in permitting cameras in and I agree with Mr. Procunier that no risk should be tolerated. Prohibition of cameras still or television from the execution witness area is a reasonable and lawful regulation.

Now, I presume for purposes of this case that the press does have more rights in witnessing an execution than every other witness. That assumption may be open to serious dispute. After all the statute permits only the attendance of witnesses. The right of a witness is simply to witness.

It doesn't necessarily encompass the right to record in any other fashion than in the mind what is witnessed. There is no custom or usage in California or elsewhere that requires cameras in the execution chamber.

In summary, Plaintiffs have failed to prove that the warden may not exclude cameras from the execution witness area.

Jeremy G. Epstein, "Require Judge and Jury to Witness Executions"

On September 1, 1995, New York's new death penalty statute took effect. It spells out the mechanics of execution with ghastly precision. Death shall be imposed by lethal injection in a "suitable and efficient facility, enclosed from public view, within the confines of the designated correctional institution for the imposition of the punishment of death."

That is not always the way it was done in New York. In 1842, Charles Dickens, only 30 years old and already a world-famous novelist, visited the United States. While in New York, Dickens visited the Tombs, which continued as a prison in lower Manhattan well into the 20th century. Executions had been conducted in public until 1835, when new legislation required that they be carried out within prison walls. Dickens described the conditions under which executions were carried out at the Tombs:

> *Into this narrow, gravelike place, men are brought out to die. The wretched creature stands beneath the gibbet on the ground; the rope around his neck; and when the sign is given, a weight at its other end comes running down and swings him up into the air—a corpse.*
>
> *The law requires that there be present at this dismal spectacle, the judge, the jury, and citizens to the amount of 25.*

Much has changed since 1842. The method of execution is different and, more "humane." The law no longer requires the judge and jury to be present. No one under the age of 18 may attend the execution. The law also expresses a touching solicitude for the privacy rights—not, as one might expect, of the defendant, but rather of those who are delicately referred to as execution technicians: "The names of the execution technicians shall never be disclosed."

I. *Make Them Attend*

New York should reinstate the practice of requiring the presence of the judge and jury at executions. If it was good enough for New York in 1842, why not now? Those to whom that argument seems absurd should know that a commonly invoked defense of the death penalty is fidelity to historical custom. Death penalty apologists frequently—and quite erroneously—claim that because the death penalty was in effect in 1791, it cannot now be deemed cruel and unusual. If this argument were correct, then whipping, the pillory, branding, ear-cropping and flogging, all common in 1791, would be acceptable today.

Historical precedents aside, requiring the presence of judge and jury at all executions would have many beneficial consequences. It would focus the attention of those imposing the punishment on the gravity of their act. Jurors could not simply depart from the courtroom and leave the state with the unpleasant task of disposing of the defendant. Now would this requirement constitute an unprecedented assault on the sensibilities of juries. During a murder trial, they are frequently exposed to as many photos of torture, mutilation, disfigurement or dismemberment as a prosecutor can persuade a judge to disclose. The only individual in the courtroom harmed by the experience is usually the defendant.

II. *A Useful Trauma*

If the experience of witnessing an execution is traumatic and leaves an impression that lasts a lifetime, so much the better. The impact of the act is at least as traumatic on the defendant and will also last what remains of his life. One of the purposes of any penal system is to teach that acts have consequences. It is fitting that judge and jury understand that their acts have consequences that reverberate far beyond the courtroom.

A judge and jury's involvement in the actual execution might also remove from public debate some of the detachment with which the death penalty is viewed. Executions are at the point of being considered routine.

The taking of a human life by the state should never be considered a routine event, no matter how often it occurs. Requiring judge and jury presence will create a body of witnesses who can inform public discourse.

What would the impact on the spectator be? Is the suggestion merely an attempt to win the death penalty debate not by reasoned argument but through physical revulsion? It is not.

Execution by lethal injection is (one is told) comparatively uneventful: there is no burning flesh, no slow and agonized asphyxiation. The defendant receives an injection and loses consciousness. If the scene remains frightening, it is not because of the overt manifestations of death, but because of what the act itself signifies. The spectator has seen the state end a life. That is an event that can be witnessed in no other Western democracy.

The most beneficial consequence of this requirement is also the most obvious. Does anyone doubt that if judge and jury knew they were required to witness an execution that there would be fewer death sentences? If the answer is no, as I believe it is, what does that say about the public's true tolerance for the death penalty?

■ Televised Executions—Perspectives

■ Issue—Should Executions Be Televised?

John Bessler, Death in the Dark: Midnight Executions in America

Executions in America are hidden from public view. Private execution laws severely restrict the number of execution witnesses, and television cameras are strictly forbidden in execution chambers. Throughout the United States, these laws effectively ensure that the vast majority of Americans will never watch an execution. Only official witnesses, hand-picked by governmental officials, will ever witness the ultimate act of the state. Many state laws also require that death row inmates be executed at night. From 1977 to 1995, over 82 percent of executions occurred between 11:00 P.M. and 7:30 A.M. These laws further inhibit the public's access to information about state-sanctioned killings because local television news programs are already over by the time many executions take place.

As Americans debate whether executions should be televised, the transition from public, daytime executions to private, nighttime executions must not be forgotten. By privatizing executions, nineteenth-century legislators, worried that executions might only incite criminal activity, sought to eliminate the spectacle of public executions. In those days, it was common knowledge that execution day crowds were often mischievous, with alcohol consumption and pickpockets regularly associated with public hangings. Rioting at public hangings also was not unknown. The "scientific" findings by skull-measuring phrenologists that public executions did not deter crime but actually caused more of it lent credence to the movement to privatize executions. The fear that well publicized executions might only cause crime certainly helps explain why many states passed laws prohibiting the publication of execution details.

By moving executions into prisons, paternalistic legislators and civic leaders also sought to protect society's sensibilities. Embarrassed by the spectacle of public hangings, and the drinking and rabble-rousing that occurred at them, legislators passed laws requiring executions to take place within the confines of prisons beginning in the 1830s. Over the next one hundred years, hangings before large, boisterous crowds gradually ebbed, as civic leaders came to view public executions as corrupting of public morals and as incongruous with the occasion's solemnity. Women and children were seen as particularly unfit execution spectators, with some private execution laws excluding these groups from executions altogether. As in England, where even newspaper publicity of executions was thought to have a demoralizing influence on the community, especially children, American legislators tried to shroud executions with secrecy to prevent what they viewed as the unhealthy effects of public executions.

Finally, private execution laws were sometimes passed to appease abolitionists after abolitionists made strong legislative efforts to abolish capital punishment. Many death penalty opponents, believing public executions would be instrumental in abolishing capital punishment, initially resisted the passage of such laws. However, abolitionists eventually relented and either acquiesced in the passage of these laws or pushed for their enactment. For instance, Minneapolis legislator John Day Smith, an ardent abolitionist, actually authored the law that privatized executions in Minnesota. He probably believed, like many other abolitionists of his time, that death penalty proponents would be deprived of their most powerful argument (that capital punishment deters crime) once executions were privatized. Ironically, the passage of private execution laws only removed the issue of capital punishment from public consciousness and made Americans apathetic toward executions.

In attempting to civilize society, private execution laws had the perverse effect of degrading America's democracy. Not only did these laws limit the number of execution spectators and restrict the public's access to information about capital punishment, but they often attempted to suppress public debate of the death penalty itself. In several states, laws were passed that prohibited newspaper reporters from attending executions or forbade newspapers from publishing any execution details. Only the bare fact that the prisoner was executed could be printed. Newspaper reporters who violated these laws could be criminally prosecuted as happened in the case of Minnesota and New York newspapers.

Laws requiring nighttime executions also were enacted with paternalistic and publicity-squelching zeal. In upholding the constitutionality of the "midnight assassination law," the Minnesota Supreme Court specifically found: "The evident purpose of the act was to surround the execution of criminals with as much secrecy as possible, in order to avoid exciting an unwholesome effect on the public mind. For that reason it must take place before dawn, while the masses are at rest, and within an inclosure, so as to debar the morbidly curious." In requiring after-dark executions, these laws only further denigrated America's democracy by suggesting that Americans have something to hide or fear carrying out their chosen public policy in broad daylight.

Today, laws requiring private, nighttime executions continue to stifle execution publicity and keep the public in the dark about the facts surrounding capital punishment. By cloaking executions in secrecy, these laws leave the public uninformed about capital punishment and unable to judge for themselves the morality of the death penalty. In addition, these laws leave politicians free to cry out for the use of capital punishment without having to live with the real life-and-death consequences of their get-tough-on-crime rhetoric. As Sister Helen Prejean aptly observes: "Beyond the rhetoric of all the legislators who score their political points for being tough on crime, what it all boils down to is that a handful of people are hired to kill a guy in the middle of the night."

To restore accountability to America's death penalty debate, several remedial steps must be taken. First, judges or jurors who sentence criminal defendants to death (or governors who refuse to exercise their clemency powers) must be required to pull the triggering switch at executions, and all of those individuals must be required to attend them. This will inject some much needed accountability and personal responsibility into capital sentencing and clemency decisions. Alex Kozinski, a conservative judge on the Ninth Circuit and a death penalty supporter, has wondered aloud whether judges "who make life-and-death decisions on a regular basis should not be required to watch as the machinery of death grinds up a human being." Kozinski writes: "I ponder what it says about me that I can, with cool precision, cast votes and write opinions that seal another human being's fate but lack the courage to witness the consequences of my actions."

Second, no longer can jurors who oppose the death penalty be excluded from jury service. The death penalty is the most severe sanction that any society can impose, so the notion of excluding potential jurors from service solely because they oppose its use is like stacking a deck of cards before playing a game of poker when the ante is a human being's life. Juries should reflect a fair cross-section of community views on this issue.

Third, the practice of allowing politically sensitive, elected state court judges to override jury verdicts of life imprisonment and impose death sentences must be outlawed via legislation. Only juries, which reflect a better sampling of a community's conscience, must be allowed to make life-and-death decisions.

Fourth, the few remaining death penalty states that do not authorize the punishment of life imprisonment without the possibility of parole for murder must do so at once, and jurors in capital cases must always be made aware of that sentencing option. It is simply unconscionable that some sentencing juries continue to be faced with the Hobson's choice of voting for death, which they might find undesirable, or returning verdicts that they fear would let violent criminals walk the streets again.

Finally, executions must be televised. Americans must acknowledge the critical role that television plays in our society and admit that printed accounts of executions are a woefully inadequate substitute for television news coverage of them. Concurrently, broadcast journalists must recognize their ethical obligation to keep the public fully informed about capital punishment issues and redouble their efforts to put executions on television so that the news is no longer sanitized. The executions-are-too-gruesome-for-television argument must be rejected. The public has a right to know when and how the state takes a human life, and both advocates and opponents of capital punishment should be able to agree that news reporting in America should not be censored by the government. If Americans want executions, they should have nothing to hide. As columnist Anna Quindlen has remarked about capital punishment, "Having it on television makes it no worse. It simply makes the reality inescapable, and our role undeniable. If we want it, we should be able to look at it. If we can't bear to look at it, maybe it's time to rethink our desires." Televised executions are necessary to let the public fully scrutinize the propriety of capital punishment. Without televised executions, Americans will always lack complete information as they debate the morality of the death penalty.

When the freedom of the press is curtailed, as it has been by private execution laws, the public is left uninformed about newsworthy events, and democracy is threatened. Indeed, it is a tragic commentary on America's democracy when governmental policies—especially those involving life and death—are carried out behind thick prison walls in the middle of the night. As James Madison warned, "A popular Government, without popular information, or the means of acquiring it, is but a Prologue to a Farce or a Tragedy; or perhaps both. Knowledge will forever govern ignorance; And a people who mean to be their own Governors, must arm themselves with the power which knowledge gives." Because an informed citizenry is essential to America's democracy, Americans can no longer afford to tolerate death in the dark. The press must be allowed to put executions on television, lest Americans relinquish to their government "the power which knowledge gives"—something that should happen only in a George Orwell novel, not in America.

George F. Will, *Washington Post* editorial, May 12, 1991

State-inflicted death used to be public theater with didactic purposes, and it may be again if KQED, the public television station here, wins its suit asserting a right to film executions.

Reporters have always attended California executions. A press sketch was made of the most recent one, in 1967. But before KQED filed suit, prison policy was changed to require reporters to be empty-handed (no note or sketch pads, tape recorders or cameras). After the suit was filed, the rules were revised again to ban all reporters from any executions.

This comprehensive ban may protect San Quentin's warden against KQED's original contention that he was unconstitutionally discriminating against graphic journalism because of its content. However, the ban opens him to another charge: He is unconstitutionally infringing the newsgathering right by abolishing a historic access to a government function without serving a compelling government interest.

The First Amendment is not a blanket freedom of information act. The constitutional newsgathering freedom means the media can go where the public can, but enjoys no superior right of access. Courts have recently protected press access to particular government functions when there is a history of openness and when openness would facilitate the function. Journalists claim no right to witness, say, Federal Reserve meetings or Supreme Court conferences. But executions are scripted rituals, not deliberative processes. Every other aspect of California's criminal justice system—trials, parole and clemency hearings, press conferences by condemned prisoners—can be televised.

The warden's real concerns, for the dignity of the occasion and for society's sensibilities, are serious. Solemnity should surround any person's death, and televised deaths might further coarsen American life.

There has not been a public execution since 1937 (a hanging in Galena, Mo.). At the time the Constitution was adopted, public executions were morality pageants, featuring civil and clerical orators, designed to buttress order and celebrate justice. But by the 1830s most states, alarmed by "animal feelings" aroused by public executions, moved executions behind prison walls, inviting representatives of the proliferating penny newspapers to be society's surrogate witnesses.

KQED says television conveys an "immediacy and reality" that is lost when events are "filtered through a reporter and conveyed only in words." It would be more accurate (and less obnoxious to writers) to say pictures have unique saliency and increasing importance in a decreasingly literate society. No camera can make capital punishment more troubling than Orwell ("A Hanging," just six pages long) and Camus ("Reflections on the Guillotine") did while working "only in words." Still, KQED could argue that Orwell and Camus are rarities and public understanding should not depend on literary genius being common in journalism.

It is dismaying but undeniable: Most Americans get most of their information, such as it is, from television. But televised executions would transmit peculiar "information," and for a problematic purpose. Information is normally valued as nourishment for reason. Many advocates of televised executions hope the horrifying sight would stir passions, particularly revulsion.

Attempts to proscribe capital punishment as unconstitutionally "cruel and unusual" have foundered on two facts: The Founders did not consider it so (the Constitution assumes its use) and society's "evolving standards of decency" have not made it so. Society's elected representatives continue to enact capital punishment.

KQED says it would not exercise a right to broadcast an execution live or without permission of the condemned. But although a court can affirm the journalistic right KQED asserts, it cannot mandate KQED's scrupulousness. Whether broadcast executions would be in bad taste or excite prurient interests are editorial concerns beyond the proper purview of government.

Televised executions might accelerate the desensitization of America. However, much death has been seen on American television: foreign executions (of the Ceausescues; a Saudi beheading), the Zapruder film of President Kennedy's exploding skull, Robert Kennedy bleeding onto a hotel kitchen floor, the explosion of the shuttle Challenger, Hank Gathers' death on a basketball court. Would tape of an execution be more lacerating to the public's sensibilities than the tape of Los Angeles police beating a motorist nearly to death?

There have been 143 executions since capital punishment was resumed in 1977. They have lost their novelty, hence much of their news value: A recent Texas execution (by lethal injection) did not even draw the permitted number of reporters. Perhaps this distresses those who support capital punishment for its deterrent power. If KQED prevails, publicity will be ample, at least for a while.

However, the dynamics of the public mind, and hence the consequences of a KQED victory, are unpredictable. Perhaps the unfiltered face of coolly inflicted death would annihilate public support for capital punishment. But perhaps society values capital punishment because of its horribleness, from which flows society's cathartic vengeance. All that is certain is that the constitutionality of capital punishment is linked to the public's values, which are malleable.

Clemency

Clemency—Introduction

Executive clemency is a last resort for death row prisoners. The U.S. Constitution vests the President with the power to commute or delay sentences, and to pardon offenses. Every state constitution has some provision for gubernatorial clemency. Most grant the governor total discretionary authority—either to act on his own or to act upon the recommendations of a clemency review board appointed by him. A governor or President may grant or withhold clemency for any reason he or she sees fit. These decisions cannot be constrained by the legislature, and are not subject to review by the courts.

States are generally free to conduct clemency proceedings in whatever manner they deem appropriate—or not to conduct them at all. In 1998, the United States Supreme Court held in *Ohio Adult Parole Authority v. Woodard* that if a state does conduct clemency proceedings, minimal due process must be accorded the inmate, though the emphasis seems to be on the word "minimal." The Court found that no further process was due Woodard, who had been given notice of the proceeding and an opportunity to be heard. In a concurrence, Justice Sandra Day O'Connor suggested that "judicial intervention might, for example, be warranted in the face of a scheme whereby a state official flipped a coin to determine whether to grant clemency." This affords the capital inmate greater protection than the ordinary prisoner, for whom due process rights are "extinguished" by conviction. The *Woodard* Court emphasized, though, that a state is not required to make clemency available at all. Whether it is defensible for the Court to offer greater, albeit thin, protection to capital inmates but not to ordinary defendants, is an interesting matter for discussion.

The concept of clemency can be traced back to the ancient Greeks. In biblical times, Pontius Pilate famously granted clemency to Barabbas, but not to Jesus. In the sixteenth century, King Henry VIII commuted the sentence of Sir Thomas More. More had been sentenced to be "drawn on a hurdle through London, after which he was to be hanged until he was 'half dead,' and then cut down alive to have 'his privy parts cut off, his belly ripped, his bowels burnt, his four quarters set up over four gates of the city, and his head upon London Bridge.'" Henry VIII reduced the sentence to "simple beheading."

The use of clemency is decreasing in the United States, a matter discussed at some length in Adam Gershowitz's article in the Perspectives section of this chapter. From the beginning of the 20th century through *Furman*, clemency is estimated to have been granted in more than 25% of capital cases. Between 1977 and 2000, juries and judges returned some 6500 death sentences. Executive clemency was granted in 87 of these cases. In 43 of these cases, governors granted clemency to avoid the cost of retrying the defendant when the Supreme Court had invalidated statutes under which the defendants were convicted. Thus, post-*Furman*, inmates have been granted clemency in less than 2% of all cases, and on the merits of their petitions less than 1% of the time.

Some notable disparities have been observed in grants of clemency. Professor Elizabeth Rappaport notes that women have been uncommonly successful in seeking clemency. Seven of the 44 grants of merit-based clemency since 1977 have been made to women—15.9%—though women constitute only about 1.4% of the death row population. The data suggests that Hispanics might do worse than average in securing clemency. The Supreme Court has not addressed whether the equal protection clause applies to clemency processes.

Clemency is controversial. Some argue that it is an anachronistic relic of monarchical times, and unjustifiable. Some defend clemency as an act of grace or mercy. Others, including the Supreme Court in *Herrera v. Collins*, regard clemency as a procedural failsafe—a final chance for the executive to correct an error that might have occurred in assessing guilt or sentence. Whether clemency is a reliable failsafe is debatable, given the absence of procedural regularities that attend it. Another view of clemency is that it allows the executive to consider factors not ordinarily taken into consideration by the courts.

The most controversial exercise of clemency in recent memory occurred in January 2003, when Illinois Governor George Ryan, as his last act in office, commuted the sentences of all 156 prisoners on death row in Illinois. Ryan was not the first governor to exercise the power of clemency broad brush. In 1970, Governor Winthrop Rockefeller of Arkansas commuted the death sentences of all 15 inmates on death row in Arkansas. Governor Rockefeller's decision, however, was grounded primarily in principled opposition to the death penalty. Governor Ryan's concerns ran more to practical concerns with the manner in which the Illinois death penalty was implemented.

Earlier in his term, Governor Ryan appointed the Illinois Commission on Capital Punishment. The Ryan Commission included academics, judges, prosecutors, and clergy. The commission issued 85 recommendations for reforming the Illinois capital sentencing system including limiting statutory aggravating factors, videotaping confessions, providing better funding for defense attorneys, and establishing guidelines for all cases. The Commission unanimously found that "no system, given human nature and frailties, could ever be devised or constructed that would work perfectly and guarantee absolutely that no innocent person is ever again sentenced to death." They cited, among other data, the study by Professor Liebman's team at Columbia, finding a 60% reversal rate in capital cases. On the basis of the commission's findings, Governor Ryan commuted the sentences of every prisoner on death row.

One line of objection to Governor Ryan's decision is procedural—clemency is about the granting of mercy in individual cases. The Ryan Commission raised systemic concerns with the Illinois capital process—it was a quintessentially legislative question whether to act on the concerns they raised. Governor Ryan might have been right, but it was for the Illinois legislature to say so. The Critical Documents section includes Governor Ryan's speech at Northwestern University College of Law in January 2003 explaining his decision to commute the sentences of the entirety of death row. The perspectives that follow offer three different views on the wisdom of Governor Ryan's actions, including an essay by Scott Turow, a member of the commission appointed by Ryan to study the death penalty in Illinois. The chapter concludes with an essay by Adam Gershowitz arguing that clemency has evolved (or devolved) in a manner that divests participants in the review process of responsibility and that this change increases the risk that an execution will be carried out in error.

■ Clemency—Critical Documents

Governor George Ryan's Speech at Northwestern University College of Law, January 11, 2003

Four years ago I was sworn in as the 39th Governor of Illinois. That was just four short years ago; that's when I was a firm believer in the American System of Justice and the death penalty. I believed that the ultimate penalty for the taking of a life was administrated in a just and fair manner.

Today, three days before I end my term as Governor, I stand before you to explain my frustrations and deep concerns about both the administration and the penalty of death. It is fitting that we are gathered here today at Northwestern University with the students, teachers, lawyers and investigators who first shed light on the sorrowful condition of Illinois' death penalty system.

Yes, it is right that I am here with you, where, in a manner of speaking, my journey from staunch supporter of capital punishment to reformer all began. But I must tell you, since the beginning of our journey, my thoughts and feelings about the death penalty have changed many, many times. I realize that over the course of my reviews I had said that I would not do blanket commutation. I have also said it was an option that was there and I would consider all options.

During my time in public office I have always reserved my right to change my mind if I believed it to be in the best public interest, whether it be about taxes, abortions or the death penalty. But I must confess that the debate with myself has been the toughest concerning the death penalty. I suppose the reason the death penalty has been the toughest is because it is so final, the only public policy that determines who lives and who dies. In addition it is the only issue that attracts most of the legal minds across the country. I have received more advice on this issue than any other policy issue I have dealt with in my 35 years of public service. I have kept an open mind on both sides of the issues of commutation for life or death.

I have read, listened to and discussed the issue with the families of the victims as well as the families of the condemned. I know that any decision I make will not be accepted by one side or the other. I know that my decision will be just that—my decision, based on all the facts I could gather over the past 3 years. I may never be comfortable with my final decision, but I will know in my heart, that I did my very best to do the right thing.

The other day, I received a call from former South African President Nelson Mandela who reminded me that the United States sets the example for justice and fairness for the rest of the world. Today the United States is not in league with most of our major allies: Europe, Canada, Mexico, most of South and Central America. These countries rejected the death penalty. We are partners in death with several third world countries. Even Russia has called a moratorium.

The death penalty has been abolished in twelve states. In none of these states has the homicide rate increased. In Illinois last year we had about 1,000 murders, only two percent of that 1,000 were sentenced to death. Where is the fairness and equality in that? The death penalty in Illinois is not imposed fairly or uniformly because of the absence of standards for the 102 Illinois State Attorneys, who must decide whether to request the death sentence. Should geography be a factor in determining who gets the death sentence? I don't think so but in Illinois it makes a difference. You are five times more likely to get a death sentence for first degree murder in the rural area of Illinois than you are in Cook County. Where is the justice and fairness in that? Where is the proportionality?

The Most Reverend Desmond Tutu wrote to me this week stating that "to take a life when a life has been lost is revenge, it is not justice." He says "justice allows for mercy, clemency and compassion. These virtues are not weakness."

"In fact the most glaring weakness is that no matter how efficient and fair the death penalty may seem in theory, in actual practice it is primarily inflicted upon the weak, the poor, the ignorant and against racial minorities." That was a quote from Former California Governor Pat Brown. He wrote that in his book "Public Justice, Private Mercy." He wrote that nearly 50 years ago; nothing has changed in nearly 50 years.

I never intended to be an activist on this issue. I watched in surprise as freed death row inmate Anthony Porter was released from jail. He was 48 hours away from being wheeled into the execution chamber where the state would kill him. It would all be so antiseptic and most of us would not have even paused, except that Anthony Porter was innocent of the double murder for which he had been condemned to die.

After Mr. Porter's case there was the report by *Chicago Tribune* reporters Steve Mills and Ken Armstrong documenting the systemic failures of our capital punishment system. Half of the nearly 300 capital cases in Illinois had been reversed for a new trial or resentencing.

Nearly half!

Thirty-three of the death row inmates were represented at trial by an attorney who had later been disbarred or at some point suspended from practicing law.

Of the more than 160 death row inmates, 35 were African American defendants who had been convicted or condemned to die by all-white juries.

More than two-thirds of the inmates on death row were African American.

Forty-six inmates were convicted on the basis of testimony from jailhouse informants.

I can recall looking at these cases and the information from the Mills/Armstrong series and asking my staff: How does that happen? How in God's name does that happen? I'm not a lawyer, so somebody explain it to me.

But no one could. Not to this day.

Then over the next few months there were three more exonerated men, freed because their sentence hinged on a jailhouse informant or new DNA technology proved beyond a shadow of doubt their innocence. We then had the dubious distinction of exonerating more men than we had executed. Thirteen men found innocent, twelve executed. That is an absolute embarrassment. How many more cases of wrongful conviction have to occur before we can all agree that the system is broken?

Throughout this process, I have heard many different points of view expressed. I have had the opportunity to review all of the cases involving the inmates on death row. I have conducted private group meetings with the surviving family members of homicide victims. Some wanted to express their grief, others wanted to express their anger. I took it all in.

My commission and my staff had been reviewing each and every case for three years. But, I redoubled my effort to review each case personally in order to respond to the concerns of prosecutors and victims' families. This individual review also naturally resulted in a collective examination of our entire death penalty system.

I also had a meeting with a group of people who are less often heard from, and who are not as popular with the media. The family members of death row inmates have a special challenge to face. Many of these families live with the twin pain of knowing not only that, in some cases, their family member may have been responsible for inflicting a terrible trauma on another family, but also the pain of knowing that society has called for another killing. These parents, siblings and children are not to blame for the crime committed, yet these innocent stand to have their loved ones killed by the state. As Mr. Mandela told me, they are also branded and scarred for life because of the awful crime committed by their family member.

In the United States the overwhelming majority of those executed are psychotic, alcoholic, drug addicted or mentally unstable. They frequently are raised in an impoverished and abusive environment. Seldom are people with money or prestige convicted of capital offenses, even more seldom are they executed.

I started with this issue concerned about innocence. But once I studied, once I pondered what had become of our justice system, I came to care above all about fairness. Fairness is fundamental to the American system of justice and our way of life.

The facts I have seen in reviewing each and every one of these cases raised questions not only about the innocence of people on death row, but about the fairness of the death penalty system as a whole. If the system was making so many errors in determining whether someone was guilty in the first place, how fairly and accurately was it determining which guilty defendants deserved to live and which deserved to die? What effect was race having? What effect was poverty having?

We not only have breakdowns in the system with police, prosecutors and judges, we have terrible cases of shabby defense lawyers. There is just no way to sugar coat it. There are defense attorneys that did not consult with their clients, did not investigate the case and were completely unqualified to handle complex death penalty cases. They often didn't put much effort into fighting a death sentence. If your life is on the line, your lawyer ought to be fighting for you. As I have said before, there is more than enough blame to go around.

I had more questions.

In Illinois, I have learned, we have 102 decision makers. Each of them is politically elected, each beholden to the demands of their community and, in some cases, to the media or especially vocal victims' families. In cases that have the attention of the media and the public, are decisions to seek the death penalty more likely to occur? What standards are these prosecutors using?

Some people have assailed my power to commute sentences, a power that literally hundreds of legal scholars from across the country have defended. But prosecutors in Illinois have the ultimate commutation power, a power that is exercised every day. They decide who will be subject to the death penalty, who will get a plea deal or even who may get a complete pass on prosecution. By what objective standards do they make these decisions? We do not know, they are not public. If you look at the cases, as I have done, both individually and collectively—a killing with the same circumstances might get 40 years in one county and death in another county. I have also seen where co-defendants who are equally or even more culpable get sentenced to a term of years, while another less culpable defendant ends up on death row.

What are we to make of the studies that showed that more than 50% of Illinois jurors could not understand the confusing and obscure sentencing instructions that were being used? What effect did that problem have on the trustworthiness of death sentences? A review of the cases shows that often even the lawyers and judges are confused about the instructions—let alone the jurors sitting in judgment.

I spent a good deal of time reviewing these death row cases. My staff, many of whom are lawyers, spent busy days and many sleepless nights answering my questions, providing me with information, giving me advice. It became clear to me that whatever decision I made, I would be criticized. It also became clear to me that it was impossible to make reliable choices about whether our capital punishment system had really done its job.

As I came closer to my decision, I knew that I was going to have to face the question of whether I believed so completely in the choice I wanted to make that I could face the prospect of even commuting the death sentence of Daniel Edwards, the man who had killed a close family friend of mine. I discussed it with my wife, Lura Lynn, who has stood by me all these years. She was angry and disappointed at my decision like many of the families of other victims will be.

I was struck by the anger of the families of murder victims. To a family they talked about closure. They pleaded with me to allow the state to kill an inmate in its name to provide the families with closure. But is that the purpose of capital punishment? Is it to soothe the families? And is that truly what the families experience?

I cannot imagine losing a family member to murder. Nor can I imagine spending every waking day for 20 years with a single-minded focus to execute the killer. The system of death in Illinois is so unsure that it is not unusual for cases to take 20 years before they are resolved. And thank God. If it had moved any faster, then the innocent men we've exonerated might be dead and buried.

But it is cruel and unusual punishment for family members to go through this pain, this legal limbo for 20 years. Perhaps it would be less cruel if we sentenced the killers to life, and used our resources to better serve victims. What kind of victims' services are we providing? Are all of our resources geared toward providing this notion of closure by execution instead of tending to the physical and social service needs of victim families? And what kind of values are we instilling in these wounded families and in the young people? As Gandhi said, an eye for an eye only leaves the whole world blind.

I have had to consider not only the horrible nature of the crimes that put men on death row in the first place, the terrible suffering of the surviving family members of the victims, the despair of the family members of the inmates, but I have also had to watch in frustration as members of the Illinois General Assembly failed to pass even one substantive death penalty reform. Not one. They couldn't even agree on one. How much more evidence is needed before the General Assembly will take its responsibility in this area seriously?

The fact is that the failure of the General Assembly to act is merely a symptom of the larger problem. Many people express the desire to have capital punishment. Few, however, seem prepared to address the tough questions that arise when the system fails. It is easier and more comfortable for politicians to be tough on crime and support the death penalty. It wins votes. But when it comes to admitting that we have a problem, most run for cover.

So when will the system be fixed? How much more risk can we afford? Will we actually have to execute an innocent person before the tragedy that is our capital punishment system in Illinois is really understood?

As I prepare to leave office, I had to ask myself whether I could really live with the prospect of knowing that I had the opportunity to act, but that I failed to do so because I might be criticized. Could I take the chance that our capital punishment system might be reformed, that wrongful convictions might not occur, that enterprising journalism students might free more men from death row? A system that's so fragile that it depends on young journalism students is seriously flawed.

"There is no honorable way to kill, no gentle way to destroy. There is nothing good in war. Except its ending." That's what Abraham Lincoln said about the bloody war between the states. It was a war fought to end the sorriest chapter in American history—the institution of slavery. While we are not in a civil war now, we are facing what is shaping up to be one of the great civil rights struggles of our time. Stephen Bright of the Southern Center for Human Rights has taken the position that the death penalty is being sought with increasing frequency in some states against the poor and minorities.

Our own study showed that juries were more likely to sentence to death if the victim were white than if the victim were black—three-and-a-half times more likely to be exact. Is our system fair to all? Is justice blind? These are important human rights issues.

The Governor has the constitutional role in our state of acting in the interest of justice and fairness. Our state constitution provides broad power to the Governor to issue reprieves, pardons and commutations. Our Supreme Court has reminded inmates petitioning them that the last resort for relief is the governor. At times the executive clemency power has perhaps been a crutch for courts to avoid making the kind of major change that I believe our system needs.

Our systemic case-by-case review has found more cases of innocent men wrongfully sentenced to death row. Because our three year study has found only more questions about the fairness of the sentencing; because of the spectacular failure to reform the system; because we have seen justice delayed for countless death row inmates with potentially meritorious claims; because the Illinois death penalty system is arbitrary and capricious—and therefore immoral—I no longer shall tinker with the machinery of death.

I cannot say it more eloquently than Justice Blackmun.

The legislature couldn't reform it.

Lawmakers won't repeal it.

But I will not stand for it.

I must act.

Our capital system is haunted by the demon of error, error in determining guilt, and error in determining whom among the guilty deserves to die. Because of all of these reasons today I am commuting the sentences of all death row inmates.

This is a blanket commutation. I realize it will draw ridicule, scorn and anger from many who oppose this decision. They will say I am usurping the decisions of judges and juries and state legislators. But as I have said, the people of our state have vested in me to act in the interest of justice. Even if the exercise of my power becomes my burden I will bear it. Our Constitution compels it. I sought this office, and even in my final days of holding it I cannot shrink from the obligations to justice and fairness that it demands.

There have been many nights where my staff and I have been deprived of sleep in order to conduct our exhaustive review of the system. But I can tell you this: I will sleep well knowing I made the right decision.

As I said when I declared the moratorium, it is time for a rational discussion on the death penalty. While our experience in Illinois has indeed sparked a debate, we have fallen short of a rational discussion. Yet if I did not take this action, I feared that there would be no comprehensive and thorough inquiry into the guilt of the individuals on death row or of the fairness of the sentences applied.

To say it plainly one more time—the Illinois capital punishment system is broken. It has taken innocent men to a hair's breadth escape from their unjust execution. Legislatures past have refused to fix it. Our new legislature and our new Governor must act to rid our state of the shame of threatening the innocent with execution and the guilty with unfairness.

In the days ahead, I will pray that we can open our hearts and provide something for victims' families other than the hope of revenge. Lincoln once said: "I have always found that mercy bears richer fruits than strict justice." I can only hope that will be so. God bless you. And God bless the people of Illinois.

■ Clemency—Perspectives

■ Issue—Was Governor Ryan Justified in Commuting the Sentences of Illinois' Death Row?

Jack Dunphy, "Cowardice Masquerading as Courage"

Illinois Governor George Ryan, his term in office drawing to a close, has commuted the death sentences for all 156 inmates awaiting execution on the state's death row. In doing so, he has apparently chosen to follow the Jimmy Carter model, which is to say he hopes to find in retirement the respectability and adulation denied to him while in office. Perhaps Matt Lauer will one day refer to him as "Illinois's greatest former governor." The cynic may argue that Ryan, under criminal investigation for corruption in both his campaign and administration, may have been moved to act as he did by the desire for a friendly reception should he someday find himself walking the yard in pressed denim. "Hi, fellas. I'm the guy who got you off the row, remember?"

Whatever his motivation, Ryan's action is an insult to the justice system, one more injurious than any of the system's flaws he cited in his speech at Northwestern University. Addressing an enthusiastic crowd of students, defense attorneys, and assorted other death penalty opponents, Ryan chided his state's legislators for failing to address the crisis. "Because the Illinois death penalty system is arbitrary and capricious—and therefore immoral—I no longer shall tinker with the machinery of death," Ryan said, bringing the crowd to its feet. Granted, there have been inmates condemned to death in Illinois only to be exonerated later, in one instance only days before the scheduled execution, and the governor has rightly criticized flaws in individual cases that raise questions as to the propriety of a death sentence. But Ryan's decision to issue a blanket commutation on 156 death sentences, even in cases where there is not a shred of doubt as to the defendant's guilt, is no less arbitrary and capricious than the "broken" system he so passionately criticizes. He had four years in office to institute reform in the system, but now leaves office on a wave of pieties and platitudes, leaving to his successor a system now, thanks to him, even more in chaos than when he was inaugurated.

Ryan trotted out many of the shibboleths so often heard from death-penalty opponents, criticisms that may make for nice sound-bites on the news or heart-wrenching quotes in the fawning op-ed pieces that will surely appear in the *New York Times* and elsewhere: The system is unfair to minorities and the poor; other Western nations have abolished the death penalty, and our continued practice of it places us in the company of barbarous regimes; only two percent of the murders in Illinois result in a death sentence; both Nelson Mandela and Bishop Desmond Tutu have beseeched him to abolish the death penalty; and on and on and on.

First, as to the supplications of Mandela and Tutu, one only need examine the ongoing carnage on the streets of South Africa, where the murder rate is roughly ten times that of the United States, to see that it is perhaps the last country in the world we should look to for guidance in the administration of justice. And if it is true that only two percent of Illinois's murders result in a death sentence, isn't that an argument that the system is anything but arbitrary and capricious, that death sentences are meted out only after careful consideration by prosecutors, judges, and above all juries, and even then only in such cases where the crime is so horrific that execution is clearly warranted?

But the greatest insult to common sense in Ryan's speech was his invocation of those last-resort weapons of the left: race and class. There is a simple reason for this, Governor Ryan: People with money and prestige, with the possible exception of some in the entertainment industry and professional sports, have acquired both their money and their prestige by conforming to society's conventions, one of the more obvious of which is refraining from the type of conduct likely to earn one a seat in the defendant's chair at a murder trial.

On Sunday, the *Chicago Tribune* published a list of the inmates spared from execution, along with a synopsis of the crime for which each was sentenced to death. Consider the following:

- Lorenzo Fayne: Stabbed or strangled four girls, ages 9 to 17. He sexually assaulted one victim and molested the body of another.
- Anthony Brown: Strangled and suffocated a 67-year-old woman in her home. He had previously served time in prison for rape.
- Lenard Johnson: Stabbed an 11-year-old boy to death and sexually assaulted three girls, ages 7, 11, and 13, while babysitting them in their home.
- Fedell Caffey and Jacqueline Williams: Shot a pregnant woman in her home, cut the nearly full-term baby from her womb, and stabbed her two children.

Ryan told his audience Saturday that he "will sleep well knowing he made the right decision." Others will not be so fortunate: They are the families of the 250 people murdered by the depraved beneficiaries of the outgoing governor's crisis of conscience.

There is a Jewish proverb in the Pirkei Avot (Ethics of the Fathers): "He who is kind to the cruel is cruel to the kind." You've made your choice, Governor Ryan. Enjoy your sleep.

"The Education of Governor Ryan," *The New York Times*, January 13, 2003

Nothing became Gov. George Ryan's term in office like his leaving it. As the clock ticked out on the Illinois governor's last days in office, he made a series of dramatic announcements that emptied his state's death row. We can only join in his hope that this sweeping, and almost shocking, gesture leads the rest of the country to reconsider whether America wants to continue to be in the business of state-sanctioned death.

Mr. Ryan, who opened a new national discussion of the death penalty in 2000 when he declared a moratorium on executions, commuted the death sentences of 163 men and 4 women to prison terms last weekend and freed four other men. It was a strange end to a political life that he began as an enthusiastic champion of capital punishment.

As governor, he was stunned by a series of close calls in which men on death row were found to be innocent—in one case just 48 hours before a scheduled execution. He determined that the death penalty was being imposed arbitrarily—a person found guilty of murder in a rural district of Illinois, he pointed out, was five times more likely to be sentenced to death than someone who committed murder in Chicago. The population on death row was overwhelmingly African-American and 35 prisoners had been condemned by all-white juries. Many of the condemned men and women were represented by incompetent or less-than-attentive attorneys.

No one will ever know how much Mr. Ryan's dramatic finale was affected by a second factor: a corruption scandal relating to his years as the Illinois secretary of state, a mess that destroyed his political career and for which he is expected to be indicted. Death penalty supporters are bound to claim that he was attempting to seize the moral high ground with a big gesture. We cannot look inside his heart. We do know his actions over the weekend were not the product of sudden desperation, but a gradual and painful re-education.

The four men Mr. Ryan pardoned outright had been condemned based on confessions elicited in a notorious Chicago police station that used torture to prod confessions from suspects. The others will continue to serve long sentences. Nevertheless, many members of the public will be horrified at the idea of showing any mercy whatsoever to some of the clearly guilty people involved. One man murdered a mother and her children, and ripped a full-term fetus from the woman's womb. And no one can be completely comfortable with this sort of sweeping use of the governor's right to pardon.

Mr. Ryan's conversion was helped along by the State Legislature, which consistently refused to consider any of the laws he promoted in an attempt to rationalize the death penalty system. It is hard to understand why supporters of capital punishment would not be eager to make sure that an innocent person is never executed. But attempts to provide everyone accused of a capital crime with competent legal defense and access to DNA evidence continue to fall short. In Washington, the Innocence Protection Act languishes in committee despite the support of more than half the House members.

This page has never seen the need to go there at all. The satisfaction of retribution that the death penalty supplies can never outweigh the danger of unfair or erroneous application as long as it exists. Virtually every country on the planet has rejected capital punishment as barbaric. Perhaps Governor Ryan, in the tortured end to his political career, can help lead the nation to a similar conclusion.

Scott Turow, "Clemency Without Clarity"

Before he left office on Monday, George Ryan, a longtime supporter of capital punishment, emptied the state's death row by pardoning four condemned men and commuting the sentences of the remaining 167 prisoners. Some are calling this an act of tremendous bravery, while prosecutors and the families of victims claim justice was thwarted. Many others believe he should have acted in the most questionable cases without providing leniency to some of the state's most brutal and unrepentant murderers.

Personally, I think the former governor did not have an easy or clear way out, and I would defend him for that reason. Yet, as a member of the governor's commission that issued a report on death-penalty reform that led to lawyers filing the clemency claims for virtually all of these prisoners, I am concerned about what we have wrought. The stability and reliability of the law as an institution are brought into question when the work of many years by the police, prosecutors, judges and juries—as well as the implied promise to victims' families—is overturned because of the actions of a single individual, no matter how well intended or even necessary.

This issue—the risk of undermining Americans' faith in the legal process—is perhaps the most overlooked aspect of the death-penalty debate. And, paradoxically, it may be the most compelling reason for those who now favor the death penalty to reconsider their position.

Governor Ryan found himself in an all-too-familiar position. Despite clear problems in the capital system, the public passion to see the worst crimes subjected to the most severe punishment makes legislators fearful of intervening, forcing executive officials or the courts to step in. Prosecutors have a natural unwillingness to undo their own work. Those with clemency powers have to steer between playing God and incurring public wrath. And the courts have given us three decades of conflicting decisions and shifting legal grounds on the issue. In short, Governor Ryan was hardly upending a stable system producing predictable results.

Rather, the 14-member commission on which I served found persistent problems: false confessions that had been coerced or dubiously reported by the police; mistaken eyewitness identifications; murderers who portrayed innocent people as accomplices; jailhouse informants who became witnesses in exchange for the kinds of favors that clearly tempted lies; and a statutory structure that provided an obvious pathway to arbitrariness in deciding who was to die.

We made 85 substantive proposals for reform, including requiring the police to videotape the full interrogation of murder suspects, reducing the number of circumstances making defendants eligible for the death penalty and establishing a statewide commission to review any case in which a local prosecutor wanted to seek a death sentence.

These proposals were greeted respectfully, although hardly with universal acclaim. Still, the state prosecutors' organization, the two candidates hoping to succeed Governor Ryan, the state's major newspapers and a host of legislators joined in the call for substantial reforms.

Yet none have been passed because of political wrangling and the chronic timidity of officials when it comes time to take positions that can later be labeled as soft on crime. When I testified last summer before the State Senate judiciary committee in favor of reducing the scope of the death penalty statute, one member confessed on the record how dangerous a yea vote might be in the hands of future political opponents.

Moreover, the failure to reform the system also left unanswered the question of how to deal with past cases. No one—not the legislature, the prosecutors, the candidates, or even the commission on which I served—offered any alternative to Governor Ryan. He either had to accept the results of a system everyone agreed needed to be fixed or exercise the clemency powers the state constitution imposed on him.

And, because a scrupulous review of the death row cases was likely to require the governor to act in some cases, it left him in the position of having to decide whether he was obliged to reduce all the state's death sentences. Knowing the details of so many of these cases, I could see how difficult it was to draw the line.

Again and again, the cases that seem to present the most compelling facts favoring execution prove, under scrutiny, to contain elements raising doubts. Probably the most dangerous man in the Illinois penitentiary system is a twice-convicted murderer, believed to have killed at least five people. He has compiled a record of repeated serious assaults on inmates and guards with a startling variety of deadly weapons. But his death sentence was based on the testimony of two eyewitnesses who now claim they implicated him falsely because of pressure from prosecutors.

Another man who murdered two police officers had been in mental institutions for more than 20 years and may well have been incompetent at the time he plead guilty. And there were also several horrible murders where one defendant was sentenced to die, while prosecutors or juries allowed a highly culpable co-defendant to live in prison. In the end, the governor says he could find no principled way to pick and choose.

What happened in Illinois is a cautionary lesson. Inaction by legislatures forces more and more of the responsibility for creating remedies into the hands of government executives or the courts. The solutions they arrive at are often unpopular, and the principles that guide them prove subject to constant change because of the irreconcilable tension between individualized decision-making and the constitutional demand that we impose this ultimate sanction on a consistent and reasoned basis.

At the end of the day, perhaps the best argument against capital punishment may be that it is an issue beyond the limited capacity of government to get things right.

■ Issue—Is Clemency a Reliable Failsafe?

Adam M. Gershowitz, "The Diffusion of Responsibility in Capital Clemency"

I. *Introduction*

The Supreme Court of the United States has described executive clemency as the "fail safe in the criminal justice system." In death-penalty cases that fail safe is essential. Capital punishment is being used more often than at any time in recent memory and, despite occasional predictions to the contrary, there is no decline on the foreseeable horizon. At the same time that the use of capital punishment has increased, the Supreme Court has "deregulated" the death penalty. The Court no longer conducts proportionality review of death sentences, habeas corpus has been scaled back, and trial courts are not obligated to instruct juries about mitigating evidence. Given the Court's hands-off approach and the more frequent use of capital punishment, executive clemency takes on even greater importance. In short, clemency truly does have the potential to be the fail safe of the criminal justice system. Unfortunately, however, that potential has not been realized. In fact, the use of executive clemency has dramatically declined in the last few decades.

What is striking about executive clemency is not that both the executive and the courts have responsibility but, rather, that neither is willing to accept that responsibility. In short, the area of capital clemency is the site of a total diffusion of responsibility: The Court will not regulate the clemency process because it is a matter for the executive and some governors will not grant clemency because the execution process belongs entirely to the courts. All the while, the use of capital punishment continues to increase, the deregulation of the death penalty continues, and the Supreme Court continues to proclaim executive clemency as the fail safe of the criminal justice system.

The diffusion of responsibility in capital clemency is dangerous. Social science and historical evidence demonstrate that when responsibility is diffused, actors will engage in behavior that they might otherwise believe to be immoral or unacceptable. An innocent defendant wrongly sentenced to death is no doubt deserving of clemency. And while most individuals sentenced to death clearly are guilty of vile acts, some guilty defendants also may be deserving of clemency. Yet, governors who have doubts about certain death sentences may not use their authority to grant clemency (or use their bully pulpits to encourage pardon boards to do so) because they believe responsibility for the execution lies elsewhere. Conversely, courts will not step forward to ensure a proper clemency system because they believe that the executive branch alone is responsible for clemency. Under these circumstances the clemency mechanism may fail to halt questionable executions.

II. *The Governors' Failure to Take Responsibility*

The most obvious evidence of the failure of chief executives to take responsibility for executive clemency is the drastic decline in the number of commutations. In the nearly twenty-five years between *Gregg* and January 2001, only forty-four death-row inmates were granted clemency for humanitarian reasons. This is a marked decrease from the number of clemencies granted prior to the Court's 1972 moratorium on capital punishment. For instance, from 1960 to 1971—only an eleven-year period, as opposed to the twenty-five years from *Gregg* to the present—204 death sentences were commuted. Before the Supreme Court's moratorium, one out of every four or five death sentences was commuted to life imprisonment. By 1990 that ratio had dwindled to one commutation for every forty death-sentences. The post-1976 decrease in commutations is even more marked when we consider that the number of executions is on the rise. While there were 191 executions in the 1960's and 3 executions in the 1970's, there were 117 executions in the 1980's and 478 in the 1990's. As the number of executions has increased the number of commutations has drastically decreased.

What explains this trend? The most optimistic answer would be that governors have found fewer legitimate reasons to grant clemency in recent years. One hypothesis might be that trials have become fairer, or that the mentally retarded and mentally ill are no longer convicted of capital offenses. Another might be that racism is no longer omnipresent in the criminal justice system or that innocent people are no longer wrongly sentenced to death. Most death-penalty experts would quickly dispose of these rosy scenarios, however. In our modern era, capital defense attorneys still sleep through trials, the merits of appeals are not considered if they are submitted a day too late, and the danger of convicting the innocent is as great as ever.

Instead, the decrease in commutations seems to be the result of political ambition. Governors secure their reputation of being tough on crime (and, by extension, their re-election) by refusing to grant clemency. Governors deftly take credit for being tough on crime while avoiding any blame for refusing to grant executive clemency. They do this in two ways. First, governors explain away their decisions not to grant clemency by saying that the prisoner had fair access to the courts. Second, governors utilize state pardon boards to insulate themselves from responsibility for declining to grant clemency.

III. *Pardon Boards and the Diffusion of Responsibility*

The existence of pardon boards unfortunately creates a diffusion of responsibility that permits governors to avoid their clemency duties. The diffusion happens as follows: pardon boards recommend that clemency not be granted. Governors then deny clemency and point to the pardon board's negative recommendation as the reason why clemency should be denied. Governors can say that they are merely following the recommendation of the pardon board and therefore are not responsible for the execution. Quantitative analysis suggests, and qualitative analysis confirms, that this diffusion of responsibility results in fewer clemencies.

All thirty-eight death-penalty states, as well as the federal government, have some type of clemency mechanism. Obviously, there are enormous political and cultural differences among the thirty-eight states that authorize the death penalty. It is therefore dangerous to over-generalize by clumping states into categories such as pardon-board states or non-pardon board states. Nevertheless, these categorizations yield interesting results. The data suggest that states in which governors have the sole responsibility for clemency decisions have considerably higher rates of commutations in comparison to the rates of executions.

In fourteen states the governor has the sole responsibility for granting or denying clemency. (In the federal government, the president has the sole responsibility for clemency decisions.) The fourteen sole-responsibility states carried out less than 24% of the nation's executions between 1976 and 2000, but they constitute more than 36% of the forty-four clemencies granted during that time-period. States in which there is a diffusion of responsibility between the governor and the pardon boards account for 70.3% of the executions but only 52.3% of the clemencies.

The conclusion that larger numbers of clemencies are granted when there is no diffusion of responsibility is further amplified when we consider the six states in which the clemency board is the sole and final decision-maker. In these states there is no diffusion of responsibility because the board has the final say on all clemencies. Adding these states to the governor-only states accounts for 29.7% of the executions but 47% of the clemencies. By way of comparison, recall that the states in which there is a diffusion of responsibility between the governor and the pardon board account for 70.3% of the executions but only 52.3% of the clemencies.

This data suggests that clemency is less likely to be granted when responsibility for its use is diffused between the governor and the pardon board. This conclusion could be challenged however because, between 1976 and 2000, Texas was responsible for 35% of the executions but only .02% of the clemencies. Texas therefore may be an outlier resulting in a false suggestion that the diffusion of responsibility between pardon boards and the governor lowers the number of clemencies.

When Texas is excluded, the data suggest that there is no substantial difference between states where there is one clemency decision-maker and states in which there is a diffusion of responsibility between the governor and the pardon boards. As a matter of statistics it may be proper to exclude Texas as an outlier. However, in an analysis of the death penalty and capital clemency, it is inconceivable that Texas—the site of half of the nation's executions in some years—should be excluded. Moreover, excluding Texas as an outlier, while not controlling for some northern states that infrequently utilize the death penalty but still actively exercise clemency, would be problematic.

One way to compensate for Texas's large number of executions, while still including it in the analysis, is to narrow the sample to the so-called "death-belt states," those southern states where most of the nation's executions are carried out. Between 1976 and 2000, the ten death-belt states—Alabama, Arkansas, Georgia, Florida, Louisiana, Missouri, Oklahoma, South Carolina, Texas, and Virginia—accounted for 83% of the nation's executions. In total, these states accounted for only 51% of the nation's commutations.

More interesting than the low percentage of clemencies in the death-belt states is the breakdown between those states in which there is a diffusion of responsibility between the governor and the pardon board and those states in which there is no diffusion of responsibility. States in which either the governor or the clemency board is the sole decision-maker account for 152 executions and 11 clemencies. States in which responsibility is diffused between the governor and the pardon board also account for 11 clemencies but 414 executions. Thus, where there is no diffusion of responsibility, clemency appears substantially more likely to be granted.

Dozens of social science studies confirm that individuals are less likely to take action when there is a diffusion of responsibility. The story of Kitty Genovese provides a powerful example. In 1964, Ms. Genovese was attacked for over thirty-five minutes outside of a New York apartment building. Nearly forty residents heard her screams, but none came to her assistance or called for help. Each witness assumed someone else had heard the screams and already had called for help. Ms. Genovese died as a result of the attacks. She was a victim of the diffusion of responsibility. Had there been only one witness, and had that witness known that he alone was in a position to help, Kitty Genovese would have been more likely to survive.

Unfortunately, in the area of capital clemency the Supreme Court and a number of governors have ignored the story of Kitty Genovese and the findings of social scientists. There is a vast diffusion of responsibility in capital clemency. In *Ohio v. Woodard*, the Court concluded that clemency is solely a matter for the executive branch. The Court refused to take responsibility and to impose procedural safeguards because it believed that someone else—the executive—was responsible. The executive branch has failed to take responsibility as well however. Governors have disclaimed responsibility for executions (and denied clemency) because the inmate had full and fair access to the courts. Essentially, governors have disclaimed responsibility because they think the courts are responsible for the execution. The situation is further complicated by the diffusion of responsibility between governors and pardon boards. Governors deny clemency because of recommendations from the pardon board; accordingly governors are not responsible because they are following the pardon boards' recommendations. At the same time, the individual members of the pardon board can believe that they are not responsible either. In some states the pardon board merely offers a recommendation, and therefore board members can have the mind-set that it is the governor who is responsible. Board members who are the final decision-makers can also avoid feeling responsible by shifting responsibility to the courts. As noted, some members of the Texas Board of Pardons and Paroles vote to deny clemency after checking to make sure that courts conducted appellate review of the prisoner's death sentence.

IV. *Conclusion*

There is a diffusion of responsibility in capital clemency. The Court has concluded that clemency is solely a matter for the executive branch. Some governors however have tried to avoid this responsibility by claiming that the matter should be left to the courts or that they are just following the pardon board. In some instances neither the governor, the pardon board, nor the courts are willing to take responsibility for clemency and executions. This diffusion of responsibility is dangerous. Governors, pardon boards, and the courts might not stop questionable executions because they believe it is someone else's responsibility to do so. If clemency is to be the fail safe against improper execution, these entities must take responsibility for denying (or granting) clemency. The first step is for the Court to take responsibility by mandating procedural safeguards: the rights of the petitioner to present evidence, to make a statement, to have the assistance of counsel, and to appear before the final decision-maker(s). These procedural safeguards will eliminate the diffusion of responsibility by forcing the final decision-makers in the executive branches to take responsibility for the substantive decision to decline (or grant) clemency.

24

The Moratorium Movement

■ Introduction—The Moratorium Movement

In 1997, the House of Delegates of the American Bar Association, describing the state of affairs as "deplorable," called for a moratorium on executions in the United States. The ABA said the moratorium should last until the jurisdictions adopted policies to: "(1) ensure that death penalty cases are administered fairly and impartially, in accordance with due process, and (2) minimize the risk that innocent persons may be executed." Specifically, the ABA expressed its continued concern that capital defendants did not receive competent counsel, that *habeas corpus* reform had restricted the ability of state and federal courts to correct injustices, that racial discrimination tainted the capital sentencing process, and that mentally retarded and juvenile offenders were not exempted. The report said, "Two decades after *Gregg*, it is apparent that the efforts to forge a fair capital punishment jurisprudence have failed. Today, administration of the death penalty, far from being fair and consistent, is instead a haphazard maze of unfair practices with no internal consistency."

The ABA resolution established some momentum for a revived moratorium movement. Several local bar associations, including those in Atlanta, Georgia; Baltimore, Maryland; Charlotte, North Carolina; Philadelphia, Pennsylvania; and San Francisco, California have followed the ABA lead and called for moratoria in their respective jurisdictions. In 1999, the Nebraska Legislature voted for a moratorium, though the governor vetoed the resolution. In 2000, Governor Ryan of Illinois imposed a moratorium, which lasted until his decision to commute the sentences of the entire death row population. Illinois remains the only state to have enacted a post-*Gregg* moratorium, but several states, including Indiana, Maryland, and Nebraska, have undertaken reviews of the administration of the death penalty in their states.

Concern with executing the innocent has fueled this movement more than any other factor. The ABA resolution expresses this explicitly. Governor Ryan's decision to impose the moratorium in Illinois was a direct response to the problem of innocence in his state. In 1999, Anthony Porter, ultimately exonerated, came within days of being executed by Illinois. At the eleventh hour, a lawyer secured a stay on the grounds that Porter might not be able to understand why he was being put to death. To this point, no one had asserted his innocence. A Northwestern University journalism class investigated Porter's case and demonstrated his innocence. A series of articles in the *Chicago Tribune* highlighted the prevalence of potentially innocent defendants on death row in Illinois. The publication of *Actual Innocence* by Jim Dwyer, Barry Scheck, and Peter Neufeld brought attention to the problem of innocence on a national level.

DNA evidence might not be the only factor contributing to this concern with innocence, but it is almost certainly the most important. For the first time, science offers the possibility of conclusively exonerating a convicted defendant. DNA evidence might be a double-edged sword, though. For the falsely convicted defendant, it is a pure godsend. But DNA evidence is available in only a small fraction of murder cases. The concern is that DNA evidence might create a false appearance of regularity, not unlike the effect that Professors Steiker and Steiker argue that *Gregg* has had on the concern with arbitrariness in death sentencing: the appearance of reform might be greater than the reality.

What are the implications of DNA evidence for the future of the moratorium movement? Ron Tabak, a leading abolitionist and president of New York Lawyers Against the Death Penalty, is buoyant about its impact. Tabak argues that DNA evidence allows prosecutors and public officials to express and act on their reservations about the death penalty without appearing weak. Professor John Wefing, also an abolitionist, argues that DNA evidence will have the opposite effect—it will assuage the public's concern with innocence, and allow prosecutors to seek the death penalty with impunity.

■ The Moratorium Movement—Critical Documents

American Bar Association Resolution Endorsing Moratoria on Executions

AS APPROVED BY THE ABA HOUSE OF DELEGATES FEBRUARY 3, 1997:
RESOLVED, That the American Bar Association calls upon each jurisdiction that imposes capital punishment not to carry out the death penalty until the jurisdiction implements policies and procedures that are consistent with the following longstanding American Bar Association policies intended to (1) ensure that death penalty cases are administered fairly and impartially, in accordance with due process, and (2) minimize the risk that innocent persons may be executed:

    (i) Implementing ABA "Guidelines for the Appointment and Performance of Counsel in Death Penalty Cases" and Association policies intended to encourage competency of counsel in capital cases;

    (ii) Preserving, enhancing, and streamlining state and federal courts' authority and responsibility to exercise independent judgment on the merits of constitutional claims in state post-conviction and federal habeas corpus proceedings;

    (iii) Striving to eliminate discrimination in capital sentencing on the basis of the race of either the victim or the defendant; and

(iv) Preventing execution of mentally retarded persons and persons who were under the age of 18 at the time of their offenses.

FURTHER RESOLVED, That in adopting this recommendation, apart from existing Association policies relating to offenders who are mentally retarded or under the age of 18 at the time of the commission of the offenses, the Association takes no position on the death penalty.

The Moratorium Movement—Perspectives

Issue—Will DNA Evidence Advance the Moratorium Movement?

Ronald J. Tabak, "Finality Without Fairness: Why We are Moving Towards Moratoria on Executions, and the Potential Abolition of Capital Punishment"

At least ninety-five people have been released from death rows since the death penalty's re-imposition in 1976—eight in 2000 and two in the first two months of 2001—due to their having been convicted erroneously. *Actual Innocence*, a book by Pulitzer-prize winner Jim Dwyer and leading DNA legal experts Barry Scheck and Peter Neufeld, had a huge impact after its early 2000 publication. Several long-standing influential supporters of capital punishment became extremely troubled about the death penalty's actual implementation after reading the book's accounts about numerous exonerations due to long after-the-fact DNA testing. For example, syndicated columnist and ABC News commentator George Will, a Pulitzer-prize winner far more conservative than Dwyer, stated, after reading *Actual Innocence*, that those who have never trusted the government to do other things properly should now also be skeptical about the government's accuracy in convicting people of crimes making them eligible for the death penalty.

What effects are these DNA-related developments beginning to have on public discourse concerning capital punishment? First, it has become obvious that the courts can make and, absent fortuitous developments, fail to correct serious factual errors in death penalty cases. Condemned inmates' claims of innocence can sometimes be validated or invalidated by subsequent fact-gathering and DNA analyses, but often the truth cannot be discerned—as where the key to the guilt determination is not physical evidence, or where no DNA analysis can be done because the physical evidence cannot be tested or does not even exist anymore. Moreover, while prisoners under lengthy sentences may be exonerated long after being convicted erroneously, thanks to newly available scientific modes of analysis such as DNA, a similarly happy fate does not await many innocent death row inmates—especially in view of the truncated legal reviews recently mandated by Congress and some state legislatures.

Second—although the great public emphasis on DNA testing may obscure this—science is often unable to provide dispositive results. Notwithstanding all the hoopla surrounding DNA testing, it can be performed only in a small minority of situations in which significant biological evidence from the real culprit is collected properly at the scene of the crime.

The public is only beginning to recognize that even good faith efforts by police to determine who has committed a crime and by prosecutors to convict only the guilty are inherently subject to error. Unfortunately, our legal system has often failed to uncover such error when it has led to a conviction and death sentence.

During the era when virtually the sole bases for identifying suspects were confessions and eyewitness testimony, people were erroneously convicted who probably would not have even been accused if law enforcement had had the ability of performing valid fingerprint analyses. Later, the initial forms of DNA analyses helped avoid certain of the mistaken convictions that had occurred when nothing more sophisticated than fingerprint analyses were available in making identifications. Now, we have more sophisticated DNA analyses, which are undoubtedly less reliable and useful in many cases than analyses that have yet to be developed.

Thus, each new analytical development enhances our ability to be accurate in criminal identifications. This means that we have convicted innocent people prior to each past analytical development whom those developments would have exonerated, and that we will inevitably convict innocent people now whom we would never even be accusing if future analytical advances had already occurred.

The public may be beginning to learn that skepticism about the legal system's ability to convict only the guilty is not limited to situations where DNA analyses can be performed. Errors can also occur in the vast majority of cases in which the physical evidence required for valid DNA analysis does not exist. Indeed, the substantial degree of errors uncovered through DNA analysis should increase concern about the accuracy of results in situations where such analysis cannot be performed. This concern should be particularly enhanced with regard to death penalty cases, because they are more likely than other cases to be investigated and tried under circumstances that can skew the efforts of fact-finders. Under these circumstances, the lawyers appointed to represent capital defendants often lack the ability, resources or investigative or expert assistance necessary to attack evidence that can lead to erroneous convictions.

The increasing public awareness of problems with the accuracy and fairness of our capital punishment systems has not yet had a discernible impact on the manner in which the courts are handling these cases. And it is not likely to begin doing so for some time.

Why? Many judges have not yet noticed the change in public concern about the death penalty system. Even when judges do notice this, they will want to see whether it is an enduring concern before they take it seriously. Even when they realize that this concern is not going to disappear, judges are not likely to respond quickly, for several reasons. First, the self-image of judges is that they do not pay attention to election returns—even though many of them obviously have done so, particularly in dealing with capital punishment cases.

Second, many trial-level judges—and almost all appellate judges—have issued rulings that have resulted in people being executed. The first reaction by many such judges to an anti-death penalty or moratorium movement would likely be to resent it, as an implicit criticism of their past rulings.

Nevertheless, judges are bound to respond in time to increased public concern about the death penalty process. Before considering why, it is important to focus on two major aspects of the public-discourse revolution that merit special attention.

I. *Two Especially Notable Aspects of the Public-Discourse Revolution*

First, the realization is growing in the United States that the death penalty is a political issue. It has been recognized as being so almost everywhere else in the world, and that has contributed to its demise in virtually all industrialized democracies in the Western world.

In the United States, the death penalty is still often considered to be a legal or a criminological policy issue. This has resulted in humanitarian and civil liberties concerns, and even values like racial equality, being subordinated to crime-control concerns from the outset. But in fact, the death penalty has no discernible impact on controlling crime, other than to expend resources that could be used to try to control crime. But while the professionals implementing capital punishment often realize this, it usually does not affect their conduct.

The very fact that the public media today is full of dramatic stories and opinionated debate about the death penalty will begin to unsettle the notion that capital punishment is a routinely functioning part of the routinely functioning criminal-justice system, and to reconceptualize it as a controversial political issue. The flash-points for discussion and the sound-bites that sum up the debate emphasize aspects of capital punishment that make it a political question rather than a question of penological policy or legal technique.

A second general point, paralleling the growing transformation of capital punishment in the public's perception from a penological issue into a political one, has been a shift in public discourse about the death penalty from incident-focused discussion to issue-focused discussion. This is epitomized by the sound-bite summations of the recent Columbia University study proclaiming the capital punishment system to be broken and "collapsing under the weight of its own mistakes." But this transformation preceded that study and is characteristic of all aspects of the discourse revolution.

Historically, public discussion and all decisions about capital punishment in this country since the middle of the nineteenth century have tended to be incident-driven and incident-focused, not issue-driven or issue-focused. Particular crimes, particular criminals, particular horror stories which capture the imagination by riveting attention on the Mansons, Gacys, and Bundys have dominated public attention and distracted it from issues centering on the ways in which the death penalty works and fails to work in general.

To the extent that public discourse about capital punishment is incident-oriented rather than issue-oriented, those opposed to the death penalty or concerned about its implementation have always suffered because the incidents that provide a focus for discussion and debate almost always enlist sympathy for the victim, horror at the perpetrator, and a punitive reaction. The most attractive condemned inmate—even Karla Faye Tucker—is less sympathetic and emotionally affecting than the innocent victim of a brutal homicide.

Conversely, when public discourse shifts away from a focus on specific incidents toward a focus on general issues, those opposed to capital punishment or concerned about its implementation gain ground. An issue transcending specific incidents emerges only when a whole group or series of cases is perceived as presenting some common feature-some common theme or collective pattern.

II. *Why the Public-Discourse Revolution Will Begin to Affect the Manner in Which Actors in the Legal System Deal with Capital Cases*

A. The Judiciary The most important effect of the public-discourse revolution regarding the death penalty is capital punishment's transformation in that discourse from a legal or criminal-policy issue into a political issue. So long as the public continued to believe that the death penalty was a strictly legal, criminal-policy issue, judges who imposed and upheld death sentences could feel that they were "just doing their jobs" in implementing capital punishment; that they were the impersonal organs of a neutral, objective system.

But as the death penalty is increasingly recognized as the political instrument it is, more and more judges will develop serious doubts about their role in implementing it. The proper function of judges, after all, is to perform necessary tasks in the service of the law or of society—not to do things for the benefit of politicians.

Judges will be more likely to develop these doubts because they have what amounts to constituencies: fellow members of religious congregations, relatives, jurists and lawyers from abroad with whom they meet, and bar leaders. Moreover, many state judges are elected. It is in their interest to read the political weather forecasts.

Another reason why judges may be receptive to adjusting their death penalty work product at this juncture is that judges tend to swing from time to time from the pole of generally being rights-oriented to the pole of generally being result-oriented—and a swing to being more rights-oriented is more likely in view of the change in public discourse on the death penalty. These two poles arise from a basic tension in the nature of judicial work: judges enforce the rules of the system by applying them to specific factual situations to decree a result. They are torn between allegiance to the rules and concerns for the results, and tend to waver between idealism on the one hand and result-orientation on the other. We are now pretty much at the end of a long-term mood swing towards result-orientation and are about due for a swing back.

The recent "themes" in public discourse about capital punishment have given judges rationales for doubting the utility of enforcing the death penalty, without being inconsistent with their judicial self-image. One example of such a theme is the point that capital punishment is taking more judicial time and effort than judges might wish to spend.

Another rationale for judicial change arises from the public's new awareness of systemic problems with the accuracy and fairness of capital punishment as implemented by our legal system—an awareness heightened by the recent Columbia University report and the many recent comprehensive media reports. As a result, capital punishment is beginning to embarrass the courts.

Moreover, advances in technology, like DNA testing, demonstrate the inevitability of mistakes at any given point in time. By showing this without impugning the good faith or capacity of those currently administering the system, DNA and other technological advances provide an additional rationale for judges to change their mind-set in dealing with capital punishment cases.

B. Prosecutors and Governors The same considerations that are beginning to affect judges are also beginning to affect prosecutors. Prosecutors have essentially the same constituencies as judges. And, being avowedly political, prosecutors can respond to these constituencies more openly than can judges. Moreover, many of the themes in the new public discourse on capital punishment permit prosecutors to opt against seeking the death penalty without conceding weakness or appearing to have lost a fight or to have shown up badly in a competition.

The same considerations are beginning to turn at least some governors around. There has been an upturn, albeit a very modest one, in commutations of death row inmates. The five in 1999, in five different states, were by far the most in a year in quite some time.

III. Why a Moratorium is Achievable and Sustainable

What reason is there to believe that a moratorium on capital punishment can be brought about, or that it will work if it is brought about in additional jurisdictions beyond Illinois? Why would the political agencies of government to whom abolition is anathema have a reason to support a moratorium? Why would a moratorium, once in place, not be ended, in the same way that the ten-year moratorium in the United States from 1967 to 1977 was ended?

A. Why a Nationwide Moratorium Is Achievable With regard to the first two questions the answer is that a moratorium differs in important ways from abolition, even though it tends in the same direction. In adopting a moratorium, the government does not have to give up the power to kill. A major allure of capital punishment is that it is the highest prerogative of sovereignty and the ultimate symbol of strength. Public support for the death penalty results more from attachment to the symbol of capital punishment as a defense against insecurity than from any practical penological objective or desire to actually use the penalty. A moratorium can be proposed on grounds and supported by arguments that do not challenge this symbol or engage the resistance of those who revere it.

Moreover, in adopting a moratorium, government does not have to give up the possibility of reinstating the actual use of capital punishment in the future. This is important because, to some extent, capital punishment represents a psychological reserve of the ultimate social defense against the ultimate imaginable threat: a response to the worst possible crime from imagination's horror chamber of the future. By preserving the potential for this response, a moratorium avoids the appearance of rendering society defenseless. Indeed, in adopting a moratorium, government does not have to give up anything forever. "Forever" is an awesome, frightening word. It imposes a nearly unbearable burden on those who appear to be urging irreversible action.

Finally, and crucially, a moratorium can enlist the support of a multitude of people who are not abolitionists, for a multitude of good reasons that do not depend on being convinced that the death penalty itself is an evil or that it should be abolished. They include concerns that the death penalty, as presently administered in this country, is applied in an arbitrary, uneven, and racially discriminatory manner; that it is applied under conditions that render it extraordinarily susceptible to the risk of killing innocent people through a variety of mistakes, often without the safeguards that could prevent or correct the grossest of those mistakes. Furthermore, it fails to assure minimal fairness in the process, such as an assurance of competent defense counsel and adequate resources to prepare a defense at trial, and the maintenance of satisfactory post-conviction procedures for hearing claims that a condemned inmate's trial was conducted in disregard of his or her constitutional rights.

The American Bar Association has found these and other reasons sufficient to warrant a moratorium, while taking no position on the death penalty as such. So, for some of the same reasons, has Governor Ryan of Illinois. Many additional people who are not convinced that the death penalty is inherently and irretrievably wrong can be moved by the concerns that have moved the ABA and Governor Ryan.

B. Why, Unlike in 1967–1977, a Moratorium Now Could Be Sustained The answer to the last question—why a new moratorium would not simply prompt the same backlash that undid its predecessor—is that there is a crucial difference between the kind of judicially-imposed moratorium that the United States had in the 1960s and 1970s and the kind of legislatively adopted or executive branch-imposed moratorium that today's moratorium movement seeks. The judicially imposed moratorium from 1967 to 1977 was a day-by-day defeat for prosecutors, a challenge to them to end it. Many of them engaged in ever-greater efforts to upset it; and those efforts broke it down.

By contrast, a politically enjoined moratorium need not be a challenge to anyone's competitive instincts. If it is adopted in a tone that says, "let us pause for a while, and take stock of where we are, and then decide where to go from here"— not "you have no legal right to do what you are doing and we defy you to try and get away with it"—there will be many fewer people with much less incentive and vastly fewer occasions to undo the moratorium than there were the last time.

IV. *Conclusion*

The climate surrounding capital punishment in the United States has begun to change significantly, in significant part because of substantial doubts about the legal system's ability to prevent innocent people from being executed. Cases involving DNA evidence have been particularly important in raising these doubts, along with some well-publicized innocence cases, that have not involved DNA.

The public is beginning to understand that the kinds of systemic problems that can lead to innocent people ending up on death row and, in some cases, being executed, even more frequently lead to the executions of people who, although guilty, would never be sentenced to death in a fair system carried out with due process, equal protection, capably performing counsel on both sides, and a judiciary functioning independently. Substantial numbers of people are also beginning to care about these "wrongful" death sentences of the guilty—and not only about wrongful convictions that can lead to executions of the innocent.

It is essential that discourse concerning DNA testing not take place in a vacuum—as if all the public need care about is that every prisoner on death row has access to DNA testing. Providing such access is the sole purported purpose of the moratorium that would be imposed under legislation introduced by Representative Jesse Jackson, Jr. The legislation introduced by Senator Leahy and Representatives LaHood and Delahunt styles itself as an "innocence" protection act, and deals only with evidence bearing on guilt or innocence, such as DNA, plus the need to provide effective counsel.

These initiatives—worthy as they may be in and of themselves—should be used as a vehicle to open up public consciousness to the broader systemic problems that lead not only to innocent people being executed but also to unfair death sentences imposed on guilty people. The same kinds of problems with the legal system can lead to both of these phenomena, and the public needs to understand that and to care about it. Such public understanding and caring is beginning to occur in Illinois, in the wake of a moratorium that was imposed solely due to concern about executing innocent people. And it is beginning to occur elsewhere, as a result of the Illinois moratorium and the revolution in the public discourse about capital punishment.

The result, within a reasonably short term, should be a growing trend toward death penalty moratoria in the United States. This should, in turn, lead to a serious consideration of whether the death penalty can serve any useful purpose in this country that is not outweighed by its inevitable social and economic costs.

John B. Wefing, "Wishful Thinking by Ronald J. Tabak: Why DNA Evidence Will Not Lead to the Abolition of the Death Penalty"

Mr. Tabak makes a number of important points about the importance of DNA in proving that there have been errors in our judicial system, which have resulted in innocent persons being convicted for crimes they did not commit. He further suggests that the errors discovered as a result of DNA testing will convince the public that there is so much danger of error that the public will turn against the death penalty. While I join in Mr. Tabak's desire to abolish the death penalty, it is my opinion that DNA evidence will in fact lead to greater support for the death penalty in the long run. Mr. Tabak's opinion that such evidence will lead to the abolition of the death penalty is simply wishful thinking. While many people in this country currently may be concerned by the potential for mistakes in determining the guilt of a defendant, once they are convinced that there is little likelihood of mistake, the majority will continue to support the death penalty.

Tabak points out that there are many cases in which DNA evidence is unavailable and thus cannot be used as proof. He argues that the dangers of incorrect verdicts, as demonstrated by DNA cases, will lead to concerns about these types of cases and to the elimination of the death penalty. He makes this argument despite the fact that DNA will now be relatively positive proof of guilt in at least some cases. The actions of the groups fighting for DNA testing of current inmates have certainly been laudable in that they have both identified a number of innocent persons who were incorrectly convicted and facilitated their release. However, this activity ultimately will make it more difficult to abolish the death penalty. With assurance that the verdict is accurate, many people who are currently hesitant about the death penalty will be reassured. A more likely result is

that the burden of proof in cases without DNA evidence will become more onerous for the prosecution as some jurors seek certitude.

Mr. Tabak says: "Moreover, recent polls have shown strong support for a moratorium on executions." Nevertheless, subsequent to testing, if guilt is confirmed, the execution will go forward. If, however, the test proves innocence,
the prisoner will be released. The release of the innocent person is, of course, an
excellent result, but it will not affect the ultimate issue of the death penalty.

As pointed out by Mr. Tabak, in January of 2000, Governor George Ryan of
Illinois ordered a moratorium on executions after it was discovered that a number of prisoners on death row had been erroneously convicted. But even more
recently, the Governor-Elect of North Carolina, Mike Easley, announced his opposition to moratoriums. "Easley is a staunch supporter of the death penalty, stating his opposition to a moratorium throughout the gubernatorial campaign." This
again demonstrates that the voters in many states continue to support the death
penalty.

While I hold little hope for total elimination of the death penalty, I still hope
that far greater attention to the process will result from a combination of concerns
for accuracy—concerns raised by the errors discovered in DNA testing—and by
continuing information about the causes of inaccurate verdicts.

I. *Mistaken Identity*

The most important cause for error in death penalty cases is mistaken identification. One of the most difficult pieces of evidence for a defense attorney to rebut is an incorrect identification. Since the witness is sincere and since juries place
great faith in eyewitness identifications, this evidence is afforded great importance. Unfortunately, the circumstances of many crimes create an atmosphere in
which it is difficult to make the careful assessment necessary to make a good identification. The witness is often upset and may even be in shock—particularly if
the witness is also the victim of the crime. The methods of identification often
unconsciously influence the witness.

Some attempts were made in the 1960s to address these problems. For example in *United States v. Wade* and *Stovall v. Denno*, the Court recognized that
the right to counsel and the due process clause have some protective role in the
procedures involved in identification. In *Wade* the Supreme Court held that the
suspect had a right to have counsel during a post-indictment line-up. That decision was limited by *Kirby v. Illinois*, which held that pre-indictment lineups did
not require a right to counsel.

In *Kirby*, the entire focus of the Court seemed to change. Rather than focusing on the "vagaries of eyewitness identification," the Court focused on the
more technical right to counsel, holding that counsel was required at a post-
indictment lineup because the right to counsel attached after an indictment, but
not at a pre-indictment lineup. As a result of the decision in *Kirby*, one potential
protection for suspects against damaging misidentifications was eliminated.

Another problem with the lineup identification arises with regard to the use
of in-court identifications. The Court may permit an in-court identification
even after an invalid out-of-court identification—if the government can show
that the in-court identification was not tainted by the out-of-court identifica-

tion. While this test may appear logical, it certainly leaves open the possibility that the in-court identification may have been tainted by the out-of-court identification. However, it is unlikely that the use of all in-court eyewitness identifications will ever be prohibited.

More recently, courts have begun to recognize and deal with the problem of cross-racial identification. The argument presented is that it is more difficult to make an accurate identification when the witness and the perpetrator are of different races. Recently the New Jersey Supreme Court held that when the major evidence in a case is a cross-racial identification, the jury must be instructed as to the difficulties of such identification. This decision appears to be unique to New Jersey. Most other states that have considered the issue have left it to the discretion of the trial court judge. Other courts have permitted expert testimony on the issue.

It is hoped that, for the benefit of all defendants, and not just for those sentenced to death, the courts will become more and more concerned with the obvious problems of eyewitness identifications and make efforts to assure the validity of such identifications. Professor Scheck says that most problems with eyewitnesses occur in cases in which only one person is an eyewitness. However, he has documented cases in which a number of eyewitnesses, and at least one case in which as many as five eyewitnesses, were subsequently shown to have been erroneous.

II. *Conclusion*

While I do not believe that many states will abolish the death penalty as a result of DNA testing, I do believe that there will be some significant reforms growing out of the concerns with accuracy demonstrated by the DNA testing. Hopefully the Innocence Protection Bill, proposed in Congress, which stresses the use of DNA evidence in death penalty cases and provides for better legal representation, will be passed. The calls for greater improvement in the quality of representation in all criminal cases, but particularly in death penalty cases, will be heeded. Judges and prosecutors will be more careful in dealing with eyewitness identification evidence. Greater stress will be placed on the instructions given to the jury regarding this type of evidence. Greater oversight over the methods of obtaining confessions and the use of informers who reveal statements made by suspects will be carried out. Greater care will be taken in instructing juries about their roles in sentencing.

Ultimately, Mr. Tabak's hopes for the abolition of the death penalty depend upon the same argument made by Justice Thurgood Marshall in his dissent in *Gregg* that an "informed" person fully aware of all the problems and factors concerning the death penalty would reject it.

Unfortunately, the vast majority of the citizens will never be as fully informed as Justice Marshall would like them to be. Perhaps Justice Blackmun is a good example. He approved numerous executions throughout his tenure on the Supreme Court and only as a last act shortly before retiring did he finally decide that the death penalty was unconstitutional because it could not be fairly applied. Additionally, it is hard to argue that the current members of the Supreme Court are not "informed," and yet they continue to support the death penalty.

There are two basic problems with the approach of Justice Marshall. First, some will never be as informed as Justice Marshall would like, and yet, as citizens, they have as much to say through the legislative process as anyone else. We are not a society ruled by the educated and elite. I have taught about the death penalty in many different contexts, from classes of law students at a number of different law schools, to programs for high school teachers who teach law courses to boy scouts taking a bill of rights course. I consistently observe support for the death penalty. Among the young it seems to be even stronger than among more mature adults. Some of these individuals are relatively informed, while others are not so informed. Some have gained much of their knowledge from recent movies like *The Green Mile*, *Dead Man Walking*, and *The Chamber*. Yet despite the fact that, in my view, those movies seemed to describe the horrors of the death penalty, most seem to watch them and their views do not change. Depth of knowledge does not seem to factor into the depth of commitment to a particular position. Many who know little about the issue are still strong in their positions.

Secondly, some informed individuals will disagree with Justice Marshall's "facts" about the death penalty. Many people would argue with these premises and say they were not true. Others would say even if all these premises were true, they would still continue to support the death penalty.

Mr. Tabak wants to add to that list provided by Justice Marshall the fact that some of the prisoners on death row are innocent, as proven by DNA evidence. While many will support efforts to use DNA to prove the innocence of individual defendants, most of American society is simply not prepared to give up their belief in the death penalty.

International Law and American Exceptionalism

■ International Law and American Exceptionalism—Introduction

The United States is in the minority of countries retaining the death penalty for ordinary crimes. According to a 2002 survey by Amnesty International, 84 nations retain the death penalty for ordinary crimes; 121 nations have abolished it. Of the abolitionist nations, 76 countries have abolished the death penalty by force of law, 20 have abolished the death penalty in practice, and 15 more have abolished the death penalty for ordinary crimes, reserving the death penalty exclusively for crimes such as treason or offenses against humanity. Tables of retentionists, abolitionist, abolitionist in practice nations are presented in the Critical Documents section of this chapter (**Tables 25-1** to **25-4**). A country is considered to have abolished the death penalty in practice if it has not executed anyone in the past 10 years or has a policy against carrying out executions or has made an international commitment not to use the death penalty.

Some notable patterns may be discerned from the lists. Every European nation except Belarus and Yugoslavia has abolished the death penalty. The same is true of Latin America with the exception of Cuba and Guatemala. The Middle East and Northern Africa are predominantly retentionists; Israel and Turkey are notable exceptions. Asia is almost entirely retentionist—China and India, the world's two largest countries included. Virtually every nation with English legal systems—including Australia, New Zealand, and Canada—have abolished the death penalty. The United States is the notable exception. Recall from the data in Chapter 12 that the United States is in an even smaller minority of nations that retain the death penalty for children.

The U.S. position on the death penalty is the source of some consternation in the international community, particularly in instances where the United States seeks to extradite persons charged with murder to the United States. In 1996, following a fact-finding mission, the International Commission of Jurists issued a report highly critical of the United States' death penalty practices and questioned whether the United States was fulfilling its obligations under international law. The United States is party to several treaties that arguably apply to the administration of the death penalty within American borders. In the early 1990s the United States ratified two treaties—the International Covenant on Civil and Political Rights (ICCPR, ratified in 1992) and the Convention Against Torture and Other Cruel, Inhuman or Degrading Treatment or Punishment (Torture Convention, 1994)—each of which prohibits the use of torture or "cruel, inhuman or degrading" punishment. In *Soering v. United Kingdom*, the Court of Human Rights held that the "death row phenomenon"—the extreme amounts of time prisoners spend on death row awaiting execution—violated the ICCPR.

No U.S. Court has considered whether the death row phenomenon violates the ICCPR and the Torture Convention, in part because the question is moot. In ratifying both treaties, the U.S. Senate issued reservations specifically stating that the U.S. did not understand the conventions to prohibit any treatment not prohibited by the U.S. Constitution including "any constitutional period of confinement prior to the imposition of the death penalty." It is questionable what force these reservations have. The United Nations Human Rights Committee declared the Senate's reservation to the ICCPR invalid because it was "incompatible with the object and purpose" of the treaty.

Some nations have declined extradition to the United States on the basis of their own national constitutions. In *Minister of Justice v. Burns*, reprinted below, the Canadian Supreme Court held that extradition of two Canadians to face murder charges in Washington State would violate the Canadian Charter of Rights and Freedom unless Washington assured that the death penalty would not be imposed. The Canadian Supreme Court attached special weight to the "death row phenomenon," the long amounts of time prisoners spend on death row awaiting execution.

Whether international opinion is of any legal consequence is open to question. In *Coker*, the Supreme Court took note of international opinion regarding the death penalty for rape: "It is not irrelevant here that out of 60 major nations in the world surveyed in 1965, only 3 retained the death penalty for rape where death did not ensue." In *Stanford*, however, the Court rejected the relevance of international opinion: "We emphasize that it is *American* conceptions of decency that are dispositive."

There is finally the question of why the United States remains so committed to the death penalty against the overwhelming weight of international opinion. The Perspectives section of this chapter offers two answers. Joshua Micah Marshall argues that European governments are less democratic on the whole than the American government. European officials are more immune to public opinion, which in the United States overwhelmingly favors the death penalty. Carol Steiker argues that no single theory is adequate for explaining "American exceptionalism," contending that a host of factors must be considered including the peculiar history of race in the American South, the area in which the death penalty is practiced with the greatest passion in the United States.

■ International Law and American Exception— Critical Documents

| Table 25-1 | Nations Abolitionist for All Crimes (76) |

Country	Date of abolition	Abolished for ordinary crimes	Date of last execution	Country	Date of abolition	Abolished for ordinary crimes	Date of last execution
Australia	1985	1984	1967	Malta	2000	1971	1943
Austria	1968	1950	1950	Marshall Islands			Ind.
Azerbaijan	1998		1993	Mauritius	1995		1987
Belgium	1996		1950	Micronesia			Ind.
Bulgaria	1998		1989	Moldova	1995		
Cambodia	1989			Monaco	1962		1847
Canada	1998	1976	1962	Mozam-bique	1990		1986
Cape Verde	1981		1835	Namibia	1990		1988[k]
Colombia	1910		1909	Nepal	1997	1990	1979
Costa Rica	1877			Netherlands	1982	1870	1952
Côte d'Ivoire	2000			New Zealand	1989	1961	1957
Croatia	1990			Nicaragua	1979		1930
Cyprus	2002	1983	1962	Norway	1979	1905	1948
Czech Republic	1990			Palau			
Denmark	1978	1933	1950	Paraguay	1992		1928
Djibouti	1995		Ind.	Poland	1997		1988
Dominican Rep.	1966			Portugal	1976	1867	1849[k]
East Timor	1999			Romania	1989		1989
Ecuador	1906			San Marino	1865	1848	1868[k]
Estonia	1998		1991	Sao Tomé and Principe	1990		Ind.
Finland	1972	1949	1944	Seychelles	1993		Ind.
France	1981		1977	Slovak Rep.	1990		
Georgia	1997		1994[k]	Slovenia	1989		
Germany	1987			Solomon	1966		Ind.
Guinea-Bissau	1993		1986[k]	South Africa	1997	1995	1991
Haiti	1987		1972[k]	Spain	1995	1978	1975
Honduras	1956		1940	Sweden	1972	1921	1910

continued

Table 25-1 Nations Abolitionist for All Crimes (76), continued

Country	Date of abolition	Abolished for ordinary crimes	Date of last execution	Country	Date of abolition	Abolished for ordinary crimes	Date of last execution
Hungary	1990		1988	Switzerland	1992	1942	1944
Iceland	1928		1830	Turkmeni-stan	1999		
Ireland	1990		1954	U.K.	1998	1973	1964
Italy	1994	1947	1947	Tuvalu			Ind.
Kiribati			Ind.	Ukraine	1999		
Liechten-stein	1987		1785	Uruguay	1907		
Lithuania	1998		1995	Vanuatu			Ind.
Luxem-bourg	1979		1949	Vatican State	1969		
Macedonia	1991			Venezuela	1863		
Panama			1903[k]	Yugoslavia	2002		

[k] refers to date of last known execution.

"Ind." means no executions since independence.

Table 25-2 Abolitionists for Ordinary Crimes (15)

Country	Date of abolition for ordinary crimes	Date of last execution	Country	Date of abolition for ordinary crimes	Date of last execution
Albania	2000		El Salvador	1983	1973 [k]
Argentina	1984		Fiji	1979	1964
Bolivia	1997	1974	Greece	1993	1972
Bosnia-Herze-govina		1997	Israel	1954	1962
Brazil	1979	1855	Latvia	1999	1996
Chile	2001		Mexico		1937
Cook Islands			Peru	1979	1979
El Salvador	1983	1973[k]	Turkey	2002	1984

Table 25-3	Nations Abolitionists in Practice (20)		
Country	**Date of last execution**	**Country**	**Date of last execution**
Bhutan	1964[k]	Nauru	Ind.
Brunei Darussalam	1957[k]	Niger	1976[k]
Burkina Faso	1988	Papua New Guinea	1950
Central African Republic	1981	Russian Federation	1996[k]
Congo (Republic)	1982	Samoa	Ind.
Gambia	1981	Senegal	1967
Grenada	1978	Sri Lanka	1976
Madagascar	1958[k]	Suriname	1982
Maldives	1952[k]	Togo	
Mali	1980	Tonga	1982

Table 25-4	Nations Retaining Capital Punishment for Ordinary Crimes (84)		
Afghanistan	Equatorial Guinea	Lesotho	Sierra Leone
Algeria	Eritrea	Liberia	Singapore
Antigua and Barbuda	Ethiopia	Libya	Somalia
Armenia	Gabon	Malawi	South Korea
Bahamas	Ghana	Malaysia	Sudan
Bahrain	Guatemala	Mauritania	Swaziland
Bangladesh	Guinea	Mongolia	Syria
Barbados	Guyana	Morocco	Taiwan
Belarus	India	Myanmar	Tajikistan
Belize	Indonesia	Nigeria	Tanzania
Benin	Iran	North Korea	Thailand
Botswana	Iraq	Oman	Trinidad and Tobago
Burundi	Jamaica	Pakistan	Tunisia
Cameroon	Japan	Palestinian Authority	United Arab Emirates
Chad	Jordan	Philippines	U.S.A
China	Kazakhstan	Qatar	Uzbekistan
Comoros	Kenya	Rwanda	Vietnam
Congo	Kuwait	St. Christopher & Nevis	Yemen
Cuba	Kyrgyzstan	Saint Lucia	Zambia
Dominica	Laos	St. Vincent & Grenadines	Zimbabwe
Egypt	Lebanon	Saudi Arabia	

Minister of Justice v. Burns
2001 SCC 7 (2001)

The Supreme Court of Canada—

I. *Facts*

The crimes alleged against the respondents were, as the Minister of Justice contends, "brutal and shocking cold-blooded murders." The father, mother and sister of the respondent Rafay were found bludgeoned to death in their home in Bellevue, Washington. Both Burns and Rafay, who had been friends at high school in British Columbia, admit that they were at the Rafay home on the night of the murders. They claim to have gone out on the evening of July 12, 1994 and when they returned, they say, they found the bodies of the three murdered Rafay family members. The house, they say, appeared to have been burgled.

However, if the confessions allegedly made by the respondents to undercover Royal Canadian Mounted Police (RCMP) officers are to be believed, the three members of the Rafay family were bludgeoned to death by the respondent Burns while the respondent Rafay watched. Burns allegedly told an undercover RCMP officer that he had killed the three victims with a baseball bat while wearing only underwear so as not to get blood on his clothes. Rafay's father, Tariq Rafay, and mother, Sultana Rafay, were beaten to death in their bedroom. The force used was so violent that blood was spattered on all four walls and the ceiling of the room. The respondent Rafay's sister, Basma Rafay, was beaten about the head and left for dead in the lower level of the house. She later died in hospital. Burns allegedly explained that following the attacks, he had a shower at the Rafay home to clean off the victims' blood. The discovery of hairs with Caucasian characteristics in the shower near the master bedroom, where the two parents were killed, supports this story. There is also evidence of dilute blood covering large sections of the shower stall.

The respondents allegedly told the police that they drove around the municipality disposing of various items used in the killings as well as some of the parents' electronic devices, apparently to feign a burglary. The respondent Rafay is also alleged to have told the officer the killings were "a necessary sacrifice in order that he could get what he wanted in life." With the death of all other members of his family, Rafay stood to inherit his parents' assets and the proceeds of their life insurance. Burns, it is alleged, participated in exchange for a share in the proceeds under an agreement with Rafay. He was, the prosecution alleges, a contract killer.

The Bellevue police suspected both of the respondents but did not have enough evidence to charge them. When the respondents returned to Canada, the Bellevue police sought the cooperation of the RCMP in their investigation of the murders. The RCMP initiated an undercover operation. An RCMP officer posed as a crime boss and subsequently testified that, after gaining the confidence of the respondents, he repeatedly challenged them to put to rest his professed skepticism about their stomach for serious violence. The respondents are alleged to have tried to reassure him by bragging about their respective roles in the Bellevue murders.

The respondents assert their innocence. They claim that in making their alleged confessions to the police they were play-acting as much as the undercover policeman to whom they confessed. At this stage of the criminal process in Washington, they are entitled to the presumption of innocence. What to make of it all will be up to a jury in the State of Washington.

The respondents were arrested in British Columbia and a committal order was issued for their extradition pending the decision of the Minister of Justice on surrender. The then Minister signed an unconditional Order for Surrender to have both of the respondents extradited to the State of Washington to stand trial without assurances in respect of the death penalty. If found guilty, the respondents will face either life in prison without the possibility of parole or the death penalty. Washington State provides for execution by lethal injection unless the condemned individual elects execution by hanging.

II. *Analysis*

The respondents' position is that the death penalty is so horrific, the chances of error are so high, the death row phenomenon is so repugnant, and the impossibility of correction is so draconian, that it is simply unacceptable that Canada should participate, however indirectly, in its imposition. While the government of Canada would not itself administer the lethal injection or erect the gallows, no executions can or will occur without the act of extradition by the Canadian government. The Minister's decision is a prior and essential step in a process that may lead to death by execution.

A. The Outcome of this Appeal is Governed by Section 7 of the Charter Section 7 of the *Canadian Charter of Rights and Freedoms* provides that: "Everyone has the right to life, liberty and security of the person and the right not to be deprived thereof except in accordance with the principles of fundamental justice." It is evident that the respondents are deprived of their liberty and security of the person by the extradition order. Their lives are potentially at risk. The issue is whether the threatened deprivation is in accordance with the principles of fundamental justice.

This Court has recognized from the outset that the punishment or treatment reasonably anticipated in the requesting country is clearly relevant. Section 7 is concerned not only with the act of extraditing, but also the potential consequences of the act of extradition.

The Minister approached this extradition decision on the basis of the law laid down in *Kindler* and *Ng* and related cases. We affirm that the "balancing process" set out in *Kindler* and *Ng* is the correct approach.

B. Factors that Arguably Favour Extradition Without Assurances Within this overall approach, a number of the "basic tenets of our legal system" relevant to this appeal may be found in previous extradition cases:

- that individuals accused of a crime should be brought to trial to determine the truth of the charges;
- that justice is best served by a trial in the jurisdiction where the crime was allegedly committed and the harmful impact felt;
- that individuals who choose to leave Canada leave behind Canadian law and procedures and must generally accept the law which the foreign state applies to its own residents;

- that extradition is based on the principles of comity and fairness to other cooperating states in rendering mutual assistance in bringing fugitives to justice.

A state seeking Canadian cooperation today may be asked to yield up a fugitive tomorrow. The extradition treaty is part of an international network of mutual assistance that enables states to deal both with crimes in their own jurisdiction and transnational crimes with elements that occur in more than one jurisdiction. Given the ease of movement of people and things from state to state, Canada needs the help of the international community to fight serious crime within our own borders. Some of the states from whom we seek cooperation may not share our constitutional values. Their cooperation is nevertheless important. The Minister points out that Canada satisfies itself that certain minimum standards of criminal justice exist in the foreign state before it makes an extradition treaty in the first place.

The Minister argues, very fairly, that the proposition that an individual (including a Canadian) who commits crimes in another state "must expect to be answerable to the justice system of that state in respect of his conduct there," provides a sufficient basis, the Minister says, for upholding the extradition without assurances.

C. Countervailing Factors that Favour Extradition Only with Assurances

The death penalty has been rejected as an acceptable element of criminal justice by the Canadian people, speaking through their elected federal representatives, after years of protracted debate. Canada has not executed anyone since 1962. Parliament abolished the last legal vestiges of the death penalty in 1998.

While government policy at any particular moment may or may not be consistent with principles of fundamental justice, the fact that successive governments and Parliaments over a period of almost 40 years have refused to inflict the death penalty reflects, we believe, a fundamental Canadian principle about the appropriate limits of the criminal justice system.

We are not called upon in this appeal to determine whether capital punishment violates section 12 of the *Charter*, and if so in what circumstances. It is, however, incontestable that capital punishment, whether or not it violates the *Charter*, engages the underlying values of the prohibition against cruel and unusual punishment. It is final. It is irreversible. Its imposition has been described as arbitrary. Its deterrent value has been doubted. Its implementation necessarily causes psychological and physical suffering. It has been rejected by the Canadian Parliament for offences committed within Canada. Its potential imposition in this case is thus a factor that weighs against extradition without assurances.

Although this particular appeal arises in the context of Canada's bilateral extradition arrangements with the United States, it is properly considered in the broader context of international relations generally, including Canada's multilateral efforts to bring about change in extradition arrangements where fugitives may face the death penalty, and Canada's advocacy at the international level of the abolition of the death penalty itself.

The United Nations Commission on Human Rights Resolutions 1999/61 and 2000/65 call for the abolition of the death penalty, and in terms of extradition state that the Commission "requests States that have received a request for extradition on a capital charge to reserve explicitly the right to refuse extradition in the absence of effective assurances from relevant authorities of the requesting State that capital punishment will not be carried out." Canada supported these initiatives.

State practice is frequently taken as reflecting underlying legal principles. To the extent this is true in the criminal justice field, it must be noted that since 1991, a greater number of countries have become abolitionist.

The existence of an international trend against the death penalty is useful in testing our values against those of comparable jurisdictions. This trend against the death penalty supports some relevant conclusions. First, criminal justice, according to international standards, is moving in the direction of abolition of the death penalty. Second, the trend is more pronounced among democratic states with systems of criminal justice comparable to our own. The United States (or those parts of it that have retained the death penalty) is the exception, although of course it is an important exception. Third, the trend to abolition in the democracies, particularly the Western democracies, mirrors and perhaps corroborates the principles of fundamental justice that led to the rejection of the death penalty in Canada.

Other factors that weigh against extradition without assurances include the growing awareness of the rate of wrongful convictions in murder cases, and concerns about the "death row phenomenon." There is an instinctive revulsion against the prospect of hanging a man after he has been held under sentence of death for many years. What gives rise to this instinctive revulsion? The answer can only be our humanity.

Concerns in the United States have been raised by such authoritative bodies as the American Bar Association which in 1997 recommended a moratorium on the death penalty throughout the United States. On August 4, 2000, the Board of Governors of the Washington State Bar Association unanimously adopted a resolution to review the death penalty process. The Governor was urged to obtain a comprehensive report addressing the concerns of the American Bar Association as they apply to the imposition of the death penalty in the State of Washington. In particular, the Governor was asked to determine "whether the reversal rate of capital cases from our state by the federal courts indicates any systemic problems regarding how the death penalty is being implemented in Washington State." Other retentionist jurisdictions have also expressed recent disquiet about the conduct of capital cases.

Finally, we note the recent study by Professor James Liebman and others, which concludes that 2 out of 3 death penalty sentences in the United States were reversed on appeal. The authors say that with "so many mistakes that it takes three judicial inspections to catch them" there must be "grave doubt about whether we do catch them all."

III. *Conclusion*

The recent and continuing disclosures of wrongful convictions for murder in Canada, the United States and the United Kingdom provide tragic testimony to the fallibility of the legal system, despite its elaborate safeguards for the protection of the innocent. When fugitives are sought to be tried for murder by a retentionist state, however similar in other respects to our own legal system, this history weighs powerfully in the balance against extradition without assurances.

A. The "Death Row Phenomenon" Is of Increasing Concern The evidence filed on this appeal includes a report by Chief Justice Richard P. Guy, Chief Justice of the State of Washington, dated March 2000. In the report the Chief Justice notes the following statistics relevant to the present discussion:

- Since 1981, 25 men have been convicted and sentenced to death. Four have had their judgments reversed by the federal courts, 2 have had their sentences reversed by the Washington State Supreme Court, and 3 have been executed.
- The case of one defendant who was sentenced to be executed 18 years ago is still pending.
- Two of the three executed defendants chose not to pursue appeals to the federal courts.
- For cases completed in the federal courts, state and federal review has taken an average of 11.2 years.
- State review after conviction has averaged 5.5 years.

These statistics are comparable to the degree of delay on "death row" that concerned the European Court of Human Rights in *Soering*. The evidence was that if Soering were to be sentenced to death under Virginia law he would face an average of six to eight years on death row. The European Court commented on the serious human rights consequences of holding a convict under the threat of death for a prolonged length of time: "However well-intentioned and even potentially beneficial is the provision of the complex of post-sentence procedures in Virginia, the consequence is that the condemned prisoner has to endure for many years the conditions on death row and the anguish and mounting tension of living in the ever-present shadow of death."

In *Pratt v. Attorney General for Jamaica*, the Judicial Committee of the Privy Council ruled against the decision of the Jamaican government which sought to carry out death sentences against two appellants who had been on death row for over 14 years. Lord Griffiths for the Committee stated that:

> *A state that wishes to retain capital punishment must accept the responsibility of ensuring that execution follows as swiftly as practicable after sentence, allowing a reasonable time for appeal and consideration of reprieve. It is part of the human condition that a condemned man will take every opportunity to save his life through use of the appellate procedure. If the appellate procedure enables the prisoner to prolong the appellate hearings over a period of years, the fault is to be attributed to the appellate system and not to the prisoner. Appellate procedures that echo down the years are not compatible with capital punishment.*

There is now, however, as is shown in the report of Chief Justice Guy of Washington a widening acceptance amongst those closely associated with the administration of justice in retentionist states that the finality of the death penalty, combined with the determination of the criminal justice system to satisfy itself fully that the conviction is not wrongful, seems inevitably to provide lengthy delays, and the associated psychological trauma. It is apposite to recall in this connection the observation of Justice Frankfurter that the "onset of insanity while awaiting execution of a death sentence is not a rare phenomenon." A Florida study of inmates showed that 35 percent of those committed to death row attempted suicide.

The death row phenomenon is not a controlling factor in the balance, but even many of those who regard its horrors as self-inflicted concede that it is a relevant consideration. To that extent, it is a factor that weighs in the balance against extradition without assurances.

Reviewing the factors for and against unconditional extradition, we conclude that to order extradition of the respondents without obtaining assurances that the death penalty will not be imposed would violate the principles of fundamental justice.

■ International Law and American Exceptionalism—Perspectives

■ Issue—How Can American Exceptionalism Be Explained?

Joshua Micah Marshall, "Death in Venice: Europe's Death Penalty Elitism"

You seldom hear conservatives note, disapprovingly, that "America is the only industrialized country in the world that doesn't have X." It's not hard to figure out why, since X usually involves European (or Canadian or Japanese) big government. But liberals sometimes imagine that America's peculiar lack of, say, nationalized health care, tough gun control, decent child care, widespread mass transport, or substantial arts funding is a sign of political underdevelopment. And so they bemoan America's uniqueness.

Particularly on the death penalty, and particularly now. The old taunt—"The only other industrialized country with the death penalty is South Africa" (recently amended to include "and now even they've abolished it")—has been hurled with particular force recently. The flood of capital punishment horror stories, combined with partial or full recantations by conservative luminaries George Will and Pat Robertson, has left anti-death-penalty liberals more convinced than ever that, on this issue at least, American political culture is inferior to its counterparts across the Atlantic.

If only it were that simple. It's true that all of America's G-7 partners, save Japan, have abolished capital punishment, but the reason isn't, as death penalty opponents usually assume, that their populations eschew vengeance. In fact, opinion polls show that Europeans and Canadians crave executions almost as much as their American counterparts do. It's just that their politicians don't listen to them. In other words, if these countries' political cultures are morally superior to America's, it's because they're less democratic.

Seen through American eyes, Canada seems almost comically nonviolent. And it's true that Ottawa administered its last execution in 1962 and formally abolished capital punishment for civilians in the mid-'70s (a ban on military executions came in 1998). But public support for the death penalty runs only slightly lower in Canada than in the United States: polls consistently show that between 60 percent and 70 percent of Canadians want it reinstated.

Differences in the way survey questions are framed complicate direct comparisons with Europe. (European polls sometimes pose the question in terms of the death penalty for terrorism, for genocide, for depraved sexual crimes, and so forth.) But, even if you ask the death-penalty question in the more restricted sense that Americans generally understand it—"Do you support the death penalty for aggravated murder?"—you find very few European countries where the public clearly opposes it, and there are a number where support is very strong. In Britain, the world headquarters of Amnesty International, opinion polls have shown that between two-thirds and three-quarters of the population favors the death penalty—about the same as in the United States. In Italy, which has led the international fight against capital punishment for much of the last decade, roughly half the population wants it reinstated. In France, clear majorities continued to back the death penalty long after it was abolished in 1981; only last year did a poll finally show that less than 50 percent wanted it restored. There is barely a country in Europe where the death penalty was abolished in response to public opinion rather than in spite of it.

How could this be? In a few cases, the reason is constitutional: Germany's and Italy's postwar constitutions abolished capital punishment outright, thus placing the issue effectively beyond public reach. Another factor is the centripetal pressure created by European integration, as cornerstone EU states like France and Germany compel smaller newcomers to adopt "European" norms. Still another factor is the lack of some equivalent to American-style federalism, which in this country allows ardently pro-death-penalty regions like the South to proceed without regard for opinion in other parts of the country.

Differences between European parliamentary government and the American separation-of-powers system also play a role. Parliamentary government may provide voters with more ideological variety, but it is much more resistant to political upstarts, outsiders, and the single-issue politics on which the death penalty thrives. In parliamentary systems, people tend to vote for parties, not individuals; and party committees choose which candidates stand for election. As a result, parties are less influenced by the odd new impulses that now and again bubble up from the electorate. In countries like Britain and France, so long as elite opinion remains sufficiently united (which, in the case of the death penalty, it has), public support cannot easily translate into legislative action. Since American candidates are largely independent and self-selected, they serve as a much more direct conduit between raw public opinion and actual political action.

Basically, then, Europe doesn't have the death penalty because its political systems are less democratic, or at least more insulated from populist impulses, than the U.S. government. And elites know it. Referring to France, a recent article in the *Unesco Courier* noted that "action by courageous political leaders has been needed to overcome local public opinion that has remained mostly in favour of the death penalty." When a 1997 poll showed that 49 percent of Swedes wanted the death penalty reinstated, the country's justice minister told a reporter: "They don't really want the death penalty; they are objecting to the increasing violence. I see this as a call to politicians and the justice system to do more."

An American attorney general—or any American politician, for that matter— could never get away with such condescension toward the public, at least not for attribution. Pundits and rival politicians would slam him, and, on most issues, liberals would be first in line. After all, liberals are rightly attached to the idea that they speak for the "little guy," the "working family," or, in Al Gore's recent phraseology, "the people, not the powerful." But, all over the industrialized world, it turns out that the men and women on the street like the death penalty. It's just that in Europe and Canada elites have exercised a kind of noblesse oblige. They've chosen a more civilized and humane political order over a fully popular and participatory one. When American liberals invoke Europe's abolition of the death penalty, that's the choice they're essentially endorsing, whether they know it or not. It's a perfectly defensible position—but it might not go over that well on "Crossfire."

Carol S. Steiker, "Capital Punishment and American Exceptionalism"

In 1931, the year before his appointment to the U.S. Supreme Court, Benjamin Cardozo predicted that "perhaps the whole business of the retention of the death penalty will seem to the next generation, as it seems to many even now, an anachronism too discordant to be suffered, mocking with grim reproach all our clamorous professions of the sanctity of life." The operative word here has turned out to be "perhaps," given that here we are in the United States almost three-quarters of a century later and still going strong. But, ironically, Cardozo's prediction proved more or less true for the rest of the Western industrialized world. Soon after World War II and the spate of executions of wartime collaborators that ensued, the use of the death penalty began to decline in Western Europe, and capital punishment for ordinary crimes has at this point been abolished, either de jure or de facto, in every single Western industrialized nation except for the United States.

At the same time, the countries that most vigorously employ the death penalty are generally ones that the United States has the least in common with politically, economically, or socially, and ones that the United States is wont to define itself against, as they are among the least democratic and the worst human rights abusers in the world. In recent years, the top four employers of capital punishment were China, Iran, Saudi Arabia—and the United States. Moreover, in the past twelve years, only seven countries in the world are known to have executed prisoners who were under eighteen-years-old at the time of their crimes: the Democratic Republic of Congo, Iran, Nigeria, Pakistan, Saudi Arabia, Yemen— and the United States. Stephen Bright, capital defense lawyer and abolitionist activist, mordantly quips that, "If people were asked thirty years ago which one of the following three countries—Russia, South Africa, and the United States— would be most likely to have the death penalty at the turn of the century, few people would have answered the United States." Yet it is true that even South Africa and Russia (and many other states of the former Soviet Union) have abandoned the death penalty, while the United States has retained it. And we have not retained it merely formally or even modestly. At the very same time that the pace of abolition quickened in Europe, the pace of executions quickened here in the United States. The rate of executions has risen precipitously since the Supreme Court reinstated the death penalty in 1976 in *Gregg*.

What accounts for this gross discrepancy in the use of capital punishment between the United States and the rest of the countries that we consider to be our "peers"? The answer to this question must be found primarily in the events of the last three decades or so, for it is only during this time period that America's use of capital punishment has diverged widely from that of Western Europe. Indeed, in the nineteenth century, to the extent that American criminal justice policy diverged from that of Europe, it was in the other direction. In his famous observations on *Democracy in America*, published in 1840, Alexis de Tocqueville commented on the "mildness" of criminal justice administration in America, noting that "whereas the English seem to want to preserve carefully the bloody traces of the Middle Ages in their penal legislation, the Americans have almost made the death penalty disappear from their codes." Tocqueville was not alone; historian Stuart Banner writes that mid-nineteenth-century movements to abolish the death penalty in the United States positively "astonished" other European visitors to America. These abolitionist movements did not turn out to be permanently successful except in a small minority of states, primarily in the Midwest and Northeast. Hence, the United States as a nation did not end up in the abolitionist vanguard, like the Scandinavian countries that led Europe in abolishing capital punishment for ordinary crimes in the first few decades of the twentieth century. But neither did the United States diverge in the other direction from the rest of Western Europe until the 1970s. As recently as the mid-1960s, the U.S. looked like most of the rest of Europe (and Canada, and most of Australia) with regard to the use of capital punishment: while most states and the federal government had the death penalty on the books, it was rarely used.

Yet in the decades that followed the 1960s, all of the other Western democracies abandoned the death penalty for ordinary crimes either de jure or de facto, and many countries that had already abandoned it for ordinary crimes abandoned it for all crimes, including such crimes as terrorism, treason, and military offenses.

This pattern—of European abolition contrasted with American enthusiasm for the death penalty—is widely remarked. Yet there is surprisingly little sustained commentary, scholarly or popular, about why it is that the U.S. differs so much from its European brethren on the issue of capital punishment. My object here is to take a sustained look at possible explanations for American exceptionalism with regard to capital punishment, with an eye for questioning and complicating what has been presented, when it has been discussed at all, as obvious or simple.

What follows is consideration of ten theories of American exceptionalism. As you will see, many of these theories are interconnected, but the disaggregation is helpful in evaluating the strengths and weaknesses of each theory.

1. *Homicide Rates*

The most common theory one encounters in writing and conversation on this issue is the fairly straightforward, sociological observation that the United States has a much higher homicide rate than that of any of our Western European (or other peer) counterparts. Notably, during the 1960s and 1970s—the period when U.S. capital punishment policy first began to diverge from that of Western Europe—the American homicide rate rose dramatically to a level much higher than that of most other Western industrialized nations. Although the rate dropped modestly in the early 1980s, it spiked again later in the decade; as of 1990, the American homicide rate was four and a half times that of Canada, nine times that of France or Germany, and thirteen times that of the United Kingdom. Although the rate fell substantially in the 1990s, as of 1998, the U.S. homicide rate was still "two to four times higher than those of most Western countries."

Often, though not always, this "homicide rates" theory for American exceptionalism regarding capital punishment is proffered with a defensive spin, the underlying implication being, "If you had our problems, you'd have our solutions, too." Of course, there is no way to test this counter-factual, short of seeing Western European homicide rates climb to American levels, and maybe not even then. However, recent studies of comparative non-capital penal policies seriously challenge the general claim that crime policy is determined primarily by crime rates. In his introductory essay to a diverse and impressive collection of studies in *Sentencing and Sanctions in Western Countries*, Michael Tonry unequivocally states his conclusion: "The evidence is clear; national differences in imprisonment rates and patterns result not from differences in crime but from differences in policy." As part of his analysis, Tonry compares violent crime rates from the 1960s to the early 1990s in three countries—the U.S., Germany, and Finland—and finds very similar rates of change in violent crime (all three curves go steeply upward) but utterly dissimilar penal policy responses. The U.S. continuously ups the ante, sending more and more offenders to prison; Finland reacts in the opposite manner, imprisoning many fewer people; and Germany reacts inconsistently, first lowering, then raising, and then lowering again its imprisonment rates, even as violent crime continues its steep rise throughout the period in question. Tonry concludes that crime rates cannot be viewed as the primary determinant of punitiveness in penal policy (at least as measured by rates of imprisonment); rather, he argues that other factors altogether—such as American moralism, history, and politics—are really at work in the divergence of American penal policy. Tonry's work has obvious implications for the question of the roots of American exceptionalism: it would be odd indeed if there were a substantial correlation between homicide rates and rates of capital punishment when there is so little correlation between violent crime rates and rates of imprisonment.

In addition, the "homicide rates" hypothesis for American exceptionalism regarding capital punishment is beset by a further difficulty: examined more closely, homicide rates and execution rates dramatically diverge at important points in the past thirty years; indeed, they diverge much more than they converge. From the mid-1960s to the mid-1970s, homicide rates roughly doubled, while execution rates fell to zero for several years preceding the Supreme Court's temporary invalidation of the death penalty in *Furman* in 1972 (though this might have been due, at least in part, to the "moratorium" strategy of the abolitionist litigators leading up to *Furman*). Even more significantly, homicide rates fell precipitously throughout most of the 1990s, while execution rates soared, reaching levels not seen since the 1950s. Moreover, there were some substantial fluctuations in homicide rates even during the 1970s and 1980s, which are not mirrored at all by fluctuations in execution rates.

These problems become only more apparent when one looks at the state and local level. On the state level, the "homicide rates" thesis gets some modest support from the generally higher homicide rates in the Southern and Border states, which also form the "death belt" primarily responsible for the nation's executions. But the thesis also suffers some embarrassment as well, in light of the fact that Texas, Virginia, Missouri, Florida, and Oklahoma—the five leading states in executions in the modern era, accounting together for almost two-thirds of the nation's executions since *Furman*—have five of the lowest homicide rates in the "death belt." Even if homicide rates somehow play a role in the formal retention of the death penalty at the state level, something else is accounting for the use of the death penalty, as reflected in execution rates, within states.

Moreover, if one widens the lens to the larger world, one finds further evidence challenging the persuasiveness of the "homicide rates" thesis. It cannot explain why a large number of countries with extremely high serious murder rates—such as South Africa, Mexico, and Brazil—have abolished the death penalty, while Japan, with a comparatively low homicide rate, continues to retain it. Obviously, each country has its own peculiar death penalty "story," as testified to by the unique experience of South Africa. But this recognition of the complex singularity of national experiences with capital punishment should only further undermine the simplistic "homicide rates" thesis as fundamentally inadequate or at the very least, incomplete.

2. Public Opinion

Related to the "homicide rates" theory is the theory that the United States has capital punishment because of strong public support for it; presumably, public support for the death penalty is bolstered, at least in part, by the fear and disgust generated by high homicide rates. There is no dearth of polling data demonstrating American public opinion in support of capital punishment.

The most problematic and little-remarked problem for the "public opinion" thesis as an explanation for American exceptionalism with regard to capital punishment is that similar levels of public support for capital punishment existed in Western European countries at the time of abolition. Majorities of roughly two-thirds opposed abolition in Great Britain in the 1960s, Canada in the 1970s, France in the 1980s, and the Federal Republic of Germany in the late 1940s (when capital punishment was abolished in Germany's post-World War II constitution). "Indeed, there are no examples of abolition occurring at a time when public opinion supported the measure." It is true that support for capital punishment has tended to fall in Europe over the last three decades—but only after abolition had already occurred, and thus more likely as a product of abolition (or the forces that produced abolition) than as cause of it. Moreover, in countries where support for capital punishment remains high, like Great Britain, efforts to reinstate the death penalty continue to fail, often by wide margins. Perhaps the question to be addressed is not, "Why does the U.S. retain the death penalty when Europe has abandoned it?" but rather, "Why did European democracies abandon the death penalty despite substantial popular support for it?" The possibility of "European exceptionalism" is discussed further below.

To be fair to the "public opinion" thesis, the polling data that shows similar levels of support for capital punishment in the United States and most European countries at the time of abolition almost never attempts to measure the comparative intensity of respondents' support for capital punishment. Yet, it is plausible, indeed even likely, that Americans care more about capital punishment than their European and other Western counterparts do (or did at the time of abolition), even when raw numbers of those who "support" or "oppose" capital punishment appear similar. There is some modest empirical support for this claim to be found in a consistent pattern of American polling data. While there is no comparable "intensity" data from Europe, the tepid popular response in Europe to abolition and the failure of movements for reinstatement to garner widespread support suggest that European voters simply do not share Americans' fervor on this issue.

3. *Salience of Crime as a Political Issue*

The most persuasive reason to believe that Americans care more intensely about capital punishment is the simple fact that crime and punishment have risen to and remained at the indisputable top of the American political agenda. Since 1968, when Richard Nixon ran for president on a largely "law and order" platform, crime policy has been a hugely salient issue in local, state, and national elections, to a degree not rivaled in any of our peer Western nations. It would not be hyperbolic to conclude that crime has been the central theme in the rhetoric of American electoral politics and in the strategies of elected officials in the decades since 1968.

Starting at the top, it is more than a little odd that we know so much about the positions of presidential candidates on capital punishment, given that ninety-nine percent of executions take place at the state level. Not only do we know about presidential positions on the issue, we really seem to care. Who can forget the pivotal moment during the 1988 presidential debates when Michael Dukakis gave an emotionless response to a question about whether his views on the death penalty would change if his wife were raped and murdered? No doubt learning from Dukakis' disastrous example, then-Governor Bill Clinton flew back to Arkansas from the campaign trail in 1992 to validate the execution of a severely mentally disabled murderer who had survived a suicide attempt during which he had fired a shotgun into his own head. The most recent presidential election in 2000 is notable for the fact that every single one of the initial eleven candidates for president, despite other ideological differences, made clear his support for the death penalty. The centrality of the death penalty as a political issue gets only more dramatic when one looks at state and local elections.

In the United States, two things are indisputably true, and "exceptional," in comparison to the rest of the industrialized West. First, crime has a political salience that is extraordinarily high, almost impossible to overstate. The designation "soft on crime" tends to be a political liability of enormous and generally untenable consequence for political actors at all levels of government. Second, the death penalty has become a potent symbol in the politics of "law and order," despite its relative insignificance as a matter of crime control policy. Political actors clearly believe, apparently correctly, that their support for capital punishment translates directly in voters' minds as support for "tough" crime control generally. This strong linkage of the death penalty to the politics of law and order renders more plausible the claim that Americans support capital punishment with a greater intensity, if not in greater numbers, than Europeans, now or in the recent past.

4. Populism

Often proffered more as an alternative than as a complement to the "intensity of preference" theory of American exceptionalism is the theory that populism in American politics, as compared to elitism in European politics, best accounts for differences in death penalty policy. As some Americans like to respond to our European detractors, it is not that Americans have different attitudes about capital punishment, it is that our political institutions are more responsive to the public will. In this vein, a provocative and much cited article in *The New Republic* sweepingly claimed, "Basically, then, Europe doesn't have the death penalty because its political systems are less democratic, or at least more insulated from populist impulses." This theory conveniently offers an explanation both for why the death penalty continues to flourish in the United States and for how Western European nations managed to achieve universal abolition despite widespread popular support for capital punishment.

The "American populism" theory has two dimensions to it, one institutional and one that might better be termed cultural. The institutional dimension emphasizes the populist features of the structures of American political organization, especially as compared to European democracies. Obviously, not all American political structures tend toward the populist, as the presidential election of 2000 amply demonstrated. The electoral college and the bicameral structure of Congress have often been noted as anti-populist, at least in the sense of anti-majoritarian. Nonetheless, there are certain features of American electoral politics that can fairly be described as distinctively populist in comparison to most European parliamentary democracies. The use of the "primary" system is one of the best examples of American political exceptionalism; in other Western democracies, political parties put up candidates for election without throwing the question open to popular intervention—a system much more likely to exclude mavericks and to insulate candidates from hot-button single issues like the death penalty. Similarly, the widespread availability and (somewhat more modest use) of direct democracy tools, such as referenda and initiatives, is another exceptional feature of American politics, that, like the "primary" system, tends to increase the power of single-issue voters and to promote populist tendencies in political debates and platforms.

While these differences in democratic organization certainly do exist, differences in political culture between the United States and the rest of the West appear even more striking. In the United States, politicians are conspicuously anti-elitist in their rhetoric and folksy in their self-presentation. Plainly spoken personal anecdotes tend to displace complex policy analysis, and rolled-up shirt-sleeves and cowboy hats are more the sartorial norm than the exception. Even though successful political candidates are frequently consummate political insiders, "it is almost obligatory for American politicians of both the right and the left to profess mistrust of government." This political culture creates a strong tendency to defer to clear majority sentiment, not merely as a matter of political expediency, but also as a reflection of the role-conception of elected officials.

Unlike the United States, most European countries have a culture of political elitism and careerism, whereby political leaders are produced in large part through education and graduated ascension through professional bureaucracies. The United States simply has no equivalent to France's Ecole Nationale d'Administration (ENA) or Britain's civil service. These institutions both reflect and reinforce a political culture in which political leaders are viewed and view themselves as educated elites who have a duty to make decisions in light of their expertise and thus, more often than in the United States, to lead the public rather than to follow it.

While the most common argument from populism is the one I have sketched above, there is an alternative argument from populism that treats America's populist political culture more as a motivation for retaining capital punishment than as a mechanism by which retention occurs. This alternative argument proposes that the inherent fragility and insecurity of the more populist versions of democracy create a demand for compelling symbols of strength and sovereignty, of which the death penalty is a potent example. There is no more vivid way for the law to be ceremoniously crowned as king than by the use of capital punishment duly authorized and channeled through the legal system.

This latter argument has a harder time establishing that American populist democracy is exceptional in its need for dramatic enactments of popular sovereignty. After all, the entire rest of the Western democratic world also moved, some nations quite dramatically, from monarchical to democratic systems of government. What reasons are there for believing that their democratic structures are any more fragile or insecure than our own? The basis for American exceptionalism here is harder to clearly identify than it is in the context of political institutions and culture.

5. *Criminal Justice Populism*

One of the most clearly "exceptional" aspects of the structure of American government is the much greater degree of both lay participation in the criminal justice system and direct political accountability of institutional actors within the criminal justice system. While many other countries use lay fact-finders to a certain extent in criminal trials, no other country authorizes such a large role for criminal trial juries as does the United States. Moreover, the extensive use of lay grand juries in the charging process in the United States is even more truly anomalous. Equally anomalous is the fact that the vast majority of American prosecutors are elected rather than appointed. Judges, too, are directly elected or otherwise politically accountable in a large number of states. This current state of affairs is the result of a uniquely American turn during the nineteenth century toward increasing and entrenching democratic control over state and local governments through state constitutionalism.

These clearly "exceptional" institutional arrangements, like populism in electoral politics, provide a mechanism through which popular support for the use of capital punishment can influence institutional decision-making. In this context, however, the influence is not on legislative decision-making but rather on prosecutorial charging decisions, judicial conducting of criminal trials, and lay rendering of verdicts and sentences—especially in highly publicized capital, or potentially capital, cases. Elected officials who campaigned on a death penalty platform, or re-elected officials who were vigorous advocates for the use of available capital sanctions while in office, no doubt perceive a mandate to use the death penalty in a way that European judges and prosecutors, more isolated products of an elite bureaucracy, could not possibly. There is thus something of a "feedback" loop between voters and elected officials that tends to reinforce and intensify tendencies toward the use of capital punishment.

6. *Federalism*

A number of other Western democracies, such as Germany, Switzerland, and Canada, are structured on a federal model, with discrete governmental units allocated some autonomous spheres of authority within the larger federal nation-state. However, the United States is the only country that gives full criminal law-making power to individual federal units. This grant cannot be superseded by Congress, as the federal constitution is structured to ensure state dominance over criminal law. As a result, criminal law-making and law enforcement are understood and experienced in the United States as primarily a state and local concern, with federal law-making and enforcement as a limited, specialized adjunct. This arrangement, unique in Western democracies, necessarily permits local or regional enthusiasts to keep the death penalty going within the United States, even when attitudes and trends are moving in the opposite direction in other parts of the country. Nationwide abolition can thus be achieved, as a legislative matter, only by convincing the legislatures of fifty different states and the federal legislature as well.

7. *Southern Exceptionalism*

The natural and intended consequence of American federalism is substantial state and regional variation, which is clearly observable in the context of capital punishment. The vast majority of executions since Furman have been carried out by a handful of states located in the American South and Southwest. Hence one theory of American exceptionalism regarding capital punishment is the thesis that the country as a whole is not exceptional; rather the South (if one expands the concept to include the Southwestern border states) is exceptional within America. This theory, of course, then requires an account of what makes the South exceptional. I will provide a brief sketch of four interrelated theories of American Southern exceptionalism.

First, perhaps the most obvious aspect of Southern exceptionalism is race. The American South has a distinctive legacy of racial inequality stemming from the widespread practice of chattel slavery and continues to have disproportionately large (though still minority) black populations. From colonial times, the capital punishment policies of the American South were deeply marked by the institution of slavery. The eighteenth century saw the widespread enactment of capital crimes targeted solely at crimes by slaves. This long-standing and close association of capital punishment with the formal and informal social control of blacks in the South may contribute to Southern unwillingness to part with the death penalty, particularly in an era, as noted above, in which the death penalty plays such a strong symbolic role in the politics of crime control. Indeed, recent empirical studies show that racial prejudice is significantly linked both to support for the death penalty and for tougher crime control policies, and that such prejudice remains stronger among native white southerners than among whites who were born and live elsewhere.

A different facet of American Southern exceptionalism is the South's distinctive embrace of Protestant fundamentalism. Indeed, the term "the death belt" is a play on "the Bible belt," with both terms designating the American South. Numerous sociological studies find a correlation between Southern fundamentalism and support for the death penalty. How exactly the dynamic works connecting Southern fundamentalism and attitudes about capital punishment is an interesting and unsettled question, about which sociologists and theologians will continue to debate. Nonetheless, whether it is fundamentalist doctrine or leadership or something else that forges the connection, it is hard to gainsay that Southern fundamentalist Protestantism plays some role in generating or reinforcing support for capital punishment in the South.

Third, there is substantial support for the view that the American South has a distinctive sub-culture of violence, whether it is measured in homicide rates, gun ownership rates, or attitudes toward defensive and retaliatory interpersonal violence. The roots of the greater violence in the South are hypothesized to stem from a Southern "honor culture" in which dueling, among other forms of interpersonal violence, was more of an accepted practice than elsewhere. The connection between the relatively more violent Southern culture and the use of capital punishment is speculative, but the Southern emphasis on defensive and retaliatory violence on the interpersonal level has some obvious connection to support for capital punishment.

Fourth and finally, the American South is exceptional in the strength and depth of its resistance to the civil rights movement of the 1950s and 1960s, to which the movement for the abolition of capital punishment has had strong connections. In the 1960s, death penalty abolition was promoted by the very same institutional actors who had promoted the end of racial segregation in the South, and through the very same means—federal constitutional imposition through litigation. It was the NAACP Legal Defense and Education Fund that litigated both the major desegregation cases and the death penalty cases. Some part of Southern enthusiasm for capital punishment in the modern, post-*Furman* era may well be a reaction to this connection and to the attempt of the federal government to impose "national" values on Southern culture.

It is a fair question whether any or all of these aspects of Southern exceptionalism fully account for the disproportionate use of the death penalty in the American South. But the biggest qualification of the "Southern exceptionalism" thesis for American exceptionalism comes from the recognition that states outside of the South still make significant use of their capital statutes in the production of death sentences, even though their execution rates are far lower than those of the South.

8. *European Exceptionalism*

This theory turns the tables and asks whether there is something distinctive about European politics, culture, or history that would lead to wholesale abolition of the death penalty in the space of only a few short decades. A version of this theory has already been explored above as a contrast to American political populism: bureaucratic elitism in European politics has allowed European political leaders to abolish the death penalty despite substantial popular support for capital punishment at the time of abolition. But this theory does not explain what has lead European political leaders to conclude that the death penalty must be abandoned at this precise point in time.

The answer to this question may lie in Europe's distinctive historical experiences during the twentieth century. Europeans and others who have recently and vividly experienced terrible abuses of state power may see more reason to remove the death penalty from the state's arsenal of sanctions. Within the last century, Europe experienced two horrific World Wars fought on its soil and witnessed the bloody rules of Mussolini, Hitler, and Stalin. These experiences may have helped to create a climate in which dramatic demonstrations of state-approved violence are disfavored. Moreover, Europe has suffered numerous violent ethnic conflicts throughout the last century, and it may fear that the use of the death penalty could play a role in exacerbating such conflicts. Thus, it is not surprising that fears of Irishmen being wrongly convicted and executed for terrorism have changed the minds of some British supporters of capital punishment.

9. *American Cultural Exceptionalism*

This theory is in some ways the inverse of the "European exceptionalism" thesis and in some ways an extension of the "Southern exceptionalism" thesis. Admittedly more popular in Europe than in the United States, this theory posits that the United States (rather than merely the American South) has a "sub-culture of violence" in the larger Western culture. Perhaps because of its relatively recent experience as a "frontier" society, the theory holds, America is simply more violent and crude than the rest of the Western industrialized world. Proponents of this theory note that America is also an outlier on the issue of gun control, and that American popular culture glorifies violence, usually by gun-toting macho men.

It is hard to prove or disprove this theory, but there are a number of reasons to be at least somewhat skeptical of it. One reason is that public opinion polls, discussed above, show that Europeans, too, support capital punishment in substantial numbers, despite any "cultural" differences that might exist. Another is that Europeans are huge consumers of exactly the media products that are noted as support for the "American violence" thesis. A third is that there is surprisingly little empirical support for a strong, generalized connection between media violence and violent attitudes or behavior, despite many attempts to forge such a link.

10. *Historical Contingency*

This last theory is like the proverbial thirteenth chime of the clock that casts doubt on all that has come before. Perhaps because it fits so poorly with all the other theories, it has been surprisingly neglected. The "historical contingency" thesis holds that the failure of the United States to abolish the death penalty was something of an historical accident—a near miss, if you will. If the Supreme Court had managed to speak more clearly, emphatically, and unanimously on the issue in the original *Furman* decision, or if the Court's membership had changed differently between 1972 and 1976, abolition might well have been permanent. But the Court's legitimacy was weakened by its decisions promoting integration, regulating the police, and legalizing abortion, and by 1976, it was willing to retrench on the issue of capital punishment in response to the outpouring of rage that *Furman* had generated.

The "historical contingency" thesis proposes that the U.S. Supreme Court is the institution most similarly situated to the abolitionist legislatures that led the rest of the Western industrialized world to abolition. Only the Court had the power to effect change throughout the United States; only the Court was sufficiently insulated from political will that it could lead rather than follow public opinion. In the aftermath of the Court's failure, the hope for abolition turned to individual state legislatures, with all of the forces noted above arrayed against abolition. In addition, the Court's hope that it could regulate and reform the death penalty through the constitution ironically added to those forces both by promising to ensure the fairness of the capital process (without actually delivering on this promise) and by rendering less powerful international claims that the death penalty violated fundamental and universal norms.

Conclusion

A quick perusal of this essay, simply by the sheer number of headings and theories, conveys a sense that powerful forces, unique to the United States, have compelled the result that we see today—anomalous American retention of capital punishment in the Western industrialized world. In fact, a careful reading should promote a much more nuanced view. Some of the most popular and easy theories of American exceptionalism with regard to capital punishment have less to recommend them than meets the eye, and a sobering recognition of the many contingencies that have attended America's recent "death penalty story" (and all of history) should temper a bleak acceptance of historical "fate."

The Future of the Death Penalty

■ The Future of the Death Penalty in America—Introduction

Some will conclude this tour and deem the state of capital punishment in America fundamentally sound. The system might have its problems, but on the whole it gives murderers what they deserve, and does more good than harm. Some might leave with the same moral objection with which they arrived— that the death penalty is an affront to human dignity. Others might wonder whether the death penalty offers any tangible benefits, and whether it is possible for this or any system to meaningfully determine who deserves to die and who does not.

For those who leave with reservations about the death penalty, and whose reservations are practical, not moral, the question is: what next? Can the system be reformed? If it is not doing a good job now of identifying for execution only those who deserve to die, is there a way to do better? This text concludes with two extraordinary views on these questions.

In *Callins v. Collins*, Justice Harry Blackmun, dissenting from a denial of *certiorari*, critiques the history of the Supreme Court's efforts since *Furman* to create a nonarbitrary capital sentencing scheme. He concludes that the effort has failed and says, famously, that he "shall no longer tinker with the machinery of death."

Judge Alex Kozinski, a member of the Ninth Circuit Court of Appeals, suggests that it is possible to create a better functioning capital sentencing system. His essay (written pre-AEDPA) calls for massive reform—for reserving the death penalty only for the absolute worst offenders and only for cases where there can be no reservations about guilt.

■ The Future of the Death Penalty in America— Critical Documents

Callins v. Collins
510 U.S. 1141 (1994)

Justice Scalia, concurring.

Justice Blackmun dissents from the denial of certiorari in this case with a statement explaining why the death penalty "as currently administered," is contrary to the Constitution of the United States. That explanation often refers to "intellectual, moral and personal" perceptions, but never to the text and tradition of the Constitution. It is the latter rather than the former that ought to control. The Fifth Amendment provides that "no person shall be held to answer for a capital crime, unless on a presentment or indictment of a Grand Jury, nor be deprived of life without due process of law." This clearly permits the death penalty to be imposed, and establishes beyond doubt that the death penalty is not one of the "cruel and unusual punishments" prohibited by the Eighth Amendment.

As Justice Blackmun describes, however, over the years since 1972 this Court has attached to the imposition of the death penalty two quite incompatible sets of commands: the sentencer's discretion to impose death must be closely confined, but the sentencer's discretion *not* to impose death (to extend mercy) must be unlimited. These commands were invented without benefit of any textual or historical support.

Though Justice Blackmun joins those of us who have acknowledged the incompatibility of the Court's *Furman* and *Lockett-Eddings* lines of jurisprudence, he unfortunately draws the wrong conclusion from the acknowledgment. He says:

> *The proper course when faced with irreconcilable constitutional commands is not to ignore one or the other, nor to pretend that the dilemma does not exist, but to admit the futility of the effort to harmonize them.*

Surely a different conclusion commends itself—to wit, that at least one of these judicially announced irreconcilable commands which cause the Constitution to prohibit what its text explicitly permits must be wrong.

Justice Blackmun begins his statement by describing with poignancy the death of a convicted murderer by lethal injection. He chooses, as the case in which to make that statement, one of the less brutal of the murders that regularly come before us—the murder of a man ripped by a bullet suddenly and unexpectedly, with no opportunity to prepare himself and his affairs, and left to bleed to death on the floor of a tavern. The death-by-injection which Justice Blackmun describes looks pretty desirable next to that. It looks even better next to some of the other cases currently before us which Justice Blackmun did not select as the vehicle for his announcement that the death penalty is always unconstitutional—for example, the case of the 11-year-old girl raped by four men and then killed by stuffing her panties down her throat. How enviable a quiet death by lethal injection compared with that! If the people conclude that such more brutal deaths may be deterred by capital punishment; indeed, if they merely conclude that justice requires such brutal deaths to be avenged by capital punishment; the creation of false, untextual and unhistorical contradictions within "the Court's Eighth Amendment jurisprudence" should not prevent them.

Justice Blackmun, dissenting.

I

On February 23, 1994, at approximately 1:00 A.M., Bruce Edwin Callins will be executed by the State of Texas. Intravenous tubes attached to his arms will carry the instrument of death, a toxic fluid designed specifically for the purpose of killing human beings. The witnesses, standing a few feet away, will behold Callins, no longer a defendant, an appellant, or a petitioner, but a man, strapped to a gurney, and seconds away from extinction.

Within days, or perhaps hours, the memory of Callins will begin to fade. The wheels of justice will churn again, and somewhere, another jury or another judge will have the unenviable task of determining whether some human being is to live or die. We hope, of course, that the defendant whose life is at risk will be represented by competent counsel—someone who is inspired by the awareness that a less-than-vigorous defense truly could have fatal consequences for the defendant. We hope that the attorney will investigate all aspects of the case, follow all evidentiary and procedural rules, and appear before a judge who is still committed to the protection of defendants' rights. In the same vein, we hope that the prosecution, in urging the penalty of death, will have exercised its discretion wisely, free from bias, prejudice, or political motive, and will be humbled, rather than emboldened, by the awesome authority conferred by the State.

But even if we can feel confident that these actors will fulfill their roles to the best of their human ability, our collective conscience will remain uneasy. Twenty years have passed since this Court declared that the death penalty must be imposed fairly, and with reasonable consistency, or not at all, and, despite the effort of the States and courts to devise legal formulas and procedural rules to meet this daunting challenge, the death penalty remains fraught with arbitrariness, discrimination, caprice, and mistake. This is not to say that the problems with the death penalty today are identical to those that were present 20 years ago. Rather, the problems that were pursued down one hole with procedural rules and verbal formulas have come to the surface somewhere else, just as virulent and pernicious as they were in their original form. Experience has taught us that the constitutional goal of eliminating arbitrariness and discrimination from the administration of death can never be achieved without compromising an equally essential component of fundamental fairness—individualized sentencing.

It is tempting, when faced with conflicting constitutional commands, to sacrifice one for the other or to assume that an acceptable balance between them already has been struck. In the context of the death penalty, however, such jurisprudential maneuvers are wholly inappropriate. The death penalty must be imposed "fairly, and with reasonable consistency, or not at all."

To be fair, a capital sentencing scheme must treat each person convicted of a capital offense with that "degree of respect due the uniqueness of the individual." That means affording the sentencer the power and discretion to grant mercy in a particular case, and providing avenues for the consideration of any and all relevant mitigating evidence that would justify a sentence less than death. Reasonable consistency, on the other hand, requires that the death penalty be inflicted evenhandedly, in accordance with reason and objective standards, rather than by whim, caprice, or prejudice.

On their face, these goals of individual fairness, reasonable consistency, and absence of error appear to be attainable: Courts are in the very business of erecting procedural devices from which fair, equitable, and reliable outcomes are presumed to flow. Yet, in the death penalty area, this Court, in my view, has engaged in a futile effort to balance these constitutional demands, and now is retreating not only from the *Furman* promise of consistency and rationality, but from the requirement of individualized sentencing as well. Having virtually conceded that both fairness and rationality cannot be achieved in the administration of the death penalty, the Court has chosen to deregulate the entire enterprise, replacing, it would seem, substantive constitutional requirements with mere aesthetics, and abdicating its statutorily and constitutionally imposed duty to provide meaningful judicial oversight to the administration of death by the States.

From this day forward, I no longer shall tinker with the machinery of death. For more than 20 years I have endeavored—indeed, I have struggled—along with a majority of this Court, to develop procedural and substantive rules that would lend more than the mere appearance of fairness to the death penalty endeavor. Rather than continue to coddle the Court's delusion that the desired level of fairness has been achieved and the need for regulation eviscerated, I feel morally and intellectually obligated simply to concede that the death penalty experiment has failed. It is virtually self-evident to me now that no combination of procedural rules or substantive regulations ever can save the death penalty from its inherent constitutional deficiencies. The basic question—does the system accurately and consistently determine which defendants "deserve" to die?—cannot be answered in the affirmative. It is not simply that this Court has allowed vague aggravating circumstances to be employed, relevant mitigating evidence to be disregarded, and vital judicial review to be blocked. The problem is that the inevitability of factual, legal, and moral error gives us a system that we know must wrongly kill some defendants, a system that fails to deliver the fair, consistent, and reliable sentences of death required by the Constitution.

I dissented in *Furman*. Despite my intellectual, moral, and personal objections to the death penalty, I refrained from joining the majority because I found objectionable the Court's abrupt change of position in the single year that had passed since *McGautha*. I objected to the "suddenness of the Court's perception of progress in the human attitude since decisions of only a short while ago." Four years after *Furman* was decided, I concurred in the judgment in *Gregg*.

A

There is little doubt now that *Furman*'s essential holding was correct. Although most of the public seems to desire, and the Constitution appears to permit, the penalty of death, it surely is beyond dispute that if the death penalty cannot be administered consistently and rationally, it may not be administered at all. I never have quarreled with this principle; in my mind, the real meaning of *Furman*'s diverse concurring opinions did not emerge until some years after *Furman* was decided. Since *Gregg*, I faithfully have adhered to the *Furman* holding and have come to believe that it is indispensable to the Court's Eighth Amendment jurisprudence.

Delivering on the *Furman* promise, however, has proved to be another matter. *Furman* aspired to eliminate the vestiges of racism and the effects of poverty in capital sentencing; it deplored the "wanton" and "random" infliction of death by a government with constitutionally limited power. *Furman* demanded that the sentencer's discretion be directed and limited by procedural rules and objective standards in order to minimize the risk of arbitrary and capricious sentences of death.

Unfortunately, all this experimentation and ingenuity yielded little of what *Furman* demanded. It soon became apparent that discretion could not be eliminated from capital sentencing without threatening the fundamental fairness due a defendant when life is at stake. Just as contemporary society was no longer tolerant of the random or discriminatory infliction of the penalty of death, evolving standards of decency required due consideration of the uniqueness of each individual defendant when imposing society's ultimate penalty.

This development in the American conscience would have presented no constitutional dilemma if fairness to the individual could be achieved without sacrificing the consistency and rationality promised in *Furman*. But over the past two decades, efforts to balance these competing constitutional commands have been to no avail. Experience has shown that the consistency and rationality promised in *Furman* are inversely related to the fairness owed the individual when considering a sentence of death. A step toward consistency is a step away from fairness.

B

There is a heightened need for fairness in the administration of death. This unique level of fairness is born of the appreciation that death truly is different from all other punishments a society inflicts upon its citizens. "Death, in its finality, differs more from life imprisonment than a 100-year prison term differs from one of only a year or two." Because of the qualitative difference of the death penalty, "there is a corresponding difference in the need for reliability in the determination that death is the appropriate punishment in a specific case."

While the risk of mistake in the determination of the appropriate penalty may be tolerated in other areas of the criminal law, "in capital cases the fundamental respect for humanity underlying the Eighth Amendment requires consideration of the character and record of the individual offender and the circumstances of the particular offense as a constitutionally indispensable part of the process of inflicting the penalty of death."

C

I believe the *Woodson-Lockett* line of cases to be fundamentally sound and rooted in American standards of decency that have evolved over time. The notion of prohibiting a sentencer from exercising its discretion "to dispense mercy on the basis of factors too intangible to write into a statute," is offensive to our sense of fundamental fairness and respect for the uniqueness of the individual.

This dilemma was laid bare in *Penry v. Lynaugh*. The defendant in *Penry* challenged the Texas death penalty statute, arguing that it failed to allow the sentencing jury to give full mitigating effect to his evidence of mental retardation and history of child abuse. The Texas statute required the jury, during the penalty phase, to answer three "special issues"; if the jury unanimously answered "yes" to each issue, the trial court was obligated to sentence the defendant to death. Only one of the three issues—whether the defendant posed a "continuing threat to society"—was related to the evidence Penry offered in mitigation. But Penry's evidence of mental retardation and child abuse was a two-edged sword as it related to that special issue: "it diminished his blameworthiness for his crime even as it indicated that there was a probability that he would be dangerous in the future." The Court therefore reversed Penry's death sentence, explaining that a reasonable juror could have believed that the statute prohibited a sentence less than death based upon his mitigating evidence.

After *Penry*, the paradox underlying the Court's post-*Furman* jurisprudence was undeniable. Texas had complied with *Furman* by severely limiting the sentencer's discretion, but those very limitations rendered Penry's death sentence unconstitutional.

D

The theory underlying *Penry* and *Lockett* is that an appropriate balance can be struck between the *Furman* promise of consistency and the *Lockett* requirement of individualized sentencing if the death penalty is conceptualized as consisting of two distinct stages. In the first stage of capital sentencing, the demands of *Furman* are met by "narrowing" the class of death-eligible offenders according to objective, fact-bound characteristics of the defendant or the circumstances of the offense. Once the pool of death-eligible defendants has been reduced, the sentencer retains the discretion to consider whatever relevant mitigating evidence the defendant chooses to offer.

Over time, I have come to conclude that even this approach is unacceptable: It simply reduces, rather than eliminates, the number of people subject to arbitrary sentencing. It is the decision to sentence a defendant to death—not merely the decision to make a defendant eligible for death—that may not be arbitrary. While one might hope that providing the sentencer with as much relevant mitigating evidence as possible will lead to more rational and consistent sentences, experience has taught otherwise. It seems that the decision whether a human being should live or die is so inherently subjective—rife with all of life's understandings, experiences, prejudices, and passions—that it inevitably defies the rationality and consistency required by the Constitution.

E

The arbitrariness inherent in the sentencer's discretion to afford mercy is exacerbated by the problem of race. Even under the most sophisticated death penalty statutes, race continues to play a major role in determining who shall live and who shall die.

A renowned example of racism infecting a capital-sentencing scheme is documented in *McCleskey v. Kemp*. Despite this staggering evidence of racial prejudice infecting Georgia's capital-sentencing scheme, the majority turned its back on McCleskey's claims, apparently troubled by the fact that Georgia had instituted more procedural and substantive safeguards than most other States since *Furman*, but was still unable to stamp out the virus of racism. Faced with the apparent failure of traditional legal devices to cure the evils identified in *Furman*, the majority wondered aloud whether the consistency and rationality demanded by the dissent could ever be achieved without sacrificing the discretion which is essential to fair treatment of individual defendants.

I joined most of Justice Brennan's significant dissent which expounded McCleskey's Eighth Amendment claim, and I wrote separately, to explain that McCleskey also had a solid equal protection argument under the Fourteenth Amendment. I still adhere to the views set forth in both dissents, and, as far as I know, there has been no serious effort to impeach the Baldus study. Nor, for that matter, have proponents of capital punishment provided any reason to believe that the findings of that study are unique to Georgia.

F

In the years since *McCleskey*, I have come to wonder whether there was truth in the majority's suggestion that discrimination and arbitrariness could not be purged from the administration of capital punishment without sacrificing the equally essential component of fairness—individualized sentencing. Viewed in this way, the consistency promised in *Furman* and the fairness to the individual demanded in *Lockett* are not only inversely related, but irreconcilable in the context of capital punishment. Any statute or procedure that could effectively eliminate arbitrariness from the administration of death would also restrict the sentencer's discretion to such an extent that the sentencer would be unable to give full consideration to the unique characteristics of each defendant and the circumstances of the offense. By the same token, any statute or procedure that would provide the sentencer with sufficient discretion to consider fully and act upon the unique circumstances of each defendant would "throw open the back door to arbitrary and irrational sentencing." All efforts to strike an appropriate balance between these conflicting constitutional commands are futile because there is a heightened need for both in the administration of death.

But even if the constitutional requirements of consistency and fairness are theoretically reconcilable in the context of capital punishment, it is clear that this Court is not prepared to meet the challenge. In apparent frustration over its inability to strike an appropriate balance between *Furman* and *Lockett*, the Court has retreated from the field, allowing relevant mitigating evidence to be discarded, vague aggravating circumstances to be employed, and providing no indication that the problem of race in the administration of death will ever be addressed. In fact some members of the Court openly have acknowledged a willingness simply to pick one of the competing constitutional commands and sacrifice the other. These developments are troubling. In my view, the proper course when faced with irreconcilable constitutional commands is not to ignore one or the other, nor to pretend that the dilemma does not exist, but to admit the futility of the effort to harmonize them. This means accepting the fact that the death penalty cannot be administered in accord with our Constitution.

II

My belief that this Court would not enforce the death penalty (even if it could) in accordance with the Constitution is buttressed by the Court's "obvious eagerness to do away with any restriction on the States' power to execute whomever and however they please." I have explained at length on numerous occasions that my willingness to enforce the capital punishment statutes enacted by the States and the Federal Government, "notwithstanding my own deep moral reservations has always rested on an understanding that certain procedural safeguards, chief among them the federal judiciary's power to reach and correct claims of constitutional error on federal habeas review, would ensure that death sentences are fairly imposed." In recent years, I have grown increasingly skeptical that "the death penalty really can be imposed fairly and in accordance with the requirements of the Eighth Amendment," given the now limited ability of the federal courts to remedy constitutional errors.

The Court's refusal last term to afford Leonel Torres Herrera an evidentiary hearing, despite his colorable showing of actual innocence, demonstrates just how far afield the Court has strayed from its statutorily and constitutionally imposed obligations. In *Herrera*, only a bare majority of this Court could bring itself to state forthrightly that the execution of an actually innocent person violates the Eighth Amendment. This concession was made only in the course of erecting nearly insurmountable barriers to a defendant's ability to get a hearing on a claim of actual innocence. Certainly there will be individuals who are actually innocent who will be unable to make a better showing than what was made by Herrera without the benefit of an evidentiary hearing. The Court is unmoved by this dilemma, however; it prefers "finality" in death sentences to reliable determinations of a capital defendant's guilt. Because I no longer can state with any confidence that this Court is able to reconcile the Eighth Amendment's competing constitutional commands, or that the federal judiciary will provide meaningful oversight to the state courts as they exercise their authority to inflict the penalty of death, I believe that the death penalty, as currently administered, is unconstitutional.

III

Perhaps one day this Court will develop procedural rules or verbal formulas that actually will provide consistency, fairness, and reliability in a capital-sentencing scheme. I am not optimistic that such a day will come. I am more optimistic, though, that this Court eventually will conclude that the effort to eliminate arbitrariness while preserving fairness "in the infliction of death is so plainly doomed to failure that it—and the death penalty—must be abandoned altogether." I may not live to see that day, but I have faith that eventually it will arrive. The path the Court has chosen lessens us all. I dissent.

■ The Future of the Death Penalty—Perspectives

■ Issue—Is the Death Penalty Beyond Repair?

Alex Kozinski and Sean Gallagher, "Death: The Ultimate Run-on Sentence"

In his last term with the Supreme Court, Justice Blackmun threw down the gauntlet on the death penalty, stating, in the great tradition of Justices Brennan and Marshall, "From this day forward, I no longer shall tinker with the machinery of death." This left many court-watchers wondering what happened to the view he stated so staunchly in *Furman* when he dissented from the Court's decision to strike down all death penalty statutes then in effect. Apparently, nothing happened to change this view except two decades of death penalty cases. Justice Blackmun concluded that the task the Court had taken on in *Furman*—overseeing the administration of the death penalty to ensure it is not "so wantonly and so freakishly imposed"—was fruitless. So he did exactly what he accused the *Furman* Court of doing: He "just decided that it was time to strike down the death penalty."

With Justice Blackmun's retirement, no sitting Supreme Court Justice, insofar as we know, holds the view that the death penalty violates the Constitution. We can take it for granted, then, that the Supreme Court will not abolish the death penalty in the United States within the foreseeable future. But that ought not to obscure other questions fairly presented by Justice Blackmun's cry of exasperation: Is the death penalty morally justified? Does it serve a legitimate societal purpose? Is it worth the resources we are devoting to it?

Death cases consume more and more of courts' time and attention these days, and no other cases are quite so grave or present quite the same mix of urgency, emotion, complexity, and drama. Somewhat less obviously, the death penalty is also a fascinating study of democracy in action. Our process for imposing and carrying out the death penalty reflects an uneasy accommodation between the will of the majority—and a fairly substantial majority at that—who favor the death penalty, and the determined resistance of a small but able minority.

The net effect is that we have little more than an illusion of a death penalty in this country. To be sure, we have capital trials; we have convictions and death sentences imposed; we have endless and massively costly reviews by the state and federal courts; and we do have a small number of people executed each year. But the number of executions compared to the number of people who have been sentenced to death is minuscule, and the gap is widening every year. Whatever purposes the death penalty is said to serve—deterrence, retribution, assuaging the pain suffered by victims' families—these purposes are not served by the system as it now operates.

If you think about it, this is a remarkable state of affairs in a country where polls consistently show that 70% or more of the people favor the death penalty, state supreme court justices are ousted on a wholesale basis when they are perceived to be too stridently opposed to the death penalty, and Congress and the state legislatures fall all over themselves adding new crimes carrying the death penalty.

I. *The Way It Works*

Leaving for others the question of how we got here, let's see if we can figure out where we are. Think of our judicial system as a large snake. It feeds largely on field mice, an occasional squirrel, maybe a game hen here and there. Then, one day, it sees a moose, and ravenously swallows it. For a long time thereafter, it lies immobilized, as the bulge slowly works its way toward the part of the snake opposite its mouth. In this metaphor, our capital cases are a herd of caribou.

To get a sense of how time consuming and expensive death penalty cases can be, let's follow a case through the entire process. It all starts, of course, with whatever act of depravity renders the criminal eligible for the death penalty. Imagine our capital defendant is someone like John Dobbert, who was convicted in Florida for the murder of his own daughter and sentenced to death because of the "premeditated and continuous torture, brutality, sadism and unspeakable horrors" he committed. He beat her, burned her, held her under water, scarred her body with a belt and board, and left her wounds to fester. After several years of this, he choked her to death, then "placed her body in a plastic garbage bag and buried her in an unmarked and unknown grave." Assume that our hypothetical defendant is, in fact, guilty, that he's not insane, and that the investigation and trial were flawless. We want to see how long it takes to process an easy case.

Within a year or two, our capital defendant will have been convicted, sentenced, and sent to death row. Post-trial proceedings begin with a mandatory appeal (everywhere except Arkansas and federal court), usually to the state supreme court. If the California Supreme Court is any indication, these appeals are backed up. The California Supreme Court currently has slightly more than 200 death cases pending, half of which are on hold because the state has been unable to find lawyers willing and able to take them. Between 1988 and 1994, roughly one-quarter of all the opinions issued by the California Supreme Court involved capital cases. In the 1993–1994 term, the California Supreme Court disposed of twenty death cases, but that was just under ten percent of the total pending.

In order to be eligible for federal habeas, our inmate must first avail himself of state post-conviction remedies and collaterally attack his conviction and sentence in state court. Assuming his guilt and penalty trials were impeccable, he loses. He then petitions the United States Supreme Court for a writ of certiorari, which is denied.

At some point, a death warrant is issued, which is often the signal for starting federal habeas proceedings. A federal stay of execution is entered while this first petition is considered, and although the district court can make a decision in as little as three months, it can take more than two years if the court decides to hold extensive evidentiary hearings, which is not at all unusual. The inmate then appeals the district court's decision, which keeps the stay of execution in place. In a death case involving a first habeas petition, it is fairly typical to consume a year on the appeal, although two years or more certainly is not unheard of. While our inmate loses this appeal, he inevitably petitions for rehearing and suggests rehearing *en banc*. At least in the Ninth Circuit, this guarantees a vote on whether to go *en banc*, which adds a few more weeks to the procedure. Our inmate then petitions the United States Supreme Court for a writ of certiorari, and for the second time his petition is denied.

In this streamlined version of events, we now stand poised for execution—maybe. The case has been reviewed at four levels of the state and federal courts and the United States Supreme Court has twice passed up the opportunity to jump in. The federal stay of execution is then lifted, and the case goes back to the state court where the government will obtain a death warrant setting a new execution date.

With an execution date in place, the petitioner's lawyers go into high gear to raise some issue that will forestall the execution. They might seek collateral relief (and a stay of execution) in state court. But, more likely, they will file a successive federal habeas petition. In the Ninth Circuit, the district court can enter a stay while the new issues raised by this petition are considered; if it refuses a stay, the appellate panel assigned to the case can enter one; and if execution is imminent, any single judge of the circuit can enter a temporary stay. Any federal stay entered can remain in effect until long after the putative execution date.

Often this successive federal petition will raise unexhausted claims, which may get shipped off to state court, with the federal stay intact. Otherwise, in this hypothetical, squeaky-clean case, the district court reaches a decision against the defendant. In the Ninth Circuit, a panel of three court of appeals judges is standing by and has been receiving the briefs at the same time as the district court. When an execution is pending, the Supreme Court also gets papers in the case as they are filed in the lower federal courts. Unique to the Ninth Circuit, there is also an eleven-judge *en banc* panel standing by. If the three-judge panel refuses to issue a stay of execution or a certification of probable cause, any active judge of the circuit can force an expedited *en banc* vote by simply requesting it. There are close to thirty active judges in the Ninth Circuit and, without exception, one of them will seek *en banc* reconsideration. The en banc panel meets to consider the case, rules against the petitioner, and dissolves the stay of execution. Within hours, sometimes within minutes, the petitioner's lawyers are before the Supreme Court with a stay petition. The Justices are polled, often at home and occasionally woken from sleep, and they deny the stay. This usually signals the end of the process.

It should come as no surprise that death penalty cases take a long time to work through the system. It takes several minutes just to walk through the steps of a streamlined case, without even discussing the many ways in which the process can be deliberately prolonged. Nor does this hypothetical case delve into the legal issues, which often pose some of the most difficult questions in the law. Putting aside the relatively few cases in which a death row inmate simply gives up, a case that comes to its conclusion within seven years of the crime is relatively rare. Ten years is about the average, and cases like that of Duncan Peder McKenzie, whose case took over two decades to shuttle its way repeatedly between the state and federal courts, are not all that atypical.

II. *What It Costs*

It's fair to ask ourselves what all this costs us. After all, the death penalty is a public good we all pay for—like roads and post offices—so we should find out whether we are getting our money's worth. This question turns out to be not all that easy to answer.

Diehard supporters of the death penalty wave aside the monetary costs. "We spend a lot of money on a lot of useless things," they say, "at least this is money spent on something I can really get behind." Although a lot of effective law enforcement could be bought for what it costs to wind up the machinery of death, let's momentarily put aside the monetary costs and look at the intangibles. A very significant one is the opportunity cost. State supreme courts find themselves flooded with mandatory death penalty appeals, and what cases these are. An average California Supreme Court opinion in a death case analyzes over three times the number of issues as in other types of cases, and four times as many issues if the court affirms the sentence. Briefs in these cases often run into the hundreds of pages, the record well into the tens of thousands of pages, and death penalty opinions comprise a striking percentage of the yearly output of the California Supreme Court.

Because direct death penalty appeals are mandatory, whereas appeals in other areas are discretionary, the time and energy devoted to death cases are often paid for by litigants whose cases cannot be considered, and indirectly by all those who must conduct their businesses or lives despite uncertainties and conflicts in the law that the state supreme court has no time to resolve. Then there's the time spent by federal district and circuit judges and Supreme Court Justices resolving federal habeas petitions in death cases. It's hard to give an accurate estimate of the judicial resources devoted to such petitions, but ten times the average case is probably a conservative estimate.

This brings us to what may be the most significant cost of the death penalty—lack of finality. Death cases raise many more issues, and more complex issues, than other criminal cases, and they are attacked with more gusto and reviewed with more vigor in the courts. This means there is a strong possibility that the conviction or sentence will be reconsidered—seriously reconsidered—five, ten, twenty years after the trial. While only a tiny percentage of state and federal criminal cases are reversed on direct appeal, the rate of reversal in death cases approaches 50%. In federal courts, habeas petitions are granted in less than 7% of cases, but the figure for death cases peaked in 1982 at 80% and averaged around 40% between 1978 and 1991. While this figure may have dropped in recent years, the fact remains that serious, sustained assaults on the validity of the conviction and death sentence continue for many years, with the case never quite reaching finality until the sentence is carried out. One has to wonder and worry about the effect this has on the families of the victims, who have to live with the possibility—and often the reality—of retrials, evidentiary hearings, and last-minute stays of execution for decades after the crime.

But let's put aside all these costs for the time being and look at the other side of the coin. What are we getting in exchange? Maybe the best way to approach this is through the following riddle: As of 1992, what was the single largest cause of death for death row inmates? It clearly was not death by firing squad, or hanging, or the gas chamber. In fact, few death row inmates die from these causes. Lethal injection, the method of execution in Texas, came in a close third. The first runner up, by a hair, was electrocution. So what's left? You guessed it, the dreaded "Other Causes." California has sentenced 512 people to death since 1973 but has executed only 2; meanwhile at least 18 have died in prison. Arizona had 1 execution between 1977 and 1992, but sentenced to death 103. Even Texas, responsible for one-third of all executions since 1977, and nearly half the executions in 1993, manages to execute only 1 in 8 death row inmates.

Nationwide, there are close to 3000 inmates on death row, and we are adding upwards of 250 more every year. The largest number of executions in any year since 1977 was 38 in 1993, and 7 of those were what we have called volunteers. This means the states would have to triple, and possibly quadruple, the number of yearly executions just to maintain the backlog at its current size. To eliminate the backlog, there would have to be 1 execution every day for the next 26 years.

Even if the machinery of death were to become this well greased, the courts could hardly keep pace. Our institutions of justice simply are not geared to handle that many executions—or anything close to it. Never mind the burden on the courts. Don't even consider that we would have to neglect every other type of civil and criminal case and devote all our time to death cases. Forget that the United States Supreme Court would have to consider daily applications for last minute stays of execution. The real sticking point is the lack of lawyers. The death penalty may be the one area of the law where there are too few lawyers willing and able to handle the available caseload. Despite a sustained and usually sincere effort over the course of many years, the state and federal courts have been unable to find enough lawyers versed in the arcane jurisprudence of death to handle the massive review process needed to make any meaningful inroad on our death row population.

The consequence of all this is that we have the worst of all possible worlds. We have capital punishment, and the enormously expensive machinery to support it, but we don't really have the death penalty.

III. *Quo Vadis?*

With remarkable consistency, our political institutions have gone about reenacting and expanding the death penalty. At the same time, the judicial system has tied itself in knots trying to carry out the popular will while also addressing the misgivings of those who have strong moral objections to having their government, their tax dollars, and their authority used to take human life.

So we are left in limbo, with machinery that is immensely expensive, that chokes our legal institutions so they are impeded from doing all the other things a society expects from its courts, that visits repeated trauma on victims' families, and that ultimately does not produce anything like the benefits we would expect from an effective death penalty. As time passes, the balance is likely to shift even farther toward the costs and away from the benefits. This is surely the worst of all worlds.

This observation does not change the fact, however, that we are devoting very substantial resources to a problem that leaves proponents and opponents of the death penalty frustrated and exhausted. From a theoretical perspective, where we are now is not really all that bad, but it is a practical mess. Is there a way out?

Only two solutions suggest themselves, one judicial and the other political. The judicial solution would require a wholesale repudiation of the Eighth Amendment case law developed by the Supreme Court over the last quarter century. This is not nearly as easy to accomplish as it might seem. The essential teaching of *Furman* is that death really is different, and that the Constitution calls for an extraordinary measure of caution before the state may take human life. The established application of the Eighth Amendment to the administration of the death penalty will continue to give opponents a legitimate platform from which to impede even the most determined efforts to carry out the death penalty on a routine basis.

The political solution is, perhaps, equally difficult to achieve, but it's really all we have left. Any hope that death penalty opponents will just go away (thus allowing the death penalty to be carried out in an assembly-line fashion) is surely unrealistic. Driven by strong moral convictions, opponents have shown they are here to stay. If we must have a death penalty, we will have to carry it out over their sustained and vigorous opposition.

The key to a solution, if there is to be one, lies in the hands of the majority, precisely those substantial numbers in our midst who strive for the application of the death penalty to an ever-widening circle of crimes. The majority must come to realize that this is a self-defeating tactic. Increasing the number of crimes punishable by death, widening the circumstances under which death may be imposed, obtaining more guilty verdicts, and expanding the population of death rows will not do a single thing to accomplish the objective, namely to ensure that the very worst members of our society—those who, by their heinous and depraved conduct have relinquished all claim to human compassion—are put to death. What the majority must come to understand is that we as a society may be willing and able to carry out thirty, forty, maybe fifty executions a year, but that we cannot and will not do a thousand a year, or even two hundred and fifty.

Once that reality is accepted, a difficult but absolutely necessary next step is to identify exactly where we want to devote our death penalty resources. To be sure, everyone on death row is very bad or else they wouldn't be there. But even within that depraved group, it is possible to make moral distinctions as to how far someone has stepped down the rungs of hell. Hitler was worse than Eichman, though both are unspeakably evil by any standard; John Wayne Gacy, with two dozen or so brutal deaths on his conscience, must be considered worse than John Spenkelink, who killed only once.

The Supreme Court already requires the states and the federal government to differentiate between murderers who deserve the death penalty and murderers who do not, and that directive has proved difficult to implement. Further differentiating only the most depraved killers would not be an easy task; it would not be pleasant; it would require some painful soul-searching about the nature of human evil. But it would have three very significant advantages. First, it would ensure that, in a world of limited resources and in the face of a determined opposition, we will run a machinery of death that only convicts about the number of people we truly have the means and the will to execute. Not only would the monetary and opportunity costs avoided by this change be substantial, but a streamlined death penalty would bring greater deterrent and retributive effect. Second, we would ensure that the few who suffer the death penalty really are the worst of the very bad—mass murderers, hired killers, terrorists. This is surely better than the current system, where we load our death rows with many more than we can possibly execute, and then pick those who will actually die essentially at random.

The third advantage of such a political solution is that it will place the process of accommodation back into the political arena where it belongs. This means that the people, through their elected representatives, will reassert meaningful control over this process, rather than letting the courts and chance perform the accommodation on an ad hoc, entirely irrational basis. Some objections to capital punishment—for example, that broadly-drafted death penalty statutes allow latent racial biases to affect sentencing decisions—might be removed by statutes that are drafted so narrowly that racial considerations become irrelevant. And death penalty opponents might react quite differently to a regime where executions are rare, extraordinary events, reserved for the most depraved in our society, rather than everyday occurrences that don't even make the morning paper. A political solution—a true compromise—might yet enable us to reach a consensus where both sides feel that their essential interests have been considered and accorded deference.

It will not be easy. It will surely take a massive act of will for the majority to admit a measure of defeat and take the initiative toward compromise. However, as in the case of democracy itself, the alternatives are all much worse.

Notes and Sources

Introduction

Furman v. Georgia, 408 U.S. 238 (1972). *Powell v. Alabama*, 287 U.S. 45 (1932). *McGautha v. California*, 402 U.S. 183 (1971). *Gregg v. Georgia*, 482 U.S. 153 (1976). *Woodson v. North Carolina*, 428 U.S. 280 (1976). **History of the death penalty in America**. The best recent history is Stuart Banner's *The Death Penalty: An American History* (Boston: Harvard University Press, 2003). **Data on the death penalty in America today**. The Bureau of Justice Statistics, a branch of the U.S. Department of Justice, maintains the most comprehensive data on the death penalty in the United States, and is the source of the table in the introduction. The most recent publication of the BJS is *Capital Punishment 2002*. It can be found online at www.ojp.usdoj.gov/bjs/cp.htm (hereafter, *Capital Punishment 2002*). **Marshall hypothesis**. Justice Marshall articulates the view that has come to be referred to as the Marshall hypothesis in *Furman*, p. 362, footnote 145. **Support in polling for the death penalty**. A good summary of polling data on the death penalty can be found at www.pollingreport.com. See also Bureau of Justice Statistics, *Sourcebook of Criminal Justice Statistics 2001*, p. 140 et seq. Also known as the BJS Sourcebook, it can be found online at www.albany.edu/sourcebook. On public opinion and the death penalty generally, see, for example, Robert M. Bohm, "American Death Penalty Opinion: Past, Present, and Future," in James Acker, Robert Bohm, and Charles Lanier, *America's Experiment With Capital Punishment* (Carolina Academic Press, 2003). **Testing the Marshall hypothesis**. See, for example, Robert Bohm, Louise Clark, and Adrian Aveni, "Knowledge and Death Penalty Opinion: A Test of the Marshall Hypothesis," *Journal of Research in Crime and Delinquency*, Vol. 28 No. 3, pp. 360–87 (August 1991). This survey is the source of the questions referred to in the text. **Educational attainment generally**. www.census.gov/population/wwz w/pop-profile/educattn.html. **Conventional explanation for support for the death penalty**. Phoebe C. Ellsworth and Samuel R. Gross, "Hardening of the Attitudes: American's Views on the Death Penalty," *Journal of Social Issues*, Vol. 50 No. 2, pp. 19–52 (1994).

Chapter 1 Retribution

Differing conceptions of retribution. John Cottingham identifies nine different theories that have been termed retributive: repayment theory, desert theory, penalty theory, minimalism, satisfaction theory, fair play theory, placation theory, annulment theory, and denunciation theory. "Varieties of Retributivism," *Philosophical Quarterly*, Vol. 29, pp. 238–46 (1979). The contrast between moral and legalistic notions of retributivism is lucidly presented by Joel Feinberg in, "What, If Anything, Justifies Legal Punishment," in Feinberg and Coleman's, *Philosophy of Law* 6th ed., (Wadsworth, 2000). **Support in polling for the death penalty based on retribution**. Again, see the useful summary of polling data found at www.pollingreport.com and the notes above. **Hugo Bedau's objection**. See Hugo Adam Bedau, "The Minimal Invasion Argument Against the Death Penalty," *Criminal Justice Ethics*, Vol. 21 No. 2, pp. 3–8 (2002). This issue of *Criminal Justice Ethics* contains an outstanding symposium from which the debate in this chapter is drawn. "**An execution is not simply death…**" A. Camus, "Reflections on the Guillotine" in *Resistance, Rebellion, and Death*, J. O'Brien trans., (1961), p. 199.

Chapter 2 Religion

Attitudes of various religions towards capital punishment. A useful summary can be found at www.religioustolerance.org/execut7.htm. **Public opinion, religion, and the death penalty**. *BJS Sourcebook*, Table 2.63, pp. 142–43. "**The first task of the biblical interpreter…**" *The Death Penalty Debate: H. Wayne House and John Howard Yoder* (Dallas: Word Publications, 1991), pp. 119–32, 139–48. **Modes of constitutional interpretation**. An excellent summary can be found in W. Murphy, J. Fleming, S. Barber, and S. Macedo, *American Constitutional Interpretation* 3rd ed., (New York: Foundation, 2003), pp. 395–413.

"**Judaism is not found in the text...**" M. Walzer, *Exodus and Revolution* (New York: Basic Books, 1985), p.144. **Ryan commission—recommended requirement of corroboration.** *Report of the Governor's Commission on Capital Punishment* (April 2002), p. ii. **Finding support in the Bible for capital punishment.** Lloyd R. Bailey, *What the Bible Says* (Abingdon Press, 1987). "**I couldn't worship a god...**" Helen Prejean, *Dead Man Walking* (New York: Vintage, 1993). "**She has abandoned biblical text...**" See Justice for All Web site, www.prodeathpenalty.com, p. 20, paragraph 21. "**To some readers...**" Bailey, *What the Bible Says.*

Chapter 3 Deterrence

Public opinion and deterrence. The *Newsweek* poll is reported on p. 8 of the summary of polling data found at www.pollingreport.com/crime.htm. **On whether deterrence is a robust explanation for public support for capital punishment.** See Phoebe C. Ellsworth and Lee Ross "Public Opinion and Capital Punishment: A Close Examination of the Views of Abolitionists and Retentionists," *Crime and Delinquency*, Vol. 29, pp. 116–69 (1983). **Bedau–van den Haag correspondence.** Cited in Earnest van den Haag, "The Death Penalty Once More" (unpublished). The article and the exchange between Professors Bedau and van den Haag is referred to in the excellent exchange by Louis P. Pojman and Jeffrey Reiman, *The Death Penalty: For and Against* (Rowman & Littlefield, 1998), p. 50. **The debate over the efficacy of harsher penalties.** Earnest van den Haag and John P. Conrad, *The Death Penalty: A Debate* (New York: Plenum, 1983), p. 326. **Murder rates in the 20th century.** See the Bureau of Justice Statistics Web site at www.ojp.usdoj.gov/bjs/homicide/homtrnd.htm. **Thorsten Sellin's studies.** Thorsten Sellin, *The Death Penalty* (Philadelphia: American Law Institute, 1959). For a summary of pre-1970 deterrence research see William C. Bailey and Ruth D. Peterson, "Murder, Capital Punishment, and Deterrence: A Review of the Evidence and an Examination of Police Killings," *Journal of Social Issues*, Vol. 50 No. 2 (1994). **Isaac Ehrlich's research.** Isaac Ehrlich, "The Deterrent Effect of Capital Punishment: A Question of Life and Death," *American Economic Review*, Vol. 65, pp. 397–417 (1975). **Pro-deterrence studies.** A summary of recent research supporting the deterrent effect of the death penalty can be found at the Justice for All Web site, www.jfa.net.

Chapter 4 Brutalization

Rational-choice theory. A useful reference on rational-choice theory and the other frameworks used to explain criminal behavior is Ronald Akers, *Criminological Theory: Introduction, Evaluation and Application* 4th ed., (Roxbury Press, 2004). **Bowers and Pierce research.** William J. Bowers and Glenn L. Pierce, "Deterrence or Brutalization: What is the Effect of Executions?" *Crime and Delinquency*, Vol. 26, pp. 453–84 (1980).

Chapter 5 Incapacitation

Recidivism rates among sex offenders. See the Web site for the Center for Sex Offender Management, www.csom.org/pubs/recidsexof.html. "**To ensure that no capital offender...**" Robert M. Bohm, *Deathquest II* (Cincinnati, OH: Anderson Publishing, 2003) p.127. "**The argument that murderers...**" www.prodeathpenalty.com, p.4. The Justice For All Web site is a useful source for pro-death penalty arguments and references. **Deterrence of LWOP-sentenced inmates as a moral consideration.** See Earnest van den Haag, "In Defense of the Death Penalty: A Legal—Practical—Moral Analysis" in *Criminal Law Bulletin*, Vol. 14 No. 1, pp. 51–68 (1978). ("I cannot see the moral or utilitarian reasons for giving permanent immunity to homicidal prisoners, thereby endangering the other prisoners and the guards.") **Recidivism and prison crime among life-sentenced inmates.** Thorsten Sellin, *The Death Penalty* (1959), ch. 3; Thomas J. Reidy, Mark D. Cunningham, and Jonathan R. Sorensen "From Death to Life: Prison Behavior of Former Death Row Inmates in Indiana," *Criminal Justice and Behavior*, Vol. 28, pp. 62–82 (2001); Hugo Adam Bedau ed., *The Death Penalty in America* 3rd ed., (New York: Oxford University Press, 1982), pp. 173–80. **Predicting behavior of life-sentenced inmates.** Jonathan R. Sorensen and Rocky L. Pilgrim "An Actuarial Risk Assessment of Violence Posed by Capital Murder Defendants," *Journal of Criminal Law and Criminology*, Vol. 90, p. 1251–70 (2000). **Behavior of *Furman*-commutees.** James W. Marquart and Jonathan R. Sorensen "A National Study of the *Furman*-Commuted Inmates: Assessing the Threat to Society from Capital Offenders," *Loyola of Los Angeles Law Review*, Vol. 23, pp. 101–20 (1989). See also D. Lester, "Suicide and Homicide on Death Row," *American Journal of Psychiatry*, Vol. 143, p. 559 et seq., (1986).

Chapter 6 Cost

Public opinion and cost. The Gallup Poll annually surveys attitudes about capital punishment. The 20% figure is derived from Jeffrey M. Jones, "Two-Thirds of Americans Support the Death Penalty," www.gallup.com/poll/releases/pr010302.asp, (2001). Dennis Longmire suggests that cost is only a secondary consideration for supporters. See Dennis R. Longmire, "American Attitudes About the Ultimate Sanction Capital Punishment," in T.J. Flanagan and D.R. Longmire eds., *Americans View Crime and Justice: A National Public Opinion Survey* (Thousand Oaks, CA: Sage, 1996) pp. 93–108. **Super due process.** For a discussion of the elements of super due process see Margaret Jane Radin, "Cruel Punishment and Respect for Persons: Super Due Process for Death," *Southern California Law Review*, Vol. 53, pp. 1143–85 (1980). **Costs of capital trials versus noncapital trials.** For a general discussion of the costs of capital trials versus noncapital trials see Robert L. Spangenberg and Elizabeth R. Walsh, "Capital Punishment or Life Imprisonment? Some Cost Considerations," *Loyola of Los Angeles Law Review*, Vol. 23, pp. 45–58 (1989). Spangenberg and Walsh state that voir dire in jury selection takes five times longer in capital cases than in ordinary felony cases. On the relative length of capital and noncapital trials see Margot Garey, "The Cost of Taking a Life: Dollars and Sense of the Death Penalty," *University of California, David Law Review*, Vol. 18, pp. 1221–73 (1985). There are also some one-time costs that attach to the death penalty, such as building death row and the electric chair. New York appropriated $1 million for start-up costs when it reinstituted the death penalty in 1995. See Justin Brooks and Jeanne Huey Erikson, "The Dire Wolf Collects His Due While the Boys Sit by the Fire: Why Michigan Cannot Afford to Buy into the Death Penalty," *Thomas Cooley Law Review*, Vol. 13, pp. 877–900 (1996). For a discussion of the notion that costs are borne regardless of outcome see J. Mark Lane and Ronald J. Tabak, "The Execution of Injustice: A Cost and Lack-of-Benefit Analysis of the Death Penalty." *Loyola of Los Angeles Law Review*, Vol. 23, p. 59 (1989). **Plea bargains.** See generally Spangenberg and Walsh, and Garey at p. 1247, note 114. **Death-sentencing rates.** Death-sentencing rates are discussed extensively in Chapter 15 in connection with the discussion of race. **Costs of incarceration.** Costs of incarceration obviously vary from state to state. Estimates generally range around $20,000 per year, somewhat more for prisoners on death row. See for example Robert M. Bohm and Keith N. Haley, *Introduction to Criminal Justice* 3rd ed., (New York: Glencoe/McGraw Hill, 2002). **Life expectancy.** Justin Brooks and Jeanne Huey Erikson estimate that a defendant sentenced to LWOP lives an average of 31 years. This figure is low in part because of the poor conditions of prison life including the risk of violence, disease, and poor nutrition. See Brooks and Erikson, p. 883. **Age of murderers.** In 2001, the median age of a death row inmate at the time of arrest was 27, the mean was 28. Tracy L. Snell, *Capital Punishment 2001*, U.S. Department of Justice, Bureau of Justice Statistics, p. 9, Table 8 (December). For murder generally, nearly half of murders are committed by men under the age of 25; U.S. Department of Justice, Bureau of Justice Statistics, *Homicide Trends in the United States, 1976–1999*. **Average time on death row.** The 66 prisoners executed in 2000 were under sentence of death an average of 11 years and 10 months. Between 1977 and 2000 the average time was approximately 10 years—9 years and 10 months for white prisoners, one year longer for black prisoners; *Capital Punishment 2001*, p. 12.

Chapter 7 Innocence

Public opinion. See generally www.pollingreport.com/crime.htm. On the belief that innocents have been executed within the past five years see CNN/*USA Today*/Gallup Poll, June 23–25, 2000. **Governor Ryan's decision.** *The Oprah Winfrey Show* (January 15, 2003) ("You know, there's a 60% error rate in the death penalty system as we speak. That means six out of ten people could be innocent. That's pretty scary." *Nightline* (January 13, 2003) ("Our capital system is haunted by the demon of error. Error in determining guilt, error in determining who among the guilty deserves to die. Because of all these reasons, today I'm commuting the sentences of all death row inmates."). **Liebman study.** Liebman, Fagan, and West, "A Broken System: Error Rates in Capital Cases, 1973–1995 (June 12, 2000) and Liebman, Fagan, Gelman, West, Davies, and Kiss, "A Broken System, Part II: Why There Is So Much Error in Capital Cases, and What Can Be Done About It," (February 11, 2002). **Response to Liebman study.** Latzer and Cauthen, "Capital Appeals Revisited," *Judicature*, Vol. 84, p. 64 (September-October 2000). **Response to Latzer and Cauthen.** Liebman, Fagan, and West, "Death Matters: A Reply to Latzer and Cauthen," *Judicature*, Vol. 84, p. 72 (September-October 2000). **"The absence of such a poster child..."** Franklin Zimring, *The Contradictions of American Capital Punishment*" (Oxford, 2003), pp. 168–69. **DNA evidence/Innocence Project.** See generally, John B. Wefing, "Wishful Thinking by Ronald J. Tabak: Why DNA Evidence Will Not Lead to the Abolition of the Death Penalty," *Connecticut Law Review*, Vol. 33, p. 861 (2001). Professor Wefing's article is excerpted in the chapter on the moratorium movement.

Chapter 8 Arbitrariness

Proportionality review and *Pulley v. Harris*. 465 U.S. 37 (1984). I have an extended discussion of the significance of *Pulley* in my article "In Defense of Specific Proportionality Review," *Albany Law Review*, Vol. 65, pp. 900–5 (2002). **Aggravating factors.** The best survey of aggravating factors employed in state statutes is James Acker and C.S. Lanier, "Parsing This Lexicon of Death: Aggravating Factors in Capital Sentencing Statutes," *Criminal Law Bulletin*, Vol. 30, p. 107 (1994).

Chapter 9 Mitigating Evidence

"The penalty of death is qualitatively different..." 428 U.S. at 305. **"We believe that in capital cases..."** *Id.* at 304. *Eddings v. Oklahoma*, 455 U.S. 104 (1982). *Skipper v. South Carolina*, 476 U.S. 1 (1986). *Hitchcock v. Dugger*, 481 U.S. 393 (1987). **Unanimity as not mitigating evidence not required.** *Mills v. Maryland*, 486 U.S. 367 (1988). **"To acknowledge that there is perhaps an inherent tension..."** *Walton*

v. Arizona, 497 U.S. 639, 664 (1990) (Scalia, J., concurring). See also *Graham v. Collins*, 506 U.S. 461, 487–500 (1993).

Chapter 10 Rape and Proportionality

Harmelin v. Michigan, 501 U.S. 957 (1991). *Solem v. Helm*, 463 U.S. 277 (1983). **"We think it enough..."** *Harmelin*, 501 U.S. at 985. **"Whether the sentence..."** *Gregg*, 428 U.S. at 198. **"Life is over for the victim of the murderer..."** *Coker*, 433 U.S. 584, 598 (1977).

Chapter 11 Felony-Murder

Felonies and homicides in Philadelphia. Kadish and Schulhofer, *Criminal Law and its Processes* 5th ed., (Boston: Little, Brown and Company, 1989), p. 512, footnote 96. **"Only about a third of American jurisdictions..."** *Enmund*, 458 U.S. 782, 792 (1982). **"The Eighth Amendment is not a ratchet..."** *Harmelin*, 501 U.S. 957, 990 (1991).

Chapter 12 Juveniles

Minimum age for execution by state. BJS, *Capital Punishment 2001*, p. 5. See also Victor L. Streib, "The Juvenile Death Penalty Today: Death Sentence and Executions for Juvenile Crimes, January 1, 1973—December 31, 2002," available at www.law.onu.edu/faculty/streib. **Public opinion.** *Sourcebook of Criminal Justice Statistics 2001*, p. 144. **International opinion.** See the Amnesty International report, "The Exclusion of Child Offenders From the Death Penalty Under General International Law," found at www.amnesty.org/library/index/engact500042003. For a response to Professor Hoffman, see Carol Steiker and Jordan Steiker, "Defending Categorical Exemptions to the Death Penalty: Reflections on the ABA's Resolution Concerning the Execution of Juveniles and Persons With Mental Retardation," *Journal of Law & Contemporary Problems*, Vol. 61, p. 89 (Autumn 1998).

Chapter 13 The Mentally Retarded

Model Penal Code definition. American Law Institute, *Model Penal Code* (1962), §4.01. **The differences between the insane and the retarded and the characteristics of the retarded.** Ellis and Luckason, "Mentally Retarded Criminal Defendants," *George Washington Law Review*, Vol. 53, pp. 414, 423

(1985). Entzeroth, "Putting the Mentally Retarded Criminal Defendant to Death: Charting the Development of a National Consensus to Exempt the Mentally Retarded from the Death Penalty," *Alabama Law Review*, Vol. 52, p. 911 (2001). Entzeroth, *Capital Punishment and the Judicial Process* 2nd ed., (Carolina Academic Press), p. 268. **"Responsibility in the criminal justice system…"** Cathleen C. Herasimchuk, *Houston Chronicle*, May 21, 1999. *Penry v. Lynaugh*, 492 U.S. 302 (1989).

Chapter 14 The Insane

"Into another world…" *Ford v. Wainwright*, 477 U.S. 399, 407 (1986). **Retribution should treat reformed persons differently.** Derek Parfit, *Reasons and Persons* (Oxford University Press, 1984). *Lowenfeld v. Butler*, 485 U.S. 995 (1988). *Washington v. Harper*, 494 U.S. 210 (1990). *Louisiana v. Perry*, 610 So. 2d 746 (La. 1992). **Charles Singleton.** Neil A. Lewis, "Justices Let Stand Ruling That Allows Forcibly Drugging an Inmate Before Execution," *The New York Times*, October 7, 2003.

Chapter 15 Race

The history of racial discrimination in capital sentencing. See generally David C. Baldus and George Woodworth, "Race Discrimination and the Death Penalty: An Empirical and Legal Overview" in James R. Acker, Robert M. Bohm, and Charles S. Lanier eds., *America's Experiment With Capital Punishment* (Carolina Academic Press, 1998); Michael Radelet and M. Vandiver, "Race and Capital Punishment: An Overview of the Issues," *Crime & Social Justice*, Vol. 25, pp. 94–113 (1986). **"If black victim cases…"** Baldus *op cit*, p. 402. **"Selectively to minorities whose numbers are few…"** *Furman*, 408 U.S. at 245. **McCleskey district court opinion.** 580 F.Supp. 338 (Ga. 1984). **Federal hearing on claim of racial discrimination.** See *Dobbs v. Zant*, 720 F.Supp. 1566 (1989). **New Jersey Supreme Court and race discrimination.** *State v. Marshall*, 613 A.2d 1059 (N.J. 1992).

Chapter 16 Victim Impact Evidence

Booth v. Maryland, 482 U.S. 496 (1987). *South Carolina v. Gathers*, 490 U.S. 805 (1989).

Chapter 17 Capital Juries

Batson v. Kentucky, 476 U.S. 79 (1986); *J.E.B. v. Alabama*, 511 U.S. 127 (1994); *Georgia v. McCollum*, 505 U.S. 42 (1992). **Baldus study of exercise of peremptory challenges.** David Baldus and George Woodworth, "The Use of Peremptory Challenges in Capital Murder Trials: A Legal and Empirical Analysis," *University of Pennsylvania Journal of Constitutional Law*, Vol. 3 (2001). **Excluding jurors who support a mandatory death penalty.** *Morgan v. Illinois*, 504 U.S. 719 (1992). *Witherspoon v. Illinois*, 391 U.S. 510 (1968). *Adams v. Texas*, 448 U.S. 38 (1980). **Conviction proneness of death-qualified juries.** See generally Marla Sandys, "Stacking the Deck for Guilt and Death: The Failure of Death Qualification to Ensure Impartiality" in Acker et al., *America's Experiment With Capital Punishment*, pp. 285–308.

Chapter 18 Sentencing Alternatives

Beliefs about life imprisonment. C. Haney, L. Sontag, and S. Costanzo, "Deciding to Take a Life: Capital Juries, Sentencing, Instructions, and the Jurisprudence of Death," *Journal of Social Issues*, Vol. 50 No. 2, pp. 170–1 (1994). *Shafer v. South Carolina*, 121 S.Ct. 1263 (2001). *Ramdass v. Angelone*, 530 U.S. 156 (2000). *Brown v. Texas*, 522 U.S. 940 (1997) (Stevens, J. respecting the denial of *certiorari*). *California v. Ramos*, 463 U.S. 992 (1983).

Chapter 19 Trial Counsel

Macias v. Collins, 979 F.2d 1067 (5th Cir. 1992). **Stephen Bright quote.** Y. Kamisar, "*Gideon v. Wainwright*: A Quarter-Century Later," *Pace Law Review*, Vol. 10, pp. 343–78 (1990). **1994 study and questionnaire of judges.** "Ineffective Assistance of Counsel," *Harvard Law Review*, Vol. 107, pp. 1923–40 (1994). **"The most pervasive right…"** David Bazelon, "The Defective Assistance of Counsel," *University of Cincinnati Law Review*, Vol. 64, pp. 1–46 (1973). **"The Constitution does not say that the lawyer has to be awake…"** See B. Shapiro, "The Sleeping Lawyer Syndrome," *The Nation* (April 7, 1997). *Burger v. Kemp*, 483 U.S. 776 (1981). *Lockhart v. Fretwell*, 506 U.S. 364 (1993). *Murray v. Giarratano*, 492 U.S. 1 (1989). **The catch-22.** See Michael Mello and Paul

J. Perkins, "Closing the Circle: The Illusion of Lawyers for People Litigating for Their Lives at the *Fin de Siecle*," in Acker et al., *America's Experiment With Capital Punishment*, pp. 245–84.

Chapter 20 Habeas Corpus and Innocence

The history of habeas corpus. LaFave and Israel, *Criminal Procedure* 2nd ed., (West, 1992), p. 1178. *Ex Parte Dorr*, 44 U.S. (3 How.) 103 (1845). *Frank v. Mangrum*, 237 U.S. 309 (1915). **The progressive restriction of habeas review.** Whitebread and Slobogin, *Criminal Procedure: An Analysis of Cases and Concepts* 3rd ed., (Foundation Press, 1993) pp. 907–8. *Brown v. Allen*, See Freedman, "Milestones in Habeas Corpus: *Brown v. Allen*: The Habeas Corpus Revolution that Wasn't," *Alabama Law Review*, Vol. 51, p. 1541 (Summer 2000). **Extra policy justifications for death penalty in capital cases.** James S. Liebman, *Federal* Habeas Corpus *Practice and Procedure* (Michie Company, 1988) Volume 1, §2.2.

Chapter 22 Televised Executions

On the history of hangings. See Stuart Banner, *The Death Penalty: An American History* (Harvard University Press, 2002), especially chapter 2. **"In the eighteenth century…"** Banner, p. 148. **Abandonment of public executions.** Banner, pp. 148–57. John Bessler's book *Death in the Dark* (Northeastern, 1997), an excerpt of which appears in the Perspectives section of the chapter, also offers an excellent history of the abandonment of public executions. **Phil Donahue and televised executions.** Transcript of Larry King Show, November 25, 1999. *KQED v. Vasquez*, 1991 U.S. Dist. LEXIS 21163.

Chapter 23 Clemency

Constitutional presidential authority. Article II, Section 2. **Survey of state clemency proceedings.** A comprehensive review of state executive clemency procedures can be found in Clifford Dorne and Kenneth Gerweth, "Mercy in a Climate of Retributive Justice: Interpretations from a National Survey of Executive Clemency Procedures," *New England Journal on Criminal and Civil Confinement*, Vol. 25, p. 413 (1999). *Ohio Adult Parole Authority v. Woodard*, 523 U.S. 272 (1998). **No due process rights for noncapital defendants in clemency proceedings.** *Connecticut Board of Pardons v. Dumschat*, 452 U.S. 458, 464 (1981). **History of clemency.** Kobil, "The Quality of Mercy Strained: Wresting the Pardoning Power from the King," *Texas Law Review*, Vol. 69, p. 569 (1991). **The declining use of clemency post-*Furman*.** Hugo Bedau, "The Decline of Clemency in Capital Cases," *New York University Review of Law and Social Change*, Vol. 18, p. 255 (1990–91); Michael L. Radelet and Barbara A. Zsembik, "Executive Clemency in Post-*Furman* Capital Cases," *University of Richmond Law Review*, Vol. 27, p. 289, 292 (1993). Professor Bedau's article also offers an interesting historical perspective on clemency. **Gender discrimination in the exercise of executive clemency.** Elizabeth Rappaport, *Buffalo Criminal Law Review*, Vol. 4, p. 967 (2001). Professor Rappaport also offers an interesting discussion of the defensibility of the Court's decision to offer marginally greater protection to capital defendants in clemency proceedings. **Governor Rockefeller's decision.** Winthrop Rockefeller, "Executive Clemency and the Death Penalty," *Catholic University Law Review*, Vol. 21, p. 94 (1971).

Chapter 24 The Moratorium Movement

ABA resolution. Recommendation No. 107 (approved February 3, 1997). **Coverage of the penalty in Illinois.** Ken Armstrong and Maurice Possley, "Trial & Error: How Prosecutors Sacrifice Justice to Win," *Chicago Tribune*, January 10–14, 1999. **Actual innocence.** *Actual Innocence: Five Days to Execution and Other Dispatches from the Wrongly Convicted* (New York: Doubleday, 2000).

Chapter 25 International Law and American Exceptionalism

International treaties and the death penalty. See generally Nina Rivkind and Steven F. Shatz, *Cases and Materials on the Death Penalty* (West, 2001), pp. 762–6. *Soering v. United Kingdom*, 11 EHRR 439 (July 7, 1989).

The Authors and Their Contributions

Chapter 1 Retribution

Claire Finkelstein is professor of law and philosophy at the University of Pennsylvania and most recently the author of *Hobbes (Philosophers and Law)* (Ashgate Publishing Co., 2003). **Michael Davis**, author of *Justice in the Shadow of Death* (Rowman and Littlefield, 1996), is senior research associate at Illinois Institute of Technology. Their exchange appeared originally in *Criminal Justice Ethics*, Vol. 21 No. 2 (Summer/Fall 2002).

Chapter 2 Religion

Kerby Anderson is the president of Probe Ministries International. He received his B.S. from Oregon State University, M.F.S. from Yale University, and M.A. from Georgetown University. He is a nationally syndicated columnist, the author of several books, including *Genetic Engineering, Origin Science, Living Ethically in the '90s, Signs of Warning, Signs of Hope,* and *Moral Dilemmas,* and the host of "Probe" (USA Radio Network). He can be reached via e-mail at kerby@probe.org. **Gardner Hanks** was the author of a series of highly readable books on the death penalty including *Against the Death Penalty: Christian and Secular Arguments Against Capital Punishment* from which the passage printed here is excerpted. Before his recent death, Mr. Hanks was the Idaho State Death Penalty Action Coordinator for Amnesty International and a spiritual adviser for death row inmates in Idaho.

Chapter 3 Deterrence

Michael Radelet is a professor in the department of sociology at the University of Colorado. **Ronald K. Akers** is a professor of criminology and sociology and director of the Center for the Studies in Criminology and Law at the University of Florida. Their study is available online at www.justice-blind.com/death/radelet.html. **Keith Harries** is professor of geography at the University of Maryland—Baltimore County. **Derral Cheatwood** is director of social sciences and professor of criminal justice at the University of Texas—San Antonio. *The Geography of Execution* (1997) was published by Rowman and Littlefield. **Hashem Dezhbakhsh, Paul H. Rubin,** and **Joanna M. Shepherd** are members of the department of economics at Emory University.

Chapter 4 Brutalization

John K. Cochran is an associate professor of criminology at the University of South Florida. **Mitchell B. Chamlin** is a professor of criminal justice at the University of Cincinnati. Their study appears in *Justice Quarterly*, Vol. 17 No. 4, (Dec. 2000). **Jon Sorensen** is an associate professor, department of criminal justice, University of Texas, Pan American. **Robert Wrinkle** is a professor in the department of political science, University of Texas, Pan American. **Victoria Brewer** is an assistant professor at the College of Criminal Justice, Sam Houston State University. **James Marquart** is a professor at the College of Criminal Justice, Sam Houston State University. Their study appeared in *Crime and Delinquency*, Vol. 45 No. 4, pp. 481–93 (1999).

Chapter 5 Incapacitation

Professor **Marquart** and **Sorensen**'s study of *Furman* commutees appeared originally in *Loyola of Los Angeles Law Review*, Vol. 23 No. 1, pp. 5–28 (November 1989). Professor **Sorensen** and **Wrinkle**'s study of disciplinary infractions among prisoners appeared originally in *Criminal Justice and Behavior*, Vol. 23 No. 4, pp. 542–53 (Dec. 1996). **Matt DeLisi** is a professor at Iowa State University. **Ed A. Munoz** is a professor at the University of Wyoming. "Future Dangerousness Revisited" was published in *Criminal Justice Policy Review*, Vol. 14, pp. 287–305 (2003).

Chapter 6 Cost

Philip J. Cook is a professor of public policy and economics at Duke University. **Donna B. Slawson** is a professor at the Terry Sanford Institute of Public Policy at Duke. **Richard C. Dieter** is executive director of the Death Penalty Information Center. **John McAdams** is an associate professor of political science at Marquette University. "It's Good and We're

Going to Keep It" can be found in the *Connecticut Law Review*, Vol. 33, p. 819 (Spring 2001).

Chapter 7 Innocence

James S. Liebman is Simon H. Rifkind Professor of Law at Columbia Law School. His coauthor **Jeffrey Fagan** is a professor at Columbia Law School and the Joseph Mailman School of Public Health. **Valerie West** is a research associate at Columbia Law School. *A Broken System* can be found at http://justice.policy.net. **Hugo Adam Bedau** is professor emeritus at Tufts University. **Michael L. Radelet** is a professor and chair of the department of sociology at University of Florida. **Stephen J. Markman** is a justice of the Michigan Supreme Court. **Paul G. Cassell** is a United States district judge in Utah. "Miscarriages of Justice" originally appeared in the *Stanford Law Review*, Vol. 40, p. 21 (1987). Markman and Cassell's response appeared in *Stanford Law Review*, Vol. 41, p. 121 (1988). Professors Bedau and Radelet's reply is at *Stanford Law Review*, Vol. 41, p. 161 (1988).

Chapter 8 Arbitrariness

Carol S. Steiker is a professor of law at Harvard Law School. **Jordan M. Steiker** is a professor of law, University of Texas School of Law. "Sober Second Thoughts" was originally published in the *Harvard Law Review*, Vol. 109, p. 355 (1995). **David McCord** is Richard and Anita Calkins Distinguished Professor of Law, Drake Law School. "Mild Success or Major Disaster" appeared in *Florida State University Law Review*, Vol. 24, p. 545 (1997).

Chapter 9 Mitigating Evidence

Jeffrey L. Kirchmeier is a professor of law at the City University of New York School of Law. His piece appeared originally in *William and Mary Bill of Rights Journal*, Vol. 6, p. 345 (Spring 1998). **Christopher Smith** is an associate professor of criminal justice at Michigan State University. His article can be found in *Drake Law Review*, Vol. 43, p. 593 (1995).

Chapter 10 Rape and Proportionality

Elizabeth Gray's article originally appeared in *Saint Louis Law Journal*, Vol. 42, p. 1443 (1998). **Pallie Zambrano**'s article can be found in *Santa Clara Law Review*, Vol. 39, p. 1267 (1999).

Chapter 11 Felony-Murder

Richard Rosen is a professor of law at the University of North Carolina—Chapel Hill Law School. "Felony-Murder and the Eighth Amendment Jurisprudence of Death" was first published in *Boston College Law Review*, Vol. 31, p. 1103 (1990). **David McCord**'s article can be found in *Arizona State Law Journal*, Vol. 32, p. 843 (Fall 2000).

Chapter 12 Juveniles

Victor L. Streib is a professor of law at the Claude W. Pettit College of Law, Ohio Northern University. His article originally appeared in *Oklahoma Law Review*, Vol. 36, p. 613 (1983). **Joseph L. Hoffmann** is Harry Pratter Professor of Law at Indiana University School of Law. His article can be found in the *Hastings Law Journal*, Vol. 40, p. 229 (1988–1989).

Chapter 13 The Mentally Retarded

The full text of Human Rights Watch's report "Beyond Reason: The Death Penalty and Offenders With Mental Retardation" can be found at http://hrw.org/reports/2001/ustat/. **Barry Latzer** is a professor at John Jay College of Criminal Justice and The Graduate Center of the City University of New York. He is the author of *Death Penalty Cases* (Butterworth, 2003). "Misplaced Compassion" originally appeared in the *Criminal Law Bulletin*, Vol. 38 No. 3, p. 327 (May/June 2002).

Chapter 14 The Insane

Charles Patrick Ewing is professor of law and psychology at State University of New York at Buffalo. His piece appears in *Behavioral Sciences and the Law*, Vol. 5, p. 175 (1987). **Barry Latzer**'s article "Between Madness and Death" was published in *Criminal Justice Ethics*, Vol. 22 No. 2, p. 3 (Summer 2003).

Chapter 15 Race

Prior to his death in 2002, **Earnest van den Haag** was John M. Olin Professor of Jurisprudence and Public Policy, Fordham University. His article appeared in *Criminal Law Bulletin*, Vol. 14 No. 1, pp. 51–68 (Jan.–Feb. 1978). **Stephen Nathanson** is professor of philosophy at Northeastern University and the author of *An Eye for an Eye? The Morality of*

Punishing By Death (Rowman and Littlefield, 1987). His article is published here for the first time.

Chapter 16 Victim Impact Evidence

Brian Johnson's article "Giving the Victim's Family a Voice in the Capital Sentencing Process" appeared in *Indiana Law Review*, Vol. 30, p. 795 (1997). The complete version of my article is published in the *Stanford Law & Policy Review*, Vol. 15 (2004).

Chapter 17 Capital Juries

"The Effects of Death Qualification on Juror's Predisposition to Convict" was published in *Law and Human Behavior*, Vol. 8 Nos. 1, 2 (1984). At the time of the writing, **Claudia Cowan** was an attorney in California, **William Thompson** was in the Program in Social Ecology at UC-Irvine, and **Phoebe Ellsworth** was a member of the department of psychology at Stanford University. **Nancy King** is professor of law at Vanderbilt University. "Silencing Nullification Advocacy" was published in *University of Chicago Law Review*, Vol. 65, p. 433 (1998).

Chapter 18 Sentencing Alternatives

Sheldon Elkand-Olson is professor and provost at the University of Texas. **John H. Blume** is co-director of the Cornell Death Penalty Project, **Stephen P. Garvey** is a professor of law, Cornell Law School. **Sheri Lynn Johnson** is a professor of law, Cornell Law School and co-director of the Cornell Death Penalty Project. "Future Dangerousness" appeared in *Cornell Law Review*, Vol. 86, p. 397 (January, 2001). "Gazing into the Crystal Ball: Can Jurors Accurately Predict Dangerousness in Capital Cases?" was published in the *Law and Society Review*, Vol. 23 No. 3, pp. 449–68 (1989). "Death by Default" was published in *Texas Law Review*, Vol. 77, p. 605 (1999). **William J. Bowers** is principal research scientist, College of Criminal Justice, Northeastern University. **Benjamin D. Steiner** is associate research scientist, College of Criminal Justice, Northeastern University.

Chapter 19 Trial Counsel

Stephen B. Bright is director of the Southern Center for Human Rights. "Counsel for the Poor" was first published in *Yale Law Journal*, Vol. 103, pp. 1835–65 (1994). **Joshua Marquis** is the district attorney in Astoria, Oregon. He has worked as a public prosecutor for 18 years and, in 1989 and 1990, spent 18 months providing indigent defense. "Not So Dire After All" was published in *National Law Journal*, Vol. 25 No. 28, p. A17 (March 31, 2003).

Chapter 20 Habeas Corpus and Innocence

Joseph Hoffmann's article "Is Innocence Sufficient" was published in *Indiana Law Journal*, Vol. 68, p. 817 (1993). **Barry Latzer**'s article "Reflections on Innocence" was published in *Criminal Law Bulletin*, Vol. 39 No. 2, pp. 133–49 (2003).

Chapter 21 Appellate Delay

Dwight Aarons is an associate professor of law at the University of Tennessee College of Law. His article was published in *Seton Hall Law Review*, Vol. 29, p. 147 (1998). **Franklin E. Zimring** is William G. Simon Professor of Law at the University of California, Berkeley. This essay has been adapted from his chapter in *The Killing State: Capital Punishment in Law, Politics, and Culture*, Austin Sarat, ed., Oxford University Press (1999).

Chapter 22 Televised Executions

John D. Bessler is an attorney and an adjunct professor of law at the University of Minnesota Law School. He is actively involved in the representation of four death row inmates. *Death in the Dark* was published in 1997 by Northeastern University Press. **George F. Will** is a syndicated columnist. **Jeremy G. Epstein**, a former assistant United States attorney, is a partner at the New York office of Shearman & Sterling.

Chapter 23 Clemency

Jack Dunphy is an officer in the Los Angeles Police Department. "Jack Dunphy" is the author's nom de cyber. His article appeared in the January 13, 2003, issue of the *National Review*. **Scott Turow** is the author, most recently, of "Reversible Errors." His op-ed appeared in the January 17, 2003, issue of *The New York Times*. **Adam Gershowitz** is an associate at Covington & Burling. His article appeared in *Journal of Law and Politics*, Vol. 17, p. 669 (Fall 2001).

Chapter 24 The Moratorium Movement

Ronald J. Tabak is special counsel to Skadden Arps Slate Meagher & Flom. He is also co-chair of the Death Penalty Committee American Bar Association Section of Individual Rights and Responsibilities, chair of the Committee on Civil Rights, Association of the Bar of the City of New York, and president of New York Lawyers Against the Death Penalty. Some of the ideas and language in Mr. Tabak's article come from discussions he had with Professor Anthony G. Amsterdam of New York University School of Law. **John B. Wefing** is Richard J. Hughes Professor of Constitutional and Public Law, Seton Hall University School of Law. Tabak and Wefing's exchange appeared in the *Connecticut Law Review*, Vol. 33, pp. 733, 861 (Spring 2001).

Chapter 25 International Law and American Exceptionalism

Joshua Micah Marshall is Washington editor of *The American Prospect*. "Death in Venice: Europe's Death Penalty Elitism" was published in *The New Republic*, p. 14 (July 13, 2000). **Carol Steiker**'s article appears in *Oregon Law Review*, Vol. 81, p. 97 (Spring 2002).

Chapter 26 The Future of the Death Penalty in America

Alex Kozinksi is a judge for the Ninth Circuit Court of Appeals. **Sean Gallagher** is an attorney. Their piece was published in *Case Western Reserve Law Review*, Vol. 46, p. 1 (1995).

Index